Western Civilizations

EIGHTH EDITION

WESTERN

EIGHTH EDITION

CIVILIZATIONS

Their History and Their Culture

EDWARD McNALL BURNS

W · W · NORTON & COMPANY · INC · NEW YORK

Eighth Edition, Copyright © 1973

FIRST EDITION, COPYRIGHT 1941
SECOND EDITION, COPYRIGHT 1947
THIRD EDITION, COPYRIGHT 1949
FOURTH EDITION, COPYRIGHT 1954
FIFTH EDITION, COPYRIGHT © 1958
SIXTH EDITION, COPYRIGHT © 1963
SEVENTH EDITION, COPYRIGHT © 1968
BY W. W. NORTON & COMPANY, INC.

Library of Congress Cataloging in Publication Data
Burns, Edward McNall, 1897–1972
     Western civilizations.
     Includes bibliographies.
     1. Civilization—History. 2. Europe—
Civilization—History. I. Title.
CB57.B8 1973b   910'.03'1821   72–13713
ISBN 0–393–09343–3

Cartography by Harold K. Faye

PRINTED IN THE UNITED STATES OF AMERICA
6 7 8 9 0

To the memory of *My Mother*
Who first inspired in me
the desire to know

Contents

Illustrations in Color

xvii

Illustrations in the Text

xxiv

Maps

Preface

To the unsophisticated, history is something fixed and permanent. Once written it is as unalterable as the Ten Commandments or the laws of the Medes and Persians. It has only to be studied and learned like the axioms of Euclid or the principles of Newton and Darwin. Probing into the factual record of history is, therefore, a waste of time; research should be confined to such fields as chemistry, astronomy, and medicine where the need for more facts is readily apparent. But facts, though indispensable, are the mere bones of any body of knowledge. The flesh and blood are provided by interpretations and conclusions as to the meaning of the facts. In few bodies of knowledge have interpretations changed more rapidly than in history. Invariably these changes have resulted from continuing research. History, as a consequence, is strewn with the wreckage of exploded theories. No longer can any responsible historian accept the oversimplification that Magna Carta laid the foundations of modern democracy; nor would he subscribe wholeheartedly to the thesis that the French Revolution was merely a struggle of a progressive and enlightened bourgeoisie against a corrupt and benighted king and aristocracy.

The main purpose of the present revision of *Western Civilizations* is to take account of the numerous discoveries and reinterpretations that have resulted from historical research during the past decade. To this end the chapters of the previous edition dealing with the Mesopotamian and Persian civilizations have been combined into one, with the deletion of outdated and surplus material. The chapters on the First and Second Industrial Revolutions have been combined to show the continuous development of man's efforts to control his environment, while a new chapter on critics and apologists of industrialization has been added. The chapter on the United States has been incorporated with material on the maturing of the European democracies, and a new chapter added, tracing the roots of the political and social revolutions of our time. The three final chapters have been expanded to reflect events and trends of the late 1960's and early 1970's. Throughout, the essential character of the book, as a history of *civilizations* rather than a mere narrative of political events, has been preserved. The author continues to believe that the effects of the Black Death were no less important than the Hundred Years' War, and that, in the long run, the teachings of Aristotle and the Stoics transcended in significance the rise of the Bourbons or the decline of the Holy Roman Empire. The facts of political history are not ignored. But they are related to the development of ideas and institutions or are presented as the groundwork of cultural, economic, and social movements.

Western Civilizations was published originally in 1941. Later editions were issued in 1947, 1949, 1954, 1958, 1963, and 1968. The present edition, the eighth, has been redesigned for easier reading and to accommodate literally hundreds of new illustrations from archives both American and European. Large portions of the older text material have been reorganized and rewritten with a view to achieving greater clarity, accuracy, and compatibility with the results of the most recent scholarship. The author believes he has thereby produced a work more adaptable to the needs of the teacher and more useful to the student. The new edition, like its predecessors, has been brought out in both a one-volume and a two-volume format. Available for use with either is a Teacher's Manual and a new Study Guide, whose most distinctive feature is the inclusion of numerous extracts from original sources.

In preparing the eighth edition the author has benefited from the assistance and counsel of many individuals whose services no words of appreciation can adequately measure. Outstanding among them are three men who offered detailed criticism of the book, Philip L. Ralph, LeRoy Dresbeck, and Maxim W. Mikulak. Deep gratitude is due also to the hundreds of college teachers throughout the world who have used the book and have contributed invaluable suggestions for its improvement. Finally, the author is indebted to his wife, Marie Bentz Burns, for her arduous labors of research, typing, proofreading, and preparing the index, and for her patience, devotion, and understanding.

Edward McNall Burns

Santa Barbara, California

Western Civilizations

PART I

The Dawn of History

No one knows the place of origin of the human species. There is evidence, however, that it may have been south central Africa or possibly central or south central Asia. Here climatic conditions were such as to favor the evolution of a variety of human types from primate ancestors. From their place or places of origin members of the human species wandered to southeastern and eastern Asia, northern Africa, Europe, and eventually, to America. For hundreds of centuries they remained primitive, leading a life which was at first barely more advanced than that of the higher animals. About 5000 B.C. a few of them, enjoying special advantages of location and climate, developed superior cultures. These cultures, which attained knowledge of writing and considerable advancement in the arts and sciences and in social organization, began in that part of the world known as the Near Orient. This region extends from the western border of India to the Mediterranean Sea and to the farther bank of the Nile. Here flourished, at different periods between 5000 and 300 B.C., the mighty empires of the Egyptians, the Babylonians, the Assyrians, the Chaldeans, and the Persians, together with the smaller states of such peoples as the Cretans, the Sumerians, the Phoenicians, and the Hebrews. In other parts of the world the beginnings of civilization were retarded. There was nothing that could be called civilized life in China until about 2000 B.C. And, except on the island of Crete, there was no civilization in Europe until more than 1000 years later.

1

A Table of Geologic Time

	ERA	PERIOD	EPOCH	CHARACTERISTIC FORMS OF LIFE	CULTURE PERIODS	AND CHARACTERISTIC ACHIEVEMENTS
3 billion years ago	Precambrian	Early Precambrian				
510 million years ago	Precambrian	Late Precambrian		One-celled organisms First invertebrates: worms, algae		
	Paleozoic	Cambrian		Mollusks, sponges		
	Paleozoic	Ordovician		Insects, first verte- brates		
	Paleozoic	Silurian		Corals, sharks, seaweed		
	Paleozoic	Devonian		Lungfish, crustaceans		
	Paleozoic	Carboniferous Pennsylvanian Mississippian		Earliest amphibians Large amphibians Ferns		
180 million years ago	Paleozoic	Permian				
	Mesozoic	Triassic		Giant reptiles		
	Mesozoic	Jurassic		Diversified reptiles, birds		
90 million years ago	Mesozoic	Cretaceous		Marsupials, bony fishes Trees		
	Cenozoic	Tertiary	Paleocene	Early mammals, first primates		
	Cenozoic	Tertiary	Eocene	Primitive apes, ancestors of monkeys		
	Cenozoic	Tertiary	Oligocene			
	Cenozoic	Tertiary	Miocene	Ancestors of great apes		
	Cenozoic	Tertiary	Pliocene	Ancestors of man, modern mammals		
	Cenozoic	Tertiary		Early human species, other primates	Lower Paleolithic	Spoken language, knowl- edge of fire, burial of dead, stone tools and weapons
500,000 years ago	Cenozoic	Quaternary	Pleistocene	Present-day animals and races of men	Upper Paleolithic	Needles, harpoons, fish- hooks, dart throwers, magic, art, social organ- ization, cooking of food
	Cenozoic	Quaternary	Recent		Neolithic	Agriculture, domestica- tion of animals, pottery, houses, navigation, in- stitutions
7000 years ago	Cenozoic	Quaternary			Civilized man	Bronze, iron, writing, technology, science, lit- erature, philosophy, etc.

CHAPTER 1

The Earliest Beginnings

As we turn to the past itself . . . we might well begin with a pious tribute to our nameless [preliterate] ancestors, who by inconceivably arduous and ingenious effort succeeded in establishing a human race. They made the crucial discoveries and inventions, such as the tool, the seed, and the domesticated animal; their development of agriculture, the "neolithic revolution" that introduced a settled economy, was perhaps the greatest stride forward that man has ever taken. They created the marvelous instrument of language, which enabled man to discover his humanity, and eventually to disguise it. They laid the foundations of civilization: its economic, political, and social life, and its artistic, ethical, and religious traditions. Indeed, our "savage" ancestors are still very near to us, and not merely in our capacity for savagery.
—Herbert J. Muller, *The Uses of the Past*

I. THE MEANING OF HISTORY

Broadly defined, history is a record and interpretation of man's achievements, hopes and frustrations, struggles and triumphs. This conception has not always been the prevailing one. At one time history was quite generally regarded as "past politics." Its content was restricted largely to battles and treaties, to the personalities and policies of statesmen, and to the laws and decrees of rulers. But important as such data are, they do not constitute the whole substance of history. Actually, history comprises a record of all of man's accomplishments in every sphere, whether political, economic, intellectual, or social. It embraces also a chronicle of his dreams and ideals, his hopes, triumphs, and failures. Perhaps most important of all, it includes an inquiry into the causes of the chief political and economic movements, a search for the forces that impelled man toward his great undertakings, and the reasons for his successes and failures.

History defined

3

Whether history is a science, and whether it can be used as an instrument for predicting the future, are questions that do not yield conclusive answers. With regard to the first, about all we can say is that both the study and the writing of history should be made as scientific as possible. This means that the scientific attitude should be brought to bear upon the solution of all of history's problems, be they political, intellectual, moral, or religious. As the American philosopher, the late John Dewey, pointed out, the scientific attitude demands a skeptical and inquiring approach toward all issues and a refusal to form conclusive judgments until all available evidence has been amassed and examined. Obviously, this approach rules out such conceptions of history as the patriotic, the racial, or the providential. Scientific history cannot be made to serve the purposes of national greatness, race supremacy, or the doctrine of a Chosen People.

History as a
chart for the
future

The value of history as a chart for the future has tormented the minds of philosophical historians for scores of centuries. The father of scientific history, Thucydides, who lived in Athens in the fifth century B.C., asserted that events do "repeat themselves at some future time—if not exactly the same, yet very similar." The British essayist Thomas Carlyle and the American philosopher William James saw in the stimulating genius of eminent individuals the motivating force of historical progress. What would have been the future of Germany, James asked, if Bismarck had died in his cradle, or of the British Empire if Robert Clive had shot himself, as he tried to do at Madras? Great stages of civilization could be accounted for only by an exceptional concourse of brilliant individuals within a limited time. But James offered no theory as to the conditions likely to produce such a concourse.

The most elaborate hypothesis in modern times concerning inevitability in history was developed by Karl Marx in the nineteenth century. Marx taught that individuals are mere instruments of forces more powerful than they. These forces, he contended, are exclusively economic and are grounded in changes in modes of production. Thus the change from a feudal economy to a commercial and industrial economy brought into existence the capitalist epoch and the rule of the bourgeois class. In time capitalism would be superseded by socialism, and, finally, by communism. The course of history was consequently predetermined, and future changes would succeed one another in the same mechanical fashion as they had in the past.

Although the theories of Marx have attracted considerable attention, they cannot be accepted as gospel by scientific historians. The motivation of human events is too complex to be forced into a single pattern. It is impossible to predict the future in terms of a single theory or thesis. No crystal ball exists which will enable anyone to foretell with certainty that every revolution must be followed by counterrevolution, that every war begets new wars, or that progress is an inescapable law. Greed is undoubtedly a powerful motive for human action, but this does not mean that economic causation must be accepted as a universal rule. Fear is also a powerful motive, in somes cases overbalancing greed. Other psychological motives, including sex and the lust for power, likewise play a part in the determination of human actions. In short, no one explanation will suffice, and a vast amount of research will be necessary before there can be any assurance that all the possible driving forces have been discovered.

One final question remains. Is history a unilinear process, an unbroken stream of progress toward higher and nobler achievements? Or is it simply a process of change marked by a general trend of advancement but with many interruptions and setbacks? Scarcely a historian would deny that some ideas and discoveries have come down through the centuries with no change except in the direction of improvement. This would be true of much of the mathematics of the ancient Egyptians, the Babylonians, and the Greeks. But other examples illustrate the opposite. Aristarchus of Samos, in the third century B.C., propounded a heliocentric theory. It was superseded, largely for religious reasons, about 400 years later by the geocentric theory. It was not reaffirmed until the time of Copernicus in the sixteenth century A.D. Although Hellenistic physicians came close to a discovery of the circulation of the blood, knowledge of their achievement lay buried for 1500 years and had to await rediscovery in the seventeenth century by Sir William Harvey, the English physician and anatomist. As with individual accomplishments, so with whole cultures. The first three millennia of written history were strewn with the wreckage of fallen empires and extinct civilizations. Egypt, Mesopotamia, Persia, Greece, and Rome fell prey one after the other to external conquest, internal conquest, or a combination of both. Many elements of the old cultures survived, but they were frequently modified or woven into quite different patterns. As Lincoln said, we cannot escape history, and the influence which history presses upon us is more complicated than we usually suspect.

The concept of a
stream of history
versus a succession
of cultures

2. HISTORY AND PREHISTORY

It is the custom among many historians to distinguish between historic and prehistoric periods in the evolution of human society. By the former they mean history based upon written records. By the latter they mean the record of man's achievements before the invention of writing. But this distinction is not altogether satisfactory. It suggests that human accomplishments before they were recorded in characters or symbols representing words or concepts were not important. Nothing could be farther from the truth. The foundations, at least, of many of the great accomplishments of modern technology, and even of social and political systems, were laid before human beings could write a word. It would seem preferable, therefore, that the whole period of man's life on earth should be regarded as historic, and that the era before the invention of writing be designated by some term such as "preliterate." The records of preliterate societies are, of course, not books and manuscripts, but tools, weapons, fossils, utensils, carvings, paintings, and fragments of jewelry and ornamentation. These, commonly known as "artifacts," are often just as valuable as the written word in providing knowledge of a people's deeds and modes of living.

The entire span of human history can be divided roughly into two periods, the Age of Stone and the Age of Metals. The former is identical with the Preliterate Age, or the period before the invention of writing. The latter coincides with the period of history based upon written records. The Preliterate Age covered at least 95 per cent of man's existence and did not come to an end until about 5000 B.C. The Age of Metals practically coincides with the history of civilized nations. The Age of Stone is subdivided into the Paleolithic, or Old Stone Age, and the Neolithic, or New Stone Age. Each takes its name from the type of stone tools and weapons characteristically manufactured during the period. Thus during the greater part of the Paleolithic Age implements were commonly made by chipping pieces off a large stone or flint and using the core that remained as a hand ax or "fist hatchet." Toward the end of the period the chips themselves were used as knives or spearheads, and the core thrown away. The Neolithic Age witnessed the supplanting of chipped stone tools by implements made by grinding and polishing stone.

Fist Hatchet

3.   THE CULTURE OF LOWER PALEOLITHIC MEN

The earliest Stone Age men

The Paleolithic period can be dated from roughly 1,750,000 B.C. to 10,000 B.C. It is commonly divided into two stages, an earlier or Lower Paleolithic and a later or Upper Paleolithic. The Lower Paleolithic was much the longer of the two, covering about 75 per cent of the entire Old Stone Age. During this time at least four species of men inhabited the earth. The oldest was apparently a creature whose skeletal remains were found in 1960–1964 by Louis S. B. Leakey in what is now Tanzania, East Africa. Leakey named this creature *Homo habilis*, or "man having ability." Estimated to be at least 1,750,000 years old, the remains included parts of the skull, hands, legs, and feet. That *Homo habilis* was a true ancestral human being is indicated by evidence that he walked erect and that he used crude tools. It must not be supposed, of course, that these tools represented any high degree of manufacturing skill or inventive talent. For the most part, they consisted of objects taken from nature:

The Skull (left) of a Young Woman of the Species Homo habilis, believed to have lived in Tanzania, East Africa, about 1,750,000 years ago. On the right is the skull of a present-day African. Though *Homo habilis* was smaller than a pygmy, the brain casing was shaped like that of modern man.

bones of large animals, limbs from trees, and chunks of stone, perhaps broken or crudely chipped.[1]

Two other early inhabitants of the Lower Paleolithic were Java man and Peking man. Java man was long thought to be the oldest of manlike creatures, but it is now generally agreed that the date of his origin was about 500,000 B.C. His skeletal remains were found on the island of Java in 1891. The remains of Peking man were found in China, about forty miles southwest of Peking between 1926 and 1930. Since the latter date, fragments of no fewer than 32 skeletons of the Peking type have been located, making possible a complete reconstruction of at least the head of this ancient species. Anthropologists generally agree that Peking man and Java man are of approximately the same antiquity, and that both probably descended from the same ancestral type.

During the last 25,000 years of the Lower Paleolithic period a fourth species of ancient man made his appearance. He was Neanderthal man, famous as an early cave man. His skeletal fragments were first discovered in the valley of the Neander, near Düsseldorf, northwestern Germany, in 1856. Since then numerous other discoveries have been made, in some cases complete skeletons, in such widely separated regions as Belgium, Spain, Italy, Yugo-

Java Man

Peking Man

[1] In 1972, near Lake Rudolf in East Africa, the remains of another manlike species were found. They were estimated to be between 2.5 and 3 million years old. The size of its brain cavity seemed to justify the species' being called the predecessor of *Homo habilis*.

7

Neanderthal Man

*Lower Paleolithic Carving
Tool and Side Scraper*

Cro-Magnon man:
physical
characteristics

8

slavia, Russia, and Palestine. So closely did Neanderthal man resemble modern man that he is classified as a member of the same genus, the genus *Homo*. The resemblance, however, was by no means perfect. Neanderthal men, on the average, were only about five feet, four inches in height. They had receding chins and heavy eyebrow ridges. Although their foreheads sloped back and their brain cases were low-vaulted, their average cranial capacity was slightly greater than that of modern Caucasians. What this may have signified with respect to their intelligence cannot be determined.

The knowledge we possess of the culture of Lower Paleolithic men is scanty indeed. The skills they achieved and the learning they acquired must have been pitiful in quantity even when compared with the accomplishments of modern primitive men. Yet Neanderthal man and his successors were not mere apes, forgetting in a moment the chance triumphs they had made. They undoubtedly had the capacity for speech, which enabled them to communicate with their fellows and to pass on what they had learned to succeeding generations. We are justified in assuming also that they possessed reasoning ability, however crudely it may have been developed. Practically from the beginning, therefore, they were probably tool-using creatures, employing their wits to fashion implements and weapons. Perhaps at first these would be nothing but limbs broken from trees to be used as clubs. Eventually it was discovered that stones could be chipped in such a way as to give them cutting edges. Thus were developed spearheads, borers, and much superior knives and scrapers. Indications have been found also of a degree of advancement in nonmaterial culture. In the entrances to caves where Neanderthal man lived, or at least took refuge, evidence has been discovered of flint-working floors and stone hearths where huge fires appear to have been made. These would suggest the origins of cooperative group life and possibly the crude beginnings of social institutions. More significance may be attached to Neanderthal man's practice of bestowing care upon the bodies of his dead, interring with them in shallow graves tools and other objects or value. Perhaps this practice indicates the development of a religious sense, or at least a belief in some form of survival after death.

4.   UPPER PALEOLITHIC CULTURE

About 30,000 B.C. the culture of the Old Stone Age passed from the Lower Paleolithic stage to the Upper Paleolithic. The Upper Paleolithic period lasted for only about 200 centuries, or from 30,000 to 10,000 B.C. A new and superior type of human being dominated the earth in this time. Biologically these men were closely related to modern man. Their foremost predecessors, Neanderthal men, had ceased to exist as a distinct variety. What became of the Neanderthalers is not known.

The name used to designate the prevailing breed of Upper Paleolithic men is Cro-Magnon, from the Cro-Magnon cave in Dordogne, France, where some of the most typical remains were discovered. Cro-Magnon men were tall, broad-shouldered, and erect, the males averaging over six feet. They had high foreheads, well-developed chins, and a cranial capacity about equal to the modern average. The heavy eyebrow ridges so typical of earlier species were absent. Whether Cro-Magnon men left any survivors is a debatable question. They do not seem to have been exterminated but appear to have been driven into mountainous regions and to have been absorbed ultimately into later breeds.

Cro-Magnon Man

Upper Paleolithic culture was markedly superior to that which had gone before. Not only were tools and implements better made, but they existed in greater variety. They were not fashioned merely from flakes of stone and an occasional shaft of bone; other materials were used in abundance, particularly reindeer horn and ivory. Examples of the more complicated tools included the bone needle, the fishhook, the harpoon, the dart thrower, and, at the very end, the bow and arrow. That Upper Paleolithic man wore clothing is indicated by the fact that he made buttons and toggles of bone and horn and invented the needle. He did not know how to weave cloth, but animal skins sewn together proved a satisfactory substitute. It is certain that he cooked his food, for enormous hearths, evidently used for roasting flesh, have been discovered. In the vicinity of one at Solutré, in southern France, was a mass of charred bones, estimated to contain the remains of 100,000 large animals. Although Cro-Magnon man built no houses, except a few simple huts in regions where natural shelters did not abound, his life was not wholly nomadic. Evidences found in the caves that were his usual homes indicate that he must have used them, seasonally at least, for years at a time.

Upper Paleolithic culture: material goods

With respect to nonmaterial elements there are also indications that Upper Paleolithic culture represented a marked advancement. Group life was now more regular and more highly organized than ever before. The profusion of charred bones at Solutré and elsewhere probably indicates cooperative enterprise in the hunt and sharing of the results in great community feasts. The amazing workmanship displayed in tools and weapons and highly developed techniques in the arts could scarcely have been achieved without some division of labor. It appears certain, therefore, that Upper Paleolithic communities included professional artists and skilled craftsmen. In order to acquire such talents, certain members of the communities must have gone through long periods of training and given all their time to the practice of their specialties.

Upper Paleolithic Fish Hook

Substantial proof exists that Cro-Magnon man had highly developed notions of a world of unseen powers. He bestowed more care upon the bodies of his dead than did Neanderthal man, painting the

9

Upper Paleolithic Engraving and Sculpture. The two objects at the top and upper right are dart throwers. At the lower left is the famous Venus of Willendorf.

corpses, folding the arms over the heart, and depositing pendants, necklaces, and richly carved weapons and tools in the graves. He formulated an elaborate system of sympathetic magic designed to increase his supply of food. Sympathetic magic is based upon the principle that imitating a desired result will bring about that result. Applying this principle, Cro-Magnon man made paintings on the walls of his caves depicting the capture of reindeer in the hunt. At other times he fashioned clay models of the bison or mammoth and mutilated them with dart thrusts. The purpose of such representations was quite evidently to facilitate the very results portrayed and thereby to increase the hunter's success and make easier the struggle for existence. Possibly incantations or ceremonies accompanied the making of the pictures or images, and it is likely that the work of

10

producing them was carried on while the actual hunt was in progress.

The supreme achievement of Cro-Magnon man was his art—an achievement so original and resplendent that it ought to be counted among the Seven Wonders of the World. Nothing else illustrates so well the great gulf between his culture and that of his predecessors. Upper Paleolithic art included nearly every branch that the material culture of the time made possible. Sculpture, painting, carving, and engraving were all represented. The ceramic arts and architecture were lacking; pottery had not yet been invented; and the only buildings erected were of simple design.

The art *par excellence* of Cro-Magnon man was painting. Here were exhibited the greatest number and variety of his talents—his discrimination in the use of color, his meticulous attention to detail, his capacity for the employment of scale in depicting a group, and above all, his genius for naturalism. Especially noteworthy was the painter's skill in representing movement. A large proportion of murals depict animals running, leaping, browsing, chewing the cud, or facing the hunter at bay. Ingenious devices were often employed to give the impression of motion. Chief among them was the drawing or painting of additional outlines to indicate the areas in which the legs or the head of the animal had moved. The scheme was so shrewdly executed that no appearance whatever of artificiality resulted.

The Venus of Laussel

Cave-man art throws a flood of light on many problems relating to primitive mentality and folkways. To a certain extent it was undoubtedly an expression of a true aesthetic sense. Cro-Magnon man did obviously take some delight in a graceful line or symmetrical pattern or brilliant color. The fact that he painted and tattooed his body and wore ornaments gives evidence of this. But his chief works of art can scarcely have been produced for the sake of creating beautiful objects. Such a possibility must be excluded for several reasons. To begin with, the best of the paintings and drawings are usually to be found on the walls and ceilings of the darkest and most inaccessible parts of the caves. The gallery of paintings at Niaux, for instance, is more than half a mile from the entrance of the cavern. No one could see the artists' creations except in the imperfect light of torches or of primitive lamps, which must have smoked and sputtered badly, for the only illuminating fluid was animal fat. Furthermore, there is evidence that Cro-Magnon man was largely indifferent toward his work of art after it was finished. Numerous examples have been found of paintings or drawings superimposed upon earlier ones of the same or of different types. Evidently the important thing was not the finished work itself, but the act of making it.

For Paleolithic man, art was a serious business. The real purpose of nearly all of it was apparently not to delight the senses but to

Cave Drawings at Lascaux, France. On the left are characteristic examples of the realism of Cro-Magnon man's art. On the right, a view of the entrance to the caves.

make easier the struggle for existence by increasing the supply of animals useful for food. The artist himself was not an aesthete but a magician, and his art was a form of magic designed to promote the hunter's success. In this purpose lay its chief significance and the foundation of most of its special qualities. It suggests, for example, the real reason why game animals were almost the exclusive subjects of the great murals and why plant life and inanimate objects were seldom represented. It aids us in understanding Cro-Magnon man's neglect of finished paintings and his predominant interest in the process of making them.

Upper Paleolithic culture came to an untimely end about 10,000 B.C. Internal decay, exemplified by the decline of art, seems to have been one of the causes. A more obvious and doubtless more effective cause was partial destruction of the food supply. As the last great glacier retreated farther and farther northward, the climate of southern Europe became too warm for the reindeer, and they gradually migrated to the shores of the Baltic. The mammoth, whether for the same or for different reasons, became extinct. Representatives of the magnificent Cro-Magnon breed probably followed the reindeer northward, but apparently they did not continue their cultural achievements.

5. NEOLITHIC CULTURE

The last stage of preliterate culture is known as the Neolithic period, or the New Stone Age. The name is applied because stone weapons and tools were now generally made by grinding and polishing instead of by chipping or fracturing as in the preceding periods. The bearers of Neolithic culture were new varieties of modern man who poured into Africa and southern Europe from western Asia. Since no evidence exists of their later extermination or wholesale migration, they must be regarded as the immediate ancestors of most of the peoples now living in Europe.

The meaning of the term Neolithic

It is impossible to fix exact dates for the Neolithic period. The culture was not well established in Europe until about 3000 B.C., though it certainly originated earlier. There is evidence that it existed in Egypt as far back as 5000 B.C., and that it probably began at an equally early date in southwestern Asia. There is also variation in the dates of its ending. It was superseded in the Nile valley by the first literate civilization soon after the year 4000.[2] Except on the island of Crete it did not come to an end anywhere in Europe before 2000, and in northern Europe much later still. In a few regions of the world it has not terminated yet. The natives of some islands of the Pacific, the Arctic regions of North America, and the jungles of Brazil are still in the Neolithic culture stage except for a few customs acquired from explorers and missionaries.

The varying dates of the Neolithic stage

In many respects the New Stone Age was the most significant in the history of the world thus far. The level of material progress rose to new heights. Neolithic man had a better mastery of his environment than any of his predecessors. He was less likely to perish from a shift in climatic conditions or from the failure of some part of his food supply. This decided advantage was the result primarily of the development of agriculture and the domestication of animals. Whereas all of the men who had lived heretofore were mere food-gatherers, Neolithic man was a *food-producer*. Tilling the soil and keeping flocks and herds provided him with much more dependable food resources and at times yielded him a surplus. These circumstances made possible a more rapid increase of population, promoted a settled existence, and fostered the growth of institutions. Such were the elements of a great social and economic revolution whose importance it would be impossible to exaggerate.

The Neolithic revolution

The new culture also derives significance from the fact that it was the first to be distributed over the *entire* world. Although some earlier cultures, especially those of Neanderthal and Cro-Magnon men, were widely dispersed, they were confined chiefly to the accessible mainland areas of the Old World. Neolithic man penetrated into every habitable area of the earth's surface—from Arctic wastes

The wide diffusion of the Neolithic culture

---

[2] All dates in Egyptian history prior to 2000 are approximations and may represent a margin of error of several centuries.

to the jungles of the tropics. He apparently made his way from a number of centers of origin to every nook and cranny of both hemispheres. He traveled incredible distances by water as well as by land, and eventually occupied every major island of the oceans, no matter how remote.

Importance of the Neolithic migrations

The historian would have difficulty in overestimating the importance of the Neolithic migrations. The net result was that they distributed a similar pattern of culture over the entire world. The few elements of earlier cultures which had managed to survive were almost completely inundated. Their disappearance means that we now have no way of discovering more than a small part of what went on in Paleolithic man's mind—whether he believed that government is an evil or that private property is sacred or that the world was created out of nothing. The fact that we find particular notions in the primitive mind of today does not prove that they are inseparable from the blood and sinew of the species, for it is necessary to remember that all existing primitive races are the beneficiaries or the victims of a common heritage.

New tools and technical skills

Migration over long distances was not the only example of Neolithic man's achievements. He developed the arts of knitting, of spinning, and of weaving cloth. He made the first pottery and knew how to produce fire artificially by friction. He built houses of wood and sun-dried mud. Toward the end of the period he discovered the possibilities of metals, and a few implements of copper and gold were added to his stock. Since nothing was yet known of the arts of smelting and refining, the use of metals was limited to the more malleable ones occasionally found in the pure state in the form of nuggets.

But the real foundation stones of the Neolithic culture were the domestication of animals and the development of agriculture. Without these it is inconceivable that the culture would have attained the complexity it did. More than anything else they made possible a settled mode of existence and the growth of villages and social

Neolithic Dwellings. Examples shown are restorations of Swiss lake dwellings. They were commonly erected on poles or stilts for purposes of defense.

institutions. The first animal to be domesticated is generally thought to have been the dog, on the assumption that he would be continually hanging around the hunter's camp to pick up bones and scraps of meat. Eventually it would be discovered that he could be put to use in hunting, or possibly in guarding the camp. After achieving success in domesticating the dog, Neolithic man would logically turn his attention to other animals, especially to those he used for food. Before the period ended, at least five species—the cow, the dog, the goat, the sheep, and the pig—had been made to serve his needs. Not all of them in all parts of the world, however. The Neolithic tribes of the New World domesticated no animals at all, except the hairless dog in some parts of Mexico, the llama and the alpaca in the Andean highland, and the guinea pig and the turkey in a few other regions.

The exact spot where agriculture originated has never been positively determined. All we know is that wild grasses which were probably the ancestors of the cereal grains have been found in a number of places. Types of wheat grow wild in Asia Minor, in the Caucasus, and in Mesopotamia. Wild ancestors of barley have been reported from North Africa, from Persia, from Asia Minor, and from Turkestan. Though it is probable that these were the first crops of Neolithic agriculture, they were by no means the only ones. Millet, vegetables, and numerous fruits were also grown. Flax was cultivated in the Old World for its textile fiber, and in some localities the growing of the poppy for opium had already begun. In the New World maize (Indian corn) was the only cereal crop, but the American Indians cultivated numerous other products, including tobacco, beans, squashes, pumpkins, and potatoes.

Historically, the most important feature of Neolithic culture was probably the development of institutions. An institution may be defined as a combination of group beliefs and activities organized in a relatively permanent fashion for the purpose of fulfilling some group need. It ordinarily includes a body of customs and traditions, a code of rules and standards, and physical extensions such as buildings, punitive devices, and facilities for communication and indoctrination. Since man is a social being, some of these elements probably existed from earliest times, but institutions in their fully developed form seem to have been an achievement of the Neolithic Age.

One of the most ancient of human institutions is the family. Sociologists do not agree upon how it should be defined. Historically, however, the family has always meant a more or less permanent unit composed of parents and their offspring, which serves the purposes of care of the young, division of labor, acquisition and transmission of property, and preservation and transmission of beliefs and customs. The family is not now, and never has been, exclusively biological in character. Like most institutions, it has evolved through a

Importance of agriculture and the domestication of animals

Neolithic Flint Sickles

The beginning of agriculture

The nature of institutions

Definition of the family

15

long period of changing conventions which have given it a variety of functions and forms. The family during Neolithic times appears to have existed in both polygamous and monogamous forms.

The nature of primitive religion; rites and ceremonies

A second institution developed in more complex form by Neolithic man was religion. On account of its infinite variations, it is hard to define, but perhaps the following would be accepted as an accurate definition of the institution in at least its basic character: "Religion is everywhere an expression in one form or another of a sense of dependence on a power outside ourselves, a power which we may speak of as a spiritual or moral power." [3] Modern anthropologists emphasize the fact that early religion was not so much a matter of belief as a matter of rites. For the most part, the rites came first; the myths, dogmas, and theologies were later rationalizations. Primitive man was universally dependent upon nature—on the regular succession of the seasons, on the rain falling when it should, on the growth of plants and the reproduction of animals. Unless he performed sacrifices and rites these natural phenomena, according to his notion, would not occur. For this reason he developed rainmaking ceremonies in which water was sprinkled on ears of corn to imitate the falling of the rain. The ceremonial dances of the American Indians often had a similar import. The members of a whole village or even a whole tribe would attire themselves in animal skins and mimic the habits and activities of some species they depended upon for food. They apparently had a vague feeling that by imitating the life pattern of the species they were helping to guarantee its continuance.

The element of fear

But there was also another element conspicuously present in primitive religion. This was the element of fear. Modern primitive men, at least, live in an almost constant state of alarm and dread. As an old Eskimo medicine man said to the explorer Knud Rasmussen: "We do not believe; we fear." [4] Everything strange and unfamiliar is fraught with danger. The savage fears not only sickness and death but also hunger, drought, storms, the spirits of the dead, and the animals he has killed.

Ceremonies to ward off evil

It follows that a large part of primitive man's religion consists of ceremonial precautions to ward off evil. For example, no savage will risk swimming across a dangerous river without first endeavoring by prayers or incantations to win its favor. An Eskimo who has killed a polar bear must present it with tools and weapons pleasing to it; if the bear is a female, women's knives and needle cases are given. Bestowal of these gifts is considered necessary to appease the wrath of the bear's soul and keep it from wreaking damage. In West Africa, the hunter who has killed a hippopotamus disembowels it, strips himself naked, crawls inside the carcass, and bathes his entire

---

[3] A. R. Radcliffe-Brown, *Structure and Function in Primitive Society,* p. 157.
[4] Lucien Lévy-Bruhl, *Primitives and the Supernatural,* p. 22.

body with the animal's blood. Throughout the procedure he prays to the spirit of the hippo that it will bear him no ill-will for having killed it, and that it will not incite other hippopotami to attack his canoe in revenge.[5]

Still another of the great institutions to be developed by Neolithic man was the state. By way of definition, the state may be described as an organized society occupying a definite territory and possessing an authoritative government independent of external control. The essence of the state is sovereignty, or the power to make and administer laws and to preserve social order by punishing men for infractions of those laws. A state must not be confused with a nation. The latter is an ethnic concept, used to designate a people bound together by ties of language, customs, or racial origin or by common memories or a belief in a common destiny. A nation may or may not occupy a definite territory and does not possess the element of sovereignty. It may not even have an independent government, as for example, the Poles during the long period when they were under Austrian, German, and Russian rule. At the present time most nations are also states, but this condition has resulted largely from the breaking up of empires in the twentieth century.

Except in time of crisis, the state does not exist in a very large proportion of preliterate societies—a fact which probably indicates that its genesis was rather late in the Neolithic culture stage. Most primitive communities have no permanent system of courts, no police agencies, and no governments with coercive power. Custom takes the place of law, the blood-feud is the mode of administering justice, and there is very little conception of crime against the community. To primitive man, offenses are mostly what we call "torts," or private wrongs between individuals or families, in the punishment of which no public authority takes part. The acceptance of *wergeld*, or blood-money, is a common practice, and even felonies such as murder are regarded merely as offenses against the victim's family. Since the family of the victim has been deprived of a valuable member, the proper satisfaction is a money payment. If this is not offered, the family may retaliate in kind by killing the offender or a member of the offender's family.

The origin of the state was probably the consequence of a variety of factors. We are certainly justified in assuming the development of agriculture to have been one of the most important. In sections like the Nile valley, where a large population lived by cultivating intensively a limited area of fertile soil, a high degree of social organization was absolutely essential. Ancient customs would not suffice for the definition of rights and duties in such a society, with its high standard of living, its unequal distribution of wealth, and its wide scope for the clash of personal interests. New measures of so-

[5] Lucien Lévy-Bruhl, *How Natives Think*, p. 238.

cial control would become necessary, which could scarcely be achieved in any other way than by setting up a government of sovereign authority and submitting to it; in other words, by establishing a state.

Origin of the state in military causes

A number of ancient states evidently owed their origin to war activities. That is, they were founded for purposes of conquest, for defense against invasion, or to make possible the expulsion of an invader from the country. The Hebrew monarchy seems to have been a product of the first of these reasons. With the war for the conquest of Canaan none too successful, the Hebrew people besought their leader Samuel to give them a king, that they might be "like all the nations" with a powerful ruler to keep them in order and to lead them to victory in battle. One has only to observe the effects of modern warfare, both offensive and defensive, in enlarging the powers of government to see how similar influences might have operated to bring the state into existence in the first place.

Other causes

Other factors undoubtedly contributed to the origin of states in various areas. A likelihood exists that one of these was religion. Medicine men, or shamans, frequently exercise a kind of sovereignty. Though they may command no physical force, their power to impose religious penalties and to strike terror into the hearts of their followers gives them a degree of coercive authority. In all probability some of them made themselves kings. It is conceivable that in other cases the state arose from the natural expansion of group life, with its resulting complexities and conflicts. As the population increased in limited areas, customary law and family administration of justice proved inadequate, and political organization became necessary as a substitute. In the domain of politics as in every other sphere concerned with social origins, no one explanation can be made to accommodate all the facts.

6. CULTURES AND CIVILIZATIONS

Culture defined

The stages of man's advancement described thus far have been referred to as *cultures*. This word is commonly used to designate societies or periods which have not yet attained to a knowledge of writing and whose general level of achievement is comparatively primitive. But the term has other meanings. It is sometimes applied to intellectual and artistic accomplishments, to literature, art, music, philosophy, and science. It is employed by some historians to designate the whole complex pattern of ideas, achievements, traditions, and characteristics of a nation or empire at a particular time.

The term *civilization* also carries a variety of meanings. The German philosopher of history Oswald Spengler referred to civilizations as decadent phases of highly developed cultures. When a great people or empire was in its prime, he characterized its social and intellectual pattern as a culture. When it passed its prime and became ossified and stagnant, he described it as a "civilization." The noted British historian, Arnold J. Toynbee, also sees world history as a succession of cultural units. But he designates each of the primary ones, throughout its development, as a "civilization." He distinguishes between civilizations and "primitive societies" largely on a quantitative basis. The latter are "relatively short-lived, are restricted to relatively narrow geographical areas, and embrace relatively small numbers of human beings." [6]

The term *civilization* has still another meaning. Since each culture has peculiar features of its own, and since some cultures are more highly developed than others, we can speak quite properly of a civilization as an advanced culture. We can say that a culture deserves to be called a civilization when it has reached a stage in which writing has come to be used to a considerable extent, some progress has been made in the arts and sciences, and political, social and economic institutions have developed sufficiently to conquer at least some of the problems of order, security, and efficiency in a complex society. This is the sense in which the term will be used throughout the remainder of this book.

7. FACTORS RESPONSIBLE FOR THE ORIGIN AND GROWTH OF CIVILIZATIONS

What causes contribute to the rise of civilizations? What factors account for their growth? Why do some civilizations reach much higher levels of development than others? Inquiry into these questions is one of the chief pursuits of social scientists. Some decide that factors of geography are the most important. Others stress economic resources, food supply, contact with older civilizations, and so on. Usually a variety of causes is acknowledged, but one is commonly singled out as deserving special emphasis.

Probably the most popular of the theories accounting for the rise of advanced cultures are those which come under the heading of geography. Prominent among them is the hypothesis of climate. The climatic theory, advocated in days past by such notables as Aristotle and Montesquieu, received its most eloquent exposition in the writings of an American geographer, Ellsworth Huntington. Huntington acknowledged the importance of other factors, but he insisted that no nation, ancient or modern, rose to the highest cultural status except under the influence of a climatic stimulus. He described the ideal climate as one in which the mean temperature seldom falls below the mental optimum of 38 degrees or rises above the physical optimum of 64 degrees. But temperature is not alone important. Moisture is also essential, and the humidity should average about 75 per cent. Finally, the weather must not be uniform: cy-

The meaning of civilization

Civilizations as advanced cultures

Origin and growth of civilizations variously explained

Geographic theories: the climatic hypothesis

[6] D. C. Somervell (ed.), A. J. Toynbee's *A Study of History*, I, 35.

clonic storms, or ordinary storms resulting in weather changes from day to day, must have sufficient frequency and intensity to clear the atmosphere every once in a while and produce those sudden variations in temperature which seem to be necessary to exhilarate and revitalize man.[7]

Much can be said in favor of the climatic hypothesis. Certainly some parts of the earth's surface, under existing atmospheric conditions, could never cradle a superior culture. They are either too hot, too humid, too cold, or too dry. Such is the case in regions beyond the Arctic Circle, the larger desert areas, and the jungles of India, Central America, and Brazil. Evidence is available, moreover, to show that some of these places have not always suffered under climate so adverse as that now prevalent. Various inhospitable sections of Asia, Africa, and America contain unmistakable traces of more salubrious days in the past. Here and there are the ruins of towns and cities where now the supply of water seems totally inadequate. Roads traverse deserts which at present are impassable. Bridges span river beds which have had no water in them for years.

The best-known evidences of the cultural importance of climatic change are those pertaining to the civilization of the Mayas. Mayan civilization flourished in Guatemala, Honduras, and on the peninsula of Yucatan in Mexico from about 400 to 1500 A.D. Numbered among its achievements were the making of paper, the invention of the zero, the perfection of a solar calendar, and the development of a system of writing partly phonetic. Great cities were built; marked progress was made in astronomy; and sculpture and architecture were advanced to high levels. At present most of the civilization is in ruins. No doubt many factors conspired to produce its untimely end, including deadly wars between tribes, but climatic change was also probably involved. The remains of most of the great cities are now surrounded by jungles, where malaria is prevalent and agriculture difficult. That the Mayan civilization or any other could have grown to maturity under conditions like these is hard to believe.

Related to the climatic hypothesis is the soil-exhaustion theory. A group of modern conservationists has hit upon this theory as the sole explanation of the decay and collapse of the great empires of the past and as a universal threat to the nations of the present and future. At best it is only a partial hypothesis, since it offers no theory of the birth or growth of civilizations. But its proponents seem to think that almost any environment not ruined by man is capable of nourishing a superior culture. The great deserts and barren areas of the earth, they maintain, are not natural but artificial, created by man through bad grazing and farming practices. Conservationists discover innumerable evidences of waste and neglect that have

Evidence in favor of the climatic hypothesis

The Mayan civilization

The soil-exhaustion theory

[7] Ellsworth Huntington, *Civilization and Climate*, 3d ed., pp. 220–23.

wrought havoc in such areas as Mesopotamia, Palestine, Greece, Italy, China, and Mexico. The majestic civilizations that once flourished in these countries were ultimately doomed by the simple fact that their soil would no longer provide sufficient food for the population. As a consequence, the more intelligent and enterprising citizens migrated elsewhere and left their inferiors to sink slowly into stagnation and apathy. But the fate that overtook the latter was not of their making alone. The whole nation had been guilty of plundering the forests, mining the soil, and pasturing flocks on the land until the grass was eaten down to the very roots. Among the tragic results were floods alternating with droughts, since there were no longer any forests to regulate the run-off of rain or snow. At the same time, much of the top soil on the close-cropped or excessively cultivated hillsides was blown away or washed into the rivers to be carried eventually down to the sea. The damage done was irreparable, since about 300 years are required to produce a single inch of top soil.

The most recent hypothesis of the origin of civilizations is Toynbee's adversity theory. According to this theory, conditions of hardship or adversity are the real causes which have brought into existence superior cultures. Such conditions constitute a *challenge* which not only stimulates men to try to overcome it but generates additional energy for new achievements. The challenge may take the form of a desert, a jungle area, rugged topography, or a grudging soil. The Hebrews and Arabs were challenged by the first, the Indians of the Andean Highland by the last. The challenge may also take the form of defeat in war or even enslavement. Thus the Carthaginians, as a result of defeat in the First Punic War, were stimulated to conquer a new empire in Spain; centuries later, Oriental captives enslaved by the Romans strengthened and propagated their religious heritage until Rome itself succumbed to it. In general it is true that the greater the challenge, the greater the achievement; nevertheless, there are limits. The challenge must not be too severe, else it will deal a crushing blow to all who attempt to meet it.

The adversity theory of Arnold J. Toynbee

8. WHY THE EARLIEST CIVILIZATIONS BEGAN WHERE THEY DID

Which of the great civilizations of antiquity was the oldest is still a sharply debated question. The judgment of some scholars inclines toward the Egyptian, though a larger body of authority supports the claims of the Tigris-Euphrates valley. These two areas were geographically the most favored sections in the general region of the so-called Fertile Crescent. The Fertile Crescent is that wide belt of productive land which extends northwestward from the Persian Gulf and then down the Mediterranean coast almost to Egypt. It

The Nile and the Tigris-Euphrates

21

forms a semicircle around the northern part of the Arabian desert. Here larger numbers of artifacts of undoubted antiquity have been found than in any other sections of the Near Orient. Furthermore, progress in the arts and sciences had reached unparalleled heights in both of these areas as early as 3000 B.C., when most of the rest of the world was steeped in ignorance. If the foundations of this progress were really laid elsewhere, it seems strange that they should have disappeared, although of course there is no telling what the spade of the archaeologist may uncover in the future.

Of the several causes responsible for the earliest rise of civilizations in the Nile and Tigris-Euphrates valleys, geographic factors would seem to have been the most important. Both regions had the notable advantage of a limited area of exceedingly fertile soil. Although it extended for a distance of 750 miles, the valley of the Nile was not more than ten miles wide in some places, and its maximum width was thirty-one miles. The total area was less than 10,000 square miles, or roughly the equivalent of the State of Maryland. Through countless centuries the river had carved a vast canyon or trench, bounded on either side by cliffs ranging in height from a few hundred to a thousand feet. The floor of the canyon was covered with a rich alluvial deposit, which in places reached a depth in excess of thirty feet. The soil was of such amazing productivity that as many as three crops per year could be raised on the same land. This broad and fertile canyon constituted the cultivable area of ancient Egypt. Here several million people were concentrated. In Roman times the population of the valley approximated seven million, and probably it was not much smaller in the days of the Pharaohs. Beyond the cliffs there was nothing but desert—the Libyan desert on the west and the Arabian on the east.

In the Tigris-Euphrates valley similar conditions prevailed. As in Egypt, the rivers provided excellent facilities for inland transportation and were alive with fish and waterfowl for a plentiful supply of protein food. The distance between the Tigris and Euphrates rivers at one point was less than twenty miles, and nowhere in the lower valley did it exceed forty-five miles. Since the surrounding country was desert, the people were kept from scattering over too great an expanse of territory. The result, as in Egypt, was the welding of the inhabitants into a compact society, under conditions that facilitated a ready interchange of ideas and discoveries. As the population increased, the need for agencies of social control became ever more urgent. Numbered among such agencies were government, schools, legal and moral codes, and institutions for the production and distribution of wealth. At the same time conditions of living became more complex and artificial and necessitated the keeping of records of things accomplished and the perfection of new techniques. Among the consequences were the invention of writing, the practice of smelting metals, the performance of mathematical operations,

A limited area of fertile soil in the Nile valley

A similar condition in Mesopotamia

22

THE FERTILE CRESCENT

and the development of astronomy and the rudiments of physics. With these achievements the first great ordeal of civilization was passed.

Climatic influences also played their part in both regions. The atmosphere of Egypt is dry and invigorating. Even the hottest days produce none of the oppressive discomfort which is often experienced during the summer seasons in more northern countries. The mean temperature in winter varies from 56 degrees in the Delta to 66 degrees in the valley above. The summer mean is 83 degrees and an occasional maximum of 122 is reached, but the nights are always cool and the humidity is extremely low. Except in the Delta, rainfall occurs in negligible quantities, but the deficiency of moisture is counteracted by the annual inundations of the Nile from July to October. Also very significant from the historical standpoint is the total absence of malaria in Upper Egypt, while even in the coastal region it is practically unknown. The direction of the prevailing winds is likewise a favorable factor of more than trivial importance. For more than three-quarters of the year the wind comes from the north, blowing in opposition to the force of the Nile current. The effect of this is to simplify immensely the problem of transportation. Upstream traffic, with the propulsion of the wind to counteract the force of the river, presents no greater difficulty than down-

Climatic advantages in Egypt

23

stream traffic. This factor in ancient times must have been of enormous advantage in promoting communication among a numerous people, some of whom were separated by hundreds of miles.

Climatic conditions in Mesopotamia do not seem to have been quite so favorable as in Egypt. The summer heat is more relentless; the humidity is somewhat higher; and tropical diseases take their toll. Nevertheless, the torrid winds from the Indian Ocean, while enervating to human beings, blow over the valley at just the right season to bring the fruit of the date palm to a full ripeness. More than anything else the excellent yield of dates, the dietary staple of the Near Orient, encouraged the settlement of large numbers of people in the valley of the two rivers. Finally, the melting of the snows in the mountains of the north produced an annual flooding of the Babylonian plain similar to that in Egypt. The effect was to enrich the soil with moisture and to cover it over with a layer of mud of unusual fertility. At the same time, it should be noted that water conditions in Mesopotamia were less dependable than in Egypt. Floods were sometimes catastrophic, a factor which left its mark on the development of culture.

Climatic influences in Mesopotamia

Most significant of all of the geographic influences, however, was the fact that the scanty rainfall in both regions provided a spur to initiative and inventive skill. In spite of the yearly floods of the rivers there was insufficient moisture left in the soil to produce abundant harvests. A few weeks after the waters had receded, the earth was baked to a stony hardness. Irrigation was accordingly necessary if full advantage was to be taken of the richness of the soil. As a result, in both Egypt and Mesopotamia elaborate systems of dams and irrigation canals were constructed as long ago as five thousand years. The mathematical skill, engineering ability, and social cooperation necessary for the development of these projects were available for other uses and so fostered the achievement of civilization.

The importance of scanty rainfall as a spur to initiative

Which of the two civilizations, the Egyptian or the Mesopotamian, was the older? Until recently most historians appeared to take it for granted that the Egyptian was the older. They based their assumption upon the conclusions of two of the world's most renowned Egyptologists, James H. Breasted and Alexandre Moret. Between the two world wars of the twentieth century, however, facts were unearthed which seemed to prove a substantial Mesopotamian influence in the Nile valley as early as 3500 B.C. This influence was exemplified by the use of cylinder seals, methods of building construction, art motifs, and elements of a system of writing of undoubted Mesopotamian origin. That such achievements could have radiated into Egypt from the Tigris-Euphrates valley at so early a date indicated beyond doubt that the Mesopotamian civilization was one of vast antiquity. It did not necessarily prove, though, that it was older than the Egyptian. For the achievements mentioned were not taken

Uncertainty as to which civilization was older

over and copied slavishly. Instead, the Egyptians modified them radically to suit their own culture pattern. On the basis of this evidence, it would seem that the only conclusion which can be safely drawn is that both civilizations were very old, and that to a large extent they developed concurrently.

SELECTED READINGS

· *Items so designated are available in paperbound editions.*

ANTHROPOLOGICAL AND ARCHAEOLOGICAL WORKS

· Boas, Franz, *The Mind of Primitive Man*, New York, 1927 (Free Press, 1965).

Breasted, James H., *The Dawn of Conscience*, New York, 1934. An excellent treatise on the origin of religious and ethical concepts.

———, *History of Egypt*, New York, 1912 (Bantam). Still one of the best.

· Ceram, C. W., *Gods, Graves and Scholars*, New York, 1951. Popular but
· scholarly.

· Childe, V. G., *Man Makes Himself*, London, 1936 (Mentor, 1952).

· ———, *New Light on the Most Ancient East*, New York, 1934 (Evergreen).

· Dawson, Christopher, *The Age of the Gods*, New York, 1937.

Herskovits, M. J., *Man and His Works*, New York, 1948. One of the best introductions to anthropology.

Lévy-Bruhl, Lucien, *How Natives Think*, London, 1926.

———, *Primitives and the Supernatural*, New York, 1935. A superlative study of primitive "Logic."

· Linton, Ralph, *The Tree of Culture*, New York, 1955 (Vintage, abr.).

MacCurdy, G. G., *Human Origins*, New York, 1924, 2 vols.

Magoffin, R. V. D., and Davis, E. C., *The Romance of Archaeology*, New York, 1929.

· Malinowski, Bronislaw, *Crime and Custom in Savage Society*, New York, 1951 (Littlefield, 1959). The most provocative and valuable study on the subject.

Osborn, H. F., *Men of the Old Stone Age*, New York, 1915.

· Radcliffe-Brown, A. R., *Structure and Function in Primitive Society*, Glencoe, Ill., 1952 (Free Press, 1952). Stimulating and informative.

· Radin, Paul, *Primitive Religion*, New York, 1937 (Dover, 1957).

Renard, Georges, *Life and Work in Prehistoric Times*, New York, 1929.

INTERPRETATIONS OF HISTORY

Butterfield, Herbert, *History and Human Relations*, New York, 1952.

· Clough, Shepard B., *The Rise and Fall of Civilization*, New York, 1951 (Columbia University Press, 1961).

· Fox, Edward W., *History in Geographic Perspective*, New York, 1971 (Norton Library).

Kahler, Erich, *The Meaning of History*, New York, 1964.

· Muller, H. J., *The Uses of the Past*, New York, 1952 (Galaxy).

· Nevins, Allan, *The Gateway to History*, New York, 1938 (Anchor, rev.).

· Somervell, D. C., ed., A. J. Toynbee, *A Study of History*, New York, 1947–57, 2 vols. (Galaxy, 6 vols.). An excellent abridgment of a monumental work.

Spengler, Oswald, *The Decline of the West*, 1-vol. ed., New York, 1934. The gist of his philosophy is contained in the Introduction.

Ancient Civilizations of the Near Orient

4000 B.C.	**POLITICAL**	**CULTURAL**

POLITICAL

CULTURAL

Pre-dynastic period in Egypt, *ca.* 4000–3100

Solar calendar in Egypt, *ca.* 4000

Sumerian supremacy in Mesopotamia, *ca.* 4000–2000

Egyptian hieroglyphic writing, *ca.* 3500

Development of irrigation, mathematics, rudimentary astronomy in Egypt and Mesopotamia, *ca.* 3500–2500

Old Kingdom in Egypt, *ca.* 3100–2200

Cuneiform writing, *ca.* 3200

Invention of principle of alphabet in Egypt, *ca.* 3000

Minoan-Mycenaean civilization, *ca.* 3000–1000

Construction of great pyramids in Egypt, *ca.* 2700

Philosophy in Egypt, *ca.* 2500

Middle Kingdom in Egypt, 2052–1786

Hittite empire, 2000–1200
Old Babylonian kingdom, 1950–1650
Hyksos conquer Egypt, 1786–1575
Kassites conquer Babylonians, *ca.* 1650
The Empire in Egypt, 1575–1087

Code of Hammurabi, *ca.* 1790

Egyptian temple architecture, 1580–1090
Development of alphabet by Phoenicians, *ca.* 1500

Hebrew conquest of Canaan, *ca.* 1300–900

Realistic sculpture of Assyrians, 1300–600

United Hebrew Monarchy, 1025–935
Secession of Ten Tribes of Israel, 935
Kingdom of Israel, 935–722
Kingdom of Judah, 935–586

Assyrian empire, 750–612
Assyrian conquest of Egypt, 670

Division of day into hours and minutes, *ca.* 600

Chaldean empire, 612–539
Babylonian captivity, 586–539
Persian empire, 559–330
Persian conquest of Egypt, 525
Persian Empire under Darius, 522–486

Calculation of length of year, *ca.* 600
Deuteronomic Code, *ca.* 600

Book of Job, *ca.* 500

*Left margin dates:*
4000 B.C.
3000 B.C.
2000 B.C.
1500 B.C.
1000 B.C.
500 B.C.

Dates are B.C. unless given as A.D.

ECONOMIC

Development of serfdom in Mesopotamia
and in Egypt, *ca.* 3500

Large-scale industry in Egypt and Crete,
ca. 2000

Slavery in Egypt, *ca.* 1580
Introduction of use of iron by Hittites,
ca. 1500

World trade of Phoenicians, *ca.* 1000–500

Slavery in Assyria, *ca.* 750

Invention of coinage by Lydians, *ca.* 600
World trade of Chaldeans, 600–500

Royal Road of Persians, *ca.* 500

RELIGIOUS

Creation and Flood epics in Mesopotamia, *ca.* 4000
Egyptian sun worship, *ca.* 3500

Ethical religion in Egypt, *ca.* 3000

Egyptian belief in personal immortality,
ca. 2500

Demon worship and witchcraft in Babylonia, *ca.* 1900

Religious revolution of Ikhnaton, 1375

Hebrew worship of Yahweh, *ca.* 1000

Ten Commandments, *ca.* 700
Prophetic Revolution, 800–600
Hebrew doctrine of universal monotheism, *ca.* 600
Astral religion of Chaldeans, 600–500
Divination and astrology, 600–500
Zoroastrianism, *ca.* 600–300
Babylonian Captivity of Jews, 586–539

Mithraism, *ca.* 300 B.C. 275 A.D.
Gnosticism, *ca.* 100 B.C.–100 A.D.
Rise of Christianity, *ca.* 25 A.D.

4000
B.C.

3000
B.C.

2000
B.C.

1500
B.C.

1000
B.C.

500
B.C.

CHAPTER **2**

The Egyptian Civilization

How great is that which thou has done, O lord of gods. Thy plans and thy counsels are those which come to pass throughout. Thou sentest me forth in valor, thy strength was with me. No land stood before me, at the mention of thee. I overthrew those who invaded my boundary, prostrated in their place. . . . It was ordained because of thy victory-bringing commands, it was given because of thy kingdom-bestowing power.

—Utterance of King Ramses III before his father, Amon-Re, ruler of the gods, from The Great Inscription in the Second Court relief in Medinet Habu temple

Although the Egyptian civilization was not necessarily the oldest in the ancient world, it was certainly of great antiquity. As we have seen, its origins went back to at least 4000 B.C. Besides, somewhat more is known about its accomplishments than about those of most other peoples. For these reasons the Egyptian civilization may be considered a kind of archetype or pattern of all the civilizations of the Near Orient.

I. POLITICAL HISTORY UNDER THE PHARAOHS

The ancient history of Egypt is commonly divided into three periods: the Old Kingdom, the Middle Kingdom, and the Empire. Even before the Old Kingdom some cultural beginnings had been made. A system of laws based upon customs had been developed and the initial stage of a system of writing. More important was the invention of the first solar calendar in the history of man. This calendar was apparently put into effect about the year 4200 B.C. It was based upon the annual reappearance of Sirius, the "Dog Star," and it provided for twelve months of thirty days each, with five feast days added at the end of the year.

Stages of Egyptian history

29

About 3100 B.C. Egypt was combined into a single unit known to historians as the Old Kingdom. From 3100 B.C. to 2200 B.C. six dynasties ruled the country. Each was headed by a "Pharaoh," from the Egyptian "per-o" meaning "great house" or "royal house." He was considered to be the son of the great sun god and he was forbidden to marry outside of his immediate family, lest the divine blood be contaminated. Moreover, his authority was limited by the ancient law. He was not above the law but subject to it. No separation of church and state existed. The Pharaoh's chief subordinates were the priests, and he himself was the chief priest.

The government of the Old Kingdom was founded upon a policy of peace and nonaggression. In this respect it was almost unique among ancient states. The Pharaoh had no standing army, nor was there anything that could be called a national militia. Each subdivision had its local militia, but it was commanded by the civil officials, and when called into active service it generally devoted its energies to labor on the public works. In case of a threat of invasion the various local units were assembled at the call of the Pharaoh and placed under the command of one of his civil subordinates. At no other time did the head of the government have a military force at his disposal. The Egyptians of the Old Kingdom were content for the most part to work out their own destinies and to let other nations alone. The reasons for this attitude are to be found in the protected position of their country, in their possession of land of inexhaustible fertility, and in the fact that their state was a product of cooperative need instead of being grounded in exploitation.

After a solid millennium of peace and relative prosperity the Old Kingdom came to an end about 2200 B.C. Several causes appear to have been responsible: the usurpation of power by the local rulers; the growth of individualism; and the financial burdens imposed upon the people by Pharaohs with grandiose schemes for national development. The period which followed is called the Feudal Age. Save for intervals of order and progress it was marked by anarchy, aggrandizement of the power of the nobles, social revolution of the masses, and invasion by desert and barbarian tribes. It did not end until the rise of the Eleventh Dynasty about 2050 B.C.—an event which ushered in the next great stage in Egyptian history, which is known as the Middle Kingdom.

The government of the Middle Kingdom was notably weaker than that of the Old Kingdom. Dynasties of Pharaohs continued a nominal rule, but extensive authority gravitated into the hands of the subordinates and nobles of lesser rank. In time they, too, were assailed by the masses, with the result that after 2000 B.C. the Pharaohs of the Twelfth Dynasty were able to regain a measure of their former power. The people themselves were rewarded by appointments to government positions and by grants of land and vested rights in particular occupations. The whole population, regardless of birth or rank, appears to have been accorded privileges hitherto reserved for the few. For this reason the government of the Twelfth Dynasty is sometimes referred to as the first democratic kingdom in history. The period of its rule was a golden age of social justice and intellectual achievement, although the forms of theocracy still survived.

With the end of the Twelfth Dynasty, Egypt entered another era of internal chaos and foreign invasion which lasted for more than two centuries, or from 1786 to 1575 B.C. The contemporary records are scanty, but they seem to show that the internal disorder was the result of a counterrevolt of the nobles. The Pharaohs were again reduced to impotence, and much of the social progress of the preceding age was destroyed. About 1750 the land was invaded by the Hyksos, or the "Shepherd Kings," a mixed horde originating in western Asia. Their military prowess is commonly ascribed to the fact that they possessed horses and war chariots, but their victory was certainly made easier by the dissension among the Egyptians themselves. Their rule had profound effects upon Egyptian history. Not only did they familiarize the Egyptians with new methods of warfare; but by providing them with a common grievance in the face of foreign tyranny they also enabled them to forget their differences and unite in a common cause.

Near the end of the seventeenth century the rulers of Upper Egypt launched a revolt against the Hyksos, a movement which was eventually joined by most of the natives of the valley. By 1575 all of the conquerors who had not been killed or enslaved had been driven from the country. The hero of this victory, Ahmose I, founder of the Eighteenth Dynasty, now made himself despot of Egypt. The regime he established was much more highly consolidated than any that had hitherto existed. In the great resurgence of nationalism which had accompanied the struggle against the Hyksos, local patriotism was annihilated, and with it the power of the nobles.

The period which followed the accession of Ahmose is called the period of the Empire. It lasted from 1575 to 1087 B.C., during which time the country was ruled by three dynasties of Pharaohs in succession, the Eighteenth, Nineteenth, and Twentieth. No longer was the prevailing state policy pacific and isolationist; a spirit of aggressive imperialism rapidly pervaded the nation. The causes of this change are not far to seek. The military ardor generated by the successful war against the Hyksos whetted an appetite for further victories. A vast military machine had been created to expel the invader, which proved to be too valuable an adjunct to the Pharaoh's power to be discarded immediately.

The first steps in the direction of the new policy were taken by the immediate successors of Ahmose in making extensive raids into Palestine and claiming sovereignty over Syria. With one of the most formidable armies of ancient times the new Pharaohs speedily annihi-

The invasion of the Hyksos

Expulsion of the Hyksos and founding of the Empire

Ramses II (XIXth Dynasty)

31

lated all opposition in Syria and eventually made themselves masters of a vast domain extending from the Euphrates to the farther cataracts of the Nile. But they never succeeded in welding the conquered peoples into loyal subjects, and weakness was the signal for widespread revolt in Syria. Their successors suppressed the uprising and managed to hold the Empire together for some time, but ultimate disaster could not be averted. More territory had been annexed than could be managed successfully. The influx of wealth into Egypt weakened the national fiber by fostering corruption and luxury, and the constant revolts of the vanquished eventually sapped the strength of the state beyond all hope of recovery. By the twelfth century most of the conquered provinces had been permanently lost.

The government of the Empire

The government of the Empire resembled that of the Old Kingdom, except for the fact that it was more absolute. Military power rather than national unity was now the basis of the Pharaoh's rule. A professional army was always available with which to overawe his subjects. Most of the former nobles now became courtiers or members of the royal bureaucracy under the complete domination of the king. The Pharaoh was not yet a divine-right monarch, but the actual extent of his power had begun to approach that of more modern despots.

The last of the Pharaohs

The last of the great Pharaohs was Ramses III, who ruled from 1182 to 1151 B.C. He was succeeded by a long line of nonentities who inherited his name but not his ability. By the middle of the twelfth century Egypt had fallen prey to numerous ills of barbarian invasion and social decadence. Libyans and Nubians were swarming over the country and gradually debasing cultural standards. About the same time the Egyptians themselves appear to have lost their creative talent; their intellects seem to have been led astray by the seductions of magic and superstition. To win immortality by magic devices was now the commanding interest of men of every class. The process of decline was hastened also by the growing power of the priests, who finally usurped the royal prerogatives and dictated the Pharaoh's decrees.

The downfall of Egypt

From the middle of the tenth century to nearly the end of the eighth a dynasty of Libyan barbarians occupied the throne of the Pharaohs. The Libyans were followed by a line of Ethiopians or Nubians, who came in from the desert regions west of the Upper Nile. In 670 Egypt was conquered by the Assyrians, who succeeded in maintaining their supremacy for only eight years. After the collapse of Assyrian rule in 662 the Egyptians regained their independence, and a brilliant renaissance of culture ensued. It was doomed to an untimely end, however, for in 525 B.C. the country was conquered by the Persians. The ancient civilization was never again revived.

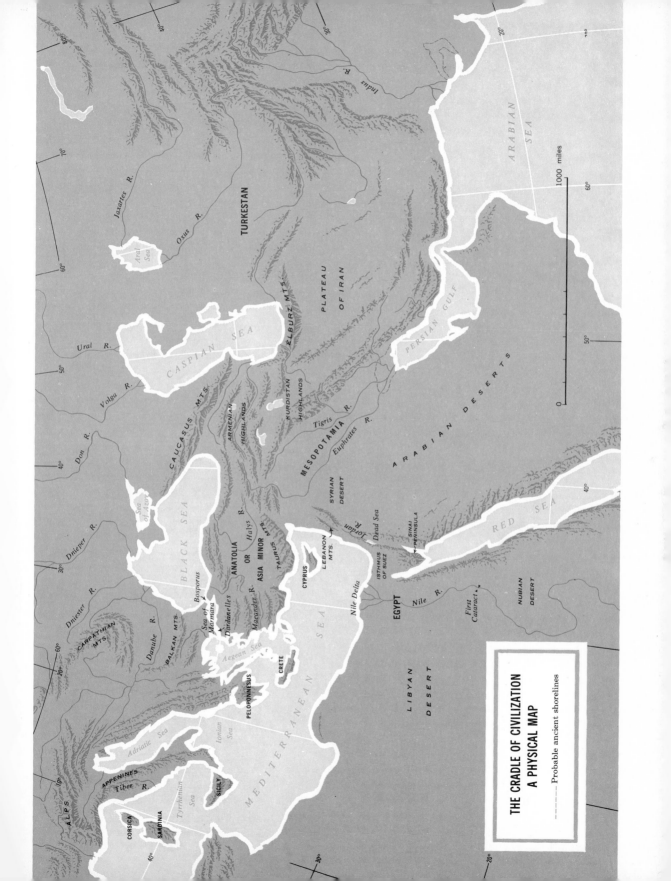

THE CRADLE OF CIVILIZATION
A PHYSICAL MAP

------- Probable ancient shorelines

Egyptian Pottery Jar, *ca.* 3600 B.C. It was filled with food or water and placed in the tomb to provide for the afterlife. (MMA)

An Egyptian Official and His Son. Painted limestone, *ca.* 2500 B.C.

Gold and Inlay Pendant of Princess Sit Hat-Hor Yunet. Egyptian, Twelfth Dynasty.

Farm Hand Plowing. Egyptian tomb figures, *ca.* 1900 B.C.

Jeweled Headdress of Gold, Carnelian, and Glass. Egyptian, 1475 B.C.

Scarab or Beetle-Shaped Charm of a Pharaoh, *ca.* 1395 B.C. The beetle was sacred in ancient Egypt.

Silversmiths Working on a Stand and a Jar. Egyptian, *ca.* 1450 B.C.

A scribe writing on a papyrus roll. Egyptian, *ca.* 1415 B.C.

Painted Wood Shrine Box for Shawabty Figures. *Ca.* 1200 B.C.

Wall painting of an Egyptian house, *ca.* 1400 B.C.

2. EGYPTIAN RELIGION

Religion played a dominant role in the life of the ancient Egyptians, leaving its impress upon almost everything. The art was an expression of religious symbolism. The literature and philosophy were suffused with religious teachings. The government of the Old Kingdom was to a large extent a theocracy, and even the military Pharaohs of the Empire professed to rule in the name of the god. Economic energy and material resources in considerable amounts were squandered in providing elaborate tombs and in maintaining a costly ecclesiastical system.

The importance of religion in Egypt

The religion of the ancient Egyptians evolved through various stages from simple polytheism to philosophic monotheism. In the beginning each city or district appears to have had its local deities, who were guardian gods of the locality or personifications of nature powers. The unification of the country under the Old Kingdom resulted not only in a consolidation of territory but in a fusion of divinities as well. All of the guardian deities were merged into the great sun god Re or Ra. In later times, with the establishment of a Theban dynasty in control of the government, this deity was commonly called Amon or Ammon-Re from the name of the chief god of Thebes. The gods who personified the vegetative powers of nature were fused into a deity called Osiris, who was also the god of the Nile. Throughout Egyptian history these two great powers who ruled the universe, Re and Osiris, vied with each other for supremacy. Other deities, as we shall see, were recognized also, but they occupied a distinctly subordinate place.

The early religious evolution

See color plates at page 64

King Mycerinus and His Queen Salet on his Right. A sculpture of the IVth Dynasty located at Gizeh.

Funerary Papyrus. The scene shows the heart of a princess of the XXIst Dynasty being weighed in a balance before the god Osiris. On the other side of the balance are the symbols for life and truth.

During the period of the Old Kingdom the solar faith, embodied in the worship of Re, was the dominant system of belief. It served as **The solar faith** an official religion whose chief function was to give immortality to the state and to the people collectively. The Pharaoh was the living representative of this faith on earth; through his rule the rule of the god was maintained. But Re was not only a guardian deity. He was in addition the god of righteousness, justice, and truth and the upholder of the moral order of the universe. He offered no spiritual blessings or even material rewards to men as individuals. The solar faith was not a religion for the masses as such, except in so far as their welfare coincided with that of the state.

The cult of Osiris, as we have already observed, began its existence as a nature religion. The god personified the growth of vegetation and the life-giving powers of the Nile. The career of Osiris was **The Osiris cult** wrapped about with an elaborate legend. In the remote past, according to belief, he had been a benevolent ruler, who taught his people agriculture and other practical arts and gave them laws. After a time he was treacherously slain by his wicked brother Set, and his body cut into pieces. His wife Isis, who was also his sister, went in search of the pieces, put them together, and miraculously restored his body to life. The risen god regained his kingdom and continued his beneficent rule for a time, but eventually descended to the nether world to serve as judge of the dead. Horus, his posthumous son, finally grew to manhood and avenged his father's death by killing Set.

Originally this legend seems to have been little more than a nature myth. The death and resurrection of Osiris symbolized the recession of the Nile in the autumn and the coming of the flood in the spring. But in time the Osiris legend began to take on a deeper significance. The human qualities of the deities concerned—the paternal solicitude of Osiris for his subjects, the faithful devotion of his wife and son—appealed to the emotions of the average Egyptian, who was now able to see his own tribulations and triumphs mirrored in the lives of the gods. More important still, the death and resurrection of Osiris came to be regarded as conveying a promise of personal immortality for man. As the god had triumphed over death and the grave, so might also the individual who followed him faithfully inherit everlasting life. Finally, the victory of Horus over Set appeared to foreshadow the ultimate ascendancy of good over evil.

Significance of
the Osiris legend

Egyptian ideas of the hereafter attained their full development in the later history of the Middle Kingdom. For this reason elaborate preparations had to be made to prevent the extinction of one's earthly remains. Not only were bodies mummified but wealthy men left munificent endowments to provide their mummies with food and other essentials. As the religion advanced toward maturity, however, a less naïve conception of the afterlife was adopted. The dead were now believed to appear before Osiris to be judged according to their deeds on earth.

Egyptian ideas of
the hereafter

All of the departed who met the tests included in this system of judgment entered a celestial realm of physical delights and simple pleasures. Here in marshes of lilies and lotus-flowers they would hunt wild geese and quail with never-ending success. Or they might build houses in the midst of orchards with luscious fruits of unfailing yield. They would find lily-lakes on which to sail, pools of sparkling water in which to bathe, and shady groves inhabited by singing birds and every manner of gentle creature. The unfortunate victims whose hearts revealed their vicious lives were condemned to perpetual hunger and thirst in a place of darkness, forever cut off from the glorious light of Re.

Rewards and
punishments

The Egyptian religion attained its highest perfection about the end of the Middle Kingdom and the beginning of the Empire. By this time the solar faith and the cult of Osiris had been merged in such a way as to preserve the best features of both. The province of Re as the god of the living, as the champion of good in this world, was accorded almost equal importance with the functions of Osiris as the giver of personal immortality and the judge of the dead. The religion was now quite clearly an ethical one. Men repeatedly avowed their desire to do justice because such conduct was pleasing to the great sun god.

The perfection of
the Egyptian
religion

Soon after the establishment of the Empire the religion which has just been described underwent a serious debasement. Its ethical significance was largely destroyed, and superstition and magic gained the ascendancy. The chief cause seems to have been that the long and bitter war for the expulsion of the Hyksos fostered the growth of irrational attitudes and correspondingly depreciated the intellect.

Priestcraft and
superstition

35

The result was a marked increase in the power of the priests, who preyed upon the fears of the masses to promote their own advantage. Greedy for gain, they inaugurated the practice of selling magical charms, which were supposed to have the effect of preventing the heart of the deceased from betraying his real character. They also sold formulas which, inscribed on rolls of papyrus and placed in the tomb, were alleged to be effective in facilitating the passage of the dead to the celestial realm. The aggregate of these formulas constituted what is referred to as the Book of the Dead. Contrary to the general impression, it was not an Egyptian Bible, but merely a collection of mortuary inscriptions.

This degradation of the religion at the hands of the priests into a system of magical practices finally resulted in a great reformation or religious revolution. The leader of this movement was the Pharaoh Amenhotep IV, who began his reign about 1375 B.C. and died or was murdered about fifteen years later. After some fruitless attempts to correct the most flagrant abuses, he resolved to crush the system entirely. He drove the priests from the temples, hacked the names of the traditional deities from the public monuments, and commanded his people to worship a new god whom he called "Aton," an ancient designation for the physical sun. He changed his own name from Amenhotep ("Amen rests") to Ikhnaton, which meant "Aton is satisfied." Ikhnaton is the name by which he is commonly known in history.

Ikhnaton and His Wife Making Offerings to Aton. A stele from the XVIIIth Dynasty.

More important than these physical changes was the new set of doctrines enunciated by the reforming Pharaoh. According to eminent authorities, he taught first of all a religion of universal monotheism; Aton, he declared, was the only god in existence, the god not merely of Egypt but of the whole universe.[1] He restored the ethical quality of the national religion at its best by insisting that Aton was the author of the moral order of the world and the rewarder of men for integrity and purity of heart. He envisaged the new god as an eternal creator and sustainer of all that is of benefit to man, and as a heavenly father who watches with benevolent care over all his creatures. Conceptions like these of the unity, righteousness, and benevolence of God were not attained again until the time of the Hebrew prophets some 600 years later.

The results of Ikhnaton's revolution

The revolution of Ikhnaton was not an enduring success. Because of its challenge to ancient myths and magical practices it was not popular with the masses. Moreover, the Pharaohs who followed Ikhnaton were not inspired by the same devoted idealism. The result was a revival and a gradual extension of the same old superstitions that had prevailed before Ikhnaton's reign. For the great masses of the nation the ethical significance of the religion was permanently lost,

[1] J. H. Breasted, *A History of Egypt*, p. 376; see also Alexandre Moret, *From Tribe to Empire*, pp. 298–300.

and they were thrown back once more to ignorance and priestly greed. Among the educated classes, however, the influence of Ikhnaton's teachings lingered for some time. Although the god Aton was no longer recognized, the qualities he represented continued to be held in high esteem. What happened was that the attributes of Aton were now transferred by the educated minority to Ammon-Re. The traditional solar deity was acclaimed as the only god and the embodiment of righteousness, justice, and truth. He was worshiped, moreover, as a merciful and loving being "who heareth prayers, who giveth the hand to the poor, who saveth the weary." [2]

The return of
decay

Adherence by the intelligent few to these noble ideas was not enough to save the religion from complete degeneracy and ruin. The spread of superstition, the popularity of magic, and the paralyzing grip of a degenerate priesthood were far too deadly in their effects to be overcome by exalted doctrines. In the end the whole system of belief and worship was engulfed by formalism and ignorance and by fetishism (worship of magical objects), animal worship, and other magical crudities. The commercialism of the priests was more rampant than ever, and the chief function of the organized religion had come to be the sale of formulas and charms which would stifle the conscience and trick the gods into granting eternal salvation. The tragedy was compounded by the fact that as the religion decayed it exerted a baneful effect upon the rest of the culture. Philosophy, art, and government were so closely linked with religion that all of them went down together.

3. EGYPTIAN INTELLECTUAL ACHIEVEMENTS

The philosophy of ancient Egypt was chiefly ethical and political, although traces of broader philosophic conceptions are occasionally to be found. The idea that the universe is controlled by mind or intelligence, for example, is a notion that appeared from time to time in the writings of priests and sages. Other philosophic ideas of the ancient Egyptians included the conception of an eternal universe, the notion of constantly recurring cycles of events, and the doctrine of natural cause and effect. Few, if any, of Egyptian writers could be classified as "pure" philosophers. They were concerned primarily with religion and with questions of individual conduct and social justice.

The general
character of
Egyptian
philosophy

The earliest examples of Egyptian ethical philosophy were maxims of sage advice similar to those of the Book of Proverbs and the Book of Ecclesiastes in the Old Testament. They went little beyond practical wisdom, but occasionally they enjoined tolerance, moderation, and justice.

The earliest
ethical
philosophy

[2] J. H. Breasted, *The Dawn of Conscience*, p. 316.

During the Middle Kingdom this practical philosophy was succeeded by a kind of epicureanism. Skepticism regarding the gods now took the place of the lofty religious conceptions of earlier times, and the life of self-indulgence was extolled as the best. Lip service, however, was also paid to the pursuit of a good name by deeds of charity and benevolence.

As political philosophers the Egyptians developed a conception of the state as a welfare institution presided over by a benevolent ruler. This conception was embodied especially in the *Plea of the Eloquent Peasant*, written about 2050 B.C. It sets forth the idea of a ruler committed to benevolence and justice for the good of his subjects. He is urged to act as the father of the orphan, the husband of the widow, and the brother of the forsaken. He is supposed to judge impartially and to execute punishment upon whom it is due; and to promote such an order of harmony and prosperity that no one may suffer from hunger or cold or thirst.

The branches of science which first absorbed the attention of the Egyptians were astronomy and mathematics. Both were developed for practical ends—to compute the time of the Nile inundations, to lay out the plans for pyramids and temples, and to solve the intricate problems of irrigation and public control of economic functions. The Egyptians were not pure sicentists; they had little interest in the nature of the physical universe as such—a fact which probably accounts for their failure to advance very far in the science of astronomy. They perfected a solar calendar, as we have already learned, mapped the heavens, identified the principal fixed stars, and achieved some success in determining accurately the positions of stellar bodies.

The science of mathematics was more highly developed. The Egyptians laid the foundations for at least two of the common mathematical subjects—arithmetic and geometry. They devised the arithmetical operations of addition, subtraction, and division, although they never discovered how to multiply except through a series of additions. They invented the decimal system, but they had no symbol for zero. Fractions caused them some difficulty: all those with a numerator greater than one had to be broken down into a series, each with *one* as the numerator, before they could be used in mathematical calculations. The only exception was the fraction two-thirds, which the scribes had learned to use as it stood. The Egyptians also achieved a surprising degree of skill in mensuration, computing with accuracy the areas of triangles, rectangles, and hexagons. The ratio of the circumference of a circle to its diameter they calculated to be 3.16. They learned how to compute the volume of the pyramid and the cylinder, and even the volume of the hemisphere.

The third branch of science in which the Egyptians did some remarkable work was medicine. Early medical practice was conservative and profusely corrupted by superstition, but a document dating from about 1700 B.C. reveals a fairly adequate conception of scientific diagnosis and treatment. Egyptian physicians were frequently specialists: some were oculists; others were dentists, surgeons, specialists in diseases of the stomach, and so on. In the course of their work they made many discoveries of lasting value. They recognized the importance of the heart and had some appreciation of the significance of the pulse. They acquired a degree of skill in the treatment of fractures and performed simple operations. Unlike some peoples of later date they ascribed disease to natural causes. They discovered the value of cathartics, noted the curative properties of numerous drugs, and compiled the first *materia medica*, or catalogue of medicines. Many of their remedies, both scientific and magical, were carried into Europe by the Greeks and are still employed by the peasantry of isolated regions.

In other scientific fields the Egyptians contributed little. Although they achieved feats which rival modern engineering, they possessed but the scantiest knowledge of physics. They knew the principle of the inclined plane, but they were ignorant of the pulley. To their credit also must be assigned considerable progress in metallurgy, the invention of the sundial, and the making of paper and glass. With all their deficiencies as pure scientists, they equaled or surpassed in actual accomplishment most of the other peoples of the ancient Near Orient.

The Egyptians developed their first form of writing during the pre-dynastic period. This system, known as the *hieroglyphic,* from the Greek words meaning sacred carving, was originally composed of pictographic signs denoting concrete objects. Gradually certain of these signs were conventionalized and used to represent abstract concepts. Other characters were introduced to designate separate syllables which could be combined to form words. Finally, twenty-four symbols, each representing a single consonant sound of the human voice, were added early in the Old Kingdom. Thus the hieroglyphic system of writing had come to include at an early date three separate types of characters, the pictographic, syllabic, and alphabetic.

The ultimate step in this evolution of writing would have been the complete separation of the alphabetic from the non-alphabetic characters and the exclusive use of the former in written communication. The Egyptians were reluctant to take this step. Their traditions of conservatism impelled them to follow old habits. Although they made frequent use of the consonant signs, they did not commonly employ them as an independent system of writing. It was left for the Phoenicians to do this some 1500 years later. Nevertheless, the Egyptians must be credited with the invention of the principle of the alphabet. It was they who first perceived the value of single symbols for the individual sounds of the human voice. The Phoenicians merely copied this principle, based their own system of writ-

Medicine

Other scientific accomplishments

The hieroglyphic system

The principle of the alphabet

ing upon it, and diffused the idea among neighboring nations. In the ultimate sense it is therefore true that the Egyptian alphabet was the parent of every other that has ever been used in the Western world.

4.   THE MEANING OF EGYPTIAN ART

*The character
of Egyptian art*

No single interpretation will suffice to explain the meaning of Egyptian art. In general, it expressed the aspirations of a collectivized national life. It was not art for art's sake, nor did it serve to convey the individual's reactions to the problems of his personal world. Yet there were times when the conventions of a communal society were broken down, and the supremacy was accorded to a spontaneous individual art that sensed the beauty of the flower or caught the radiant idealism of a youthful face. Seldom was the Egyptian genius for faithful reproduction of nature entirely suppressed. Even the rigid formalism of the official architecture was commonly relieved by touches of naturalism—columns in imitation of palm trunks, lotus-blossom capitals, and occasional statues of Pharaohs that were not conventionalized types but true individual portraits.

Architecture

In most civilizations where the interests of society are exalted above those of its members, architecture is at once the most typical and the most highly developed of the arts. Egypt was no exception. Whether in the Old Kingdom, Middle Kingdom, or Empire it was the problems of building construction that absorbed the talent of the artist. Although painting and sculpture were by no means primitive, they nevertheless had as their primary function the embellishment of temples. Only at times did they rise to the status of independent arts.

The Pyramids of Gizeh with the Sphinx in the Foreground. The pyramid on the right is the Great Pyramid of Khufu or Cheops.

Detail of the Temple of Karnak. Most of this building has collapsed or been carried away, but the huge pylons and statues give an idea of the massiveness of Egyptian temples.

The characteristic examples of Old Kingdom architecture were the pyramids, the first of which were built at least as early as 2700 B.C. An amazing amount of labor and skill were expended in their construction. The Greek historian Herodotus estimated that 100,000 men must have been employed for twenty years to complete the single pyramid of Khufu at Gizeh. Its total height exceeds 480 feet, and the more than two million limestone blocks it contains are fitted together with a precision which few modern masons could duplicate. Each of the blocks weighs about two and a half tons. They were evidently hewn out of rock cliffs with drills and wedges and then dragged up earthen ramps by gangs of men and pried into place.

The pyramids

The significance of the pyramids is not easy to comprehend. They may have been intended for the economic purpose of providing employment opportunities. Such a theory would assume that the population had increased to overcrowding, and that the resources of agriculture, mining, industry, and commerce were no longer adequate to provide a livelihood for all the people. This theory doubtless had some validity. But for propaganda purposes it was glossed over with a political and religious significance. The construction of the pyramids was held to be an act of faith, the expression of an ambition to endow the state with permanence and stability. As indestructible tombs of the rulers they were believed to guarantee immortality to the people, for the Pharaoh was the embodiment of the national life. It is possible also that they were intended to serve as symbols of sun worship. As the tallest structures in Egypt they would catch the first light of the rising sun and reflect it to the valley below.

Significance of the pyramids

During the Middle Kingdom and the Empire the temple displaced the pyramid as the leading architectural form. The most noted

41

The Temple at Karnak. Hypostyle columns are shown at the left. Details of wall construction on the right.

The temples

examples were the great temples at Karnak and Luxor, built during the period of the Empire. Many of their gigantic, richly carved columns still stand as silent witnesses of a splendid architectural talent. Egyptian temples were characterized by massive size. The temple at Karnak, with a length of about 1300 feet, covered the largest area of any religious edifice ever built. Its central hall alone could contain almost any of the Gothic cathedrals of Europe. The columns used in the temples had stupendous proportions. The largest of them were seventy feet high, with diameters in excess of twenty feet. It has been estimated that the capitals which surmounted them could furnish standing room for a hundred men.

Egyptian sculpture

As already mentioned, Egyptian sculpture and painting served primarily as adjuncts to architecture. The former was heavily laden with conventions that restricted its style and meaning. Statues of Pharaohs were commonly of colossal size. Those produced during the Empire ranged in height from seventy-five to ninety feet. Some of them were colored to resemble life, and the eyes were frequently inlaid with rock crystal. The figures were nearly always rigid, with the arms folded across the chest or fixed to the sides of the body and with the eyes staring straight to the front. Countenances were generally represented as impassive, utterly devoid of emotional expression. Anatomical distortion was frequently practiced: the natural length of the thighs might be increased, the squareness of the shoulders accentuated, or all of the fingers of the hand made equal in length. A familiar example of non-naturalistic sculpture was the Sphinx. This represented the head of a Pharaoh on the body of a lion. The purpose was probably to symbolize the notion that the Pharaoh possessed the lion's qualities of strength and courage. The figures of sculpture in relief were even less in conformity with na-

See color plates at pages 33, 64

42

ture. The head was presented in profile, with the eye fullface; the torso was shown in the frontal position, while the legs were rendered in profile. Such were the general tendencies, but it should be noted that they were not universal. Occasionally the artist succeeded in a partial defiance of conventions, as is evidenced by the production of some highly individual likenesses of the later Pharaohs.

The meaning of Egyptian sculpture is not hard to perceive. The colossal size of the statues of Pharaohs was doubtless intended to symbolize their power and the power of the state they represented. It is significant that the size of these statues increased as the empire expanded and the government became more absolute. The conventions of rigidity and impassiveness were meant to express the timelessness and stability of the national life. Here was a nation which, according to the ideal, was not to be torn loose from its moorings by the uncertain mutations of fortune but was to remain fixed and imperturbable. The portraits of its chief men consequently must betray no anxiety, fear, or triumph, but an unvarying calmness throughout the ages. In similar fashion, the anatomical distortion can probably be interpreted as a deliberate attempt to express some national ideal. The most eloquent device for this purpose was representation of the body of a Pharaoh with the head of a god, but the other examples of non-naturalistic portrayal probably had a similar object.

The meaning of Egyptian sculpture

Egyptian painting developed late and did not have time to become weighted down with a mass of traditions. Religion did exert its influence, but in a positive manner. The best paintings were those created during the reign of Ikhnaton and immediately after. The gospel of the reforming king, with its reverence for nature as the handiwork of God, fostered a revival of realism in art which was particularly evident in painting. As a result, the murals of this period exhibit a decided talent for representation of the striking phenomena of the world of experience. They have particular merit as examples of the portrayal of movement. They caught the instant action of the wild bull leaping in the swamp, the headlong flight of the frightened stag, and the effortless swimming of ducks in the pond.

Queen Hat-shepsut. Limestone statue about 1485 B.C.

5. SOCIAL AND ECONOMIC LIFE

During the greater part of the history of Egypt the population was divided into five classes: the royal family; the priests; the nobles; the middle class of scribes, merchants, artisans, and farmers; and the serfs. During the Empire a sixth class, the professional soldiers, was added, ranking immediately below the nobles. Thousands of slaves were captured in this period also, and these formed for a time a seventh class. Despised by freemen and serfs alike, they were forced to labor in the government quarries and on the temple estates. Gradually, however, they were enrolled in the army and

The principal classes

43

Fishing and Fowling: Wall Painting Thebes, XVIIIth Dynasty. Most of the women appear to belong to the prosperous classes, while the simple garb and insignificant size of the men indicates that they are probably slaves.

even in the personal service of the Pharaoh. With these developments they ceased to constitute a separate class. The position of the various ranks of society shifted from time to time. In the Old Kingdom the nobles and priests among all of the Pharaoh's subjects held the supremacy. During the Middle Kingdom the classes of commoners came into their own. Scribes, merchants, artisans, and serfs rebelled against the nobles and wrested concessions from the government. Particularly impressive is the dominant role played by the merchants and industrialists in this period. The establishment of the Empire, accompanied as it was by the extension of government functions, resulted in the ascendancy of a new nobility, made up primarily of bureaucrats. The priests also waxed in power with the growth of magic and superstition.

The gulf that separated the standards of living of the upper and lower classes of Egypt was perhaps even wider than it is today in Europe and America. The wealthy nobles lived in splendid villas that opened into fragrant gardens and shady groves. Their food had all the richness and variety of sundry kinds of meat, poultry, cakes, fruit, wine, beer, and sweets. They ate from vessels of alabaster, gold, and silver, and adorned their persons with expensive fabrics and costly jewels. By contrast, the life of the poor was wretched indeed. The laborers in the towns inhabited congested slums composed of mud-brick hovels with roofs of thatch. Their only furnishings were stools and boxes and a few crude pottery jars. The peasants on the great estates enjoyed a less crowded but no more abundant life.

The basic social unit among the Egyptians was the monogamous family. No man, not even the Pharaoh, could have more than one lawful wife. Concubinage, however, was a socially reputable institu-

The gulf between rich and poor

44

tion. Women occupied an unusually enviable status. Wives were not secluded, and there is no record of any divorce. Women could own and inherit property and engage in business. Almost alone among Oriental peoples the Egyptians permitted women to succeed to the throne. Another extraordinary social practice was close inbreeding. The ruler as son of the great sun god was required to marry his sister or some other female of his immediate family lest the divine blood be contaminated. There is evidence that many of his subjects followed the identical custom. As yet, historians have been unable to discover any positive traces of racial degeneration produced by this practice, probably for the reason that the Egyptian stock was genetically sound to begin with.

The Egyptian economic system rested primarily upon an agrarian basis. Agriculture was diversified and highly developed, and the soil yielded excellent crops of wheat, barley, millet, vegetables, fruits, flax, and cotton. Theoretically the land was the property of the king, but in the earlier periods he granted most of it to his subjects, so that in actual practice it was largely in the possession of individuals. Commerce did not amount to much before 2000 B.C., but after that date it grew rapidly to a position of first-rate importance. A flourishing trade was carried on with the island of Crete, with Phoenicia, Palestine, and Syria. The chief articles of export consisted of wheat, linen fabrics, and fine pottery. Imports were confined largely to gold, silver, ivory, and lumber. Of no less significance than commerce was manufacturing as a branch of economic life. As early as 3000 B.C. large numbers of people were already engaged in industrial pursuits, mostly in separate crafts. In later times factories were established, employing twenty or more persons under one roof, and with some degree of division of labor. The leading industries were quarrying, shipbuilding, and the manufacture of pottery, glass, and textiles.

Left: *Making Sun-dried Bricks*. Nile mud (generally mixed with chaff or straw) is being worked with a hoe, carried away in buckets and dumped in a pile. Lying on the ground in a row are three bricks, from the last of which a wooden mold, used in shaping them, is being lifted. An overseer with a stick is seated close by. The finished bricks are carried off by means of a yoke across the shoulders. From a wall-painting at Thebes about 1500 B.C.
Right: *Stonecutters Dressing Blocks*. Men with mallets and chisels are dressing down blocks to true surfaces. Below, two of them test the accuracy of the dressed surface. After two edges of the block are determined, a cord is stretched between two pegs to help gauge how much remains to be chiseled away.

Sowing Seed and Working It into the Soil. From a bag which he wears over his left shoulder, the sower casts seed under the feet of cattle yoked to a plow. The plow is here used to harrow the soil. While one laborer guides the cows with a stick, another guides the plow straight and keeps the plow-share in the ground by bearing down on the handles. Sheep are then driven across the field to trample in the seed. From wall paintings at Sheikh Saïd, about 2700 B.C.

From an early date the Egyptians made progress in the perfection of instruments of business. They knew the elements of accounting and bookkeeping. Their merchants issued orders and receipts for goods. They invented deeds for property, written contracts, and wills. While they had no system of coinage, they had nevertheless attained a money economy. Rings of copper or gold of definite weight circulated as media of exchange. This Egyptian ring-money is apparently the oldest currency in the history of civilizations. Probably it was not used except for larger transactions. The simple dealings of the peasants and poorer townsfolk doubtless continued on a basis of barter.

The Egyptian economic system was always collectivistic. From the very beginning the energies of the people had been drawn into socialized channels. The interests of the individual and the interests of society were conceived as identical. The productive activities of the entire nation revolved around the huge state enterprises, and the government remained by far the largest employer of labor. But this collectivism was not all-inclusive; a considerable sphere was left for private initiative. Merchants conducted their own businesses; many of the craftsmen had their own shops; and as time went on, larger and larger numbers of peasants gained the status of independent farmers. The government continued to operate the quarries and mines, to build pyramids and temples, and to farm the royal estates.

The extreme development of state control came with the founding of the Empire. The growth of a military absolutism and the increasing frequency of wars of conquest augmented the need for revenue and for unlimited production of goods. To fulfill this need the government extended its control over every department of economic life. The entire agricultural land became the property of the Pharaoh. Although large sections of it were granted to favorites of the king, most of it was worked by royal serfs and slaves. The free middle class largely disappeared. The services of craftsmen were conscripted for the erection of magnificent temples and for the manufacture of implements of war, while foreign trade became a state monopoly. As the Empire staggered toward its downfall, the government absorbed more and more of the economic activities of the people.

Except during the reign of Ikhnaton, a corrupt alliance existed between the Pharaohs of the Empire and the priests. Greedy for power and plunder, the members of the ecclesiastical hierarchy supported the kings in their ambitions for despotic rule. As a reward they were granted exemption from taxation and a generous share of the national wealth. War captives were turned over to them in such numbers that they actually held two per cent of the population of the country as temple slaves. They employed a great host of artisans in the manufacture of amulets and funerary equipment, which they sold at tremendous profit to the worshipers. Without question these priestly enterprises meant a serious drain on the national resources and thereby contributed to economic and social decay. Too large a proportion of the wealth of Egypt was being squandered on sterile projects of the church and the state and on the conquest of an empire.

Defects in the economic system

6. THE EGYPTIAN ACHIEVEMENT AND ITS IMPORTANCE TO US

Few civilizations of ancient times surpassed the Egyptian in importance to the modern world. Even the influence of the Hebrews was not much greater. From the land of the Pharaohs came the germ and the stimulus for numerous intellectual achievements of later centuries. Important elements of philosophy, mathematics, science, and literature had their beginnings there. The Egyptians also developed one of the oldest systems of jurisprudence and political theory. They perfected the achievements of irrigation, engineering, and the making of pottery, glass, and paper. They were one of the first peoples to have any clear conception of art for other than utilitarian purposes, and they originated architectural principles that were destined for extensive use in subsequent history.

Egyptian contributions: (1) intellectual and artistic

More significant still were the Egyptian contributions in the fields of religion and individual and social ethics. Aside from the Persians, the dwellers on the banks of the Nile were the only people of the ancient world to build a national religion around the doctrine of personal immortality. Egyptian priests and sages likewise were the first to preach universal monotheism, the providence of God, forgiveness of sins, and rewards and punishments after death. Finally, Egyptian ethical theory was the source from which various nations derived standards of personal and social morality; for it embraced not only the ordinary prohibitions of lying, theft, and murder, but included also the exalted ideals of justice, benevolence, and the equal rights of all men.

(2) religious and ethical

47

SELECTED READINGS

· *Items so designated are available in paperbound editions.*

· Alfred, Cyril, *The Egyptians,* New York, 1963 (Praeger).

Breasted, James H., *The Dawn of Conscience,* New York, 1934. An excellent account of the development of religious and ethical concepts.

———, *History of Egypt,* New York, 1912. Still one of the best histories of ancient Egypt.

· Childe, V. G., *New Light on the Most Ancient East,* New York, 1969 (Norton Library).

· Cottrell, Leonard, *Life under the Pharaohs,* New York, 1960 (Tempo, 1964).

· Desroches-Noblecourt, Christiane, *Egyptian Wall Paintings,* New York, 1962 (Mentor).

· Edwards, I. E. S., *The Pyramids of Egypt,* Baltimore, 1962 (Penguin).

· Emery, W. B., *Archaic Egypt,* Baltimore, 1961 (Penguin).

· Frankfort, Henri, *et al., Before Philosophy,* Baltimore, 1949 (Penguin). A splendid account of early man's thinking.

Giles, F. J., *Ikhnaton,* London, 1970.

Glanville, S. R. K., *The Legacy of Ancient Egypt,* Oxford, 1957.

· Kramer, S. N., *Mythologies of the Ancient World,* New York, 1961 (Anchor).

· Lloyd, Seton, *The Art of the Ancient Near East,* New York, 1962 (Praeger).

Moret, Alexandre, *The Nile and Egyptian Civilization,* New York, 1928. Interesting in its contrast with Breasted.

· Moscati, Sabatino, *The Face of the Ancient Orient,* New York, 1962 (Anchor).

Shorter, A. W., *Everyday Life in Ancient Egypt,* London, 1932. One of the few works of its kind, therefore valuable.

· Smith, W. S., *Art and Architecture of Ancient Egypt,* Baltimore, 1958 (Penguin).

· Steindorff, G., and Steele, K. C., *When Egypt Ruled the East,* Chicago, 1942 (Phoenix). A useful supplement to Breasted.

· Wilson, J. A., *The Burden of Egypt,* Chicago, 1951. An excellent interpretation. Also available in paperback under the title, *The Culture of Ancient Egypt* (Phoenix).

SOURCE MATERIALS

Breasted, J. H., *Ancient Records of Egypt,* Chicago, 1929, 5 vols.

· ———, *Development of Religion and Thought in Ancient Egypt,* Gloucester, Mass., 1959 (Torchbook).

Budge, E. A. W., *Osiris and the Egyptian Resurrection,* New York, 1911, 2 vols.

· Pritchard, J. B., ed., *Ancient Near Eastern Texts,* Princeton, 1950 (Princeton University Press).

CHAPTER 3

The Mesopotamian and Persian Civilizations

If a son strike his father, they shall cut off his fingers.

If a man destroy the eye of another man, they shall destroy his eye.

If one break a man's bone, they shall break his bone.

If one destroy the eye of a freeman or break the bone of a freeman, he shall pay one mina of silver.

If one destroy the eye of a man's slave or break a bone of a man's slave he shall pay one-half his price.

—The Code of Hammurabi, lines 195–199.

The other of the most ancient civilizations was that which began in the Tigris-Euphrates valley at least as early as 4000 B.C. This civilization was formerly called the Babylonian or Babylonian-Assyrian civilization. It is now known, however, that the civilization was not founded by either the Babylonians or the Assyrians but by an earlier people called the Sumerians. It seems better, therefore, to use the name Mesopotamian to cover the whole civilization, even though Mesopotamia is sometimes applied only to the northern portion of the land between the two rivers. The Mesopotamian civilization was unlike the Egyptian in many respects. Its political history was marked by sharper interruptions. Its ethnic composition was less homogeneous, and its social and economic structure gave wider scope to individual initiative.

Origin and comparison with Egypt

The differences in ideals and in religious and social attitudes were perhaps more fundamental. The Egyptian culture was predominantly ethical, the Mesopotamian legalistic. The Egyptian outlook on life, except during the Middle Kingdom, was generally one of cheerful resignation, comparatively free from the cruder superstitions. By contrast, the Mesopotamian view was gloomy, pessimistic, and enthralled by morbid fears. Where the native of Egypt believed in immortality and dedicated a large part of his energy to preparation for the life to come, his Mesopotamian contemporary lived in the present and cherished few hopes regarding his fate beyond the

Religious and social differences

grave. Finally, the civilization of the Nile valley embodied concepts of monotheism, a religion of love, and of social equalitarianism; that of the Tigris-Euphrates was more selfish and practical. Its religion seldom evolved beyond the stage of primitive polytheism, and its arts bore few of the natural and personal qualities of the Egyptian.

On the other hand, there were similarities too striking to be ignored. Both civilizations made progress in ethical theory and in concepts of social justice. Both had their evils of slavery and imperialism, of oppressive kings and greedy priests. Both had common problems of irrigation and land boundaries; and, as a result, both made
notable progress in the sciences, especially in mathematics. Finally,
rivalry among small states led eventually to consolidation and to the
growth of mighty empires, especially in the case of Mespotamia.

Similarities

I. FROM THE SUMERIAN TO THE PERSIAN CONQUEST

The pioneers in the development of the Mesopotamian civilization were the people known as Sumerians, who settled in the lower Tigris-Euphrates valley between 5000 and 4000 B.C. Their precise origin is unknown, but they seem to have come from the plateau of central Asia. They spoke a language unrelated to any now known, although their culture bore a certain resemblance to the earliest civilization of India. With little or no difficulty they subjugated the natives already in the lower valley, a mysterious people who were just emerging from the Neolithic stage.

The Sumerians

The new Sumerian empire did not survive long. It was annexed by the Elamites in the twenty-first century and about 1950 B.C. was conquered by a Semitic people known as the Amorites, who had come in from the fringes of the Arabian desert. Since they made the village of Babylon the capital of their empire they are commonly called the Babylonians, or the Old Babylonians, to distinguish them from the Neo-Babylonians or Chaldeans who occupied the valley much later. The rise of the Old Babylonians inaugurated the second important stage of the Tigris-Euphrates civilization. Although most of the Sumerian culture survived, Sumerian dominance was now at an end. The Babylonians established an autocratic state and during the reign of their most famous king, Hammurabi, extended their dominion north to Assyria. But after his time their empire gradually declined until it was finally overthrown by the Kassites about 1650 B.C.

The rise and fall of the Old Babylonians

With the downfall of Old Babylonia a period of retrogression set in which lasted for 600 years. The Kassites were barbarians with no interest in the cultural achievements of their predecessors. Their lone contribution was the introduction of the horse into the Tigris-Euphrates valley. The old culture would have died out entirely had it not been for its partial adoption by another Semitic people who,

The Kassites and the Assyrians

as early as 3000 B.C., had founded a tiny kingdom on the plateau of Assur some 500 miles up the Tigris River. These people came to be called the Assyrians, and their ultimate rise to power marked the beginning of the third stage in the development of the Mesopotamian civilization. They began to expand about 1300 B.C. and soon afterward made themselves masters of the whole northern valley. In the tenth century they overturned what was left of Kassite power in Babylonia. Their empire reached its height in the eighth and seventh centuries under Sargon II (722–705 B.C.), Sennacherib (705–681), and Assurbanipal (668–626). It had now come to include nearly all of the civilized world of that time. One after another, Syria, Phoenicia, the Kingdom of Israel, and Egypt had fallen victims to Assyrian military prowess. Only the little Kingdom of Judah was able to withstand the hosts of Nineveh, probably because of an outbreak of pestilence in the ranks of Sennacherib's army.[1]

Brilliant though the successes of the Assyrians were, they did not endure. So rapidly were new territories annexed that the empire soon reached an unmanageable size. The Assyrians' genius for government was far inferior to their appetite for conquest. Subjugated nations chafed under the cruel despotism that had been forced upon them and, as the empire gave signs of cracking from within, determined to regain their freedom. The death blow was delivered by the Kaldi or Chaldeans, a nation of Semites who had settled southeast of the valley of the two rivers. Under the leadership of Nabopolassar, who had served the Assyrian emperors in the capacity of a provincial governor, they organized a revolt and finally captured Nineveh in 612 B.C.

The downfall of the Assyrians and the rise of the Chaldeans

In 539 B.C. the empire of the Chaldeans fell, after an existence of less than a century. It was overthrown by Cyrus the Persian, as he himself declared, "without a battle and without fighting." The easy victory appears to have been made possible by assistance from the Jews and by a conspiracy of the priests of Babylon to deliver the city to Cyrus as an act of vengeance against the Chaldean king, whose policies they did not like. Members of other influential classes appear also to have looked upon the Persians as deliverers.

Although the Persian state incorporated all of the territories that had once been embraced by the Mesopotamian empires, it included many other provinces besides. It was the vehicle, moreover, of a new and different culture. The downfall of Chaldea must therefore be taken as marking the end of Mesopotamian political history.

2. SUMERIAN ORIGINS OF THE CIVILIZATION

More than to any other people, the Mesopotamian civilization owed its character to the Sumerians. Much of what used to be

Assurbanipal and His Armies Storming the Elamite Capital

[1] Hebrew prophets declared that an angel of the Lord visited the camp of the Assyrians by night and slew 185,000 of them. II Kings 19:35.

ascribed to the Babylonians and Assyrians is now known to have been developed by the nation that preceded them. The system of writing was of Sumerian origin; likewise the religion, the laws, and a great deal of the science and commercial practice. Only in the evolution of government and military tactics and in the development of the arts was the originating talent of the later conquerors particularly manifest.

The Sumerian political system

Through the greater part of their history the Sumerians lived in a loose confederation of city-states, united only for military purposes. At the head of each was a *patesi*, who combined the functions of chief priest, commander of the army, and superintendent of the irrigation system. Occasionally one of the more ambitious of these rulers would extend his power over a number of cities and assume the title of king. Not until about 2000 B.C., however, were all of the Sumerian people united under a single authority of the same nationality as themselves.

The Sumerian economic pattern

The Sumerian economic pattern was relatively simple and permitted a wider scope for individual enterprise than was generally allowed in Egypt. The land was never the exclusive property of the king either in theory or in practice. Neither was trade or industry a monopoly of the government. The temples, however, seem to have fulfilled many of the functions of a collectivist state. They owned a large portion of the land and operated business enterprises. Because the priests alone had the technical knowledge to calculate the seasons and lay out canals, they controlled the irrigation system. The masses of the people had little they could call their own. Many of them were serfs, but even those who were technically free were little better off, forced as they were to pay high rents and to labor on public works. Slavery in the strict sense of the word was not an important institution.

Agriculture was the chief economic pursuit of most of the citizens, and the Sumerians were excellent farmers. By virtue of their

Diorama of a Part of Ur about 2000 B.C. A modern archaeologist's conception. Walls are omitted to show interiors at left.

knowledge of irrigation they produced amazing crops of cereal grains and subtropical fruits. Since most of the land was divided into large estates held by the rulers, the priests, and the army officers, the average rural citizen was either a tenant farmer or a serf. Commerce was the second most important source of the nation's wealth. A flourishing trade was established with all of the surrounding countries, revolving around the exchange of metals and timber from the north and west for agricultural products and manufactured goods from the lower valley. Nearly all of the familiar adjuncts of business were highly developed; bills, receipts, notes, and letters of credit were regularly used.

The most distinctive achievement of the Sumerians was their system of law. It was the product of a gradual evolution of local usage, but it was finally incorporated into a comprehensive code after the middle of the third millennium. Only a few fragments of this law have survived in their original form, but the famous code of Hammurabi, the Babylonian king, is now recognized to have been little more than a revision of the code of the Sumerians. Ultimately this code became the basis of the laws of nearly all of the Semites— Babylonians, Assyrians, Chaldeans, and Hebrews.

The following may be regarded as the essential features of the Sumerian law:

(1) The *lex talionis*, or law of retaliation in kind—"an eye for an eye, a tooth for a tooth, a limb for a limb," etc.

(2) Semiprivate administration of justice. It was incumbent upon the victim himself or his family to bring the offender to justice. The court served principally as an umpire in the dispute between the plaintiff and defendant, not as an agency of the state to maintain public security, although constables attached to the court might assist in the execution of the sentence.

(3) Inequality before the law. The code divided the population into three classes: patricians or aristocrats; burghers or commoners; serfs and slaves. Penalties were graded according to the rank of the victim, but also in some cases according to the rank of the offender. The killing or maiming of a patrician was a much more serious offense than a similar crime committed against a burgher or a slave. On the other hand, when a patrician was the offender he was punished *more severely* than a man of inferior status would be for the same crime. The origin of this curious rule was probably to be found in considerations of military discipline. Since the patricians were army officers and therefore the chief defenders of the state, they could not be permitted to give vent to their passions or to indulge in riotous conduct.

(4) Inadequate distinction between accidental and intentional homicide. A person responsible for killing another accidentally did not escape penalty, as he would under modern law, but had to pay a fine to the family of the victim, apparently on the theory that chil-

Male Votive Figure, Sumer.
This statue of white gypsum
colored with bitumen shows
the huge staring eyes characteristic of Mesopotamian art.

A religion
neither ethical
nor spiritual

dren were the property of their fathers and wives the property of
their husbands.

Quite as much as their law, the religion of the Sumerians illumi-
nates their social attitudes and the character of their culture. They
did not succeed in developing a very exalted religion; yet it occupied an important place in their lives. To begin with, it was
polytheistic and anthropomorphic. They believed in a number of
gods and goddesses, each a distinct personality with human attributes. Shamash, the sun god; Enlil, the lord of the rain and wind;
and Ishtar, the goddess of the female principle in nature, were only
a few of them. Although the Sumerians had a special deity of the
plague in the person of the god Nergal, their religion was really
monistic in the sense that they regarded all of their deities as capable
of both good and evil.

The Sumerian religion was a religion for this world exclusively; it
offered no hope for a blissful, eternal afterlife. The afterlife was a
mere temporary existence in a dreary, shadowy place which later
came to be called Sheol. Here the ghosts of the dead lingered for a
time, perhaps a generation or so, and then disappeared. No one
could look forward to resurrection in another world and a joyous
eternal existence as a recompense for the evils of this life; the victory of the grave was complete. In accordance with these beliefs the
Sumerians bestowed only limited care upon the bodies of their
dead. No mummification was practiced, and no elaborate tombs
were built. Corpses were commonly interred beneath the floor of
the house without a coffin and with comparatively few articles for
the use of the ghost.

Spiritual content had no place of conspicuous importance in this
religion. As we have seen, the gods were not spiritual beings but
creatures cast in the human mold, with most of the weaknesses and
passions of mortal men. Nor were the purposes of the religion any
more spiritual. It provided no blessings in the form of solace, uplift
of the soul, or oneness with God. If it benefited man at all, it did so
chiefly in the form of material gain—abundant harvests and prosperity in business. At the same time, the religion did, at least, have an
ethical content. All the major deities in the Sumerian pantheon were
extolled in hymns as lovers of truth, goodness, and justice. The goddess Nanshe, for example, was said "to comfort the orphan, to make
disappear the widow, to set up a place of destruction for the
mighty." Yet the same deities who personified these noble ideals
created such evils as falsehood and strife, and endowed every human
being with a sinful nature. "Never," it was said, "has a sinless child
been born to its mother." [2]

A dominant idea in the Sumerian religion was the notion that man
was created in order that he might serve the gods—not merely by
worshipping them, but also by giving them food. This notion was

[2] S. N. Kramer, *History Begins at Sumer,* pp. 106–107.

revealed in the famous Creation and Flood epics, which provided the framework for the much later Hebrew stories in the Old Testament. The Creation epic related the magic triumph of the god Marduk over the jealous and cowardly gods who had created him, the formation of the world out of the body of one of his slain rivals, and finally, in order that the gods might be fed, the making of man out of clay and dragon's blood. The whole account was crude and revolting, with nothing in it to appeal to a spiritual or moral sense. Almost as barbarous was the Sumerian version of the Flood. Grown jealous of man, the gods decided to destroy the whole race of mortals by drowning. One of their number, however, betrayed the secret to a favorite inhabitant of the earth, instructing him to build an ark for the salvation of himself and his kind. The flood raged for seven days, until the whole earth was covered with water. Even the gods "crouched like a dog on the wall." Finally the tumult was stilled and the waters subsided. The favored man came forth from the ark and offered grateful sacrifice. As a reward he was given "life like a god" and translated to "the place where the sun rises."

In the field of intellectual endeavor the Sumerians achieved no small distinction. They produced a system of writing which was destined to be used for a thousand years after the downfall of their nation. This was the celebrated *cuneiform* writing, consisting of wedge-shaped characters imprinted on clay tablets with a square-tipped reed. At first a pictographic system, it was gradually transformed into an aggregate of syllabic and phonetic signs, some 350 in number. No alphabet was ever developed out of it. The Sumerians wrote nothing that could be called philosophy, but they did make some notable beginnings in science. In mathematics, for example, they surpassed the Egyptians in every field except geometry. They discovered the processes of multiplication and division and even the extraction of square and cube root. Their systems of numeration and of weights and measures were duodecimal, with the number sixty as the most common unit. They invented the water clock and the lunar calendar, the latter an inaccurate division of the year into months based upon cycles of the moon. In order to bring it into harmony with the solar year, an extra month had to be added from time to time. Astronomy was little more than astrology, and medicine was a curious compound of herbalism and magic. The repertory of the physician consisted primarily of charms to exorcise the evil spirits which were believed to be the cause of the disease.

Gudea of Lagash. A black diorite statue of the late Sumerian ruler.

As artists, the Sumerians excelled in metalwork, gem carving, and sculpture. They produced some remarkable specimens of naturalistic art in their weapons, vessels, jewelry, and animal representations, which revealed alike a technical skill and a gift of imagination. Evidently religious conventions had not yet imposed any paralyzing influence, and consequently the artist was still free to follow his own impulses. Architecture, on the other hand, was distinctly inferior, probably because of the limitations enforced by the scarcity of

Left: *The Great Ziggurat, or Flat-topped Temple at Ur.* Right: *Fragments of Jewelry Found at Ur in Two Graves of Ladies-in-waiting to the Queen.* The gold jewelry is the oldest in the world.

good building materials. Since there was no stone in the valley, the architect had to depend upon sun-dried brick. The characteristic Sumerian edifice, extensively copied by their Semitic successors, was the *ziggurat*, a terraced tower set on a platform and surmounted by a shrine. Its construction was massive, its lines were monotonous, and little architectural ingenuity was exhibited in it. The royal tombs and private houses showed more originality. It was in them that the Sumerian inventions of the arch, the vault, and the dome were regularly employed, and the column was used occasionally.

3. OLD BABYLONIAN "CONTRIBUTIONS"

The shortcomings of the Old Babylonians

Although the Old Babylonians were an alien nation, they had lived long enough in close contact with the Sumerians to be influenced profoundly by them. They had no culture of their own worthy of the name when they came into the valley, and in general they simply appropriated what the Sumerians had already developed. With so excellent a foundation to build upon, they should have made remarkable progress; but such was not the case. When they ended their history, the state of civilization in the Tigris-Euphrates valley was little more advanced than when they began.

Changes in the system of law

First among the significant changes which the Old Babylonians made in their cultural inheritance may be mentioned the political and legal. As military conquerors holding in subjection numerous vanquished nations, they found it necessary to establish a consolidated state. Vestiges of the old system of local autonomy were swept away, and the power of the king of Babylon was made supreme. Kings became gods, or at least claimed divine origin. A system of royal taxation was adopted as well as compulsory military service. The system of law was also changed to conform to the new condition of centralized despotism. The list of crimes against the state was enlarged, and the king's officers assumed a more active role

56

in apprehending and punishing offenders, although it was still impossible for any criminal to be pardoned without the consent of the victim or the victim's family. The severity of penalties was decidedly increased, particularly for crimes involving any suggestion of treason or sedition. Such apparently trivial offenses as "gadding about" and "disorderly conduct of a tavern" were made punishable by death, probably on the assumption that they would be likely to foster disloyal activities. Whereas under the Sumerian law the harboring of fugitive slaves was punishable merely by a fine, the Babylonian law made it a capital crime. According to the Sumerian code, the slave who disputed his master's rights over him was to be sold; the Code of Hammurabi prescribed that he should have his ear cut off. Adultery was also made a capital offense, whereas under the Sumerian law it did not even necessarily result in divorce. In a few particulars the new system of law revealed some improvement. Wives and children sold for debt could not be held in bondage for longer than four years, and a female slave who had borne her master a child could not be sold at all.

The Old Babylonian laws also reflect a more extensive development of business than that which existed in the preceding culture. That a large middle class traded for profit and enjoyed a privileged position in society is evidenced by the fact that the commercial provisions of Hammurabi's code were based upon the principle of "Let the buyer beware." The Babylonian rulers did not believe in a regime of free competition, however. Trade, banking, and industry were subject to elaborate regulation by the state. There were laws regarding partnership, storage, and agency; laws respecting deeds, wills, and the taking of interest on money; and a host of others. For a deal to be negotiated without a written contract or without witnesses was punishable by death. Agriculture, which was still the occupation of a majority of the citizens, did not escape regulation. The code provided penalties for failure to cultivate a field and for neglect of dikes and canals. Both government ownership and private tenure of land were permitted; but, regardless of the status of the owner, the tenant farmer was required to pay two-thirds of all he produced as rent.

Religion at the hands of the Old Babylonians underwent numerous changes both superficial and profound. Deities that had been venerated by the Sumerians were now neglected and new ones exalted in their stead. They carried no spiritual significance, however, conveying no promise of the resurrection of man from the dead or of personal immortality. The Old Babylonians were no more otherworldly in their outlook than the Sumerians. The religions of both peoples were fundamentally materialistic.

Equally noteworthy was an increase in superstition. Astrology, divination, and other forms of magic took on added significance. A morbid consciousness of sin gradually displaced the essentially

Gold Jewelry from Ur, ca. 3500–2800 B.C.

Changes in religion

57

The increase in
superstition

The decline
of intellect and
the arts

amoral attitude of the Sumerians. In addition, an increased emphasis was placed upon the worship of demons. Nergal, the god of the plague, came to be envisaged as a hideous monster seeking every chance to strike down his victims. Hordes of other demons and malevolent spirits lurked in the darkness and rode through the air bringing terror and destruction to all in their path. Against them there was no defense except sacrifices and magic charms. If the Old Babylonians did not invent witchcraft, they were at least the first "civilized" people to magnify it to serious proportions. Their laws invoked the death penalty against it, and there is evidence that the power of witches was widely feared. Whether the growth of demonology and witchcraft was a result of the increasing unhealthfulness of the climate of the Tigris-Euphrates valley, or of the needs of a centralized, conquering state to inspire fear in its subjects is a question which cannot be answered; but it is probable that the latter is the chief explanation.

There seems to be little doubt that intellectually and artistically the Mesopotamian civilization suffered a partial decline during the period of Babylonian rule. This was not the first instance of cultural retrogression in history, but it was one of the most pronounced. Nothing of great importance was added to the scientific discoveries of the Sumerians, except for advancement in mathematics; they discovered, for example, the solution of quadratic equations. Literature showed some improvement over the earlier writings. A kind of prototype of the Book of Job, the so-called *Babylonian Job,* was written in this period. It relates the story of a pious sufferer who is afflicted he knows not why, and it contains some mature reflections on the helplessness of man and the impenetrable mysteries of the universe. As an example of Oriental philosophy it is not without merit. The graphic arts, on the other hand, definitely deteriorated. The Babylonians lacked the creative interest and talent to

Panel of Glazed Brick, Babylon, Sixth Century B.C. An ornamental relief on a background of earth brown. The lion is in blue, white, and yellow glazes.

surpass the fresh and ingenious carving and engraving of the Sumerians. Moreover, sculpture fell under the domination of religious and political conventions, with the result that originality was stifled.

4. THE METAMORPHOSIS UNDER ASSYRIA

Of all the peoples of the Mesopotamian area after the time of the Sumerians, the Assyrians went through the most completely independent evolution. For several centuries they had lived a comparatively isolated existence on top of their small plateau in the upper valley of the Tigris. Eventually they came under the influence of the Babylonians, but not until after the course of their own history had been partially fixed. As a consequence, the period of Assyrian supremacy (from about 1300 B.C. to 612 B.C.) had more nearly a peculiar character than any other era of Mesopotamian history.

The evolution of Assyrian supremacy

The Assyrians were preeminently a nation of warriors; not because they were racially different from any of the other Semites, but because of the special conditions of their own environment. The limited resources of their original home and the constant danger of attack from hostile nations around them forced the development of warlike habits and imperial ambitions. It is therefore not strange that their greed for territory should have known no limits. The more they conquered, the more they felt they had to conquer, in order to protect what they had already gained. Every success excited ambition and riveted the chains of militarism more firmly than ever. Disaster was inevitable.

A nation of warriors

The exigencies of war determined the whole character of the Assyrian system. The state was a great military machine. The army commanders were at once the richest and the most powerful class in the country. Not only did they share in the plunder of war, but they were frequently granted huge estates as rewards for victory. At least one of them, Sargon II, dared to usurp the throne. The military establishment itself represented the last word in preparedness. The standing army greatly exceeded in size that of any other nation of the Near Orient. New and improved armaments and techniques of fighting gave to the Assyrian soldiers unparalleled advantages. Iron swords, heavy bows, long lances, battering rams, fortresses on wheels, and metal breastplates, shields, and helmets were only a few examples of their superior equipment.

Features of the Assyrian militarism

But swords and spears and engines of war were not their only instruments of combat. As much as anything else the Assyrians depended upon frightfulness as a means of overcoming their enemies. Upon soldiers captured in battle, and sometimes upon noncombatants as well, they inflicted unspeakable cruelties—skinning them alive, impaling them on stakes, cutting off ears, noses, and sex organs, and then exhibiting the mutilated victims in cages for the

Terrorism

59

benefit of cities that had not yet surrendered. Accounts of these cruelties are not taken from atrocity stories circulated by their enemies; they come from the records of the Assyrians themselves. Their chroniclers boasted of them as evidences of valor, and the people believed in them as guaranties of security and power. It is clear why the Assyrians were the most hated of all the nations of antiquity.

The tragedy of Assyrian militarism

Seldom has the decline of an empire been so swift and so complete as was that of Assyria. In spite of her magnificent armaments and her wholesale destruction of her foes, Assyria's period of imperial splendor lasted little more than a century. Nation after nation conspired against her and finally accomplished her downfall. Her enemies took frightful vengeance. The whole land was so thoroughly sacked and the people so completely enslaved or exterminated that it has been difficult to trace any subsequent Assyrian influence upon history. The power and security which military strength was supposed to provide proved a mockery in the end. If Assyria had been utterly defenseless, her fate could hardly have been worse.

Assyrian political and economic achievements

With so complete an absorption in military pursuits, it was inevitable that the Assyrians should have neglected in some measure the arts of peace. Industry and commerce appear to have declined under the regime of the Assyrians; for such pursuits were generally scorned as beneath the dignity of a soldierly people. The minimum of manufacturing and trade which had to be carried on was left quite largely to the Arameans, a people closely related to the Phoenicians and the Hebrews. The Assyrians themselves preferred to derive their living from agriculture. The land system included both public and private holdings. The temples held the largest share of the landed wealth. Although the estates of the crown were likewise extensive, they were constantly being diminished by grants to army officers.

Defects in the economic system

Neither the economic nor the social order was sound. The frequent military campaigns depleted the energies and resources of the nation. In the course of time the army officers became a pampered aristocracy, delegating their duties to their subordinates and devoting themselves to luxurious pleasures. The stabilizing influence of a prosperous and intelligent middle class was precluded by the rule that only foreigners and slaves could engage in commercial activities. Yet more serious was the treatment accorded to the lower classes, the serfs and the slaves. The former comprised the bulk of the rural population. Some of them cultivated definite portions of their master's estates and retained a part of what they produced for themselves. Others were "empty" men, without even a plot to cultivate and dependent on the need for seasonal labor to provide for their means of subsistence. All were extremely poor and were subject to the additional hardships of labor on public works and compulsory military service. The slaves, who were chiefly an urban working class, were of two different types: the domestic slaves, who performed household duties and sometimes engaged in business for their masters; and the war captives. The former were not numerous and were allowed a great deal of freedom, even to the extent of owning property. The latter suffered much greater miseries. Bound by heavy shackles, they were compelled to labor to the point of exhaustion in building roads, canals, and palaces.

Whether the Assyrians adopted the law of the Old Babylonians has never been settled. Undoubtedly they were influenced by it, but several of the features of Hammurabi's code are entirely absent. Notable among these are the *lex talionis* and the system of gradation of penalties according to the rank of the victim and the offender. Whereas the Babylonians prescribed the most drastic punishments for crimes suggestive of treason or sedition, the Assyrians reserved theirs for such offenses as abortion and unnatural vice, probably for the military reason of preventing a decline in the birth rate. Another contrast is the more complete subjection of Assyrian women. Wives were treated as chattels of their husbands, the right of divorce was placed entirely in the hands of the male, a plurality of wives was permitted, and all married women were forbidden to appear in public with their faces unveiled. Here, according to Professor Olmstead, was the beginning of the Oriental seclusion of women.[3]

Assyrian law

That a military nation like the Assyrians should not have taken first rank in intellectual achievement is easily understandable. The atmosphere of a military campaign is not favorable to reflection or disinterested research. Yet the demands of successful campaigning may lead to a certain accumulation of knowledge, for practical problems have to be solved. Under such circumstances the Assyrians accomplished some measure of scientific progress. They appear to have divided the circle into 360 degrees and to have estimated locations on the surface of the earth in something resembling latitude and longitude. They recognized and named five planets and achieved some success in predicting eclipses. Since the health of armies is important, medicine received considerable attention. More than 500 drugs, both vegetable and mineral, were catalogued and their uses indicated. Symptoms of various diseases were described and were generally interpreted as due to natural causes, although incantations and the prescription of disgusting compounds to drive out demons were still commonly employed as methods of treatment.

*Scientific
achievements*

In the domain of art the Assyrians surpassed the Old Babylonians and at least equaled the work of the Sumerians, although in different form. Sculpture was the art most highly developed, particularly in the low reliefs. These portrayed dramatic incidents of war and the hunt with the utmost fidelity to nature and a vivid description of movement. The Assyrians delighted in depicting the cool bravery of

*The excellence
of Assyrian art*

[3] A. T. E. Olmstead, *History of Assyria*, p. 553.

Assyrian Relief Sculpture. This panel depicts Assurbanipal hunting lions.

the hunter in the face of terrific danger, the ferocity of lions at bay, and the death agonies of wounded beasts. Unfortunately this art was limited almost entirely to the two themes of war and sport. Its purpose was to glorify the exploits of the ruling class. Architecture ranked second to sculpture from the standpoint of artistic excellence. Assyrian palaces and temples were built of stone, obtained from the mountainous areas of the north, instead of the mud brick of former times. Their principal features were the arch and the dome. The column was also used but never very successfully. The chief demerit of this architecture was its hugeness, which the Asyrians appeared to regard as synonymous with beauty.

5. THE CHALDEAN RENASCENCE

The Chaldean or final stage in Mesopotamian civilization

The Mesopotamian civilization entered its final stage with the overthrow of Assyria and the establishment of Chaldean supremacy. This stage is often called the Neo-Babylonian, because Nebuchadnezzar and his followers restored the capital at Babylon and attempted to revive the culture of Hammurabi's time. As might have been expected, their attempt was not wholly successful. The Assyrian metamorphosis had altered that culture in various profound and ineffaceable ways. Besides, the Chaldeans themselves had a history of their own which they could not entirely escape. Nevertheless, they did manage to revive certain of the old institutions and ideals. They restored the ancient law and literature, the essentials of the Old Babylonian form of government, and the economic system of their supposed ancestors with its dominance of industry and trade. Farther than this they were unable to go.

It was in religion that the failure of the Chaldean renascence was most conspicuous. Although Marduk was restored to his traditional place at the head of the pantheon, the system of belief was little more than superficially Babylonian. What the Chaldeans really did was to develop an astral religion. The gods were divested of their limited human qualities and exalted into transcendent, omnipotent beings. They were actually identified with the planets themselves. Marduk became Jupiter, Ishtar became Venus, and so on. Though still not entirely aloof from man, they certainly lost their character as beings who could be cajoled and threatened and coerced by magic. They ruled the universe almost mechanically. While their immediate intentions were sometimes discernible, their ultimate purposes were inscrutable.

Two significant results flowed from these amazing conceptions. The first was an attitude of fatalism. Since the ways of the gods were past finding out, all that man could do was to resign himself to his fate. It behooved him therefore to submit absolutely to the gods, to trust in them implicitly, in the vague hope that the results in the end would be good. Thus arose for the first time in history the conception of piety as submission—a conception which was adopted in several other religions, as we shall see in succeeding chapters. For the Chaldeans it implied no otherwordly significance; one did not resign himself to calamities in this life in order to be justified in the next. The Chaldeans had no interest in a life to come. Submission might bring certain earthly rewards, but in the main, as they conceived it, it was not a means to an end at all. It was rather the expression of an attitude of despair, of humility in the face of mysteries that could not be fathomed.

The second great result which came from the growth of an astral religion was the development of a stronger spiritual consciousness. This is revealed in the penitential hymns of unknown authors and in the prayers which were ascribed to Nebuchadnezzar and other kings as the spokesmen for the nation. In most of them the gods are addressed as exalted beings who are concerned with justice and righteous conduct on the part of men, although the distinction between ceremonial and genuine morality is not always sharply drawn. It has been asserted by one author that these hymns could have been used by the Hebrews with little modification except for the substitution of the name of Yahweh for that of the Chaldean god.[4]

With the gods promoted to so lofty a plane, it was perhaps inevitable that man should have been abased. Creatures possessed of mortal bodies could not be compared with the transcendent, passionless beings who dwelt in the stars and guided the destinies of the earth. Man was a lowly creature, sunk in iniquity and vileness, and hardly even worthy of approaching the gods. The consciousness of sin already present in the Babylonian and Assyrian religions now reached a stage of almost pathological intensity. In the hymns the sons of men are compared to prisoners, bound hand and foot, lan-

THE CHALDEAN
RENASCENCE

The astral religion
of the Chaldeans

The growth of
fatalism

The development
of a spiritual
consciousness

The abasement
of man

[4] Morris Jastrow, *The Civilization of Babylonia and Assyria*, p. 217.

63

guishing in darkness. Their transgressions are "seven times seven." Their misery is increased by the fact that their evil nature has prompted them to sin unwittingly.[5] Never before had men been regarded as so hopelessly depraved, nor had religion been fraught with so gloomy a view of life.

Curiously enough, the pessimism of the Chaldeans does not appear to have affected their morality very much. So far as the evidence reveals, they indulged in no rigors of asceticism. They did not mortify the flesh, nor did they even practice self-denial. Apparently they took it for granted that man could not avoid sinning, no matter how hard he tried. They seem to have been just as deeply engrossed in the material interests of life and in the pursuit of the pleasures of the senses as any of the earlier nations. Indeed, it seems that they were even more greedy and sensual. Occasional references were made in their prayers and hymns to reverence, kindness, and purity of heart as virtues, and to oppression, slander, and anger as vices, but these were intermingled with ritualistic conceptions of cleanness and uncleanness and with expressions of desire for physical satisfactions. When the Chaldeans prayed, it was not always that their gods would make them good, but more often that they would grant long years, abundant offspring, and luxurious living.

Aside from religion, the Chaldean culture differed from that of the Sumerians, Babylonians, and Assyrians chiefly in regard to scientific achievements. Without doubt the Chaldeans were the most capable scientists in all of Mesopotamian history, although their accomplishments were limited primarily to astronomy. They worked out the most elaborate system for recording the passage of time that had yet been devised, with their invention of the seven-day week and their division of the day into twelve double-hours of 120 minutes each. They kept accurate records of their observation of eclipses and other celestial occurrences for more than 350 years—until long after the downfall of their empire. The motivating force behind Chaldean astronomy was religion. The chief purpose of mapping the heavens and collecting astronomical data was to discover the future the gods had prepared for the race of men. Since the planets were gods themselves, that future could best be divined in the movements of the heavenly bodies. Astronomy was therefore primarily astrology.

Sciences other than astronomy continued in a backward state. There is evidence that the Chaldeans knew the principle of the zero and laid at least some of the foundations of algebra. Medicine showed little advance beyond the stage it had reached under the Assyrians. The same was true of the remaining aspects of Chaldean culture. Art differed only in its greater magnificence. Literature, dominated by the antiquarian spirit, revealed a monotonous lack of

Chaldean morality

Chaldean achievements in astronomy

Other aspects of Chaldean culture

[5] *Ibid.*, pp. 471–74.

Stele or Grave Marker. It shows the deceased being presented to the Sun god on his throne. She is holding her heart in her hand.

Head of Ramses II, 1324–1258 B.C.

Shawabty ("to answer") Figures, *ca.* 1400 B.C. These were put in the tomb to do any degrading work the rich man might be called upon to do in the next world.

Part of the Egyptian "Book of the Dead." A collection of magic formulas to enable the deceased to gain admission to the realm of Osiris and to enjoy its eternal benefits.

Painted limestone figures, *ca.* 1300 B.C.

A hieroglyphic character for the idea "Millions of Years," 500–330 B.C.

carved sandstone capital, *ca.* 370 B.C., representing a bundle of papyrus reeds.

Thutmose III as Amon, 1450 B.C. The Pharaoh wears the crown and the beard of the god, and carries a scimitar and the symbol of "life."

Bronze Bull, Symbol of Strength. Arabian, VI cent. B.C.

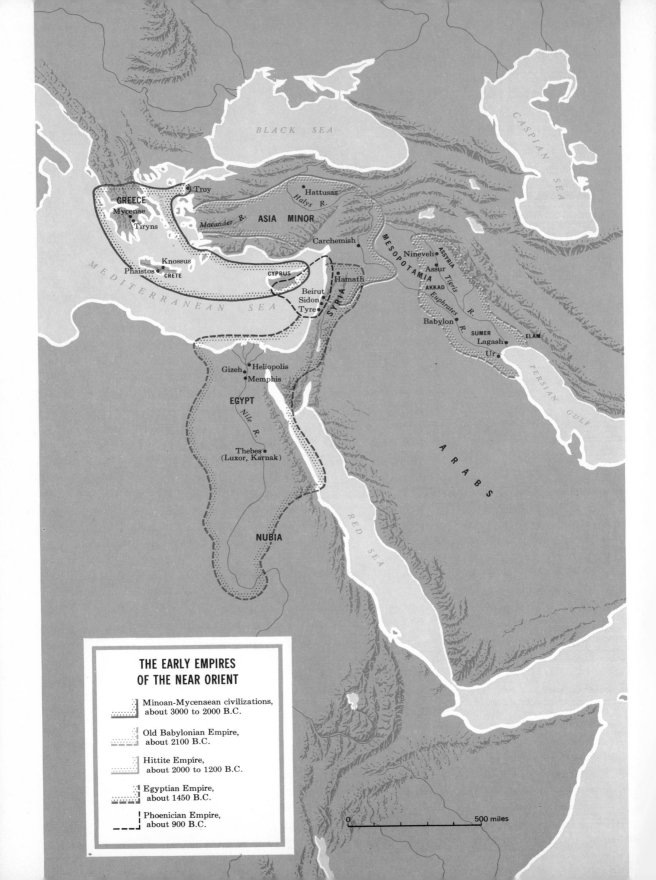

BLACK SEA

CASPIAN SEA

GREECE

Troy

Mycenae

Tiryns

Maeander R.

ASIA MINOR

Hattusas

Halys R.

Carchemish

MESOPOTAMIA

Nineveh

Assur

ASSYRIA

Tigris R.

AKKAD

Euphrates R.

Babylon

SUMER

Lagash

ELAM

Ur

Knossus

Phaistos

CRETE

CYPRUS

Hamath

Beirut

Sidon

Tyre

SYRIA

MEDITERRANEAN SEA

PERSIAN GULF

Gizeh

Heliopolis

Memphis

EGYPT

Nile R.

Thebes
(Luxor, Karnak)

A R A B S

RED SEA

NUBIA

THE EARLY EMPIRES
OF THE NEAR ORIENT

Minoan-Mycenaean civilizations,
about 3000 to 2000 B.C.

Old Babylonian Empire,
about 2100 B.C.

Hittite Empire,
about 2000 to 1200 B.C.

Egyptian Empire,
about 1450 B.C.

Phoenician Empire,
about 900 B.C.

0   500 miles

originality. The writings of the Old Babylonians were extensively copied and reedited, but they were supplemented by little that was new.

6. THE PERSIAN EMPIRE AND ITS HISTORY

Comparatively little is known of the Persians before the sixth century B.C. Up to that time they appear to have led an obscure and peaceful existence on the eastern shore of the Persian Gulf. Their homeland afforded only modest advantages. On the east it was hemmed in by high mountains, and its coast line was destitute of harbors. The fertile valleys of the interior, however, were capable of providing a generous subsistence for a limited population. Save for the development of an elaborate religion, the people had made little progress. They had no system of writing, but they did have a spoken language closely related to Sanskrit and to the languages of ancient and modern Europe. It is for this reason alone and not because of race that they are accurately referred to as an Indo-European people. At the dawn of their history they were not an independent nation but were vassals of the Medes, a kindred people who ruled over a great empire north and east of the Tigris River.

The Persian background

In 559 B.C. a prince by the name of Cyrus became king of a southern Persian tribe. About five years later he made himself ruler of all the Persians and then developed an ambition for dominion over neighboring peoples. As Cyrus the Great he has gone down in history as one of the most sensational conquerors of all time. Within the short space of twenty years he founded a vast empire, larger than any that had previously existed.

The rise of Cyrus

The first of the real conquests of Cyrus was the kingdom of Lydia, which occupied the western half of Asia Minor and was separated from the lands of the Medes only by the Halys River, in what is now northern Turkey. Perceiving the ambitions of the Persians, Croesus, the famous Lydian king, determined to wage a preventive war to preserve his own nation from conquest. He formed alliances with Egypt and Sparta and then consulted the Greek oracle at Delphi as to the advisability of an immediate attack. According to Herodotus, the oracle replied that if he would cross the Halys and assume the offensive he would destroy a great army. He did, but that army was his own. His forces were completely overwhelmed, and his prosperous little kingdom was annexed as a province of the Persian state. Seven years later, in 539 B.C., Cyrus took advantage of discontent and conspiracies in the Chaldean empire to capture the city of Babylon. His victory was an easy one, for he had the assistance of the Jews within the city and of the Chaldean priests, who were dissatisfied with the policies of their king. The conquest of the Chaldean capital made possible the rapid extension of control over

The conquests of Cyrus

the whole empire and thereby added the Fertile Crescent to the domains of Cyrus.

The great conqueror died in 529 B.C., apparently as the result of wounds received in a war with barbarian tribes. Soon afterward a succession of troubles overtook the state he had founded. Like so many other empire builders both before and since, he had devoted too much energy to conquest and not enough to internal development. He was succeeded by his son Cambyses, who conquered Egypt in 525 B.C. During the new king's absence revolt spread throughout his Asiatic possessions. Chaldeans, Elamites, and even the Medes strove to regain their independence. The chief minister of the realm, abetted by the priests, organized a movement to gain possession of the throne for a pretender who was one of their puppets. Upon learning of conditions at home, Cambyses set out from Egypt with his most dependable troops, but he was murdered on the way. The most serious of the revolts was finally crushed by Darius, a powerful noble, who killed the pretender and seized the throne for himself.

Darius I, or the Great, as he has been called by his admirers, ruled the empire from 522 to 486 B.C. The early years of his reign were occupied in suppressing the revolts of subject peoples and in improving the administrative organization of the state. He completed the division of the empire into satrapies, or provinces, and fixed the annual tribute due from each province. He standardized the currency and weights and measures. He repaired and completed a primitive canal from the Nile to the Red Sea. He followed the example of Cyrus in tolerating and protecting the institutions of subject peoples. Not only did he restore ancient temples and foster local cults, but he ordered his satrap of Egypt to codify the Egyptian laws in consultation with the native priests. But in some of his military exploits Darius overreached himself. In order to check the incursions of the Scythians, he crossed the Hellespont, conquered a large part of the Thracian coast, and thereby aroused the hostility of the Athenians. In addition, he increased the oppression of the Ionian Greeks on the shore of Asia Minor, who had fallen under Persian domination with the conquest of Lydia. He interfered with their trade, collected heavier tribute from them, and forced them to serve in his armies. The immediate result was a revolt of the Ionian cities with the assistance of Athens. And when Darius attempted to punish the Athenians for their part in the rebellion, he found himself involved in a war with nearly all the states of Greece.

Darius the Great died while the war with the Greeks was still raging. The struggle was prosecuted vigorously but ineffectively by his successors, Xerxes I and Artaxerxes. By 479 B.C. the Persians had been driven from all of Greece. Though they recovered temporarily possession of the Ionian islands and continued to hold sway as a major power in Asia, their attempt to extend their dominion into

THE PERSIAN EMPIRE UNDER DARIUS I • 521-486 B.C.

Europe had come to an end. The last century and a half of the empire's existence was marked by frequent assassinations, revolts of provincial governors, and barbarian invasions, until finally, in 330 B.C., its independence was annihilated by the armies of Alexander the Great.

Although the Persian government had its defects, it was certainly superior to most of the others that had existed in the Near Orient. The Persian kings did not imitate the terrorism of the Assyrians. They levied tribute upon conquered peoples, but they generally allowed them to keep their own customs, religions, and laws. Indeed, it may be said that the chief significance of the Persian empire lay in the fact that it resulted in a synthesis of Near Eastern cultures, including those of Persia itself, Mesopotamia, Asia Minor, the Syria-Palestine coast, and Egypt.

Significance of
the Persian empire

The Persian kings built excellent roads to help hold their empire together. Most famous was the Royal Road, some 1600 miles in length. It extended from Susa near the Persian Gulf to Ephesus on the coast of Asia Minor. So well kept was this highway that the king's messengers, traveling day and night, could cover its entire length in less than a week. Other roads linked the various provinces with one or another of the four Persian capitals: Susa, Persepolis, Babylon, and Ecbatana. Although they naturally contributed to ease of trade, the highways were all built primarily to facilitate control over the outlying sections of the empire.

Persian
government

67

7. PERSIAN CULTURE

The eclectic culture of Persia

The culture of the Persians, in the narrower sense of intellectual and artistic achievements, was largely derived from that of previous civilizations. Much of it came from Mesopotamia, but a great deal of it from Egypt, and some from Lydia and northern Palestine. Their system of writing was originally the Babylonian cuneiform, but in time they devised an alphabet of thirty-nine letters, based upon the alphabet of the Arameans who traded within their borders. In science they accomplished nothing, except to adopt with some slight modifications the solar calendar of the Egyptians and to encourage exploration as an aid to commerce. They deserve credit also for diffusing a knowledge of the Lydian coinage throughout many parts of western Asia.

The eclectic character of Persian architecture

It was the architecture of the Persians which gave the most positive expression of the eclectic character of their culture. They copied the raised platform and the terraced building style that had been so common in Babylonia and Assyria. They imitated also the winged bulls, the brilliantly colored glazed bricks, and other decorative motifs of Mesopotamian architecture. But at least two of the leading features of Mesopotamian construction were not used by the Persians at all—the arch and the vault. In place of them they adopted the column and the colonnade from Egypt. Such matters as interior arrangement and the use of palm and lotus designs at the base of columns also point very distinctly toward Egyptian influence. On the other hand, the fluting of the columns and the volutes or scrolls beneath the capitals were not Egyptian but Greek, adopted not from the mainland of Greece itself but from the Ionian

The Great Palace of Darius and Xerxes at Persepolis. Persian architecture made use of fluted columns, probably copied from the Greeks, and reliefs resembling those of the Assyrians.

Two Reliefs from the Staircase of the Great Palace at Persepolis

cities of Asia Minor. If there was anything unique about Persian architecture, it was the fact that it was purely secular. The great Persian structures were not temples but palaces. They served to glorify not gods, but the "King of Kings." The most famous were the magnificent residences of Darius and Xerxes at Persepolis. The latter, built in imitation of the temple at Karnak, had an enormous central audience-hall containing a hundred columns and surrounded by innumerable rooms which served as offices and as quarters for the eunuchs and members of the royal harem.

8. THE ZOROASTRIAN RELIGION

By far the most enduring influence left by the ancient Persians was that of their religion. Their system of faith was of ancient origin. It was already highly developed when they began their conquests. So strong was its appeal, and so ripe were the conditions for its acceptance, that it spread through most of western Asia. Its doctrines turned other religions inside out, displacing beliefs which had been held for ages.

The religion of the Persians

Although the roots of this religion can be traced as far back as the fifteenth century B.C., its real founder was Zoroaster,[6] who appears to have lived in the early sixth century B.C. From him the religion derives its name of Zoroastrianism. He seems to have conceived it to be his mission to purify the traditional beliefs of his people—to eradicate polytheism, animal sacrifice, and magic—and to establish their worship on a more spiritual and ethical plane. In spite of his reforming efforts many of the old superstitions survived and were gradually fused with the new ideals.

The founding of Zoroastrianism

[6] "Zoroaster" is the corrupt Greek form of the Persian name Zarathustra.

69

Characteristics
of Zoroastrianism:
(1) dualism

In many respects Zoroastrianism had a character unique among
the religions of the world up to that time. First of all, it was
dualistic—not monistic like the Sumerian and Babylonian religions,
in which the same gods were capable of both good and evil; nor did
it make any pretensions to monotheism, or belief in a single divinity,
as did the Egyptian and Hebrew religions. Two great deities
ruled over the universe: one, Ahura-Mazda,[7] supremely good and
incapable of any wickedness, embodied the principles of light, truth,
and righteousness; the other, Ahriman, treacherous and malignant,
presided over the forces of darkness and evil. The two were engaged in a desperate struggle for supremacy. Although they were
about evenly matched in strength, the god of light would eventually
triumph, and the world would be saved from the powers of darkness.

(2) messianism

Zoroastrianism included such ideas as the coming of a messiah, the
resurrection of the dead, a last judgment, and the translation of the
redeemed into a paradise eternal. According to the Zoroastrian belief
the world would endure for 12,000 years. At the end of 9000 years
the second coming of Zoroaster would occur as a sign and a promise
of the ultimate redemption of the good. This would be followed in
due course by the miraculous birth of a messiah, whose work would
be the perfection of the good as a preparation for the end of the
world. Finally the last great day would arrive when Ahura-Mazda
would overpower Ahriman and cast him down into the abyss. The
dead would then be raised from their graves to be judged according
to their deserts. The righteous would enter into immediate bliss,
while the wicked would be sentenced to the flames of hell. Ultimately, though, all would be saved; for the Persian hell, unlike the
Christian, did not last forever.

(3) an ethical
religion

The Zoroastrian religion was definitely an ethical one. Although it
contained suggestions of predestination, of the election of some
from all eternity to be saved, in the main it rested upon the assumption that men possessed free will, that they were free to sin or not to
sin, and that they would be rewarded or punished in the afterlife in
accordance with their conduct on earth. Ahura-Mazda commanded
that men should be truthful, that they should love and help one
another to the best of their power, that they should befriend the
poor and practice hospitality. The essence of these broader virtues
was perhaps expressed in another of the god's decrees: "Whosoever
shall give meat to one of the faithful . . . he shall go to Paradise."
The forms of conduct forbidden were sufficiently numerous and
varied to cover the whole list of the Seven Cardinal Sins of medieval
Christianity and a great many more. Pride, gluttony, sloth, covetous-
ness, wrathfulness, lust, adultery, abortion, slander, and waste were
among the more typical. The taking of interest on loans to others of
the same faith was described as the "worst of sins," and the accumulation of riches was strongly discountenanced. The restraints which

[7] The name was frequently abbreviated to Mazda.

men were to practice included also a kind of negative Golden Rule: "That nature alone is good which shall not do unto another whatever is not good for its own self." [8]

9. THE MYSTICAL AND OTHERWORLDLY HERITAGE FROM PERSIA

The religion of the Persians as taught by Zoroaster did not long continue in its original state. It was corrupted, first of all, by the persistence of primitive superstitions, of magic and priestcraft. The farther the religion spread, the more of these relics of barbarism were engrafted upon it. As the years passed, additional modification resulted from the influence of alien faiths, particularly that of the Chaldeans. The outcome was the growth of a powerful synthesis in which the primitive priestliness, messianism, and dualism of the Persians were combined with the pessimism and fatalism of the Neo-Babylonians.

The fusion of Zoroastrianism with alien faiths

Out of this synthesis gradually emerged a profusion of cults, alike in their basic dogmas but according them different emphasis. The oldest of these cults was Mithraism, deriving its name from Mithras, the chief lieutenant of Mazda in the struggle against the powers of evil. At first only a minor deity in the religion of Zoroastrianism, Mithras finally won recognition in the hearts of many of the Persians as the god most deserving of worship. The reason for this change was probably the emotional appeal made by the incidents of his career. He was believed to have lived an earthly existence involving great suffering and sacrifice. He performed miracles giving bread and wine to man and ending a drought and also a disastrous flood. Finally, he created much of the ritual of Zoroastrianism, proclaiming Sunday as the most sacred day of the week and the twenty-fifth of December as the most sacred day of the year. Since the sun was the giver of light and the faithful ally of Mithras, his day was naturally the most sacred. The twenty-fifth of December also possessed its solar significance: as the approximate date of the winter solstice it marked the return of the sun from his long journey south of the Equator. It was in a sense the "birthday" of the sun, since it connoted the revival of his life-giving powers for the benefit of man.

Mithraism

Exactly when the worship of Mithras became a definite cult is unknown, but it was certainly not later than the fourth century B.C. Its characteristics became firmly established during the period of social ferment which followed the collapse of Alexander's empire, and its spread at that time was exceedingly rapid. In the last century B.C. it was introduced into Rome, although it was of little importance in Italy itself until after 100 A.D. It drew its converts especially from the lower classes, from the ranks of soldiers, foreigners, and slaves. Ultimately it rose to the status of one of the most popular religions

The spread and influence of Mithraism

[8] The quotations in the last paragraph are taken from J. O. Hertzler, *The Social Thought of the Ancient Civilizations*, pp. 149–158.

of the Empire, the chief competitor of Christianity and of old Roman paganism itself. After 275, however, its strength rapidly waned. How much influence this astonishing cult exerted is impossible to say. Its superficial resemblance to Christianity is certainly not hard to perceive, but this does not mean, of course, that the two were identical, or that one was an offshoot of the other. Nevertheless, it is probably true that Christianity as the younger of the two rivals borrowed a good many of its externals from Mithraism, at the same time preserving its own philosophy essentially untouched.

Manicheism

One of the principal successors of Mithraism in transmitting the legacy from Persia was Manicheism, founded by Mani, a high-born priest of Ecbatana, about 250 A.D. Like Zoroaster he conceived it to be his mission to reform the prevailing religion, but he received scant sympathy in his own country and had to be content with missionary ventures in India and western China. About 276 A.D. he was condemned and crucified by his Persian opponents. Following his death his teachings were carried by his disciples into practically every country of western Asia and finally into Italy about 330 A.D. Large numbers of western Manicheans, the great Augustine among them, eventually became Christians.

The strict dualism of the Manicheans

Of all the Zoroastrian teachings, the one that made the deepest impression upon the mind of Mani was dualism. But Mani gave to this doctrine a broader interpretation than it had ever received in the earlier religion. He conceived not merely of two deities engaged in a relentless struggle for supremacy, but of a whole universe divided into two kingdoms, each the antithesis of the other. The first was the kingdom of spirit ruled over by a God eternally good. The second was the kingdom of matter under the dominion of Satan. Only spiritual" substances such as fire, light, and the souls of men were created by God. Darkness, sin, desire, and all things bodily and material owed their origin to Satan.

The moral implications of dualism

The moral implications of this rigorous dualism were readily apparent. Since everything connected with sensation or desire was the work of Satan, man should strive to free himself as completely as possible from enslavement to his physical nature. He should refrain from all forms of sensual enjoyment, the eating of meat, the drinking of wine, the gratification of sexual desire. Even marriage was prohibited, for this would result in the begetting of more physical bodies to people the kingdom of Satan. In addition, man should subdue the flesh by prolonged fasting and infliction of pain. Recognizing that this program of austerities would be too difficult for ordinary mortals, Mani divided the race of mankind into the "perfect" and the "secular." Only the former would be obliged to adhere to the full program as the ideal of what all should hope to attain. To aid the children of men in their struggle against the powers of darkness, God had sent prophets and redeemers from time to time to comfort and inspire them. Noah, Abraham, Zoroaster, Jesus, and Paul were numbered among these divine emissaries; but the last and greatest of them was Mani.

The influence of Manicheism is very difficult to estimate, but it was undoubtedly considerable. People of all classes in the Roman Empire, including some members of the Christian clergy, embraced its doctrines. In its Christianized form it became one of the principal sects of the early Church,[9] and it exerted some influence upon the development of the Albigensian heresy as late as the twelfth and thirteenth centuries.

The influence of Manicheism

The third most important cult which developed as an element in the Persian heritage was Gnosticism (from the Greek *gnosis*, meaning knowledge). The name of its founder is unknown, and likewise the date of its origin, but it was certainly in existence as early as the first century A.D. It reached the height of its popularity in the latter half of the second century. Although it gained some followers in Italy, its influence was confined primarily to the Near East.

Gnosticism

The feature which most sharply distinguished this cult from the others was mysticism. The Gnostics denied that the truths of religion could be discovered by reason or could even be made intelligible. They regarded themselves as the exclusive possessors of a secret spiritual knowledge revealed to them directly by God. This knowledge was alone important as a guide to faith and conduct.

The mysticism of the Gnostics

The combined influence of these several Persian religions was enormous. Most of them were launched at a time when political and social conditions were particularly conducive to their spread. The breakup of Alexander's empire about 300 B.C. inaugurated a peculiar period in the history of the ancient world. International barriers were broken down; there was an extensive migration and intermingling of peoples; and the collapse of the old social order gave rise to profound disillusionment and a vague yearning for individual salvation. Men's attentions were centered as never before since the downfall of Egypt upon compensations in a life to come. Under such circumstances religions of the kind described were bound to flourish like the green bay tree. Otherwordly, mystical, and messianic, they offered the very escape that men were seeking from a world of anxiety and confusion.

The combined influence of the several off-shoots of Zoroastrianism

Although not exclusively religious, the heritage left by the Persians contained few elements of a secular nature. Their form of government was adopted by the later Roman monarchs, not in its purely political aspect, but in its character of a divine-right despotism. When such emperors as Diocletian and Constantine I invoked divine authority as a basis for their absolutism and required their subjects to prostrate themselves in their presence, they were really submerging the state in the religion as the Persians had done from the time of Darius. At the same time the Romans were impressed by

Persian Legacy

[9] See pp. 226–27

73

the Persian idea of a world empire. Darius and his successors conceived of themselves as the rulers of the whole civilized world, with a mission to reduce it to unity and, under Ahura-Mazda, to govern it justly. For this reason they generally conducted their wars with a minimum of savagery and treated conquered peoples humanely. Their ideal was a kind of prototype of the *Pax Romana*. Traces of Persian influence upon certain Hellenistic philosophies are also discernible; but here again it was essentially religious, for it was confined almost entirely to the mystical theories of the Neo-Platonists and their philosophical allies.

SELECTED READINGS

• *Items so designated are available in paperbound editions.*

Burn, A. R., *Persia and the Greeks*, New York, 1962.
• Chiera, Edward, *They Wrote on Clay*, Chicago, 1956 (Phoenix).
• Childe, V. G., *What Happened in History*, Baltimore, 1946 (Penguin).
• Contenau, G., *Everyday Life in Babylonia and Assyria*, New York, 1954 (Norton Library). Based on archaeological evidence and well illustrated.
• Cumont, Franz, *The Mysteries of Mithra*, Chicago, 1903 (Dover). A thorough analysis, interestingly presented.
• Frankfort, Henri, *The Birth of Civilization in the Near East*, Bloomington, Ind., 1951 (Anchor). Brief but useful.
• _____, *The Intellectual Adventure of Ancient Man*, Chicago, 1946. Contains evidence of the pessimism of the Mesopotamian peoples.
• Frye, R. N., *The Heritage of Persia*, New York, 1962 (Mentor).
• Ghirshman, Roman, *Iran*, Baltimore, 1954 (Penguin).
• Kramer, S. N., *History Begins at Sumer*, New York, 1959 (Anchor).
• _____, *Sumerian Mythology*, New York, 1961 (Torchbook).
_____, *The Sumerians, Their History, Culture, and Character*, Chicago, 1963.
• Lloyd, Seton, *Foundations in the Dust*, Baltimore, 1955 (Penguin).
• Neugebauer, Otto, *The Exact Sciences in Antiquity*, New York, 1969 (Dover).
Olmstead, A. T. E., *History of Assyria*, New York, 1923. The standard work. Perhaps a little too favorable.
• _____, *History of the Persian Empire (Achaemenid Period)*, Chicago, 1948 (Phoenix). Detailed and complete but somewhat uncritical.
Openheim, A. L., *Ancient Mesopotamia: Portrait of a Dead Civilization*, Chicago, 1964.
• Woolley, C. L., *The Sumerians*, New York, 1928 (Norton Library). A pioneer work, brief and interestingly written.
• _____, *Ur of the Chaldees*, New York, 1965 (Norton Library).
Zaehner, R. C., *The Dawn and Twilight of Zoroastrianism*, New York, 1961.

SOURCE MATERIALS

Barton, G. A., *The Royal Inscriptions of Sumer and Akkad*, New Haven, 1929.
Harper, R. F., ed., *The Code of Hammurabi*, Chicago, 1904.
• Herodotus, *The Persian Wars*, Baltimore, 1954 (Penguin).
Hertzler, J. O., *The Social Thought of the Ancient Civilizations*, New York, 1961, pp. 149–68.
Luckenbill, D. D., ed., *Ancient Records of Assyria and Babylonia*, Chicago, 1926, 2 vols.

CHAPTER 4

The Hebrew Civilization

I am the Lord thy God, which brought thee out of the land of
Egypt from the house of bondage.
Thou shalt have none other Gods before me.
Thou shalt not make thee any graven image, or any likeness of
any thing that is in heaven above, or that is in the earth beneath,
or that is in the waters beneath the earth:
Thou shalt not bow down thyself unto them, nor serve them: for
I the Lord thy God am a jealous God, visiting the iniquity of the
fathers upon the children unto the third and fourth generation of
them that hate me . . .

—*Deuteronomy* v. 6-9

Of all the peoples of the ancient Orient, none, with the possible exception of the Egyptians, has been of greater importance to the
modern world than the Hebrews. It was the Hebrews, of course,
who provided much of the background of the Christian religion—
its Commandments, its stories of the Creation and the Flood, its concept of God as lawgiver and judge, and more than two-thirds of its
Bible. Hebrew conceptions of morality and political theory have
also profoundly influenced modern nations, especially those in
which the Calvinist faith has been strong. On the other hand, it is
necessary to remember that the Hebrews themselves did not develop their culture in a vacuum. No more than any other people
were they able to escape the influence of nations around them.

Importance of the Hebrew civilization

1. HEBREW ORIGINS AND RELATIONS WITH OTHER PEOPLES

The origin of the Hebrew people is still a puzzling problem. Certainly they were not a separate race, nor did they have any physical
characteristics sufficient to distinguish them clearly from other nations around them.

Origin of the Hebrews and their name

Most scholars agree that the original home of the Hebrews was
the Arabian Desert. The first definite appearance of the founders of
the nation of Israel, however, was in northwestern Mesopotamia.

Apparently as early as 1800 B.C. a group of Hebrews under the leadership of Abraham had settled there. Later Abraham's grandson Jacob led a migration westward and began the occupation of Palestine. It was from Jacob, subsequently called Israel, that the Israelites derived their name. Sometime after 1600 B.C. certain tribes of Israelites, together with other Hebrews, went down into Egypt to escape the consequences of famine. They appear to have settled in the vicinity of the Delta and to have been enslaved by the Pharaoh's government. Around 1300–1250 B.C. their descendants found a new leader in the indomitable Moses, who freed them from bondage, led them to the Sinai Peninsula, and persuaded them to become worshipers of Yahweh, a god whose name is sometimes written erroneously as Jehovah. Hitherto Yahweh had been the deity of Hebrew shepherd folk in the general locality of Sinai. Making use of a Yahwist cult as a nucleus, Moses welded the various tribes of his followers into a confederation, sometimes called the Yahweh Amphictyony. It was this confederation which played the dominant role in the conquest of Palestine, or the Land of Canaan.

Hebrew migrations

With its scanty rainfall and rugged topography, Palestine as a haven for the Children of Israel left much to be desired. For the most part it was a barren and inhospitable place. But compared with the arid wastes of Arabia it was a veritable paradise, and it is not surprising that the leaders should have pictured it as a "land flowing with milk and honey." Most of it was already occupied by the Canaanites, another people of Semitic speech who had lived there for centuries. Through contact with the Babylonians, Hittites, and Egyptians they had built up a culture which was no longer primitive. They practiced agriculture and carried on trade. They knew the use of iron and the art of writing, and they had adapted the laws of Hammurabi's code to the needs of their simpler existence. Their religion, which was also derived in large part from Babylonia, was cruel and sensual, including human sacrifice and temple prostitution.

The Promised Land

The Hebrew conquest of the land of Canaan was a slow and difficult process. Seldom did the tribes unite in a combined attack, and even when they did, the enemy cities were well enough fortified to resist capture. After several generations of sporadic fighting the Hebrews had succeeded in taking only the limestone hills and a few of the less fertile valleys. In the intervals between wars they mingled freely with the Canaanites and adopted no small amount of their culture. Before they had a chance to complete the conquest, they found themselves confronted by a new and more formidable enemy, the Philistines, who had come into Palestine from Asia Minor and from the islands of the Aegean Sea. Stronger than either the Hebrews or Canaanites, the new invaders rapidly overran the country and forced the Hebrews to surrender much of the territory they had already gained. It is from the Philistines that Palestine derives its name.

Efforts to conquer the Promised Land

2. THE RECORD OF POLITICAL HOPES
AND FRUSTRATIONS

The crisis produced by the Philistine conquests served not to dis- The founding of the Hebrew monarchy courage the Hebrews but to unite them and to intensify their ardor for battle. Moreover, it led directly to the founding of the Hebrew monarchy about 1025 B.C. Up to this time the nation had been ruled by "judges," who possessed little more than the authority of reli- gious leaders. But now with a greater need for organization and dis- cipline, the people demanded a king to rule them and to go out before them and fight their battles. The man selected as the first in- cumbent of the office was Saul, "a choice young man and a goodly," a member of the tribe of Benjamin.

In spite of his popularity at the start, the reign of King Saul was not a happy one, either for the nation or for the ruler himself. Only a few suggestions of the reasons are given in the Old Testament ac- The reign of King Saul count. Evidently Saul incurred the displeasure of Samuel, the last of the great judges, who had expected to remain the power behind the throne. Before long there appeared on the scene the ambitious David, who, with the encouragement of Samuel, carried on skillful maneuvers to draw popular support from the king. Waging his own military campaigns, he achieved one bloody triumph after another. By contrast, the armies of Saul met disastrous reverses. Finally the king himself, being critically wounded, requested his armor-bearer to kill him. When the latter would not, he drew his own sword, fell upon it, and died.

David now became king and ruled for forty years. His reign was one of the most glorious periods in Hebrew history. He smote the Philistines hip and thigh and reduced their territory to a narrow The mighty David strip of coast in the south. He united the Twelve Tribes into a con- solidated state under an absolute monarch, and he began the con- struction of a magnificent capital at Jerusalem. But strong govern- ment, military glory, and material splendor were not unmixed bless- ings for the people. Their inevitable accompaniments were high taxation and conscription. As a consequence, before David died, rumblings of discontent were plainly to be heard in certain parts of his kingdom.

David was succeeded by his son Solomon, the last of the kings of the united monarchy. As a result of the nationalist aspirations of later times, Solomon has been pictured in Hebrew lore as one of the Solomon aspires to Oriental magnificence wisest, justest, and most enlightened rulers in all history. The facts of his career furnish little support for such a belief. About all that can be said in his favor is that he was a shrewd diplomat and an ac- tive patron of trade. Most of his policies were oppressive, although of course not deliberately so. Ambitious to copy the luxury and magnificence of other Oriental despots, he established a harem of 700 wives and 300 concubines and completed the construction of

The Entrance to King David's Tomb on Mount Zion, Jerusalem

sumptuous palaces, stables for 4000 horses, and a costly temple in Jerusalem. Since Palestine was poor in resources, most of the materials for the building projects had to be imported. Gold, silver, bronze, and cedar were brought in in such quantities that the revenues from taxation and from the tolls levied upon trade were insufficient to pay for them. To make up the deficit Solomon ceded twenty towns and resorted to the corvée, or the system of conscripting labor. Every three months 30,000 Hebrews were drafted and sent into Phoenicia to work in the forests and mines of King Hiram of Tyre, from whom the most expensive materials had been purchased.

The secession of the Ten Tribes

Solomon's extravagance and oppression produced acute discontent among his subjects. His death in 935 B.C. was the signal for open revolt. The ten northern tribes, refusing to submit to his son Rehoboam, seceded and set up their own kingdom. Sectional differences played their part also in the disruption of the nation. The northern Hebrews were sophisticated and accustomed to urban living. They benefited from their location at the crossroads of Near Eastern trade. While this factor increased their prosperity, it also caused them to be steeped in foreign influences. By contrast, the two southern tribes were composed very largely of pastoral and agricultural folk, loyal to the religion of their fathers, and hating the ways of the foreigner. Perhaps these differences alone would have been sufficient in time to break the nation asunder.

The fate of Israel and Judah

After the secession the ten northern tribes came to be known as the Kingdom of Israel [1] while the two southern tribes were called henceforth the Kingdom of Judah. For more than two centuries the two little states maintained their separate existences. But in 722 B.C. the Kingdom of Israel was conquered by the Assyrians. Its inhabit-

[1] Or the Kingdom of Samaria, from the name of its capital city.

ants were scattered throughout the vast empire of their conquerors and were eventually absorbed by the more numerous population around them. They have ever since been referred to as the Lost Ten Tribes of Israel. The Kingdom of Judah managed to survive for more than a hundred years longer, successfully defying the Assyrian menace. But in 586 B.C., as we have already learned, it was overthrown by the Chaldeans under Nebuchadnezzar. Jerusalem was plundered and burned, and its leading citizens were carried off into captivity in Babylon. When Cyrus the Persian conquered the Chaldeans, he freed the Jews and permitted them to return to their native land. Few were willing to go, and considerable time elapsed before it was possible to rebuild the temple. From 539 to 332 B.C. Palestine was a vassal state of Persia. In 332 B.C. it was conquered by Alexander and after his death was placed under the rule of the Ptolemies of Egypt. In 63 B.C. it became a Roman protectorate. Its political history as a Jewish commonwealth was ended in 70 A.D. after a desperate revolt which the Romans punished by destroying Jerusalem and annexing the country as a province. The inhabitants were gradually diffused through other parts of the Empire.

The destruction of Jerusalem and annexation of the country by the Romans were the principal factors in the so-called *Diaspora*, or dispersion of the Jews from Palestine. Even earlier large numbers of them had fled into various parts of the Greco-Roman world on account of difficulties in their homeland. In their new environment they rapidly succumbed to foreign influences, a fact which was of tremendous importance in promoting a fusion of Greek and Oriental ideas. It was a Hellenized Jew, St. Paul, who was mainly responsible for remolding Christianity in accordance with Greek philosophical doctrines.

The *Diaspora*

Model of King Solomon's Temple. Significant details are: A, royal gates; B, treasury; C, royal palace; D, people's gate; E, western (wailing) wall; F, priests' quarters; G, courthouse; H, Solomon's porch.

PALESTINE AFTER THE DEATH OF KING SOLOMON

3. THE HEBREW RELIGIOUS EVOLUTION

Few peoples in history have gone through a religious evolution comparable to that of the Hebrews. Its cycle of development ranged all the way from the crudest superstitions to the loftiest spiritual and ethical conceptions. Part of the explanation is doubtless to be found in the peculiar geographic position occupied by the Hebrew people. Located as they were after their conquest of Canaan on the highroad between Egypt and the major civilizations of Asia, they were bound to be affected by an extraordinary variety of influences.

At least four different stages can be distinguished in the growth of the Hebrew religion. The first we can call the pre-Mosaic stage, from the earliest beginnings of the people to approximately 1100 B.C. This stage was characterized at first by animism, the worship of

Reasons for the varied evolution of Hebrew religion

80

spirits that dwelt in trees, mountains, sacred wells and springs, and even in stones of peculiar shape. Diverse forms of magic were practiced also at this time—necromancy, imitative magic, scapegoat sacrifices, and so on. Numerous relics of these early beliefs and practices are preserved in the Old Testament.

The pre-Mosaic stage

Gradually animism gave way to anthropomorphic gods. How this transition occurred cannot be determined. Perhaps it was related to the fact that Hebrew society had become patriarchal, that is, the father exercised absolute authority over the family and descent was traced through the male line. The gods may have been thought to occupy a similar position in the clan or tribe. Apparently few of the new deities were as yet given names; each was usually referred to merely by the generic name of "El," that is, "God." They were guardian deities of particular places and probably of separate tribes. No *national* worship of Yahweh was known at this time.

Anthropomorphic gods

The second stage, which lasted from the twelfth century B.C. to the ninth, is frequently designated the stage of national monolatry. The term may be defined as the exclusive worship of one god but without any denial that other gods exist. Due chiefly to the influence of Moses, the Hebrews gradually adopted as their national deity during this period a god whose name appears to have been written "Jhwh" or "Yhwh." How it was pronounced no one knows, but scholars generally agree that it was probably uttered as if spelled "Yahweh." The meaning is also a mystery. When Moses inquired of Yahweh what he should tell the people when they demanded to know what god had sent him, Yahweh replied: "I AM THAT I AM: and he said, Thus shalt thou say unto the children of Israel, I AM hath sent me unto you." [2]

The stage of national monolatry

During the time of Moses and for two or three centuries thereafter Yahweh was a somewhat peculiar deity. He was conceived almost exclusively in anthropomorphic terms. He possessed a physical body and the emotional qualities of men. He was capricious, on occasions, and somewhat irascible—as capable of evil and wrathful judgments as he was of good. His decrees were often quite arbitrary, and he would punish the man who sinned unwittingly just about as readily as him whose guilt was real.[3] Omnipotence was scarcely an attribute that Yahweh could claim, for his power was limited to the territory occupied by the Hebrews themselves.

Characteristics of Yahweh

The religion of this stage was neither primarily ethical nor profoundly spiritual. Yahweh was revered as a supreme lawgiver and as the stern upholder of the moral order of the universe. According to Biblical account, he issued the Ten Commandments to Moses on top of Mount Sinai. Old Testament scholars, however, do not generally accept this tradition. They admit that a primitive Decalogue may

The supremacy of law and ritual

[2] Exodus 3:13-14.
[3] By way of illustration, he struck Uzza dead merely because that unfortunate individual placed his hand upon the Ark of the Covenant to steady it while it was being transported to Jerusalem. I Chronicles 13:9-10.

have existed in Mosaic times, but they doubt that the Ten Commandments in the form in which they are preserved in the Book of Exodus go back any farther than the seventh century. In any event, it is clear that Moses' God was interested just about as much in sacrifice and in ritualistic observances as he was in good conduct or in purity of heart. Moreover, the religion was not vitally concerned with spiritual matters. It offered naught but material rewards in this life and none at all in a life to come. Finally, the belief in monolatry was corrupted by certain elements of fetishism, magic, and even grosser superstitions that lingered from more primitive times or that were gradually acquired from neighboring peoples. These varied all the way from serpent worship to bloody sacrifices and licentious fertility orgies.

The stage of the prophetic revolution

The really important work of religious reform was accomplished by the great prophets—Amos, Hosea, Isaiah,[4] and Micah. And their achievements represented the third stage in the development of the Hebrew religion, the stage of the prophetic revolution, which occupied the eighth and seventh centuries B.C. The great prophets were men of broader vision than any of their forerunners. Their outlook was progressive; they did not demand a return to some age of simplicity in the past but taught that the religion should be infused with a new philosophy and a new conception of the ends it was supposed to serve. Three basic doctrines made up the substance of their teachings: (1) rudimentary monotheism—Yahweh is the Lord of the universe; He even makes use of nations other than the Hebrews to accomplish his purposes; the gods of other peoples are false gods and should not be worshiped for any reason; (2) Yahweh is a god of righteousness exclusively; He is not really omnipotent, but His power is limited by justice and goodness; the evil in the world comes from man not from God; (3) the purposes of religion are chiefly ethical; Yahweh cares nothing for ritual and sacrifice, but that men should "seek justice, relieve the oppressed, judge the fatherless, plead for the widow." Or as Micah expressed it: "What doth the Lord require of thee, but to do justly, and to love mercy, and to walk humbly with thy God?"[5]

Contrasts with the older religion; political and social aspects

These doctrines contained a definite repudiation of nearly everything that the older religion had stood for. Such, however, was apparently not the intention of the prophets. They conceived it rather as their mission to restore the religion to its ancient purity. The crudities within it they regarded as foreign corruptions. But like many such leaders, they builded better than they knew. Their actual accomplishments went so far beyond their original objectives that

---

[4] Many Old Testament authorities consider the Book of Isaiah the work of two authors. They ascribe the first part to Isaiah, and the second part, beginning with Chapter 40, to Deutero-Isaiah, or the Second Isaiah. The Second Isaiah is more emphatic than the first in denying the existence of the gods of other peoples. It dates from the period of the Exile.

[5] Micah 6:8.

Remains of an Ancient Synagogue at Capernaum. Capernaum was supposed to have been the scene of many of the miracles attributed to Jesus. Here also he called out Peter, Andrew, and Matthew to be his disciples.

they amounted to a religious revolution. To a considerable extent this revolution also had its social and political aspects. Wealth had become concentrated in the hands of a few. Thousands of small farmers had lost their freedom and had passed under subjection to rich proprietors. If we can believe the testimony of Amos, bribery was so rife in the law courts that the plaintiff in a suit for debt had merely to give the judge a pair of shoes and the defendant would be handed over as a slave.[6] Overshadowing all was the threat of Assyrian domination. To enable the nation to cope with that threat, the prophets believed that social abuses should be stamped out and the people united under a religion purged of its alien corruptions.

The results of this revolution must not be misinterpreted. It did eradicate some of the most flagrant forms of oppression, and it rooted out permanently most of the barbarities that had crept into the religion from foreign sources. But the Hebrew faith did not yet bear much resemblance to modern orthodox Judaism. It contained little of a spiritual character and hardly a trace of the mystical. Instead of being otherwordly, it was oriented toward this life. Its purposes were social and ethical—to promote a just and harmonious society and to abate man's inhumanity to man—not to confer individual salvation in an afterlife. As yet there was no belief in heaven and hell or in Satan as a powerful opponent of God. The shades of the dead went down into Sheol to linger there for a time in the dust and gloom and then disappear.

The religion not yet otherworldly or mystical

The final significant stage in Hebrew religious evolution was the post-Exilic stage or the period of Persian influence. This period may be considered to have covered the years from 539 to about 300 B.C. Perhaps enough has been said already to indicate the character of the influence from Persia. It will be recalled from the preceding

The post-Exilic stage

[6] Amos 2:6. This, of course, was poetic propaganda and may have been slightly exaggerated.

chapter that Zoroastrianism was a dualistic, messianic, otherwordly, and esoteric religion. In the period following the Exile these ideas gained wide acceptance among the Jews. They adopted a belief in Satan as the Great Adversary and the author of evil. They developed an eschatology, including such notions as the coming of a spiritual savior, the resurrection of the dead, and a last judgment. They turned their attention to salvation in an afterworld as more important than enjoyment of this life. Lastly, they embraced the conception of a revealed religion. The Book of Ezekiel, for example, was asserted to have been prepared by God in heaven and given to the man whose name it bears with instruction to "eat" it.[7]

4. HEBREW CULTURE

The limitations of the Hebrew genius

In certain respects the Hebrew genius was inferior to that of some other great nations of antiquity. In the first place, it revealed no talent for science. Not a single important discovery in any scientific field has ever been traced to the ancient Hebrews. Nor were they particularly adept in appropriating the knowledge of others. They could not build a bridge or a tunnel except of the crudest sort. Whether it was from lack of interest in these things or whether it was because of too deep an absorption in religious affairs is not clear. In the second place, they seem to have been almost entirely devoid of artistic skill. Their only examples of the glyptic arts were engraved seals similar to those made by the Sumerians and Hittites and used for the purpose of affixing signatures. They had no architecture, sculpture, or painting worthy of mention. The famous temple at Jerusalem was not a Hebrew building at all but a product of Phoenician skill, for Solomon imported artisans from Tyre to finish the more complicated tasks.

Hebrew law

It was rather in law, literature, and philosophy that the Hebrew genius was most perfectly expressed. Although all of these subjects were closely allied with religion, they did have their secular aspects. The finest example of Jewish law was the Deuteronomic Code, which forms the core of the Book of Deuteronomy. Despite claims of its great antiquity, it was probably an outgrowth of the prophetic revolution. It was based in part upon an older Code of the Covenant, which was derived in considerable measure from the laws of the Canaanites and the Old Babylonians.[8] In general, its provisions were more enlightened than those of Hammurabi's code. One of them enjoined liberality to the poor and to the stranger. Another commanded that the Hebrew slave who had served six years should be freed, and insisted that he must not be sent away empty. A third provided that judges and other officers should be chosen by the peo-

[7] Ezekiel 3:1-4.
[8] C. F. Kent, *The Message of Israel's Lawgivers*, p. 24.

ple and forbade them to accept gifts or to show partiality in any form. A fourth condemned witchcraft, divination, and necromancy. A fifth denounced the punishment of children for the guilt of their fathers and affirmed the principle of individual responsibility for sin. A sixth prohibited the taking of interest on any kind of loan made by one Jew to another. A seventh required that at the end of every seven years there should be a "release" of debts. "Every creditor that lendeth aught unto his neighbour shall release it; he shall not exact it of his neighbour, or of his brother . . . save when there shall be no poor among you." [9]

The literature of the Hebrews was by far the best that the ancient Orient ever produced. Nearly all of it now extant is preserved in the Old Testament and in the books of the so-called Apocrypha. Except for a few fragments like the Song of Deborah in Judges 5, it is not really so ancient as is commonly supposed. Scholars now recognize that the Old Testament was built up mainly through a series of collections and revisions (redactions) in which the old and new fragments were merged and generally assigned to an ancient author, Moses, for example. But the oldest of these redactions was not prepared any earlier than 850 B.C. The majority of the books of the Old Testament were of even more recent origin, with the exception, of course, of certain of the chronicles. As one would logically expect, the philosophical books were of late authorship. Although the bulk of the Psalms were ascribed to King David, a good many of them actually refer to events of the Captivity. It seems certain that the collection as a whole was the work of several centuries. Most recent of all were the books of Ecclesiastes, Esther, and Daniel, composed no earlier than the third century B.C. Likewise, the Apocrypha, or books of doubtful religious authority, did not see the light of day until Hebrew civilization was almost extinct. Some, like Maccabees I and II, relate events of the second century B.C. Others including the Wisdom of Solomon and the Book of Enoch were written under the influence of Greco-Oriental philosophy.

Not all of the writings of the Hebrews had high literary merit. A considerable number were dull, repetitious chronicles. Nevertheless, most of them, whether in the form of battle song, prophecy, love lyric, or drama, were rich in rhythm, concrete images, and emotional vigor. Few passages in any language can surpass the scornful indictment of social abuses voiced by the prophet Amos:

> Hear this, O ye that swallow up the needy, even to make the
>   poor of the land to fail,
> Saying, when will the new moon be gone, that we may sell
>   corn?
> And the sabbath that we may set forth wheat,
> Making the ephah small, and the shekel great,

Hebrew literature

The Shekel of Ancient Israel. Struck between 141 and 137 B.C., this silver coin is approximately half the weight of a United States silver dollar.

Amos' indictment of social abuses

And falsifying the balances by deceit?
That we may buy the poor for silver, and the needy for a pair
    of shoes;
Yea, and sell the refuse of the wheat?

The most beautiful of Hebrew love lyrics was the Song of Songs, or the Song of Solomon. Its theme was quite probably derived from an old Canaanite hymn of spring, celebrating the passionate affection of the Shulamith or fertility goddess for her lover, but it had long since lost its original meaning. The following verses are typical of its sensuous beauty:

The Song of Songs

I am the rose of Sharon
and the lily of the valleys.
As the lily among thorns,
so is my love among the daughters.

.   .   .   .

My beloved is white and ruddy,
the chiefest among ten thousand.
His head is as the most fine gold;
his locks are bushy and black as a raven:
His eyes are as the eyes of doves by the rivers of waters,
washed with milk and fitly set.
His cheeks are as a bed of spices, as sweet flowers;
his lips like lilies, dropping sweet smelling myrrh.

.   .   .   .

How beautiful are thy feet with shoes, O prince's daughter!
The joints of thy thighs are like jewels,
the work of the hands of a cunning workman.

Few authorities would deny that the supreme achievement of the Hebrew literary genius was the Book of Job. In form the work is a drama of the tragic struggle between man and fate. Its central theme is the problem of evil: how it can be that the righteous suffer while the eyes of the wicked stand out with fatness. The story was an old one, adapted very probably from the Babylonian writing of similar content, but the Hebrews introduced into it a much deeper realization of philosophical possibilities. The main character, Job, a man of unimpeachable virtue, is suddenly overtaken by a series of disasters: he is despoiled of his property, his children are killed, and his body is afflicted with a painful disease. His attitude at first is one of stoic resignation; the evil must be accepted along with the good. But as his sufferings increase he is plunged into despair. He curses the day of his birth and delivers an apostrophe to death, where "the wicked cease from troubling and the weary be at rest."

The Book of Job

Then follows a lengthy debate between Job and his friends over the meaning of evil. The latter take the traditional Hebraic view that all suffering is a punishment for sin, and that those who repent are forgiven and strengthened in character. But Job is not satisfied with any of their arguments. Torn between hope and despair, he strives to review the problem from every angle. He even considers the possibility that death may not be the end, that there may be some adjustment of the balance hereafter. But the mood of despair returns, and he decides that God is an omnipotent demon, destroying without mercy wherever His caprice or anger directs. Finally, in his anguish he appeals to the Almighty to reveal Himself and make known His ways to man. God answers him out of the whirlwind with a magnificent exposition of the tremendous works of nature. Convinced of his own insignificance and of the unutterable majesty of God, Job despises himself and repents in dust and ashes. In the end no solution is given of the problem of individual suffering. No promise is made of recompense in a life hereafter, nor does God make any effort to refute the hopeless pessimism of Job. Man must take comfort in the philosophic reflection that the universe is greater than himself, and that God in the pursuit of His sublime purposes cannot really be limited by human standards of equity and goodness.

The problem of evil

As philosophers the Hebrews surpassed every other people before the Greeks, including the Egyptians. Although they were not brilliant metaphysicians and constructed no great theories of the universe, they did concern themselves with most of the problems relating to the life and destiny of man. Their thought was essentially personal rather than abstract. Probably the earliest of their writings of a distinctly philosophical character were the Book of Proverbs and the Book of Ecclesiasticus. In their final form both were of late composition, but much of the material they contain was doubtless quite ancient. Not all of it was original, for a considerable portion had been taken from Egypt sources as early as 1000 B.C. The books have as their essential teaching: be temperate, diligent, wise, and honest, and you will surely be rewarded with prosperity, long life, and a good name among men. Only in such isolated passages as the following is any recognition given to higher motives of sympathy or respect for the rights of others: "Whoso mocketh the poor reproacheth his Maker; and he that is glad at calamities shall not be unpunished." [10]

Hebrew philosophy: early examples

A much more profound and critical philosophy is contained in Ecclesiastes, an Old Testament book, not to be confused with the Ecclesiasticus mentioned above. The author of Ecclesiastes is unknown. In some way it came to be attributed to Solomon, but he certainly did not write it, for it includes doctrines and forms of

Ecclesiastes

[10] Proverbs 17:5.

expression unknown to the Hebrews for hundreds of years after his death. Modern critics date it no earlier than the third century B.C. The basic ideas of its philosophy may be summarized as follows:

(1) Mechanism. The universe is a machine that rolls on forever without evidence of any purpose or goal. Sunrise and sunset, birth and death are but separate phases of constantly recurring cycles.

(2) Fatalism. Man is a victim of the whims of fate. There is no necessary relation between effort and success. "The race is not to the swift, nor the battle to the strong, neither yet bread to the wise . . . but time and chance happeneth to them all."

(3) Pessimism. All is vanity and vexation of spirit. Fame, riches, extravagant pleasure are snares and delusions in the end. Although wisdom is better than folly, even it is not a sure key to happiness, for an increase in knowledge brings a keener awareness of suffering.

(4) Moderation. Extremes of asceticism and extremes of indulgence are both to be avoided. "Be not righteous over much . . . be not over much wicked: why shouldest thou die before thy time?" [11]

5. THE MAGNITUDE OF THE HEBREW INFLUENCE

The influence of the Hebrews, like that of most other Oriental peoples, has been chiefly religious and ethical. While it is true that the Old Testament has served as a source of inspiration for much of the literature and art of the Renaissance and early modern civilizations, this has resulted largely because the Bible was already familiar material as a part of the religious heritage. The same explanation can be applied to the use of the Old Testament as a source of law and political theory by the Calvinists in the sixteenth century, and by many other Christians both before and since.

The nature of the Hebrew influence

But these facts do not mean that the Hebrew influence has been slight. On the contrary, the history of nearly every Western civilization during the past two thousand years would have been radically different without the heritage from Israel. For it must be remembered that Hebrew beliefs were among the principal foundations of Christianity. The relationship between the two religions is frequently misunderstood. The movement inaugurated by Jesus of Nazareth is commonly represented as a revolt against Judaism; but such was only partly the case. On the eve of the Christian era the Jewish nation had come to be divided into three main sects: a majority sect of Pharisees, and two minority sects of Sadducees and Essenes. The Pharisees represented the middle classes and some of the better educated common folk. They believed in the resurrection, in rewards and punishments after death, and in the coming of a political messiah. Intensely nationalistic, they advocated participation in government and faithful observance of the ancient ritual.

Hebrew foundations of Christianity: the beliefs of the Pharisees

[11] For a more complete analysis of the philosophy of Ecclesiastes see Morris Jastrow, *A Gentle Cynic.*

They regarded all parts of the law as of virtually equal importance, whether they applied to matters of ceremony or to obligations of social ethics.

Representing altogether different strata of society, the minority sects disagreed with the Pharisees on both religious and political issues. The Sadducees, including the priests and the wealthier classes, were most famous for their denial of the resurrection and of rewards and punishments in an afterlife. Although temporarily, at least, they favored the acceptance of Roman rule, their attitude toward the ancient law was even more inflexible than that of the Pharisees. The sect of Essenes, the smallest of them all, was possibly the most influential. Its members, who were drawn from the lower classes, practiced asceticism and preached otherworldliness as means of protest against the wealth and power of priests and rulers. They ate and drank only enough to keep themselves alive, held all their goods in common, and looked upon marriage as a necessary evil. Far from being fanatical patriots, they regarded government with indifference and refused to take oaths under any conditions. They emphasized the spiritual aspects of religion rather than the ceremonial, and stressed particularly the immortality of the soul, the coming of a religious messiah, and the early destruction of the world.

Until recently scholars were dependent for their knowledge of the Essenes almost entirely upon secondary sources. But in 1947 an Arab shepherd unwittingly opened the way to one of the most spectacular discoveries of documentary evidence in world history. Searching for a lost sheep on the western shore of the Dead Sea, he threw a stone that entered a hole in the rocks and made such a peculiar noise that he ran away in fright. He returned, however, with a friend to investigate and discovered a cave in which were stored

The Sadducees
and the Essenes

The Dead Sea
scrolls

The Dead Sea Scrolls. Now on display in an underground vault at the Hebrew University in Jerusalem. The oldest extant examples of Hebrew religious literature, they furnish us with evidence of the activities of the Essenes and mystical and other worldly sects about the beginning of the Christian era.

about fifty cylindrical earthen jars stuffed with writings on leather scrolls. Studied by scholars, the scrolls revealed the existence of a monastic community which flourished from about 130 B.C. to 67 A.D. Its members lived a life of humility and self-denial, holding their goods in common, and devoting their time to prayer and sacraments and to studying and copying Biblical texts. They looked forward confidently to the coming of a messiah, the overthrow of evil, and the establishment of God's kingdom on earth. That they belonged to the same general movement that fostered the growth of the Essenes seems almost beyond question.

Hebrew influence upon Christianity

All branches of Judaism except the Sadducees strongly influenced the development of Christianity. From Jewish sources Christianity obtained its cosmogony, or theory of the origin of the universe; the Ten Commandments; and a large portion of its theology. Jesus himself, although he condemned the Pharisees for their legalism and hypocrisy, did not repudiate all of their tenets. Instead of abolishing the ancient law, as he is popularly supposed to have done, he demanded its fulfillment, insisting, however, that it should not be made the essential part of religion. To what extent the beliefs and practices of the Christian religion were molded by the more radical Judaism of the Essenes and kindred sects is a question whose answer must await further research. Nonetheless, we know that many early Christians practiced asceticism, regarded government with indifference and the Roman Empire with hostility, held all their goods in common, and believed in the imminent end of the world. These parallels do not mean, of course, that Christianity was a mere adaptation of beliefs and practices emanating from Judaism. There was much in it that was unique; but that is a subject which can be discussed more conveniently in another connection.[12]

Ethical and political influence of the Hebrews

The ethical and political influence of the Hebrews has also been substantial. Their moral conceptions have been a leading factor in the development of the negative approach toward ethics which has prevailed for so long in Western countries. For the early Hebrews, "righteousness" consisted primarily in the observance of taboos. Although a positive morality of charity and social justice made rapid headway during the time of the prophets, this in turn was partly obscured by the revival of priestly influence in the period that followed. With respect to political influence, the record is more impressive. Hebrew ideals of limited government, the sovereignty of law, and regard for the dignity and worth of the individual have been among the major formative influences which have shaped the growth of modern democracy. It is now almost universally recognized that the traditions of Judaism contributed equally with the influence of Christianity and Stoic philosophy in fostering recognition of the rights of man and in promoting the development of the free society.

[12] See chapter on The Civilization of the Early Middle Ages.

· *Items so designated are available in paperbound editions.*

· Albright, W. F., *The Archaeology of Palestine*, Baltimore, 1960 (Penguin).

Anderson, B. W., *Rediscovering the Bible*, New York, 1951.

Bertholet, Alfred, *A History of Hebrew Civilization*, London, 1926.

· Chase, Mary E., *Life and Language in the Old Testament*, New York, 1955 (Norton Library).

· Davies, A. P., *The Meaning of the Dead Sea Scrolls*, New York, 1956 (Mentor).

· De Burgh, W. G., *The Legacy of the Ancient World*, 3d ed., New York, 1960 (Penguin). A good survey of the influence of Hebrew thought.

Finegan, Jack, *Light from the Ancient Past*, Princeton, 1946.

Fritsch, C. T., *The Qumrān Community*, New York, 1956. Relates the importance of the Dead Sea Scrolls.

· Frye, R. N., *The Heritage of Persia*, Cleveland, 1963 (Mentor).

· Kenyon, K. M., *Archaeology in the Holy Land*, New York, 1960 (Praeger).

Klausner, Joseph, *The Messianic Idea in Israel*, New York, 1955.

Lods, Adolphe, *Israel from Its Beginnings to the Middle of the Eighth Century*, New York, 1932. Excellent on religious, intellectual, and social history.

· Meek, T. J., *Hebrew Origins*, rev., New York, 1951 (Torchbook).

Oesterley, W. O. E., and Robinson, T. H., *Hebrew Religion, Its Origin and Development*, New York, 1932. One of the best interpretations.

Olmstead, A. T. E., *History of Palestine and Syria*, New York, 1931.

· Orlinsky, H. M., *Ancient Israel*, Ithaca, 1956 (Cornell). Brief but good.

· Roth, Cecil, *The Dead Sea Scrolls*, New York, 1965 (Norton Library). Author contends that the scrolls were not produced by the Essenes but by the Zealots, a warlike sect deeply involved in the rebellion against Rome in 66 A.D.

Smith, J. M. P., *The Moral Life of the Hebrews*, Chicago, 1923.

———, *The Origin and History of Hebrew Law*, Chicago, 1931.

Vaux, Roland de, *Ancient Israel: Its Life and Institutions*, New York, 1962. Especially valuable for archaeological data.

SOURCE MATERIALS

The Apocrypha, Ancient Hebrew writings of doubtful authorship. Not recognized as scriptural by Hebrew and Protestant theologians.

· Gaster, T. H., trans., *The Dead Sea Scriptures in English Translation*. New York, 1964 (Anchor).

The Old Testament, especially the following books and portions of books: Deuteronomy 5, 12–21; Ecclesiastes; Amos; I Samuel 8–31; II Samuel; I Kings 1–12; Job; Proverbs; Isaiah 1–12, 40–66; Micah; Psalms.

Pritchard, J. B., ed., *Ancient Near Eastern Texts Relating to the Old Testament*, rev. ed., Princeton, 1955.

CHAPTER 5

The Hittite, Minoan-Mycenaean,
and Lesser Cultures

But for them among these gods will be bled for annual food:
to the god Karnua one steer and one sheep;
to the goddess Kupapa one steer and one sheep;
to the divinity Sarku one sheep;
and a Kutupalis sheep to the male divinities.
——Hittite sacrifice formula, translated
from a hieroglyph by
H. T. Bossert

A few other ancient cultures of the Near Orient require more than passing attention. Chief among them are the Hittite, Minoan-Mycenaean, Phoenician, and Lydian cultures. The Hittites are important primarily as intermediaries between East and West. They were one of the main connecting links between the civilizations of Egypt, the Tigris-Euphrates valley, and the region of the Aegean Sea. It appears certain also that they were the original discoverers of iron. The Minoan-Mycenaean civilization is significant for its remarkable achievements in the arts and for its quality of freedom and courage for experimentation. Though many of its achievements perished, there is evidence that the Greeks owed to these Aegean peoples a considerable debt. The Greek religion, for example, contained numerous Minoan-Mycenaean elements. Of the same origin were probably the devotion of the Greeks to athletics, their system of weights and measures, their knowledge of navigation, and perhaps also a great many of their artistic traditions. As for the Phoenicians, no one could overlook the importance of their distribution of a knowledge of the alphabet and a primitive commercial law to the surrounding civilized world. The Lydians have gone down in history as the originators of the first system of coinage.

Importance of these cultures

93

1. THE HITTITES AND THE PHRYGIANS

The discovery
of remains
of the Hittite
civilization

Until about a century ago little was known of the Hittites except their name. They were commonly assumed to have played no role of any significance in the drama of history. The slighting references to them in the Bible give the impression that they were little more than a half-barbarian tribe. But in 1870 some curiously inscribed stones were found at Hamath in Syria. This was the beginning of an extensive inquiry which has continued with a few interruptions to the present day. It was not long until scores of other monuments and clay tablets were discovered over most of Asia Minor and through the Near East as far as the Tigris-Euphrates valley. In 1907 some evidences of an ancient city were unearthed near the village of Boghaz-Keui in the province of Anatolia. Further excavation eventually revealed the ruins of a great fortified capital which was known as Hattusas or Hittite City. Within its walls were discovered more than 20,000 documents and fragments, most of them apparently laws and decrees.

The Hittite empire

On the basis of these finds and other evidences gradually accumulated, it was soon made clear that the Hittites were once the rulers of a mighty empire covering most of Asia Minor and extending to the upper reaches of the Euphrates. Part of the time it included Syria as well and even portions of Phoenicia and Palestine. The Hittites reached the zenith of their power during the years from 2000 to 1200 B.C. In the last century of this period they waged a long and exhausting war with Egypt, which had much to do with the downfall of both empires. Neither was able to regain its strength. After 1200 B.C. Carchemish on the Euphrates River became for a time the leading Hittite city, but as a commercial center rather than as the capital of a great empire. The days of imperial glory were over. Finally, after 717 B.C., all the remaining Hittite territories were conquered and absorbed by the Assyrians, Lydians, and Phrygians.

The mystery of
the race and
language of the
Hittites

Where the Hittites came from and what were their relationships to other peoples are problems which still defy a perfect solution. As depicted by the Egyptians, some of them appear to have been of a Mongoloid type. All had enormous hooked noses, receding foreheads, and slanting eyes. Most modern scholars trace their place of origin to Turkestan and consider them related to the Greeks. Their language was Indo-European. Its secret was unlocked during World War I by the Czech scholar Bedrich Hrozny. Since then thousands of clay tablets making up the laws and official records of the emperors have been deciphered. They reveal a civilization resembling more closely the Old Babylonian than any other.

Hardly enough evidence has yet been collected to make possible an accurate appraisal of Hittite civilization. Some modern historians refer to it as if it were on a level with the Mesopotamian or even with the Egyptian civilization. Such may have been the case from the material standpoint, for the Hittites undoubtedly had an extensive knowledge of agriculture and a highly developed economic life in general. They mined great quantities of silver, copper, and lead, which they sold to surrounding nations. They discovered the mining and use of iron and made that material available for the rest of the civilized world. Trade was also one of their principal economic pursuits. In fact, they seem to have depended almost as much upon commercial penetration as upon war for the expansion of their empire.

The literature of the Hittites consisted chiefly of mythology, including adaptations of creation and flood legends from the Old Babylonians. They had nothing that could be described as philosophy, nor is there any evidence of scientific originality outside of the metallurgical arts. They evidently possessed some talent for the perfection of writing, for in addition to a modified cuneiform adapted from Mesopotamia they also developed a hieroglyphic system which was partly phonetic in character.

One of the most significant achievements of the Hittites was their system of law. Approximately two hundred separate paragraphs or decrees, covering a great variety of subjects, have been translated. They reflect a society comparatively urbane and sophisticated but subject to minute governmental control. The title to all land was vested in the king or in the governments of the cities. Grants were made to individuals only in return for military service and under the strict requirement that the land be cultivated. Prices were fixed in the laws themselves for an enormous number of commodities—not only for articles of luxury and the products of industry, but even for food and clothing. All wages and fees for services were likewise minutely prescribed, with the pay of women fixed at less than half the rate for men.

On the whole, the Hittite law was more humane than that of the Old Babylonians. Death was the punishment for only eight offenses —such as witchcraft, and theft of property from the palace. Even premeditated murder was punishable only by a fine. Mutilation was not specified as a penalty at all except for arson or theft when committed by a slave. The contrast with the cruelties of Assyrian law was more striking. Not a single example is to be found in the Hittite decrees of such fiendish punishments as flaying, castration, and impalement, which the rulers at Nineveh seemed to think necessary for maintaining their authority.

The art of the Hittites was not of outstanding excellence. So far as we know, it included only sculpture and architecture. The former was generally crude and naïve, but at the same time it revealed a freshness and vigor all too uncommon in the work of Oriental peoples. Most of it was in the form of reliefs depicting scenes of war and mythology. Architecture was ponderous and huge. Temples and palaces were squat, unadorned structures with small, two-columned porches and great stone lions guarding the entrance.

The economic life of the Hittites

The intellectual level of Hittite culture

Hittite law

Humane character of Hittite law

The art of the Hittites

Hittite Sculpture. Perhaps the most highly conventionalized sculpture of the ancient world is found in Hittite reliefs.

Hittite religion

Not a great deal is known about the Hittite religion except that it had an elaborate mythology, innumerable deities, and forms of worship of Mesopotamian origin. A sun god was worshiped, along with a host of other deities, some of whom appear to have had no particular function at all. The Hittites seem to have welcomed into the divine company practically all of the gods of the peoples they conquered and even of the nations that bought their wares. The practices of the religion included divination, sacrifice, purification ceremonies, and the offering of prayers. Nothing can be found in the records to indicate that the religion was in any sense ethical.

The importance of the Hittites

The chief historical importance of the Hittites probably lies in the role which they played as intermediaries between the Tigris-Euphrates valley and the westernmost portions of the Near East. Doubtless in this way certain culture elements from Mesopotamia were transmitted to the Canaanites and Hyksos and perhaps to the peoples of the Aegean islands.

2. THE MINOAN-MYCENAEAN CIVILIZATION

A long-forgotten civilization

By a strange coincidence the discovery of the existence of the Hittite and Minoan-Mycenaean civilizations was made at just about the same time. Before 1870 scarcely anyone dreamed that great civilizations had flourished on the Aegean islands and on the shores of Asia Minor for hundreds of years prior to the rise of the Greeks. Students of the *Iliad* knew, of course, of the references to a strange people who were supposed to have dwelt in Troy, to have kidnaped the fair Helen, and to have been punished by the Greeks for this act by the siege and destruction of their city; but it was commonly supposed that these accounts were mere figments of a poetical imagination.

The first discovery of a highly developed Aegean culture center was made not by a professional archaeologist but by a retired German businessman, Heinrich Schliemann. Fascinated from early youth by the stories of the Homeric epics, he determined to dedicate his life to archaeological research as soon as he had sufficient income to enable him to do so. Luckily for him and for the world he accumulated a fortune in Russian petroleum and then retired from business to spend both time and money in the pursuit of his boyhood dreams. In 1870 he began excavating at Troy. Within a few years he had uncovered portions of nine different cities, each built upon the ruins of its predecessor. The second of these cities he identified as the Troy of the *Iliad*, although it has been proved since that Troy was the seventh city. After fulfilling his first great ambition, he started excavations on the mainland of Greece and eventually uncovered two other Aegean cities, Mycenae and Tiryns. The work of Schliemann was soon followed by that of other investigators, notably the Englishman Sir Arthur Evans, who discovered Knossos, the resplendent capital of the Minoan kings of Crete. Up to the present time more than half of the ancient Aegean sites have been carefully searched, and a wealth of knowledge has been accumulated about various aspects of the culture.

The discoveries by Schliemann and others

The Minoan-Mycenaean civilization appears to have originated on the island of Crete, from which it spread to the mainland of Greece and to Asia Minor. In few other cases in history does the geographic interpretation of culture origins fit so neatly. Crete has a benign and equable climate, neither so hot as to make men lazy nor so cold as to require a life of unceasing struggle. While the soil is fertile, it is not of unlimited area; consequently, as the population increased, men were impelled to sharpen their wits and to contrive new means of earning a living. Some emigrated; others took to the sea; but a larger number remained at home and developed articles for export. The latter included, especially, wine and olive oil, pottery, gems and seals, knives and daggers, and objects of skilled craftsmanship. The chief imports were foodstuffs and metals. As a result of such trade, the country became an industrial and commercial nation with pros-

The favorable natural environment of Crete

The Goddess Cybele. A Roman statue depicting the Phrygian goddess on a processional cart drawn by lions.

perous cities and extensive contacts with the surrounding civilized world. Added to these factors of a favorable environment were the beauties of nature, which abounded almost everywhere, stimulating the development of a marvelous art.

The Minoan civilization was one of the earliest in the history of the world. As far back as 3000 B.C. the natives of Crete had made the transition from the Neolithic stage to the age of metals and probably to the age of writing. The first peak of advancement was attained under the leadership of the cities of Knossos and Phaistos about 1800 B.C. Recently evidence has been found of the existence of another great city, Kato Zakros, on the east coast of Crete. Here was a huge palace of 250 rooms, with a swimming pool, parquet floors, and thousands of decorated vases. About 1450 B.C. this palace was destroyed by volcanic eruptions followed by violent earthquakes. Other cities probably suffered a similar fate, although Knossos and Phaistos were rebuilt. A new dynasty came to the throne of Crete. A new system of writing was adopted, and a new cycle of civilization began which carried Minoan culture to its greatest heights.

After about fifty years of uncertainty the Minoan-Mycenaean civilization rose to new heights of brilliance and strength. Troy and the cities of Crete were rebuilt, and other great centers were established at Mycenae and Tiryns. Soon afterward Cretan hegemony was extended over the remaining portions of the Aegean world. But the new age of power and splendor was not destined for long duration. The island's resources were substantially depleted, and commerce with Egypt had diminished. In the sixteenth century B.C. a group of barbarian Greeks subsequently known as Achaeans expanded from their original home in the northern Peloponnesus and eventually conquered Mycenae. Gradually absorbing the material culture of the vanquished, they became rich and powerful sea lords. About 1400 B.C. they overwhelmed the city of Knossos, and soon the whole island of Crete passed under their sway. Although they were no longer a primitive people, they seem never to have appreciated the finer aspects of Cretan culture. As a result this period of Mycenaean supremacy was marked by a decline in art and probably in intellect as well. In the thirteenth century the Mycenaeans waged their successful war with the Trojans, but less than 200 years later they themselves fell the victims of barbarian invasion. The new hordes that came in were also Greeks, but they belonged to the group known as Dorians (originally from somewhere on the Balkan peninsula). Their culture was relatively primitive, except for the fact that they had iron weapons. For centuries they had lived on the mainland of Greece, gradually penetrating farther southward. About 1250 B.C. they began their conquest of the Mycenaean cities. Two hundred years later the Minoan-Mycenaean civilization had passed into the limbo of history.

The racial character of the Minoan people has been determined with substantial accuracy. Archaeological data from Crete have been found in sufficient profusion to leave little doubt that its ancient inhabitants were a composite nation. Their ancestors appear to have come from Syria and Anatolia and were closely related to the Hittites and to the earliest invaders of India. At the same time there is evidence—from the fact that their artists depicted them with long heads, short, slender bodies, and dark, wavy hair—that they bore a relationship to the Egyptians. Although they occupied Greek territory, they were not Greeks at all in the historic meaning of that name. The true Greeks, as we shall presently see, were of altogether different ethnic origin.

The Minoan civilization was probably one of the freest and most progressive in all the Near Orient. The ruler was known by the title of Minos, which was roughly the equivalent of Pharaoh (hence the name *Minoan*). That it was a title of divinity is shown by the fact that it was occasionally used as if it referred to a god. But the Minos was no bristling war lord like the Assyrian and Persian kings. He did have a large and efficient navy, but this was for defense against external attack and for the protection of trade, not to overawe the citizens at home.

On the other hand, there was some regimentation of industry. The king was the chief capitalist and entrepreneur in the country. The factories in connection with his palace turned out great quantities of fine pottery, textiles, and metal goods. Although private enterprise was not prohibited, the owners of smaller establishments were naturally at some disadvantage in competing with the king. Nevertheless, numerous privately owned factories did flourish, especially in cities other than the capital, and agriculture and trade were also in private hands. It must be understood that these establishments, both royal and private, were factories in nearly every modern sense of the word. While they did not use power-driven machinery, they were engaged in large-scale production, and there was division of labor and centralized control and supervision of workers. The hundreds of women employed in the royal textile factory worked under the supervision of the queen.

The Aegean people of nearly all classes appear to have led happy and fairly prosperous lives. If slavery existed at all, it certainly occupied an unimportant place. The dwellings in the poorest quarters of great industrial towns such as Gournia were substantially built and commodious, often with as many as six or eight rooms, but we do not know how many families resided in them. If we can judge from the number of inscriptions found in the homes of the common people, literacy was well-nigh universal. Women enjoyed complete equality with men. Regardless of class there was no public activity from which they were debarred, and no occupation which they could not enter. Crete had its female bull fighters and even female

Scenes from the Bull Ring, Cretan Painting, about 1500 B.C. Evident are the Cretans' devotion to sport and the skill and agility of their athletes. The body and horns of the bull, however, are exaggerated as are the slenderness of the athletes and their full-face eyes in profile heads.

pugilists. Ladies of the upper strata devoted much time to fashion. Dressed in their tight-fitting bodices and bell-shaped skirts with flounces which would not have been much out of style in nineteenth-century Europe, they vied with each other for attention in the theaters and at public entertainments of numerous kinds.

The natives of the Aegean area delighted in games and sports of every description. Chess, dancing, running matches, and boxing rivaled each other in their attraction for the people. The Cretans were the first to build stone theaters where processions and music entertained large audiences.

The religion of the subjects of Minos was a medley of strange characteristics. First of all it was matriarchal. The chief deity was not a god but a goddess, who was the ruler of the entire universe—the sea and the sky as well as the earth. Originally no male deity appears to have been worshiped, but later a god was associated with the goddess as her son and lover. Although, like the divine sons in several other religions, he apparently died and rose from the dead, he was never regarded by the Cretans as of particular importance.

In the second place, the Minoan religion was thoroughly monistic. The mother goddess was the source of evil as well as of good, but not in any morbid or terrifying sense. Though she brought the storm and spread destruction in her path, these served for the replenishment of nature. Death itself was interpreted as the condition prerequisite for life. Whether the religion had any ethical purposes is unknown.

Other rather curious features included the worship of animals and birds (the bull, the snake, and the dove); the worship of sacred trees; the veneration of sacred objects which were probably reproductive symbols (the double-axe, the pillar, and the cross); and the employment of priestesses instead of priests to administer the rites of the cult. By far the most important act of worship was sacrifice. At the great religious festivals hundreds of animals and large quantities of grain and fruit were brought as grateful offerings to the goddess and her son.

For many years after the discovery of the Minoan-Mycenaean civilization its system of writing remained a complete enigma. At length, however, Sir Arthur Evans succeeded in showing that these Aegean people produced not only one system of writing but three—a hieroglyphic script and two linear scripts, which were used in successive periods. One script, used during the Mycenaean stage, was actually a form of Greek. The other continues to belong to the realm of mystery.[1] No literary texts of the Minoan-Mycenaean civilization have yet been unearthed. It is impossible therefore to tell whether any literature or philosophy had been written. The problem of scientific achievements is easier to solve, since we have material remains for our guidance. Archaeological discoveries on the island of Crete indicate that the ancient inhabitants were gifted inventors and engineers. They built excellent roads of concrete about eleven feet wide. Nearly all the basic principles of modern sanitary engineering were known to the designers of the palace of Knossos, with the result that the royal family of Crete in the seventeenth century B.C. enjoyed comforts and conveniences that were not available to the wealthiest rulers of Western countries in the seventeenth century A.D.

Minoan-Mycenaean writing and scientific achievements

If there was any one achievement of these Aegean people that appears more than others to emphasize the vitality and freedom of their culture, it was their art. With the exception of the Greek, no other art of the ancient world was quite its equal. Its distinguishing features were delicacy, spontaneity, and naturalism. It served not to glorify the ambitions of an arrogant ruling class or to inculcate the doctrines of a religion, but to express the delight of the ordinary man in the world of beauty around him. As a result, it was remarkably free from the retarding influence of ancient tradition. It was unique, moreover, in the universality of its application, for it extended not merely to paintings and statues but even to the humblest objects of ordinary use.

Minoan-Mycenaean art

Of the major arts, architecture was the least developed. The great palaces were not remarkably beautiful buildings but rambling structures designed primarily for capaciousness and comfort. As more and more functions were absorbed by the state, the palaces were enlarged to accommodate them. New quarters were annexed to those already built or piled on top of them without regard for order or symmetry. The interiors, however, were decorated with beautiful paintings and furnishings. The architecture of Crete may be said to have resembled the modern international style in its subordination

Architecture

---

[1] Although his findings are widely disputed, one scholar, Cyrus H. Gordon, maintains that it derives from a Semitic script.

Central Staircase of the Palace of Minos.

of form to utility and in its emphasis upon a pleasing and livable interior as more important than external beauty.

Painting

Painting was the art supreme of the Aegean world. Nearly all of it consisted of murals done in fresco, although painted reliefs were occasionally to be found. The murals in the palaces of Crete were by all odds the best that have survived from ancient times. They revealed almost perfectly the remarkable gifts of the Minoan artist— his instinct for the dramatic, his sense of rhythm, his feeling for nature in her most characteristic moods.

Sculpture, pottery, and engraving

Sculpture and the ceramic and gem-carving arts were also developed to a high stage of perfection. The sculpture of the Cretans differed from that of any other people in the ancient Near Orient. It never relied upon size as a device to convey the idea of power. The Cretans produced no colossi like those of Egypt or reliefs like those of Babylonia depicting a king of gigantic proportions smiting his puny enemies. Instead, they preferred sculpture in miniature. Nearly all of the statues of human beings or of deities that the archaeologists have found are smaller than life-size.

The more barbarous character of Mycenaean culture

The point must be emphasized that the Minoan achievements in the arts, government, and social life were not equaled in the Mycenaean stage. Compared with the Cretans, the Mycenaeans were barbarians who failed to appreciate the subtle refinements of Minoan culture.

Much has been written about the significance of the Minoan-Mycenaean civilization and its relation to the surrounding cultures. By some historians it is regarded as a mere offshoot of the civilization of Egypt. A number of facts can be adduced to support this view. Both civilizations were ethnically similar. Their governments were alike in their theocratic character. Both societies contained elements of matriarchy and economic collectivism. But that is about as far as the comparison can be carried. The differences were just as marked. The Aegean people built no great pyramids or magnificent temples. Only in painting did their art resemble that of Egypt very closely. The systems of writing of the two civilizations appear to have been of entirely independent origin, as is evidenced by the fact that a knowledge of Egyptian helps very little in deciphering Cretan. Whereas the Egyptian religion was an elaborate ethical system based upon the worship of a sun god of righteousness and justice, the religion of the Aegean venerated a goddess of nature with no evidence of a concept of ethical purpose. Finally, the two peoples differed in their basic philosophies of life. The Egyptians believed in the sacrifice of personal interests to the glory and eternity of the state and looked to rewards in an after-existence as a just compensation for good deeds on earth. The people of the Aegean were individualists, intent upon living their own lives of pleasurable activity and concerned with the hereafter merely as an extension of their pleasant and satisfying earthly careers.

The influence of the Minoan-Mycenaean civilization is not easy to estimate. The Philistines, who came from some part of the Aegean world, introduced certain aspects of the culture into Palestine and Syria. There is reason to believe that various elements of Phoenician art and the Samson legends of the Old Testament were really acquired from the Philistines. It is probable also that the religious and aesthetic traditions of the Cretans and perhaps something of their spirit of freedom influenced the Greeks. But a considerable part of the Minoan-Mycenaean civilization was lost or destroyed following the downfall of Knossos. The conquerors were barbarians who were unable to appreciate much of the culture of the people they conquered and consequently allowed it to perish.

Despite its limited influence the Minoan-Mycenaean civilization, especially in its Minoan form, is not without importance for the student of history; for it was one of the few in ancient times which assured to most of its citizens a reasonable share of happiness and prosperity, free from the tyranny of a despotic state and a crafty priesthood. The apparent absence of slavery, brutal punishments, forced labor, and conscription, together with the substantial equality of classes and the dignified status accorded to women, all point to a social regime in striking contrast with those of the Asiatic empires. If additional evidence of this contrast is needed, it can be found in the art of the various nations. The Cretan sculptor or painter gloried not in portraying the slaughter of armies or the sacking of cities but in picturing flowery landscapes, joyous festivals, thrilling exhibitions of athletic prowess, and similar scenes of a free and peaceful existence. Last of all, the Minoan-Mycenaean civilization is significant for its worldly and progressive outlook. This is exemplified in the devotion of the people to comfort and opulence, in their love of amusement, in their individualism, zest for life, and courage for experimentation.

THE MINOAN-MYCENAEAN CIVILIZATION

Relation of the Minoan-Mycenaean to other civilizations

A Minoan Vase. From the Palace of Phaistos, Crete, it was decorated with stalks of grass or cereal.

Gold Pendant from Crete, Seventeenth Century B.C.

103

Throne Room in the Palace of Minos. The throne and bench are original; the fresco has been restored in accordance with fragments found on the site which are now in the Candia Museum on the island of Crete. A remarkable grace characterizes the lilies and the body and head of the mythical animal.

3. THE LYDIANS AND THE PHOENICIANS

When the Hittite empire fell in the eighth century B.C., its successor in its main areas of power was the kingdom of Lydia. The Lydians established their rule in what is now the territory of the Turkish Republic in Anatolia. They quickly secured control of the Greek cities on the coast of Asia Minor and of the entire plateau west of the Halys River. But their power was short-lived. In 550 B.C. their fabulous king, Croesus, fancied he saw a good opportunity to add to his domain the territory of the Medes east of the Halys. The Median king had just been deposed by Cyrus the Persian. Thinking this meant an easy triumph for his own armies, Croesus set out to capture the territory beyond the river. After an indecisive battle with Cyrus, he returned to his own capital (Sardis) for reinforcements. Here Cyrus caught him unprepared in a surprise attack and captured and burned the city. The Lydians never recovered from the blow, and soon afterward all of their territory, including the Greek cities on the coast, passed under the dominion of Cyrus the Great.

The Lydians were a people of Indo-European speech, who were probably a mixture of native peoples of Asia Minor with migrant stocks from eastern Europe. Benefiting from the advantages of

The kingdom of Lydia

favorable location and abundance of resources, they enjoyed one of the highest standards of living of ancient times. They were famous for the splendor of their armored chariots and the quantities of gold and articles of luxury possessed by the citizens. The wealth of their kings was legendary, as attested by the simile "rich as Croesus." The chief sources of this prosperity were gold from the streams, wool from the thousands of sheep on the hills, and the profits of the extensive commerce which passed overland from the Tigris-Euphrates valley to the Aegean Sea. But with all their wealth and opportunities for leisure, they succeeded in making only one original contribution to civilization. This was the coinage of money from electrum or "white gold," a natural mixture of gold and silver found in the sands of one of their rivers. Hitherto all systems of money had consisted of weighed rings or bars of metal. The new coins, of varying sizes, were stamped with a definite value more or less arbitrarily given by the ruler who issued them.

In contrast with the Lydians, who gained their ascendancy as a result of the downfall of the Hittites, were the Phoenicians, who benefited from the break-up of Aegean supremacy. But the Phoenicians were neither conquerors nor the builders of an empire. They exerted their influence through the arts of peace, especially through commerce. During most of their history their political system was a loose confederation of city-states, which frequently bought their security by paying tribute to foreign powers. The territory they occupied was the narrow strip between the Lebanon Mountains and the Mediterranean Sea and the islands off the coast. With good harbors and a central location, it was admirably situated for trade. The great centers of commerce included Tyre, Sidon, and Beirut. Under the leadership of the first, Phoenicia reached the zenith of her cultural brilliance, from the tenth to the eighth century B.C. During the sixth century she passed under the domination of the Chaldeans and then of the Persians. In 332 B.C. Tyre was destroyed by Alexander the Great after a siege of seven months.

The Phoenicians were a people of Semitic language, closely related to the Canaanites. They displayed very little creative genius, but were remarkable adapters of the achievements of others. They produced no original art worthy of the name, and they made but slight contributions to literature. Their religion, like that of the Canaanites, was characterized by human sacrifice to the god Moloch and by licentious fertility rites. They excelled, however, in specialized manufactures, in geography and navigation. They founded colonies at Carthage and Utica in North Africa, at Palermo on the island of Sicily, on the Balearic Islands, and at Cadiz and Malaga in Spain. They were renowned throughout the ancient world for their glass and metal industries and for their purple dye obtained from a mollusk in the adjacent seas. They developed the art of navigation to such a stage that they could sail by the stars at

The Lydian people and their culture

The Phoenician cities and confederation

Achievements of the Phoenicians

night. To less venturesome peoples, the North Star was known for some time as the Phoenicians' star. A company of Phoenicians is believed to have circumnavigated Africa. Phoenician ships and sailors were recruited by all the great powers. The most lasting achievement of the Phoenicians, however, was the completion and diffusion of an alphabet based upon principles discovered by the Egyptians. The Phoenician contribution was the adoption of a system of signs representing the sounds of the human voice, and the elimination of all pictographic and syllabic characters. The Egyptians, as we have seen, had accomplished the first of these steps but not the second.

4. LESSONS FROM THE HISTORY OF THE NEAR EASTERN STATES

Like most other periods in world history, the period of the states we have studied thus far was an era of contention and strife. Nearly all of the great empires, and the majority of the smaller states as well, devoted their energies most of the time to policies of expansion and aggression. The only notable exceptions were the Minoan and Egyptian, but even the Egyptians, in the later period of their history, yielded to no one in their addiction to imperialism. The causes were largely geographic. Each nation grew accustomed to the pursuit of its own interests in some fertile river valley or on some easily defended plateau. Isolation bred fear of foreigners and an incapacity to think of one's own people as members of a common humanity. The feelings of insecurity that resulted seemed to justify aggressive foreign policies and the annexation of neighboring states to serve as buffers against a hostile world.

Defects of the Near Orient empires

It seems possible to trace nearly all of the woes of the Near Eastern nations to wars of aggression and imperialist greed. Arnold J. Toynbee has shown this in devastating fashion in the case of the Assyrians. He contends that it was no less true of such later peoples as the Spartans, the Carthaginians, the Macedonians, and the Ottoman Turks. Each made militarism and conquest its gods and wrought such destruction upon itself that when it made its last heroic stand against its enemies, it was a mere "corpse in armor." Not death by foreign conquest but national suicide was the fate which befell it.[2] The way of the warrior brought race intolerance, a love of ease and luxury, crime and racketeering, and crushing burdens of taxation. Expansion of empire promoted a fictitious prosperity, at least for the upper classes, and aroused enough envy among poorer nations to make them willing conspirators against a rich neighbor who could easily be portrayed as an oppressor. The use of hungry and discontented allies against powerful rivals is not new in history.

Results of Near Orient imperialism

[2] D. C. Somervell (ed.), A. J. Toynbee's *A Study of History*, I, 338-43.

· *Items so designated are available in paperbound editions.*

· Blegen, C. W., *Troy*, London and New York, 1963 (Cambridge University Press).

Burn, A. R., *Minoans, Philistines and Greeks*, New York, 1930.

Ceram, C. W., *The Secret of the Hittites*, New York, 1956. The best of recent works.

· Chadwick, John, *The Decipherment of Linear B*, New York, 1958 (Vintage).

· Gordon, Cyrus H., *The Ancient Near East*, New York, 1965 (Norton Library).

· ———, *The Common Background of Greek and Hebrew Civilizations*, New York, 1965 (Norton Library).

· Gurney, O. R., *The Hittites*, Baltimore, 1962 (Penguin).

· Harden, Donald, *The Phoenicians*, New York, 1962 (Praeger).

· Hutchinson, R. W., *Prehistoric Crete*, Baltimore, 1962 (Penguin).

· Lloyd, Seton, *Early Anatolia*, Baltimore, 1956 (Penguin).

· MacDonald, William A., *Progress into the Past: The Rediscovery of Mycenaean Civilization*, New York, 1967.

Moscati, Sabatino, *The World of the Phoenicians*, New York, 1968.

· Nilsson, M. P., *The Mycenaean Origin of Greek Mythology*, New York, 1963 (Norton Library).

Palmer, L. R., *Mycenaeans and Minoans*, New York, 1962. Must be read with care. Author is not entirely impartial.

· Pendlebury, J. D. S., *The Archaeology of Crete*, New York, 1965 (Norton Library).

Wace, A. J. B., *Mycenae*, Princeton, 1949.

Willetts, R. F., *Aristocratic Society in Ancient Crete*, London, 1955.

SOURCE MATERIALS

Evans, Sir Arthur, *Scripta Minoa; the Written Documents of Minoan Crete*.

Hertzler, J. O., *The Social Thought of the Ancient Civilizations*, New York, 1961, pp. 135–44.

Ventris, M., and Chadwick, J., *Documents in Mycenaean Greek*, Cambridge, 1956.

PART II

The Classical Civilizations
of Greece and Rome

After 600 B.C. the centers of civilization in the Western world were no longer confined to the Near East. By that time new cultures were already growing to maturity in Greece and in Italy. Both had started their evolution considerably earlier, but the civilization of Greece did not begin to ripen until about 600 B.C., while the Romans showed little promise of original achievement before 500. About 300 B.C. Greek civilization, properly speaking, came to an end and was superseded by a new culture representing a fusion of elements derived from Greece and from the Near Orient. This was the Hellenistic civilization, which lasted until about the beginning of the Christian era and included not only the Greek peninsula but Egypt and most of Asia west of the Indus River. The outstanding characteristic which serves to distinguish these three civilizations from the ones that had gone before is secularism. No longer does religion absorb the interests of man to the extent that it did in ancient Egypt or in the nations of Mesopotamia. The state is now above the church, and the power of the priests to determine the direction of cultural evolution has been greatly reduced. Furthermore, ideals of human freedom and an emphasis on the welfare of man as an individual have largely superseded the despotism and collectivism of the ancient Near East.

109

A Chronological Table *Dates are B.C. unless given as A.D.*

POLITICS	ARTS AND LETTERS

800 B.C.

Mycenaean stage, *ca.* 1500–1100
Dark Ages of Greek history, 1100–800
Beginning of city-states in Greece, *ca.* 800 *Iliad* and *Odyssey*, *ca.* 800
Rome founded, *ca.* 750

500 B.C.

Age of the Tyrants in Greece, 650–500
Reforms of Solon, 594–560 Doric architecture, 650–500
Reforms of Cleisthenes, 508–502
Overthrow of monarchy in Rome and establish- Aeschylus, 525–456
 ment of republic, *ca.* 500 Phidias, 500?–432?
Patrician-plebeian struggle in Rome, 500–287 Ionic architecture, *ca.* 500–400
Greco-Persian War, 493–479

  Sophocles, 496–406
Delian League, 479–404 Herodotus, 484–425
  Euripides, 480–406
Perfection of Athenian democracy, 461–429 Thucydides, 471?–400?
Law of the Twelve Tables (Rome), *ca.* 450 Parthenon, *ca.* 460

400 B.C.

Peloponnesian War, 431–404 Aristophanes, 448?–380?
Decline of democracy in Greece, 400 Corinthian architecture, *ca.* 400–300
Theban supremacy in Greece, 371–362 Praxiteles, 370?–310?
Macedonian conquest of Greece, 338–337
Conquests of Alexander the Great, 336–323
Division of Alexander's empire, 323

300 B.C.

Hortensian Law (Rome), 287
Punic Wars, 264–146

200 B.C.

Revolt of the Gracchi, 133–121

100 B.C.

  Vergil, 70–19
  Horace, 65–8
Dictatorship of Julius Caesar, 46–44
Principate of Augustus Caesar, 27 B.C.–14 A.D.

  Tacitus, 55?–117? A.D.
  Colosseum, *ca.* 80 A.D.

100 A.D.

Barbarian invasions of Rome, *ca.* 100–476 A.D.
Completion of Roman law by the great jurists,
 ca. 200 A.D.

300 A.D.

Diocletian, 284–305 A.D.
Constantine I, 306–337 A.D.

476 A.D.

Theodosius I, 379–395 A.D.

Deposition of last of Roman emperors, 476 A.D.

PHILOSOPHY AND SCIENCE	ECONOMICS	RELIGION	
		Development of worldly, non-ethical religion of the Greeks, 1200–800	800 B.C.
	Economic Revolution and colonization in Greece, 750–600 Rise of middle class in Greece, 750–600		
Thales of Miletus, 640?–546 Pythagoras, 582?–507?			
		Orphic and Eleusinian mystery cults, 500–100	500 B.C.
Protagoras, 490?–420? Socrates, 469–399 Hippocrates, 460–377? Democritus, 470?–362? Sophists, *ca.* 450–400 Plato, 427–347 Aristotle, 384–322 Epicurus, 342–270			400 B.C.
Zeno (the Stoic), 320?–250? Euclid, 323?–285 Aristarchus, 310–230	Growth of advertising and insurance, 300 B.C.–100 A.D. Hellenistic world trade, 300 B.C.–100 A.D. International money economy, 300 B.C.–100 A.D. Growth of serfdom in Hellenistic empires, 300 B.C.–100 A.D. Growth of metropolitan cities, 300 B.C.–100 A.D.		300 B.C.
Archimedes, 287?–212 Eratosthenes, 276?–195?	Growth of slavery in Rome, 250–100 Rise of middle class in Rome, 250–100	Oriental mystery cults in Rome, 250–50	
Herophilus, 220?–150? Polybius, 205?–118	Decline of small farmer in Rome, 250–100 Depressions and unemployment in Hellenistic world, 200 B.C.–100 A.D		200 B.C.
Skeptics, 200–100	Decline of slavery in Hellenistic world 200 B.C.–100 A.D.	Development of mysticism and otherworldliness, 200	
Introduction of Stoicism into Rome, *ca.* 140 Cicero, 106–43 Lucretius, 98–55			100 B.C.
Seneca, 34 B.C.–65 A.D.	Decline of slavery in Rome, 27 B.C.–476 A.D.	Spread of Mithraism in Rome, 27 B.C.–270 A.D. First persecution of Christians in Rome, *ca.* 65 A.D.	
Marcus Aurelius, 121–180 A.D. Galen, 130–200? A.D. Neo-Platonism, 250–600 A.D.			100 A.D.
	Growth of serfdom and extralegal feudalism in Rome, 300–500 A.D.	Beginning of toleration of Christians in Rome, 311 A.D.	300 A.D.
		Christianity made official religion of Roman Empire, 380 A.D.	476 A.D.

CHAPTER 6

The Hellenic Civilization

There Lawfulness dwells and her sisters,
Safe foundation of cities,
Justice and Peace, who was bred with her,
Dispensers of wealth to men
Golden daughters of wise-counselling Right.
—Pindar, on the city of Corinth, *Olympian Ode XIII*

Now, what is characteristic of any nature is that which is best
for it and gives most joy. Such to man is the life according to reason, since it is this that makes him man.
—Aristotle, *Nichomachean Ethics*

Among all the peoples of the ancient world, the one whose culture
most clearly exemplified the spirit of Western man was the Hellenic
or Greek. No other of these nations had so strong a devotion to
liberty, at least for itself, or so firm a belief in the nobility of
human achievement. The Greeks glorified man as the most important creature in the universe and refused to submit to the dictation
of priests or despots or even to humble themselves before their gods.
Their attitude was essentially secular and rationalistic; they exalted
the spirit of free inquiry and made knowledge supreme over faith. It
was largely for these reasons that they advanced their culture to the
highest stage which the ancient world was destined to reach. But the
Greeks did not begin without foundations. It is necessary to remember that the groundwork for many of their achievements had already been laid by certain of the Oriental peoples. The rudiments of
their philosophy and science had been prepared by the Egyptians.
The Greek alphabet was derived from Phoenicia. And probably to a
larger extent than we shall ever realize the Hellenic appreciation of
beauty and freedom was a product of Minoan-Mycenaean influence.

The character of Hellenic civilization

1. EARLY STAGES

The early history of Greece is divided into two basic periods, the
Mycenaean from about 1500 to 1100 B.C. and the Dark Ages from
about 1100 to 800 B.C. In the sixteenth century a Greek people

113

known subsequently as Achaeans burst the confines of their original home and expanded southward. In time they conquered Mycenae and made it their principal stronghold. They were henceforth called in Greek history Mycenaeans, although they had other important centers at Athens, Thebes, Pylos, and elsewhere. In 1400 B.C. they conquered Knossos. The Mycenaeans were a semibarbarous people whose social and political systems resembled those of the Orient. The great lords or kings who ruled in the fortified strongholds seemed to wield a monopoly over production, trade, and artistic activity. The chief function of their subjects was to work and strive for the king's enrichment. These officials resided in magnificent palaces surrounded by objects of gold, bronze, and ivory, skillfully fashioned by talented workmen. To obtain these riches traders and colonizers roamed the whole world of the Aegean and penetrated as far as Italy and Central Europe.

The arts of the Mycenaeans never equaled the delicacy and grace of the painting and sculpture of the Minoans. Much of it was copied boldly from the Orient, and for the most part it remained stilted and lifeless. They did, nevertheless, produce some excellent pottery and exquisitely inlaid daggers. Their massive palaces and tombs indicate that they understood stresses and how to counteract them. The Mycenaeans had a system of writing, which has been definitely established as an early form of Greek. But they seem to have used it almost exclusively for keeping the fiscal records of their all-encompassing governments. No trace of anything resembling literature, history, or philosophy has thus far been found.

The fall of the Mycenaean civilization was a major catastrophe for the Greek world. It ushered in a period now called by historians the Dark Ages, which lasted from about 1100 to 800 B.C. Written records disappeared, except where accidentally preserved, and culture reverted to simpler forms than had been known for centuries. Whether the collapse came as a result of foreign invasion or of internal revolt against oppression has not been determined. Perhaps it

Ruins of the Palace of Nestor at Pylos. See the opposite page for an artist's conception of the original.

A Reconstruction of the Palace of Nestor. Shown here is the central court and the hearth.

was a combination of both. According to tradition, about 1200 B.C. the cities were attacked by an invading horde of more primitive Greeks known as Dorians. They were illiterate, and though they possessed weapons of iron, their knowledge of the arts and crafts was no more than rudimentary. They burned the palace at Mycenae and sacked a number of the others. Some historians maintain that the destruction of despotic Mycenae was a necessary prelude to the emergence of the freer and more enlightened Hellenic outlook.

The culture of many of the Greeks had always been rudimentary. That of the Mycenaeans rapidly deteriorated following the destruction of Mycenae. We can therefore conclude that cultural achievement in most of Greece remained at a low ebb throughout the period from 1100 to 800 B.C. Toward the end some decorated pottery and skillfully designed metal objects began to appear on the islands of the Aegean Sea, but essentially the period was a long night. Aside from the development of writing at the very end, intellectual accomplishment was limited to folk songs, ballads, and short epics sung and embellished by bards as they wandered from one village to another. A large part of this material was finally woven into a great epic cycle by one or more poets in the ninth century B.C. Though not all the poems of this cycle have come down to us, the two most important, the *Iliad* and the *Odyssey*, the so-called Homeric epics, provide us with a rich store of information about many of the customs and institutions of the Dark Ages.

The political institutions of the Dark Ages were exceedingly primitive. Each little community of villages was independent of external control, but political authority was so tenuous that it would not be too much to say that the state scarcely existed at all. The *basileus* or ruler was not much more than a tribal leader. He could not make or enforce laws or administer justice. He received no

115

Mycenean Stirrup Jar, Twelfth Century B.C.

The rudimentary pattern of social and economic life

Religious conceptions in the Dark Ages

remuneration of any kind, and had to cultivate his farm for a living the same as any other citizen. Practically his only functions were military and priestly. He commanded the army in time of war and offered sacrifices to keep the gods on the good side of the community. Although each little community had its council of nobles and assembly of warriors, neither of these bodies had any definite membership or status as an organ of government. The duties of the former were to advise and assist the ruler and prevent him from usurping despotic powers. The functions of the latter were to ratify declarations of war and assent to the conclusion of peace. Almost without exception custom took the place of law, and the administration of justice was private. Even willful murder was punishable only by the family of the victim. While it is true that disputes were sometimes submitted to the ruler for settlement, he acted in such cases merely as an arbitrator, not as a judge. As a matter of fact, the political consciousness of the Greeks of this time was so poorly developed that they had no conception of government as an indispensable agency for the preservation of social order. When Odysseus, ruler of Ithaca, was absent for twenty years, no regent was appointed in his place, and no session of the council or assembly was held. No one seemed to think that the complete suspension of government, even for so long a time, was a matter of critical importance.

The pattern of social and economic life was amazingly simple. Though the general tone of the society portrayed in the epics is aristocratic, there was actually no rigid stratification of classes. Manual labor was not looked upon as degrading, and there were apparently no idle rich. That there were dependent laborers of some kind who worked on the lands of the nobles and served them as faithful warriors seems clear from the Homeric epics, but they appear to have been serfs rather than slaves. The slaves were chiefly women, employed as servants, wool processors, or concubines. Many were war captives, but they do not appear to have been badly treated. Agriculture and herding were the basic occupations of free men. Except for a few skilled crafts like those of wagonmaker, swordsmith, goldsmith, and potter, there was no specialization of labor. For the most part every household made its own tools, wove its own clothing, and raised its own food. So far were the Greeks of this time from being a trading people that they had no word in their language for "merchant," and barter was the only method of exchange that was practiced.

To the Greeks of the Dark Ages religion meant chiefly a system for: (1) explaining the physical world in such a way as to remove its awesome mysteries and give man a feeling of intimate relationship with it; (2) accounting for the tempestuous passions that seized man's nature and made him lose that self-control which the Greeks considered essential for success as a warrior; and (3) obtaining such tangible benefits as good fortune, long life, skill in craftsmanship, and abundant harvests. The Greeks did not expect that their religion would save them from sin or endow them with spiritual blessings. As they conceived it, piety was neither a matter of conduct nor of faith. Their religion, accordingly, had no commandments, dogmas, or sacraments. Every man was at liberty to believe what he pleased and to conduct his own life as he chose without fear of the wrath of the gods.

As is commonly known, the deities of the early Greek religion were merely human beings writ large. It was really necessary that this should be so if the Greek was to feel at home in the world over which they ruled. Remote, omnipotent beings like the gods of most Oriental religions would have inspired fear rather than a sense of security. What the Greek wanted was not necessarily gods of great power, but deities he could bargain with on equal terms. Consequently he endowed his gods with attributes similar to his own—with human bodies and human weaknesses and wants. He imagined the great company of divinities as frequently quarreling with one another, needing food and sleep, mingling freely with men, and even procreating children occasionally by mortal women. They differed from men only in the fact that they subsisted on ambrosia and nectar, which made them immortal. They dwelt not in the sky or in the stars but on the summit of Mount Olympus, a peak in northern Greece with an altitude of about 10,000 feet.

The deities of the early Greek religion

The religion was thoroughly polytheistic, and no one deity was elevated very high above any of the others. Zeus, the sky god and wielder of the thunderbolt, who was sometimes referred to as the father of the gods and of men, frequently received less attention than did Poseidon, the sea god, Aphrodite, goddess of love, or Athena, variously considered goddess of wisdom and war and patroness of handicrafts. Since the Greeks had no Satan, their religion cannot be described as dualistic. Nearly all of the deities were capable of malevolence as well as good, for they sometimes deceived men and caused them to commit wrongs. The nearest approach to a god of evil was Hades, who presided over the nether world. Although he is referred to in the Homeric poems as "implacable and unyielding" and the most hateful of gods to mortals, he was never assumed to have played an active role in affairs on earth. He was not considered as the source of pestilence, earthquake, or famine. He did not tempt men or work to defeat the benevolent designs of other gods. In short, he was really not regarded as anything more than the guardian of the realm of the dead.

Poseidon

The Greeks of the Dark Ages were almost completely indifferent to what happened to them after death. They did assume, however, that the shades or ghosts of men survived for a time after the death of their bodies. All, with a few exceptions, went to the same abode —to the murky realm of Hades situated beneath the earth. This was neither a paradise nor a hell: no one was rewarded for his good deeds, and no one was punished for his sins. Each of the shades ap-

Battle between the Gods and the Giants. This frieze dates from before 525 B.C. and is from the sanctuary of Apollo at Delphi.

peared to continue the same kind of life its human embodiment had lived on earth. The Homeric poems make casual mention of two other realms, the Elysian Plain and the realm of Tartarus, which seem at first glance to contradict the idea of no rewards and punishments in the hereafter. But the few individuals who enjoyed the ease and comfort of the Elysian Plain had done nothing to deserve such blessings; they were simply persons whom the gods had chosen to favor. The realm of Tartarus was not really an abode of the dead but a place of imprisonment for rebellious deities.

The external
and mechanical
character of
worship

Worship in early Greek religion consisted primarily of sacrifice. The offerings were made, however, not as an atonement for sin, but chiefly in order to please the gods and induce them to grant favors. In other words, religious practice was external and mechanical and not far removed from magic. Reverence, humility, and purity of heart were not essentials in it. The worshiper had only to carry out his part of the bargain by making the proper sacrifice, and the gods would fulfill theirs. For a religion such as this no elaborate institutions were required. Even a professional priesthood was unnecessary. Since there were no mysteries and no sacraments, one man could perform the simple rites about as well as another. The Greek temple was not a church or place of religious assemblage, and no ceremonies were performed within it. Instead it was a shrine which the god might visit occasionally and use as a temporary house.

Conceptions of
virtue and evil

As intimated already, the morality of the Greeks in the Dark Ages had only the vaguest connection with their religion. While it is true that the gods were generally disposed to support the right, they did not consider it their duty to combat evil and make righteousness prevail. In meting out rewards to men, they appear to have been influenced more by their own whims and by gratitude for sacrifices offered than by any consideration for moral character.

The only crime they punished was perjury, and that none too consistently. Nearly all the virtues extolled in the epics were those which would make the individual a better soldier—bravery, self-control, patriotism, wisdom (in the sense of cunning), love of one's friends, and hatred of one's enemies. There was no conception of sin in the Christian sense of wrongful acts to be repented of or atoned for.

At the end of the Dark Ages the Greek was already well started along the road of social ideals that he was destined to follow in later centuries. He was an optimist, convinced that life was worth living for its own sake, and he could see no reason for looking forward to death as a glad release. He was an egoist, striving for the fulfillment of self. As a consequence, he rejected mortification of the flesh and all forms of denial which would imply the frustration of life. He could see no merit in humility or in turning the other cheek. He was a humanist, who worshiped the finite and the natural rather than the otherworldly or sublime. For this reason he refused to invest his gods with awe-inspiring qualities, or to invent any conception of man as a depraved and sinful creature. Finally, he was devoted to liberty in an even more extreme form than most of his descendants in the classical period were willing to accept.

The basic Greek ideals

2. THE EVOLUTION OF THE CITY-STATES

About 800 B.C. the village communities which had been founded mainly upon tribal or clan organization, began to give way to larger political units. As the need for defense increased, an acropolis or citadel was built on a high location, and a city grew up around it as the seat of government for a whole community. Thus emerged the city-state, the most famous unit of political society developed by the Greeks. Examples were to be found in almost every section of the Hellenic world. Athens, Thebes, and Megara on the mainland; Sparta and Corinth on the Peloponnesus; Miletus on the shore of Asia Minor; and Mitylene and Samos on the islands of the Aegean Sea were among the best known. They varied enormously in both area and population. Sparta with more than 3000 square miles and Athens with 1060 had by far the greatest extent; the others averaged less than a hundred. At the peak of their power Athens and Sparta, each with a population of about 400,000, had approximately three times the numerical strength of most of their neighboring states.

The origin and nature of the city-states

More important is the fact that the Greek city-states varied widely in cultural evolution. From 800 to 500 B.C., commonly called the Archaic period, the Peloponnesian cities of Corinth and Argos were leaders in the development of literature and the arts. In the seventh century Sparta outshone many of her rivals. Preeminent above all were the Ionian cities on the coast of Asia Minor and the islands of the Aegean Sea. Foremost among them was Miletus,

Variations among the city-states

where, as we shall see, a brilliant flowering of philosophy and science occurred as early as the sixth century. Athens lagged behind until at least 100 years later.

With a few exceptions the Greek city-states went through a similar political evolution. They began their histories as monarchies. During the eighth century they were changed into oligarchies. About a hundred years later, on the average, the oligarchies were overthrown by dictators, or "tyrants," as the Greeks called them, meaning usurpers who ruled without legal right whether oppressively or not. Finally, in the sixth and fifth centuries, democracies were set up, or in some cases "timocracies," that is, governments based upon a property qualification for the exercise of political rights, or in which love of honor and glory was the ruling principle.

On the whole, it is not difficult to determine the causes of this political evolution. The first change came about as a result of the concentration of landed wealth. As the owners of great estates waxed in economic power, they determined to wrest political authority from the ruler, now commonly called king, and vest it in the council, which they generally controlled. In the end they abolished the kingship entirely. Then followed a period of sweeping economic changes and political turmoil.

These developments affected not only Greece itself but many other parts of the Mediterranean world. For they were accompanied and followed by a vast overseas expansion. The chief causes were an increasing scarcity of agricultural land, internal strife, and a general temper of restlessness and discontent. The Greeks rapidly learned of numerous areas, thinly populated, with climate and soil similar to those of the homelands. The parent states most active in the expansion movement were Corinth, Chalcis, and Miletus. Their citizens founded colonies along the Aegean shores and even in Italy and Sicily. Of the latter the best known were Tarentum and Syracuse. They also established trading centers on the coast of Egypt and as far east as Babylon. The results of this expansionist movement can only be described as momentous. Commerce and industry grew to be leading pursuits, the urban population increased, and wealth assumed new forms. The rising middle class now joined with dispossessed farmers in an attack upon the landholding oligarchy. The natural fruit of the bitter class conflicts that ensued was dictatorship. By encouraging extravagant hopes and promising relief from chaos, ambitious demagogues attracted enough popular support to enable them to ride into power in defiance of constitutions and laws. Ultimately, however, dissatisfaction with tyrannical rule and the increasing economic power and political consciousness of the common citizens led to the establishment of democracies or liberal oligarchies.

Unfortunately space does not permit an analysis of the political history of each of the Greek city-states. Except in the more back-

The evolution of the city-states

The causes of the political cycle; the growth of colonization

The results of Greek expansion

ward sections of Thessaly and the Peloponnesus, it is safe to conclude that the internal development of all of them paralleled the account given above, although minor variations due to local conditions doubtless occurred. The two most important of the Hellenic states, Sparta and Athens, deserve more detailed study.

3. THE ARMED CAMP OF SPARTA

The history of Sparta [1] was the great exception to the political evolution of the city-states. Despite the fact that her citizens sprang from the same origins as most of the other Greeks, she failed to make any progress in the direction of democratic rule. Instead, her government gradually degenerated into a form more closely resembling a modern élite dictatorship. Culturally, also, the nation stagnated after the seventh century. The causes were due partly to isolation. Hemmed in by mountains on the northeast and west and lacking good harbors, the Spartan people had little opportunity to profit from the advances made in the outside world. Besides, no middle class arose to aid the masses in the struggle for freedom.

The major explanation is to be found, however, in militarism. The Spartans had come into the eastern Peloponnesus as an invading army. At first they attempted to amalgamate with the Mycenaeans they found there. But conflicts arose, and the Spartans resorted to conquest. Though by the end of the ninth century they had gained dominion over all of Laconia, they were not satisfied. West of the Taygetus Mountains lay the fertile plain of Messenia. The Spartans determined to conquer it. The venture was successful, and the Messenian territory was annexed to Laconia. About 640 B.C. the Messenians enlisted the aid of Argos and launched a revolt. The war that followed was desperately fought, Laconia itself was invaded, and apparently it was only the death of the Argive commander and the patriotic pleas of the fire-eating poet Tyrtaeus that saved the day for the Spartans. This time the victors took no chances. They confiscated the lands of the Messenians, murdered or expelled their leaders, and forced the masses into serfdom. The Spartans' appetite for conquest was not unlimited, however. Following the Messenian wars they devoted themselves to keeping what they had already gained.

There was scarcely a feature of the life of the Spartans that was not the result of their wars with the Messenians. In subduing and despoiling their enemies they unwittingly enslaved themselves; for they lived through the remaining centuries of their history in deadly fear of insurrections. It was this fear which explains their

The peculiar development of Sparta

The Spartan desire for conquest

The results of Spartan militarism

[1] Sparta was the leading city of a district called Laconia or Lacedaemonia; sometimes the *state* was referred to by one or the other of these names. The people, also, were frequently called Laconians or Lacedaemonians.

121

conservatism, their stubborn resistance to change, lest any innovation result in a fatal weakening of the system. Their provincialism can also be attributed to the same cause. Frightened by the prospect that dangerous ideas might be brought into their country, they discouraged travel and prohibited trade with the outside world. The necessity of maintaining the absolute supremacy of the citizen class over an enormous population of serfs required an iron discipline and a strict subordination of the individual; hence the Spartan collectivism, which extended into every branch of the social and economic life. Finally, much of the cultural backwardness of Sparta grew out of the atmosphere of coarseness and hate which inevitably resulted from the bitter struggle to conquer the Messenians and hold them under stern repression.

The Spartan government

The Spartan constitution, which tradition ascribed to an ancient lawgiver, Lycurgus, provided for a government preserving the forms of the old system of the Dark Ages. Instead of one king, however, there were two, representing separate families of exalted rank. The Spartan sovereigns enjoyed but few powers and those chiefly of a military and priestly character. A second and more authoritative branch of the government was the council, composed of the two kings and twenty-eight nobles sixty years of age and over. This body supervised the work of administration, prepared measures for submission to the assembly, and served as the highest court for criminal trials. The third organ of government, the assembly, approved or rejected the proposals of the council and elected all public officials except the kings. But the highest authority under the Spartan constitution was vested in a board of five men known as the ephorate. The ephors virtually were the government. They presided over the council and the assembly, controlled the educational system and the distribution of property, censored the lives of the citizens, and exercised a veto power over all legislation. They had power also to determine the fate of newborn infants, to conduct prosecutions before the council, and even to depose the kings if the religious omens appeared unfavorable. The Spartan government was thus very decidedly an oligarchy. In spite of the fact that the ephors were chosen for one-year terms by the assembly, they were indefinitely reeligible, and their authority was so vast that there was hardly any ramification of the system they could not control. Moreover, it should be borne in mind that the assembly itself was not a democratic body. Not even the whole citizen class, which was a small minority of the total population, was entitled to membership in it, but only those males of full political status who had incomes sufficient to qualify them for enrollment in the heavy infantry.

The population of Sparta was divided into three main classes. The ruling element was made up of the Spartiates, or descendants of the original conquerors. Though never exceeding one-twentieth of the total population, the Spartiates alone had political privileges. Next in order of rank were the perioeci, or "dwellers around." The origin of this class is uncertain, but it was probably composed of peoples that had at one time been allies of the Spartans or had submitted voluntarily to Spartan domination. In return for service as a buffer population between the ruling class and the serfs, the perioeci were allowed to carry on trade and to engage in manufacturing. At the bottom of the scale were the helots, or serfs, bound to the soil and despised and persecuted by their masters.

Among these classes only the perioeci enjoyed any appreciable measure of comfort and freedom. While it is true that the economic condition of the helots cannot be described in terms of absolute misery, since they were permitted to keep for themselves a good share of what they produced on the estates of their masters, they were personally subjected to such shameful treatment that they were constantly wretched and rebellious. On occasions they were compelled to give exhibitions of drunkenness and lascivious dances as an example to the Spartan youth of the effects of such practices. At the beginning of each year, if we can believe the testimony of Aristotle, the ephors declared war upon the helots, presumably for the purpose of giving a gloss of legality to the murder of any by the secret police upon suspicion of disloyalty.

Those who were born into the Spartiate class were doomed to a respectable slavery for the major part of their lives. Forced to submit to the severest discipline and to sacrifice individual interests, they were little more than cogs in a vast machine. Their education was limited almost entirely to military training, supplemented by exposure and merciless floggings to harden them for the duties of war. Between the ages of twenty and sixty they gave all their time to service to the state. Although marriage was practically compulsory, no family life was permitted. Husbands carried off their wives on the wedding night by a show of force. But they did not live with them. Instead, they were supposed to contrive means of escaping at night to visit them secretly. According to Plutarch, it thus sometimes happened that men "had children by their wives before ever they saw their faces by daylight." [2] No jealousy between marital partners was allowed. The production of vigorous offspring was all-important. Whether they were born within the limits of strict monogamy was a secondary consideration. In any case, children were the property not of their parents but of the state. It may be doubted that the Spartiates resented these hardships and deprivations. Pride in their status as the ruling class probably compensated in their minds for harsh discipline and denial of privileges.

The economic organization of Sparta was designed almost solely for the ends of military efficiency and the supremacy of the citizen class. The best land was owned by the state and was originally

The class system in Sparta

Perioeci and helots

Discipline for the benefit of the state

[2] Plutarch, "Lycurgus," *Lives of Illustrious Men*, I, 81.

divided into equal plots which were assigned to the Spartiate class as inalienable estates. Later these holdings as well as the inferior lands were permitted to be sold and exchanged, with the result that some of the citizens became richer than others. The helots, who did all the work of cultivating the soil, also belonged to the state and were assigned to their masters along with the land. Their masters were forbidden to emancipate them or to sell them outside of the country. The labor of the helots provided for the support of the whole citizen class, whose members were not allowed to be associated with any economic enterprise other than agriculture. Trade and industry were reserved exclusively for the perioeci.

The Spartan economic system is frequently described by modern historians as communistic. It is true that some of the means of production (the helots and the land) were collectively owned, in theory at least, and that the Spartiate males contributed from their incomes to provide for a common mess in the clubs to which they belonged. But with these rather doubtful exceptions the system was as far removed from communism as it was from anarchy. Essentials of the communist ideal include the doctrines that all the instruments of production shall be owned by the community, that no one shall live by exploiting the labor of others, and that all shall work for the benefit of the community and share the wealth in proportion to need. In Sparta commerce and industry were in private hands; the helots were forced to contribute a portion of what they produced to provide for the subsistence of their masters; and political privileges were restricted to an hereditary aristocracy, most of whose members performed no socially useful labor whatever. With its militarism, its secret police, its minority rule, and its closed economy, the Spartan system would seem to have resembled fascism more nearly than true communism. But even with respect to fascism the resemblance was not complete. The Spartan system was not revolutionary, as fascism usually is in the beginning, but was always rather strongly conservative.

4. THE ATHENIAN TRIUMPH AND TRAGEDY

Athens began her history under conditions quite different from those which prevailed in Sparta. The district of Attica had not been the scene of an armed invasion or of bitter conflict between opposing peoples. As a result, no military caste imposed its rule upon a vanquished nation. Furthermore, the wealth of Attica consisted of mineral deposits and splendid harbors in addition to agricultural resources. Athens, consequently, never remained a predominantly agrarian state but rapidly developed a prosperous trade and a culture essentially urban.

Until the middle of the eighth century B.C. Athens, like the other Greek states, had a monarchical form of government. During the century that followed, the council of nobles, or Council of the Areopagus, as it came to be called, gradually divested the king of his powers. The transition to rule by the few was both the cause and the result of an increasing concentration of wealth. The introduction of vine and olive culture about this time led to the growth of agriculture as a great capitalistic enterprise. Since vineyards and olive orchards require considerable time to become profitable, only those farmers with abundant resources were able to survive in the business. Their poorer and less thrifty neighbors sank rapidly into debt, especially since grain was now coming to be imported at ruinous prices. The small farmer had no alternative but to mortgage his land, and then his family and himself, in the vain hope that some day a way of escape would be found. Ultimately many of his class became serfs when the mortgages could not be paid.

Bitter cries of distress now arose and threats of revolution were heard. The middle classes in the towns espoused the cause of the peasant in demanding liberalization of the government. Finally, in 594 B.C., all parties agreed upon the appointment of Solon as a magistrate with absolute power to carry out reforms. The measures Solon enacted provided for both political and economic adjustments. The former included: (1) the establishment of a new council, the Council of Four Hundred, and the admission of the middle classes to membership in it; (2) the enfranchisement of the lower classes by making them eligible for service in the assembly; and (3) the organization of a supreme court, open to all citizens and elected by universal manhood suffrage, with power to hear appeals from the decisions of the magistrates. The economic reforms benefited the poor farmers by canceling existing mortgages, prohibiting enslavement for debt in the future, and limiting the amount of land any one individual could own. Nor did Solon neglect the middle classes. He introduced a new system of coinage designed to give Athens an advantage in foreign trade, imposed heavy penalties for idleness, ordered every man to teach his son a trade, and offered full privileges of citizenship to alien craftsmen who would become permanent residents of the country.

Significant though these reforms were, they did not allay the discontent. The nobles were disgruntled because some of their privileges had been taken away. The middle and lower classes were dissatisfied because they were still excluded from the offices of magistracy, and because the Council of the Areopagus was left with its powers intact. Worse still was the fact that Solon, like many rulers in all times, attempted to divert the people from their domestic troubles by persuading them to embark upon military adventures abroad. An old quarrel with Megara was revived, and Athens committed her fate to the uncertainties of war. The chaos and disillusionment that followed paved the way in 560 B.C. for the triumph of the first of the Athenian tyrants. Although he proved to be a benevo-

From monarchy to oligarchy in Athens

Threats of revolution and the reforms of Solon

The rise of dictatorship

lent despot, one of his two sons who succeeded him was a ruthless and spiteful oppressor.

In 510 B.C. tyranny was overthrown by a group of nobles with aid from Sparta. Factional conflict raged anew until Cleisthenes, an intelligent aristocrat, enlisted the support of the masses to eliminate his rivals from the scene. Having promised concessions to the people as a reward for their help, he proceeded to reform the government in so sweeping a fashion that he has since been known as the father of Athenian democracy. He greatly enlarged the citizen population by granting full rights to all free men who resided in the country at that time. He established a new council and made it the chief organ of government with power to prepare measures for submission to the assembly and with supreme control over executive and administrative functions. Members of this body were to be chosen by lot. Any male citizen over thirty years of age was eligible. Cleisthenes also expanded the authority of the assembly, giving it power to debate and pass or reject the measures submitted by the Council, to declare war, to appropriate money, and to audit the accounts of retiring magistrates. Lastly, Cleisthenes is believed to have instituted the device of ostracism, whereby any citizen who might be dangerous to the state could be sent into honorable exile for a ten-year period. The device was quite obviously intended to eliminate men who were suspected of cherishing dictatorial ambitions. Too often its effect was to eliminate exceptional men and to allow mediocrity to flourish.

The Athenian democracy attained its full perfection in the Age of Pericles (461–429 B.C.). It was during this period that the assembly acquired the authority to initiate legislation in addition to its power to ratify or reject proposals of the council. It was during this time also that the famous Board of Ten Generals rose to a position roughly comparable to that of the British cabinet. The Generals were chosen by the assembly for one-year terms and were eligible for reelection indefinitely. Pericles held the position of Chief Strategus or President of the Board of Generals for more than thirty years. The Generals were not simply commanders of the army but the chief legislative and executive officials in the state. Though wielding enormous power, they could not become tyrants, for their policies were subject to review by the assembly, and they could easily be recalled at the end of their one-year terms or indicted for malfeasance at any time. Finally, it was in the Age of Pericles that the Athenian system of courts was developed to completion. No longer was there merely a supreme court to hear appeals from the decisions of magistrates, but an array of popular courts with authority to try all kinds of cases. At the beginning of each year a list of 6000 citizens was chosen by lot from the various sections of the country. From this list separate juries, varying in size from 201 to 1001, were made up for particular trials. Each of these juries constituted a court with power to decide by majority vote every question involved in the case. Although one of the magistrates presided, he had none of the prerogatives of a judge; the jury itself was the judge, and from its decision there was no appeal. It would be difficult to imagine a system more thoroughly democratic.

The Athenian democracy differed from the modern form in various ways. First of all, it did not extend to the whole population, but only to the citizen class. While it is true that in the time of Cleisthenes (508–502 B.C.) the citizens probably included a majority of the inhabitants because of his enfranchisement of resident aliens, in the Age of Pericles they were distinctly a minority. It may be well to observe, however, that within its limits Athenian democracy was more thoroughly applied than is the modern form. The choice by lot of nearly all magistrates except the Ten Generals, the restriction of all terms of public officials to one year, and the uncompromising adherence to the principle of majority rule even in judicial trials were examples of a serene confidence in the political capacity of the average man which few modern nations would be willing to accept. The democracy of Athens differed from the contemporary ideal also in the fact that it was direct, not representative. The Athenians were not interested in being governed by men of reputation and ability; what vitally concerned them was the assurance to every citizen of an actual voice in the control of all public affairs. Nevertheless, their democracy did not last much longer than a hundred years.

In the century of her greatest expansion and creativity, Athens fought two major wars. The first, the war with Persia, was an outgrowth of the expansion of that empire into the eastern Mediterranean area. The Athenians resented the conquest of their Ionian kinsmen in Asia Minor and aided them in their struggle for freedom. The Persians retaliated by sending a powerful army and fleet to attack the Greeks. Although all Greece was in danger of conquest, Athens bore the chief burden of repelling the invader. The war, which began in 493 B.C. and lasted with interludes of peace for about fourteen years, is commonly regarded as one of the most significant in the history of the world. The decisive victory of the Greeks put an end to the menace of Persian conquest and forestalled at least for a time the submergence of Hellenic ideals of freedom in Near Eastern despotism. The war also had the effect of strengthening democracy in Athens and making that state the leading power in Greece.

The other of the great struggles, the Peloponnesian War with Sparta, had results of a quite different character. Instead of being another milestone in the Athenian march to power, it ended in tragedy. The causes of this war are of particular interest to the student of the downfall of civilizations. First and most important was the growth of Athenian imperialism. In the last year of the war with Persia, Athens had joined with a number of other Greek states in the formation of an offensive and defensive alliance known as the Delian League. When peace was concluded the league was not dissolved, for many of the Greeks feared that the Persians might come back. As time went on, Athens gradually transformed the league into a naval empire for the advancement of her own interests. She used some of the funds in the common treasury for her own purposes. She tried to reduce all the other members to a condition of vassalage, and when one of them rebelled, she overwhelmed it by force, seized its navy, and imposed tribute upon it as if it were a conquered state. Such high-handed methods aroused the suspicions of the Spartans, who feared that an Athenian hegemony would soon be extended over all of Greece.

Other causes of the Peloponnesian War

A second major cause was to be found in the social and cultural differences between Athens and Sparta. Athens was democratic, progressive, urban, imperialistic, and intellectually and artistically advanced. Sparta was aristocratic, conservative, agrarian, provincial, and culturally backward. Where such sharply contrasting systems exist side by side, conflicts are almost bound to occur. The attitude of the Athenians and Spartans had been hostile for some time. The former looked upon the latter as uncouth barbarians. The Spartans accused the Athenians of attempting to gain control over the northern Peloponnesian states and of encouraging the helots to rebel. Economic factors also played a large part in bringing the conflict to a head. Athens was ambitious to dominate the Corinthian Gulf, the principal avenue of trade with Sicily and southern Italy. This made her the deadly enemy of Corinth, the chief ally of Sparta.

The defeat of Athens

The war, which broke out in 431 B.C. and lasted until 404, was a record of frightful calamities for Athens. Her trade was destroyed, her democracy overthrown, and her population decimated by a terrible pestilence. Quite as bad was the moral degradation which followed in the wake of the military reverses. Treason, corruption, and brutality were among the hastening ills of the last few years of the conflict. On one occasion the Athenians even slaughtered the whole male population of the state of Melos, and enslaved the women and children, for no other crime than refusing to abandon neutrality. Ultimately, deserted by all her allies except Samos and with her food supply cut off, Athens was left with no alternative but to surrender or starve. The terms imposed upon her were drastic enough: destruction of her fortifications, surrender of all foreign possessions and practically her entire navy, and submission to Sparta as a subject state. Though Athens recovered her leadership for a time in the fourth century, her period of glory was approaching its end.

5. POLITICAL DEBACLE—THE LAST DAYS

Not only did the Peloponnesian War put an end, temporarily, to the supremacy of Athens; it annihilated freedom throughout the Greek world and sealed the doom of the Hellenic political genius. Following the war Sparta asserted her power over all of Hellas. Oli-

PHYSICAL MAP OF EUROPE, WESTERN ASIA,
AND NORTHERN AFRICA

Geometric Horse, VIII cent. B.C. Greek art of this early period was angular, formal, and conventionalized.

Geometric Jar, VIII cent. B.C. Another example of the stylized decorative patterns of early Greek art.

Sphinx, *ca.* 540–530 B.C. Though doubtless of Oriental derivation, Greek sphinxes had a softer and more human aspect than the Oriental.

Statue of an Amazon, one of the fabled tribe of women warriors, V cent. B.C. (Roman copy)

Departure of a Warrior. Gravestone, *ca.* 530 B.C., a period when naturalism was the dominant note of Greek art.

Athena, *ca.* 460 B.C. The young, graceful patron-goddess of Athens is about to send forth an owl as a sign of victory.

Jar, 500–490 B.C. The figures depicted in a fine black glaze on the natural red clay show athletes in the Panathenaic games.

Chorus of Satyrs, *ca.* 420 B.C. The background is black with the figures in red clay. The satyrs, dressed in fleecy white, with flowing tails, are the chorus of a play.

Toilet Box, 465–460 B.C., showing the Judgment of Paris, an early incident in the Trojan War.

GREECE AT THE END OF THE AGE OF PERICLES

Map legend:
- Sparta and allies
- Athens and allies
- Neutral Greek states

0 ———— 100 miles

garchies supported by Spartan troops replaced democracies wherever they existed. Confiscation of property and assassination were the methods regularly employed to combat opposition. Although in Athens the tyrants were overthrown after a time and free government restored, Sparta was able to dominate the remainder of Greece for more than thirty years. In 371 B.C., however, Epaminondas of Thebes defeated the Spartan army at Leuctra and thereby inaugurated a period of Theban supremacy. Unfortunately Thebes showed little more wisdom and tolerance in governing than Sparta, and nine years later a combination was formed to free the Greek cities from their new oppressor. Failing to break up the alliance, the Thebans gave battle on the field of Mantinea. Both sides claimed the victory, but Epaminondas was slain, and the power of his empire soon afterward collapsed.

Continuing conflict among the city-states

The long succession of wars had now brought the Greek states to the point of exhaustion. Though the glory of their culture was yet undimmed, politically they were prostrate and helpless. Their fate

129

was soon decided for them by the rise of Philip of Macedon. Except for a thin veneer of Hellenic culture, the Macedonians were barbarians; but Philip, before becoming their king, had learned how to lead an army while a hostage at Thebes. Perceiving the weakness of the states to the south, he determined to conquer them. A series of early successes led to a decisive victory in 338 B.C. and soon afterward to dominion over all of Greece except Sparta. Two years later Philip was murdered as the sequel to a family brawl.

Rule over Hellas now passed into the hands of his son Alexander, a youth of twenty years. After putting to death all possible aspirants to the throne and quelling some feeble revolts of the Greeks, Alexander conceived the grandiose scheme of conquering Persia. One victory followed another until in the short space of twelve years the whole ancient Near Orient from the Indus River to the Nile had been annexed to Greece as the personal domain of one man. Alexander did not live to enjoy it long. In 323 B.C. he fell ill of Babylonian swamp fever and died at the age of thirty-two.

It is difficult to gauge the significance of Alexander's career. Historians have differed widely in their interpretations. Some have seen him as one of the supreme galvanizing forces in history. Others would limit his genius to military strategy and organization and deny that he made a single major contribution of benefit to humanity.[3] There can be no doubt that he was a master of the art of war (he never lost a battle), and that he was intelligent and endowed with charm and physical courage. Unquestionably, also, he was a man of vibrant energy and overpowering ambitions. Just what these ambitions were is not certain. Evidence eludes us that he aspired to conquer the world or to advance the Hellenic ideals of freedom and justice. It seems doubtful that he had much interest in lofty ideals or in using military force to extend them. As the British historian A. R. Burn has said: "His abiding ideal was the glory of Alexander."[4] Nevertheless, he did introduce Macedonian standards of administrative efficiency into the government of the Near East. Aside from this, the primary significance of the great conqueror seems to lie in the fact that he carried the Hellenic drive into Asia farther and faster than would otherwise have occurred. He undoubtedly caused the Greek influence to be more widely felt. At the same time he appears to have placed too great a strain upon Hellenism with the result of encouraging a sweeping tide of Oriental influences into the West. Within a short period Hellenic and Oriental cultures interpenetrated to such an extent as to produce a new civilization. This was the Hellenistic civilization to be discussed in the chapter that follows.

[3] Compare W. W. Tarn, *Alexander the Great*, and A. R. Burn, *Alexander the Great and the Hellenistic World*.
[4] *Alexander the Great and the Hellenistic World*, p. 23.

Marble Stele with Law against Tyranny, 338 B.C. Sculptured relief shows a woman (Democracy) crowning an aged man (the people of Athens). The law provides that if anyone establishes a dictatorship in Athens, a person who kills him shall be held guiltless.

6. HELLENIC THOUGHT AND CULTURE

From what has been said in preceding chapters it should be clear that the popular notion that all philosophy originated with the Greeks is fallacious. Centuries earlier the Egyptians had given much thought to the nature of the universe and to the social and ethical problems of man. The achievement of the Greeks was rather the development of philosophy in a more inclusive meaning than it had ever possessed before. They attempted to find answers to every conceivable question about the nature of the universe, the problem of truth, and the meaning and purpose of life. The magnitude of their accomplishment is attested by the fact that philosophy ever since has been largely a debate over the validity of their several conclusions.

The antecedents of Greek philosophy

Greek philosophy had its origins in the sixth century B.C. in the work of the so-called Milesian school, whose members were natives of the great commercial city of Miletus on the shore of Asia Minor. Their philosophy was fundamentally scientific and materialistic. The problem which chiefly engaged their attention was to discover the nature of the physical world. They believed that all things could be reduced to some primary substance or original matter which was the source of worlds, stars, animals, plants, and men, and to which all would ultimately return. Thales, the founder of the school, perceiving that all things contained moisture, taught that the primary substance is water. Anaximander insisted that it could not be any particular thing such as water or fire but some substance "ungendered and imperishable" which "contains and directs all things."

The philosophy of the Milesian school

131

He called this substance the Infinte or the Boundless. A third member of the school, Anaximenes, declared that the original material of the universe is air. Air when rarefied becomes fire; when condensed it turns successively to wind, vapor, water, earth, and stone.

Although seemingly naïve in its conclusions the philosophy of the Milesian school was of real significance. It broke through the mythological beliefs of the Greeks about the origin of the world and substituted a purely rational explanation. It revived and expanded the Egyptian ideas of the eternity of the universe and the indestructibility of matter. It suggested very clearly, especially in the teachings of Anaximander, the concept of evolution in the sense of rhythmic change, of continuing creation and decay.

Before the end of the sixth century Greek philosophy developed a metaphysical turn; it ceased to be occupied solely with problems of the physical world and shifted its attention to abstruse questions about the nature of being, the meaning of truth, and the position of the divine in the scheme of things. First to exemplify the new tendency were the Pythagoreans, who interpreted philosophy largely in terms of religion. Little is known about them except that their leader, Pythagoras, migrated from the island of Samos to southern Italy and founded a religious community at Croton. He and his followers apparently taught that the speculative life is the highest good, but that in order to pursue it, man must purify himself from the evil desires of the flesh. They held that the essence of things is not a material substance but an abstract principle, number. Their chief significance lies in the sharp distinctions they drew between spirit and matter, harmony and discord, good and evil. Perhaps it is accurate to regard them as the real founders of dualism in Greek thought.

Renewal of the
debate over the
nature of the
universe

A consequence of the work of the Pythagoreans was to intensify the debate over the nature of the universe. Some of their contemporaries, notably Parmenides, argued that stability or permanence is the real nature of things; change and diversity are simply illusions of the senses. Directly opposed to this conception was the position taken by Heracleitus, who argued that permanence is an illusion, that change alone is real. The universe, he maintained, is in a condition of constant flux; therefore "it is impossible to step twice into the same stream." Creation and destruction, life and death, are but the obverse and reverse sides of the same picture. In affirming such views Heracleitus was really contending that the things we see and hear and feel are all that there is to reality. Evolution or constant change is the law of the universe. The tree or the stone that is here today is gone tomorrow; no underlying substance exists immutable through all eternity.

The eventual answer to the question of the underlying character of the universe was provided by the atomists. The philosopher chiefly responsible for the development of the atomic theory was

Democritus, who lived in Abdera on the Thracian coast in the second half of the fifth century. As their name implies, the atomists held that the ultimate constituents of the universe are atoms, infinite in number, indestructible, and indivisible. Although these differ in size and shape, they are exactly alike in composition. Because of the motion inherent in them, they are eternally uniting, separating, and reuniting in different arrangements. Every individual object or organism in the universe is thus the product of a fortuitous concourse of atoms. The only difference between a man and a tree is the difference in the number and arrangement of their atoms. Here was a philosophy which represented the final fruition of the materialistic tendencies of early Greek thought. Democritus denied the immortality of the soul and the existence of any spiritual world. Strange as it may appear to some people, he was a moral idealist, affirming that "Good means not merely not to do wrong, but rather not to desire to do wrong." [5]

About the middle of the fifth century B.C. an intellectual revolution began in Greece. It accompanied the high point of democracy in Athens. The rise of the common man, the growth of individualism, and the demand for the solution of practical problems produced a reaction against the old ways of thinking. As a result philosophers abandoned the study of the physical universe and turned to consideration of subjects more intimately related to man himself. The first exponents of the new intellectual trend were the Sophists. Originally the term meant "those who are wise," but later it came to be used in the derogatory sense of men who employ specious reasoning. Since most of our knowledge of the Sophists was derived, until comparatively recently, from Plato, one of their severest critics, they were commonly considered to have been the enemies of all that was best in Hellenic culture. Modern research has exposed the fallacy of so extreme a conclusion. Some members of the group, however, did lack a sense of social responsibility and were quite unscrupulous in "making the worse appear the better cause." It is said that a few of them charged the equivalent of $10,000 to educate a single individual.

The greatest of the Sophists was undoubtedly Protagoras, a native of Abdera who did most of his teaching in Athens. His famous dictum, "Man is the measure of all things," comprehends the essence of the Sophist philosophy. By this he meant that goodness, truth, justice, and beauty are relative to the needs and interests of man himself. There are no absolute truths or eternal standards of right and justice. Since sense perception is the exclusive source of knowledge, there can be only particular truths valid for a given time and place. Morality likewise varies from one people to another. The Spartans encourage adultery in certain cases on the part of wives as well as

[5] Quoted by Frank Thilly, *History of Philosophy*, p. 40.

husbands; the Athenians seclude their women and refuse even to allow them a normal social life. Which of these standards is right? Neither is right in any absolute sense, for there are no absolute canons of right and wrong eternally decreed in the heavens to fit all cases; yet both are right in the relative sense that the judgment of man alone determines what is good.

Some of the later Sophists went far beyond the teachings of their great master. The individualism which was necessarily implicit in the teachings of Protagoras was twisted by Thrasymachus into the doctrine that all laws and customs are merely expressions of the will of the strongest and shrewdest for their own advantage, and that therefore the wise man is the "perfectly unjust man" who is above the law and concerned with the gratification of his own desires.

Yet there was much that was admirable in the teachings of all the Sophists, even of those who were the most extreme. Without exception they condemned slavery and the racial exclusiveness of the Greeks. They were champions of liberty, the rights of the common man, and the practical and progressive point of view. They perceived the folly of war and ridiculed the silly chauvinism of many of the Athenians. Perhaps their most important work was the extension of philosophy to include not only physics and metaphysics, but ethics and politics as well. As Cicero expressed it, they "brought philosophy down from heaven to the dwellings of men."

It was inevitable that the relativism, skepticism, and individualism of the Sophists should have aroused strenuous opposition. In the judgment of the more conservative Greeks these doctrines appeared to lead straight to atheism and anarchy. If there is no final truth, and if goodness and justice are merely relative to the whims of the individual, then neither religion, morality, the state, nor society itself can long be maintained. The result of this conviction was the growth of a new philosophic movement grounded upon the theory that truth is real and that absolute standards do exist. The leaders of this movement were perhaps the three most famous individuals in the history of thought—Socrates, Plato, and Aristotle.

Socrates was born in Athens in 469 B.C. of humble parentage; his father was a sculptor, his mother a midwife. How he obtained an education no one knows, but he was certainly familiar with the teachings of earlier Greek thinkers, presumably from extensive reading. The impression that he was a mere gabbler in the market place is quite unfounded. He became a philosopher on his own account chiefly to combat the doctrines of the Sophists. In 399 B.C. he was condemned to death on a charge of "corrupting the youth and introducing new gods." The real reason for the unjust sentence was the tragic outcome for Athens of the Peloponnesian War. Overwhelmed by resentment and despair, the people turned against Socrates because of his associations with aristocrats, including the traitor Alcibiades, and because of his criticism of popular belief.

The extremist doctrines of the later Sophists

The valuable contributions of the Sophists

The reaction against Sophism

The career of Socrates

There is evidence that he disparaged democracy and contended that no government was worthy of the name except intellectual aristocracy.

For the reason that Socrates wrote nothing himself, historians have been faced with a problem in determining the scope of his teachings. He is generally regarded as primarily a teacher of ethics with no interest in abstract philosophy or any desire to found a new school of thought. Certain admissions made by Plato, however, indicate that a large part of the famous doctrine of Ideas was really of Socratic origin. At any rate we can be reasonably sure that Socrates believed in a stable and universally valid knowledge, which man could possess if he would only pursue the right method. This method would consist in the exchange and analysis of opinions, in the setting up and testing of provisional definitions, until finally an essence of truth recognizable by all could be distilled from them. Socrates argued that in similar fashion man could discover enduring principles of right and justice independent of the selfish desires of human beings. He believed, moreover, that the discovery of such rational principles of conduct would prove an infallible guide to virtuous living, for he denied that anyone who truly knows the good can ever choose the evil.

The philosophy of Socrates

By far the most distinguished of Socrates' pupils was Plato, who was born in Athens in 427 B.C., the son of noble parents. His real name was Aristocles, "Plato" being a nickname supposedly given to him by one of his teachers because of his broad frame. When he was twenty years old he joined the Socratic circle, remaining a member until the tragic death of his teacher. He seems to have drawn inspiration from other sources also, notably from the teachings of Parmenides and the Pythagoreans. Unlike his great master he was a prolific writer, though some of the works attributed to him are of doubtful authorship. The most noted of his writings are such dialogues as the *Apology*, the *Protagoras*, the *Phaedrus*, the *Timaeus*, and the *Republic*. He was engaged in the completion of another great work, the *Laws*, when death overtook him in his eighty-first year.

Plato

Plato's objectives in developing his philosophy were similar to those of Socrates although somewhat broader: (1) to combat the theory of reality as a disordered flux and to substitute an interpretation of the universe as essentially spiritual and purposeful; (2) to refute the Sophist doctrines of relativism and skepticism; and (3) to provide a secure foundation for ethics. In order to realize these objectives he developed his celebrated doctrine of Ideas. He admitted that relativity and constant change are characteristics of the world of physical things, of the world we perceive with our senses. But he denied that this world is the complete universe. There is a higher, spiritual realm composed of eternal forms or Ideas which only the mind can conceive. These are not, however, mere abstractions in-

Plato's philosophy of Ideas

vented by the mind of man, but spiritual things. Each is the pattern of some particular class of objects or relation between objects on earth. Thus there are Ideas of man, tree, shape, size, color, proportion, beauty, and justice. Highest of them all is the Idea of the Good, which is the active cause and guiding purpose of the whole universe. The things we perceive with our senses are merely imperfect copies of the supreme realities, Ideas.

Plato's ethical and religious philosophy was closely related to his doctrine of Ideas. Like Socrates he believed that true virtue has its basis in knowledge. But the knowledge derived from the senses is limited and variable; hence true virtue must consist in rational apprehension of the eternal Ideas of goodness and justice. By relegating the physical to an inferior place, he gave to his ethics a mildly ascetic tinge. He regarded the body as a hindrance to the mind and taught that only the rational part of man's nature is noble and good. In contrast with some of his later followers, he did not demand that appetites and emotions should be denied altogether, but urged that they should be strictly subordinated to the reason. Plato never made his conception of God entirely clear. Sometimes he referred to the Idea of the Good as if it were a divine power of subordinate rank, at other times as if it were the supreme creator and ruler of the universe. Probably the latter is what he really meant. At any rate it is certain that he conceived of the universe as spiritual in nature and governed by intelligent purpose. He rejected both materialism and mechanism. As for the soul, he regarded it not only as immortal but as preexisting through all eternity.

As a political philosopher Plato was motivated by the ideal of constructing a state which would be free from turbulence and self-seeking on the part of individuals and classes. Neither democracy nor liberty but harmony and efficiency were the ends he desired to achieve. Accordingly, he proposed in his *Republic* a famous plan for society which would have divided the population into three principal classes corresponding to the functions of the soul. The lowest class, representing the appetitive function, would include the farmers, artisans, and merchants. The second class, representing the spirited element or will, would consist of the soldiers. The highest class, representing the function of reason, would be composed of the intellectual aristocracy. Each of these classes would perform those tasks for which it was best fitted. The function of the lowest class would be the production and distribution of goods for the benefit of the whole community; that of the soldiers, defense; the aristocracy, by reason of special aptitude for philosophy, would enjoy a monopoly of political power. The division of the people into these several ranks would not be made on the basis of birth or wealth, but through a sifting process that would take into account the ability of each individual to profit from education. Thus the farmers, artisans, and merchants would be those who had shown the least intellectual

Plato's ethical and religious philosophy

Plato as a political philosopher

capacity, whereas the philosopher-kings would be those who had shown the greatest.

The last of the great champions of the Socratic tradition was Aristotle, a native of Stagira, born in 384 B.C. At the age of seventeen he entered Plato's Academy,[6] continuing as student and teacher there for twenty years. In 343 he was invited by King Philip of Macedon to serve as tutor to the young Alexander. Perhaps history affords few more conspicuous examples of wasted talent, except for the fact that the young prince acquired an enthusiasm for science and for some other elements of Hellenic culture. Seven years later Aristotle returned to Athens, where he conducted a school of his own, known as the Lyceum, until his death in 322 B.C. Aristotle wrote even more voluminously than Plato and on a greater variety of subjects. His principal works include treatises on logic, metaphysics, rhetoric, ethics, natural sciences, and politics. A considerable number of the writings credited to him have never been found.

Though Aristotle was as much interested as Plato and Socrates in absolute knowledge and eternal standards, his philosophy differed from theirs in several outstanding respects. To begin with, he had a higher regard for the concrete and the practical. In contrast with Plato, the aesthete, and Socrates, who declared he could learn nothing from trees and stones, Aristotle was a scientist with a compelling interest in biology, medicine, and astronomy. Moreover, he was less inclined than his predecessors to a spiritual outlook. And lastly, he did not share their strong aristocratic sympathies.

Aristotle agreed with Plato that universals, Ideas (or forms as he called them), are real, and that knowledge derived from the senses is limited and inaccurate. But he refused to go along with his master in ascribing an independent existence to universals and in reducing material things to pale reflections of their spiritual patterns. On the contrary, he asserted that form and matter are of equal importance; both are eternal, and neither can exist inseparable from the other. It is the union of the two which gives to the universe its essential character. Forms are the causes of all things; they are the purposive forces that shape the world of matter into the infinitely varied objects and organisms around us. All evolution, both cosmic and organic, results from the interaction of form and matter upon each other. Thus the presence of the form *man* in the human embryo molds and directs the development of the latter until it ultimately evolves as a human being. Aristotle's philosophy may be regarded as halfway between the spiritualism and transcendentalism of Plato, on the one hand, and the mechanistic materialism of the atomists on the other. His conception of the universe was *teleological*—that is, governed by purpose; but he refused to regard the spiritual as completely overshadowing its material embodiment.

[6] So called from the grove of Academus, where Plato and his disciples met to discuss philosophic problems.

That Aristotle should have conceived of God primarily as a First Cause is no more than we should expect from the dominance of the scientific attitude in his philosophy. Unlike Plato's Idea of the Good, Aristotle's God did not fulfill an ethical purpose. His character was that of a Prime Mover, the original source of the purposive motion contained in the forms. In no sense was he a personal God, for his nature was pure intelligence, devoid of all feelings, will, or desire. Aristotle seems to have left no place in his religious scheme for individual immortality: all the functions of the soul, except the creative reason which is not individual at all, are dependent upon the body and perish with it.

Aristotle's ethical
philosophy of the
golden mean

Aristotle's ethical philosophy was less ascetic than Plato's. He did not regard the body as the prison of the soul, nor did he believe that physical appetites are necessarily evil in themselves. He taught that the highest good for man consists in self-realization, that is, in the exercise of that part of man's nature which most truly distinguishes him as a human being. Self-realization would therefore be identical with the life of reason. But the life of reason is dependent upon the proper combination of physical and mental conditions. The body must be kept in good health and the emotions under adequate control. The solution is to be found in the *golden mean,* in preserving a balance between excessive indulgence on the one hand and ascetic denial on the other. This was simply a reaffirmation of the characteristic Hellenic ideal of *sophrosyne,* "nothing too much."

Although Aristotle included in his *Politics* much descriptive and analytical material on the structure and functions of government, he dealt primarily with the broader aspects of political theory. He considered the state as the supreme institution for the promotion of the good life among men, and he was therefore vitally interested in its origin and development and in the best forms it could be made to assume. Declaring that man is by nature a political animal, he denied that the state is an artificial product of the ambitions of the few or of the desires of the many. On the contrary, he asserted that it is rooted in the instincts of man himself, and that civilized life outside of its limits is impossible. He considered the best state to be neither a monarchy, an aristocracy, nor a democracy, but a *polity*—which he defined as a commonwealth intermediate between oligarchy and democracy. Essentially it would be a state under the control of the middle class, but Aristotle intended to make sure that the members of that class would be fairly numerous, for he advocated measures to prevent the concentration of wealth. He defended the institution of private property, but he opposed the heaping up of riches beyond what is necessary for intelligent living. He recommended that the government should provide the poor with money to buy small farms or to "make a beginning in trade and husbandry" and thus promote their prosperity and self-respect.[7]

[7] *Politics,* Maurice Francis Egan (ed.), pp. 158–59.

Contrary to a popular belief, the period of Hellenic civilization, strictly speaking, was not a great age of science. The vast majority of the scientific achievements commonly thought of as Greek were made during the Hellenistic period, when the culture was no longer predominantly Hellenic but a mixture of Hellenic and Oriental.[8] The interests of the Greeks in the Periclean age and in the century that followed were chiefly speculative and artistic; they were not deeply concerned with material comforts or with mastery of the physical universe. Consequently, with the exception of some important developments in mathematics, biology, and medicine, scientific progress was relatively slight.

Hellenic science

The founder of Greek mathematics was apparently Thales of Miletus, who is supposed to have originated several theorems which were later included in the geometry of Euclid. Perhaps more significant was the work of the Pythagoreans, who developed an elaborate theory of numbers, classifying them into various categories, such as odd, even, prime, composite, perfect, and so forth. They are also supposed to have discovered the theory of proportion and to have proved for the first time that the sum of the three angles of any triangle is equal to two right angles. But the most famous of their achievements was the discovery of the theorem attributed to Pythagoras himself: the square of the hypotenuse of any right-angled triangle is equal to the sum of the squares on the other two sides. The Greek who first developed geometry as a science is now considered to have been Hippocrates of Chios, not to be confused with the physician, Hippocrates of Cos.[9]

Mathematics

The first of the Greeks to manifest an interest in biology was the philosopher Anaximander, who developed a crude theory of organic evolution based upon the principle of survival through progressive adaptations to the environment. The earliest ancestral animals, he asserted, lived in the sea, which originally covered the whole face of the earth. As the waters receded, some organisms were able to adjust themselves to their new environment and became land animals. The final product of this evolutionary process was man himself. The real founder of the science of biology, however, was Aristotle. Devoting many years of his life to painstaking study of the structure, habits, and growth of animals, he revealed many facts which were not destined to be discovered anew until the seventeenth century or later. The metamorphoses of various insects, the reproductive habits of the eel, the embryological development of the dog-fish—these are only samples of the amazing extent of his knowledge. Unfortunately he committed some errors. He denied the sexuality of plants, and although he subscribed to the general theory of evolution, he believed in the spontaneous generation of certain species of worms and insects.

Biology

[8] See the chapter on The Hellenistic Civilization.
[9] George Sarton, *An Introduction to the History of Science*, I, 92.

Medicine

Greek medicine also had its origin with the philosophers. A pioneer was Empedocles, exponent of the theory of the four elements (earth, air, fire, and water). He discovered that blood flows to and from the heart, and that the pores of the skin supplement the work of the respiratory passages in breathing. More important was the work of Hippocrates of Cos in the fifth and fourth centuries. By general consensus he is still regarded as the father of medicine. He dinned into the ears of his pupils the doctrine that "Every disease has a natural cause, and without natural causes, nothing ever happens." In addition, by his methods of careful study and comparison of symptoms he laid the foundations for clinical medicine. He discovered the phenomenon of crisis in disease and improved the practice of surgery. Though he had a wide knowledge of drugs, his chief reliances in treatment were diet and rest. The main fact to his discredit was his development of the theory of the four humors—the notion that illness is due to excessive amounts of yellow bile, black bile, blood, and phlegm in the system. The practice of bleeding the patient was the regrettable outgrowth of this theory.

Generally the most common medium of literary expression in the formative age of a people is the epic of heroic deeds. It is a form well adapted to the pioneering days of battle and lusty adventure when men have not yet had time to be awed by the mystery of things. The most famous of the Greek epics, the *Iliad* and the *Odyssey*, were put into written form at the end of the Dark Ages and commonly attributed to Homer. The first, which deals with the Trojan War, has its theme in the wrath of Achilles; the second describes the wanderings and return of Odysseus. Both have supreme literary merit in their carefully woven plots, in the realism of their character portrayals, and in their mastery of the full range of emotional intensity. They exerted an almost incalculable influence upon later writers. Their style and language inspired the fervid emotional poetry of the sixth century, and they were an unfailing source of plots and themes for the great tragedians of the Golden Age of the fifth and fourth centuries.

The three centuries which followed the Dark Ages were distinguished, as we have already seen, by tremendous social changes. The rural pattern of life gave way to an urban society of steadily increas-

Homer

140

ing complexity. The founding of colonies and the growth of commerce provided new interests and new habits of living. Individuals hitherto submerged rose to a consciousness of their power and importance. It was inevitable that these changes should be reflected in new forms of literature, especially of a more personal type. The first to be developed was the elegy, which was probably intended to be declaimed rather than sung to the accompaniment of music. Elegies varied in theme from individual reactions toward love to the idealism of patriots and reformers. Generally, however, they were devoted to melancholy reflection on the disillusionments of life or to bitter lament over loss of prestige. Outstanding among the authors of elegiac verse was Solon the legislator.

Development
of the elegy

In the sixth century and the early part of the fifth, the elegy was gradually displaced by the lyric, which derives its name from the fact that it was sung to the music of the lyre. The new type of poetry was particularly well adapted to the expression of passionate feelings, the violent loves and hates engendered by the strife of classes. It was employed for other purposes also. Both Alcaeus and Sappho used it to describe the poignant beauty of love, the delicate grace of spring, and the starlit splendor of a summer night. Meanwhile other poets developed the choral lyric, intended to express the feelings of the community rather than the sentiments of any one individual. Greatest of all the writers of this group was Pindar of Thebes, who wrote during the first half of the fifth century. The lyrics of Pindar took the form of odes celebrating the victories of athletes and the glories of Hellenic civilization. They are significant also for their religious and moral conceptions. Pindar had accepted the idea that Zeus is a god of righteousness, and that he will punish the wicked with the "direst doom" and reward the good with a life "that knows no tears."

Lyric poetry

The supreme literary achievement of the Greeks was the tragic drama. Like so many of their other great works, it had its roots in religion. At the festivals dedicated to the worship of Dionysus, the god of spring and of wine, a chorus of men dressed as satyrs, or goatmen, sang and danced around an altar, enacting the various parts of

The origins of
tragic drama

Interior of a Greek Cup. Depicted here is Achilles bandaging the wound of Patrokolus. Ca. 500 B.C.

a dithyramb or choral lyric that related the story of the god's career. In time a leader came to be separated from the chorus to recite the main parts of the story. The true drama was born about the beginning of the fifth century when Aeschylus introduced a second "actor" and relegated the chorus to the background. The name "tragedy," which came to be applied to this drama, was probably derived from the Greek word *tragos* meaning "goat."

Greek tragedy stands out in marked contrast to the tragedies of Shakespeare, Eugene O'Neill, or Arthur Miller. There was, first of all, little action presented on the stage; the main business of the actors was to recite the incidents of a plot which was already familiar to the audience, for the story was drawn from popular legends. Secondly, Greek tragedy devoted little attention to the study of complicated individual personality. There was no unfoldment of personal character as shaped by the vicissitudes of a long career. Those involved in the plot were scarcely individuals at all, but types. On the stage they wore masks to disguise any characteristics which might serve to distinguish them too sharply from the rest of humanity. In addition, Greek tragedies differed from the modern variety in having as their theme the conflict between man and the universe, not the clash of individual personalities, or the conflict of man with himself. The tragic fate that befell the main characters in these plays was external to man himself. It was brought on by the fact that someone had committed a crime against society, or against the gods, thereby offending the moral scheme of the universe. Punishment must follow in order to balance the scale of justice. Finally, the purpose of Greek tragedies was not merely to depict suffering and to interpret human actions, but to purify the emotions of the audience by representing the triumph of justice.

As already indicated, the first of the tragic dramatists was Aeschylus (525–456 B.C.). Though he is supposed to have written about eighty plays, only seven have survived in complete form, among them *The Persians, Seven against Thebes, Prometheus Bound*, and a trilogy known as *Oresteia*. Guilt and punishment is the recurrent theme of nearly all of them. The second of the dramatists, Sophocles (496–406), is often considered the greatest. His style was more polished and his philosophy more profound than that of his predecessor. He was the author of over a hundred plays. More than any other writer in Greek history, he personified the Hellenic ideal of "nothing too much." His attitude was distinguished by love of harmony and peace, intelligent respect for democracy, and profound sympathy for human weakness. The most famous of his plays now extant are *Oedipus Rex, Antigone*, and *Electra*.

The work of the last of the tragedians, Euripides (480–406), reflects a far different spirit. He was a skeptic, an individualist, a humanist, who took delight in ridiculing the ancient myths and the "sacred cows" of his time. An embittered pessimist who suffered from the barbs of his conservative critics, he loved to humble the

Greek tragedy compared with modern tragedy

Aeschylus and Sophocles

Greek Theater in Epidauros. The construction, to take advantage of the slope of the hill, and the arrangement of the stage are of particular interest. Greek dramas were invariably presented in the open air.

proud in his plays and to exalt the lowly. He was the first to give the ordinary man, even the beggar and the peasant, a place in the drama. Euripides is also noted for his sympathy for the slave, for his condemnation of war, and for his protests against the exclusion of women from social and intellectual life. Because of his humanism, his tendency to portray men as they actually were (or even a little worse), and his introduction of the love *motif* into drama, he is often considered a modernist. It must be remembered, however, that in other respects his plays were perfectly consistent with the Hellenic model. They did not exhibit the evolution of individual character or the conflict of egos to any more notable extent than did the works of Sophocles or Aeschylus. Nevertheless, he has been called the most tragic of the Greek dramatists because he dealt with situations having analogues in real life. Among the best-known tragedies of Euripides are *Alcestis*, *Medea*, and *The Trojan Women*.

Euripides

Epidaros Plan

Hellenic comedy was definitely inferior to tragedy. In common with tragedy it appears to have grown out of the Dionysiac festivals, but it did not attain full development until late in the fifth century B.C. Its only outstanding representative was Aristophanes (448?–380?), a somewhat coarse and belligerent aristocrat who lived in Athens. Most of his plays were written to satirize the political and intellectual ideals of the radical democracy of his time. In *The Knights* he pilloried the incompetent and greedy politicians for their reckless adventures in imperialism. In *The Frogs* he lampooned

Hellenic comedy

143

Euripides for the innovations the latter had made in the drama. *The Clouds* he reserved for ridicule of the Sophists, ignorantly or maliciously classifying Socrates as one of them. While he was undoubtedly a clever poet with a mastery of subtle humor and imaginative skill, his ideas were founded largely upon prejudice. He is deserving of much credit, however, for his sharp criticisms of the stupid policies of the war-hawks of Athens during the struggle with Sparta. Though written as a farce, his *Lysistrata* cleverly pointed a way—however infeasible—to the termination of any war.

No account of Greek literature would be complete without some mention of the two great historians of the Golden Age. Herodotus, the "father of history" (484–425), was a native of Halicarnassus in Asia Minor. He traveled extensively through the Persian empire, Egypt, Greece, and Italy, collecting a multitude of interesting data about various peoples. His famous account of the great war between the Greeks and the Persians included so much background that the work seems almost a history of the world. He regarded that war as an epic struggle between East and West, with Zeus giving victory to the Greeks against a mighty host of barbarians.

The Greek historians: Herodotus

If Herodotus deserves to be called the father of history, much more does his younger contemporary, Thucydides, deserve to be considered the founder of scientific history. Influenced by the skepticism and practicality of the Sophists, Thucydides chose to work on the basis of carefully sifted evidence, rejecting opinion, legends, and hearsay. The subject of his *History* was the war between Sparta and Athens, which he described scientifically and dispassionately, emphasizing the complexity of causes which led to the fateful clash. His aim was to present an accurate record which could be studied with profit by statesmen and generals of all time, and it must be said that he was in full measure successful. If there were any defects in his historical method, they consisted in overemphasizing political factors to the neglect of the social and economic and in failing to consider the importance of emotions in history. He also had a prejudice against the democratic factions in Athens after the death of Pericles.

7. THE MEANING OF GREEK ART

Art even more than literature probably reflected the true character of Hellenic civilization. The Greek was essentially a materialist who conceived of his world in physical terms. Plato and the followers of the mystic religions were, of course, exceptions, but few other Greeks had much interest in a universe of spiritual realities. It would be natural therefore to find that the material emblems of architecture and sculpture should exemplify best the ideals the Greek held before him.

What did Greek art express? Above all, it symbolized humanism —the glorification of man as the most important creature in the uni-

Marble Statue of the Apollo Type. Probably end of seventh century B.C. At this time Greek sculpture was still under Egyptian influence.

Young Men Playing a Ball Game. This relief, ca. 510 B.C., depicts what may have been a forerunner of modern field hockey.

verse. Though much of the sculpture depicted gods, this did not detract in the slightest from its humanistic quality. The Greek deities existed for the benefit of man; in glorifying them he thus glorified himself. Both architecture and sculpture embodied the ideals of balance, harmony, order, and moderation. Anarchy and excess were abhorrent to the mind of the Greek, but so was absolute repression. Consequently, his art exhibited qualities of simplicity and dignified restraint—free from decorative extravagance, on the one hand, and from restrictive conventions on the other. Moreover, Greek art was an expression of the national life. Its purpose was not merely aesthetic but political: to symbolize the pride of the people in their city and to enhance their consciousness of unity. The Parthenon at Athens, for example, was the temple of Athena, the protecting goddess who presided over the corporate life of the state. In providing her with a beautiful shrine which she might frequently visit, the Athenians were giving evidence of their love for their city and their hope for its continuing welfare.

The ideals embodied in Greek art

See color plates at pages 129, 160

The art of the Hellenes differed from that of nearly every people since their time in an interesting variety of ways. Like most of the tragedies of Aeschylus and Sophocles, it was universal. It included few portraits of personalities either in sculpture or in painting.[10] The human beings depicted were generally types, not individuals. Again, Greek art differed from that of most later peoples in its ethical purpose. It was not art for the sake of mere decoration or for the expression of the artist's individual philosophy, but a medium for the ennoblement of man. This does not mean that it was didactic in the sense that its merit was determined by the moral lesson it taught, but rather that it was supposed to exemplify qualities of living essen-

Greek art compared with that of later peoples

[10] Most of the portraits in sculpture commonly considered Greek really belong to the Hellenistic Age, although a few were produced at the end of the fourth century B.C.

145

Corinthian

Ionic

Doric

*Details of the Three Famous
Orders of Greek Architecture*

tially artistic in themselves. The Athenian, at least, drew no sharp distinction between the ethical and aesthetic spheres; the beautiful and the good were really identical. True morality, therefore, consisted in rational living, in the avoidance of grossness, disgusting excesses, and other forms of conduct aesthetically offensive. Finally, Greek art may be contrasted with most later forms in the fact that it was not "naturalistic." Although the utmost attention was given to the depiction of beautiful bodies, this had nothing to do with fidelity to nature. The Greek was not interested in interpreting nature for its own sake, but in expressing *human* ideals.

The history of Greek art divides itself naturally into three great periods. The first, which can be called the archaic period, covered the seventh and sixth centuries. During the greater part of this age sculpture was dominated by Egyptian influence, as can be seen in the frontality and rigidity of the statues, with their square shoulders and one foot slightly advanced. Toward the end, however, these conventions were thrown aside. The chief architectural styles also had their origin in this period, and several crude temples were built. The second period, which occupied the fifth century, witnessed the full perfection of both architecture and sculpture. The art of this time was completely idealistic. During the fourth century, the last period of Hellenic art, architecture lost some of its balance and simplicity and sculpture assumed new characteristics. It came to reflect more clearly the reactions of the individual artist, to incorporate traces of realism, and to lose some of its quality as an expression of civic pride.

For all its artistic excellence, Greek temple architecture was one of the simplest of structural forms. Its essential elements were really only five in number: (1) the cella or nucleus of the building, which was a rectangular chamber to house the statue of the god; (2) the columns, which formed the porch and surrounded the cella; (3) the entablature or lintel, which rested upon the columns and supported the roof; (4) the gabled roof itself; and (5) the pediment or triangular section under the gable of the roof. Two different architectural styles were developed, representing modifications of certain of these elements. The more common was the Doric, which made use of a rather heavy, sharply fluted column surmounted by a plain capital. The other, the Ionic, had more slender and more graceful columns with flat flutings, a triple base, and a scroll or volute capital. The so-called Corinthian style, which was chiefly Hellenistic, differed from the Ionic primarily in being more ornate. The three styles differed also in their treatment of the entablature or lintel. In the Ionic style it was left almost plain. In the Doric and Corinthian styles it bore sculptured reliefs. The Parthenon, the best example of Greek architecture, was essentially a Doric building, but it reflected some of the grace and subtlety of Ionic influence.

According to the prevailing opinion among his contemporaries, Greek sculpture attained its acme of development in the work of

The Parthenon. The largest and most famous of Athenian temples, the Parthenon is considered the classic example of Doric architecture. Its columns were made more graceful by tapering them in a slight curve toward the top. Its friezes and pediments were decorated with lifelike sculptures of prancing horses (see below), fighting giants, and benign and confident deities.

Phidias (500?–432?). His masterpieces were the statue of Athena in the Parthenon and the statue of Zeus in the Temple of Olympian Zeus. In addition, he designed and supervised the execution of the Parthenon reliefs. The main qualities of his work are grandeur of conception, patriotism, proportion, dignity, and restraint. Nearly all of his figures are idealized representations of deities and mythological creatures in human form. The second most renowned fifth-century sculptor was Myron, noted for his statue of the discus thrower and for his glorification of other athletic types. The names of three great sculptors in the fourth century have come down to us. The most gifted of them was Praxiteles, renowned for his portrayal of humanized deities with slender, graceful bodies and countenances of philosophic repose. The best known of his works is the statue of Hermes with the infant Dionysus. His older contemporary, Scopas, gained distinction as an emotional sculptor. One of his most successful creations was the statue of a religious ecstatic, a worshiper of Dionysus, in a condition of mystic frenzy. At the end of the century Lysippus introduced even stronger qualities of realism and individualism into sculpture. He was the first great master of the realistic portrait as a study of personal character.

Parthenon Frieze

8.   ATHENIAN LIFE IN THE GOLDEN AGE

The population of Athens in the fifth and fourth centuries was divided into three distinct groups: the citizens, the metics, and the slaves. The citizens, who numbered at the most about 160,000, included only those born of citizen parents, except for the few who were occasionally enfranchised by special law. The metics, who probably did not exceed a total of 100,000, were resident aliens, chiefly non-Athenian Greeks, although some were Phoenicians and Jews. Save for the fact that they had no political privileges and generally were not permitted to own land, the metics had equal opportunities with citizens. They could engage in any occupation they desired and participate in any social or intellectual activities. Contrary to a popular tradition, the slaves in Athens were never a majority of the population. Their maximum number does not seem to have exceeded 140,000. Urban slaves, at least, were very well treated and were sometimes rewarded for faithful service by being set free. They could work for wages and own property, and some of them held responsible positions as minor public officials and as managers of banks. The treatment of slaves who worked in the mines, however, was often cruel.

Life in Athens stands out in rather sharp contrast to that in most other civilizations. One of its leading features was the amazing degree of social and economic equality that prevailed among all the inhabitants. Although there were many who were poor, there were few who were very rich. Nearly everyone, whether citizen, metic, or slave, ate the same kind of food, wore the same kind of clothing, and participated in the same kind of amusement. This substantial equality was enforced in part by the system of *liturgies*, which were services to the state rendered by wealthy men, chiefly in the form of contributions to support the drama, equip the navy, or provide for the poor.

A second outstanding characteristic of Athenian life was its poverty in comforts and luxuries. Part of this was a result of the low

The amazing degree of social and economic equality

Porch of the Maidens of the So-Called Erechtheum, a Temple of Athena on the Acropolis

Left: *The Discobolus or Discus Thrower of Myron*. The statue reflects the glorification of the human body characteristic of Athens in the Golden Age. Now in the Vatican Museum. Right: *Hermes with the Infant Dionysus, by Praxiteles, Fourth Century* B.C. Original in the Olympia Museum, Greece.

income of the mass of the people. Teachers, sculptors, masons, carpenters, and common laborers all received the same standard wage of one drachma per day. Part of it may have been a consequence also of the mild climate, which made possible a life of simplicity. But whatever the cause, the fact remains that, in comparison with modern standards, the Athenians endured an exceedingly impoverished existence. They knew nothing of such common commodities as watches, soap, newspapers, cotton cloth, sugar, tea, or coffee. Their beds had no springs, their houses had no drains, and their food consisted chiefly of barley cakes, onions, and fish, washed down with diluted wine. From the standpoint of clothing they were no better off. A rectangular piece of cloth wrapped around the body and fastened with pins at the shoulders and with a rope around the waist served as the main garment. A larger piece was draped around the body as an extra garment for outdoor wear. No one wore either stockings or socks, and few had any footgear except sandals.

But lack of comforts and luxuries was a matter of little consequence to the Athenian citizen. He was totally unable to regard

The poverty of Athenian life

149

these as the most important things in life. His aim was to live as interestingly and contentedly as possible without spending all his days in grinding toil for the sake of a little more comfort for his family. Nor was he interested in piling up riches as a source of power or prestige. What each citizen really wanted was a small farm or business that would provide him with a reasonable income and at the same time allow him an abundance of leisure for politics, for gossip in the market place, and for intellectual or artistic activities if he had the talent to enjoy them.

It is frequently supposed that the Athenian was too lazy or too snobbish to work hard for luxury and security. But this was not quite the case. True, there were some occupations in which he would not engage because he considered them degrading or destructive of moral freedom. He would not break his back digging silver or copper out of a mine; such work was fit only for slaves of the lowest intellectual level. On the other hand, there is plenty of evidence to show that the great majority of Athenian citizens did not look with disdain upon manual labor. Most of them worked on their farms or in their shops as independent craftsmen. Hundreds of others earned their living as hired laborers employed either by the state or by their fellow Athenians. Cases are on record of citizens, metics, and slaves working side by side, all for the same wage, in the construction of public buildings; and in at least one instance the foreman of a crew was a slave.[11]

In spite of expansion of trade and increase in population, the economic organization of Athenian society remained comparatively simple. Agriculture and commerce were by far the most important enterprises. Even in Pericles' day the majority of the citizens still lived in the country. Industry was not highly developed. Very few examples of large-scale production are on record, and those chiefly in the manufacture of pottery and implements of war. The largest establishment that ever existed was apparently a shield factory owned by a metic and employing 120 slaves. No other was more than half as large. The enterprises which absorbed the most labor were the mines, but they were owned by the state and were leased in sections to petty contractors to be worked by slaves. The bulk of industry was carried on in small shops owned by individual craftsmen who produced their wares directly to the order of the consumer.

Religion underwent some notable changes in the Golden Age of the fifth and fourth centuries. The primitive polytheism and anthropomorphism of the Homeric myths were largely supplanted, among intellectuals at least, by a belief in one God as the creator and sustainer of the moral law. Such a doctrine was taught by many of the philosophers, by the poet Pindar, and by the

[11] A. E. Zimmern, *The Greek Commonwealth*, p. 258.

dramatists Aeschylus and Sophocles. Other significant consequences flowed from the mystery cults. These new forms of religion first became popular in the sixth century because of the craving for an emotional faith to make up for the disappointments of life. The more important of them was the Orphic cult, which revolved around the myth of the death and resurrection of Dionysus. The other, the Eleusinian cult, had as its central theme the abduction of Persephone by Hades, god of the nether world, and her ultimate redemption by Demeter, the great Earth Mother. Both of these cults had as their original purpose the promotion of the lifegiving powers of nature, but in time they came to be fraught with a much deeper significance. They expressed to their followers the ideas of vicarious atonement, salvation in an afterlife, and ecstatic union with the divine. Although entirely inconsistent with the spirit of the ancient religion, they made a powerful appeal to certain classes and were largely responsible for the spread of the belief in personal immortality. The more thoughtful Greeks, however, seem to have persisted in their adherence to the worldly, optimistic, and mechanical faith of their ancestors and to have shown little concern about a conviction of sin or a desire for salvation in a life to come.

It remains to consider briefly the position of the family in Athens in the fifth and fourth centuries. Though marriage was still an important institution for the procreation of children who would become citizens of the state, there is reason to believe that family life had declined. Men of the more prosperous classes, at least, now spent the greater part of their time away from their families. Wives were relegated to an inferior position and required to remain secluded in their homes. Their place as social and intellectual companions for their husbands was taken by alien women, the famous *hetaerae*, many of whom were highly cultured natives of the Ionian cities. Marriage itself assumed the character of a political and economic arrangement devoid of romantic elements. Men married wives so as to ensure that at least some of their children would be legitimate and in order to obtain property in the form of a dowry. It was important also, of course, to have someone to care for the household. But husbands did not consider their wives as their equals and did not appear in public with them or encourage their participation in any form of social or intellectual activity.

9. THE GREEK ACHIEVEMENT AND ITS SIGNIFICANCE FOR US

No historian would deny that the achievement of the Greeks was one of the most remarkable in the history of the world. With no great expanse of fertile soil or abundance of mineral resources, they succeeded in developing a higher and more varied civilization than

The family in Athens in the Golden Age

any of the most richly favored nations of Africa and Western Asia. With only a limited cultural inheritance from the past to build upon as a foundation, they produced intellectual and artistic achievements which have served ever since as the chief inspiration to man in his quest for wisdom and beauty. It seems reasonable to conclude also that they achieved a more normal and more rational mode of living than most other peoples who strutted and fretted their hour upon this planet. The absence of violent revolution, except in the earlier period, and during the Peloponnesian War, the infrequency of brutal crimes, and the contentment with simple amusements and modest wealth all point to a comparatively happy and satisfied existence. Moreover, the sane moral attitude of the Greek helped to keep him almost entirely free from the nervous instability and emotional conflicts which wreak so much havoc in modern society. Suicide, for example, was exceedingly rare in Greece.[12]

It is necessary to be on our guard, however, against uncritical judgments that are sometimes expressed in reference to the achievement of the Greeks. We must not assume that all of the natives of Hellas were as cultured, wise, and free as the citizens of Athens and of the Ionian states across the Aegean. The Spartans, the Arcadians, the Thessalians, and probably the majority of the Boeotians remained untutored and benighted from the beginning to the end of their history. Further, the Athenian civilization itself was not without its defects. It permitted some exploitation of the weak, especially of the ignorant slaves who toiled in the mines. It was based upon a principle of racial exclusiveness which reckoned every man a foreigner whose parents were not both Athenians, and consequently denied political rights to the majority of the inhabitants. Its statecraft was not sufficiently enlightened to avoid the pitfalls of imperialism and even of aggressive war. Finally, the attitude of its citizens was not always tolerant and just. Socrates was put to death for his opinions, and two other philosophers, Anaxagoras and Protagoras, were forced to leave the country. The former was condemned to death by the assembly, and the books of the latter were ordered to be burned. It must be conceded, however, that the record of the Athenians for tolerance was better than that of most other nations, both ancient and modern. There was probably more freedom of expression in Athens during the war with Sparta than there was in the United States during World War I.

Nor is it true that the Hellenic influence has really been as great as is commonly supposed. No intelligent student could accept the sentimental verdict of Shelley: "We are all Greeks; our laws, our literature, our religion, our arts have their roots in Greece." Our laws do not really have their roots in Greece but chiefly in Hellenistic and Roman sources. Much of our poetry is undoubtedly Greek

[12] For a discussion of this point see E. A. Westermarck, *The Origin and Development of Moral Ideas*, pp. 247 ff.

in inspiration, but such is not the case with most of our prose literature. Our religion is no more than partly Greek; except as it was
influenced by Plato, Aristotle, and the Romans, it reflects primarily
the spirit of Western Asia. Even our arts take their form and meaning
from Rome almost as much as from Greece. Actually, modern civilization has been the result of the convergence of several influences
coming from a variety of sources. The influence from Greece has
been partly overshadowed by heritages from Western Asia and
from the Romans and the Germans. Philosophy appears to have
been the only important segment of Greek civilization that has been
incorporated into modern culture virtually intact.

In spite of all this, the Hellenic adventure was of profound significance for the history of the world. For the Greeks were the founders of nearly all those ideals we commonly think of as peculiar to
the West. The civilizations of ancient Western Asia, with the exception, to a certain extent, of the Hebrew and Egyptian, were
dominated by absolutism, supernaturalism, ecclesiasticism, the denial
of both body and mind, and the subjection of the individual to the
group. Their political regime was the reign of force as expressed in
an absolute monarch supported by a powerful priesthood. Their
religion in many cases was the worship of omnipotent gods who demanded that man should humble and despise himself for the purpose
of their greater glory. Culture in these mighty empires served mainly
as an instrument to magnify the power of the state and to enhance
the prestige of rulers and priests.

By contrast, the civilization of Greece, notably in its Athenian
form, was founded upon ideals of freedom, optimism, secularism,
rationalism, the glorification of both body and mind, and a high regard for the dignity and worth of the individual man. Insofar as the
individual was subjected at all, his subjection was to the rule of the
majority. This, of course, was not always good, especially in times

The influence of
the Greeks on the
West

Contrast of
Greek and
Oriental ideals

The Acropolis Today. Occupying the commanding position is the Parthenon.
To the left is the Erechtheum with its Porch of the Maidens facing the
Parthenon.

of crisis, when the majority might be swayed by prejudice. Religion was worldly and practical, serving the interests of human beings. Worship of the gods was a means for the ennoblement of man. As opposed to the ecclesiasticism of the Orient, the Greeks had no organized priesthood at all. They kept their priests in the background and refused under any circumstances to allow them to define dogma or to govern the realm of intellect. In addition, they excluded them from control over the sphere of morality. The culture of the Greeks was the first to be based upon the primacy of intellect— upon the supremacy of the spirit of free inquiry. There was no subject they feared to investigate, or any question they regarded as excluded from the province of reason. To an extent never before realized, mind was supreme over faith, logic and science over superstition.[13]

The tragedy of
Hellenic history

The supreme tragedy of the Greeks was, of course, their failure to solve the problem of political conflict. To a large degree, this conflict was the product of social and cultural dissimilarities. Because of different geographic and economic conditions the Greek city-states developed at an uneven pace. Some went forward rapidly to high levels of cultural superiority, while others lagged behind and made little or no intellectual progress. The consequences were discord and suspicion, which gave rise eventually to hatred and fear. Though some of the more advanced thinkers made efforts to propagate the notion that the Hellenes were one people who should reserve their contempt for non-Hellenes, or "barbarians," the conception never became part of a national ethos. Athenians hated Spartans, and *vice versa*, just as vehemently as they hated Lydians or Persians. Not even the danger of Asian conquest was sufficient to dispel the distrust and antagonism of Greeks for one another. The war that finally broke out between Athenians and Spartans sealed the doom of Hellenic civilization just as effectively as could ever have resulted from foreign conquest. For a time it appeared as if a new world, largely devoid of ethnic distinctions, might emerge from the ruins of the Greek city-states as a result of the conquests of Alexander the Great. Alexander dreamed of such a world, in which there would be neither Athenian nor Spartan, Greek nor Egyptian, but unfortunately neither he nor his generals knew any means of achieving it except to impose it by force. The parallels between the last phases of Hellenic history and the developments in our own time are at least interesting, if not conclusive.

SELECTED READINGS

· *Items so designated are available in paperbound editions.*

· Agard, Walter, *What Democracy Meant to the Greeks,* Chapel Hill, 1942 (University of Wisconsin).

[13] For further discussion of the contrast between Hellas and the Orient see the admirable study by Edith Hamilton, *The Greek Way.*

Andrewes, Antony, *The Greeks*, New York, 1967.

· Barker, Ernest, *Greek Political Theory: Plato and His Predecessors*, New York, 1919, 2 vols. (Barnes & Noble). One of the best of the commentaries.

· Boardman, John, *Greek Art*, New York, 1964 (Praeger).

· ———, *The Greeks Overseas*, Baltimore, 1964 (Penguin).

· Burn, A. R., *Pericles and Athens*, New York, 1962 (Collier).

· Clagett, Marshall, *Greek Science in Antiquity*, New York, 1963 (Collier).

· Dickinson, G. L., *The Greek View of Life*, New York, 1927 (Ann Arbor, Collier). An excellent interpretation.

· Dodds, E. R., *The Greeks and the Irrational*, Berkeley, 1963 (Univ. of California).

· Ehrenberg, Victor, *The Greek State*, New York, 1960 (Norton Library).

· Farrington, Benjamin, *Greek Science*, Baltimore, 1961 (Penguin).

· Finley, M. I., *The Ancient Greeks: An Introduction to Their Life and Thought*, New York, 1963 (Compass).

· Forrest, W. G., *A History of Sparta, 950–152 B.C.*, London, 1968 (Norton Library).

· Freeman, Kathleen, *The Greek City-States*, New York, 1963 (Norton Library).

· Glotz, Gustave, *Ancient Greece at Work*, London, 1927 (Norton Library).

· Hamilton, Edith, *The Greek Way*, New York, 1930 (Norton Library). Thoughtful and stimulating.

· Kitto, H. D. F., *The Greeks*, Baltimore, 1957 (Penguin). Probably the best one-volume survey in English.

· Larsen, J. A. O., *Representative Government in Greek and Roman History*, Berkeley, 1955 (University of California).

· MacKendrick, Paul, *The Greek Stones Speak*, New York, 1962 (Mentor).

· Marrou, H. I., *A History of Education in Antiquity*, New York, 1964 (Mentor).

· Mitchell, H., *Sparta*, New York, 1952 (Cambridge).

· Nilsson, M. P., *A History of Greek Religion*, New York, 1964 (Norton Library). Interesting and authoritative.

Richter, G. M. A., *Greek Art*, New York, 1963.

Ridder, A. H. P. de, and Deonna, Waldemar, *Art in Greece*, New York, 1927. An excellent one-volume account.

· Rose, H. J., *A Handbook of Greek Literature*, New York, 1960 (Dutton).

· ———, *A Handbook of Greek Mythology*, New York, 1959 (Dutton).

· Snell, Bruno, *The Discovery of the Mind*, New York, 1960 (Torchbook).

Starr, C. G., *The Origins of Greek Civilization*, New York, 1961.

· Webster, T. B. L., *From Mycenae to Homer*, New York, 1964 (Norton Library).

· Zimmern, A. E., *The Greek Commonwealth*, New York, 1911 (Galaxy). Good, though perhaps a bit too laudatory of the Athenians.

SOURCE MATERIALS

Most Greek authors have been translated in the appropriate volumes of the Loeb Classical Library, Harvard University Press.

In addition the following may be helpful:

· Barnstone, Willis (trans.), *Greek Lyric Poetry*, New York, 1962 (Bantam).

· Kagan, Donald, *Sources in Greek Political Thought*, Glencoe, Ill., 1965 (Free Press).

· Kirk, G. S., and Raven, J. E., *The Presocratic Philosophers*, Cambridge, 1957 (Cambridge University Press).

CHAPTER 7

The Hellenistic Civilization

Beauty and virtue and the like are to be honored, if they give pleasure, but if they do not give pleasure, we must bid them farewell.

———Epicurus, "On the End of Life"

I agree that Alexander was carried away so far as to copy oriental luxury. I hold that no mighty deeds, not even conquering the whole world, is of any good unless the man has learned mastery of himself.

—Arrian, *Anabasis of Alexander*

The death of Alexander the Great in 323 B.C. constituted a watershed in the development of world history. Hellenic civilization as it had existed in its prime now came to an end. Of course, the old institutions and ways of life did not suddenly disappear, but Alexander's career had cut so deeply into the old order that it was inconceivable that it could be restored intact. The fusion of cultures and intermingling of peoples resulting from Alexander's conquests accomplished the overthrow of many of the ideals of the Greeks in their Golden Age of the fifth and fourth centuries. Gradually a new pattern of civilization emerged, based upon a mixture of Greek and Oriental elements. To this new civilization, which lasted until about the beginning of the Christian era, the name Hellenistic is the one most commonly applied.

A new stage in world history

Though the break between the Hellenic and Hellenistic eras was as sharp as that between any two other civilizations, it would be a mistake to deny all continuity. The language of the new cultured classes was predominantly Greek, and even the hordes of people whose heritage was non-Greek considered it desirable to have some Hellenic culture. Hellenic achievements in science provided a foundation for the great scientific revolution of the Hellenistic Age. Greek emphasis upon logic was likewise carried over into Hellenistic philosophy, though the objectives of the latter were in many cases quite different. In the spheres of the political, social, and eco-

Comparison of the Hellenistic Age with the Golden Age of Greece nomic the resemblances were few indeed. The classical ideal of democracy was now superseded by despotism perhaps as rigorous as any that Egypt or Persia had ever produced. The Greek city-state survived in some parts of Greece itself, but elsewhere it was replaced by the big monarchy, and in the minds of some leaders by notions of a world state. The Hellenic devotion to simplicity and the golden mean gave way to extravagance in the arts and to a love of luxury and riotous excess. Golden Age intensity of living was superseded by a craving for novelty and breadth of experience. In the economic realm the Athenian system of small-scale production was supplanted largely by the growth of big business and vigorous competition for profits. In view of these changes it seems valid to conclude that the Hellenistic Age was sufficiently distinct from the Golden Age of Greece to justify its being considered the era of a new civilization.

1. POLITICAL HISTORY AND INSTITUTIONS

The Hellenistic
states

When Alexander died in 323 B.C., he left no legitimate heir to succeed him. His nearest male relative was a feeble-minded half-brother. Tradition relates that when his friends requested him on his deathbed to designate a successor, he replied vaguely, "To the best man." After his death his highest-ranking generals proceeded to divide the empire among them. Some of the younger commanders contested this arrangement, and a series of wars followed which culminated in the decisive battle of Ipsus in 301 B.C. The result of this battle was a new division among the victors. Seleucus took possession of Persia, Mesopotamia, and Syria; Lysimachus assumed control over Asia Minor and Thrace; Cassander established himself in Madeconia; and Ptolemy added Phoenicia and Palestine to his original domain of Egypt. Twenty years later these four states were reduced to three when Seleucus defeated and killed Lysimachus in battle and appropriated his kingdom. In the meantime most of the Greek states had revolted against the attempts of the Macedonian king to extend his power over them. By banding together in defensive leagues several of them succeeded in maintaining their inde-

Scythian Pectoral Found at Ordzhonikidze in Southern Russia. The Scythians were supposedly a warlike people living on the fringes of Greece. However, the pectoral shows pastoral activities. The heavy gold jewelry exhibits a great skill and workmanship.

pendence for nearly a century. Finally, between 146 and 30 B.C. nearly all of the Hellenistic territory passed under Roman rule.

The dominant form of government in the Hellenistic Age was the despotism of kings who represented themselves as at least semi-divine. Alexander himself was recognized as a son of God in Egypt and was worshiped as a god in Greece. His most powerful successors, the Seleucid kings in western Asia and the Ptolemies in Egypt, made systematic attempts to deify themselves. A Seleucid monarch, Antiochus IV, adopted the title "Epiphanes" or "God Manifest." The later members of the dynasty of the Ptolemies signed their decrees "Theos" (God) and revived the practice of sister marriage which had been followed by the Pharaohs as a means of preserving the divine blood of the royal family from contamination. Only in the kingdom of Macedonia was despotism tempered by a modicum of respect for the liberties of the citizens.

Two other political institutions developed as by-products of Hellenistic civilization: the Achaean and Aetolian Leagues. We have already seen that most of the Greek states rebelled against Macedonian rule following the division of Alexander's empire. The better to preserve their independence, several of these states formed alliances among themselves, which were gradually expanded to become confederate leagues. The organization of these leagues was essentially the same in all cases. Each had a federal council composed of representatives of the member cities with power to enact laws on subjects of general concern. An assembly which all of the citizens in the federated states could attend decided questions of war and peace and elected officials. Executive and military authority was vested in the hands of a general, elected for one year and eligible for reelection only in alternate years. Although these leagues are frequently described as federal states, they were scarcely more than confederacies. The central authority, like the government of the American States under the Articles of Confederation, was dependent upon the local governments for contributions of revenue and troops. Furthermore, the powers delegated to the central government were limited primarily to matters of war and peace, coinage, and weights and measures. The chief significance of these leagues is to be found in the fact that they embodied the principle of representative government and constituted the nearest approach ever made in Greece to voluntary national union.

2. SIGNIFICANT ECONOMIC AND SOCIAL DEVELOPMENTS

The history of the Hellenistic civilization was marked by economic developments second only in magnitude to the Commercial and Industrial Revolutions of the modern era. Several important causes can be distinguished: (1) the opening up of a vast area of

Alexander the Great. Shown here is a tetradrachma struck in Thrace at the order of King Lysimachus, ca. 300 B.C.

The Achaean and Aetolian Leagues

159

trade from the Indus River to the Nile as a result of the Alexandrian conquests; (2) the rise in prices as a consequence of the release of the enormous Persian hoard of gold and silver into the channels of circulation, resulting in an increase in investment and speculation; and (3) the promotion of trade and industry by governments as a means of augmenting the revenues of the state. The net result was the growth of a system of large-scale production, trade, and finance, with the state as the principal capitalist and entrepreneur.

Agriculture was as profoundly affected by the new developments as any other branch of the economic life. The most striking phenomena were the concentration of holdings of land and the degradation of the agricultural population. One of the first things the successors of Alexander did was to confiscate the estates of the chief landowners and add them to the royal domain. The lands thus acquired were either granted to the favorites of the king or leased to tenants under an arrangement calculated to ensure an abundant income for the crown. The tenants were generally forbidden to leave the lands they cultivated until after the harvest and were not allowed to dispose of their grain until after the king had had a chance to sell the share he received as rent at the highest price the market

The economic revolution and its causes

The concentration of land ownership

160

Bronze Mirror Case, V cent. B.C. Greek articles of everyday use were commonly finished with the same delicacy and precision as major works of art.

Diadoumenos, after Polykleitos, V cent. B.C. An idealized statue of a Greek athlete tying the "diadem," or band of victory, around his head.

Bracelet Pendant, IV–III cent. B.C. This tiny figure of the god Pan is a masterpiece of detail and expression.

Woman Arranging Her Hair, 400–300 B.C. Sculptors of antiquity took pride in these statuettes of ordinary people in ordinary activities, which were usually made of terra cotta painted soft blue, pink, or yellow.

Head of an Athlete, *ca.* 440–420 B.C. The sculptor aimed to express manly beauty in perfect harmony with physical and intellectual excellence.

Comic Actor, 200–100 B.C. Hellenistic realism often included portrayal of ugly and even deformed individuals.

Sleeping Eros, 250–150 B.C. Along with a penchant for realism, Hellenistic sculptors were fond of portraying serenity or repose.

Statuette of Hermarchos, III cent. B.C. An example of the realism of Hellenistic sculpture.

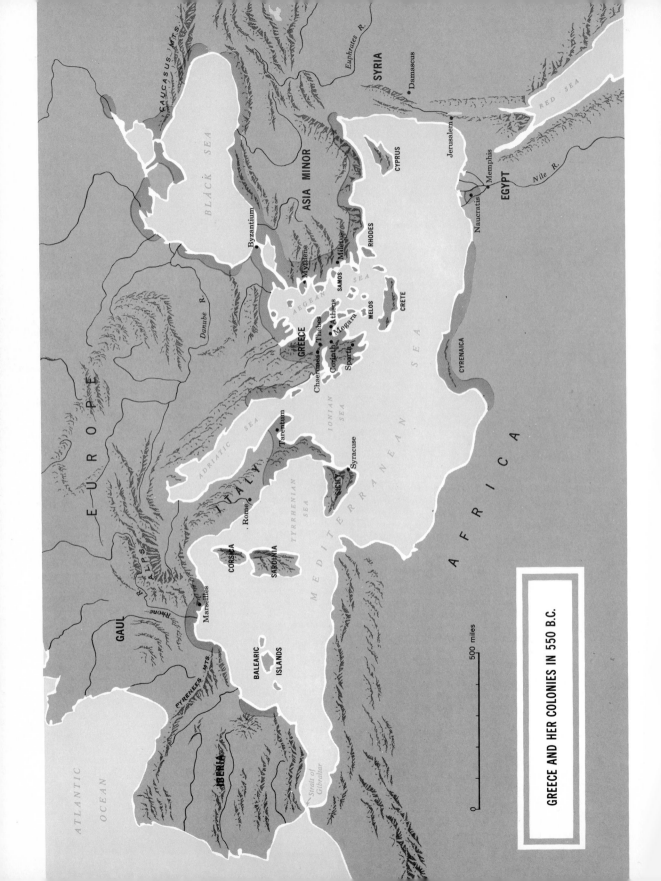

GREECE AND HER COLONIES IN 550 B.C.

500 miles

ATLANTIC
OCEAN

E U R O P E

GAUL

Rhone

Marseilles

Pyrenees Mts.

IBERIA

BALEARIC
ISLANDS

A L P S

CORSICA

SARDINIA

ITALY

Rome

TYRRHENIAN
SEA

SICILY

Syracuse

Strait of Gibraltar

M E D I T E R R A N E A N   S E A

Tarentum

ADRIATIC
SEA

Danube R.

CAUCASUS MTS.

B L A C K   S E A

Byzantium

AEGEAN SEA

Mytilene

GREECE

Thebes
Chaeronea
Athens
Corinth
Megara
Sparta

Samos

MELOS

IONIAN
SEA

Miletus

SAMOS

RHODES

CRETE

A F R I C A

CYRENAICA

Euphrates R.

SYRIA

Damascus

CYPRUS

Jerusalem

RED SEA

Nile R.

Memphis

EGYPT

Naucratis

ASIA MINOR

would bring. When some of the tenants went on srike or attempted to run away, they were all bound to the soil as hereditary serfs. Many of the small independent farmers also became serfs when they got into debt as a result of inability to compete with large-scale production.

In an effort to make all of the resources of the state contribute to the profit of the government, the rulers of Egypt and the Seleucid empire promoted and regulated industry and trade. The Ptolemies established factories and shops in nearly every village and town to be owned and operated by the government for its own financial benefit. In addition, they assumed control over all of the enterprises that were privately owned, fixing the prices the owners could charge and manipulating markets to the advantage of the crown. A similar plan of regimentation for industry, although not on quite so ambitious a scale, was enforced by the Seleucid rulers of western Asia. Trade was left by both of these governments very largely in private hands, but it was heavily taxed and regulated in such a way as to make sure that an ample share of the profits went to the king. Every facility was provided by the government for the encouragement of new trading ventures. Harbors were improved, warships were sent out to police the seas, and roads and canals were built. Moreover, the Ptolemies employed famous geographers to discover new routes to distant lands and thereby gain access to valuable markets. As a result of such methods Egypt developed a flourishing commerce in the widest variety of products. Into the port of Alexandria came spices from Arabia, copper from Cyprus, gold from Abyssinia and India, tin from Britain, elephants and ivory from Nubia, silver from the northern Aegean and Spain, fine carpets from Asia Minor, and even silk from China. Profits for the government and for some of the merchants were often as high as 20 or 30 per cent.

Further evidence of the significant economic development of the Hellenistic Age is to be found in the growth of finance. An international money economy, based upon gold and silver coins, now became general throughout the Near East. Banks, usually owned by the government, developed as the chief institutions of credit for business ventures of every description. Speculation, cornering of markets, intense competition, the growth of large business houses, and the development of insurance and advertising were other significant phenomena of this remarkable age.

According to the available evidence, the Hellenistic Age, during the first two centuries at least, was a period of prosperity. Although serious crises frequently followed the collapse of speculative booms, they appear to have been of short duration. But the prosperity that existed seems to have been limited chiefly to the rulers, the upper classes, and the merchants. It certainly did not extend to the peasants or even to the workers in the towns. The daily wages of both

State regimentation of industry and trade

The growth of finance

The disparity between rich and poor

161

Hellenistic Coins. Obverse and reverse sides of the silver tetradrachma of Macedon, 336–323 B.C. Objects of common use from this period often show as much beauty of design as formal works of art.

skilled and unskilled workers in Athens in the third century had dropped to less than half of what they had been in the Age of Pericles. The cost of living, on the other hand, had risen considerably. To make matters worse, unemployment in the large cities was so serious a problem that the government had to provide free grain for many of the inhabitants. Slavery declined in the Hellenistic world, partly because of the influence of the Stoic philosophy, but mainly for the reason that wages were now so low that it was cheaper to hire a free laborer than to purchase and maintain a slave.

An interesting result of social and economic conditions in the Hellenistic Age was the growth of metropolitan cities. Despite the fact that a majority of the people still lived in the country, there was an increasing tendency for men to become dissatisfied with the dullness of rural living and to flock into the cities, where life, if not easier, was at least more exciting. But the chief reasons are to be found in the expansion of industry and commerce, in the enlargement of governmental functions, and in the desire of former independent farmers to escape the hardships of serfdom. Cities multiplied and grew in the Hellenistic empires almost as rapidly as in nineteenth- and twentieth-century America. Antioch in Syria quadrupled its population during a single century. Seleucia on the Tigris grew from nothing to a metropolis of several hundred thousand in less than two centuries. The largest and most famous of all the Hellenistic cities was Alexandria in Egypt, with over 500,000 inhabitants and possibly as many as 1,000,000. No other city in ancient times, not even Rome, surpassed it in size or in magnificence. Its streets were well paved and laid out in regular order. It had splendid public buildings and parks, a museum, and a library of 750,000 volumes. It was the most brilliant center of Hellenistic cultural achievement, especially in the field of scientific research. The masses of its people, however, were a disorganized mob without any share in the brilliant and luxurious life around them, although it was paid for in part out of the fruits of their labor.

The growth of metropolitan cities

162

3. HELLENISTIC CULTURE: PHILOSOPHY, LITERATURE, AND ART

Hellenistic philosophy exhibited two trends that ran almost parallel throughout the civilization. The major trend, exemplified by Stoicism and Epicureanism, showed a fundamental regard for reason as the key to the solution of man's problems. This trend was a manifestation of Greek influence, though philosophy and science, as combined in Aristotle, had now come to a parting of the ways. The minor trend, exemplified by the Skeptics, Cynics, and various Asian cults, tended to reject reason, to deny the possibility of attaining truth, and in some cases to turn toward mysticism and a reliance upon faith. Despite the differences in their teachings, the philosophers of the Hellenistic Age were generally agreed upon one thing: the necessity of finding some way of salvation for man from the hardships and evils of his existence.

Trends in philosophy

The first of the Hellenistic philosophers were the Cynics, who had their origin about 350 B.C. Their foremost leader was Diogenes, who won fame by his perpetual quest for an "honest" man. Essentially this meant the adoption of the "natural" life and the repudiation of everything conventional and artificial. The Cynics adopted as their principal goal the cultivation of "self-sufficiency": every man should cultivate within himself the ability to satisfy his own needs. Obviously the Cynics bore some resemblance to other movements that have cropped up through the ages—the hippie movement of our own day, for example. There were notable differences, however. The Cynics spurned music and art as manifestations of artificiality, and they were not representative of a youth generation. But all such movements seem to reflect a sense of frustration and hopeless conflict in society.

The Cynics

Epicureanism and Stoicism both originated about 300 B.C. The founders were, respectively, Epicurus (342–270) and Zeno (fl. after 300), who were residents of Athens; the former was born on the island of Samos, and the latter was a native of Cyprus, probably of Phoenician descent. Epicureanism and Stoicism had several features in common. Both were individualistic, concerned not with the welfare of society primarily, but with the good of the individual. Both were materialistic, denying categorically the existence of any spiritual substances; even divine beings and the soul were declared to be formed of matter. In Stoicism and Epicureanism alike there were definite elements of universalism, since both implied that men are the same the world over and recognized no distinctions between Greeks and "barbarians."

Epicureanism and Stoicism

But in many ways the two systems were quite different. Zeno and his principal disciples taught that the cosmos is an ordered whole in which all contradictions are resolved for ultimate good. Evil is, therefore, relative; the particular misfortunes which befall human beings are but necessary incidents to the final perfection of the universe. Everything that happens is rigidly determined in accordance with rational purpose. Man is not master of his fate; his destiny is a link in an unbroken chain. He is free only in the sense that he can accept his fate or rebel against it. But whether he accepts or rebels, he cannot overcome it. The supreme duty of man is to submit to the order of the universe in the knowledge that that order is good; in other words, to resign himself as graciously as possible to his fate. Through such an act of resignation he will attain to the highest happiness, which consists in tranquillity of mind. The individual who is most truly happy is therefore the man who by the assertion of his rational nature has accomplished a perfect adjustment of his life to the cosmic purpose and has purged his soul of all bitterness and whining protest against evil turns of fortune.

The ethical and
social teachings of
the Stoics

The Stoics developed an ethical and social theory that accorded well with their general philosophy. Believing that the highest good consists in serenity of mind, they naturally emphasized duty and self-discipline as cardinal virtues. Recognizing the prevalence of particular evil, they taught that men should be tolerant and forgiving in their attitudes toward one another. Unlike the Cynics, they did not recommend that man should withdraw from society but urged participation in public affairs as a duty for the citizen of rational mind. They condemned slavery and war, but it was far from their purpose to preach any crusade against these evils. They were disposed to think that the results that would flow from violent measures of social change would be worse than the diseases they were supposed to cure. Besides, what difference did it make if the body were in bondage so long as the mind was free? Despite its negative character, the Stoic philosophy was the noblest product of the Hellenistic Age. Its equalitarianism, pacifism, and humanitarianism were important factors in mitigating the harshness not only of that time but of later centuries as well.

Whereas the Stoics went back to Heracleitus for much of their conception of the universe, the Epicureans derived their metaphysics chiefly from Democritus. Epicurus taught that the basic ingredients of all things are minute, indivisible atoms, and that change and growth are the results of the combination and separation of these particles. Nevertheless, while accepting the materialism of the atomists, Epicurus rejected their absolute mechanism. He denied that an automatic, mechanical motion of the atoms can be the cause of all things in the universe. Though he taught that the atoms move downward in perpendicular lines because of their weight, he insisted upon endowing them with a spontaneous ability to swerve from the perpendicular and thereby to combine with one another. The chief reason for this peculiar modification of the atomic theory was to make possible a belief in human freedom. If the atoms were capable only of mechanical motion, then man, who is made up of atoms, would be reduced to the status of an automaton, and fatalism would be the law of the universe. In this repudiation of the mechanistic interpretation of life, Epicurus was probably closer to the Hellenic spirit than either Democritus or the Stoics.

The ethical philosophy of the Epicureans was based upon the doctrine that the highest good for man is pleasure. But they did not include all forms of indulgence in the category of genuine pleasure. The so-called pleasures of the debauched man should be avoided, since every excess of carnality must be balanced by its portion of pain. On the other hand, a moderate satisfaction of bodily appetites is permissible and may be regarded as a good in itself. Better than this is mental pleasure, sober contemplation of the reasons for the choice of some things and the avoidance of others, and mature reflection upon satisfactions previously enjoyed. The highest of all pleasures, however, consists in serenity of soul, in the complete absence of both mental and physical pain. This end can be best achieved through the elimination of fear, especially fear of the supernatural, since that is the sovereign source of mental pain. Man must recognize from the study of philosophy that the soul is material and therefore cannot survive the body, that the universe operates of itself, and that the gods do not intervene in human affairs. The gods live remote from the world and are too intent upon their own happiness to bother about what takes place on earth. Since they do not reward or punish men either in this life or in a life to come, there is no reason why they should be feared. The Epicureans thus came by a different route to the same general conclusion as the Stoics—the supreme good is tranquillity of mind.

The ethics of the Epicureans as well as their political theory rested squarely upon a utilitarian basis. In contrast with the Stoics, they did not insist upon virtue as an end in itself but taught that the only reason why man should be good is to increase his own happiness. In like manner, they denied that there is any such thing as absolute justice; laws and institutions are just only in so far as they contribute to the welfare of the individual. Certain rules have been found necessary in every complex society for the maintenance of security and order. Men obey these rules solely because it is to their advantage to do so. Generally speaking, Epicurus held no high regard for either political or social life. He considered the state as a mere convenience and taught that the wise men should take no active part in public life. Unlike the Cynics, he did not propose that man should abandon civilization and return to nature; yet his conception of the happiest life was essentially passive and defeatist. The wise man will recognize that he cannot eradicate the evils in the world no matter how strenuous and intelligent his efforts; he will therefore withdraw to "cultivate his garden," study philosophy, and enjoy the fellowship of a few congenial friends.

A more radically defeatist philosophy was that propounded by the Skeptics. Skepticism reached the zenith of its popularity about 200 B.C. under the influence of Carneades. The chief source of its inspiration was the Sophist teaching that all knowledge is derived from sense perception and therefore must be limited and relative. From this was deduced the conclusion that we cannot prove anything. Since the impressions of our senses deceive us, no truth can be certain. All we can say is that things *appear* to be such and such; we do not know what they really *are*. We have no definite knowledge of the supernatural, of the meaning of life, or even of right and wrong. It follows that the sensible course to pursue is suspension of judgment; this alone can lead to happiness. If man will abandon the fruitless quest for absolute truth and cease worrying about good and evil, he will attain that equanimity of mind which is the highest satisfaction that life affords. The Skeptics were even less concerned than the Epicureans with political and social problems. Their ideal was the typically Hellenistic one of escape for the individual from a world he could neither understand nor reform.

The nonrational trend in Hellenistic thought reached its farthest extreme in the philosophies of Philo Judaeus and the Neo-Pythagoreans in the last century B.C. and the first century A.D. The proponents of the two systems were in general agreement as to their basic teachings, especially in their predominantly religious viewpoint. They believed in a transcendent God so far removed from the world as to be utterly unknowable to mortal minds. They conceived the universe as being sharply divided between spirit and matter. They considered everything physical and material as evil; man's soul is imprisoned in his body, from which an escape can be effected only through rigorous denial and mortification of the flesh. Their attitude was mystical and nonintellectual: truth comes neither from science nor from reason but from revelation. Philo maintained that the books of the Old Testament were of absolute divine authority and contained all truth; the ultimate aim in life is to accomplish a mystic union with God, to lose one's self in the divine. Both Philo and the Neo-Pythagoreans influenced the development of Christian theology—Philo, in particular, with his dualism of matter and spirit and his doctrine of the Logos, or highest intermediary between God and the universe.

Hellenistic literature is significant mainly for the light it throws upon the character of the civilization. Most of the writings showed little originality or depth of thought. But they poured forth from the hands of the copyists in a profusion that is almost incredible when we consider that the art of printing by movable type was unknown. The names of at least 1100 authors have been discovered already, and more are being added from year to year. Much of what they wrote was trash, comparable to some of the cheap novels of our own day. Nevertheless, there were several works of more than mediocre quality and a few which met the highest standards ever set by the Greeks.

The leading types of Hellenistic poetry were the drama, the pastoral, and the mime. Drama was almost exclusively comedy, represented mainly by the plays of Menander. His plays were entirely different from the comedy of Aristophanes. They were distinguished by naturalism rather than by satire, by preoccupation with the seamy side of life rather than with political or intellectual issues. Their dominant theme was romantic love, with its pains and pleasures, its intrigues and seductions, and its culmination in happy marriage. The greatest author of pastorals and mimes was Theocritus of Syracuse, who wrote in the first half of the third century B.C. His pastorals, as the name implies, celebrate the charm of life in the country and idealize the simple pleasures of rustic folk. The mimes, on the other hand, portray in colorful dialogue the squabbles, ambitions, and varied activities of the bourgeoisie in the great metropolitan cities.

The field of prose literature was dominated by the historians, the biographers, and the authors of utopias. By far the ablest of the writers of history was Polybius of Megalopolis, who lived during the second century B.C. From the standpoint of his scientific approach and his zeal for truth, he probably deserves to be ranked second only to Thucydides among all the historians in ancient times; but he excelled Thucydides in his grasp of the importance of social and economic forces. Although most of the biographies were of a light and gossipy character, their tremendous popularity bears eloquent testimony to the literary tastes of the time. Even more significant was the popularity of the utopias, or descriptive accounts of ideal states. Virtually all of them depicted a life of social and economic equality, free from greed, oppression, and strife, on an imaginary island or in some distant, unfamiliar region. Generally in these paradises money was considered to be unknown, trade was prohibited, all property was held in common, and all men were required to work with their hands in producing the necessaries of life. We are probably justified in assuming that the profusion of this utopian literature was a direct result of the evils and injustices of Hellenistic society and a consciousness of the need for reform.

Hellenistic art did not preserve all of the characteristic qualities of the art of the Greeks. In place of the humanism, balance, and restraint which had distinguished the architecture and sculpture of the Golden Age, qualities of exaggerated realism, sensationalism, and voluptuousness now became dominant. The simple and dignified Doric and Ionic temples gave way to luxurious palaces, costly mansions, and elaborate public buildings and monuments symbolical of power and wealth. A typical example was the great lighthouse of Alexandria, which rose to a height of nearly 400 feet, with three diminishing stories and eight columns to support the light at the top. Sculpture likewise exhibited tendencies in the direction of extravagance and sentimentality. Many of the statues and figures in relief were huge and some of them almost grotesque. Violent emotionalism and exaggerated realism were features common to the majority. But by no means all of Hellenistic sculpture was over-wrought and

Hellenistic poetry

Historians, biographers, and authors of utopias

Hellenistic art

See color plates at page 160

167

The Dying Gaul. A good example of Hellenistic realism in sculpture, which often reflected a preoccupation with the morbid and sensational. Every detail of the warrior's agony is dramatically portrayed. Now in the Capitoline Museum, Rome.

grotesque. Some of it was distinguished by a calmness and poise and compassion for human suffering reminiscent of the best work of the great fourth-century artists. Statutes which exemplify these superior qualities include the *Aphrodite of Melos* (*Venus de Milo*) and the *Winged Victory of Samothrace.*

4. THE FIRST GREAT AGE OF SCIENCE

Factors responsible for the remarkable progress of science

The most brilliant age in the history of science prior to the seventeenth century A.D. was the period of the Hellenistic civilization. Indeed, many of the achievements of the modern age would scarcely have been possible without the discoveries of the scientists of Alexandria, Syracuse, Pergamum, and other great cities of the Hellenistic world. The reasons for the phenomenal development of science in the centuries after the downfall of Alexander's empire are not difficult to discover. Alexander himself had given some financial encouragement to the progress of research. More important was the stimulus provided for intellectual inquiry by the fusion of Chaldean and Egyption science with the learning of the Greeks. Possibly a third factor was the new interest in luxury and comfort and the demand for practical knowledge which would enable man to solve the problems of a disordered and unsatisfying existence.

The most popular sciences

The sciences which received major attention in the Hellenistic Age were astronomy, mathematics, geography, medicine, and physics. Chemistry, aside from metallurgy, was practically unknown. Except for the work of Theophrastus, who was the first to

168

recognize the sexuality of plants, biology was also largely neglected. Neither chemistry nor biology bore any definite relationship to trade or to the forms of industry then in existence, and apparently they were not regarded as having much practical value.

The most renowned of the earlier astronomers of this time was Aristarchus of Samos (310–230 B.C.), who is sometimes called the "Hellenistic Copernicus." His chief title to fame comes from his deduction that the earth and the other planets revolve around the sun. Unfortunately this deduction was not accepted by his successors. It conflicted with the teachings of Aristotle and with the anthropocentric ideas of the Greeks. Besides, it was not in harmony with the beliefs of the Jews and other Orientals who made up so large a percentage of the Hellenistic population. The only other astronomer of much importance in the Hellenistic Age was Hipparchus, who did his most valuable work in Alexandria in the latter half of the second century B.C. His chief contributions were the invention of the astrolabe and the approximately correct calculation of the diameter of the moon and its distance from the earth. His fame was eventually overshadowed, however, by the reputation of Ptolemy of Alexandria, the last of the Hellenistic astronomers. Although Ptolemy made few original discoveries, he systematized the work of others. His principal writing, the *Almagest*, based upon the geocentric theory, was handed down to medieval Europe as the classic summary of ancient astronomy.

Astronomy

The Winged Victory of Samothrace. In this figure and in the *Venus de Milo*, Hellenistic sculptors preserved some of the calmness and devotion to grace and proportion characteristic of Hellenic art in the Golden Age. Now in the Louvre.

Closely allied with astronomy were two other sciences, mathematics and geography. The Hellenistic mathematician of greatest renown was, of course, Euclid (*ca.* 323–*ca.* 285 B.C.), erroneously considered the founder of geometry. Until the middle of the nineteenth century his *Elements of Geometry* remained the accepted basis for the study of that branch of mathematics. Much of the material in this work was not original but was a synthesis of the discoveries of others. The most original of the Hellenistic mathematicians was probably Hipparchus, who laid the foundations of both plane and spherical trigonometry. Hellenistic geography owed most of its development to Eratosthenes (*ca.* 276–*ca.* 195 B.C.), astronomer, poet, philologist, and librarian of Alexandria. By means of sun dials placed some hundreds of miles apart, he calculated the circumference of the earth with an error of less than 200 miles. He produced the most accurate map that had yet been devised, with the surface of the earth divided into degrees of latitude and longitude. He propounded the theory that all of the oceans are really one, and he was the first to suggest the possibility of reaching India by sailing west. One of his successors divided the earth into the five climatic zones which are still recognized, and explained the ebb and flow of the tides as due to the influence of the moon.

Perhaps none of the Hellenistic advances in science surpassed in importance the progress in medicine. Especially significant was the work of Herophilus of Chalcedon, who conducted his researches in Alexandria about the beginning of the second century. Without question he was the greatest anatomist of antiquity and, according to Galen, the first to practice human dissection. Among his most important achievements were a detailed description of the brain, with an attempt to distinguish between the functions of its various parts; the discovery of the significance of the pulse and its use in diagnosing illness; and the discovery that the arteries contain blood alone, not a mixture of blood and air as Aristotle had taught, and that their function is to carry blood from the heart to all parts of the body. The value of this last discovery in laying the basis for a knowledge of the circulation of the blood can hardly be overestimated.

The ablest of the colleagues of Herophilus was Erasistratus, who flourished in Alexandria about the middle of the third century. He is considered the founder of physiology as a separate science. Not only did he practice dissection, but he is believed to have gained a great deal of his knowledge of bodily functions from vivisection. He discovered the valves of the heart, distinguished between motor and sensory nerves, and taught that the ultimate branches of the arteries and veins are connected. He was the first to reject absolutely the humoral theory of disease and to condemn excessive blood-letting as a method of cure. Unfortunately this theory was revived by Galen, the great encyclopedist of medicine who lived in the Roman Empire in the second century A.D.

Prior to the third century B.C. physics had been a branch of philosophy. It was made a separate experimental science by Archimedes of Syracuse (*ca.* 287–212 B.C.). Archimedes discovered the law of floating bodies, or specific gravity, and formulated with scientific exactness the principles of the lever, the pulley, and the screw. Among his memorable inventions were the compound pulley, the tubular screw for pumping water, the screw propeller for ships, and the burning lens. Although he has been called the "technical Yankee of antiquity," there is evidence that he set no high value upon his ingenious mechanical contraptions and preferred to devote his time to pure scientific research.

Certain other individuals in the Hellenistic Age were quite willing to give all their attention to applied science. Preeminent among them was Hero or Heron of Alexandria, who lived in the last century B.C. The record of inventions credited to him almost passes belief. The list includes a fire engine, a siphon, a jet engine, a hydraulic organ, a slot machine, and a catapult operated by compressed air. How many of these inventions were really his own is impossible to say, but there appears to be no question that such contrivances were actually in existence in his time or soon thereafter. Nevertheless, the total progress in applied science was comparatively slight, probably for the reason that human labor continued to be so abundant and cheap that it was not worthwhile to substitute the work of machines.

5. RELIGION IN THE HELLENISTIC AGE

If there was one aspect of the Hellenistic civilization which served more than others to accent the contrast with Hellenic culture, it was the new trend in religion. The civic religion of the Greeks as it was in the age of the city-states had now almost entirely disappeared. For the majority of the intellectuals its place was taken by the philosophies of Stoicism, Epicureanism, and Skepticism. Some who were less philosophically inclined turned to the worship of Fortune or became followers of dogmatic atheism.

Among the masses a tendency to embrace emotional religions was even more clearly manifest. The Orphic and Eleusinian mystery cults attracted more votaries than ever before. The worship of the Egyptian mother-goddess, Isis, threatened for a time to become dominant throughout the Near Orient. The astral religion of the Chaldeans likewise spread rapidly, with the result that its chief product, astrology, was received with fanatical enthusiasm throughout the Hellenistic world. But the most powerful influence of all came from the offshoots of Zoroastrianism, especially from Mithraism and Gnosticism. While all of the cults of Oriental origin resembled each other in their promises of salvation in a life to come, Mithraism and Gnosticism had a more ethically significant mythology, a deeper contempt for this world, and a more clearly defined doctrine of redemption through a personal savior. These were the ideas which satisfied the emotional cravings of the common people, convinced as they were of the worthlessness of this life and ready to be lured by extravagant promises of better things in a world to come. If we can judge by conditions in our own time, some of the doctrines of these cults must have exerted their influence upon members of the upper classes also. Even the most casual observer of modern society knows that pessimism, mysticism, and otherworldliness are not confined to the downtrodden. In some cases the keenest disgust with this life and the deepest mystical yearnings are to be found among those whose pockets bulge with plenty.

The influence of the Jews

A factor by no means unimportant in the religious developments of the Hellenistic Age was the dispersion of the Jews. As a result of Alexander's conquest of Palestine in 332 B.C. and the Roman conquest about three centuries later, thousands of Jews migrated to various sections of the Mediterranean world. It has been estimated that 1,000,000 of them lived in Egypt in the first century A.D. and 200,000 in Asia Minor. They mingled freely with other peoples, adopting the Greek language and no small amount of the Hellenic culture which still survived from earlier days. At the same time they played a major part in the diffusion of Oriental beliefs. Their religion had already taken on a spiritual and messianic character as a result of Persian influence. Their leading philosopher of this time, Philo Judaeus of Alexandria, developed a body of doctrine representing the farthest extreme which mysticism had yet attained. Many of the Hellenistic Jews eventually became converts to Christianity and were largely instrumental in the spread of that religion outside of Palestine. A notable example, of course, was Saul of Tarsus, known in Christian history as the Apostle Paul.

6.   A FORETASTE OF MODERNITY?

Hellenistic civilization compared with that of the modern age

With the possible exception of the Roman, no great culture of ancient times appears to suggest the spirit of the modern age quite so emphatically as does the Hellenistic civilization. Here as in the world of the twentieth century were to be found a considerable variety of forms of government, the growth of militarism, a decline of respect for democracy, and a trend in the direction of authoritarian rule. Many of the characteristic economic and social developments of the Hellenistic Age are equally suggestive of contemporary experience: the growth of big business, the expansion of trade, the zeal for exploration and discovery, the interest in mechanical inventions, the devotion to comfort and the craze for material prosperity, the growth of metropolitan cities with congested slums, and the widening gulf between rich and poor. In the realms of intellect and art the Hellenistic civilization also bore a distinctly modern flavor. This was exemplified by the exaggerated emphasis upon sci-

Statue of an Old Market Woman. In the Hellenistic Age the idealism and restraint of Hellenic art were succeeded by a tendency to portray the humble aspects of life and to express compassion for human suffering. Original in the Metropolitan Museum of Art, New York.

ence, the narrow specialization of learning, the penchant for realism and naturalism, the vast production of mediocre literature, and the popularity of mysticism side by side with extreme skepticism and dogmatic unbelief.

Because of these resemblances there has been a tendency among certain writers to regard our own civilization as decadent. But this is based partly upon the false assumption that the Hellenistic culture was merely a degenerate phase of Greek civilization. Instead, it was a new social and cultural organism born of a fusion of Greek and Near Eastern elements. Moreover, the differences between the Hellenistic civilization and that of the contemporary world are perhaps just as important as the resemblances. The Hellenistic political outlook was essentially cosmopolitan; nothing comparable to the national patriotism of modern times really prevailed. Despite the remarkable expansion of trade in the Hellenistic Age, no industrial revolution ever took place, for reasons which have already been noted. Finally, Hellenistic science was somewhat more limited than that of the present day. Modern pure science is to a very large extent a species of philosophy—an adventure of the mind in the realm of the unknown. Notwithstanding frequent assertions to the contrary, much of it is gloriously impractical and will probably remain so.

Basic differences

173

SELECTED READINGS

· Items so designated are available in paperbound editions.

Bamm, Peter, *Alexander the Great: Power as Destiny*, New York, 1968.
· Burn, A. R., *Alexander the Great and the Hellenistic World*, New York, 1962 (Collier).
· Bury, J. B., and others, *The Hellenistic Age*, New York, 1923.
Cary, Max, *The Legacy of Alexander: A History of the Greek World from 323 to 146 B.C.*, New York, 1932.
· Clagett, Marshall, *Greek Science in Antiquity*, New York, 1963 (Collier).
Festugière, A. J., *Epicurus and His Gods*, Cambridge, Mass., 1956.
· Finley, M. I., *The Ancient Greeks: An Introduction to Their Life and Thought*, New York, 1963 (Compass).
· Grant, F. C., *Hellenistic Religions*, New York, 1963 (Library of Liberal Arts).
· Hadas, Moses, *Hellenistic Culture*, New York, 1959 (Norton Library).
· Hamilton, Edith, *The Echo of Greece*, New York, 1964 (Norton Library).
· Larsen, J. A. O., *Representative Government in Greek and Roman History*, Berkeley, 1955 (University of California).
Starr, C. G., *A History of the Ancient World*, New York, 1964.
· Tarn, W. W., *Alexander the Great*, Boston, 1956 (Beacon).
· ———, *Hellenistic Civilization*, New York, 1952 (Meridian).
Vermeule, Emily, *Greece in the Bronze Age*, Chicago, 1964.
· Wilcken, Ulrich, *Alexander the Great*, New York, 1967 (Norton Library).

SOURCE MATERIALS

Greek source materials for the Hellenistic period are available in the appropriate volumes of the Loeb Classical Library, Harvard University Press.

CHAPTER 8

Roman Civilization

Like Hercules, citizens, they said just now
He had sought the laurel at the cost of death:
Returning from Spain, seeking his household gods,
    Caesar has conquered.

After sacrifice to the just gods, let his
wife come forth, happy for her matchless husband,
And the sister of our famous leader, and,
    Wearing the bands of

Suppliants, mothers of young men and maidens
Who are now safe . . .
                    —Horace, *Odes,* III.xiv

Long before the glory of Greece had begun to fade, another civilization, derived in large measure from that of the Greeks, had started its growth on the banks of the Tiber in Italy. In fact, by the time the Greeks had entered their Golden Age, Rome was already a dominant power on the Italian peninsula. For more than six centuries thereafter her might increased, and she still maintained her supremacy over the civilized world when the glory of Greece was no more than a memory.

The rise of Rome

But the Romans never equaled the Greeks in intellectual or artistic accomplishments. The reasons may have been partly geographic. Except for some excellent marble and small quantities of copper, gold, and iron, Italy has no mineral resources. Her extensive coast line is broken by only two good harbors, Tarentum and Naples. On the other hand, the amount of her fertile land is much larger than that of Greece. As a consequence, the Romans were destined to remain a predominantly agrarian people through the greater part of their history. They never enjoyed the intellectual stimulus which comes from extensive trading with other nations. In addition, the topography of Italy is such that the peninsula was more easily accessible to invasion than was Greece. The Alps opposed no effectual barrier to the influx of peoples from central Europe, and the

Why Roman civilization was generally inferior to that of the Greeks low-lying coast in many places invited conquest by sea. As a result, domination of the country by force was more common than peaceful intermingling of immigrants with original settlers. The Romans became absorbed in military pursuits almost from the moment of their settlement on Italian soil, for they were forced to defend their own conquests against other invaders.

1. FROM THE BEGINNING TO THE OVERTHROW OF THE MONARCHY

The earliest inhabitants of Italy

Archaeological evidence indicates that Italy was inhabited at least as far back as the Upper Paleolithic Age. At this time the territory was occupied by a people closely related to the Cro-Magnon race of southern France. In the Neolithic period people of Mediterranean stock entered the land, some coming in from northern Africa and others from Spain and Gaul. The beginning of the Bronze Age witnessed several new incursions. From north of the Alps came the first of the immigrants of the Indo-European language group. They were herdsmen and farmers, who brought the horse and the wheeled cart into Italy. Their culture was based upon the use of bronze, although after 1000 B.C. they appear to have acquired a knowledge of iron. These Indo-Europeans seem to have been the ancestors of most of the so-called Italic peoples, including the Romans. Racially they were probably related to the Hellenic invaders of Greece.

The Etruscans and the Greeks

Probably during the eighth century B.C. two other nations of immigrants occupied different portions of the Italian peninsula: the Etruscans and the Greeks. Where the Etruscans came from is a question which has never been satisfactorily answered. Most authorities believe that they were natives of some part of the Near Orient, probably Asia Minor. Although their writing has never been completely deciphered, enough materials survive to indicate the nature of their culture. They had an alphabet based upon the Greek, a high degree of skill in the metallurgical arts, a flourishing trade with the East, and a religion based upon the worship of gods in hu-

An Etruscan Sarcophagus. The Etruscans often depicted social events, sports, funeral banquets, and processions, either in painting or relief, on their tombs. Seen here are preparations for a funeral.

Sarcophagus. This Etruscan work of the fourth century B.C., located in the Museum of Fine Arts, Boston, depicts a husband and wife.

man form. They bequeathed to the Romans a knowledge of the arch and the vault, the practice of divination, and the cruel amusement of gladiatorial combats. The Etruscans established a great empire in the sixth century that included Latium, the Po valley, and Campania. The Greeks located mainly along the southern and southwestern shores of Italy and on the island of Sicily. Their most important settlements were Tarentum, Syracuse, and Naples, each of which was an entirely independent city-state. From the Greeks the Romans derived their alphabet, a number of their religious concepts, and much of their art and mythology.

The actual founders of Rome were Italic peoples who lived in the district of Latium south of the Tiber River. Though the exact year of the founding of the city is unknown, recent archaeological research places the event quite near the traditional date of 753 B.C. Latium included a number of towns, but Rome, by reason of its strategic location, soon came to exercise an effective suzerainty over several of the most important of them. One conquest followed another until, by the end of the sixth century B.C., the territory dominated by the Roman state was probably coextensive with the whole Latin plain from the slopes of the Apennines to the Mediterranean Sea.

The founding of Rome

Etruscan Bust of Jove

The political evolution of Rome in this early period resembled in some ways the governmental development of the Greek communities in the formative stage of their history. But it was far from being the same. The Romans appear from the first to have had a much stronger interest in authority and stability than in liberty or democracy. Their state was essentially an application of the idea of the patriarchal family to the whole community, with the king exercising a jurisdiction over his subjects comparable to that of the head of the family over the members of his household. But just as the authority of the father was limited by custom and by the requirement

177

The government
of Rome under
the monarchy;
the powers of the
king

that he respect the wishes of his adult sons, the sovereignty of the king was limited by the ancient constitution, which he was powerless to change without the consent of the chief men of the realm. His prerogatives were not primarily legislative but executive and judicial. He punished men for infractions of order, usually by infliction of the death penalty or by flogging. He judged all civil and criminal cases, but he had no authority to pardon without the consent of the assembly. Although his accession to office had to be confirmed by the people, he could not be deposed, and there was no one who could really challenge the exercise of his regal powers.

In addition to the kingship the Roman government of this time included an assembly and a Senate. The former was composed of all the male citizens of military age. As one of the chief sources of sovereign power, according to the theory, this body had an absolute veto on any proposal for a change in the law which the king might make. Besides, it determined whether pardons should be granted and whether aggressive war should be declared. But it was essentially a ratifying body with no right to initiate legislation or recommend changes of policy. Its members could not even speak except when invited to do so by the king. The Senate, or council of elders, comprised in its membership the heads of the various clans which formed the community. Even more than the common citizens, the rulers of the clans embodied the sovereign power of the state. The king was only one of their number to whom they had delegated the active exercise of their authority. When the royal office became vacant, the powers of the king immediately reverted to the Senate until the succession of a new monarch had been confirmed by the people. In ordinary times the chief function of the Senate was to examine proposals of the king which had been ratified by the assembly and to veto them if they violated rights established by ancient custom. It was thus almost impossible for fundamental changes to be made in the law even when the majority of the citizens were ready to sanction them. This extremely conservative attitude of the ruling classes persisted until the end of Roman history.

Toward the end of the sixth century B.C. senatorial jealousy of the kings increased to such a point that the monarchy was overthrown and an oligarchic republic set up. While the real nature of this revolution was doubtless a movement of the aristocracy to gain supreme power for itself, factors of nationalism may also have played some part in it. Tradition relates that the last of the Roman kings was an Etruscan, whose family, the Tarquins, had usurped the royal office some years before. The Romans of later centuries described in lurid fashion the wicked deeds of these rulers and implied that the overthrow of the monarchy was due primarily to a revolt against alien oppressors. In any event the Etruscan empire was already in a state of decay. Its collapse made easier the establishment of Roman dominance in Italy.

2. THE EARLY REPUBLIC

The history of the Roman Republic for more than two centuries after its establishment was one of almost constant warfare. The causes which led to the series of conflicts are not easy to untangle. It is possible that the overthrow of the Tarquins resulted in acts of reprisal by their kinsmen in neighboring countries. It is conceivable also that other nations on the borders took advantage of the confusion accompanying the revolution to slice off portions of Roman territory. But doubtless the compelling reason was desire for more land. The Romans were already a proud and aggressive people with a rapidly growing population. As the number of the inhabitants increased, the need for outlets into new territory became ever more urgent. Their final conquests included the Greek cities in the southernmost portion of Italy. Not only did these add to the Roman domain, but they also brought the Romans into fruitful contact with Greek culture. The Romans were then frequently confronted with revolts of peoples previously conquered. The suppression of these revolts awakened the suspicions of surrounding states and sharpened the appetite of the victors for further triumphs. New wars followed each other in what seemed an unending succession, until by 265 B.C. Rome had conquered the entire Italian peninsula, with the exception of the Po valley.

The origins of Roman imperialism

This long series of military conflicts had profound social and economic effects upon the subsequent history of Rome. It affected adversely the interests of the poorer citizens and furthered the concentration of land in the possession of wealthy proprietors. Long service in the army forced the ordinary farmers to neglect the cultivation of the soil, with the result that they fell into debt and frequently lost their farms. Many took refuge in the city, until they were settled later as tenants on great estates in the conquered territories. The wars had the effect also of confirming the agrarian character of the Roman nation. The repeated acquisition of new lands made it possible to absorb the entire population into agricultural pursuits. As a consequence there was no need for the development of industry and commerce as means of earning a livelihood. Lastly, as in the case of Sparta, the Roman wars of conquest enslaved the nation to the military ideal.

Effects of the early military conflicts

During this same period of the early Republic, Rome underwent some significant political changes. These were not products so much of the revolution of the sixth century as of the developments of later years. The revolution which overthrew the monarchy was about as conservative as it is possible for a revolution to be. Its chief effect was to substitute two elected consuls for the king and to exalt the position of the Senate by vesting it with control over the public funds and with a veto on all actions of the assembly. The consuls themselves were usually senators and acted as the agents of their

Political changes following the overthrow of the monarchy

class. They did not rule jointly, but each was supposed to possess the full executive and judicial authority which had previously been wielded by the king. If a conflict arose between them, the Senate might be called upon to decide; or, in time of grave emergency, a dictator might be appointed for a term not greater than six months. In other respects the government remained the same as in the days of the monarchy.

Not long after the establishment of the Republic a struggle began by the common citizens for a larger share of political power. Before the end of the monarchy the Roman population had come to be divided into two great classes—the patricians and the plebeians. The former were the aristocracy, wealthy landowners, who were apparently the descendants of the old clan leaders. They monopolized the seats in the Senate and the offices of magistracy. The plebeians were the common people—small farmers, craftsmen, and tradesmen. Many were clients or dependents of the patricians, obliged to fight for them, to render them political support, and to cultivate their estates in return for protection. The grievances of the plebeians were numerous. Compelled to pay heavy taxes and forced to serve in the army in time of war, they were nevertheless excluded from all part in the government except membership in the assembly. Moreover, they felt themselves the victims of discriminatory decisions in judicial trials. They did not even know what legal rights they were supposed to enjoy, for the laws were unwritten, and no one but the consuls had the power to interpret them. In suits for debt the creditor was frequently allowed to sell the debtor into slavery. It was in order to obtain a redress of these grievances that the plebeians rebelled soon after the beginning of the fifth century B.C.

The plebeians gained their first victory about 470 B.C., when they forced the patricians to agree to the election of a number of tribunes with power to protect the citizens by means of a veto over unlawful acts of the magistrates. This victory was followed by a successful demand for codification of the laws about 450 B.C. The result was the publication of the famous Law of the Twelve Tables, so called because it was written on tablets of wood. Although the Twelve Tables came to be revered by the Romans of later times as a kind of charter of the people's liberties, they were really nothing of the sort. For the most part they merely perpetuated ancient custom without even abolishing enslavement for debt. They did, however, enable the people to know where they stood in relation to the law, and they permitted an appeal to the assembly against a magistrate's sentence of capital punishment. About a generation later the plebeians won eligibility to positions as lesser magistrates, and about 366 B.C. the first plebeian consul was elected. Since ancient custom provided that, upon completing their term of office, consuls should automatically enter the Senate, the patrician monopoly of seats in that body was broken. The final plebeian victory came in 287 B.C. with the passage of the Hortensian Law (named for the dictator Quintus Hortensius), which provided that measures enacted by the assembly should become binding upon the state whether the Senate approved them or not.

The significance of these changes must not be misinterpreted. They did not constitute a revolution to gain more liberty for the individual but merely to curb the power of the magistrates and to win for the common man a larger share in government. The state as a whole remained as despotic as ever, for its authority over the citizens was not even challenged. As Theodor Mommsen says, the Romans from the time of the Tarquins to that of the Gracchi "never really abandoned the principle that the people were not to govern but to be governed." [1] Because of this attitude the grant of full legislative powers to the assembly seems to have meant little more than a formality; the Senate continued to rule as before. Nor did the admission of plebeians to membership in the Senate have any effect in liberalizing that body. So high was its prestige and so deep was the veneration of the Roman for authority, that the new members were soon swallowed up in the conservatism of the old. Moreover, the fact that the magistrates received no salaries prevented most of the poorer citizens from seeking public office.

Significance of the plebeian victories

Intellectually and socially the Romans appear to have made but slow advancement as yet. The times were still harsh and crude. Though writing had been adopted as early as the sixth century, little use was made of it except for the copying of laws, treaties, and funerary inscriptions and orations. Inasmuch as education was limited to instruction imparted by the father in manly sports, practical arts, and soldierly virtues, probably the great majority of the people were still illiterate. War and agriculture continued as the chief occupations for the bulk of the citizens. A few craftsmen were to be found in the cities, and a minor development of trade had occurred, evidenced by the founding of a maritime colony at Ostia on the coast in the fourth century. But the comparative insignificance of Roman commerce at this time is pretty clearly revealed by the fact that the country had no standard system of coinage until 269 B.C.

Roman society and culture still rather primitive

The period of the early Republic was the period when the Roman religion assumed the character it was destined to retain through the greater part of the nation's history. In several ways this religion resembled the religion of the Greeks, partly for the reason that the Etruscan religion was deeply indebted to the Greek, and the Romans, in turn, were influenced by the Etruscans. Both the Greek and Roman religions were worldly and practical with neither spiritual nor ethical content. The relation of man to the gods was external and mechanical, partaking of the nature of a bargain or contract

The religion of the Romans compared with that of the Greeks

[1] *The History of Rome*, I. 313.

between two parties for their mutual advantage. The deities in both religions performed similar functions: Jupiter corresponded roughly to Zeus as god of the sky, Minerva to Athena as goddess of wisdom and patroness of craftsmen, Venus to Aphrodite as goddess of love, Neptune to Poseidon as god of the sea, and so on. The Roman religion no more than the Greek had any dogmas or sacraments or belief in rewards and punishments in an afterlife.

But there were significant differences also. The Roman religion was distinctly more political and less humanistic in purpose. It served not to glorify man or to make him feel at home in his world but to protect the state from its enemies and to augment its power and prosperity. The gods were less anthropomorphic; indeed, it was only as a result of Greek and Etruscan influences that they were made personal deities at all, having previously been worshiped as *numina* or animistic spirits. The Romans never conceived of their deities as quarreling among themselves or mingling with human beings after the fashion of the Homeric divinities. Finally, the Roman religion contained a much stronger element of priestliness than the Greek. The priests, or pontiffs as they were called, formed an organized class, a branch of the government itself. They not only supervised the offering of sacrifices, but they were guardians of an elaborate body of sacred traditions and laws which they alone could interpret. It must be understood, however, that these pontiffs were not priests in the sense of intermediaries between the individual Roman and his gods; they heard no confessions, forgave no sins, and administered no sacraments.

The morality of the Romans in this as in later periods had almost no connection with religion. The Roman did not ask his gods to make him good, but to bestow upon the community and upon his family material blessings. Morality was a matter of patriotism and of respect for authority and tradition. The chief virtues were bravery, honor, self-discipline, reverence for the gods and for one's ancestors, and duty to country and family. Loyalty to the state took precedence over everything else. For the good of the state the citizen must be ready to sacrifice not only his own life but, if necessary, the lives of his family and friends. The courage of certain consuls who dutifully put their sons to death for breaches of military discipline was a subject of profound admiration. Few peoples in European history with the exception of the Spartans and perhaps the modern Germans have ever taken the problems of national interest so seriously or subordinated the individual so completely to the good of the state.

3. THE FATEFUL WARS WITH CARTHAGE

By 265 B.C., as we have already learned, Rome had conquered and annexed the whole of Italy, except for the Po valley. Proud and confident of her strength, she was almost certain to strike out into new fields of empire. The prosperous island of Sicily was not yet within her grasp, nor could she regard with indifference the situation in other parts of the Mediterranean world. She was now prone to interpret almost any change in the *status quo* as a threat to her own power and security. It was for such reasons that Rome after 264 B.C. became involved in a series of wars with other great nations which decidedly altered the course of her history.

The first and most important of these wars was the struggle with Carthage, a great maritime empire that stretched along the northern coast of Africa from Numidia to the Strait of Gibraltar. Carthage had originally been founded about 800 B.C. as a Phoenician colony. In the sixth century it severed its ties with the homeland and gradually developed into a rich and powerful nation. The prosperity of its upper classes was founded upon commerce and upon exploitation of the silver and tin resources of Spain and Britain and the tropical products of north central Africa. Conditions within the country were far from ideal. The Carthaginians appear to have had no conception of free and orderly government. Bribery and oppression were methods regularly employed by the plutocracy to maintain its dominant position. The form of government itself can best be described as an oligarchy. At the head of the system were two magistrates, or *suffetes,* who exercised powers approximating those of the Roman consuls. The real governors, however, were thirty merchant princes who constituted an inner council of the Senate. These men controlled elections and dominated every other branch of the government. The remaining 270 members of the Senate appear to have been summoned to meet only on special occasions. In spite of these political deficiencies and a gloomy and cruel religion, Carthage had a civilization superior in luxury and scientific attainment to that of Rome when the struggle between the two countries began.

The beginning of imperialism on a major scale

Carthage

The initial clash with Carthage began in 264 B.C.[2] The primary cause was Roman jealousy over Carthaginian expansion in Sicily. Carthage already controlled the western portion of the island and was threatening the Greek cities of Syracuse and Messana on the eastern coast. If these cities should be captured, all chances of Roman occupation of Sicily would be cut off. Faced with this danger, Rome declared war upon Carthage with the hope of forcing her back into her African domain. Twenty-three years of fighting finally brought victory to the Roman generals. Carthage was compelled to surrender her possessions in Sicily and to pay an indemnity of 3200 talents, or about 2½ million dollars at present silver prices.

Causes of the
First Punic War

But the Romans were unable to stand the strain of this triumph. They had had to put forth such heroic efforts to win that when victory was finally secured it made them more arrogant and greedy than ever. As a result, the struggle with Carthage was renewed on

The Second
Punic War

[2] The wars with Carthage are known as the Punic Wars. The Romans called the Carthaginians *Poeni,* i.e., Phoenicians, whence is derived the adjective "Punic."

A Roman Battle Sarcophagus Depicts the Horrors of War

two different occasions thereafter. In 218 B.C. the Romans interpreted the Carthaginian attempt to rebuild an empire in Spain as a threat to their interests and responded with a declaration of war. This struggle raged through a period of sixteen years. Italy was ravaged by the armies of Hannibal, the famous Carthaginian commander, whose tactics have been copied by military experts to the present day. Rome escaped defeat by the narrowest of margins. Only the durability of her system of alliances in Italy saved the day. As long as these alliances held, Hannibal dared not besiege the city of Rome itself for fear of being attacked from the rear. In the end Carthage was more completely humbled than before. She was compelled to abandon all her possessions except the capital city and its surrounding territory in Africa, and to pay an indemnity of 10,000 talents.

The Third Punic War and the destruction of Carthage

Roman vindictiveness and avarice reached their zenith about the middle of the second century B.C. By this time Carthage had recovered a modicum of her former prosperity—enough to excite the envy and fear of her conquerors. Nothing would now satisfy the senatorial magnates but the complete destruction of Carthage and the expropriation of her land. In 149 B.C. the Senate dispatched an ultimatum demanding that the Carthaginians abandon their city and settle at least ten miles from the coast. Since this demand was tantamount to a death sentence for a nation dependent upon commerce, it was refused—as the Romans probably hoped it would be. The result was the Third Punic War, which was fought between 149 and 146 B.C. Seldom has the world witnessed a more desperate and more barbarous struggle. The final assault upon the city was carried into the houses of the natives themselves, and a frightful butchery took place. When the resistance of the Carthaginians was finally broken, the few citizens who were left to surrender were sold into slavery, and their once magnificent city was razed to the ground. The land was organized into a Roman province with the best areas parceled out as senatorial estates.

The wars with Carthage had momentous effects upon Rome. First, they brought her into conflict with eastern Mediterranean powers and thereby paved the way for world dominion. During the Second Punic War, Philip V of Macedon had entered into an alliance with Carthage and had plotted with the king of Syria to divide Egypt between them. In order to punish Philip and to forestall the execution of his plans, Rome sent an army into the East. The result was the conquest of Greece and Asia Minor and the establishment of a protectorate over Egypt. Thus before the end of the second century B.C. virtually the entire Mediterranean area had been brought under Roman dominion. The conquest of the Hellenistic East led to the introduction of semi-Oriental ideas and customs into Rome. Despite formidable resistance, these ideas and customs exerted considerable influence in changing some aspects of social and cultural life.

By far the most important effect of the Punic Wars was a great social and economic revolution that swept over Rome in the third and second centuries B.C. The incidents of this revolution may be enumerated as follows: (1) a marked increase in slavery due to the capture and sale of prisoners of war; (2) the decline of the small farmer as a result of the establishment of the plantation system in conquered areas and the influx of cheap grain from the provinces; (3) the growth of a helpless city mob composed of impoverished farmers and workers displaced by slave labor; (4) the appearance of a middle class comprising merchants, moneylenders, and "publicans" or men who held government contracts to operate mines, build roads, or collect taxes; and (5) an increase in luxury and vulgar display, particularly among the *parvenus* who fattened on the profits of war.

As a consequence of this social and economic revolution, Rome was changed from a republic of yeoman farmers into a nation with a complex society and new habits of luxury and indulgence. Though property had never been evenly distributed, the gulf which separated rich and poor now yawned more widely than before. The old-fashioned ideals of discipline and devotion to the service of the state were sadly weakened, and men began to make pleasure and wealth their gods. A few members of the senatorial aristocracy exerted efforts to check the evil tendencies and to restore the homely virtues of the past. The eminent leader of this movement was Cato the Elder, who inveighed against the new rich for their soft living and strove to set an example to his countrymen by performing hard labor on his farm and dwelling in a house with a dirt floor and no plaster on the walls. But his efforts had little effect, perhaps because of his own inconsistencies. He fought everything new, the good as well as the evil. He staunchly defended slavery and condemned the humane philosophy of Stoicism. The rich continued to indulge their expensive tastes and to rival each other in vulgar consumption of

Results of the wars with Carthage: (1) conquest of the Hellenistic East

(2) a social and economic revolution

The transformation of Roman society

185

wealth. At the same time public morality decayed. Tax gatherers plundered the provinces and used their illicit gains to purchase the votes of the poor. The anarchic masses in the city came to expect that politicians would feed them and provide for their amusement with ever more brutal shows. The total effect was so serious that some authorities date the beginning of Rome's decline from this period.[3]

4. THE REVOLUTION OF THE LATE REPUBLIC

The period from the end of the Punic Wars in 146 B.C. to about 30 B.C. was one of the most turbulent in the history of Rome. It was between these years that the nation reaped the full harvest of the seeds of violence sown during the wars of conquest. Bitter class conflicts, assassinations, desperate struggles between rival dictators, wars, and insurrections were the all too common occurrences of this time. Even the slaves contributed their part to the general disorder: first, in 104 B.C. when they ravaged Sicily; and again in 73 B.C. when 70,000 of them under the leadership of Spartacus held the consuls at bay for more than a year. Spartacus was finally slain in battle and 6000 of his followers were captured and crucified.

The first stage in the conflict between classes of citizens began with the revolt of the Gracchi. The Gracchi were leaders of the liberal, pro-Hellenic elements in Rome and had the support of the middle classes and a number of influential senators as well. Though of aristocratic lineage themselves, they earnestly strove for a program of reforms to alleviate the country's ills. They considered these to be a result of the decline of the free peasantry, and proposed the simple remedy of dividing state lands among the landless. The first of the brothers to take up the cause of reform was Tiberius. Elected tribune in 133 B.C., he proposed a law that restricted the current renters or holders of state lands to a maximum of 620 acres. The excess was to be confiscated by the government and given to the poor in small plots. Conservative aristocrats bitterly opposed this proposal and brought about its veto by Tiberius' colleague in the tribunate, Octavius. Tiberius removed Octavius from office, and when his own term expired, determined to stand for re-election. Both of these moves were unconstitutional and gave the conservative senators an excuse for violence. Armed with clubs and legs of chairs, they went on a rampage during the elections and murdered Tiberius and 300 of his followers.

Nine years later Gaius Gracchus, the younger brother of Tiberius, renewed the struggle for reform. Though Tiberius' land law had finally been enacted by the Senate, Gaius believed that the crusade must go further. Elected tribune in 123 B.C., and reelected in

[3] See D. C. Somervell (ed.), A. J. Toynbee's *A Study of History*, I, 258.

122, he procured the enactment of various laws for the benefit of the less privileged. The first provided for stabilizing the price of grain in Rome. For this purpose great public granaries were built along the Tiber River. A second law proposed to extend the franchise to Roman allies, giving them the rights of Latin citizens. Still a third gave the middle class the right to make up the juries that tried governors accused of exploiting the provinces. These and similar measures provoked so much anger and contention among the classes that civil war broke out. Gaius was proclaimed an enemy of the state, and the Senate authorized the consuls to take all necessary steps for the defense of the Republic. In the ensuing conflict Gaius and 3000 of his followers were killed.

The Gracchan revolt had a broad significance. It demonstrated, first of all, that the Roman Republic had outgrown its constitution. The assembly had gained, over the years, *de facto* powers almost equal to those of the Senate. Instead of working out a peaceful accommodation to these changes, both sides resorted to violence. By so doing they set a precedent for the unbridled use of force by any politician ambitious for supreme power and thereby paved the way for the destruction of the Republic. The Romans had shown a remarkable capacity for organizing an empire and for adapting the Greek idea of a city-state to a large territory, but the narrow conservatism of their upper classes was a fatal hindrance to the health of the state. They appeared to regard all change as evil. They failed to understand the reasons for internal discord and seemed to think that repression was its only remedy.

From 146 B.C. to the downfall of the Republic, Rome engaged in a series of wars. The victorious commanders in these wars frequently made themselves rulers of the state. The first of these conquering heroes to make capital out of his military reputation was Marius, who was elevated to the consulship by the masses in 107 B.C. and reelected six times thereafter. Unfortunately Marius was no statesman and accomplished nothing for his followers beyond demonstrating the ease with which a military leader with an army at his back could override opposition. Following his death in 86 B.C. the aristocrats took a turn at government by force. Their champion was Sulla, another victorious commander. Appointed dictator in 82 B.C. for an unlimited term, Sulla proceeded to exterminate his opponents and to restore to the Senate its original powers. Even the senatorial veto over acts of the assembly was revived, and the authority of the tribunes was sharply curtailed. After three years of rule Sulla decided to exchange the pomp of power for the pleasures of the senses and retired to a life of luxury and ease on his Campanian estate.

It was not to be expected that the "reforms" of Sulla would stand unchallenged after he had relinquished his office, for the effect of his decrees was to give control to a bigoted and selfish aristocracy. Several new leaders now emerged to espouse the cause of the people. The most famous of them were Pompey (106–48 B.C.) and

Pompey

Caesar's
triumph and
downfall

Julius Caesar

Julius Caesar (100–44 B.C.). For a time they pooled their energies and resources in a plot to gain control of the government, but later they became rivals and sought to outdo each other in bids for popular support. Pompey won fame as the conqueror of Syria and Palestine, while Caesar devoted his talents to a series of brilliant forays against the Gauls, adding to the Roman state the territory of modern Belgium and France. In 52 B.C., after a series of mob disorders in Rome, the Senate turned to Pompey and caused his election as sole consul. Caesar was eventually branded an enemy of the state, and Pompey conspired with the senatorial faction to deprive him of political power. The result was a deadly war between the two men. In 49 B.C. Caesar began a march on Rome. Pompey fled to the East in the hope of gathering a large enough army to regain control of Italy. In 48 B.C. the forces of the two rivals met at Pharsalus in Thessaly. Pompey was defeated and soon afterward was murdered by agents of the king of Egypt.

After dallying for a season at the court of Cleopatra in Egypt, Caesar returned to Rome. There was now no one who dared to challenge his power. With the aid of his veterans he cowed the Senate into granting his every desire. In 46 B.C. he became dictator for ten years, and two years later for life. In addition, he assumed nearly every other magisterial title that would augment his power. He was consul, censor, and supreme pontiff. He obtained from the Senate full authority to make war and peace and to control the revenues of the state. For all practical purposes he was above the law, and the other agents of the government were merely his servants. It seems unquestionable that he had little respect for the constitution, and there were rumors that he intended to make himself king. At any rate, it was on such a charge that he was assassinated in 44 B.C. by a group of conspirators, under the leadership of Brutus and Cassius, representing the old aristocracy.[4]

Through the centuries ever since, students of history have been blinded by hero worship in estimating Caesar's political career. It is undoubtedly erroneous to acclaim him as the savior of his country or to praise him as the greatest statesman of all time. For he treated the Republic with contempt and made the problem of governing more difficult for those who came after him. What Rome needed at this time was not the rule of force, however efficiently it might be exercised, but an enlightened attempt to correct the inequities of her political and economic regime. Though it is true that Caesar carried out numerous reforms, not all of them were really fundamental. With the aid of a Greek astronomer he revised the official calendar so as to bring it into harmony with the Egyptian solar calendar of 365 days, with an extra day added every fourth year. He

[4] During the last few months of his life Caesar became more ill-tempered and domineering than ever. Perhaps this change was due to the fact that he was really a sick man, his old affliction of epilepsy having returned. W. E. Heitland, *The Roman Republic*, III, 355.

investigated extravagance in the distribution of public grain and reduced the number of recipients by more than 50 per cent. He made plans for codification of the law and increased the penalty for criminal offenses. By conferring citizenship upon thousands of Spaniards and Gauls he took an important step toward eliminating the distinction between Italians and provincials. He settled a great many of his veterans and a considerable proportion of the urban poor on unused lands not only in Italy but throughout the empire, and he ordered the proprietors of large estates to employ at least one free citizen to every two slaves. It seems fair to say that his greatest fault lay in his exercise of dictatorial power. By ignoring the Senate entirely he destroyed the main foundation on which the Republic rested.

Caesar's
achievements

5 . ROME BECOMES SOPHISTICATED

During the last two centuries of republican history Rome came under the influence of Hellenistic civilization. The result was a modest flowering of intellectual activity and a further impetus to social change beyond what the Punic Wars had produced. The fact must be noted, however, that several of the components of the Hellenistic pattern of culture were never adopted by the Romans at all. The science of the Hellenistic Age, for example, was largely ignored, and the same was true of some of its art.

Rome under the
influence of
Hellenistic civilization

One of the most notable effects of Hellenistic influence was the adoption of Epicureanism and Stoicism by numerous Romans of the upper classes. The most renowned of the Roman exponents of the Epicurean philosophy was Lucretius (98–55 B.C.), author of a didactic poem entitled *On the Nature of Things*. In writing this work Lucretius was moved to explain the universe in such a way as to liberate man from all fear of the supernatural, which he regarded as the chief obstacle to peace of soul. Worlds and all things in them, he taught, are the results of fortuitous combinations of atoms. Though he admitted the existence of the gods, he conceived of them as living in eternal peace, neither creating nor governing the universe. Everything is a product of mechanical evolution, including man himself and his habits, institutions, and beliefs. Since mind is indissolubly linked with matter, death means utter extinction; consequently, no part of the human personality can survive to be rewarded or punished in an afterlife. Lucretius' conception of the good life was perhaps even more negative than that of Epicurus: what man needs, he asserted, is not enjoyment but "peace and a pure heart."

Roman
Epicureanism:
Lucretius

Stoicism was introduced into Rome about 140 B.C. Although it soon came to include among its coverts numerous influential leaders of public life, its most distinguished representative was Cicero (106–43 B.C.), the famous orator and statesman. Although Cicero adopted doctrines from a number of philosophers, including both Plato and Aristotle, the fact remains that he derived more of his

The Stoic
philosophy of
Cicero

ideas from the Stoics than from any other source. Certainly his chief ethical writings reflect substantially the doctrines of Zeno and his school. The basis of Cicero's ethical philosophy was the premise that virtue is sufficient for happiness, and that tranquillity of mind is the highest good. He conceived of the ideal man as one who has been guided by reason to an indifference toward sorrow and pain. In political philosophy Cicero went considerably beyond the earlier Stoics. He was one of the first to deny that the state is superior to the individual and taught that government had its origin in a compact among men for their mutual protection. In his *Republic* he set forth the idea of a higher law of eternal justice which is superior to the statutes and decrees of governments. This law is not made by man but is a product of the natural order of things and is discoverable by reason. It is the source of those rights to which all men are entitled as human beings and which governments must not assail. As we shall see presently, this doctrine influenced considerably the development of the Roman law by the great jurists of the second and third centuries A.D. By reason of his contributions to political thought, and by virtue of his urbanity and tolerance, Cicero deserves to be ranked as one of the greatest men Rome produced. He typified the genius of the nation at its best. It was his misfortune that, as a defender of the old Republic, he came to be associated in the public mind with the leaders of the aristocracy who had assassinated Julius Caesar. In 43 B.C. he was proscribed by Mark Antony, Caesar's friend, and hunted down and killed.

Roman literary progress

Hellenistic influence was in large measure responsible for Roman literary progress in the last two centuries of the Republic. It now became the fashion among the upper classes to learn the Greek language and to strive to reproduce in Latin some of the more popular forms of Hellenistic literature. Noteworthy results were some excellent comedy, lyric poetry, and above all, the letters, essays, and orations of Cicero, which are generally regarded as the finest examples of Latin prose.

Social conditions in the late Republic

The conquest of the Hellenistic world accelerated the process of social change which the Punic Wars had begun. The effects were most clearly evident in the growth of luxury, in a widened cleavage between classes, and in a further increase in slavery. The Italian people, numbering about 2,000,000 at the end of the Republic, had come to be divided into four main castes: the aristocracy, the equestrians, the common citizens, and the slaves.[5] The aristocracy included the senatorial class with a total membership of 300 citizens and their families. The majority of them inherited their status, although occasionally a plebeian would gain admission to the Senate through serving a term as consul or quaestor. Most of the aristocrats

---

[5] In addition, of course, there were numerous aliens, who really did not constitute a separate class. Many were on about the same level as the common citizens. Others were slaves.

gained their living as office holders and as owners of great landed estates. The equestrian order was made up of government contractors, bankers, and the wealthier merchants. Originally this class had been composed of those citizens with incomes sufficient to enable them to serve in the cavalry at their own expense, but the term *equites* had now come to be applied to all outside of the senatorial class who possessed property in substantial amount. The equestrians were the chief offenders in the indulgence of vulgar tastes and in the exploitation of the poor and the provincials. As bankers they regularly charged interest rates of 12 per cent and three or four times that much when they could get it. By far the largest number of the citizens were mere commoners or plebeians. Some of these were independent farmers, a few were industrial workers, but the majority were members of the city mob. When Julius Caesar became dictator, 320,000 citizens were actually being supported by the state.

The Roman slaves were scarcely considered people at all but instruments of production like cattle or horses to be worked for the profit of their masters. Notwithstanding the fact that some of them were refined and intelligent foreigners, they had none of the privileges granted to slaves in Athens. The policy of many of their owners was to get as much work out of them as possible during the years of their prime and then to turn them loose to be fed by the state when they became old and useless. Of course, there were exceptions, especially as a result of the civilizing effects of Stoicism. Cicero, for example, reported himself very fond of his slaves. It is, nevertheless, a sad commentary on Roman civilization that nearly all of the productive labor in the country was done by slaves. They produced practically all of the nation's food supply, for the amount contributed by the few surviving independent farmers was quite insignificant. At least 80 per cent of the workers employed in shops were slaves or former slaves. But many of the members of the

The status of the slaves

Atrium of an Upper-class House in Pompeii, seen from the Interior. Around the atrium or central court were grouped suites of living rooms. The marble columns and decorated walls still give an idea of the luxury and refinement enjoyed by the privileged minority.

servile population were engaged in nonproductive activities. A lucrative form of investment for the business classes was ownership of slaves trained as gladiators, who could be rented to the government or to aspiring politicians for the amusement of the people. The growth of luxury also required the employment of thousands of slaves in domestic service. The man of great wealth must have his doorkeepers, his litter-bearers, his couriers (for the government of the Republic had no postal service), his valets, and his pedagogues or tutors for his children. In some great mansions there were special servants with no other duties than to rub the master down after his bath or to care for his sandals.

The religious beliefs of the Romans were altered in various ways in the last two centuries of the Republic—again mainly because of the extension of Roman power over most of the Hellenistic states. There was, first of all, a tendency of the upper classes to abandon the traditional religion for the philosophies of Stoicism and Epicureanism. But many of the common people also found worship of the ancient gods no longer satisfying. It was too formal and mechanical and demanded too much in the way of duty and self-sacrifice to meet the needs of the masses, whose lives were now empty and meaningless. Furthermore, Italy had attracted a stream of immigrants from the East, most of whom had a religious background totally different from that of the Romans. The result was the rapid spread of Oriental mystery cults, which satisfied the craving for a more emotional religion and offered the reward of a blessed immortality to the wretched and downtrodden of earth. From Egypt came the cult of Isis and Osiris (or Sarapis, as the god was now more commonly called), while from Phrygia was introduced the worship of the Great Mother, with her eunuch priests and wild, symbolic orgies. So strong was the appeal of these cults that the decrees of the Senate against them proved almost impossible to enforce. In the last century B.C. the Persian cult of Mithraism, which came to surpass all the others in popularity, gained a foothold in Italy.

6. THE PRINCIPATE OR EARLY EMPIRE (27 B.C.–284 A.D.)

Shortly before his death in 44 B.C., Julius Caesar had adopted as his sole heir his grandnephew Octavian (63 B.C.–14 A.D.), then a young man of eighteen quietly pursuing his studies in Illyria across the Adriatic Sea. Upon learning of his uncle's death, Octavian hastened to Rome to take over control of the government. He soon found that he must share his ambition with two of Caesar's powerful friends, Mark Antony and Lepidus. The following year the three men formed an alliance for the purpose of crushing the power of the aristocratic clique responsible for Caesar's murder. The methods employed were not to the new leaders' credit. Prominent members of the aristocracy were hunted down and slain and their

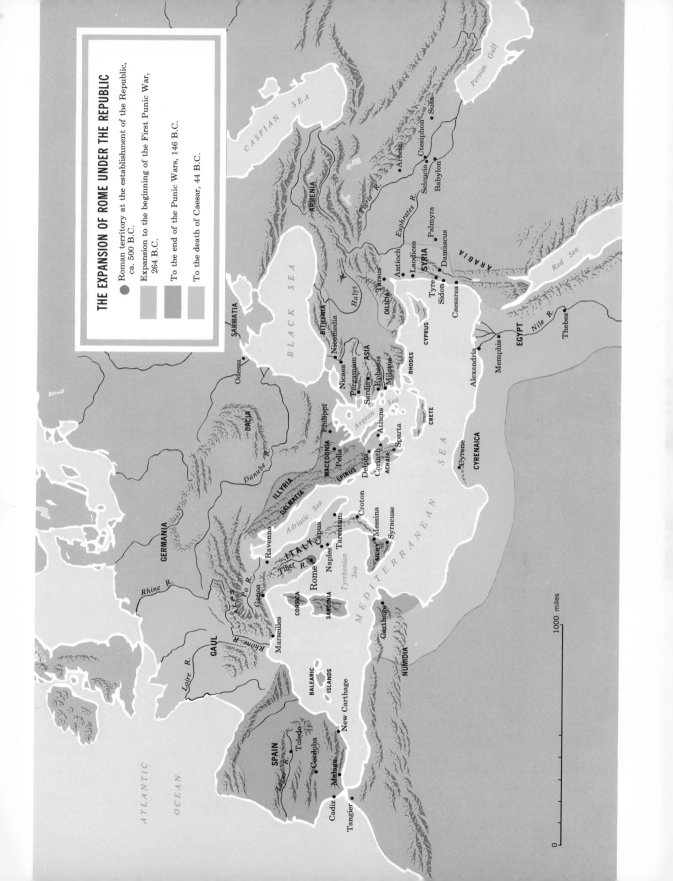

THE EXPANSION OF ROME UNDER THE REPUBLIC

- ● Roman territory at the establishment of the Republic, ca. 500 B.C.
- Expansion to the beginning of the First Punic War, 264 B.C.
- To the end of the Punic Wars, 146 B.C.
- To the death of Caesar, 44 B.C.

GERMANIA

GAUL

SPAIN

Rhine R.

Loire R.

Rhône R.

Tagus R.

ALPS

Po R.

Danube R.

DACIA

SARMATIA

ILLYRIA

DALMATIA

MACEDONIA

EPIRUS

ITALY

Tiber R.

Rome

Naples

Capua

Tarentum

Croton

Messina

SICILY

Syracuse

CORSICA

SARDINIA

Genoa

Ravenna

Marseilles

BALEARIC
ISLANDS

New Carthage

Cadiz

Tangier

Málaga

Córdoba

Toledo

Carthage

NUMIDIA

MEDITERRANEAN SEA

Tyrrhenian
Sea

Adriatic Sea

CYRENAICA

Cyrene

Alexandria

Memphis

EGYPT

Nile R.

Thebes

Red Sea

ARABIA

SYRIA

Antioch

Laodicea

Tyre

Sidon

Damascus

Caesarea

Palmyra

Seleucia

Ctesiphon

Babylon

Susa

Arbela

Euphrates R.

Tigris R.

ARMENIA

Tarsus

CILICIA

CYPRUS

CRETE

RHODES

Miletus

Ephesus

Sardis

ASIA

Pergamum

Nicaea

Nicomedia

BITHYNIA

Halys R.

BLACK SEA

CASPIAN SEA

Odessa

Philippi

Pella

Delphi

Athens

Corinth

Sparta

ACHAIA

Aegean
Sea

Persian Gulf

ATLANTIC
OCEAN

0   1000 miles

Unidentified Man, I cent. B.C. The Romans excelled in portraits of sharp individuality.

Augustus, Reigned 31 B.C.–14 A.D. This portrait suggests the contradictory nature of the genius who gave Rome peace after years of strife.

Constantine, Reigned 306–337 A.D. The head is from a statue sixteen feet in height.

Mummy Portrait, II cent. A.D. A Roman woman buried in Egypt.

Mosaic, I cent. A.D. A floor design composed of small pieces of colored marble fitted together to form a picture.

Wall Painting of a Satyr Mask, I cent. B.C. The belief in satyrs, thought to inhabit forests and pastures, was taken over from the Greeks.

Architectural Wall Painting from a Pompeiian Villa, I cent. B.C., suggesting the Greek origin of Roman forms of architecture.

property confiscated. The most noted of the victims was Cicero, brutally slain by Mark Antony's soldiers though he had taken no part in the conspiracy against Caesar's life. The real murderers, Brutus and Cassius, escaped and organized an army of 80,000 republicans, but were finally defeated by Octavian and his colleagues in 42 B.C. About eight years later a quarrel developed among the members of the alliance themselves, inspired primarily by Antony's jealousy of Octavian. The ultimate outcome in 31 B.C. was the triumphant emergence of Caesar's heir as the most powerful man in the Roman state.

The victory of Octavian ushered in a new period in Roman history, the most glorious and the most prosperous that the nation experienced. Although problems of peace and order were still far from being completely solved, the deadly civil strife was ended, and the people now had their first decent opportunity to show what their talents could achieve. Unlike his great uncle, Octavian seems to have entertained no monarchical ambitions. He was determined, at any rate, to preserve the forms if not the substance of constitutional government. He accepted the titles of Augustus and Imperator conferred upon him by the Senate and the army.[6] He held the authority of proconsul and tribune permanently; but he refused to make himself dictator or even consul for life, despite the pleas of the populace that he do so. In his view the Senate and the people were the supreme sovereigns, as they had been under the early Republic. The title by which he preferred to have his authority designated was Princeps, or First Citizen of the State. For this reason the period of his rule and that of his successors is properly called the Principate, or early Empire, to distinguish it from the period of the Republic (sixth century B.C. to 27 B.C.) and from the period of the late Empire (284 A.D. to 476 A.D.)

Octavian, or Augustus as he was now more commonly called, ruled over Italy and the provinces for forty-four years (31 B.C.–14 A.D.). At the beginning of the period he governed by military power and by common consent, but in 27 B.C. the Senate bestowed upon him the series of offices and titles described above. His work as a statesman at least equaled in importance that of his more famous predecessor. Among the reforms of Augustus were the establishment of a new coinage system, the creation of a centralized system of courts under his own supervision, and the bestowal of a large measure of local self-government upon cities and provinces. For the nation as a whole he laid the foundations for an elaborate postal service. He insisted upon experience and intelligence as qualifications for appointment to administrative office. By virtue of his proconsular authority he assumed direct control over the provincial governors and punished them severely for graft and extortion. He

See color plates at page 193

The revival of constitutional government

The reforms of Augustus

---

[6] The title Augustus signified "consecrated" and implied the idea that its bearer was specially favored by the gods. Imperator meant "victorious general."

Augustus

abolished the old system of farming out the collection of taxes in the provinces, which had led to such flagrant abuses, and appointed his own personal representatives as collectors at regular salaries. But he did not stop with political reforms. He procured the enactment of laws designed to check the more glaring social and moral evils of the time. By his own example of temperate living he sought to discourage luxurious habits and to set the precedent for a return to the ancient virtues.

After the death of Augustus in 14 A.D. Rome had few enlightened and capable rulers. Several of his successors were brutal tyrants who squandered the resources of the state and kept the country in an uproar by their deeds of bloody violence. As early as 68 A.D. the army began to take a hand in the selection of the Princeps, with the result that on several occasions thereafter the head of the government was little more than a military dictator. Between 235 and 284 A.D. sheer anarchy prevailed: of the twenty-six men who were elevated to power in that time only one escaped violent death. As a matter of fact, in the 270 years which followed the demise of Augustus, Rome had scarcely more than four or five rulers of whom much good could be said. The list would include Nerva (96–98 A.D.), Trajan (98–117), Antoninus Pius (138–161), and Marcus Aurelius (161–180).

The Pax Romana

These rulers and their great predecessor, Augustus, succeeded in maintaining, for about two centuries, the celebrated *Pax Romana*. On three occasions Augustus himself ceremonially closed the doors of the temple of Janus to symbolize the reign of absolute peace in the Empire. Yet the *Pax Romana* was primarily a peace of subjugation. Augustus added more territory to the empire than did any other Roman ruler. His stepsons pushed the frontiers into central and eastern Europe, conquering the territories known today as Switzerland, Austria, and Bulgaria. They attempted the subjugation of the territory occupied by modern Germany, but met with only minimal success. The *Pax Romana* rested upon an efficient navy and a vast imperial army. Though comparatively small, the navy performed its functions so well that the Romans maintained their control over the Mediterranean Sea for 200 years without fighting a battle. The army, numbering about 300,000 men, was much less successful. It was badly defeated in Germany and eventually lost nearly all of the territory it had conquered there. To prevent revolts, more than twenty of its twenty-eight legions were pinned down in Spain, Syria, and Egypt and on the Rhine and the Danube. Feeding and supplying these hordes of armed men put a constant strain on the resources of the state. Even a sales tax had to be adopted to supplement the usual sources of revenue.

How can this comparative failure of the political genius of the Romans in the very best period of their history be accounted for? The assertion is frequently made that it was due to the absence of any definite rule of hereditary succession to the office of Princeps.

But this answer rests upon a misconception of the nature of the Roman constitution at this time. The government Augustus established was not intended to be a monarchy. Although the Princeps was virtually an autocrat, the authority he possessed was supposed to be derived exclusively from the Senate and the people of Rome; he could have no inherent right to rule by virtue of royal descent. The explanation must therefore be sought in other factors. The Romans were now reaping the whirlwind which had been sown in the civil strife of the late Republic. They had grown accustomed to violence as the way out when problems did not admit of an easy solution. Furthermore, the long wars of conquest and the suppression of barbarian revolts had cheapened human life in the estimation of the people themselves and had fostered the growth of crime. As a consequence it was practically inevitable that men of vicious character should push their way into the highest political office.

CULTURE AND LIFE IN
THE PERIOD OF THE
PRINCIPATE

Reasons for the
political troubles
in Rome

7.   CULTURE AND LIFE IN THE PERIOD OF THE PRINCIPATE

From the standpoint of variety of intellectual and artistic interests the period of the Principate outshone all other ages in the history of Rome. Most of the progress took place, however, in the years from 27 B.C. to 200 A.D. It was between these years that Roman philosophy attained its characteristic form. This period witnessed also the feeble awakening of an interest in science, the growth of a distinctive art, and the production of the best literary works. After 200 A.D. economic and political decay stifled all further cultural growth.

Cultural progress
under the
Principate

Trajan Addressing His Troops. This relief on the Column of Trajan dates to the first century A.D.

Stoicism was now the prevailing philosophy of the Romans. Much of the influence of Epicureanism lingered and found occasional expression in the writings of the poets, but as a system it had ceased to be popular. The reasons for the triumph of Stoicism are not hard to discover. With its emphasis upon duty, self-discipline, and subjection to the natural order of things, it accorded well with the ancient virtues of the Romans and with their habits of conservatism. Moreover, its insistence upon civic obligations and its doctrine of cosmopolitanism appealed to the Roman political-mindedness and pride in world empire. Epicureanism, on the other hand, was a little too negative and individualistic to agree with the social consciousness of Roman tradition. It seemed not only to repudiate the idea of any purpose in the universe, but even to deny the value of human effort. Since the Romans were men of action rather than speculative thinkers, the Epicurean ideal of the solitary philosopher immersed in the problem of his own salvation could have no permanent attraction for them. It is necessary to observe, however, that the Stoicism developed in the days of the Principate was somewhat different from that of Zeno and his school. The old physical theories borrowed from Heracleitus were now discarded, and in their place was substituted a broader interest in politics and ethics. There was a tendency also for Roman Stoicism to assume a more distinctly religious flavor than that which had characterized the original philosophy.

Three eminent apostles of Stoicism lived and taught in Rome in the two centuries that followed the rule of Augustus: Seneca (4 B.C.–65 A.D.), millionaire adviser for a time to Nero; Epictetus, the slave (60?–120 A.D.); and the Emperor Marcus Aurelius (121–180 A.D.). All of them agreed that inner serenity is the ultimate goal to be sought, that true happiness can be found only in surrender to the benevolent order of the universe. They preached the ideal of virtue for virtue's sake, deplored the sinfulness of man's nature, and urged obedience to conscience as the voice of duty. Seneca and Epictetus adulterated their philosophy with such deep mystical yearnings as to make it almost a religion. They worshiped the cosmos as divine, governed by an all-powerful Providence who ordains all that happens for ultimate good. The last of the Roman Stoics, Marcus Aurelius, was more fatalistic and less hopeful. Although he did not reject the conception of an ordered and rational universe, he shared neither the faith nor the dogmatism of the earlier Stoics. He was confident of no blessed immortality to balance the sufferings of one's earthly career. Living in a melancholy time, he was inclined to think of man as a creature buffeted by evil fortune for which no distant perfection of the whole could fully atone. He urged, nevertheless, that men should continue to live nobly, that they should neither abandon themselves to gross indulgence nor break down in angry protest, but that they should derive what contentment they could from dignified resignation to suffering and tranquil submission to death.

Marcus Aurelius. The mounted figure of the great emperor-philosopher is one of the few equestrian statues surviving from the ancient world. It was originally entirely gilded. Now on the Piazza del Campidoglio, Rome.

The literary achievements of the Romans bore a definite relation to their philosophy. This was especially true of the works of the most distinguished writers of the Augustan Age. Horace (65–8 B.C.), for example, in his famous *Odes* drew copiously from the teachings of both Epicureans and Stoics. He confined his attention, however, to their doctrines of a way of life, for like most of the Romans he had little curiosity about the nature of the world. He developed a philosophy which combined the Epicurean justification of pleasure with the Stoic bravery in the face of trouble. While he never reduced pleasure to the mere absence of pain, he was sophisticated enough to know that the highest enjoyment is possible only through the exercise of rational control.

Vergil (70–19 B.C.) likewise reflects a measure of the philosophical temper of his age. Though his *Eclogues* convey something of the Epicurean ideal of quiet pleasure, Vergil was much more of a Stoic. His utopian vision of an age of peace and abundance, his brooding sense of the tragedy of human fate, and his idealization of a life in harmony with nature indicate an intellectual heritage similar to that of Seneca and Epictetus. Vergil's most noted work, the *Aeneid*, like several of the *Odes* of Horace, was a purposeful glorification of Roman imperialism. The *Aeneid* in fact was an epic of empire recounting the toils and triumphs of the founding of the state, its glorious traditions, and its magnificent destiny. The only other major writers of the Augustan Age were Ovid (43 B.C.?–17 A.D.) and Livy (59 B.C.–17 A.D.). The former, the greatest of Roman elegiac poets, was the chief representative of the cynical and individualist tendencies of his day. His writings, although brilliant and witty, often reflected the dissolute tastes of the time, and their popularity gives evidence of the failure of the efforts of Augustus to regenerate Roman society. The chief claim of Livy to fame rests upon his skill as a prose stylist. As a historian he was woefully deficient. His main work, a history of Rome, is replete with dramatic and picturesque

197

narrative, designed to appeal to the patriotic emotions rather than to present the impartial truth.

The literature of the period which followed the death of Augustus also exemplified conflicting social and intellectual tendencies. The novels of Petronius and Apuleius and the epigrams of Martial are specimens of individualist writing generally descriptive of the meaner aspects of life. The attitude of the authors is unmoral; their purpose is not to instruct or uplift but chiefly to tell an entertaining story or turn a witty phrase. An entirely different viewpoint is presented in the works of the other most important writers of this age: Juvenal, the satirist (60?–140 A.D.), and Tacitus, the historian (55?–117? A.D.). Juvenal wrote under the influence of the Stoics but with little intelligence and narrow vision. Laboring under the delusion that the troubles of the nation were due to moral degeneracy, he lashed the vices of his countrymen with the fury of an evangelist. A somewhat similar attitude characterized the writing of his younger contemporary, Tacitus. The best-known of Roman historians, Tacitus described the events of his age not entirely with a view to scientific analysis but largely for the purpose of moral indictment. His description of the customs of the ancient Germans in his *Germania* served to heighten the contrast between the manly virtues of an unspoiled race and the effeminate vices of the decadent Romans. Whatever his failings as a historian, he was a master of ironic wit and brilliant aphorism. Referring to the boasted *Pax Romana*, he makes a barbarian chieftain say: "They create a wilderness and call it peace." [7]

Floor Plan of the Baths of Caracalla

The period of the Principate was the period when Roman art first assumed its distinctive character as an expression of the national life. Before this time what passed for an art of Rome was really an importation from the Hellenistic East. Conquering armies brought back to Italy wagonloads of statues, reliefs, and marble columns as part of the plunder from Greece and Asia Minor. These became the

[7] Tacitus, *Agricola*, p. 30.

The Baths of Caracalla, Rome. The gigantic scale is typical of late Empire buildings. Elaborate and luxurious public baths like these were often presented to the public by the emperor or rich citizens. The floor plan above indicates the separate chambers for hot tub baths.

property of wealthy publicans and bankers and were used to embellish their sumptuous mansions. As the demand increased, hundreds of copies were made, with the result that Rome came to have by the end of the Republic a profusion of objects of art which had no more cultural significance than the Rembrandts or Botticellis in the home of some modern broker. The aura of national glory which surrounded the early Principate stimulated the growth of an art more nearly indigenous. Augustus himself boasted that he found Rome a city of brick and left it a city of marble. Nevertheless, much of the old Hellenistic influence remained until the talent of the Romans themselves was exhausted.

The arts most truly expressive of the Roman character were architecture and sculpture. Both were monumental, designed to symbolize power and grandeur rather than freedom of mind or contentment with life. Architecture contained as its leading elements the round arch, the vault, and the dome, although at times the Corinthian column was employed, especially in the construction of temples. The materials most commonly used were brick, squared stone blocks, and concrete, the last generally concealed with a marble facing. As a further adornment of public buildings, sculptured entablatures and façades, built up of tiers of colonnades or arcades, were frequently added. Roman architecture was devoted primarily to utilitarian purposes. The foremost examples were government buildings, amphitheaters, baths, race courses, and private houses. Nearly all were of massive proportions and solid construction. Among the largest and most noted were the Pantheon, with its dome having a diameter of 142 feet, and the Colosseum, which could accommodate 65,000 spectators at the gladiatorial combats. Roman sculpture included as its main forms triumphal arches and columns, narrative reliefs, altars, and portrait busts and statues. Its distinguishing characteristics were individuality and naturalism. Even more than architecture it served to express the vanity and love of power of the Roman aristocracy, although some of it was marked by unusual qualities of harmony and grace.[8]

As scientists the Romans accomplished comparatively little in this period or in any other. Scarcely an original discovery of fundamental importance was made by a man of Latin nationality. This fact seems strange when we consider that the Romans had the advantage of Hellenistic science as a foundation upon which to build. But they neglected their opportunity almost completely. Why should this have been so? It was due, first of all, to the circumstance that the Romans were absorbed in problems of government and military conquest. Forced to specialize in law, politics, and military strategy, they had very little time for investigation of nature. A reason of

[8] A great many of the best examples of both architecture and sculpture were produced not by Romans at all but by Greeks resident in Italy.

Architecture and sculpture

Head of a Young Man, ca. 140 A.D.

Why the Romans accomplished little as scientists

The Pantheon in Rome. Built by the emperor Hadrian and dedicated to the deities of the seven planets.

more vital importance was the fact that the Romans were too practical-minded. They had none of that divine fire which impels man to lose himself in the quest for unlimited knowledge. They had no vigorous intellectual curiosity about the world in which they lived. In short, they were not philosophers.

Mainly because of this lack of talent for pure science, the achievements of the Romans were limited almost entirely to engineering and the organization of public services. They built marvelous roads, bridges, and aqueducts. They provided the city of Rome with a water supply of 300,000,000 gallons daily. They established the first hospitals in the Western world and the first system of state medicine for the benefit of the poor. But their own writers on scientific subjects were hopelessly devoid of critical intelligence. The most renowned and the most typical of them was Pliny the Elder (23-79 A.D.), who completed about 77 A.D. a voluminous encyclopedia of "science" which he called *Natural History*. The subjects discussed varied from cosmology to economics. Despite the wealth of material

Lack of scientific originality

it contains, the work is of limited value. Pliny was totally unable to distinguish between fact and fable. In his estimation, the weirdest tales of wonders and portents were to be accepted as of equal value with the most solidly established facts. The other best-known author of an encyclopedia of science was Seneca (4 B.C.?–65 A.D.), the Stoic philosopher, who took his own life at Nero's command in 65 A.D. Seneca was less credulous than Pliny but no more original. Besides, he maintained that the purpose of all scientific study should be to divulge the moral secrets of nature. If there was any Latin who could be considered an original scientist, the title would have to be given to Celsus, who flourished during the reign of Tiberius. Celsus wrote a comprehensive treatise on medicine, including an excellent manual of surgery, but there is, a strong suspicion that the entire work was compiled, if not actually translated, from the Greek. Among the operations he described were tonsillectomy, operations for cataracts and goiter, and plastic surgery.

No account of the scientific aspects of Roman civilization would be complete without some mention of the work of Hellenistic scientists who lived in Italy or in the provinces during the period of the Principate. Nearly all of them were physicians. The most distinguished, although apparently not the most original, was Galen of Pergamum, who was active in Rome at various times during the latter half of the second century. While his fame rests primarily upon his medical encyclopedia, systematizing the learning of others, he is

Hellenistic scientists in Italy

Roman Aqueduct at Segovia, Spain. Aqueducts conveyed water from mountains to the larger cities.

The Colosseum. The Colosseum was built by the Roman emperors as a place of entertainment and public exhibition. It was the scene of gladiatorial combats and of the throwing of Christians to the lions.

deserving of more credit for his own experiments which brought him close to a discovery of the circulation of the blood. He not only taught but proved that the arteries carry blood, and that severance of even a small one is sufficient to drain away all of the blood of the body in little more than half an hour. But Galen was not the only Hellenistic physician who made important contributions in this time. At least one other is entitled to more recognition than is commonly given to him: Rufus of Ephesus, who wrote the first accurate description of the liver and of the rhythm of the pulse, and was the first to recommend boiling of suspicious water before drinking it.

Roman society exhibited the same general tendencies under the Principate as in the last days of the Republic. A few significant differences, however, can be noted. Owing in part to the influence of the Stoic philosophy and in part to the abundance of free labor, slavery began to decline. Despite the efforts of Augustus to limit the manumission of slaves, the number of freedmen steadily increased. They crowded into every field of employment, including the civil service. Many succeeded in becoming proprietors of small shops, and some even became rich. Related to these developments was the

Social tendencies under the Principate

202

growth of the institution of clientage. Members of the citizen class who had lost their property or who had been driven out of business by the competition of enterprising freedmen now frequently became "clients" or dependents of wealthy aristocrats. In return for pittances of food and money these "shabby genteel" served the great magnates by applauding their speeches and fawning before them when they appeared in public. Custom made it practically obligatory for every man of great wealth to maintain a retinue of these miserable flatterers.

Although the evidence has frequently been exaggerated, the period of the Principate was apparently marked by changing morals. According to the records there were 32,000 prostitutes in Rome during the reign of Trajan, and, if we can judge from the testimony of some of the most noted writers, homosexuality was exceedingly common and even fashionable. While political corruption had been subjected to more stringent control, crimes of violence appear to have increased. But the most serious moral indictment which can be brought against the age would seem to have been a further growth of the passion for cruelty. The great games and spectacles became bloodier and more disgusting than ever. The Romans could no longer obtain a sufficient thrill from mere exhibitions of athletic prowess; pugilists were now required to have their hands wrapped with thongs of leather loaded with iron or lead. The most popular amusement of all was watching the gladiatorial combats in the Colosseum or in other amphitheaters capable of accommodating thousands of spectators. Fights between gladiators were nothing new, but they were now presented on a much more elaborate scale. Not only the ignorant rabble attended them, but wealthy aristocrats also, and frequently the head of the government himself. The gladiators fought to the accompaniment of savage cries and curses from the audience. When one went down with a disabling wound, it was the privilege of the crowd to decide whether his life should be spared or whether the weapon of his opponent should be plunged into his heart. One contest after another was staged in the course of a single exhibition. Should the arena become too sodden with blood, it was covered over with a fresh layer of sand, and the revolting performance went on. Most of the gladiators were condemned criminals or slaves, but some were volunteers even from the respectable classes. The Princeps Commodus, the worthless son of Marcus Aurelius, entered the arena several times for the sake of the plaudits of the mob.

Notwithstanding its low moral tone, the age of the Principate was characterized by an even deeper interest in salvationist religions than that which had prevailed under the Republic. Mithraism now gained adherents by the thousands, absorbing most of the followers of the cults of the Great Mother and of Isis and Sarapis. About 40 A.D. the first Christians appeared in Rome. The new sect grew rapidly and eventually succeeded in displacing Mithraism as the most popular of the mystery cults. For some time the Roman gov-

Signs of moral change

The spread of Mithraism and Christianity

The Maison Carrée at Nîmes, France. The most perfect example of Roman temple extant. Reflecting possible Etruscan influence, it was built on a high base or podium with great steps leading to the entrance. It dates from the beginning of the Christian era.

ernment was no more hostile toward Christianity than it was toward the other mystery religions. While some members of the sect were put to death by Nero in response to the demand for a scapegoat for the disastrous fire of 64 A.D., there was no systematic persecution of Christians as such until the reign of Decius nearly 200 years later. Even then the persecution was inspired by political and social considerations more than by religious motives. Because of their otherworldliness and their refusal to take the customary oaths in the courts or participate in the civic religion, the Christians were regarded as disloyal citizens and dangerous characters. Moreover, their ideals of meekness and nonresistance, their preaching against the rich, and their practice of holding what appeared to be secret meetings made the Romans suspect them as enemies of the established order. In the end, persecution defeated its own purpose. It intensified the zeal of those who survived, with the result that the new faith spread more rapidly than ever.

The establishment of stable government by Augustus ushered in a period of prosperity for Italy which lasted for more than two centuries. Trade was now extended to all parts of the known world, even to Arabia, India, and China. Manufacturing reached more than insignificant proportions, especially in the production of pottery, textiles, and articles of metal and glass. As a result of the development of rotation of crops and the technique of soil fertilization, agriculture flourished as never before. In spite of all this, the economic order was far from healthy. The prosperity was not evenly distributed but was confined primarily to the upper classes. Since the stigma attached to manual labor persisted as strong as ever, production was bound to decline as the supply of slaves diminished. Perhaps worse was the fact that Italy had a decidedly unfavorable balance of trade. The meager industrial development was by no means sufficient to provide enough articles of export to meet the demand for luxuries imported from the provinces and from the outside world. As a consequence, Italy was gradually drained of her supply of precious metals. By the third century signs of economic collapse were already abundant.

8. ROMAN LAW

There is general agreement that the most important legacy which the Romans left to succeeding cultures was their system of law. This system was the result of a gradual evolution which may be considered to have begun with the publication of the Twelve Tables about 450 B.C. In the later centuries of the Republic the law of the Twelve Tables was modified and practically superseded by the growth of new precedents and principles. These emanated from different sources: from changes in custom, from the teachings of the Stoics, from the decisions of judges, but expecially from the edicts of the praetors. The Roman praetors were magistrates who had authority to define and interpret the law in a particular suit and issue instructions to the jury for the decision of the case. The jury merely decided questions of fact; all issues of law were settled by the praetor, and generally his interpretations became precedents for

A Street in Ostia. This town was the seaport of ancient Rome. The round arches and masonry columns form the balcony of a rich man's house.

205

the decision of similar cases in the future. Thus a system of judicial practice was built up in somewhat the same fashion as the English common law.

It was under the Principate, however, that the Roman law attained its highest stage of development. This later progress was the result in part of the extension of the law over a wider field of jurisdiction, over the lives and properties of aliens in strange environments as well as over the citizens of Italy. But the major reason was the fact that Augustus and his successors gave to certain eminent jurists the right to deliver opinions, or *responsa* as they were called, on the legal issues of cases under trial in the courts. The most prominent of the men thus designated from time to time were Gaius, Ulpian, Papinian, and Paulus. Although most of them held high judicial office, they had gained their reputations primarily as lawyers and writers on legal subjects. The responses of these jurists came to embody a science and philosophy of law and were accepted as the basis of Roman jurisprudence. It was typical of the Roman respect for authority that the ideas of these men should have been adopted so readily even when they upset, as they occasionally did, time-honored beliefs.

Roman law under the Principate; the great jurists

The Roman law as it was developed under the influence of the jurists comprised three great branches or divisions: the *jus civile*, the *jus gentium*, and the *jus naturale*. The *jus civile*, or civil law, was essentially the law of Rome and her citizens. As such it existed in both written and unwritten forms. It included the statutes of the Senate, the decrees of the Princeps, the edicts of the praetors, and also certain ancient customs operating with the force of law. The *jus gentium*, or law of peoples, was the law that was held to be common to all men regardless of nationality. It was the law which authorized the institutions of slavery and private ownership of property and defined the principles of purchase and sale, partnership, and contract. It was not superior to the civil law but supplemented it as especially applicable to the alien inhabitants of the empire.

The three divisions of Roman law

The most interesting and in many ways the most important branch of the Roman law was the *jus naturale*, or natural law. This was not a product of judicial practice, but of philosophy. The Stoics had developed the idea of a rational order of nature which is the embodiment of justice and right. They had affirmed that all men are by nature equal, and that they are entitled to certain basic rights which governments have no authority to transgress. The father of the law of nature as a legal principle, however, was not one of the Hellenistic Stoics, but Cicero. "True law," he declared, "is right reason consonant with nature, diffused among all men, constant, eternal. To make enactments infringing this law, religion forbids, neither may it be repealed even in part, nor have we power through Senate or people to free ourselves from it." [9] This law is prior to

The jus naturale

[9] *The Republic*, III, 22.

the state itself, and any ruler who defies it automatically becomes a tyrant. With the exception of Gaius, who identified the *jus naturale* with the *jus gentium*, all of the great jurists subscribed to conceptions of the law of nature very similar to those of the philosophers. Although the jurists did not regard this law as an automatic limitation upon the *jus civile*, they thought of it nevertheless as a great ideal to which the statutes and decrees of men ought to conform. This development of the concept of abstract justice as a legal principle was one of the noblest achievements of the Roman civilization.

9. THE LATE EMPIRE (284–476 A.D.)

The last period of Roman history, from 284 to 476 A.D., is properly called the period of the late Empire. With the accession of Diocletian in 284, the government of Rome finally became an undisguised autocracy. It is true, of course, that constitutional government had been little more than a fiction for some time, but now all pretense of maintaining the Republic was thrown aside. Both in theory and in practice the change was complete. No longer was the doctrine advanced that the ruler was the mere agent of the Senate and the people; he was now held to be absolutely sovereign on the assumption that the people had surrendered all power to him. Diocletian adopted the regalia and ceremony of an Oriental despot. In place of the simple military garb of the Princeps he substituted a purple robe of silk interwoven with gold. He required all his subjects who were admitted to an audience with him to prostrate themselves before him. Needless to say, the Senate was now completely excluded from participation in the government. It was not formally abolished, but it was reduced to the status of a municipal council and a social club for the plutocracy. The chief reason for these political changes is undoubtedly to be found in the economic decline of the third century. The people had lost confidence in themselves, as they frequently do under such circumstances, and were ready to sacrifice all of their rights for the faint hope of security.

The triumph of absolute autocracy

Diocletian's successors continued his system of absolutism. The most famous of them were Constantine I (306–337), Julian (361–363), and Theodosius I (379–395). Constantine is best known for his establishment of a new capital, called Constantinople, on the site of ancient Byzantium, and for his policy of religious toleration toward Christians. Contrary to a common belief, he did not make Christianity the official religion of the Empire; his various edicts issued in 313 simply gave Christianity equal status with the pagan cults, thereby terminating the policy of persecution. Later in his reign he bestowed upon the Christian clergy special privileges and caused his sons to be brought up in the new faith, but he continued to maintain the imperial cult. Although he was acclaimed by historians of the Church as Constantine the Great, his practice of favoring Christianity was dictated primarily by political motives. A

Diocletian's successors

207

generation after Constantine's death the Emperor Julian attempted to stimulate a pagan reaction. He was a devoted admirer of Hellenic culture and thought of Christianity as an alien and enemy religion. His attempt to accomplish a pagan revival ended in failure, partly because Christianity was too firmly entrenched, and partly because his reign was too short. The last of the noted pagan emperors, he has been branded by Christian historians as Julian the Apostate. The other most prominent of the rulers of Rome in its dying stage was Theodosius I, who, in spite of his butchery of thousands of innocent citizens on imaginary charges of conspiracy, is also known as "the Great." The chief importance of his reign comes from his decree of 380 commanding all of his subjects to become orthodox Christians. A few years later he classified participation in any of the pagan cults as an act of treason.

From the standpoint of cultural achievement the period of the Empire is of little significance. With the establishment of a despotic state and the degradation of intellect by mystical and otherworldly religions, creative talent was destroyed. The few literary works produced were characterized by an overemphasis upon form and a neglect of content. A barren and artificial rhetoric took the place of the study of the classics in the schools, and science died out completely. Aside from the teachings of the Christian Fathers, which will be discussed later, the prevailing philosophy of the age was Neo-Platonism. This philosophy, purporting to be a continuation of the system of Plato, was really an outgrowth of the doctrines of the Neo-Pythagoreans and of Philo Judaeus.[10] The first of its basic teachings was emanationism: everything that exists proceeds from God in a continuing stream of emanations. The initial stage in the process is the emanation of the world-soul. From this come the divine Ideas or spiritual patterns, and then the souls of particular things. The final emanation is matter. But matter has no form or quality of its own; it is simply the privation of spirit, the residue which is left after the spiritual rays from God have burned themselves out. It follows that matter is to be despised as the symbol of evil and darkness. The second major doctrine was mysticism. The soul of man was originally a part of God, but it has become separated from him through its union with matter. The highest goal of life should be mystic reunion with the divine, which can be accomplished through contemplation and through emancipation of the soul from bondage to matter. Man should be ashamed of the fact that he possesses a physical body and should seek to subjugate it in every way possible. Asceticism was therefore the third main teaching of this philosophy.

The real founder of Neo-Platonism was Plotinus, who was born in Egypt about 204 A.D. In the later years of his life he taught in Rome and won many followers among the upper classes. His princi-

Gold Medallion of Constantine I

Neo-Platonism

[10] See pp. 166–67

pal successors diluted the philosophy with more and more bizarre superstitions. In spite of its anti-intellectual viewpoint and its utter indifference to the state, Neo-Platonism became so popular in Rome in the third and fourth centuries A.D. that it almost completely supplanted Stoicism. No fact could have expressed more eloquently the extent of the social and intellectual decline that the Roman nation had experienced.

10. DECAY AND DECLINE

In 476 A.D. the last of the emperors in the West, the insignificant Romulus Augustulus, was deposed, and a barbarian chieftain assumed the title of King of Rome. Though this event is commonly taken to have marked the end of Roman history, it was really only the final incident in a long process of disintegration. The fall of Rome did not occur with dramatic suddenness, but extended over a period of approximately two centuries. A large part of the civilization was already dead before the Empire collapsed. Indeed, for all practical purposes the pagan culture of Rome from the middle of the third century on could be considered as belonging to a dark age.

More has been written on the fall of Rome than on the death of any other civilization. The theories offered to account for the tragedy have been many and various. Moralist historians have found the explanation in the evidences of lechery unearthed at Pompeii or revealed in the satires of Juvenal and Martial. They overlook the fact, however, that nearly all of this evidence comes from the early Principate, and that in the centuries preceding the collapse of the Empire, morality became more austere through the influence of ascetic religions. Historians of a sociological bent have attributed the downfall to a declining birth rate. But there is little to indicate that Rome could have been saved by greater numbers. The Athenian civilization reached the height of its glory during the very centuries when growth of population was most strictly limited.

If there was one primary factor which operated more than others to accomplish the downfall of Roman civilization, it was probably imperialism. Nearly all of the troubles that beset the country were traceable in some measure to the conquest of a great empire. It was this which was largely responsible for the creation of the city mob, for the growth of slavery, for the strife between classes and the widespread political corruption. It was also imperialism that was partly responsible for the barbarian invasions, for the exhaustion of the resources of the state to maintain a huge military machine, and for the influx of alien ideas which the Romans could not readily assimilate. The idea that Rome became a civilized nation as a result of her conquests is undoubtedly a fallacy. Instead, her repeated victories caused her ruling population to become greedy and domineering. It is true that she appropriated much of the Hellenistic culture after her conquest of the Near East; but the really valuable elements

The Arch of Titus

of this culture would eventually have been acquired anyway through the normal expansion of trade, while the evil consequences of domination of vast areas by force would have been avoided.

(2) revolution in economic and social conditions

Another important cause, closely related to imperialism, deserves analysis: namely, the revolution in economic and social conditions that swept over Italy in the third and fourth centuries A.D. This revolution, which differed radically from the one that had occupied the third and second centuries B.C., had the following features: (1) the disappearance of money from circulation and the return to a natural economy; (2) the decline of industry and commerce; (3) the growth of serfdom and the rise of an extralegal feudalism; (4) the extension of government control over a large portion of the economic sphere; and (5) the transition from a regime of individual initiative to a regime of hereditary status. The primary cause of this revolution seems to have been the unfavorable balance of trade that Italy suffered in her commerce with the provinces. In order to check the withdrawal of precious metals from the country, the government, instead of encouraging manufactures for export, resorted to the hazardous expedient of debasing the coinage. Nero began the practice, and his successors continued it until the proportion of baser metal in the Roman coins had increased to 98.5 per cent. The inevitable result was disappearance of money from circulation. Commerce could no longer be carried on, salaries had to be paid in food and clothing, and taxes collected in produce. The scarcity of money in turn led to a decline in production, until the government intervened with a series of decrees binding peasants to the soil and compelling every townsman to follow the occupation of his father. The great landlords, now that they had control over a body of serfs, entrenched themselves on their estates, defied the central government, and ruled as feudal magnates. So close were the peasants to the margin of starvation that some of them sold their newborn children or gave them up for adoption in order to escape from the burden of supporting them.

No one can present an exhaustive list of causes of Rome's decline. Among others of at least minor significance were the following: (1) the unjust policy of taxation, which rested most heavily on the business and farming classes and resulted in the discouragement of productive enterprise; (2) the social stigma attached to work, resulting in the deliberate choice by thousands of the debasing relationship of clientage in preference to useful labor; (3) exhaustion of the soil, resulting in part from unscientific farming and in part from the attempt of too many people to make a living from the land; and (4) the disastrous plagues of Asiatic origin which broke out in 166 and 252 A.D., resulting in depopulating whole sections of Italy and thereby opening the way for barbarian incursions. To the last of these causes should be appended the fact that as lands along the low-lying coast were withdrawn from cultivation because of the competition of grain from the provinces, malaria spread. The effect of this disease in undermining the vigor of the Italian population is impossible to estimate, but it must have been considerable.

11.   THE ROMAN HERITAGE

It is tempting to believe that the modern world owes a vast debt to the Romans: first of all, because Rome is nearer to us in time than any of the other civilizations of antiquity; and secondly, because Rome seems to bear such a close kinship to the modern temper. The resemblances between Roman history and the history of Great Britain or the United States in the nineteenth and twentieth centuries have often been noted. The Roman economic evolution progressed all the way from a simple agrarianism to a complex urban system with problems of unemployment, monopoly, gross disparities of wealth, and financial crises. The Roman Empire, in common with the British and the American, was founded upon conquest and upon visions of Manifest Destiny. It must not be forgotten, however, that the heritage of Rome was an ancient heritage and that consequently, the similarities between the Roman and modern civilizations are not so important as they seem. As we have noted already, the Romans disdained industrial activities, and they were incredibly naïve in matters of science. Neither did they have any idea of the modern national state; the provinces were mere appendages, not integral parts of a body politic. It was largely for this reason that the Romans never developed an adequate system of representative government. Finally, the Roman conception of religion was vastly different from our own. Their system of worship, like that of the Greeks, was external and mechanical, not inward or spiritual in any

The Forum, the Civic Center of Ancient Rome. In addition to public squares, the Forum included triumphal arches, magnificent temples, and government buildings. In the foreground is the Temple of Saturn. Behind it is the Temple of Antoninus and Faustina. The three columns at the extreme right are what is left of the Temple of Castor and Pollux, and in the farthest background is the arch of Titus.

sense. What Christians consider the highest ideal of piety—an emotional attitude of love for the divine—the Romans regarded as gross superstition.

Nevertheless, the civilization of Rome was not without a definite influence upon later cultures. The form, if not the spirit, of Roman architecture was preserved in the ecclesiastical architecture of the Middle Ages and survives to this day in the design of most of our government buildings. The sculpture of the Augustan Age also lives on in the equestrian statues, the memorial arches and columns, and in the portraits in stone of statesmen and generals that adorn our boulevards and parks. Although subjected to new interpretations, the law of the great jurists became an important part of the Code of Justinian and was thus handed down to the later Middle Ages. Modern lawyers and especially American judges frequently cite maxims originally invented by Gaius or Ulpian. Further, the legal systems of nearly all Continental European countries today incorporate much of the Roman law. This law was one of the grandest of the Romans' achievements and reflected their genius for governing a vast and diverse empire. It should not be forgotten either that Roman literary achievements furnished much of the inspiration for the revival of learning that spread over Europe in the

The influence of Roman civilization

twelfth century and reached its zenith in the Renaissance. Nor should the debt of the Western world to Rome for the transmission of Greek culture be overlooked. Perhaps not so well known is the fact that the organization of the Catholic Church, to say nothing of part of its ritual, was adapted from the structure of the Roman state and the complex of the Roman religion. For example, the Pope still bears the title of Supreme Pontiff (*Pontifex Maximus*), which was used to designate the authority of the emperor as head of the civic religion. But the most important element in the Roman influence has probably been the idea of the absolute authority of the state. In the judgment of nearly all Romans, with the exception of philosophers such as Cicero and Seneca, the state was legally omnipotent. However much the Roman may have detested tyranny, it was really only *personal* tyranny that he feared; the despotism of the Senate as the organ of popular sovereignty was perfectly proper. This conception survives to our own day in the popular conviction that the state can do no wrong, and especially in the doctrines of absolutist political philosophers that the individual has no rights except those which the state confers upon him.

One other political conception, emanating from the Romans, has had lasting significance. This is the conception of a world empire established and maintained by a single people by virtue of its martial prowess and its superior civilization. The Romans brought to a temporary end the regime of local independence that had prevailed during most of previous history except during the brief rule of the Hellenistic empires. Under the *Pax Romana* none of the smaller states was really master of its own fate. All were mere appendages of Rome, in theory if not in actuality. They had not chosen this fate for themselves but had been obliged to accept it because of the overwhelming power of their mighty neighbor. As a consequence, the Mediterranean Sea, which washed the shores of most of what was then the civilized Western world, had become a Roman lake. This same *Pax Romana* provided much of the inspiration for the *Pax Britannica* of the nineteenth century. Controlling a population amounting to one-fourth of the world's total and maintaining a navy equal in strength to the combined navies of any two other powers, Great Britain molded the destinies of most of the Western world. In this way she succeeded in preventing major wars and in acquiring cultural and economic supremacy. At the end of the nineteenth century many Americans also fell under the spell of the *Pax Romana*. Politicians and propagandists such as Albert J. Beveridge, William Allen White, and Theodore Roosevelt proclaimed it the mission of the American people to become the "master organizers" of the world, to enforce peace, and to advance the cause of human welfare. They insisted that their country had been given a divine appointment as "trustee of the civilization of the world." [11]

The Roman conception of a world empire

[11] For an extended discussion of this subject see E. M. Burns, *The American Idea of Mission*, pp. 206–10.

SELECTED READINGS

· Items so designated are available in paperbound editions.

POLITICAL HISTORY

· Adcock, F. E., *Roman Political Ideas and Practice*, Ann Arbor, 1964 (University of Michigan).

Bloch, Raymond, *The Origins of Rome*, New York, 1960.

Boak, A. E. R., *A History of Rome to 565 A.D.*, New York, 1929. Clear and concise.

· Cowell, F. R., *Cicero and the Roman Republic*, New York, 1948 (Penguin). A good account of the fall of the Republic.

· Haywood, R. M., *The Myth of Rome's Fall*, New York, 1962 (Apollo).

· Katz, Solomon, *The Decline of Rome*, Ithaca, 1955 (Cornell).

· Mommsen, Theodor, *The History of Rome*, Chicago, 1957 (Meridian, Wisdom Library). A reprint of a great masterpiece.

· Scullard, H. S., *From the Gracchi to Nero*, New York, 1959 (Barnes & Noble).

· Starr, C. G., *The Emergence of Rome*, Ithaca, 1953 (Cornell).

· Syme, Ronald, *The Roman Revolution*, New York, 1939 (Oxford, 1960).

· Warmington, B. H., *Carthage*, Baltimore, 1965 (Penguin).

CULTURAL AND SOCIAL HISTORY

Arnold, E. V., *Roman Stoicism*, New York, 1911.

Badian, Ernst, *Roman Imperialism in the Late Republic*, Oxford, 1967.

Bailey, Cyril, ed., *The Legacy of Rome*, New York, 1924.

Balston, J. P. V. D., *Life and Leisure in Ancient Rome*, New York, 1969.

· Carceopino, Jerome, *Daily Life in Ancient Rome*, New Haven, 1960 (Yale University Press).

· Clagett, Marshall, *Greek Science in Antiquity*, New York, 1963 (Collier). Includes developments in late antiquity.

· Dill, Samuel, *Roman Society from Nero to Marcus Aurelius*, New York, 1905 (Meridian). Old but still highly regarded.

· Duff, J. W., *A Literary History of Rome in the Golden Age*, New York, 1964 (Barnes & Noble).

· ———, *A Literary History of Rome in the Silver Age*, New York, 1960 (Barnes & Noble, 1964).

Earl, Donald, *The Moral and Political Tradition of Rome*, Ithaca, 1967.

· Fowler, W. W., *Social Life at Rome in the Age of Cicero*, New York, 1915 (St. Martin's Library).

———, *The Religious Experience of the Roman People*, London, 1911.

Frank, Tenney, *Economic History of Rome*, Baltimore, 1927. Perhaps the best economic history.

· Hamilton, Edith, *The Roman Way*, New York, 1932 (Norton Library).

· Laistner, M. L. W., *The Greater Roman Historians*, Berkeley, 1947 (University of California, 1963).

· Lot, Ferdinand, *The End of the Ancient World*, New York, 1931 (Torchbook).

· Mattingly, Harold, *Christianity in the Roman Empire*, New York, 1967 (Norton Library).

· ———, *The Man in the Roman Street*, New York, 1947 (Norton Library).

Rostovtzev, M. I., *Social and Economic History of the Roman Empire*, New York, 1957, 2 vols. Has become almost a classic.

Scullard, H. H., *The Etruscan Cities and Rome*, Ithaca, 1967.

· Starr, C. G., *Civilization and the Caesars*, New York, 1954 (Norton Library).
Westermann, W. L., *The Slave Systems of Greek and Roman Antiquity*, Philadelphia, 1955.
· Wheeler, Mortimer, *The Art of Rome*, New York, 1964 (Praeger).
White, Lynn T., Jr., ed., *Transformation of the Roman World*, Berkeley, 1966.

SOURCE MATERIALS

Translations of Roman authors are available in the appropriate volumes of the Loeb Classical Library.
See also:
Lewis, Naphtali, and Reinhold, M., *Roman Civilization*, New York, 1955, 2 vols.

PART III

The Early Middle Ages

During the period from 284 to 476 A.D. Roman civilization was strongly influenced by a revival of Oriental ideals of despotism, otherworldliness, pessimism, and fatalism. In the midst of economic distress and cultural decay men lost interest in earthly achievement and began to yearn for spiritual blessings in a life after death. This change in attitude was due primarily to the spread of Near Eastern religions, especially Christianity. When the Roman Empire finally collapsed, the victory of Orientalism was almost complete. The result was the evolution of new civilizations, compounded in part of elements taken from Greece and from Rome but with religion as a dominant factor behind most of their achievements. Altogether three new cultures finally emerged: the civilization of western Europe in the early Middle Ages, the Byzantine civilization, and the Saracenic civilization. The periods covered by the history of all three overlapped. The civilization of western Europe in the early Middle Ages extended from about 400 to 1000. Although Constantine established his capital on the site of ancient Byzantium in the fourth century A.D., Byzantine civilization did not begin its independent evolution until after 500. It survived until the capture of Constantinople by the Turks in 1453. The Saracenic civilization flourished from the seventh century to the end of the thirteenth.

A Chronological Table

	WESTERN EUROPE	**BYZANTINE EMPIRE**

Germanic migrations and invasions,
  100 B.C.–600 A.D.
Rise of the Papacy, 50–300
Growth of the colonate, *ca.* 200–500

300

Rise of monasticism, *ca.* 300
Council of Nicaea, 325
Constantinople established as capital, 330

Invasions of England by Angles and Saxons, 400–600
Decline of industry and commerce, 400–800
Capture of Rome by Visigoths, 410
St. Augustine's *City of God*, 413–426
Merovingian dynasty in France, 481–751
Ostrogothic rule in Italy, 493–552
Boethius' *Consolation of Philosophy*, 523
Origin of Seven Liberal Arts, *ca.* 550

Monophysite movement, 450–565

500

Justinian's empire, 527–565
Revision and codification of Roman law, 527–535
Construction of church of Santa Sophia, 532–537
Byzantine conquest of Italy, 535–552

Lombard invasion of Italy, 568

Iconoclastic movement, 725–850

Battle of Tours, 732
Carolingian dynasty, 751–887
Development of feudalism, 800–1300
Charlemagne's empire, 800–814
Unification of England under Saxon Kings, 802–1066
Treaty of Verdun, 843
Holy Roman Empire, 962–
Founding of national monarchy in France, 987

800

Separation of Eastern and Western churches, 1054
Battle of Manzikert, 1071

1100

The Crusades, 1096–1204

Capture of Constantinople by Crusaders of Fourth Crusade, 1204

1453

Capture of Constantinople by Ottoman Turks, 1453

THE SARACENS

Mohammed, 570?–632

The Hegira, 622
Capture of Mecca, 630
Conquest of Persia, Egypt, Palestine, Syria,
North Africa, Spain, 632–732
Division of Islam into sects—Sunnites,
Shiites, and Sufis, *ca.* 640

Development of steel manufacturing, textile manufacturing, leather tooling, and
paper making, *ca.* 800–1400

Hindu-Arabic system of numerals, *ca.* 1000
Saracenic world trade, *ca.* 1000–1500

Cultivation of cotton, sugar, oranges, lemons, bananas, coffee, *ca.* 1100
Transmission of complete works of Aristotle to Europe, *ca.* 1150

Transmission of compass and astrolabe to
Europe, *ca.* 1400

CHAPTER 9

The Civilization of the Early Middle Ages

Think not that I am come to destroy the law, or the prophets:
I am not come to destroy, but to fulfill.
—Jesus of Nazareth, The Sermon on the Mount, *Matthew* v.17

Although checked for the time, this pernicious susperstition
[Christianity] broke out again . . . throughout the City, in which
the atrocities and shame from all parts of the world center and
flourish. Therefore those who confessed were first seized, then on
their information a great multitude were convicted, not so much
of the crime of incendiarism, as of hatred of the human race.
—Tacitus on Nero's persecution of Christians

Sometime during the Renaissance the practice arose of dividing the
history of the world into three great epochs: ancient, medieval, and
modern. This classification has come to be accepted with almost
dogmatic finality. It ties in with the average man's belief that this
planet of ours has witnessed only two great periods of progress: the
time of the Greeks and the Romans and the age of modern invention. Between these two periods were the Middle Ages, popularly
regarded as an interlude of abysmal ignorance and superstition when
man lived enveloped in a cowl, oblivious of the wonders of knowledge, and concerned only with escape from the miseries of this
world and the torments of hell. The very word "medieval" has an
odious meaning in the average mind of today. It has come to be a
synonym for reactionary or unprogressive. Thus when a modern
reformer wishes to cast reproach upon the ideas of his conservative
opponent, all he has to do is to brand them as "medieval."

The reason for such erroneous judgments lies in the conventional
notion that the entire medieval period from the fall of Rome to the
beginning of the Renaissance was a cultural unit, that the ideals and

*Misinterpreta-
tion of the word
"medieval"*

221

Only the period
from 400 to
1000 A.D. really
dark

institutions of the sixth century, for example, were the same as those of the thirteenth. Nothing could be farther from the truth. The medieval period, in western Europe, really encompassed two civilizations, as different from each other as Greece from Rome or the Renaissance from the nineteenth and twentieth centuries. The first of these civilizations, beginning about 400 A.D., when the process of Roman decay was nearly complete, and extending until 1000, was that of the early Middle Ages. It was this period alone which was really distinguished by most of those attributes commonly referred to as "medieval." The culture of the early Middle Ages undoubtedly represented in certain respects a reversion to barbarism. Intellect did not merely stagnate but sank to very low depths of ignorance and credulity. Economic activity declined to primitive levels of barter and ruralism, while morbid asceticism and contempt for this world superseded more normal social attitudes. With the Carolingian Renaissance of the ninth century, however, a brief intellectual revival occurred in Europe. In the eleventh, twelfth, and thirteenth centuries the human spirit soared to much greater heights. The result was another of the world's great cultures, distinguished alike by intellectual progress and a high degree of prosperity and freedom. Indeed, this later medieval civilization, which endured until the end of the thirteenth century, was more nearly similar to the modern age than most people realize.

I. THE CHRISTIAN FOUNDATION OF EARLY MEDIEVAL CULTURE

Factors influ-
encing early
medieval culture

Three main factors combined to produce the civilization of early medieval Europe: the Christian religion, the influence of the Germanic barbarians, and the heritage from the classical cultures. The effect of the third was probably less than that of the others. Outside the realm of philosophy the influence of the Greek and Hellenistic civilizations was comparatively slight. While the Roman heritage was still powerful, the men of the early Middle Ages rejected some portions of it as inconsistent with Christianity and barbarized much of the remainder.

The career of
Jesus of
Nazareth

The most important foundation of the new culture was the Chrisian religion, whose founder, Jesus of Nazareth, was born in a small town of Judea some time near the beginning of the Christian era. Judea was then under Roman rule, though the Jews themselves recognized only their own king, Herod I, as their rightful sovereign. The atmosphere of the country was charged with religious emotionalism and political discontent. Some of the people, notably the Pharisees, looked forward to the coming of a political messiah, a son of David, who would rescue the country from foreign rule. Others, for example, the Essenes, thought in terms of spiritual deliverance through asceticism, repentance, and mystical union with God. It was this latter sect, together with others of a similar character, which prepared the way for the ministry of Jesus. When he was about twenty-eight years old, he was acclaimed by an ascetic evangelist, John the Baptist, as one "mightier than I, whose shoes I am not worthy to bear." [1] Thenceforth for about three years the career of Jesus, according to the New Testament accounts, was a continuous course of preaching and teaching and of healing the sick, "casting out devils," restoring sight to the blind, and raising the dead. He not only denounced shame, greed, and licentious living but set the example himself by a life of humility and self-denial. Though the conception he held of himself is somewhat obscure, he apparently believed· that he had a mission to oppose Roman rule and to save mankind from error and sin. His preaching and other activities eventually aroused the antagonism of some of the chief priests and conservative rabbis. They disliked his caustic references to the legalism of the Pharisees, his contempt for form and ceremony, and his scorn for pomp and luxury. They feared also that his active leadership would cause trouble with the Romans. Accordingly, they brought him into the highest court in Jerusalem, where he was solemnly condemned for blasphemy and for setting himself up as "King of the Jews" and turned over to Pontius Pilate, the Roman governor, for execution of the sentence. After hours of agony he died on the cross between two thieves on the hill of Golgotha outside Jerusalem.

The crucifixion of Jesus marked a great climax in Christian history. At first his death was viewed by his followers as the end of their hopes. Their despair soon vanished, however, for rumors began to spread that the Master was alive, and that he had been seen

The crucifixion

[1] Matthew 3:11.

Nazareth. A modern view of the small town in Judea where Jesus spent his early life, where he worked for a time as a carpenter and began his career of preaching.

by certain of his faithful disciples. The remainder of his followers were quickly convinced that he had risen from the dead, and that he was truly a divine being. With their courage restored, they organized their little band and began preaching and testifying in the name of their martyred leader. Thus another of the world's great religions was launched on a career that would ultimately shake the foundations of no less an empire than mighty Rome.

There has never been perfect agreement among Christians as to the precise teachings of Jesus of Nazareth. The only dependable records are the four Gospels, but the oldest of these was not written until at least a generation after Jesus' death. According to the beliefs of his orthodox followers, the founder of Christianity revealed himself as the Christ, the divine Son of God, who was sent on this earth to suffer and die for the sins of mankind. They were convinced that after three days in the tomb, he had risen from the dead and ascended into heaven, whence he would come again to judge the world. The Gospels at least make it clear that he included the following among his basic teachings: (1) the fatherhood of God and the brotherhood of man; (2) the Golden Rule; (3) forgiveness and love of one's enemies; (4) repayment of evil with good; (5) self-denial; (6) condemnation of hypocrisy and greed; (7) opposition to ceremonialism as the essence of religion; (8) the imminent approach of the end of the world; and (9) the resurrection of the dead and the establishment of the kingdom of Heaven.

Christianity was broadened and invested with a more elaborate theology by some of the successors of Jesus. Chief among them was the Apostle Paul, originally known as Saul of Tarsus. Although of Jewish nationality, Paul was not a native of Palestine but a Jew of the Diaspora,[2] born in the city of Tarsus in southeastern Asia Minor. Here he came into contact with the Stoic philosophy, but he was possibly more deeply influenced by Gnosticism. Eventually converted to Christianity, he devoted his limitless energy to propagating that faith throughout the Near East. It would be almost impossible to overestimate the significance of his work. Denying that Jesus was sent merely as the redeemer of the Jews, he proclaimed Christianity to be a universal religion. But this was not all. He gave major emphasis to the idea of Jesus as the Christ, as the God-man who existed from the foundation of the world and whose death on the cross was an atonement for the sins of mankind. Not only did he reject the works of the Law (i.e., Jewish ritualism) as of primary importance in religion, but he declared them to be utterly worthless in procuring salvation. Man is a sinner by nature, and he can therefore be saved only by faith and by the grace of God "through the redemption that is in Christ Jesus." It follows, according to Paul, that man's fate in the life to come is almost entirely de-

The teachings of Jesus

The influence of Paul

[2] See pp. 78–79

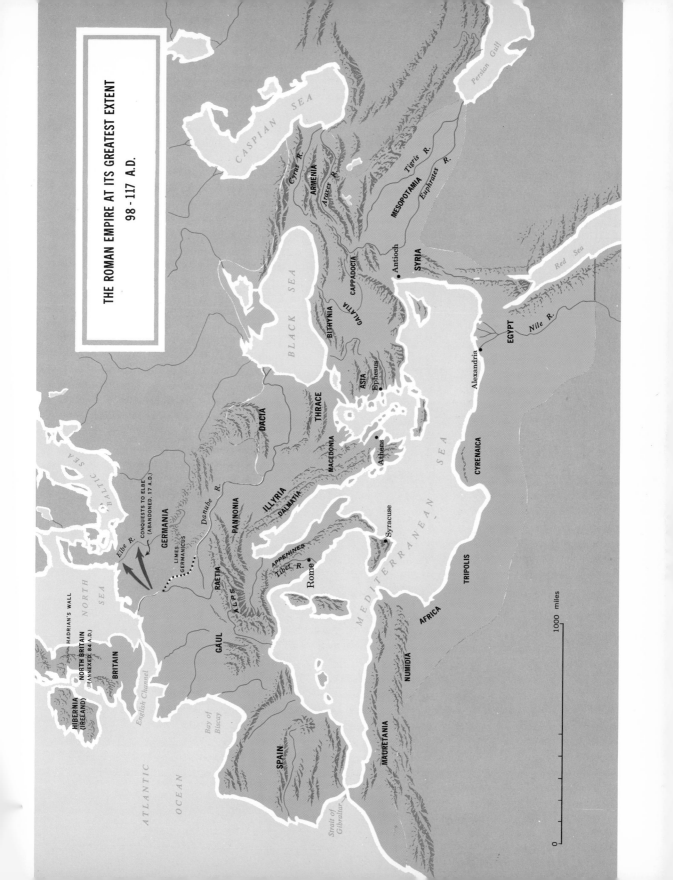

THE ROMAN EMPIRE AT ITS GREATEST EXTENT
98 - 117 A.D.

CASPIAN SEA

Cyrus R.

ARMENIA

Araxes R.

Tigris R.

Euphrates R.

MESOPOTAMIA

CAPPADOCIA

Antioch

SYRIA

BITHYNIA

GALATIA

Red Sea

EGYPT

Nile R.

ASIA

Ephesus

BLACK SEA

Alexandria

DACIA

THRACE

MACEDONIA

Athens

CYRENAICA

ILLYRIA

DALMATIA

PANNONIA

MEDITERRANEAN SEA

Danube R.

GERMANIA

CONQUESTS TO ELBE
(ABANDONED, 17 A.D.)

Elbe R.

LIMES
GERMANICUS

RAETIA

ALPS

APPENINES

Syracuse

Tiber R.

Rome

TRIPOLIS

BALTIC SEA

NORTH SEA

HADRIAN'S WALL

NORTH BRITAIN
(ANNEXED, 84 A.D.)

BRITAIN

HIBERNIA
(IRELAND)

English Channel

GAUL

AFRICA

NUMIDIA

MAURETANIA

ATLANTIC OCEAN

Bay of Biscay

SPAIN

Strait of Gibraltar

Persian Gulf

1000 miles

0

Gold Cup, Byzantine, VI–IX cent. The figure is a personification of Constantinople, a queen or goddess holding the scepter and orb of imperial rule. (MMA)

Saint John Writing His Gospel. From an Anglo-Frankish illuminated manuscript, *ca.* 850, produced in a Carolingian monastery. The unknown artist knew nothing of perspective, but excelled in coloring and conveying a sense of vitality and energy. (Morgan Library)

Enthroned Madonna and Child, Byzantine School, XIII cent. The painters of Siena followed the opulent and brilliant style of Byzantine art. Their madonnas were not earthly mothers, but celestial queens reigning in dignified splendor. (National Gallery)

Merovingian Fibula or Brooch, VII cent. A fabulous gold-plated animal set with garnets and colored paste reveals the lively imagination of the early Middle Ages. (MMA)

pendent upon the will of God; for "Hath not the potter power over the clay, of the same lump to make one vessel unto honour, and another unto dishonour?" [3] He has mercy "on whom he will have mercy, and whom he will he hardeneth." [4]

By the beginning of the Middle Ages the triumph of Christianity over its rivals was almost complete. The Emperor Galerius' edict of toleration in 311 was already an admission that the religion was too strong to be stamped out by persecution. By a series of decrees between 380 and 392 Christianity was recognized as the only lawful faith of the Roman Empire. How is this triumph to be explained? Perhaps as much as anything else it was a result of the composite character of Christianity. Here was a religion which ultimately came to embody elements from a wide variety of sources. A large number of them were taken from Judaism: the name of the deity, the cosmogony, the world history, the Ten Commandments, and such doctrines as original sin and the providence of God. In addition, several of the ethical doctrines were really of Jewish origin. Although many of these elements were modified by Jesus and his followers, there can be no doubt that the Hebrew contributions to Christianity were of great importance.

But obviously Christianity derived much from other than Jewish sources. Some idea of the debt it owed to religions of Persian origin has been indicated in a preceding chapter.[5] Zoroastrianism had already made the ancient world familiar with such concepts as otherworldliness and an eternal conflict between good and evil. Suggested also was the belief in secret revelation and the notion of a primal man or God-man becoming incarnate in human form. Supplementing these influences was that of the philosophy of Stoicism, which had familiarized the educated classes with ideals of cosmopolitanism and the brotherhood of man. In short, mystery religions and Hellenistic philosophy had already brought into existence a large deposit of doctrines and practices upon which Christianity could draw, at the same time preserving its distinctive character. The early Church was an organism that fed upon the whole pagan world, selecting and incorporating a wide variety of ideas and practices which were not inconsistent with its own nature. The appeal of Christianity was therefore more nearly universal than that of any other of the ancient religions.

The other main reasons for the triumph of Christianity can be summarized briefly. It admitted women to full rights of participation in worship, whereas Mithraism, the strongest of its early competitors, excluded them. It enjoyed the advantage for about fifty years of systematic persecution by the Roman government, a factor which enormously strengthened the cohesiveness of the

Reasons for the triumph of Christianity

A Carved Tablet, ca. 400 A.D., Depicting Christ's Tomb and Ascension into Heaven

Other reasons for the Christian triumph

[3] Romans 9:21.
[4] Romans 9:18.
[5] See pp. 69–74

movement, since those who remained in the faith had to be ready to die for their convictions. While most of the other religions revolved around imaginary figures, the creatures of grotesque legends, Christianity possessed as its founder a historic individual of clearly defined personality. Lastly, the triumph of Christianity is partly explained by the fact that it made a stronger appeal to the poor and oppressed than did any of the other mystery religions. Although it included the ideal of the equality of all men in the sight of God, its founder and some of his followers had condemned the rich and exalted the lowly. It propagated a new and exceedingly democratic morality, with meekness, self-effacement, and love of one's enemies as primary virtues. Perhaps these were the qualities most likely to find ready acceptance among the helpless masses who had long since abandoned hope of bettering their material condition.

The division of Christians into rival sects: Arians, Athanasians, and Nestorians

Hardly had Christianity emerged victorious over its rivals than disaffection developed within its own ranks. This was due partly to the heterogeneous elements out of which the religion had been formed, and partly also to the compromising attitudes displayed by the leaders as the success of the movement increased. A more fundamental reason seems to have been the conflict between the intellectual and emotional tendencies within the religion. Representing the former were the Arians and the Nestorians. Both of these sects agreed in their refusal to accept what has since become the orthodox doctrine of the Trinity. Under the influence of Greek philosophy they rejected the idea that the Christ could be the equal of God. The Arians maintained that the Son was created by the Father and therefore was not co-eternal with him or formed of the same substance. Their chief opponents were the Athanasians, who held that Father, Son, and Holy Ghost were all absolutely equal and composed of identical substance. The Nestorians broke away from the rest of the Church with the contention that Mary should be called the mother of Christ but not the mother of God, implying of course that they considered the Christ something less than divine.

Gnostics and Manicheans

The most important of the sects that emphasized the emotional character of Christianity were the Gnostics and the Manicheans. Both were extreme ascetics and mystics. Believing that genuine religious truth was a product of revelation exclusively, they were inclined to be strongly suspicious of any attempt to rationalize the Christian faith. They were opposed also to the tendency toward worldliness which was making itself evident among many of the clergy. The Gnostics and the Manicheans were not originally sects of Christianity at all, but eventually many of them went over to that faith. Those who became Christians retained their old doctrines of exaggerated spiritualism and contempt for matter as evil. Naturally, along with these went an abiding distrust of every variety of human knowledge. The doctrines of all these sects, with the exception of the Athanasian, were eventually condemned by Church councils as heresies.

Notwithstanding the condemnation of many beliefs as heresies, the body of Christian doctrine was never very firmly fixed during the early Middle Ages. Of course, all Christians believed in a God who was the creator and governor of the universe, in salvation from sin, and in rewards and punishments after death. But as regards many other questions of dogma there was confusion and uncertainty. Even the concept of the Trinity continued to be an issue of debate for several centuries. Many of the Eastern Christians never accepted the extreme Athanasian view of the relation of the Father and the Son adopted by the Council of Nicaea (325). Further, there was no clearly formulated theory at this time of the number and the precise nature of the sacraments, nor was the doctrine of the powers of the priesthood definitely established. The theory of the Mass was not formally defined until 1215. In general, there were two main points of disagreement affecting all of these issues. Some very devout believers clung to an ideal of Christianity similar to that of the Apostolic age, when the Church was a community of mystics, each of them guided by the Inner Light in matters of faith and conduct. Others envisaged the Christian Church as an organized society prescribing its own rules for the government of its members in accordance with the practical requirements of the time.

The growth of Christian organization was one of the outstanding developments of the whole medieval era. Even during the first few centuries of that period the Church and its related institutions evolved into an elaborate structure which ultimately became the principal framework of society itself. As the Roman Empire in the West decayed, the Church took over many of its functions and helped to preserve order amid the deepening chaos. That anything at all was saved out of the wreckage was due in large part to the stabilizing influence of the organized Church. It aided in civilizing the barbarians, in promoting ideals of social justice, and in preserving and transmitting the antique learning.

The organization of the Church was at first quite simple. The early Christian congregations met in the homes of their members and listened to the spiritual testimony of various of the brethren who were believed to have been in direct communication with the Holy Ghost. No distinction between laymen and clergy was recognized. Each independent church had a number of officers, generally known as bishops and elders, whose functions were to preside at the services, discipline members, and dispense charity. Gradually, under the influence of the pagan mystery religions, the ritual of Christianity increased to such a stage of complexity that a professional priesthood seemed to become necessary. The need for defense against persecution and the desire to attain uniformity of belief also favored the development of ecclesiastical organization. The consequence was that about the beginning of the second century one bishop in each important city came to be recognized as supreme over all the clergy in that vicinity. The sphere of his jurisdiction corresponded

The persistence of doctrinal disputes

The importance of Christian organization

The evolution of Church organization

227

A Fourth Century A.D. Sarcophagus Depicting Stories and Lessons from the Bible

to the *civitas*, the smallest administrative unit of the Roman state. As the number of congregations multiplied, and as the influence of the Church increased due to the adoption of Christianity as the official religion of Rome, distinctions of rank among the bishops themselves began to appear. Those who had their headquarters in the larger cities came to be called metropolitans, with authority over the clergy of an entire province. In the fourth century the still higher dignity of patriarch was established to designate those bishops who ruled over the oldest and largest of Christian communities—such cities as Rome, Constantinople, Antioch, and Alexandria, with their surrounding districts. Thus the Christian clergy by 400 A.D. had come to embrace a definite hierarchy of patriarchs, metropolitans, bishops, and priests.

The rise of the papacy

The climax of all this development was the growth of the primacy of the bishop of Rome, or in other words the rise of the papacy. For several reasons the bishop of Rome enjoyed a preeminence over the other patriarchs of the Church. The city in which he ruled was venerated by the faithful as a scene of the missionary activities of the Apostles Peter and Paul. The tradition was widely accepted that Peter had founded the bishopric of Rome, and that therefore all of his successors were heirs of his authority and prestige. This tradition was supplemented by the theory that Peter had been commissioned by the Christ as his vicar on earth and had been given the keys of the Kingdom of Heaven with power to punish men for their sins and even to absolve them from guilt.[6] This theory, known as the doctrine of the Petrine Succession, has been used by Popes ever since as a basis for their claims to authority over the

228   [6] See Matthew 16:18–19.

Church. The bishops of Rome had an advantage also in the fact that after the transfer of the imperial capital to Constantinople there was seldom any emperor with effective sovereignty in the West. Finally, in 455 the Emperor Valentinian III issued a decree commanding all Western bishops to submit to the jurisdiction of the Pope. It must not be supposed, however, that the Church was yet under a monarchical form of government. The patriarchs in the East regarded the extreme assertions of the papal claims as a brazen effrontery, and even many bishops in the West continued to ignore them for some time.

The organization of the Church was by no means confined to an ecclesiastical hierarchy. In any study of Christian institutions a prominent place must be given to monasticism. Since monasticism was originally an outgrowth of asceticism, it becomes necessary, first of all, to examine the relationship between that ideal and the Christian religion. Original Christianity was only mildly ascetic. Neither Jesus nor his immediate followers practiced any extremes of self-torture. To be sure, Jesus did not marry; he declared that he had no place to lay his head; and he was supposed to have fasted for forty days in the wilderness; but these examples could scarcely have encouraged the pathological excesses of mortification of the flesh indulged in by the hermits of the third and fourth centuries. We must therefore look for additional causes of the growth of this later asceticism. Perhaps the following may be considered fundamental:

Reasons for the
popularity of
asceticism

(1) The choice of morbid self-torture as a substitute for martyrdom. With the abandonment of persecution by the Romans all chances of winning a crown of glory in heaven by undergoing death for the faith were eliminated. But the desire to give evidence of one's religious ardor by self-abasement and suffering was still present and demanded an outlet.

(2) The desire of some Christians who were sincerely devoted to the faith to set an example of exalted piety and unselfishness as an inspiration to their weaker brethren. Even though most men should fail to attain the ideal, the general level of morality and piety would be raised.

(3) The influence of other Near Eastern religions, especially Gnosticism and Manicheism, with their exaggerated spiritualism, contempt for this world, and degradation of the body.

The earliest Christian ascetics were hermits, who withdrew from the world to live in seclusion in some wilderness or desert. This form of asceticism seems to have originated in Egypt in the third century. From there it spread into other provinces of the eastern section of the Empire and continued to be popular for more than 100 years. It developed into a kind of religious mania characterized by morbid excesses. We read of hermits or anchorites grazing in the fields after the manner of animals, rolling naked in thorn bushes, or living in swamps infested with snakes. The famous St. Simeon

The asceticism of
Christian hermits

Stylites passed a whole summer "as a rooted vegetable in a garden" and then began the construction of his celebrated pillar. He built it to a height of sixty feet and spent the remaining thirty years of his life on the top. Such absurdities as these, while certainly not typical of the attitude of the majority of Christians at this time, were probably the natural fruit of too strong an emphasis upon the spiritual way of life.

The rise of monasticism

In time the force of the anchorite hysteria subsided. Certain of the more practical Christian ascetics came to the conclusion that the solitary life of the hermit was not good for the soul, since it sometimes drove men insane. The result of this conclusion was the origin of monasticism. The most prominent early leader of monasticism was St. Basil, a bishop of Cappadocia, who was the first to issue a set of rules for the government of a monastic order. Disapproving of extreme self-torture, St. Basil required his monks to discipline themselves by useful labor. They were not to engage in prolonged fasting or in degrading laceration of the flesh, but they were compelled to submit to obligations of poverty and humility and to spend many hours of the day in silent religious meditation. The Basilian type of monasticism came to be adopted universally in the eastern areas of Christendom. Many of its units are still to be seen perched on lofty crags to which access can be gained only by climbing long rope ladders or being hauled up in a basket. There was no important monasticism in the West until the sixth century, when St. Benedict drafted his famous rule which ultimately became the guide for nearly all the monks of Latin Christendom. The Benedictine rule imposed obligations similar to those of the rule of St. Basil— poverty, obedience, labor, and religious devotion. Yet there was an

A Monastery of the Basilian Order on Mt. Athos. The asceticism of the Basilian monks caused them to build their monasteries in almost inaccessible places on lofty crags or on the steep sides of rugged mountains.

absence of severe austerities. The monks were allowed a sufficiency of simple food, good clothing, and enough sleep. They were permitted to have wine but no meat. They were allowed no recreation and few baths, unless they were sick. They were subject to the absolute authority of the abbot, who could flog them for disobedience. The original Benedictine monastery was established at Monte Cassino, halfway between Rome and Naples. Eventually it came to possess one of the finest libraries in medieval Europe. It was destroyed by Allied bombing during World War II, but has since been rebuilt.

The influence of monasticism upon the society of the early Middle Ages would be difficult to exaggerate. The monks were generally the best farmers in Europe; they reclaimed waste lands, drained swamps, and made numerous discoveries relating to the improvement of the soil. They preserved some of the building skill of the Romans and achieved noteworthy progress in many of the industrial arts, especially in wood carving, metal-working, weaving, glass-making, and brewing. It was monks, furthermore, who wrote most of the books, copied the ancient manuscripts, and maintained the majority of the schools and libraries and nearly all of the hospitals that existed during the early Middle Ages. The growth of monasticism also profoundly affected the history of the Church. It led to a division in the ranks of the clergy. Living according to a definite rule or *regula*, the monks came to be called the *regular* clergy; while the priests, bishops, and archbishops, who carried on their activities in the midst of the affairs of the world (*saeculum*), were henceforth known as the *secular* clergy. Between the two groups intense rivalry developed, with the monks sometimes organizing reform movements against the worldliness of the priests. The Benedictine monks enjoyed the special favor of the Popes, and it was partly on account of an alliance between the papacy and monasticism that the former was able to extend its power over the Church.

The results of monasticism

2. THE GERMANIC FOUNDATIONS OF THE NEW CULTURE

The second most important of the factors which combined to produce the civilization of early medieval Europe was the influence of the Germanic barbarians. They were not the only northern peoples who helped to mold the pattern of early medieval society; the contributions of the Celts in Brittany and Ireland and of the Slavs in central and eastern Europe were by no means insignificant. Nevertheless, the Germanic influence appears to have been the most extensive. Where the Germans came from originally is a problem upon which scholars disagree, but they seem to have migrated into northern Europe from western Asia. By the beginning of the Christian

The ancient Germans

era they had come to be divided into several peoples: Scandinavians, Vandals, Goths, Franks, Burgundians, Anglo-Saxons, Dutch, and so on. Both in language and in physical characteristics they bore some affinity to the Greeks and the Romans.

For centuries different nations of Germanic barbarians had been making incursions into Roman territory. At times they came as invading armies, but generally they filtered in slowly, bringing their families and belongings with them and occupying depopulated or abandoned areas. Many were brought in by Roman commanders and rulers. Julius Caesar was impressed by their value as warriors and enrolled thousands of them in his armies. They were to be found in the bodyguard of nearly every Princeps and Emperor. Finally, by the time of Constantine, they formed the bulk of the soldiers in the entire Roman army. Many were also drawn into the civil service and thousands were settled by the government as *coloni* or serfs on the great estates. In view of these conditions it is not surprising that Rome should eventually have been taken over by the Germans. As more and more of them gained a foothold in Italy, others were bound to be tempted by the opportunities for plunder. It must be emphasized that many of the supposed invasions were mere "folk wanderings," and not necessarily motivated by a desire for conquest. Although armed invasions of Italy began as early as the second century B.C., and were repeated several times thereafter, there were no really disastrous incursions until the fourth and fifth centuries A.D. In 378 the Visigoths, angered by the oppression of imperial governors, raised the standard of revolt. They overwhelmed a Roman army at Adrianople and then marched westward into Italy. In 410 under Alaric they captured and plundered Rome, later moving on into southern Gaul. In 455 Rome was sacked by the Vandals, who had migrated from their original home between the Oder and Vistula rivers and established a kingdom in the province of Carthage. Other Germanic peoples also made their way into Italy, and before the end of the fifth century the Roman Empire in the West had passed completely under the domination of the barbarians.

For our knowledge of ancient Germanic society we are dependent primarily upon the *Germania* of Tacitus, written in 98 A.D. The literature and the laws of the Germans themselves also contain much information, but these were not put into written form until after Roman and Christian influences had begun to exert their effect. When Tacitus wrote, the Germanic barbarians had attained a cultural level about equal to that of the early Greeks. They were illiterate and ignorant of any knowledge of the arts. Their houses were built of rough timber plastered over with mud. While they had achieved some development of agriculture, they preferred the risks of plundering expeditions to the prosaic labor of tilling the soil. Nearly all of the work was done by the women and old men and other dependents. When not fighting or hunting, the warriors spent most of their time sleeping and carousing. Gambling and drunken-

CHRISTIANITY IN 500 A.D. AND THE BARBARIAN INVASIONS

ness were glaring vices, but, if we can believe the testimony of Tacitus, sex morality was singularly pure. Monogamous marriage prevailed, except in those cases where a chief might be permitted to take more than one wife for political reasons. Adultery was rare and was severely punished; divorce was almost unknown. In some tribes even widows were forbidden to remarry.

The economic and political institutions of the Germans were such as befitted a people who were just emerging into a settled existence. The tiny proportion of trade carried on rested solely upon a basis of barter, while cattle were still the main article of wealth. Whether the agricultural land was individually or collectively owned is still a debated question, but there seems little doubt that the forests and pastures were held and used in common. Possibly the community controlled the distribution of new lands as they were acquired, allotting the arable portions as individual farms. There is evidence

Economic and political institutions

233

that a class of wealthy proprietors had grown up as an aristocracy in certain of the tribes. Although Tacitus states that the Germans had slaves, it seems probable that most of their dependents were serfs, since they had houses of their own and paid their masters only a portion of what they produced. Their servitude in some cases was a result of capture in war but in others of indebtedness and especially reckless gambling, in which men staked their own liberty when everything else had been lost. The state scarcely existed at all. Law was a product of custom, and the administration of justice remained largely in private hands. While the Germans had their tribal courts, the function of these bodies was chiefly to mediate between plaintiff and defendant. Judicial procedure consisted mainly of oaths and ordeals, both of which were considered as appeals to the judgment of the gods. The most important of the remaining political institutions was the primary assembly of the warriors. But this body had no lawmaking powers beyond those involved in the interpretation of custom. Its main function was to decide questions of war and peace and whether the tribe should migrate to some new locality. Originally the German tribes had no kings. They had chiefs elected by the freemen, but these were little more than ceremonial officials. In time of war a military leader was elected and endowed with considerable power, but as soon as the campaign was over his authority lapsed. Nevertheless, as wars increased in frequency and duration, some of the military leaders actually became kings. The formality of election, however, was generally retained.

The Germanic influence

The influence of the Germans upon the Middle Ages, while not so important as is sometimes imagined, was extensive enough to deserve consideration. Above all, they were largely responsible for several of the elements of feudalism: (1) the conception of law as an outgrowth of custom and not as the expression of the will of a sovereign; (2) the idea of law as a personal possession of the individual which he could take with him wherever he went, in contrast to the Roman conception of law as limited to a definite territory; (3) the notion of a contractual relationship between rulers and subjects, involving reciprocal obligations of protection and obedience; (4) the theory of an honorable relationship between lord and vassal, growing out of the Germanic institution of the *comitatus* or military band, in which the warriors were bound by pledges of honor and loyalty to fight for and serve their leader; (5) trial by ordeal as a prevailing mode of procedure in the feudal courts; and (6) the idea of elective kingship.

3. POLITICAL AND ECONOMIC DEVELOPMENTS IN THE EARLY MIDDLE AGES

Between 500 and 700 A.D. most of western Europe languished in a kind of backward age. The barbarian kings who usurped the authority of the Roman Emperors proved themselves wholly incapable of maintaining the administrative organization that passed into their hands. They appeared to have no conception of efficient government for the public welfare and regarded their kingdoms as private estates to be exploited for their own benefit. They allowed the Roman tax system to break down and delegated much of their political authority to the nobility and the Church. Although many of the old Roman towns survived, they declined in importance, and the ancient urban culture largely disappeared. The characteristic institutions were now the monastery, the peasant village, and the great villa or semifeudal estate cultivated by tenant farmers. No longer was the economy international as it had been in the heyday of Rome. Except for the exchange of a few luxury items, it sank rapidly into localism or rural self-sufficiency.

The only barbarian ruler who did anything in Italy to check the progress of deterioration was Theodoric the Ostrogoth, who conquered the peninsula in 493. Until nearly the end of his reign of thirty-three years, he gave Italy a more enlightened rule than it had known under many of the Caesars. He fostered agriculture and commerce, repaired public buildings and roads, patronized learning, and enforced religious toleration. But in his last years he became querulous and suspicious, accusing some of his faithful subordinates of plotting with the Roman aristocracy to overthrow him. Several were put to death, including the philosopher Boethius. After the death of Theodoric decay set in once more, hastened this time by new wars of conquest. When Justinian became Emperor at Constantinople in 527 he determined to reconquer Italy and the provinces in the West. Not until 552 was the project completed. The devastation of the long war was so great that Italy was opened for invasion by the Lombards in 568. The Lombards succeeded in holding most of the peninsula under the rule of semi-independent dukes until the conquest of Charlemagne in the late eighth century.

Deterioration continued apace in Spain. The Spanish Church was corrupt, and the barbarian (Visigothic) kings were ignorant and predatory. By allowing their power to slip into the hands of an oppressive nobility they made their country an easy prey for Moslem conquest in the eighth century. Deterioration was also evident in France. In 481 a youth by the name of Clovis became king of an important tribe of the Salian Franks, who dwelt on the left bank of the Rhine. The Merovingian dynasty,[7] which he founded, occupied the throne of the Frankish state until 751. Eventually, however, the royal line began to degenerate. A series of short-lived weaklings, the so-called do-nothing kings, inherited the crown of their lusty forebears. Absorbed in the pursuit of pleasure, these worthless youths delegated most of their authority to their chief subordinates, the mayors of the palace. Nothing more natural could have happened

POLITICAL AND ECONOMIC DEVELOPMENT

Decline in western Europe

Theodoric in Italy

Spain and France

---

[7] So called from Merovech, the half-mythical founder of the family to which Clovis belonged.

Charlemagne, Painting by
Dürer

than the eventual displacement of the Merovingian kings by these very officials to whom they had entrusted their powers. The most capable and aggressive of the mayors of the palace was Charles Martel ("the Hammer"), who may be considered a second founder of the Frankish state. He won fame in 733 by defeating the Moors at Poitiers, a town a little more than 100 miles from Paris. Although his opponents were merely a marauding band, the Battle of Poitiers is nevertheless important as the high-water mark of Moorish invasion of France. Yet, even after his victory, Charles was content with the substance of power and did not bother to assume the royal title. It was left for his son, Pepin the Short, to have himself elected king of the Franks in 751 and thereby to put an end to Merovingian rule. the new dynasty became known as the Carolingian from the name of its most famous member, Carolus Magnus or Charlemagne (742–814).

In the minds of most students of history Charlemagne stands out as one of the two or three most important individuals in the whole medieval period. By some of his contemporaries he was acclaimed as a new Augustus who would bring peace and prosperity to western Europe. There can be no question that he established more efficient government, and that he did much to combat the centrifugal tendencies which had gathered momentum during the reigns of the later Merovingians. Not only did he abolish the office of mayor of the palace, but he eliminated the tribal dukes and bestowed all the powers of local government upon his own appointees, the counts. He modified the old system of private administration of justice by authorizing the counts to summon accused persons to court and by vesting the magistrates with more control over judicial procedure. He revived the Roman institution of the sworn inquest, in which a number of persons were summoned by agents of the king and bound by oath to tell what they knew of any crimes committed in their locality. This institution survived the downfall of the Carolingian state and was carried by the Normans to England, where it eventually became an important factor in the origin of the grand-jury system. Although much of the remainder of the political structure Charlemagne established perished with the end of his dynasty, the precedent that he set for strong government undoubtedly influenced many of the French kings in the later Middle Ages and the German emperors as well. There was scarcely a people of western Europe against whom he did not fight, except the English. Since most of his campaigns were successful, he annexed to the Frankish domain the greater part of central Europe and northern and central Italy. But some of these conquests were made possible only by a fearful sacrifice of blood and a resort to measures of the harshest cruelty. The campaign against the Saxons met with such stubborn opposition that Charlemagne finally ordered the beheading of 4500 of them. It is typical of the spirit of the times that all of this was done under the pretext of inducing the pagans to adopt Christianity.

THE EMPIRE OF CHARLEMAGNE • 814 A.D.

In fact, it was Charlemagne's constant intervention in religious affairs which led to the climax of his whole career—his coronation as Roman Emperor by Pope Leo III. Leo had been in trouble for some time. Accused of being a tyrant and a rake, he so aroused the indignation of the people of Rome that in 799 they gave him a severe beating and forced him to flee from the city. Struggling over the mountains to Germany, he implored the aid of Charlemagne. The great king sent him back to Italy and was instrumental in restoring him to the papal throne. On Christmas Day, 800, as Charles knelt in prayer in St. Peter's Church, the grateful Pope placed a crown on his head while the assembled multitude hailed him as "Augustus, crowned of God, great and pacific Emperor of the Romans." The significance of this event is rather hard to appraise. It seems doubtful that Charles was under any illusions as to the nature of the act. For all practical purposes it was merely the recognition of an accomplished fact. By his conquests Charles had made himself ruler of nearly all of western and central Europe. In 794 he established a permanent capital at Aachen that was called "New Rome." He never acknowledged any sovereignty of the Pope over him. In his view ecclesiastical affairs were as much a part of his domain as

Charlemagne becomes emperor

237

Charlemagne Weeping for His Knights. A panel commissioned by Frederick Barbarosa for the shrine of Charlemagne at Aachen.

were secular matters. Though he did not attempt to prescribe Church doctrine, he displayed an interest in maintaining uniformity of both discipline and theology. He summoned a number of Church synods during his reign and presided over one of them. In the eyes of the Pope the coronation had a quite different significance. He regarded all kings as his stewards exercising their authority for the benefit of the Church. True, Charles was now an emperor, but it was the Pope who had given him this dignity; and what the Pope could grant he could also take away. This conflict of views foreshadowed the great struggle of the eleventh, twelfth, and thirteenth centuries—a struggle over who should be supreme in western Europe, the Emperor or the Pope.

At the beginning of the early Middle Ages a large part of what is now England was still under Roman rule. But in the fifth century the Romans were forced to withdraw on account of increasing trouble with Germanic invasions into Italy. Soon afterward England was overrun by hordes of Saxons, Angles, and Jutes from the Continent. They brought with them the customs and institutions of their homeland, which were similar to those of the other Germanic barbarians. Driving the original Celtic natives into the mountains of Wales and Cornwall, they quickly established their own kingdoms. At one time there were seven, mutually suspicious and hostile. In the ninth century tribes of Danes took advantage of the strife among the Saxon kingdoms and attempted their conquest. Efforts to defeat the new enemy brought the seven kingdoms into a strong confederation under the leadership of Wessex and its celebrated ruler, Alfred the Great (849–899). King Alfred reorganized the army, infused new vigor into local government, and revised and broadened the laws. In addition, he founded schools and fostered an interest in literature and other elements of a national culture.

King Alfred's successors were men of weaker fiber. One of them, Ethelred the Unready, surrendered his kingdom to the powerful Danish King Canute. For eighteen years England was ruled as part of a North Sea empire which also included Norway and Denmark. But in 1035 Canute died, and the Saxon dynasty regained control of England. It was not for long. Ethelred's son, Edward the Confessor, was more interested in cultivating a reputation for piety than he was in statecraft, and allowed affairs of his country to be regulated by the Duchy of Normandy, across the Channel. Upon Edward's death the Duke of Normandy, subsequently known as William the Conqueror (1027–1087), laid claim to the crown of England. Landing an army in Sussex in 1066, he caught the English monarch, Harold, unprepared and defeated him in the Battle of Hastings. Harold fell mortally wounded, and his forces disintegrated. Apparently regarding discretion as the better part of valor, the surviving magnates offered the crown to Duke William. The Battle of Hastings is considered a turning point in English history, for it ended the period of Anglo-Saxon supremacy and prepared the way for the ultimate establishment of a nation state under William the Norman's successors.

Most of the records of economic life in the early Middle Ages present a mournful picture of return to primitive conditions and, in some cases, actual misery. The decline of Italy in the second half of the fifth century was especially swift. The forces that were set in motion by the economic revolution of the preceding 200 years had now attained their full momentum. Commerce and industry were rapidly becoming extinct, lands that were formerly productive were

Duke William of Normandy Crossing the Channel to Conquer England, from the Bayeux Tapestry. The Bayeux Tapestry depicts, in needlework on linen, 72 scenes of the Norman Conquest. It was probably completed under the direction of Bishop Odo of Bayeux, the Conqueror's half-brother.

growing up in briars and brambles, and the population was declining
so noticeably that a law was enacted forbidding any woman under
forty years of age to enter a convent. While the proprietors of the
great landed estates extended their control over agriculture and over
many of the functions of government as well, larger and larger
numbers of the masses of the people became serfs. During the reign
of Theodoric this process of economic decline was arrested in some
measure as a result of the benefits he extended to agriculture and
commerce and his reduction of taxes. But Theodoric was unable to
eliminate serfdom or to reverse the concentration of landed wealth,
for he felt that he needed the support of the aristocracy. After his
death the forces of decay again became operative; yet had it not
been for Justinian's war of reconquest, Italy might still have preserved a degree of the prosperity she had gained under the Ostrogothic king. The long military conflict brought the country to the
verge of stark barbarism. Pestilence and famine completed the havoc
wrought by the contending armies. Fields were left untilled, and
most of the activities in the towns were suspended. Wolves penetrated into the heart of the country and fattened on the corpses that
remained unburied. So great was the widespread hunger that canni-
balism appeared in some areas. Only in the larger cities were the
normal functions of civilization continued to any appreciable extent.

Economic change in what is now France followed a pattern very
similar to that in Italy, but it proceeded at a slower rate. In Roman
times southern Gaul had had a flourishing commerce and considerable industry. By the end of the ninth century, however, stagnation
was almost complete. The streets of the city of Marseilles were
grown over with grass and weeds, and the port itself was deserted
for over 200 years. In some other Mediterranean towns and in the
interior of the country, trade on a petty scale continued to be carried on, mostly by Jews and Syrians and later by Lombards; but
even the activities of these men became steadily more difficult as
brigandage increased, the roads deteriorated, and money disappeared
from general circulation. The economic history of France was also
characterized by the growth of an irregular feudalism similar to that
which had sprung up in Italy. Several of the causes were closely related to the policies of the Merovingian and Carolingian kings.
Nearly all of these rulers compensated their officials by grants of
land. Both Pepin the Short and Charlemagne adhered to the example
of Charles Martel in expropriating lands of the Church and turning
them over to their chief followers as rewards for military services.
More serious was the practice of granting *immunities*, or exemptions
from the jurisdiction of the king's agents. Their legal effect was to
make the holder subject to the exclusive jurisdiction of the king; but
as the king was far away and generally preoccupied with other matters, the nobles took advantage of the opportunity to increase their
own independence. Wars, brigandage, and oppression also contributed to the growth of a largely feudal structure of society by forcing

Economic
conditions
in France;
the foundations
of feudalism

the weaker citizens to seek the protection of their more powerful neighbors. The result was a tendency toward a division of the population into two distinct classes: a landed aristocracy and serfs.

4. INTELLECTUAL ATTAINMENTS OF THE EARLY MIDDLE AGES

Generally speaking, the intellectual culture of early medieval Europe was not of a high order. Superstition and credulity frequently characterized the work even of many of the outstanding writers. A fondness for compilation rather than for original achievement was also a distinguishing feature of much of the intellectual endeavor. Few men any longer had much interest in philosophy or science, except insofar as these subjects could be made to serve religious purposes. Such an attitude often led to mystical interpretations of knowledge and to the acceptance of fables as fact when they appeared to be freighted with symbolical significance for the sphere of religion. In spite of all this, the mind of the times was not hopelessly submerged in darkness. The light of antique learning was never entirely extinguished; even some of the most pious of Church Fathers recognized the value of classical literature. Moreover, there were a few men in the period who, if not creative geniuses, at least had abilities of scholarship which would not have been rated inferior in the best days of Greece.

Nearly all of the philosophers of the early Middle Ages may be classified as either Christians or pagans, although a few seem to have been nominal adherents of the Church who wrote in the spirit of pagan thought. The Christian philosophers tended to divide into two different schools: (1) those who emphasized the primacy of authority; and (2) those who believed that the doctrines of the faith should be illumined by the light of reason and brought into harmony with the finest products of pagan thinking. The authoritarian tradition in Christian philosophy stemmed originally from Tertullian, a priest of Carthage who lived about the beginning of the third century. For him, Christianity was a system of sacred law to be accepted entirely upon faith. The wisdom of men was mere foolishness with God, and the more a tenet of the faith contradicted reason the greater was the merit in accepting it. Even today theologians can be found who insist upon this absolute supremacy of authority over intellect, of faith over the powers of reason.

While few of the Christian Fathers went as far as Tertullian in despising intellectual effort, there were several who adhered to his general principle that the dogmas of the faith were not to be tested by reason. The most influential was Pope Gregory I (540–604), known in Church history as Gregory the Great. The scion of a rich senatorial family, Gregory scorned the seductions of wealth and power in order that he might dedicate his life to the Church. He turned his father's palace into a convent and gave all of the remainder of the wealth he had inherited to the poor. In his work as a theologian he laid great stress upon the idea of penance as essential to the remission of sins and strengthened the notion of purgatory as a place where even the righteous must suffer for minor offenses in order to be purified for admission to heaven.

The most eminent of the Christian philosophers who may be described as representatives of a rationalist tradition were Clement of Alexandria and Origen. Both lived in the third century and were deeply influenced by Neo-Platonism and Gnosticism. Far from despising all human knowledge, they taught that the best of the Greek thinkers had really anticipated the teachings of Jesus, and that Christianity is improved by being brought into harmony with pagan learning. While Clement and Origen would not qualify as rationalists in the modern sense, inasmuch as they took a great many of their beliefs on faith, they nevertheless recognized the importance of reason as a fundamental basis of knowledge, whether religious or secular. They denied the omnipotence of God and taught that God's power is limited by His goodness and wisdom. They rejected the fatalism of many of their opponents and insisted that man by his own free will molds his course of action while on earth. Both Clement and Origen condemned the extreme asceticism of some of their more zealous brethren; in particular, they deplored the tendency of such men as Tertullian to speak of marriage as simply a legalized form of carnality. Finally, they maintained that the purpose of all future punishment is purification and not revenge. Consequently, punishment in hell cannot be eternal, for even the blackest of sinners must eventually be redeemed. If it were not so, God would not be a God of goodness and mercy.

The most erudite and perhaps the most original of all the early Christian philosophers was St. Augustine. Insofar as it is possible to classify him at all, he occupied an intermediate position between Clement and Origen, on the one hand, and Tertullian and Gregory on the other. Though contending that truths of revelation were above natural reason, he perceived the need for an intellectual understanding of what he believed. Born in 354, the son of a pagan father and a Christian mother, Augustine was torn by conflicting impulses throughout the greater part of his life. As a young man he was addicted to sensual pleasures, from which he tried vainly to escape, though he admits in his *Confessions* that his efforts were not wholly sincere. Even after his engagement to marry he could not resist the temptation to take a new mistress. Meanwhile, when he was about eighteen years old, he was attracted to philosophy by reading Cicero's *Hortensius*. He passed from one system of thought to another, unable to find spiritual satisfaction in any. For a brief period he considered the possibilities of Christianity, but it impressed him as too crude and superstitious. Then for nine years he was a Manichean, but ultimately he became convinced that that faith was decadent. Next he was attracted to Neo-Platonism, and then finally returned to Christianity. Though already in his thirty-third year when he was baptized, Augustine advanced rapidly in ecclesiastical positions. In 395 he became Bishop of Hippo in northern Africa, an office he held until his death in 430.

Augustine believed that the supremely important knowledge is knowledge of God and His plan of redemption for mankind. Though most of this knowledge must be derived from the revelation contained in the Scriptures, it is nevertheless the duty of man to understand as much of it as possible in order to strengthen his belief. On the basis of this conclusion St. Augustine developed his conception of human history as the unfoldment of the will of God. Everything that has happened or ever will happen represents but an episode in the fulfillment of the divine plan. The whole race of human beings comprises two great divisions: those whom God has predestined to eternal salvation constitute the City of God; all others belong to the Earthly City. The end of the drama of history will come with the Day of Judgment, when the blessed few who compose the City of God will put on the garment of immortality, while the vast multitude in the earthly kingdom will be cast into the fires of hell. This, according to St. Augustine, is the whole meaning of human existence.

St. Augustine's theology was an integral part of his philosophy. Believing as he did in a deity who controls the operation of the universe down to the smallest detail, he naturally emphasized the omnipotence of God and set limits to the freedom of the will. Since man is sinful by nature, the will has to struggle against an inclination to commit evil. Although man has the power to choose between good and bad, it is God who provides the motive or "inspiration" for the choice. God created the world in the knowledge that some men would respond to the divine "invitation" to lead holy lives, and that others would resist or refuse to cooperate. In this way God *predestined* a portion of the human race to be saved and left the remainder to perish; in other words, He fixed for all time the number of inhabitants of the heavenly city. It was not that He elected some for salvation and denied to all others the opportunity to be saved. Rather, He knew that some would not *wish* to be saved. The influence of St. Augustine was enormous. In spite of the fact that his teachings were modified considerably by the theologians of the later Middle Ages, he is revered to this day as one of the most important Fathers of the Roman Catholic religion. Lutheran and other Protestant Reformers also held him in the highest esteem, although the interpretations they gave to his teachings frequently differed from those of the Catholics.

Practically the only pagan school of philosophy in early medieval Europe was that of the Neo-Platonists, whose doctrines were discussed in a preceding chapter. There was one other individual thinker, however, who cannot be positively classified as either a pagan or a Christian. It is quite probable that he was a Christian,

The philosophy of St. Augustine

St. Augustine theology

The Neo-Platonists and Boethius

243

though he makes no reference to the Church or to the name of Christ in his chief work. The name of this man was Boethius. Born about 480 of aristocratic parentage, Boethius eventually became principal adviser to Theodoric, the Ostrogothic king. Later he fell out with that monarch, was accused of treason, and thrown into prison. In 524 he was put to death. The chief philosophical work of Boethius, which he wrote while languishing in prison, is entitled *The Consolation of Philosophy*. Its dominant theme is the relation of man to the universe. The author considers such problems as fate, the divine government of the world, and individual suffering. After carefully weighing the various conceptions of fortune, he comes to the conclusion that true happiness is synonymous with philosophic understanding that the universe is really good, and that evil is only apparent. Although he seems to assume the immortality of the soul, he refers to no definitely Christian belief as a source of consolation. His attitude is essentially that of the Stoics, colored by a trace of Neo-Platonist mysticism. Few treatises on philosophy were more popular in medieval Europe than Boethius' *Consolation of Philosophy*. Not only was it ultimately translated into nearly every vernacular language, but numerous imitations of it also were written.

Literature in the early Middle Ages

The history of literature in the early Middle Ages was marked, first of all, by a decline of interest in the classical writings and later by the growth of a crude originality that ultimately paved the way for the development of new literary traditions. By the fifth century the taste for good Latin literature had already begun to decline. Some of the Christian Fathers who had been educated in pagan schools were inclined to apologize for their attachment to the ancient writings; others expressly denounced them; but the attitude that generally prevailed was that of St. Augustine. The great bishop of Hippo declared that men should continue to study the pagan classics, not for their aesthetic value or their human appeal, but "with a view to making the wit more keen and better suited to penetrate the mystery of the Divine Word."[8] Toward the close of the period the vernacular languages, which had been slowly evolving from a fusion of barbarian dialects, with some admixture of Latin elements, began to be employed for crude poetic expression. The consequence was a new and vigorous literary growth which attained its full momentum about the thirteenth century.

Beowulf and other examples of vernacular literature

The best-known example of this literature in the vernacular is the Anglo-Saxon epic poem *Beowulf*. First put into written form about the eighth century, this poem incorporates ancient legends of the Germanic peoples of northwestern Europe. It is a story of fighting and seafaring and of heroic adventure against deadly dragons and the forces of nature. The background of the epic is heathen, but the author of the work introduced into it some qualities of Christian

[8] Quoted by Thompson and Johnson, *An Introduction to Medieval Europe*, p. 221.

idealism. *Beowulf* is important, not only as one of the earliest specimens of Anglo-Saxon or Old English poetry, but also for the picture it gives of the society of the English and their ancestors in the early Middle Ages. No account of the vernacular literature of this time would be complete without some mention of the achievements of the Irish. Ireland in the late sixth and early seventh centuries experienced a brilliant renaissance which made that country one of the brightest spots in the early Middle Ages. Irish monks and bards wrote stories of fantastic adventure on land and sea and hundreds of poems of remarkable sensitivity to natural beauty. The Irish monasteries of this time were renowned centers of learning and art. Their inmates excelled in illuminating manuscripts and in composing both religious and secular verse. As missionaries, under the leadership of St. Columban, they conveyed their influence to Scotland and to many parts of the Continent.

Aside from theological works, the leading productions of authors who wrote in Latin during the early Middle Ages were the histories of Gregory of Tours and Bede. Bishop Gregory of Tours, a near-contemporary of Clovis, wrote with a view to defense of the faith. In his *History of the Franks* he condoned the murders of Clovis on the ground that they were committed in the service of the Church. Although his work contains interesting information about the events of his time, he tended to give a supernatural interpretation to every occurrence. By far the best of the historical writings of the early medieval period was the Venerable Bede's *Ecclesiastical History of the English Nation*. Bede, an English monk, lived between 673 and 735. Apparently more interested in scholarship than in pious meditation, he pursued his studies so assiduously that he gained a reputation as one of the most learned men of his time. In collecting material for his history he devoted careful attention to sources. He did not hesitate to reject the statements of some of the most respectable authorities when he found them to be in error; and when the evidence was a matter of mere oral tradition, he was honest enough to say so.

No account of intellectual attainments in the early Middle Ages would be complete without some reference to developments in education. After the reign of Theodoric, the old Roman system of state schools rapidly disappeared. Throughout the remainder of western Europe the monasteries had a practical monopoly of education. The man who did most to establish the monasteries as institutions of learning was Cassiodorus, formerly chief secretary to Theodoric. Following his retirement from official service, Cassiodorus founded a monastery on his ancestral estate in Apulia and set the monks to work copying manuscripts. The precedent he established was gradually adopted in nearly all the Benedictine institutions. Cassiodorus also insisted that his monks should be trained as scholars, and for this purpose he prepared a curriculum based upon seven subjects, which

The historians

Developments in education; the Seven Liberal Arts

came to be called the Seven Liberal Arts. These subjects were divided, apparently by Boethius, into the *trivium* and the *quadrivium*. The former included grammar, rhetoric, and logic, which were supposed to be the keys to knowledge; the *quadrivium* embraced subjects of more definite content—arithmetic, geometry, astronomy, and music.

The textbooks used in the monastic schools were for the most part elementary. In some of the best schools, however, translations of Aristotle's logical works were studied. But nowhere was attention given to laboratory science, and history was largely neglected. Learning was largely memorization, with limited opportunity for criticism or refutation. No professional training of any kind was provided, except for careers in the Church. Learning was, of course, a privilege for the few; the masses as a rule received no education, save what they acquired incidentally, and even most members of the secular aristocracy were illiterate. Yet, with all of its shortcomings, this system of education did help to save European culture from complete eclipse. And it is worth remembering that the best of the monastic and cathedral schools—notably those at Yarrow and York in England—provided the main impetus for the first of the revivals of learning which occurred in the later Middle Ages.

SELECTED READINGS

· *Items so designated are available in paperbound editions.*

· Artz, F. B., *The Mind of the Middle Ages,* New York, 1954.

· Bark, W. C., *Origins of the Medieval World,* Stanford, 1958 (Doubleday).

· Bury, J. B., *The Invasion of Europe by the Barbarians,* London, 1928 (Norton Library).

· Chadwick, Henry, *The Early Church,* Baltimore, 1967 (Penguin).

· Chambers, Mortimer, *The Fall of Rome: Can It Be Explained?* New York, 1963 (European Problem Series, Holt, Rinehart & Winston).

Deanesley, Margaret, *A History of Early Medieval Europe,* New York, 1960.

· Dill, Samuel, *Roman Society in the Last Century of the Western Empire,* London, 1921 (Meridian). Valuable for excerpts from the writers of the fifth century.

· ———, *The Wandering Saints of the Middle Ages,* New York, 1959 (Norton Library).

· Ganshof, Francois Louis, *Frankish Institutions under Charlemagne,* Providence, 1968 (Norton Library).

Hearnshaw, F. J. C., *The Social and Political Ideas of Some Great Medieval Thinkers,* New York, 1923.

Laistner, M. L. W., *Thought and Letters in Western Europe, A.D. 500–900,* rev. ed., New York, 1957.

Latouche, Robert, *The Birth of Western Economy,* New York, 1960.

Latourette, K. S., *A History of Christianity,* New York, 1953.

· Lot, Ferdinand, *The End of the Ancient World and the Beginning of the Middle Ages,* New York, 1931 (Torchbook). An excellent account of the decline of Rome and the transition to the Middle Ages.

· Lyon, Bryce, *The Origins of the Middle Ages,* New York, 1971 (Norton).

· Moss, H. St. L. B., *The Birth of the Middle Ages, 395–814,* New York, 1935 (Galaxy). Clear and concise.

Patch, R. R., *The Tradition of Boethius,* New York, 1935.

· Rand, E. K., *Founders of the Middle Ages,* Cambridge, Mass., 1928 (Dover). A very good presentation of the contributions of individuals.

· Rops, Daniel, *Jesus and His Times,* New York, 1954 (Doubleday).

Russell, J. B., *A History of Medieval Christianity,* New York, 1968.

· Taylor, H. O., *The Classical Heritage of the Middle Ages,* New York, 1925 (Torchbook).

———, *The Medieval Mind,* New York, 1927, 2 vols.

· Wallace-Hadrill, J. M., *The Barbarian West,* New York, 1962 (Torchbook).

SOURCE MATERIALS

· Boethius, *The Consolation of Philosophy,* New York, 1962 (Library of Liberal Arts, Ungar).

· Brentano, Robert, *The Early Middle Ages, 500–1000,* 1964, Glencoe, Ill. (Free Press).

COLUMBIA RECORDS OF CIVILIZATIONS

· Gregory of Tours, *History of the Franks,* New York, 1965 (Norton).

King, J. E., ed., *The Historical Works of Bede,* 2 vols., Harvard.

St. Augustine, *The City of God,* especially Books IV, VII, X, XII, XIV, XV, XVII.

———, *Confessions.*

———, *Enchiridion,* especially Chs. XXVI, XXVII, XXX–XXXIII, XLI, L, LI, XCVIII, XCIX.

Shotwell, J. T., and Loomis, L. R., eds., *The See of Peter,* New York, 1927.

CHAPTER 10

The Byzantine and Saracenic Civilizations

What is there greater, what more sacred than imperial majesty? Who so arrogant as to scorn the judgment of the Prince, when lawgivers themselves have precisely and clearly laid down that imperial decisions have the force of law?

—Justinian

Muhammad is the messenger of Allah. And those with him are hard against the disbelievers and merciful among themselves. Allah hath promised, unto such of them as believe and do good works, forgiveness and immense reward.

—*The Koran*, Sûrah XLVIII

The so-called medieval period of history does not concern Europe alone. In addition to the cultures of the European Middle Ages, medieval history includes two other civilizations, the Byzantine and the Saracenic or Islamic. Although each occupied territory on the European continent, the larger portions of their empires were located in Africa and in Asia. Of greater significance is the fact that the features of both civilizations were largely those of the Near East. While the Saracens were Moslems and the Byzantine people Christians, religion was a dominant factor in the lives of both. The two states were so closely linked with the religious organizations that their governments appeared more theocratic than many of those in the West. Moreover, both civilizations were characterized by attitudes of pessimism and fatalism and by a tendency for the mystical point of view to gain supremacy over the rational. It should be noted, however, that the Saracens especially made distinctive contributions to philosophy and science, while the Byzantine Empire was exceedingly important for its art and for its work in preserving innumerable achievements of the Greeks and Romans.

The semi-Oriental character of the Byzantine and Saracenic civilizations

249

I.   THE BYZANTINE EMPIRE AND ITS CULTURE

The founding of
the Byzantine
Empire

In the fourth century the Emperor Constantine established a new capital for the Roman Empire on the site of the old Greek colony of Byzantium. When the western division of the Empire collapsed, Byzantium (or Constantinople, as the city was now more commonly called) survived as the capital of a powerful state which included the Near Eastern provinces of the Caesars. Gradually this state came to be known as the Byzantine Empire, although the existence of a Byzantine civilization was not clearly recognized before the sixth century. Even after that there were many who believed that Rome had merely shifted its center of gravity to the East.

Byzantine culture
more distinctly
Near Eastern
than that of
Latin Europe

Although Byzantine history covered a period similar to that of the Middle Ages, the cultural pattern was far different from the one which prevailed in western Europe. Byzantine civilization had a more pronounced Near Eastern character. Indeed, most of the territories of the Empire actually lay outside of Europe. The most important among them were Syria, Asia Minor, Palestine, and Egypt. Furthermore, Greek and Hellenistic elements entered into the formation of Byzantine culture to a greater extent than was ever true in western Europe. The language of the eastern state was predominantly Greek, while the traditions in literature, art, and science were largely Hellenistic. Lastly, the Christianity of the Byzantine Empire differed from that of Latin Europe in being more mystical, abstract, and pessimistic, and more completely subject to political control. Notwithstanding all these differences, Byzantine civilization was distinctly superior to that of western Europe.

Nationalities in
the Byzantine
Empire

The population of the territories under Byzantine rule comprised a great number of nationalities. The majority of the inhabitants were Greeks and Hellenized Orientals—Syrians, Jews, Armenians, Egyptians, and Persians. In addition, the European sections of the Empire included numerous barbarians, especially Slavs and Mongols. There were some Germans also, but the emperors at Constantinople were generally able to divert the German invasions to the west. The encroachments of the Slavs and the Mongols, on the other hand, proved to be much more difficult to deal with. The original home of the Slavs, a round-headed people of Alpine stock, was apparently the region northeast of the Carpathian Mountains, principally in what is now southwestern Russia. A peaceful agricultural folk, they seldom resorted to armed invasion but gradually expanded into thinly settled territories whenever the opportunity arose. Not only did they move into the vast empty spaces of central Russia, but they occupied many of the regions vacated by the Germans and then slowly filtered through the frontiers of the Eastern Empire. By the seventh century they were the most numerous people in the entire Balkan peninsula, as well as in the whole region of Europe east of the Germans. The Mongolian inhabitants of the Empire came into

Europe from the steppes of what is now Asiatic Russia. They were herdsmen, with the furious energy and warlike habits characteristic of that mode of existence. After entering the valley of the Danube, many of them forced their way into Byzantine territory. It was a fusion of some of these Mongolian peoples with Slavs which gave rise to such modern nations as the Bulgarians and the Serbs.

The early history of the Byzantine Empire was marked by struggles to repel the Germanic barbarians. The confidence inspired by the success of these struggles encouraged the Emperor Justinian to begin the reconquest of Italy and North Africa, but most of Italy was soon afterward abandoned to the Lombards, and Norh Africa to the Moslems. In the early seventh century Byzantium became involved in a great war with Persia, which eventually exhausted both empires and laid their territories open to Saracenic conquest. By 750 the Byzantine state had lost all of its possessions outside of Europe with the exception of Asia Minor. After the tide of Saracenic advance had spent its force, Byzantium enjoyed a brief recovery and even regained the province of Syria, the island of Crete, and some portions of the Italian coast, as well as certain territories on the Balkan peninsula which had been lost to the barbarians. In the eleventh century, however, the Empire was attacked by the Seljuk Turks, who rapidly overran the eastern provinces and in 1071 annihilated a Byzantine army of 100,000 men at Manzikert. The Emperor Romanus Diogenes was taken prisoner and held for a ransom of one million pieces of gold. Soon afterward the government sent an appeal for aid to the West. The result was the Crusades, launched originally against the Moslems but eventually turned into plundering attacks upon Byzantine territory. In 1204 the Crusaders captured Constantinople and treated that city "with more barbarity than the barbarian Alaric had treated Rome eight hundred years before."[1] But even these disasters did not prove fatal. During the late thirteenth and early fourteenth centuries the Empire once again recovered some measure of its former strength and prosperity. Its history was finally brought to an end with the capture of Constantinople by the Ottoman Turks in 1453.

During this long period of approximately 1000 years the stability of Byzantine rule was frequently menaced not only by foreign aggression but also by palace intrigues, mutinies in the army, and violent struggles between political factions. How then can it be explained that the Empire survived so long, especially in view of the rapid decay of the West during the early centuries of this period? Geographic and economic factors were probably the major causes. The location of Constantinople made it almost impregnable. Surrounded on three sides by water and on the fourth by a thick, high wall, the city was able to resist capture practically as long as any

Byzantine political history

Factors in the stability of the Byzantine Empire

[1] J. B. Bury, *History of the Later Roman Empire* (1931 ed.), I, 3.

The government
of the Byzantine
Empire

State control of
the economic
system

will to defend it remained. Furthermore, the Near East suffered no
decay of industry and commerce like that which had occurred in
Italy during the last centuries of the empire in the West. Last of all,
the Byzantine government had a well-filled treasury which could
be drawn upon for purposes of defense. The annual revenues of the
state have been estimated as high as $167 million (1972 dollars).

The government of the Byzantine Empire was similar to that of
Rome after the time of Diocletian, except that it was even more
despotic and theocratic. The emperor was an absolute sovereign
with unlimited power over every department of national life. His
subjects not only fell prostrate before him, but in petitioning his
grace they customarily referred to themselves as his slaves. Moreover, the spiritual dignity of the emperor was in no sense inferior to
his temporal power. He was the vicar of God with a religious authority supposed to be equal to that of the Apostles. Although some
of the emperors were able and hard-working officials, most of the
actual functions of the government were performed by an extensive
bureaucracy, many of whose members were highly trained. A great
army of clerks, inspectors, and spies maintained the closest scrutiny
over the life and possessions of every inhabitant.

The economic system was as strictly regulated as in Hellenistic
Egypt. In fact, the Byzantine Empire has been described as a "paradise of monopoly, of privilege, and of paternalism." [2] The state exercised a thorough control over virtually every activity. The wage
of every workman and the price of every product were fixed by
government decree. In many cases it was not even possible for the
individual to choose his own occupation, since the system of guilds
which had been established in the late Roman Empire was still maintained. Each worker inherited his status as a member of one guild or
another, and the walls which surrounded these organizations were
hermetically sealed. Nor did the manufacturer enjoy much greater
freedom. He could not choose for himself what quantity or quality
of raw materials he would purchase, nor was he permitted to buy
them directly. He could not determine how much he would produce or under what conditions he would sell his product. A number
of large industrial enterprises were owned and operated by the state.
Chief among them were the murex or purple fisheries, the mines,
the armament factories, and the establishments for the weaving of
cloth. An attempt was made at one time to extend monopolistic
control over the silk industry, but the government factories were
unable to supply the demand, and permission had to be given to
private manufacturers to resume production.

The agricultural regime developed under the late Roman Empire
was also perpetuated and extended in the Byzantine territories. Most
of the land was divided into great estates operated by feudal magnates. Except in the hilly and mountainous regions, there were

[2] J. W. Thompson, *Economic and Social History of the Middle Ages*, p. 336.

few independent farmers left. In the richest areas the agricultural population was made up almost entirely of tenant farmers and serfs. The number of the latter was increased in the fifth century, when the Emperor Anastasius issued a decree forbidding all peasants who had lived on a particular farm for thirty years ever to remove therefrom. The purpose of the decree was to ensure a minimum of agricultural production, but its natural effect was to bind the peasants to the soil and make them actual serfs of their landlords. Another of the significant agricultural developments in the Byzantine Empire was the concentration of landed wealth in the hands of the Church. The monasteries, especially, came to be included among the richest proprietors in the country. With the increasing difficulty of making a living from the soil and the growing popularity of asceticism, more and more farmers sought refuge in the cloister and made gifts of their lands to the institutions which admitted them. The estates acquired by the Church were cultivated, not by the monks or the priests, but by serfs. During the seventh and eighth centuries many of the serfs gained their freedom and became owners of the lands they cultivated. But by the eleventh century the great estates had reappeared, and the independent peasantry virtually ceased to exist.

The agricultural regime

No subject appears to have absorbed the interest of the Byzantine people more completely than religion. They fought over religious questions as vehemently as citizens of the modern world quarrel over issues of government control versus private ownership or democracy versus totalitarianism. They took great delight in theological subtleties which would impress most people in our time as barren and trivial. Gregory of Nyssa, one of their own Church Fathers, thus described Constantinople in the fourth century: "Everything is full of those who are speaking of unintelligible things. I wish to know the price of bread; one answers: 'The Father is greater than the Son'; I inquire whether my bath is ready; one says, 'The Son has been made out of nothing.' " [3]

The absorbing interest in religion

The most crucial of the religious issues, however, were those which grew out of the Monophysite and Iconoclastic movements, although neither of these movements was exclusively religious in character. The Monophysites derived their name from their contention that the Christ was composed of only one nature, and that that nature was divine. This doctrine, which was probably a reflection of the Neo-Platonist contempt for everything physical or material, flatly contradicted the official theology of Christianity. Having begun as early as the fifth century, the Monophysite movement reached its height during the reign of Justinian (527–565). Its strength lay chiefly in Syria and in Egypt, where it served as an expression of nationalist resentment against subjection to Constantinople. In dealing with the sect Justinian was caught between two fires. Not only was he ambitious to unite his subjects in allegiance to

Religious controversies; the Monophysite movement

[3] A. A. Vasiliev, *History of the Byzantine Empire*, I, 99 f.

a single faith, but he was anxious to win the support of Rome. On the other hand, he was reluctant to take any steps for the suppression of the Monophysites, partly because of their strength and also because his wife, the popular actress Theodora, was a member of the sect. It was her will that finally prevailed. During the seventh century the Monophysites broke away from the Eastern Church. The sect survives to this day as an important branch of Christendom in Egypt, Syria, and Armenia. They are now commonly called Coptic Christians.

The Iconoclastic movement was launched about 725 by a decree of the Emperor Leo III forbidding the use of images in the Church.

The Iconoclasts In the Eastern Church any image of God, the Christ, or a saint was called an icon. Those who condemned the use of icons in worship were known as Iconoclasts, or image-breakers. The Iconoclastic movement was a product of several factors. First of all, it had a certain affinity with the Monophysite movement in its opposition to anything sensuous or material in religion. Secondly, it was a protest against paganism and worldliness in the Church. But perhaps more than anything else it represented a revolt of certain of the emperors against the increasing power of the ecclesiastical system. The monasteries in particular were absorbing so large a proportion of the national wealth and enticing so many men away from service in the army and from useful occupations that they were undermining the economic vitality of the Empire. Since the monks derived a large part of their income from the manufacture and sale of icons, it was logical that the reforming emperors should center their attacks upon the use of images in the Church. Naturally they had the support of many of their pious subjects, who resented what they considered a corruption of their religion by idolatrous practices.

Although the struggle against the worship of images was continued until well into the ninth century, it really accomplished no more than the elimination of sculptured representations; the flat or painted icons were eventually restored. Nevertheless, the Iconoclas-

Significance of
the Iconoclastic
controversy tic controversy had more than a trivial significance. It may be said to have represented an important stage in the irrepressible conflict between Roman and Near Eastern traditions, which occupied so large a place in Byzantine history. Those who upheld the use of images generally believed in an ecclesiastical religion in which symbols and ceremony were regarded as indispensable aids to worship. Most of their opponents were mystics and ascetics who condemned any form of institutionalism or veneration of material objects and advocated a return to the spiritualism of primitive Christianity. Many of the ideals of the Iconoclasts were similar to those of the Protestant Reformers of the sixteenth century, and the movement itself may be said to have foreshadowed the great revolt of Luther and Calvin against what were considered pagan elements in the Roman Catholic religion. Finally, the Iconoclastic controversy was a potent cause of the separation of the Greek and Roman branches of the Church in

1054. Even though the attack upon the use of images was not entirely successful, it went far enough to arouse much antagonism between Eastern and Western Christians. The Pope excommunicated the Iconoclasts and turned from the Byzantine emperors to the Frankish kings for support. From this point on the East and the West drew farther apart.

Social conditions in the Byzantine Empire presented a marked contrast with western Europe during the early Middle Ages. Whereas large sections of Italy and France sank to almost primitive levels in the ninth and tenth centuries, Byzantine society continued to maintain its essentially urban and luxurious character. Approximately a million people lived in the city of Constantinople alone, to say nothing of the thousands who dwelt in Nicaea, Edessa, Thessalonica, and other great urban centers. Merchants, bankers, and manufacturers ranked with the great landlords as members of the aristocracy, for there was no tendency in Byzantium as there had been in Rome to despise the man who derived his income from industry or trade. The rich lived in elegance and ease, cultivating the indulgence of opulent tastes as a fine art. A large part of the industrial activity of the nation was absorbed in the production of articles of luxury to meet the demand of the wealthier classes. Magnificent garments of wool and silk interwoven with gold and silver thread, gorgeously colored tapestries of brocaded or damasked stuffs, exquisite glass and porcelain ware, illuminated gospels, and rare and costly jeweled ornaments composed only a small part of the sumptuous output of factories and shops, both public and private.

A Silver Byzantine Plate Portraying David and Goliath

The life of the lower classes was poor and mean by comparison. And yet the common man in the Byzantine Empire was probably better off than the average citizen in most other parts of the Christian world at that time. The extensive industrial and commercial development and the high degree of economic stability provided opportunities for employment for thousands of urban workers. Even the lot of the serf who was attached to the estate of some one of the great secular proprietors was probably superior to that of the peasants in western Europe, since the landlord's powers of exploitation were at least regulated by law.

A Byzantine Plate of Gold and Enamel Portraying the Christ

The tone of morality in the Empire exhibited sharp contrasts. The Byzantine people, in spite of their Greek antecedents, apparently had no aptitude for the typical Hellenic virtues of balance and restraint. In place of the golden mean they seemed always to prefer the extremes. Consequently, the most extravagant self-indulgence was frequently to be found side by side with the humblest self-denial or laceration of the flesh. The contradictory qualities of sensuality and piety, charity and heartless cruelty, were commonly evident in the same stratum of society or even in the same individuals. For example, the great reform Emperor, Leo III, tried to improve the lot of the peasants, but he also introduced mutilation as a punishment for crime. Life at the imperial court and among some

Extremes of asceticism and sensual indulgence

255

members of the higher clergy appears to have been characterized by indolence, luxurious vice, and intrigue. As a consequence, the very word "Byzantine" has come to be suggestive of elegant sensuality and refinements of cruelty.

Revision and codification of the Roman law

In the intellectual realm the Byzantine people won little distinction for originality. Comparatively few discoveries or contributions in any of the fields of knowledge can actually be credited to them. Probably their most noteworthy achievement was the revision and codification of the ancient Roman law. After the time of the great jurists (second and third centuries A.D.) the creative genius of the Roman lawyers subsided, and nothing new was added to the philosophy or the science of law. The volume of statutory enactments, however, continued to grow. By the sixth century Roman law had come to contain numerous contradictory and obsolete provisions. Moreover, conditions had changed so radically that many of the old legal principles could no longer be applied, particularly on account of the establishment of an Oriental despotism and the adoption of Christianity as the official religion. When Justinian came to the throne in 527, he immediately decided upon a revision and codification of the existing law to bring it into harmony with the new conditions and to establish it as an authoritative basis of his rule. To carry out the actual work he appointed a commission of lawyers under the supervision of his minister, Tribonian. Within two years the commission published the first result of its labors. This was the Code, a systematic revision of all of the statutory laws which had been issued from the reign of Hadrian to the reign of Justinian. The Code was later supplemented by the Novels, which contained the legislation of Justinian and his immediate successors. By 532 the commission had completed the Digest, representing a summary of all of the writings of the great jurists. The final product of the work of revision was the Institutes, a textbook of the legal principles which were reflected in both the Digest and the Code. The combination of all four of these results of the program of revision constitutes the *Corpus Juris Civilis*, or the body of the civil law.

The Institutes and the Digest

From the historical standpoint the two most important sections of the *Corpus Juris* were unquestionably the Institutes and the Digest. It was these which contained the philosophy of law and of government which had come to prevail in Justinian's time. There is a popular but inaccurate belief that this philosophy was the same as that of Ulpian, Papinian, and the other great jurists of 300 years before. While it is true that most of the old theory was preserved, a few fundamental changes were introduced. First, the *jus civile* was more completely denationalized than it had ever been during Roman times and was now made applicable to citizens of a great many divergent nationalities. The *jus naturale* was now declared to be divine and consequently superior to all of the enactments of men—a conception which was destined to become exceedingly popular in later medieval philosophy. There was a tendency also for Justinian's jurists to speak of the emperor as the sole legislator, on the assumption that the people had surrendered all of their power to him. In other words, the classical Roman law was being revised to make it fit the needs of an Oriental monarch whose sovereignty was limited only by the law of God.

The supreme artistic achievement of the Byzantine civilization was its architecture. Its finest example was the Church of Santa Sophia (Holy Wisdom), built at enormous cost by the Emperor Justinian. Although designed by architects of Hellenic descent, it was vastly different from any Greek temple. Its purpose was not to express man's pride in himself or his satisfaction with this life, but to symbolize the inward and spiritual character of the Christian religion. It was for this reason that the architects gave little attention to the external appearance of the building. Nothing but plain brick covered with plaster was used for the exterior walls; there were no marble facings, graceful columns, or sculptured entablatures. The interior, however, was decorated with richly colored mosaics, gold leaf, colored marble columns, and bits of tinted glass set on edge to refract the rays of sunlight after the fashion of sparkling gems. It was for this reason also that the building was constructed in such a way that no light appeared to come from the outside at all but to be manufactured within.

The structural design of Santa Sophia was something altogether new in the history of architecture. Its central feature was the application of the principle of the dome to a building of square shape. The church was designed, first of all, in the form of a cross, and then over the central square was to be erected a magnificent dome, which would dominate the entire structure. The main problem was how to fit the round circumference of the dome to the square area it

The Church of
Santa Sophia

Plan of Santa Sophia Dome

The Church of Santa Sophia in Constantinople. Built by Justinian in the sixth century A.D., it is an outstanding example of Byzantine architectural design. As the diagram shows, the central dome rests upon four massive arches. Its tremendous downward thrust necessitates buttressing with enormous masonry piles and half-domes. The minarets were added later by the Moslems.

was supposed to cover. The solution consisted in having four great arches spring from pillars at the four corners of the central square. The rim of the dome was then made to rest on the keystones of the arches, with the curved triangular spaces between the arches filled in with masonry. The result was an architectural framework of marvelous strength, which at the same time made possible a style of imposing grandeur and even some delicacy of treatment. The great dome of Santa Sophia has a diameter of 107 feet and rises to a height of nearly 180 feet from the floor. So many windows are placed around its rim that the dome appears to have no support at all but to be suspended in mid-air.

Other Byzantine arts

See color plates at page 225

The other arts of Byzantium included ivory-carving, the making of embossed glassware and brocaded textiles, the illumination of manuscripts, the goldsmith's and jeweler's arts, and considerable painting. The last, however, was not so highly developed as some of the others. In place of painting, the Byzantine artist generally preferred mosaics. These were designs produced by fitting together small pieces of colored glass or stone to form a geometric pattern, symbolical figures of plants and animals, or even an elaborate scene of theological significance. Representations of saints and of the Christ were commonly distorted to create the impression of extreme piety.

The Byzantine influence in eastern Europe

The importance of the Byzantine civilization is usually underestimated. It was undoubtedly the most powerful factor in determining the course of development of eastern Europe. To a large extent the civilization of imperial Russia was founded upon the institutions and achievements of Byzantium. The Russian Orthodox Church was an offshoot of the so-called Greek Orthodox or Eastern church, which broke away from Rome in 1054. The Tsar as the head of the religion as well as the state occupied a position analogous to that of the emperor at Constantinople. The architecture of the Russians, their calendar, and a large part of their alphabet were also of Byzantine origin. Perhaps even the despotism of the Soviet regime can be traced in some measure to the long-standing tradition of absolute rule in Russia, which ultimately goes back to Byzantine influence.

The Byzantine influence in the West

But the influence of the Byzantine civilization was not limited to eastern Europe. It would be hard to overestimate the debt of the West to scholars in Constantinople and the surrounding territory who copied and preserved manuscripts, prepared anthologies of Greek literature, and wrote encyclopedias embodying the learning of the ancient world. Moreover, Byzantine scholars exerted a notable influence upon the Italian Renaissance. The extensive trade between Venice and Constantinople in the late Middle Ages fostered cultural relations between East and West. Consequently, long before the fifteenth century when eminent Greek scholars arrived in Italy, a foundation for the revival of interest in the Greek classics had already been laid. Likewise, Byzantine art exerted its effect upon the art of western Europe. Several of the most famous churches in Italy,

A Byzantine Mosaic Depicting Jesus Entering Jerusalem

for example St. Mark's in Venice, were built in close imitation of the Byzantine style. Byzantine painting also influenced the painting of the Renaissance, especially of the Venetian school. Finally, it was the *Corpus Juris* of Justinian which really made possible the transmission of the Roman law to the late Middle Ages and to the modern world.

2. ISLAM AND THE SARACENIC CIVILIZATION

The history of the Saracenic or Arabian civilization began a little later than the history of Byzantium and ended a short time earlier. The dates were roughly 630 A.D. to 1300. In many ways the Saracenic civilization was one of the most important in the Western world—not only because it was the orbit of a new religion, which has attracted converts by the hundreds of millions, but mainly because its impact upon Christian Europe was responsible for social and intellectual changes that can only be described as revolutionary. The term "Saracen" originally meant an Arab, but later it came to be applied to any member of the Islamic faith, regardless of his nationality. Some of the Saracens were Jews, some were Persians, some were Syrians. Nevertheless, the founders of the civilization were Arabs, and it therefore becomes necessary to examine the culture of that people on the eve of their expansion beyond the borders of their homeland.

Toward the end of the sixth century the people of Arabia had come to be divided into two main groups: the urban Arabs and the Bedouins. The former, who dwelt in such cities as Mecca and Yathrib, were traders and petty craftsmen. Many were literate, and some were comparatively wealthy. The Bedouins were mostly nomads, subsisting on dates and the flesh and milk of their animals. Ignorant and superstitious, they practiced infanticide and occasional human sacrifice. They were frequently involved in bloody warfare over possession of wells and oases. Neither Bedouins nor urban

259

St. Mark's Church, Venice. The most splendid example of Byzantine architecture in Italy.

Arabs had any organized government. The clan and the tribe took the place of the state. When a member of one clan committed a crime against a member of another, the issue was settled by means of the blood feud, which sometimes raged until scores had been killed on each side. The religion was generally polytheistic, although some of the better educated townsmen had adopted a belief in Allah as the only God. From time immemorial Mecca had been a sacred city. Here was the shrine known as the Kaaba, containing a sacred black stone which was supposed to have been miraculously sent down from heaven. The men who controlled this shrine formed the tribe of the Kuraish, the nearest approach to an Arabian aristocracy that ever existed before the migrations.

The Islamic religion as a driving force in the civilization

Whether the Saracenic civilization would ever have originated without the development of the Islamic religion is a question almost impossible to answer. It is commonly assumed that a new religion was necessary to unite the people and to imbue them with ardor in a common cause. Yet other nations had expanded before this and had accomplished great things without the influence of any particularly inspiring system of belief. Nevertheless, in the case of the Arabs it was a new religion which undoubtedly provided much of the driving force behind the development of their civilization. The origin and nature of that religion must therefore be given attention.

The founder of the new faith was born in Mecca about the year 570. The child of parents who belonged to one of the poorest clans of the Kuraish tribe, he was given the common Arabic name of Muhammad or Mohammed. Little is known about his early life. He was left an orphan while still very young and was reared by his grandfather and his uncle. When he was about twenty-five years old, he entered the employment of a rich widow and accompanied her caravans, perhaps as far north as Syria. Soon afterward he became her husband, thereby acquiring leisure and security to devote all of his time to religious interests.

Exactly what influences led Mohammed to become the founder of a new religion, no one knows. He was apparently of a highly emotional nature. At times he seems to have believed that he heard voices from heaven. Quite early in his life he became acquainted with numerous Jews and Christians who lived in the cities of northern Arabia, and he appears to have been deeply impressed by their religious beliefs. In addition, he seems to have developed the idea that social and moral conditions in his country were badly in need of reform. He began to denounce the plutocrats of Mecca for their greed and to reproach his people for their bloody feuds and their practice of infanticide. Gradually he came to conceive of himself as the appointed instrument of God to rescue the Arabian people from the path of destruction.

Mohammed's preaching was not at first particularly successful. After almost nine years of communicating the revelations of Allah to all who would listen, he had managed to win very few converts outside of his immediate family. The wealthy Kuraish were naturally against him, and even the common people of Mecca were generally indifferent. In 619 he decided to seek a more promising field for the propagation of his teachings. He had learned that the city of Yathrib on the caravan route to the north had been torn for some time by factional strife, and that there might be some chance for a neutral leader to step in and assume control. In 622, he and the

The early life of Mohammed

Mohammed's character and beliefs

Founding the new religion

The Interior of St. Mark's Cathedral in Venice

The Kaaba. It contains the black stone which was supposed to have been miraculously sent down from heaven, and rests in the courtyard of the great mosque in Mecca.

remainder of his followers decided to abandon the sacred city of Mecca and to risk their future in the new location. This migration to Yathrib is known to Mohammedans as the Hegira, from the Arabic word meaning "flight," and is considered by them so important that they regard it as the beginning of their era and date all their records from it.

The conquest of Mecca

Mohammed changed the name of Yathrib to Medina (the "city of the Prophet"), and quickly succeeded in establishing himself as ruler of the city. But to obtain means of support for his followers was a somewhat more difficult matter. Besides, the Jews in Medina rejected his leadership. Under these circumstances Mohammed began to enlist the support of the Bedouins for a holy war against his enemies. In a single year approximately 600 Jews were massacred, and then the followers of the Prophet launched their plundering attacks upon the caravans of the merchants of Mecca. When the latter took up arms to resist, they were badly defeated in battle. In 630 Mohammed entered Mecca in triumph. He murdered a few of his leading opponents and smashed the idols in the temple, but the Kaaba itself was preserved, and Mecca was established as a sacred city of the Islamic faith. Two years later Mohammed died, but he lived to see the religion he had founded a militant and successful enterprise.

The doctrines of the Islamic religion

The doctrines of the Islamic religion as developed by the Prophet are really quite simple. They revolve around a belief in one God, who is called by the old Arabic name Allah, and in Mohammed as His Prophet. This God desires that men shall be kind to their neighbors, lenient toward debtors, honest, and forgiving; and that they shall refrain from infanticide, eating swine's flesh, drinking intoxicating beverages, and waging the blood feud. The religion also enjoins the faithful observance of certain obligations. Chief among these are the giving of alms to the poor, fasting during the day throughout the sacred month of Ramadan, praying five times a day, and making a pilgrimage, if possible, at least once in a lifetime to Mecca. Almost as much emphasis is placed upon purity of heart and practical benevolence as in Christianity or Judaism. Several passages in the Koran, which constitutes the Islamic Scriptures, provide ample warrant for such a conclusion. One of them declares that "There is no piety in turning your faces toward the east or the west, but he is pious who believeth in God, and the last day, and the angels, and the Scriptures, and the prophets; who for the love of God disburseth his wealth to his kindred, and to the orphans, and the needy, and the wayfarer and those who ask, and for ransoming." [4] Another affirms that the highest merit is "to free the captive; or to feed, in a day of famine, the orphan who is of kin, or the poor man who lieth on the ground." [5] There are no sacraments in the system of worship taught by Mohammed, and there are no priests. The religion itself is officially known as "Islam," a word meaning "to submit, or to surrender oneself absolutely to God." The official designation of a believer is a "Moslem," which is the participle of the same verb of which "Islam" is the infinitive.

The sources of the religion of Islam are somewhat in doubt. Judaism was unquestionably one of them. Mohammed taught that the Arabs were descendants of Ishmael, Abraham's oldest son. Moreover, a good many of the teachings of the Koran are quite similar to doctrines in the Old Testament: strict monotheism, the sanction of polygamy, and the prohibition of usury and the eating of pork. Christianity was also an exceedingly important source. Mohammed considered the New Testament as well as the Old to be a divinely inspired book, and he regarded Jesus as one of the greatest of a long line of prophets. Besides, the Islamic doctrines of the resurrection of the body, the last judgment, rewards and punishments after death, and the belief in angels were more probably derived from Christianity than from any other system of belief. On the other hand, it is necessary to remember that the Christianity with which Mohammed was acquainted was far from the orthodox variety. Nearly all of the Christians who lived in Syria as well as those in Arabia itself were Ebionites or Nestorians. It is perhaps for this reason that Mohammed always thought of Jesus as human, the son of Joseph and Mary, and not as a god.

It was not long after the origin of Islam that its followers split into a number of sects not entirely dissimilar to some of the off-shoots of Christianity. The three most important of the Islamic sects were the Sunnites, the Shiites, and the Sufis. The first two had a political as well as a religious character. The Sunnites maintained that the head of the Islamic state and successor to the Prophet should be elected by representatives of the whole body of believers, in accord-

The probable
sources of Islam

The principal
Islamic sects

[4] Sura 2:v. 172.
[5] Sura 90:v. 12.

ance with the ancient Arabian custom of election of tribal chiefs. In matters of religion they contended that the *sunna*, or traditions which had grown up outside of the Koran, should be accepted as a valid source of belief. The Shiites were opposed to the elevation of anyone to the highest political and religious office who was not related to the Prophet himself, either by blood or by marriage. In general, they represented the absolutist ideal in Islam as distinct from the democratic ideal of the Sunnites. What is more, the Shiites were against the acceptance of anything but the Koran as a source of religious belief. The Sufis adhered to a mystical and ascetic ideal. Denying absolutely the validity of rational judgment, they maintained that the only truth of any worth is that which proceeds from divine revelation. They believed that it is possible for man to partake of this divine revelation through torturing his body and thereby releasing the soul for a mystic union with God. Many of the fakirs and dervishes in India, Pakistan, and Iran today are members of the Sufi sect.

Political history of the Islamic state: the caliphs

The political history of the Saracenic civilization is closely interwoven with the growth of the religion. As we have already seen, Mohammed became the founder not merely of a religion but also of an Arabic state with its capital at Medina. Following his death in 632 his companions chose as his successor Abu-Bekr, one of the earliest converts to the faith and the father-in-law of Mohammed. The new ruler was given the title of *caliph*, that is, successor to the Prophet. After Abu-Bekr's death two other caliphs were chosen in succession from among the earlier disciples of Mohammed. In 656, however, a long struggle began for possession of the supreme power in Islam. First the Shiites succeeded in deposing a member of the Ommiad family and in electing Ali, the husband of Mohammed's daughter Fatima, as caliph. Five years later Ali was murdered, and the Ommiads came back into power. Soon afterward they transferred the capital to Damascus and established their family as a reigning dynasty with a luxurious court in imitation of the Byzantine model. In 750 the Shiites revolted again, this time under the leadership of a member of the Abbasid family, who was a distant relative of the Prophet. The Abbasids seized the throne and moved the capital to the city of Baghdad on the Tigris River, where they ruled as Oriental despots for more than three centuries. A few of them were enlightened patrons of learning, especially Harun-al-Raschid (786–809) and Al-Mamun (813–33).

The Saracenic conquests

In the meantime, a great wave of Saracenic expansion had swept over Asia, Africa, and Europe. When Mohammed died in 632, the authority of his little state probably did not extend over more than one-third of the Arabian peninsula. A hundred years later at least one-third of the civilized world was under Moslem domination. The Saracenic empire extended from the borders of India to the Strait of Gibraltar and the Pyrenees Mountains. One after another, with

1000 miles

*ARAL
SEA*

CASPIAN SEA

PERSIA

Indus R.

PERSIAN GULF

ARABIA

CAUCASUS MTS.

ARMENIA

Tigris R.

Euphrates R.

• Baghdad

• Medina

• Mecca

RED SEA

SYRIA

• Damascus

• Jerusalem

BLACK SEA

MAGYARS

BULGARIANS

Constantinople

Danube R.

AVARS

Ravenna

LOMBARDS

Rome •

CORSICA

SARDINIA

FRANKS

PYRENEES

Barcelona

SPAIN

Toledo •

• Cordova

Cadiz •

Tangier •

ATLANTIC OCEAN

CYPRUS

CRETE

B Y Z A N T I N E   E M P I R E

M E D I T E R R A N E A N   S E A

SICILY

Tunis •

Tripoli •

• Barca
(Barce, Al Marj)

Alexandria •

Cairo •

EGYPT

Nile R.

BERBERS

THE EXPANSION OF ISLAM AND THE SARACENIC EMPIRE

At the death of Mohammed, 632 A.D.

After the conquests of the first four caliphs, 661 A.D.

After the conquests of the Ommiad caliphs, 750 A.D.

——·——·—— Outer limits of the Byzantine Empire

startling rapidity, Persia, Syria, Egypt, North Africa, and Spain had been conquered. How can this prodigious expansion be explained? Contrary to common belief, it was not the result primarily of religious ardor. The Saracens were not engaged in a great crusade to impose their beliefs upon the rest of the world. Naturally there were outbreaks of fanaticism from time to time, but as a rule the Moslems of this period did not really care very much whether the nations they conquered accepted their religion or not. Subject peoples were usually quite leniently treated. As long as they refrained from the possession of arms and paid the tribute levied upon them, they were permitted to retain their own beliefs and customs. Jews and Christians lived unmolested in the Saracenic empire for centuries, and some rose to positions of prominence in political and intellectual circles.

In truth, economic and political factors were much more important than religion in causing the Saracenic expansion. First of all, it **Reasons for the** must be borne in mind that the majority of the Arabs were a prolific **Saracenic ex-** race of nomads. Since the men were polygamists, the occasional **pansion** practice of infanticide was far from sufficient to prevent a rapid increase in population. Arabia, moreover, was suffering from a serious drought, which extended over a number of years shortly after the beginning of the seventh century. Oases that had formerly provided good crops of dates and good pasturage for flocks and herds were gradually being absorbed by the surrounding desert. Discontent among the famished tribes increased to such a point that they would probably have seized upon almost any excuse to plunder neighboring countries. The initial attacks upon Byzantine territory appear to have grown out of a revolt of Arab mercenaries in Syria. The leaders of the rebellion appealed to the followers of the Prophet in Medina, who already had some reputation for military prowess as a result of their conquest of Mecca. The outcome of this appeal was a great wave of military invasion which soon made the Arabs masters not merely of Syria, but also of Persia, Palestine, and Egypt. Finally, it should be noted that the conquests of the Moslems were facilitated by the fact that the Byzantine and Persian empires had fought each other to the point of exhaustion in the previous century, and their governments were now attempting to replenish their treasuries by heavier taxation. As a consequence, many of the inhabitants of these empires were disposed to welcome the Arabs as deliverers.

The decline of the Saracenic empire was almost as swift as its rise. The Arabs themselves lacked political experience; besides, the empire **The decline of** they conquered was too vast in extent and too heterogeneous in pop-**the Saracenic** ulation ever to be welded into a strong and cohesive political unit. But **empire** a more decisive reason for its downfall was sectarian and factional strife. Sunnites and Shiites were never able to reconcile their differences, and widening cleavages between the mystics and rationalists also helped weaken the religion, which was the basis of the state. In

929 members of the Ommiad family succeeded in establishing an independent caliphate at Cordova in Spain. Soon afterward descendants of Ali and Fatima proclaimed themselves independent rulers of Morocco and Egypt. Meanwhile, the caliphs at Baghdad were gradually succumbing to the debilitating effects of Oriental customs. Aping the practices of Eastern monarchs, they retired more and more into the seclusion of the palace and soon became the puppets of their Persian viziers and later of their Turkish mercenary troops. In 1057 they surrendered all of their temporal power to the Sultan of the Seljuk Turks, who two years before had taken possession of Baghdad. For all practical purposes this marked the extinction of the Saracenic empire, although much of the territory continued to be ruled by peoples who had adopted the Islamic faith—the Seljuk Turks until the middle of the twelfth century and the Ottoman Turks from the fifteenth century to 1918.

The intellectual achievements of the Saracens were far superior to any in Christian Europe before the twelfth century. In conquering Persia and Syria the Saracens came into possession of a brilliant intellectual heritage. In both of these countries traditions of Greek learning had survived. Numerous physicians of Greek nationality had been attracted to the court of the Persian kings, while in Syria there were excellent schools of philosophy and rhetoric and several libraries filled with copies of writings of the Hellenic philosophers, scientists, and poets. Of course, it would be foolish to suppose that very many of the Arabs themselves were able to appreciate this cultural heritage; their function was rather to provide the encouragement and the facilities for others to make use of it.

The intellectual
achievements of
the Saracens

Saracenic philosophy was essentially a compound of Aristotelianism and Neo-Platonism. Its basic teachings may be set forth as follows: Reason is superior to faith as a source of knowledge; the doctrines of religion are not to be discarded entirely, but should be interpreted by the enlightened mind in a figurative or allegorical sense; when thus interpreted they can be made to yield a pure philosophical knowledge which is not in conflict with reason but supplementary to it. The universe never had a beginning in time but is created eternally; it is a series of emanations from God. Everything that happens is predetermined by God; every event is a link in an unbroken chain of cause and effect; both miracles and divine providence are therefore impossible. Although God is the First Cause of all things, He is not omnipotent; His power is limited by justice and goodness. There is no immortality for the individual soul, for no spiritual substance can exist apart from its material embodiment; only the soul of the universe goes on forever, since its primal substance is eternal.

Saracenic phi-
losophy

The development of Saracenic philosophy was limited to two brief periods of brilliance: the ninth and tenth centuries in the Baghdad caliphate and the twelfth century in Spain. Among the philosophers in the East three great names stand out—Al Kindi, Al Farabi, and Avicenna. The first of them died about 870, and the last was born in 980. All seem to have been of Turkish or Persian nationality. In the eleventh century Saracenic philosophy in the East degenerated into religious fundamentalism and mysticism. Like the Sufis, from whom they derived a great many of their doctrines, the Eastern philosophers denied the competence of reason and urged a reliance upon faith and revelation. After their time philosophy died out in the Baghdad caliphate. The most renowned of the philosophers in the West, and probably the greatest of all the Saracenic thinkers, was Averroës of Cordova (1126–98). His influence upon the Christian Scholastics of the thirteenth century was especially profound.

In no subject were the Saracens farther advanced than in science. In fact, their achievements in this field were the best the world had seen since the end of the Hellenistic civilization. The Saracens were brilliant astronomers, mathematicians, physicists, chemists, and physicians. Despite their reverence for Aristotle, they did not hesitate to criticize his notion of a universe of concentric spheres with the earth at the center, and they admitted the possibility that the earth rotates on its axis and revolves around the sun. Their celebrated poet, Omar Khayyàm, developed one of the most accurate calendars ever devised. The Saracens were also capable mathematicians and developed algebra and trigonometry considerably beyond the stage these had reached in Hellenistic times. Although they did not invent the celebrated "Arabic" system of numerals, they were nevertheless responsible for adapting it from the Indian system and making it available to the West. Saracenic physicists founded the science of optics and drew a number of significant conclusions regarding the theory of magnifying lenses and the velocity, transmission, and refraction of light. As is commonly known, the chemistry of the Moslems was an outgrowth of alchemy, the famous pseudoscience that was based upon the principle that all metals were the same in essence, and that baser metals could therefore be transmuted into gold if only the right instrument, the philosopher's stone, could be found. But the efforts of scientists in this field were by no means confined to this fruitless quest. Some even denied the whole theory of transmutation of metals. As a result of innumerable experiments by chemists and alchemists alike, various new substances and compounds were discovered; among them carbonate of soda, alum, borax, bichloride of mercury, nitrate of silver, saltpeter, and nitric and sulphuric acids. In addition, Saracenic scientists were the first to describe the chemical processes of distillation, filtration, and sublimation.

The accomplishments in medicine were just as remarkable. Saracenic physicians appropriated the knowledge contained in the medical writings of the Hellenistic Age, but some of them were not content with that. Avicenna (980–1037) discovered the contagious nature of tuberculosis, described pleurisy and several varieties of nervous ailments, and pointed out that disease can be spread through contamination of water and soil. His chief medical writing, the *Canon*, was venerated in Europe as an authoritative work until late in the seventeenth century. Avicenna's older contemporary, Rhazes (850–923), was the greatest clinical physician of the medieval world. His supreme achievement was the discovery of the true nature of smallpox. Other Saracenic physicians discovered the value of cauterization and of styptic agents, diagnosed cancer of the stomach, prescribed antidotes for cases of poisoning, and made notable progress in treating diseases of the eyes. In addition, they recognized the highly infectious character of the plague, pointing out that it could be transmitted by garments, by eating utensils and drinking cups, as well as by personal contact. Finally, the Saracens excelled all other medieval peoples in the organization of hospitals and in the control of medical practice. Authentic records indicate that there were at least thirty-four great hospitals located in the principal cities of Persia, Syria, and Egypt. They appear to have been organized in a strikingly modern fashion. Each had its wards for particular cases, its dispensary, and its library. The chief physicians and surgeons lectured to the students and graduates, examined them, and issued diplomas or licenses to practice. Even the owners of leeches, who in most cases were also barbers, had to submit them for inspection at regular intervals.

So far as literature was concerned, the Saracens derived their inspiration almost entirely from Persia. If they knew anything about the classic poetry of the Greeks, they evidently found it of little interest. As a result, their own writings are colorful, imaginative, sensuous, and romantic; but with a few exceptions they make no very strong appeal to the intellect. The best-known example of their poetry is the *Rubáiyát* by Omar Khayyàm (*ca.* 1048–*ca.* 1124). The *Rubáiyát*, as it is preserved for us in the translation by Edward Fitzgerald, appears to reflect the qualities of an effete Persian culture much more than the ideals of the Arabs themselves. Its philosophy of mechanism, skepticism, and hedonism is quite similar to that of the Book of Ecclesiastes in the Old Testament. The most notable example of Saracenic literature in prose is the so-called *Arabian Nights*, or *Book of the 1001 Nights*, written mainly during the eighth and ninth centuries. The material of the collection includes fables, anecdotes, household tales, and stories of erotic adventures derived from the literatures of various nations from China to Egypt. The chief significance of the collection of tales is to be found in the picture they present of the sophisticated life of the Moslems in the best days of the Baghdad caliphate.

Since the Arabs themselves had scarcely any more of an artistic background than the Hebrews, it was necessary that the art of the Saracenic civilization should be an eclectic product. Its primary sources were Byzantium and Persia. From the former came many of

Saracenic contributions to medicine

Saracenic literature

the structural features of the architecture, especially the dome, the column, and the arch. Persian influence was probably responsible for the intricate, nonnaturalistic designs which were used as decorative motifs in practically all of the arts. From both Persia and Byzantium came the tendency to subordinate form to rich and sensuous color. Architecture is generally considered the most important of the Saracenic arts; the development of both painting and sculpture was inhibited by religious prejudice against representation of the human form. By no means all of the examples of this architecture were mosques or churches; many were palaces, schools, libraries, private mansions, and hospitals. Indeed, Saracenic architecture had a much more decidedly secular character than any in medieval Europe. Among its principal elements were bulbous domes, minarets, horseshoe arches, and twisted columns, together with the use of tracery in stone, alternating stripes of black and white, mosaics, and Arabic script as decorative devices. As in the Byzantine style, comparatively little attention was given to exterior ornamentation. The so-called minor arts of the Saracens included the weaving of gorgeous pile carpets and rugs, magnificent leather tooling, and the making of brocaded silks and tapestries, inlaid metal work, enameled glassware, and painted pottery. Most of the products of these arts were embellished with complicated patterns of interlacing geometric designs, plants and fruits and flowers, Arabic script, and fantastic animal figures. The richness and variety of these works of art, produced in defiance of a religion which often displayed a puritanical trend, afford most convincing proof of the vitality of Saracenic civilization.

The economic development of the Saracenic civilization remains to this day one of the marvels of history. In areas which had produced practically nothing for centuries, the Saracens literally made the desert to blossom as the rose. Where only squalid villages encumbered the landscape, they built magnificent cities. The products of their industries were known from China to France and from the interior of Africa to the shores of the Baltic. As the builders of a vast commercial empire, they excelled the Carthaginians. The reasons for this astounding economic development do not lend themselves to easy explanation. Perhaps it was the result in some measure of the long experience with trade which many of the Arabs had had in their homeland. When a wider field opened up, they made the most of their skill. The diffusion of the Arabic language over a vast expanse of territory also helped to extend the avenues of trade. In addition, the great variety of resources in the various sections of the empire served to stimulate exchange of the products of one region for those of another. The principal reason, however, was probably the advantageous location of the Saracenic empire at the crossroads of the world. It lay athwart the major trade routes between Africa, Europe, India, and China.

The Court of the Lions in the Alhambra, Granada, Spain. The palace-fortress of the Alhambra is one of the finest monuments to Saracenic architectural style. Notable are the graceful columns, the horseshoe arches, and the delicate tracery in stone that surmounts the arches.

Commerce and manufacturing were the main foundations of the national wealth. Both were developed in extraordinary degree. The Saracens made use of a great many of the instruments of commerce familiar to the modern world: checks, receipts, bills of lading, letters of credit, trade associations, joint-stock companies, and various others. Saracenic merchants penetrated into southern Russia and even into the equatorial regions of Africa. Caravans of thousands of camels traveled overland to the gates of India and China. Saracenic ships furrowed new paths across the Indian Ocean, the Persian Gulf, and the Caspian Sea. Except for the Aegean Sea and the route from Venice to Constantinople, the Saracens dominated the Mediterranean almost as if it were a private lake. But so vast an expansion of commerce would scarcely have been possible without a corresponding development of industry. It was the ability of the people of one region to turn their natural resources into finished products for sale to other regions which provided a basis for a large part of the trade. Nearly every one of the great cities specialized in some particular variety of manufactures. Mosul was a center of the manufacture of cotton cloth; Baghdad specialized in glassware, jewelry, pottery, and silks; Damascus was famous for its fine steel and for its "damask," or woven-figure silk; Morocco was noted for the manufacture of leather; and Toledo for its excellent swords. The products of these cities, of course, did not exhaust the list of Saracenic manufactures. Drugs, perfumes, carpets, tapestries, brocades, woolens, satins, metal products and a host of others were turned out by the craftsmen of many cities. From the Chinese the Saracens learned the art of paper-making, and the products of that industry were in great demand, not

Commerce and industry

271

only within the empire itself but in Europe as well. The men engaged in the various industries were organized into guilds, over which the government exercised only a general supervision for the prevention of fraudulent practices. For the most part, the guilds themselves regulated the conduct of business by their own members. Control by the state over economic affairs was much less rigid than in the Byzantine Empire.

Agriculture

The Saracens developed farming to as high a level as did any other people of the medieval world. They repaired and extended the irrigation systems originally built by the Egyptians, the Sumerians, and the Babylonians. They terraced the slopes of the mountains in Spain in order to plant them with vineyards, and here as elsewhere they converted many barren wastes into highly productive lands by means of irrigation. Experts attached to the imperial palaces and the mansions of the rich devoted much attention to ornamental gardening, to the cultivation of shrubs and flowers of rare beauty and delightful fragrance. The variety of products of the Saracenic farms and orchards almost passes belief. Cotton, sugar, flax, rice, wheat, spinach, asparagus, apricots, peaches, lemons, and olives were cultivated as standard crops almost everywhere, while bananas, coffee, and oranges were grown in the warmer regions. Some of the farms were great estates, worked in part by serfs and slaves and in part by free peasants as tenants, but the major portion of the land was divided into small holdings cultivated by the owners themselves.

The intellectual and artistic influence of the Saracenic civilization

The influence of the Saracenic civilization upon medieval Europe and upon the Renaissance was almost incalculable, and some of that influence has, of course, persisted until the present time. The philosophy of the Saracens was almost as important as Christianity in providing a basis for the Scholastic thought of the thirteenth century; for it was the Saracens who made available to the West most of the works of Aristotle and indicated more thoroughly than ever before the use to which those writings could be put as a support for religious doctrine. The scientific achievements of the Saracens furnished even more enduring contributions. Though the activity of the Saracens in literature was not as extensive as in science, their literary influence has been important. The songs of the troubadours and some other examples of the love poetry of medieval France were partly inspired by Saracenic writings. Some of the stories in the *Book of the 1001 Nights* found their way into Boccaccio's *Decameron* and Chaucer's *Canterbury Tales*. The art of the Saracens has likewise had an influence of deep significance. A considerable number of the elements in the design of Gothic cathedrals were apparently derived from the mosques and palaces of the Saracens. A partial list would include the cusped arches, the traceried windows, the pointed arch, the use of script and arabesques as decorative devices, and possibly ribbed vaulting. The architecture

Interior of the Great Mosque at Córdoba, Spain. This splendid specimen of Moorish architecture gives an excellent view of the cusped arches and alternating stripes of black and white so commonly used by Saracenic architects.

of late medieval castles was even more closely copied from the design of Saracenic buildings, especially the fortresses of Syria.[6]

Finally, the Saracens exerted a profound influence upon the economic development of late medieval and early modern Europe. The revival of trade which took place in western Europe in the eleventh, twelfth, and thirteenth centuries would scarcely have been possible without the development of Saracenic industry and agriculture to stimulate the demand for new products in the West. From the Saracens, western Europeans acquired a knowledge of the compass, the astrolabe, the art of making paper, and possibly the production of silk, although knowledge of the last may have been obtained somewhat earlier from the Byzantine Empire. Furthermore, it seems probable that the development by the Saracens of the joint-stock company, checks, letters of credit, and other aids to business transactions had much to do with the beginning of the Commercial Revolution in Europe about 1300. Perhaps the extent of Saracenic economic influence is most clearly revealed in the enormous number of words now in common usage which were originally of Arabic or Persian origin. Among them are "traffic," "tariff," "risk," "check," "magazine," "alcohol," "cipher," "zero," "algebra," "muslin," and "bazaar."[7]

Economic contributions

[6] For a more complete discussion of the influence of Saracenic literature and art, see Arnold and Guillaume, (eds.), *The Legacy of Islam.*

[7] It must not be supposed, of course, that Saracenic influence upon medieval Europe was entirely one-sided. There was also a reverse influence of substantial proportions.

273

The Saracenic civilization has significance also for the modern world from the standpoint of international relations. The Saracenic empire was itself an international state. Though loosely organized, it united peoples as diverse as Persians, Arabs, Turks, and Berbers. Its binding cement was a great religion. The spread of this empire and religion constituted the first threat from the Orient that the Western world had faced since the destruction of Carthage. The long conflict between East and West, which extended at least from the Battle of Tours to the end of the Crusades, was commonly represented as a struggle of ideals. The rise and expansion of the Saracens anticipated in several respects the dynamism of such twentieth-century movements as Nazism and communism. There was one outstanding difference, however. Despite their fanaticism at times, the Saracens devoted only part of their energies to military objectives. They adopted the cultures of the peoples they conquered, built a civilization that surpassed in magnificence any that then existed, and left a splendid legacy of original discoveries and achievements.

SELECTED READINGS

· *Items so designated are available in paperbound editions.*

BYZANTINE CIVILIZATION

Baynes, N. H., *The Byzantine Empire,* London, 1925. Compact and interestingly written.

· ———, and Moss, H. St. L. B., eds., *Byzantium,* New York, 1948 (Oxford).

Diehl, Charles, *History of the Byzantine Empire,* New Brunswick, N. J., 1956. Perhaps the definitive work.

Kaegi, Walter E., *Byzantium and the Decline of Rome,* Princeton, 1968.

Ostrogorsky, George, *History of the Byzantine State,* New Brunswick, N. J., 1957.

· Runciman, Steven, *Byzantine Civilization,* New York, 1933 (Meridian). Complete and thorough; easily readable.

· Vasiliev, A. A., *History of the Byzantine Empire, 324–1453,* Madison, Wisc., 1928–1929, 2 vols. (University of Wisconsin).

Vryonis, Speros, *Byzantium and Europe,* New York, 1967.

SARACENIC CIVILIZATION

Arnold, Thomas, and Guillaume, Alfred, eds., *The Legacy of Islam,* New York, 1931. Excellent as a study of Saracenic influence.

De Boer, T. J., *History of Philosophy in Islam,* London, 1903. The best account; concise and clear.

· Gibb, H. A. R., *Mohammedanism: An Historical Survey,* New York, 1953 (Oxford).

· Hitti, P. K., *The Arabs, A Short History,* Princeton, 1946 (Gateway, new ed.).

· Lewis, Bernard, *The Arabs in History,* New York, 1960 (Torchbook).

Margoliouth, D. S., *Mohammed and the Rise of Islam*, New York, 1927. Complete and interesting.

· Pirenne, Henri, *Mohammed and Charlemagne*, New York, 1939 (Meridian).

Saunders, J. J., *A History of Medieval Islam*, New York, 1965.

· von Grunebaum, G. E., *Medieval Islam*, 2d ed., New York, 1961 (Phoenix).

SOURCE MATERIALS

Dewing, H. B., tr., *Procopius: History of the Wars*, Harvard, 1915. 7 vols.

Lane-Poole, Stanley, ed., *Speeches and Table Talk of the Prophet Mohammed*, London, 1882.

Sanders, T. C., tr., *The Institutes of Justinian*, New York, 1924.

· *The Koran* (Penguin).

PART IV

The Later Middle Ages
and the Transition
to the Modern World

Soon after 1000 A.D. there began in Europe several movements of intellectual awakening which culminated finally in a brilliant flowering of culture in the twelfth and thirteenth centuries. In fact, so remarkable was the progress in western Europe from the eleventh century to the end of the thirteenth that the achievements of that period can justifiably be called a new civilization. While some of these achievements were discarded during the subsequent period of the Renaissance, quite a few were preserved and have exerted their influence to the present day. Indeed, the civilization of the later Middle Ages and that of the Renaissance had more in common than is usually suspected. Both were distinguished by humanism, by a new interest in man as the most important creature in the universe. Both were concerned quite largely with affairs of this world, as opposed to the otherworldliness of the early Middle Ages. In the later Middle Ages and the Renaissance alike there was a tendency to glorify the life of adventure and of conquest in place of the early Christian ideals of humility and self-effacement. It should be noted, however, that before the end of the Renaissance a religious revolution known as the Reformation began, which in some respects attempted to turn the clock back to the very beginning of the Middle Ages.

277

A Chronological Table

	EUROPE AS A WHOLE	SOUTHERN EUROPE	NORTHERN EUROPE
1050	Cluny movement, 950–1100 Romanesque architecture, 1000–1150 Scholasticism, 1050–1300 Revival of trade with the East, 1050–1150 Struggle between secular and spiritual powers, 1050–1350 Separation between Eastern and Western churches, 1054 Establishment of the College of Cardinals, 1059 The Crusades, 1096–1204 Rise of merchant and craft guilds, 1100–1300 Growth of cities, 1100–1300 Development of the sacramental system of the Church, 1100–1300 First universities, *ca.* 1150 Gothic architecture, 1150–1300		Norman Conquest of England, 1066 Romances of chivalry, 1100–1300 Holy Roman (Hohenstaufen) Empire, 1152–1254
1200	Orders of friars, 1200– Fourth Lateran Council, 1215	St. Francis of Assisi, 1182–1226 Dante, 1265–1321	Roger Bacon, 1214?–1294 Magna Charta, 1215 St. Thomas Aquinas, 1225–1274 Origin of Parliament in England, 1265–1295 Hanseatic League, 1300–1500
	Feudalism declines, 1300–1500 Rise of capitalism, 1300–1500 Growth of banking and development of money economy, 1300–1600 Black Death, 1347–1349	Boccaccio, 1313–1375 Savonarola, 1452–1498 Leonardo da Vinci, 1452–1519 Machiavelli, 1469–1527 Michelangelo, 1475–1564 Unification of Spain, 1492 Cervantes, 1547–1616 Galileo, 1564–1642	Establishment of Estates-General in France, 1302 Hundred Years' War, 1337–1453 Christian Renaissance, 1400–1500 War of the Roses in England, 1455–1485. Erasmus, 1466?–1536 Copernicus, 1473–1543 Tudor dynasty in England, 1485–1603
1600			Montaigne, 1533–1592 Sir Francis Bacon, 1561–1626 Shakespeare, 1564–1616 Sir William Harvey, 1578–1657

CHAPTER 11

The Later Middle Ages (1050-1350): Political and Economic Institutions

> The count asked if he was willing to become completely his man, and the other replied "I am willing," and with clasped hands, surrounded by the hands of the count, they were bound together by a kiss. Secondly, he who had done homage gave his fealty to the representative of the count in these words, "I promise on my faith that I will in future be faithful to count William and will observe my homage to him completely against all persons in good faith and without deceit," and thirdly, he took his oath to this upon the relics of the saints.
>
> —Description of Ceremony of Homage and Fealty
> at court of Count of Flanders, twelfth century

Long before the famous Renaissance of the fourteenth and succeeding centuries, western Europe began slowly to emerge from the backwardness of earlier times. The start of this gradual awakening can be dated as far back as 1050 A.D. During the three centuries that followed, the people of Latin Christendom cast off at least some of their winter garments of repentance and other-worldliness and put on the less restrictive attire of the man who is determined to live in this world and mold his environment to his own advantage. The causes of this change in attitude were many and various: among them were the influence of contact with the Saracenic and Byzantine civilizations, the increase in economic security, and the influence of monastic education. In addition, the revival of trade in the eleventh and twelfth centuries and the growth of cities led to an increase in prosperity and sophistication which greatly stimulated the progress of enlightenment. The results of these several causes were reflected in a brilliant intellectual and artistic civilization which reached the zenith of its development in the thirteenth century. Probably the most distinctive element in the social and political structure of this civilization was the feudal regime.

The cultural revival of the later Middle Ages

279

We must not overlook the fact, however, that from the twelfth century on the role of the commercial and industrial classes in the cities was an exceedingly important one.

I.   THE ORIGINS OF THE FEUDAL REGIME

The meaning of
feudalism

Feudalism may be defined as a structure of society in which the powers of government are exercised by private barons over persons economically dependent upon them. It is a system of overlordship and vassalage in which the right to govern is conceived as a property right belonging to anyone who is the holder of a fief. The relationship between the overlord and his vassals is a contractual relationship involving reciprocal obligations. In return for the protection and economic assistance they receive, the vassals are bound to obey their lord or suzerain, to serve him faithfully, and generally to compensate him by dues or taxes for the services he renders in their interest. Defined in this fashion, feudalism was not limited to the later Middle Ages. Examples of it had existed in several other periods of world history—in many parts of the Roman Empire, for instance, and throughout the early Middle Ages. Late medieval feudalism, however, differed from the earlier specimens in being a legally recognized framework of society. Men did not apologize for it as a crude substitute for centralized government but glorified it as an ideal system, much as we idealize democracy and the national state at the present time.

Roman origins of
feudalism

How did late medieval feudalism originate? To some extent it was the outgrowth of ancient Roman institutions. One of these was *clientage*. From very early times Roman citizens who had fallen upon evil days had sought the protection of wealthy patrons, becoming their clients or personal dependents. During the confusion that accompanied the decline of the Empire, clientage was greatly extended. A second of these Roman institutions was the *colonate*. In a desperate attempt to check the decline of agricultural production during the economic revolution of the third and fourth centuries, the government of the Empire bound many of the agricultural laborers and tenants to the soil as *coloni* or serfs, and in effect placed them under the control of the proprietors of large estates. The *colonate* had much to do with the growth of an extralegal feudalism in late Roman history, for it increased the wealth and importance of the great landed proprietors. As time went on, the tendency of these men was to ignore or defy the central government and to arrogate to themselves the powers of sovereign rulers over their estates. They levied taxes upon their dependents, made laws for the regulation of their affairs, and administered what passed for justice.

Feudalism was also derived in part from significant economic and political developments of the early Middle Ages. One of these was the growth of the institution of *beneficium*. *Beneficium* consisted in the grant of a *benefice*, or the right to use land in return

EXPANSION OF THE NORSEMEN

for rent or services. In the seventh century the Merovingian kings adopted the practice of rewarding their counts and dukes with benefices, thereby cementing a bond between public office and land-holding. Not long afterward Charles Martel and the Carolingian kings resorted to the granting of benefices to local nobles in return for furnishing mounted troops to fight against the Moors. The result was to increase the dependence of the central government upon the principal landowners throughout the country. The bestowal of *immunities* by the Frankish kings upon some of the holders of bene-fices also accelerated the growth of a feudal regime. Immunities were exemptions of the lands of a secular or ecclesiastical noble from the jurisdiction of the king's agents. The natural outcome was the exercise of public authority by the noble himself as a virtually independent sovereign, subject only to the nominal overlordship of the king. These developments were accentuated by the chaos that accompanied the breakup of Charlemagne's empire following his death in 814. Yet another important development in the early Middle Ages which hastened the growth of a feudal organization of society was the invasions of the Norsemen, the Magyars, and the Moslems. In the eighth and ninth centuries these peoples began mak-

Other origins of feudalism

281

ing swift incursions into the settled portions of western Europe, plundering the richer areas and occasionally massacring the inhabitants. The attacks of the Norsemen in particular were widely feared. As a consequence, many small farmers who had hitherto maintained their independence now sought the protection of their more powerful neighbors, who frequently had armed retainers and strongholds in which men could take refuge.

2. FEUDALISM AS A POLITICAL, SOCIAL, AND ECONOMIC STRUCTURE

As a system of government, feudalism embodied a number of basic conceptions. First of all, as we have seen, it included the notion that the right to govern was a privilege belonging to any man who was the holder of a fief; but it was a privilege entailing very definite obligations, the violation of which might be followed by loss of the fief. Secondly, it included the notion that all government rests upon contract. Rulers must agree to govern justly in accordance with the laws, both human and divine. Subjects must pledge themselves to obey so long as their rulers govern justly. If either party violates the contract, the other is absolved from his obligations and has the right to take action for redress. In the third place, feudalism was based upon the ideal of limited sovereignty, upon opposition to absolute authority no matter by whom it might be exercised. Feudal government was supposed to be a government of laws and not of men. No ruler, regardless of his rank, had any right to impose his personal will upon his subjects in accordance with the dictates of his own whims. Indeed, under feudal theory, no ruler had the right to make law at all; law was the product of custom or of the will of God. The authority of the king or the baron was limited to the issuance of what might be called administrative decrees to put the law into effect. Whether the ideals of feudalism were carried out less successfully in practice than the ideals of political systems generally is a very hard question to answer. Yet organized revolts against political oppression were not of frequent occurrence in the later Middle Ages, notwithstanding the fact that the existence of the *right* to revolt against a ruler who had made himself a tyrant was commonly taught.

Not only in theory but also in practice the feudal regime was a system of overlordship and vassalage, based upon the granting and holding of fiefs. In the main, a fief was a benefice that had become hereditary. It was not always an area of land, however; it might be an office or position, or the right to collect tolls at a bridge, or even the right to coin money or to establish markets and enjoy the profits therefrom. The man who granted the fief was a lord or suzerain, irrespective of his rank; the man who received the fief to hold and transmit to his descendants was a vassal, whether he was a knight, count, or duke. As a rule, the king was the highest suzerain.

Feudalism as a system of government

Fiefs, vassals, and overlords

Immediately below him were the great nobles, who were variously known as dukes, counts, earls, or margraves. These nobles in turn had acquired vassals of their own through dividing their fiefs and granting them to lesser nobles, who were commonly called viscounts or barons. At the bottom of the scale were the knights, whose fiefs could not be divided. Thus, according to the general pattern, every lord except the king was the vassal of some other lord, and every vassal except the knight was a lord over other vassals. But this apparently logical and orderly arrangement was broken by numerous irregularities. There were vassals who held fiefs from a number of different lords, not all of them of the same rank. There were lords some of whose vassals held fiefs from the same overlord as they themselves did. And in some cases there were kings who actually held fiefs from certain of their counts or dukes and were therefore to some extent vassals of their own vassals.

Moreover, the fact must be borne in mind that feudalism was not the same in all countries of western Europe. Many of its features commonly assumed to have been universal were found only in France, where the system was most fully developed, or in one or two other countries at the most. For example, the rule of primogeniture, under which the fief descended intact to the oldest son, was not in force in Germany; nor were social distinctions so sharply defined there as in France. Further, not all of the lands and not all of the inhabitants of any European country were included under the feudal regime. Most of the farmers in the hilly and mountainous regions of France, Italy, and Germany did not hold their lands as fiefs but owned them outright, as their ancestors had for centuries.

Feudalism not the same in all countries

Each member of the feudal nobility was involved in an elaborate network of rights and obligations which varied with his status as a suzerain or a vassal. The most important rights of the suzerain were the right to serve as legal guardian in case any of the fiefs he had granted should be inherited by a minor; the right of escheat, or the right to take back the fief of a vassal who had died without heirs; and the right of forfeiture, or the right to confiscate a vassal's fief for violation of contract. The last of these rights could be exercised, however, only after the vassal had been condemned by a court composed of his own equals. The suzerain himself merely presided over this court. Aside from this privilege of being judged only by his equals, the noble in his capacity as a vassal had only one other important right. That was the right to repudiate his lord for acts of injustice or failure to provide adequate protection. The obligations of the vassal were more numerous than his rights. He was required to render military service for a number of days each year, attend the lord's court, ransom his lord if he were captured, and pay a heavy tax if he inherited or sold a fief.

Feudal rights and obligations

Feudal society was, of course, highly aristocratic. It was a regime of status, not of individual initiative. In almost all cases the members

A regime of
status, with a
few exceptions

of the various ranks of the nobility owed their positions to heredity, although occasionally noble rank would be conferred upon a commoner for his services to the king. Seldom was it possible for a man to win advancement under the system by his own efforts or intelligence. Nevertheless, an important exception was to be found in the case of the *ministeriales* in Germany and in the Low Counties. The *ministeriales*, as their name implies, formed a class of administrative officials under feudal rule. They had charge of castles, toll gates, bridges, market places, and so on. Some of the most capable rose to be bailiffs or administrators of towns or districts, serving under a great prince or bishop or even under the emperor himself. Their position was of such high advantage that ultimately they invaded the ranks of the lesser nobility and came to form a subordinate class of knights.

The life of the
feudal nobles

The life of the feudal nobility was scarcely the idyllic existence frequently described in romantic novels. While there was undoubtedly plenty of excitement, there was also much hardship, and death took its toll at an early age. From a study of medieval skeletons a modern scientist has estimated that the peak of the mortality rate in feudal times came at the age of forty-two,[1] whereas at the present time it occurs at about seventy-five. Moreover, conditions of living even for the richest nobles were comparatively poor. Until almost the end of the eleventh century the feudal castle was nothing but a crude blockhouse of timber. Even the great stone castles of later date were far from being models of comfort and convenience. Rooms were dark and damp, and the bare stone walls were cold and cheerless. Until after the revival of trade with the Orient, which led to the introduction of carpets and rugs, floors were generally covered with rushes or straw, a new layer being put down from time to time as the old became vile from the filth of hunting dogs. The food of the noble and his family, though plentiful and substantial, was neither particularly varied nor appetizing. Meat and fish, cheese, cabbages, turnips, carrots, onions, beans, and peas were the staples of their diet. The only fruits obtainable in abundance were apples and pears. Coffee and tea were unknown, and so were spices until after trade with the Orient had continued for some time. Sugar was eventually introduced, but for a long time it remained so rare and costly that it was often sold as a drug.

*See color
plates at page
320*

Feudal warfare

Although the nobles did not work for a living, their days were not spent in idleness. The conventions of their society dictated an active life of war, high adventure, and sport. Not only did they wage war on flimsy pretexts for the conquest of neighboring fiefs, but they fought for the sheer love of fighting as an exciting adventure. So much violence resulted that the Church intervened with the Peace of God in the tenth century and supplemented this with the Truce

[1] J. W. Thompson, *An Economic and Social History of the Middle Ages*, p. 718.

The World of Sports in the Later Middle Ages. Among the activities shown are fishing, bird netting, archery, and boar sticking. From *A Book of Rural Profits* by Petrus Crescentius.

of God in the eleventh. The Peace of God pronounced the solemn anathemas of the Church against any who did violence to places of worship, robbed the poor, or injured members of the clergy. Later the same protection was extended to merchants. The Truce of God prohibited fighting entirely from "vespers on Wednesday to sunrise on Monday" and also from Christmas to Epiphany (January 6) and throughout the greater part of the spring, late summer, and early fall. The purpose of the last regulation was obviously to protect the peasants during the seasons of planting and harvesting. The penalty against any noble who violated this truce was excommunication. Perhaps if rules such as these could really have been maintained, human beings would eventually have abandoned war as senseless and unprofitable. But the Church itself, in launching the Crusades, was largely responsible for making the rules a dead letter. The holy wars against the infidel were fought with a great deal more barbarity than had ever resulted from the petty squabbles among feudal nobles.

Feudalism flourished throughout the Middle Ages, but until after 1000 its customs were crude and barbaric. In the earlier period gluttony was a common vice, and the quantities of wine and beer consumed at a medieval castle brawl would stagger the imagination of a modern toper. At dinner everyone carved his meat with his own dagger and ate it with his fingers. Bones and scraps were thrown on the floor for the omnipresent dogs to fight over. Women were treated with indifference and sometimes with contempt and brutality, for this was a world dominated by men. During the eleventh century, however, the manners of the aristocratic classes were softened and improved considerably by the growth of what is known as chivalry. Chivalry was the social and moral code of feudalism, the embodiment of its highest ideals and the expression of its virtues. The origins of this code were mainly Germanic and Christian, but Saracenic influence also played some part in its development. Chivalry set forth the ideal of a knight who is not only

Early and later feudalism; chivalry

285

Tournament with Lances. Engraving by Lucas Cranach. Tournaments, imitating the conditions of medieval warfare but with blunted spears and lances, were among the principal recreational pursuits of the feudal aristocracy.

brave and loyal but generous, truthful, reverent, kind to the poor and defenseless, and disdainful of unfair advantage or sordid gain. Above all, perhaps, the perfect knight must be the perfect lover. The chivalric ideal made the lofty love of ladies a veritable cult with an elaborate ceremonial which the hot-blooded young noble had to be careful to follow. As a result, women in the later Middle Ages were elevated to a much higher status than they had enjoyed in early medieval Europe. Chivalry also imposed upon the knight the obligation of fighting in defense of noble causes. It was especially his duty to serve as the champion of the Church and to further its interest with sword and spear.

The manorial estate; systems of agriculture

The basic economic unit that served as an adjunct to the feudal regime was the manorial estate, although manorialism itself had a political as well as an economic aspect. The manor, or manorial estate, was generally the fief of an individual knight. Lords of higher rank held many manors, the number frequently running into the hundreds or thousands. No one knows even the average size of these economic units, but the smallest appear to have included at least 300 or 400 acres. Each manorial estate comprised one or more villages, the lands cultivated by the peasants, the common forest and pasture lands, the land belonging to the parish church, and the lord's demesne, which included the best farm land on the manor. With minor exceptions, all of the arable land was divided into three main blocks: the spring planting ground, the autumn planting ground, and the fallow. These were rotated from year to year, so that the spring planting ground one year would become the autumn planting ground the next, and so on. Such was the famous *three-field system*, which seems to have originated in western Europe toward the end of the eighth century. Manorial agriculture was also conducted largely under the *open-field system*. The holding allotted to each peasant was not a compact area of the manor, but consisted of a number of strips located in each of the three main blocks of arable land. These strips, averaging about an acre in size, were generally separated only by a narrow band of unplowed turf. The main object of the system was apparently to give to each serf his fair share of the three different kinds of land. In cultivating these strips the peasants worked cooperatively, chiefly because their holdings were scattered, and it was therefore logical for a number of men to combine their efforts in farming all the strips in a particular area. Besides, no one peasant had enough oxen to draw the crude wooden plows through the stubborn soil.

Except for the noble and his family, the parish priest, and possibly a few administrative officials, the entire population of the manor consisted of persons of servile status. These might be embraced in as many as four different classes: villeins; serfs; crofters and cotters; and slaves. Though villeins and serfs eventually came to be almost indistinguishable, there were at one time several important differences between them. Villeins were originally small farmers who had surrendered their lands as individuals to some powerful neighbor. The ancestors of the serfs had frequently been subjected *en masse*, whole villages of them at once. The villeins were perpetual tenants, not bound in person to the soil, whereas the serfs were bought and sold with the land to which they were attached. Another difference was that the villein was liable to obligations only within the definite terms of his customary contract, while the labor of the serf could be exploited virtually as his owner saw fit. Finally, the villein could be taxed only within limits fixed by custom, but the serf was taxable at the lord's mercy. By the thirteenth century, however, most of these differences had disappeared. And it is a notable fact that the villeins were not degraded to the level of serfs; instead, the serfs rose to the level of villeins. Neither serfs nor villeins were included in the personal relations of feudalism. They had numerous obligations of a servile character, but they shared none of the political or social privileges of the lords and vassals.

The servile classes; villeins and serfs

Although the other dependent classes on the manor were much less numerous than the villeins and serfs, a word or two must be said about them. The crofters and cotters were wretchedly poor men who had no definite status under the feudal regime at all. Unlike even the meanest of the serfs, they had no strips of land which they could cultivate for their living. They occupied small cottages or

Crofters, cotters, and slaves

Diagram of a Manor

The image contains the following labels: WASTE, WOOD LOT, AUTUMN PLANTING, FALLOW, SPRING PLANTING, VILLAGE, CHURCH, PARSON'S HOUSE, Parson's Fields or God's Acre, COMMON PASTURE, MILL, BARN, OVEN, POND, MANOR HOUSE, LORD'S CLOSE, Showing parcellation, MEADOW, Showing meadow lots, MARSH.

Legend:
- Glebe lands of parish church in open fields
- Lord's demesne in open fields
- Strip fields of a single peasant

shanties and hired themselves out to the richer villeins or did odd jobs for the lord of the manor. A few slaves continued to be held throughout the later Middle Ages, but in steadily diminishing numbers. They did not fit in well with the manorial type of economy, for the manor was not a plantation but an aggregate of petty farms cultivated under perpetual lease. The few slaves who were to be found were employed mainly as household servants. After the year 1000 slavery as an institution became practically extinct in western Europe.

Like all other members of the subject classes under feudalism, the villeins and serfs were liable for numerous obligations. Although these appear at first glance to have been exceedingly oppressive, it is necessary to remember that they took the place of both rent and

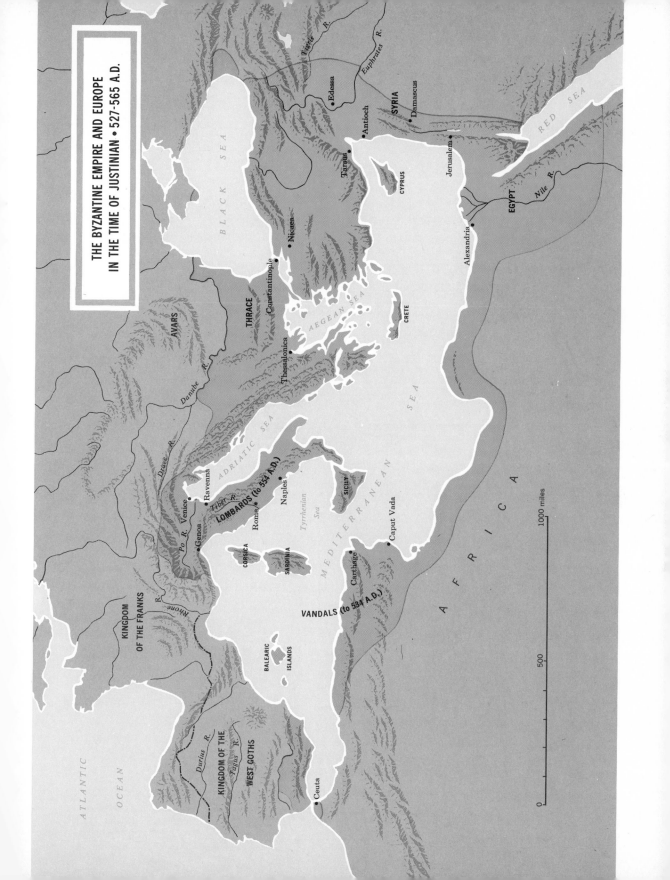

THE BYZANTINE EMPIRE AND EUROPE
IN THE TIME OF JUSTINIAN • 527-565 A.D.

ATLANTIC OCEAN

KINGDOM OF THE FRANKS

KINGDOM OF THE WEST GOTHS

Durius R.

Tagus R.

Ceuta

Rhone R.

R.

BALEARIC ISLANDS

VANDALS (to 534 A.D.)

Carthage

CORSICA

SARDINIA

MEDITERRANEAN SEA

Tyrrhenian Sea

Rome

Naples

SICILY

Caput Vada

AFRICA

1000 miles

500

0

Genoa

Po R.

Venice

Ravenna

LOMBARDS (to 554 A.D.)

Tiber R.

ADRIATIC SEA

Drave R.

Danube R.

AVARS

Thessalonica

THRACE

Constantinople

Nicaea

AEGEAN SEA

CRETE

BLACK SEA

Tarsus

Antioch

Edessa

Tigris R.

Euphrates R.

SYRIA

Damascus

Jerusalem

CYPRUS

Alexandria

EGYPT

Nile R.

RED SEA

The Young King, Louis IX, XIII cent. Though Louis was widely revered as a saint, the artist has endowed him with distinctively human features. (Morgan Library)

Aquamanile, German, XII–XIII cent. Aquamaniles were water jugs used for hand-washing during church ritual, or at meal times. (MMA)

Ivory Plaque, German, X cent. The plaque shows Otto the Great presenting a church to Christ while St. Peter watches, a reference to Otto's building an empire by co-operating with the Church. (MMA)

Kings in Battle, French, *ca.* 1250. A scene depicting, with the trappings of knighthood, Joshua's fight against the five kings of Canaan. In the center Joshua raises his hand, commanding the sun and moon to stand still to enable him to complete his victory. (Morgan Library)

Chalice, German, XIII cent. A beautifully embellished wine cup used in the sacrament of the Eucharist. (MMA)

taxes. The most important of these obligations were the following: the *capitatio*, the *cens*, the *taille*, the *banalités* and the *corvée*. The *capitatio* was a head tax imposed only upon serfs. The *cens* was a species of rent paid only by villeins and freemen. The *taille* was a percentage of nearly everything produced on the lands of both villeins and serfs. The *banalités* were fees paid to the lord for the use of the village mill, winepress, brewery, bake-oven, and sometimes even for the use of the village well. The final form of peasant obligations, the *corvée* consisted of forced labor which the villeins and serfs were required to perform in cultivating the lord's demesne and in building and repairing roads, bridges, and dams.

By no stretch of the imagination could the lot of the medieval peasant be considered an enviable one. During the planting and harvesting seasons, at least, he toiled from sunrise to sunset, and the rewards of his labor were few. His home was generally a miserable hovel constructed of wattle plastered over with mud. A hole in the thatched roof served as the only outlet for smoke. The floor was the bare earth, which was often cold and damp from the infalling rain and snow. For a bed the peasant had a box filled with straw, and his easy chair was a three-legged stool. His food was coarse and monotonous—black or brown bread, a few vegetables from his garden in the summer and fall, cheese and porridge, and salt meats and fish, which were often badly cured and half putrid. When crops were bad, he suffered from famine, and death from starvation was by no means unknown. He was, of course, invariably illiterate and was commonly the victim of superstitious fears and sometimes of the dishonesty of unscrupulous stewards. Perhaps the most lamentable aspect of the peasant's life was the fact that he was a despised and degraded creature. Spokesmen for the nobles and townsmen alike seldom referred to him except in the most scornful and odious terms.

Obligations of the villeins and serfs

The lot of the medieval peasant

Scene in a Medieval Village. Among the activities shown are plowing, grinding grain, and slaughtering a boar for meat. In the lower right two friars are dispensing bread and soup to the poor.

Yet the medieval peasant enjoyed some advantages which undoubtedly helped to redress the balance of his miseries. Many of the fears and uncertainties that plague the lowly in modern times meant nothing to him. He was in very little danger of loss of employment or of insecurity in old age. It was an established principle of feudal law that the peasant could not be deprived of his land. If the land was sold, the serf went with it and retained the right to cultivate his holdings as before. When he became too old or too feeble to work, it was the duty of the lord to care for him through the remainder of his days. Although he worked hard during the busiest seasons, he had at least as many holidays as are allowed to the laborer today. In some parts of Europe these amounted to about sixty out of the year, not counting Sundays. Moreover, it was customary for the lord of the manor to feast his peasants after the spring planting was completed and after the harvest was gathered, as well as during the principal religious holidays. Last of all, the peasant was under no obligation to render military service. His crops might be trampled and his cattle driven off by the armies of warring nobles, but at least he could not be compelled to sacrifice his life for the benefit of some ruler with questionable motives.

No sooner had feudalism reached the height of its development than it began to show signs of decay. The decline was already noticeable in France and Italy by the end of the twelfth century. The system continued longer in Germany and England, but by 1500 it was almost extinct in all countries of western Europe. Many relics of it, of course, survived until much later—some till the middle of the nineteenth century in central and eastern Europe. The causes of the decline of the feudal regime are not far to seek. Many of them were closely associated with the revolutionary economic changes of the eleventh and succeeding centuries. The revival of trade with the Near East and the growth of cities led to an increased demand for products of the farms. Prices rose, and as a consequence some peasants were able to buy their freedom. Moreover, the expansion of commerce and industry created new opportunities for employment and tempted many serfs to flee to the towns. Once they had made good their escape, it was almost impossible to bring them back. Still another economic cause was the opening up of new lands to agricultural production, mainly on account of the higher prices for products of the soil. In order to get peasants to clear forests and drain swamps, it was frequently necessary to promise them their freedom. The Black Death, which swept over Europe in the fourteenth century, while not exactly an economic factor, had results similar to those of the causes already mentioned. It produced a scarcity of labor and thereby enabled the serfs who survived to enforce their demands for freedom. With the peasant a free man, the manorial system was practically impossible to operate.

The political causes of the downfall of feudalism were also of major significance. One was the establishment of professional armies and the inducements offered to the peasants to become mercenary soldiers. Another was the adoption of new methods of warfare (especially firearms) which rendered the knights somewhat less indispensable as a military class. A third was the condition of chaos produced by the Hundred Years' War and the peasant insurrections resulting therefrom. A fourth was the influence of the Crusades in eliminating powerful nobles, in promoting the adoption of direct taxation, and in compelling the sale of privileges to communities of serfs as a means of raising money to equip armies. But probably the most important political cause was the rise of strong national monarchies, especially in France and England. By various means the ambitious kings of these countries in the later Middle Ages gradually deprived the nobles of all of their political authority.

3. THE RISE OF NATIONAL MONARCHIES

Soon after the death of Charlemagne in 814 the strong government which he had built up in western Europe collapsed. In 843, by the Treaty of Verdun, his grandsons agreed to divide the Carolingian Empire into three separate parts. The two largest portions became the kingdoms of East Francia and West Francia, corresponding roughly to the modern states of Germany and France. A wide belt of land between the two was formed into a middle kingdom including the territories of modern Belgium, Holland, Alsace, and Lorraine. Such was the beginning of some of the most important political divisions in the map of Europe today.

Meanwhile all three of these kingdoms passed rapidly under feudal domination. The real rulers were not the descendants of the great Carolingian king, but a host of petty princes, counts, and dukes. The kings themselves sank to the level of mere feudal overlords, dependent upon the local nobles for their soldiers and their revenues. While as kings their moral preponderance was still very great, their actual authority over the people was practically nonexistent. By the end of the tenth century, however, signs of change in this condition began to appear in France. In 987 the last of the weak Carolingian monarchs was displaced by the Count of Paris, Hugh Capet. The direct descendants of this man were to occupy the throne of France for more than 300 years. Although neither Hugh nor any of his immediate successors exercised the degree of sovereignty commonly associated with the royal office, several of the later Capetians were powerful rulers. A number of factors aided these kings in establishing their dominant position. First of all, they were fortunate enough for hundreds of years to have sons to succeed them, and often an only son. Consequently there were no deadly quarrels over the right of succession, nor was there any necessity of dividing the royal property among disgruntled relatives who might be able to defend a claim to the throne. In the second place, most of these kings lived to an advanced age, with the result

Political causes

The division of the Carolingian Empire

The rise of a national monarchy in France

that their sons were already mature men when they came to the throne. There were therefore no regencies to haggle the royal power away during the minority of a prince. Another factor was the growth of trade, which afforded the kings new sources of revenue and enabled them to find powerful allies among the bourgeoisie for their struggle against the nobles. Finally, considerable credit must be given to the shrewdness and vigor of several of the kings themselves.

Founders of the French monarchy

France developed into a national monarchy between the beginning of the eleventh century and the middle of the fifteenth. This development was enhanced by a number of outstanding royal personalities. Foremost among them were Philip Augustus (1180–1223), Louis IX (1226–1270), and Philip IV (1285–1314), or Philip the Fair. These kings instituted numerous changes that undermined feudalism and paved the way for royal autocracy. By one device or another they appropriated the domains of powerful nobles. They commuted feudal dues into money payments, employed mercenary soldiers, and sold charters to cities. They established their own systems of coinage for the whole realm and limited the right of the feudal courts to hear appeals in cases involving treason and breaches of the peace. They issued ordinances and proclaimed them as law, without the consent of their vassals. The culmination of these usurpations of authority by the kings was the creation of the Estates General by Philip IV in 1302. He included in it not only the clergy and the higher nobility but also representatives of the towns. Its main purpose was to approve new forms of taxation. Originally it was not a legislative body but a council of advisers to the king. As time went on, however, it came to be regarded as a true legislative assembly, and was so regarded by the leaders of the great Revolution of 1789 in their eagerness to find precedents for limitations upon the power of the king. Of greater significance, undoubtedly, was its inclusion of commoners in the government.

A Coin Depicting Philip Augustus

Monarchical power in France underwent still further consolidation as a result of the Hundred Years' War (1337–1453). This war grew out of a number of causes. The primary one was probably the long-standing conflict between the French and English kings over territory in France. At the beginning of the fourteenth century, English monarchs still held portions of two provinces in southwestern France as vassals of the French crown. The French monarchs resented the presence of a foreign power on their soil. Moreover, they feared that the English interest in the woolen trade of Flanders might lead to an alliance with the Flemish burghers against the king of France.

The course and climax of the conflict

The Hundred Years' War actually covered more than a century, although the fighting was by no means continuous. At first the English armies were generally victorious. They were better organized, better disciplined, and better equipped. Besides, England did not suffer from the extremes of internal discord which plagued the French. By 1420 the Duke of Burgundy had deserted the French cause, and all of the

NORTHUMBRIA

• Whitby

NORTH
SEA

ENGLAND

WALES

MERCIA

EAST
ANGLIA

ESSEX
London

WESSEX

KENT

SUSSEX

CORNWALL

	Royal domain
	Ecclesiastical seignories
━━	Boundary of the Holy Roman Empire

ENGLISH

CHANNEL

COUNTY OF FLANDERS

Seine
R.

H
O
L
Y

DUCHY OF NORMANDY

• Paris

COUNTY OF
CHAMPAGNE

COUNTY OF BRITTANY

COUNTY OF MAINE

COUNTY
OF BLOIS

COUNTY
OF
NEVERS

DUCHY OF BURGUNDY

R
O
M
A
N

COUNTY OF ANJOU

Loire R.

ATLANTIC

COUNTY OF
BOURBON

DUCHY OF GUIENNE
(AQUITAINE)

KINGDOM OF BURGUNDY

E
M
P
I
R
E

OCEAN

Garonne
R.

C. OF ROUERGUE

C. OF GEVAUDAN

DUCHY OF GASCONY

COUNTY
OF
TOULOUSE

MARQUISATE OF GOTHIA

MEDITERRANEAN SEA

COUNTY OF BARCELONA

SPAIN

0   200 miles

ENGLAND AND FRANCE ca. 1000 A.D.

Statue of Joan of Arc, Orléans. A modern idealization of the French heroine of the 15th century.

Jeanne d'Arc

northern half of France had been occupied by English soldiers. Soon afterward occurred the most dramatic incident of the war, which infused new confidence into the French armies and paved the way for their ultimate victory. A devout but simple peasant girl, Jeanne d'Arc or Joan of Arc, came forward with the declaration that she had been commissioned by God to "drive the English out of the whole kingdom of France." Though she was completely uneducated, "knowing neither A nor B," her piety and sincerity made such a strong impression upon the French soldiers that they firmly believed they were being led by an angel from heaven. In a few months she had liberated most of central France and had brought the dauphin Charles VII to Reims, where he was crowned King of France. But in May 1430, she was captured by the Burgundians and turned over to the English. The latter regarded her as a witch and set up a special court of the clergy to try her for heresy. Found guilty, she was given over to the secular government on May 30, 1431, and burned in the public square of Rouen.

Effects of the Hundred Years' War

As is often true of martyrs, Jeanne d'Arc was more powerful dead than alive. Her memory lingers in France to this day as the spiritual embodiment of a patriotic cause. The years that followed her death witnessed a series of uninterrupted triumphs for the French armies. In 1453 the capture of Bordeaux, the last of the English strongholds, brought the war to an end. Only the port of Calais remained of the once extensive English holdings in France. But the Hundred Years' War did more than expel the English from French territory. It added the capstone to the consolidation of royal power in the kingdom of France. The attempts of both the Estates General and the great nobles to control the government had proved abortive. In spite of the confusion and sufferings of the greater part of the war, France had emerged with enough of a national consciousness to enable her kings to centralize their power in accordance with a pattern of absolute monarchy. The completion of this process marked the final transition from feudalism to something resembling a modern state.

The development of a national monarchy in England goes back to the reign of William the Conqueror. His conquest of the island in 1066 resulted in the establishment of a stronger monarchy than had previously existed under the Saxon rulers. The enlargement of power thus effected was not necessarily deliberate. King William made few sweeping changes. For the most part he preserved Anglo-Saxon laws and institutions. He brought over certain elements of feudalism from the Continent, but he took care to prevent too great a degree of decentralization. By the Salisbury Oath he required his vassals to swear allegiance to him directly instead of to their immediate overlords. He prohibited private warfare and retained the right to coin money as a royal prerogative. When he granted lands to his followers, he rarely gave any of them large estates composed of compact territory. He transformed the old advisory council of the Anglo-Saxon kings into a royal court, composed primarily of his own retainers and administrative subordinates. By the end of his reign the constitution of England had been markedly changed, but the alterations had been so gradual that few were aware of their significance.

Foundations of national monarchy in England

William the Conqueror's immediate successors continued their father's policies, but after the death of Henry I in 1135 a violent quarrel broke out between rival claimants for the throne, and the country was plunged into anarchy. When Henry II (1133–1189) became king in 1154, he found the treasury depleted and the barons entrenched in power. His first objectives, therefore, were to increase the royal revenues and to reduce the power of the nobles. In pursuance of the former, he made a regular practice of commuting the feudal obligation of military service to a money payment, and levied the first English taxes on personal property and on incomes. In his war against the nobles he demolished hundreds of castles that had been built without authorization and curtailed the jurisdiction of the feudal courts. But he apparently realized that the power of the barons could not be permanently restricted without thoroughgoing changes in the law and in judicial procedure. Accordingly, he gathered around him a staff of eminent lawyers to advise him regarding the laws that ought to be in force. In addition, he followed a practice already established of appointing itinerant judges to administer justice in the various parts of the realm. These judges, traveling from one region to another, applied a

The reforms of Henry II

uniform law throughout the kingdom. The precedents laid down by their decisions gradually supplanted local customs and came to be recognized as the Common Law of England. Henry also issued writs commanding the sheriffs to bring before the judges as they went from shire to shire groups of men who were familiar with local conditions. Under oath these men were required to report every case of murder, arson, robbery, or similar crime they knew to have occurred since the judges' last visit. This was the origin of the grand jury. Another of Henry's reforms made it possible for either party to a civil dispute to purchase a writ which would order the sheriff to bring both plaintiff and defendant, together with twelve citizens who knew the facts, before the judge. The twelve were then asked under oath if the plaintiff's statements were true, and the judge rendered his decision in accordance with the answer. Out of this practice grew the institution of the trial jury.

There was one branch of the administration of justice which Henry failed to bring under royal control, though he made strenuous efforts to do so. This was the judging and punishing of members of the clergy. Priests and other members of the ecclesiastical hierarchy were not tried in ordinary courts but in Church courts under the rules of the canon law. Punishment was notoriously lax. A priest, for instance, convicted of murder, was deprived of his clerical status but was rarely given any further penalty. Not only this, but decisions handed down in any English courts on ecclesiastical matters could be appealed to the papal court in Rome. In an effort to eradicate these practices Henry issued the Constitutions of Clarendon in 1164. The Constitutions provided that any clergyman accused of crime must be taken into a royal court first. If the royal court found that a crime had been committed, the defendant would be sent to a Church court for trial. If found guilty he would be sent back to the royal court to be sentenced. From such judgments no appeal could be taken to Rome without the king's consent. In attempting to enforce the constitutions, Henry ran afoul of the Archbishop of Canterbury. The latter, Thomas à Becket, was as devoted to the interests of the Church as Henry was to the strengthening of the monarchy. The quarrel reached a tragic climax when the Archbishop was murdered by a band of Henry's knights after the king, in an outburst of anger, had rebuked his followers for doing nothing to rid him of "a turbulent priest." The crime so shocked the English public that the whole program of bringing the ecclesiastical courts under royal control was largely abandoned. The Archbishop was revered as a martyr and eventually canonized by the Pope.

During the reigns of Henry's sons, Richard I and John, feudalism enjoyed a partial recovery. For all but six months of his ten-year reign Richard was absent from England waging the Third Crusade or defending his possessions on the Continent. Moreover, the heavy

Henry's quarrel with Thomas à Becket

taxation which had to be imposed to defray his military expenses angered many of the barons. The feudal revolt reached its height during the reign of King John, who was perhaps not much worse a tyrant than some of his predecessors. But John had the misfortune to have two powerful enemies in King Philip Augustus of France and Pope Innocent III; and when he lost most of his possessions in France to Philip and suffered a humiliating defeat at the hands of the Pope, it was inevitable that the barons would take advantage of the opportunity to regain their power. In 1215 they compelled John to sign the famous Magna Carta, a document which remains to this day an important part of the British Constitution. The popular interpretation placed upon Magna Carta is really erroneous. It was not intended to be a Bill of Rights or a charter of liberties for the common man. On the contrary, it was a feudal document, a written feudal contract in which the king as an overlord pledged himself to respect the traditional rights of his vassals. It was chiefly important at the time as an expression of the principle of limited government, of the idea that the king is bound by the law.

The opposition of the barons continued during the reign of John's son, Henry III (1216–1272). They now drew considerable support from the middle class and found a new leader in Simon de Montfort. Civil war broke out, in which the king was taken prisoner. In 1265 Simon de Montfort, wishing to secure popular support for his plans to limit the powers of the crown, called together an assembly or parliament which included not only the higher nobles and churchmen but also two knights from each shire, and two citizens from each of the more important towns. Thirty years later this device of a parliament composed of members of the three great classes became a regular agency of the government when Edward I (1272–1307) convoked the so-called Model Parliament in 1295. Edward's purpose in summoning this parliament was not to inaugurate democratic reform but merely to broaden the political structure and thereby make the king less dependent upon the nobles. Nevertheless, a precedent was established that representatives of the commons should always meet with the two higher classes to advise the king. By the end of the reign of Edward III (1327–1377) Parliament had divided for all practical purposes into two houses, and they had increased their control over taxation and were assuming lawmaking authority. The subsequent evolution of the English Parliament into the sovereign power in the country will be discussed in later chapters. The last feudal levy was written in 1381.

During the fourteenth century England was profoundly affected by economic changes which had begun somewhat earlier on the Continent. The development of commerce and industry, the growth of cities, the greater use of money, the scarcity of labor—all of these seriously weakened the manorial system and consequently undermined feudal power. In addition, the Hundred Years' War in-

Revolt of the barons against King John

King John. An effigy in Worchester Cathedral.

Origin of the English Parliament

The extinction of feudalism in England

297

creased the military and financial powers of the kings and tended to make them more independent of baronial support. Feudalism in England was finally extinguished in a great struggle among rival factions for control of the crown. This struggle, known as the War of the Roses, lasted from 1455 to 1485. The death of a great many of the nobles in this war and the disgust of the people with continual disorder enabled the new king, Henry Tudor, or Henry VII (1485–1509), to establish a more highly consolidated rule than the country had known up to this time.

Although the feudal regime became extinct in Germany by the fifteenth century and in Italy somewhat earlier, in neither of these countries was a national monarchy set up until long after the close of the Middle Ages. The power of the dukes in Germany and the power of the Pope always proved too strong to overcome. Some of the German emperors might have succeeded in building up centralized rule if they had been content to remain in their own country, but they persisted in interfering in Italy, thereby antagonizing the Popes and encouraging revolts at home.

The failure of Germany and Italy to form national states

When the eastern branch of the Carolingian dynasty died out in 911, the Germans returned to their ancient practice of electing a king. The most noted of the rulers thus chosen was Otto the Great, who became king in 936. From the beginning of his reign Otto apparently entertained ambitions of becoming something more than a mere king of Germany. He had himself crowned at Aachen, probably to convey the idea that he was the rightful successor of Charlemagne. Soon afterward he intervened in Italian affairs and assumed the title of King of the Lombards. From this it was only a step to becoming involved with the papacy. In 961 Otto responded to an appeal from Pope John XII for protection against his enemies, and in January of the following year he was rewarded by being crowned Roman Emperor.

The empire of Otto the Great

In the twelfth century the crown of Otto the Great came into possession of the Hohenstaufen family, whose most powerful representatives were Frederick Barbarossa (1152–1190) and Frederick II (1220–1250). Both of these rulers were outspoken in asserting their claims to imperial dignity. Frederick Barbarossa called the empire of Germany and Italy the Holy Roman Empire on the theory that it was a universal empire established directly by God and coordinate in rank with the Church. Frederick II, who was king of Sicily and southern Italy as well as Holy Roman Emperor, was much more interested in his southern kingdom than he was in Germany. Nevertheless, he believed just as firmly as did his grandfather Barbarossa in a universal empire as the highest secular power in western Europe. But he considered that the only possible way to make the claims of the Emperor a reality was to build a strong state in Sicily and southern Italy and then extend its power northward. He swept away the vestiges of feudalism almost at a single stroke. Like William the Conqueror, he required all nobles, regardless

The Holy Roman Empire of Frederick Barbarossa and Frederick II

THE HOLY ROMAN EMPIRE ca. 1200 A.D.

of rank, to swear allegiance to him directly. He established a professional army, introduced direct taxation, and abolished trial by ordeal and by combat. He appointed traveling judges to promote the development of a uniform law and judicial procedure. He decreed it to be an act of sacrilege even to discuss the Emperor's statutes or judgments. He set up rigid control over commerce and industry and founded government monopolies of the grain trade, the exchange of money, and the manufacture of textiles and other commodities. He even anticipated modern dictators in a campaign for racial purity, declaring that "When the men of Sicily ally themselves with the daughters of foreigners, the purity of the race becomes besmirched." He seemed to forget the fact that the

299

The Emperor Frederick Barbarossa (Frederick I) and His Two Sons. A miniature dating from about 1180.

blood of most of his people was already mixed with Saracenic, Greek, Italian, and Norman infusions, and that he himself was half German and half Norman.

The succession of the Hapsburgs to the throne

Frederick II was no more successful than any of his predecessors in increasing the power of the Holy Roman Empire. His great mistake was his failure to enlist the support of the middle class in the cities, as the Capetian monarchs in France had done. Without this it was impossibe to break through the wall of papal opposition. After Frederick died the Popes proceeded to eliminate the remaining contenders of the Hohenstaufen line. In 1273 Rudolf of Hapsburg was elected to the imperial throne, but the Holy Roman Empire over which he and his descendants ruled was seldom very powerful. When finally abolished in 1806 by Napoleon, it was little more than a political fiction.

4. URBAN LIFE IN THE LATER MIDDLE AGES

Importance of the cities

By no means all of the inhabitants of western Europe in the later Middle Ages lived in castles, manor houses, or peasant villages. Thousands of others dwelt in cities and towns; and from the eleventh century on, at least, the activities of the urban classes were just as important as the fighting and love-making of nobles or the toiling and roistering of peasants. Indeed, the cities were the real centers of most of the intellectual and artistic progress of the later Middle Ages.

Origins of the medieval cities

The oldest of the medieval cities in western Europe were undoubtedly those which had survived from Roman times. But outside of Italy these were few indeed. Others came into being through a variety of causes. By far the greatest number originated as a result of the revival of trade which began in the eleventh century. The leaders in this revival were the Italian towns of Venice, Genoa, and Pisa. Their merchants rapidly built up a flourishing commerce with the Byzantine Empire and with the great Saracenic cities of Baghdad, Damascus, and Cairo. The products brought in by these merchants stimulated a brisk demand not only in Italy but also in Germany, France, and England. As a result, new markets were opened up, and many people turned to manufacturing to imitate products imported from the Near East. Cities and towns multiplied so rapidly that in some regions half the population had been drawn from agriculture into commercial and industrial pursuits by the fourteenth century.

As one would expect, the largest cities during the late Middle Ages were located in southern Europe. Palermo on the island of Sicily, with possibly 300,000 inhabitants, surpassed all the others in size and probably in magnificence also. The metropolis of northern Europe was Paris, with a population of about 240,000 in the thirteenth century. The only other cities with a population of 100,000 or over were Venice, Florence, and Milan. Although England doubled the number of her inhabitants between the eleventh century and the fourteenth, only about 45,000 of them lived in London in the thirteenth century. By the end of the Middle Ages nearly all of the cities of western Europe had gained some degree of exemption from feudal control. Their citizens had complete freedom to dispose of their property as they saw fit, to marry whom they pleased, and to go and come as they liked. All feudal dues were either abolished or commuted to monetary payments; provision was made for cases involving townsmen to be tried in the municipal courts. Some of the largest and wealthiest towns were almost entirely free, having organized governments with elected officials to administer their affairs. This was especially true in northern Italy, Provence, northern France, and Germany. The great cities of Ghent, Bruges, and Ypres, grown rich from trade and woolen manufactures, virtually dominated all of Flanders. The freedom of the medieval cities was secured in a variety of ways—frequently by purchase, occasionally by violence, and sometimes by taking advantage of the weakness of the nobles or their preoccupation with quarrels of their own. The governments of these cities were generally dominated by an oligarchy

The cities and their governments

Pont Valentre. A medieval bridge on the Lot River (tributary of the Garonne in southwest France). The town in the background is Cahors.

A Section of the Medieval Town of Nordlingen, Germany. The need for protection against invaders led to congested housing conditions inside the walls.

of merchants, but in some cases forms of democracy prevailed. Annual elections of magistrates were relatively common; universal suffrage was occasionally employed; in a few towns the rich were disfranchised entirely, and the government was controlled by the masses.

Social problems in the cities

Most of the medieval cities grew so rapidly that it would have been almost impossible to provide optimum standards of healthfulness and comfort for the inhabitants even if there had been sufficient knowledge and inclination to do so. Overcrowding was so bad that sometimes as many as sixteen people lived in three rooms. Part of this congestion was due to the need of the cities for protection against nobles and brigands. To fulfill this need, fortified walls had to be built around each city with gates that could be securely barred to shut out marauders. Naturally, it was too much trouble to tear down these walls and build new ones with every substantial increase in the population, although eventually this had to be done several times in a great many of the principal towns. Land values within these walls rose to fantastic heights and brought into existence a wealthy rent-collecting class. Because of the high cost of land, houses were built with upper stories that projected over the street, and even space on the walls was utilized for cottages and gardens. Streets were narrow and crooked and generally remained unpaved for centuries. The practice of paving began in Italy in the eleventh century and then gradually spread northward, but no thoroughfare in Paris had a hard surface until 1184 when Philip Augustus paved a single roadway in front of the Louvre. With space in the cities so limited, the streets served as the common playgrounds for boys and young men. Many were the protests voiced by their elders and by the clergy against wrestling, bowling, and pitching of quoits in the

302

streets. "Football was constantly denounced, with good reason, as it was not an orderly game with a fixed number of players . . . but a wild struggle between opposing parties to force the ball through the streets from one end of the town to the other, frequently resulting in broken legs." [2]

Prominent among the economic institutions in the medieval cities were the guilds. Of the two, the merchant and the craft guilds, the merchant organizations were the older, having developed as far back as the eleventh century. At first these included both traders and artisans, and then as industry became more specialized, the original guilds were split into separate organizations of craftsmen and merchants. The main functions of the merchant guild were to maintain a monopoly of the local market for its own members and to preserve a stable, noncompetitive economic system. To accomplish these ends the guild severely restricted trading by foreign merchants in the city, guaranteed to every member the right to participate in every purchase of goods made by any other member, required all of its members to charge uniform prices for the goods they sold, drastically punished cornering of the market, and prohibited many forms of advertising. It should be borne in mind that the merchant guilds were involved primarily in local trade. They had little or nothing to do with international commerce. This was conducted by large commercial firms, chiefly in Italy and Flanders. Their methods were not dissimilar to those of modern capitalism. Vigorous competition, adjustment of prices to market conditions, and use of the credit facilities of banks were typical examples.

The merchant guilds

A Medieval Tailor

Each of the craft guilds had three different classes of members—the master craftsmen, the journeymen, and the apprentices. Only the first two had any voice in the management of guild affairs, and toward the close of the Middle Ages even the journeymen lost most of their privileges. The master craftsmen were always the aristocrats of medieval industry; they owned their shops, employed other workers, and were responsible for the training of apprentices. The

The craft guilds

[2] L. F. Salzman, *English Life in the Middle Ages*, pp. 82–83.

The Walls of Avila, Central Spain. Medieval cities were generally surrounded by fortified walls. The apse of the cathedral built into the massive walls is the supposed birthplace of St. Theresa (1515–1582).

A Medieval Baker

A Medieval Shoemaker

whole craft guild system operated largely for their benefit. The journeymen (from the French *journée* meaning "day" or "day's work") were craftsmen who worked in the masters' shops for wages. In some parts of Germany it was customary for the young journeyman to spend a year wandering about the country picking up casual employment, the so-called *Wanderjahr*, before settling down in any particular place. But in most other sections of Europe he seems to have lived with the master's family. The industrious and intelligent journeyman could eventually become a master craftsman by accumulating enough money to set up his own shop and by passing an examination, which sometimes included the submission of a masterpiece. As in many specialized trades today, entrance into the medieval craft could be accomplished only through serving an apprenticeship, varying in length from two to seven years. The apprentice was entirely under the control of the master craftsman, who was commonly held responsible for the boy's education in elementary subjects and for the development of his character as well as for teaching him his trade. Usually the apprentice received no compensation except his food, lodging, and clothing. When the period of training was over, he became a journeyman. During the waning of the Middle Ages the craft guilds grew more and more exclusive. Terms of apprenticeship were lengthened, and it was made increasingly difficult for journeymen ever to become masters.

The functions of the craft guilds were similar to those of the related organizations of merchants, except for the additional responsibility of maintaining standards of quality. The craftsmen were just as ambitious as the merchants to preserve monopolies in their particular fields and to prevent any real competition among those producing the same article. Consequently, they required uniformity of prices and wages, prohibited working after hours, and set up elaborate regulations governing methods of production and the quality of materials used. They even went to the extreme of discouraging new inventions and discoveries unless they were made available to all and everyone adopted them. As a rule, no one was permitted to practice his trade in a town without first becoming a member of the guild. But in spite of all these regulations there were evidently a good many "chiselers." We read of millers who stole part of their customers' grain, of upholsterers who stuffed their mattresses with thistledown, and of metal-workers who substituted iron for copper and covered it over with gilt.

The medieval craft guilds bore no actual relationship to the labor unions of today, despite a superficial resemblance to those modern unions which are organized on the basis of separate crafts, such as the associations of carpenters, plumbers, and electricians. But the differences are more fundamental. Unlike the modern labor union, the craft guilds were not strictly confined to the working class; the master craftsmen were capitalists, owners of the means of production, and employers as well as workers. Furthermore, they included not only men who worked with their hands but some who would now be classified as professional men entirely outside the ranks of labor. For example, there were guilds of notaries, physicians, and pharmacists. Finally, the craft guild had a much greater breadth of purpose. It was really a miniature industrial system in itself, combining the functions of the modern corporation, the trade association, and the labor union.

A Medieval Weaver

Both the craft and merchant guilds performed other functions besides those directly related to production and trade. They served the purposes of religious associations, benevolent societies, and social clubs. Each guild had its patron saint and chapel, and its members celebrated together the chief religious holidays and Church festivals. With the gradual secularization of the drama, the miracle and mystery plays were transferred from the church to the market place, and the guilds assumed charge of presenting them. In addition, each organization ministered to the needs of its members who were sick or in distress of any kind. Money was appropriated to provide for the care of widows and orphans. A member who was no longer able to work or who had been thrown into jail by his enemies could look to his colleagues for assistance. Even an unfortunate brother's debts might be assumed by the guild if his financial plight was serious.

The economic theory upon which the guild system rested was vastly different from that which prevails in capitalist society. It reflected, first of all, some of the ascetic flavor of Christianity. In the eyes of the Church the vitally important aim in life should be the salvation of one's soul. Everything else should be kept in a subordinate place. It was not proper that men should expend their energies in the pursuit of luxury, or even that they should strive to become too comfortable. Moreover, the religion had been founded upon the idea that riches are a hindrance to the welfare of the soul. St. Ambrose, one of the most influential of the Christian Fathers, had even referred to private property as "a damnable usurpation." However, the economic theory of the later Middle Ages was influenced not only by Christianity but by Aristotle's doctrines of the golden mean and the just price and by his condemnation of usury. This theory included the following basic assumptions:

The economic theory of the guild system

(1) The purpose of economic activity is to provide goods and services for the community and to enable each member of society to live in security and freedom from want. Its purpose is not to furnish opportunities for the few to get rich at the expense of the many.

Basic doctrines

(2) Every commodity has its "just price," which is equal to its cost of production, plus expenses and a reasonable profit. The contract price and the true economic value of the product must be equivalent. Generally speaking, the just price was simply the price for which goods could be sold without fraud.

(3) No man is entitled to a larger share of this world's goods than

305

PRINCIPAL TRADE ROUTES ca. 1400 A.D.

Map legend:

✦ Major cities in the Hanseatic League
—— Land routes   - - - Sea routes

Map labels: NORTH SEA, ATLANTIC OCEAN, BALTIC SEA, MEDITERRANEAN SEA, BLACK SEA, CASPIAN SEA, ADRIATIC SEA

Cities and features: Bergen, Stockholm, Novgorod, Nizhni Novgorod, Kazan, Moscow, Riga, Chester, Amsterdam, Lübeck, Danzig, Bremen, Hamburg, Brunswick, Magdeburg, London, Antwerp, Bruges, Cologne, Warsaw, Kiev, Chapaev, Calais, Rhine R., Breslau, Oder R., Bug R., Don R., Volga R., Seine R., Paris, Elbe R., Cracow, Rostov, Astrakhan, Vienna, Bordeaux, Garonne R., Lyon, Milan, Venice, Odessa, Leon, Marseilles, Genoa, Pisa, Florence, Ragusa, Danube R., Trebizond, Barcelona, Tag R., Lisbon, Toledo, Valencia, Cordova, Rome, Constantinople, Fez, Tunis, Syracuse, Antioch, Baghdad, Beirut, Tripoli, Alexandria

0 ——— 500 miles

is necessary for his reasonable needs. Any surplus that may come
into his possession is not rightfully his but belongs to society. St.
Thomas Aquinas, the greatest of all the medieval philosophers,
taught that if a rich man refuses to share his wealth with the poor, it
is entirely justifiable that his surplus should be taken from him.

(4) No man has a right to financial reward unless he engages in
socially useful labor or incurs some actual risk in an economic venture. The taking of interest on loans where no genuine risk is involved constitutes the sin of usury.

It would be foolish, of course, to suppose that these lofty ideals
were ever carried out to perfection. As we have seen, manifestations

**Exceptions to the
ideal**

of greed were not lacking among many members of the guilds. But
more than this, the noncapitalistic guild system did not extend into
every sphere of medieval economic activity. For example, long-
distance trade, as we have seen, was carried on by great mercantile
establishments in Flanders and in the cities of Italy. In other cases it
was in the hands of *associations* of merchants. Characteristic of the
latter were the Teutonic Hanse, or associations of German merchants engaged in exchanging the furs, fish, amber, leather, salt, and

grain from the Baltic region for the wines, spices, textiles, fruits, and other products of the west and the south. By the fourteenth century these associations had developed into the powerful Hanseatic League with a membership of about eighty towns under the leadership of Lübeck, Hamburg, and Bremen. The Hanse was essentially a profit-making organization, and the activities of its members foreshadowed the growth of a capitalist economy in northern Europe.

SELECTED READINGS

· *Items so designated are available in paperbound editions.*

Barraclough, Geoffrey, ed., *Medieval Germany*, New York, 1961, 2 vols.

· ———, *Origins of Modern Germany*, New York, 1946 (Capricorn).

· Bloch, Marc, *Feudal Society*, Chicago, 1961 (Phoenix, 2 vols.).

· Boissonnade, Prosper, *Life and Work in Medieval Europe*, New York, 1927 (Torchbook). Interesting and dependable.

· Brooke, Christopher, *From Alfred to Henry III, 1871–1272*, London, 1961 (Norton Library History of England).

· Bryce, James, *The Holy Roman Empire*, New York, 1919 (Schocken).

Buchan, Alice, *Joan of Arc and the Recovery of France*, New York, 1948.

Clough, S. B., and Cole, C. W., *Economic History of Europe*, Boston, 1947. Contains excellent chapters on medieval economy.

· Fawtier, Robert, *The Capetian Kings of France*, New York, 1960 (St. Martin's Library).

· Ganshof, F. L., *Feudalism*, New York, 1952 (Torchbook). A high-level and somewhat technical account. Valuable for a clear understanding of feudal theory and institutions.

· Haskins, Charles H., *The Normans in European History*, Boston, 1915 (Norton Library).

· Hollister, C. W., *Medieval Europe: A Short History*, New York, 1964 (Wiley). Concise, authoritative, and delightfully written.

· Holmes, *The Later Middle Ages*, 1272–1485 (Norton Library, History of England).

Kantorowicz, Ernst, *Frederick II*, New York, 1957.

· Labarge, M. W., *A Baronial Household of the Thirteenth Century*, New York, 1965 (Barnes & Noble).

Loyn, H. R., *Anglo-Saxon England and the Norman Conquest*, New York, 1963.

Luchaire, A., *Social France in the Time of Philip Augustus*, New York, 1912.

· Mundy, J. H., and Riesenberg, Peter, *The Medieval Town*, Princeton, 1958 (Anvil). A valuable supplement to Pirenne.

· Myers, A. R., *England in the Late Middle Ages*, London, 1952 (Penguin).

· Painter, Sidney, *The Rise of Feudal Monarchies*, Ithaca, 1951 (Cornell).

· ———, *Medieval Society*, 1951 (Cornell). A brief but scholarly survey.

· Pirenne, Henri, *Economic and Social History of Medieval Europe*, New York, 1956 (Harvest). Stimulating and authoritative.

· ———, *Medieval Cities*, Princeton, 1925 (Anchor). The most highly regarded book on the subject.

· Power, Eileen, *Medieval People*, London, 1924 (Anchor).

· Runciman, Steven, *A History of the Crusades, The First Crusade and the Foundation of the Kingdom of Jerusalem*, New York, 1951, Vol. 1 (Torchbook).

· Sayles, G. O., *The Medieval Foundations of England*, London, 1952 (Perpetua).

READINGS

· Stephenson, Carl, *Medieval Feudalism*, New York, 1935 (Cornell).

· Tawney, R. H., *Religion and the Rise of Capitalism*, New York, 1947 (Mentor). Interesting for the light it throws on medieval economic theory under the influence of the Church.

Ziegler, Philip, *The Black Death*, New York, 1969.

SOURCE MATERIALS

Coulton, G. G., *Life in the Middle Ages*, New York, 1955, 4 vols.

· ———, *The Medieval Village, Manor, and Monastery*, New York, 1960 (Torchbook).

· Dante, *De Monarchia (On World Government)*, 2d rev. ed., New York, 1957 (Library of Liberal Arts).

John of Salisbury, *Policraticus*, New York, 1909, 2 vols.

· Johnes, Thomas, *Froissart's Chronicles of England, France, Spain and the Adjoining Countries*, Vol. I, 240–41; Vol. II, 94–95, New York, 1961 (Dutton).

· Lopez, Robert S., and Raymond, Irving W., *Medieval Trade in the Mediterranean World*, New York, 1955 (Norton).

McKechnie, W. S., *Magna Carta*, 2d rev. ed., New York, 1914.

Marsiglio of Padua, *Defensor Pacis (Defender of the Peace)*, especially Book I, Chs. IV, XII, XV.

· Otto of Freising, *The Deeds of Frederick Barbarossa*, New York, 1953 (Norton).

· *Portable Medieval Reader* (Viking).

CHAPTER 12

The Later Middle Ages (1050-1350): Religious and Intellectual Developments

> Now in those things which we hold about God there is truth in two ways. For certain things that are true about God wholly surpass the capability of human reason, for instance that God is three and one; while there are certain things to which even natural religion can attain, for instance that God is, that God is one, and others like these, which even the philosophers proved demonstratively of God, being guided by the light of natural reason.
> —St. Thomas Aquinas, *Summa Contra Gentiles*, Book I

It has already been mentioned more than once that the civilization of western Europe between 1050 and 1350 was vastly different from that which had existed at the beginning of the medieval period. Nowhere was the contrast more striking than in the spheres of religion and the intellect. The religious and intellectual attitudes of the early Middle Ages were products of a time of transition and of considerable chaos. The Roman political and social structure had disintegrated, and no new regime had yet emerged to take its place. As a consequence, the thinking of this time was directed toward pessimism and otherworldly concerns. But after the tenth century these attitudes gradually gave way to more optimistic sentiments and to an increasing interest in worldly affairs. The original causes were directly related to the progress of monastic education, to the rise of more stable government, and to an increase in economic security. Later such factors as the influence of the Saracenic and Byzantine civilizations and the growth of cities brought the culture of the later Middle Ages to a magnificent climax of intellectual achievement in the twelfth and thirteenth centuries. At the same time religion took on a less otherworldly aspect and evolved into an institution more deeply concerned with the affairs of this life.

The change in religious and intellectual attitudes

I. THE NEW CHRISTIANITY

During the later Middle Ages, Christianity underwent so many significant developments from its early medieval character that it seemed in some respects to be almost a new religion. To be sure, such cardinal features as faith in one God, the belief in the Trinity, and the hope for salvation in a world to come continued to be accepted in their original form, but other elements in the religion of St. Augustine and Gregory the Great were modified or eliminated and different ones substituted for them. The transformation began about 1050 and reached its zenith in the thirteenth century under the influence of such leaders as St. Thomas Aquinas, St. Francis, and Innocent III.

Late medieval Christianity

Perhaps the most important developments were in matters of doctrine and religious attitudes. The religion of the early Middle Ages had been pessimistic, fatalistic, and, theoretically at least, opposed to everything worldly as a compromise with the devil. Man was considered to be inherently wicked and incapable of any good works except as the beneficiary of God's grace. God Himself was omnipotent, selecting for reasons of His own those human beings who would enter His paradise, and leaving the rest to follow the path to destruction. By the thirteenth century quite different religious conceptions had come to prevail. Life in this world was now held to be exceedingly important, not only as a preparation for eternity but for its own sake as well. No longer was human nature regarded as totally evil. Man could therefore cooperate with God in achieving the salvation of his soul. Instead of emphasizing the omnipotence of God, philosophers and theologians now stressed the divine justice and mercy.

New doctrines and new attitudes

The most inclusive statements of late medieval theology were contained in the *Summa theologica* of St. Thomas Aquinas and in the pronouncements issued by Church councils, especially the Fourth Lateran Council of 1215. New elements in this theology included the theory of the priesthood and the theory of the sacraments. There had, of course, been priests and sacraments in the Church long before the eleventh century, but neither the exact functions of the priests nor the precise nature of the sacraments had ever been clearly formulated. The theory now came to be held that the priest, by virtue of his ordination by a bishop and the latter's confirmation by the Pope, was the inheritor of a portion of the authority conferred by the Christ upon the Apostle Peter. In effect, this meant that the priest had the power to cooperate with God in performing certain miracles and in releasing sinners from the temporal consequences of their wickedness.

The new theology: (1) the theory of the priesthood

By the end of the twelfth century the number of sacraments had come to be accepted as seven. The seven were and still are: baptism; confirmation; penance; the Eucharist, or Lord's Supper; marriage; ordination; and extreme unction, or the last rites administered to the dying. The Roman Church defines a sacrament as an instrumentality whereby divine grace is communicated to men. The sacramental theory as it came to be accepted during the last centuries of the Middle Ages included a number of separate doctrines. First, there was the doctrine that the sacraments were indispensable means of procuring God's grace, that no individual could be saved without them. Second, there was the principle that the sacraments were automatic in their effects. In other words, it was held that the efficacy of the sacraments did not depend upon the character of the priest who administered them. The priest might be a very unworthy man, but the sacraments in his hands would remain as unpolluted as if they were administered by a saint. Finally, at the Fourth Lateran Council, the doctrine of transubstantiation was made an integral part of the sacramental theory. This doctrine means that the priest, at a given moment in the Eucharistic ceremony, actually cooperates with God in the performance of a miracle whereby the bread and wine of the sacrament are changed or transubstantiated into the body and blood of Christ. The change, of course, is considered a change in essence only; the "accidents" of taste and appearance remain the same.

(2) the theory of the sacraments

The adoption of these two fundamental theories, the theory of the priesthood and the theory of the sacraments, had potent effects in exalting the power of the clergy and in strengthening the formal and mechanical elements in the Latin Church. However, medieval Catholicism was revitalized and made into a civilizing influence by two other developments that marked the later Middle Ages. One was the adoption of a rationalist philosophy by the leading theologians, and the other was the growth of a humanizing attitude. The influence of rationalist philosophy will be discussed farther on in this chapter. The humanizing element in religion expressed itself in a variety of ways—in the revolt against the selfish asceticism of monks and hermits, in the naturalism of St. Francis, and perhaps most of all in the veneration of saints and the Virgin Mary. All through the later medieval period, the veneration or "invocation" of saints was a popular practice, especially among the common people. For the average person God and Christ were remote and sublime beings who could hardly be bothered with the petty problems of men. But the saints were human; one could ask them for favors which one would hesitate to request of God. For example, a woman could implore the aid of St. Agnes in helping her find a husband. Even more popular than the invocation of saints was reverence for the Virgin Mary, which came to be almost a religion in itself during the twelfth and thirteenth centuries. Devotion to Mary as the beautiful and compassionate Mother undoubtedly served as one of the strongest expressions of the humanizing tendency in medieval religion. For she was venerated not only as the ideal woman but also as Our Lady of Sorrows. The grief that she experienced over the tragic death of her Son was believed to endow her with a special

Mechanical religion modified by rationalism and a humanizing attitude

Changes in the
organization of
the Church

sympathy for the sorrows of mankind. Though revered as the Queen of Heaven, she was, above all, the goddess of this life.

Significant developments in ecclesiastical organization and the adoption of new forms of religious discipline also occurred during the later Middle Ages. In 1059 the College of Cardinals was established as a papal electoral college. Originally the members of this body were the deacons, priests, and bishops of certain churches in the city of Rome. Later high ranking clergy from nearly all countries of the Western world were appointed to membership, although the College included a majority of Italians until 1946. At present there are 134 members, and a two-thirds vote is necessary to elect the Pope, who is invariably a cardinal himself. Prior to 1059 Popes were chosen in a variety of ways. In the early days they had been elected by the clergy of the diocese of Rome, but later they were often appointed by powerful nobles and frequently by the German emperors. The vesting of the sole right of election in the College of Cardinals was part of a great reform movement to free the Church from political control. The other main development in religious organization was the growth of the papal monarchy. The first of the Popes to achieve much success in extending his supremacy over the whole ecclesiastical hierarchy was Nicholas I (858–867). Intervening in disputes between bishops and archbishops, he forced all of them to submit to his own direct authority. Nicholas was followed, however, by a series of weak successors, and the papal monarchy was not revived until the reign of Gregory VII (1073–1085). It reached the highest stage of its medieval developments during the pontificate of Innocent III (1198–1216).

New methods of
discipline

During the later centuries of the Middle Ages the Church made systematic attempts to extend its moral authority over all of its lay members, whether of high or of low degree. The chief methods adopted were excommunication and the requirement of oral confession. Excommunication was not used to any extent before the eleventh century. Its effect was to expel an individual from the Church and to deprive him of all the privileges of a Christian. His body could not be buried in consecrated ground, and his soul was temporarily consigned to hell. All other Christians were forbidden to associate with him, under penalty of sharing his fate. Sometimes a decree of excommunication against a king or a powerful noble was fortified by placing an *interdict* upon the area over which he ruled. The interdict, by withholding most of the benefits of religion from a ruler's subjects, was intended to kindle their resentment against him and force him to submit to the Church. Both excommunication and the interdict proved to be powerful weapons until about the end of the thirteenth century; after that their effectiveness waned. By a decree of the Fourth Lateran Council in 1215 the Church adopted the requirement that every individual must make an oral confession of his sins to a priest at least once a year, and then undergo the punishment imposed before becoming eligible to partake of the Eucharist. The result of this decree was to give the priest the authority of a moral guardian over every individual in his parish.

As the Church became more successful, it tended to become more worldly. Long before the great Reformation of the sixteenth century, medieval Catholicism went through a series of reformations calculated to restore the institutions of the Church to some earlier state of purity or to make them more useful to society. The first of these reform movements was the Cluny movement or the Cluniac revival, which derived its name from the French monastery of Cluny founded in 910. The original purpose of the Cluny movement was simply to reform monasticism. The Benedictine monasteries, which were practically the only ones in existence by the tenth century in western Europe, had grown corrupt and were rapidly passing under the control of feudal nobles. Consequently the Cluniac leaders took as their objectives the enforcement of the rules of piety and chastity upon the monks and the liberation of the monasteries themselves from feudal domination. But by the eleventh century the movement had gained a much broader significance. In fact, its purposes were now so different from the original ones that it is often referred to as the New Cluny movement. No longer were the reformers content merely to purify monasticism and free it from the clutches of the lay feudality; their primary aims were now to eliminate corruption and worldliness from the entire Church, to abolish feudal control over the secular clergy as well as over monks, and to establish the absolute supremacy of the Pope in ecclesiastical matters. They centered their attacks, first of all, upon *simony*, which was interpreted to include the buying and selling of Church offices, any form of appointment to Church offices contrary to the canon law, and the investing of bishops and abbots with the symbols of their spiritual power by secular authorities. In addition, the reformers demanded celibacy for all grades of the clergy. Nearly all of these elements in their program were directed toward making the Church entirely independent of the great nobles, especially by depriving them of their power to dictate the appointment of bishops, abbots, and priests. The movement aroused bitter opposition, for it struck at the very basis of the feudal relationship which had been established between secular rulers and the clergy. But most of the program was eventually put into effect, due in large part to the fanatical zeal of such leaders as Hildebrand, the "holy Satan" who in 1073 became Pope Gregory VII.

By the middle of the eleventh century the Cluniac monks had begun to sink into the same morass of worldliness as their older Benedictine brothers whom they had set out to reform. The result was the launching of new movements to set an even stronger example of purity and austerity for the regular clergy. In 1084 the Carthusian order was established with a set of rules more rigorous than any hitherto adopted in the West. The Carthusian monks were required to live in cells, to fast three days each week on bread and water, to wear hair shirts, and to spend all their time in prayer, meditation, and manual labor. A few years later the Cistercian order was founded at Citeaux in Burgundy and soon proved to be one of the most popular of them all. By the middle of the twelfth century more than 300 Cistercian monasteries were receiving converts from all over western Europe. Although not so strict in their requirements of individual asceticism as the Carthusians, the founders of the Cistercian order saw to it that the rules would be puritanical enough to constitute an emphatic protest against the luxury and idleness of the Cluniac monks. Only a vegetarian diet was allowed, and manual labor was strictly enforced.

Undoubtedly the most significant reform movement of the later Middle Ages was the rise of the friars in the thirteenth century. Though the friars are often regarded as simply another species of monks, they were really quite different. Originally they were not members of the clergy at all but laymen. Instead of shutting themselves up in monasteries, they devoted all of their time to social welfare work and to preaching and teaching. The growth of the new orders was symptomatic of an attempt to bring religion into harmony with the needs of a world which had completely outgrown the so-called Dark Ages. Men were now coming to realize that the main business of religion was not to enable a few self-serving monks to save their own souls at the expense of society, but to help make this world a happier place in which to live and to rescue the great mass of mankind from ignorance and sin.

(3) the rise of the orders of friars: the Franciscan order

The founder of the original order of friars was St. Francis of Assisi (1182–1226). The son of a rich merchant, the young Francis became dissatisfied with the values of his social class and determined to become a servant of the poor. Giving away all of his property and donning the rags of a beggar, he set out on his great mission of preaching salvation in the darkest corners of the Italian cities and ministering to the needs of helpless outcasts. The philosophy of St. Francis was different from that of many other Christian leaders. The major portion of it was founded almost literally upon the gospel of Jesus. St. Francis followed Jesus in his selflessness, in his devotion to poverty as an ideal, in his indifference to doctrine, and in his contempt for form and ceremony. In addition he had a profound love not merely for man but for every creature around him, and even for the objects of inanimate nature. He found God revealed in the sun, the wind, the flowers, and everything that existed for the use or delight of man. His disciples related how he would never put out a fire, but "treated it reverently," and how "he directed the brother who cut and fetched the fire wood never to cut a whole tree, so that some part of it might remain untouched for the love of Him who was willing to work out our salvation upon the wood of the cross." [1] Finally, it should be made clear that St. Francis was not an ascetic in the

St. Francis of Assisi

[1] Quoted by H. O. Taylor, *The Medieval Mind*, I, 454–55.

Illuminated Manuscript from *Les Belles Heures de Jean, Duc de Berry*, a book of hours. Monks reading prayers at the bier of their deceased brother, St. Anthony. Illuminated manuscripts have value not merely as works of art but for their portrayals of medieval life and culture.

accurate meaning of that term. Although he denied himself comforts and pleasures, he did not despise the body or practice laceration of the flesh to achieve the salvation of his soul. His abandonment of earthly possessions was done primarily to conquer pride and bring himself down to the level of the people whom he wished to help.

The second of the orders of friars was the Dominican order, founded about 1215 by St. Dominic, a Castilian noble who lived in southern France. The Dominicans adopted as their principal task the combating of heresy. Believing that an effective means to this end was education, they prepared themselves by diligent study to refute the arguments of pagans and skeptics. Many members of the order gained teaching positions in the universities and contributed much to the development of philosophy and theology. Unfortunately, they were carried away at times by a zeal for persecuting; they were active leaders of the medieval, or Papal Inquisition. By the fourteenth century both the Dominican and Franciscan orders had departed widely from the teachings of their founders, but they continued to exert a strong influence upon late medieval civilization. The majority of the philosophers and scientists of the thirteenth and fourteenth centuries were either Dominicans or Franciscans.

The Dominican order

2. THE STRUGGLE BETWEEN THE SECULAR AND SPIRITUAL AUTHORITIES

As it happened, the growth of the Church in the later Middle Ages was accompanied by the rise of ambitious political leaders. A

315

The overlapping
of jurisdiction

conflict between secular and spiritual authorities was practically unavoidable, since the jurisdictions claimed by each frequently overlapped. The struggle began about 1050 and continued with varying
intensity until well into the fourteenth century.

The two great opponents in the early stages of the struggle were
Pope Gregory VII and the German emperor, Henry IV. The quarrel
between these powerful rivals was related to the New Cluny
movement, of which Gregory had been the leader for some time before he became Pope. As noted previously, one of the fundamental
aims of this movement was to free the Church from secular control.
During a period of many years the practice had been established
that a bishop, abbot, or priest who held his position as a fief should
be invested with the symbols of his office by the king or noble who
granted the fief. This practice, known as lay investiture, was a thorn
in the side of such zealous reformers as Gregory; they feared that as
long as the clergy owed allegiance in any degree to secular overlords, papal supremacy would be impossible. But this was not the
only issue involved; there was also the question of the Pope's right
to exercise temporal authority. Just how much temporal jurisdiction
Gregory intended to claim is not clear. Sometimes it appears from
his decrees that he regarded himself as the supreme ruler of the
world and thought of all princes and kings as his vassals. But leading
scholars of medieval political theory have denied that this was the
case. They contend that Gregory's conception of his authority was
merely that of *pastor of the Christian flock*, and that he never
claimed an unlimited right to create and depose secular rulers or
annul their decrees. He would intervene only to protect the interests of the Church and the religious rights of Christians.[2] Naturally,
this was a rather extensive authority, but it would still fall short of
the right to rule as an autocrat over the whole world.

The quarrel between Henry and Gregory was one of the most
bitter in the Middle Ages. When Henry refused to obey decrees of
the Pope prohibiting lay investiture, Gregory threatened to excom-
municate him. The king retaliated by denouncing the Pope as a false
monk and ordering him to descend from the throne "to be damned
throughout the ages." Whereupon Gregory not only excommunicated Henry but declared his throne vacant and released all his subjects from allegiance to him. Faced with revolt by his vassals, Henry
had no alternative but to make peace with the Pope. He journeyed
over the Alps in the depth of winter to Canossa in northern Italy and
implored the Pope's forgiveness. Later on, he had his revenge when
he led an army into Italy, set up an anti-pope, and compelled
Gregory to flee from Rome. The great apostle of reform died in
exile in 1085.

Before the struggle ended in the fourteenth century, nearly all of
the monarchs of western Europe had been involved. Among them

The struggle
between Gregory
VII and Henry IV

[2] *Cf.* C. H. McIlwain, *The Growth of Political Thought in the West*, pp.
208 ff.

Shrine of the Three Kings, Cologne Cathedral. Richly decorated shrines are one of the principal forms of interior ornamentation in Gothic cathedrals. The cathedral of Cologne (Köln) in western Germany contains the Shrine of the Three Kings, or the Three Wise Men of the East, who are supposed to have brought gifts to the infant Jesus. According to legend, the bones of the Three Kings were brought from Italy in the twelfth century by Frederick Barbarossa and buried in Cologne.

were the Holy Roman Emperors, Frederick Barbarossa and Frederick II; the French kings, Philip Augustus and Philip the Fair; and the English king, John. The leading contenders on the papal side were Innocent III, Innocent IV, and Boniface VIII. The issues included the right of the Holy Roman Emperors to rule over Italy, the freedom of Italian towns from German domination, and the right of kings to tax the property of the Church. Furthermore, the Popes were now extending their claims to temporal authority a degree or two beyond what had been asserted by Gregory VII. Innocent III declared that "it is the business of the pope to look after the interests of the Roman empire, since the empire derives its origin, and its final authority from the papacy."[3] Innocent IV appears to have gone a step further and to have claimed jurisdiction over all temporal affairs and over all human beings, whether Christians or not. Nevertheless, it must be borne in mind that none of these Popes was really demanding absolute power. What they were insisting upon was not legislative but a judicial authority, an authority to judge and punish rulers for their sins. The fundamental issue was whether rulers were directly responsible to God for their official acts or indirectly through the Pope.

Issues of the struggle

The conflict between Popes and secular authorities had momentous results not only for medieval Europe but for subsequent ages as well. For a time the Popes were almost uniformly successful. With the aid of the Lombard cities and the rebellious dukes in Germany, they checked the ambitions of the Holy Roman Emperors and finally broke the power of the Empire entirely. By means of interdicts Innocent III compelled Philip Augustus to take back the wife he had repudiated and forced King John to recognize England and Ireland as fiefs of

Results of the conflict

[3] O. J. Thatcher and E. H. McNeal, *A Source Book for Medieval History,* p. 220.

the papacy. At the beginning of the fourteenth century, however, Boniface VIII went down to humiliating defeat at the hands of King Philip the Fair of France. As the outcome of a quarrel over Philip's attempt to tax the property of the Church, Boniface was taken prisoner by the king's soldiers, and a month later he died. The Archbishop of Bordeaux was chosen to succeed him, and the papal capital was transferred to Avignon in France, where it remained for seventy years. There were also other results. Many pious Christians now came to believe that the Popes were carrying their ambitions for political power too far and were forgetting their spiritual functions. As a consequence, the papacy lost prestige, and the way was opened for repudiation of its leadership even in religious affairs. In like manner, papal meddling in the internal politics of different countries tended to strengthen the growth of national feeling, particularly in England and France. Finally, the struggle led to a quickening of intellectual activity. As each side attempted to justify its position, interest was awakened in ancient writings, an incentive was provided for the study of Roman law, and many valuable contributions were made to political theory.

3. THE CRUSADES

It is probably not inaccurate to regard the Crusades as the chief expression of medieval expansionism. Unfortunately it appears to be true that nearly every civilization sooner or later develops imperialist tendencies. Certain ones, of course, have been much worse offenders than others, but expansionism in some degree has been characteristic of nearly all of them. It seems to be the natural fruit of the increasing complexity of economic life and of the growth of pride in the real or fancied superiority of a system.

The Crusades an expression of medieval imperialism

Although the Crusades were by no means exclusively a religious movement, there can be no denying the importance of the religious factor in producing them. The century in which they were launched was an age when religion occupied a predominant place in men's thinking. The medieval Christian had a deep conviction of sin. He feared its consequences in the form of eternal damnation and was anxious to avert them by acts of penance. For hundreds of years the most popular type of penance had been the making of pilgrimages to sacred places. A trip to the Holy Land, if at all possible, had been the cherished ambition of every Christian. By the eleventh century the religious revivalism generated by the Cluniac reform movement, combined with the opening up of trade with the Near East, had made pilgrimages to Palestine especially appealing. Hundreds of people now joined the roving bands that trailed across central and eastern Europe on their way to the Levant. In 1065 the Bishop of Bamberg led a horde of 7000 Germans to visit the holy places in and around Jerusalem. Of course, not everyone who joined these mass migrations was inspired by religious ardor. Pil-

Religious causes of the Crusades: (1) mass pilgrimages

grimages afforded an opportunity for adventure and sometimes even for profit. Besides, what better chance was there to escape the responsibilities of life for a season and have a good time in the bargain? Every pilgrim who returned brought back stories of the wonderful sights he had seen and thereby aroused the desire of others to follow his example. Without these mass pilgrimages, interest in conquest of the Holy Land would probably never have developed.

Other religious causes must also be mentioned. For a time during the late eleventh century, prospects for papal supremacy did not look bright. Gregory VII had been driven from the throne and had died in exile. His successor was an aged friend who went to his own grave after a year of failure. The cardinals then chose a younger and more vigorous man, who adopted the name of Urban II. Urban had been a French noble who had renounced the world to become a monk at Cluny. Subsequently he became the talented assistant of Gregory VII. Elected Pope himself in 1088, he turned his attention to the glorious dream of uniting all classes of Christians in support of the Church. Perhaps he might even force a reunion of the Eastern and Western branches of Christendom. At any rate, a war against the infidel to rescue the Holy Places from desecration would enable Latin Christians to forget their differences and to rally behind the Pope. The papacy had already inspired or given its blessing to wars on behalf of religion. Predecessors of Urban II had blessed the Norman conquest of England, the campaigns of Robert Guiscard against heretical Greeks in Italy, the wars of Teutons against Slavs on Germany's northern and eastern borders, and the crusades of Christians against Moors in Spain. To merge these efforts in a grand enterprise against the whole unbelieving world must have seemed like a logical climax to what had already occurred.

(2) religious wars as means of promoting unity

For more than a century religious leaders in Europe had been disturbed by the prevalence of fighting among the feudal nobles. Despite the Peace of God and the Truce of God, the warfare of barons and knights continued to be a menace to the security of the Church. The rights of clergy, peasants, and other noncombatants were often trampled upon, merchants were robbed, and religious edifices pillaged and burned. Against these depredations the penalty of excommunication was of little avail. Small wonder, therefore, that Popes should have turned to the idea of protecting the Church and its members by diverting the military ardor of the nobles into a holy war against the heathen. Still another religious cause was surplus idealism left over from the New Cluny movement. Movements of this kind, which strike deeply into the emotional nature of man, generally stir up more enthusiasm than is necessary for their immediate objectives. Some of this surplus must then find new outlets, just as in later years the fanaticism engendered by the Crusades themselves burst forth into persecution of the Jews.

(3) other religious causes

To discover some of the most important economic causes of the Crusades, one has only to read the speech of Pope Urban II at the

THE MAJOR CRUSADES ca. 1096 A.D.

Economic causes

Council of Clermont inviting the nobles of France to take up arms for the conquest of Palestine. He urged them to let nothing detain them, "since this land which you inhabit, shut in on all sides by the sea and surrounded by mountain peaks, is too narrow for your large population; nor does it abound in wealth; and it furnishes scarcely enough food for its cultivators. . . . Enter upon the road to the Holy Sepulchre; wrest that land from the wicked race and subject it to yourselves. That land which, as the Scripture says, 'floweth with milk and honey,' was given by God into the possession of the children of Israel. Jerusalem is the navel of the world; the land is fruitful above others, like another paradise of delights." [4] There is evidence also that a good many nobles, because of extravagance or poor

[4] O. J. Thatcher and E. H. McNeal, *A Source Book for Medieval History*, pp. 519-20.

320

Building Operations. From a French picture Bible, *ca.*
1250. Note the treadmill, with wheel, ropes, and pulley,
by means of which a basket of stones is brought to the
construction level. (Morgan Library)

Above: Siege of a City. From the *Universal Chronicle* by
Jean de Courcy, Flemish, *ca.* 1470. The cannon meant the
end of feudal knights and medieval towered fortresses.
(Morgan Library) Below: A Scholar at Work. From the
Flemish manuscript *The Golden Legend*, 1445–1460.
(Morgan Library)

Stained Glass, German, *ca.* 1300.
Some stained-glass windows were
purely decorative; others told a
story. (MMA)

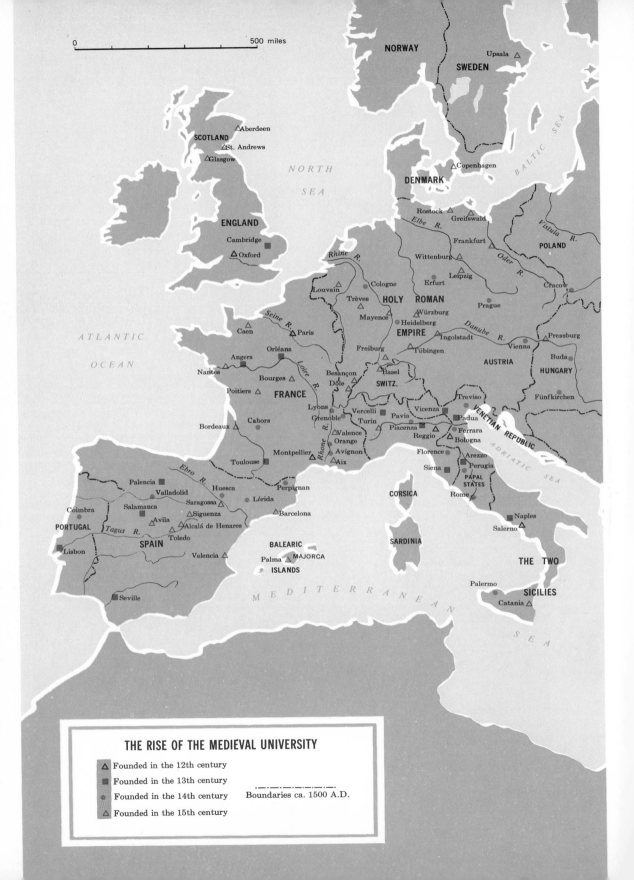

THE RISE OF THE MEDIEVAL UNIVERSITY

△ Founded in the 12th century
■ Founded in the 13th century
● Founded in the 14th century
△ Founded in the 15th century

Boundaries ca. 1500 A.D.

French Knights about to Depart on a Crusade. Their chief weapons are the long bow and the spear.

management of their estates had fallen into debt. Further, the rule of primogeniture in France and in England created the problem of what to do with the younger sons. New fiefs were hard to obtain, and positions in the Church were becoming scarce. As a result, these surplus offspring of the nobles tended to form a rebellious and disorderly class, alert for any opportunity to despoil a weak neighbor of his property. Confronted by such problems as these, the nobles of western Europe needed no second invitation to respond to Pope Urban's plea.

But the catalyst or immediate cause of the Crusades was the advance of the Seljuk Turks in the Near East. In about 1050 these people had come down into western Asia and had gained control over the Baghdad caliphate. Soon afterward they conquered Syria, Palestine, and Egypt. In 1071 they slaughtered a Byzantine army at Manzikert and then swept through Asia Minor and captured Nicaea, within a few miles of Constantinople. After the death of the great Sultan, Malik Shah, in 1092 the Seljuk empire began to disintegrate. The time now seemed ripe for the Byzantine Emperor, Alexius Comnenus, to attempt the reconquest of his lost possessions. Realizing the difficulty of this task, since his own government was exhausted from previous struggles, he sent an appeal in 1095 to the Pope, probably for aid in recruiting mercenary soldiers. Urban II, the reigning pontiff, took full advantage of this opportunity. He summoned a council of French nobles and clergy at Clermont and exhorted them in a fiery speech to make war upon the accursed race of Turks. He employed every artful device of eloquence to arouse the fury and cupidity of his hearers, emphasizing especially the horrible atrocities which he declared the Turks were committing upon Christians. When he had finished, it is reported that all who were present cried out with one accord, "It is the will of God," and rushed forward to take the crusader's oath.

The first of the organized Crusades was not actually started until late in 1096. The majority of those who participated in it were

The immediate cause of the Crusades

321

The major
Crusades

Frenchmen and Normans. Altogether, between 1096 and 1244, three other major Crusades and a number of minor ones were launched. Only the first achieved much success in destroying Turkish control over Christian territory. By 1098 most of Syria had been captured, and a year later Jerusalem was taken. But these gains were only temporary. In 1187 Jerusalem was recaptured by the Moslems under Saladin, Sultan of Egypt. Before the end of the thirteenth century every one of the petty states established by the crusaders in the Near East had been wiped out.

Reasons for the
failure of the
Crusades

The ultimate failure of the Crusades resulted from several causes. To begin with, the expeditions were frequently badly managed; there was seldom any unified command, and rival leaders quarreled among themselves. In some of the later expeditions the original purpose of conquering the Holy Land from the Turks was lost sight of altogether. The Fourth Crusade, for example, turned out to be a gigantic plundering foray against Constantinople. There was also another cause which cannot be overlooked: the conflicting ambitions of the East and the West. According to the evidence, the Byzantine Emperor, Alexius Comnenus, in appealing to the Pope for aid, professed a desire to protect the Christian churches of the Orient. But this was not his primary objective. He had come to the conclusion that the time was ripe for a major offensive against the Turks. He was not interested simply or even primarily in driving them out of the Holy Land but in reconquering all of the Asiatic provinces of his empire. By contrast, Pope Urban II had the grandiose dream of a holy war of all of Latin Christendom to expel the infidel from Palestine. His underlying purpose was not to rescue the Byzantine Empire but to strengthen Latin Christianity, to exalt the papacy, and perhaps to restore the union of the Eastern and Western churches.

Exaggeration of
the importance of
the Crusades

In line with a common tendency to overestimate the importance of wars, the Crusades were at one time considered as the primary cause of nearly all of European progress in the later Middle Ages. It was assumed that they led to the growth of cities, to the overthrow of feudalism, and to the introduction of Saracenic philosophy and science into Latin Europe. For several reasons most historians now regard this assumption as being of limited validity. First, the progress of civilization in the later Middle Ages was already well under way before the Crusades began. Second, the educated classes in Europe did not generally take part in the military expeditions; as a result, the soldiers who actually went were totally devoid of the intellectual background necessary for an appreciation of Saracenic learning. Third, very few of the armies ever reached the real centers of Saracenic civilization, which were not Jerusalem or Antioch, but Baghdad, Damascus, Toledo, and Cordova. European intellectual progress in the twelfth and thirteenth centuries was due far more to the revival of trade with the Near East and to the work of scholars and translators in Spain and Sicily than to any influence of holy wars against the Turks. Nor were the Crusades primarily responsi-

Krak des Chevaliers, Northern Syria. This Castle of the Knights is considered the most magnificent of all the Crusader fortresses and one of the best-preserved relics of the Middle Ages.

ble for the political and economic changes at the end of the Middle Ages. The decline of feudalism, for instance, occurred chiefly because of the Black Death, the growth of an urban economy, and the rise of national monarchies; and these in turn were only in minor degree the results of the Crusades.

What effects, then, is it possible to ascribe to the great holy wars against Islam? To some extent they hastened the emancipation of the common people. Nobles who were hard pressed for money sold privileges to townsmen and to communities of serfs somewhat earlier than they would otherwise have done. Further, many peasants took advantage of the absence of the nobles to break away from bondage to the soil. Among other economic effects were an increased demand for products of the East, the growth of banking, and the elimination of Constantinople as the middleman in the trade between East and West. Venice, Genoa, and Pisa now gained a virtual monopoly of commerce in the Mediterranean area. In addition, the Crusades had some influence in strengthening the monarchies of France and England by eliminating powerful nobles and providing a pretext for direct taxation; but the political consequences were relatively slight. In the domain of religion, where we would normally expect the most profound results, few positive effects can be discovered. It is impossible to prove that the Popes enjoyed any increase in power or repute as a result of having launched the Crusades. On the contrary, as the true character of the expeditions became more and more transparent, the papacy seems rather to have suffered a loss of prestige. There was, however, an increase in religious fanaticism, which expressed itself particularly in savage persecution of the Jews. These unfortunate people suffered

The actual results of the Crusades

323

nearly everywhere. They were cruelly beaten, sometimes killed in mob attacks, and expelled from several countries. Naturally, the fury against them was partly economic in origin, since they were the chief moneylenders of the time; nevertheless, it is a significant fact that hostility to Jews had one of its chief sources in the holy wars against Islam. Finally, it is doubtless true that the Crusades had some effect in widening geographic knowledge and in encouraging travel and exploration, but these developments were more the result of the gradual expansion of trade.

4.   THE LATE MEDIEVAL MIND

The revival of learning in western Europe

Intellectual progress in the later Middle Ages received its original stimulus from the so-called Carolingian Renaissance of the ninth century. This was a movement initiated by Charlemagne when he brought to his court at Aachen the most distinguished scholars he could find. In doing this the emperor was prompted partly by his own interest in learning but also by his desire to find uniform standards of orthodoxy which could be imposed upon all of his subjects. Fortunately he seems to have allowed the scholars he imported a generous freedom to pursue their own inclinations. The result was a brilliant though superficial revival of learning which continued for some years after the death of its sponsor. After the Carolingian Renaissance intellectual progress in western Europe was interrupted for some time on account of the Norse and Saracenic invasions. A brief revival in Germany in the tenth century was followed by a more virile growth of classical studies in Italy and France after the year 1000. But the climax of intellectual achievement in the later Middle Ages was not reached until the twelfth and thirteenth centuries.

Philosophy:
Scholasticism

The outstanding intellectual achievement of the late Middle Ages was the famous system of dialectics known as Scholasticism. This system is usually defined as the attempt to harmonize reason and faith or to make philosophy serve the interest of theology. But no such definition is sufficient to convey an adequate conception of the Scholastic mind. The great thinkers of the Middle Ages did not limit their interests to problems of religion. On the contrary, they were just as anxious as philosophers in any period to answer the great questions of life, whether they pertained to religion, politics, economics, or metaphysics. Perhaps the best way to explain the true nature of Scholasticism is to define it in terms of its characteristics. In the first place, it was rationalistic, not empirical; in other words, it was based primarily upon logic rather than upon science or experience. The Scholastic philosophers, like the Greek thinkers of the Socratic school, did not believe that the highest truth could be derived from sense perception. They admitted that the senses could provide man with a knowledge of the appearances of things, but they maintained that reality or the essential nature of the universe is discoverable mainly by reason. In the second place, Scholastic philosophy was authoritarian. Even reason was not considered a sufficient instrument for the discovery of all knowledge, but the deductions of logic needed to be buttressed by the authority of the Scriptures, of the Church Fathers, and especially of Plato and Aristotle. Third, Scholastic philosophy had a predominantly ethical approach. Its cardinal aim was to discover how man could improve this life and insure salvation in the life to come. Fourth, Scholastic thought, unlike modern philosophy, was not mainly concerned with causes and underlying relationships. Its purpose was rather to discover the attributes of things; the universe was assumed to be static, and therefore it was only necessary to explain the meaning of things and what they were good for, not to account for their origin and evolution.

The primary development of the Scholastic philosophy began with the teachings of Peter Abelard (1079–1142), one of the most interesting figures in the history of thought. This handsome and talented Frenchman was educated in the best schools of Paris and gained a wide reputation for dialectical skill before he was out of his twenties. For a number of years he taught in Paris, drawing great crowds to his lectures on philosophy and theology. Despite the fact that he was a monk, his habits of life were far from ascetic. He was proud, belligerent, and egotistical—boastful of his intellectual triumphs and even of his prowess in love. He avowed that he possessed such advantages of comeliness and youth that "he feared no repulse from whatever woman he might deign to honor with his love." His tragic affair with Heloïse, which he poignantly describes in his autobiography, *The Story of My Misfortunes*, contributed to his downfall. But he had already incurred the enmity of some powerful theologians who regarded him as a heretic. As a philosopher Abelard had accomplishments to his credit for which he had a right to be proud. He was probably the most critical of all the medieval thinkers. In his most famous philosophical work, *Sic et Non* (*Yes and No*), he exposed many of the shabby arguments based on authority that were commonly accepted in his time. The preface to this work contains a statement which expresses clearly his conviction about the vital importance of critical reasoning: "For the first key to wisdom is called interrogation, diligent and unceasing. . . . By doubting we are led to inquiry; and from inquiry we perceive the truth."

The heyday of Scholasticism came in the thirteenth century, as a result of the labors of numerous intellectuals in various fields of learning. Two of the greatest were Albertus Magnus and his renowned pupil, St. Thomas Aquinas. These men had the advantage of being able to study most of the works of Aristotle, recently translated from copies in the possession of the Saracens. Albertus Magnus, the only scholar ever to be honored with the title of Great, was born in Germany in 1193. During a long and active career he

Peter Abelard

The heyday of Scholasticism; Albertus Magnus

St. Thomas Aquinas (1225–1274).

served as a teacher, especially at Cologne and at the University of Paris. A profound admirer of Aristotle, he strove to emulate the example of that ancient master by taking the whole field of knowledge as his province. His writings included more than twenty volumes on subjects ranging from botany and physiology to the soul and the creation of the universe. He was often skeptical of ancient authorities, and he attempted to found his conclusions upon reason and experience. In referring to hoary myths, such as the one about ostriches eating iron, he would frequently say: "but this is not proved by experience." He defined natural science "as not simply receiving what one is told, but the investigation of causes in natural phenomena." [5]

Thomas Aquinas, the most noted of all the Scholastic philosophers, was born in southern Italy in 1225. Following the example of the great Albert, he entered the Dominican order and devoted his life to teaching. He was a professor at the University of Paris by the time he was thirty-one. His most famous work was his *Summa theologica,* but he wrote on many other subjects as well, including politics and economics. The fundamental aims of St. Thomas were, first, to demonstrate the rationality of the universe, and second, to establish the primacy of reason. He believed that the universe is an ordered whole governed by intelligent purpose. All things were created in order to make possible the fulfillment of the great Christian plan for the promotion of justice and peace on earth and the salvation of mankind in a world to come. The philosophy of St. Thomas implied a serene confidence in the ability of man to know and understand his world. He regarded the intellectual faculties of man and also his senses as God-given. The great *Summaries* he wrote were attempts to build up out of logic and the wisdom of the past comprehensive systems of knowledge which would leave no mysteries unsolved. Though he leaned heavily upon the authority of Aristotle and the Church Fathers he regarded reason as the primary key to truth. Even his attitude toward religion was essentially intellectual rather than emotional; piety to him was a matter of knowledge more than of faith. He admitted that a few doctrines of Christianity, such as the belief in the Trinity and the creation of the world in time, could not be proved by the intellect; but he denied that they were contrary to reason, for God Himself is a rational being. The influence of St. Thomas was not only of cardinal importance in his own time, but it survives to this day. In the late nineteenth century Pope Leo XIII exhorted the bishops of the Church "to restore the golden wisdom of St. Thomas and to spread it far and wide for the defense of the faith, for the good of society, and for the advantage of all the sciences." He recommended St. Thomas as a master and guide for everyone interested in scholarly studies.

[5] Lynn Thorndike, *A History of Magic and Experimental Science,* II, ch. 59.

By the end of the thirteenth century Scholasticism had begun to decline. Its decay was due partly to the teachings of the last of the Scholastics, John Duns Scotus. A member of the Franciscan order, Duns Scotus was inclined to emphasize the emotional and practical side of religion in place of the intellectual. He conceived of piety as an act of will rather than an act of intellect. Less confident of the powers of reason than St. Thomas, he excluded a large number of the doctrines of religion from the sphere of philosophy altogether. From this it was only a step to denial that any religious beliefs were capable of rational demonstration; all would have to be accepted on faith or rejected entirely. When this step was finally taken by Duns Scotus' successors, the overthrow of Scholasticism was speedily accomplished.

The decay of Scholasticism

The other main reason for the decline of Scholasticism was the growing popularity of nominalism. Although nominalism is often considered a form of Scholasticism, actually the nominalists were fundamentally opposed to nearly everything the Scholastics taught. They denied that concepts or class names have any reality, insisting that they are nothing but abstractions invented by the mind to express the qualities common to a number of objects or organisms. Only individual things are real. Far from accepting the Scholastic confidence in reason, the nominalists contended that all knowledge has its source in experience. Anything beyond the realm of concrete experience must be taken on faith, if it is to be accepted at all; the truths of religion cannot be demonstrated by logic. Although some of the earlier nominalists inclined toward religious skepticism, the majority became mystics. Nominalism flourished in the fourteenth century and for some time was the most popular philosophy in western Europe. Nominalism is especially important for having laid the foundations for the scientific progress of the Renaissance and for the mystical religious movements which helped to bring on the Protestant Revolution.

The growth of nominalism

A good many medieval philosophers devoted earnest attention to questions of political authority; a few, in fact, were primarily concerned with such questions. The political theorists of the later Middle Ages were in substantial agreement on a large part of their philosophy. Practically all of them had abandoned the idea of the Church Fathers that the state was established by God as a remedy for sin, and that men must therefore render faithful obedience even to the tyrant. It was now commonly held that the state is a product of man's social nature, and that when justice is the guiding principle of the ruler, government is a positive good, not a necessary evil. In the second place, it was generally agreed by the philosophers of the later Middle Ages that all of western Europe should constitute a single commonwealth under one supreme ruler. There might be many subordinate kings or princes in the different parts of the continent, but one supreme overlord, either the Pope or the Holy Roman Em-

The political theory of the later Middle Age

Opposition to
absolutism

peror, should have the highest jurisdiction. The most noted of those who defended the supremacy of the Emperor was Dante in his *De Monarchia*. On the papal side were the Englishman John of Salisbury (*ca.* 1115–1180) and Thomas Aquinas. Virtually without exception the political theorists of the later Middle Ages believed in limited government. They had no use for absolutism in any form. John of Salisbury even went so far as to defend the right of the subjects of a tyrant to put him to death. Practically all of late medieval theory was based upon the assumption that the authority of every ruler, whether pope, emperor, or king, was essentially judicial in character. His function was merely to apply the law, not to make or alter it in accordance with his will. Indeed, the medievalists did not conceive of law as the command of a sovereign at all, but as the product of custom or of the divine order of nature. On the other hand, the medieval political theorists were not democrats, for not one of them believed in the doctrine of majority rule. The man who came closest to an exposition of the democratic ideal was Marsiglio of Padua in the fourteenth century. He advocated that the people should have the right to elect the monarch and even to depose him if necessary. He believed also in a representative body with power to make laws. But Marsiglio was no champion of unlimited popular sovereignty. In fact, he defined democracy as a degraded form of government. His idea of representative government was representation of the citizens according to quality rather than mere numbers, and the law-making powers of his representative body would be confined to the enactment of statutes regulating the structure of the government.

Progress in
science

The record of scientific achievements in the later Middle Ages can scarcely be considered an imposing one. Yet it was probably about all we should expect in view of the absorption of interest in other fields. The names of only a few individual scientists need to be mentioned. One of the most original was Adelard of Bath, who lived in the early years of the twelfth century. Not only did he condemn reliance upon authority, but he devoted many years of his life to direct investigation of nature. He discovered some important facts about the causes of earthquakes, the functions of different parts of the brain, and the processes of breathing and digestion. He was probably the first scientist since the Hellenistic Age to affirm the indestructibility of matter.

Frederick II as
a scientist

The toughest-minded of all the medieval scientists was the notorious Holy Roman Emperor, Frederick II, whose reign occupied the first part of the thirteenth century. Frederick was skeptical of almost everything. He denied the immortality of the soul, and he was accused of having written a brochure entitled *Jesus, Moses and Mohammed: The Three Great Impostors*. But he was not satisfied merely to scoff. He performed various experiments of his own to gratify his boundless curiosity, testing the artificial incubation of eggs, for example, and sealing the eyes of vultures to determine whether they found their food by sight or by smell. His most important scientific contributions were made, however, as a patron of learning. An ardent admirer of Saracenic culture, he brought distinguished scholars to Palermo to translate the writings of the Saracens into Latin. He subsidized leading scientists, especially Leonard of Pisa, the most brilliant mathematician of the thirteenth century. In addition, Frederick instituted measures for the improvement of medical practice. He legalized the practice of dissection, established a system of examining and licensing physicians, and founded the University of Naples with one of the best medical schools in Europe.

By far the best known of medieval scientists was Roger Bacon (*ca.* 1214–1294), possibly because he predicted certain modern inventions such as horseless carriages and flying machines. In reality, Bacon was less critical than Frederick II; he believed that all knowledge must enhance the glory of theology, the queen of the sciences. Moreover, Adelard of Bath preceded him by more than a century in advocating and using the experimental method. Nevertheless, Bacon, by virtue of his strong insistence upon accurate investigation, deserves a high place among medieval scientists. He denied that either reason or authority could furnish valid knowledge unless supported by experimental research. Besides, he himself did some practical work of great value. His writings on optics remained authoritative for several centuries. He discovered much about magnifying lenses, and it seems more than probable that he invented the simple microscope. He demonstrated that light travels faster than sound, and he was apparently the first scientist to perceive the inaccuracy of the Julian calendar and to advocate its revision.

Much of the advancement in philosophy and science in the later Middle Ages would have been quite impossible without the educational progress which marked the centuries from the ninth to the fourteenth. The Carolingian Renaissance resulted in the establishment of better schools and libraries in several of the

Roger Bacon

Alchemists in Their Laboratory. Note the great variety of instruments used and the spectacles worn by the experimenter.

The transfer of
education from
the monasteries
to the cathedral
schools

See color map
at page 289

monasteries of western Europe. Many of these institutions, however, were destroyed during the chaos of the ninth century. As a consequence of the religious reform movements of the eleventh century, the monasteries tended to neglect education, with the result that the monastic schools that had survived were gradually overshadowed by the cathedral schools. Some of the latter developed into what would now be considered the equivalent of colleges, providing excellent instruction in the so-called liberal arts. This was notably true of the cathedral schools located at Canterbury, Chartres, and Paris. But by far the most important educational development of the Middle Ages was the rise of the universities.

The term university (from the Latin, *universitas*) originally meant a corporation or guild. In fact, many of the medieval universities were very much like craft guilds, organized for the purpose of training and licensing teachers. Gradually the word came to have the meaning of an educational institution with a school of liberal arts and one or more faculties in the professional subjects of law, medicine, and theology. No one knows which of the universities was the oldest. It may have been Salerno, which was a center of medical study as far back as the tenth century. The universities of Bologna and Paris are also very ancient, the former having been established about 1150 and the latter before the end of the twelfth century. The next oldest included such famous institutions as the universities of Oxford, Cambridge, Montpellier, Salamanca, and Naples. There were no universities in Germany until the fourteenth century, when schools of this type were organized at Prague, Vienna, Heidelberg, and Cologne. By the end of the Middle Ages some eighty universities had been established in western Europe.

Practically every university in medieval Europe was patterned after one or the other of two different models. Throughout Italy, Spain, and southern France the standard was generally the University of Bologna, in which the students themselves constituted the guild or corporation. They hired the teachers, paid their salaries, and fined or discharged them for neglect of duty or inefficient instruction. Nearly all of these southern institutions were secular in character, specializing in law or medicine. The universities of northern Europe were modeled after the one at Paris, which was not a guild of students but of teachers. It included the four faculties of arts, theology, law, and medicine, each headed by an elected dean. In the great majority of the northern universities arts and theology were the leading branches of study. Before the end of the thirteenth century separate colleges came to be established within the University of Paris. The original college was nothing more than an endowed home for poor students, but the discovery was soon made that discipline could best be preserved by having all of the students live in colleges. Eventually the colleges became centers of instruction as well as residences. While on the Continent of Europe most

A Noted Teacher, Henricus de Alemania, Lecturing in a Medieval University.
Some interesting comparisons and contrasts may be observed between his students and those in a modern classroom.

of these colleges have ceased to exist, in England the universities of Oxford and Cambridge still retain the pattern of federal organization copied from Paris. The colleges of which they are composed are practically independent educational units.

Though modern universities have borrowed much of their organization from their medieval prototypes, the course of study has been radically changed. No curriculum in the Middle Ages included much history or natural science, nor any great amount of mathematics. The student in the Middle Ages was required, first of all, to spend four or five years in studying the *trivium*—grammar, rhetoric, and logic, or dialectic. If he passed his examinations he received the preliminary degree of bachelor of arts, which conferred no particular distinction. To assure himself a place in professional life he must devote some additional years to the pursuit of an advanced degree, such as master of arts, doctor of laws, or doctor of medicine. For the master's degree three or four years had to be given to study of the *quadrivium*—arithmetic, geometry, astronomy, and music. These subjects were not quite what their names imply now. Their content was highly philosophical; arithmetic, for example, included primarily a study of the theory of numbers, while music was concerned largely with the properties of sound. The requirements for the doctor's degree were generally more severe and included more specialized training. By the end of the Middle Ages the course for the doctorate of theology at Paris had been extended to fourteen years, and the degree could not be conferred unless the candidate was at least thirty-five years of age. Both the master's and

The course of study

331

The university
students

The humanistic
quality of late
medieval
literature

doctor's degrees were teaching degrees; even the title of doctor of medicine meant a teacher of medicine, not a practicing physician.

The life of medieval students differed in many ways from that of their modern descendants. The student body in any one university was not a homogeneous group but was composed of diverse nationalities. The young Frenchman or German who wanted to study law would almost certainly go to Bologna or Padua, just as the young Italian with an interest in theology would probably enroll at Paris. The entire university was usually an independent community, and the students were consequently exempt from the jurisdiction of political authorities. A relic of this ancient autonomy is to be found in the fact that some of the German universities still have their own jails. The learning process consisted primarily in taking down copious notes on wax tablets from the master's lecture and then analyzing and discussing them afterwards. The young man's education was supposed to be acquired through logic and memory rather than from extensive reading or research. In other respects, however, student life in the Middle Ages was not so far different from what it is now. If the medieval student knew nothing of intercollegiate sports, he at least had his violent fights with the hoodlums of the town to absorb his surplus energy. In the medieval universities as in those of today there were the sharply contrasting types of sincere, intelligent scholars and frank and frivolous loafers. We hear much about radicalism and activism in modern colleges, but these tendencies were certainly not absent in the universities of the Middle Ages. Many of these institutions were roundly denounced as breeding places of heresy, paganism, and worldliness. It was said that young men "seek theology at Paris, law at Bologna, and medicine at Montpellier, but nowhere a life that is pleasing to God." The students at Paris even had to be admonished to stop playing dice on the altar of Notre Dame after one of their holiday celebrations.

No one who has more than a casual acquaintance with the literature of the later Middle Ages could ever imagine the whole medieval period to have been an era of darkness and otherworldliness. For much of this literature expresses a zest for living as spontaneous, joyous, and free as any attitude revealed in the writings of the Renaissance of the fourteenth and succeeding centuries. Indeed, the spirit of late medieval literature was even closer to that of the modern age than most people realize. Probably the actual amount of religious literature in the later Middle Ages did not bear a much larger ratio to the total quantity of writings produced than would be true at the present time.

Late medieval writings can be classified, first of all, as either Latin or vernacular literature. The revival of classical studies in the cathedral schools and in the earliest universities led to the production of some excellent Latin poetry. The best examples of this were the secular lyrics, especially those written by a group of poets known as the Goliards or *Goliardi*. The Goliards derived their name from the fact that they commonly referred to themselves as disciples of Golias. Who Golias was, no one knows, but one scholar thinks that he was probably the devil.[6] Such a choice of a master would undoubtedly have been appropriate enough, for most of the Goliard poets were regarded by the Church as lewd fellows of the baser sort for whom nothing was too sacred to be ridiculed. They wrote parodies of the creeds, travesties of the mass, and even burlesques of the Gospels. Their lyrics were purely pagan in spirit, celebrating the beauties of the changing seasons, the carefree life of the open road, the pleasures of drinking and gambling, and especially the joys of love. The authors of these rollicking and satirical songs were mostly wandering students, although some appear to have been men more advanced in years. The names of nearly all of them are unknown. Their poetry is particularly significant as the first emphatic protest against the ascetic ideal of Christianity. The following stanzas taken from *The Confession of Golias* may be considered typical of what they wrote:

Latin literature: the poetry of the Goliards

> Prelate, most discreet of priests,
> Grant me absolution!
> Dear's the death whereof I die,
> Sweet my dissolution;
> For my heart is wounded by
>
> Beauty's soft suffusion;
> All the girls I come not nigh
> Mine are in illusion.
> 'Tis most arduous to make
>
> Nature's self-surrender;
> Seeing girls, to blush and be
> Purity's defender!
> We young men our longings ne'er
> Shall to stern law render,
> Or preserve our fancies from
> Bodies smooth and tender.[7]

By no means all of medieval literature was written in Latin. As the Middle Ages waned, the vernacular languages of French, German, Spanish, English, and Italian became increasingly popular as media of literary expression. Until the beginning of the twelfth century nearly all of the literature in the vernacular languages assumed the form of the heroic epic. Among the leading examples were the French *Song of Roland*, the German *Song of the Nibelungs*, the eddas and sagas of the Norsemen, and the Spanish *Poem of My Cid*. These epics picture a virile but unpolished feudal

The growth of vernacular literature

[6] C. H. Haskins, *The Renaissance of the Twelfth Century*, p. 177.
[7] J. A. Symonds, *Wine, Women and Song*, p. 66.

society in its earlier stage of evolution, when valorous deeds in battle on behalf of one's suzerain represented the fulfillment of the highest knightly ideal. Heroism, honor, and loyalty were practically the exclusive themes. The tone of the epics was almost entirely masculine. If women were mentioned at all, it was generally in a condescending fashion. The hero must show the utmost devotion to his superior, but it was not considered inappropriate that he should beat his wife.

The literature of chivalry: (1) the songs of the troubadours

During the twelfth and thirteenth centuries feudal society in western Europe attained the full flower of its growth. As a result of the progress of learning and of contact with the higher civilization of the Saracens, the feudal aristocracy adopted new attitudes and interests. Chivalry, with its glorification of woman and its emphasis upon kindness and refinement of manners, tended to displace the older conception of a feudal ideal limited to the virtues of the battlefield. The first literary works to reflect and in part to inspire this change in ideals were the songs of the troubadours. The original home of the troubadours was southern France, especially the region known as Provence. Here was one of the most highly civilized areas of feudal Europe. It received the full impact of Saracenic influence from Spain, and it seems to have preserved an extensive inheritance from ancient Rome. Whatever the reasons, there can be no doubt that the troubadours of Provence initiated a movement of profound importance in late medieval literature. The central theme of their songs was romantic love. Woman was idealized now as never before. The virtues of her who had once been condemned by monks and Church Fathers as the very incarnation of evil were extolled to the skies. But the love of the troubadours for the ladies of the feudal courts was not supposed to be sensual; it was a rarefied, almost mystical emotion which could be satisfied by a smile or some trifling memento from the haughty goddesses who were the objects of the singers' affection. The fact must be emphasized also that romantic love was not the only topic in which the troubadours were interested. Many wrote acrid satires against the rapacity and hypocrisy of the clergy, and one even addressed a powerful "poem of blame" to God. The literary tradition originated by the troubadours was continued by the *trouvères* in northern France and by the *minnesingers* in Germany.

(2) the romances of the Arthurian cycle

The most important of all the writings which expressed the ideals of the feudal aristocracy were the romances of the Arthurian cycle. The material of these romances consisted of legends woven about the career of a Celtic chieftain by the name of Arthur, who had been the hero of the struggle against the Anglo-Saxon invaders of Britain. In the twelfth century certain Norman and French writers, especially Marie de France and Chrétien de Troyes, became interested in these legends as a background for the chivalric ideal. The result was the composition of a number of romances of love and adventure, famous alike for their colorful narrative and their poetic beauty. Later the best known of these romances were adapted and completed by German poets. Wolfram von Eschenbach developed what is usually considered the most perfect version of the Parzival legend, while Gottfried von Strassburg gave to the story of Tristan and Isolde its classic medieval form. Although these romances differed in form and in substance, they may yet be said to have had features in common. All of them glorified adventure for its own sake, and taught that experience of the deepest and most varied kind is the only sure road to wisdom. All of them strove to inculcate gentleness, protection of the weak, and rescue of those in distress as knightly obligations, in addition to honor, truthfulness, and bravery. The redeeming power of love was another universal element, although not all of the authors agreed as to the form which this love should assume. Some maintained that it ought to be the faithful affection between husband and wife, but others insisted that it must be love unsustained by wedlock. In the minds of the latter group true love was possible only between knight and mistress, never between husband and wife. Finally, in the best of these romances an element of tragedy was nearly always present. Indeed, such a work as Gottfried von Strassburg's *Tristan* might almost be regarded as the prototype of modern tragic literature. He was certainly one of the first to develop the idea of individual suffering as a literary theme and to point out the indistinct dividing line which separates pleasure from pain. For him, to love is to yearn, and suffering and death are integral chapters of the book of life.

By the thirteenth century the merchants and craftsmen of the towns had risen to a position of power and influence equal if not superior to that of the feudal nobles. We can therefore logically expect that some literature would be written to appeal to burgher tastes. Among the foremost examples of such writings were the romance of *Aucassin and Nicolette* and the short stories in verse known as the *fabliaux*. The romance of *Aucassin and Nicolette* resembles in some ways the romances of chivalry. The hero Aucassin is a young noble, and the main theme of the romance is the imperious demands of love; but the plot is frequently turned into channels distinctly at variance with the chivalric ideal. Aucassin has fallen desperately in love, not with the high-born wife of some noble, but with Nicolette, a Saracen slave girl. Warned that he will suffer in hell if he does not give up his beloved, the hero replies that he does not mind, for in hell he will enjoy the company of all who have really lived. The story is also quite different from the romances of chivalry in its occasional expression of sympathy for the peasant. But the writings which undoubtedly made the strongest appeal to the urban classes were the *fabliaux*. These were stories written not to edify or instruct but chiefly to amuse. Often richly spiced with indecency, they reveal a contempt for the trappings of

Literature of the
urban classes

335

chivalry, with its romanticized love and idiotic pursuit of adventure. Most of them are also strongly anti-clerical and indicate no high regard for the religious spirit. Nearly always it is monks and priests who are made the butts of the jokes. The *fabliaux* are significant as expressions of the growing worldliness of the urban classes and as forerunners of the robust realism which was later to appear in the works of such writers as Chaucer and Boccaccio.

The supreme achievements of medieval literary talent were two great masterpieces written in the thirteenth and fourteenth centuries. The first was the *Romance of the Rose* of William of Lorris and John of Meun, and the second was Dante's *Divine Comedy*. Each in its own way is a kind of summary of late medieval civilization. The *Romance of the Rose* consists of two parts: the first 4000 lines were begun by William of Lorris about 1230; the other part, nearly three times as long, was finished by John of Meun about 1265. The two parts are entirely different, the first being an allegory dealing with the cult of chivalric love, while the second is a eulogy of reason. John of Meun was quite skeptical of the value of the feudal aristocracy to medieval society; he hated superstition; and he satirized the monastic orders, the papacy, and many other established institutions of his time. He embodied the mocking, realistic attitude of the bourgeoisie, as his predecessor, William of Lorris, symbolized the romantic, mystical spirit of chivalry. The work of the two men taken together furnishes a kind of guidebook to the later Middle Ages.

The Romance of the Rose

Without doubt the most profound of the medieval summaries was the *Divine Comedy* of Dante Alighieri (1265–1321). Not a great deal is known about the life of Dante except that he was the son of a Florentine lawyer and was active during the early part of his career in the political affairs of his city. Despite his absorption in politics he managed to acquire a full mastery of the philosophic and literary knowledge of his time. In 1302 the party to which he belonged was ousted from power in Florence, and he was compelled to live the remainder of his years outside of his native city. Most of his writings were apparently produced during this period of exile. Dante called his chief work simply the *Comedy*, but his admirers during the Italian Renaissance always spoke of it as the *Divine Comedy*, and that is the title which has come down to us. In form the work may be considered a drama of the struggles, temptations, and ultimate redemption of the soul. But of course it is much more than this; for it embraces a complete summation of medieval culture, a magnificent synthesis of the Scholastic philosophy, the science, the religion, and the economic and ethical ideals of the later Middle Ages. Its dominant theme is the salvation of mankind through reason and divine grace, but it includes many other ideas as well. The universe is conceived as a finite world of which the earth is the center and in which everything exists for the benefit of man. All natural phe-

The Divine Comedy

Left: *Romanesque Houses in Brussels.* Right: *Worms Cathedral, Eleventh-Century Romanesque.* It still stands although most of the city was destroyed in World War II.

nomena have their meaning in relation to the divine scheme for peace and justice on earth and salvation in the life beyond. Human beings possess free will to choose the good and avoid the evil. The worst of the sins which man can commit is treason or betrayal of trust; the least serious are those which proceed from weakness of the flesh. Dante took earnest pleasure in the classical authors, almost worshiping Aristotle, Seneca, and Vergil. He chose Vergil rather than some Christian theologian to personify philosophy. By reason of his imaginative power and the warmth and vigor of his style, he deserves to be ranked as one of the greatest poets of all time, but he is especially important to the historian because of the well-rounded picture he presents of the late medieval mind.

5. ART AND MUSIC IN THE LATER MIDDLE AGES

The later Middle Ages produced two great styles of architecture, the Romanesque and the Gothic. The Romanesque was mainly a product of the monastic revival and attained its full development in the century and a half following the year 1000. Fundamentally it was an ecclesiastical architecture, symbolizing the pride of the monastic orders at the height of their power. Naturally, since the Cluniac revival affected the entire Church, the Romanesque style was not confined to monasteries. Nevertheless, it is significant that some of the most impressive Romanesque buildings were houses of the Cluniac order. The essential features of this building style were

Architecture: the Romanesque style

337

the round arch, massive walls, enormous piers, small windows, gloomy interiors, and the predominance of horizontal lines. The plainness of interiors was sometimes relieved by mosaics or by frescoing in bright colors, but the style of construction was not such as to encourage elaborate ornamentation. Moreover, the strong religious spirit in which this architecture was conceived did not generally foster an appeal to the senses. Some of the architects of southern Europe, however, succeeded in breaking away from this somber monastic tradition and often decorated their churches with an elaborate symbolic sculpture.

In the late twelfth and thirteenth centuries the Romanesque architecture was superseded in popularity by the Gothic. The increase in wealth, the advancement of learning, the growth of secular interests, and the pride of the cities in their newly acquired freedom and prosperity led to a demand for a more elaborate architectural style to express the ideals of the new age. Besides, the monastic revival had now spent its force. Gothic architecture was almost exclusively urban. Its monuments were not monasteries situated on lonely crags but cathedrals, bishops' churches, located in the largest cities and towns. It must be understood, though, that the medieval cathedral was not simply a church but a center of the community life. It generally housed a school and a library and was sometimes used as a town hall. It was often large enough to accommodate the whole population of the town. The people of the entire community participated in erecting it, and they rightfully regarded it as civic property. Indeed, many of the Gothic cathedrals were the outcome of town rivalry. For example, the people of Siena became dissatisfied with their modest church after the cathedral at Florence was completed and determined to build a new one on a much more pretentious scale. Frequently the citizens' ambitions got far out of bounds, with the result that many of the buildings were left unfinished. The architects of the Cathedral of Chartres, for instance, planned for several more lofty towers than were ever completed.

Gothic architecture was one of the most intricate of building styles. Its basic elements were the pointed arch, groined and ribbed vaulting, and the flying buttress. These devices made possible a much lighter and loftier construction than could ever have been achieved with the round arch and the engaged pier of the Romanesque. In fact, the Gothic cathedral could be described as a skeletal framework of stone enclosed by enormous windows. Other features included lofty spires, rose windows, delicate tracery in stone, elaborately carved façades, multiple columns, and the use of gargoyles, or representations of mythical monsters, as decorative devices. Ornamentation in the best of the cathedrals was generally concentrated on the exterior. Except for the stained glass windows and the intricate carving on woodwork and altars, interiors were kept rather simple and occasionally almost severe. But the inside of

Quarter Barrel Vaults, Typical of Romanesque Architecture. St. Etienne, Nivers.

See color plates at pages 289, 320

338

Amiens, Floor Plan

Amiens Cathedral. The floor plan to the right shows features which were typical of thirteenth century Gothic—the side aisles continue around the elongated choir and apse, forming the ambulatory, off which radiate the chapels. The transepts are fully developed with side aisles.

the Gothic cathedral was never somber or gloomy. The stained glass windows served not to exclude the light but to glorify it, to catch the rays of sunlight and suffuse them with a richness and warmth of color which nature herself could hardly duplicate even in her gayest moods.

The significance of Gothic architecture is frequently misunderstood. As a matter of fact, its very name, implying that the art was of barbarian origin, was originally a term of reproach given to it by the men of the Renaissance, who wanted to express their contempt for everything medieval. Many people still think of the Gothic cathedral as a product of an ascetic and otherworldly civilization. Nothing could be more inaccurate. Insofar as Gothic architecture was spiritual at all, it was the symbol of a religion which had come to recognize the importance of this life. But as we have already seen, the cathedral was more than a church. It was in large part an expression of the new secular spirit which had grown out of the rise of cities and the progress of enlightenment. Many of the scenes depicted on the stained glass windows—a medieval bakeshop in operation, for instance—had no direct religious significance whatever. The definite appeal to the senses revealed in the sparkling radiance of colored glass and in the naturalistic sculpture of saints

Amiens, Cross Section. Note the pointed Gothic arch which allows for a higher nave vaulting. Note also the typical flying buttresses which take the thrust of the nave vaulting clear of the main structure to the great masonry buttress piers.

339

The High Chapel of La Sainte-Chapelle, Paris. High Gothic is here carried to its logical extreme. Slender columns, tracery, and stained-glass windows take the place of walls.

and the Virgin gives positive proof that man's interest in his human self and in the world of natural beauty was no longer considered a sin. Last of all, Gothic architecture was an expression of the medieval intellectual genius. Each cathedral, with its detailed mass of carvings of plant and animal life and symbolic figures, was a kind of encyclopedia of medieval knowledge—a culture epic in stone.

Music in the later Middle Ages

Music in the later Middle Ages was the product of an evolution extending far back into the early history of medieval Europe. The beginning of this evolution was the development of the so-called plain chant, a vast body of melodies that is virtually an anthology of folk, cultic, and composed music of many centuries. Its collection and organization took a long time, though it is ascribed by tradition to Pope Gregory the Great—hence its name: Gregorian chant. The Gregorian chant is a single, unaccompanied line of music of great melodic and rhythmic subtlety, much of which is lost on us, accustomed as we are to a harmonic background. By the tenth century we encounter the first written monuments of music for more than one line, which consisted of another line running parallel with the first at the distance of a fourth or fifth. The next step in evolution was the introduction of the principle of contrary motion; the second part asserted its independence by not running parallel with the first but following its own bent. It is significant, however, that the modern concept of *harmony*, that is, a vertical organization of sounds (melody with accompaniment) was lacking. The new line of music (called "voice" or "part") was set *against* the existing one, dot against dot, *punctus contra punctum* ("dot" standing for "note") —hence the term counterpoint. Thus the development was linear, each melodic line was largely independent. This type of music is called polyphonic in contrast to homophonic, the harmonically ordered style. The twelfth and thirteenth centuries produced great schools of musical composition that demonstrated considerable skill in weaving together two, three, and even four independent voice-parts. A particular manifestation of music in the later Middle Ages was the art of the troubadours, *trouvères*, and minnesingers. With them a new and altogether Western conception enters music: individual invention. Troubadour comes from the French verb *trouver*, to find (invent); this kind of musician does not use inherited, traditional tunes but "finds" his own. Among the kings and knights of France of the north and of Provence, there were many fine creative artists. The German minnesingers (from the Middle High German word *minne*, "love") patterned themselves after the composing French aristocracy. Secular music was kept under wraps by the Church, but it was nevertheless well developed and by 1300 we come across reliable descriptions of its nature. Music also formed part of the liberal arts as taught at the university, but its study was purely mathematical and philosophical.

SELECTED READINGS

· *Items so designated are available in paperbound editions.*

· Adams, Henry, *Mont-Saint-Michel and Chartres*, New York, 1913 (Mentor). Stimulating and provocative.

Artz, F. B., *The Mind of the Middle Ages*, New York, 1954. Brief but scholarly and interesting.

· Bainton, R. H., *The Medieval Church*, Princeton, 1964 (Anvil).

· Brundage, J. A., *The Crusades: Motives and Achievements*, New York, 1964 (Heath).

· Cheyney, E. P., *The Dawn of a New Era, 1250–1453*, New York, 1936 (Torchbook). Written in a clear and interesting style.

· Copleston, F. C., *Medieval Philosophy*, New York, 1961 (Torchbook).

Crombie, A. C., *From Augustine to Galileo*, Cambridge, 1961.

Crump, C. G., and Jacob, E. F., *The Legacy of the Middle Ages*, New York, 1926. Especially good on medieval arts and crafts.

Easton, Stewart C., *Roger Bacon and His Search for a Universal Science*, New York, 1952.

Evans, Joan, *Art in Medieval France*, London, 1948.

Gardner, Helen, *Art through the Ages*, New York, 1948. Comprehensive and valuable.

Gilson, E. H., *The Philosophy of St. Thomas Aquinas*, Cambridge, Mass., 1924.

· ——, *Dante the Philosopher*, London, 1948 (Torchbook).

READINGS   Haskins, C. H., *Studies in Medieval Culture*, New York, 1929.

· ———, *The Renaissance of the Twelfth Century*, Cambridge, Mass., 1928 (Meridian). Excellent.

Hearnshaw, F. J. C., *The Social and Political Ideas of Some Great Medieval Thinkers*, New York, 1923.

· Heer, Friedrich, *The Medieval World*, New York, 1964 (Mentor).

· Huizinga, J., *The Waning of the Middle Ages*, New York, 1954 (Anchor). A provocative interpretation.

Jones, Charles W., ed., *Medieval Literature in Translation*, New York, 1950.

Lang, Paul, *Music in Western Civilization*, New York, 1941.

Latourette, K. S., *A History of Christianity*, New York, 1953.

Leff, Gordon, *Heresy in the Later Middle Ages*, New York, 1967, 2 vols.

· ———, *Medieval Thought*, Baltimore, 1958 (Penguin).

Luscombe, D. E., *The School of Peter Abelard*, New York, 1969.

Mazzeo, J. A., *The Medieval Cultural Tradition in Dante's Comedy*, Ithaca, N.Y., 1960.

· McGiffert, A. C., *History of Christian Thought*, New York, 1932, Vol. II (Scribner Library).

McIlwain, C. H., *The Growth of Political Thought in the West*, New York, 1932. Perhaps the best interpretation.

Morey, C. R., *Medieval Art*, New York, 1942.

· Panofsky, Erwin, *Gothic Architecture and Scholasticism*, Cleveland, 1957 (Meridian).

Rashdall, Hastings, *The Universities of Europe in the Middle Ages*, New York, 1936, 2 vols. The standard work.

Reese, Gustave, *Music in the Middle Ages*, New York, 1940.

Setton, K. M., ed., *A History of the Crusades*, Philadelphia, 1955. Vol. 1.

· Southern, R. W., *The Making of the Middle Ages*, New Haven, 1953 (Yale University Press).

Taylor, H. O., *The Medieval Mind*, New York, 1927, 2 vols. Good for interpretation.

Vossler, Karl, *Medieval Culture: An Introduction to Dante and His Times*, New York, 1929, 2 vols. Profound and very valuable for the student with a good background of medieval knowledge.

· Waddell, Helen, *The Wandering Scholars*, London, 1927 (Anchor). A vivid and sympathetic account.

· ———, *Peter Abelard*, New York, 1933 (Compass). Valuable not only as biography but for its grasp of the spirit of medieval culture.

SOURCE MATERIALS

Abelard, Peter, *The Story of My Misfortunes*.

Baumer, F. L. V., *Main Currents of Western Thought*, New York, 1952.

Coulton, G. G., *A Medieval Garner*, London, 1910.

Jones, C. W., ed., *Medieval Literature in Translation*, New York, 1950.

Krey, A. C., *The First Crusade; The Accounts of Eyewitnesses and Participants*.

· Marzialis, F. T., tr., *Memoirs of the Crusades*, for *Villehardouin's Chronicle of the Fourth Crusade* and *Joinville's Chronicle of the Crusade of St. Louis* (Dutton).

Pegis, A. C., ed., *Basic Writings of St. Thomas Aquinas*, 2 vols.

· Polo, Marco, *Travels* (Dell and others).

· Poole, R. L., *Illustrations of the History of Medieval Thought and Learning* (Dover).

Robinson, Paschal, tr., *The Writings of St. Francis of Assisi*.

Thatcher, O. J., and McNeal, E. H., *A Source Book for Medieval History*, pp. 513–21, Speech of Urban at Council of Clermont.

CHAPTER 13

The Civilization of the Renaissance:
In Italy

> Wherefore it may be surely said that those who are the possessors of such rare and numerous gifts as were seen in Raphael of Urbino, are not merely men, but, if it not be a sin to say it, mortal gods . . .
>
> —Giorgio Vasari, *Lives of the Painters*

Soon after 1300 the majority of the characteristic institutions and ideals of the Middle Ages had begun to decay. Chivalry, feudalism, the Holy Roman Empire, the universal authority of the papacy, the guild system of trade and industry were all gradually being weakened and would eventually disappear. The great age of the Gothic cathedrals was practically over, the Scholastic philosophy was beginning to be ridiculed and despised, and the supremacy of the religious and ethical interpretations of life was being slowly but effectively undermined. In place of all these there gradually emerged new institutions and ways of thinking of sufficient importance to stamp the centuries that followed with the character of a different civilization. The traditional name applied to this civilization, which extended from 1300 to approximately 1650, is the Renaissance.

The transition from the Middle Ages to the Renaissance

The term Renaissance leaves much to be desired from the standpoint of historical accuracy. Literally it means rebirth, and it is commonly taken to imply that in the fourteenth century, or Trecento,[1] there was a sudden revival of interest in the classical learning of Greece and Rome. But this implication is far from strictly true. Interest in the classics was by no means rare in the

Meaning of the term Renaissance

[1] So called from the Italian word for three hundred, *trecento*, used to designate the century which followed 1300. Quattrocento, from the word four hundred, is applied to the period of the fifteenth century and Cinquecento to the sixteenth.

later Middle Ages. Such writers as John of Salisbury, Dante, and the Goliard poets were just as enthusiastic admirers of Greek and Latin literature as any who lived in the fourteenth century. Indeed, the so-called Renaissance was in considerable measure simply the culmination of a series of revivals which began as far back as the tenth century. All of these movements were characterized by a reverence for the ancient authors. Even in the cathedral and monastic schools Cicero, Vergil, Seneca, and, later on, Aristotle frequently received as much worshipful adoration as was given to any of the saints.

The Renaissance was a great deal more than a mere revival of pagan learning. It embraced, first of all, an impressive record of new achievements in art, literature, science, philosophy, education, and religion. Although the foundation of many of these was classical, they soon expanded beyond the measure of Greek and Roman influence. Indeed, many of the achievements in painting, science, politics, and religion bore little relation to the classical heritage. Secondly, the Renaissance incorporated a number of dominant ideals and attitudes that gave it the impress of a unique society. Notable among these in general were optimism, secularism, and individualism; but the most significant of them all was humanism. In its broadest meaning humanism may be defined as emphasis on the human values implicit in the writings of the ancient Greeks and Romans. It was a term derived from Cicero, who used it in the sense of devotion to the liberal arts, or the subjects most compatible with the dignity of man. The humanists rejected the Scholastic philosophy with its preoccupation with theology and logic. They strove for a smooth and elegant style that would appeal more to the aesthetic than to the rational side of man's nature. Though the viewpoint of many of them was pagan, this was not always the case. A large number took Christianity for granted, and some extolled it as the noblest of moral philosophies.

Not only culturally but socially, economically, and politically the Renaissance constituted a new society which differed in many ways from the social pattern of the Middle Ages. To begin with, it was nonecclesiastical. Its great accomplishments were chiefly the work of laymen, not of monks or priests. Such arenas of achievement as the universities, hitherto dominated by the clergy, now went into temporary decline. Gothic and Romanesque architectures, preeminently associated with the medieval church, were superseded by a new style based upon classical models. Latin as a medium of literary expression survived, of course, for it was Roman in origin. But gradually literature in the vernacular acquired a status at least equal to that in Latin. Renaissance society took on an urban rather than a predominantly rural character. The centers of both social and economic life were no longer castles of the feudal nobility or manorial estates but rich cities such as Florence, Milan, Venice, and Rome. Politically, also, the changes were momentous. The decentralized

The Renaissance
more than a
revival of pagan
learning

feedal regime gave way to consolidated government in either large or small units. The rule of dukes and counts was succeeded by that of monarchs, or in some cases by that of oligarchs whose power sprang from their wealth as bankers or merchants. As a noted authority points out, "the fifteenth and sixteenth centuries were the age of kings." [2]

I. THE CAUSES OF THE RENAISSANCE

To determine the causes of a movement as complex as the Renaissance is not an easy task. In large measure it was a result of the disintegration of a medieval society that was no longer in harmony with changed economic and cultural conditions. The growth of commerce and the rise of national monarchies made the decentralized feudal regime obsolete. The self-sufficient manorial system decayed with the development of trade between distant regions and the appearance of new employment opportunities for villeins and serfs. As cities multiplied the nobles suffered a loss of power to the emerging middle class. Culturally, also, there was radical change. Medieval Scholasticism failed to satisfy the growing interest in natural science. Gothic architecture, which had reached its zenith of harmony and restraint in the thirteenth century, became exaggerated and flamboyant. Asceticism as an ideal was losing its appeal as men uncovered a greater variety of worldly satisfactions. Nearly everywhere, especially in southern Europe, there was a demand for a broader expanse of knowledge, a new style of living, and a greater recognition of the status of the individual. One factor, it may be said, was primarily responsible for nearly all these changes. That factor was the growth of cities, with their stimulating influence and the tendency of their populations to be impatient with old ways of living. But the cities themselves were chiefly the product of the revival of commerce. As far back as the eleventh century a flourishing trade had begun with the Saracenic and Byzantine empires. Material commodities were not the only things exchanged. There was a prosperous commerce also in ideas, manuscripts, and artistic influences. By the fourteenth century the Italian cities engaged in this trade had reached such a state of affluence that they were well adapted to becoming the centers of a cultural revival.

The main causes

Soon after the Renaissance got under way, its progress was accelerated by the influence of secular and ecclesiastical patrons of learning. Outstanding among the former were the Medici family in Florence and the Sforza family in Milan. Most of these patrons were wealthy merchants who had become despots of the city republics in which they lived. The ecclesiastical patrons included such Popes as Nicholas V, Pius II, Julius II, and Leo X. The

Influence of patrons of learning

[2] Denys Hay, *The Italian Renaissance in Its Historical Background*, p. 15.

attitude of these men was singularly at variance with what is normally expected of occupants of the fisherman's throne. They displayed no interest in theology or in the conversion of the ungodly. They kept on the payroll of the Church men who openly attacked fundamental Christian doctrines. Nicholas V, for example, employed as a papal secretary the celebrated Lorenzo Valla, who exposed an important document of the Church as a forgery and preached a philosophy of carnal pleasure. Whatever the incongruity of their attitude, the work of these Popes was of inestimable value to cultural progress, for they bestowed their patronage upon some of the most brilliant artists and literary men of the Italian Renaissance.

Before leaving this subject of factors responsible for the Renaissance, it will be desirable to dispose of two alleged causes commonly believed to have been of decisive importance. One of these is the Crusades, and the other is the invention of printing. In a preceding chapter we observed that the intellectual influence of the Crusades was slight. The introduction of Saracenic learning into Europe came about as a result of the work of scholars in the libraries of Toledo and Cordova and as a consequence of the trade revival between the Italian cities and the Near East. Only to the extent that the Crusades weakened feudalism, diminished the prestige of the papacy, and helped to give the Italian cities a monopoly of Mediterranean trade may they be considered as in any way responsible for the beginning of Renaissance civilization. And even these results can be ascribed in large part to other factors.

Alleged causes of the Renaissance: The Crusades

Although the invention of printing was an achievement of the utmost importance, it was perhaps even less than the Crusades a direct cause of the Renaissance. For one thing, it came too late. So far as the evidence shows, no printing press was in operation much before the middle of the fifteenth century. The earliest work known to have been printed from movable type actually dates from 1454.[3] By this time the Renaissance in Italy was already well under way, having started about a century and a half before. Furthermore, many of the early humanists were decidedly hostile toward the new invention. They regarded it as a barbarous German contraption and refused to allow their works to be printed lest they obtain too wide a circulation and be misunderstood by the common people. It should also be noted that the earliest publishing firms were far more interested in turning out religious books and popular stories than in printing the writings of the new learning. The conclusion seems amply justified that the invention of printing served chiefly to accelerate the Renaissance in its later stages, particularly in northern

Printing in the Sixteenth Century

[3] This was an indulgence issued from the press of Johann Gutenberg at Mainz, who is commonly credited with the invention of printing, though it is somewhat doubtful that he did more than perfect the technique developed by others, perhaps as early as 1445.

Europe. Most of the great benefits of the invention came after the Renaissance had ended.

2. THE RENAISSANCE IN ITALY

Reference has already been made to the fact that the Renaissance had its beginning in Italy. Why should this have been so? For one reason, Italy had a stronger classical tradition than any other country of western Europe. All through the medieval period the Italians had managed to preserve the belief that they were descendants of the ancient Romans. They looked back upon their ancestry with pride, ignoring of course the infiltrations of Lombard, Byzantine, Saracenic, and Norman blood that had been poured into the people from time to time. In some of the Italian cities traces of the old Roman system of education still survived in the municipal schools. It is likewise true that Italy had a more thoroughly secular culture than most other regions of Latin Christendom. The Italian universities were founded primarily for the study of law or medicine rather than theology, and, with the exception of the University of Rome, few of them had any ecclesiastical connections whatever. In addition to all this, Italy received the full impact of cultural influences from the Byzantine and Saracenic civilizations. Finally, and perhaps most important of all, the Italian cities were the main beneficiaries of the revival of trade with the East. For years the seaport towns of Venice, Naples, Genoa, and Pisa enjoyed a virtual monopoly of the Mediterranean trade, while the merchants of Florence, Bologna, Piacenza, and other cities of the Lombard plain served as the chief middlemen in the commerce between northern and southern Europe. The economic prosperity thus acquired was the principal foundation of the intellectual and artistic progress.

Why the Renaissance began in Italy

1. THE POLITICAL BACKGROUND   It is generally assumed that orderly and efficient government is a necessary condition for the development of a superior culture; but such was not the case with the civilization we are now considering. The Renaissance was born in the midst of political turmoil. Italy was not a unified state when the Renaissance began, and throughout the period the country remained in a turbulent condition. The reasons for this chaos were several. The first was the failure of universal government. In common with the rest of central Europe, Italy was supposed to be part of the Holy Roman Empire. But after the death of Conrad IV in 1254 the imperial throne was vacant for nineteen years. When successors were finally chosen, they proved to be too weak to wield any effective authority beyond their own family domains. The Pope also lost his power as a political ruler over the Italian peninsula. As a result of a quarrel between Pope Boniface VIII and King Philip IV of France the papacy was transferred to Avignon, France, where it remained under greater or less subjection to the French king for

The political crisis in Italy

347

Gattamelata. This statue of the famous condottiere by Donatello stands outside St. Anthony's basilica in Padua.

Francesco Sforza

seventy years. By the time a Pope was finally crowned again in Rome in 1378, the political authority of the universal Church had been eroded. The dozen or more petty states into which Italy was divided had grown accustomed to managing their own affairs. Politically, the Pope was little more than another Italian prince with an uncertain authority limited to a belt of land stretching across the peninsula.

The remainder of the Italian states rapidly solidified their rule as a means of preserving their power. But stability was not easily accomplished. Interstate rivalries, internal revolts, wars of conquest, and threats of invasion combined to continue the enveloping chaos. At the beginning of the Renaissance most of the Italian states were nominally republics. As conflicts increased and ambitions grew, many of them evolved into tyrannies or oligarchies. As early as 1311 the government of Milan became a dictatorship under the head of the Visconti family. In 1450 the Visconti were succeeded by Francesco Sforza, notorious as a *condottiere*, or leader of a band of mercenary soldiers. The new despotism was no less tyrannical than the old and was tolerated by its subjects chiefly because of its success in maintaining order and prosperity.

Despotism in Venice differed from that in Milan in being collective rather than individual. Although a *doge* was the nominal head of the state, he was hemmed in by so many restrictions that he was little·more than a figurehead. The real power rested with the heads of the chief business houses, who constituted a tight little oligarchy. They wielded effective authority through the Council of Ten, which took swift and merciless action against suspected enemies of the government. Politically as well as culturally, the most progressive of the Italian states was Florence. But even the Florentines were by no means entirely free from oligarchic evils. Though a constitution adopted in 1282 vested the government in an elected council whose members served short terms, restrictions on the suffrage ensured control of this body by the dominant business interests. Defeat in war and failure to maintain unbroken prosperity discredited this oligarchy, and in 1434 it was replaced by the rule of Cosimo de' Medici. Although Cosimo held no official title, he was accepted by the people as a virtual dictator, mainly because he ruled with an eye to their welfare. He and his descendants, the most famous of whom was his grandson Lorenzo the Magnificent, controlled the political life of Florence for sixty years. To the heads of the Medici family must be given a large measure of credit for the fact that Florence remained for so long the most brilliant center of the Italian Renaissance.

In the view of a number of historians the origins of the modern state system can be traced to Renaissance Italy. The rulers of such states as Milan, Florence, and Venice repudiated the conception of the state as existing for religious purposes and gave it a secular character. They emphasized civic responsibility, loyalty, and concern for the public welfare. They developed a strong notion of the end of the state as the advancement of its own interests. They invented procedures of diplomacy, including a system of permanent ambassadors in foreign capitals. They fostered alliances and toyed with the idea of a balance of power to keep the peace. The balance never really worked, however. Ambitious politicians in some of the states, notably Milan, disturbed it by soliciting help for their schemes from powerful nations outside the peninsula. A tragic consequence was the invasion of Italy by the French in 1494, followed soon afterward by a Spanish invasion from the Kingdom of Aragon. Henceforth the peninsula was at the mercy of competing armies of major European powers.

Perhaps the most "modern" of the activities of the Italian Renaissance states were their ventures in "imperialism." Before the end of the fourteenth century Milan reached out and annexed nearly the whole of the Lombard plain. Needing an agricultural province as a source of food supply and coveting control of mainland trade routes, Venice conquered nearly all of northeastern Italy, including the cities of Padua and Verona. Nor did the republic of Florence lag behind in the development of expansionist ambitions. Before the end of the fourteenth century practically all of the territory of Tuscany had been taken, and in 1406 the great mercantile city of Pisa succumbed to Florentine domination. The papacy also took part in the general movement of territorial aggrandizement. Under such worldly and aggressive Popes as Alexander VI (1492–1503) and Julius II (1503–1513) the dominion of the Papal States was ex-

Venice and Florence

Lorenzo de' Medici by Raphael

Possible origins of the modern state system

Expansionism

349

THE STATES OF ITALY DURING THE RENAISSANCE ca. 1494

tended over most of central Italy. By the early 1500's nearly the whole peninsula had been brought under the five most powerful states: Milan, Venice, Florence, the Kingdom of Naples, and the States of the Church.

II. THE LITERARY AND ARTISTIC CULTURE No wide gulf separated Italian Renaissance literature from the literature of the later Middle Ages. The majority of the literary achievements between 1300 and 1550 were already foreshadowed in one or another of the different trends initiated in the twelfth and thirteenth centuries. The so-called father of Italian Renaissance literature, Francesco Petrarca or Petrarch (1304–1374), was himself very close to the medieval temper. He employed the same Tuscan dialect that Dante had chosen as the basis of an Italian literary language. Moreover, he believed firmly in Christianity as the way of salvation for man, and he was addicted at times to a monkish asceticism. His best-known writings, the sonnets he addressed to his beloved Laura, partook of the same flavor as the chivalrous love poetry of the thirteenth-century troubadours.

The second of the great figures in the Italian literary Renaissance, Giovanni Boccaccio (1313–1375), was scarcely more of an original genius. Like Petrarch, Boccaccio was a Florentine, the illegitimate son of a prosperous merchant. His father having planned for him a business career, he was sent to Naples to serve an apprenticeship in a branch of the great Florentine banking house of the Bardi. But the young Boccaccio soon displayed more ardor in worshiping in the temple of the Muses than in computing the interest on loans. It was perhaps natural that this should be so, for Naples was a center of gracious living under languorous skies and of strong poetic traditions emanating from the lands of the Saracens and the troubadours. It was an environment especially fitted to stimulate the poetic fancies of youth. Boccaccio was also inspired by a passionate love for the beautiful wife of a Neapolitan citizen. Nearly all of his earlier works were poems and romances dealing with the triumphs and tortures of this love. Gradually his skill in the story-telling art attained perfection, and he eventually found prose a more suitable medium for his purposes. By far the most notable of Boccaccio's writings was his *Decameron*, which he wrote after his return to Florence about 1348. The *Decameron* consists of 100 stories which the author puts into the mouths of seven young women and three young men. The stories do not form a novel revolving about a continuous theme but are united by the artificial plot of having been told by a group of people who are concerned merely with passing the time during their sojourn at a villa outside of Florence to escape the ravages of the Black Death. Though some of the tales were probably invented by Boccaccio, most of them were drawn from the *fabliaux*, from the *Book of the 1001 Nights*, and from other medieval sources. In general, they differ from their medieval prototypes in being slightly more ribald, egoistic, and anticlerical and more deeply concerned with a frank justification of the carnal life. Yet the *Decameron* certainly does not represent, as many people think, the first emphatic protest against the ascetic and impersonal ideals of the early Middle Ages. Its real significance lies in the fact that it set the pattern for Italian prose and exerted considerable influence upon Renaissance writers in other countries.

The character of
literature in the
Quattrocento

The death of Boccaccio in 1375 marks the end of the first period of the Italian Renaissance in literature, the Trecento. The age which followed, known as the Quattrocento, was characterized by a more zealous devotion to the Latin language and a broader conception of humanistic studies. The Italian of Dante and Boccaccio was regarded now by many writers as an inferior language unsuited to the perfection of an elegant style and the expression of noble ideas. No longer were the humanities thought of as synonymous with rhetoric, oratory, grammar, ethics, and poetry, but were held to include history, philosophy, and religion as well. In fine, they embraced every subject considered by the ancients as a proper medium for the study of man. As a third difference, the men of the Quattrocento turned away from the asceticism of Petrarch. They taught that nature had endowed man for action, for usefulness to his family and society, not for religious seclusion. Passion, ambition, and the quest for glory are noble impulses and ought to be encouraged. They refused to condemn the striving for material possessions, for they argued that the history of man's progress is inseparable from his success in gaining mastery over the earth and its resources. A few of the writers of the Quattrocento were completely pagan or atheistic, but most of them were neither religious nor antireligious. They took Christianity for granted and were concerned primarily with worldly interests.

The passion for
Greek studies

The Quattrocento was also the period when the passion for Greek studies was at its zenith. Prior to this time the Italian humanists had achieved but indifferent success in their attempts to learn the Greek language and to discover the treasures of Hellenic culture. But in 1393 a famous scholar of Constantinople, Manuel Chrysaloras, arrived in Venice on a mission from the Byzantine emperor to implore the aid of the West in a war against the Turks. Almost immediately acclaimed by the Italians as an apostle of the glorious Hellenic past, he was eventually persuaded to accept a professorship of the Greek classics at the University of Florence. About the beginning of the fifteenth century several other Byzantine scholars, notably Platonist philosophers, migrated to Italy. The influence of these men in providing information about the achievements of the ancient Greeks seems to have been considerable. At any rate, it was not long until Italian scholars began to make trips to Constantinople and other Byzantine cities in search of manuscripts. Between 1413 and 1423 a certain Giovanni Aurispa, for example, brought back nearly 250 manuscript books, including works of Sophocles, Euripides, and Thucydides. It was in this way that many of the Hellenic classics, particularly the writings of the dramatists, historians, and earlier philosophers, were first made available to the modern world.

The last great age in the development of Italian Renaissance literature was the Cinquecento, the period from 1500 to about 1550.

Vespers of the Holy Ghost, with a View of Paris, Jean Fouquet. From the *Book of Hours* of Etienne Chevalier, 1461. Demons in the sky are sent flying by the divine light from Heaven. The cathedral is Notre Dame. (Robert Lehman)

A Sixteenth-Century Map of the World by Paolo dal Toscanelli, Adviser to Columbus. The European continent is in the upper left. (Scala)

St. Lawrence Enthroned, Fra Lippo Lippi (1406–1469). One of the first of the psychological painters, Fra Lippo Lippi exhibited in this work his gift for portraying pensive melancholy. (MMA)

The Flight into Egypt, Giotto (1276–1337). Giotto is regarded as the founder of the modern tradition in painting. A fresco in the Arena Chapel, Padua. (MMA)

The Birth of Venus, Sandro Botticelli (1444–1510). Botticelli was a mystic as well as a lover of beauty whose works suggest a longing for the glories of the classical world. (Scala)

Mona Lisa, Leonardo da Vinci (1452–1519). Unlike most other Renaissance painters who sought to convey an understandable message, Leonardo created questions to which he gave no answer. Nowhere is this more evident than in the enigmatic countenance of Mona Lisa. (Louvre)

The Virgin of the Rocks, Leonardo da Vinci. This painting reveals not only Leonardo's interest in human character, but also his absorption in the phenomena of nature. (Louvre)

The Last Supper, Leonardo da Vinci. This great fresco depicts the varying reactions of Jesus' disciples when He announces that one of them will betray Him. (Santa Maria della Grazie, Milan)

Above: *The Madonna of the Chair*, Raphael (1483–1520). Raphael's art was distinguished by warmth and serenity, and by an uncritical acceptance of the traditions and conventions of his time. (Pitti Palace, Florence) Right: "Christ and Madonna." From *The Last Judgment*, Michelangelo (1475–1564). This painting above the altar in the Sistine Chapel, Rome, shows Christ as judge condemning sinners to perdition. Even the Madonna at His side seems to shrink from His wrath. (Sistine Chapel)

Charles V, Titian (1488–1576). (Alte Pinakothek)

Pope Paul III and His Nephews, Titian (1477–1576). This painting, with its rich harmony of color, is unusual in being both a group portrait and a study of action. (National Museum, Naples)

Italian was now raised to a full equality with Greek and Latin, classical and modern influences were more perfectly blended, and a deeper originality of both form and content was achieved. But the literary capital of the Renaissance was no longer Florence. In 1494 that city came under the rule of the fanatical reformer Savonarola; and, while the Medici were restored to power about eighteen years later, the brilliant Tuscan metropolis soon afterward fell a victim of factional disputes and foreign invasion. During the first half of the sixteenth century the city of Rome gradually rose to a position of cultural leadership, mainly because of the patronage of the Church, especially during the reign of Pope Leo X (Giovanni de' Medici), the son of Lorenzo the Magnificent. When he was only fourteen years old, his father's influence had been sufficient to procure his appointment as a cardinal. Elevated to St. Peter's throne in 1513, he is reported to have said, "Let us enjoy the papacy since God has given it to us." There can be little doubt that he did enjoy it, for he was a magnificent spendthrift, lavishing rewards upon artists and writers and financing the construction of beautiful churches.

The chief forms of literature developed in the Cinquecento were epic and pastoral poetry, drama, and history. The most eminent of the writers of epics was Ludovico Ariosto (1474–1533), author of a lengthy poem entitled *Orlando Furioso*. Although woven largely of materials taken from the romances of adventure and the legends of the Arthurian cycle, this work differed radically from any of the medieval epics. It incorporated much that was derived from classical sources; it lacked the impersonal quality of the medieval romances; and it was totally devoid of idealism. Ariosto wrote to make men laugh and to charm them with felicitous descriptions of the quiet splendor of nature and the passionate beauty of love. His work represents the disillusionment of the late Rennaissance, the loss of hope and faith, and the tendency to seek consolation in the pursuit of aesthetic pleasure. The development of pastoral poetry at this time probably reflects a similar attitude of disenchantment and loss of confidence. As the name implies, the pastoral romance glorifies the simple life amid rustic surroundings and expresses the yearning for a golden age of unspoiled pleasures and freedom from the worries and frustrations of artificial urban society. The chief author of this type of literature in the Italian Renaissance was Jacopo Sannazaro (1458–1530), who gave to his main work the title of *Arcadia*.

In the field of the drama the Italians never achieved more than moderate success. Their failure as writers of tragedy was particularly noticeable, despite the fact that they had considerable knowledge of classical models from which to profit. The Italian was apparently too much of an individualist to be influenced profoundly by the Greek conception of a tragic conflict between man and society and too much of an optimist to brood over personal suffering. His mind was fixed upon the compensations of life rather than upon

The Cinquecento

The epic and the pastoral romance

Drama

its grim and terrifying aspects. His real talents lay in naturalistic description, in the development of light and joyous themes, and in the expression of personal egotism. It was natural, therefore, that the best of his dramas should have been comedies, especially satirical comedies, rather than tragedies. The first and the greatest of the Italian comedians was a man who is far better known as a political philosopher—Niccolò Machiavelli (1469–1527). The finest product of his dramatic skill was a work entitled *Mandragola*, which has been called "the ripest and most powerful play in the Italian language." [4] Sparkling with salacious wit and based upon incidents typical of life in the author's native city of Florence, it is a lurid satire of Renaissance society. In this as in his other writings, Machiavelli reveals his cynical views of human nature. He appears to believe that all human beings are knaves and fools at heart, with their meanness and stupidity only partly concealed by a thin veneer of refinement and learning.

History

The historians of the High Renaissance in Italy displayed a critical spirit and a degree of objectivity which had not been seen since the end of the ancient world. First among them in order of time although not in order of greatness was Machiavelli. In his main historical work, an account of the evolution of the Florentine republic to the death of Lorenzo de' Medici, he rigidly excluded all theological interpretations and sought to discover the natural laws which govern the life of a people. More scientific in his methods of analysis was Machiavelli's younger contemporary, Francesco Guicciardini (1483–1540). Having served many years as an ambassador of Florence and as a governor of papal territories, Guicciardini enjoyed a unique advantage in acquiring familiarity with the cynical and tortuous political life of his day. His special gifts as a historian were a capacity for minute and realistic analysis and an uncanny ability in disclosing the springs of human action. His masterpiece was his *History of Italy*, a detailed and dispassionate account of the varying fortunes of that country from 1492 to 1534. No study of Renaissance historians would be complete without some mention of Lorenzo Valla (1406–1457), who may properly be regarded as the father of historical criticism. By careful scrutiny of their literary style he challenged the authenticity of a number of accepted documents. He proved the famous "Donation of Constantine" to be a forgery, thereby demolishing one of the principal bases of papal supremacy, since this document purported to have been a grant by the Emperor Constantine of the highest spiritual and temporal power in the West to the Pope. In addition, Valla denied that the so-called Apostles' Creed had ever been written by the Apostles, and he pointed out numerous corruptions in the Vulgate edition of the New Testament as compared with the earlier Greek texts. His critical methods served later on to stimulate a much broader attack by

[4] J. A. Symonds, "Machiavelli," *Encyclopedia Britannica* (14th ed.), XIV, 577.

the northern humanists upon the doctrines and practices of the organized Church.

Despite the wealth of brilliant accomplishments in literature, the proudest achievements of the Italian Renaissance were made in the realm of art. Of all the arts, painting was undoubtedly supreme. The evolution of Italian painting followed a course of development which roughly paralleled the history of literature. During the initial period of the Trecento, however, there was only one artist of distinction worthy to be compared to Petrarch and Boccaccio in literature. His name was Giotto (1276–1337). With him, painting definitely took on the status of an independent art, although his master Cimabue had already made some beginnings in this direction. Giotto was preeminently a naturalist. So skillful was he in depicting the semblance of life that, according to the story, one of his drawings of a fly so completely deceived Cimabue that he attempted to brush the creature away with his hand. Giotto also displayed more than ordinary talent in the portrayal of action, especially in such frescoes as *Saint Francis Preaching to the Birds*, *The Massacre of the Innocents,* and his scenes from the life of Christ.

It was not till the Quattrocento, however, that Italian Renaissance painting really attained its majority. By this time the increase in wealth and the partial triumph of the secular spirit had freed the domain of art to a large extent from the service of religion. The Church was no longer the only patron of artists. While subject matter from Biblical history was still commonly employed, it was frequently infused with nonreligious themes. The painting of portraits for the purpose of revealing the hidden mysteries of the soul now became popular. Paintings intended to appeal primarily to the intellect were paralleled by others whose only purpose was to delight the eye with gorgeous color and beauty of form. The Quattrocento was characterized also by the introduction of painting in oil, probably from Flanders. The use of the new technique doubtless had much to do with the artistic advance of this period. Since oil does not dry so quickly as water, the painter could now work more leisurely, taking his time with the more difficult parts of the picture and making corrections if necessary as he went along.

The majority of the painters of the Quattrocento were Florentines. First among them was a precocious youth known as Masaccio (1401–1428). Although he died at the age of twenty-seven, Masaccio inspired the work of Italian painters for a hundred years. He is commonly considered the first of the realists in Renaissance art. Besides, he introduced a tactile quality into his work which profoundly influenced many of his successors. The greatest of his paintings, *The Expulsion of Adam and Eve from the Garden* and *The Tribute Money,* dealt not with specific themes but with the simple emotions common to mankind in all ages. Masaccio was also the first to achieve any notable success in imparting unity of action to

Italian painting in the Trecento: Giotto the naturalist

See color plates between pages 352 and 353

The Expulsion of Adam and Eve from the Garden. Masaccio's painting departed from the tradition of Giotto by introducing emotion and psychological study.

Botticelli

*See color
plates between
pages 352 and
353*

Leonardo da
Vinci

*See color
plates between
pages 352 and
353*

Leonardo's artis-
tic approach

groups of figures and in giving the effect of thickness to objects by the use of light and shade.

The best known of the painters who followed directly the paths marked out by Masaccio was Sandro Botticelli (1444–1510), who specialized in depicting both religious and classical themes. He excelled in representing human emotions, but always with an eye for harmony and rhythm. In spite of his sensitive feeling for nature which led him to paint with such delicate skill the subtle loveliness of youth, the summer sky, and the tender bloom of spring, Botticelli was really more deeply interested in the spiritual beauty of the soul. Like others of his time, he was strongly influenced by Neo-Platonism and dreamed of the reconciliation of pagan and Christian thought. As a consequence many of the countenances he painted reveal a pensive sadness, a mystic yearning for the divine. By no means all of his work had a religious import. His *Allegory of Spring* and *Birth of Venus* are based entirely upon classical mythology and suggest little more than an absorbing pleasure in the unfolding of life and a romantic longing for the glories of ancient Greece and Rome.

Perhaps the greatest of the Florentine painters was Leonardo da Vinci (1452–1519), one of the most talented and versatile geniuses who ever lived. Not only was he a gifted painter but a sculptor, musician, and architect of outstanding ability and a brilliant engineer and philosopher. The son of an illicit union of a prominent lawyer and a woman of humble station, he was placed by his father at an early age under the instruction of Verrocchio, a sculptor and painter of some renown and the most celebrated teacher of art in Florence. By the time he was twenty-five Leonardo was already sufficiently distinguished as a painter to win the favor of Lorenzo the Magnificent. But after five or six years he appears to have become dissatisfied with the intellectual and artistic views of the Medici and gladly accepted an offer of regular employment at the court of the Sforza in Milan. It was under the patronage of the Sforza that he produced some of the finest achievements of his life. His work, which embraces the late years of the fifteenth century and the first two decades of the sixteenth, marks the beginning of the so-called High Renaissance in Italy.

As a painter Leonardo da Vinci was impatient with the established tradition of striving to imitate classical models. He believed that all art should have as its basis a scientific study of nature. But he had no intention of confining his interests to the mere surface appearances of things. He was convinced that the secrets of nature are deeply hidden, and that the artist must examine the structure of a plant or probe into the emotions of a human soul as painstakingly as the anatomist would dissect a body. He appears especially to have been fascinated by the grotesque and unusual in nature. Yawning fissures in the earth, jagged pinnacles of rocks, rare plants and animals, embryos, and fossils—these were the phenomena he loved to ponder, evidently in the belief that this mysterious universe yields more of its secrets in the fantastic and unaccustomed than in the things that are commonplace and obvious. For the same reason he devoted much time to the study of exceptional human types, often wandering the streets for hours in quest of some face that would reveal the beauty or terror, the sincerity or hypocrisy, of the personality behind it. As a result of this deliberate selection of subjects, the paintings of Leonardo have a quality of realism decidedly at variance with the ordinary type. He did not generally portray the aspects of nature as they appear to the casual observer but strove to present them as symbols of his own philosophic reflections. He was one of the most profoundly intellectual of painters.

It is generally agreed that Leonardo da Vinci's masterpieces are his *Virgin of the Rocks*, his *Last Supper*, and his *Mona Lisa*. The first represents not only his marvelous technical skill but also his passion for science and his belief in the universe as a well-ordered place. The figures are arranged in geometric composition with every rock and plant depicted in accurate detail. The *Last Supper*, painted on the walls of the rectory of Santa Maria delle Grazie in Milan, is a study of psychological reactions. A serene Christ, resigned to his terrible fate, has just announced to his disciples that one of them will betray him. The purpose of the artist is to portray the mingled emotions of surprise, horror, and guilt revealed in the faces of the disciples as they gradually perceive the meaning of their master's statement. The third of Leonardo's major triumphs, the *Mona Lisa*, reflects a similar interest in the varied moods of the human soul. Although it is true that the *Mona Lisa* (or *Monna Lisa*, i.e., "my Lady Lisa") is a portrait of an actual woman, the wife of Francesco del Giocondo, a Neapolitan, it is more than a mere photographic likeness. The distinguished art critic and historian Bernard Berenson has said of it, "Who like Leonardo has depicted . . . the inexhaustible fascination of the woman in her years of mastery? . . . Leonardo is the one artist of whom it may be said with perfect literalness: 'Nothing that he touched but turned into a thing of eternal beauty.' " [5]

The late Quattrocento, or the beginning of the High Renaissance, was marked by the rise of another celebrated school of Italian painting, the so-called Venetian school. Its chief representatives included Giorgione (1478–1510), Titian (*ca.* 1488–1576), and Tintoretto (1518–1594). Of the three, Titian was perhaps the greatest. The work of all these men reflected the luxurious life and the pleasure-loving interests of the thriving commercial city of Venice. The Venetian painters had none of the preoccupation with philosophical and psychological themes that had characterized the Florentine

Bust of a Warrior by Leonardo da Vinci

See color plates at page 353

The Venetian painters

school. Their aim was to appeal to the senses rather than to the mind. They delighted in painting idyllic landscapes and gorgeous symphonies of color. For their subject matter they chose not merely the opulent beauty of Venetian sunsets and the shimmering silver of lagoons in the moonlight but also the man-made splendor of sparkling jewels, richly colored satins and velvets, and gorgeous palaces. Their portraits were invariably likenesses of the rich and the powerful. In the subordination of form and meaning to color and elegance there were mirrored not only the sumptuous tastes of a wealthy bourgeoisie but also definite traces of Oriental influence which had filtered through from Byzantium during the late Middle Ages.

The painters of the late Renaissance: Raphael

The remaining great painters of the High Renaissance all lived their active careers in the Cinquecento. It was in this period that the evolution of art reached its peak, and the first signs of decay began to appear. Rome was now almost the only artistic center of importance on the mainland of the Italian peninsula, although the traditions of the Florentine school still exerted a potent influence. Among the eminent painters of this period at least two must be given more than passing attention. One of the most noted was Raphael (1483–1520), a native of Urbino, and perhaps the most popular artist of the entire Renaissance. The lasting appeal of his style is due primarily to his intense humanism. He developed a conception of a spiritualized and ennobled humanity. He portrayed the members of the human species, not as dubious, tormented creatures, but as temperate, wise, and dignified beings. Although he was influenced by Leonardo da Vinci and copied many features of his work, he cultivated to a much greater extent than Leonardo a symbolical or allegorical approach. His *Disputá* symbolized the dialectical relationship between the church in heaven and the church on earth. In a worldly setting against a brilliant sky, doctors and theologians ve-

See color plates at page 353

Michelangelo, *The Creation of Adam*. One of a series of frescoes on the ceiling of the Sistine Chapel in Rome. Suggesting philosophical inquiries into the meaning of life and the universe, it represents Renaissance realism at its height.

hemently debate the meaning of the Eucharist, while in the clouds above saints and the Trinity repose in the possession of a holy mystery. The *School of Athens* is an allegorical representation of the conflict between the Platonist and Aristotelian philosophies. Plato is shown pointing upward to emphasize the spiritual basis of his world of Ideas, while Aristotle gestures toward the earth to exemplify his belief that concepts or ideas are inseparably linked with their material embodiments. Raphael is noted also for his portraits and Madonnas. To the latter, especially, he gave a softness and warmth that seemed to endow them with a sweetness and piety quite different from the enigmatic and analytical portraits of Leonardo da Vinci.

Another towering giant of the Cinquecento in painting was Michelangelo (1475–1564). Beset by the hardships of poverty, harassed by grasping relatives, and torn by the emotional conflicts of his own tempestuous nature, Michelangelo appears as one of the most tragic figures in the history of art. His dark presentiments were often reflected in his work, with the result that some of his paintings are overwrought and almost morbidly pessimistic. Nevertheless, the sense of tragedy he implanted in the scenes he portrayed was not really personal but universal. After the manner of the Greek dramatists he conceived of the tragic fate of mortals as something external to man himself, a product of the cosmic order of things. If there was any one theme that dominated all of his work, it was humanism in its most intense and eloquent form. He considered the pathos and nobility of man as the only legitimate subjects of art. Rocks and trees and flowers meant nothing to him, not even as background. Michelangelo's grandest achievement as a painter was the series of frescoes he produced on the ceiling of the Sistine Chapel and on the wall above the altar. The sheer physical labor required to complete the task was prodigious. For four and a half years he toiled on a lofty scaffold, most of the time face upward, covering the 6000 square feet of ceiling with nearly 400 figures, many of them as much as ten feet in stature. The series embraces a number of scenes in the mighty epic of the human race according to Christian legend. Among them are *God Dividing the Light from the Darkness, God Creating the Earth, The Creation of Adam, The Fall of Man, The Deluge,* and so on. The culminating scene is *The Last Judgment,* which Michelangelo finished some thirty years later on the wall back of the altar. Sometimes referred to as the most famous painting in the world, this scene depicts a Herculean Christ damning the great mass of mankind to perdition. Although the subject matter is Christian, the spirit is pagan, as indicated by the naked and muscular figures and the suggestion of a ruthless deity who punishes men beyond their deserts. Nowhere else is Michelangelo's conception of universal tragedy more strongly expressed than in this work of his lonely old age.

Michelangelo

See color plates at page 353

359

Italian Renais-
sance sculpture:
Donatello

David by Donatello

Michelangelo's
allegorical
sculpture

360

Medieval sculpture, as we have already seen, was not an independent art but a mere adjunct of architecture. During the Italian Renaissance a gradual evolution began which ultimately had the effect of freeing sculpture from its bondage to architecture and establishing its status as a separate art frequently devoted to secular purposes.

The first great master of Renaissance sculpture was Donatello (1386?–1466). He emancipated his art from Gothic mannerisms and introduced a more vigorous note of individualism than did any of his predecessors. His statue of David standing triumphant over the body of the slain Goliath established a precedent of naturalism and of glorification of the nude which sculptors for many years afterward were destined to follow. Donatello also produced the first monumental equestrian statue in bronze since the time of the Romans, a commanding figure of the *condottiere*, Gattamelata.

One of the greatest sculptors of the Italian Renaissance, and probably of all time, was Michelangelo. Sculpture, in fact, was the artistic field of Michelangelo's personal preference. Despite his success as a painter he considered himself unfitted for that work. Whether he was ever particularly happy as a sculptor might be open to debate, for he smashed some of the works upon which he had spent months of labor and invested others with the same quality of pessimism that characterized much of his painting. The dominant purpose which motivated all of his sculpture was the expression of thought in stone. His art was above mere naturalism, for he subordinated nature to the force and sweep of his ideas. Other features of his work included the use of distortion for powerful effect, preoccupation with themes of disillusionment and tragedy, and a tendency to express his philosophical ideas in allegorical form. Most of his great masterpieces were done for the embellishment of tombs, a fact significantly in harmony with his absorbing interest in death, especially in his later career. For the tomb of Pope Julius II, which was never finished, he carved his famous figures of the *Bound Slave* and *Moses*. The first, which is probably in some degree autobiographical, represents tremendous power and talent restrained by the bonds of fate. The statue of Moses is perhaps the leading example of Michelangelo's sculpture showing his use of anatomical distortion to heighten the effect of emotional intensity. Its purpose was evidently to express the towering rage of the prophet on account of the disloyalty of the children of Israel to the faith of their fathers.

Some other examples of Michelangelo's work as a plastic artist create an even more striking impression. On the tombs of the Medici in Florence he produced a number of allegorical figures representing such abstractions as sorrow and despair. Two of them are known by the traditional titles of *Dawn* and *Sunset*. The first is that of a female figure, turning and raising her head like someone called from a dreamless sleep to awake and suffer. *Sunset* is the figure of a powerful man who appears to sink under the load of human misery around him. Whether these allegorical figures were intended to symbolize the disasters that had overtaken the republic of Florence or merely to express the artist's own sense of the repletion of disappointment and defeat in the world is unknown. As Michelangelo's life drew toward its close, he tended to introduce into his sculpture a more exaggerated and spectacular emotional quality. This was especially true of the *Pietà* intended for his own tomb. The *Pietà* is a statue of the Virgin Mary grieving over the body of the dead Christ. The figure standing behind the Virgin is possibly intended to represent Michelangelo himself, contemplating the stark tragedy which seemed to epitomize the reality of life. It is perhaps fitting that this profound but overwrought interpretation of human existence should have brought the Renaissance epoch in sculpture to a close.

To a much greater extent than either sculpture or painting, Renaissance architecture had its roots in the past. The new building style was eclectic, a compound of elements derived from the Middle Ages and from pagan antiquity. It was not the Hellenic or the Gothic, however, but the Roman and the Romanesque which provided the inspiration for the architecture of the Italian Renaissance. Neither the Greek nor the Gothic had ever found a congenial soil in Italy. The Romanesque, by contrast, was able to flourish there, since it was more in keeping with Italian traditions, while the persistence of a strong admiration for Latin culture made possible a revival of the Roman style. Accordingly, the great architects of the Renaissance generally adopted their building plans from the Romanesque churches and monasteries and copied their decorative devices from the ruins of ancient Rome. The result was an architecture based upon the cruciform floor plan of transept and nave and embodying the decorative features of the column and arch, or the column and lintel, the colonnade, and frequently the dome. Horizontal lines predominated; and, though many of the buildings were churches, the

Gattamelata by Donatello (see also p. 348)

Pietà by Michelangelo. This portrayal of tragedy was made by the sculptor for his own tomb. Note the distortion for effect exemplified by the elongated body and left arm of the Christ. The figure in the rear is Nicodemus, but was probably intended to stand as a symbol of Michelangelo himself. Original in the Cathedral of Florence.

The Villa Rotunda of Palladio. A Renaissance building near Vicenza combining the Roman features of a square floor plan and a central dome with the Greek features of Ionic columns and colonnades.

ideals they expressed were the purely secular ones of joy in this life and pride in human achievement. Renaissance architecture emphasized harmony and proportion to a much greater extent than did the Romanesque style. Under the influence of Neo-Platonism, Italian architects concluded that perfect proportions in man reflect the harmony of the universe, and that, therefore, the parts of a building should be related to each other and to the whole in the same way as the parts of the human body. A fine example of Renaissance architecture is St. Peter's Church in Rome, built under the patronage of Popes Julius II and Leo X and designed by some of the most celebrated architects of the time, including Donato Bramante and Michelangelo. Profusely decorated with costly paintings and sculpture, it remains to this day the most magnificent church in the world.

III. PHILOSOPHY AND SCIENCE   The popular impression that the Renaissance represented in every way a marked improvement over the Middle Ages is not strictly true. It was certainly not more than half true in the realm of philosophy. The early humanists scorned logic and even the rationalism of Scholastic philosophy. Such disciplines they regarded as formal and mechanical hindrances to a fine literary style and to the enhancement of the nobility of man. Instead of Aristotle they chose Cicero as their idol and centered their interest almost exclusively upon moral philosophy. During the Quattrocento many became Platonists after the founding of the Platonic Academy by Cosimo de' Medici in Florence. Outstanding among the philosophers of the Academy were Marsilio Ficino (1433–1499) and Pico della Mirandola (1463–1494). Both were deeply pious and sought to reconcile Christianity with philosophy and even to show the basic harmony of all religions and philosophies. They rejected some of the cardinal tenets of humanism—the indissoluble unity of mind and body and the high valuation of material goods—and preached an asceticism that harked back to the Middle Ages. They adulterated their Platonism with some elements taken from Neo-Platonism and even from astrology and other occult pseudosciences.

Italian Renaissance philosophy: the Platonists

362

But not all the Italian humanists were ecstatic worshipers of Plato. In their zeal for a revival of pagan culture some sought to reawaken an interest in Aristotle for his own sake and not as a bulwark of Christianity. Others became Stoics, Epicureans, or Skeptics. The most original philosophers of the Italian Renaissance were Lorenzo Valla, Leonardo da Vinci, and Niccolò Machiavelli. The fearless and sensational ventures of Lorenzo Valla into the field of historical criticism have already been noted. He was equally unconventional as a philosopher. Defending the principles of Epicurus, he avowed the highest good to be tranquil pleasure, condemned asceticism as utterly vain and worthless, and insisted that it is irrational to die for one's country. Although Leonardo da Vinci wrote nothing that could be called a philosophical treatise, he may yet be considered a philosopher in the broad meaning of the word. He was one of the first to condemn unequivocally reliance upon authority as a source of truth, and he urged the use of the inductive method. It may be worthwhile also to take note of his strictures on war, which he called "that most bestial madness." He wrote that "It is an infinitely atrocious thing to take away the life of a man," and he even refused to divulge the secret of one of his inventions for fear it might be used by unscrupulous rulers to increase the barbarity of war.[6]

Niccolò Machiavelli is by far the most famous—and also the most infamous—political philosopher of the Italian Renaissance. No man did more than he to overturn the basic political conceptions of the Middle Ages, the ideas of universalism, limited government, and the ethical basis of politics. He was the first to conceive of the state in its modern form as a completely sovereign and independent unit. In

[6] Edward MacCurdy (ed.), *The Notebooks of Leonardo da Vinci*, I, 24.

St. Peter's, Rome. Built to a square cross plan originally conceived by Bramante and revised by Michelangelo. Substantially completed by 1603, the church rises to a total height of 450 feet.

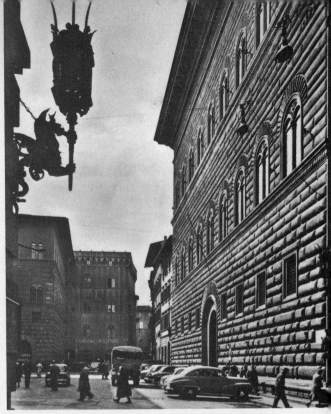

Left: *The Tempietto*. Designed in 1500 by Bramante, its Roman lines represent a turning point in Italian Renaissance architecture. Right: *The Strozzi Palace in Florence*. The heavy rustication of the walls with windows set into wide arches is a typical feature of Italian Renaissance palaces.

his *Discourses on Livy* he praised the ancient Roman republic as a model for all time. He lauded constitutionalism, equality, liberty in the sense of freedom from outside interference, and subordination of religion to the interests of the state. But Machiavelli also wrote *The Prince*. More than the *Discourses* it reflects the unhappy condition of Italy in his time. At the end of the fifteenth century Italy had become the cockpit of international struggles. Both France and Spain had invaded the peninsula and were competing with each other for the allegiance of the Italian states. The latter, in many cases, were torn by internal dissension which made them an easy prey for foreign conquerors. In 1498 Machiavelli entered the service of the republic of Florence as Second Chancellor and Secretary. His duties largely involved diplomatic missions to other states. While in Rome he became fascinated with the achievements of Cesare Borgia, son of Pope Alexander VI, in cementing a solidified state out of scattered elements. He noted with approval Cesare's combination of ruthlessness with shrewdness and his complete subordination of morality to political ends. In 1512 the Medici overturned the government of Florence, and Machiavelli was deprived of his position. Disappointed and embittered, he spent the remainder of his life in exile, devoting his time primarily to writing. In his books, especially in *The Prince,* he described the policies and practices of government, not in accordance with some lofty ideal, but as they actually were. The supreme obligation of the ruler, he avowed, was to maintain the power and safety of the country over which he ruled. No consideration of justice or mercy or the sanctity of treaties should be allowed to stand in his way. Cynical in his views of human nature, Machiavelli maintained that all men are prompted exclusively by motives of self-interest, particularly by desires for personal power and material prosperity. The head of the state should therefore take nothing for granted as to the loyalty or affection of his subjects. Machiavelli was the first important realist in political theory since the time of Polybius. The one ideal he kept before him in his later years was the unification of Italy. But this he believed had no chance of accomplishment except by the methods of the hard-core realist.

Not only did the narrow attitude of the early humanists in Italy retard the progress of philosophy; it also hindered for some time the advancement of science. The early humanists, as we have seen, were not critical minded. They accepted revered authorities of classical antiquity much too readily. Moreover, their interests were in art and literature, not in science. Part of this emphasis may undoubtedly be attributed to the fact that the leaders of the Renaissance for some time had only a limited knowledge of Greek achievements. The early pagan revival was predominantly a revival of Latin antiquity. And it will be recalled that the contributions of the Romans to science were few and mediocre. But in spite of the unfavorable influence of early humanism, Italy became by the fifteenth century the most important center of scientific discovery in Renaissance Europe. Much of the work was done, however, by non-Italians. Men from all over the Continent came to study in Italy and to profit from the researches of her eminent scholars. They laid the foundations for nearly every major discovery of the fifteenth and sixteenth centuries. Such was notably the case in the fields of astronomy, mathematics, physics, and medicine.

The achievement *par excellence* in astronomy was the revival and demonstration of the heliocentric theory. Contrary to popular opinion, this was the work not of any one man but of several. It will be remembered that the idea of the sun as the center of our universe had originally been set forth by the Hellenistic astronomer Aristarchus in the third century B.C. But then, some 400 years later, the theory of Aristarchus had been superseded by the geocentric explanation of Ptolemy. For more than twelve centuries thereafter the Ptolemaic theory was the universally accepted conclusion as to the nature of the physical universe. The Romans seem never to have questioned it, and it was adopted as a cardinal dogma by the Saracenic and Scholastic philosophers. It was first openly challenged about the middle of the fifteenth century by Nicholas of Cusa, who argued that the earth is not the center of the universe. Soon after-

Science in the Italian Renaissance

Niccolò Machiavelli

The revival of the heliocentric theory

ward Leonardo da Vinci taught that the earth rotates on its axis and denied that the apparent revolutions of the sun actually occur. In 1496 the now famous Pole, Nicholas Copernicus (1473–1543), came down into Italy to complete his education in civil and canon law. For ten years he studied in the universities of Bologna, Padua, and Ferrara, adding to his course in the law such subjects as mathematics and medicine. He also acquired an interest in astronomy and studied and worked for some years with the leading professors of that science. But he made no significant discoveries of his own. In the main, he was content to rely upon the observations of others, especially the ancients. His approach was not really scientific. It contained elements of the mystical and such Neo-Platonic assumptions as the notion that the sphere is the perfect shape and the idea that motion is more nearly divine than rest. He accepted most of Ptolemy's premises but denied that they pointed to Ptolemy's conclusion of a geocentric universe. On account of timidity he refrained from publishing his book, *On the Revolutions of the Heavenly Spheres*, until 1543. The proof sheets were brought to him on his deathbed.

The most important astronomical evidence for the heliocentric theory was furnished by the greatest of Italian scientists, Galileo Galilei (1564–1642). With a telescope which he had perfected to a magnifying power of thirty times, he discovered the satellites of Jupiter, the rings of Saturn, and spots on the sun.[7] He was able also to determine that the Milky Way is a collection of celestial bodies independent of our solar system and to form some idea of the enormous distances of the fixed stars. Though there were many who held out against them, these discoveries of Galileo gradually convinced the majority of scientists that the main conclusion of Copernicus was true. The final triumph of this idea is commonly called the Copernican Revolution. Few more significant events have occurred in the intellectual history of the world; for it overturned the medieval world-view and paved the way for modern conceptions of mechanism, skepticism, and the infinity of time and space. Some thinkers believe that it contributed also to the degradation of man, since it swept man out of his majestic position at the center of the universe and reduced him to a mere particle of dust in an endless cosmic machine.

In the front rank among the physicists of the Renaissance were Leonardo da Vinci and Galileo. If Leonardo da Vinci had failed completely as a painter, his contributions to science would entitle him to considerable fame. Not the least of these were his achievements in physics. Though he actually made few complete discoveries, his conclusion that "every weight tends to fall toward the center by

"A Perfect Description of the Celestial Orbes." A diagram by Copernicus showing the relationship of stars, the planets, and the sun.

Leonardo da Vinci and Galileo as physicists

---

[7] Galileo was not the original inventor of the telescope. That honor is usually accorded to Johannes Lippershey, an obscure optician who lived in the Low Countries about the beginning of the seventeenth century. Galileo learned of Lippershey's invention and improved upon it in a single night.

the shortest way" contained the kernel of the law of gravitation.[8] In addition, he worked out the principles of an astonishing variety of inventions, including a diving boat, a steam engine, an armored fighting car, and a marble saw. Galileo is especially noted as a physicist for his law of falling bodies. Skeptical of the traditional theory that bodies fall with a speed directly proportional to their weight, he taught that bodies dropped from various heights would fall at a rate of speed which increases with the square of the time involved. Rejecting the Scholastic notions of absolute gravity and absolute levity, he taught that these are purely relative terms, that all bodies have weight, even those which like the air are invisible, and that in a vacuum all objects would fall with equal velocity. Galileo seems to have had a broader conception of a universal force of gravitation than Leonardo da Vinci, for he perceived that the power which holds the moon in the vicinity of the earth and causes the satellites of Jupiter to circulate around that planet is essentially the same as the force which enables the earth to draw bodies to its surface. He never formulated this principle as a law, however, nor did he realize all of its implications, as did Newton some fifty years later. Galileo's reputation as a scientist is somewhat exaggerated. He was inclined toward intellectual arrogance and not always willing to recognize the merit in his opponents' arguments.

Galileo

The record of Italian achievements in the various sciences related to medicine is also an impressive one. A number of Italian physicians contributed valuable information pertaining to the circulation of the blood. One of them described the valves of the heart, the pulmonary artery, and the aorta, while another located the valves in the veins. Equally significant was the work of certain foreigners who lived and taught in Italy. Andreas Vesalius (1514–1564), a native of Brussels, issued the first careful description of the human body based upon actual investigation. As a result of his extensive dissections he was able to correct many ancient errors. He is commonly considered the father of the modern science of anatomy. Nevertheless, there is danger in giving him too much credit. He was almost as conservative as Copernicus. Whereas the Polish astronomer could not refrain from worshiping Ptolemy, Vesalius revered Galen and deviated from him with great reluctance. Fortunately, Galen was a better physician than Ptolemy was an astronomer. Two other physicians of foreign nationality who were heavily indebted to Italian progress in medicine were the Spaniard Michael Servetus (1511–1553) and the Englishman William Harvey (1578–1657). Servetus discovered the lesser or pulmonary circulation of the blood. In his work entitled *Errors concerning the Trinity* (his major interest was theology, but he practiced medicine for a living), he described how the blood leaves the right chambers of the heart, is carried to the lungs to be purified,

Progress in anatomy and medicine

[8] Edward MacCurdy (ed.), *The Notebooks of Leonardo da Vinci*, I, 18.

367

Notebook Sketches by Leonardo da Vinci. Left: A cannon foundry. Right: A mechanical mace. As the vehicle is drawn by horses, the steel balls rotate.

Studies of the Shoulder by Leonardo da Vinci

then returns to the heart and is conveyed from that organ to all parts of the body. But he had no idea of the return of the blood to the heart through the veins. It was left for William Harvey, who had studied under Italian physicians at Padua, to complete the discovery. This he did after his return to England about 1610. In his *Dissertation upon the Movement of the Heart* he described how an artery bound by a ligature would fill with blood in the section nearer the heart, while the portion away from the heart would empty, and how exactly the opposite results would occur when a ligature was placed on a vein. By such experiments he reached the conclusion that the blood is in constant process of circulation from the heart to all parts of the body and back again.

3.   THE WANING OF THE ITALIAN RENAISSANCE

About 1550 the Renaissance in Italy came to an end after two and a half centuries of glorious history. The causes of its sudden demise are by no means perfectly clear. Possibly at the head of the list should be placed the French invasion of 1494 and the chaos that quickly ensued. The French monarch, Charles VIII, ruled over the richest and most powerful kingdom in Europe. Italy, weak and divided, seemed an easy prey for his grandiose ambitions. Accordingly, in 1494, he led an army of 30,000 well-trained troops across the Alps. The Medici of Florence fled before him, leaving their city to immediate capture. Halting only long enough to establish a puppet government, the French resumed their advance and conquered Naples. By so doing they aroused the suspicions of the rulers of

Invasion and conquest

368

Spain, who feared an attack on their own possession of Sicily. An alliance of Spain, the Papal States, the Holy Roman Empire, and Venice finally forced Charles to abandon his project. Upon his death in 1498 his successor, Louis XII, repeated the invasion of Italy. Alliances and counteralliances succeeded one another in bewildering confusion. Louis himself formed a combination with Ferdinand of Spain, Pope Julius II, and the Holy Roman Emperor to despoil Venice of her rich lands in the Po valley, but it foundered on the rocks of distrust and perfidy. In 1511 the Pope, fearful of French domination, organized a new "Holy League" with Venice and Spain, which was joined later by Henry VIII of England and the Emperor Maximilian. The French were defeated on two fronts and left Italy in 1512 to the miseries of her own weakness and internal squabbles. In 1530 the peninsula was conquered by the Emperor Charles V after a series of struggles involving pillage and wholesale destruction.

Charles made a practice of restoring favorite princes to the nominal headship of Italian states in order to win their support in his unending struggle with France. They continued to preside over their courts, to patronize the arts, and to adorn their cities with luxurious buildings. But the great days of Italy were over. To the political disorders was added a waning of prosperity. It apparently brought no severe hardship until after 1600, but the shift of trade routes from the Mediterranean to the Atlantic region, following the discovery of America, was bound ultimately to have its effect. Italian cities

The Entrance of Charles VIII into Florence. Painting by Francesco Granacci.

gradually lost their supremacy as the centers of world trade. The prosperity they had enjoyed from a monopoly of trade with the Near East had been one of the chief nourishing influences in the development of their brilliant culture. A source of strength and of great expectations for the future was now being drained away. Yet another cause of cultural decline would seem to have been the Catholic Reformation. During the first half of the sixteenth century the Roman Church was engulfed by waves of intolerance, dogmatism, and asceticism. The objects were partly to combat increasing worldliness and sensuality and partly to strengthen the Church in its campaigns against heresy. In 1542 the Inquisition was established in Rome and soon afterward an Index of Prohibited Books was issued. The arts were censored, publication was controlled, and heretics were burned at the stake. Such procedures could hardly be other than inimical to the free spirit of Renaissance culture.

A glaring symptom of the flimsy foundations of much of Renaissance civilization may be found in the Savonarola affair. Underneath the proud structure of Italian art and learning were smoldering embers of ignorance and superstition ready to be kindled into flame by the first bigot or fanatic who happened along. Girolamo Savonarola was born in Ferrara in 1452, the son of a shiftless and spendthrift father. Though he lived in a gay and worldly city, his early education, directed by his mother and grandfather, seems to have been chiefly religious. At the age of nineteen he fell passionately in love with the daughter of an aristocratic neighbor. The young lady spurned him contemptuously, and soon afterward he decided to renounce the world and fled to a Dominican monastery in Bologna. In 1482 he was transferred to Florence, where Lorenzo the Magnificent was then at the height of his power. The longer Savonarola remained in Florence, the more he was dismayed by the frivolity and paganism he saw all around him. Within two or three years he began preaching in the cloister garden and in the churches of the city, burning into the hearts of his hearers the terrible wrath that would overtake them if they did not flee from their sins. His fiery eloquence and gaunt and unearthly appearance attracted hordes of frightened people. By 1494 his power over the mob had reached such proportions that he became virtual dictator of Florence. For four long years the gay Tuscan metropolis was then subjected to a puritanical rule surpassing in austerity anything that Italy had witnessed since the days of Gregory the Great. Half the year was devoted to Lenten abstinence, and even marriage was discouraged. Citizens were commanded to surrender their articles of luxury and their books and paintings alleged to be immoral; all of these works of the devil were cast into the flames in the public square in the celebrated "burning of the vanities." Though he claimed the gift of prophecy and the ability to work miracles, he finally ran into trouble when he agreed under pressure to go through an ordeal by fire to prove the truth of his doctrines. In

The Savonarola affair

The Burning of Savonarola.
In this view of Florence, the
Palazzo Vecchio is in the right
center and a portion of the
cathedral is at the extreme left.

April 1498, an immense throng gathered in the Piazza della Signoria
to witness the grisly spectacle. A sudden rainstorm, however, caused
the authorities to postpone the ordeal on the ground that God had
interposed against it. Deprived of its cruel diversion, the mob turned
in rage against Savonarola and forced his arrest and imprisonment.
Pope Alexander VI, whose sins he had condemned, took advantage
of the opportunity to demand that he be destroyed as a heretic. After a month of excruciating tortures resulting in forced confessions,
he was sentenced to death. He was burned in front of the Medici
palace and his remains thrown into the Arno River. His career may
be regarded not only as a symptom of the weakness of Renaissance
society, but as a forerunner of the fanatical zeal of the Reformation.

SELECTED READINGS

· *Items so designated are available in paperbound editions.*

GENERAL

· Allen, J. W., *Political Thought in the Sixteenth Century*, London, 1951
(Barnes & Noble). The standard work on the subject.
· Becker, Marvin B., *Florence in Transition*, Baltimore, 1967–1968, 2 vols.
· Berenson, Bernard, *The Italian Painters of the Renaissance*, New York, 1957
(Meridian). Accurate and interesting.
· Butterfield, Herbert, *The Origins of Modern Science*, New York, 1951
(Collier).
Cronin, Vincent, *The Florentine Renaissance*, New York, 1967.
· Ferguson, W. K., *The Renaissance*, New York, 1940 (Torchbook). A splen-
did introduction.

READINGS   Gilbert, Felix, *Machiavelli and Guicciardini: Politics and History in Sixeenth-century Florence*, Princeton, 1965.

· Gilmore, M., *The World of Humanism*, New York, 1952 (Torchbook). An excellent general account.

Gould, Cecil, *An Introduction to Italian Renaissance Painting*, London, 1957. Discerning and authoritative.

· Hall, A. R., *The Scientific Revolution, 1450–1650*, Boston, 1956 (Beacon).

Hay, Denys, *The Italian Renaissance in Its Historical Background*, New York, 1961.

· ———, *The Renaissance Debate*, New York, 1965 (European Problem Series).

· Huizinga, J., *The Waning of the Middle Ages*, London, 1924 (Anchor). A good analysis of the decline of feudalism.

· Kristeller, Paul, *Renaissance Thought*, New York, 1961–65, 2 vols. (Torchbook).

Lang, Paul, *Music in Western Civilization*, New York, 1941. The best survey yet published.

Lopez, Robert S., *The Three Ages of the Italian Renaissance*, Charlottesville, Va., 1970.

· Mattingly, Garrett, *Renaissance Diplomacy*, Baltimore, 1964 (Penguin).

Owen, John, *The Skeptics of the Italian Renaissance*, London, 1893.

· Pater, Walter, *The Renaissance*, New York (Mentor, 1959, Meridian, 1961). Interesting interpretations.

Ridolfi, R., *The Life of Girolamo Savonarola*, New York, 1959.

———, *The Life of Niccolò Machiavelli*, Chicago, 1963. Presents Machiavelli in a new and more favorable light.

· Roeder, R., *The Man of the Renaissance*, New York, 1933 (Meridian).

Schevill, Ferdinand, *The First Century of Italian Humanism*, New York, 1928. Scholarly and stimulating.

· Smith, Preserved, *A History of Modern Culture*, New York, 1930, Vol. I (Collier). Thorough and scholarly.

· Taylor, H. O., *Thought and Expression in the Sixteenth Century*, London, 1920. Reliable and suggestive. Also available in paperback under the title, *The Humanism of Italy* (Collier, 2 vols.).

Thorndike, Lynn, *Science and Thought in the Fifteenth Century*, New York, 1929.

· Vallentin, Antonina, *Leonardo da Vinci*, New York, 1938 (Grosset and Dunlap).

Wilkins, Ernest H., *A History of Italian Literature*, Cambridge, Mass., 1954. One of the best accounts of Italian writing since Dante.

· Woodward, G. W. O., *A Short History of Sixteenth-century England*, New York, 1963 (Mentor).

SOURCE MATERIALS

Baumer, F. L. V., *Main Currents of Western Thought*, New York, 1952.

Galileo Galilei, *The Sidereal Messenger.*

MacCurdy, Edward, ed., *The Notebooks of Leonardo da Vinci*, 2 vols. New York, 1955.

· Machiavelli, Niccolo, *The Prince*, especially Chs. 15–21, 26 (Modern Library College Edition).

· ———, *Discourses on Livy*, especially Book I, Chs. 3, 4, 6, 9, 11, 12, 25, 32, 33, 34, 47, 53, 55, 58, 59; Book II, Chs. 2, 5, 13, 19, 22 (Modern Library College Editions).

Robinson, J. H., and Rolfe, H. W., *Petrarch, the First Modern Scholar and Man of Letters.*

Willis, Robert, tr., *The Works of William Harvey, M. D.*

CHAPTER 14

The Expansion of the Renaissance

Art and sciences are not cast in a mould, but are formed and perfected by degrees, by often handling and polishing, as bears leisurely lick their cubs into form.

—Michel de Montaigne, *Works*, II.xii

If a rock falls on your head, that is clearly painful; but shame,
disgrace, and curses hurt only so far as they are felt. What isn't
noticed isn't troublesome. So long as you applaud yourself what
harm are the hisses of the world? And folly is the only key to
this happiness.

—Erasmus, *The Praise of Folly*, II, *The Powers
and Pleasures of Folly*

That a movement as vigorous as the Italian Renaissance should have
spread into other countries was a result no less than inevitable. For
years there had been a continuous procession of northern European
students coming down into Italy to bask in the genial intellectual
climate of Florence, Milan, and Rome. Moreover, the economic and
social changes in northern and western Europe had roughly paralleled those of Italy for some time. Everywhere feudalism was being
supplanted by a capitalist economy, and a new individualism was
superseding the corporate structure of society sanctified by the
Church in the Middle Ages. Common economic and social interests
fostered the growth of a similar culture. But it must not be supposed
that the Renaissance in northern and western Europe was exactly
the same as that in the south. The Italian and the Teuton differed
markedly in temperament and in historical background. More
deeply affected by Saracenic and Byzantine influences, the Italian
was disposed to find in art and literature the most suitable media of
self-expression. Besides, he was the heir of classical traditions, which
also enhanced his aesthetic interests. The northern European tended
to view the problems of life from a moral or religious angle. As a
result of these differences the northern European Renaissance was

The spread of
the Renaissance

less distinctly an artistic movement than the Renaissance in the south. Though painting flourished in the Low Countries, elsewhere it had no more than a limited scope, and sculpture was largely neglected. The main efforts of the northern peoples were concentrated in literature and philosophy, often with some religious or practical purpose. It may be added that there was less paganism in the northern Renaissance than there was in the Renaissance in Italy. Perhaps this condition reflected the fact that theological studies predominated in the curricula of the northern universities as late as 1550.

The political history of the countries of northern and western Europe during the age of the Renaissance was characterized by developments somewhat similar to those which had occurred in Italy. There was the same transition from a weak and decentralized feudal regime to the concentrated rule of despotic princes. There was also the destruction of the political power of the guilds and the absorption of their prerogatives of sovereignty by the state. The chief difference was to be found in the fact that many of the states outside of Italy were beginning to take on the character of national units. Each of them occupied a territory of considerable size and embraced a population knit together by bonds of language and a vague consciousness of unity as a people. But for the most part these great political organisms were the creations of ambitious monarchs, who broke the power of local nobles and welded their petty principalities into huge dynastic empires. In England this process was abetted by the so-called Wars of the Roses, a series of bloody struggles beginning about 1455 between rival factions of barons. So many were the nobles killed in these wars and so profound was the disgust with the long period of disorder that the Tudor dynasty, founded by Henry VII in 1485, was soon able to crush completely the rem-

The political background of the Renaissance outside of Italy; conditions in England

Portrait of Henry VIII by Hans Holbein the Younger. In the Palazzo Corsini, Rome.

Louis XI as Founder of the Order of St. Michael. A French miniature ca. 1470.

nants of feudal power. The most noted members of this dynasty, Henry VIII and Queen Elizabeth I, were the real founders of despotic government in England—with the support of the middle classes, who desired more protection for their commercial interests than the feudal regime could give.

In the case of France it was also a war which led to the establishment of a consolidated state—but an international war rather than an internal squabble. The struggle which enabled the French kings to stamp out feudal sovereignty was the Hundred Years' War (1337–1453), fought primarily to expel the English from France and to break their commercial alliance with the Flemish cities. As a result of this conflict a national consciousness was aroused in the French people, the nobles who had followed their own selfish ambitions were discredited, and the monarchy was extolled for having saved the country from ruin. Within thirty years the shrewd but unscrupulous Louis XI (1461–1483) extended the royal domain over all of France with the exception of Flanders and Brittany. His policies paved the way for the absolute rule of the Bourbons. Still another important country of western Europe began its emergence as a nation-state toward the end of the fifteenth century. This country was Spain, united partly as a result of the marriage of Ferdinand of Aragon and Isabella of Castile in 1469 and partly through the exigencies of the long war against the Moors. Under Philip II (1556–1598) Spain rose to a place in the very front rank of European powers. Aside from Italy, the only major country of western Europe which was not united into a consolidated state during the age of the Renaissance was Germany. Though it is true that political authority in some of the individual German kingdoms was solidified, the country as a whole remained a part of the Holy Roman Empire, now headed by the Hapsburg monarchs of Austria. The sovereignty

Conditions in France, Spain, and Germany

Philip II of Spain

375

of the Holy Roman Emperors was a mere fiction, mainly because during the Middle Ages they had wasted their energies in a vain attempt to extend their control over Italy, thereby enabling the German dukes to entrench themselves in power.

I. THE INTELLECTUAL AND ARTISTIC RENAISSANCE IN GERMANY

One of the first countries to receive the full impact of the Italian humanist movement was Germany. This was a natural development, not only because of the proximity of the two countries, but also because of the large-scale migration of German students to the Italian universities. But the influence of this humanism was short-lived and its fruits rather scanty and mediocre. What the results might have been if Germany had not been hurled so soon into the maelstrom of religious contention cannot be determined. The fact remains, however, that the Protestant Revolution stirred up passions of hate and intolerance which could not be other than inimical to the humanist ideal. A premium was now set upon bigotry and faith, while anything resembling the worship of man or reverence for pagan antiquity was almost certain to be regarded as a work of the devil.

To fix a date for the beginning of the German Renaissance is practically impossible. In such prosperous cities of the south as Augsburg, Nuremberg, Munich, and Vienna there was a lively humanist movement, imported from Italy, as early as 1450. By the beginning of the sixteenth century it had taken firm root in university circles, particularly in the cities of Heidelberg, Erfurt, and Cologne. Its most notable representatives were Ulrich von Hutten (1488–1523) and Crotus Rubianus (1480–1539). Both were less interested in the literary aspects of humanism than in its possibilities as an expression of religious and political protest. Von Hutten, especially, made use of his gifts as a writer to satirize the worldliness and greed of the clergy and to indite fiery defenses of the German people against their enemies. He was himself an embittered rebel against almost every institution of the established order. The chief title of von Hutten and Rubianus to fame is their authorship of the *Letters of Obscure Men,* one of the wittiest satires in the history of literature. The circumstances under which it was written are so strikingly like those which frequently occur in the evolution of nations that they deserve to be recounted here. A learned humanist at the University of Heidelberg by the name of Johann Reuchlin had developed a passionate enthusiasm for the study of Hebrew writings. Because he criticized some of the theologians' interpretations of the Old Testament, he was savagely attacked by Christian fanatics and was finally haled before the Inquisitor-General for the Catholic Church in Germany. Numerous pamphlets were published on both

The limited scope of the German Renaissance

German humanism: the Letters of Obscure Men

sides of the controversy, and the issue was soon sharply drawn between freedom and tolerance, on the one hand, and authoritarianism and bigotry on the other. When it became apparent that rational argument was accomplishing nothing, the friends of Reuchlin decided to make use of ridicule. Rubianus and von Hutten published a series of letters purporting to have been written by some of Reuchlin's opponents, with such ridiculous signatures as Ziegenmelker (Goat-milker), Honiglecker (Honey-licker), and Mistlader (Dung-loader). Heinrich Shafmaul (Sheep's mouth), the supposed writer of one of the letters, professed to be worried lest he had sinned grievously by eating an egg which contained a chick on Friday. The author of another of the letters boasted of his brilliant "discovery" that Julius Caesar could not have written the *Commentaries on the Gallic Wars* because he was too busy with his military exploits ever to have learned the Latin language. How much effect these letters had in undermining the influence of the Catholic hierarchy in Germany is impossible to say, but it must have been considerable, for they enjoyed a wide circulation.

The German Renaissance in art was limited entirely to painting and engraving, represented chiefly by the work of Albrecht Dürer (1471–1528) and Hans Holbein (1497–1543). Both of these artists were profoundly influenced by Italian traditions, though much of

Melancholy. A Famous Engraving from a Series by Albrecht Dürer. In the National Gallery, Washington, D.C.

the Germanic spirit of somber realism is also expressed in their work. Dürer's best-known paintings are his *Adoration of the Magi,* the *Four Apostles,* and *The Crucified Christ.* The last is a study in tragic gloom. It shows the body of the pale Galilean stretched on the cross against a bleak and sinister sky. The glimmer of light on the horizon merely adds to the somber effect of the scene. Some of Dürer's best-known engravings exhibit similar qualities. His *Melancholy* represents a female figure, with wings too small to lift her body, meditating hopelessly on the problems of life, which appear to defy all solution. A compass is in her hand, and various other implements upon which man has relied for the control of his environment lie strewn about the floor. Hans Holbein the elder, the other great artist of the German Renaissance, derives his renown primarily from his portraits and drawings. His portraits of Erasmus and of Henry VIII are among the most famous in the world. An impressive example of his drawings is the one known as *Christ in the Tomb.* It depicts the body of the Son of God, with staring eyes and mouth half open, as neglected in death as the corpse of an ordinary criminal. The artist's purpose was probably to express the utter degradation which the Savior had suffered for the redemption of man. In his later career Holbein also drew many religious pictures satirizing the abuses in the Catholic Church which were believed to be the chief justification for the Protestant Revolution. He was one of the few prominent artists to devote his talents to the Protestant cause.

The only German during the age of the Renaissance to make any significant contribution to science was Johann Kepler (1571–1630). His interest aroused by the work of Copernicus, he improved the theory of the distinguished Pole by proving that the planets move in elliptical, rather than circular, orbits around the sun. Thus he may be said to have destroyed the last important vestige of the Ptolemaic astronomy, which had assumed the planets to be imbedded in perfect crystalline spheres. In addition, the laws of planetary motion which Kepler formulated were of tremendous value in suggesting to Newton his principle of universal gravitation. There was another scientist of German nationality whose work can be appropriately discussed in this connection, though he was actually born in the vicinity of Zürich, about the end of the fifteenth century. The name of this man was Theophrastus von Hohenheim, but he chose to call himself Paracelsus to indicate his own belief in his superiority to Celsus, the great Roman physician. Although Paracelsus is often referred to as a quack and an impostor, there is really comparatively little evidence that this was the case. He was at least sufficiently skillful as a practitioner of healing to be appointed professor of medicine at the University of Basel and town physician in 1527. Moreover, it is his special merit that he went straight to the book of experience for his knowledge of diseases and their cures. Instead of following the teachings of ancient authorities, he traveled widely, studying cases of illness in different environments and experimenting with innumerable drugs. He denied that the quest for the philosopher's stone should be the function of the chemist and insisted upon the close interrelation of chemistry and medicine. Perhaps his most important specific contribution was his discovery of the relation between cretinism in children and the presence of goiter in their parents.

2. RENAISSANCE CULTURE IN THE LOW COUNTRIES

Despite the fact that the Low Countries did not win independence of foreign domination until the seventeenth century,[1] they were nevertheless one of the most splendid centers of Renaissance culture on the Continent of Europe outside of Italy. The explanation is to be found primarily in the wealth of the Dutch and Flemish cities and in the important trade connections with southern Europe. As early as 1450 there were significant attainments in art in the Low Countries, including the development of painting in oil. Here also some of the first books were printed. While it is true that the Renaissance in the Low Countries was no broader in scope than in several other areas of northern Europe, its achievements were generally of surpassing brilliance.

The derivation and character of Renaissance culture in the Low Countries

The history of Renaissance literature and philosophy in the Low Countries begins and ends with Desiderius Erasmus, universally acclaimed as the Prince of the Humanists. The son of a priest and a servant girl, Erasmus was born near Rotterdam, probably in the year 1466. For his early education he had the benefit of the excellent training given in the school of the Brethren of the Common Life at Deventer.[2] Later, after his father and mother were both dead, his guardians placed him in an Augustinian monastery. Here the young Erasmus found little religion or formal instruction of any kind but plenty of freedom to read what he liked. He devoured all the classics he could get his hands on and the writings of many of the Church Fathers. When he was about thirty years of age, he obtained permission to leave the monastery and enroll in the University of Paris, where he completed the requirements for the degree of bachelor of divinity. But Erasmus never entered into the active duties of a priest, choosing rather to make his living by teaching and writing. By extensive reading of the classics he achieved a style of Latin expression so remarkable for its wit and urbanity that everything he wrote was widely read. But Erasmus' love of the classics was not born of pedantic interest. He admired the ancient authors because

Erasmus. A woodcut by Hans Holbein the Younger.

Erasmus, Prince of the Humanists

---

[1] They were ruled by the Duchy of Burgundy until 1506 when they were inherited by Charles, the young king of Spain, whose grandfather had married the sole heiress of the Burgundian duke.

[2] See The Renaissance in Religion, §7 in this chapter.

they gave voice to the very ideals of naturalism, tolerance, and humanitarianism which held so exalted a place in his own mind. He was wont to believe that such pagans as Cicero and Socrates were far more deserving of the title of Saint than many a Christian canonized by the Pope. In 1536 Erasmus died in Basel at the end of a long and unfaltering career in defense of scholarship, high standards of literary taste, and the life of reason. He has rightfully been called the most civilized man of his age.

The liberal philosophy of Erasmus

As a philosopher of humanism Erasmus was the incarnation of the finest ideals of the northern Renaissance. Convinced of the inherent goodness of man, he believed that all misery and injustice would eventually disappear if only the pure sunlight of reason could be allowed to penetrate the noisome caverns of ignorance, superstition, and hate. With nothing of the fanatic about him, he stood for liberality of mind, for reasonableness and conciliation, rather than for fierce intolerance of evil. He shrank from the violence and passion of war, whether between systems, classes, or nations. Much of his teaching and writing was dedicated to the cause of religious reform. The ceremonial, dogmatic, and superstitious extravagances in sixteenth-century Catholic life repelled him. But it was alien to his temper to lead any crusade against them. He sought rather by gentle irony, and occasionally by stinging satire, to expose irrationalism in all of its forms and to propagate a humanist religion of simple piety and noble conduct based upon what he called the "philosophy of Christ." Although his criticism of the Catholic faith had considerable effect in hastening the Protestant Revolution, he recoiled in disgust from the bigotry of the Lutherans. Neither did he have much sympathy for the scientific revival of his time. Like most of the humanists he believed that an emphasis upon science would serve to promote a crude materialism and to detract men's interests from the ennobling influences of literature and philosophy. The chief writings of Erasmus were his *Praise of Folly*, in which he satirized pedantry, the dogmatism of theologians, and the ignorance and credulity of the masses, and his *Familiar Colloquies* and *The Handbook of the Christian Knight*, in which he condemned ecclesiastical Christianity and argued for a return to the simple teachings of Jesus, "who commanded us nothing save love for one another." In a less noted work entitled *The Complaint of Peace*, he expressed his abhorrence of war and his contempt for despotic princes.

A Peasant. Drawing by Peter Breughel the Elder.

The artistic Renaissance in the Low Countries was confined almost entirely to painting; and in this field the outstanding achievements were those of the Flemish school. Flemish painting derived no small measure of its excellence from the fact that it was an indigenous art. Here there were no classical influences, no ancient statues to imitate, and no living traditions from the Byzantine or Saracenic cultures. Until comparatively late, even the Italian influence was of little consequence. The painting of Flanders was rather the spontaneous product of a virile and prosperous urban society

The Massacre of the Innocents. This painting by Peter Breughel the Elder pictures the slaughter of women and children by Spanish soldiers. Seldom has great art been used more effectively as a weapon of political protest.

dominated by aspiring merchants interested in art as a symbol of luxurious tastes. The work of nearly all the leading painters—the van Eycks, Hans Memling, and Roger van der Weyden—betrayed this flair for depicting the solid and respectable virtues of their patrons. It was distinguished also by powerful realism, by a relentless attention to the details of ordinary life, by brilliant coloring, and by a deep and uncritical piety. Hubert and Jan van Eyck are noted for their *Adoration of the Lamb,* an altarpiece produced for a church in Ghent soon after the beginning of the fifteenth century. Described by some critics as the noblest achievement of the Flemish school, it portrays a depth of religious feeling and a background of ordinary experience unmatched in Italian art. It was the first great work of the Renaissance to be done by the new method of painting in oil, a process believed to have been invented by the van Eycks. The other two Flemish painters of the fifteenth century, Hans Memling and Roger van der Weyden, are noted, respectively, for naturalism and for the expression of emotional intensity. About 100 years later came the work of Peter Breughel the elder, the most independent and

381

the most socially conscious of the northern artists. Spurning the religious and bourgeois traditions of his predecessors, Breughel chose to depict the life of the common man. He loved to portray the boisterous pleasures of peasant folk at their wedding feasts and village fairs or to illustrate proverbs with scenes from the lives of humble people close to the earth. While he was enough of a realist never to idealize the characters in his paintings, his attitude toward them was definitely sympathetic. He employed his talents for the purpose also of condemning the tyranny of the Spanish regime in the Low Countries.

3.   THE FRENCH RENAISSANCE

French
achievements in
art and science

Despite the strong aesthetic interests of the French people, as evidenced by their perfection of Gothic architecture during the Middle Ages, the achievements of their artists in the age of the Renaissance were of comparatively little importance. There was some minor progress in sculpture and a modest advancement in architecture. It was during this time that the Louvre was built, on the site of an earlier structure bearing the same name, while numerous châteaux erected throughout the country represented a more or less successful attempt to combine the grace and elegance of the Italian style with the solidity of the medieval castle. Nor was science entirely neglected, although the major accomplishments were few. They included the contributions of François Viète (1540–1603) to mathematics and of Ambroise Paré (1517?–1590) to surgery. The former invented modern algebraic symbols and elaborated the theory of equations. Paré improved upon the method of treating gunshot wounds by substituting bandages and unguents for applications of boiling oil. He was also responsible for introducing the ligature of arteries as a means of controlling the flow of blood in major

The Château of Chenonceaux in Central France as It Appears Today. Built during the sixteenth century, it represents a transitional type of architecture between Gothic and Renaissance.

amputations. He has rightfully been called the father of modern surgery.

But the outstanding achievements of the French Renaissance were in literature and philosophy, illustrated especially by the writings of François Rabelais (1490?–1553) and Michel de Montaigne (1533–1592). Like Erasmus, Rabelais was educated as a monk, but soon after taking holy orders he left the monastery to study medicine at the University of Montpellier. He finished the course for tne bachelor's degree in the short space of six weeks and obtained his doctorate about five years later, in the meantime having served for a period as public physician in Lyon in addition to lecturing and editing medical writings. He seems from the start to have interspersed his professional activities with literary endeavors of one sort or another. He wrote almanacs for the common people, satires against quacks and astrologers, and burlesques of popular superstitions. In 1532 Rabelais published his first edition of *Gargantua*, which he later revised and combined with another book bearing the title of *Pantagruel*. Gargantua and Pantagruel were originally the names of legendary medieval giants noted for their prodigious strength and their gross appetites. Rabelais' account of their adventures served as a vehicle for his robust, sprawling wit and for the expression of his philosophy of exuberant naturalism. In language far from delicate he satirized the practices of the Church, ridiculed Scholasticism, scoffed at superstitions, and pilloried every form of bigotry and repression. No man of the Renaissance was a more uncompromising individualist or exhibited more zeal in glorifying the human and the natural. For him every instinct of man was healthy, provided it was not directed toward tyranny over others. In common with Erasmus he believed in the inherent goodness of man, but unlike the great Prince of the Humanists he was a thoroughgoing pagan, rejecting not only Christian dogma but Christian morality as well. Any degree of restraint, intellectual or moral, was repugnant to Rabelais. His celebrated description of the abbey of Theleme, built by Gargantua, was intended to show the contrast between his conception of freedom and the Christian ascetic ideal. At Theleme there were no clocks summoning to duties and no vows of celibacy or perpetual membership. The inmates could leave when they liked; but while they remained they dwelt together "according to their own free will and pleasure. They rose out of their beds when they thought good; they did eat, drink, labour, sleep, when they had a mind to it, and were disposed for it. None did awake them, none did offer to constrain them . . . for so Gargantua had established it. In all their Rule and strictest tie of their order there was but this one clause to be observed, *Do what thou wilt*." [3]

A man of far different temperament and background was Michel de Montaigne (1533–1592). His father was a Catholic, his mother a

Achievements in literature and philosophy; Rabelais

Rabelais

[3] Urquhart and Motteux (trans.), *Works of Rabelais*, First Book, p. 165.

Jewess who had become a Protestant. Almost from the day of his birth their son was subjected to an elaborate system of training. Every morning he was awakened by soft music, and he was attended throughout the day by servants who were forbidden to speak any language but Latin. When he was six years old he was ready for the College of Guienne at Bordeaux and at the age of thirteen began the study of law. After practicing law for a time and serving in various public offices, he retired at thirty-seven to his ancestral estate to devote the remainder of his life to study, contemplation, and writing. Always in delicate health, he found it necessary now more than ever to conserve his strength. Besides, he was repelled by the bitterness and strife he saw all around him and was for that reason all the more anxious to find a refuge in a world of intellectual seclusion.

Montaigne's ideas are contained in his famous *Essays,* written during his years of retirement. The essence of his philosophy is skepticism in regard to all dogma and final truth. He knew too much about the diversity of beliefs among men, the welter of strange customs revealed by geographic discoveries, and the disturbing conclusions of the new science ever to accept the idea that any one sect had exclusive possession of "the Truth delivered once for all to the saints." It seemed to him that religion and morality were as much the product of custom as styles of dress or habits of eating. He taught that God is unknowable, and that it is as foolish to "weep that we shall not exist a hundred years hence as it would be to weep that we had not lived a hundred years ago." Man should be encouraged to despise death and to live nobly and delicately in this life rather than to yearn piously for an afterlife that is doubtful at best. Montaigne was just as skeptical in regard to assumptions of final truth in philosophy or science. The conclusions of reason, he taught, are sometimes fallacious, and the senses often deceive us. The sooner men come to realize that there is no certainty anywhere the better chance they will have to escape the tyranny which flows from superstition and bigotry. The road to salvation lies in doubt, not in faith.

A second element in Montaigne's philosophy was cynicism. He could see no real difference between the morals of Christians and those of infidels. All sects, he pointed out, fight each other with equal ferocity, except that "there is no hatred so absolute as that which is Christian." Neither could he see any value in crusades or revolutions for the purpose of overthrowing one system and establishing another. All human institutions in his judgment were about equally futile, and he therefore considered it fatuous that man should take them so seriously as to wade through slaughter in order to substitute one for its opposite. No ideal, he maintained, is worth burning your neighbor for. In his attitude toward questions of ethics Montaigne was not so ribald a champion of carnality as

Montaigne

Montaigne's
cynicism

The Harvesters, Peter Breughel the Elder (1520–1569). Breughel chose to depict the life of humble people. (MMA)

The Virgin and Chancellor Rolin, Jan van Eyck (1390–1444). The early Flemish painters loved to present scenes of piety in the sumptuous surroundings of wealthy burghers. (Louvre)

Erasmus, Hans Holbein the Younger (1497–1543). This portrait is generally regarded as the best representation of the character and personality of the Prince of the Humanists. (Louvre)

St. Andrew and St. Francis, EL Greco
(1541–1614). (The Prado)

Burial of the Count of Orgaz, El Greco
(1541–1614). El Greco's masterpiece im-
mortalizes the character of the people
among whom he dwelt. The elongated
figures, gaunt faces, and bold and dramatic colors are typical of his work.
(Iglesia S. Tomé, Toledo, Spain)

Rabelais, yet he had no sympathy for asceticism. He believed it ridiculous that men should attempt to deny their physical natures and pretend that everything connected with sense is unworthy. "Sit we upon the highest throne in the world," he declared, "yet we do but sit upon our own behind." The philosophy of Montaigne, tinctured as it was with escapism and disenchantment, marked a fitting close of the Renaissance in France. But in spite of his negative attitude he did more good in the world than most of his contemporaries who founded new faiths or invented new excuses for absolute monarchs to enslave their subjects. Not only did his ridicule help to quench the flames of the cruel hysteria against witches, but the influence of his skeptical teachings had no small effect in combating fanaticism generally and in paving the way for a more generous tolerance in the future.

4. THE SPANISH RENAISSANCE

During the sixteenth and early seventeenth centuries Spain was at the height of her glory. Her conquests in the Western Hemisphere brought wealth to her nobles and merchants and gave her a proud position in the front rank of European states. Notwithstanding these facts the Spanish nation was not one of the leaders in Renaissance culture. Apparently her citizens were too deeply absorbed in plundering the conquered territories to devote much attention to intellectual or artistic pursuits. Moreover, the long war with the Moors had engendered a spirit of bigotry, the position of the Church was too strong, and the expulsion of the Jews at the end of the fifteenth century had deprived the country of talent it could ill afford to lose. For these reasons the Spanish Renaissance was limited to a few achievements in painting and literature, albeit some of these rank in brilliance with the best that other countries produced.

Spanish painting bore the deep impression of the bitter struggle between Christian and Moor. As a result it expressed an intense preoccupation with religion and with themes of anguish and tragedy. Its background was medieval; upon it were engrafted influences from Flanders and from Italy. The first of the eminent Spanish painters was Luis de Morales (1517–1586), frequently called "The Divine." His Madonnas, Crucifixions, and Mater Dolorosas typified that earnest devotion to Catholic orthodoxy regarded by many Spaniards of this time as a duty both religious and patriotic. But the most talented artist of the Spanish Renaissance was not a native of Spain at all, but an immigrant from the island of Crete. His real name was Domenico Theotocopuli, but he is commonly called El Greco (1541?–1614?). After studying for some time under Titian in Venice, El Greco settled in Toledo about 1575, to live there until his death. A stern individualist in temperament, he seems to have

Reasons for the backwardness of Spain in the Renaissance

The character of Spanish painting; El Greco

imbibed little of the warmth of color and serene joy in satin splendor of the Venetian school. Instead, nearly all of his art is characterized by fevered emotionalism, stark tragedy, or enraptured flights
into the supernatural and mystical. His figures are often those of
gaunt, half-crazed fanatics; his colors sometimes are cold and severe.
His scenes of suffering and death seem deliberately contrived to
produce an impression of horror. Among his famous works are *The
Burial of the Count of Orgaz, Pentecost,* and *The Apocalyptic
Vision.* Better than any other artist, El Greco expresses the fiery
religious zeal of the Spanish people during the heyday of the Jesuits
and the Inquisition.

Literature in the Spanish Renaissance displayed tendencies not
dissimilar to those in painting. This was notably true of drama,
which frequently took the form of allegorical plays depicting the
mystery of transubstantiation or appealing to some passion of religious fervor. Others of the dramatic productions dwelt upon themes
of political pride or sang the praises of the bourgeoisie and expressed contempt for the dying world of feudalism. The colossus
among the Spanish dramatists was Lope de Vega (1562–1635), the
most prolific author of plays the literary world has seen. He is supposed to have written no fewer than 1500 comedies and more than
400 religious allegories. Of the total about 500 survive to this day.
His secular dramas fall mainly into two classes: (1) the "cloak and
sword plays," which depict the violent intrigues and exaggerated
ideals of honor among the upper classes; and (2) the plays of national greatness, which celebrate the glories of Spain in her prime
and represent the king as the protector of the people against a
vicious and degenerate nobility.

Cervantes

Few would deny that the most gifted writer of the Spanish Renaissance was Miguel de Cervantes (1547–1616). His great masterpiece, *Don Quixote,* has even been described as "incomparably the
best novel ever written." Composed in the best tradition of Spanish
satirical prose, it recounts the adventures of a Spanish gentleman
(Don Quixote) who has been slightly unbalanced by constant reading of chivalric romances. His mind filled with all kinds of fantastic
adventures, he finally sets out at the age of fifty upon the slippery
road of knight-errantry. He imagines windmills to be glowering
giants and flocks of sheep to be armies of infidels, whom it is his
duty to rout with his spear. In his disordered fancy he mistakes inns
for castles and the serving-wenches within them for courtly ladies on
fire with love of him. Set off in bold contrast to the ridiculous knight-
errant is the figure of his faithful squire, Sancho Panza. The latter
represents the ideal of the practical man, with his feet on the ground
and content with the substantial pleasures of eating, drinking, and
sleeping. The book as a whole is a pungent satire on feudalism, especially on the pretensions of the nobles as the champions of honor
and right. Its enormous popularity was convincing proof that
medieval civilization was approaching extinction even in Spain.

The satirical
novel of Cer-
vantes

5. THE RENAISSANCE IN ENGLAND

In common with Spain, England also enjoyed a golden age in the sixteenth and early seventeenth centuries. Though her vast colonial empire had not yet been established, she was nevertheless reaping big profits from the production of wool and from her trade with the Continent. Her government, recently consolidated under the rule of the Tudors, was making the prosperity of the middle class the object of its special solicitude. Through the elimination of foreign traders, the granting of favors to English shipping, and the negotiation of reciprocal commercial treaties, the English merchant classes were given exceptional advantages over their rivals in other countries. The growth of a national consciousness, the awakening of pride in the power of the state, and the spread of humanism from Italy, France, and the Low Countries also contributed toward the flowering of a brilliant culture in England. Nevertheless, the English Renaissance was confined primarily to philosophy and literature. The arts did not flourish; perhaps because of the Calvinist influence, which began to make itself felt in Britain by the middle of the sixteenth century.

The economic and political foundations of the Renaissance in England

The earliest philosophers of the English Renaissance may best be described simply as humanists. Although they were not unmindful of the value of classical studies, they were interested chiefly in the more practical aspects of humanism. Most of them desired a simpler and more rational Christianity and looked forward to an educational system freed from the dominance of medieval logic. Others were concerned primarily with individual freedom and the correction of social abuses. The greatest of these early thinkers was Sir Thomas More (1478–1535), esteemed by contemporary humanists as "excellent above all his nation." Following a successful career as a lawyer and as Speaker of the House of Commons, More was appointed in 1529 Lord Chancellor of England. He was not long in this position, however, before he incurred the enmity of his royal master, Henry VIII. More was loyal to Catholic universalism and did not sympathize with the king's design to establish a national church under subjection to the state. When, in 1534, he refused to take the Oath of Supremacy acknowledging the king as the head of the Church of England, he was thrown into the Tower. A year later he was tried before a packed jury, convicted, and beheaded. More's philosophy is contained in his *Utopia*, which he published in 1516. Purporting to describe an ideal society on an imaginary island, the book is really an indictment of the glaring abuses of the time—of poverty undeserved and wealth unearned, of drastic punishments, religious persecution, and the senseless slaughter of war. The inhabitants of Utopia hold all their goods in common, work only six hours a day so that all may have leisure for intellectual pursuits, and practice the natural virtues of wisdom, moderation, fortitude, and justice. Iron is the precious metal "because it is useful," war and

Sir Thomas More. Painting by Holbein.

The early English humanists; Thomas More

387

The Title Page of Sir Francis Bacon's *Novum Organum*, Printed in 1620

monasticism are abolished, and tolerance is granted to all creeds that recognize the existence of God and the immortality of the soul. Despite criticism of the *Utopia* as deficient in wit and originality, the conclusion seems justified that the author's ideals of humanity and tolerance were considerably in advance of those of most other men of his time.

The thinker who has gone down in history as the greatest of all English Renaissance philosophers is Sir Francis Bacon. Born in 1561, the son of a high government official, Bacon was nurtured in the lap of luxury until the age of seventeen when the death of his father compelled him to work for a living. Thereafter the dominating ambition of his life was to obtain some profitable position with the government which would enable him to pursue his intellectual interests. Probably it was this mania for security which accounts for the shady morality of his public career. When occasion arose, he did not shrink from concealing his true beliefs, from disloyalty to his friends, or from sharing in graft. In 1618 he was appointed Lord Chancellor, but after a scant three years in this office he was impeached for accepting bribes. Despite his protestations that the taking of money from litigants had never influenced his decisions, he was convicted and sentenced to pay a fine of $200,000 and to undergo imprisonment in the Tower "at the king's pleasure." King James I remitted the fine and limited the term of imprisonment to four days. Bacon devoted the remaining five years of his life to writ-

Sir Francis Bacon

388

ing, especially to the completion of the third and enlarged edition of his essays. Among his most valuable works are the *Novum Organum* and *The Advancement of Learning.*

Bacon's monumental contribution to philosophy was the glorification of the inductive method. He was by no means the discoverer of that method, but he trumpeted it forth as the indispensable ground of accurate knowledge. He believed that all seekers of truth in the past had stumbled in darkness because they were slaves of preconceived ideas or prisoners in the dungeons of Scholastic logic. He argued that in order to overcome these obstacles the philosopher should turn to the direct observation of nature, to the accumulation of facts about things and the discovery of the laws that govern them. Induction alone, he believed, was the magic key that would unlock the secrets of truth. Authority, tradition, and syllogistic logic should be as sedulously avoided as the plague. Admirable as these teachings are, they were honored by Bacon himself almost as much in the breach as in the observance. He believed in astrology, divination, and witchcraft. Moreover, the distinction he drew between ordinary knowledge and the truths of religion was hardly in keeping with his staunch defense of induction. "The senses," he wrote, "are like the sun, which displays the face of the earth, but shuts up that of the heavens." For our voyage to the realm of celestial truth, we must "quit the small vessel of human reason and put ourselves on board the ship of the Church, which alone possesses the divine needle for justly shaping the course. The stars of philosophy will be of no further service to us. As we are obliged to obey the divine law, though our will murmur against it, so we are obliged to believe in the word of God, though our reason is shocked at it. The more absurd and incredible any divine mystery is, the greater honor we do God in believing it." It was not such a far cry after all from Roger Bacon in the thirteenth century to Francis Bacon in the seventeenth.

In literature, also, the English followed much more closely in the footsteps of their medieval forerunners than did the Renaissance writers in any other country with the exception of Italy. Indeed, it is difficult to say just when the English Renaissance in literature began. Chaucer's great work, the *Canterbury Tales,* written toward the end of the fourteenth century, is commonly considered medieval; yet it breathed a spirit of earthiness and of lusty contempt for the mystical quite as pronounced as anything to be found in the writings of Shakespeare. If there were any essential dfferences between the English literature of the Renaissance and that produced during the late Middle Ages, they would consist in a bolder individualism, a stronger sense of national pride, and a deeper interest in themes of philosophic import. The first great poet in England after the time of Chaucer was Edmund Spenser(1552?–1599). His immortal creation, *The Faërie Queene,* is a colorful epic of England's

Bacon's inductive philosophy

English Renaissance literature

389

greatness in the days of Queen Elizabeth. Though written as a moral allegory to express the author's desire for a return to the virtues of chivalry, it celebrates also the joy in conquest and much of the gorgeous sensuousness typical of Renaissance humanism.

The Elizabethan dramatists; Marlowe

But the most splendid achievements of the English in the Elizabethan Age were in the realm of drama. Not since the days of the Greeks had the writing of tragedies and comedies attained such heights as were reached in England during the sixteenth and early seventeenth centuries. Especially after 1580 a galaxy of playwrights appeared whose work outshone that of all their predecessors in 2000 years. Included in this galaxy were such luminaries as Christopher Marlowe (1564–1593), Beaumont and Fletcher (1584–1616; 1579–1625), Ben Jonson (1573?–1637), and Shakespeare (1564–1616), of whom the first and the last are chiefly significant to the historian. Better than anyone else in his time, Christopher Marlowe embodies the insatiable egoism of the Renaissance—the everlasting craving for the fullness of life, for unlimited knowledge and experience. His brief but stormy career was a succession of scandalous escapades and fiery revolts against the restraints of convention until it was terminated by his death in a tavern brawl before he was thirty years old. The best known of his plays, entitled *Doctor Faustus*, is based upon the legend of Faust, in which the hero sells his soul to the devil in return for the power to feel every possible sensation, experience every possible triumph, and know all the mysteries of the universe.

Mr. WILLIAM
SHAKESPEARES
COMEDIES,
HISTORIES, &
TRAGEDIES.

Publiſhed according to the True Originall Copies.

William Shakespeare. Portrait made for the First Folio edition of his works, 1623.

William Shakespeare, the most talented genius in the history of drama since Euripides, was born into the family of a petty trades-man in the provincial market town of Stratford-on-Avon. His life is enshrouded in more mists of obscurity than the careers of most other great men. It is known that he left his native village when he was about twenty years old, and that ultimately he drifted to Lon-don to find employment in the theater. Tradition relates that for a time he earned his living by holding the horses of the more prosper-ous patrons of the drama. How he eventually became an actor and still later a writer of plays is unknown, but there is evidence that by the time he was twenty-eight he had already acquired a reputation as an author sufficient to excite the jealousy of his rivals. Before he retired to his native Stratford about 1610 to spend the rest of his days in ease, he had written or collaborated in writing nearly forty plays, to say nothing of 150 sonnets and two narrative poems.

THE RENAISSANCE IN ENGLAND

The life and writings of William Shakespeare

In paying homage to the universality of Shakespeare's genius, we must not lose sight of the fact that he was also a child of the Renais-sance. His work bore the deep impression of most of the virtues and defects of Renaissance humanism. Almost as much as Boccaccio or Rabelais, he personified that intense love of things human and earthly which had characterized most of the great writers since the close of the Middle Ages. Moreover, like the majority of the human-ists, he showed a limited concern with the problems of politics and the values of science. Virtually the only political theory that inter-ested him greatly was whether a nation had a better chance of pros-pering under a good king who was weak or under a bad king who was strong. Though his knowledge of the sciences of his time was extensive, he regarded them as consisting primarily of alchemy, astrology, and medicine.[4] But the force and range of Shakespeare's intellect were far from bounded by the narrow horizons of the age in which he lived. While few of the works of his contemporaries are now widely read, the plays of Shakespeare still hold their rank as a kind of secular Bible wherever the English language is spoken. The reason lies not only in the author's unrivaled gift of expression, but especially in his scintillating wit and his profound analysis of human character assailed by the storms of passion and tried by the whims of fate.

The character of Shakespeare's work

Shakespeare's dramas fall rather naturally into three main groups. Those written during his earlier years conformed to the traditions of existing plays and generally reflected his own confidence in per-sonal success. They include such comedies as *A Midsummer Night's Dream* and *The Merchant of Venice*, a number of historical plays, and the lyrical tragedy, *Romeo and Juliet*. Shortly before 1600 Shakespeare seems to have experienced a change of mood. The re-

The main groups of Shakespeare's plays

[4] In psychology, however, he gives evidence of having been ahead of his time, especially in his treatment of mental illness. Perhaps this was natural in view of his profound interest in human emotions, in man's conflict with himself and with the universe of which he is a part.

strained optimism of his earlier plays was supplanted by some deep disillusion which led him to distrust human nature and to indict the whole scheme of the universe. The result was a group of dramas characterized by bitterness, overwhelming pathos, and a troubled searching into the mysteries of things. The series begins with the tragedy of intellectual idealism represented by *Hamlet*, goes on to the cynicism of *Measure for Measure* and *All's Well That Ends Well*, and culminates in the cosmic tragedies of *Macbeth* and *King Lear*. Perhaps the famous speech of Gloucester in the last of these plays may be taken to illustrate the depths of the author's pessimism at this time:

> As flies to wanton boys are we to the gods;
> They kill us for their sport.[5]

The final group of dramas includes those written during the closing years of Shakespeare's life, probably after his retirement. Among them are *The Winter's Tale* and *The Tempest*. All of them may be described as idyllic romances. Trouble and grief are now assumed to be only the shadows in a beautiful picture. Despite individual tragedy, the divine plan of the universe is somehow benevolent and just.

6. RENAISSANCE DEVELOPMENTS IN MUSIC

The evolution of music as an independent art

Music in western Europe in the fifteenth and sixteenth centuries reached such a high point of development that it constitutes, together with painting and sculpture, one of the most brilliant aspects of Renaissance activity. While the visual arts were stimulated by the study of ancient models, music flowed naturally from an independent evolution which had long been in progress in medieval Christendom. As earlier, leadership was supplied by men trained in the service of the Church, but the value of secular music was now appreciated, and its principles were combined with those of sacred music to bring a decided gain in color and emotional appeal. The distinction between sacred and profane became less sharp; most composers did not restrict their activities to either field. Music was no longer regarded merely as a diversion or an adjunct to worship but as an independent art.

Leadership provided by Italy and France

Different sections of Europe vied with one another for musical leadership. As with the other arts, advance was related to the increasingly generous patronage made possible by the expansion of commerce, and was centered in the prosperous towns. During the fourteenth century a pre- or early Renaissance musical movement called Ars Nova (new art) flourished in Italy and France. Its outstanding composers were Francesco Landini (*ca.* 1325–1397) and Guillaume de Machaut (1300–1377). The madrigals, ballads, and

[5] *King Lear*, Act IV, scene 1.

Left: *Musical Instruments in the Sixteenth Century.* Right: *A Print Showing Palestrina Presenting His First Printed Work to Pope Julius III*

other songs composed by the Ars Nova musicians testify to a rich secular art, but the greatest achievement of the period was a highly complicated yet delicate contrapuntal style adapted for motet and chanson. With Machaut we reach the first integral polyphonic setting of the Ordinary of the Mass.

The fifteenth century was ushered in by a synthesis of English, French, Flemish, and Italian elements that took place in the Duchy of Burgundy. It produced a remarkable school of music inspired by the cathedral of Cambrai and the ducal court at Dijon. This music was gentle, melodious, and euphonious, but in the second half of the century it hardened a little as the northern Flemish element gained in importance. As the sixteenth century opened we find these Franco-Flemish composers in every important court and cathedral choir all over Europe, gradually establishing regional-national schools, usually in attractive combinations of Flemish with German, Spanish, and Italian musical cultures. The various genres thus created show a close affinity with Renaissance art and poetry. In the second half of the sixteenth century the leaders of the nationalized Franco-Flemish style were the Italian Palestrina (*ca.* 1525–1594), who, by virtue of his position as papal composer and his devotion to a subtle and crystal-clear vocal style, became the venerated symbol of church music; the Flemish Roland de Lassus (1532–1594), the most versatile composer of the age; and Tomas

Synthesis of national elements

393

Luis de Victoria (*ca.* 1540–1611), the glowing mystic of Spanish music. Music also flourished in England, for the Tudor monarchs were not behind the Medici or the Bavarian dukes in patronizing the arts; several of them were accomplished musicians. It was inevitable that the reigning Franco-Flemish style should reach England, where it was superimposed upon an ancient and rich musical culture. The Italian madrigal, imported toward the end of the sixteenth century, found a remarkable second flourishing in England, but songs and instrumental music of an original cast anticipated future developments on the Continent. In William Byrd (1543–1623) English music produced a master fully the equal of the great Flemish, Roman, and Spanish composers of the Renaissance. The general level of music proficiency seems to have been higher in Queen Elizabeth's day than in ours: the singing of part-songs was a popular pastime in homes and at informal social gatherings, and the ability to read a part at sight was expected of well-bred persons.

The greatness of the Renaissance achievement

In conclusion, it may be observed that while counterpoint had matured, our modern harmonic system had been born, and thus a way was opened for fresh experimentation. At the same time one should realize that the music of the Renaissance constitutes not merely a stage in evolution but a magnificent achievement in itself, with masters who rank among the great of all time. The composers Palestrina and Lassus are as truly representative of the artistic triumph of the Renaissance as are the painters Raphael and Michelangelo. Their heritage, long neglected except at a few ecclesiastical centers, has within recent years begun to be appreciated, and is now gaining in popularity as interested groups of musicians devote themselves to its revival.

7. THE RENAISSANCE IN RELIGION

No account of the age of the Renaissance would be complete without some attention to the Renaissance in religion, or the Christian Renaissance as it is commonly called. This was a movement almost entirely independent of the Protestant Revolution, which will be discussed in the next chapter. The leaders of the Christian Renaissance were generally humanists, not Protestants. Few of them ever deserted the Catholic faith; their aim was to purify that faith from within, not to overthrow it. Most of them found the bigotry of early Protestantism as repugnant to their religious ideals as any of the abuses in the Catholic Church. The original impetus for the Christian Renaissance appears to have come from the Brethren of the Common Life, a group of pious laymen who maintained schools in the Low Countries and in western Germany. Their aim was to propagate a simple religion of practical piety, as free as possible from dogmatism and ritual. The most noted of their early followers was Thomas a Kempis (1380–1471) who wrote or edited about 1425 a book entitled *The Imitation of Christ*. Though profoundly

The Christian Renaissance

mystical in tone, the book nevertheless repudiated the extreme otherworldliness of medieval mystics and urged a life of simple devotion to the teachings of Jesus. For over a century the *Imitation* was more widely read in Europe than any other book with the exception of the Bible.

By 1500 the Christian Renaissance had become definitely associated with northern humanism. Writers and philosophers in every country lent their support to the movement. Prominent among them were Sebastian Brant in Germany, Sir Thomas More in England, Erasmus in the Low Countries, and figures of lesser renown in France and Spain. The religious teachings of these men were thoroughly in keeping with the humanist ideal as it was understood in northern Europe. Believing that religion should function for the good of man and not for the benefit of an organized church or even for the glory of an ineffable God, they interpreted Christianity primarily in ethical terms. Many of the theological and supernatural elements in it they regarded as superfluous, if not positively harmful. They likewise had little use for ceremonies of any kind, and they ridiculed the superstitions connected with the veneration of relics and the sale of indulgences. While they recognized the necessity of a limited amount of ecclesiastical organization, they denied the absolute authority of the Pope and refused to admit that priests were really essential as intermediaries between man and God. In fine, what most of these Christian humanists really desired was the superiority of reason over faith, the primacy of conduct over dogma, and the supremacy of the individual over the organized system. They believed that this simple and rational religion could best be achieved, not through violent revolt against the Catholic Church, but through the gradual conquest of ignorance and the elimination of abuses.

The ideals of the Christian Renaissance

The decline of Renaissance culture in the countries of northern and western Europe came much less abruptly than in Italy. Indeed, the change in some respects was so gradual that there was simply a fusion of the old with the new. The achievements in science, for example, were merely extended, although with a definite shift of emphasis as time went on from the mathematical and physical branches to the biological. The Renaissance art of northern Europe, moreover, gradually evolved into the baroque, which dominated the seventeenth and early eighteenth centuries. On the other hand, humanism, in its Renaissance meaning of the worship of man and indifference to everything else, practically died out after the sixteenth century. In philosophy there has since been a tendency to exalt the universe and to relegate man to a place of insignificance as the helpless victim of an all-powerful destiny. When the end of the northern Renaissance did finally come, it probably resulted chiefly from the heritage of bitterness and unreason left by the Protestant Revolution. But that is a subject which can be discussed more appropriately in the chapter that follows.

The decline of the Renaissance outside of Italy

SELECTED READINGS

· Items so designated are available in paperbound editions.

· Beard, M. R., *A History of the Business Man*, New York, 1938 (Ann Arbor). Interesting sketches of Renaissance capitalists.

Benesch, Otto, *The Art of the Renaissance in Northern Europe*, Cambridge, Mass., 1945.

· Bush, D., *The Renaissance and English Humanism*, Toronto, 1939 (University of Toronto Press). A brief but excellent introduction.

Curtis, Mark H., *Oxford and Cambridge in Transition, 1558–1642*, Oxford, 1959.

Elton, G. R., *England Under the Tudors*, London, 1955.

· Gilmore, M., *The World of Humanism*, New York, 1952 (Torchbook). An excellent general account.

· Hay, Denys, *The Renaissance Debate*, New York, 1965 (European Problem Series).

· Huizinga, Johan, *The Waning of the Middle Ages*, London, 1924 (Anchor).

Hyma, Albert, *The Christian Renaissance*, New York, 1924. The most authoritative work on this subject.

———, *Erasmus and the Humanists*, New York, 1930.

Lang, Paul, *Music in Western Civilization*, New York, 1941. The best survey yet published.

McGinn, D. F., *Shakespeare and the Drama of His Age*, New Brunswick, N.J., 1938.

Oxford History of Music, Vols. I–II.

Panofsky, E., *Early Netherlandish Painting; Its Origins and Character*, Cambridge, Mass., 1954. Valuable for an understanding of Flemish painters.

Reese, Gustave, *Music in the Renaissance*, rev. ed., New York, 1959.

· Smith, Preserved, *A History of Modern Culture*, New York, 1930, Vol. I (Collier). Thorough and scholarly.

· ———, *Erasmus, A Study of His Life, Ideals and Place in History*, New York, 1923 (Dover).

· Taylor, H. O., *Thought and Expression in the Sixteenth Century*, London, 1920. Also available in paperback under the title *Humanism of Italy* (Collier, 2 vols.). Reliable and suggestive.

Thorndike, Lynn, *A History of Magic and Experimental Science in the Fourteenth and Fifteenth Centuries*, New York, 1934, 2 vols. Detailed and authoritative.

———, *Science and Thought in the Fifteenth Century*, New York, 1929.

SOURCE MATERIALS

· Bacon, Sir Francis, *The Great Instauration*, Preface (Washington Square Press and others).

Erasmus, Desiderius, *The Complaint of Peace*.

———, *The Handbook of a Christian Knight*.

· ———, *The Praise of Folly* (Ann Arbor, Bantam).

· Montaigne, Michel de, *Essays* (Penguin).

· More, Sir Thomas, *Utopia*, especially Book II (Penguin and others).

· Rabelais, François, *Gargantua and Pantagruel*, especially Book I (Penguin).

CHAPTER 15

The Age of the Reformation
(1517-*ca*.1600)

> For the word of God cannot be received and honored by any works, but by faith alone.
> —Martin Luther, *On Christian Liberty*

> In conformity to the clear doctrine of the Scripture, we assert that by an eternal and immutable counsel, God has once for all determined both whom he would admit to salvation and whom he would condemn to destruction. . . . In the elect, we consider calling as an evidence of election, and justification as another token of its manifestation, till they arrive in glory, which constitutes its completion.
> —John Calvin, *Institutes* III.xxi

Preceding chapters have described the unfolding of a marvelous culture which marked the transition from the Middle Ages to the modern world. It became apparent that this culture, known as the Renaissance, was almost as peculiarly an echo of the past as a herald of the future. Much of its literature, art, and philosophy, and all of its superstitions, had roots that were deeply buried in classical antiquity or in the fabulous centuries of the Middle Ages. Even its humanism breathed veneration for the past. Only in science and politics and in the vigorous assertion of the right of the individual to pursue his own quest for freedom and dignity was there much that was really new. But the Renaissance in its later stages was accompanied by the growth of another movement, the Reformation, which somewhat more accurately foreshadowed the modern age. This movement included two principal phases: the Protestant Revolution, which broke out in 1517 and resulted in the secession of most of northern Europe from the Roman faith; and the Catholic Reformation, which reached its height about 1560. Although the latter is not called a revolution, it really was such in nearly every sense of

The later stages of the Renaissance accompanied by a religious revolution

397

the term; for it effected a profound alteration of some of the notable features of late medieval Catholicism.

In a number of ways the Renaissance and the Reformation were closely related. Both were products of that powerful current of individualism which wrought such havoc to the established order in the fourteenth and fifteenth centuries. Each had a similar background of economic causes in the growth of capitalism and in the rise of a bourgeois society. Both partook of the character of a return to original sources: in the one case, to the literary and artistic achievements of the Greeks and Romans; in the other, to the Scriptures and the doctrines of the Church Fathers. But in spite of these important resemblances, it is misleading to think of the Reformation as merely the religious aspect of the Renaissance. The guiding principles of the two movements had comparatively little in common. The essence of the Renaissance was devotion to the human and the natural, with religion relegated to a subordinate place. The spirit of the Reformation was otherworldliness and contempt for the things of this life as inferior to the spiritual. In the mind of the humanist, man's nature was generally considered good; in the view of the Reformer it was unspeakably corrupt and depraved. The leaders of the Renaissance believed in urbanity and tolerance; the followers of Luther and Calvin emphasized faith and conformity. While both the Renaissance and the Reformation aimed at a recovery of the past, they were really oriented in different directions. The past the humanists strove to revive was Greek and Roman antiquity, though a few were concerned with the original Gospels as sources of an unspoiled religion. The Reformers, by contrast, were interested chiefly in a return to the teachings of St. Paul and St. Augustine. It goes without saying that the Renaissance, being an aristocratic movement, had less influence on the common man than did the Reformation.

For reasons such as these it seems justifiable to conclude that the Reformation was not really a part of the Renaissance movement. In actual fact, it represented a much sharper break with the civilization of the later Middle Ages than ever did the movement led by the humanists. The radical Reformers would have nothing to do with the basic theories and practices of thirteenth-century Christianity. Even the simple religion of love and selflessness for the betterment of man, as taught by St. Francis of Assisi, appeared to repel them almost as much as the mysteries of the sacramental theory or the bombastic claims of Innocent III to spiritual and temporal power. In the main, the religious results of this clash with medieval Christianity have endured to this day. Moreover, the Reformation was intimately bound up with certain political trends which have persisted throughout the modern era. National consciousness, as we shall see, was one of the principal causes of the Protestant Revolution. While it is true that several of the humanists wrote under the influence of national pride, perhaps the majority were swayed by altogether different considerations. Many were scornful of politics, being interested solely in man as an individual; others, the great Erasmus among them, were thoroughly international in their outlook. But the Protestant Reformers could scarcely have gained much of a hearing if they had not associated their cause with the powerful groundswell of national resentment in northern Europe against an ecclesiastical system that had come to be recognized as largely Italian in character. For this reason as well as for the reasons mentioned previously, it would seem not unwarranted to regard the Reformation as a gateway to the modern world. And when we speak of the Renaissance in religion, we should think, not of the Reformation, but of the so-called Christian Renaissance, initiated by the Brethren of the Common Life and carried to its highest fulfillment in the teachings of Sir Thomas More and Erasmus. The common assumption that Luther hatched the egg which Erasmus had laid is true only in a very limited sense. The bird which Luther hatched belonged to a much tougher and wilder breed than any that could have descended from the Prince of the Humanists.

1. THE PROTESTANT REVOLUTION

The Protestant Revolution sprang from a multiplicity of causes, most of them closely related to the political and economic conditions of the age. Nothing could be more inaccurate than to think of the revolt against Rome as exclusively a religious movement, though doubtless religious ideas occupied a large place in the mind of sixteenth-century man. But without the basic political changes in northern Europe and the growth of new economic interests, Roman Catholicism would probably have undergone no more than a gradual evolution, perhaps in line with the teachings of the Christian Renaissance. Nevertheless, since religious causes were the most obvious ones, it will be appropriate to consider them first.

The multiplicity of causes of the Protestant Revolution

To the majority of Luther's early followers the movement he launched was chiefly a rebellion against abuses in the Catholic Church. That such abuses existed no careful historian would deny, regardless of his religious affiliations. For example, numerous of the Roman clergy at this time were ignorant. Some, having obtained their positions through irregular means, were unable to understand the Latin of the Mass they were required to celebrate. Further, a considerable number of the clergy led scandalous lives. While some of the Popes and bishops were living in princely magnificence, the lowly priests occasionally sought to eke out the incomes from their parishes by keeping taverns, gaming houses, or other establishments for profit. Not only did some monks habitually ignore their vows of chastity, but a few indifferent members of the secular clergy surmounted the hardships of the rule of celibacy by keeping mistresses. Pope Innocent VIII, who reigned about twenty-five years before the beginning of the Protestant Revolution, was known to have had

Religious causes: abuses in the Catholic Church

Leo X. From an Italian minia-ture.

The sale
of indulgences

Abuses connected
with the venera-
tion of sacred
relics

eight illegitimate children, several of them born before his election to the papacy. There were numerous evils also in connection with the sale of religious offices and dispensations. As in the case of most civil positions, offices in the Church during the Renaissance period were commonly sold to the highest bidder. It is estimated that Pope Leo X enjoyed an income of more than a million dollars a year from the sale of more than 2000 ecclesiastical offices. This abuse was rendered more serious by the fact that the men who bought these positions were under a strong temptation to make up for their investment by levying high fees for their services. The sale of dispensations was a second malodorous form of ecclesiastical graft. A dispensation may be defined as an exemption from a law of the Church or from some vow previously taken. On the eve of the Reformation the dispensations most commonly sold were exemptions from fasting and from the marriage laws of the Church. By way of illustration, first cousins would be permitted to marry for the payment of a fee of one ducat.

But the abuses which seemed to arouse the most ardent pressure for reform were the sale of indulgences and the superstitious veneration of relics. An indulgence is a remission of all or of part of the temporal punishment due to sin—that is, of the punishment in this life and in purgatory; it is not supposed to have anything to do with punishment in hell. The theory upon which the indulgence rests is the famous doctrine of the Treasure of Merit developed by Scholastic theologians in the thirteenth century. According to this doctrine, Jesus and the saints, by reason of their "superfluous" virtues on earth, accumulated an excess of merit in heaven. This excess constitutes a treasure of grace upon which the Pope can draw for the benefit of ordinary mortals. Originally indulgences were not issued for payments of money, but only for works of charity, fasting, going on crusades, and the like. It was the Renaissance Popes, with their insatiable greed for revenue, who first embarked upon the sale of indulgences as a profitable business. The methods they employed were far from scrupulous. The traffic in "pardons" was often turned over to bankers on a commission basis. As an example, the Fuggers in Augsburg had charge of the sale of indulgences for Leo X, with permission to pocket one-third of the proceeds. Naturally, but one motive dominated the business—to raise as much money as possible.

For centuries before the Reformation the veneration of sacred relics had been an important element in Catholic worship. It was believed that objects used by the Christ, the Virgin, or the saints possessed a miraculous healing and protective virtue for anyone who touched them or came into their presence. It was inevitable that this belief should open the way for innumerable frauds. Superstitious peasants could be easily convinced that almost any ancient splinter of wood was a fragment of the true cross. And there was evidently no dearth of relic-mongers quick to take advantage of such credulity. The results were fantastic. According to Erasmus, the churches of Europe contained enough wood of the true cross to build a ship. No fewer than five shinbones of the ass on which Jesus rode to Jerusalem were on exhibition in different places, to say nothing of twelve heads of John the Baptist. Martin Luther declared in a pamphlet lampooning his enemy, the Archbishop of Mainz, that the latter claimed to possess "a whole pound of the wind that blew for Elijah in the cave on Mount Horeb and two feathers and an egg of the Holy Ghost."[1]

Modern historians agree, however, that abuses in the Catholic Church were not the primary religious cause of the Protestant Revolution. It was medieval Catholicism itself, not the abuses therein, to which the Reformers objected. Moreover, just before the revolt broke out, conditions had begun to improve. Many pious Catholics themselves had started an agitation for reform, which in time would probably have eliminated most of the glaring evils in the system. But as so often happens in the case of revolutions, the improvement had come too late. Other forces more irresistible in character had been gradually gathering momentum. Conspicuous among these was the growing reaction against late medieval theology, with its elaborate sacramental theory, its belief in the necessity of good works to supplement faith, and its doctrine of divine authority in the hands of the priests.

Abuses not the primary causes of the Protestant Revolution

From preceding chapters the reader will recall that two different systems of theology had developed within the medieval Church.[2] The first was formulated mainly by followers of St. Augustine in the early Middle Ages, on the basis of teachings in the Pauline Epistles. It was predicated on the assumption of an omnipotent God, who sees the whole drama of the universe in the twinkling of an eye. Not even a sparrow falls to the ground except in accordance with the divine decree. Human nature is hopelessly depraved, and it is therefore as impossible for man to perform good works as for thistles to bring forth figs. Man is absolutely dependent upon God, not only for grace to keep him from sin but also for his fate after death. Only those mortals can be saved whom God for reasons of His own has predestined to inherit eternal life. Such in its barest outlines was the system of doctrine commonly known as Augustinianism. It was a theology well suited to the age of chaos which followed the breakup of the classical world. Men in this time were prone to fatalism and otherworldliness, for they seemed to be at the mercy of forces beyond their control. But the system never wholly died out. It was preserved intact for centuries in certain areas, especially in parts of Germany, where the progress of late medieval civilization was comparatively slow. To Luther and many of his followers it seemed the most logical interpretation of Christian belief.

The clash between two different systems of theology: the Augustinian system

[1] Preserved Smith, *The Age of the Reformation*, pp. 495–96.
[2] See the chapters on The Early Middle Ages and The Later Middle Ages: Religious and Intellectual Developments.

With the growth of a more abundant life in the cities of southern and western Europe, it was natural that the pessimistic philosophy of Augustinianism should have been replaced by a system which would restore to man some measure of pride in his own estate. The change was accelerated also by the growth of a dominant Church organization. The theology of Augustinianism, by placing man's fate entirely in the hands of God, had seemed to imply that the functions of an organized Church were practically unnecessary. Certainly no sinner could rely upon the ministrations of priests to improve his chances of salvation, since those who were to be saved had already been "elected" by God from all eternity. The new system of belief was finally crystallized in the writings of Peter Lombard and St. Thomas Aquinas in the twelfth and thirteenth centuries. Its cardinal premise was the idea that man had been endowed by God with freedom of will, with power to choose the good and avoid the evil. However, man could not make this choice entirely unaided, for without the support of heavenly grace he would be likely to fall into sin. It was therefore necessary for him to receive the sacraments, the indispensable means for communicating the grace of God to man. Of the seven sacraments of the Church, the three most important for the layman were baptism, penance, and the Eucharist. The first wiped out the stain of previous sin; the second absolved the contrite sinner from guilt; the third was especially significant for its effect in renewing the saving grace of Christ's sacrifice on the cross. Except in emergencies, none of the sacraments could be administered by persons outside the ranks of the priesthood. The members of the clergy, having inherited the power of the keys from the Apostle Peter, alone had the authority to cooperate with God in forgiving sins and in performing the miracle of the Eucharist, whereby the bread and wine were transubstantiated into the body and blood of the Savior.

The Protestant
Revolution a rebellion against
the late medieval system of
theology

The Protestant Revolution was in large measure a rebellion against the second of these systems of theology. Although the doctrines of Peter Lombard and St. Thomas Aquinas had virtually become part of the theology of the Church, they had never been universally accepted. To Christians who had been brought up under Augustinian influence, they seemed to detract from the sovereignty of God and to contradict the plain teachings of Paul that man's will is in bondage and his nature unspeakably vile. Worse still, in the opinion of these critics, was the fact that the new theology greatly strengthened the authority of the priesthood. In sum, what the Reformers wanted was a return to a more primitive Christianity than that which had prevailed since the thirteenth century. Any doctrine or practice not expressly sanctioned in the Scriptures, especially in the Pauline Epistles, or not recognized by the Fathers of the Church, they were strongly inclined to reject. It was for this reason that they condemned not only the theory of the priesthood and the sacramental system of the Church, but also such medieval additions to the faith as the worship of the Virgin, the belief in purgatory, the invocation of saints, the veneration of relics, and the rule of celibacy for the clergy. Motives of rationalism or skepticism had comparatively little to do with it. While it is true that Luther ridiculed the worship of relics as a form of superstition, in the main the early Protestants were even more suspicious of reason than the Catholics. Their religious ideal rested upon the Augustinian dogmas of original sin, the total depravity of man, predestination, and the bondage of the will—which were certainly more difficult to justify on a rational basis than the liberalized teachings of St. Thomas.

A few remaining religious causes deserve at least passing mention. One was the decline of respect for the papacy in consequence of the so-called "Babylonian Captivity" of the papacy. The "Babylonian Captivity" grew out of a quarrel between King Philip IV of France and Pope Boniface VIII at the beginning of the fourteenth century. The soldiers of the king arrested the Pope, and soon afterward Boniface died from the effects of the humiliation. A short time later King Philip's own candidate was elected to St. Peter's throne, and the papal capital was transferred to Avignon in the Rhone valley, where it remained for nearly seventy years. Surrounded by French influences, the Popes who reigned at Avignon were unable to escape the charge of subservience to French interests. In the minds of many Christians the papacy had ceased to be an international institution and had been degraded into the mere plaything of a secular power. In 1378 the head of the Church suffered an even greater loss of prestige. An effort to restore the papacy to its original capital led to the election of two Popes, one at Avignon and one at Rome, each loudly proclaiming himself the rightful successor of the Apostle Peter. The resulting division of the Church into two factions, supporting respectively the claims of the French and Italian Popes, is known as the Great Schism. Though finally healed by the Council of Constance in 1417, its effect in weakening the position of the papacy could hardly be overestimated.

Influence of
the "Babylonian
Captivity" of the
papacy and the
Great Schism

Still another factor of some importance in hastening the Protestant Revolution was the influence of the mystics and early reformers. For more than two centuries before the time of Luther, mysticism had become one of the most popular forms of religious expression in northern Europe. And it is not without significance that the vast majority of the mystics were Germans or natives of the Low Countries. Though none of the mystics preached open rebellion against the Catholic system, they were vehemently opposed to the ritualistic route to salvation sponsored by the medieval Church. Their version of religion was one in which the individual would attain the highest heaven through extinction of selfish desires and absolute surrender of the soul to God. No sacraments or priestly miracles would be necessary. Faith and a deep

Influence of
the mystics and
early reformers

St. John Lateran, the Pope's Cathedral in Rome. The "Mother Church" of Catholic Christendom, it derives its name from Plautius Lateranus, a rich nobleman whose property in this area was confiscated by Nero.

emotional piety would accomplish more wonders in reconciling sinful man to God than all the Masses in the calendar of the Church. Along with the mystics a number of pre-Reformation reformers exerted considerable influence in preparing the ground for the Protestant Revolt. At the end of the fourteenth century an Oxford professor by the name of John Wyclif launched an attack upon the Catholic system which anticipated much of the thunder of Luther and Calvin. He denounced the immorality of the clergy, condemned indulgences and the temporal power of the Church, recommended marriage of the clergy, insisted upon the supreme authority of the Scriptures as the source of belief, and denied transubstantiation. Most of Wyclif's teachings were ultimately carried to central Europe by Czech students from Oxford. They were actively propagated in Bohemia by John Huss, who was burned at the stake in 1415. Luther acknowledged his deep indebtedness to the Bohemian martyr.

As a political movement the Protestant Revolt was mainly the result of two developments: first, the growth of a national consciousness in northern Europe; and second, the rise of absolute monarchs. Ever since the late Middle Ages there had been a growing spirit of independence among many of the peoples outside of Italy. They had come to regard their own national life as unique and to resent interference from any external source. Although they were not nationalists in the modern sense, they tended to view the Pope as a foreigner who had no right to meddle with local affairs in England, France, or Germany. This feeling was manifested in England as early as the middle of the fourteenth century, when the famous Statutes of Provisors and Præmunire were passed. The first prohibited appointments by the Pope to Church offices in England; the

The political causes of the Protestant Revolution: the growth of national consciousness

second forbade the appeal of cases from the English courts to Rome. A law more extreme than either of these was issued by the king of France in 1438. The French law practically abolished all papal authority in the country, including the appointive authority and the right to raise revenue. To the civil magistrates was given the power to regulate religious affairs within their own districts. In Germany, despite the fact that there was no solid political unity, national feeling was by no means absent. It expressed itself in violent attacks upon the clergy by the Imperial Diet and in numerous decrees by the rulers of separate states prohibiting ecclesiastical appointments and the sale of indulgences without their consent.

The growth of a national consciousness in all of these countries went hand in hand with the rise of absolute monarchs. Indeed, it would be difficult to say how much of the sense of nationality was spontaneous and how much of it was stimulated by ambitious princes intent upon increasing their power. At any rate it is certain that the claims of rulers to absolute authority were bound to result in defiance of Rome. No despot could be expected to tolerate long the exclusion of religion from his sphere of control. He could not *be* a despot so long as there was a double jurisdiction within his realm. The appetite of princes for control over the Church was whetted originally by the revival of the Roman law, with its doctrine that the people had delegated *all* of their power to the secular ruler. From this doctrine it was a comparatively easy step to the idea that all of the Pope's authority could be properly assumed by the head of the state. But whatever the reasons for its growth, there can be no doubt that the ambition of secular princes to establish churches under their own control was a primary cause of the mounting antagonism against Rome.

The rise of absolute monarchs

Historians disagree as to the importance of economic causation of the Protestant Revolution. Those who conceive of the movement as primarily a religious one think of the sixteenth century as a period of profound and agonized concern over spiritual problems. Such a condition may well have characterized the mass of the people. But it does not alter the fact that in the sixteenth century, as in all ages, there were ruling groups greedy for wealth and quite willing to use and even to cultivate mass ideologies for their own advantage. Prominent among the economic objectives of such groups were acquisition of the wealth of the Church and elimination of papal taxation. In the course of its history from the beginning of the Middle Ages, the Church had grown into a vast economic empire. It was by far the largest landowner in western Europe, to say nothing of its enormous movable wealth in the form of rich furnishings, jewels, precious metals, and the like. Some of these possessions had been acquired by the Church through grants by kings and nobles, but most of them came from the gifts and bequests of pious citizens. Religious restrictions on taxation were also a galling grievance to

Economic causes: the desire to confiscate the wealth of the Catholic Church secular rulers. Kings, panting for big armies and navies, had an urgent need for more revenue. But Catholic law prohibited the taxing of Church property. The exemption of episcopal and monastic property from taxation meant a heavier burden on the possessions of individual owners, especially on the property of merchants and bankers. Moreover, the lesser nobles in Germany were being threatened with extinction on account of the collapse of the manorial economy. Many of them looked with covetous eyes upon the lands of the Church. If only some excuse could be found for expropriating these, their difficult situation might be relieved.

Resentment
against
papal taxation

Papal taxation, by the eve of the Protestant Revolution, had assumed a baffling variety of irritating forms. The most nearly universal, if not the most burdensome, was the so-called *Peter's pence*, an annual levy on every household in Christendom.[3] It must be understood that this tax was in addition to the *tithe*, which was supposed to be one-tenth of every Christian's income paid for the support of the parish church. Then there were the innumerable fees paid into the papal treasury for indulgences, dispensations, appeals of judicial decisions, and so on. In a very real sense the moneys collected for the sale of Church offices and the *annates*, or commissions levied on the first year's income of every bishop and priest, were also forms of papal taxation, since the officials who paid them eventually reimbursed themselves through increased collections from the people. But the main objection to these taxes was not that they were so numerous and burdensome. The real basis of grievance against the papal levies was their effect in draining the northern countries of so much of their wealth for the enrichment of Italy. Economically the situation was almost exactly the same as if the nations of northern Europe had been conquered by a foreign prince and tribute imposed upon them. Some Germans and Englishmen were scandalized also by the fact that most of the money collected was not being spent for religious purposes, but was being squandered by worldly Popes to maintain luxurious courts. The reason for the resentment, however, was probably as much financial as moral.

Conflicts between middle-class ambitions and the ascetic ideals of the Church

A third important economic cause of the Protestant Revolution was the conflict between the ambitions of the new middle class and the ascetic ideals of medieval Christianity. It was shown in a preceding chapter that the Catholic philosophers of the later Middle Ages had developed an elaborate theory designed for the guidance of the Christian in matters of production and trade.[4] This theory was founded upon the assumption that business for the sake of profit is

[3] Peter's pence derived its name from the fact that it was a tax of one penny. But the English penny at the end of the Middle Ages was the equivalent in purchasing power of slightly more than one dollar of our money. H. E. Barnes, *An Economic History of the Western World*, p. 121.

[4] See the chapter on The Later Middle Ages: Political and Economic institutions.

essentially immoral. No one has a right to any more than a reasonable wage for the service he renders to society. All wealth acquired in excess of this amount should be given to the Church to be distributed for the benefit of the needy. The merchant or craftsman who strives to get rich at the expense of the people is really no better than a common thief. To gain an advantage over a rival in business by cornering the market or beating down wages is contrary to all law and morality. Equally sinful is the damnable practice of usury—the charging of interest on loans where no actual risk is involved. This is sheer robbery, for it deprives the person who uses the money of earnings that are justly his; it is contrary to nature, for it enables the man who lends the money to live without labor.

While it is far from true that these doctrines were universally honored even by the Church itself, they nevertheless remained an integral part of the Catholic ideal, at least to the end of the Middle Ages. Even to this day they have not been entirely abandoned, as our study of liberal Catholicism in the nineteenth and twentieth centuries will show.[5] However, the age of the Renaissance was accompanied by the growth of an economic pattern distinctly incompatible with most of these doctrines. A ruthless, dynamic capitalism, based upon the principle of "dog eat dog," was beginning to supplant the old static economy of the medieval guilds. No longer were merchants and manufacturers content with a mere "wage" for the services they rendered to society. They demanded profits, and they could not see that it was any business of the Church to decide what a man's earnings should be. Wages were fit only for hirelings, who had neither the wit nor the industry to go after the big rewards. In addition to all this, the growth of banking meant an even more violent conflict with the ascetic ideal of the Church. As long as the business of moneylending was in the hands of Jews and Moslems, it mattered little that usury should be branded as a sin. But now that Christians were piling up riches by financing the exploits of kings and merchants, the shoe was on another foot. The new crop of bankers resented being told that their lucrative trade in cash was contrary to the laws of God. This seemed to them an attempt of spokesmen for an outmoded past to dictate the standards for a new age of progress. But how was it that Italy did not break with the Catholic Church in view of the extensive development of banking and commerce in such cities as Florence, Genoa, Milan, and Venice? Perhaps one explanation is to be found in the fact that such business activities had taken earlier and deeper roots in Italy than in most parts of Germany. They had been established for so long a time that any possible conflict between them and religious ideals had been largely ignored. Besides, the religion of many Italians, espe-

Effects of the rise of competitive capitalism

---

[5] See the paragraph on Christian Socialism in the chapter on Critics and Apologists of Industrialization.

cially during the Renaissance period, tended to approximate that of the ancient Romans; it was external and mechanical rather than profoundly spiritual. To many northern Europeans, by contrast, religion had a deeper significance. It was a system of dogmas and commandments to be observed literally under pain of the awful judgment of a wrathful God. They were, therefore, more likely to be disturbed by inconsistencies between worldly practices and the doctrines of the faith.

Why the Protestant Revolution began in Germany

The full story of why the Protestant Revolution began in Germany is so complex that only a few of the possible reasons can be suggested as topics for the student to ponder. Was Germany relatively more backward than most other areas of western Europe? Had the Renaissance touched her so lightly that medieval religiosity remained quite pervasive? Or did economic factors operate more strongly in Germany than elsewhere? The Church in Germany held an enormous proportion of the best agricultural lands, and evidence exists that the country was seething with discontent on account of a too rapid transition from a feudal society to an economy of profits and wages. It seems to be true, finally, that Germany was the victim of Catholic abuses to a greater extent than most other countries. How crucial was the shock resulting from these is impossible to say, but at least they provided the immediate impetus for the outbreak of the Lutheran revolt. Unlike England and France, Germany had no powerful king to defend her interests against the papacy. The country was weak and divided. At least partly for this reason, Pope Leo X selected German territory as the most likely field for the sale of indulgences.

I. THE LUTHERAN REVOLT IN GERMANY   By the dawn of the sixteenth century Germany was ripe for religious revolution. All that was necessary was to find a leader who could unite the dissatisfied elements and give a suitable theological gloss to their grievances. Such a leader was not long in appearing. His name was Martin Luther, and he was born in Thuringia in 1483. His parents were originally peasants, but his father had left the soil soon after his marriage to work in the mines of Mansfeld. Here he managed to become moderately prosperous and served in the village council. Nevertheless, young Martin's early environment was far from ideal. He was whipped at home for trivial offenses until he bled, and his mind was filled with hideous terrors of demons and witches. Some of these superstitions clung to him until the end of his life. His parents intended that he should become a lawyer, and with this end in view they placed him at the age of eighteen in the University of Erfurt. During his first four years at the university, Luther worked hard, gaining more than an ordinary reputation as a scholar. But in 1505, while returning from a visit to his home, he was overtaken by a violent storm and felled to the ground by a bolt of lightning. In terror lest an angry God strike him dead, he vowed to St. Anne to become

Martin Luther by Lucas Cranach the Elder, 1520

a monk. Soon afterward he entered the Augustinian monastery at Erfurt.

Here he gave himself up to earnest reflection on the state of his soul. Obsessed with the idea that his sins were innumerable, he strove desperately to attain a goal of spiritual peace. He engaged in long vigils and went for days on end without a morsel of food. But the more he fasted and tortured himself, the more his anguish and depression increased. Told that the way of salvation lies in love of God, he was ready to give up in despair. How could he love a Being who is not even just, who saves only those whom it pleases Him to save? "Love Him?" he said to himself, "I do not love Him. I hate Him." But in time, as he pondered the Scriptures, especially the story of the Crucifixion, he gained a new insight into the mysteries of the Christian theology. He was profoundly impressed by the humiliation of the Savior's death on the cross. For the benefit of sinful humanity, the Christ, the God-man, had shared the fate of common criminals. Why had He done so except out of love for His creatures? The God of the storm whose chief attribute appeared to be anger had revealed Himself as a Father who pities His children. Here was a miracle which no human reason could understand. It must be taken on faith; and by faith alone, Luther concluded, can man be justified in the sight of God. This doctrine of justification by faith alone, as opposed to salvation by "good works," quickly became the central doctrine of the Lutheran theology.

But long before Luther had completed his theological system, he was called to lecture on Aristotle and the Bible at the University of Wittenberg, which had recently been founded by Frederick the Wise of Saxony. While serving in this capacity, he was confronted by an event which furnished the spark for the Protestant Revolution. In 1517 an unprincipled Dominican friar by the name of Tetzel appeared in Germany as a hawker of indulgences. Determined to raise as much money as possible for Pope Leo X and the Archbishop

The doctrine of justification by faith alone

Luther's revolt against the sale of indulgences

Luther Preaching. With one hand he points to popes, monks, and cardinals going down hell's mouth. Hell is a beast with a snout, tusk, and eye. With the other hand, Luther points to the crucifix. The Lord's Supper is being administered, both the bread and the wine, to the laity. The chalice on the table emphasizes the evangelical practice of giving the cup to the laity.

of Mainz who had employed him, Tetzel deliberately represented
the indulgences as tickets of admission to heaven. Though forbidden
to enter Saxony, he came to the borders of that state, and many natives of Wittenberg rushed out to buy salvation at so attractive a
price. Luther was appalled by such brazen deception of ignorant
people. Accordingly, he drew up a set of ninety-five theses or statements attacking the sale of indulgences, and posted them, after the
manner of the time, on the door of the castle church on October 31,
1517. Later he had them printed and sent to his friends in a number
of cities. Soon it became evident that the Ninety-five Theses had
voiced the sentiments of a nation. All over Germany, Luther was
hailed as a leader whom God had raised to break the power of an
arrogant and hypocritical clergy. A violent reaction against the sale
of indulgences was soon in full swing. Tetzel was mobbed and
driven from the country. The revolt against Rome had begun.

With the revenue from indulgences cut off, it was inevitable that
the Pope should take action. Early in 1518 he commanded the general of the Augustinian order to make the rebellious friar recant.
Luther not only refused but published a sermon stating his views
more strongly than ever. Forced by his critics to answer questions on many points other than indulgences, he gradually came
to realize that his own religion was utterly irreconcilable with
that of the Roman Church. There was no alternative except to
break with the Catholic faith entirely. In 1520 his teachings were formally condemned in a bull promulgated by Leo
X, and he was ordered to recant within sixty days or be dealt with
as a heretic. Luther replied by publicly burning the Pope's proclamation. For this he was excommunicated and ordered to be turned
over to the secular arm for punishment. Germany at this time was
still under the technical rule of the Holy Roman Empire. Charles V,
who had recently been elevated to the throne of this ramshackle
state, was anxious to be rid of the insolent rebel at once, but he
dared not act without the approval of the Imperial Diet. Accordingly, in 1521, Luther was summoned to appear before a meeting of
this body at Worms. Since many of the princes and electors who
composed the Diet were themselves hostile toward the Church,
nothing in particular was done, despite Luther's stubborn refusal to
retract any of the things he had said. Finally, after a number of the
members had gone home, the Emperor forced through an edict
branding the obstreperous friar as an outlaw. But Luther had already been hidden away in the castle of his friend, the Elector of
Saxony. Here he remained until all danger of arrest by the Emperor's soldiers had passed. Charles soon afterward withdrew to
conduct his war with France, and the Edict of Worms was never
enforced.

Thenceforth until his death in 1546 Luther was occupied with his
work of building an independent German church. Despite the fun-

The condem-
nation and ex-
communication
of Luther

damental conflict between his own beliefs and Catholic theology, he nevertheless retained a good many of the elements of the Roman system. With the passing of the years he became more conservative than many of his own followers and compared some of them to Judas betraying his Master. Though he had originally denounced transubstantiation, he eventually came around to adopting a doctrine which bore at least a superficial resemblance to the Catholic theory. He denied, however, that any change in the substance of the bread and wine occurs as the result of a priestly miracle. The function of the clergyman is simply to *reveal* the presence of God in the bread and wine. Still, the changes he made were drastic enough to preserve the revolutionary character of the new religion. He substituted German for Latin in the services of the church. He rejected the entire ecclesiastical system of Pope, archbishops, bishops, and priests as custodians of the keys to the kingdom of heaven. By abolishing monasticism and insisting upon the right of priests to marry, he went far toward destroying the barrier which had separated clergy from laity and given the former their special status as representatives of God on earth. He recognized only baptism and the Eucharist as sacraments, and he denied that even these had any supernatural effect in bringing down grace from heaven. Since he continued to emphasize faith rather than good works as the road to salvation, he naturally discarded such formalized practices as fasts, pilgrimages, the veneration of relics, and the invocation of saints. On the other hand, the doctrines of predestination and the supreme authority of the Scriptures were given in the new religion a higher place than they had ever enjoyed in the old. Last of all, Luther abandoned the Catholic idea that the Church should be supreme over the state. Instead of having bishops subject to the Pope as the Vicar of Christ, he organized his church under superintendents who were essentially agents of the government.

Of course, Luther was not alone responsible for the success of the Protestant Revolution. The overthrow of Catholicism in Germany was also abetted by the outbreak of social revolt. In 1522–1523 there occurred a ferocious rebellion of the knights. These petty nobles were being impoverished by competition from the great estates and by the change to a capitalist economy. They saw as the chief cause of their misery the concentration of landed wealth in the hands of the great princes of the Church. Obsessed with national sentiments they dreamed of a united Germany free from the domination of powerful landlords and grasping priests. The leaders of the movement were Ulrich von Hutten, who had turned from a humanist into a fierce partisan of Luther, and Franz von Sickingen, a notorious robber baron and soldier of fortune. To these men the gospel of Luther seemed to provide an excellent program for a war on behalf of German liberty. Although their rebellion was speedily crushed by the armies of the archbishops and richer nobles, it apparently had considerable effect

Founding the Lutheran church; Luther's doctrines

The outbreak of social revolution; the revolt of the knights

411

in persuading the pillars of the old regime that too much resistance to the Lutheran movement would scarcely be wise.

The revolt of the knights was followed by a much more violent uprising of the lower classes in 1524–1525. Though most who took part were peasants, a great many poor workmen from the cities were attracted to the movement also. The causes of this second rebellion were somewhat similar to those of the first: the rising cost of living, the concentration of holdings of land, and the religious radicalism inspired by Luther's teachings. But the peasants and urban workers were stirred to action by many other factors as well. The decay of the feudal regime had eliminated the paternal relationship between noble and serf. In its place had grown up a mere cash nexus between employer and worker. The sole obligation now of the upper classes was to pay a wage. When sickness or unemployment struck, the laborer had to make shift with his slender resources as best he could. Furthermore, most of the old privileges which the serf had enjoyed on the manorial estate, of pasturing his flocks on the common lands and gathering wood in the forest, were being rapidly abolished. To make matters worse, landlords were attempting to meet advancing prices by exacting higher rents from the peasants. Finally, the lower classes were angered by the fact that the revival of the Roman law had the effect of bolstering property rights and of strengthening the power of the state to protect the interests of the rich.

Many of the downtrodden folk who participated in the so-called Peasants' Revolt belonged to a religious sect known as the Anabaptists. The name means "re-baptizers," and was derived from the fact that the members of the sect held infant baptism to be ineffectual and insisted that the rite should be administered only when the individual had reached the age of reason. But a belief in adult baptism was not really their principal doctrine. The Anabaptists were extreme individualists in religion. Luther's teaching that every man has a right to follow the dictates of his own conscience they took exactly as it stood. Not only did they reject the Catholic theory of the priesthood, but they denied the necessity of any clergy at all, maintaining that every individual should follow the guidance of the "inner light." They refused to admit that God's revelation to man had ceased with the writing of the last book of the New Testament, but they insisted that He continues to speak directly to certain of His chosen followers. They attached much importance to literal interpretation of the Bible, even of its most occult portions. They believed that the church should be a community of saints and required of their followers abstention from lying, profanity, gluttony, lewdness, and drinking intoxicating liquors. Many of the members looked forward to the early destruction of this world and the establishment of Christ's kingdom of justice and peace, in which they would have a prominent place. But the Anabaptists were not merely a group of religious extremists; they represented as well the most radical social tendencies of their time. Though it is certainly an exaggeration to call them communists, they did denounce the accumulation of wealth and taught that it was the duty of Christians to share their goods with one another. In addition, they declined to recognize any distinctions of rank or class, declaring all men equal in the sight of God. Many also abominated the taking of oaths, condemned military service, and refused to pay taxes to governments that engaged in war. They abstained in general from political life and demanded the complete separation of church and state. Their doctrines represented the extreme manifestation of the revolutionary fervor generated by the Protestant movement.

The Peasants' Revolt of 1524–1525 began in southern Germany and spread rapidly to the north and west until most of the country was involved. At first it had more of the character of a strike than a revolution. The rebels contented themselves with drafting petitions and attempting peaceably to persuade their masters to grant them relief from oppression. But before many months had passed, the movement came under the control of such fanatics as Thomas

Pages from a Bible Translated by Martin Luther, 1534. Left: The title page. Right: An illustration showing several episodes from the story of Jonah in a single composite picture.

The Siege of Münster in 1534

Münzer, who urged the use of fire and sword against the wicked nobles and clergy. In the spring of 1525 the misguided rustics began

Suppression of the Peasants' Revolt

plundering and burning cloisters and castles and even murdering some of their more hated opponents. The nobles now turned against them with fiendish fury, slaughtering indiscriminately both those who resisted and those who were helpless. Strange as it may seem, the lords were encouraged in this savagery by several of the Reformers, including the great Luther himself. In a pamphlet *Against the Thievish, Murderous Hordes of Peasants* he urged everyone who could to hunt the rebels down like mad dogs, to "strike, strangle, stab secretly or in public, and let him remember that nothing can be more poisonous, harmful, or devilish than a man in rebellion." [6] To Luther's credit, it should perhaps be added that he feared anarchy more than he did the particular doctrines of the Anabaptists. He believed that the use of force by anyone except the lawful authorities would result in the destruction of the social order.

But the brutal suppression of the Peasants' Revolt did not mark the end of revolutionary activities on the part of the submerged classes. In 1534 a group of Anabaptists gained control of the episcopal city of Münster in Westphalia. Thousands of their fellow believers from the surrounding country came pouring in, and Münster became a New Jerusalem where all of the accumulated vagaries of the lunatic fringe of the movement were put into practice. The property of unbelievers was confiscated, and polygamy was introduced. A certain John of Leyden assumed the title of king, proclaiming himself the successor of David with a mission to conquer

The Siege of Münster

[6] Quoted by H. S. Lucas, *The Renaissance and the Reformation*, p. 457.

the world and destroy the heathen. But after a little more than a year of this, Münster was recaptured by its bishop, and the leaders of Zion were put to death by horrible tortures. This second disaster proved to be the turning point in the revolt of the have-nots of the sixteenth century. Convinced of the futility of violence, they now abandoned the fanatical dogmas of their fallen leaders and returned to the religious quietism of earlier years. Most of the radical economic teachings were also dropped. Some of the survivors of the persecutions now joined the sect of Mennonites, so called from Menno Simons (1492–1559), whose teachings were partly derived from those of the original Anabaptists. Others fled to England to become the spiritual ancestors of the Quakers.

II. THE ZWINGLIAN AND CALVINIST REVOLTS IN SWITZERLAND The special form of Protestantism developed by Luther did not prove to be particularly popular beyond its native environment. Outside of Germany, Lutheranism became the official religion only in Denmark, Norway, and Sweden. But the force of the Lutheran revolt made itself felt in a number of other lands. Such was especially the case in Switzerland, where national consciousness had been gathering strength for centuries. At the close of the Middle Ages the gallant herdsmen and peasants of the Swiss cantons had challenged the right of the Austrians to rule over them, and finally in 1499 had compelled the Emperor Maximilian to recognize their independence, not only of the house of Hapsburg but of the Holy Roman Empire as well. Having thrown off the yoke of a foreign Emperor, the Swiss were not likely to submit indefinitely to an alien Pope. Moreover, the cities of Zürich, Basel, Berne, and Geneva had grown into flourishing centers of trade. Their populations were dominated by solid burghers who were becoming increasingly contemptuous of the Catholic ideal of glorified poverty. Here also northern humanism had found welcome lodgment in cultivated minds, with the effect of creating a healthy distrust of priestly superstitions. Erasmus had lived for a number of years in Basel. Lastly, Switzerland had been plucked by the indulgence peddlers to an extent only less grievous than that in Germany, while the city of Berne had been the scene of some particularly flagrant monkish frauds.

> **Causes of
> the Protestant
> Revolution in
> Switzerland**

The father of the Protestant Revolution in Switzerland was Ulrich Zwingli (1484–1531). Only a few weeks younger than Luther, he was the son of a well-to-do magistrate, who was able to provide him with an excellent education. As a student he devoted nearly all of his time to philosophy and literature, with no interest in religion save in the practical reforms of the Christian humanists. Although he took holy orders at the age of twenty-two, his purpose in entering the priesthood was mainly the opportunity it would give him to cultivate his literary tastes. Ultimately, he turned his interest to religion and devoted his energies to reform of the Church. He accepted nearly all of the teachings of Luther except that he regarded

Ulrich Zwingli. A sixteenth-century woodcut.

415

the bread and wine as mere symbols of the body and blood, and he reduced the sacrament of Holy Communion to a simple memorial service. So ably did he marshal the anti-Catholic forces that by 1528 nearly all of northern Switzerland had deserted the ancient faith.

From the northern cantons the Protestant Revolution in Switzerland spread to Geneva. This beautiful city, located on a lake of the same name near the French border, had the doubtful advantage of a double government. The people owed allegiance to two feudal suzerains, the local bishop and the Count of Savoy. When these high-born chieftains conspired to make their power more absolute, the citizens rebelled against them. The result was their expulsion from the town about 1530 and the establishment of a free republic. But the movement could hardly have been successful without some aid from the northern cantons. Thus it was not long until Protestant preachers from Zürich and Berne began arriving in Geneva.

It was soon after these events that John Calvin (1509–1564) arrived in Geneva. Although destined to play so prominent a role in the history of Switzerland, he was not a native of that country but of France. He was born at Noyon in Picardy. His mother died when he was very young, and his father, who did not like children, turned him over to the care of an aristocratic friend. For his higher education he was sent to the University of Paris, where, because of his bilious disposition and fault-finding manner, he was dubbed "the accusative case." Later he shifted at his father's wish to study of law at Orléans. Here he came under the influence of disciples of Luther, evidently to a sufficient extent to cause him to be suspected of heresy. Consequently, in 1534, when the government began an attack on the wavering ones, Calvin fled to Switzerland. He settled for a time in Basel and then moved on to Geneva, which was still in the throes of political revolution. He began preaching and organizing at once, and by 1541 both government and religion had fallen completely under his sway. Until his death from asthma and dyspepsia in 1564 he ruled the city with a rod of iron. History contains few examples of men more dour in temperament and more stubbornly convinced of the rightness of their own ideas.

Under Calvin's rule Geneva was transformed into a religious oligarchy. The supreme authority was vested in the Congregation of the Clergy, who prepared all legislation and submitted it to the Consistory to be ratified. The latter body, composed, in addition to the clergy, of twelve elders representing the people, had as its principal function the supervision of public and private morals. This function was carried out, not merely by the punishment of antisocial conduct but by a persistent snooping into the private life of every individual. The city was divided into districts, and a committee of the Consistory visited each household without warning to conduct an in-

John Calvin

The spread of the Protestant Revolution to Geneva

Calvin's rule at Geneva

An Interior with a Woman Drinking, with Two Men and a Maidservant, Pieter de Hooch (1629–1677?). The subjects and setting contrast strongly with those of the Italian artists. (National Gallery, London) Below: *Crucifixion*, Matthias Grünewald (?–1528). This work is the central panel of the Isenheim Altarpiece, in the Unterlinden Museen, Colmar. (Scala)

THE RELIGIOUS SITUATION IN EUROPE
AT THE HEIGHT OF THE REFORMATION

PRINCIPAL CHRISTIAN CHURCHES IN 1560:

Lutherans   Anglicans

Calvinists and   Roman
Zwinglians   Catholics

MINORITIES:

L   Lutherans   RC Roman Catholics   WM Waldensians,
CZ   Calvinists,   Moravians
     Zwinglians
ASA Anabaptists, Socinians, Antitrinitarians

- - - Approximate extent of the revolt
       from the Roman Church

quisition into the habits of its members. Even the mildest forms of human folly were strictly prohibited. Dancing, card-playing, attending the theater, working or playing on the Sabbath—all were outlawed as works of the Devil. Innkeepers were forbidden to allow anyone to consume food or drink without first saying grace, or to permit any patron to sit up after nine o'clock unless he was spying on the conduct of others. Needless to say, penalties were severe. Not only murder and treason were classified as capital crimes, but also adultery, witchcraft, blasphemy, and heresy; and the last of these especially was susceptible to a broad interpretation. During the first four years after Calvin became ruler of Geneva, there were no fewer than fifty-eight executions out of a total population of only 16,000.[7] The good accomplished by all of this harshness seems to have been small indeed. There were more cases of vice in Geneva after the Reformation than before.[8]

The essentials of Calvin's theology are contained in his *Institutes of the Christian Religion*, which was published originally in 1536 and revised and enlarged several times thereafter. His ideas resemble those of St. Augustine more than any other theologian. He conceived of the universe as utterly dependent upon the will of an Almighty God, who created all things for His greater glory. Because of Adam's transgression all men are sinners by nature, bound hand and foot to an evil inheritance they cannot escape. Nevertheless, God for reasons of His own has predestined some for eternal salvation and damned all the rest to the torments of hell. Nothing that human beings may do can alter their fate; their souls are stamped with God's blessing or curse before they are born. But this did not mean, in Calvin's opinion, that the Christian could be indifferent to his conduct on earth. If he were among the elect, God would have implanted in him the desire to live right. Abstemious conduct is a sign, though not an infallible one, that he who practices it has been chosen to sit at the throne of glory. Public profession of faith and participation in the sacraments are also presumptive evidences of election to be saved. But most of all, the Calvinists required an active life of piety and good morality as a solemn obligation resting upon members of the Christian Commonwealth. Like the ancient Hebrews, they conceived of themselves as chosen instruments of God with a mission to help in the fulfillment of His purposes on earth. Their duty was not to strive for their soul's salvation but for the glory of God. Thus it will be seen that the Calvinist system did not encourage its followers to sit with folded hands serene in the knowledge that their fate was sealed. No religion has fostered a more abundant zeal in the conquest of nature, in missionary activity,

Calvin's theology

---

[7] Preserved Smith, *The Age of the Reformation*, p. 171.
[8] *Ibid.*, p. 174.

or in the struggle against political tyranny. Doubtless the reason lies in the Calvinist's belief that as the chosen instrument of God he must play a part in the drama of the universe worthy of his exalted status. And with the Lord on his side he was not easily frightened by whatever lions lurked in his path.

The religion of Calvin compared with that of Luther

The religion of Calvin differed from that of Luther in a number of ways. First, it was more legalistic. Whereas the Wittenberg Reformer had emphasized the guidance of individual conscience, the dictator of Geneva stressed the sovereignty of law. He thought of God as a mighty legislator who had handed down a body of rules in the Scriptures which must be followed to the letter. Secondly, the religion of Calvin was more nearly an Old Testament faith than that of Luther. This can be illustrated in the attitude of the two men toward Sabbath observance. Luther's conception of Sunday was similar to that which prevails in modern Continental Europe. He insisted, of course, that his followers should attend church, but he did not demand that during the remainder of the day they should refrain from all pleasure or work. Calvin, on the other hand, revived the old Jewish Sabbath with its strict taboos against anything faintly resembling worldliness. In the third place, the religion of Geneva was more closely associated with the ideals of the new capitalism. Luther's sympathies lay with the nobles, and on at least one occasion he sharply censured the tycoons of finance for their greed. Calvin sanctified the ventures of the trader and the moneylender and gave an exalted place in his ethical system to the business virtues of thrift and diligence. Finally, Calvinism as compared to Lutheranism represented a more radical phase of the Protestant Revolution. As we have seen, the Wittenberg friar retained a good many features of Roman worship and even some Catholic dogmas. Calvin rejected everything he could think of that smacked of "popery." The organization of his church was constructed in such a way as to exclude all traces of the episcopal system. Congregations were to choose their own elders and preachers, while an association of ministers at the

The Reformation Unleashes its Fury on Calvin, Luther, and Beza. A contemporary anti-reform woodcut.

top would govern the entire church. Ritual, instrumental music, stained glass windows, pictures, and images were ruthlessly eliminated, with the consequence that the religion was reduced to "four bare walls and a sermon." Even the observance of Christmas and Easter was sternly prohibited.

The popularity of Calvinism was not limited to Switzerland. It spread into most countries of western Europe where trade and finance had become leading pursuits. The Huguenots of France, the Puritans of England, the Presbyterians of Scotland, and the members of the Reformed church in Holland were all Calvinists. It was preeminently the religion of the bourgeoisie; though, of course, it drew converts from other strata as well. Its influence in molding the ethics of modern times and in bolstering the revolutionary courage of the middle class was enormous. Members of this faith had much to do with the initial revolts against despotism in England and France, to say nothing of their part in overthrowing Spanish tyranny in the Netherlands.

III. THE PROTESTANT REVOLUTION IN ENGLAND The original blow against the Roman Church in England was not struck by a religious enthusiast like Luther or Calvin but by the head of the government. This does not mean, however, that the English Reformation was exclusively a political movement. Henry VIII could not have succeeded in establishing an independent English church if such action had not had the endorsement of large numbers of his subjects. And there were plenty of reasons why this endorsement was readily given. Though the English had freed themselves in some measure from papal domination, national pride had reached such a point that any degree of subordination to Rome was resented. Besides, England had been the scene for some time of lively agitation for religious reform. The memory of Wyclif's scathing attacks upon the avarice of the priests, the temporal power of Popes and bishops, and the sacramental system of the Church had lingered since the fourteenth century. The influence of the Christian humanists, notably Sir Thomas More, in condemning the superstitions in Catholic worship, had also been a factor of considerable importance. Finally, soon after the outbreak of the Protestant Revolution in Germany, Lutheran ideas were brought into England by wandering preachers and through the circulation of printed tracts. As a result, the English monarch, in severing the ties with Rome, had no lack of sympathy from some of the most influential of his subjects.

The clash with the Pope was precipitated by Henry VIII's domestic difficulties. For eighteen years he had been married to Catherine of Aragon and had only a sickly daughter to succeed him. The death of all the sons of this marriage in infancy was a grievous disappointment to the king, who desired a male heir to perpetuate the Tudor dynasty. But this was not all, for Henry later became deeply infatuated with the dark-eyed lady-in-waiting, Anne Boleyn,

The spread of Calvinism

Underlying causes of the Protestant Revolution in England

and determined to make her his queen. He therefore appealed in 1527 to Pope Clement VII for an annulment of the marriage to Catherine. The law of the Church did not sanction divorce, but it did provide that a marriage could be annulled if proof could be presented that conditions existing at the time of the marriage made it unlawful. Queen Catherine had previously been married to Henry's older brother, Arthur, who had died a few months after the ceremony was performed. Recalling this fact, Henry's lawyers found a passage in the Book of Leviticus which pronounced a curse of childlessness upon the man who should marry his deceased brother's wife. The Pope was now in a difficult position. If he rejected the king's appeal, England would probably be lost to the Catholic faith, for Henry was apparently firmly convinced that the Scriptural curse had blighted his chances of perpetuating his dynasty. On the other hand, if the Pope granted the annulment he would provoke the wrath of the Emperor Charles V, who was a nephew of Catherine. Charles had already invaded Italy and was threatening the Pope with a loss of his temporal power. There seemed nothing for Clement to do but to procrastinate. At first he made a pretense of having the question settled in England, and empowered his own legate and Cardinal Wolsey to hold a court of inquiry to determine whether the marriage to Catherine had been legal. After long delay the case was suddenly transferred to Rome. Henry lost patience and resolved to take matters into his own hands. In 1531 he convoked an assembly of the clergy and, by threatening to punish them for violating the Statute of Praemunire in submitting to the papal legate, he induced them to recognize himself as the head of the English church, "as far as the law of Christ allows." Next he persuaded Parliament to enact a series of laws abolishing all payments of revenue to the Pope and proclaiming the Anglican church an independent, national unit, subject to the exclusive authority of the king. By 1534 the last of the bonds uniting the English church to Rome had been cut.

But the enactments put through by Henry VIII did not really make England a Protestant country. Though the abolition of papal authority was followed by the gradual dissolution of the monasteries and confiscation of their wealth, the church remained Catholic in doctrine. The Six Articles, adopted by Parliament at the king's behest in 1539, left no room for doubt as to official orthodoxy. Auricular confession, Masses for the dead, and clerical celibacy were all confirmed; death by burning was made the penalty for denying the Catholic dogma of the Eucharist. Yet the influence of a minority of Protestants at this time cannot be ignored. Their numbers were steadily increasing, and during the reign of Henry's successor, Edward VI (1547–1553), they actually gained the ascendancy. Since the new king was only nine years old when he inherited the crown, it was inevitable that the policies of the government should be dictated by powers behind the throne. The men most active in this work were Thomas Cranmer, Archbishop of Canterbury, and the Dukes of Somerset and Northumberland, who successively dominated the council of regency. All three of these officials had strong Protestant leanings. As a result, the creeds and ceremonies of the Church of England were given some drastic revision. Priests were permitted to marry; English was substituted for Latin in the services; the use of images was abolished; and new articles of belief were drawn up repudiating all sacraments except baptism and the Lord's Supper and affirming the Lutheran dogma of justification by faith. When the youthful Edward died in 1553, it looked as if England had definitely entered the Protestant camp.

Surface appearances, however, are frequently deceiving. They were never more so than in England at the end of Edward's reign. The majority of the people had refused to be weaned away from the usages of their ancient faith, and a reaction had set in against the high-handed methods of the radical Protestants. Moreover, the English during the time of the Tudors had grown accustomed to obeying the will of their sovereign. It was an attitude fostered by national pride and the desire for order and prosperity. The successor of Edward VI was Mary (1553–1558), the forlorn and graceless daughter of Henry VIII and Catherine. It was inevitable that Mary should have been a Catholic, and that she should have abhorred the revolt against Rome, for the origin of the movement was painfully associated with her mother's sufferings. Consequently, it is not strange that upon coming to the throne she should have attempted to turn the clock back. Not only did she restore the celebration of the Mass and the rule of clerical celibacy, but she prevailed upon Parliament to vote the unconditional return of England to papal allegiance. But her policies ended in lamentable failure for several reasons. First of all, she fell into the same error as her predecessors in forcing through changes that were too radical for the temper of the times. The people of England were not ready for a Lutheran or Calvinist revolution, but neither were they in a mood to accept immediate subjection to Rome. Probably a more serious cause of her failure was her marriage to Philip, the ambitious heir to the Spanish throne. Her subjects feared that this union might lead to foreign complications, if not actual domination by Spain. When the queen allowed herself to be drawn into a war with France, in which England was compelled to surrender Calais, her last foothold on the Continent of Europe, the nation was almost ready for rebellion. Death ended Mary's inglorious reign in 1558.

The question whether England was to be Catholic or Protestant was left to be settled by Mary's successor, her half-sister Elizabeth (1558–1603), daughter of the vivacious Anne Boleyn. Though reared as a Protestant, Elizabeth had no deep religious convictions. Her primary interest was statecraft, and she did not intend that her kingdom should be rent in twain by sectarian strife. Therefore she decided upon a policy of moderation, refusing to ally herself with either the extreme Catholics or the fanatical Protestants. So carefully did she hew to this line that for some years she deceived the Pope into thinking that she might turn Catholic. Nevertheless, she was enough of a nationalist to refuse even to consider a revival of allegiance to Rome. One of the first things she did after becoming queen was to order the passage of a new Act of Supremacy declaring the English sovereign to be the "supreme governor" of the independent Anglican church. The final settlement, completed about 1570, was a typical English compromise. The church was made Protestant, but certain articles of the creed were left vague enough so that a moderate Catholic might accept them without too great a shock to his conscience. Moreover, the episcopal form of organization was retained and much of the Catholic ritual. Long after Elizabeth's death this settlement remained in effect. Indeed, most elements in it have survived to this day. And it is a significant fact that the modern Church of England is broad enough to include within its ranks such diverse factions as the Anglo-Catholics, who differ from their Roman brethren only in rejecting papal supremacy, and the "low-church" Anglicans, who are as radical in their Protestantism as the Lutherans.

2. THE CATHOLIC REFORMATION

As noted at the beginning of this chapter, the Protestant Revolution was only one of the phases of the great movement known as the Reformation. The other was the Catholic Reformation, or the Counter Reformation as it used to be called, on the assumption that the primary purpose of its leaders was to cleanse the Catholic Church in order to check the growth of Protestantism. Modern historians have shown, however, that the beginings of the movement for Catholic reform were entirely independent of the Protestant Revolt. In Spain, during the closing years of the fifteenth century, a religious revival inaugurated by Cardinal Ximenes, with the approval of the monarchy, stirred that country to the depths. Schools were established, abuses were eliminated from the monasteries, and priests were goaded into accepting their responsibilities as shepherds of their flocks. Though the movement was launched primarily for the purpose of strengthening the Church in the war against heretics and infidels, it nevertheless had considerable effect in regenerating the spiritual life of the nation. In Italy also, since the beginning of the sixteenth century, a number of earnest clerics had been laboring to make the priests of their Church more worthy of their Christian calling. The task was a difficult one on account of the paganism of the Renaissance and the example of profligacy set by the papal court. In spite of these obstacles the movement did lead to the founding of several religious orders dedicated to high ideals of piety and social service.

The beginnings of Catholic reform

But the fires of Catholic reform burned rather low until after the Protestant Revolution began to make serious inroads upon the ancient faith. Not until it appeared that the whole German nation was likely to be swept into the Lutheran orbit did any of the Popes become seriously concerned about the need for reform. The first of the Holy Fathers to attempt a purification of the Church was Adrian VI of Utrecht, the only non-Italian to be elected to the papal throne in nearly a century and a half, and the last in history. But his reign of only twenty months was too short to enable him to accomplish much, and in 1523 he was succeeded by a Medici (Clement VII), who ruled for eleven years. The campaign against abuses in the Church was not renewed until the reign of Paul III (1534–1549). He and three of his successors, Paul IV (1555–1559), Pius V (1566–1572), and Sixtus V (1585–1590), were the most zealous crusaders for reform who had presided over the See of Peter since the days of Gregory VII. They reorganized the papal finances, filled the Church offices with priests renowned for austerity, and dealt drastically with those clerics who persisted in idleness and vice. It was under these Popes that the Catholic Reformation reached its height. Unfortunately, they were also responsible for reviving the Inquisition, which had fallen into disuse during the Italian Renaissance.

These direct activities of the Popes were supplemented by the decrees of a great Church council convoked in 1545 by Paul III, which met in the city of Trent (modern Trento), at intervals between 1545 and 1563. This council was one of the most important in the history of the Church. The main purpose for which it had been summoned was to redefine the doctrines of the Catholic faith, and several of the steps in this direction were highly significant. Without exception the dogmas challenged by the Protestant Reformers were reaffirmed. Good works were held to be as necessary for salvation as faith. The theory of the sacraments as indispensable means of grace was upheld. Likewise, transubstantiation, the apostolic succession of the priesthood, the belief in purgatory, the invocation of saints, and the rule of celibacy for the clergy were all confirmed as essential elements in the Catholic system. On the much-debated question as to the proper source of Christian belief, the Bible and the traditions of apostolic teaching were held to be of equal authority. Not only was papal supremacy over every bishop and priest expressly maintained, but there was more than a faint suggestion that the authority of the Pope transcended that of the Church council itself. By this admission the government of the Church was reconstituted as monarchical in form. The great movement of the fourteenth and fifteenth centuries which had attempted to establish the superior authority of the general council was ignored entirely.

The Council of Trent did not confine its attention to matters of dogma. It passed important legislation also for the elimination of

Reforms of
the Council of
Trent

abuses and for reinforcing the discipline of the Church over its members. The sale of indulgences was flatly prohibited, and even their issuance for considerations other than money was restricted temporarily. Bishops and priests were forbidden to hold more than one benefice, so that none could grow rich from a plurality of incomes. To eliminate the evil of an ignorant priesthood it was provided that a theological seminary must be established in every diocese. Toward the end of its deliberations the Council decided upon a censorship of books to prevent heretical ideas from corrupting the minds of those who still remained in the faith. A commission was appointed to draw up an index or list of writings which ought not to be read. The publication of this list by the Pope in 1564 resulted in the formal establishment of the Index of Prohibited Books as a part of the machinery of the Church. Later a permanent agency known as the Congregation of the Index was set up to revise the list from time to time. Altogether more than forty such revisions have been made. The majority of the books condemned have been theological treatises, and probably the effect in retarding the progress of learning has been slight. Nonetheless, the establishment of the Index must be taken as a symptom of the intolerance which had come to infect both Catholics and Protestants.

The founding of
the Society of
Jesus by Loyola

The Catholic Reformation would never have been as thorough or as successful as it was if it had not been for the activities of the Jesuits, or members of the Society of Jesus. They did most of the rough political work in the Council of Trent, which enabled the Popes to dominate that body in its later and more important sessions. The Jesuits also were largely responsible for winning Poland and southern Germany back into the Catholic fold. The founder of the Society of Jesus was Ignatius of Loyola (1491–1556), a Spanish nobleman from the Basque country. His early career seems not to have been particularly different from that of other Spaniards of his class—a life of philandering and marauding as a soldier of the king. But about the time the Protestant Revolution was getting well under way in Germany, he was painfully wounded in a battle with the French. While waiting for his injuries to heal, he read a pious biography of Jesus and some legends of the saints which profoundly changed his emotional nature. Overwhelmed by a consciousness of his wasted life, he determined to become a soldier of Christ. After a period of morbid self-tortures, in which he saw visions of Satan, Jesus, and the Trinity, he went to the University of Paris to learn more about the faith he intended to serve. Here he gathered around him a small group of devoted disciples, with whose aid in 1534 he founded the Society of Jesus. The members took monastic vows and pledged themselves to go on a pilgrimage to Jerusalem. In 1540 their organization was approved by Pope Paul III. From then on it grew rapidly. When Loyola died it could boast of no fewer than 1500 members.

Ignatius Loyola. Engraving by Lucas Vorstiman, 1621.

The Society of Jesus was by far the most militant of the religious orders fostered by the spiritual zeal of the sixteenth century. It was not merely a monastic society but a company of soldiers sworn to defend the faith. Their weapons were not to be bullets and spears but eloquence, persuasion, instruction in the right doctrines, and if necessary more worldly methods of exerting influence. The organization was patterned after that of a military company, with a general as commander-in-chief and an iron discipline enforced on the members. All individuality was suppressed, and a soldierlike obedience to the general was exacted of the rank and file. Only the highest of the four classes of members had any share in the government of the order. This little group, known as the Professed of the Four Vows, elected the general for life and consulted with him on important matters. They were also bound to implicit obedience.

As suggested already, the activities of the Jesuits were numerous and varied. First and foremost, they conceived of themselves as the defenders of true religion. For this object they obtained authority from the Pope to hear confessions and grant absolution. Many of them became priests in order to gain access to the pulpit and expound the truth as the oracles of God. Still others served as agents of the Inquisition in the relentless war against heresy. In all of this work they followed the leadership of Mother Church as their infallible guide. They raised no questions and attempted to solve no mysteries. Loyola taught that if the Church ruled that white was black, it would be the duty of her sons to believe it. But the Jesuits were not satisfied merely to hold the field against the attacks of Protestants and heretics; they were anxious to propagate the faith in the farthest corners of the earth—to make Catholics out of Buddhists, Moslems, the Parsees of India, and even the untutored savages of the newly discovered continents. Long before the Reformation had ended, there were Jesuit missionaries in Africa, in Japan and China, and in North and South America. Yet another important activity of Loyola's soldiers of Christ was education. They founded colleges and seminaries by the hundreds in Europe and America and obtained positions in older institutions as well. Until the Society ran into conflict with several monarchs and was finally suppressed by the Pope in 1773, it had a monopoly of education in Spain and a near-monopoly in France. That the Catholic Church recovered so much of its strength in spite of the Protestant secession was due in large measure to the manifold and aggressive activities of the Jesuits.

3. THE REFORMATION HERITAGE

The most obvious result of the Reformation was the division of western Christendom into a multitude of hostile sects. No longer was there one fold and one shepherd for the whole of Latin and Teutonic Europe as had been true in the Middle Ages. Instead, northern

Results of the
Reformation:
the effect in
promoting re-
ligious tolera-
tion

Germany and the Scandinavian countries had become Lutheran; England had adopted a compromise Protestantism of her own; Calvinism had triumphed in Scotland, Holland, and French Switzerland. In the vast domain once owing allegiance to the Vicar of Christ only Italy, Austria, France, Spain and Portugal, southern Germany, Poland, and Ireland were left; and even in several of these countries aggressive Protestant minorities were a thorn in the side of the Catholic majority. Strange as it may seem, this splintering of Christianity into rival factions was, indirectly at least, a source of some good to man. It worked in the long run to curb ecclesiastical tyranny and thereby to promote religious freedom. As the sects multiplied in various countries, it gradually became evident that no one of them could ever become strong enough to enforce its will upon the rest. Mutual toleration was made necessary in order for any of them to survive. To be sure, this was an incidental and long-delayed result, but its importance cannot be denied.

Effects in
promoting in-
dividualism
and mass
education

The Reformation also gave an added momentum to individualism and to the expansion of popular education. By asserting the right of private judgment and by simplifying ritual and organization, the leaders of the Protestant Revolution liberated man from some of the constraints of medieval ecclesiasticism. It would be a mistake, however, to assume that Lutherans, Calvinists, and Anglicans really believed at this time in genuine religious freedom. They had no interest whatever in tolerating anyone who disagreed with their own respective orthodoxies. About all they did was to set a new and stronger precedent for challenging the authority and beliefs of a universal church. By so doing they promoted self-assertion in the religious sphere in somewhat the same degree as it already existed in the political and economic spheres. In addition, the Reformation had some effect in promoting the education of the masses. The Renaissance, with its absorbing interest in the classics, had had the unfortunate result of distorting the curricula of the schools into an exaggerated emphasis upon Greek and Latin and of restricting education to the aristocracy. The Lutherans, Calvinists, and Jesuits changed all of this. Ambitious to propagate their respective doctrines, they established schools for the masses, where even the son of the cobbler or peasant might learn to read the Bible and theological tracts in the vernacular. Practical subjects were often introduced in place of Greek and Latin, and it is a significant fact that some of these schools eventually opened their doors to the new science.

Limitation upon
the power of
rulers

A good case can be made for the theory that the Reformation furthered democracy, in the form, at least, of limited government. Every one of the sects, whether Protestant or Catholic, raised arguments against the absolute state. Even the Lutherans, despite their adoption of St. Paul's doctrine that "the powers that be are ordained of God," nevertheless recognized the right of the German princes to rebel against the Holy Roman Empire. Luther wrote that disobedience was a greater sin than murder, unchastity, dishonesty, or

NORWAY SWEDEN RUSSIA

TEUTONIC ORDER

IRELAND

NORTH SEA

DENMARK PRUSSIA

ENGLAND

London

BRANDENBURG

Warsaw

POLAND LITHUANIA

NETHERLANDS

Cologne

SAXONY

ATLANTIC

Aachen

HOLY ROMAN

LUXEMBOURG

Prague

OCEAN

Paris Verdun

Seine R.

Rhine R.

EMPIRE

BOHEMIA

FRANCE

Augsburg

Vienna

AUSTRIA

HUNGARY

Rhone R.

Milan

Po R.

Venice

VENETIAN

Danube R.

Valladolid

Marseilles

Genoa

PAPAL STATES

REPUBLIC OF GENOA

Florence

SPAIN

Toledo

CORSICA

Rome

REPUBLIC

Constantinople

BALEARIC ISLANDS

SARDINIA

Naples

NAPLES

PORTUGAL

Seville

MEDITERRANEAN

Palermo

SICILY

SEA

O T T O M A N   E M P I R E

0 — 500 miles

EUROPE ca. 1550 A.D.

theft; but what he meant was the disobedience of the common man. He generally held that the authority of kings and princes was absolute and never to be questioned by their subjects. Some observers see in Luther's influence a powerful stimulus to the growth of authoritarian government in Germany. A more critical attitude toward secular rulers was taken by the Calvinists. In France, England, and the Low Countries they not only asserted the right of revolution but actively practiced it. Jesuit philosophers taught that the authority of the secular ruler is derived from the people, and some even affirmed the right of the ordinary citizen to kill a tyrant. Among the leaders of many sects, efforts were made to revive the medieval idea of a higher law of nature, embodying principles of right and justice, which should be recognized as an automatic limitation upon the power of rulers.

427

The St. Bartholomew's Day Massacre. Thousands of Huguenots were killed in the continuing religious strife of the sixteenth century.

The Reformation resulted in a series of religious wars which kept Europe in turmoil for two score years. The first to break out was the Schmalkaldic War (1546–1547), waged by Charles V in an effort to restore the unity of the Holy Roman Empire under the Catholic faith. In a few months he succeeded in cowing the Protestant princes of Germany into submission, but he was unable to force their subjects back into the Roman religion. The strife was ultimately settled by a compromise treaty, the Religious Peace of Augsburg (1555), under which each German prince was to be free to choose either Lutheranism or Catholicism as the faith of his people. The religion of each state was thus made to depend upon the religion of its ruler. A much more sanguinary struggle took place in France between 1562 and 1593. Here the Protestants, or Huguenots

428

as they were called, were decidedly in the minority, but they included some of the ablest and most influential members of the commercial and financial classes. Besides, they composed a political party involved in machinations against the Catholics for control of the government. In 1562 a faction of ultra-Catholics under the leadership of the Duke of Guise forced their way into power and, by their threats of persecution of the Huguenots, plunged the country into civil war. The struggle culminated ten years later in the frightful massacre of St. Bartholomew's Day. The regent, Catherine de' Medici, in a desperate effort to put an end to the strife, plotted with the Guises to murder the Protestant chiefs. The conspiracy unloosed the ugly passions of the Paris mob, with the result that in a single night 2000 Huguenots were slain. The war dragged on until 1593 when Henry IV became a Catholic in order to please the majority of his subjects, but the religious issue did not approach a settlement until 1598 when Henry issued the Edict of Nantes guaranteeing freedom of conscience to Protestants.

To a large extent the Revolt of the Netherlands was also an episode in the religious strife stirred up by the Reformation. Long after the Protestant Revolution began in Germany, the countries now known as Belgium and Holland were still being governed as dominions of the Spanish crown. Though Lutheranism and Calvinism had gained a foothold in the cities, the Protestants of the Netherlands were yet but a fraction of the total population. With the passage of time, however, the numbers of Calvinists increased until they included a majority of the townsmen, at least, in the Dutch provinces of the north. Interference by the Spanish government with their freedom of religion led to a desperate revolt in 1565. Religious causes were, of course, not the only ones. Nationalist feeling was a leading factor also, particularly since the Spanish king, Philip II, persisted in treating the Netherlands as mere subject provinces. In addition, there were serious economic grievances—high taxation and the restriction of commerce for the benefit of Spanish merchants. On the other hand, it was religious hatred that was largely responsible for the bitterness of the struggle. Philip II regarded all Protestants as traitors, and he was determined to root them out of every territory over which he ruled. In 1567 he sent the bigoted Duke of Alva with 10,000 soldiers to quell the revolt in the Netherlands. For six years Alva terrorized the land, putting hundreds of the rebels to death and torturing or imprisoning thousands of others. The Protestants retaliated with almost equal savagery, and the war continued its barbarous course until 1609. It ended in victory for the Protestants, largely through the bravery and self-sacrifice of their original leader, William the Silent. The chief result of the war was the establishment of an independent Dutch Republic comprising the territories now included in Holland. The southern or Belgian prov-

The Cities of Schmalkaldic League Surrendering to Charles V. Engraving by Hieronymus Cock, 1560.

inces, where the majority of the people were Catholics, returned to Spanish rule.

Actual warfare between nations and sects was not the only type of barbarity which the Reformation directly encouraged. For other examples we need only recall the atrocities perpetrated by the Catholic Inquisition, the savage persecution of Anabaptists in Germany, and the fierce intolerance of Calvinists against Catholics. The horrible witchcraft persecution, which will be discussed in the next chapter, was also in some measure the product of the seeds of fanaticism sown by the Reformation. On the whole, the amount of intolerance was now much greater than at any other time in the history of Christianity, not excepting the age of the Crusades. In more than one instance the victims of persecution were distinguished philosophers or scientists, whose talents the world of that day could ill afford to lose. The most eminent of the martyrs to the new learning put to death by the Catholics was Giordano Bruno. Despite his philosophy of mystical pantheism, Bruno set forth in startling fashion a number of the cardinal axioms of modern science. He taught the eternity of the universe, revived the atomic theory of matter, and denied that the heavenly bodies contain any superior element not found in the earth. Partly for these teachings and partly also for his pantheism and for his rejection of miracles, he was haled before the Inquisition and burned at the stake in 1600. One of the victims of Calvinist persecution at Geneva was Michael Servetus, the discoverer of the lesser circulation of the blood. Servetus was convicted of rejecting the doctrines of the Trinity and predestination and of teaching that Palestine is a barren country in defiance of the Old Testament description of it as a land flowing with milk and honey. In 1553 he was condemned to be burned at the stake by slow fire. Some admirers of Calvin have argued that the Genevan Reformer opposed the burning of Servetus: he wanted him beheaded! But even the evidence for this rather doubtful display of mercy is not conclusive.

Bigotry, witchcraft, and persecution

430

SELECTED READINGS

· *Items so designated are available in paperbound editions.*

· Bainton, R. H., *The Age of the Reformation*, New York, 1956 (Anvil). The best short treatise. Half of it consists of documents.

· ———, *Here I Stand: A Life of Martin Luther*, Nashville, 1950 (Apex).

Bax, E. B., *The Peasants' War in Germany*, New York, 1899. The best account in English but not especially scholarly.

· Beard, C., *The Reformation of the Sixteenth Century in Its Relation to Modern Thought and Knowledge*, New York, 1927 (Ann Arbor).

· Burns, E. M., *The Counter Reformation*, Princeton, 1964 (Anvil).

Bury, J. B., *History of the Freedom of Thought*, New York, 1913.

Cohn, Norman, *The Pursuit of the Millennium*, Oxford, 1970.

· Erikson, E. H., *Young Man Luther*, New York, 1961 (Norton Library).

· Harkness, G. E., *John Calvin: the Man and His Ethics*, New York, 1931 (Apex).

· Huizinga, Johan, *Erasmus and the Age of Reformation*, New York, 1957 (Torchbook).

Janelle, Pierre, *The Catholic Reformation*, Milwaukee, 1949.

Jenkins, B. A., *The World's Debt to Protestantism*, Boston, 1930.

· Jones, R. M., *The Spiritual Reformers of the Sixteenth and Seventeenth Centuries*, New York, 1914 (Beacon).

Kidd, B. J., *The Counter-Reformation, 1550–1600*, New York, 1933. A complete account of the Jesuits, the Inquisition, and the Council of Trent.

Latourette, K. S., *A History of Christianity*, New York, 1953.

Lindsay, T. M., *History of the Reformation*, New York, 1928, 2 vols. Complete and scholarly.

Lucas, H. S., *The Renaissance and the Reformation*, New York, 1934.

· McGiffert, A. C., *Protestant Thought before Kant*, New York, 1911 (Torchbook).

McNeill, J. T., *The History and Character of Calvinism*, New York, 1954.

Marti, O. A., *The Economic Causes of the Reformation in England*, New York, 1930.

Nelson, E. N., *The Idea of Usury*, Princeton, 1949.

Randall, J. H., Jr., *The Making of the Modern Mind*, New York, 1926. Ch. VII.

Schwiebert, E. G., *Luther and His Times*, St. Louis, 1952.

· Smith, Preserved, *The Age of the Reformation*, New York, 1920 (Collier, 2 vols.). The best general survey.

———, *The Life and Letters of Martin Luther*, New York, 1914.

Smithson, Robert, *The Anabaptists*, London, 1935.

· Tawney, R. H., *Religion and the Rise of Capitalism*, New York, 1926 (Mentor). Thoughtful and provocative.

Van Dyke, P., *Ignatius Loyola, The Founder of the Jesuits*, New York, 1926.

· Weber, Max, *The Protestant Ethic and the Spirit of Capitalism*, New York, 1948 (Scribner Library). A stimulating sociological interpretation.

SOURCE MATERIALS

· Calvin, John, *Institutes of the Christian Religion*, especially Book II, Chs. 1–3; Book III, Chs. 19, 21–25; Book IV, Chs. 3, 14, 17, 20 (Wm. B. Eerdmans Publishing Co., 2 vols.).

Catechism of the Council of Trent.

Luther, Martin, *Works* (Jacobs, tr.), "On Trade and Usury," Vol. IV.

· ———, *On Christian Liberty* (Fortress, 1940).

———, *Address to the Christian Nobility of the German Nation.*

PART V

The Early Modern World
1400-1789

We have already learned that in 1517 a religious upheaval, known as the Protestant Revolution, began in Germany and eventually spread to many other countries. Some historians regard this revolution as the beginning of the modern age since it helped to bring to a close the civilization of the Middle Ages and was accompanied by an upsurge of individualism and national consciousness. But in some respects the Protestant Revolution looked back to the Middle Ages, especially to the early Middle Ages when the Christian religion was supposed to have flourished in its purest form. Moreover, the secular culture which developed after 1500 had an even more distinctively modern character than that relating to religion. The period from 1400 to 1700 was the heyday of the Commercial Revolution, which overthrew the static economy of the medieval guilds and established a dynamic regime of business for profit. The entire era was marked by the growth of absolute governments, headed in some instances by kings who equated themselves with the state and professed to rule by divine right. States increased in size and in power and gradually absorbed the feudal duchies and principalities. The medieval Empire even more than the medieval Church shrank to a shadow of its former existence. Finally, during the years from 1600 to 1789, there occurred an intellectual revolution, culminating in the enthronement of reason and in the development of the concept of a mechanistic universe governed by inflexible laws.

A Chronological Table

	EUROPE AS A WHOLE	WESTERN EUROPE	CENTRAL AND EASTERN EUROPE
1400	Rise of a capitalist economy, 1400–1500 Growth of banking, 1400–1600 Development of a money economy, 1400–1600 The Great Schism, 1379–1417 The domestic system, 1400–1750 The enclosure movement, 1400–1800 Voyages of discovery and exploration, 1450–1600	Erasmus, 1466?–1536 Machiavelli, 1469–1527 Michelangelo, 1475–1564 Tudor dynasty in England, 1485–1603 Rabelais, *ca.* 1490–1553	Copernicus, 1473–1543 Martin Luther, 1483–1546
1500	Catholic Reformation, 1500–1563		John Calvin, 1509–1564 Beginning of Protestant Revolution, 1517 Zwinglian movement in Switzerland, 1519–1529 Rise of the Anabaptists, *ca.* 1520 Revolt of the knights, 1522–1523 Peasants' Revolt, 1524–1525
1550	Founding of Society of Jesus, 1534 Council of Trent, 1545–1563 Joint stock companies, 1550	Montaigne, 1533–1592 Henry VIII establishes Anglican Church, 1534 Cervantes, 1547–1616 Sir Francis Bacon, 1561–1626 Shakespeare, 1564–1616 Galileo, 1564–1642 Revolt of the Netherlands, 1565–1609 Monteverdi, 1567–1643 The Elizabethan Compromise, 1570 Massacre of St. Bartholomew's Day, 1572 Rubens, 1577–1640	
	Beginning of International Law: Hugo Grotius, 1583–1645	Sir William Harvey, 1578–1657 Spanish Armada, 1588 Bourbon dynasty in France, 1589–1792 Edict of Nantes, 1598 Velasquez, 1599–1660	

EUROPE AS A WHOLE	WESTERN EUROPE	CENTRAL AND EASTERN EUROPE	
Baroque architecture, 1600–1750			**1600**
Classicism in literature and the arts, 1600–1750		Cameralism, 1600–1800	
Mercantilism, 1600–1789			
Chartered companies, 1600–1850			
Thirty Years' War, 1618–1648	Rembrandt, 1606–1669		
Deism, 1630–1800	Colbert, 1619–1683		
	Rationalism in philosophy, 1630–1700		
	Puritan Revolution in England, 1640–1659		
Beginning of modern state system, 1648			
Treaty of Westphalia, 1648			
	Commonwealth and Protectorate in England, 1649–1659		
	Restoration of the Stuart dynasty, 1660–1688		
	John Milton, *Paradise Lost,* 1667		
The Enlightenment, 1680–1800	Revocation of Edict of Nantes, 1685		
	Newton's law of gravitation, 1687	J. S. Bach, 1685–1750	
War of the League of Augsburg, 1688–1697	Glorious Revolution in England, 1688–1689		**1688**
	John Locke, *Two Treatises of Civil Government,* 1690	Peter the Great, of Russia, 1682–1725	
	Voltaire, 1694–1778		
	Bank of England, 1694		
Agricultural Revolution, 1700–1800			
Rococo architecture, 1700–1800			
War of the Spanish Succession, 1702–1714	Union of England and Scotland, 1707		
Age of the Enlightened Despots, 1740–1796		Frederick the Great, of Prussia, 1740–1786	
Romanticism, 1750–1800	Rousseau, *The Social Contract,* 1762	Mozart, 1756–1791	
Seven Years' War, 1756–1763	Beginning of the factory system, *ca.* 1770	Catherine the Great, of Russia, 1762–1796	
	Joseph Priestley discovers oxygen, 1774		
	Adam Smith, *The Wealth of Nations,* 1776		
	Lavoisier discovers indestructibility of matter, 1789	Kant, *The Critique of Pure Reason,* 1781	**1789**
	Edward Jenner develops vaccination for smallpox, 1796	Goethe, *Faust,* 1790–1808	

CHAPTER 16

The Commercial Revolution
and the New Society (ca. 1300-1700)

Although a Kingdom may be enriched by gifts received, or by purchases taken from some other Nations, yet these are things uncertain and of small consideration when they happen. The ordinary means therefore to encrease our wealth and treasure is by *Forraign Trade*, wherein wee must ever observe this rule: to sell more to strangers yearly than wee consume of theirs in value.
—Thomas Mun, *England's Treasure by Forraign Trade*

The last three chapters described the intellectual and religious transition from the medieval to the modern world. It was observed that the Renaissance, despite its kinship in many ways with the Middle Ages, spelled the doom of Scholastic philosophy, undermined the supremacy of Gothic architecture, and overthrew medieval conceptions of politics and the universe. Likewise, it was noted that, before the Renaissance had completed its work, a mighty torrent of religious revolution had swept Christianity from it medieval foundations and cleared the way for spiritual and moral attitudes in keeping with the trends of the new age. That both the Renaissance and the Reformation should have been accompanied by fundamental economic changes goes without saying. Indeed, the intellectual and religious upheavals would scarcely have been possible had it not been for drastic alterations in the medieval economic pattern. This series of changes, marking the transition from the semistatic, localized, nonprofit economy of the late Middle Ages to the dynamic, worldwide, capitalistic regime of the fourteenth and succeeding centuries, is what is known as the Commercial Revolution.

The meaning of the Commercial Revolution

437

1. THE CAUSES AND INCIDENTS OF THE COMMERCIAL REVOLUTION

Causes of
the Commercial
Revolution

The causes which led to the beginning of the Commercial Revolution about 1300 are none too clear. This arises from the fact that the initial stage of the movement was more gradual than is commonly supposed. In so far as it is possible to isolate particular causes, the following may be said to have been basic: (1) the capture of a monopoly of Mediterranean trade by the Italian cities; (2) the development of a profitable commerce between the Italian cities and the merchants of the Hanseatic League in northern Europe; (3) the introduction of coins of general circulation, such as the ducat of Venice and the florin of Florence; (4) the accumulation of surplus capital in trading, shipping, and mining ventures; (5) the demand for war materials and the encouragement given by the new monarchs to the development of commerce in order to create more taxable wealth; and (6) the desire for the products of the Far East stimulated by the reports of travelers, especially the fascinating account of the wealth of China published by Marco Polo upon his return from a trip to that country toward the end of the thirteenth century. This combination of factors gave to the men of the early Renaissance new visions of riches and power and furnished them with some of the equipment necessary for an expansion of business. Henceforth they were bound to be dissatisfied with the restricted ideal of the medieval guilds with its ban upon trading for unlimited profit.

See color map
at page 464

The voyages of
overseas discov-
ery

About two centuries after it began, the Commercial Revolution received a powerful stimulus from the voyages of overseas discovery. The reasons why these voyages were undertaken are not hard to perceive. They were due primarily to Spanish and Portuguese ambitions for a share in the trade with the Orient. For some time this trade had been monopolized by the Italian cities, with the consequence that the people of the Iberian peninsula were compelled to pay high prices for the silks, perfumes, spices, and tapestries imported from the East. It was therefore quite natural that attempts should be made by Spanish and Portuguese merchants to discover a new route to the Orient independent of Italian control. A second cause of the voyages of discovery was the missionary fervor of the Spaniards. Their successful crusade against the Moors had generated a surplus of religious zeal, which spilled over into a desire to convert the heathen. To these causes should be added the fact that advances in geographical knowledge and the introduction of the compass and the astrolabe [1] gave mariners more courage to venture into the open

A Moslem Astrolabe, Thir-teenth Century

---

[1] The astrolabe is a device for measuring the altitude or position of heavenly bodies. It was invented by Hellenistic astronomers and perfected by the Saracens. Especially useful in determining locations at sea, it has since been replaced by the sextant.

sea. But the effect of these things must not be exaggerated. The popular idea that all Europeans before Columbus believed that the earth was flat is simply not true. From the twelfth century on it would be almost impossible to find an educated man who did not accept the fact that the earth is a sphere. Furthermore, the compass and the astrolabe were known in Europe long before any mariners ever dreamed of sailing the Atlantic, with the exception of the Norsemen. The compass was brought in by the Saracens in the twelfth century, probably from China. The astrolabe was introduced even earlier.

If we except the Norsemen, who discovered America about 1000 A.D., the pioneers in oceanic navigation were the Portuguese. By the middle of the fifteenth century they had discovered and settled the islands of Madeira and the Azores and had explored the African coast as far south as Guinea. In 1497 their most successful navigator, Vasco da Gama, rounded the tip of Africa and sailed on the next year to India. In the meantime, the Genoese mariner, Christopher Columbus, became convinced of the feasibility of reaching India by sailing west. Rebuffed by the Portuguese, he turned to the Spanish sovereigns, Ferdinand and Isabella, and enlisted their support of his plan. The story of his epochal voyage and its result is a familiar one and need not be recounted here. Though he died ignorant of his real achievement, his discoveries laid the foundations for the Spanish claim to nearly all of the New World. Other discoverers representing the Spanish crown followed Columbus, and soon afterward the conquerors, Cortes and Pizarro. The result was the establishment of a vast colonial empire including what is now the southwestern portion of the United States, Florida, Mexico, and the West Indies, Central America, and all of South America with the exception of Brazil.

The English and the French were not slow in following the Spanish example. The voyages of John Cabot and his son Sebastian in 1497–1498 provided the basis for the English claim to North America, though there was nothing that could be called a British empire in the New World until after the settlement of Virginia in 1607. Early in the sixteenth century the French explorer Cartier sailed up the St. Lawrence, thereby furnishing his native land with some shadow of a title to eastern Canada. More than a hundred years later the explorations of Joliet, La Salle, and Father Marquette gave the French a foothold in the Mississippi valley and in the region of the Great Lakes. Following their victory in their war for independence the Dutch also took a hand in the struggle for colonial empire. The voyage of Henry Hudson up the river which bears his name enabled them to found New Netherland in 1623, which they were forced to surrender to the English some forty years later. But the most valuable possessions of the Dutch were Malacca, the Spice Islands, and the ports of India and Africa taken from Portugal in the early seventeenth century.

The Spaniards
and Portuguese

Hernando Cortes

The British,
French, and
Dutch

439

The results of these voyages of discovery and the founding of colonial empires were almost incalculable. To begin with, they expanded commerce from its narrow limits of Mediterranean trade into a world enterprise. For the first time in history the ships of the great maritime powers now sailed the seven seas. The tight little monopoly of Oriental trade maintained by the Italian cities was thoroughly punctured. Genoa, Pisa, and Venice sank henceforth into relative obscurity, while the harbors of Lisbon, Bordeaux, Liverpool, Bristol, and Amsterdam were crowded with vessels and the shelves of their merchants piled high with goods. A second result was a tremendous increase in the volume of commerce and in the variety of articles of consumption. To the spices and textiles from the Orient were now added potatoes, tobacco, and maize from North America; molasses and rum from the West Indies; cocoa, chocolate, quinine, and the cochineal dye from South America; and ivory, slaves, and ostrich feathers from Africa. In addition to these commodities hitherto unknown or obtainable only in limited quantities, the supply of certain older products was greatly increased. This was especially true of sugar, coffee, rice, and cotton, which were brought in in such amounts from the Western Hemisphere that they ceased to be articles of luxury.

Another significant result of the discovery and conquest of lands overseas was an expansion of the supply of precious metals. When Columbus discovered America, the quantities of gold and silver in Europe were scarcely sufficient to support a dynamic economy. Indeed, it was nearly fifty years before the full impact of wealth from America made itself felt. For some time gold was the more abundant metal and was relatively cheap in relation to silver. The white metal, which came chiefly from the mines of Germany, was more highly prized than gold. About 1540 this relation was reversed. Massive im-

Aden. A sixteenth-century woodcut of the seaport which was a base for merchants and travelers sailing to India.

ports of silver from the mines of Mexico, Bolivia, and Peru produced such a depreciation in the value of silver that quantities of gold had to hoarded for critical transactions. Henceforth, for about eighty years, the European economy ran on silver. The result was a tremendous inflation. Prices and wages rose to fantastic heights in what may be considered an artificial prosperity. It did not affect all parts of Europe alike. The German mines were ruined by the flood of silver from the Americas. As a consequence, the position of Germany declined, while England and the Netherlands rose to preeminence. For a brief period Spain shared this preeminence, but she was ill-fitted to continue it. Her industrial development was too feeble to supply the demand for manufactured products from the European settlers in the Western Hemisphere. Accordingly, they turned to the north of Europe for the textiles, cutlery, and similar products they urgently needed. About 1535 Spain suffered a severe crisis which gradually spread to other countries.

The incidents or features of the Commercial Revolution have been partly suggested by the foregoing discussion of causes. The outstanding one was the rise of capitalism. Reduced to its simplest terms, capitalism may be defined as a system of production, distribution, and exchange in which accumulated wealth is invested by private owners for the sake of gain. Its essential features are private enterprise, competition for markets, and business for profit. Generally it involves also the wage system as a method of payment of workers; that is, a mode of payment based not upon the amount of wealth they create, but rather upon their ability to compete with one another for jobs. As indicated already, capitalism is the direct antithesis of the semistatic economy of the medieval guilds, in which production and trade were supposed to be conducted for the benefit of society with only a reasonable charge for the service rendered, instead of unlimited profits. Although capitalism did not come to its full maturity until the nineteenth century, nearly all of its cardinal features were developed during the Commercial Revolution.

A second important incident of the Commercial Revolution was the growth of banking. Because of the strong disapproval of usury, banking had scarcely been a respectable business during the Middle Ages. For centuries the little that was carried on was virtually monopolized by Moslems and Jews. Nevertheless, exceptions did exist. Descendants of the Lombards ignored the prohibitions of the Church. The rise of national monarchies toward the end of the Middle Ages led to borrowing on contract to pay for wars or for the operations of government. Lending money for interest on such contracts was not considered sinful if the king took the guilt upon himself in a special clause of the contract. By the fourteenth century the business of lending money for profit was an established business. The rate on loans to governments was often 15 per cent, and in times of crisis much higher. The real founders of banking were certain of the great commercial houses of the Italian cities. Most of them com-

Incidents of the Commercial Revolution: (1) the rise of capitalism

(2) the growth of banking

441

Jacob Fugger

(3) the expansion of credit facilities

bined money lending with the management of manufacturing enterprises in their localities. Notable among them was the Medici firm, with its headquarters in Florence, but with branches throughout Italy and as far north as Bruges. By the fifteenth century the banking business had spread to southern Germany and France. The leading firm in the north was that of the Fuggers of Augsburg, with a capital of $40,000,000. The Fuggers lent money to kings and bishops, served as brokers for the Pope in the sale of indulgences, and provided the funds that enabled Charles V to buy his election to the throne of the Holy Roman Empire. The rise of these private financial houses was followed by the establishment of government banks, intended to serve the monetary needs of the national states. The first in order of time was the Bank of Sweden (1657), but the one which was destined for the role of greatest importance in economic history was the Bank of England, founded in 1694. Although not technically under government control until 1946, it was the bank of issue for the government and the depositary of public funds.

The growth of banking was necessarily accompanied by the adoption of various aids to financial transactions on a large scale. Credit facilities were extended in such a way that a merchant in Amsterdam could purchase goods from a merchant in Venice by means of a bill of exchange issued by an Amsterdam bank. The Venetian merchant would obtain his money by depositing the bill of exchange in his local bank. Later the two banks would settle their accounts by comparing balances. Among the other facilities for the expansion of credit were the adoption of a system of payment by check in local transactions and the issuance of bank notes as a substitute for gold and silver. Both of these devices were introduced by the Italians and were gradually adopted in nothern Europe. The system of payment by check was particularly important in increasing the volume of trade, since the credit resources of the banks

The Antwerp Bourse. Built in the sixteenth century, it was the place of exchange for merchants from all countries.

THE COMMERCIAL REVOLUTION IN CENTRAL AND WESTERN EUROPE ca. 1500

could now be expanded far beyond the actual amounts of cash in their vaults.

The Commercial Revolution was not confined, of course, to the growth of trade and banking. Included in it also were fundamental changes in methods of production. The system of manufacture developed by the craft guilds in the later Middle Ages was rapidly becoming defunct. The guilds themselves, dominated by the master craftsmen, had grown selfish and exclusive. Membership in them was commonly restricted to a few privileged families. Besides, they were so completely choked by tradition that they were unable to

(4) the decline of the craft guilds and the rise of new industries

443

*Printing Plant in the Late
Seventeenth Century*

(5) the domes-
tic, or putting-out
system

Advantages and
disadvantages
of the domestic
system

444

make adjustments to changing conditions. Moreover, new industries had sprung up entirely outside the guild system. Characteristic examples were mining and smelting and the woolen industry. The rapid development of these enterprises was stimulated by technical advances, such as the invention of the spinning wheel and the stocking frame and the discovery of a new method of making brass, which saved about half of the fuel previously used. In the mining and smelting industries a form of organization was adopted similar to that which has prevailed ever since. The tools and plant facilities belonged to capitalists, while the workers were mere wage laborers subject to hazards of accident, unemployment, and occupational disease.

But the most typical form of industrial production in the Commercial Revolution was the domestic system, developed first of all in the woolen industry. The domestic system derives its name from the fact that the work was done in the homes of individual artisans instead of in the shop of a master craftsman. Since the various jobs in the manufacture of a product were given out on contract, the system is also known as the putting-out system. Notwithstanding the petty scale of production, the organization was basically capitalistic. The raw material was purchased by an entrepreneur (known as a clothier in the woolen industry) and assigned to individual workers, each of whom would complete his allotted task for a stipulated payment. In the case of the woolen industry the yarn would be given out first of all to the spinners, then to the weavers, fullers, and dyers in succession. When the cloth was finally finished, it would be taken by the clothier and sold in the open market for the highest price it would bring. The domestic system was, of course, not restricted to the manufacture of woolen cloth. As time went on, it was extended into many other fields of production. It tied in well with the new glorification of riches and with the conception of a dynamic economy. The capitalist could now thumb his nose at the old restrictions on profits. No association of his rivals could judge the quality of his product or the wages he paid to his workers. Perhaps best of all he could expand his business as he saw fit and introduce new techniques that would reduce costs or increase the volume of production.

Undoubtedly the domestic system had advantages for the workers themselves, especially as compared to its successor, the factory system. Though wages were low, there was no regular schedule of hours, and it was generally possible for the laborer to supplement his family income by cultivating a small plot of land and raising a few vegetables, at least. Furthermore, conditions of work in the homes were more healthful than in factories, and the artisan had his family to assist him with the simpler tasks. Freedom from the supervision of a foreman and from the fear of discharge for petty reasons must also be accounted definite advantages. On the other hand, it must not be forgotten that the workers were too widely scattered to organize effectively for common action. As a consequence they had

Merchants' Houses in Amsterdam, 17th Century. Several of the principal streets of Amsterdam are canals.

no means of protecting themselves from dishonest employers, who cheated them out of part of their wages or forced them to accept payment in goods. It is also true that toward the end of the Commercial Revolution the workers became more and more dependent upon the capitalists, who now furnished not only the raw materials but the tools and equipment as well. In some cases the laborers were herded into large central shops and compelled to work under a fixed routine. The difference between this and the high-pressure methods of the factory system was only a matter of degree.

That the Commercial Revolution would involve extensive changes in business organization was practically assured from the start. The prevailing unit of production and trade in the Middle Ages was the shop or store owned by an individual or a family. The partnership was also quite common, in spite of its grave disadvantage of unlimited liability of each of its members for the debts of the entire firm. Obviously no one of these units was well adapted to business involving heavy risks and a huge investment of capital. The first result of the attempt to devise a more suitable business organization was the formation of *regulated companies.* The regulated company was an association of merchants banded together for a common venture. The members did not pool their resources but agreed merely to cooperate for their mutual advantage and to abide by certain definite regulations. Usually the purpose of the combination was to maintain a monopoly of trade in some part of the world. Assessments were often paid by the members for the upkeep of docks and warehouses and especially for protection against "interlopers," as those traders were called who attempted to break into the monopoly. A leading example of this type of organization was

(6) changes in business organization; the growth of regulated companies

445

an English company known as the Merchant Adventurers, established for the purpose of trade with the Netherlands and Germany.

In the seventeenth century the regulated company was largely superseded by a new type of organization at once more compact and broader in scope. This was the *joint-stock company*, formed through the issuance of shares of capital to a considerable number of investors. Those who purchased the shares might or might not take part in the work of the company, but whether they did or not they were joint owners of the business and therefore entitled to share in its profits in accordance with the amount they had invested. The joint-stock company had numerous advantages over the partnership and the regulated company. First, it was a permanent unit, not subject to reorganization every time one of its members died or withdrew. And second, it made possible a much larger accumulation of capital, through a wide distribution of shares. In short, it possessed nearly every advantage of the modern corporation except that it was not a person in the eyes of the law with the rights and privileges guaranteed to individuals. While most of the early joint-stock companies were founded for commercial ventures, some were organized later in industry. A number of the outstanding trading combinations were also *chartered companies*. This means that they held charters from the government granting a monopoly of the trade in a certain locality and conferring extensive authority over the inhabitants. Through a charter of this kind the British East India Company ruled over India as if it were a private estate until 1784, and even in a sense until 1858. Other famous chartered companies were the Dutch East India Company, the Hudson's Bay Company, the Plymouth Company, and the London Company. The last of these founded the colony of Virginia and governed it for a time as company property.

The remaining feature of the Commercial Revolution which needs to be considered was the growth of a more efficient money economy. Money, of course, had been in use ever since the revival of trade in the eleventh century. Nevertheless, there were few coins with a value that was recognized other than locally. By 1300 the ducat of Venice and the florin of Florence, each with a value of about $4.00, had come to be accepted in Italy and also in the international markets of northern Europe. But no country could be said to have had a uniform monetary system. Nearly everywhere there was great confusion. Coins issued by kings circulated side by side with the money of local nobles and even with Saracenic currency. Moreover, the types of currency were modified frequently, and the coins themselves were often debased. A common method by which kings expanded their own personal revenues was to increase the proportion of cheaper metals in the coins they minted. But the growth of trade and industry in the Commercial Revolution accentuated the need for more stable and uniform monetary systems. The problem was solved by the adoption of a standard system of money by every

The Spanish Milled Dollar or "Piece of Eight." It was one of the first coins to have its circumference scored or "milled." It was cut into halves and quarters to make change.

important state to be used for all transactions within its borders. Much time elapsed, however, before the reform was complete. England began the construction of a uniform coinage during the reign of Queen Elizabeth, but the task was not finished until late in the seventeenth century. The French did not succeed in reducing their money to its modern standard of simplicity and convenience until the time of Napoleon. In spite of these long delays it appears safe to conclude that national currencies were really an achievement of the Commercial Revolution.

2. MERCANTILISM IN THEORY AND PRACTICE

The Commercial Revolution in its later stages was accompanied by the adoption of a new set of doctrines and practices known as mercantilism. In its broadest meaning, mercantilism may be defined as a system of government intervention to promote national prosperity and increase the power of the state. Though frequently considered as a program of economic policy exclusively, its objectives were quite largely political. The purpose of the intervention in economic affairs was not merely to expand the volume of manufacturing and trade, but also to bring more money into the treasury of the king, which would enable him to build fleets, equip armies, and make his government feared and respected throughout the world. Because of this close association with the ambitions of princes to increase their own power and the power of the states over which they ruled, mercantilism has sometimes been called *statism*. Certainly the system would never have come into existence had it not been for the growth of absolute monarchy in place of the weak, decentralized structure of feudalism. But kings alone did not create it. Naturally

The meaning of mercantilism

Coining Money in the Sixteenth Century. These coins were not "milled" and therefore were easily "clipped," a process of scraping portions of the valuable metal from the edges of the coin.

the new magnates of business lent support, since they would obviously derive great advantages from active encouragement of trade by the state. The heyday of mercantilism was the period between 1600 and 1700, but many of its features survived until the end of the eighteenth century.

If there was any one principle which held the central place in mercantilist theory, it was the doctrine of bullionism. This doctrine means that the prosperity of a nation is determined by the quantity of precious metals within its borders. The greater the amount of gold and silver a country contains, the more money the government can collect in taxes, and the richer and more powerful the state will become. The growth of such an idea was fostered by knowledge of the prosperity and power of Spain, which seemed to be the direct results of the flood of precious metals pouring in from her American colonies. But what of those countries that owned no bullion-producing colonies? How were *they* to achieve riches and power? For these questions the mercantilists had a ready answer. A nation without access to gold and silver directly should attempt to increase its trade with the rest of the world. If its government took steps to ensure that the value of exports would always exceed the value of imports, more gold and silver would come into the country than would have to be shipped out. This was called maintaining a "favorable balance of trade." To preserve this balance, three main devices would be necessary: first, high tariffs to reduce the general level of imports and to shut out some products entirely; second, bounties on exports; and third, extensive encouragement of manufactures in order that the nation might have as many goods to sell abroad as possible.

Other elements
of mercantilism:
economic na-
tionalism, pa-
ternalism, and
imperialism

The theory of mercantilism also included certain elements of economic nationalism, paternalism, and imperialism. By the first is meant the ideal of a self-sufficient nation. The policy of fostering new industries was not intended merely as a device for increasing exports, but also as a means of making the nation independent of foreign supplies. In similar fashion, the mercantilists argued that the government should exercise the functions of a watchful guardian over the lives of its citizens. Generous relief should be provided for the poor, including free medical attention if they were unable to pay for it. These things were to be done, however, not with any view to charity or justice, but mainly in order that the state might rest upon a secure economic foundation and have the support of a numerous and healthy citizenry in case of war. Finally, the mercantilists advocated the acquisition of colonies. Again, the primary purpose was not to benefit individual citizens of the mother country, but to make the nation strong and independent. The types of possessions most ardently desired were those that would enlarge the nation's hoard of bullion. If these could not be obtained, then colonies providing tropical products, naval stores, or any other commodities which the mother country could not produce would be acceptable. The theory which underlay this imperialism was the notion that colonies existed for the benefit of the state that owned them. For this reason they were not allowed to engage in manufacturing or shipping. Their function was to produce raw materials and to consume as large a proportion of manufactured products as possible. In this way they would infuse lifeblood into the industries of the mother country and thus give her an advantage in the struggle for world trade.

The majority of those who wrote on mercantilist theory were not professional economists but philosophers and men of action in the world of business. Among the political philosophers were such advocates of absolute monarchy as the Frenchman Jean Bodin (1530–1596) and the Englishman Thomas Hobbes (1588–1679), who were naturally disposed to favor any policy that would increase the wealth and power of the ruler. While most of the apologists for mercantilism were interested in it mainly as a device for promoting a favorable balance of trade, others conceived it as a species of paternalism for increasing prosperity within the country. For example, the Englishman Edward Chamberlayne advocated a policy somewhat similar to contemporary ideas of government spending. He recommended that the state should appropriate a huge fund for the relief of the poor and for the construction of public works as a means of stimulating business.

The defenders of mercantilism

Attempts to put various mercantilist doctrines into practice characterized the history of many of the nations of western Europe in the sixteenth and seventeenth centuries. The theories, however, were not universally applied. Spain, of course, had the initial advantage by reason of the flow of bullion from her American empire. And while the Spaniards did not need to resort to artificial devices in order to bring money into their country, their government nevertheless maintained a rigid control over commerce and industry. The policies of other nations were designed to make up for the lack of bullion-producing colonies by capturing a larger share of export trade. This naturally involved a program of bounties, tariffs, and extensive regulation of manufacturing and shipping. Mercantilist policies were largely adopted in England during the reign of Queen Elizabeth I and were continued by the Stuart monarchs and by Oliver Cromwell. Most of these rulers engaged in a furious scramble for colonies, bestowed monopolistic privileges upon trading companies, and sought in a wide variety of ways to control the economic activities of the citizens. The most interesting examples of mercantilist legislation in England were, first, the Elizabethan laws designed to eliminate idleness and stimulate production and, second, the Navigation Acts. By a series of laws enacted toward the end of the sixteenth century, Queen Elizabeth gave to the justices of the peace the authority to fix prices, regulate hours of labor, and compel every able-bodied citizen to work at some useful trade. The first of the Navigation Acts was passed in 1651 under Oliver Cromwell.

Mercantilism in practice: in Spain and in England

With the aim of destroying Dutch predominance in the carrying trade, it required that all colonial exports to the mother country should be carried in English ships. A second Navigation Act was passed in 1660, which provided not merely that colonial exports should be shipped in British vessels but prohibited the sending of certain "enumerated articles," especially tobacco and sugar, directly to Continental European ports. They were to be sent first of all to England, whence, after the payment of customs duties, they could be reshipped elsewhere. Both of these laws were based upon the principle that colonies should serve for the enrichment of the mother country.

The Germanic states during the Commercial Revolution were too completely occupied with internal problems to take an active part in the struggle for colonies and overseas trade. As a consequence, German mercantilism was concerned primarily with increasing the strength of the state from within. It partook of the dual character of economic nationalism and a program for a planned society. But, of course, the planning was done chiefly for the benefit of the government and only incidentally for that of the people as a whole. Because of their dominant purpose of increasing the revenues of the state, the German mercantilists are known as cameralists (from *Kammer*, a name given to the royal treasury). Most of them were lawyers and professors of finance. Cameralist ideas were put into practice by the Hohenzollern kings of Prussia, notably by Frederick William I (1713–1740) and Frederick the Great (1740–1786). The policies of these monarchs embraced a many-sided scheme of intervention and control in the economic sphere for the purpose of increasing taxable wealth and bolstering the power of the state. Marshes were drained, canals dug, new industries established with the aid of the government, and farmers instructed as to what crops they should plant. In order that the nation might become self-sufficient as soon as possible, exports of raw materials and imports of manufactured products were prohibited. The bulk of the revenues gained from these various policies went for military purposes. The standing army of Prussia was increased by Frederick the Great to 160,000 men.

The most thorough, if not the most deliberate, application of mercantilism was probably to be found in France during the reign of Louis XIV (1643–1715). This was due partly to the fact that the French state was the complete incarnation of absolutism and partly to the policies of Jean Baptiste Colbert (1619–1683), chief minister under *le grand monarque* from 1661 until his death. Colbert was no theorist but a practical politician, ambitious for personal power and intent upon magnifying the opportunities for wealth of the middle class, to which he belonged. He accepted mercantilism, not as an end in itself, but simply as a convenient means for increasing the wealth and power of the state and thereby gaining the approval of his sovereign. He firmly believed that France must acquire as large

Mercantilism in Germany: the cameralists

Jean Baptiste Colbert

an amount of the precious metals as possible. To this end he prohibited the export of money, levied high tariffs on foreign manufactures, and gave liberal bounties to encourage French shipping. It was largely for this purpose also that he fostered imperialism, hoping to increase the favorable balance of trade through the sale of manufactured goods to the colonies. Accordingly, he purchased islands in the West Indies, encouraged settlements in Canada and Louisiana, and established trading posts in India and in Africa. Furthermore, he was as devoted to the ideal of self-sufficiency as any of the cameralists in Prussia. He gave subsidies to new enterprises, established a number of state-owned industries, and even had the government purchase goods which were not really needed in order to keep struggling companies on their feet. But he was determined to keep the manufacturing industry under strict control, so as to make sure that companies would buy their raw materials only from French or colonial sources and produce the commodities necessary for national greatness. Consequently he clamped upon industry an elaborate set of regulations prescribing nearly every detail of the manufacturing process. Finally, it should be mentioned that Colbert took a number of steps to augment the political strength of the nation directly. He provided France with a navy of nearly 300 ships, drafting citizens from the maritime provinces and even criminals to man them. He sought to promote a rapid growth of population by discouraging young people from becoming monks or nuns and by exempting families with ten or more children from taxation.

3. THE RESULTS OF THE COMMERCIAL REVOLUTION

It goes without saying that the Commercial Revolution was one of the most significant developments in the history of the Western world. The whole pattern of modern economic life would have been impossible without it, for it changed the basis of commerce from the local and regional plane of the Middle Ages to the world-wide scale it has occupied ever since. Moreover, it exalted the power of money, inaugurated business for profit, sanctified the accumulation of wealth, and established competitive enterprise as the foundation of production and trade. In a word, the Commercial Revolution was responsible for a large number of the elements that go to make up the capitalist regime.

The foundation for modern capitalism

But these were not the only results. The Commercial Revolution brought into being wide fluctuations of economic activity. What we now call booms and recessions alternated with startling rapidity. The inflow of precious metals, combined with a "population explosion" which doubled the inhabitants of Europe between 1450 and 1650, led to rising prices and an unprecedented demand for goods. Businessmen were tempted to expand their enterprises too rapidly;

Booms and recessions

451

bankers extended credit so liberally that their principal borrowers, especially nobles, often defaulted on loans. Spain and Italy were among the first to suffer setbacks. In both, failure of wages to keep pace with rising prices brought incredible hardships to the lower classes. Impoverishment was rife in the cities, and banditry flourished in the rural areas. In Spain some ruined aristocrats were not too proud to join the throngs of vagrants who wandered from city to city. At the end of the fifteenth century the great Florentine bank of the Medici, with its branches in Venice, Rome, and Naples, closed its doors. The middle of the century that followed saw numerous bankruptcies in Spain and the decline of the Fuggers in Germany. Meanwhile, England, Holland, and to some extent France, waxed prosperous. This prosperity was especially characteristic of the "age of silver," which lasted from about 1540 to 1620. In the seventeenth century decline set in once more after inflation had spent its force, and as a consequence of religious and international wars and civil strife.

The alternation of booms and recessions was followed by orgies of speculation. These reached their climax early in the eighteenth century. The most notorious were the South Sea Bubble and the Mississippi Bubble. The former was the result of inflation of the stock of the South Sea Company in England. The promoters of this company agreed to take over a large part of the national debt and in return received from the English government an exclusive right to trade with South America and the Pacific islands. The prospects for profit seemed almost unlimited. The stock of the company rose rapidly in value until it was selling for more than ten times its original price. The higher it rose, the more gullible the public became. But gradually suspicion developed that the possibilities of the enterprise had been overrated. Buoyant hopes gave way to fears, and investors made frantic attempts to dispose of their shares for whatever they would bring. A crash was the inevitable result.

During the very same years when the South Sea Bubble was being inflated in England, the French were going through a similar wave of speculative madness. In 1715 a Scotsman by the name of John Law, who had been compelled to flee from British soil for killing his rival in a love intrigue, settled in Paris, after various successful gambling adventures in other cities. He persuaded the regent of France to adopt his scheme for paying off the national debt through the issuance of paper money and to grant him the privilege of organizing the Mississippi Company for the colonization and exploitation of Louisiana. As the government loans were redeemed, the persons who received the money were encouraged to buy stock in the company. Soon the shares began to soar, ultimately reaching a price forty times their original value. Nearly everyone who could scrape together a few livres of surplus cash rushed forward to participate in the scramble for riches. Stories were told of butchers and tailors who were supposed to have become millionaires by buying a few shares and holding them for a rise in price. But as the realization grew that the company would never be able to pay more than a nominal dividend on the stock at its inflated value, the more cautious investors began selling their holdings. The alarm spread, and soon everyone was as anxious to sell as he had been to buy. In 1720 the Mississippi Bubble burst in a wild panic. Thousands of people who had sold good property to buy the shares at fantastic prices were ruined. The collapse of the South Sea and Mississippi companies gave a temporary chill to the public ardor for gambling. It was not long, however, until the greed for speculative profits revived, and the stock-jobbing orgies that followed in the wake of the Commercial Revolution were repeated many times over during the nineteenth and twentieth centuries.

Among other results of the Commercial Revolution were the rise of the bourgeoisie to economic power, the beginning of Europeanization of the world, and the revival of slavery. Each of these requires brief comment. By the end of the seventeenth century the bourgeoisie had become an influential class in nearly every country of western Europe. Its ranks included the merchants, the bankers, the shipowners, the principal investors, and the industrial entrepreneurs. Their rise to power was mainly the result of increasing wealth and their tendency to ally themselves with the king against the remnants of the feudal aristocracy. But as yet their power was purely economic. Not until the nineteenth century did middle-class supremacy in politics become a reality. By the Europeanization of the world is meant the transplanting of European manners and culture in other continents. As a result of the work of traders, missionaries, and colonists, North and South America were rapidly stamped with the character of appendages of Europe. No more than a beginning was made in the transformation of Asia, but enough was done to foreshadow the trend of later times when even Japanese and Chinese would adopt Western locomotives and shell-rimmed spectacles. The most regrettable result of the Commercial Revolution was the revival of slavery. As we learned in our study of the Middle Ages, slavery practically disappeared from European civilization about the year 1000. But the development of mining and plantation farming in the English, Spanish, and Portuguese colonies led to a tremendous demand for unskilled labor. At first an attempt was made to enslave the American Indians, but they usually proved too hard to manage. The problem was solved in the sixteenth century by the importation of African Negroes. For the next 200 years and more, Negro slavery was an integral part of the European colonial system, especially in those regions producing tropical products.

Europeanization of the world and the revival of slavery

Finally, the Commercial Revolution was exceedingly important in preparing the way for the Industrial Revolution. This was true for a number of reasons. First, the Commercial Revolution created a class

Effects of the
Commercial
Revolution in
preparing
the way for the
Industrial
Revolution

of capitalists who were constantly seeking new opportunities to invest their surplus profits. Second, the mercantilist policy, with its emphasis upon protection for infant industries and production of goods for export, gave a powerful stimulus to the growth of manufactures. Third, the founding of colonial empires flooded Europe with new raw materials and greatly increased the supply of certain products which had hitherto been luxuries. Most of these required fabrication before they were available for consumption. As a consequence, new industries sprang up wholly independent of any guild regulations that still survived. The outstanding example was the manufacture of cotton textiles, which, significantly enough, was one of the first of the industries to become mechanized. Last of all, the Commercial Revolution was marked by a trend toward the adoption of factory methods in certain lines of production, together with technological improvements, such as the invention of the spinning wheel and the stocking frame, and the discovery of more efficient processes of refining ores. The connection between these developments and the mechanical progress of the Industrial Revolution is not hard to perceive.

4. REVOLUTIONARY DEVELOPMENTS IN AGRICULTURE

To a large extent the sweeping changes that occurred in agriculture between the fourteenth century and the eighteenth may be regarded as effects of the Commercial Revolution. For example, the rise in prices and the increase in urban population eventually made agriculture a profitable business and thus tended to promote its absorption into the capitalist system. In addition, the development of the woolen industry in England caused many landowners of that country to substitute the pasturing of flocks for ordinary farming as their principal source of income. But there were also other causes not directly connected with the Commercial Revolution at all. One was the influence of the Crusades and the Hundred Years' War in weakening the power of the nobles and in undermining the structure of the old society. Another was the reduction of the supply of agricultural labor on account of the Black Death and the influx of peasants into the cities and towns to take advantage of the new opportunities for a living resulting from the revival of trade with the Near East. A third was the opening up of new farms to cultivation under a system of free labor and individual enterprise. The combined effect of these factors was the destruction of the manorial system and the establishment of agriculture on something like its modern foundations. The transformation was most complete in England, but there were similar developments in other countries also.

An important development of the agricultural revolution was the enclosure movement, which was of notable importance in

England. This movement had two main aspects: first, the enclosing of the common wood and pasture lands of the manor, thereby abolishing the communal rights which the peasants had enjoyed of pasturing their flocks and gathering wood on the untilled portions of the lord's estate; and second, the eviction of large numbers of peasants from their leaseholds or other rights of tenantry on the arable lands. Both of these forms of enclosure resulted in much hardship for the rural population. For centuries the peasant's rights in the common pasture and woodlot had formed an essential element in his scheme of subsistence, and it was difficult for him to get along without them. But the fate of those peasants who were dispossessed entirely of their rights of tenantry was much more serious. In most cases they were forced to become landless wage earners or to make their way in the world as helpless beggars. The chief reason for the enclosures was the desire of the former feudal proprietors to convert as large an area of their estates as possible into pasturage for sheep, on account of the high price which could now be obtained for wool. Usually they began by fencing in the common lands as their own property. This was frequently followed by the conversion of many of the grain fields into pastures also, resulting in the eviction especially of those peasants whose leaseholds were none too secure. Enclosures began in the fifteenth century and were continued beyond the period of the Commercial Revolution. Even as late as 1819 hundreds of acts were still being passed by the British Parliament authorizing the eviction of tenants and the closing in of great estates. In the eighteenth and nineteenth centuries the process was accelerated by the ambition of capitalists to push their way into the aristocracy by becoming gentleman farmers. The enclosure movement completed the transformation of English agriculture into a capitalistic enterprise.

The enclosure movement

The final stage in the agricultural upheaval which accompanied or followed the Commercial Revolution was the introduction of new crops and improvements in mechanical equipment. Neither of these developments was conspicuous until the beginning of the eighteenth century. It was about this time that Lord Townshend in England discovered the value of raising clover as a means of preventing exhaustion of the soil. Not only is the effect of clover in reducing fertility much less than that of the cereal grains, but it actually helps to improve the quality of the soil by gathering nitrogen and making the ground more porous. The planting of this crop from time to time made unnecessary the old system of allowing one-third of the land to lie fallow each year. Further, the clover itself provided an excellent winter feed for animals, thereby aiding the production of more and better livestock. Only a small number of mechanical improvements were introduced into farming at this time, but they were of more than trivial significance. First came the adoption of the metal plowshare, which made possible a deeper and wider fur-

A Ball and Chain Pump. Men walking in the treadmill to the left powered this mid-sixteenth-century irrigation device.

row than could ever be accomplished with the primitive wooden plows handed down from the Middle Ages. For a time farmers were reluctant to use the new device in the belief that iron would poison the soil, but this superstition was eventually abandoned. The other most important mechanical improvement of this period was the drill for planting grain. The adoption of this invention eliminated the old wasteful method of sowing grain broadcast by hand, most of it remaining on top of the ground to be eaten by crows. Significant as these inventions were, however, the real mechanization of agriculture did not come until well along in the nineteenth century.

5. THE NEW SOCIETY

Profound changes in the texture of society inevitably accompany economic or intellectual revolutions. The society which was brought into being by the Renaissance, the Reformation, and the Commercial Revolution, though retaining characteristics of the Middle Ages, was really quite different in its underlying features. For one thing, the population of Europe was now considerably larger. The number of inhabitants of both Italy and England increased by approximately one-third during the single century from 1500 to 1600. In the same period the estimated population of Germany grew from 12,000,000 to 20,000,000. In 1378 London had a population of about 46,000; by 1605 the total had grown to about 225,000.[2] The reasons for these increases are closely related to the religious and economic developments of the time. Un-

Significant social changes: (1) a more rapid growth of population

[2] J. W. Thompson, *Economic and Social History of Europe in the Later Middle Ages,* p. 461; Preserved Smith, *The Age of the Reformation,* pp. 453–458.

Interior of a French Peasant's Cottage, Seventeenth Century. Virtually all activities centered about the hearth, the only source of heat for the entire dwelling.

doubtedly in nothern countries the overthrow of clerical celibacy and the encouragement of marriage were factors partly responsible. But far more important was the increase in means of subsistence brought about by the Commercial Revolution. Not only were new products, such as potatoes, maize, and chocolate, added to the food supply, but older commodities, especially sugar and rice, were now made available to Europeans in much larger quantities. In addition, the growth of new opportunities for making a living in industry and commerce enabled most countries to support a larger population than would ever have been possible under the predominantly agrarian economy of the Middle Ages. It is significant that the bulk of the increases occurred in the cities and towns.

A development of even greater consequence than the growth in population was the increasing equality and fluidity of classes. The Renaissance, the Reformation, and the accompanying Commercial Revolution were all, in some degree, leveling movements. It is an impressive fact that the majority of the men who rose to positions of leadership in Renaissance culture were not scions of the nobility. A few, Shakespeare among them, sprang from humble families and at least three men were of illegitimate birth—Boccoccio, Leonardo da Vinci, and Erasmus. The influence of the Renaissance in promoting social equality is illustrated also by the rise of the professions to a higher dignity than they had ever enjoyed in the Middle Ages. The artist, the writer, the lawyer, the university professor, and the physician emerged into a position of importance roughly comparable to that which they hold in modern society. This is confirmed by the incomes which many are known to have received. Michelangelo enjoyed a pension of thousands of dollars a year from the Pope. Raphael left an estate which even by modern standards would be considered princely.[3] Erasmus was able to live in luxury from the gifts and favors received from his patrons. Although few historians would now subscribe to Nietzsche's dictum that the Reformation was simply a revolt of the ignorant masses against their betters, the influence of that movement in weakening the old aristocracy cannot be ignored. By sanctifying the accumulation of wealth it did much to enthrone the middle class. As for the third of the great leveling movements, the Commercial Revolution, we need only recall its effects in providing the opportunities for any lucky or ambitious burgher to pile up a fortune and thereby to climb some of the higher rungs of the social ladder.

The condition of the lower classes did not improve at a rate commensurate with that of the bourgeoisie. Some historians deny that there was any improvement at all, but this view is open to debate. It is true that real wages remained very low: English masons and carpenters were paid the modern equivalent of not more than a dollar a day about 1550. Attempts were even made to prohibit by law any

(2) an increasing equality and fluidity of classes

(3) the modest gains of the lower classes

---

[3] Preserved Smith, *The Age of the Reformation*, p. 472.

The Peasants Revolt in Germany. This drawing shows the plunder of the monastery of Weissenau in 1525.

rise in the level of wages, as in the English Statute of Laborers of 1351. It is also true that there were numerous strikes and insurrections of the lower classes. The most serious were the Great Revolt in England in 1381 and the so-called Peasants' Revolt in Germany in 1524–1525. In both, large numbers of workers from the towns took part along with the peasants. But there were also uprisings of the urban proletariat alone. An example is furnished by the revolt of the workers of Florence between 1379 and 1382 against the denial of their right to form unions and to participate in the government of the city. This revolt, like the others, was put down with merciless severity. Desperate though these uprisings were, we cannot be sure that they indicate a condition of absolute wretchedness among the

lower classes. It must be understood that in a time of transition the
spirit of revolution is in the air. Indeed, the fact that revolts occurred may perhaps be taken as a sign that the lot of the workers
was not always deplorable. Men do not generally rebel unless their
economic condition has improved sufficiently to give them some
confidence of success. Finally, it is almost impossible to believe
that none of the working classes would share in the increasing
prosperity of the age. It is probably never strictly true that all of
the poor grow poorer while the rich grow richer.

Notwithstanding the cultural and economic progress of the period under review, social and moral conditions do not appear to
have sustained much improvement. For one thing, the new egoism
that characterized the middle and upper classes stood as a barrier to
more generous treatment of the least fortunate human beings. Hearing a disturbance outside his quarters, the Emperor Charles V, in
1552, was reported to have asked who were causing the commotion.
When told that they were poor soldiers, he said, "Let them die,"
and compared them to caterpillars, locusts, and June bugs that eat
the sprouts and other good things of the earth. As a rule, the most
pitiable fate was reserved for slaves and demented persons. For the
sake of big profits Negroes were hunted like beasts on the coast of
Africa and shipped to the American colonies. It may be of interest
to note that the Englishman who originated this body-snatching
business, Captain John Hawkins, called the ship in which he transported the victims the *Jesus*. In view of the fact that insanity was
regarded as a form of demonic possession, it is not strange that the
sufferers from this disease should have been cruelly treated. They
were generally confined in filthy barracks and flogged unmercifully
to drive the demons out of their bodies. A favorite diversion of
some of our ancestors was to organize parties to visit the madhouses
and tease the insane.

The immediate effect of the Reformation in improving conditions
of morality appears to have been almost negligible. Perhaps this is
explainable in part by the return to the legalism of the Old Testament. But probably the chief cause was the fierce antagonism between sects. A condition of war is never favorable to the growth of
a high morality. Whatever the reasons, the licentiousness and brutality continued unchecked. Even some of the clergy who were
closely identified with the work of religious reform could scarcely
be said to have been armored with the breastplate of righteousness.
An acquaintance of Luther's seems to have experienced no difficulty
in getting a new pastorate after he had been dismissed from an earlier one on charges of seduction. Several of the Protestant Reformers
considered polygamy less sinful than divorce, on the ground that
the former was recognized in the Old Testament while the latter
was prohibited in the New. So doubtful was the quality of moral
standards among the Catholic clergy that the Reformers of that

Social and moral
conditions

The effect of
the Reforma-
tion upon mor-
al standards

faith found it necessary to introduce the closed confessional box for the protection of female penitents. Formerly women as well as men had been required to kneel at the knees of the priest while confessing their sins. The effects of the Reformation upon the virtues of truthfulness and tolerance were woeful indeed. Catholic and Protestant Reformers alike were so obsessed with the righteousness of their own particular cause that they did not hesitate to make use of almost any extreme of falsehood, slander, or repression that seemed to guarantee victory for their side. For example, Luther expressly justified lying in the interests of religion, and the Jesuits achieved a reputation for tortuous reasoning and devious plotting for the advantage of the Church. No one seemed to have the slightest doubt that in the sphere of religion the end justified the means.

Effects of the coffee and tobacco habits

The widespread adoption of the tobacco and coffee habits in the seventeenth century ultimately had interesting social and perhaps physiological effects. Although the tobacco plant was brought into Europe by the Spaniards about fifty years after the discovery of America, another half century passed before many Europeans adopted the practice of smoking. At first the plant was believed to possess miraculous healing powers and was referred to as "divine tobacco" and "our holy herb nicotian." [4] The habit of smoking was popularized by English explorers, especially by Sir Walter Raleigh, who had learned it from the Indians of Virginia. It spread rapidly through all classes of European society despite the condemnation of the clergy and the "counterblaste" of King James I against it. The enormous popularity of coffee drinking in the seventeenth century had even more important social effects. Coffee houses or "cafes" sprang up all over Europe and rapidly evolved into leading institutions. They provided not merely an escape for the majority of men from a cribbed and monotonous home life, but they took others away from the sordid excesses of the tavern and the gambling-hell. In addition, they fostered a sharpening of wits and promoted more polished manners, especially inasmuch as they became favorite rendezvous for the literary lions of the time. If we can believe the testimony of English historians, there was scarcely a social or political enterprise which did not have its intimate connections with the establishments where coffee was sold. Some, indeed, were the rallying places of rival factions, which may in time have evolved into political parties. In London, according to Macaulay,

> There were coffee houses where the first medical men might be consulted. . . . There were Puritan coffee houses where no oath was heard and where lank-haired men discussed election and reprobation through their noses; Jew coffee houses where dark-eyed money-changers from Venice and Amsterdam

[4] The word "nicotian" or "nicotine" is derived from Jean Nicot, the French ambassador to Portugal who introduced the tobacco plant into France.

greeted each other; and Popish coffee houses where, as good
Protestants believed, Jesuits planned, over their cups, another
great fire, and cast silver bullets to shoot the king.[5]

Despite its remarkable attainments in intellect and the arts, the
period was by no means free from superstitions. Even at the peak
of the Renaissance numerous quaint and pernicious delusions continued to be accepted as valid truths. The illiterate masses clung to
their beliefs in goblins, satyrs, and wizards and to their fear of the
devil, whose malevolence was assumed to be the cause of diseases,
famine, storms, and insanity. But superstition was not harbored in the
minds of the ignorant alone. The famous astronomer, Johann Kepler, believed in astrology and depended upon the writing of almanacs, with predictions of the future according to signs and
wonders in the heavens, as his chief source of income. Not only did
Sir Francis Bacon accept the current superstition of astrology, but
he also contributed his endorsement of the witchcraft delusion.
Eventually the enlightenment of the Renaissance might have eliminated most of the harmful superstitions if a reaction had not set in
during the Reformation. The emphasis of the Reformers upon faith,
their contempt for reason and science, and their incessant harping
on the wiles of the devil fostered an attitude of mind decidedly
favorable to prejudice and error. Besides, the furor of hate stirred
up by religious controversy made it almost impossible for the average man to view his social and individual problems in a calm and intelligent spirit.

The persistence of superstitions

The worst of all the superstitions that flourished in this period
was unquestionably the witchcraft delusion. Belief in witchcraft
was by no means unknown in the Middle Ages or even in the early
Renaissance, but it never reached the proportions of a dangerous
madness until after the beginning of the Protestant Revolution. And
it is a significant fact that the persecutions attained their most
virulent form in the very countries where religious conflict raged
the fiercest, that is, in Germany and France. The witchcraft superstition was a direct outgrowth of the belief in Satan which obsessed
the minds of so many of the Reformers. Luther maintained that he
often talked with the Evil One and sometimes put him to rout after
a session of argument by calling him unprintable names.[6] Calvin insisted that the Pope never acted except on the advice of his patron
the devil. In general, the tendency of each camp of theologians was
to ascribe all the victories of their opponents to the uncanny powers
of the Prince of Darkness. With such superstitions prevailing among
religious leaders, it is not strange that the mass of their followers
should have harbored bizarre and hideous notions. The belief grew
that the devil was really more powerful than God, and that no man's
life or soul was safe from destruction. It was assumed that Satan not

The witch-craft delusion

[5] Thomas Babington Macaulay, *History of England*, I, 335.
[6] Preserved Smith, *The Age of the Reformation*, p. 653.

461

only tempted mortals to sin, but actually forced them to sin by sending his minions in human form to seduce men and women in their sleep. This was the height of his malevolence, for it jeopardized chances of salvation.

According to the definition of the theologians, witchcraft consisted in selling one's soul to the devil in return for supernatural powers. It was believed that a woman who had concluded such a bargain was thereby enabled to work all manner of spiteful magic against her neighbors—to cause their cattle to sicken and die, their crops to fail, or their children to fall into the fire. But the most valuable gifts bestowed by Satan were the power to blind husbands to their wives' misconduct or to cause women to give birth to idiots or deformed infants. It is commonly assumed that the so-called witches were toothless old hags whose cranky habits and venomous tongues had made them objects of suspicion and dread to all who knew them. Undoubtedly a great many of the victims of the Salem trials in Massachusetts in 1692 did belong to this class. However, the writers on the Continent of Europe generally imagined the witch to be a "fair and wicked young woman," and a large percentage of those put to death in Germany and France were adolescent girls and matrons not yet thirty.[7]

The earliest persecutions for witchcraft were those resulting from the crusades launched against heretics by the Papal Inquisition in the thirteenth century. With the growth of intolerance of heresy it was probably inevitable that members of sects like the Albigenses should be accused of trafficking with the devil. But the amount of persecution in this period was comparatively small. A second campaign against witches was initiated by Pope Innocent VIII in 1484, who instructed his inquisitors to use torture in procuring convictions. But, as we have already seen, it was not until after the beginning of the Protestant Revolution that witchcraft persecution became a mad hysteria. Luther himself provided some of the impetus by recommending that witches should be put to death with fewer considerations of mercy than were shown to ordinary criminals. Other Reformers quickly followed Luther's example. Under Calvin's administration in Geneva thirty-four women were burned or quartered for the alleged crime in 1545.[8] From this time on the persecutions spread like a pestilence. Women, young girls, and even mere children were tortured by driving needles under their nails, roasting their feet in the fire, or crushing their legs under heavy weights until the marrow spurted from their bones, in order to force them to confess filthy orgies with demons. To what extent the persecutions were due to sheer sadism or to the greed of magistrates, who were sometimes permitted to confiscate the property of those convicted, is impossible to say. Certainly there were few people who

The definition of witchcraft

Hanging Witches. A woodcut from the late sixteenth century.

---

[7] Preserved Smith, *A History of Modern Culture*, I, 436–37.
[8] Preserved Smith, *The Age of the Reformation*, p. 656.

did not believe that the burning of witches was justifiable. One of the most zealous defenders of the trials was the political philosopher, Jean Bodin. As late as the eighteenth century John Wesley declared that to give up the belief in witchcraft was to give up the Bible.

The witchcraft persecutions reached their peak during the later years of the sixteenth century. The number of victims will never be known, but it was certainly not fewer than 30,000. We read of cities in Germany in which as many as 900 were put to death in a single year, and of whole villages in which practically no women were left alive.

The peak of the witchcraft persecutions

After 1600 the mania gradually subsided on the Continent of Europe, though it continued for some years longer in England. The reasons for the decline are not far to seek. In some measure it was the consequence of a recovery of sanity by the people themselves, particularly as the fogs of suspicion and hate produced by religious warfare gradually lifted. But the principal causes were the revival of reason and the influence of scientists and skeptical philosophers. At the very zenith of the witch-burning frenzy certain lawyers began to have doubts as to the value of the evidence admitted at the trials. In 1584 an English jurist by the name of Reginald Scott published a book condemning the belief in witchcraft as irrational and asserting that most of the lurid crimes confessed by accused women were mere figments of disordered minds. Such eminent scientists as Pierre Gassendi (1592–1655) and William Harvey also denounced the persecutions. But the most effective protest of all came from the pen of Montaigne. This distinguished French skeptic directed the shafts of his most powerful ridicule against the preposterous nonsense of the sorcery trials and the cruelty of men like Bodin who would have witches killed on mere suspicion.

The end of the witchcraft persecutions

From what has been said in preceding paragraphs the conclusion must not be drawn that the period of the Renaissance, the Reformation, and the Commercial Revolution was an age of universal depravity. Of course, there were numerous individuals as urbane and tolerant as any who lived in less boisterous times. It must be remembered also that this was the age of Sir Thomas More and Erasmus, who were at least as civilized as the majority of men historians have chosen to honor. The enormous popularity of Castiglione's *Book of the Courtier* may likewise be taken to indicate that the period was not hopelessly barbarous. This treatise, which ran through more than 100 editions, set forth the ideal of a knight who was not merely brave in battle and accomplished in the social graces, but courteous, unaffected, and just. In spite of all this, the dolorous fact remains that for large numbers of men ethics had lost their true meaning. The cardinal aims were now gratification of self and victory in the struggle to make the whole world conform to one's own set of dogmas. Perhaps these were inevitable accompaniments of the chaotic transition from the impersonal society of the Middle Ages.

The age not one of universal depravity

463

SELECTED READINGS

· *Items so designated are available in paperbound editions.*

· Burckhardt, Jacob, *The Civilization of the Renaissance in Italy*, London, 1890 (Mentor, Torchbook, 2 vols.) No longer considered authoritative.

· de Roover, Raymond, *The Rise and Decline of the Medici Bank, 1397–1494*, Cambridge, 1964 (Norton Library).

· Ford, Franklin, *Robe and Sword*, Cambridge, 1953 (Torchbook).

· Haring, C. H., *The Spanish Empire in America*, New York, 1947 (Harbinger). One of the best studies of the subject.

Heaton, Herbert, *Economic History of Europe*, New York, 1936.

Heckscher, E. E., *Mercantilism*, New York, 1935, 2 vols.

Kimble, G. H. T., *Geography in the Middle Ages*, London, 1938. A graphic account of geographic notions before the time of Columbus.

Morison, S. E., *Admiral of the Ocean Sea; A Life of Christopher Columbus*, Boston, 1942, 2 vols.

· Nowell, C. E., *The Great Discoveries and the First Colonial Empires*, Ithaca, N.Y., 1954 (Cornell). Brief but good.

Ogg, F. A., and Sharp, W. R., *Economic Development of Modern Europe*, New York, 1929.

Packard, L. B., *The Commercial Revolution*, New York, 1927.

Parr, C. M., *So Noble a Captain: The Life and Times of Ferdinand Magellan*, New York, 1953. Scholarly.

· Penrose, Boies, *Travel and Discovery in the Renaissance (1420–1620)*, Cambridge, Mass., 1952 (Atheneum).

Randall, J. H., Jr., *The Making of the Modern Mind*, New York, 1926, Chs. VI–X.

Rees, William, *Industry before the Industrial Revolution*, Cardiff, 1968, 2 vols.

Sée, Henri, *Modern Capitalism: Its Origin and Evolution*, London, 1928.

· Smith, Preserved, *The Age of the Reformation*, New York, 1920 (Collier, 2 vols.).

· ———, *A History of Modern Culture*, New York, 1930, Vol. I (Collier).

Sombart, Werner, *The Quintessence of Capitalism*, London, 1915. A suggestive interpretation.

· Sykes, P., *A History of Exploration from the Earliest Times to the Present*, London, 1934 (Torchbook). Comprehensive.

· Tawney, R. H., *Religion and the Rise of Capitalism*, New York, 1926 (Mentor).

Wrong, G. M., *The Rise and Fall of New France*, New York, 1928, 2 vols. A thorough account.

SOURCE MATERIALS

· More, Sir Thomas, *Utopia*, Part I, pp. 175–78, the Enclosure Movement (Penguin and others).

· Mun, Thomas, *England's Treasure by Foreign Trade*, Chs. I–IV, XX, XXI.

Richter, J. P., *The Literary Works of Leonardo da Vinci*, Vol. II, pp. 304–5, Leonardo da Vinci on Witchcraft, New York, 1939, 2 vols.

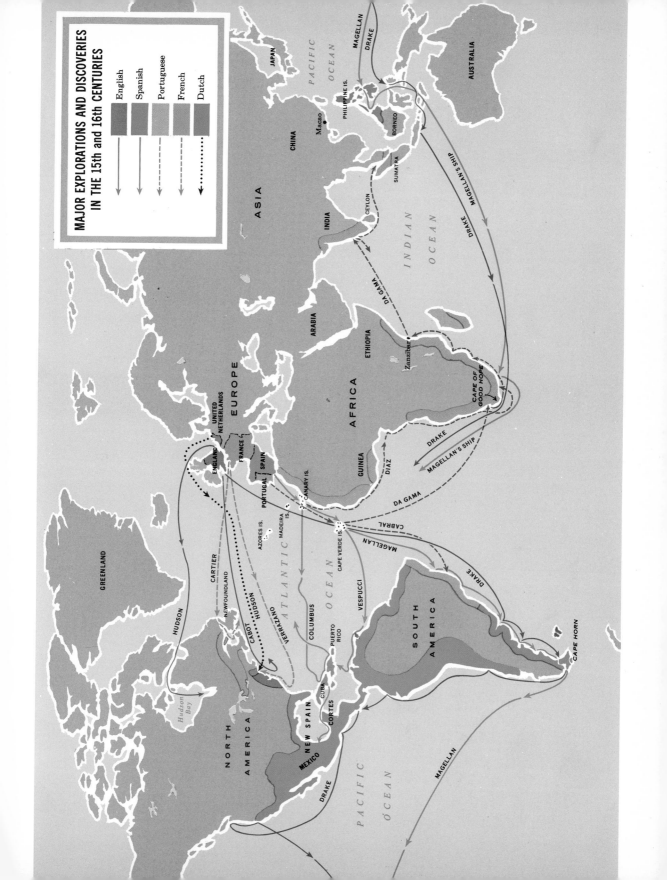

MAJOR EXPLORATIONS AND DISCOVERIES
IN THE 15th and 16th CENTURIES

English
Spanish
Portuguese
French
Dutch

RUSSIA

SWEDEN

Stockholm

Christiania

DENMARK

Copenhagen

BALTIC SEA

POLAND

Kiev

Warsaw

Danzig

E. PRUSSIA

Vistula R.

BRANDENBURG

Berlin

MECKLEN-BURG

HANOVER

Hamburg

HESSE

SAXONY

Elbe R.

WÜRTEN-BERG

BAVARIA

AUSTRIA

Vienna

Budapest

HUNGARY

Danube R.

SWITZ.

Rhine R.

MILAN

VENICE

Venice

(To Venice)

Zara

Adriatic Sea

OTTOMAN EMPIRE

BLACK SEA

Constantinople

AEGEAN SEA

CYPRUS
(To Ottoman Empire)

CRETE
(To Venice)

UNITED PROVINCES

Amsterdam

NETH.

SPANISH NETH.

LORRAINE

FRANCHE-COMTÉ

SAVOY

PIEDMONT

GENOA

PARMA

MODENA

TUSCANY

Florence

PAPAL STATES

Rome

Naples

KINGDOM OF THE
TWO SICILIES

Ragusa

Cattaro

(To Venice)

Paris

Seine R.

FRANCE

AVIGNON

Marseilles

Loire R.

Garonne R.

Bordeaux

CORSICA
(To Genoa)

SARDINIA
(To Spain)

BALEARIC
ISLANDS

MEDITERRANEAN SEA

ALGERIA

TUNIS

OTTOMAN EMPIRE

SCOTLAND

Edinburgh

ENGLAND

London

Liverpool

Bristol

IRELAND

Dublin

English Channel

NORTH SEA

ATLANTIC OCEAN

PORTUGAL

Lisbon

SPAIN

Madrid

Tagus R.

Ebro R.

Strait of Gibraltar

500 miles

Le Mezzetin, Antoine Watteau (1684–1721). Mezzetin was a popular character in Italian comedy who was much liked in France. Watteau enjoyed portraying the make-believe world of the court with its festivals and formalized elegance. (MMA)

The Blue Boy, Thomas Gainsborough (1727–1788). Though the costume suggests the romantic ideal of Prince Charming, the face is a penetrating study of the moodiness and uncertainty of adolescence. (Huntington Library)

Sarah Siddons as the Tragic Muse, Sir Joshua Reynolds (1723–1792). Mrs. Siddons, a famous actress of the XVIII cent., is here portrayed as the Queen of Tragedy, in accordance with Reynolds' habit of depicting wealthy patrons in impressive classical poses. (Huntington Library)

Above: *Landscape with the Burial of Phocion*, Nicolas Poussin (1594–1665). Many consider his paintings of the Roman hills to be models of French classicism. (Louvre) Left: *The Calling of St. Matthew*, Caravaggio (1573–1610). Painted for the altarpiece of the Church of San Luigi dei Francesci, Rome. (Scala)

CHAPTER 17

The Age of Absolutism (1485-1789)

> There are four essential characteristics or qualities of royal authority.
> First, royal authority is sacred.
> Second, it is paternal.
> Third, it is absolute.
> Fourth, it is subject to reason.
>
> —Jacques Bossuet, *Politics Drawn from the Very Words of Holy Scripture*

It becomes necessary now to go back and attempt to analyze the major political developments which accompanied the birth of modern civilization. During the fourteenth and fifteenth centuries the decentralized feudal regime of the Middle Ages broke down and was gradually replaced by dynastic states with governments of absolute power. For this there were numerous causes, some of which have already been discussed.[1] The position of the nobles was weakened by the growth of an urban economy, by the decay of the manorial system, and by the effects of the Crusades, the Black Death, and the Hundred Years' War. But these factors would not necessarily have laid the foundations for absolute monarchy. They might just as conceivably have resulted in chaos or in the democratic rule of the masses. We must therefore look for other causes to account for the rise of despotic governments. Apparently the most significant of these causes were the wars of the sixteenth and seventeenth centuries. These wars were themselves a product of a variety of factors. With the decay of feudalism, great struggles occurred between the forces of centralization and the forces of localism or decentralization. Ambitious kings sought to eliminate powerful princes and dukes who in some cases were their overlords. Struggles for empire also resulted from the geographic expansion incident to the Commercial Revolution. From the

The rise of the new absolutism

[1] See especially the paragraphs on the decline of feudalism in the chapter on The Later Middle Ages: Political and Economic Institutions.

colonies and into the royal coffers flowed wealth which was used in many cases to build navies and to hire professional soldiers. To organize and equip armies and fleets, large bureaucracies of civil servants became necessary. These also aided in the consolidation of monarchical power. Finally, the Protestant Revolution contributed not a little to the growth of royal omnipotence. It broke the unity of the Christian Church, abolished papal overlordship over secular rulers, fostered nationalism, revived the doctrine of the Apostle Paul that "the powers that be are ordained of God," and encouraged the kings of northern Europe to extend their authority over religious as well as over civil affairs.

1. THE GROWTH AND DECAY OF ABSOLUTE GOVERNMENT IN ENGLAND

Absolutism in England founded by the Tudor monarchs

The real founders of despotic government in England were the Tudors. The first of the kings of this line, Henry VII, came to the throne in 1485 at the end of the Wars of the Roses, in which rival factions of nobles had fought each other to the point of exhaustion. So great was the disgust on account of the turmoil of these wars that many of the citizens welcomed the establishment of absolute monarchy as an alternative to anarchy. The middle class, especially, desired the protection of consolidated government. This factor more than anything else accounts for the remarkable success of the Tudors in regulating the consciences of their subjects and in binding the nation to their will. It should be added that the most celebrated members of the dynasty, Henry VIII (1509–1547) and Elizabeth I (1558–1603), gained some of their power through shrewdly maintaining a semblance of popular government. When they desired to enact measures of doubtful popularity, they regularly went through the formality of obtaining parliamentary approval. Or when they wanted more money, they manipulated procedure in such a way as to make the appropriations appear to be voluntary grants by the representatives of the people. But the legislative branch of the government under these sovereigns was little more than a rubber stamp. They convoked Parliament irregularly and limited its sessions to very brief periods;[2] they interfered with elections and packed the two houses with their own favorites; and they cajoled, flattered, or bullied the members as the case might require in order to obtain their support.

The establishment of divine-right monarchy by James I

In 1603 Elizabeth I, the last of the Tudors, died, leaving no direct descendants. Her nearest relative was her cousin, King James VI of Scotland, who now became the sovereign of both England and Scotland under the name of James I. His accession marks the beginning of the troubled history of the Stuarts, the last of

---

[2] During Elizabeth's reign it was in session on the average only three or four weeks out of the year.

Queen Elizabeth I (1558–1603).
In this regal portrait the queen
is shown armed with the two
symbols of power and justice,
the scepter and the orb. A
touch of cynicism seems to be
revealed in her face.

the absolute dynasties in England. A curious mixture of stubbornness, vanity, and erudition, King James was appropriately
called by Henry IV of France "the wisest fool in Christendom."
Though he loved to have his courtiers flatter him as the English
Solomon, he did not even have sense enough to emulate his Tudor
predecessors in being satisfied with the substance of absolute power;
he insisted upon the theory as well. From France he appropriated
the doctrine of the divine right of kings, contending that "as it is
atheism and blasphemy to dispute what God can do, so it is pre-
sumption and high contempt in a subject to dispute what a king can
do." In his speech to Parliament in 1609, he declared that "Kings are
justly called gods, for they exercise a manner of resemblance of Divine power upon earth." [3]

That such ridiculous pretensions to divine authority would arouse
opposition among the English people was a result which even James
himself should have been able to foresee. Despite the clever machinations of the Tudor sovereigns and the desire of the middle class
for stable government, England still had traditions of liberty which
could not be ignored. The feudal ideal of limited government expressed in Magna Carta had never been entirely destroyed. Moreover, the policies of the new king were of such a character as to
antagonize even some of his most conservative subjects. He insisted
upon supplementing his income by modes of taxation which had
never been sanctioned by Parliament; and when the leaders of that
body remonstrated, he angrily tore up their protests and dissolved

The high-
handed policies
of James I

[3] Quoted by R. G. Gettell, *History of Political Thought*, p. 201.

the two houses. He interfered with the freedom of business by granting monopolies and extravagant privileges to favored companies. He conducted foreign relations in disregard for the economic interests of some of the most powerful citizens. Ever since the days of Hawkins and Drake, English merchants had been ambitious to destroy the commercial empire of Spain. They openly desired a renewal of the war, begun during Elizabeth's reign, for that purpose. But James made peace with Spain and entered into negotiations for marriage alliances favorable to Catholic sovereigns.

It was not marriage alliances alone that involved King James in religious troubles. The Elizabethan Compromise, which brought the Reformation in England to a close, had not been satisfactory to the more radical Protestants. They believed that it did not depart widely enough from the forms and doctrines of the Roman Church. During the reign of Queen Mary many of them had been in exile in France and had come under the influence of Calvinism. When Elizabeth's compromise policy took shape, they denounced it as representing too great a concession to Catholicism. Gradually they came to be called Puritans from their desire to "purify" the Anglican church of all traces of "Popish" ritual and observances. In addition, they preached an ascetic morality and condemned the episcopal system of church government. However, they did not form a united group. One faction believed that it could transform the Anglican church by working within that organization. The other preferred to withdraw from the Anglican fold and establish separate congregations where they could worship as they pleased. The members of this latter group came to be designated Separatists. They achieved fame in American history as the so-called Pilgrims, who founded Plymouth Colony.

Any brand or faction of Puritans was anathema to King James. Though not much interested in theology, he distrusted any religion that did not fit in with his own ideas of relations between church and state. In his estimation the Puritans, by repudiating the episcopal system of church government, were threatening to pull down one of the chief pillars of monarchy itself. Refusal to submit to the authority of bishops appointed by the king was identical in his mind with disloyalty to the sovereign. For this reason he regarded the Puritans as the equivalent of traitors and threatened to "harry them out of the land." He showed little more wisdom or discretion in his dealings with the Catholics. For the most part, he favored them, though he could not resist the temptation to levy fines upon them from time to time for violating the severe code which came down from the Reformation. In 1605 a group of fanatical adherents of the Roman faith organized the Gunpowder Plot. They planned to blow up the Parliament building while the king and the legislators were assembled in it, and in the resulting confusion, seize control of the government. The plot was discovered, and Parliament enacted even

Religious dissension during the reign of James I

Relations with Puritans and Catholics

more stringent laws against the Catholics. James, however, allowed the measures to go unenforced. Needless to say, his persistent leniency antagonized his Protestant subjects and made him more unpopular than ever.

From 1611 to 1621 King James ruled virtually without Parliament. But this did not mean that his troubles were over. In 1613 the rights of the people found a new champion when Sir Edward Coke was appointed Chief Justice. Coke was no democrat, but he did have a profound reverence for the common law and for the basic liberties inferred from Magna Carta. Moreover, he was a staunch defender of the privileged position of lawyers and judges. When the king insisted that he also had the faculty of reason and could interpret the law as well as the judges, Coke reminded him that he was not learned in the law, and that causes which concerned the lives and fortunes of his subjects were not be be decided by natural reason but only on the basis of long study and experience. Furthermore, the Chief Justice developed a rudimentary concept of judicial review. In the celebrated Dr. Bonham's case, he held that "when an act of Parliament is against common right and reason, or repugnant, or impossible to be performed, the common law will control it, and adjudge such act to be void." [4] There is evidence that this opinion was highly regarded in colonial America, and that it was one of the factors which later gave rise to the idea that the Supreme Court of the United States has the authority to nullify laws of Congress which conflict with the Constitution.

The revolt of the judiciary

The first of the Stuart kings died in 1625 and was succeeded by his son as Charles I (1625–1649). The new monarch was more regal in appearance than his father, but he held the same inflated notions of royal power. As a consequence he was soon in hot water with the Puritans and the leaders of the parliamentary opposition. As in the case of his father, the conflict was precipitated by questions of taxation. Soon after his accession to the throne Charles became involved in a war with France. His need for revenue was desperate. When Parliament refused to make more than the customary grants, he resorted to forced loans from his subjects, punishing those who failed to comply by quartering soldiers upon them or throwing them into prison without a trial. The upshot of this tyranny was the famous Petition of Right, which Charles was compelled by the leaders of Parliament to agree to in 1628. This document declared all taxes not voted by Parliament illegal. It condemned also the quartering of soldiers in private houses and prohibited arbitrary imprisonment and the establishment of martial law in time of peace.

Charles I and the Petition of Right

But acceptance of the Petition of Right did not end the conflict. Charles soon resumed his old tricks of raising money by various irregular means. He revived obsolete feudal laws and collected fines

[4] Quoted by George H. Sabine, *A History of Political Theory*, p. 452.

from all who violated them. He compelled rich burghers to apply for knighthood and then charged them high fees for their titles. He sold monopolies at exorbitant rates and admonished his judges to increase the fines in criminal cases. But the most unpopular of all his

The continued tyranny of Charles I

expedients for raising revenue was his collection of ship money. Under an ancient custom the English seaboard towns had been required to contribute ships for the royal navy. Since the needs of the fleet were now provided for in other ways, Charles maintained that the towns should contribute money; and he proceeded to apply the new tax not merely to the coastal cities but to the inland counties as well. The levies of ship money were particularly irritating to the middle class and served to crystallize the opposition of that group to monarchical tyranny. Many refused to pay, and the king's attorney-general finally decided to prosecute. A wealthy squire by the name of John Hampden was haled into court in a test case. When convicted by a vote of seven to five, he acquired a sort of martyrdom. For years he was venerated by the middle class as a symbol of resistance to royal autocracy.

Like his blundering father before him, Charles also aroused the antagonism of the Calvinists. He appointed as Archbishop of Canterbury a clergyman by the name of William Laud, whose sympa-

Conflict with the Calvinists

thies were decidedly high-Anglican. He outraged the Sabbatarianism of the Puritans by authorizing public games on Sunday. Worse still, he attempted to impose the episcopal system of church government upon the Scottish Presbyterians, who were even more radical Calvinists than the Puritans. The result was an armed rebellion by his northern subjects.

In order to get money to punish the Scots for their resistance, Charles was finally compelled in 1640 to summon Parliament, after

The outbreak of civil war

more than eleven years of autocratic rule. Knowing full well that the king was helpless without money, the leaders of the House of Commons determined to take the government of the country into their own hands. They abolished ship money and the special tribunals which had been used as agencies of tyranny. They impeached and sent to the Tower the king's chief subordinates, Archbishop Laud and the Earl of Strafford. They enacted a law forbidding the monarch to dissolve Parliament and requiring sessions at least every three years. Charles replied to these invasions of his prerogative by a show of force. He marched with his guard into the House of Commons and attempted to arrest five of its leaders. All of them escaped, but the issue was now sharply drawn between king and Parliament, and an open conflict could no longer be avoided. Both sides collected troops and prepared for an appeal to the sword.

These events ushered in a period of civil strife, which lasted from 1642 to 1649. It was a struggle at once political, economic, and religious. Arrayed on the side of the king were most of the chief nobles and landowners, the Catholics, and the staunch Anglicans. The followers of Parliament included, in general, the small landholders, tradesmen, and manufacturers. The majority were Puritans and Presbyterians. The members of the king's party were commonly known by the aristocratic name of Cavaliers. Their opponents, who cut their hair short in contempt for the fashionable custom of wearing curls, were called in derision Roundheads. At first the party of the royalists, having obvious advantages of military experience, won most of the victories. In 1644, however, the parliamentary army was reorganized, and soon afterward the fortunes of battle shifted. The Cavalier forces were badly beaten, and in 1646 the king was compelled to surrender. The struggle would now have ended had not a quarrel developed within the parliamentary party. The majority of its members, who were now Presbyterians, were ready to restore Charles to the throne as a limited monarch under an arrangement whereby the Presbyterian faith would be imposed upon England as the state religion. But a radical minority of Puritans, made up principally of Separatists but now more commonly known as Independents, distrusted Charles and insisted upon religious toleration for themselves and all other Protestants. Their leader was Oliver Cromwell (1599–1658), who had risen to command of the Roundhead army. Taking advantage of the dissension within the ranks of his opponents, Charles renewed the war in 1648 but after a brief campaign was forced to concede that his cause was hopeless.

The second defeat of the king gave an indisputable mastery of the situation to the Independents. Cromwell and his friends now resolved to put an end to "that man of blood," the Stuart monarch, and remodel the political system in accordance with their own desires. They conducted a purge of the legislative body by military force, ejecting 143 Presbyterians from the House of Commons; and then with the "Rump Parliament" that remained—numbering about sixty members—they proceeded to eliminate the monarchy. An act was passed redefining treason so as to apply to the offenses of the king. Next a special High Court of Justice was established, and Charles was brought to trial before it. His conviction was a mere matter of form. On January 30, 1649, he was beheaded in front of his palace of Whitehall. A short time later the House of Lords was abolished, and England became an oligarchic republic. The first stage in the so-called Puritan Revolution was now completed.

The work of organizing the new state, which was given the name of the Commonwealth, was entirely in the hands of the Independents. Since the Rump Parliament continued as the legislative body, the really fundamental change was in the nature of the executive. In place of the king there was set up a Council of State composed of forty-one members. Cromwell, with the army at his back, soon came to dominate both of these bodies. However, as time went on he became exasperated by the attempts of the legislators to perpetuate themselves in power and to profit from confiscation of the wealth of their opponents. Accordingly, in 1653, he marched a

Cavaliers and
Roundheads

The defeat and
execution of
the king

Oliver Cromwell

471

The Trial of Charles I, King of Great Britain and Ireland, 1625–1649. His armies defeated by the forces of Cromwell and himself a prisoner, Charles was tried by a special court in Westminster Hall and convicted of treason "by levying war against the parliament and kingdom of England." Soon afterward he was beheaded. His dignity in his last hours fitted Shakespeare's lines: "Nothing in his Life became him, like the leaving it."

The Commonwealth and Protectorate

detachment of troops into the Rump and ordered the members to disperse, informing them that the Lord Jehovah had no further use for their services. This action was followed by the establishment of a virtual dictatorship under a constitution drafted by officers of the army. Called the Instrument of Government, it was the nearest approach to a written constitution Britain has ever had. Extensive powers were given to Cromwell as Lord Protector for life, and his office was made hereditary. At first a Parliament exercised limited authority in making laws and levying taxes, but in 1655 its members were abruptly dismissed by the Lord Protector. Thereafter the government was but a thinly disguised autocracy. Cromwell now wielded a sovereignty even more despotic than any the Stuart monarchs would have dared to claim. In declaring his authority to be from God he even revived what practically amounted to the divine right of kings.

Cromwell's opponents

That Cromwell's regime would have its difficulties was certainly to be expected, since it rested upon the support of only a small minority of the British nation. He was opposed not only by royalists and Anglicans but by various dissenters more radical than he. Like all upheavals of a similar character, the Puritan Revolution tended to move farther and farther in an extremist direction. Many of the Puritans became Levellers, who derived their name from their advocacy of equal political rights and privileges for all classes. Expressly disclaiming any intention of equalizing property, they confined their radicalism to the political sphere. They insisted that sovereignty inheres in the people and that government should rest upon the consent of the governed. Long in advance of any other party, they demanded a written constitution, universal manhood suffrage, and the supremacy of Parliament. The Levellers were especially powerful in the army and through it exerted some influence upon the government. Still farther to the left were the Diggers, so called from their attempt to seize and cultivate unenclosed common land and distribute the produce to the poor. Though in common with the Levellers the Diggers appealed to the law of nature as a source of rights, they were more interested in economic than in political equality. They espoused a kind of primitive communism based upon the idea that the land is the "common treasury" of all. Every ablebodied man would be required to work at productive labor, and all persons would be permitted to draw from the common fund of wealth produced in proportion to their needs. The church would be transformed into an educational institution and the clergy would become schoolmasters, giving instruction every seventh day in public affairs, history, and the arts and sciences. "To know the secrets of nature is to know the works of God" was one of the Digger mottoes.

In September 1658, the stout-hearted Protector died. He was succeeded by his well-meaning but irresolute son Richard, who managed to hold office only until May of the following year. Perhaps even a man of much sterner fiber would also have failed eventually, for the country had grown tired of the austerities of Calvinist rule. Neither the Commonwealth nor the Protectorate had ever had the support of a majority of the English nation. Royalists regarded the Independents as usurpers. Republicans hated the disguised monarchy which Oliver Cromwell had set up. Catholics and Anglicans resented the branding of their acts of worship as criminal offenses. Even some members of the middle class gradually came to suspect that Cromwell's war with Spain had done more harm than good by endangering English commerce with the West Indies. For these and similar reasons there was general rejoicing when in 1660 a newly elected Parliament proclaimed Prince Charles king and invited him to return to England and occupy the throne of his father. The new king had gained a reputation for joyous living and easy morality, and his accession was hailed as a welcome relief from the somber rule of soldiers and zealots. Besides, he pledged himself not to reign as a despot, but to respect Parliament and to observe Magna Carta and the Petition of Right; for he admitted that he was not anxious to "resume his travels." England now entered upon a period known as the Restoration, covered by the reigns of Charles II (1660–1685) and his brother James II (1685–1688). Despite its

Charles II

473

auspicious beginning, many of the old problems had not really been solved but were simply concealed by the fond belief that the nation had regained its former stability.

Toward the end of the seventeenth century England went through a second political upheaval, the so-called Glorious Revolution of 1688–1689. Several of the causes were grounded in the policies of Charles II. That amiable sovereign was extravagant and lazy but determined on occasion to let the country know whose word was law. His strongly pro-Catholic attitude aroused the fears of patriotic Englishmen that their nation might once again be brought into subservience to Rome. Worse still, he showed a disposition, in spite of earlier pledges, to defy the authority of Parliament. In 1672 he suspended the laws against Catholics and other Dissenters and nine years later resolved to dispense with the legislative branch entirely. The policies of Charles II were continued in more insolent form by his brother, who succeeded him in 1685. King James II was an avowed Catholic and seemed bent upon making that faith the established religion of England. He openly violated an act of Parliament requiring that all holders of public office should adhere to the Anglican church, and proceeded to fill important positions in the army and the civil service with his Romanist followers. He continued his brother's practice of exempting Catholics from the disabilities imposed upon them by Parliament, even going so far as to demand that the Anglican bishops should read his decrees for this purpose in their churches. As long as his opponents could expect that James II would be succeeded by one of his two Protestant daughters, they were inclined to tolerate his arbitrary rule, lest the country be plunged again into civil war. But when the king acquired a son by his second wife, who was a Catholic, the die of revolution was cast. It was feared that the young prince would be infected with his father's doctrines, and that, as a consequence, England would be fettered with the shackles of despotic and papist rule for an indefinite time to come. To forestall such a result it seemed necessary to depose the king.

The "Glorious Revolution" of 1688–1689 was an entirely bloodless affair. A group of politicians from both the upper and middle classes secretly invited Prince William of Orange and his wife Mary, the elder daughter of James II, to become joint rulers of England.[5] William crossed over from Holland with an army and occupied London without firing a shot. Deserted even by those whom he had counted as loyal supporters, King James took refuge in France. The English throne was now declared vacant by Parliament and the crown presented to the new sovereigns. But their enthronement did not complete the revolution. Throughout the year 1689 Parliament

The failure of the Puritan Revolution paves the way for the Glorious Revolution of 1688–1689

Results of the Glorious Revolution

[5] There is evidence that William himself was a party to the secrets of the dissatisfied Englishmen, and he may even have inspired the invitation. Threatened with war by the king of France, he could make very good use of the resources and military power of England.

passed numerous laws designed to safeguard the rights of Englishmen and to protect its own power from monarchical invasion. First came an act requiring that appropriations should be made for one year only. Next the Toleration Act was passed, granting religious liberty to all Christians except Catholics and Unitarians. Finally, on the sixteenth of December the famous Bill of Rights was enacted into law. It provided for trial by jury and affirmed the right of Englishmen to petition the government for a redress of grievances. It condemned excessive bail, cruel punishments, and exorbitant fines. And it forbade the king to suspend laws or to levy taxes without the consent of Parliament. More sweeping in its provisions than the Petition of Right of 1628, it was backed by a Parliament that now had the power to see that it was obeyed.

The significance of the revolution of 1688–1689 would be almost impossible to exaggerate. Since it marked the final triumph of Parliament over the king, it therefore spelled the doom of absolute monarchy in England. Never again was any crowned head in Britain able to defy the legislative branch of the government as the Stuart monarchs had done. The revolution also dealt the *coup de grâce* to the theory of the divine right of kings. It would have been impossible for William and Mary to have denied the fact that they received their crowns from Parliament. And the authority of Parliament to determine who should be king was made more emphatic by the passage of the Act of Settlement in 1701. This law provided that upon the death of the heiress-presumptive Anne, younger sister of Mary, the crown should go to the Electress Sophia of Hanover or to the eldest of her heirs who might be Protestant.[6] There were some forty men or women with a better claim to the throne than Sophia, but all were eliminated arbitrarily by Parliament on the ground of their being Catholics. Finally, the Glorious Revolution contributed much to the American and French revolutions at the end of the eighteenth century. The example of the English in overthrowing absolute rule was a powerful inspiration to the opponents of despotism elsewhere. It was the British revolutionary ideal of limited government which furnished the substance of the political theory of Voltaire, Jefferson, and Paine. And a considerable portion of the English Bill of Rights was incorporated in the French Declaration of the Rights of Man in 1789 and in the first ten amendments to the American Constitution.

Significance of the Glorious Revolution

2. ABSOLUTE MONARCHY IN FRANCE AND SPAIN

The development of absolutism in France followed a course quite similar in some respects to that in England. Although France remained Catholic, her rulers had to contend with a Calvinist (Hugue-

---

[6] In this way the House of Hanover, the ruling dynasty until 1901, came to the English throne. The first Hanoverian king was Sophia's son, George I (1714–1727).

not) opposition almost as formidable as that of the Puritans in England. They also had a prosperous middle class to which they could look for support, on occasions, against the nobility. Both nations had their staunch defenders of absolutism among lawyers and political philosophers. But there was one notable difference. England enjoyed an advantage of geographic isolation that sheltered her from foreign danger. Her soil had not been invaded since the Norman Conquest in 1066. As a consequence her people felt secure, and her rulers found it difficult to justify a huge professional army. They did, of course, maintain large fleets of war vessels, but a "blue-water" navy could not be used in the same manner as an army stationed in inland garrisons to overawe subjects or to stifle incipient revolutions. France, on the other hand, like most Continental nations, faced almost constant threats of invasion. Her northeastern and eastern frontiers were poorly protected by geographic barriers and had been penetrated several times. As a result, it was easy for the French kings to argue the need for massive armies of professional soldiers. And such troops could readily be utilized to nip domestic disturbances in the bud. It would doubtless be a mistake to give all of the credit to this difference in geographic position for the longer persistence of absolute government in France, but it was certainly a major factor.

The growth of royal despotism in France was the product of a gradual evolution. Some of its antecedents went back to the reigns of Philip Augustus, Louis IX, and Philip IV in the thirteenth and fourteenth centuries. These kings solidified royal power by hiring mercenary soldiers, subsituting national taxation for feudal dues, arrogating to themselves the power to administer justice, and restricting the authority of the Pope to regulate ecclesiastical affairs in their kingdom. The Hundred Years' War (1337–1453) produced an even further accretion of power for the kings of France. They were now able to introduce new forms of taxation, to maintain a huge standing army, and to abolish the sovereignty of the feudal nobles. The members of this latter class were gradually reduced to the level of courtiers, dependent mainly upon the monarch for their titles and prestige.

The trend toward absolutism was interrupted during the sixteenth century when France was involved in a war with Spain and torn by a bloody struggle between Catholics and Huguenots at home. Ambitious nobles took advantage of the confusion to assert their power and contested the succession to the throne. Peace was restored to the distracted kingdom in 1593 by Henry of Navarre (1589–1610), who four years before had proclaimed himself king as Henry IV. He was the founder of the Bourbon dynasty. Though at one time a leader of the Huguenot faction, Henry perceived that the nation would never accept him unless he renounced the Calvinist religion. Flippantly remarking that Paris was worth a Mass, he formally

Contrasting conditions in England and France

The origins of absolutism in France

Henry IV and the Duke of Sully

adopted the Catholic faith. In 1598 he issued the Edict of Nantes, guaranteeing freedom of conscience and political rights to all Protestants. With the grounds for religious controversy thus removed, Henry could turn his attention to rebuilding his kingdom. In this work, he had the able assistance of his chief minister, the Duke of Sully. Grim, energetic, and penurious, Sully was a worthy forerunner of Colbert in the seventeenth century. For years the king and his faithful servant labored to repair the shattered fortunes of France. Sully devoted his efforts primarily to fiscal reform, so as to eliminate corruption and waste and bring more revenue into the royal treasury. He endeavored also to promote the prosperity of agriculture by draining swamps, improving devastated lands, subsidizing stock-raising, and opening up foreign markets for the products of the soil. The king gave most of his attention to fostering industry and commerce. He introduced the manufacture of silk into France, encouraged other industries by subsidies and monopolies, and made favorable commercial treaties with England and Spain. But Henry did not stop with economic reforms. He was deeply concerned with crushing the renascent power of the nobility, and so successful were his efforts in this direction that he restored the monarchy to the dominant position it had held at the end of the Hundred Years' War. He was active also in sponsoring the development of a colonial empire in America. During his reign the French acquired a foothold in Canada and began their exploration in the region of the Great Lakes and the Mississippi Valley. His rule was intelligent and benevolent but none the less despotic.

The reign of Henry IV was brought to an end by the dagger of a crazed fanatic in 1610. Since the new king, Louis XIII, was only

The Assassination of Henry IV. This contemporary engraving shows the manner in which Rivaillic, a Catholic monk, climbed upon the wheel of Henry's carriage in order to stab the French ruler.

Cardinal Richelieu

nine years old, the country was ruled by his mother, Marie de Médicis, as regent. In 1624 Louis XIII, no longer under the regency, entrusted the management of his kingdom to a brilliant but domineering cleric, Cardinal Richelieu, whom he made his chief minister. Richelieu dedicated himself to two objectives: (1) to destroy all limitations upon the authority of the king; and (2) to make France the chief power in Europe. In the pursuit of these aims he allowed nothing to stand in his way. He ruthlessly suppressed the nobility, destroying its most dangerous members and rendering the others harmless by attaching them as pensioners to the royal court. Though he fostered education and patronized literature, he neglected the interests of commerce and allowed graft and extravagance to flourish in the government. His main constructive achievements were the creation of a postal service and the establishment of a system under which *intendants,* or agents of the king, took charge of local government. Both were conceived as devices for consolidating the nation under the control of the crown, thereby eradicating surviving traces of feudal authority.

Richelieu's foreign policy

Richelieu's ambitions were not limited to domestic affairs. To make France the most powerful nation in Europe was alleged to require an aggressive diplomacy and eventual participation in war. France was still surrounded by what Henry IV had referred to as a "Hapsburg ring." On her southern border was Spain, ruled since 1516 by a branch of the Hapsburg family. To the north, less than 100 miles from Paris, were the Spanish Netherlands. Other centers of Hapsburg power included Alsace, the Franche-Comté, Savoy, Genoa, and Milan, and still farther to the east the great Austrian Empire itself. Cardinal Richelieu eagerly awaited an opportunity to break this ring. As we shall see, he finally found it in the Thirty Years' War. Though engaged in suppressing Protestants at home, he did not hesitate to ally himself with Gustavus Adolphus, king of

The Inauguration of the Invalides. A detail from the painting by Martin the Younger shows Louis XIV arriving at the site of the home for war heroes.

Sweden and leader of a coalition of Protestant states. Long before his death in 1642 the great cardinal-statesman had forged to the front as the most powerful individual in Europe.

Absolute monarchy in France attained its zenith during the reigns of the last three Bourbon kings before the Revolution. The first of the monarchs of this series was Louis XIV (1643–1715), who epitomized the ideal of absolutism more completely than any other sovereign of his age. Proud, extravagant, and domineering, Louis entertained the most exalted notions of his position as king. Not only did he believe that he was commissioned by God to reign, but he regarded the welfare of the state as intimately bound up with his own personality. The famous phrase imputed to him, *l'état c'est moi* (I am the state), may not represent his exact words, but it expresses very clearly the conception he held of his own authority. He chose the sun as his official emblem to indicate his belief that the nation derived its glory and sustenance from him as the planets do theirs from the actual sun. He gave personal supervision to every department and regarded his ministers as mere clerks with no duty but to obey his orders. In general, he followed the policies of Henry IV and Richelieu in consolidating national power at the expense of local officials and in trying to reduce the nobles to mere parasites of the court. But any possible good he may have done was completely overshadowed by his extravagant wars and his reactionary policy in religion. In 1685 he revoked the Edict of Nantes, which had granted freedom of conscience to the Huguenots. As a result, large numbers of his most intelligent and prosperous subjects fled from the country.

Until the beginning of the Revolution in 1789 the form of the French government remained essentially as Louis XIV had left it. His successors, Louis XV (1715–1774) and Louis XVI (1774–1792), also professed to rule by divine right. But neither of these kings had the desire to emulate the Grand Monarch in his enthusiasm for work and his meticulous attention to the business of state. Louis XV was lazy and incompetent and allowed himself to be dominated by a succession of mistresses. Problems of government bored him incredibly, and when obliged to preside at the council table he "opened his mouth, said little, and thought not at all." His grandson, who succeeded him, the ill-fated Louis XVI, was weak in character and mentally dull. Indifferent to politics, he amused himself by shooting deer from the palace window and playing at his hobbies of lock-making and masonry. On the day in 1789 when mobs stormed the Bastille, he wrote in his diary "Nothing." Yet both of these monarchs maintained a government which, if not more despotic, was at least more arbitrary than had ever been the case before. They permitted their ministers to imprison without a trial persons suspected of disloyalty; they suppressed the courts for refusing to approve their decrees; and they brought the country to

Louis XIV, the supreme incarnation of absolute rule

Louis XIV by Rigaud

Louis XV and Louis XVI

Versailles. This seventeenth-century painting shows the château which was the focus of social life during the reign of Louis XIV.

the verge of bankruptcy by their costly wars and by their reckless extravagance for the benefit of mistresses and worthless favorites. If they had deliberately planned to make revolution inevitable, they could scarcely have succeeded better.

The growth of absolute monarchy in Spain was swifter and less interrupted than was true of its development in France. As late as the thirteenth century what is now Spain was divided into five parts. Four Christian kingdoms—Aragon, Castile, León, and Navarre—maintained a precarious existence in the north, while the southern half of the country was in the possession of the Moors. In the fifteenth century *de facto* unification was accomplished by the marriage of Ferdinand of Aragon and Isabella of Castile. Though ruling nominally as independent monarchs, for all practical purposes they were sovereigns of a united Spain. Like their predecessors, they continued the crusade against the Moors, completing as their major achievement the conquest of Granada, last stronghold of Moorish power on the Iberian peninsula. The surviving Moors were expelled from the country, along with the Jews, for in the desperate struggle to drive out an alien invader all forms of non-Christian belief had come to be regarded as treason.

Queen Isabella died in 1504, and King Ferdinand in 1516. Their entire kingdom was inherited by their daughter Joanna, who had married into the Hapsburg family. Her son succeeded to the throne of Spain as Charles I in 1516. Three years later he was elected Holy Roman Emperor as Charles V, thereby uniting Spain with Central Europe and southern Italy. Charles was interested not merely in the destinies of Spain but in the welfare of the Church and in the politics of Europe as a whole. He dreamed that he might be the instrument of restoring the religious unity of Christendom, broken by the Protestant Revolution and of making the empire over which he pre-

The rise of absolutism in Spain

The empire of Charles V

sided a worthy successor of Imperial Rome. Though successful in holding his disjointed domain together and in fighting off attempts of the French to conquer his Italian possessions and of the Turks to overrun Europe, he failed in the achievement of his larger objectives. At the age of fifty-six, overcome with a sense of discouragement and futility, he abdicated and retired into a monastery. The German princes chose his brother, Ferdinand I, to succeed him as Holy Roman Emperor. His Spanish and Italian possessions, including the colonies overseas, passed to his son, who became king as Philip II.

Philip II came to the throne of Spain at the height of its glory. But he also witnessed, and to a considerable extent was responsible for, the beginning of its decline. His policies were mainly an intensification of those of his predecessors. He was narrow, despotic, and cruel. Determined to enforce a strict conformity in matters of religion upon all of his subjects, he is reputed to have boasted that he would gather faggots to burn his own son if the latter were guilty of heresy. Reference has already been made to the horrors of the Spanish Inquisition and of the war for suppression of the revolt in the Netherlands. Philip was equally shortsighted in his colonial policy. Natives were butchered or virtually enslaved. Their territories were greedily despoiled of their gold and silver, which were dragged off to Spain in the mistaken belief that this was the surest means of increasing the nation's wealth. No thought was given to the development of new industries in either the colonies or the mother country. Instead, the gold and silver were largely squandered in furthering Philip's military and political ambitions. It can be said, however, in the king's defense that he was following the accepted theories of the time. Doubtless most other monarchs with a like opportunity would have imitated his example. Philip II's crowning stupidity was probably his war against England. Angered by the

ABSOLUTE MONARCHY IN FRANCE AND SPAIN

Philip II of Spain. This painting by Coello shows the famous protruding chin and lower lip which were characteristic features of the Hapsburg family.

The Escorial. Built in the sixteenth century by Philip II of Spain, it originally served as his retreat.

attacks of English privateers upon Spanish commerce, and frustrated in his schemes to bring England back into the Catholic faith, he sent a great fleet in 1588, the "Invincible Armada," to destroy Queen Elizabeth's navy. But Philip had little knowledge of either the new techniques of naval warfare or of the robust patriotism of the English. A combination of fighting seamanship and disastrous storms sent most of his 132 ships to the bottom of the Channel. Spain never recovered from the blow. Though a brilliant afterglow, exemplified in the work of the Renaissance artists and dramatists, continued for some years, the greatness of Spain as a nation was approaching its end.

3.   ABSOLUTISM IN CENTRAL EUROPE

The chief countries of Central Europe where despotism flourished on its most grandiose scale were Prussia and Austria. The founder of absolute rule in Prussia was the Great Elector, Frederick William, a contemporary of Louis XIV. Not only was he the first member of the Hohenzollern family to acquire full sovereignty over Prussia, but he brought all of his dominions under centralized rule, abolishing their local Diets and merging their petty armies into a national military force. The work of the Great Elector was continued and extended by his grandson, known as Frederick William I (1713–1740), since he now had the title of *King* of Prussia. This miserly monarch ruled over his people like a Hebrew patriarch, regulating their private conduct and attending personally to the correction of their short-comings. His consuming passion was the army, which he more than doubled in size and drilled to a machine-like efficiency. He even sold the furniture in the palace to hire recruits for his famous regiment of Potsdam Giants. Those whom money could not buy he is alleged to have kidnaped. He traded musicians and prize stallions for soldiers who were well over six feet in height.

Frederick William I

The most noted of the Prussian despots was Frederick II (1740–1786), commonly known as Frederick the Great. An earnest disciple of the reformist doctrines of the new rationalist philosophy, Frederick was the leading figure among the "enlightened despots" of the eighteenth century. Declaring himself not the master but merely the "first servant of the state," he wrote essays to prove that Machiavelli was wrong and rose at five in the morning to begin a Spartan routine of personal management of public affairs. He made Prussia in many ways the best-governed state in Europe, abolishing torture of accused criminals and bribery of judges, establishing elementary schools, and promoting the prosperity of industry and agriculture. He fostered scientific forestry and imported crop rotation, iron plows, and clover from England. He opened up new lands in Silesia and brought in hundreds of thousands of immigrants to cultivate them. When wars ruined their farms, he supplied the

The Spanish Armada. This contemporary engraving shows the defeat of the Spanish by the English in the Channel.

peasants with new livestock and tools. As an admirer of Voltaire, whom he entertained for some time at his court, he tolerated all sorts of religious beliefs. He declared that he would build a mosque in Berlin if enough Moslems wished to locate there. Yet he was perversely anti-Semitic. He levied special taxes on the Jews and made efforts to close the professions and the civil service to them. Moreover, such benevolence as he showed in internal affairs was not carried over into foreign relations. Frederick robbed Austria of Silesia, conspired with Catherine of Russia to dismember Poland, and contributed at least his full share to the bloody wars of the eighteenth century.

The full bloom of absolutism in Austria came during the reigns of Maria Theresa (1740–1780) and Joseph II (1780–1790). Under the rule of the beautiful but high-strung empress a national army was established, the powers of the Church were curtailed in the interest of consolidated government, and elementary and higher education was greatly expanded. Unlike the despots of most other countries, Maria Theresa was sincerely devoted to Christian morality. Though she participated in the dismemberment of Poland to make up for the loss of Silesia, she did so with grave misgivings—an attitude which prompted the scornful remark of Frederick the Great: "She weeps, but she takes her share." The reforms of Maria Theresa were extended, at least on paper by her son Joseph II. Inspired by the teachings of French philosophers, Joseph determined to remake his empire in accordance with the highest ideals of justice and reason. Not only did he plan to reduce the powers of the Church by confiscating its lands and abolishing monasteries, but he aspired to humble the nobles and improve the condition of the masses. He decreed that the serfs should become free men and promised to relieve them of the feudal obligations owed to their masters. He aimed

Absolutism in Austria

483

to make education universal and to force the nobles to pay their proper share of taxes. But most of his magnificent plans ended in failure. He antagonized not merely the nobles and clergy but also the proud Hungarians, who were deprived of all rights of self-government. He alienated the sympathies of the peasants by making them liable to compulsory military service. He was scarcely any more willing than Louis XIV or Frederick the Great to sacrifice personal power and national glory even for the sake of his lofty ideals.

4.   ABSOLUTISM IN RUSSIA

Russia at the beginning of the early modern age was a composite of European and Oriental characteristics. Much of her territory had been colonized by the Norsemen in the early Middle Ages. Her religion, her calendar, her system of writing had been derived from Byzantium. Even her feudal regime, with its boyars, or magnates, and serfs, was not greatly dissimilar to that of western Europe. On the other hand, much of Russia's culture, and many of her customs, were distinctly not European. Her arts were limited almost entirely to icon painting and an onion-domed religious architecture. There was no literature in the Russian language, arithmetic was barely known, Arabic numerals were not used, and bankers and merchants made their calculations with the abacus. Nor were manners and customs comparable to those of the West. Women of the upper classes were veiled and secluded. Flowing beards and skirted garments were universal for men. Knives and forks were considered superfluous. Seasons of wild revelry alternated with periods of repentance and morbid atonement. Geographically, also, Russia had an Asiatic orientation. The Russian heartland looked out upon Siberia, Persia, and China, with Europe in the rear. It would be a mistake, however, to suppose that Russia was totally cut off from Europe. As early as the fourteenth century, German merchants of the Hanse conducted some trade in Russian furs and amber. In the 1550's English merchants discovered the White Sea and made Archangel a port of entry through which military supplies could be exchanged for a few Russian goods and even products from Persia and China. But with Archangel frozen most of the year, the volume of this trade was undoubtedly small.

As late as the thirteenth century Russia was a collection of small principalities. They were besieged from the west by Swedes, Lithuanians, Poles, and the Teutonic Knights, or members of the Teutonic Order. The Teutonic Order was one of several religious and military organizations that sprang from the Crusades. Established originally for charitable purposes, it developed into a military club whose members adopted as their mission the conquest of lands on Germany's eastern frontier. Their operations set a precedent for the famous *Drang nach Osten* (Drive to the East) which later occu-

Russia at the beginning of the modern age

Foreign invaders; the Mongols

484

pied such a prominent place in German history. From the east Russia was threatened by the Mongols (Tartars) or the Golden Horde, who had established a great empire in central Asia, eventually including both northern India and China. In 1237 the Mongols began an invasion which led to their conquest of nearly all of Russia. Mongol rule was in several ways a disaster. It marked the development of a stronger Asiatic orientation. Henceforth Russia turned more and more away from Europe and looked beyond the Urals as the arena of her future development. Her citizens intermarried with Mongols and adopted many elements of their way of life.

Eventually, Mongol power declined, in accordance with the common fate of vast empires. In 1380 a Russian army defeated the Tartars and thus initiated a movement to drive them back into Asia. The state which assumed the leadership of this movement was the Grand Duchy of Moscow. Under strong rulers it had been increasing its power for some time. Located near the sources of the great rivers flowing both north and south, it had geographic advantages surpassing those of the other states. Moreover, it had recently been made the headquarters of the Russian church. The first of the princes of Moscow to put himself forward as Tsar (Caesar) of Russia was Ivan the Great (1462–1505). Taking as his bride the niece of the last of the Byzantine Emperors, who had perished in the capture of Constantinople in 1453, he proclaimed himself his successor by the grace of God. He adopted as his insignia the Byzantine double-headed eagle and imported Italian architects to build him an enormous palace, the Kremlin, in imitation of the one in Constantinople. Avowing his intention to recover the ancient lands that had been lost to foreign invaders, he forced the Prince of Lithuania to acknowledge him as sovereign of "all the Russias" and pushed the Tartars out of northern Russia and beyond the Urals.

The rise of Moscow; Ivan the Great

The first of the Tsars to attempt the Europeanization of Russia was Peter the Great (1682–1725). He stands out as the most powerful and probably the most intelligent autocrat yet to occupy the Russian throne. With a reckless disregard for ancient customs, Peter endeavored to force his subjects to change their ways of living. He forbade the Oriental seclusion of women and commanded both sexes to adopt European styles of dress. He made the use of tobacco compulsory among the members of his court. He summoned the great nobles before him and clipped their flowing beards with his own hand. In order to make sure of his own absolute power he abolished all traces of local self-government and established a system of national police. For the same reason he annihilated the authority of the patriarch of the Orthodox church and placed all religious affairs under a Holy Synod subject to his own control. Profoundly interested in Western science and technology, he made journeys to Holland and England to learn about shipbuilding and industry. He imitated the mercantilist policies of Western nations by improving

Peter the Great. An eighteenth-century mosaic.

485

agriculture and fostering manufactures and commerce. In order to get "windows to the west" he conquered territory along the Baltic shore and transferred his capital from Moscow to St. Petersburg, his new city at the mouth of the Neva. But the good that he did was greatly outweighed by his extravagant wars and his fiendish cruelty. He put thousands to death for alleged conspiracies against him. He murdered his own son and heir because the latter boasted that when *he* became Tsar he would return Russia to the ways of her fathers. To raise money for his expensive wars he debased the currency, sold valuable concessions to foreigners, established government monopolies on the production of salt, oil, caviar, and coffins, and imposed taxes on almost everything, from baths to beehives.

The significance of Peter the Great

The significance of Peter the Great is not easy to evaluate. He did not singlehandedly transform Russia into a Western nation. Western influences had been seeping into the country as a consequence of trade contacts for many years. But Peter accelerated the process and gave it a more radical direction. Evidence abounds that he really did aim to remake the nation and to give it at least a veneer of civilization. He sent many of his countrymen abroad to study. He simplified the ancient alphabet and established the first newspaper to be published in Russia. He ordered the publication of a book on polite behavior, teaching his subjects not to spit on the floor or to scratch themselves or gnaw bones at dinner. He encouraged exports, built a fleet on the Baltic, and fostered new industries such as textiles and mining. Though a reaction set in after Peter's death against many of his innovations, some of them survived for at least two centuries. The church, for example, continued as essentially an arm of the state, governed by a Procurator of the Holy Synod appointed by the Tsar himself. Serfdom not only survived but continued in the extended forms required or authorized by Peter. No longer were serfs bound to the soil; they could be bought and sold at any time, even for work in factories and mines. Finally, the absolutism devel-

The Winter Palace. This contemporary engraving shows the palace built by Peter the Great in the town that bore his name, St. Petersburg.

oped by Peter showed few signs of abating until the twentieth century. It was an absolutism based upon force, with a secret police, an extensive bureaucracy, and a subordinated church as instruments for imposing the autocrat's will.

The other most noted of the Russian monarchs in the age of absolutism was Catherine the Great (1762–1796), who before her marriage was a German princess. Frequently classified as one of the "enlightened despots," Catherine corresponded with French philosophers, founded hospitals and orphanages, and expressed the hope that someday the serfs might be liberated. Ambitious to gain for herself a place in the Enlightenment, she purchased Diderot's library and rose at five in the morning to dabble in scholarship. She wrote plays, published a digest of Blackstone's *Commentaries on the Laws of England,* and even began a history of Russia. Her accomplishments as a reformer, however, had only a limited scope. She took steps toward a codification of the Russian laws, restricted the use of torture, and remodeled and consolidated local government. Any plans she may have had, however, for improving the lot of the peasants were abruptly canceled after a violent serf rebellion in 1773–1774. Landlords and priests were murdered and the ruling classes terrified as the revolt swept through the Urals and the valley of the Volga. Catherine responded with stern repression. The captured leader of the peasants was drawn and quartered, and as a guaranty against future outbreaks, the nobles were given increased powers over their serfs. They were permitted to deal with them virtually as if they were chattel slaves. Catherine's chief significance lies in the fact that she continued the work of Peter the Great in introducing Russia to Western ideas and in making the country a formidable power in European affairs. She managed to extend the boundaries of her country to include not only eastern Poland but lands on the Black Sea.

Catherine the Great

5 · THE WARS OF THE DESPOTS

Between 1485 and 1789 the years of peace in Europe were actually outnumbered by the years of war. The earlier conflicts were largely religious in character and have already been dealt with in the chapter on the Reformation. The majority of the wars after 1600 partook of the nature of struggles for supremacy among the powerful despots of the principal countries. But religion was also a factor in some of them, and so was the greed of the commercial classes. In general, nationalistic motives were much less important than in the wars of the nineteenth and twentieth centuries. Peoples and territories were so many pawns to be moved back and forth in the game of dynastic aggrandizement.

The major warfare of the seventeenth century revolved around a titanic duel between Hapsburgs and Bourbons. Originally the rulers of Austria, the Hapsburgs had gradually extended their power over

Character of the wars in the age of the despots

Hungary and Bohemia as well. In addition, the head of the family enjoyed what was left of the distinction of being Holy Roman Emperor. Since the time of Charles V (1519–1556) branches of the Hapsburgs had ruled over Spain, the Netherlands, the Franche-Comté, Alsace, Savoy, Genoa, Milan, and the Kingdom of the Two Sicilies.[7] For many years this expansion of Hapsburg power had been a source of profound disturbance to the rulers of France. They regarded their country as encircled and longed to break through the enclosing ring. But tensions were building up in other parts of Europe also. The princes of Germany looked with alarm upon the growing power of the Holy Roman Emperor and sought opportunities to restrict him in ways that would increase their own stature. The kings of Denmark and Sweden were also developing expansionist ambitions, which could hardly be realized except at the expense of the Hapsburg Empire. Finally, the seeds of religious conflict, sown by the Reformation, were about ready to germinate in a new crop of hostilities. In 1608–1609 two opposing alliances had been formed, based upon principles of religious antagonism. The existence of these mutually hostile leagues added to the tension in central Europe and contributed toward making an eventual explosion almost a certainty. The conflict that followed, known as the Thirty Years' War (1618–1648), was one of the most tragic in history.

The immediate cause of the Thirty Years' War was an attempt of the Holy Roman Emperor, Matthias, to consolidate his power in Bohemia. Though the Hapsburgs had been overlords of Bohemia for a century, the Czech inhabitants of the country had retained their own king. When the Bohemian throne became vacant in 1618, Matthias conspired to obtain the position for one of his kinsmen, Duke Ferdinand of Styria. By exerting pressure he induced the Bohemian Diet to elect Ferdinand king. The Czech leaders resented this since both nationalist and Protestant traditions were strong in the country. The upshot was the invasion of the Emperor's headquarters in Prague by Czech noblemen and the proclamation of Bohemia as an independent state with Frederick, the Calvinist Elector Palatine, as king. The war now began in earnest. The success of the Hapsburgs in suppressing the Bohemian revolt and in punishing Frederick by seizing his lands in the valley of the Rhine galvanized the Protestant rulers of northern Europe into action. Not only the German princes but King Christian IV of Denmark and Gustavus Adolphus of Sweden joined the crusade against Austrian aggression —with the additional purpose, of course, of expanding their own dominions. In 1630 the French intervened with donations of arms

Gustavus Adolphus

[7] Charles V was the grandson of Ferdinand and Isabella of Spain and became king of that country as Charles I in 1516. Three years later he was made Holy Roman Emperor. He was also the grandson of Maximilian I of Austria and therefore a Hapsburg. When Charles abdicated as Emperor in 1556, his realm was divided. The Spanish and Italian dominions and the colonies in America went to his son Philip II and his central European possessions to his brother, Ferdinand I.

and money to the Protestant allies, and after 1632, when Gustavus Adolphus was killed in battle, France bore the brunt of the struggle. The war was no longer a religious conflict, but essentially a contest between the Bourbon and Hapsburg houses for mastery of the Continent of Europe. The immediate objectives of Cardinal Richelieu, who was directing affairs for Louis XIII, were to wrest the province of Alsace from the Holy Roman Empire and to weaken the hold of the Spanish Hapsburgs on the Netherlands and on Italy. For a time the French armies suffered reverses, but the organizing genius of Richelieu and of Cardinal Mazarin, who succeeded him in 1643, ultimately brought victory to France and her allies. Peace was restored to a distracted Europe by the Treaty of Westphalia in 1648.

Most of the results of the Thirty Years' War were unmitigated evils. By the Treaty of Westphalia France was confirmed in the possession of Alsace and other smaller territories. Sweden received territory in Germany; the independence of Holland and Switzerland was formally acknowledged; and the Holy Roman Empire was reduced to a mere fiction, since each of the German princes was now recognized as a sovereign ruler with power to make war and peace and to govern his state as he chose. But most of these changes merely laid the foundations for bitter international squabbles in the future. In addition, the war wrought terrible havoc in central Europe. Probably few military conflicts since the dawn of history had caused so much misery to the civilian population. It is estimated that fully one-third of the people in Germany and Bohemia lost their lives as a consequence of famine and disease and the marauding attacks of brutal soldiers. The armies of both sides pillaged, tortured, burned, and killed in such manner as to convert whole regions into veritable desert. In Saxony one-third of the land went out of cultivation, and packs of wolves roamed through areas where thriving villages once had stood. In the midst of such misery, education and intellectual achievement of every description were bound to decline, with the result that civilization in Germany was retarded by at least a century.

In 1700 the French king saw what appeared to be a new opportunity for expanding Bourbon power. In that year Charles II, king of Spain, died with neither children nor brothers to succeed him, and willed his dominion to the grandson of Louis XIV. The Austrians denounced this settlement, and formed a new alliance with England, Holland, and Brandenburg. The War of the Spanish Succession, which broke out in 1702 when Louis attempted to enforce the claim of his grandson, was the last important stage in the struggle between Bourbons and Hapsburgs.[8] By the Peace of Utrecht (1713–1714) the grandson of Louis XIV was permitted to occupy the

Results of the Thirty Years' War

Final stage: the War of the Spanish Succession

[8] The War of the Austrian Succession (1740–1748), in which France fought on the side of Prussia against Great Britain and Austria, also involved a struggle between Bourbons and Hapsburgs. But the results for France were indecisive: the war was mainly a duel between Prussia and Austria.

Spanish throne, on condition that France and Spain should never be united. Nova Scotia and Newfoundland were transferred to England from France, and Gibraltar from Spain. The Belgian Netherlands, Naples, and Milan were given to the Austrian Hapsburgs.

It would be difficult to exaggerate the significance of the War of the Spanish Succession. Since it involved most of the nations of Europe and also the lands overseas, it was the first of what can be called "world wars." It was fought, however, not by mass armies but chiefly by professional soldiers. It was the prototype, therefore, of most of the wars of the eighteenth century. These were wars among kings, in which the masses of the people were little involved. Among large-scale conflicts the War of the Spanish Succession was the first in which religion played almost no part. Secular rivalries over commerce and sea power were the major bones of contention. The war disposed of the claims of the smaller states to equal rank with their larger neighbors. Brandenburg and Savoy were the only important exceptions. The first came to be called Prussia and the second, Sardinia. Aside from Sardinia, the rest of the Italian states dwindled into insignificance. Austria henceforth was overshadowed by Prussia. Holland suffered such a strain from the war that she ceased to be a prime factor in the competition for world power. With a Bourbon king on the throne, Spain was reduced to subservience to France. Her Bourbon dynasty continued to rule, with brief interruptions, until the overthrow of Alphonso XIII in 1931. The War of the Spanish Succession left France and Great Britain as the two major powers in Europe. Of these, the latter was the principal victor. Not only did she acquire valuable possessions, but she muscled her way into the Spanish commercial empire. By an agreement known as the Asiento she gained the privilege of providing Spanish America with African slaves. This privilege opened the way to the smuggling of all kinds of goods into the Spanish colonies, and contributed toward making Great Britain the richest nation on earth.

The most important of the wars of the despots in the eighteenth century was the Seven Years' War (1756–1763), known in American history as the French and Indian War. The causes of this struggle were closely related to some of the earlier conflicts already discussed. A chief factor in several of these wars had been commercial rivalry between England and France. Each had been striving for supremacy in the development of overseas trade and colonial empires. The Seven Years' War was simply the climax of a struggle which had been going on for nearly a century. Hostilities began, appropriately enough, in America as the result of a dispute over possession of the Ohio valley. Soon the whole question of British or French domination of the North American continent was involved. Eventually, nearly every major country of Europe was drawn in on one side or the other. Louis XV of France enlisted the aid of his kinsman, the Bourbon king of Spain. A struggle begun in 1740 between Frederick

Significance of the War of the Spanish Succession

The Seven Years' War

the Great and Maria Theresa over possession of Silesia was quickly merged with the larger contest. The Seven Years' War thus reached the proportions of what virtually amounted to a world conflict, with France, Spain, Austria, and Russia arrayed against Great Britain and Prussia in Europe, and with English and French colonial forces striving for mastery not only in America but also in India.

The outcome of the Seven Years' War was exceedingly significant for the later history of Europe. Frederick the Great won a decisive victory over the Austrians and forced Maria Theresa to surrender all claims to Silesia. The acquisition of this territory increased the area of Prussia by more than a third, thereby raising the Hohenzollern kingdom to the status of a first-rank power. In the struggle for colonial supremacy the British emerged with a sensational triumph. Of her once magnificent empire in America, France lost all but two tiny islands off the coast of Newfoundland, Guadeloupe and a few other possessions in the West Indies, and a portion of Guiana in South America.[9] She was allowed to retain her trading privileges in India, but she was forbidden to build any forts or maintain any troops in that country. France was now crippled beyond much hope of a quick recovery. Her treasury was depleted, her trade almost ruined, and her chances of dominance on the Continent of Europe badly shattered. These disasters, brought on by the stupid policies of her rulers, had much to do with preparing the ground for the great revolution of 1789. By contrast, Britain was now riding the crest of the wave—in a literal as well as a figurative sense, for her triumph in the Seven Years' War was a milestone in her struggle for supremacy on the seas. The wealth from her expanded trade enriched her merchants, thereby enhancing their prestige in political and social affairs. But perhaps most important of all, her victory in the struggle for colonies gave her an abundance of raw materials which enabled her to take the lead in the Industrial Revolution.

6. THE POLITICAL THEORY OF ABSOLUTISM

The autocratic behavior of the despots in the sixteenth, seventeenth, and eighteenth centuries was not all of their own making. As indicated at the beginning of this chapter, they were encouraged by various economic and political factors for which they were not solely responsible. To these causes must be added another: the influence of political theory. Several of the Stuart and Bourbon kings, for example, derived justification for their policies from philosophers who expressed the prevailing ideas of their time in systematic and forceful writings. These ideas were, of course, not those of the

---

[9] All of the territory given up by the French was acquired by Great Britain, with the exception of Louisiana, which France turned over to Spain as a reward for her part in the war.

Jean Bodin

The Title Page of *Leviathan*

common people, but they did reflect the desires of those whom John Adams used to call "the rich, the well-born, and the able."

One of the first of the philosophers to lend encouragement to the absolutist ambitions of monarchs was Jean Bodin (1530–1596), whose zeal in the persecution of witches had earned for him the title of "Satan's Attorney-General." Bodin was not quite so extreme as some of his colleagues in exalting monarchical power. He agreed with the medieval philosophers that rulers were bound by the law of God, and he even acknowledged that the prince had a moral duty to respect the treaties he had signed. But Bodin had no use for parliaments of any description. He emphatically denied the right of a legislative body to impose any limits upon royal power. And while he admitted that princes who violated the divine law or the law of nature were tyrants, he refused to concede that their subjects would have any right of rebellion against them. The authority of the prince is from God, and the supreme obligation of the people is passive obedience. Revolution must be avoided at all costs, for it destroys that stability which is a necessary condition for progress. The main contribution of Bodin, if such it can be called, was his doctrine of sovereignty, which he defined as "supreme power over citizens and subjects, unrestrained by the laws." By this he meant that the prince, who is the only sovereign, is not bound by man-made laws. There is no *legal* restriction upon his authority whatever—nothing except obedience to the natural or moral law ordained by God.

The most noted of all the apostles of absolute government was the Englishman Thomas Hobbes (1588–1679). Writing during the Puritan Revolution and in close association with the royalists, Hobbes was disgusted with the turn which events had taken in his native country and longed for a revival of the monarchy. However, his materialism and his doctrine of the secular origin of the kingship made him none too popular with the Stuarts. For the title of his chief work Hobbes chose the name *Leviathan*, to indicate his conception of the state as an all-powerful monster.[10] All associations within the state, he declared, are mere "worms in the entrails of Leviathan." The essence of Hobbes' political philosophy is directly related to his theory of the origin of government. He taught that in the beginning all men lived in a state of nature, subject to no law but brutal self-interest. Far from being a paradise of innocence and bliss, the state of nature was a condition of universal misery. Every man's hand was against his neighbor. Life for the individual was "solitary, poor, nasty, brutish, and short." [11] In order to escape from this war of each against all, men eventually united with one another to form a civil society. They drew up a contract surrendering all of their rights to a sovereign, who would be strong enough to

[10] In the Book of Job, Leviathan is the monster that ruled over the primeval chaos. Job 41:1.

[11] *Leviathan* (Routledge ed.), p. 81.

protect his subjects from violence. Thus the sovereign, while not a party to the contract, was made the recipient of absolute authority. The people gave up *everything* for the one great blessing of security. In contrast with Bodin, Hobbes did not recognize any law of nature or of God as a limitation upon the authority of the prince. Absolute government, he maintained, had been established by the people themselves, and therefore they would have no ground for complaint if their ruler became a tyrant. On the basis of pure deduction, without any appeal to religion or history, Hobbes arrived at the conclusion that the king is entitled to rule despotically—not because he has been appointed by God, but because the people have *given* him absolute power.

In a sense the great Dutchman, Hugo Grotius (1583–1645), may also be considered an exponent of absolutism; though with him the question of power within the state was more or less incidental to the larger question of relations among the states. Living during the period of religious strife in France, the revolt of the Netherlands, and the Thirty Years' War, Grotius was impressed by the need for a body of rules that would reduce the dealings of governments with one another to a pattern of reason and order. He wrote his famous *Law of War and Peace* to prove that the principles of elemental justice and morality ought to prevail among nations. Some of these principles he derived from the Roman *jus gentium* and some from the medieval law of nature. So well did he present his case that he has been regarded ever since as one of the chief founders of international law. Grotius' revulsion against turbulence also inspired him to advocate despotic government. He did not see how order could be preserved within the state unless the ruler possessed unlimited authority. He maintained that in the beginning the people had either surrendered to a ruler voluntarily or had been compelled to submit to superior force; but in either case, having once established a government, they were bound to obey it unquestioningly forever.

Hugo Grotius

The theories just discussed were not simply those of a few ivory-tower philosophers, but rather the widely accepted ideas of an age when order and security were considered more important than liberty. They reflected the desire of the commercial classes, especially, for the utmost degree of stability and protection in the interest of business. Mercantilism and the policies of the despots went hand in hand with the new theories of absolute rule. The dictum, "I am the state," attributed to Louis XIV, was not just the brazen boast of a tyrant, but came close to expressing the prevailing conception of government—in Continental Europe at least. Those who had a stake in society really believed that the king *was* the state. They could hardly conceive of a government able to protect and assist their economic activities except in terms of centralized and despotic authority. Their attitude was not so far different from

The significance of philosophers' attempts to justify absolutism

493

that of some people today who believe that a dictatorship of one form or another is our only means for security and plenty.

7. SIGNIFICANCE OF THE AGE OF ABSOLUTISM

The age of absolutism was important not merely for the establishment of absolute monarchies. It bears even greater significance for its effects upon international relations. It was during this period that the modern state system came into existence. During the era of approximately 1000 years after the fall of Rome, states, in the sense in which we now understand the term, scarcely existed in Europe west of the Byzantine Empire. True, there were kings in England and France, but until almost the end of the Middle Ages, their relations with their subjects were essentially those of lords with their vassals. They had *dominium* but not sovereignty. In other words, they had the highest proprietary rights over the lands which constituted their fiefs; they did not necessarily possess supreme political authority over all the persons who lived on their lands. Only through extension of the taxing power, the judicial power, and the establishment of professional armies did such rulers as Philip Augustus of France, Henry II of England, and Frederick II of the Holy Roman Empire take steps toward becoming sovereigns in the modern sense. Even so, their domains continued their essentially feudal character for several more centuries. In yet another respect these rulers were not sovereign: they were not free from external control. In theory, they were subject to the Holy Roman Emperor, who was supposed to have a universal secular authority over Western Christendom. More important, they were responsible for their personal conduct and even for their relations with their subjects to the spiritual authority of the Pope. For example, Pope Innocent III compelled King Philip Augustus of France, by means of an interdict on his kingdom, to take back the wife he had repudiated. The same Pope forced King John of England to acknowledge England and Ireland as fiefs of the papacy.

By some historians the beginnings of the modern state system are considered to date from the invasion of Italy in 1494 by King Charles VIII of France. Involved in this war for conquest of foreign territory were considerations of dynastic prestige, the balance of power, elaborate diplomacy, and alliances and counteralliances. It was in no sense a religious or ideological war but a struggle for power and territorial aggrandizement. Other historians conceive of the Reformation as the primary cause of the modern state system. The Protestant Revolution broke the unity of Western Christendom. It facilitated the determination of kings and princes to make their own power complete by repudiating the authority of a universal Church. As early as 1555 the Peace of Augsburg gave to each German prince the right to decide whether Lutheranism or Catholicism should be the faith of his people. It was probably the Treaty of

Westphalia, however, that played the dominant role in making the modern state system a political reality. This treaty, which ended the Thirty Years' War in 1648, transferred territories from one rule to another with no regard for the nationality of their inhabitants. It recognized the independence of Holland and Switzerland and reduced the Holy Roman Empire to a fiction. Each of the German princes was acknowledged as a sovereign ruler with power to make war and peace and to govern his domain as he chose. Finally, the treaty introduced the principle that *all* states, regardless of their size or power, were equal under international law and endowed with full and complete control over their territories and inhabitants.

Whatever its origins, the modern state system may be considered to embody the following elements: (1) the equality and independence of all states; (2) the right of each state to pursue a foreign policy of its own making, to form alliances and counteralliances, and to wage war for its own advantage; (3) the use of diplomacy as a substitute for war, often involving intrigue, espionage, and treachery to the extent necessary for political advantage; (4) the balance of power as a device for preventing war or for assuring the support of allies if war becomes necessary. Most of these elements of the state system have continued to the present day. Even the establishment of the League of Nations and the United Nations brought no substantial change, for both were founded upon the principle of the sovereign equality of independent states. Some observers believe that there will be no genuine prospect of world peace until the system of sovereign independent states is recognized as obsolete and is replaced by a world community of nations organized on a federal basis.

SELECTED READINGS

· *Items so designated are available in paperbound editions.*

HISTORICAL AND BIOGRAPHICAL

Adams, G. B., *Constitutional History of England*, New York, 1921. A standard work, still highly regarded.

·Aylmer, G. E., *A Short History of Seventeenth-Century England*, New York, 1963 (Mentor).

·Beloff, Max, *The Age of Absolutism*, New York, 1962 (Torchbook).

Bruun, Geoffrey, *The Enlightened Despots*, New York, 1929. The best short treatise.

Carston, F. L., *The Origins of Prussia*, London, 1954.

Coles, Paul, *The Ottoman Impact on Europe*, New York, 1968.

· Elliott, J. H., *Imperial Spain, 1469–1716*, New York, 1964 (Mentor).

·Elton, G. R., *The Tudor Revolution in Government*, New York, 1959 (Cambridge University Press). A thoughtful interpretation.

·Ford, Franklin L., *Strasbourg in Transition, 1648–1789*, Cambridge, (Norton Library).

·Gardiner, S. R., *Oliver Cromwell*, New York, 1901 (Collier).

Gipson, L. H., *The Great War for the Empire*, New York, 1954.

READINGS • Harris, R. W., *A Short History of Eighteenth-Century England*, New York, 1963 (Mentor).

• Hill, Cristopher, *The Century of Revolution, 1603–1714*, London, 1963 (Norton Library).

Holborn, Hajo, *A History of Modern Germany: 1648–1840*, New York, 1964.

• Keir, D. L., *The Constitutional History of Modern Britain, Since 1485*, Princeton, 1960 (Norton Library). An excellent introductory survey.

• Neale, J. E., *Queen Elizabeth*, New York, 1931 (Anchor).

Nowak, Frank, *Medieval Slavdom and the Rise of Russia*, New York, 1930.

Ogg, David, *Louis XIV*, New York, 1951. A good brief account.

Packard, L. B., *The Age of Louis XIV*, New York, 1929. An excellent short treatise.

• Pares, Sir Bernard, *A History of Russia*, New York, 1965 (Vintage).

Petrie, C., *Earlier Diplomatic History, 1492–1713*, New York, 1949. Valuable for origins of the state system.

• Pollard, A. F., *Henry VIII*, New York, 1951 (Torchbook).

Riasanovsky, N. V., *A History of Russia*, New York, 1963.

Schenk, W., *The Concern for Social Justice in the Puritan Revolution*, New York, 1948. Valuable and interesting.

Scherger, G. L., *The Evolution of Modern Liberty*, New York, 1904.

• Sumner, B. H., *Peter the Great and the Emergence of Russia*, London, 1950 (Collier).

• Trevelyan, G. M., *England under the Stuarts*, New York, 1904 (Barnes & Noble). Thoughtful and very readable.

• ———, *The English Revolution 1688–1689*, London, 1938 (Galaxy). Emphasizes results.

Trevor-Davies, R., *The Golden Century of Spain*, London, 1937. A good brief account.

• Wedgwood, C. V., *The Thirty Years' War*, London, 1938 (Anchor). A complete and well-reasoned account.

———, *Richelieu and the French Monarchy*, New York, 1950.

• Wolf, John B., *The Emergence of the Great Powers, 1685–1715*, New York, 1951 (Torchbook).

• ———, *Louis XIV*, New York, 1968 (Norton).

POLITICAL THEORY

• Allen, J. W., *History of Political Thought in the Sixteenth Century*, New York, 1928 (Barnes & Noble). The standard work, still unsurpassed.

• Figgis, J. N., *The Divine Right of Kings*, Cambridge, 1922 (Torchbook).

• Friedrich, C. J., *The Age of the Baroque, 1610–1660*, New York, 1952 (Torchbook). Emphasizes political theory.

Sabine, G. H., *A History of Political Theory*, New York, 1961. Especially good on sixteenth and seventeenth centuries.

SOURCE MATERIALS

Bodin, Jean, *Six Books Concerning the State*, especially Book I, Chs. I, VI, VIII, X, Cambridge, 1962.

• Grotius, Hugo, *The Law of War and Peace*, especially Prolegomena and Book I, Ch. I, New York, 1963 (Library of Liberal Arts).

• Hobbes, Thomas, *Leviathan*, Part I, Chs. XIII–XV; Part II, Chs. XIII, XVIII, XIX, XXI, XXVI, New York (Library of Liberal Arts and others).

Webster, Hutton, *Historical Selections*, pp. 640–42, "The Bill of Rights."

CHAPTER 18

The Intellectual Revolution
of the Seventeenth and
Eighteenth Centuries

> I wish we could derive the rest of the phenomena of nature . . .
> from mechanical principles, for I am induced by many reasons
> to suspect that they may all depend upon certain forces by which
> the particles of bodies, by some causes hitherto unknown, are
> either mutually impelled towards one another, and cohere in reg-
> ular figures, or are repelled and recede from one another. These
> forces being unknown, philosophers have hitherto attempted the
> search of Nature in vain; but I hope the principles here laid down
> will afford some light either to this or some truer method of
> philosophy.
>
> —Sir Isaac Newton, Preface to the First Edition,
> *Mathematical Principles* (*Principia Mathematica*)

By one of the ironies of history, the period when arrogant despots bestrode the nations of the European continent was a period of stupendous intellectual achievement. To one who understands the underlying forces at work in this and in preceding ages, however, the cultural progress of the seventeenth and eighteenth centuries is not particularly mysterious. The absolute monarchs, of course, had nothing to do with it. Though a few, like Frederick the Great, dabbled in philosophy and science, not one of them could accurately be described as a patron of learning. The intellectual advance of their time was due rather to factors growing out of the principal economic and cultural movements in European history after the end of the Middle Ages. Characteristic examples were the influence of the Renaissance, the increasing prosperity of the middle and lower classes, and the widened intellectual horizons produced by the new knowledge of distant lands and strange peoples.

Causes of intellectual advance in the 17th and 18th centuries

497

Character of
the Intellectual
Revolution

See color map
at page 528

The achievements in philosophy and science in the seventeenth and eighteenth centuries, together with the new attitudes resulting therefrom, constitute what is commonly known as the Intellectual Revolution. But to speak of this revolution as if it were an event without precedent in the records of man leads to an erroneous conception. On several occasions before this, developments had occurred which went quite as far in upsetting old habits of thinking as did any of the discoveries of the seventeenth and eighteenth centuries. Illustrations may be found in the radicalism and individualism of the Sophists in fifth-century Athens and in the disturbing effects of the revival of paganism and worldliness in the later Middle Ages. Nevertheless, the Intellectual Revolution of the seventeenth and eighteenth centuries was somewhat broader in scope than any of these earlier upheavals, and its results were perhaps more significant for our own generation.

1. PHILOSOPHY IN THE SEVENTEENTH CENTURY

The rationalism
and dualism of
René Descartes

Perhaps without straining the imagination too much, we can say that the Intellectual Revolution had a triple paternity. Its fathers were René Descartes, Sir Isaac Newton, and John Locke. More will be said later about Newton and Locke. For the present we need to examine the teachings of the renowned Frenchman who initiated the dominant philosophic trend of the seventeenth century. René Descartes (1596–1650), soldier of fortune, mathematician, and physicist, was an unswerving advocate of rationalism in philosophy. He was, of course, not the first exponent of reason as the pathway to knowledge; but his rationalism differed from that of most earlier thinkers—the medieval Scholastics, for instance—in his rigid exclusion of authority. He scorned reliance upon books, no matter how venerable the reputation of their authors. Convinced that both traditional opinion and the ordinary experiences of mankind are untrustworthy guides, he determined to adopt a new method entirely unprejudiced by either. This method was the mathematical instrument of pure deduction. It would consist in starting with simple, self-evident truths or axioms, as in geometry, and then reasoning from these to particular conclusions. Descartes believed that he had found such an axiom in his famous principle: "I think, therefore I am." From this he maintained that it is possible to deduce a sound body of universal knowledge—to prove, for example, that God exists, that man is a thinking animal, and that mind is distinct from matter. These "truths," he declared, are just as infallible as the truths of geometry, for they are products of the same unerring method.

But Descartes is important not only as the father of the new rationalism. He was also partly responsible for introducing the conception of a mechanistic universe. He taught that the whole world of matter, organic and inorganic alike, could be defined in terms of extension and motion. "Give me extension and motion," he once boldly declared, "and I will construct the universe." Every individual thing—a solar system, a star, the earth itself—is a self-operating machine propelled by a force arising from the original motion given to the universe by God. Descartes did not even exclude the bodies of animals and of men from this general mechanistic pattern. The whole world of physical nature is one. The behavior of animals and the emotional reactions of men flow automatically from internal or external stimuli. He insisted, however, that man is distinct from all other creatures in the possession of a reasoning faculty. Mind is not a form of matter, but an entirely separate substance implanted in the body of man by God. Along with this dualism of mind and matter, Descartes also believed in *innate* ideas. He taught that self-evident truths having no relation to sensory experience must be inherent in the mind itself. Man does not learn them through the use of his senses, but perceives them instinctively because they have been part of his mental equipment from birth.

Of the several teachings of Descartes the new rationalism and mechanism were by far the most influential. In fact, these two doctrines were almost sufficient in themselves to have produced a revolution, for they involved the rejection of nearly all the theological bias of the past. No longer need the philosopher pay homage to revelation as a source of truth; reason was now held to be the solitary fount of knowledge, while the whole idea of spiritual meaning in the universe was cast aside like a worn-out garment. Descartes' principles of rationalism and mechanism were adopted in some form or other by the majority of the philosophers of the seventeenth century. The most noted of his intellectual successors were the Dutch Jew Benedict Spinoza and the Englishman Thomas Hobbes, whom we have already encountered as a political theorist. Benedict (or Baruch) Spinoza was born in Amsterdam in 1632 and died an outcast from his native community forty-five years later. His parents were members of a group of Jewish immigrants who had fled from persecution in Portugal and Spain and had taken refuge in the Netherlands. At an early age Spinoza came under the influence of a disciple of Descartes and as a result grew critical of some of the dogmas of the Hebrew faith. For this he was expelled from the synagogue, cursed by the chief priests and elders, and banished from the community of his people. From 1656 till his death he lived in various cities of Holland, eking out a meager existence by grinding lenses. During these years he developed his philosophy, incorporating the rationalism and mechanism but not the dualism of Descartes. Spinoza maintained that there is only one essential substance in the universe, of which mind and matter are but different aspects. This single substance is God, who is identical with nature itself. Such a conception of the universe was, of course, pure pantheism; but it

An Illustration from Descartes' *De Homine*, Showing the Relationship between Perception and Motion of the Hand

Descartes' intellectual successors: Benedict Spinoza

was grounded upon reason rather than upon faith, and it was intended to express the scientific notions of the unity of nature and the continuity of cause and effect. It is not without significance that one of the greatest of modern scientists, Albert Einstein, declared that his idea of God was the same as that of Spinoza.

Much more than Descartes, Spinoza was interested in ethical questions. Having come to the conclusion early in life that the things men prize most highly—wealth, pleasure, power, and fame—are empty and vain, he set out to inquire whether there was any perfect good which would give lasting and unmitigated happiness to all who attained it. By a process of geometric reasoning he attempted to prove that this perfect good consists in "love of God"—that is, in worship of the order and harmony of nature. If men will but realize that the universe is a beautiful machine, whose operation cannot be interrupted for the benefit of particular persons, they will gain that serenity of mind for which philosophers have yearned through the ages. We can only be delivered from impossible hopes and cringing fears by acknowledging to ourselves that the order of nature is unalterably fixed, and that man cannot change his fate. In other words, we gain true freedom by realizing that we are not free. But with all his determinism, Spinoza was an earnest apostle of tolerance, justice, and rational living. He wrote in defense of religious liberty and, in the face of cruel mistreatment, set a noble example in his personal life of kindliness, humanity, and freedom from vengeful passions.

The third of the great rationalists of the seventeenth century was Thomas Hobbes. Born before either Descartes or Spinoza, he outlived both. Hobbes agreed with his two contemporaries in the belief that geometry furnished the only proper method of discovering philosophic truth. But he denied the doctrine of innate ideas, maintaining that the *origin* of all knowledge is in sense perception. He likewise refused to accept either the dualism of Descartes or the pantheism of Spinoza. According to Hobbes, absolutely nothing exists except matter. Mind is simply motion in the brain or perhaps a subtle form of matter, but in no sense a distinct substance. God, also, if we can believe that He exists, must be assumed to have a physical body. There is nothing spiritual anywhere in the universe of which the mind can conceive. This was the most thoroughgoing materialism to make its appearance since the days of Lucretius. Naturally it was combined with mechanism, as materialism usually is. Hobbes contended that not only the universe but man himself can be explained mechanically. All that man does is determined by appetites or aversions, and these in turn are either inherited or acquired through experience. In similar fashion, Hobbes maintained that there are no absolute standards of good and evil. Good is merely that which gives pleasure; evil, that which brings pain. Thus did Hobbes combine with materialism and mechanism a thoroughgoing philosophy of hedonism.

2. THE ENLIGHTENMENT

The climax of the Intellectual Revolution in philosophy was a movement known as the Enlightenment. Beginning in England about 1680, it quickly spread into most of the countries of northern Europe and was not without influence in America. The supreme manifestation of the Enlightenment, however, was in France, and the period of its real importance was the eighteenth century. Few other movements in history have had such profound effects in molding men's thoughts or in shaping the course of their actions. The philosophy of the Enlightenment was built around a number of significant concepts, chief among which were the following:

(1) Reason is the only infallible guide to wisdom. All knowledge has its roots in sense perception, but the impressions of our senses are but the raw material of truth, which has to be refined in the crucible of reason before it can have value in explaining the world or in pointing the way to the improvement of life.

(2) The universe is a machine governed by inflexible laws which man cannot override. The order of nature is absolutely uniform and not subject in any way to miracles or to any other form of divine interference.

(3) The future is bright with promise if men will abandon old superstitions and prejudices and live in accordance with the dictates of reason. The leaders of the Enlightenment believed in the possibility of a "heavenly city" delivered from ignorance, intolerance, and oppression. It would be purged also of artificiality and enslavement to outworn conventions. Religion, government, and economic institutions would be reduced to their simplest and most natural forms in order to lessen the possibility of tyranny and greed.[1]

(4) There is no such thing as original sin. Men are not inherently depraved but are driven to acts of cruelty and meanness by scheming priests and war-making despots. The infinite perfectibility of human nature, and therefore of society itself, would become easily realized if men were free to follow the guidance of reason and their own instincts.

The inspiration for the Enlightenment came partly from the rationalism of Descartes, Spinoza, and Hobbes, but the real founders of the movement were Sir Isaac Newton (1642–1727) and John Locke (1632–1704). Although Newton was not a philosopher in the ordinary sense, his work has the deepest significance for the history of thought. His majestic achievement was to bring the whole world of nature under a precise mechanical interpretation. His celebrated principle that "every particle of matter in the universe attracts every other particle with a force varying inversely as the square of the distance between them and directly proportional to

Sir Isaac Newton

The chief philosophical concepts of the Enlightenment

The founders of the Enlightenment: (1) Sir Isaac Newton

[1] The political and economic doctrines of the Enlightenment will be treated more fully in the following chapter on The French Revolution.

the product of their masses" was held to be valid not only on this earth but throughout the endless expanse of solar systems. From this it was an easy step to the conclusion that every event in nature is governed by universal laws, which can be formulated as precisely as mathematical principles. The discovery of these laws is the chief business of science, and the duty of man is to allow them to operate unhindered. Gone was the medieval conception of a universe guided by benevolent purpose; men now dwelt in a world in which the procession of events was as automatic as the ticking of a watch. Newton's philosophy did not rule out the idea of a God, but it deprived Him of His power to guide the stars in their courses or to command the sun to stand still.

The influence of John Locke was quite different from that of Newton, but it was no less important. Locke was the father of a new theory of knowledge, which served as the keynote of the philosophy of the Enlightenment. Rejecting Descartes' doctrine of innate ideas, he maintained that all of man's knowledge originates from sense perception. This theory had already been asserted by Hobbes; but Locke systematized and enlarged it. He insisted that the human mind at birth is a blank tablet, a "white paper," upon which absolutely nothing is inscribed. It does not even contain the idea of a God or any notions of right and wrong. Not until the newborn child begins to have experiences, to perceive the external world with its senses, is anything registered in its mind. But the simple ideas which result directly from sense perception are merely the foundations of knowledge; no human being could live intelligently on the basis of them alone. These simple ideas must be integrated and fused into *complex ideas*. This is the function of the reason or understanding, which has the power to combine, coordinate, and organize the impressions received from the senses and thus to build a usable body of general truth. Sensation and reason are both indispensable—the one for furnishing the mind with the raw materials of knowledge and the other for working them into meaningful form. It was this modification of rationalism which became a leading element in the philosophy of the Enlightenment. Locke is significant also for his defense of religious toleration and for his liberal political theory, which will be discussed in the chapter on the French Revolution.

The Enlightenment blossomed forth in its fullest glory in France during the eighteenth century under the leadership of Voltaire and other like-minded critics of the established order. Voltaire, or François Marie Arouet as he was originally named, epitomized the Enlightenment in somewhat the same way as Luther did the Reformation or Leonardo da Vinci the Italian Renaissance. A son of the bourgeoisie, Voltaire was born in 1694 and, despite his delicate physique, lived to within eleven years of the outbreak of the French Revolution. He developed a taste for satiric writing early in his life and got himself into numerous scrapes by his ridicule of noblemen

An Illustration from *Candide* by Voltaire

and pompous officials. As a consequence of one of his lampoons he was sent to the Bastille and afterwards exiled to England. Here he remained for three years, acquiring a deep admiration for British institutions, and composing his first philosophic work, which he entitled *Letters on the English*. In this work he popularized the ideas of Newton and Locke, whom he had come to regard as two of the greatest geniuses who ever lived. Most of his later writings—the *Philosophical Dictionary*, *Candide*, his histories, and many of his poems and essays—were also concerned with exposition of the doctrine that the world is governed by natural laws, and that reason and concrete experience are the only dependable guides for man to follow. Voltaire had contempt for the smug optimism which taught that the ills of each make up the good of all, and that everything is for the best in the best of all possible worlds. He saw, on the contrary, universal misery, hatred, strife, and oppression. Only in his utopia of El Dorado, which he placed somewhere in South America, were freedom and peace conceivable. Here there were no monks, no priests, no lawsuits, and no prisons. The inhabitants dwelt together without malice or greed, worshiping God in accordance with the dictates of reason, and solving their problems by logic and science. But this idyllic life was made possible only by the fact that the land was cut off by impassable mountains from the "regimented assassins of Europe."

Voltaire is best known as a champion of individual freedom. He regarded all restrictions upon liberty of speech and opinion as barbarous. In a letter to one of his opponents he wrote what has often been quoted as the highest criterion of intellectual tolerance: "I do not agree with a word that you say, but I will defend to the death your right to say it." [2] But if there was any one form of repression that Voltaire abhorred more than others, it was the tyranny of organized religion. He blasted with fire and brimstone

[2] E. B. Hall, *Voltaire in His Letters*, p. 65.

against the monstrous cruelty of the Church in torturing and burning intelligent men who dared to question its dogmas. With reference to the whole system of persecuting and privileged orthodoxy, he adopted as his slogan, "Crush the infamous thing." He was almost as unsparing in his attacks upon political tyranny, especially when it resulted in the slaughter of thousands to glut the ambitions of despots. "It is forbidden to kill," he sarcastically asserted: "therefore all murderers are punished unless they kill in large numbers and to the sound of trumpets." [3]

Among the other philosophers of the Enlightenment in France were Denis Diderot and Jean d'Alembert, both of whom lived in the latter part of the eighteenth century. Diderot and d'Alembert were the chief members of a group known as the Encyclopedists, so-called from their contributions to the *Encyclopedia*, which was intended to be a complete summation of the philosophic and scientific knowledge of the age. In general, both of them agreed with the rationalism and liberalism of Voltaire. Diderot, for example, maintained that "men will never be free till the last king is strangled with the entrails of the last priest." D'Alembert, while accepting the rationalist and individualist tendencies of the Enlightenment, differed from most of his associates in advocating a diffusion of the new doctrines among all the people. The general attitude of his contempo-

Other philosophers of the Enlightenment: the Encyclopedists

[3] *Philosophical Dictionary*, article on "War."

A Gathering of the Philosophes. The seated figures are Voltaire with his left hand raised, then moving to his left, Diderot, Père Adam, Condorcet, d'Alembert, Abbé Maury, and Laharpe.

raries, notably Voltaire, was to despise the common man, to regard him as a mere clodhopper beyond redemption from ignorance and grossness. But for d'Alembert the only assurance of progress lay in universal enlightenment. Accordingly, he maintained that the truths of reason and science should be taught to the masses in the hope that eventually the whole world might be freed from darkness and tyranny.

Although the Enlightenment was of much less importance in Germany than in France or England, it did give birth to some progressive ideas. The most widely recognized of its German leaders was Gotthold Lessing (1729–1781), primarily a dramatist and critic but also a philosopher of humane and far-sighted views. The essence of his philosophy is tolerance, founded upon a sincere conviction that no one religion has a monopoly of truth. In his play, *Nathan the Wise,* he expounded the idea that nobility of character has no particular relation to theological creeds. He maintained that, historically, men of charitable spirit were as often found among Jews and Moslems as among Christians. Largely for this reason he condemned adherence to any one system of dogma and taught that the development of each of the world's great religions (Christianity included) was simply a step in the spiritual evolution of mankind. One of Lessing's friends and disciples turned out to be the foremost Jewish philosopher of the Enlightenment. His name was Moses Mendelssohn (1729–1786), and he was a sickly product of the ghetto in the German town of Dessau. Agreeing with Lessing that religions should be judged by their effects upon the conduct of their followers, Mendelssohn urged his Jewish brethren to give up their notion of themselves as the Chosen People of God. They should look upon Judaism merely as one of a number of good religions. He recommended also that Jews should renounce their clannishness, that they should cease to long for a return to Zion, and that they should adapt themselves to the civic requirements of the countries in which they lived. His teachings, along with those of Moses Maimonides, the great rationalist Jew of the twelfth century, were among the principal sources of what has since come to be known as Reform Judaism.

The Enlightenment in Germany

Two other philosophers are commonly given a place in the Enlightenment—the Scotsman David Hume (1711–1776) and the Frenchman Rousseau (1712–1778).[4] Neither, however, was in full agreement with the majority of his contemporaries. Hume is noted above all for his skepticism. He taught that the mind is a mere bundle of impressions, derived exclusively from the senses and tied together by habits of association. That is, we learn from experience to associate warmth with fire and nourishment with bread. If we had never actually experienced the sensation of warmth, no reasoning faculty in our minds would enable us to draw the conclusion

David Hume, the foremost skeptic of the Enlightenment

[4] By birth Rousseau was French Swiss, a native of Geneva, but he lived the greater part of his life in France.

that fire produces heat. But constant repetition of the fact that when we see a flame we generally experience warmth leads to the habit of associating the two in our minds. Impressions and associations are all that there is to knowing. Since every idea in the mind is nothing but a copy of a sense impression, it follows that we can know nothing of final causes, the nature of substance, or the origin of the universe. We cannot be sure of any of the conclusions of reason except those which, like the principles of mathematics, can be verified by actual experience. All others are likely to be the products of feelings and desires, of animal urges and fears. In thus denying the competence of reason, Hume placed himself almost entirely outside the main intellectual trend of the Enlightenment. As a matter of fact, he helped to prepare its death.

In similar measure Jean Jacques Rousseau repudiated many of the basic assumptions which had stemmed from Newton and Locke. A hopeless misfit wallowing in the mire of his emotions, Rousseau would have been a marvel indeed if he had championed the rationalist doctrines of the Enlightenment. Whole segments of his personality appear to have been out of joint. He failed in nearly every occupation he undertook. He preached lofty ideals of educational reform, but abandoned his own children to a foundling asylum. He quarreled wih everybody and reveled in morbid self-disclosures. Undoubtedly it was these qualities of temperament which were largely responsible for his revolt against the coldly intellectual doctrines of his contemporaries. He maintained that to worship reason as the infallible guide to conduct and truth is to lean upon a broken reed. Reason, of course, has its uses, but it is not the whole answer. In the really vital problems of life it is much safer to rely upon feelings, to follow our instincts and emotions. These are the ways of nature and are therefore more conducive to happiness than the artificial lucubrations of the intellect. The "thinking man is a depraved animal." [5] Yet notwithstanding his contempt for reason, Rousseau was in other ways thoroughly in agreement with the viewpoint of the Enlightenment. He extolled the life of the "noble savage" even more fervently than did any of his associates. In his prize-winning essay, the *Discourse on the Arts and Sciences*, he contrasted the freedom and innocence of primitive men with the tyranny and wickedness of civilized society, even insisting that the progress of learning is destructive of human happiness. He shared the impatience of the Enlightenment with every sort of restriction upon individual freedom, though he was much more concerned about the liberty and equality of the masses than were the other reformers of his time. He regarded the origin of private property as the primary source of misery in human society.

It would be almost impossible to fix limits to the influence of Rousseau. As the first significant writer to uphold the validity of

Rousseau's antirationalism

[5] *A Discourse on the Origin of Inequality* (Everyman Library ed.), p. 181.

conclusions dictated by emotion and sentiment he is commonly considered the father of romanticism. For fifty years after his time Europe was bathed in literary tears, and it was difficult to find a philosopher who would boldly assert the inerrancy of reason. His slogan, "Back to nature," furnished the foundation for a veritable cult dedicated to the pursuit of the simple life. The new fashion spread even to the simpering courtiers at Versailles. The queen herself designed a dainty rural village in a corner of the palace grounds and diverted herself by playing milkmaid. But Rousseau's influence was not limited to the founding of romanticism and the encouragement of sentimental devotion to nature. His dogmas of equality and popular sovereignty, though frequently misinterpreted, became the rallying cries of revolutionaries and of thousands of more moderate opponents of the existing regime. And, as the chapter on the French Revolution will show, it was Rousseau's political philosophy that provided the real inspiration for the modern ideal of majority rule.

Rousseau Playing a Hurdy-Gurdy

The most typical religious philosophy of the Enlightenment was deism. The originator of this philosophy appears to have been an Englishman by the name of Lord Herbert of Cherbury (1583–1648). In the eighteenth century deistic doctrines were propagated by such men as Voltaire, Diderot, and Rousseau in France; Alexander Pope, Lord Bolingbroke, and Lord Shaftesbury in England; and Thomas Paine, Benjamin Franklin, and Thomas Jefferson in America. Not satisfied with condemning the irrational elements in religion, the deists went on to denounce every form of organized faith. Christianity was spared no more than the others. Institutionalized religions were branded as instruments of exploitation, devised by wily scoundrels to enable them to prey upon the ignorant masses. As Voltaire expressed it, "the first divine was the first rogue who met the first fool." [6] But the aims of the deists were not all destructive. They were interested not merely in demolishing Christianity but in constructing a simpler and more natural religion to replace it. The fundamental tenets of this new religion were about as follows: (1) there is one God who created the universe and ordained the natural laws that control it; (2) God does not intervene in the affairs of men in this world: He is not a capricious deity, like the God of the Christians and Jews, making "one vessel unto honour and another unto dishonour" in accordance with His peculiar whims; (3) prayer, sacraments, and ritual are mere useless mumbo jumbo; God cannot be wheedled or bribed into setting aside natural law for the benefit of particular persons; (4) man is endowed with freedom of will to choose the good and avoid the evil; there is no predestination of some to be saved and others to be damned, but rewards and punishments in the life hereafter are determined solely by the individual's conduct on earth.

The religious doctrines of the Enlightenment: deism

[6] *Philosophical Dictionary*, article on "Religion."

507

The influence
of the
Enlightenment

Naïve though many of its assumptions were, the influence of the Enlightenment was tremendous. No other movement, with the possible exception of humanism, had done more to dispel the accumulated fogs of superstition and illogical restraint that still enveloped the Western world. The rationalism of the Enlightenment helped to break the shackles of political tyranny and to weaken the power of conscienceless priests. Its ideal of religious freedom was a leading factor in the ultimate separation of church and state and in the liberation of the Jews from ancient restrictions. The humanitarianism implied in the opposition to oppression carried over into agitation for penal reform and for the abolition of slavery. The desire for a natural order of society contributed to a demand for the overthrow of relics of feudalism and for the destruction of monopoly and unearned privilege. If there was any evil result of the Enlightenment, it probably consisted in an exaggerated development of individualism. Liberty of the individual against political and religious tyranny was sometimes easily translated into the right of the strong to satisfy economic greed at the expense of the weak.

3. REVOLUTIONARY SCIENTIFIC DISCOVERIES

Achievements
in the physical
sciences:
(1) physics

The major scientific interests of the Intellectual Revolution followed very largely the paths marked out during the late Renaissance. Accordingly, primary attention was given to the physical sciences. Unquestionably the most illustrious physicist of the Intellectual Revolution was Sir Isaac Newton. His conclusions molded men's thinking in philosophy for a hundred years. His influence upon science was even more lasting; the Newtonian physics stood virtually unchallenged until the twentieth century. It was in 1687 that Newton published his renowned law of universal gravitation. Based in part upon the work of Galileo, this law provided a single unifying principle for the entire world of matter. Besides, it re-

The Manuscript of Newton's *Philosophie Naturalis Principia Mathematica*. The first edition was published in 1687.

An Early Eighteenth-Century Laboratory as Seen in Diderot's *Encyclopedia*

moved all doubt as to the validity of the Copernican hypothesis. But Newton's researches in physics were not confined to the problem of gravitation. He devised a series of tables, of great value to navigation, by which the changing positions of the moon among the stars could be accurately predicted. He invented the sextant for measuring these positions and thereby determining latitude and longitude. Some of his other achievements proved of substantial value in paving the way for later discoveries regarding the nature of light. He shares with Galileo the honor of being the father of modern physics.

Some preliminary progress was made during the Intellectual Revolution in connection with the understanding of electrical phenomena. At the beginning of the seventeenth century the Englishman William Gilbert (1540–1603), discovered the properties of lodestones and introduced the word "electricity" into the language.[7] Other scientists quickly became interested, and sensational results were anticipated from experiments with the marvelous "fluid." A learned Jesuit even suggested that two persons might communicate at a distance by means of magnetized needles which would point simultaneously to identical letters of the alphabet. Late in the eighteenth century Alessandro Volta (1745–1827) constructed the first battery. Still another important achievement in electrical physics was the invention in 1746 of the Leyden jar for the storage of electric energy. It was mainly as a result of this invention that Benjamin Franklin was able to show that lightning and electricity are identical. In his celebrated kite experiment in 1752 he succeeded in charging a Leyden jar from a thunderstorm.

(2) progress in the understanding of electrical phenomena

[7] "Electric" comes from the Greek word for amber. Gilbert and others had observed that amber rubbed on fur will attract paper, hair, straw, and various other things. Preserved Smith, *A History of Modern Culture*, I, 63–64.

Almost as spectacular as the progress in physics was the development of chemistry. If any one scientist can be called the founder of modern chemistry, the title must be given to Robert Boyle (1627–1691). The son of an Irish nobleman, Boyle achieved distinction in 1661 with the publication of his *Sceptical Chymist, or Chymico-Physical Doubts and Paradoxes*. In this work he rejected the theories of the alchemists and thereby contributed toward the establishment of chemistry as a pure science. In addition, he distinguished between a mixture and a compound, learned a great deal about the nature of phosphorus, produced alcohol from wood, suggested the idea of chemical elements, and reviewed the atomic theory. No scientist before his time had foreshadowed so much of the knowledge of modern chemistry.

Despite the work of Boyle, little further development of chemistry occurred for almost 100 years. The reason lay partly in the wide acceptance of errors concerning such matters as heat, flame, air, and the phenomenon of combustion. The most common of these errors was the so-called phlogiston theory. Phlogiston was the fire substance. When an object burned, phlogiston was supposed to be given off. The remaining ash was said to be the true material. In the second half of the eighteenth century important discoveries were made which ultimately overthrew this theory and cleared the way for a true understanding of some of the most familiar chemical reactions. In 1766 Henry Cavendish, one of the richest men in England, reported the discovery of a new kind of gas obtained by treating iron, zinc, and other metals with sulphuric acid. He showed that this gas, now known as hydrogen, would not of itself support combustion, and yet would be rapidly consumed by a fire with access to the air. In 1774 oxygen was discovered by Joseph Priestley, who had managed for some years to squeeze enough time out of his profession of Unitarian minister to perform some extensive experiments in natural science. He found that a candle would burn with extraordinary vigor when placed in the new gas—a fact which indicated clearly that combustion was not caused by any mysterious principle in the flame itself. A few years after this discovery Cavendish demonstrated that air and water, long supposed to be elements, are a mixture and a compound, respectively, the first being composed principally of oxygen and nitrogen and the second of oxygen and hydrogen.

The final blow to the phlogiston theory was administered by Antoine Lavoisier (1743–1794), one of the greatest of all scientists of the Intellectual Revolution. By some he has been called "the Newton of Chemistry." Lavoisier proved that both combustion and respiration involve oxidation, the one being rapid and the other slow. He provided the names for oxygen and hydrogen, demonstrated that the diamond is a form of carbon, and argued that life itself is essentially a chemical process. But undoubtedly his greatest accomplishment was his discovery of the law of the conservation of mass. He found evidence that "although matter may alter its state in a series of chemical actions, it does not change in amount; the quantity of matter is the same at the end as at the beginning of every operation, and can be traced by its weight." This "law" has, of course, been modified by later discoveries regarding the structure of the atom and the conversion of some forms of matter into energy. It is hardly too much to say that as a result of Lavoisier's genius chemistry became a true science. To the lasting shame of the French Revolutionists, he was put to death on the guillotine at the age of fifty-one, a victim of the Reign of Terror.

Although it was the physical sciences that received the major attention in the Intellectual Revolution, the biological sciences were by no means neglected. One of the greatest of the early biologists was Robert Hooke (1635–1703), the first man to see and describe the cellular structure of plants. This achievement was soon followed by the work of Marcello Malpighi (1628–1694) in demonstrating the sexuality of plants and in comparing the function of vegetable leaves with that of the lungs of animals. About the same time a Dutch businessman and amateur scientist, Anthony van Leeuwenhoek (1632–1723), discovered protozoa and bacteria and wrote the first description of human spermatozoa. The seventeenth century also witnessed some progress in embryology. About 1670 the Dutch physician, Jan Swammerdam (1637–1680), carefully described the life history of certain insects from the caterpillar stage to maturity and compared the change of tadpole into frog with the development of the human embryo.

In many ways the end of the seventeenth century appeared to mark a decline of originality in the sciences that deal with living things. During the next 100 years biologists were inclined more and more to center their efforts upon description and classification of knowledge already in existence. The most brilliant classifier of biological knowledge was the Swedish scientist, Carl von Linné (1707–1778), more commonly known by his Latinized name of Linnaeus. In his *System of Nature* and in his *Botanical Philosophy* Linnaeus divided all natural objects into three kingdoms: stone, animal, and vegetable. Each of these kingdoms he subdivided into classes, genera, and species. He invented the system of biological nomenclature still in use, by which every plant and animal is designated by two scientific names, the first denoting the genus and the second the species. Thus he called man *Homo sapiens*. Though some people condemned Linnaeus for presuming to rename the animals that Adam had named, his classification was nevertheless widely adopted even in his own time. Despite certain defects which have had to be corrected, it still has its value.

The second great genius of descriptive biology in the eighteenth century was the Frenchman Georges Buffon (1707–1788). His *Natural History* in forty-four volumes, though intended as a summation of practically all science, dealt mainly with man and other

Lavoisier's Apparatus for the Decomposition of Air

The biological scientists: Hooke, Malpighi, Leeuwenhoek, and Swammerdam

Linnaeus

vertebrates. While much of the material in this work was taken from the writings of other scientists and from the accounts of travelers, the author did have a unique ability in reducing a vast body of knowledge to orderly arrangement and in enlivening it with his own interpretations. The chief importance of Buffon to us lies in his recognition of the close relationship between man and the higher animals. Though he could never quite bring himself to accept the full implications of the evolutionary theory, he was nonetheless strongly impressed by the striking resemblances among all of the higher species. He admitted the possibility that the entire range of organic forms had descended from a single species.

The paucity of
medical
achievements in
the 17th century

The development of physiology and medicine progressed rather slowly during the seventeenth century. Among the several reasons, one was the inadequate preparation of physicians, many of whom had begun their professional careers with little more training than a kind of apprenticeship under an older practitioner. Another was the common disrepute in which surgery was held as a mere trade, like that of barber or blacksmith.[8] Perhaps the most serious of all was the prejudice against dissection of human bodies as a basis of anatomical study. As late as 1750 medical schools which engaged in this practice were in danger of destruction by irate mobs. Despite these obstacles some progress was still possible. About 1670 Malpighi and Leeuwenhoek confirmed the famous discovery of Sir William Harvey by observing the actual flow of blood through the network of capillaries connecting the arteries and veins. At approximately the same time an eminent physician of London, Thomas Sydenham, proposed a new theory of fever as nature's attempt to expel diseased material from the system. The substance of this theory is still quite generally accepted; in fact, new evidence has been discovered which strongly confirms it.

Medical progress during the eighteenth century was somewhat more rapid. Among the noteworthy achievements were the discovery of blood pressure, the founding of histology or microscopic anatomy, the development of the autopsy as an aid to the study of disease, and the recognition of scarlet fever as a malady distinct from smallpox and measles. But the chief milestones of medical advancement in this period were the adoption of inoculation and the development of vaccination for smallpox. Knowledge of inoculation came originally from the Near East, where it had long been employed by the Saracens. Information concerning its use was relayed to England in 1717 through the letters of Lady Montagu, wife of the British ambassador to Turkey. The first systematic application of the practice in the Western world, however, was due to the efforts of the great Puritan leaders, Cotton and Increase Mather, who implored the physicians of Boston to inoculate their patients in

---

[8] As a matter of fact, surgery in northern Europe was very commonly left in the hands of barbers. Surgeons in England are still referred to as "Mr."

the hope of curbing an epidemic of smallpox which had broken out in 1721. By the middle of the century inoculation was quite generally employed by physicians in Europe and in America. In 1796 the milder method of vaccination was discovered by Edward Jenner. It was now revealed that direct inoculation of human beings with the deadly virus of smallpox was unnecessary: a vaccine manufactured in the body of an animal would be just as effective and much less likely to have disastrous results. Vast possibilities were thus opened up for the elimination of contagious diseases.

4. CLASSICISM IN ART AND LITERATURE

In so far as there was any one purpose dominating the art and literature of the seventeenth and eighteenth centuries, it was the desire to preserve or recapture the spirit of ancient Greece and Rome. The artists and writers of the Intellectual Revolution strove to imitate classical models. They chose classical titles and themes for many of their works and embellished them wherever possible with allusions to antique mythology. Deploring the destruction of ancient civilization by "Christian barbarians," they were unable to see much value in the cultural achievements of later centuries. In particular, they despised the Middle Ages as a long night of barbaric darkness. Doubtless most of them would have agreed with the dictum of Rousseau that the Gothic cathedrals were "a disgrace to those who had the patience to build them." In all of these attitudes the men of the Intellectual Revolution were following in the footsteps of the humanists. Devotion to the achievements of classical antiquity was at least one important element of Renaissance culture that had not

The nature of the new classicism

Below: *The Petit Trianon.* Designed by J. A. Gabriel and completed in 1768, it was Louis XV's gift to Madame Pompadour. It was later given by Louis XVI to Marie Antoinette. Right: *St. Paul's Cathedral, London.* Designed by Christopher Wren and completed in 1710, its dome measures 112 feet in diameter. The stone cross at its top is 366 feet above the ground.

St. Peter's, Rome. A contemporary print showing the colonnades designed by Bernini.

yet died out. Nevertheless, it must not be forgotten that the classicism of the seventeenth and eighteenth centuries was by no means exactly the same as that of the humanists. As a rule, it was more sentimental, grandiose, and extravagant. Besides, it was less sincere, since it was frequently employed for the glorification of cynical monarchs and their corrupt and frivolous dependents. Finally, classicism was now perhaps even less a universal theme than it had been during the age of the Renaissance. A number of the great artists and writers of the seventeenth and eighteenth centuries sought to escape from its influence entirely.

Classicism in architecture: the baroque style

The leading arts to be developed during the age of the Intellectual Revolution were architecture and painting. Sculpture ceased to be an independent art, as it had been in the Renaissance, and was relegated to its earlier function of a mere aid to the adornment of buildings. The prevailing style of architecture in the seventeenth century was the so-called baroque. Originating in Italy, it spread to France, England, and Spain and was eventually adopted for churches, palaces, opera houses, museums, and government buildings in practically every Western country. In European capitals to this day it meets the eye in every direction. Among its celebrated monuments still standing are the Luxembourg palace and the main palaces at Versailles in France, St. Paul's Cathedral in London, the government buildings in Vienna and Brussels, and the palaces of the Tsars at Peterhof near Leningrad in Russia. The most noted of the baroque architects were Giovanni Lorenzo Bernini (1598–1680), who designed the colonnade and square in front of St. Peter's Church in Rome, and Sir Christopher Wren (1632–1723), whose masterpiece was St. Paul's Cathedral. The baroque style was supposed to be founded upon the architecture of ancient Rome, but it was much more lavish than anything the Romans produced. Its principal features were hugeness, artificiality, extravagance of ornamentation, and the extensive use of such "classical" elements as the column, the dome, and sculptured representations of mythological scenes. So much detail was added to the surface of the buildings that they often give the impression of having been carved, like the altars in medieval churches. A similar passion for splendor and magnificence was reflected in the enrichment of interiors with gilt and silver, flashing mirrors, and colored marble. Originally, baroque architecture was a style inspired by the Catholic Reformation. It represented an attempt by the Church to strengthen its hold upon Catholics through manifestations of grandeur and magnificence. Later it was used by rulers of the chief dynastic states to symbolize their power and opulence.

During the eighteenth century the heavy and pompous architectural style of the age of Louis XIV gave way to still other adaptations of the classical. The first to be developed was the rococo architecture in France, so called from the fantastic scrolls and shell-like designs that were commonly employed for ornamentation. The rococo differed from the baroque not only in being lighter but also in the impression of grace and sumptuous refinement it was intended to create. In place of a struggle for dynastic power and for colonial empire, it was now the indolent ease and elegant manners of the court of Louis XV which set the standard for French society. A

CLASSICISM IN ART AND LITERATURE

The rococo and Georgian styles

St. Nicholas' Cathedral, Prague. This photo shows the interior of the baroque masterpiece.

Venus and Adonis by Peter Paul Rubens. Rubens often painted classical themes, which he conceived on a grand scale and executed with sweeping vigor.

Rubens' Portrait of His Son Nicolaus

more delicate and effeminate architecture seemed to be necessary to accompany this change. Well-known examples of the rococo style are the Petit Trianon at Versailles and the palace of Sans Souci at Potsdam, built by Frederick the Great. About the middle of the eighteenth century a reaction set in against both the rococo and the baroque, and efforts were made to produce a truer and less flamboyant imitation of the classical. Perhaps the best results were achieved in England and in the American colonies with the development of the so-called Georgian style, named from the era when the four Georges reigned successively as kings of England (1714–1830) and known on this side of the ocean as colonial architecture. Though the Georgian retained certain elements of the baroque—the columns, the dormer windows, and often the cupola or dome—it at least had the classical merit of simplicity.

To a certain extent the evolution of painting during the seventeenth and eighteenth centuries paralleled that of architecture. The greatest of the painters who may be considered to have expressed the baroque tradition were the Flemings, Peter Paul Rubens (1577–1640) and Anthony Van Dyck (1599–1641), and the Spaniard, Diego Velásquez (1599–1660). Rubens was not merely the outstanding genius among these three, but he was the greatest of all the Flemish painters. In such famous works as *The Fates Spinning* and *Venus and Adonis* he combined classical themes with the sumptuous color and richness so pleasing to the affluent burghers and nobles of his day. The pink and rounded flesh of his full-blown nudes is thoroughly in keeping with the robust vitality of the age. Both Rubens and his gifted pupil, Anthony Van Dyck, are noted for their portraits of rulers and nobles. These were done in highly aristocratic fashion with full attention to the gorgeous details of elegant apparel and opulent furnishings in the background. Van Dyck's best-known portraits are those of the English kings, James I and Charles I, and their families. Velásquez, the third great artist of the baroque tradition, was the court painter to Philip IV of Spain. Much of his work consisted of paintings of royal faces, suffused in soft and silvery light but empty of meaning or emotional expression.

All of the painters mentioned thus far were exponents in some degree of the classical influence. But there were others in both the seventeenth and eighteenth centuries who refused to be bound by the prevailing artistic conventions. Foremost among them was Rembrandt van Rijn (1606–1669), now universally acclaimed as one of the greatest painters of all time. The son of a well-to-do miller of Leyden, Rembrandt was allowed to begin his artistic education at an early age. Under a series of native masters he learned the technique of subtle coloring and skillful depiction of the unusual in nature. Famous by the time he was twenty-five, he fell upon evil days later in his life, mainly as a consequence of bad investments and the failure of critics to appreciate his more recondite works. In 1656 he was stripped by his creditors of all he possessed, even to his table linen, and driven from his house. Apparently these reverses served mainly to broaden and deepen his philosophy, for in this very same year he

See color plates between pages 528 and 529

Self-Portrait by Rembrandt

The painters who defied classical conventions: (1) Rembrandt

The Return of the Prodigal Son by Rembrandt. The painting now hangs in the Hermitage Museum in Leningrad.

See color
plates between
pages 528 and
529

(2) Hals and
Goya

See color
plates at page
593

Classicism in
literature: the
French poets
and dramatists

produced some of his greatest achievements. As a painter Rembrandt surpassed all the other members of the Dutch school and deserves to be ranked with the great masters of the High Renaissance in Italy. No artist had a keener understanding of the problems and trials of human nature or a stronger perception of the mysteries of this life. His portraits, including those of himself, are imbued with an introspective quality and with a suggestion that the half is not being told. The subjects he delighted to paint were not the incidents of classical mythology but solemn rabbis, tattered beggars, and scenes from the Old and New Testaments, rich in drama and in human interest. Some of his best-known works include *The Good Samaritan, The Woman Taken in Adultery, The Marriage of Samson,* and *The Night Watch.*

Two other noted artists of the period of the Intellectual Revolution also departed widely from the classical tradition. The first was the Dutchman Frans Hals (1580–1666) and the second was the Spaniard Francisco Goya (1746–1828). Like his great contemporary Rembrandt, Hals insisted upon choosing the subjects he liked, regardless of whether they conformed to the notions of genteel critics. Most of his works are realistic portraits. He loved to depict the imbecilic grin in the face of the tavern drunkard, the naïve enthusiasm of itinerant singers and players, or the bewildered misery of some beaten and hopeless derelict. Goya was not merely a rebel against accepted artistic standards but a political and social revolutionary as well. He detested the aristocracy, despised the Church, and ridiculed the hypocrisy of respectable society. But he reserved his deepest contempt for absolute monarchy. His *Charles IV on Horseback* has been called "the most impudent portrait of royalty ever painted." Goya also made use of his talents to indict the cruelty of war, especially during the period when Europe was ravaged by Napoleon's armies.

The history of literature in the seventeenth and eighteenth centuries exhibited tendencies quite similar to those of art. The most popular literary ideal was classicism, which generally meant not only a studied imitation of classical forms but also an earnest devotion to reason as a way of life, on the assumption that the Greeks and Romans had been rationalists above everything else. Although classicism was not confined to any one country, its principal center was France. Here lived during the reign of Louis XIV a distinguished company of poets and dramatists, who gave more genuine luster to their country than had ever been won by the Grand Monarch in his boldest exploits of diplomacy and war. The most noted member of this company was Jean-Baptiste Poquelin (1622–1673), who is much better known by his adopted name of Molière. Much of the work of these writers was marked by qualities similar to those of the baroque in art: it was decorative, turgid, affected, artificial, and in general expressive of a tendency to subordinate content to form. The writings of Molière, however, stand out as a brilliant exception.

Less respectful of ancient formalism than any of his associates, Molière was the most original of French comedians. Few keener critics of human nature have ever lived. "The business of comedy," he once declared, "is to represent in general all the defects of men and especially of the men of our time." The mortal weakness he delighted most to ridicule was pretentiousness. But with all of his penchant for satire, Molière had a measure of pity for the evil fortunes of men. In a number of his plays sympathy and even melancholy go hand in hand with clever wit and pungent scorn. His genius was probably broader in scope than that of any other dramatist since Shakespeare.

England also had a luxuriant growth of literary effort in the classical style. The first great master of this style as applied to English literature was the renowned Puritan poet, John Milton (1608–1674). The leading philosopher of the Puritan Revolution, Milton wrote the official defense of the beheading of Charles I and later held the position of Secretary for Foreign Tongues under Cromwell's Commonwealth. Nearly all of his writings were phrased in the rich and stately expression of the classical tradition, while many of the lesser ones revolved about themes from Greek mythology. But Milton was as much a Puritan as he was a classicist. He could never quite get away from the idea that the essence of beauty is morality. Moreover, he was deeply interested in theological problems. His greatest work, *Paradise Lost*, is a synthesis of the religious beliefs of his age, a majestic epic of the Protestant faith. In spite of the fact that Milton was a Puritan, his views in this work departed widely from Calvinist dogma. Its principal themes are the moral responsibility of the individual and the importance of knowledge as an instrument of virtue. Paradise is lost repeatedly in human life to the extent that man allows passion to triumph over reason in determining the course of his actions. Milton also threw Calvinist doctrine to the winds in his *Areopagitica*, perhaps the most eloquent defense of freedom of speech in the English language.

Classicism in English literature reached its zenith in the eighteenth century in the poetry of Alexander Pope (1688–1744) and in the writings of a score of masters of prose. Pope was the great exponent in verse of the mechanistic and deistic doctrines of the Enlightenment. In such works as his *Essay on Man* and his *Essay on Criticism* he set forth the view that nature is governed by inflexible laws, and that man must study and follow nature if he would bring any semblance of order into human affairs. The chief masters of prose who wrote under classicist influence were the journalist and writer of popular fiction Daniel Defoe (1660?–1731); the satirist Jonathan Swift (1667–1745); and the historian Edward Gibbon (1737–1794), author of *The Decline and Fall of the Roman Empire*.

The age of classicism in English prose was also the period that witnessed the origin of the modern novel. To some extent the new literary form was anticipated by Daniel Defoe's *Robinson Crusoe*,

John Milton

Alexander Pope
and the masters
of English prose

a story based upon the fictional adventures of a shipwrecked sailor who had spent five years on a desolate island off the coast of Chile. But the true modern novel, with its more or less elaborate plot of human behavior and its psychological analysis of life and love, springs from the work of Henry Fielding (1707–1754). His *History of Tom Jones* has been acclaimed by some critics as the greatest novel in the English language. Rich in humor and in colorful description of manners and customs, it provided the inspiration for innumerable others, not only in England but on the Continent of Europe as well.

The beginning
of romanticism
in literature

Earlier in this chapter we learned that the rationalistic and mechanistic philosophy of the Enlightenment was followed by a romantic revolt, expressed first of all in the teachings of Rousseau. We have now to observe that an almost identical development took place in literature. Beginning about 1750 a reaction set in against the intellectualism and high-flown formalism involved in the classical tradition. A group of writers now demanded a return to simplicity and naturalism with less attention to man as a rational creature and more to his instincts and feelings. No longer was it considered disgraceful for the poet to show sympathy or pity or to display any other of his deepest emotions; the heart should rule the head, at least in all cases where problems vital to man's happiness were concerned. No longer was nature regarded as a cold, automatic machine but worshiped as the embodiment of beauty, sublimity, and charm, or tenderly revered as a source of protection and solace. God now ceased to be a mere First Cause and came to be identified with the universe itself or mystically adored as the soul of nature. Still another element in the romantic ideal was glorification of the common man, often accompanied by a generous compassion for the weak and oppressed. Although some of this regard for the lowly had been implied in the humanitarianism of the Enlightenment, most of the leaders of that movement had little respect for the masses. Now under the influence of romanticism the humble herdsman and peasant were given a recognition in literature long overdue.

Goethe

The early romantic poets in
Britain: Gray,
Goldsmith, and
Burns

Though literary romanticism had its roots in France in such sentimental works as *Émile* and *The New Héloïse* of Rousseau, the movement attained its most vigorous development in Great Britain and Germany. Among the eighteenth-century romantic poets in Britain were Thomas Gray (1716–1771), author of the *Elegy Written in a Country Churchyard;* and, to a certain extent, Oliver Goldsmith (1728–1774), who celebrated the rustic innocence of Auburn, "loveliest village of the plain." The most original of them all, however, was the Scotsman Robert Burns (1759–1796). In his homely dialect verse the romantic feeling for nature and sympathy for the common man received their finest expression. No writer has inspired more tenderness for the humblest things of this earth or filled the world with a deeper respect for those who toil for their bread. Moreover, Burns was unique among poets of his age in combining an extraordinary pathos with a delicate touch of humor. He had the rare gift of being passionately earnest without being solemn. In the very last years of the eighteenth century two other romantic poets began their literary activities on British soil. Their names were William Wordsworth and Samuel Taylor Coleridge. But since most of the work of these men was done in the nineteenth century, they can be discussed more appropriately in a later chapter.

The romantic movement in German literature developed primarily under the brilliant guidance of Friedrich Schiller (1759–1805) and Johann Wolfgang von Goethe (1749–1832). Schiller grew up during the period of the *Sturm und Drang* (Storm and Stress), when writers all over Germany were denouncing restraints and conventions and attempting to free the culture of their country from foreign domination. As a consequence his romanticism generally embraced as its important elements the idealization of heroic deeds and the glorification of struggles for freedom. While a strong quality of individualism pervades a number of his plays, Schiller's conception of liberty seems to have been closely akin to nationalism. This is revealed quite clearly in his *William Tell*, a drama of the struggle of the Swiss against Austrian tyranny. This natonalistic aspect of Schiller's work was probably the one which had the major influence upon later German writers.

The greatest name in the history of German literature is unquestionably that of Schiller's older contemporary, Johann Wolfgang von Goethe. The two men were associated for a number of years at the court of the Duke of Weimar. Born in Frankfurt, the son of a family of ample means, Goethe was educated for the law but soon found the limits of knowledge in that profession unsatisfying. His indefatigable spirit drove him to the study of medicine, and then of the fine arts and the natural sciences. His first important literary production was *The Sorrows of Young Werther*, a romantic novel about a love-sick youth who takes his own life with the pistol of his rival and friend. Written in dashing sentimental style, it attained an enormous popularity not only in Germany but also in England and France. Though the author apparently intended that it should express the idea that weakness of character is the greatest of sins, it came to be taken as a symbol of profound dissatisfaction with the world and as a basis of fiery revolt. In 1790 Goethe published the first part of his drama *Faust*, which he finally completed in 1831, a year before his death. Universally acknowledged as his grandest achievement, *Faust* not only epitomizes the personal philosophy of the author but expresses the spirit of the modern age as few other writings have done. Part I reflects some of the quality of rebellion in the *Sturm und Drang*, but in Part II the conviction grows that freedom from restraint is not enough; the individual must go on in an endless quest for mastery of all knowledge and for enrichment of life through unlimited experience. Considered as a whole, the drama is a symbol of perpetual unrest, of that ceaseless yearning for the

An Illustration from *The Sorrows of Young Werther* by Goethe

Goethe

fullness of life which has come to be one of the most distinctive traits of modern civilization.

5. MUSIC IN THE SEVENTEENTH AND EIGHTEENTH CENTURIES

The birth of opera and the concerto

As was observed in a preceding chapter,[9] the sixteenth century marked the culmination of a long era of music illustrated by choral works of polyphonic structure. The seventeenth opens with a general rebellion against polyphony, a rebellion so powerful and pervasive that the Palestrinian style became completely archaic within twenty-five years of the death of its creator. The new ideal, a primary voice *accompanied* by one or several instruments, which swept Italy in an incredibly short time, became known as *monody*. One of the main reasons for this radical change was the Italians' powerful dramatic instinct; they realized that the feelings of an individual cannot be expressed by a many-voiced chorus. The same trends that created modern theater and the dramatic architecture of the Jesuits invaded music and led to the creation of opera, which reached its first magnificent manifestation in *Orfeo* (1607) by Claudio Monteverdi (1567–1643), the dominating musical personality in the first half of the new century. Within a generation operas were performed in most important cities in Italy, and by 1736 Venice boasted an opera house for every parish. Now the already respectable instrumental music of the Renaissance began to make rapid gains and a fine literature arose for beautifully constructed instruments—organ, harpsichord, and the various string and wind instruments. In the last third of the century instrumental music created the concerto, along with opera one of the greatest original stylistic accomplishments of the Italian baroque. Both opera and concerto spread beyond the Alps and conquered every country, producing national offshoots. Though the seventeenth century was preoccupied with experiments, it created an impressive synthesis upon which the first half of the eighteenth century could build the final great edifices of the late baroque.

Johann Sebastian Bach

The origin of the modern novel

The late baroque culminated in two towering figures: Johann Sebastian Bach (1685–1750) and George Frederick Handel (1685–1759). Though both were born in Saxony, Bach became the epitome of German musical genius, while Handel, who lived for almost half a century in London and became a British subject, embodied an English national style. Bach combined an unbounded imagination and a capacious intellect with heroic powers of discipline and an unquenchable zeal for work. By lifelong study he made himself the master of most existing types and styles of music, from little

[9] See §6 in the chapter on The Expansion of the Renaissance.

dance pieces for the clavichord to gigantic choral works. Being a church musician, Bach's duty was to provide new music for the elaborate Sunday and holy day services. Therefore the bulk of his work is made up of cantatas (over 200 preserved), oratorios, Passions, and Masses. His settings of the Gospel according to St. John and St. Matthew represent the unsurpassable peak of this genre. Fundamentally, though, Bach was an instrumental composer, the creator of tremendous works for the organ and harpsichord. Then there are his spacious concertos, sonatas for various combinations of instruments, and suites for orchestra. Bach was still steeped in an almost medieval German Protestant mysticism that no longer fitted the age of the Enlightenment. Thus it happened that soon after his death he was overshadowed by a musical world devoted to more mundane aims. But when the nineteenth century rediscovered him his influence became paramount; to this day composers have been known to "return" to Bach for inspiration and guidance.

Handel was the absolute antithesis of his great fellow-Saxon. After four years spent in Italy he completely absorbed Italian techniques and modes of composition, subsequently settling in England where for years he ran an opera company that produced nothing but Italian operas, mostly his own. Though many of these are masterpieces that we are just beginning to appreciate, the fact remains that Italian opera did not suit the taste of the large English middle class public, and after decades spent in composing and producing dozens of operas, Handel finally realized that he must turn to something more acceptable to the English mind. This he found in the "oratorio," a rather loose definition for the English music drama intended for an ideal theater. With the exception of *Messiah*, the most famous of the oratorios, these works were not religious music,

"The Charming Brute." A contemporary caricature of Handel, engraved by Joseph Groupy, 1754.

although the themes came from the Old Testament. Undoubtedly one reason for Handel's success in his adopted country was the fact that his virile and heroic oratorios symbolized the English people, their pride in their institutions and their attainment of national greatness. Handel lived in circumstances wholly different from those permitted to Bach and most other Continental composers. He was not a salaried artisan but a free citizen, an English squire who ran his own business and left behind a respectable estate.

The birth of classicism in music

After a transition era in music led by J.S. Bach's gifted sons we reach the period dominated by the Viennese School, so called because its leading masters were active in or near the Austrian capital. By about 1770 a remarkable stylistic synthesis reconciled baroque weightiness, rococo charm, and pre-romantic excitement. This peace between warring extremes created an island in the romantic stream, an art that truly deserves the term applied to it: classicism. Vienna now assimilated every musical thought, from Naples to Hamburg. Christoph Willibald Gluck (1714–1787) reformed the declining "serious" opera into a noble drama that recalls the tone of classical antiquity. But the mischievous, Italian comic opera, the *opera buffa*, was victorious in the end and forced a fusion with the serious opera which reached its unsurpassable height in the operas of Wolfgang Amadeus Mozart (1756–1791), while chamber and orchestral music reached a new formal and expressive level under the leadership of Joseph Haydn (1732–1809).

Mozart; his early life

The eighteenth century was full of music, but its social organization was as cruel to the creative artist as is our own free society. If the artist was not employed by a court, noble house, church, or municipality, if he was not an internationally acclaimed virtuoso or a renowned teacher, he was ground up in the effort to make a living. Mozart was among the first to shed the security of the "musical

Left: *Mozart and His Sister at the Piano*. In this painting of somewhat dubious authenticity, their father is seen holding the violin while their mother's portrait hangs above the piano. Right: *A Portion of the Original Score for Mozart's Quartet in C Major, K 465*

lackey" and try the free artistic economy of the metropolis. While a child prodigy he was adored and admired, but when he left the employ of the Archbishop of Salzburg to take up the career of a free lance artist in Vienna, a shadow fell over him that he was not able to elude. The remaining ten years of his life were spent in bountiful productivity. Yet he had to live from hand to mouth—the world was not yet ready for the independent artist.

When appraising the music of the classical era we must realize that in spite of the magnificent sonatas and symphonies, the stylistic core of the era was still in dramatic music. This classical music, with its clear, absolute forms, emphasized on the stage everything that is permanent and finite. Mozart used these forms to shape the characters, fates, and conflicts of human beings in a way that they too became permanent and finite. Drama and melody, characterization and absolute form evolve simultaneously on Mozart's stage. Each great opera—*The Marriage of Figaro, Don Giovanni, The Magic Flute*—provides a center around which cluster piano sonatas, quartets, quintets, concertos, and symphonies. The nineteenth century's likening of Mozart to Apollo was neither an accident nor a mistake, but men failed to understand that hidden behind the Appollonian poise and smile were deep wounds.

Mozart's operas

Haydn was carved from harder timber than Mozart; his peasant background made him tenacious and stubborn. If Mozart embodied the aristocratic spirit, Haydn did that of the liberated plebeian. It was because of their diametrically opposed personalities that the two musicians got along so well; they complemented each other, learned from each other, and fulfilled the hopes and aspirations of the second half of the eighteenth century. Haydn had a sharp intellect and he acquired his extensive knowledge of music through incessant study and experimentation. His art conveys the impressions of the village and the countryside, but also the elegance of the princely household that employed him for many years, as well as the solemnity of the cathedral. Haydn's compositions are so numerous that a complete edition of them has never been made. They include many operas and Masses, oratorios, concertos, over eighty string quartets, and more than 100 symphonies. It was Haydn who firmly established the technical and stylistic principles of symphonic construction, creating, with Mozart, the pattern of the symphony orchestra which remained the basis for all future developments.

Joseph Haydn

6. SOCIAL IDEALS AND REALITIES DURING THE AGE OF THE ENLIGHTENMENT

A movement as profoundly disturbing to Western society as the Intellectual Revolution was bound to have its effects upon social customs and individual habits. These effects were especially discernible during the bloom of the Enlightenment in the eighteenth century. Of course, not all of the social progress of this time can be traced to intellectual influences; much of it derived from the bulging prosperity induced by the expansion of trade in the Commercial Revolution. Nevertheless, the progress of philosophy and science had more than incidental effects in clearing away the cobwebs of ancient prejudice and in building a more liberal and humane society.

Social idealism:
(1) the reform
of criminal
codes

Mention has already been made of the influence of the Enlightenment in promoting the cause of social reform. A characteristic expression of this influence was agitation for revision of drastic criminal codes and for more liberal treatment of prisoners. In regard to both, the need for reform was urgent. Penalties even for minor offenses were exceedingly severe in practically all countries, death being the punishment for stealing a horse or a sheep or for the theft of as little as five shillings in money. During the first half of the eighteenth century no fewer than sixty crimes were added to the capital list in England. The treatment accorded to bankrupts and debtors was also a standing disgrace. Beaten and starved by cruel jailers, they died by the thousands in filthy prisons. Conditions such as these eventually challenged the sympathies of several reformers. Foremost among them was Cesare Beccaria, a jurist of Milan, who had been deeply influenced by the writings of French rationalist philosophers. In 1764 he published his famed treatise on *Crimes and Punishments*, in which he condemned the common theory that penalties should be made as horrible as possible in order to deter potential offenders. Insisting that the purpose of criminal codes should be the prevention of crime and the reform of the wayward rather than vengeance, he urged the abolition of torture as unworthy of civilized nations. He likewise condemned capital punishment as contrary to the natural rights of man, since it cannot be revoked in case of error. Beccaria's book created a veritable sensation. It was translated into a dozen languages, and it stimulated efforts to improve conditions in many lands. By the end of the eighteenth century considerable progress had been made in reducing the severity of penalties, in relieving debtors from punishment, and in providing work and better food for prisoners.

(2) opposition
to slavery and
war

The humanitarian spirit of the Enlightenment found an outlet also in other directions. Several of the scientists and philosophers, notably Buffon and Rousseau, denounced the evils of slavery. Many more condemned the slave trade. The efforts of intellectuals in this regard were warmly seconded by the leaders of certain religious groups, especially by prominent Quakers in America. Even John Wesley, conservative as he was on many social issues, branded slavery as an abomination. Pacifism was another ideal of many of the new liberal thinkers. Voltaire's strictures on war were by no means the only example of such sentiments. Even the sentimental Rousseau could perceive the illogic in Grotius' attempt to draw a distinction been just and unjust wars. From the pens of other *philosophes* emanated various ingenious plans of insuring perpetual peace, including a scheme for a league of nations with power to take concerted action against aggressors.[10]

Perhaps it was natural that humanitarian agitation for reform should be accompanied by an increase of sympathy for the lower classes. This was especially true during the final stage of the Enlightenment. With the progress of reason and the increasing emphasis upon the natural rights of man, the strong reaction against the evils of slavery and war was eventually translated into a protest against every form of suffering and oppression. Thus the hardships of the poor came in for a larger share of attention than they had received since the time of the Sophists. Besides, the middle class, in the pursuit of its ambition to dethrone the aristocracy, needed the support of the peasants and urban workers. Out of such factors there developed a tendency on the part of leading thinkers to espouse the cause of the common man. In some quarters, it became popular to despise aristocratic lineage or royal birth. Thomas Paine echoed the sentiments of many when he declared that a single honest plowman was worth more than all the crowned ruffians who ever lived. The great Scottish economist, Adam Smith, deplored the habit of feeling more pity for a royal scoundrel like Charles I than for the thousands of common citizens slaughtered in the civil war. Several of the French philosophers of the Enlightenment went considerably farther in professions of sympathy for the masses. Gabriel de Mably (1709–1785), the Marquis de Condorcet (1743–1794), and Rousseau advocated an absolute equality of freedom and privileges for every man. Mably and Condorcet, at least, perceived that this could not be attained except by a redistribution of wealth.

[10] This was the famous scheme of the Abbé de Saint-Pierre (1658–1743).

Canvassing for Votes by William Hogarth. Hogarth's satirical engravings give us insights into the social life of the eighteenth century. Here, bribery seems to be the chief lubricant of the electoral process.

Morality as
exemplified in
the customs
and practices of
the upper
classes

The more vio-
lent and brut-
ish aspects of
18th-century
society

While they did not propose socialism, they nevertheless argued that landed property should be held in substantially equal amounts, so that exploitation of the poor by the rich would be practically impossible.

The moral ideals of the Enlightenment were reflected not only in the books of the philosophers; they were also revealed in the principal customs and social practices of the time. The eighteenth century, in particular, was an age of pampered elegance and gracious living decidedly at variance with the ascetic taboos of the church. The houses of the nobles were resplendently furnished with shining mirrors, crystal chandeliers, and graceful sofas and chairs richly upolstered in brocaded silk. Men of the upper classes arrayed themselves in powdered wigs, velvet coats with lace at the cuffs, silk stockings, and knee breeches of delicate hue. Not since the days of the Renaissance had fashion played so dominant a part in the lives of both sexes. Habits of personal behavior were also characterized by similar qualities of elegance and artificiality. Form was everything; motive, nothing. The ladies and gentlemen of the best society addressed even those whom they cordially hated with the most fulsome compliments and groveled disgustingly in the presence of higher rank.

Among the upper classes, manners very largely took the place of morals. The ladies and gentlemen who danced the stately minuet and deported themselves with such charming grace quite commonly ridiculed married love as a relic of a benighted past. Adultery became fashionable and almost a virtue. A husband sometimes lived on friendly terms with his wife's lovers, for no one in this cultivated society would be so uncouth as to display any sentiment of jealousy. Prostitution had not only its apologists but also its defenders, and brothels were quite commonly permitted to remain open on Sundays, though theaters had to be closed. A prevailing attitude toward relations between the sexes appears to have been that of Buffon, who declared that "there is nothing good in love but the physical."

Eighteenth-century society also had its more violent and brutish aspects, which were largely survivals from the turbulent days of the Renaissance. Despite the severity of penal laws, vicious crimes were still very common. In many large cities bands of hooligans roamed the streets at night, while footpads infested the highways in the open country. In London such hoodlums were known as Mohawks, and their favorite diversions, aside from robbery, were beating constables, "turning women upside down," and gouging out the eyes of any who tried to restrain them. Drunkenness continued in much the same measure as before, though the consumption of hard liquor by the poorer classes appears to have increased. About this time gin became popular, especially in England, as the poor man's drink. Gambling and cruel games and sports likewise survived unabated. Yet

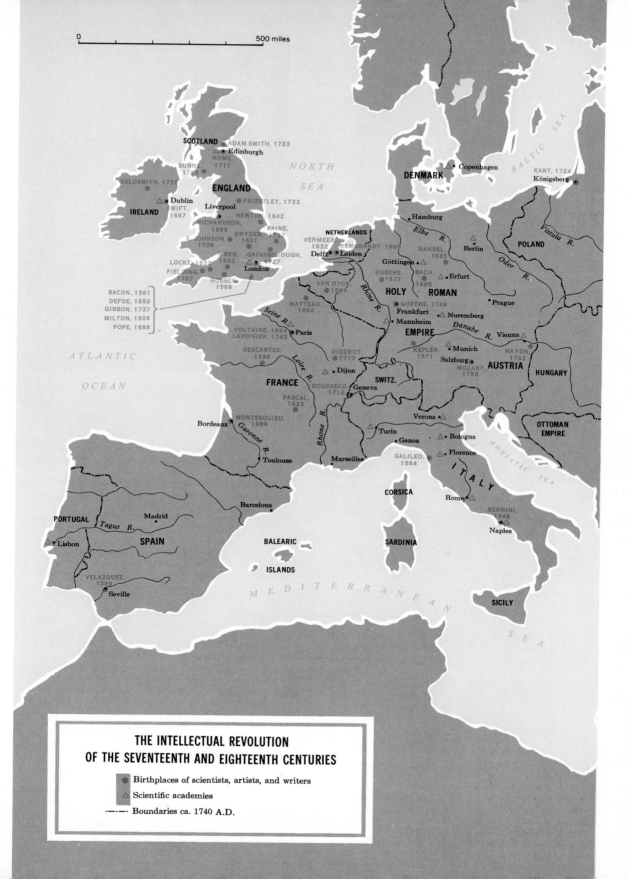

THE INTELLECTUAL REVOLUTION
OF THE SEVENTEENTH AND EIGHTEENTH CENTURIES

● Birthplaces of scientists, artists, and writers

△ Scientific academies

-·-·- Boundaries ca. 1740 A.D.

Left: *The Last Judgment*, Peter Paul Rubens (1577–1640). Vivid colors, voluptuous figures, and classical themes are typical of Rubens' work. (Alte Pinakothek, Munich) Above: *England and Scotland Crowning Charles I*, Rubens. This scene was part of a series painted in Whitehall Palace, London, to glorify the Stuart family. (Minneapolis Institute of Art)

Above: *The Marchessa Durazzo*, Anthony Van Dyck (1599–1641). This portrait of a Genoese noblewoman suggests the Italian Renaissance sophistication admired by the Flemish burghers. (MMA) Right: *Pope Innocent X*, Velásquez. (Doria-Pamphili Collection)

The Night Watch, Rembrandt. (The Rijksmuseum)

The Anatomy Lesson, Rembrandt van Rijn (1606–1669). Rembrandt scorned the classical themes of most of his contemporaries and turned to character analysis and the portrayal of life. (Mauritshuis, The Hague)

The Stonemason's Yard,
Canaletto (1697–1768). A
quiet scene of everyday life,
in strong contrast to the portrait below. (National Gallery, London)

Madame de Pompadour,
François Boucher (1703–
1770). This portrait idealizes
the favorite mistress of Louis
XV. (The Wallace Collec-
tion, London)

another of the prevailing vices of this period was dueling, although it was confined primarily to the upper and middle classes. The gentleman of spirit was still supposed to avenge any real or imaginary insult by challenging the offender to a mortal combat with sword or pistol. Even so prominent a statesman as William Pitt the younger felt obliged to meet an opponent on the so-called field of honor.

It is necessary to observe, however, that the picture of social conditions in the eighteenth century was not altogether dark. For one thing, there was a definite improvement in the standard of living, certainly for the middle classes and probably even for some of the poor. This is evidenced by the increasing per capita consumption of sugar, chocolate, coffee, and tea, which were not merely substituted for other foods and beverages but were additions to the average diet. The growing demand for linen and cotton cloth, and for such articles of luxury as mahogany furniture designed by such masters as Chippendale, Hepplewhite, and Sheraton, may be taken as a further indication of rising prosperity. Such evidences applied, however, only to a small proportion of the population, chiefly to the nobles and to the merchants, bankers, and lawyers in the larger cities. The life of the peasants, with a few exceptions, was still one of privation. In England large tenant farmers enjoyed some luxuries, but the condition of the small, independent yeomen was far from prosperous. Because of instability of prices, increasing taxes, and the costs of new farming methods, many were forced down into the ranks of agricultural wage earners. In France the peasants constituted about 80 per cent of the population, but less than one-twentieth of them owned their land. The remainder were serfs, tenant farmers, and *métayers*, who were required to surrender half of the produce of the lands they occupied to the lord. Most wretched of all were the peasants of eastern Europe. In East Prussia peasants often had to work from three to six days a week for their lord, and some had only late evening or night hours to cultivate their own lands. In Russia landlords had the power of life and death over their serfs, and could sell them apart from the land and even apart from their families.

The other of the more favorable aspects of social life during the age of the Enlightenment was a sharp reduction of the death rate. This came about as the result of several causes. Probably the most important was the effective control of smallpox as a consequence of inoculation and vaccination. A second factor was the establishment of maternity hospitals, which, in combination with improved obstetrical methods, reduced the mortality among infants in the second half of the century by more than 50 per cent and among mothers by an even larger proportion. Finally, advancement in sanitation, together with the adoption of more hygienic habits by people of all classes, contributed not a little to the conquest of various diseases and to lengthening the span of life.

Evidences of improvement in standards of living

Improvements in health and sanitation

529

SELECTED READINGS

· *Items so designated are available in paperbound editions.*

PHILOSOPHY

· Artz, F. B., *The Enlightenment in France,* Kent, Ohio, 1968 (Kent State).

· ———, *From the Renaissance to Romanticism: 1300–1820,* Chicago, 1962

· Becker, C. L., *The Heavenly City of the Eighteenth Century Philosophers,* New Haven, 1932 (Yale University Press).

Brandes, Georg, *Voltaire,* New York, 1930, 2 vols. A brilliant evaluation by a distinguished critic.

Chapman, J. W., *Rousseau—Totalitarian or Liberal?* New York, 1956.

· Church, W. F., *The Influence of the Enlightenment on the French Revolution,* New York, 1964 (Heath).

· Crocker, Lester G., *The Age of Enlightenment,* New York, 1970 (Torchbook).

· Gay, Peter, *The Enlightenment: The Rise of Modern Paganism,* New York, 1970 (Vintage).

Green, F. C., *Jean-Jacques Rousseau: A Critical Study of His Life and Writings,* New York, 1955.

· Hazard, Paul, *European Thought in the Eighteenth Century,* New York, 1954 (Meridian).

Hertzberg, Arthur, *The French Enlightenment and the Jews,* New York, 1968.

Kropotkin, Peter, *Ethics: Origin and Development,* New York, 1924. Stimulating and suggestive.

Lecky, W. E. H., *History of the Rise and Influence of the Spirit of Rationalism in Europe,* New York, 1914, 2 vols. A classic.

· Lovejoy, Arthur, *Essays in the History of Ideas,* Baltimore, 1948 (Capricorn). Includes good chapters on the Intellectual Revolution.

· McGiffert, A. C., *Protestant Thought before Kant,* New York, 1915 (Torchbook). An excellent survey.

· Manuel, Frank E., *The Age of Reason,* Ithaca, 1951 (Cornell).

· Martin, Kingsley, *The Rise of French Liberal Thought,* New York, 1954, 2d. rev. edn. A brilliant but somewhat biased account. Also available in paperback under the title, *French Liberal Thought in the Eighteenth Century: A Study of Political Ideas from Bayle to Condorcet.* (Torchbook).

Morais, H. M., *Deism in Eighteenth Century America,* New York, 1934.

Morley, John, *Rousseau,* New York, 1891, 2 vols.

———, *Voltaire,* New York, 1871.

Mowat, R. B., *The Age of Reason,* New York, 1934. A good general account.

· Muller, H. J., *Religion and Freedom in the Modern World,* Chicago, 1963 (Phoenix).

· Plumb, J. H., *et al.,* James L. Clifford, ed., *Man versus Society in Eighteenth Century Britain,* New York, 1968.

Randall, J. H., Jr., *The Making of the Modern Mind,* New York, 1926. Chs. XI, XII, XVI.

· Rossi, Paoli, *Francis Bacon: From Magic to Science.* Trans. by Saca Rabinovitch, Chicago, 1968 (University of Chicago).

Rowe, Constance, *Voltaire and the State,* New York, 1955.

· Rudé, George, *The Crowd in History: A Study of Popular Disturbances in France and England, 1730–1848,* New York, 1964 (Wiley).

Schapiro, J. S., *Condorcet and the Rise of Liberalism in France,* New York, 1934.

· Smith, Preserved, *A History of Modern Culture,* New York, 1934, Vol. II (Collier).

· Snyder, L. L., *The Age of Reason*, Princeton, 1953 (Anvil). Includes a good interpretive essay as well as selections from original sources.
· Stephen, Leslie, *History of English Thought in the Eighteenth Century*, New York, 1927 (Harbinger, 2 vols.).
Vaughan, C. E., *The Romantic Revolt*, New York, 1930.

SCIENCE

· Butterfield, Herbert, *The Origins of Modern Science*, New York, 1951 (Collier).
· Hall, A. R., *The Scientific Revolution, 1500–1800*, Boston, 1956 (Beacon).
· Hogben, Lancelot, *Mathematics for the Million*, New York, 1937. (Pocket Book).
Nordenskiöld, Erik, *The History of Biology*, New York, 1928.
Singer, Charles, *A Short History of Medicine*, New York, 1928.
· Smith, Preserved, *History of Modern Culture*, New York, 1934, Vol. II (Collier).
Taylor, Frank, *Galileo and the Freedom of Thought*, London, 1938.

LITERATURE, ART, AND MUSIC

Bukofzer, Manfred F., *Music in the Baroque Era*, New York, 1947.
Davenport, Marcia, *Mozart*, New York, 1932.
· Guérard, A. L., *France in the Classical Age: Life and Death of an Ideal*, New York, 1928 (Torchbook).
Lang, Paul, *Music in Western Civilization*, New York, 1941.
———, *George Friedrich Handel*, New York, 1966.
Machlis, Joseph, *The Enjoyment of Music*, 3rd. ed., New York, 1970. Excellent.
Robertson, J. G., *A History of German Literature*, New York, 1930.
· Schweitzer, Albert, *J. S. Bach*, London, 1923, 2 vols. (Bruce Humphries, 2 vols.).
· Stephen, Leslie, *English Literature and Society in the Eighteenth Century*, New York, 1907 (Barnes & Noble).
Vaughan, C. E., *The Romantic Revolt*, New York, 1930.
Wright, C. H. C., *French Classicism*, Cambridge, Mass., 1920.

SOURCE MATERIALS

Baumer, F. L. V., *Main Currents of European Thought*, New York, 1952.
· Milton, John, *Areopagitica; The Tenure of Kings and Magistrates*. (Appleton-Century-Crofts, Inc.).
Newton, Sir Isaac, *Principia, Third Book*. Rules of Reasoning in Philosophy.
Spinoza, Benedict, *A Theological-Political Treatise*.
Voltaire, *Philosophical Dictionary; Candide; Essay on Toleration*.
· Redman, B. R., ed., *The Portable Voltaire*, New York, 1949 (Viking).

PART VI

The Later Modern World
(1789-1914)

A second stage in the history of the world in modern times was ushered in by the French Revolution. This event, which occupied the years from 1789 to 1799, had a profound influence upon modern civilizations. It overthrew mercantilism and the surviving relics of feudalism and contributed to the political supremacy of the middle class. Besides, it was a cardinal source of militant nationalism, of economic individualism, and of the sovereignty of the masses. Several of these results—especially nationalism, democracy, and middle-class supremacy—persisted throughout the nineteenth and early twentieth centuries and were among the dominant characteristics of that era. At the same time, it must not be forgotten that the history of Western nations from the French Revolution to the outbreak of World War I was radically conditioned by other factors. Chief among these was the Industrial Revolution, which began about 1760 and has continued into the present age. Included among its significant results were the urbanization of modern life, the creation of new social classes and new economic and political philosophies, the revival of imperialism, and a general improvement in standards of living. In addition, by enabling countries to support a much larger population than would ever have been possible under an agricultural economy, the Industrial Revolution was partly responsible for the fact that the number of inhabitants of Europe more than doubled between 1789 and 1914.

A Chronological Table

	AMERICA	BRITAIN
	Great Awakening, 1740–1810	Development of steam engine, 1769 William Wordsworth, 1770–1850 Beginning of factory system, *ca.* 1770
1775	American Revolution, 1775–1783 Declaration of Independence, 1776	Adam Smith, *The Wealth of Nations,* 1776 Classical economics, 1776–1880
	Adoption of the Constitution of the U.S., 1787 John Fitch's steamboat, 1787	
	The Bill of Rights, 1791 Thomas Paine, *The Rights of Man,* 1791	Utilitarianism, 1790–1870 Edward Jenner develops vaccination for smallpox, 1796
1800	Jeffersonian Revolution, 1800–1801	
		Revival of atomic theory, 1810 Charles Dickens, 1812–1870
	Monroe Doctrine, 1823	
1825		First railroad, 1825
	Jacksonian Revolution, 1828–1837	
		First Reform Act, 1832
	Mechanization of agriculture, 1835–	
		Chartist Movement, 1838–1848
	Use of ether as an anesthetic, 1842 Telegraph, 1844	
		Repeal of Corn Laws, 1846
1850		Law of dissipation of energy, 1851
	First oil well, 1859	Bessemer process, 1856 Charles Darwin, *Origin of Species,* 1859 J. S. Mill, *On Liberty,* 1859

WESTERN EUROPE	CENTRAL AND EASTERN EUROPE	
Physiocrats, 1750–1800		
	Beethoven, 1770–1827	
		1775
	Immanuel Kant, *Critique of Pure Reason*, 1781	
	Friedrich List, 1789–1846	
French Declaration of Rights of Man, 1789 French Revolution, 1789–1799		
Coup d'état of Napoleon, 1799 Romanticism in literature and arts, 1800–1900 Victor Hugo, 1802–1885 First Empire in France, 1804–1814	Franz Schubert, 1797–1828	1800
Battle of Waterloo, 1815	Richard Wagner, 1813–1883 Congress of Vienna, 1814–1815 Carlsbad Decrees, 1819 Feodor Dostoievski, 1821–1881	
		1825
Henrik Ibsen, 1828–1906 July Revolution in France, 1830 Realism in literature and arts, 1830–1914 Independence of Belgium, 1831	Leo Tolstoi, 1828–1910 Independence of Greece, 1829 Unification of Germany, 1833–1871	
Émile Zola, 1840–1902	Tchaikovsky, 1840–1893	
February Revolution in France, 1848 Second Republic in France, 1848–1852 Second Empire in France, 1852–1870	Law of conservation of energy, 1847 *Communist Manifesto*, 1848 Unification of Italy, 1848–1870 Crimean War, 1854–1856	1850

	AMERICA	BRITAIN
	Civil War, 1861–1865	
		Antiseptic surgery, 1865
		Second Reform Act, 1867
1875	Telephone, 1876	
		Herbert Spencer, *Data of Ethics*, 1879
	Pragmatism, 1880–1930	
		Third Reform Act, 1884
	Beginning of finance capitalism, 1890	
	Populism, 1890–1897	
	William James, *The Will to Believe*, 1897	
	Spanish-American War, 1898	Boer War, 1899–1902
1900	Progressive movement, 1901–1916	
	First airplane flight, 1903	
	Model T Ford, 1908	
		Parliament Act of 1911

| | CENTRAL AND EASTERN | |
WESTERN EUROPE	EUROPE	

Emancipation of serfs in Russia, 1861

Austro-Prussian War, 1866
Ausgleich establishes Dual Monarchy, 1867

Franco-Prussian War, 1870–1871
Impressionism, 1870–1890
Paris Commune, 1871

Law of Papal Guaranties, 1871
German Empire, 1871–1918
Kulturkampf, 1872–1886

Development of dynamo, 1873
Germ theory of disease, 1875
Third Republic in France, 1875–1940

Internal-combustion engine, 1876
Russo-Turkish War, 1877–1878
Congress of Berlin, 1878

1875

Triple Alliance, 1882–1914

Post-impressionism, 1890
Dreyfus affair, 1894–1905
Discovery of X-ray, 1895

Berlin-to-Baghdad Railway, 1890–1907
Ivan Pavlov discovers conditioned reflex, *ca.* 1895
Diesel engine, 1897

First Hague Conference, 1899

Wireless telegraph, 1899

1900

Hugo DeVries, mutation theory, 1901
Cubism, 1903–
Entente Cordiale, 1904
Separation of church and state in France, 1905

Russo-Japanese War, 1904–1905
Russian Revolution of 1905
Einstein theories, 1905–1910

Second Hague Conference, 1907
Triple Entente, 1907
Discovery of protons and electrons, *ca.* 1910

Young Turk Revolution, 1908
Bosnian crisis, 1908

Balkan wars, 1912–1913

CHAPTER 19

The French Revolution (1789-1799)

> Today the third estate is everything, the nobility but a word. . . .
> —Abbé Sieyès, *What Is the Third Estate?*

> France, when she let loose the reins of regal authority, doubled
> the licence of a ferocious dissoluteness in manners, and of an in-
> solent irreligion in opinions and practices; and has extended
> through all ranks of life, as if she were communicating some
> privilege, or laying open some secluded benefit, all the unhappy
> corruptions that usually were the disease of wealth and power.
> —Edmund Burke, *Reflections on the Revolution in France*

Profound changes were wrought in the political history of the
Western world in the latter part of the eighteenth century. This
period witnessed the death throes of that peculiar system of government and society which had grown up during the age of the
despots. In England this system had already been largely overthrown by 1689, but in other nations of Europe it lingered on,
growing more and more ossified and corrupt with the passing of the
years. It flourished in every major country of Europe under the
combined influence of militarism and the ambitions of monarchs to
consolidate their power at the expense of the nobles. But scarcely
anywhere did it exist in so deplorable a form as in France during
the reigns of the last three Bourbon kings. Louis XIV was the supreme incarnation of absolute rule. His successors, Louis XV and
Louis XVI, dragged the government to very low depths of extravagance and irresponsibility. Moreover, their subjects were sufficiently enlightened to be keenly aware of their disadvantages. Yet
the French Revolution was not an isolated event. In many ways it
was simply the French aspect of a great Western revolution which
had begun in the American Colonies in the 1770's, had spread to Ireland in 1782–1783, to the Low Countries, and to Hungary and
Poland. The French outbreak was the climax of this widespread
Western revolution. Moreover, it was the broadest and most significant. It involved not merely the king and the nobility but the

*The era of rev-
olution*

539

middle class, the peasants, and even the "little people" of the cities and towns.

1. THE CAUSES OF THE FRENCH REVOLUTION

For convenience we can divide the causes of the French Revolution into three main classes: political, economic, and intellectual. Naturally, this division is somewhat arbitrary, for none of these classes was entirely distinct. The intellectual causes, for example, and to some extent the political also, were largely economic in origin. Nevertheless, for purposes of simplification it will be best to keep them separate. One of the major political causes has already been mentioned. This was the despotic rule of the Bourbon kings. For nearly 200 years government in France had been largely a one-man institution. During the fourteenth, fifteenth, and sixteeth centuries a kind of parliament known as the Estates General, composed of representatives of the clergy, the nobility, and the common people, had met at irregular intervals. But after 1614 it was no longer summoned. Henceforth the king was the sole repository of sovereign power. In a very real sense the king was the state. He could do almost anything his imperious will might dictate, without fear of impeachment or legislative restrictions of any kind. No questions of constitutionality or the natural rights of his subjects need trouble him. He could throw men into prison without a trial by means of royal orders, or *lettres de cachet*. He could prevent any criticism of his policies by clamping a rigid censorship on the press or by restricting freedom of speech. It must be conceded, however, that the tyranny of the French kings has often been exaggerated. In actual practice there was comparatively little interference with what men wrote or said, particularly during the reigns of Louis XV and Louis XVI. No action of these monarchs inhibited the mordant wit of Voltaire or suppressed the radical books of Rousseau.[1] On the contrary, the attacks by these and other philosophers increased in virulence the nearer the Revolution approached. The explanation, of course, is not to be found in any liberalism of Louis XV and his dull-witted grandson but rather in their indifference to politics.

A second political cause of the French Revolution was the illogical and unsystematic character of the government. Confusion reigned in nearly every department. The political structure was the product of a long and irregular growth extending back into the Middle Ages. New agencies had been established from time to time to meet some particular condition, with a total disregard for those already in existence. As a result there was much overlapping of functions, and numerous useless officials drew salaries from the pub-

Louis XV

Louis XVI

[1] Voltaire was imprisoned for a time and afterwards exiled to England for one of his vitriolic lampoons, but this was early in his career. Most of his trenchant criticisms of the government and the Church were written *after his return* from England.

lic purse. Conflicts of jurisdiction between rival departments frequently delayed action on vital problems for months at a stretch. Almost everywhere inefficiency, waste, and graft were the ruling qualities of the system. Even in financial matters there was no more regularity than in other branches of public policy. The collection of public revenues was exceedingly haphazard. Instead of appointing official collectors, the king employed the old Roman system of farming out the collection of taxes to private corporations and individuals, permitting them to retain as profit all that they could gouge from the people in excess of a stipulated amount. Similar disorganized conditions prevailed in the realm of law and judicial procedure. Nearly every province of France had its special code based upon local custom. As a consequence an act punishable as a crime in southern France, where the Roman influence was strongest, might be no concern of the law in a central or northern province.

Probably the most decisive of the political causes was the disastrous wars into which France was plunged during the eighteenth century. Revolutions are not made by sporadic attacks upon a system still in its prime, no matter how oppressive some of its policies may be. Before a great political and social upheaval (which is the way we must define a true revolution) can occur, it seems to be necessary that there shall be a near collapse of the existing order. Something must happen to produce a condition of chaos, to reveal the incompetence and corruption of the government, and to create such disgust and hardship that many of those who formerly supported the old regime shall now turn against it. Nothing could be better calculated to achieve these ends than conflict with foreign powers resulting in humiliating defeat or at least in serious reverses. As a matter of fact, it is almost impossible to conceive of any of the great revolutions of modern times except as a consequence of long and disastrous wars.[2] The first of the wars that prepared the ground for the French Revolution was the Seven Years' War (1756–1763), fought during the reign of Louis XV. In this struggle France was pitted against England and Prussia and, in spite of aid from Austria and also for a time from Russia, went down to overwhelming defeat. As a result, the French were compelled to surrender nearly all of their colonial possessions. It was natural and, on the whole quite justifiable, that the blame for this catastrophe should be placed on the incompetence of the government. The effects of this blow were made worse when Louis XVI decided in 1778 to intervene in the American War for Independence. Though France was now on the winning side, the cost of maintaining fleets and armies in the Western Hemisphere for more than three years virtually bankrupted the government. As we shall see, it was this condition of financial helplessness in the face of an impossible burden of

The costly wars of the French kings

[2] A distinction, of course, must be drawn between true revolutions and those of the "palace" variety, so common in Africa, Southeast Asia, and in Latin America, which are really very little more than substitutes for elections.

The French
Revolution not
the result of
misery and
poverty among
the people

debt which led directly to the quarrel between the king and the middle class and the consequent outbreak of revolution.

In turning to the economic causes of the French Revolution, we must note first of all that universal wretchedness among the mass of the people was not one of them. The popular notion that the Revolution occurred because the majority of the people were starving for want of bread, and because the queen said, "Let them eat cake," is far from historically accurate. Despite the loss of her colonial empire, France on the eve of the Revolution was still a rich and prosperous nation. Some conditions were critical, however. The government was so close to bankruptcy that it could pay its debts only by borrowing money at ruinous rates of interest. Though some industries were prospering, others were scraping the bottom of the barrel to make ends meet. As for the bulk of the rural population, it is the opinion of some modern scholars that the French peasants in the eighteenth century were better off than the rural folk in any other country of Europe except England.[3] Only about one-twentieth of the French population still languished in serfdom, and the proportion was gradually diminishing. What the downtrodden classes did in 1789 was not to initiate the Revolution, but to provide an army of followers after it had been started by others. The fact cannot be emphasized too strongly that the French Revolution was launched as a middle-class movement. Its original objectives were primarily for the benefit of the bourgeoisie. Since the leaders of this class needed the support of a larger percentage of the people, they naturally took some notice of the grievances of the peasants, and eventually of the proletarians.

What then were the real economic causes? Perhaps we should place at the head of the list the rise of the middle class to a position of extraordinary affluence and prestige. The emergence of a new economic group with a sense of grievances and a consciousness of its own strength and importance seems to be a necessary condition to the outbreak of any revolution. This class is never composed of miserable dregs of humanity—wretched, starving, and hopeless. On the contrary, its ranks must be permeated by a sense of confidence inspired by previous success and strengthened by the belief that additional effort will being greater gains in the future. During the years preceding the Revolution the French bourgeoisie had grown to be the dominant economic class. It controlled the resources of trade, manufacturing, and finance. Moreover, its members appear to have been growing richer year by year. In 1789 the foreign commerce of France reached the unprecedented total of 1,153,000,000 francs.[4] But the chief effect of this rising prosperity was to sharpen bourgeois discontent. No matter how much money a merchant,

The real economic causes:
(1) the rise of
the middle class

[3] L. R. Gottschalk, *The Era of the French Revolution*, pp. 30–31.
[4] *Ibid.*, p. 44.

manufacturer, banker, or lawyer might acquire, he was still excluded from political privileges. He had almost no influence at the court; he could not share in the highest honors; and, except in the choice of a few petty local officers, he could not even vote. Besides, he was looked down upon as an inferior by the idle and frivolous nobility. As the middle class rose in affluence and in consciousness of its own importance, its members were bound to resent such attempts at social discrimination. But above all it was the demand of the commercial, financial, and industrial leaders for political power commensurate with their economic position that made the bourgeoisie a revolutionary class.

A demand for political power was not the only consequence of the growing prosperity of the middle class; there was also an increasing clamor for the abandonment of mercantilist policies. In earlier times mercantilism had been welcomed by merchants and manufacturers because of its effects in procuring new markets and fostering trade. But those times were at the beginning of the Commercial Revolution when business was still in its swaddling clothes. As commerce and industry flourished through succeeding centuries, the bourgeoisie became increasingly confident of its ability to stand on its own feet. The result was a growing tendency to look upon the regulations of mercantilism as oppressive restrictions. Merchants disliked the special monopolies granted to favored companies and the interference with their freedom to buy in foreign markets. Manufacturers chafed under the laws controlling wages, fixing prices, and restricting the purchase of raw materials outside of France and her colonies. These were only a few of the more annoying regulations enforced by a government operating under the twin objectives of paternalism and economic self-sufficiency. Perhaps it is not strange that the middle class should have come to think of pure economic liberty as a paradise, worthy to be gained at terrific cost. At any rate, it can scarcely be doubted that the desire of businessmen to be rid of mercantilism was one of the principal causes of the French Revolution.

(2) opposition to mercantilism

A third factor, mainly economic in character, which contributed much to the outbreak of the French Revolution was the system of privilege entrenched in the society of the *ancien régime*. Prior to the Revolution the population of France was divided into three great classes or estates: the first was composed of the clergy; the second, of the nobles; and the third, of the common people. The first estate really included two different ranks: (1) the higher clergy, made up of cardinals, archbishops, bishops, and abbots; and (2) the lower clergy or parish priests. Though all of these servants of the Church were supposed to be members of a privileged group, in actual fact a wide gulf separated the two ranks. The lower clergy were frequently as poor as their humblest parishioners and were generally disposed to sympathize with the common man. By

(3) the survival of privilege: the first estate

contrast, the higher clergy lived on the fattest fruits of the land and moved in the gay and sophisticated circle of the king and his court. Including no more than 1 per cent of the total population, they nevertheless owned about 20 per cent of all the land, to say nothing of vast wealth in the form of castles, paintings, gold, and jewels. Several of the bishops and archbishops had incomes running into hundreds of thousands of francs. Naturally, most of these gilded prelates gave little attention to religious affairs. Some of them dabbled in politics, aiding the king in maintaining his absolute rule. Others gambled or devoted their energies to more scandalous vices. Though it cannot be assumed that all of them were depraved and neglectful of their professional duties, a sufficient number were corrupt, domineering, and vicious to convince many people that the Church was rotten to the core and that its leaders were guilty of robbing the people and wasting the nation's resources.

The second
estate

The second estate, comprising the secular nobility, was also divided into two subordinate castes. At the top were the *nobles of the sword*, whose titles went all the way back to the feudal suzerains of the Middle Ages. Beneath them were the *nobles of the robe*, whose immediate ancestors had acquired some judicial office conferring a title of nobility; the "robe" was the magistrate's or judge's gown. Though commonly despised by their brethren of more ancient lineage, the nobles of the robe were by far the most intelligent and progressive members of the upper classes. Several of their number became ardent reformers, while a few played prominent roles in the Revolution itself. Their ranks included such famous critics of the established order as Montesquieu, Mirabeau, and Lafayette. It was the nobles of the sword who really constituted the privileged class in the second estate. Together with the higher clergy they monopolized the leading positions in the government, usually delegating the actual work to subordinates. While they owned vast estates, they customarily resided at Versailles and depended upon stewards or bailiffs to extort enough from the peasants to provide for their luxurious needs. Few, indeed, of these high-born wastrels performed any useful function. They acted as if they believed that their only responsibilities to society were to flatter the king, to cultivate the graces of courtly life, and occasionally to patronize the decadent classical art. In a very real sense, most of them were worthless parasites consuming the wealth which others labored hard to produce.

(4) the inequi-
table system of
taxation

Among the most valuable privileges of clerics and nobles were those relating to taxation. And the inequitable system of taxation may well be considered a fourth economic cause of the French Revolution. Taxes in France, long before 1789, had come to consist of two main types. First, there were the direct taxes, which included the *taille*, or tax on real and personal property; the poll tax; and the tax on incomes, originally at the rate of 5 per cent, but in the eighteenth century more commonly 10 or 11 per cent. The indirect taxes, or taxes added to the price of commodities and paid

Le Hameau. This rustic villa was constructed in the English style on the grounds of the Petit Trianon at Versailles. Here Marie Antoinette and ladies of the court mimicked peasant life.

by the ultimate consumer, embraced mainly the tariffs on articles imported from foreign countries and the tolls levied on goods shipped from one province of France to another. In addition, the *gabelle*, or tax on salt, may also be considered a form of indirect tax. For some time the production of salt had been a state monopoly in France, and every individual inhabitant was required to buy at least seven pounds a year from the government works. To the cost of production was added a heavy tax, with the result that the price to the consumer was often as much as fifty or sixty times the actual value of the salt. While exceedingly burdensome, the indirect taxes were not as a rule unfairly distributed. It was difficult, of course, for anyone, regardless of his social status, to avoid paying them. The case of most of the direct taxes, however, was far otherwise. The clergy, by virtue of the medieval rule that the property of the Church could not be taxed by the state, escaped payment of both the *taille* and the income tax. The nobles, especially those of higher rank, made use of their influence with the king to obtain exemption from practically all direct levies. As a result, the main task of providing funds for the government fell upon the common people, or members of the third estate. And since few of the artisans and laborers had much that could be taxed, the chief burden had to be borne by the peasants and the bourgeoisie.

A final economic cause of the Revolution was the survival of relics of feudalism in France as late as 1789. While the feudal system itself had long since become extinct, vestiges of it remained and served as convenient instruments for maintaining the power of the king and the privileged position of the nobles. In some backward

545

areas of the country serfdom still lingered, but the prevalence of this institution must not be exaggerated. The highest estimate ever given of the number of peasants who were serfs is 1,500,000, out of a total rural population of at least 15,000,000. The vast majority of the peasants were free men. A considerable proportion owned the lands they cultivated. Others were tenants or hired laborers, but the largest percentage appear to have been sharecroppers, farming the lands of the nobles for a portion of the harvest, generally ranging from a third to a half. However, even those peasants who were entirely free were still required to perform obligations which had come down from the later Middle Ages. One of the most odious of these was the payment of an annual rental to the lord who had formerly controlled the land. Another was the donation to the local noble of a share of the price received whenever a tract of land was sold. In addition, the peasants were still required to contribute the *banalités*, or fees supposedly for the use of various facilities owned by the noble. During the Middle Ages *banalités* had been paid for the use of the lord's flour mill, his wine press, and his bake oven. In spite of the fact that by the eighteenth century many of the peasants owned such equipment themselves and no longer benefited by the services provided by the noble, the *banalités* were still collected in the original amounts.

Probably the most exasperating of all the relics of feudalism were the *corvée* and the hunting privileges of the nobility. The *corvée*, formerly a requirement of labor on the lord's demesne and in the building of roads and bridges on the manorial estate, was now an obligation to the government. For several weeks each year the peasant was forced to put his own work aside and devote his labor to maintaining the public highways. No other class of the population was required to perform this service. Even greater inconvenience was suffered by the rural citizens as a result of the hunting privileges of the nobles. From time immemorial the right to indulge in the diversions of the chase had been regarded as a distinctive badge of aristocracy. The man of gentle birth must have unlimited freedom to pursue this exciting pastime wherever he wished. Naturally, nothing so trivial as the property rights of the peasants should be allowed to stand in the way. In some parts of France the peasants were forbidden to weed or mow in breeding time lest they disturb the nests of the partridges. Rabbits, crows, and foxes could not be killed regardless of how much damage they did to the crops or to domestic fowl and young animals. Furthermore, the peasant was supposed to resign himself to having his fields trampled at any time by the horses of some thoughtless crew of noble hunters.

Every great social upheaval of modern times has developed out of a background of intellectual causes. Before a movement can reach the proportions of an actual revolution, it is necessary that it be supported by a body of ideas, providing not only a program of action but a glorious vision of the new order that is finally to be achieved. To a large extent these ideas are the product of political and economic ambitions, but in time they take on the significance of independent factors. Eventually the fulfillment of the ideas is accepted as an end in itself and draws the allegiance of men like the gospel of a new religion. The intellectual causes of the French Revolution were mainly an outgrowth of the Enlightenment. This movement produced two interesting political theories, which have exerted influence ever since. The first was the *liberal* theory of such writers as Locke and Montesquieu; and the second was the *democratic* theory of Rousseau. While the two were fundamentally opposed, they nevertheless had elements in common. Both were predicated upon the assumption that the state is a necessary evil and that government rests upon a contractual basis. Each had its doctrine of popular sovereignty, although with contrasting interpretations. And, finally, both upheld in some measure the fundamental rights of the individual.

The father of the liberal theory of the seventeenth and eighteenth centuries was John Locke (1632–1704). Locke's political philosophy is contained chiefly in his *Second Treatise of Civil Government,* published in 1690. In this he developed a theory of limited government which was used to justify the new system of parliamentary rule set up in England as a result of the Glorious Revolution. He maintained that originally all men had lived in a state of nature in which absolute freedom and equality prevailed, and there was no government of any kind. The only law was the law of nature, which each individual enforced for himself in order to protect his natural rights to life, liberty, and property. It was not long, however, until men began to perceive that the inconveniences of the state of nature greatly outweighed its advantages. With every individual attempting to enforce his own rights, confusion and insecurity were the unavoidable results. Accordingly, the people agreed among themselves to establish a civil society, to set up a government, and to surrender certain powers to it. But they did not make that government absolute. The only power they conferred upon it was the executive power of the law of nature. Since the state is nothing but the joint power of all the members of society, its authority "can be no more than those persons had in a state of nature before they entered into society, and gave it up to the community." [5] All powers not expressly surrendered are reserved to the people themselves. If the government exceeds or abuses the authority explicitly granted in the political contract, it becomes tyrannical; and the people then have the right to dissolve it or to rebel against it and overthrow it.

Locke condemned absolutism in every form. He denounced despotic monarchy, but he was no less severe in his strictures against the absolute sovereignty of parliaments. Though he defended the

[5] *Second Treatise of Civil Government* (Everyman Library ed.), p. 184.

supremacy of the law-making branch, with the executive primarily an agent of the legislature, he nevertheless refused to concede to the representatives of the people an unlimited power. Arguing that government was instituted among men for the preservation of property (which he generally defined in the inclusive sense of life, liberty, and estate),[6] he denied the authority of any political agency to invade the natural rights of a single individual. The law of nature, which embodies these rights, is an automatic limitation upon every branch of the government. Regardless of how large a majority of the people's representatives should demand the restriction of freedom of speech or the confiscation and redistribution of property, no such action could legally be taken. If taken illegally it would justify effective measures of resistance on the part of the majority of citizens. Locke was much more concerned with protecting individual liberty than he was with promoting stability or social progress. If forced to make a choice, he would have preferred the evils of anarchy to those of despotism in any form.

Locke's condemnation of absolutism

The influence of few political philosophers in the history of the world has exceeded that of Locke. Not only were his doctrines of natural rights, limited government, and the right of resistance against tyranny an important source of French Revolutionary theory, but they found ready acceptance in American thought as well. They furnished most of the theoretical foundation for the colonial revolt against British oppression. They were reflected so clearly in the Declaration of Independence that whole passages of that document might almost have been copied from the *Second Treatise of Civil Government*. Lockian principles also influenced the drafting of the Constitution and especially the arguments advanced by Hamilton, Madison, and Jay in the *Federalist* urging its ratification. Later, when the new government enacted the Alien and Sedition laws, it was mainly on the basis of Lockian theory that Madison and Jefferson in the Virginia and Kentucky Resolutions appealed to the several States to resist the usurpation of power.

Locke's influence

In France the foremost exponents of the liberal political theory were Voltaire (1694–1778) and Baron de Montesquieu (1689–1755). As was indicated earlier, Voltaire considered orthodox Christianity to be the worst of the enemies of mankind, but he reserved plenty of contempt for tyrannical government. During his exile in England he had studied the writings of Locke and had been deeply impressed by their vigorous assertions of individual freedom. Returning to France while still a comparatively young man, he devoted a large part of the remainder of his life to the fight for intellectual, religious, and political liberty. In common with Locke he conceived of government as a necessary evil, with powers which ought to be limited to the enforcement of natural rights. He main-

The liberal political theory of Voltaire

[6] *Ibid.*, p. 159.

tained that all men are endowed by nature with equal rights to liberty, property, and the protection of the laws. But Voltaire was no democrat. He was inclined to think of the ideal form of government as either an enlightened monarchy or a republic dominated by the middle class. To the end of his life he continued to be more than a little afraid of the masses. He was even fearful that his attacks upon organized religion might serve to incite the multitude to deeds of violence. It is related that after he had been robbed by some peasants, he attended church for a season in order to persuade the country bumpkins that he still believed in God.

A more systematic political thinker than Voltaire was his older contemporary, Baron de Montesquieu. Though, like Voltaire, a student of Locke and an ardent admirer of British institutions, Montesquieu was a unique figure among the political philosophers of the eighteenth century. In his celebrated *Spirit of Laws* he brought new methods and new conceptions into the theory of the state. Instead of attempting to found a science of government by pure deduction, he followed the Aristotelian method of studying actual political systems as they were supposed to have operated in the past. He denied that there is any one perfect form of government suitable for all peoples under all conditions. He maintained, on the contrary, that political institutions in order to be successful must harmonize with the physical conditions and the level of social advancement of the nations they are intended to serve. Thus he declared that despotism is best suited to countries of vast domain; limited monarchy to those of moderate size; and republican government to those of small extent. For his own country, France, he was disposed to think that a limited monarchy would be the most appropriate form, since he regarded the nation as too large to be made into a republic unless on some kind of federal plan.

Montesquieu

Montesquieu is especially famous for his theory of the separation of powers. He avowed that it is a natural tendency of man to abuse any extent of power entrusted to him, and that consequently every government, regardless of its form, is liable to degenerate into despotism. To prevent such a result he argued that the authority of government should be broken up into its three natural divisions of legislative, executive, and judicial. Whenever any two or more of these are allowed to remain united in the same hands, liberty, he declared, is at an end. The only effective way to avoid tyranny is to enable each branch of the government to act as a check upon the other two. For example, the executive should have the power by means of the veto to curb the encroachments of the lawmaking branch. The legislature, in turn, should have the authority of impeachment in order to restrain the executive. And, finally, there should be an independent judiciary vested with power to protect individual rights against arbitrary acts of either the legislature or the executive. This favorite scheme of Montesquieu was not intended,

The separation of powers and checks and balances

of course, to facilitate democracy. In fact, its purpose was largely the opposite: to prevent the absolute supremacy of the majority, expressed as it normally would be through the people's representatives in the legislature. It was a typical illustration of that strong dislike which the bourgeoisie had come to have for despotic government in any form, whether of the few or of the many. Montesquieu's principle of the separation of powers was none the less influential. It was incorporated in the first of the governments set up during the French Revolution, and it found its way with very few changes indeed into the Constitution of the United States.[7]

The democratic political theory

The second of the great political ideals which occupied an important place in the intellectual background of the French Revolution was the ideal of democracy. In contrast with liberalism, democracy, in its original meaning, was much less concerned with the defense of individual rights than with the enforcement of popular rule. What the majority of the citizens wills is the supreme law of the land, for the voice of the people is the voice of God. It is generally assumed that under democracy the minority will continue to enjoy full liberty of expression, but this assumption does not necessarily hold. The only sovereign right of the minority is the right to become the majority. As long as a particular group remains a minority, its members cannot claim any rights of individual action beyond the control of the state. Exponents of democracy today commonly maintain their devotion to freedom of speech and freedom of the press as rights which the government cannot legally infringe. But this attitude springs from the fact that the current ideal is generally combined with liberalism. Indeed, democracy and liberalism have now come to be used as if they were identical in meaning. Originally, however, they were entirely separate ideals. Historic democracy also included a belief in the natural equality of all men, opposition to hereditary privilege, and an abiding faith in the wisdom and virtue of the masses.

Rousseau, the founder of democracy

The founder of democracy as described above was Jean Jacques Rousseau (1712–1778). Since Rousseau was also the father of romanticism, we can expect that sentiment should have deeply colored his political judgments. Consistency, moreover, was not always his crowning virtue. The most significant of his writings on political theory were his *Social Contract* and his *Discourse on the Origin of Inequality*. In both of these he upheld the popular thesis that men had originally lived in a state of nature. But in contrast with Locke he regarded this state of nature as a veritable paradise. No one suffered inconvenience from maintaining his own rights against others. Indeed, there were very few chances of conflict of any sort; for private property did not exist for a long time, and every man was the equal of his neighbor. Eventually, however,

[7] For the influence of Montesquieu upon the founders of the American government, see E. M. Burns, *James Madison: Philosopher of the Constitution*, pp. 180–83.

evils arose, due primarily to the fact that some men staked off plots of land and said to themselves, "This is mine." It was in such manner that various degrees of inequality developed; and, as a consequence, "cheating trickery," "insolent pomp," and "insatiable ambition" soon came to dominate the relations among men.[8] The only hope of security was now for men to establish a civil society and to surrender all of their rights to the community. This they did by means of a social contract, in which each individual agreed with the whole body of individuals to submit to the will of the majority. Thus the state was brought into existence.

Rousseau developed an altogether different conception of sovereignty from that of the liberals. Whereas Locke and his followers had taught that only a portion of sovereign power is surrendered to the state, the rest being retained by the people themselves, Rousseau contended that sovereignty is indivisible, and that all of it became vested in the community when civil society was formed. He insisted further that each individual in becoming a party to the social contract gave up all of his rights to the people collectively and agreed to submit absolutely to the general will. It follows that the sovereign power of the state is subject to no limitations whatever. The general will, expressed through the vote of the majority, is the court of final appeal. What the majority decides is always right in the political sense and is absolutely binding upon every citizen. The state, which in actual practice means the majority, is legally omnipotent. But this does not really imply, according to Rousseau, that the liberty of the individual is entirely destroyed. On the contrary, subjection to the state has the effect of enhancing *genuine* liberty. Individuals in surrendering their rights to the community merely exchange the animal liberty of the state of nature for the true freedom of reasoning creatures in obedience to law. Compelling an individual to abide by the general will is therefore merely "forcing him to be free." It must be understood, also, that when Rousseau referred to the state he did not mean the government. He regarded the state as the politically organized community, which has the sovereign function of expressing the general will. The authority of the state cannot be represented, but must be expressed directly through the enactment of fundamental laws by the people themselves. The government, on the other hand, is simply the executive agent of the state. Its function is not to formulate the general will but merely to carry it out. Moreover, the community can set the government up or pull it down "whenever it likes."[9]

The influence of Rousseau's political theory would be hard to exaggerate. His dogmas of equality and the supremacy of the majority were the chief inspiration for the second stage of the French

Rousseau's conception of sovereignty

---

[8] *Discourse on the Origin of Inequality* (Everyman Library ed.), p. 207.

[9] *The Social Contract* (Everyman Library ed.), p. 88.

The influence
of Rousseau

Revolution. Doctrinaire radicals like Robespierre were among his most fervent disciples. But Rousseau's influence was not confined to his own country. Some of his theories made their way to America and found an echo in certain of the principles of Jacksonian Democracy–although, of course, it is extremely improbable that many of Jackson's followers had ever heard of Rousseau. The German Romantic Idealists, who, in the early nineteenth century, glorified the state as "God in history," would also appear to have been indebted to the philosophy of *The Social Contract*. From Rousseau's doctrines that the state is legally omnipotent, and that true liberty consists in submission to the general will, it was not a very difficult step to exalting the state as an object of worship and reducing the individual to a mere cog in the political machine.[10] Even though Rousseau suggested that the majority would be limited by moral restraints and insisted upon the right of the people to "pull down" their government, these limitations were not enough to counteract the effect of his stress upon absolute sovereignty.

The influence
of the new eco-
nomic theory

As a final intellectual cause of the French Revolution, the influence of the new economic theory must be given at least passing attention. In the second half of the eighteenth century a number of brilliant writers began attacking the traditional assumptions in regard to public control over production and trade. Their special target of criticism was mercantilist policy. To a large extent the new economics was founded upon the basic conceptions of the Enlightenment, particularly the idea of a mechanistic universe governed by inflexible laws. The notion now came to prevail that the sphere of the production and distribution of wealth was subject to laws just as irresistible as those of physics and astronomy. The new economic theory may also be regarded as the counterpart of political liberalism. The cardinal aims of the two were quite similar: to reduce the powers of government to the lowest minimum consistent with safety and to preserve for the individual the largest possible measure of freedom in the pursuit of his own devices.

The economics
of Adam Smith

The greatest of all the economists of the age of the Enlightenment and one of the most brilliant of all time was Adam Smith (1723–1790). A native of Scotland, Smith began his career as a lecturer on English literature at the University of Edinburgh. From this he was soon advanced to a professorship of logic at Glasgow College. He first won fame in 1759 with the publication of his *Theory of Moral Sentiments*. In 1776 he published his *Inquiry into the Nature and Causes of the Wealth of Nations*, generally considered the foundation of modern economic theory. In this work he maintained that labor, rather than agriculture or the bounty of nature, is the real source of wealth. While in general he accepted the principle of *laissez faire*, avowing that the prosperity of all can best be promoted

[10] For a discussion of the political theory of the Romantic Idealists see §3 in the chapter on The Age of Romanticism and Reaction.

by allowing each individual to pursue his own interest, he neverthe-less recognized that certain forms of governmental interference would be desirable. The state should intervene for the prevention of injustice and oppression, for the advancement of education and the protection of public health, and for the maintenance of necessary enterprises which would never be established by private capital. Notwithstanding these rather broad limitations upon the principle of laissez faire, Smith's *Wealth of Nations* was adopted as Holy Writ by the economic individualists of the eighteenth and nine-teenth centuries. Its influence in causing the French Revolution was indirect but none the less profound. It furnished the final answer to mercantilist argument and thereby strengthened the ambition of the bourgeoisie to have done with a political system which continued to block the path to economic freedom.

2. THE DESTRUCTION OF THE ANCIEN RÉGIME

Early in the year 1789 the volcano of discontent in France burst forth into revolution. The immediate causes were a series of eco-nomic troubles for which no one seemed to be able to find an ac-ceptable remedy. As a consequence of bad harvests bread prices al-most doubled. In December 1788, 80,000 workers were reported unemployed in Paris. Most serious of all was the near bankruptcy of the French government. To meet the mounting deficit, the king's finance ministers proposed new taxes, notably a stamp duty and a direct tax on the annual production of the soil. Mean-while, such earlier impositions as the *taille* and the *gabelle* would continue in effect. Additional taxation might well have provided the government with the revenue it so desperately needed had there not been confusion and discord in the administration of fiscal policies. Every proposed reform threatened the interests of some powerful group. Conditions moved rapidly from bad to worse as the government continued its makeshift policy of borrowing and spending. Prices rose so rapidly that the cost of bread alone consumed more than 50 per cent of the poor man's income. In 1787 the king summoned an Assembly of Notables in the hope that the chief magnates of the realm might consent to bearing a larger share of the fiscal burden. Factional discord soon split the Assembly. The nobles of the sword and the higher clergy staunchly supported the monarchy and demanded retention of their privileges. The judicial oligarchy, or nobles of the robe, took a broader view. In-spired by the philosophy of the Enlightenment and the American Revolution, they argued not merely in favor of fiscal revision but of governmental reform. Specifically, they demanded convocation of the Estates General to deal with the national crisis.

Although the Estates General had not met for 175 years, the be-lief prevailed widely that it alone could save the country in a dire

The immediate causes of the French Revolution

553

FRANCE IN 1789 · THE "GOVERNMENTS"

emergency. As its name implies, the Estates General was supposed to represent the three great estates or classes of the nation. During the period when it was convoked more or less regularly, the representatives of each estate had met and voted as a body. Generally this meant that the first and second estates combined against the third. By the late eighteenth century the third estate had attained such importance that it was not willing to tolerate such an arrangement. Consequently its leaders demanded that the three orders should sit together and vote as individuals. Leaving this issue unresolved, King Louis XVI, in the summer of 1788, yielded to popular clamor and summoned the Estates General to meet in May of the following year. After weeks of wrangling, the third estate, on June 17, boldly proclaimed itself the National Assembly and invited the representatives of the privileged orders to join in its work. Many of them actually did so. Within two days a

The first stage of the Revolution

554

majority of the clergy went over and a sprinkling of the nobles also. But then the king intervened. When the rebellious deputies assembled at their hall on the morning of June 20, they found its doors guarded by troops. There were now no alternatives but to submit or to defy the sovereign power of the monarch himself. Confident of the support of a majority of the people, the commoners and their allies withdrew to a near-by hall, variously used as a riding academy and a tennis court. Here under the leadership of Mirabeau and the Abbé Sieyès they bound themselves by a solemn oath not to separate until they had drafted a constitution for France. This Oath of the Tennis Court, on June 20, 1789, was the real beginning of the French Revolution. By claiming the authority to remake the government in the name of the people, the Estates General was not merely protesting against the arbitrary rule of Louis XVI but asserting its right to act as the highest sovereign power in the nation. On June 27 the king virtually conceded this right by ordering the remaining delegates of the privileged classes to meet with the third estate as members of a National Assembly.

The course of the French Revolution was marked by three great stages, the first of which extended from June 1789 to August 1792. During most of this period the destinies of France were in the hands of the National Assembly, dominated by the leaders of the third

The Opening of the Estates General in Versailles, May 5, 1789

The Tennis Court Oath by David. In the hall where royalty played a game known as *jeu de paume* (similar to tennis) leaders of the Revolution swore to draft a constitution. In the center of this painting with his arm extended is Jean Bailly, president of the National Assembly. Seated at the table below him is Abbé Sieyès. Somewhat to the right of Sieyès with both hands on his chest is Robespierre. Mirabeau, with hat in his left hand and wearing a black coat, stands somewhat farther to the right.

estate. In the main, this stage was a moderate, middle-class stage. The masses had not yet gained any degree of political power, nor were they in a position to seize control of the economic system. Aside from the destruction of the Bastille on July 14, 1789, and the murder of a few members of the royal guard, there was comparatively little violence in Paris or Versailles. In certain of the country districts, however, a more unruly spirit prevailed. Many of the peasants grew impatient over the delay in granting reforms and determined to deal with the situation directly. Arming themselves with pitchforks and scythes, they set out to destroy what they could of the *ancien régime*. They demolished *châteaux* of hated nobles, plundered monasteries and residences of bishops, and murdered some of the lords who offered resistance. Most of this violence occurred during the summer of 1789 and had much to do with frightening the upper classes into surrendering some of their privileges.

The most significant developments of the first stage of the Revolution were the achievements of the National Assembly between 1789 and 1791. The initial one of these achievements was the destruction of most of the relics of feudalism. This came about largely

> The triumph of the third estate

as a result of the rebellious temper displayed by the peasants. By the beginning of August 1789, such alarming reports of anarchy in the villages had reached the National Assembly that an urgent need for concessions soon came to be recognized by many of the members. On the fourth of August a certain noble proposed in an eloquent speech that all of his brethren should renounce their feudal privileges. His plea stirred the Assembly to a wild enthusiasm, compounded partly of fear and partly of revolutionary zeal. Nobles, churchmen, and burghers vied with each other in suggesting reforms. Before the night had ended, numerous remnants of the hoary structure of vested rights had been swept away. Ecclesiastical tithes and the *corvée* were formally abolished. Serfdom was eliminated. The hunting privileges of the nobles were declared at an end. Exemption from taxation and monopolies of all kinds were sacrificed as contrary to natural equality. While the nobles did not surrender all of their rights, the ultimate effect of these reforms of the "August Days" was to annihilate distinctions of rank and class and to make all Frenchmen citizens of an equal status in the eyes of the law.[11]

Achievements of the first stage: (1) the destruction of feudal privileges

Following the destruction of privilege the Assembly turned its attention to preparing a charter of liberties. The result was the Declaration of the Rights of Man and of the Citizen, issued in September 1789. Modeled in part after the English Bill of Rights and embodying the teachings of liberal political philosophers, the French Declaration was a typical middle-class document. Property was declared to be a natural right as well as liberty, security, and "resistance to oppression." No one was to be deprived of anything he possessed except in case of public necessity, and then only on condition that he should have been "previously and equitably indemnified." Proper consideration was also to be given to personal rights. Freedom of speech, religious toleration, and liberty of the press were held to be inviolable. All citizens were declared to be entitled to equality of treatment in the courts. No one was to be imprisoned or otherwise punished except in accordance with due process of law. Sovereignty was affirmed to reside in the people, and officers of the government were made subject to deposition if they abused the powers conferred upon them. Nothing was said about any right of the common man to an adequate share of the wealth he produced or even to protection by the state in case of inability to earn a living. The authors of the Declaration of Rights were not socialists, nor were they interested particularly in the economic welfare of the masses.

(2) the Declaration of the Rights of Man

ON NE CONNOÎT ICI

QUE LA DÉNOMINATION

DE CITOYEN.

"Only the Title of Citizen Is Employed Here." A placard from the revolutionary period.

The next of the main accomplishments of the National Assembly was the secularization of the Church. Under the *ancien régime* the higher clergy had been a privileged caste, rewarding the king for his favors by a staunch support of absolute rule. As a result, the Church

[11] Along with these reforms in connection with the destruction of monopolies and feudal privileges, the guilds were also abolished and workers were forbidden to form unions.

557

THE FRENCH REVOLUTION
(1789—1799)

(3) the secular-
ization of the
Church

Assignat

(4) the Consti-
tution of 1791

had come to be regarded as an instrument of greed and oppression almost as odious as the monarchy itself. Moreover, the ecclesiastical institutions were the possessors of vast estates, and the new Revolutionary government was desperately in need of funds. Accordingly, in November 1789, the National Assembly resolved to confiscate the lands of the Church and to use them as collateral for the issue of *assignats,* or paper money. In July of the following year the Civil Constitution of the Clergy was enacted, providing that all bishops and priests should be elected by the people and should be subject to the authority of the state. Their salaries were to be paid out of the public treasury, and they were required to swear allegiance to the new legislation. The secularization of the Church also involved a partial separation from Rome. The aim of the Assembly was to make the Catholic Church of France a truly national institution with no more than a nominal subjection to the papacy.

Not until 1791 did the National Assembly manage to complete its primary task of drafting a new constitution for the nation. Too many other problems of more immediate concern had absorbed its attention. Besides, autocratic government was already a thing of the past. The constitution as it finally emerged gave eloquent testimony to the dominant position now held by the bourgeoisie. France was not made a democratic republic, but the government was converted merely into a limited monarchy, with the supreme power virtually a monopoly of the well-to-do. The privilege of voting was restricted to those who paid a direct tax equal to three days' wages, while eligibility for holding office was limited to citizens of comparative wealth. As to the structure of the government, the principle of the separation of powers was to be the basic feature. For this the founders of the new system went back to Montesquieu's idea of independent legislative, executive, and judicial departments. The lawmaking powers were bestowed upon a Legislative Assembly chosen indirectly by the people through a process somewhat similar to that by which the President of the United States was originally supposed to be selected. The king was deprived of the control he had formerly exercised over the army, the Church, and local government. His ministers were forbidden to sit in the Assembly, and he was shorn of all power over the legislative process except a suspensive veto, which in fact could be overridden by the issuance of proclamations. Thus the new system, although far removed from absolute monarchy, was decidedly not a government the masses could claim as their own.

In the summer of 1792 the French Revolution entered a second stage, which lasted for about two years. This stage differed from the first in a number of ways. To begin with, France was now a republic. On the tenth of August the Legislative Assembly voted to suspend the king and ordered the election, by universal manhood suffrage, of a National Convention to draft a new constitution. Soon

The Execution of Louis XVI. The event took place on what is now the Place de la Concorde in Paris, on January 21, 1793.

afterward Louis XVI was brought to trial on charges of plotting with foreign enemies of the Revolution, and on January 21, 1793, he was beheaded. In addition to its republican character, the second stage differed from the first in the fact that it was dominated by the lower classes. No longer was the course of the Revolution dictated by relatively conservative members of the bourgeoisie. Instead, it was extremists representing the proletariat of Paris who were largely responsible for determining the nature of the movement. The liberal philosophy of Voltaire and Montesquieu was now replaced by the radical, equalitarian doctrines of Rousseau. Yet another difference was the more violent and bloody character of the second stage. This was the period not only of the execution of the king but also of the September massacres (1792) and of the Reign of Terror from the summer of 1793 to the summer of 1794.

The second or radical stage of the Revolution

What factors may be taken to explain this spectacular transition from a comparatively moderate, middle-class phase to a stage of radicalism and turmoil? First of all may be mentioned the disappointed hopes of the proletariat. The Revolution in its beginning had held out what appeared to be glorious promises of equality and justice for every citizen. Hope had been built particularly on the Declaration of Rights, in spite of its emphasis upon the sanctity of private property. But now after more than three years of social and political upheaval it was just as hard for the urban worker to earn his bread as it had been before. In actual fact, it was probably

Causes of the transition to a radical stage

559

A Contemporary Engraving of the September Massacres in Paris

harder. In the spring of 1791 the government abolished the public workshops which had provided employment for thousands who had been left jobless by the disruption of business. Moreover, new laws were passed prohibiting the formation of unions, collective bargaining, picketing, and strikes. Another disappointment developed when the common man discovered after the adoption of the Constitution of 1791 that he was not even to be allowed to vote. Ever more clearly the realization dawned that he had simply exchanged one set of masters for another. In such a state of mind he was bound to be attracted by the preaching of extremists, who offered to lead him into the Promised Land of security and plenty. A second cause of the transition to a radical stage was the accumulated momentum of the Revolution itself. Every great movement of this kind generates an atmosphere of discontent, which is breathed more deeply by some men than by others. The result is the emergence of a kind of professional revolutionist, who is eternally dissatisfied no matter how much has been accomplished. He denounces the leaders of the revolution in its preliminary stage even more scathingly than he condemns the adherents of the old order. For him, no price of slaughter and chaos is too great to pay in order to purchase the fulfillment of his own ideals. He will murder his closest associates, the moment they disagree with him, just as readily as he will consign the most hated reactionary to outer darkness. He is the political counterpart of the religious fanatic who believes that sword and faggot are proper instruments for hastening the reign of God's righteousness and peace.

Yet perhaps the most important cause of the triumph of the radicals was the outbreak of war between France and foreign states. In several European countries the progress of the French Revolution was coming to be viewed with increasing alarm by reactionary

EUROPE • 1789

Hapsburg possessions

Boundary of the Holy Roman Empire

Volga R.

RUSSIAN EMPIRE

Sea of Azov

BLACK SEA

O T T O M A N   E M P I R E

Constantinople

Dnieper R.

AEGEAN SEA

Dniester R.

SWEDEN

Stockholm

BALTIC SEA

P R U S S I A

POLAND

Warsaw

Vistula R.

Budapest

Danube R.

Athens

NORWAY

DENMARK

Oder R.

Berlin

Prague

Vienna

VENETIAN REP.

ADRIATIC SEA

KINGDOM

OF THE

TWO SICILIES

IONIAN IS.
(To Venice)

Elbe R.

HOLY ROMAN
EMPIRE

Venice

PAPAL
STATES

MEDITERRANEAN

NORTH SEA

UNITED
NETHERLANDS

Amsterdam

Brussels

Rhine R.

Berne

SWITZ.

GENOA

Rome

(Fr.)

SEA

OTTOMAN
EMPIRE

GREAT
BRITAIN

London

Thames R.

Seine R.

Paris

FRANCE

KINGDOM OF SARDINIA

English Channel

Loire R.

Garonne R.

IRELAND
(Br.)

Dublin

*Bay of
Biscay*

Madrid

Tagus R.

SPAIN

Gibraltar (Br.)

*ATLANTIC
OCEAN*

PORTUGAL

Lisbon

*Strait of
Gibraltar*

500 miles

Madame Recamier, Jacques Louis David (1748–1825). David was the exponent of a new classicism during and after the French Revolution. The couch, the lamp, and the costume are copied from Rome and Pompeii. (Louvre)

Napoleon's Coronation, David. (Versailles Museum)

rulers. The fear was particularly strong in Austria and Prussia, where numerous *émigrés*, or French royalists, had taken refuge and were convincing the monarchs of those countries of the danger that the Revolution might spread. Besides, the French queen, Marie Antoinette, was a member of the Hapsburg family and was making frenzied appeals to the Emperor to come to the aid of her husband. In August 1791, the Austrian and Prussian rulers joined in issuing the Declaration of Pillnitz, in which they boldly avowed that the restoration of order and of the rights of the monarch in France was a matter of "common interest to all sovereigns of Europe." Naturally this pronouncement was keenly resented by the French, since it could hardly be interpreted in any other way than as a threat of intervention. Moreover, there was a tendency on the part of many of the revolutionists to welcome a conflict with a foreign enemy. While the moderate faction expected that military success would solidify the loyalty of the people to the new regime, many of the radicals were clamoring for war in the secret hope that the armies of France would suffer defeat, and that the monarchy would thereby be discredited. A republic could then be set up, and the heroic soldiers of the people would turn defeat into victory and carry the blessings of freedom to all the oppressed of Europe. With such considerations in mind, the Assembly voted for war on April 20, 1792. As the radicals had hoped, the forces of the French met serious reverses. By August the allied armies of Austria and Prussia had crossed the frontier and were threatening the capture of Paris. A fury of rage and despair seized the capital. The belief prevailed that the military disasters had been the result of treasonable dealings with the enemy on the part of the king and his conservative followers. As a consequence, a vigorous demand arose for drastic action against all who were suspected of disloyalty to the Revolution. It was this situation more than anything else which brought the extremists to the fore and enabled them to gain control of the Legislative Assembly and to put an end to the monarchy.

From 1792 to 1795—that is, during the second stage of the Revolution and for more than a year longer—the governing power of France was the National Convention. As originally set up, this body was supposed to draft a new constitution and then surrender its authority to a regular government. In 1793 a new constitution was actually drawn up, the most democratic in history thus far. It provided for universal manhood suffrage and the right of referendum. It declared that society owes a living to the poor, either by finding work for them or giving them the means of subsistence. It made the provision of education an obligation of the state. Never before had the needs of social democracy been so clearly recognized in an instrument of government. But on account of the disordered conditions of the time, the Constitution of 1793 was never put into effect. With the justification that a national

The threat of
foreign inter-
vention

The govern-
ment of France
during the
second stage:
the National
Convention

561

emergency existed, the Convention simply prolonged its life from year to year. After the spring of 1793 it delegated its executive functions to a group of nine (later twelve) of its members, known as the Committee of Public Safety. This agency conducted foreign relations, supervised the command of the armies, and enforced the Reign of Terror. The Convention itself was composed of a number of factions representing various shades of radical opinion. The most important were the Girondists and the Jacobins. The Girondists drew their support largely from regions outside of Paris and were inclined to distrust the proletariat. They were republicans but not extreme democrats. Their Jacobin opponents were among the most thoroughgoing radicals of the Revolution.[12] Though most of them sprang from the middle class, they were ardent disciples of Rousseau and militant champions of the urban workers. They accused the Girondists of desiring an "aristocratic republic" and of plotting to destroy the unity of France by putting into effect some kind of federal plan in which the *départements* or provinces would be exalted at the expense of Paris.

Leadership in the National Convention was furnished by some of the most interesting and dramatic personalities of modern history. Famous among those who usually identified themselves with the Girondists were Thomas Paine (1737–1809) and the Marquis de Condorcet (1743–1794). Following his brilliant work as a pamphleteer in the American Revolution, Paine sailed for England, determined to open the eyes of the people of that country "to the madness and stupidity of the government." In 1791 he published his celebrated *Rights of Man*, a blistering attack upon Edmund Burke's *Reflections on the Revolution in France*, issued the previous year. *The Rights of Man* created a sensation, especially after the bungling attempts of the government to suppress it. The author was indicted for treason, but he escaped to France before he could be seized for trial. In 1792 he was elected to the National Convention and immediately began an active career as one of the more moderate leaders of that body. He urged the destruction of the monarchy but opposed the execution of the king on the ground that it would alienate American sympathy. Ultimately he incurred the suspicion of some of the extremists and escaped the guillotine by the sheerest accident.

A man of milder temperament than Paine but of similar philosophic interests was the Marquis de Condorcet. Originally a disciple of Voltaire and Turgot, he eventually went considerably beyond these bourgeois liberals in his demands for reform. He condemned not only the evils of absolutism, mercantilism, slavery, and war, as did many of the enlightened thinkers of his time, but he was one of the first to insist that the elimination of poverty should be a cardinal

Thomas Paine

The moderate leaders in the National Convention: (1) Thomas Paine

(2) Condorcet

[12] The Jacobin Club had not always been radical. During the earlier years of the Revolution it had numbered among its members such well-known moderates as Mirabeau, Sieyès, and Lafayette. In 1791, however, it had come under the domination of extremists led by Maximilien Robespierre.

purpose of statecraft. He thought that this end could be largely attained through the destruction of monopoly and privilege and the abolition of primogeniture and entail. The removal of these obstacles would permit a wide distribution of property, especially land, and thereby enable most individuals to achieve economic independence. He also advocated old-age pensions and cooperative banking to provide cheap credit.[13] At the height of the Terror, Condorcet was outlawed for denouncing the violence of the Jacobins and was compelled to flee for his life. Disguised as a carpenter, he wandered half-starved through the country until one night he aroused suspicion, was apprehended, and thrown into prison. The next morning he was found dead on the floor. Whether he collapsed from suffering and exposure or swallowed poison he was supposed to have carried in a ring is unknown.

Foremost among the leaders of the extremist factions were Marat, Danton, and Robespierre. Jean Paul Marat (1743–1793) was educated as a physician, and, by 1789, had already earned enough distinction in that profession to be awarded an honorary degree by St. Andrews University in Scotland. Almost from the beginning of the Revolution he stood as a champion of the common people. He opposed nearly all of the dogmatic assumptions of his middle-class colleagues in the Assembly, including the idea that France should pattern her government after that of Great Britain, which he recognized to be oligarchic in form. He was soon made a victim of persecution and was forced to find refuge in sewers and dungeons, but this did not stop him from his efforts to rouse the people to a defense of their rights. In 1793 he was stabbed through the heart by Charlotte Corday, a young woman who was fanatically devoted to the Girondists. In contrast with Marat, Georges Jacques Danton (1759–1794) did not come into prominence until the Revolution was three years old, but, like Marat, he directed his activities toward goading the masses into rebellion. Elected a member of the Committee of Public Safety in 1793, he had much to do with organizing the Reign of Terror. As time went on he appears to have wearied of ruthlessness and displayed a tendency to compromise. This gave his opponents in the Convention their opportunity, and in April 1794, he was sent to the guillotine. Upon mounting the scaffold he is reported to have said: "Show my head to the people; they do not see the like every day."

The most famous and perhaps the greatest of all the extremist leaders was Maximilien Robespierre (1758–1794). Born of a family reputed to be of Irish descent, Robespierre was trained for the law and speedily achieved a modest success as an advocate. In 1782 he was appointed a criminal judge, but soon resigned because he could not bear to impose a sentence of death. Of a nervous and timid disposition, he was never able to display much executive ability, but he

The extremist leaders: Marat and Danton

Robespierre

Robespierre

[13] J. S. Schapiro, *Condorcet and the Rise of Liberalism*, pp. 142–55.

made up for this lack of talent by fanatical devotion to principle. He had adopted the belief that the philosophy of Rousseau held the one great hope of salvation for all mankind. To put this philosophy into practice he was ready to employ any means that would bring results, regardless of the cost to himself or to others. This passionate loyalty to a gospel that exalted the masses eventually won him a following. Indeed, he was so lionized by the public that he was allowed to wear the knee breeches, silk stockings, and powdered hair of the old society until the end of his life. In 1791 he was accepted as the oracle of the Jacobin Club, now purged of all but its most radical elements. Later he became president of the National Convention and a member of the Committee of Public Safety. Though he had little or nothing to do with originating the Reign of Terror, he was nevertheless responsible for enlarging its scope. He actually came to justify ruthlessness as a necessary and therefore laudable means to revolutionary progress. In the last six weeks of his virtual dictatorship, no fewer than 1285 heads rolled from the scaffold in Paris. But sooner or later such methods were bound to bring his own doom. On July 28, 1794, he and twenty-one of his lieutenants were beheaded, after no more pretense of a trial than Robespierre himself had allowed to his opponents.

Jacobins. Contemporary drawings by Heuriot.

The actual extent of violence during the second stage of the Revolution will probably never be known. Many of the stories of horrible butchery that circulated then and later were highly exaggerated. No streets ran red with blood and no rivers were clogged with corpses. Nevertheless, an appalling amount of bloodshed did actually occur. During the period of the Terror, from September 1793 to July 1794, the most reliable estimates place the number of executions at approximately 20,000 in France as a whole. A law of September 17, 1793, made every person who had been identified in any way with the Bourbon government or with the Girondists an object of suspicion; and no one who was a suspect or who was suspected of being a suspect was entirely safe from persecution. When some time later the Abbé Sieyès was asked what he had done to distinguish himself during the Terror, he responded dryly, "I lived." Yet when all is said, it must be conceded that the slaughter during the French Revolution was much less than that which has accompanied most civil and international wars. The 20,000 victims of the Reign of Terror can hardly be compared, for example, to the hundreds of thousands slain during the American War between the States. Napoleon Bonaparte, whom many people worship as a hero, was responsible for at least twenty times as many deaths as all of the members of the Committee of Public Safety. This comparison is not meant to condone the savagery of the Terror, but it may serve to correct a distorted picture.

Despite the violence of the Reign of Terror, the second stage of the French Revolution was marked by some worthy achievements.

*Meeting of a Revolution-
ary Committee during the
Reign of Terror*

Such leaders as Robespierre, fanatical though they might have been,
were nevertheless sincere humanitarians, and it was not to be expected that they would ignore the opportunity to inaugurate reforms. Among their most significant accomplishments were the
abolition of slavery in the colonies; the prohibition of imprisonment
for debt; the establishment of ·the metric system of weights and
measures; and the repeal of primogeniture, so that property might
not be inherited exclusively by the oldest son but must be divided in
substantially equal portions among all of the immediate heirs. The
Convention also attempted to supplement the decrees of the National Assembly in abolishing the remnants of feudalism and in providing for greater freedom of economic opportunity. The property
of enemies of the Revolution was confiscated for the benefit of the
government and the lower classes. Great estates were broken up and
offered for sale to poorer citizens on easy terms. The indemnities
hitherto promised to the nobles for the loss of their privileges were
abruptly canceled. To curb the rise in the cost of living, maximum
prices for grain and other necessities were fixed by law, and merchants who profiteered at the expense of the poor were threatened
with the guillotine. Still other measures of reform were those in the
sphere of religion. At one time during the Terror an effort was
made to abolish Christianity and to substitute the worship of Reason
in its place. In accordance with this purpose a new calendar was
adopted, dating the year from the birth of the republic (September
22, 1792) and dividing the months in such a way as to eliminate the
Christian Sunday. When Robespierre came to power, he supplanted
this cult of Reason by a deistic religion dedicated to the worship of
a Supreme Being and to the belief in the immortality of the soul.
Finally, in 1794, the Convention took the more sensible step of mak-

Reforms
achieved during
the second stage

565

The Death of Marat. Painting by David.

ing religion a private concern of the individual. It was decided that church and state should be entirely separate, and that all beliefs not actually hostile to the government should be tolerated.

In the summer of 1794 the Reign of Terror came to an end, and soon afterward the Revolution passed into its third and final stage. The event which inaugurated the change was the Thermidorian Reaction, so called from the month of Thermidor (heat month—July 19 to August 18) in the new calendar. The execution of Robespierre on July 28, 1794 represented the completion of a cycle. The Revolution had now devoured its own children. One after another the radical giants had fallen—first Marat, then Hébert and Danton, and now finally Robespierre and Saint-Just. The only remaining leaders in the Convention were men of moderate sympathies. As time went on they inclined toward increasing conservatism and toward any kind of political chicanery which would serve to keep them in power. Gradually the Revolution came once more to reflect the interests of the bourgeoisie. Much of the extremist work of the radicals was now undone. The law of maximum prices and the law against "suspects" were both repealed. Political prisoners were freed, the Jacobins were driven into hiding, and the Committee of Public Safety was shorn of its despotic powers. The new situation made possible the return of priests, royalists, and other *émigrés* from abroad to add the weight of their influence to the conservative trend.

In 1795 the National Convention adopted a new constitution, which lent the stamp of official approval to the victory of the prosperous classes. The new organic law, known as the Constitution of the Year III, granted suffrage to all adult male citizens who could read and write, but they were permitted to vote only for electors, who in turn would choose the members of the Legislative Body; and in order to be an elector, one had to be the proprietor of a farm or other establishment with an annual income equivalent to at least 100 days of labor. It was thus made certain that the authority of the government would actually be derived from citizens of considerable wealth. Since it was not practicable to restore the monarchy, lest the old aristocracy also come back into power, executive authority was vested in a board of five men known as the Directory, chosen by the legislative body. The new constitution included not only a bill of rights but also a declaration of the *duties* of the citizen. Conspicuous among the latter was the obligation to bear in mind that "it is upon the maintenance of property . . . that the whole social order rests."

The third stage of the French Revolution was of little historical importance compared with the other two. In general it was a period of stagnation, wholesale corruption, and cynicism. The burning zeal for reform that had characterized the other two stages now disappeared into thin air. The members of the new government were interested much more in opportunities for personal profit than in the shining ideals of philosophers for remaking the world. Graft was a familiar accompaniment of the levying and collecting of taxes and the disbursement of public funds. Even some members of the Directory coolly demanded bribes as the price of favors which the duties of their office should normally have required them to bestow. This cynical greed in high places was bound to have its effect upon the tone of society. It is therefore not surprising that the age of the Di-

The Death of Robespierre

The end of the
Revolution: the
coup d'état of
Napoleon
Bonaparte

rectory should have been a period of riotous extravagance, dissipation, and frenzied pursuit of wealth. Speculation and gambling tended to crowd legitimate business into a secondary place. While famine stalked the slums of Paris, profiteers accumulated fortunes and flaunted their gains at the expense of the people in senseless display. Thus were the glorious promises of the Revolution trailed in the mud, even by some who had originally sworn to uphold them.

In the fall of 1799 the Revolution in France came to a close. The event that marked its end was the *coup d'état* of Napoleon Bonaparte on the eighteenth Brumaire (November 9). This, however, was merely the final blow. For some time the regime set up by the Constitution of the Year III had been hovering on the verge of collapse. Though for a while it was bolstered up by victories in the war which was still going on against foreign enemies of the Revolution, eventually even this support was torn away. In 1798–1799 the aggressive policy of the Directory had involved France in a struggle with a new combination of powerful foes—Great Britain, Austria, and Russia. The fortunes of battle soon shifted. One after another the satellite states the French had erected on their eastern frontier collapsed. The armies of the republic were driven from Italy. Soon it appeared as if all the gains of previous years were to be blotted out. Meanwhile the Directory had been suffering an even greater loss of prestige from its conduct of internal affairs. Thousands of people were disgusted with the shameful corruption of public officials and their indifference to the needs of the poor. To make matters worse, the government was partly responsible for a serious financial crisis. In order to defray the cost of wars and to make up for the extravagance of incompetent officials, the issuance of *assignats* or paper money was increased. The inevitable results were wild inflation and utter chaos. Within a short time the *assignats* had depreciated until they were actually worth no more

The Eighteenth Brumaire: A Detail of Napoleon. Painting by Bronchot.

than 1 per cent of their face value. By 1797 conditions had grown so hopeless that the only alternative was to repudiate all of the outstanding paper currency. During the period of financial chaos millions of cautious and respectable citizens who had managed to accumulate some property were reduced to the level of proletarians. The effect was naturally to turn them into bitter enemies of the existing government.

Under these deplorable circumstances the accession of Napoleon Bonaparte was rendered comparatively easy. Disgust with the banality and indifference of the Directory, resentment on account of the hardships suffered from the inflation, the sense of being humiliated as a result of defeat in the war—these were the factors which encouraged a widespread conviction that the existing regime was intolerable, and that only the appearance of a "man on horseback" could save the nation from ruin. In other words, Napoleon rose to power under conditions quite similar to those which presided at the birth of more recent dictatorships in Germany and Italy. But, of course, young Bonaparte was a military hero, which Hitler and Mussolini were not. In 1795 he had endeared himself to the friends of law and order by defending the National Convention with a "whiff of grapeshot" against an uprising of Parisian insurgents. Later he had come trailing clouds of glory from his campaigns in Italy and in Egypt. True, his reports of success in the latter country were slightly colored, but they convinced patriotic Frenchmen that here at last was a general in whose skill they could place absolute trust. Besides, no one could doubt the fact that he had driven the Austrians from Italy and had added Savoy and Nice and the Austrian Netherlands to France. It is no wonder that he should have come to be regarded as the man of the hour. His name became a symbol of national greatness and the glorious achievements of the Revolution. And as the revulsion of feeling against the Directory increased, he was hailed more than ever as the incorruptible hero who would deliver the nation from shame and disaster.

3. THE GOOD AND EVIL FRUITS OF THE REVOLUTION

While the coming to power of Napoleon Bonaparte as a military dictator marked the beginning of a new era, it by no means erased the influence of the French Revolution. Indeed, as will subsequently be shown, Napoleon himself preserved quite a few of the Revolutionary achievements and posed as an embattled champion of Equality and Fraternity, if not of Liberty. But even if he had done none of these things, the heritage of the Revolution would most certainly have survived. No movement which had so thoroughly shaken the foundations of society could ever have passed into history without leaving a train of momentous results. Its influence reverberated through most of the years of the nineteenth century

"Am I Not Your Brother?" An antislavery woodcut from the revolutionary period in France.

and was felt in a score of nations of the Western world. The new passion for liberty was the activating force behind numerous insurrections and so-called revolutions which punctuated the period between 1800 and 1850. First came the uprising of the Spaniards against Joseph Bonaparte in 1808. This was followed by a veritable epidemic of revolutionary disturbances between 1820 and 1831 in such countries as Greece, Italy, Spain, France, Belgium, and Poland. Finally, the revolutionary movements of 1848 were far from unrelated to the great French upheaval of 1789, since most of them were infused with the same nationalist enthusiasm and with similar ideals of political liberty.

The French Revolution also had other results of more enduring character and of greater benefit to mankind as a whole. It dealt, first of all, a powerful blow to absolute monarchy. Thenceforth few kings dared to claim an unlimited authority. Even though a Bourbon was restored to the throne of France in 1814, he made no pretensions to a divine appointment to rule as he liked. Secondly, the French Revolution was responsible for the destruction of most of the remnants of a decadent feudalism, including serfdom and the feudal privileges of the nobles. The guilds also were abolished, never to be revived. Though a few of the elements of mercantilism still survived, its days as a recognized policy of governments were numbered. Although the separation of church and state, accomplished in 1794, was eventually nullified by Napoleon, it nevertheless furnished a precedent for an ultimate divorce of religion from politics, not only in France but in other countries as well. Among the remaining beneficial results of the Revolution may be mentioned the abolition of slavery in the French colonies, the elimination of imprisonment for debt, the overthrow of the rule of primogeniture, and a wider distribution of land through the breaking up of great estates. Finally, the groundwork of two of Napoleon's most significant achievements, his educational reforms and his codification of the laws, was actually prepared by Revolutionary leaders.

On the other hand, the fact cannot be ignored that the French Revolution bore some bitter fruit. It was largely responsible for the growth of jingoistic nationalism as a dominant ideal. Nationalism, of course, was nothing new. It can be traced almost as far back as the unfoldment of the earliest civilizations. It manifested itself in the Chosen People belief of the Hebrews and in the racial exclusiveness of the Greeks. Nevertheless, nationalism did not really become an all-pervading force until after the French Revolution. It was the pride of the French people in what they had achieved and their determination to protect those achievements that gave rise to a fanatical patriotism exemplified in the stirring battle song, the *Marseillaise*. For the first time in modern history a whole nation was girded for war. In contrast to the relatively small professional armies of former days, the National Convention in 1793 enrolled a force of

The legacy of evil results

nearly 800,000 men, while millions behind the lines devoted their energies to the task of suppressing disaffection at home. Workers, peasants, and bourgeois citizens alike rallied to the slogan of "Liberty, Equality, and Fraternity" as to a holy cause. The cosmopolitanism and pacifism of the philosophers of the Enlightenment were completely forgotten. Later this militant patriotism infected other lands, contributing the weight of its influence to notions of national superiority and to racial hatreds. Finally, the French Revolution resulted in a deplorable cheapening of human life. The butchery of thousands during the Reign of Terror, often for no crime at all but merely as a method of striking fear into the hearts of enemies of the Revolution, tended to create the impression that the life of a man was of very small worth compared to the noble aims of the faction in power. Perhaps this impression helps to explain the comparative indifference with which France accepted, a few years later, the sacrifice of hundreds of thousands of her citizens to satisfy the boundless ambitions of Napoleon.

SELECTED READINGS

· *Items so designated are available in paperbound editions.*

Aldridge, A. D., *Man of Reason: the Life of Thomas Paine*, London, 1960.
• Arendt, Hannah, *On Revolution*, New York, 1963 (Compass).
Barber, E. G., *The Bourgeoisie in Eighteenth-Century France*, Princeton, 1955.
• Brinton, C. C., *A Decade of Revolution, 1789–1799*, New York, 1934 (Torchbook). Stimulating and critical.
——, *The Jacobins: An Essay in the New History*, New York, 1930.
• Cobban, Alfred, *Aspects of the French Revolution*, New York, 1970 (Norton Library).
——, *In Search of Humility; the Role of the Enlightenment in Modern History*, London, 1960.
Cone, Carl B., *The English Jacobins*, New York, 1968.
• Ford, Franklin, *Robe and Sword: The Regrouping of the French Aristocracy after Louis XIV*, Cambridge, Mass., 1953 (Torchbook).
Gershoy, Leo, *The French Revolution, 1789–1799*, New York, 1932. A dependable summary.
•——, *From Despotism to Revolution*, New York, 1944 (Torchbook). Valuable for background of the Revolution.
• Geyl, Pieter, *Napoleon, For and Against*, New Haven, 1949 (Yale University Press).
• Gooch, G. P., *English Democratic Ideas in the Seventeenth Century*, New York, 1962 (Torchbook).
Gooch, R. K., *Parliamentary Government in France, Revolutionary Origins, 1781–1791*, Ithaca, N.Y., 1960.
Gottschalk, L. R., *The Era of the French Revolution*, New York, 1929.
——, *Jean Paul Marat; a Study in Radicalism*, New York, 1927.
Hampson, Norman, *A Social History of the French Revolution*, Toronto, 1963.
Kerr, W. B., *The Reign of Terror, 1793–94*, Toronto, 1927.
• Lefebvre, Georges, *The Coming of the French Revolution*, Princeton, 1947 (Vintage). An excellent study of the causes and early events of the Revolution.

READINGS · Martin, Kingsley, *French Liberal Thought in the Eighteenth Century*, Boston, 1929 (Torchbook).

· Mathiez, Albert, *The French Revolution*, New York, 1928 (Universal Library). A liberal interpretation.

Moore, J. M., *The Roots of French Republicanism*, New York, 1962.

O'Gorman, F., *The Whig Party and the French Revolution*, New York, 1967.

Palmer, R. R., *The Age of the Democratic Revolution: A Political History of Europe and America, 1760–1800*, Princeton, 1964.

· ———, *Twelve Who Ruled*, Princeton, 1941 (Atheneum). Excellent biographical and interpretive studies.

———, *The World of the French Revolution*, New York, 1970.

· Rudé, George, *The Crowd in History: A Study of Popular Disturbances in France and England, 1730–1848*, New York, 1964 (Wiley).

Schapiro, J. S., *Condorcet and the Rise of Liberalism in France*, New York, 1934. A splendid study of revolutionary idealism.

Sée, Henri, *Economic and Social Conditions in France during the Eighteenth Century*, New York, 1927.

Sydenham, M. J., *The Girdondins*, London, 1961. A reinterpretation of the significance of this faction.

Thompson, J. M., *Leaders of the French Revolution*, New York, 1929.

· ———, *Robespierre and the French Revolution*, New York, 1953 (Collier). An excellent short biography.

SOURCE MATERIALS

Higgins, E. L., *The French Revolution as Told by Contemporaries*, Boston, 1938.

Locke, John, *Second Treatise on Civil Government* (Everyman Library ed.), London, 1924.

· Montesquieu, Baron de, *The Spirit of Laws*, especially Books, I, II, III, XI (Hafner Library of World Classics).

Rousseau, J. J., *The Social Contract* (Everyman Library ed.), London, 1913.

Sieyès, Abbé, *What Is the Third Estate?*

Smith, Adam, *The Wealth of Nations*, Introduction and Books I, IV.

Stewart, J. H., *A Documentary Survey of the French Revolution*, New York, 1951.

· Tocqueville, Alexis de, *The Old Regime and the French Revolution*, Garden · City, L. I., 1955 (Anchor).

University of Pennsylvania Translations and Reprints, Vol. I, No. 5, Declaration of the Rights of Man and of the Citizen.

Young, Arthur, *Travels in France during the Years 1787, 1788, 1789*, New York, 1929. A contemporary account of the life of the peasants.

CHAPTER 20

Romanticism and Reaction
(1800-1830)

The principle of non-intervention is very popular in England; false in its essence, it may be maintained by an island-state. New France has not failed to appropriate this principle and to proclaim it loudly. It is brigands who object to police, and incendiaries who complain about firemen. We can never admit a claim as subversive as this is of all social order; we recognize, however, that we always have the right to answer any appeal for help addressed to us by a legitimate authority, just as we recognize that we have the right of extinguishing the fire in a neighbor's house in order to prevent its catching our own.

—Prince Metternich, 1830

The century that followed the French Revolution was a period of rapid and tremendous change. By comparison, life in preceding ages seems almost static. Never before in so short a time had there been such radical alteration of modes of living or such wholesale destruction of venerable tradition. As a result of a welter of inventions the speed of living was accelerated to a pace which would have startled Leonardo da Vinci or Sir Isaac Newton. The population of Europe increased from 180 million at the close of the French Revolution to the almost incredible total of 460 million by 1914. Never before in little more than a century had anything like such an increase occurred. As a result life for modern man took on a degree of complexity and variety hitherto unknown. New political and social ideals multiplied in bewildering confusion. The entire age was an age of flux, of conflicting tendencies and sharp disagreements over the problems of society. We must not suppose, however, that the nineteenth century was totally unrelated to preceding periods. Although Napolean declared after his *coup d'état* of 1799 that the great aims of the years of turbulence had been accomplished, such was not really the case. In the minds of a great many people

Character
of the new age

573

the objectives of the French Revolution remained as goals worth striving for. Through a period of thirty years and more the Western world was disturbed by what virtually amounted to a civil war between the defenders of those goals and those who would repudiate freedom and equality and force men back under obedience to authority. It was a condition not unlike that which followed the Russian revolution of 1917 when a conflict between Communists and their opponents fanned out into other countries and eventually took on global dimensions.

1. THE SIGNIFICANCE OF NAPOLEON

We have seen that the *coup d'état* of the eighteenth Brumaire dealt what seemed to be a final blow to the French Revolution. Therefore, the period of Napoleon's rule, from November 1799 to April 1814 and during the Hundred Days from March until June 1815, may properly be regarded as the initial stage of the nineteenth-century reaction against the liberal ideals which had made the Revolution possible. To be sure, Napoleon professed to be in sympathy with some of these ideals, but he established a form of government scarcely compatible with any of them. His real aim, so far as it concerned the work of the Revolution, was to preserve those achievements which comported with national greatness and with his own ambitions for military glory. In other words, he fostered and strengthened Revolutionary patriotism and continued those accomplishments of his predecessors which could be adapted to the purposes of concentrated government. But liberty in the sense of the inviolability of personal rights meant nothing to him; in fact, he declared that what the French people needed was not liberty but equality. Moreover, he interpreted equality as meaning little more than a fair opportunity for all regardless of birth. That is, he did not propose to restore serfdom or to give back the land to the old nobility, but neither did he plan any restrictions upon the economic activities of the rich.

Napoleon not a true son of the French Revolution

In order to understand the historical significance of Napoleon, it is necessary to know something of his personal life and of the part he played in the dramatic events preceding his rise to power. Born in 1769 in a little town in Corsica just a year after the island had been ceded to France, Napoleon was the son of a proud but impoverished family that held a title of nobility from the republic of Genoa. In 1779 he entered a school at Brienne in France and five years later was admitted to the military academy in Paris. As a student he appears to have led an unhappy existence, abstaining from all social pleasures, eating dry bread to save expenses, and growing ever more bitter against the French, whom he accused of enslaving his fellow Corsicans. He achieved no distinction in any academic subject except mathematics, but he applied himself so assiduously to

The early career of Napoleon

military science that he won a commission as a sub-lieutenant of artillery at the age of sixteen. The progress of the Revolution and the outbreak of foreign war brought rapid promotion, since many of the officers appointed under the *ancien régime* fled from the country. By 1793 he had become Colonel Bonaparte and had been entrusted with the difficult task of expelling the British from Toulon. Soon afterward he was rewarded with a promotion to brigadier-general. In 1795 he defended the National Convention against an uprising of reactionaries in Paris and was placed in command the following year of the expedition against the Austrians in Italy. His brilliant success in this campaign elevated him to the status of a national hero. His name was on everybody's lips. Politicians feared him and tumbled over one another to grant his every desire. While the comfortable classes adored him as a bulwark against radicalism, many ordinary folk were deceived by his honeyed pledges of devotion to Revolutionary doctrine. To all whose emotions had been set aflame by the new patriotism he loomed as the symbol of victory and of hope for a glorious future.

Had conditions in France been more stable than they were in 1799, it is probable that Napoleon Bonaparte would have lived out his days as no more than a talented army officer. But we have seen that conditions in this and in preceding years were exceedingly chaotic. Corruption, profiteering, and financial ruin added to the woes of a people already bowed down by the miseries of a long revolution. So profound was the mood of despair that thousands welcomed a new despotism as the only hope of relief. Besides, the government of the Directory was shot through with intrigue. One of its members, the Abbé Sieyès, was actually conspiring to overthrow it and was casting about for a popular hero to assist him. Napoleon had the advantage of being married to the mistress of one of the Directors, but his triumph was due also to certain qualities of his own personality. He was shrewd, egotistical, and unscrupulous. He had the sagacity to perceive that the people were tired of disorder and corruption, and that they longed for the return of stability. Convinced that destiny had touched his brow, he determined to let nothing stand in the way of fulfillment of his lofty ambitions. Moreover, he was endowed with an indefatigable energy. He endeared himself to his soldiers by his ability to withstand hardships and by his infinite capacity for personal attention to every detail necessary to the success of a military campaign. Lastly, Napoleon had a keen instinct for the dramatic, a gift of eloquence, and a magnetic ability to exact from his followers the highest measure of devotion. He knew how to make the most of an inspiring setting and to fill the imaginations of all around him with magnificent visions of glory and power.

The new regime set up by Napoleon after the *coup d'état* of the eighteenth Brumaire was a thinly disguised autocracy. The constitution, drafted by the conspirators themselves, bore some of the hall-

THE SIGNIFICANCE OF NAPOLEON

Napoleon. A famous unfinished painting by David.

Napoleon's triumph

575

The Empress Josephine

marks of democracy, but the whole system depended in last analysis upon the will of the executive. Yet the framers of the constitution made a pretense of deferring to popular sovereignty, since the principle of universal manhood suffrage was revived. In December 1799, the new instrument of government was submitted to a popular referendum and was approved by a stupendous majority. When the votes were finally counted, it was found (or at least it was claimed) that only 1562 out of more than 3,000,000 had been cast in the negative. However, 4,000,000 eligible voters had abstained. The constitution thus adopted went into effect on January 1, 1800; but since the Revolutionary calendar was still technically in force, it is known as the Constitution of the Year VIII.

Though Napoleon was now an absolute monarch in nearly everything but name, he still was not satisfied. In 1802 he obtained the consent of the people to extend his term of office from ten years to life. All that then remained was to make his position hereditary. In 1804 by another plebiscite he won permission to convert the government into an empire. Soon afterward, in the midst of impressive ceremonies in the Cathedral of Notre Dame, he placed a crown upon his own head and assumed the title of Napoleon I, Emperor of the French. His action in making this change was influenced partly by the growth of opposition. Several attempts had recently been made to take his life, and royalist plots were being hatched against him. Napoleon proceeded against the conspirators with characteristic ruthlessness. Scores were arrested upon mere suspicion, and some of the most prominent were singled out for execution. Having thus disposed of his chief enemies, Napoleon evidently concluded that the best way to guard against future trouble would be to establish a dynasty of his own and thereby cut the ground from under all Bourbon pretenders. Especially if he could obtain for his rule the benediction of the Church, there would be few who would dare to oppose him. For this reason, he brought Pope Pius VII all the way from Rome to officiate at his coronation, though he was careful to produce the impression that His Holiness was acting as the mere agent of God and not as an international sovereign who could create and depose the emperor.

It is unfortunately true that most of the fame of Napoleon Bonaparte rests upon his exploits as a soldier. His work as a statesman was much more important. In the latter capacity he made at least a few notable contributions to civilization. He confirmed the redistribution of land accomplished by the Revolution, thereby permitting the average peasant to remain an independent farmer. He eliminated graft and waste from the government, reformed the system of taxation, and established the Bank of France to promote a more efficient control over fiscal affairs. He drained marshes, enlarged harbors, built bridges, and constructed a network of roads and canals. Most of these achievements were completed mainly for military purposes,

Napoleon's
constructive
work as a states-
man

but partly also in order to win the support of the commercial classes. In addition, he centralized the government of France, dividing the country into uniform districts or *départements*, each under a prefect taking orders from Paris.[1] Perhaps his accomplishment of greatest significance was his completion of the educational and legal reforms begun during the Revolution. He ordered the establishment of *lycées* or high schools in every important town, and a normal school in Paris for the training of teachers. To supplement these changes, he brought the military and technical schools under control of the state and founded a national university to exercise supervision over the entire system. But he was never willing to allocate more than a small fraction of his budget for educational purposes, with the consequence that only a tiny proportion of the children of France received instruction at the expense of the state. In 1810, with the aid of a staff of jurists, he completed his famous Code Napoléon, a revision and codification of the civil and criminal laws on the basis of plans worked out by the National Convention. Despite its harsh provisions—the death penalty, for example, was retained for theft, parricides were to have their hands cut off before execution, and slavery was reestablished in the colonies—the Code Napoléon was hailed as the work of a second Justinian. With modifications it remained the law of France and Belgium for more than a century, and substantial portions of it were incorporated in the legal systems of Germany, Italy, Switzerland, Japan, and the French colony of Louisiana, where it was to persist even after the purchase of that territory by the United States.

Napoleon's work as a statesman included many other changes in the political system of France. For one thing, he restored the union between the Catholic Church and the state. In 1801 he signed a Concordat with the Pope, which provided that bishops be nominated by the First Consul and that the salaries of the clergy be paid by the government. Even if the Catholic Church did not regain the legal monopoly it had enjoyed under the *ancien régime*, since other religions were also to be tolerated, it was nevertheless placed in a position of decided advantage and was thereby able to increase its power in succeeding years. Not until 1905, when the Concordat of 1801 was finally broken, was Catholicism again reduced to equality with other faiths. Napoleon was responsible also for curtailing the liberties of his subjects almost from the moment he came into power. He abolished trial by jury in certain cases, imposed a strict censorship on the press, and suspended many journals that he suspected of being hostile toward his policies.

Although a detailed account of Napoleon's campaigns must be left to the military historian, the subject cannot be ignored. His ex-

*Other results
of Napoleon's
statecraft*

---

[1] The *départments* were originally established by the Revolutionary National Assembly, but not under a centralized arrangement. Their officers were to be elected by the people.

The Battle of Trafalgar. This engraving by Pollard after a painting by Serres depicts one of the decisive events in British history. It was in this battle that Napoleon's naval power was destroyed, along with any hope that he might have had of conquering Britain.

The beginning of Napoleon's wars: the destruction of the Second Coalition

ploits as a military commander had considerable effect in shaping the course of history. To his credit it should perhaps be said that the wars in which he engaged were not all of his own making. Upon his accession to power in 1799 he inherited from the Directory the struggle with the Second Coalition, composed of Great Britain, Austria and Russia.[2] By a series of brilliant forays he eliminated Austria and Prussia from the war and neutralized Italy and the Netherlands. Russia withdrew, while Britain bided her time.

Napoleon at the zenith of his power

By 1808 the star of Napoleon was at its zenith. He was master of nearly all of the Continent of Europe west of Russia. He had destroyed what was left of the Holy Roman Empire and had brought most of the German states outside of Austria into a Confederation of the Rhine of which he himself was Protector. He had not only extended the boundaries of France, but he had created as his personal domain a new kingdom of Italy including the Po valley and what had once been the republic of Venice. In addition, he had placed relatives and friends on several of the remaining thrones of Europe. His brother Joseph had been made king of Naples, his brother Louis king of Holland, and his brother Jerome king of Westphalia. He had selected his friend, the king of Saxony, to be the ruler of the duchy of Warsaw, a new Poland created mainly out of territories taken from Prussia. Not since the days of Charles V had so much of Europe been dominated by any one man. Yet Napoleon's position was far from secure, for he still had the "contemptible nation of shopkeepers" across the English Channel to deal with.

See color map at page 592

[2] The First Coalition was the original combination of European powers formed in opposition to the French Revolution. It was organized in 1793 and was made up of Austria, Prussia, Great Britain, Spain, Holland, and some lesser states.

Having lost to the British in the great naval battle of Trafalgar (October 1805), he determined to wear them down by the indirect method of ruining their commerce. In 1806 and the years following he established his famous Continental System, a scheme by which his various puppet states were obliged to cooperate with France in excluding British goods from the whole of Continental Europe. By depriving the English nation of its markets, Napoleon hoped that he could eventually sap its wealth to such a degree that the people would turn against their government and force it to capitulate. By the Treaty of Tilsit he even managed to bring Russia into the scheme.

The story of Napoleon's career from 1808 to 1815 is a record of the gradual decay of his fortunes. From his overthrow of the Directory in 1799 to the Peace of Tilsit in 1807 he had steadily climbed to an eminence which even an Alexander or a Caesar might well have envied. But soon after the latter event his difficulties began to multiply until finally they overwhelmed him in disaster. The explanation is to be found in several factors. First of all, with the passage of the years, he grew more egotistical, and therefore less inclined to accept advice even from his most capable subordinates. He kept nurturing the idea that he was a man of destiny until it developed into an obsession, a superstitious fatalism that destroyed the resiliency of his mind. Second, his aggressive militarism provoked an inevitable reaction among its victims. The more it became evident that Napoleon's conquests were the sordid fruits of a maniacal ambition for power, the stronger was the determination of the vanquished to regain their freedom. Peoples that had at one time mistakenly welcomed him as an apostle of Revolutionary liberty now turned against him as a hated foreign oppressor. In addition, militarism was producing its effect upon France itself. The bones of hundreds of thousands of the best young men of the nation had been strewn in the dust of battlefields all over Europe. The problem not merely of filling their places in the ranks of the army but also of maintaining the levels of

The causes of Napoleon's downfall

See color plates at page 561

agricultural and industrial production was becoming more and more serious. Finally, the Continental System proved to be a boomerang. It actually inflicted more damage upon France and her allies than it did upon England. Napoleon found it impossible to enforce the exclusion of British products from the Continent, since most of the countries he dominated were agricultural nations and insisted upon trading the things they produced for manufactured goods from England. Moreover, the British retaliated with a series of Orders in Council making all vessels trading with France or her allies subject to capture. The effect was to cut Napoleon's empire off from sources of supply in neutral countries.

The Spanish revolt

The first episode of Napoleon's downfall was the Spanish revolt which broke out in the summer of 1808. In May of that year Napoleon had tricked the Spanish king and the crown prince into resigning their claims to the throne and had promoted his brother Joseph from king of Naples to king of Spain. But scarcely had the new monarch been crowned than the people rose in revolt. Though Napoleon sent an army against them, he was never able to crush the rebellion entirely. With encouragement and assistance from the British, the Spaniards kept up a series of guerilla attacks which caused no end of expense and annoyance to the great warlord of France. Further, the courage of Spain in resisting the invader promoted a spirit of defiance elsewhere, with the result that Napoleon could no longer count upon the docility of any of his victims.

The disastrous campaign against Russia

The second stage in the downfall of the Corsican adventurer was the disruption of his alliance with Russia. As a purely agricultural country, Russia had suffered a severe economic crisis when she was no longer able, as a result of the Continental System, to exchange her surplus grain for British manufactures. The consequence was that the Tsar Alexander began to wink at trade with Britain and to ignore or evade the protests from Paris. By 1811 Napoleon decided that he could endure this flouting of the Continental System no longer. Accordingly, he collected an army of 600,000 men and set out in the spring of 1812 to punish the Tsar. The project ended in disaster. The Russians refused to make a stand, thereby leading the French farther and farther into the heart of their country. They finally permitted Napoleon to occupy their ancient capital. But on the very night of his entry, fire of suspicious origin broke out in the city. When the flames subsided, little but the blackened walls of the Kremlin remained to shelter the invading troops. Hoping that the Tsar would eventually surrender, Napoleon lingered amid the ruins for more than a month, finally deciding on October 22 to begin the homeward march. The delay was a fatal blunder. Long before he had reached the border, the terrible Russian winter was upon him. Swollen streams, mountainous drifts of snow, and bottomless mud slowed the retreat almost to a halt. To add to the miseries of bitter cold, disease, and starvation, Cossacks rode out of the blizzard to harry the exhausted troops. Each morning the miserable remnant

The Retreat from Russia. In this painting by Charlet, the horrors of the Russian winter can be seen.

that pushed on left behind circles of corpses around the campfires of the night before. On December 13 a few thousand broken, starved, and half-demented soldiers crossed the frontier into Germany—a miserable fraction of what had once been proudly styled the *Grande Armée*. The lives of nearly 300,000 men had been sacrificed in the Russian adventure.

The disastrous outcome of the Russian campaign destroyed the myth that Napoleon was invincible. Soon the Prussians and the Austrians regained their courage and, with Russian aid, joined in a War of Liberation. Napoleon hastily collected a new army and marched to suppress the revolts. He won a few modest victories in the spring and summer of 1813 but was finally cornered at Leipzig by an allied army of 500,000 men. Here on October 16–19 was fought the celebrated Battle of the Nations, in which Napoleon was decisively beaten. His grand empire now collapsed like a house of cards; his vassal states deserted him; and France itself was invaded. On March 31, 1814, the victorious allies entered Paris. Thirteen days later Napoleon signed the Treaty of Fontainebleau, renouncing all of his claims to the throne of France. In return he was granted a pension of two million francs a year and full sovereignty over the island of Elba, located in the Mediterranean Sea within sight of his native Corsica. The victors then took up with the French Senate the problem of reorganizing the government of France. It was agreed that the Bourbon line should be restored in the person of Louis XVIII, brother of the king who had been sent to the guillotine in 1793. It was carefully stipulated, however, that there was not to be a full restoration of the *ancien régime*. Louis XVIII was made to

The Battle of Leipzig

581

Napoleon's es-
cape from
Elba; the Battle
of Waterloo

understand that he must not interfere with the political and economic reforms which still survived as fruits of the Revolution. In accordance with this requirement the new sovereign issued a charter confirming the Revolutionary liberties of the citizen and providing for a limited monarchy.

But the restoration of 1814 proved to be short-lived. The exiled emperor was growing impatient with his tiny island kingdom and eagerly awaiting the first opportunity to escape. His chance came in the spring of 1815. The French people were showing signs of disgust with the prosaic rule of Louis XVIII and with the effrontery of returning nobles of the *ancien régime*. Under these circumstances Napoleon slipped away from Elba and landed on the coast of southern France on March 1. Everywhere he was received by peasants and former soldiers in a delirium of joy. Officers sent to arrest him went over to his side with whole regiments of his former comrades in arms. On March 20, after a journey of triumph across the country, Napoleon entered Paris. Louis XVIII, who had sworn that he would die in defense of his throne, was already on his way to Belgium. But Napoleon was not to enjoy his new triumph long. Almost immediately upon learning of the escape from Elba, the allies proclaimed the Corsican an outlaw, and prepared to depose him by force. On June 12, 1815, Napoleon set out from Paris with the largest army he could gather in the

The French Campaign. A painting by Meissonier hanging in the Louvre. After his escape from exile on Elba, Napoleon leads his loyal troops to Paris.

Louis XVIII Leaves the Tuileries. A painting by Gros showing Louis, surrounded by family and those loyal to him, preparing to leave Paris as Napoleon returns to power.

hope of routing the enemy forces before they could invade his country. Six days later at Waterloo in Belgium he suffered a crushing defeat at the hands of the Duke of Wellington in command of an army of British, Dutch, and Germans. With all hope lost, Napoleon returned to Paris, abdicated his throne a second time, and made plans to escape to America. Finding the coast too heavily guarded, he was compelled to take refuge on a British ship. He was subsequently exiled by the British government to the rocky South Atlantic island of St. Helena. There he died, on May 5, 1821, a lonely and embittered man.

In attempting a final estimate of the significance of Napoleon Bonaparte, we must not lose sight of the fact that his name has been richly embellished with legend. The myth-mongering of patriots and hero-worshipers has raised his reputation almost to supernatural proportions. With the single exception of Jesus of Nazareth, he is actually the most written-about figure in history. But whether he deserves so exalted a fame is at least debatable. He was by no means a universal genius with a mastery of all knowledge or a patent on wisdom. Aside from mathematics, he knew little about any of the sciences, and his grasp of economics was too feeble to save him from the colossal errors of the Continental System. Though he was undoubtedly a clever tactician, the blunders of his Russian campaign indicate that even in military affairs he was not infallible. But worse than any other of his shortcomings were his defects of character. He was unscrupulous and unprincipled. Moreover, his boundless egotism made him coldly indifferent to the shedding of blood. His real significance lies in the fact that he helped to preserve some of the major results of the French Revolution. Though he

583

might easily have done so, he refused to restore the regime of
privilege which had flourished in the days of the Bourbons. He
confirmed the abolition of serfdom and the repeal of primogeniture,
and he allowed the peasants to keep the lands they had acquired
through the breakup of the great estates. What is more, he was at
least indirectly responsible for spreading Revolutionary ideals into
other countries. For example, it was his smashing defeat of Prussia
in 1806 which finally persuaded the leading men of that nation of
the necessity of adopting the main reforms of the French Revolution as the only means by which their state could rise again to
smite the oppressor. The Prussian government in 1807–1808
abolished serfdom and threw open the various occupations and
professions to men in all ranks of society. Unfortunately these
measures were accompanied by an outburst of extreme nationalism, which found characteristic expression in the adoption of
compulsory military service, one of the tyrannical devices employed by Napoleon himself. True, he did not invent it. It had been
initiated by the Revolution before him. But he continued it, as he
did the whole Revolutionary concept of a nation in arms and of war
as a mass endeavor rather than a game of kings and generals.

2.   THE NEW EUROPE

The movement
to return to
the *status quo*

Following the overthrow of Napoleon, an overwhelming desire
for peace and order seized the minds of the conservative classes in
the victorious countries. Nearly everything that had happened since
the Corsican had come into power now came to be regarded as a
horrible nightmare. In some quarters there was a desire to return to
the *status quo* of 1789, to undo the work of the Great Revolution,
and to revive the power and the glamour of the *ancien régime*. The
government of the Papal States proceeded to abolish street lighting
in Rome as a dangerous novelty, while the Elector of Hesse restored
pigtails to the freshly-powdered heads of his faithful soldiers. The
leading statesmen realized, however, that a complete restoration of
the old order would not be possible. For example, it was perfectly
evident that the French people would not tolerate a revival of serfdom or the return of confiscated lands to the nobles and clergy.
Therefore, while the portly Louis XVIII was put back on the
throne, it was understood that he would continue to rule in conformity with the Charter of 1814. Furthermore, some of the victorious powers were not ready to give up the conquests they had
made at the expense of France. Hence it was found necessary to
modify suggestions frequently made for redrawing the map of Europe in accordance with the form it had had in the days of Louis
XVI.

Most of the work of deciding the fate of Europe at the conclusion
of the long war which had involved nearly the whole of the Western world was done at the so-called Congress of Vienna. To refer to

this body as a "Congress" is to be guilty of a misnomer, for, as a matter of fact, no plenary session of all the delegates was ever held. As in the drafting of the Versailles Treaty more than a hundred years later, the vital decisions were really made by small committees. Nevertheless, the assemblage at Vienna was staged with such pomp and splendor that even the most neglected member was made to feel that he was participating in events of epochal importance. No fewer than six monarchs attended: the Tsar of Russia, the Emperor of Austria, and the kings of Prussia, Denmark, Bavaria, and Württemberg. Great Britain was represented by Lord Castlereagh and the "Iron Duke" of Wellington. From France came the subtle intriguer Talleyrand, who had served as a bishop under Louis XVI, as foreign minister at the court of Napoleon, and who now stood ready to espouse the cause of reaction.

The dominant roles at the Congress of Vienna were played by Alexander I and Metternich. The dynamic Tsar was one of the most baffling figures in history. Reared at the voluptuous court of Catherine the Great, he imbibed the doctrines of Rousseau from a French Jacobin tutor. In 1801 he succeeded his murdered father as Tsar and for the next two decades disturbed the dreams of his fellow sovereigns by becoming the most liberal monarch in Europe. After the defeat of Napoleon in the Russian campaign, his mind turned more and more into mystical channels. He conceived of a mission to convert the rulers of all countries to the Christian ideals of justice and peace. But the chief effect of his voluble expressions of devotion to "liberty" and "enlightenment" was to frighten conservatives into suspecting a plot to extend his power over all of Europe. He was accused of intriguing with Jacobins everywhere to substitute an all-powerful Russia for an all-powerful France.

The most commanding figure at the Congress was Klemens von Metternich, born in 1773 at Coblenz in the Rhine valley, where his father was Austrian ambassador at the courts of three small German

The Congress of Vienna. The figure to the left of center is Metternich. Seated at the right with his arm on the table is Talleyrand.

states. As a student at the University of Strassburg the young Metternich witnessed some excesses of mob violence connected with the outbreak of the French Revolution, and to these he attributed his life-long hatred of political innovation. After completing his education he entered the field of diplomacy and served for nearly forty years as Minister of Foreign Affairs. He was active in fomenting discord between Napoleon and the Tsar Alexander, after the two became allies in 1807, and he played some part in arranging the marriage of Napoleon to the Austrian archduchess, Marie Louise. In 1813 he was made a hereditary prince of the Austrian Empire. At the Congress of Vienna Metternich distinguished himself for charm of manner and skillful intrigue. His two great obsessions were hatred of political and social change and fear of Russia. Actually the two were related. It was not simply that he feared revolutions as such; he feared even more revolutions inspired by the "Jacobin" Tsar for the sake of establishing Russian supremacy in Europe. For this reason he favored moderate terms for France in her hour of defeat, and was ready at one time to sponsor the restoration of Napoleon as Emperor of the French under the protection and overlordship of the Hapsburg monarchy.

Legitimacy

The basic idea that guided the work of the Congress of Vienna was the principle of *legitimacy*. This principle was invented by Talleyrand as a device for protecting France against drastic punishment by her conquerors, but it was ultimately adopted by Metternich as a convenient expression of the general policy of reaction. Legitimacy meant that the dynasties of Europe that had reigned in pre-Revolutionary days should be restored to their thrones, and that each country should regain essentially the same territories it had held in 1789. In accordance with this principle Louis XVIII was recognized as the "legitimate" sovereign of France, and the restoration of Bourbon rulers in Spain and the Two Sicilies was also confirmed. France was compelled to pay an indemnity of 700,000,000 francs, but her boundaries were to remain essentially the same as in 1789. Other territorial arrangements likewise adhered to the idea of a return to the *status quo*. The Pope was allowed to recover his temporal possessions in Italy; Switzerland was restored as an independent confederation under guaranties of neutrality by the principal powers; while the Polish kingdom set up by Napoleon was abolished and the country again divided among Russia, Austria, and Prussia.

Violations of
legitimacy

But the Congress of Vienna was a bit cynical in applying the principle of legitimacy. Before the lace-cuffed princes had gone very far in restoring the old map of Europe, they diluted the principle of legitimacy with their curious system of compensations. The real purpose of this system was to enable certain of the major powers to gratify their hunger for spoils. For example, Great Britain was permitted to keep the valuable territories she had taken from the Dutch, who had fought for a time on the side of France. Among these rich prizes were South Africa, a portion of Guiana in South America, and the island of Ceylon. Then to compensate the Dutch for the loss of so large a part of their empire, provision was made for transferring the Austrian Netherlands, or Belgium, to Holland. Since this involved a sacrifice on the part of Austria, the Hapsburgs were rewarded with an extensive foothold in Italy. They received the republic of Venice and the duchy of Milan, and members of the family were placed on the thrones of Tuscany, Parma, and Modena. Thus Austria profited by gaining a compact empire occupying a commanding position in central Europe. A similar series of compensations was provided to reward Russia for her part in conquering Napoleon. The Tsar was allowed to retain Finland, which he had seized from Sweden in 1809. Sweden, in turn, was compensated by the acquisition of Norway from Denmark. All of these arrangements were put through with a total disregard for the interests of the peoples concerned.

One of the cardinal purposes of Metternich and his conservative colleagues was to erect the Vienna settlement into a permanent bulwark of the *status quo*. With this end in view they established the Quadruple Alliance of Great Britain, Austria, Prussia, and Russia as an instrument for maintaining the settlement intact. In 1818 France was admitted to the combination, thereby making it a Quintuple Alliance. For some years this aggregate of powers functioned as a kind of League of Nations to enforce the system of Metternich. It is also frequently referred to as the Concert of Europe, for its members were pledged to cooperate in suppressing any disturbances which might arise from the attempts of peoples to throw off their "legitimate" rulers or to change international boundaries. In the minds of liberals and nationalists of this period the Quintuple Alliance was often confused with another combination that also grew out of the settlement at Vienna. This was the so-called Holy Alliance, a product of the sentimental idealism of the Tsar Alexander I. In September 1815, Alexander proposed that the monarchs of Europe should "take as their sole guide . . . the precepts of Justice, Christian Charity, and Peace," and that they should base international relations as well as the treatment of their subjects "upon the sublime truths which the Holy Religion of our Savior teaches. . . ." But none of the Tsar's fellow sovereigns took him seriously. Though most of them signed the agreement he proposed, they were inclined to regard it as so much mystical verbiage. As a matter of fact, the Holy Alliance was never anything more than a series of pious pledges. The real weapon for preserving the triumph of reaction was not the Holy Alliance but the Quintuple Alliance.

The purposes of the Quintuple Alliance were achieved primarily through a series of international congresses which met between 1818 and 1822. It was at the second of these conferences, the Congress of Troppau, that the true character of the Alliance was most clearly revealed. Here the assembled delegates drew up an agreemnt avow-

The system of alliances

EUROPE AFTER THE CONGRESS OF VIENNA · 1815

Legend:
- Boundary of the Germanic Confederation
- Austrian Empire
- France
- Prussia

The activities of the Quintuple Alliance

ing the intention of the great powers to intervene by force of arms
to suppress any revolution that might threaten the stability of Europe. In two different instances the policy of intervention was actually carried out. After an uprising in the Kingdom of the Two
Sicilies, in which the Bourbon monarch, Ferdinand I, was compelled
to swear allegiance to a liberal constitution, Metternich convoked
the Congress of Laibach in 1821. King Ferdinand was summoned
before it, commanded to disavow his oath, and persuaded to invite
an Austrian army to march into Naples. As a result, the constitution
was revoked, and Ferdinand was restored to his position as an
autocratic sovereign. In 1822 the Congress of Verona was summoned to deal with an insurrection in Spain, which also had had the
effect of forcing the king to subscribe to a liberal constitution.

588

After considerable wrangling among the powers as to the measures which should be taken to crush the revolt, it was finally decided that the king of France should send an army into Spain to support his Bourbon kinsman. Not only was the revolt speedily crushed, but intervention was followed by the blackest reaction Europe had yet seen. Hundreds of devoted liberals were put to death; even greater numbers were chained in prison. And it is not without interest that some of the ruthless measures of the Spanish king were the result of direct encouragement from the leaders of the Quintuple Alliance.

Although foreign intervention was confined to Spain and the Kingdom of the Two Sicilies, these were by no means the only countries where violent conflicts occurred between liberals and conservatives. The system of Metternich involved a regime of stern repression in domestic affairs by the governments of the great powers as well as the suppression of revolutions in the lesser states. But the more blind and bitter the policy of repression, the greater was the number of uprisings against it. In Great Britain the rule of the Tories for the benefit of the landed aristocracy evoked powerful opposition from intellectual radicals like William Godwin, from the poets Shelley and Byron, and from the new industrial classes. When the protests of these groups were silenced by laws prohibiting public meetings and muzzling the press, some of the more desperate leaders organized the Cato Street Conspiracy in 1820 to murder the whole Tory Cabinet. Discovery of the plot was a foregone conclusion, and five of the conspirators were hanged. In France the modest compromise with progressive ideas which Louis XVIII incorporated in his Charter of 1814 proved to be more than his die-hard followers were willing to stand. As a result, the years between 1815 and 1820 were fraught with savage and sometimes bloody strife between Ultra-Royalists and their liberal and moderate opponents. In 1824 the victory of the forces of reaction was strengthened further when Louis XVIII died and was succeeded by his brother, Charles X, the leader of the Ultra-Royalists.

Similar struggles occurred in central and eastern Europe with almost identical results. In Germany students in the universities organized secret societies and participated in stormy agitation against conservative regimes. These activities convinced Metternich, who dominated the Germanic Confederation, that all of central Europe was about to be engulfed by a radical revolution. Accordingly, he forced through the federal Diet a program of repressive measures known as the Carlsbad Decrees (1819). By the terms of these it was provided that every university should have a government supervisor; rebellious professors were to be removed from their positions; student societies were ordered to be dissolved; and the press was to be subject to a strict censorship. Vigorous enforcement of the Carlsbad Decrees put the liberal movement in Germany under a cloud, from which it did not emerge until 1848.

The clash of liberals and conservatives: (1) in Great Britain and France

(2) in Germany

589

Meanwhile, the change in the attitude of Tsar Alexander I had produced some rumblings of discontent in Russia. Time was when Alexander had been one of the most enlightened monarchs of Europe. He had founded schools and universities. He had emancipated a few of the serfs and had considered plans for freeing the remainder. He had even toyed with the idea of granting a written constitution. But after 1818 he turned reactionary. This change of heart of the Tsar was the signal for the growth of an opposition movement among officers of the army and the intellectual classes. When Alexander died in 1825, the leaders of this movement determined to prevent the reaction from going any farther. They organized the Dekabrist revolt (from the Russian word for December) to compel the accession to the throne of the liberal Grand Duke Constantine in place of his hard-shell brother, Nicholas. Unfortunately Constantine would have nothing to do with the rebellion, and Nicholas speedily crushed it. The ensuing reign was one of the worst in Russian history. Not only did Nicholas abolish freedom of the press, but he established a system of secret police and converted the nation into a huge military camp where every move of the citizen could be watched and controlled by the government.

In spite of what semed to be enduring victories for the cause of reaction, by 1830 the system of Metternich had begun to break down. The initial step in the process was the withdrawal of Great Britain from the Quintuple Alliance. As early as 1822 the British refused to participate in Metternich's scheme for suppression of the revolution in Spain. Soon afterward they flatly repudiated the entire policy of intervention in the internal affairs of foreign states. It was not that the British of this time were more liberal than their allies on the Continent; it was rather that the Industrial Revolution was forcing Britain to seek new markets for the things she produced. Therefore she was strongly opposed to a foreign policy that would antagonize other nations and cut off her channels of trade. She had developed a lucrative commerce with the states of Central and South America, which had lately thrown off their allegiance to Spain, and she was fearful that the system of Metternich might be used to force these former colonies back under Spanish rule.

About the same time that Great Britain was weakening her ties with the Concert of Europe, Russia began to develop ambitions which also threatened the supremacy of Metternich's system. For some years the Russians had been greedily awaiting the breakup of the Ottoman Empire in the hope that that would pave the way for an easy expansion into the Balkans. The Russian opportunity came after 1821 when the Greeks launched a rebellion against Turkish rule. Since the Tsar, Alexander I, was still bound by loyalty to the doctrine of legitimacy, nothing was done until after his death in 1825. His successor, Nicholas I, entertained no such scruples. Especially when he observed in England and France expressions of the profoundest sympathy for the Greeks in their heroic struggle against an infidel oppressor, he determined to go to their rescue. Accordingly, in 1828, he declared war against Turkey. In a little more than a year a Russian army fought its way almost to the gates of the Turkish capital and forced the Sultan to sign the Treaty of Adrianople. By the terms of this treaty Turkey was compelled to acknowledge the independence of Greece, to grant autonomy to Serbia, and to permit the establishment of a Russian Protectorate over the provinces which later became the kingdom of Rumania. In thus contributing to the dismemberment of the empire of a "legitimate" ruler, Russia, with considerable encouragement from England and France, dealt a powerful blow to the system of political stagnation which Metternich was striving to maintain. For all practical purposes the empire of the Tsars had ceased to be a member of the Quintuple Alliance.

The system of Metternich was weakened still further by the series of revolutions that broke out in western Europe in 1830. The first in the series was the July Revolution in France, which resulted in the overthrow of Charles X, the last of the regular line of Bourbon kings. As was indicated previously, Charles X, who had suc-

(3) the July Revolution in France

The July Revolution of 1830. Charles X was overthrown in favor of Louis Philippe, upon whom hopes of popular sovereignty were based.

ceeded Louis XVIII in 1824, was the perfect embodiment of the spirit of reaction. His stubborn and vindictive attitude inspired relentless hatred, especially among the ranks of the bourgeoisie, who resented his reduction of the interest on government bonds and his attempt to disfranchise three-fourths of the voters. As evidence accumulated that the king was determined to rule in complete defiance of Parliament, barricades were thrown up in the streets. After futile efforts to quell the insurrection with a remnant of loyal troops, Charles abdicated his throne and fled to England. The leaders of the bourgeoisie then chose as his successor Louis Philippe, a member of the Orleanist branch of the Bourbon family and a former Jacobin who had taken an active part in the revolution of 1789. The new government was proclaimed to be a constitutional monarchy founded upon the principle of popular sovereignty; and the white flag of the Bourbons was replaced by the tricolor originally invented by the apostles of Liberty, Equality, and Fraternity.

(4) the revolt
of the Belgians

Soon after the July Revolution in France a revolt broke out in the Belgian Netherlands. It will be recalled that in the Vienna settlement of 1815 the Belgian or Austrian Netherlands had been subjected to the rule of Holland in defiance of the obvious differences of language, nationality, and religion between the Belgians and the Dutch. An additional basis of friction was the divergent economic interests of the two peoples. Whereas the Dutch were engaged primarily in commerce and agriculture, the occupations of the Belgians were largely industrial. These differences, combined with the stupid tyrannies of the Dutch king, incited the Belgians in the fall of 1830 to strike a blow for independence. The revolt was regarded with favor by the new government in France and also by the British, who hoped that it might benefit their trade. Consequently, the following year, an international agreement was signed in London that recognized the independence of Belgium as a constitutional monarchy. The Dutch had no alternative but to acquiesce in an accomplished fact. In 1839 the independence and neutrality of Belgium were guaranteed by all the great powers.

The unsuccessful
revolt of the Poles

The revolutionary movement of 1830 spread into a number of other countries, but the results were not so successful. The major one of serious dimensions was the insurrection of the Poles in 1831, a desperate attempt of that harassed people to regain independence from Russia. Had the Poles been as fortunate as the Belgians in obtaining aid from foreign nations, they might have won. But the British and the French were now too busy with affairs in western Europe and gave nothing more than verbal support. As a consequence, the Tsar Nicholas I was able to crush the revolt with murderous severity. Hundreds of the rebellious leaders were shot or exiled to the dreary wastes of Siberia, and Poland was governed henceforth as a conquered province.

THE EMPIRE OF NAPOLEON
AT ITS GREATEST EXTENT · 1812

French territory

French dependencies

Allied with Napoleon

Independent states

× Battle sites

Moscow

Borodino

NAPOLEON, 1812

RUSSIA

BLACK SEA

OTTOMAN EMPIRE

AEGEAN SEA

Warsaw

DUCHY OF WARSAW

AUSTRIAN EMPIRE

Tilsit

Friedland

PRUSSIA

BALTIC SEA

SWEDEN

NORWAY

Berlin

Elbe R.

Austerlitz ×

Vienna

ILLYRIAN PROVINCES

ADRIATIC SEA

KINGDOM OF NAPLES

KDM. OF SICILY

Copenhagen

DENMARK

Leipzig

CONFEDERATION OF THE RHINE

Ulm

KINGDOM OF ITALY

Po R.

PAPAL STATES

Rome

Naples

MEDITERRANEAN SEA

HOLLAND

Amsterdam

Rhine R.

HELVETIC REPUBLIC

CORSICA

KDM. OF SARDINIA

NORTH SEA

Waterloo ×

Brussels

★ Paris

FRENCH EMPIRE

Marseille

IRELAND

ENGLAND

London

English Channel

Bordeaux

ATLANTIC OCEAN

Madrid

SPAIN

KDM. OF PORTUGAL

Lisbon

500 miles

Execution of the Rioters, Francisco Goya (1746–1828). Unlike most artists of his time, Goya dealt unflinchingly with suffering, violence, fear, and death. Depicted here is the execution of Spanish rebels by Napoleon's soldiers in 1808. This harshness caused the rebellion to spread over the whole peninsula. (Prado)

The Raft of the Medusa, Théodore Géricault. Agony and suffering is vividly portrayed in Géricault's realistic figures. (Louvre)

Rue Transnonain. Drawn by Honoré Daumier in 1834. A typically powerful statement on a series of insurrections.

3.   EFFORTS TO RESTORE THE STATUS QUO

Just as there was a struggle in the years from 1800 to 1830 between liberals and conservatives in the political sphere, so there was a similar clash in the realm of ideas. And the outcome of this second struggle was not so far different from that of the first. In general, throughout the period, the doctrines of intellectual conservatives enjoyed supremacy. Order was exalted above liberty. The interests of groups, of society, and especially of the state were given pre-eminence over those of the individual. An emphasis upon faith, authority, and tradition superseded the eighteenth-century belief in the primacy of reason and science. A group of French philosophers under the leadership of Joseph de Maistre (1754–1821) sought to inaugurate a Catholic revival in which mystical piety, supernaturalism, and the belief in an infallible Church would serve as the lamps to guide men's feet from the pitfalls of anarchy. Maistre acclaimed obedience as the first political virtue and regarded the executioner as the bulwark of social order.

For this ascendancy of conservative patterns of thought various factors were responsible. Probably the major factor, in the beginning at least, was the strong revulsion of feeling which had set in against the horrors of the French Revolution. All who had been frightened by the violence of that movement were inclined to blame it on the rationalism, materialism, and individualism of the age of the Enlightenment. Hence they were disposed to swing to the opposite extreme of glorifying faith, authority, and tradition. Such in particular was the attitude expressed by Edmund Burke (1729–1797), the renowned British orator and Whig statesman of the late eighteenth century. Although he did not live to see the end of the French Revolution, Burke denounced that movement with all the

The ascendancy of the conservative attitude

Revulsion at excesses of French Revolution; Edmund Burke

593

fiery eloquence he could command. To him the Revolution was an attempt to repudiate the accumulated wisdom of the ages. This world, he averred, cannot be made over in a single night. No one generation has the right to set itself up as the judge of society's future needs. The institutions and traditions which have come down to us from the past have an enduring value. To lay violent hands upon them is to threaten the vital elements of civilization itself.

The body of thought that stands as the most perfect expression of the age of reaction was the German philosophy of Romantic Idealism. This philosophy derives its name from the fact that it was a combination of the romanticist theory of truth with the idealist conception of the universe. The Romantic Idealists deviated sharply from the individualism and humanism of eighteenth-century philosophy. They regarded the individual as totally devoid of significance except insofar as he was a member of some social group. Therefore, they argued, the welfare of the group must come first, and that of the individual will automatically follow. Society and the state are social organisms, products of a *natural* evolution, and not the artificial creations of man himself for his own convenience. No such thing as a state of nature ever existed, nor was political society founded by a social compact. Consequently the individual cannot claim any inviolable sphere of rights beyond the jurisdiction of organized society. His duty is rather to submerge his own interests in those of the group and thereby gain the true liberty which consists in obedience to law and in respect for accumulated tradition.

The philosopher who provided the original inspiration for Romantic Idealism was a methodical little German who lived most of his life in the eighteenth century. His name was Immanuel Kant, and he was born in Königsberg in 1724; there he died in 1804 without once having left his native city, except for a brief period of tutoring in a neighboring village. Devoting most of his life to teaching, he matured his philosophic ideas very slowly. Not until he was fifty-seven years old did he finish his first great work, the *Critique of Pure Reason*. As a philosopher, Kant owed considerable to the great minds of the Enlightenment. They contributed particularly to his political ideas. Unlike most of his followers, he believed in the natural rights of man and even defended the separation of powers as a necessary protection for the liberty of the citizen. But in the field of general philosophy Kant departed widely from the rationalism of the eighteenth century. He divided the entire universe into two worlds: one, the realm of physical nature, or the world of *phenomena;* and the other, the realm of ultimate reality, or the world of *noumena.* The methods of knowing applicable to these realms are entirely different. Sense perception and reason can give us knowledge only of the realm of *phenomena,* of the world of physical things. But in the higher realm of the spiritual, which is the world of ultimate reality, such methods have no value. Since all ordinary knowledge rests in final analysis upon sense perception, we cannot prove by reason or science that God exists, that the human will is free, or that the soul is immortal. Nevertheless, we are justified in assuming that these things are true. In the realm of *noumena*, faith, intuition, and deep conviction are just as valid instruments of knowledge as logic and science in the realm of *phenomena*.

Undoubtedly the most influential philosopher of the Romantic Idealist movement was Georg Wilhelm Hegel (1770–1831). Professor of philosophy for a considerable period at the University of Berlin, Hegel won a great number of adherents, and through them exerted a potent force in shaping intellectual currents for many years. The central doctrine of Hegel's philosophy is the idea of purposive evolution. He regarded the universe as in a condition of flux, with everything tending to pass over into its opposite. In particular, each institution or social or political organism grows to maturity, fulfills its mission, and then gives way to something different. But the old itself is never entirely destroyed; the clash of opposites results eventually in a fusion, in the creation of a new organism made up of elements taken from the two opposites themselves. Then the process is repeated over and over again with each new stage representing an improvement over that which has gone before. But Hegel's conception of evolution was not mechanistic. He believed the whole process to be guided by the universal reason or God. Evolution, he maintained, is the unfoldment of God in history. Further, he argued that the war of opposites would ultimately lead to a beneficent goal. This goal he described as the perfect state, in which the interests of every citizen would be perfectly blended with the interests of society. Actually, Hegel worshiped the state in a much more

Hegel

Hegel Lecturing to His Students at the University of Berlin

The influence
of Romantic
Idealism

Utilitarianism,
founded by
Jeremy Ben-
tham

ecstatic fashion than did any of the other Romantic Idealists. He held that true liberty consists in subjection to political society, and that the individual has no rights which the state is bound to respect, for without the state the individual would be nothing but an animal. "The State is the Divine Idea as it exists on earth." [3]

Romantic Idealism cast its influence in many directions. In one or another of its forms it was adopted as the principal gospel of nearly all in the conservative camp. Churchmen who had been disturbed by the attacks of deists and skeptics were delighted to find a philosophy that recognized the merits of faith and exalted the world of spirit. People with a stake in the maintenance of order rejoiced in the new worship of tradition and authority and in the implied condemnation of revolution. Especially pleasing to the ruling class were the political teachings of Hegel, who enjoyed such prestige at the Prussian court that his enemies called him "the official philosopher." The doctrines of Hegel and Fichte strengthened the rising tide of nationalism and ultimately contributed their quota to the devastating flood of fascism.[4] But Romantic Idealism also bore certain other fruits not exactly to the liking of its principal exponents. One of their younger contemporaries, Arthur Schopenhauer (1788–1860), developed the notion of a universal force, directing all growth and movement, into a philosophy of stark pessimism. He taught that this force is *will*—a blind, unconscious craving of individuals and species to survive. Since the will to live is present in all animate forms, and since it leads the strong to devour the weak, this world is the worst of all possible worlds. Selfishness, pain, and misery are inseparable from life, and therefore the only road to happiness for man consists in as complete a denial of life as possible after the manner of an Oriental ascetic. Still another of the strange offshoots of Romantic Idealism was the philosophy of history of Karl Marx. For his celebrated doctrine of dialectical materialism, Marx was heavily indebted to Hegel. Both believed in a progressive evolution through a clash of opposing systems, resulting finally in a perfect society. But whereas Hegel assumed that the ultimate goal would be a perfect state, Marx argued that it would be communism. It was the proud boast of the great socialist leader that he turned Hegel right side up.

Romantic Idealism was most popular in Germany. In other countries, especially in England and France, where the influence of the Enlightenment had taken deeper root, philosophy was generally more liberal in tone. The leading system of thought in England in the early nineteenth century was Utilitarianism, founded by Jeremy Bentham (1748–1832). Despite a frail and nervous physique, Bentham displayed prodigious intellectual talent throughout the greater part of his long life. He began the study of Latin when he

[3] Hegel, *Philosophy of History* (J. Sibree, trans.), p. 87.
[4] Hegelian ideas influenced the growth of fascism not only in Germany but also in Italy. See H. W. Schneider, *Making the Fascist State*, pp. 20–24.

was only three years old and was graduated from Oxford at the age of fifteen. When he was nearly seventy he was still propounding schemes for prison reform and for cutting canals across the Isthmus of Panama and the Isthmus of Suez. His chief philosophical work, the *Principles of Morals and Legislation*, was published in 1789. Bentham's Utilitarianism derives its name from his cardinal teaching that the supreme test to which every belief and institution should be made to conform is the test of utility or usefulness. This test he defined as contributing to the greatest happiness of the greatest number. Any doctrine or practice which fails to meet this requirement should be rejected forthwith, regardless of how much hoary tradition may stand behind it. Despite its social connotations, Bentham's ideal was the acme of individualism. Not only did he maintain that the interest of the community is simply the sum of the interests of the several members who compose it, but he was quite frank in admitting that the motives of individuals are purely selfish. The mainspring of human action is the desire to secure pleasure and to avoid pain. Therefore society should leave to each of its members complete freedom to follow his own enlightened self-interest. Since every individual knows better than anyone else what constitutes his own good, the welfare of society can best be promoted by allowing to each of its members the maximum liberty of action. Bentham was firmly convinced that granting this concession would not mean a reversion to the ways of the jungle. He insisted that every man would be obliged to respect his neighbor's rights through fear of retaliation; that men would obey the laws for the simple reason that the "probable mischiefs of obedience are less than the probable mischiefs of disobedience." [5]

Bentham's most faithful disciple was James Mill (1773–1836), but the greatest of all the Utilitarian philosophers was James Mill's oldest son, John Stuart Mill (1806–1873). Educated exclusively by his father, John Stuart Mill surpassed even Bentham as an intellectual prodigy. He learned the Greek alphabet at the age of three, and by the time he was eight had read all of Herodotus and a considerable portion of Plato in the original. When scarcely thirteen he had completed a rigorous course of training in history, Scholastic logic, and Aristotelian philosophy. His greatest works are his *Logic*, his *Principles of Political Economy*, his essay *On Liberty*, and his *Representative Government*. As a philosopher, John Stuart Mill summed up nearly all of the major tendencies in English thought initiated by Locke, Hume, and Bentham. He was a skeptic in regard to final truth and a champion of the liberal and practical point of view. But he was also an original and independent thinker and made a number of distinct contributions of his own. He founded a new system of logic, based upon experience as the origi-

John Stuart Mill

[5] W. A. Dunning, *History of Political Theories*, III, 216.

nal ground of all knowledge. All of the so-called self-evident truths, even the axioms of mathematics, he argued, are simply inferences derived from the observed facts that nature is uniform and that every effect has a cause. Knowledge comes neither from inborn ideas nor from mystic intuition. Though Mill agreed with the general purport of Bentham's teachings, he rejected the doctrine that the pursuit of pleasure and the avoidance of pain are the sole determinants of human conduct (the "pig philosophy," as Thomas Carlyle once called it). According to Mill the conduct of individuals is often influenced by mere habit and by the desire for unity with their fellow beings. Further, he maintained that pleasures themselves differ in quality, arguing that it is better to be "Socrates dissatisfied than a fool satisfied." In his later years Mill also modified much of Bentham's individualism. While repudiating socialism on the ground that it would involve the destruction of personal liberty, he nevertheless advocated a considerable degree of intervention by the state for the benefit of its less fortunate members. He looked forward to a time "when society will no longer be divided into the idle and the industrious; when the rule that they who do not work shall not eat, will be applied not to paupers only, but impartially to all. . . ." [6]

Positivism

The nearest approach to a liberal and practical philosophy on the Continent of Europe was the Positivism of Auguste Comte (1798–1857). Positivism takes its name from Comte's doctrine that the only knowledge of any value is *positive* knowledge, or knowledge which comes from the sciences. Comte's philosophy may therefore be placed, along with Utilitarianism, in the classification of *empirical* philosophies, which includes those deriving all truth from experience or from observation of the physical world. Comte rejected metaphysics as utterly futile; no man can discover the hidden essences of things—why events happen as they do, or what is the ultimate meaning and goal of existence. All we really know is how things happen, the laws which control their occurrence, and the relations existing between them. If there was any one purpose preeminent over others in Comte's philosophy, it was to devise means for improving relations among men. He did not agree with Bentham that the actions of individuals are motivated exclusively by self-interest. He avowed, on the contrary, that men are influenced by nobler impulses of *altruism*, or feelings for others, as well as by instincts of selfishness. The great object of all social teaching should be to promote the supremacy of altruism (a word invented by Comte) over egoism. Believing that this purpose could be achieved only through an appeal to the emotions of love and self-sacrifice, Comte developed what he called the Religion of Humanity, which was supposed to bring men together in a common devotion to justice, charity, and benevolence. Although this religion included no

[6] J. S. Mill, *Autobiography* (Uniform Library ed.), p. 231.

belief in the supernatural, it was provided with an extensive ritual and even with a Trinity and a priesthood. Ridiculed by its critics as "Catholicism minus Christianity," it nevertheless represented an attempt to build a system of belief dedicated to the aim of social progress.

4· ROMANTICISM IN LITERATURE AND THE ARTS

In the chapter on the Intellectual Revolution it was observed that toward the end of the eighteenth century a romantic revolt set in against the dominant classical tendencies in literature. The essence of romanticism was the glorification of the instincts and emotions as opposed to a worship of the intellect. Included in it also were such elements as a deep veneration for nature, a contempt for formalism, a sentimental love for humble folk, and often a flaming zeal to remake the world. Among the leaders of the new movement in its infancy were Rousseau, Thomas Gray, Oliver Goldsmith, Robert Burns, and Friedrich Schiller. Romanticism flourished after the beginning of the nineteenth century, attaining the zenith of its growth about 1830. No longer was it confined to literature; it was a vital force in painting and to a considerable extent also in music. Though it still had to compete in some fields with classicism, especially in France during the era of Napoleon, it was by far the most vigorous literary and artistic influence in the first three decades of the nineteenth century. Its kinship with the revolt of youth in our own time is fairly obvious.

The nature of the romantic revolt

Romanticism in literature had its deepest and longest roots in England. Its two great prophets at the beginning of the nineteenth century were the poets William Wordsworth (1770–1850) and Samuel Taylor Coleridge (1772–1834). Wordsworth is noted for his mystical adoration of nature, not alone in its surface beauties but especially as the embodiment of a universal spirit which unites all living things in a kinship of divinity. He believed that a sensuous worship of nature would bring man to a deeper awareness of the nobility of life, that it would enable him to hear "the still sad music of humanity" and thereby increase his love and compassion for his fellow creatures. The special gift of Coleridge was an ability to make the weird and fantastic credible. Though he sometimes wandered into the dense jungles of metaphysics, he succeeded in the magic stanzas of *The Ancient Mariner* in producing some of the most colorful imaginative writing in the English language. This work reveals his unusual power of combining tender, almost womanly sentiment with witching descriptions of strange, supernatural terrors, of phantoms and specters that rise out of the murky depths of the emotions to torment man with a sense of his helplessness.

Romanticism in English literature: Wordsworth and Coleridge

Perhaps the most typical of the English romantic poets were John Keats (1795–1821), Percy Bysshe Shelley (1792–1822), and

Lord Byron

George Gordon, Lord Byron (1788–1824). Keats differed from most of his contemporaries in identifying beauty with intellectual passion in somewhat the same way as the Greeks identified the beautiful with the good. The substance of his creed is expressed in the well-known lines from the *Ode on a Grecian Urn:* "Beauty is truth, truth beauty,—that is all ye know on earth, and all ye need to know." His conception was one of ideal beauty, which endures independently of the fading of the flower or the passing of the loveliness of youth. The other two short-lived poets of the English romantic circle were much more interested in political and social questions. In spite of their upper-class origins, both were rebels against stubborn conservatism and employed their talents in passionate appeals for justice and freedom. Shelley was expelled from Oxford on a charge of atheism and then for some years was a disciple of William Godwin, the philosophical anarchist. Though he eventually modified some of his youthful radicalism and allowed his thoughts to wander more and more into vaporous abstractions, he never relinquished his hatred of injustice or his hopes for a golden dawn of happiness and freedom. Lord Byron, who inherited the title of baron at the age of ten, was even more than Shelley a poet of stormy defiance, of romantic daring, and of sardonic laughter at the hypocrisy and arrogance of the human race. Not only in the qualities of his proud personality, but also in the scandals which enveloped his career and in the directness and audacity of his poetic style he typified for the age the spirit of romantic man. His death while aiding the Greeks in their war for independence was a fitting climax to his brief, adventurous life.

Except for the dramas of Schiller and Goethe, discussed in a preceding chapter,[7] romantic literature in Continental countries is scarcely to be compared with that in England. The only other important writer in Germany was Heinrich Heine (1797–1856), born of orthodox Jewish parents but later a convert to Christianity for the sake of expediency. Like Shelley and Byron, Heine was an individualist and a relentless critic of conservatism. He devoted nearly the whole of his active life to what he loved to call "humanity's war of liberation." But he was not merely a witty satirist and pungent critic of smugness and reaction. In his *Book of Songs* he displayed lyric gifts of tenderness and melancholy and a haunting charm of melody which few other poets of his day could surpass. He has been aptly called "a nightingale nesting in the wig of a Voltaire."

Romanticism in France as in England wavered between a mystic irrationalism, on the one hand, and a gallant defense of individual liberty and social reform on the other. The chief exponent of the irrational tendency was François de Chateaubriand (1768–1848). Chateaubriand found in the mysteries of Christianity and in the

[7] See p. 521.

"holy innocence" of simple folk the sublimest beauty in the universe. He was the prophet of a Catholic revival designed to guide men back to an age of faith and thus save them from the perils of reason. The libertarian and individualist aspect of French romanticism was best exemplified by the work of George Sand (1804–1876) and Victor Hugo (1802–1885). The former, whose real name was Aurore Dupin, wrote novels of country life with an idyllic charm that has endeared them to countless readers. She was one of the first to make peasants and humble laborers the heroes of fiction. Later she became a zealous advocate of republicanism and of the rights of women to a love untrammeled by marital convention. A novelist of much wider influence was Victor Hugo, who for many years was the living voice of French romanticism. Intensely interested in public affairs, he was an eloquent champion of political freedom and of justice for those who were caught in the web of fate. His best-known work is *Les Miserables*, an epic of the redemption of a soul purified by heroism and suffering and a powerful indictment of social cruelty.

In attempting to judge the importance of literary romanticism as a factor of social and intellectual progress, we should note, first of all, its grave limitations. The disdain for reason and scientific analysis by even the most liberal of the romanticists was certainly a handicap to any permanent solution of humanity's problems. Excesses of sentimentality are not easily controlled. To allow free reign to the emotions in one direction is to run the risk of an impairment of judgment in others. Thus we find Victor Hugo hurling bitter invectives against Napoleon III, whom he called "Napoleon the Little," but singing paeans of praise to Napoleon I. It was perhaps for this reason also that the liberalism of so many of the romanticists eventually gave way to nationalism, as in the case of Schiller, or even to hopeless reaction, as in the case of Wordsworth. Yet, notwithstanding these weaknesses, literary romanticism accomplished no small amount of good in combating repression in many of its forms and in proclaiming the nobility of the common man. And probably it is safe to say that it was these elements of strength which really survived to influence the work of such writers as Dickens, George Eliot, and John Ruskin in the middle and later years of the nineteenth century.

The growth of a romantic movement in art was scarcely noticeable until after the downfall of Napoleon. This was especially true in France. With the outbreak of the French Revolution a strong reaction set in against the elegant rococo style of the old order. But instead of launching a new tradition, the artists of the Revolution simply went back to what was supposed to be a *pure* classicism, on the assumption that this would be in harmony with the rationalist ideals of the new order. The advent of Napoleon made no perceptible change. The Little Corporal liked to think of himself as a modern Caesar or Alexander the Great. Accordingly, he adopted the

Studies for a Sculpture of Victor Hugo by Rodin

The importance of literary romanticism

The revival of classicist art

601

Roman imperial eagle as one of his emblems, invested his son with the title of King of Rome, and erected arches, columns, and temples of triumph in the city of Paris. Under such influences it is not surprising that a classicist movement in art of more than ordinary vitality should have crystallized in France in the first two decades of the nineteenth century. It reached its apex in painting under the leadership of Jacques David (1748–1825) and Jean Auguste Ingres (1780–1867). The work of both of these men was characterized by order and restraint, by a strict attention to form, and by a liberal choice of themes from Greek and Roman mythology.

The eventual triumph of romanticism in painting

Notwithstanding the vigor of the classical revival, the force of the romantic influence, overflowing from the channels of literature and philosophy, was not to be denied. After the defeat of Napoleon at Waterloo the period of the Enlightenment and the Revolution was definitely accepted as a closed chapter. There seemed to be no longer any reason for trying to preserve the ideals of a bygone age. As a consequence, classicism in painting was quickly supplanted by romanticism. The foremost champion of the new style in France was Eugène Delacroix (1798–1863), who gloried in portraying struggles for freedom and other dramatic scenes from history. In place of the restraint and sobriety of classical painting, he substituted an emotionalism in some cases as overwrought as that of Michelangelo. Inspired also by Rubens and the Venetians, he employed small strokes of pure color that seem to merge into the actual flesh of his subjects. The work of Delacroix was paralleled to a certain distance by that of the romantic landscape painters. Their chief representative was Camille Corot (1796–1875), leader of the Barbizon school, so called from the village of Barbizon near Paris. Among others who followed the same tradition was the Englishman J. M. W. Turner (1775–1851). The romantic landscape painters were just as addicted to effusive displays of emotionalism as Delacroix, but it was an emotionalism of a quieter tone. They were poets of nature who suffused forests and streams and mountains with a gentle haze of tender worship.

See color plates at pages 593, 625, 656, 657

Architecture not greatly affected by romanticism

From what we have learned about the influence of romanticism upon literature and painting, we should normally expect that architecture also would be deeply affected. Such, however, was not the case. While it is true that, under romantic inspirations, a movement was started about 1840 to revive the medieval Gothic, the results were only moderately significant. A large number of churches with soaring spires and pointed arches were built, and even some government buildings also; but not infrequently what was supposed to be pure Gothic turned out to be a crude eclecticism made up of elements taken only partly from the Gothic. In general, the classical influence was still too strong to be overcome, with the result that throughout the greater part of the nineteenth century variations of the baroque continued to be the most popular building styles. Not

A Page from the Score of Beethoven's Piano Sonata Opus 109 in E Major
Right: *Ludwig van Beethoven*

until about 1900 was there much evidence of a desire to create a new and original architecture more truly expressive of our own civilization.

In music, as in painting and literature, the first decades of the nineteenth century saw the rise of romanticism. The romanticists regarded music not essentially as objective beauty but mainly as a medium for expressing man's inner moods. It must not merely please but must stir a sympathetic vibration in the listener. Attempts were made to capture in tone the various aspects of nature and, above all, human sentiments and passions. To some extent the composers, like the poets, responded to the exciting political drama about them. It is significant that at first musical romanticism found its congenial expression in lyricism—piano pieces and songs. This represents a rebellion against the logical architecture of the large symphonic forms. Since the redoubtable guardian of the latter, Ludwig van Beethoven (1770–1827), stood there as a formidable sentinel, the spirit of romanticism moved into chamber and orchestral music only gradually.

Ludwig van Beethoven was born in the west German town of Bonn but spent most of his productive years in Vienna, then regarded as the musical capital of Europe. Poverty and a harsh father made his childhood unhappy, and his adult life was a succession of difficulties, largely occasioned by his impractical nature and irascible temper. He was not only coarse in manner, careless in

603

dress, and blunt to the point of rudeness, but overly sensitive and suspicious, frequently injuring his closest friends bceause of resentment toward some imaginary slight. In spite of such traits he was able to retain the loyalty of his friends and to fascinate and humble the Viennese aristocracy, both male and female. The crowning source of Beethoven's suffering was his deafness, which began to trouble him before he was thirty and became total in his later years. As a result, he was not only forced to give up playing in public, but was never able to hear many of his greatest works.

The first two decades of Beethoven's life in Vienna saw the composition of dozens of piano sonatas, much chamber music, eight symphonies, overtures, one opera, and one Mass. The most remarkable thing about these works is their uniqueness: each represents a new solution of the problems of the respective genre. In the Fifth Symphony Beethoven reaches the summit of symphonic logic, the Sixth is a glorification of nature, the Seventh a Dionysian revelry, the Eighth a genial conjuring up of the spirit of the eighteenth-century symphony. Then Beethoven embarks on his last artistic journey; the deaf composer takes us into the world of visions, though everything remains ordered by an iron will. Five piano sonatas, five string quartets, the Ninth Symphony and the great Mass called *Missa Solemnis* constitute his final legacy. They fill the listener with awe not so much because of their unusual form or their vast proportions, but because of their tone, a tone altogether new in the history of music. It expresses boundless will and power and ecstasy, the tone of unspeakable solitude breaking into the open. It is this tone and harnessed power that made Beethoven the Titan of music.

Franz Schubert (1797–1828), the Viennese schoolteacher's son, does not fit very well into any scheme or schedule. He was no one's disciple; he just assimilated music that was around him and by his eighteenth year composed masterpieces—surely the embodiment of what is called "God-given" natural talent. But this was a dangerous precocity. Perhaps Schubert felt that he must hasten, for he died in his thirty-first year. After he left the paternal home he lived a romantic bohemian life with a group of like-minded poets, painters, and singers, eternally poor, eternally working, and eternally hoping. In this genial company perhaps three friends shared one hat and five one purse, but the world was wrong in construing from this carefree existence the parochial picture of unfortunate derelicts perishing in the adventure. These people lived a life congenial to them, but it was a life that did not agree with the pattern set by the ruling Biedermeier bourgeoisie. They did not need much, they got together in the evenings to make music, and on nice days went out into the country where Schubert would compose on the back of a country-inn menu half a dozen songs and waltzes in one afternoon. It is thus that Schubert's music came to reflect Vienna's grace and the rhythm of its life. Schubert was the greatest of song composers, but he was also the only one of the age who could be ranked next to Beethoven as an instrumental composer. Though they lived in the same town, Schubert was so overawed by Beethoven that he never dared to address him. Among his eight symphonies, numerous chamber music works, piano sonatas and Masses there are many incomparable masterpieces. Only his operas failed to show the full weight of his genius.

SELECTED READINGS

· *Items so designated are available in paperbound editions.*

THE AGE OF NAPOLEON

· Brinton, Crane, *The Lives of Talleyrand*, New York, 1932 (Norton Library).
· Bruun, Geoffrey, *Europe and the French Imperium*, New York, 1938 (Torchbook).
  Gershoy, Leo, *The French Revolution and Napoleon*, New York, 1933. A brief but excellent account.
· Geyl, Pieter, *Napoleon, For and Against*, New Haven, 1949 (Yale University Press).
  Gottschalk, L. R., *The Era of the French Revolution, 1715–1815*, New York, 1929. Thorough and scholarly.
  Kircheisen, F. M., *Napoleon*, New York, 1932.
  Tarle, Eugene, *Napoleon's Invasion of Russia*, New York, 1942. An exciting account.
  Thompson, J. M., *Napoleon Bonaparte*, New York, 1952. A recent evaluation.

THE AGE OF REACTION

· Artz, F. B., *Reaction and Revolution, 1814–1832*, New York, 1934 (Torchbook).
· Gulick, E. V., *Europe's Classical Balance of Power*, Ithaca, N.Y., 1955 (Norton Library).
· May, A. J., *The Age of Metternich, 1814–1848*, New York, 1933 (Holt, Rinehart & Winston). A good summary.
· Nicholson, Harold, *The Congress of Vienna*, London, 1946 (Compass).

INTELLECTUAL AND ARTISTIC DEVELOPMENTS, 1800–1830

  Artz, F. B., *France under the Bourbon Restoration, 1814–1830*, New York, 1963. Emphasizes social and intellectual developments.
  Bell, Clive, *Landmarks in Nineteenth Century Painting*, New York, 1927.
  Boas, George, *French Philosophies of the Romantic Period*, Baltimore, 1934.
  Brandes, Georg, *Main Currents in Nineteenth Century Literature*, New York, 1901–06.
· Brinton, Crane, *English Political Thought in the Nineteenth Century*, New York, 1962 (Torchbook). A new edition.
  ———, *Political Ideas of the English Romanticists*, London, 1926.
  Davidson, W. L., *Political Thought in England from Bentham to Mill*, New York, 1916.
  Einstein, Alfred, *Music in the Romantic Era*, New York, 1947.
  Lang, Paul, *Music in Western Civilization*, New York, 1941.
  Machlis, Joseph, *The Enjoyment of Music*, 3rd ed., New York, 1970.

READINGS   Randall, J. H., Jr., *The Making of the Modern Mind*, New York, 1926. Chs.
XVI, XVII.
Wright, C. H. C., *A History of French Literature*, New York, 1925.

SOURCE MATERIALS

Bentham, Jeremy, *A Fragment on Government*.

———, *Principles of Penal Law*, Part II, Book II, Ch. XII.

· Burke, Edmund, *Reflections on the Revolution in France* (Holt, Rinehart &
Winston and others).

· de Caulaincourt, A. A. L., *With Napoleon in Russia*, New York, 1935 (Universal Library). An eye-witness account by one of Napoleon's officers.

· Herold, J. C., ed., *The Mind of Napoleon*, New York, 1955 (Collier).

Johnston, R. M., ed., *The Corsican: A Diary of Napoleon in His Own Words*.

· Kant, Immanuel, *Plan for Perpetual Peace* (Library of Liberal Arts).

· Mill, John Stuart, *Autobiography*, New York, 1924 (Library of Liberal Arts
and others).

Thompson, J. M., ed., *Napoleon Self-Revealed*, Boston, 1934.

CHAPTER 21

The Early Industrial Revolutions

It may not be true, in spite of *Punch* cartoons, that coal-miners drank champagne in 1871–1873; but certainly many wage-earners were getting more cake as well as tea, cocoa, meat, sugar, rice, and fats. They might return home a little earlier for the evening meal, as trade union pressure was chipping the working .week from sixty (or more) hours down toward fifty-five, with a Saturday half-holiday. If they lived in Britain the public health service was beginning to make their living environment a bit better. . . . Parliament had given them a vote in 1867, and in 1870 it finally insisted that the children it had shut out of the factories must go to school. Things had moved since the Hungry Forties.
—Herbert Heaton, "Economic Change and Growth,"
The New Cambridge Modern History, X

The years from about 1760 to 1860 were marked by economic changes so sweeping in character as to deserve the label Industrial Revolution. Actually they continued beyond this time until well into the twentieth century. Many historians divide the movement into two stages, with the year 1860 marking the approximate boundary between them. The stage from 1860 to 1914 is often referred to as the Second Industrial Revolution. It differed from the first primarily in being based on electricity and the internal combustion engine instead of their more cumbersome predecessors, coal and the steam engine.

The First and Second Revolutions

I. CAUSES AND EARLY BEGINNINGS

The First Industrial Revolution sprang from a multitude of causes. It may be well to consider first the early improvements in technology. The marvelous inventions of the late eighteenth century did not spring full-blown like Athena from the brow of Zeus. On the contrary, there had been a more or less fruitful interest in mechanical innovations for some time. The period of the Commercial Revolution had witnessed the invention of the pendulum clock, the thermometer, the air pump, and the spinning wheel, to say nothing of improvements in the techniques of smelting ores and making brass. About 1580 a mechanical loom was devised, capable of weaving several strands of ribbon at the same time. There were also important technological advances in such industries as glass blowing, clock making, and wood finishing. Several of the early inventions made necessary the use of factory methods. For example, the silk-throwing machine invented in Italy about 1500 had to be housed in a large building and required a considerable corps of workers. In the Temple Mills on the Thames above London, according to a description by Daniel Defoe in 1728, brass was beaten into kettles and pans by enormous hammers operated by water power. These early technological improvements are hardly to be compared in significance with those made after 1760, but they do indicate that the machine age did not burst upon the world out of a clear sky.

Among other causes of paramount importance were several more direct consequences of the Commercial Revolution. That movement brought into existence a class of capitalists who were constantly seeking new opportunities to invest their surplus wealth. At first this wealth could be readily absorbed by trade or by mining, banking, and shipbuilding ventures; but as time went on the opportunities in such fields became limited. As a consequence more and more capital was made available for the development of manufacturing. But a rapid development of manufacturing would scarcely have occurred had there not been a growing demand for industrial products. This demand grew largely from the establishment of colonial empires and from the marked increase in the population of Europe. It will be recalled that one of the primary objects in the acquisition of colonies was to expand the market for manufactured goods from the mother country. At the same time the potential markets at home were being rapidly enlarged by the large increase of population in western European countries. In England the number of inhabitants rose from 4,000,000 in 1600 to 6,000,000 in 1700 and to 9,000,000 by the end of the eighteenth century. The population of France grew from 17,000,000 in 1700 to 26,000,000 about a hundred years later. Finally, the Commercial Revolution gave a stimulus to the growth of manufactures through its basic gospel of mercantilism. The mercantilist policy was designed, as much as for any other purpose, to increase the quantity of manufactured goods available for export and thereby to ensure a favorable balance of trade.

Despite the importance of the causes already mentioned, the Industrial Revolution would undoubtedly have been delayed had there not been a need for fundamental mechanical improvements in certain fields of production. By 1700 the demand for charcoal for smelting iron had so depleted the resources of timber that several of

The Staffordshire Collieries. In the building to the right is a whimsey, or coal-powered steam engine, used to lift loads of coal from mines.

the nations of western Europe were threatened with deforestation. A partial solution was found about 1709 when Abraham Darby discovered that coke could be used for smelting. But in order to obtain sufficient coke it was necessary that coal be mined in much larger quantities than ever before. Since the chief obstacle to the extraction of coal was the accumulation of water in the mines, the need for the new fuel led to a search for some convenient source of power to drive the pumps. Various experiments in connection with this search finally resulted in the invention of the steam engine. An even more crucial need for mechanization existed in the textile industry. With the increasing popularity of cotton clothing in the seventeenth and eighteenth centuries, it was simply impossible to provide enough yarn with the primitive spinning wheels still in use. Even when every available woman and child was pressed into service, the demand could not be met. The result was the development later of the spinning jenny and the water frame, the forerunners of a series of important inventions in the textile industry. As the practicability of these machines was soon demonstrated, mechanization was bound to be extended to other manufactures.

The need for fundamental mechanical improvements in certain industries

2. WHY INDUSTRIALIZATION BEGAN IN BRITAIN

At first thought it may seem strange that a small island kingdom should not only have become the industrial leader of the world but should have held that leadership for more than a century.

609

Possibly we should place first as a primary cause the fact that Britain had profited most from the Commercial Revolution. Though it is true that about 1750 France had a foreign trade 25 per cent larger than that of Britain, it must be remembered that the French population was at least three times as large as the British. Moreover, France had reached her limit of imperial aggrandizement, while much of the profit of her world trade was being diverted through loans and taxes to the upkeep of a costly army and a frivolous and extravagant court. Britain, on the other hand, was just on the brink of a golden age of power and prosperity. She had already acquired the most valuable colonies in the Western Hemisphere, and she was soon to clinch her imperial and commercial supremacy by defeating the French in the Seven Years' War. In addition, a much larger proportion of Britain's gains from overseas trade was available for productive investment. Her government was comparatively free from corruption and wasteful expenditure. Her military establishment cost less than that of the French, and her revenues were much more efficiently collected. As a result, her merchants and shipowners were left with a larger share of surplus earnings, which they were eager to invest in any conceivable business venture that might be the source of additional profit.

Favorable factors operating in Britain

See color map at page 624

In view of these facts it is not strange that Britain should have emerged as the leading capitalist nation in the early eighteenth century. Nowhere was the joint-stock company more highly developed. Trading in securities was organized as a legitimate business when the London Stock Exchange was chartered in 1698. Britain, moreover, had perhaps the best banking system in Europe. At its apex was the Bank of England, founded in 1694. Though established for the purpose of raising funds for the government, it was organized as a private corporation. Its stock was privately owned, and its management was not subject to any official control by the state. Nevertheless, it always operated in close association with the government, and even in its early days served as an important stabilizing factor in public finance. With the financial stability of the government thus assured, leaders of business enterprise could carry on their activities unhindered by fear of national bankruptcy or ruinous inflation.

**Britain the
leading capitalist nation**

Political and social factors were not alone important in accounting for the beginning of the Industrial Revolution in Britain. Although the British government of the eighteenth century was far from democratic, it was at least more liberal than most of the governments on the Continent. The Glorious Revolution of 1688–1689 had done much to establish the conception of limited sovereignty. The doctrine was now widely accepted that the power of the state should extend no farther than the protection of man's natural rights to liberty and to the enjoyment of property. Under

**Favorable
political and social conditions in Britain**

the influence of this doctrine Parliament repealed old laws providing for special monopolies and interfering with free competition. Mercantilist principles continued to be applied to trade with the colonies, but in the sphere of domestic business many restrictions were gradually abolished. Furthermore, Britain was already coming to be recognized as a haven for refugees from other countries. More than 40,000 Huguenots settled in her villages and cities after being driven from France in 1685 by the revocation of the Edict of Nantes. Thrifty, energetic, and ambitious, these people instilled new vigor into the British nation. Social conditions also were distinctly favorable to the industrial development of Britain. Her nobility had ceased to be a hereditary caste exclusively and was rapidly becoming an aristocracy of wealth. Almost anyone who had made a fortune could rise to the highest levels of social distinction.

A few other causes must be added to complete the picture. First may be mentioned the fact that the damp climate of the British Isles was singularly favorable for the manufacturing of cotton cloth, since the thread would not become brittle and break easily when woven by machines. And it is sufficient to call to mind that it was the mechanization of the textile industry which ushered in the age of machines. Second, the guild system of production, with its elaborate restrictions, had never become so firmly implanted in Britain as on the Continent. Even the regulations that were established had been thrown off, especially in the northern counties, by the end of the seventeenth century. Lastly, since wealth was more evenly distributed in Britain than in most other nations at that time, her manufacturers could devote their attention to the production of large quantities of cheap and ordinary wares instead of to the making of limited supplies of luxury goods. This factor had considerable influence in promoting the adoption of factory methods in the hope of achieving a larger output. In France, by contrast, the demand was for articles *de luxe* to gratify the tastes of a small class of elegant wastrels. Since quality of workmanship was a primary consideration in this type of goods, there was little incentive to invent machines.

Other favorable factors in Britain

3. THE PROGRESS AND SPREAD OF INDUSTRIALIZATION

The initial stage of the Industrial Revolution, from about 1760 to 1860, witnessed a phenomenal development of the application of machinery to industry that laid the foundations for our modern mechanical civilization. As we have seen, the first of the branches of industry to be mechanized was the manufacture of cotton cloth. The first invention essential to the development of this industry was the spinning jenny invented by James Hargreaves in 1767. The spinning "jenny," so called from the name of the inventor's wife,

The application of machinery to cotton manufactures

611

The Spinning Jenny Invented by James Hargreaves in 1767

was really a compound spinning wheel, capable of producing sixteen threads at once. Unfortunately the threads it spun were not strong enough to be used for the longitudinal fibers, or warp, of cotton cloth. It was not until the invention of the water frame by Richard Arkwright about two years later that quantity production of both kinds of cotton yarn became possible.

The power loom and the cotton gin

The problems of the cotton industry were still not entirely solved. The invention of spinning machines had more than made up for the deficiency of yarn, but now there was a scarcity of weavers. It soon became obvious that the only remedy for this shortage would be the invention of some kind of automatic machine to take the place of the hand loom. Many declared such a contrivance impossible, but a Kentish clergyman, the Reverend Edmund Cartwright, was not to be discouraged so easily. He reasoned that if automatic machinery could be applied to spinning, it could be just as logically extended to weaving. Knowing little about mechanics himself, he hired a carpenter and a smith to put his ideas into effect. The result was the power loom, which Cartwright patented in 1785. A good many years elapsed, however, before it was sufficiently improved to be more than a modest success. Not until about 1820 did it largely displace more primitive methods of weaving. Meanwhile, the invention of a machine for separating the seeds from the cotton fiber made possible a much more abundant supply of raw cotton at a lower price. This machine was the cotton gin, invented by a Yankee schoolteacher, Eli Whitney, in 1792.

Origin of the factory system

Several of the new inventions in the textile industry contributed to the growth of the factory system. The water frame and the automatic loom were large and heavy machines which could not possibly be set up in the cottages of individual workers. All were eventually designed to be driven by power, and, besides, they cost so much that no one but a wealthy capitalist could afford to buy them. It was therefore inevitable that they should be installed in large buildings, and that the workers employed to operate them should be brought under the supervision of the owner or of a manager acting for him. Such were the essentials of the factory system in its original form. Appropriately enough, the real founder of this system was Richard Arkwright, inventor of the water frame. By indomitable perseverance and shrewd management, Arkwright rose from the status of an obscure barber and wigmaker to that of a captain of industry. Commonly working from five in the morning until nine at night, he struggled against obstacles for years. He was accused, perhaps with some truth, of stealing his ideas for the water frame from others. Altogether he is said to have spent some $60,000 before his plans brought him any profit. He established his first factory, operated by water power, in 1771.

It is difficult to believe that the factory system would ever have assumed much importance had it not been for the perfection of the steam engine. That steam could be employed as a means of power had been known for centuries. Crude steam engines had been devised by Hero of Alexandria in the first century B.C., by Leonardo da Vinci during the Renaissance, and by various individuals in the early modern period. None of these, however, had been put to any practical use. The first man to apply the power of steam to industrial purposes was Thomas Newcomen, who in 1712 devised a crude but effective engine for pumping water from the British coal mines. By the middle of the century nearly 100 of his engines were in use.

Newcomen's steam engine

Though of great value to the coal mining industry, Newcomen's engine suffered from defects which prevented its being widely used for industrial purposes. For one thing, it wasted both fuel and power. It was constructed in such a way that after each stroke of the piston, the steam had to be condensed by spraying cold water into the cylinder. This meant that the cylinder had to be heated again before the next stroke, and this alternate heating and cooling greatly retarded the speed of the engine. In the second place, Newcomen's "Miner's Friend" was adaptable only to the straight-line motion necessary for pumping; the principle of converting the straight-line action of the piston into a rotary motion had not been discovered. Both of these defects were eventually remedied by James Watt, a maker of scientific instruments at the University of Glasgow. In 1763 Watt was asked to repair a model of the Newcomen engine. While engaged in this task he conceived the idea that the machine would be greatly improved if a separate chamber were added to condense the steam, so as to eliminate the necessity of cooling the cylinder. He patented his first engine incorporating this device in 1769. Unfortunately Watt's genius as an inventor was not matched by his business ability. He admitted that he would "rather face a loaded cannon than settle a disputed account or make a bargain." As a consequence he fell into debt in attempting to place his machines on the market. He was rescued by Matthew Boulton, a wealthy hardware manufacturer of Birmingham. The two men formed a partnership, with Boulton providing the capital. By 1800 the firm had sold 289 engines for use in factories and mines.

Newcomen's engine greatly improved by James Watt

613

James Watts' Steam Engine

Few single inventions have had greater influence upon the history of modern times than the steam engine. Contrary to popular opinion, it was not the initial cause of the Industrial Revolution; instead, it was partly an effect. Watt's engine, at least, would never have become a reality if there had not been a demand for an effective source of power to operate the heavy machines already invented in the textile industry. On the other hand, the perfection of the steam engine was certainly a cause of the more rapid growth of industrialization. It raised the production of coal and iron to a new importance. It made possible a revolution in transportation. It provided almost unlimited opportunities for accelerating the manufacture of goods, thereby making the industrialized nations the richest and most powerful in the world. Before the development of the steam engine, the resources of power were largely at the mercy of the weather. In time of drought, low water in the streams would probably force the mills to curtail operations or even to shut down entirely. Ships on ocean voyages might be delayed for weeks by lack of wind. Now, however, there was a constant supply of energy, which could be tapped and used when needed. It is therefore not too much to say that the invention of Watt's engine was the real beginning of the age of power.

One of the industries that owed its rapid development to the improvement of the steam engine was the manufacture of iron and iron products. While many of the new machines, such as the spinning jenny and the water frame, could be constructed of wood, steam engines required a more substantial material. Moreover, the cylinders of these engines needed to be bored as accurately as possible in order to prevent a loss of power. This made necessary a considerable advance in the production of machine tools and in scientific methods of iron manufacture. The pioneer in this work was John Wilkinson, a manufacturer of cannon. In 1774 Wilkinson patented a method of boring cylinders which reduced the percentage of error to a very small amount for that day. Even more important than the achievements of Wilkinson were the accomplishments of another Englishman, who devised the method of puddling, or stirring the molten iron to eliminate a larger percentage of its carbon content. This process made possible the production in quantity of the tougher grade of metal known as wrought iron. A few years later came the invention of the rolling mill for the manufacture of sheet iron. These two achievements revolutionized the industry. Within less than twenty years the production of iron in England quadrupled, and the price dropped to a fraction of what it had been.

The first signs of a definite improvement in methods of travel began to appear about 1780. It was about that time that the construction of turnpikes and canals in England was started in earnest. By 1830 nearly all of the highways had been drained and covered with a surface of broken stone, while the principal streams had been linked together by a network of 2500 miles of canals. The improvement of roads made possible a faster stagecoach service. In 1784 the postmaster general inaugurated a mail service with coaches that ran continuously day and night, covering a distance of 120 miles in twenty-four hours. By the end of the century special stages, known as "flying machines," operated between all of the principal cities, sometimes achieving the sensational speed of nine or ten miles per hour.

But the really significant progress in transportation did not come until after the steam engine had been generally accepted as a dependable source of power. Attempts were first made to adapt the use of steam to stagecoaches, and several of these ancestors of the modern automobile were actually put on the highways. Gradually the opinion grew that it would be more profitable to use the steam engine to draw a train of cars over iron rails. A number of such railroads were already in existence for the purpose of transporting coal, but the cars were drawn by horses. The man primarily responsible for the first steam railway was George Stephenson, a self-made engineer who had not even learned to read until he was seventeen years of age. In 1822 he convinced a group of men who were projecting a coal railroad from Stockton to Darlington of the merits of steam traction, and was appointed engineer for the line with full liberty to carry out his plans. The result was the opening three

Early developments in transportation: (1) roads and canals

(2) the first railroads

Puffing Billy. Built by Timothy Hackworth in 1813, it was the first commercially successful railway engine and a predecessor of George Stephenson's famous *Rocket*.

The Crimple Valley Viaduct. Located in York, England, and built during the 1840's, this and others like it were essential to the rapid development of British railroads in the early part of the nineteenth century.

years later of the first railway operated entirely by steam. The locomotives he built for this line attained a speed of fifteen miles an hour, the fastest rate at which human beings had yet traveled.

(3) the beginning of steam navigation

Meanwhile the steam engine was being gradually applied to water transportation. Here it was Americans rather than Englishmen who took the lead. Precisely who should receive credit for inventing the steamboat is a matter of dispute. There is evidence that a number of men had something to do with it. About 1787 an American metal worker, John Fitch, constructed a boat that actually carried passengers on the Delaware for several months. But Fitch was never able to make his craft a financial success. After vainly attempting to persuade governments to adopt his invention, he committed suicide in 1798. Another American, Robert Fulton, is given the credit for having made the steamboat commercially successful. That Fulton was any more ingenious than Fitch is open to doubt, but he was a good enough salesman and promoter to secure the backing of a wealthy capitalist, and he knew how to keep himself in the public eye. In April 1838, the first steamships, the *Sirius* and the *Great Western,* crossed the Atlantic. Two years later Samuel Cunard founded the famous Cunard Line, providing a regular transoceanic service with vessels propelled entirely by steam.

The invention of the telegraph

The one significant improvement in communications, during the first stage of the Industrial Revolution was the invention of the telegraph. As early as 1820 the French physicist Ampère discovered that electromagnetism could be used for sending messages by wire between distant points. About all that remained was to devise effective instruments for transmitting and receiving the messages. Experiments for this purpose were carried on by a number of individuals. Three of them succeeded almost simultaneously. In 1844 a telegraph line efficient enough for commercial purposes was established. This was the line between Baltimore and Washington, which an American, Samuel Morse, succeeded in having built on the strength of improvements in his own invention. Once started, telegraph systems multiplied all over the world. Soon all important cities were linked, and in 1866 the first Atlantic cable was laid under the direction of the American capitalist, Cyrus Field.

The Industrial Revolution also had its agricultural aspects. They were especially noticeable in the first sixty years of the nineteenth century. Among them were the production of better breeds of livestock; the introduction of new crops, such as the sugar beet, which was now being extensively cultivated in Germany and France; and the development of agricultural chemistry by Justus von Liebig, which made possible the production of artificial fertilizers. Agriculture in this period also came under the influence of mechanization. Better plows and harrows were designed, and the threshing machine was quite generally adopted. In 1834 the American farmer, Cyrus McCormick, patented his mechanical reaper and soon afterward began its manufacture in Chicago. By 1860 these machines were being sold at the rate of 20,000 a year. As a result of these various improvements, agriculture all over the world rejoiced in an unprecedented prosperity, which lasted until the great depression of 1873.

Improvements in agriculture

As early as the year 1000 the Saracens were producing excellent steel swords at Damascus. Beginning with the later Middle Ages, Europeans had also known how to manufacture the desirable material. But the methods were slow and difficult and the product expensive. In 1856 Sir Henry Bessemer discovered that the introduction of a jet of air into the molten iron in a blast furnace would eliminate all but the tiniest percentage of carbon and thereby convert the iron into steel. The result was to reduce the price of steel to less than a seventh of its former cost. By 1878 a method was discovered whereby even low-grade iron with a heavy content of phosphorus could also be converted into steel. The consequences of this advance were astounding. Not only was the phosphoric iron of England brought into production, but enormous deposits in Lorraine, in Belgium, and in the United States now became immensely valuable. Between 1880 and 1914 the output of steel in Great Britain rose from 2,000,000 tons to 7,000,000, in Germany from 1,000,000 to 15,000,000, and in the United States from 1,600,000 to 28,000,000. Steel almost entirely supplanted iron for railroad rails, for the framework of large buildings, for bridges, and for other purposes where a cheap metal with a high degree of tensile strength was desired.

The Bessemer Process of Manufacturing Steel. This process involved the introduction of a jet of air into the molten iron to reduce its impure elements and thereby toughen it for the production of steel.

The partial displacement of coal as a basic source of power resulted, first of all, from the invention of the dynamo, a machine for converting mechanical energy into electrical energy. Although the principle of the dynamo was formulated by Michael Faraday in 1831, no machine of this kind capable of practical use was available

617

until 1873. From that time on the harnessing of electrical energy to the mechanism of industry went rapidly ahead. The steam engine came to be relegated gradually to the background, to be used primarily for driving dynamos. The electric energy thus generated is converted by electric motors into mechanical energy. In some areas, especially where coal is scarce, the steam engine for driving dynamos has been superseded by water power. By 1914 electricity provided more than half of the power required by industry in Great Britain and an even larger proportion in Germany.[1] The German A.E.G. (Allgemeine Elektrizitäts Gesellschaft), manufacturing motors, generators, and other electrical equipment, had evolved into the largest industrial unit in Europe.

An Early Dynamo Used for Lighting

A second revolutionary development making available new sources of power was the utilization of petroleum products to add to the supply of energy. The existence of petroleum had been known for some time before its value was discovered. Until the middle of the nineteenth century it was regarded as a curiosity. Labeled as Indian Oil or Seneca Oil, it was sold in the United States for its alleged medicinal properties. Even after its value for lubricating purposes was revealed, its use was limited by scarcity. In 1859 Edwin L. Drake solved the problem of an inadequate supply by drilling the first oil well near Titusville, Pennsylvania. New uses for the product were gradually found, although for many years most of it went into the manufacture of kerosene for lamps. In 1876, however, Nikolaus Otto invented the first successful internal-combustion engine. This was the starting point of a series of developments which heralded the dawn of a motorized age.

The internal-combustion engine

The growth of mass production and the adoption of automatic and highly specialized processes in industry

Among the most typical features of the Second Industrial Revolution were the introduction of automatic machinery, an enormous increase in mass production, and a division of the tasks of labor into minute segments of the manufacturing process. All three of these things date from the years just preceding World War I. A characteristic example of the development of automatic machinery was the invention of the photoelectric cell, or the "electric eye," which could be used to throw switches, to open doors, to sort eggs, to inspect tin cans, to count sheets of paper and measure their thickness, and even to eliminate counterfeit bills. Machines were invented to direct and operate other machines and to complete whole series of manufacturing processes which formerly required much human labor. Not only did automatic machinery result in a marked increase in mass production, but the volume of goods turned out by industry was also greatly expanded by the adoption of the endless conveyor belt. The idea for this was copied originally by Henry Ford about 1908 from the Chicago packers, who used an overhead trolley to move carcasses of beef along a line of butchers. Ford gradually im-

[1] Herbert Heaton, *Economic History of Europe*, p. 518.

proved the device to a point where he could assemble a complete chassis of his famous Model T in an hour and thirty-three minutes. The principle of the conveyor belt and the assembly line, which requires each worker to toil all day at a simple, monotonous task, was subsequently adopted in every automobile factory in the United States and in many other industries as well. It provided the world with a staggering abundance of goods and reduced the prices of some articles which were formerly luxuries for the rich, but no one was then able to foresee how serious might be its effects upon society.

Radical changes in methods of production came not only from the invention of intricate machines but also from a growing domination of industry by science. Actually, the significant discoveries of the Second Industrial Revolution emanated more often from the laboratory of the physicist or chemist than from the brain of the individual inventor. The supremacy of science in the realm of industry was originally foreshadowed in 1856 when William Henry Perkin produced the first aniline or coal-tar dyes. This was the beginning of a marvelous development of synthetic chemistry. From this same coal tar it was discovered that literally hundreds of dyes could be derived, together with an infinite variety of other products, such as aspirin, oil of wintergreen, essence of orange blossoms, saccharine, carbolic acid, and vanilla. As the years passed, many additional subtances were added to the list of synthetic products. Methods were devised for manufacturing nitric acid out of the nitrogen in the air, for making glucose from corn, and for pro-

The growing domination of industry by science

An Early Assembly Line of the Ford Motor Co., 1913. Bodies were slid down the ramp and attached to the chassis as they passed through the line below. Production amounted to 1000 cars a day.

ducing textile fibers from wood and from minerals. Chemists likewise came to the aid of many of the older industries, discovering methods of utilizing hitherto worthless by-products or of increasing the yield from available supplies of raw materials. For example, cotton seeds were turned into celluloid, cosmetics, smokeless powder, and salad oil, while the cracking process of refining gasoline greatly increased the yield from a given quantity of petroleum. Though not recognized at the time, many of these products of industrial chemistry were not biologically degradable. They therefore constituted a problem in helping nature to maintain a balance of forces.

The second stage of the Industrial Revolution saw perhaps an even greater revolution in transportation and communication than did the first. The years after 1860 were marked by feverish activity in railroad building. Before that date there were hardly more than 30,000 miles of railroad in the entire world. By 1890 there were 20,000 miles in Great Britain alone, 26,000 in Germany, and 167,000 in the United States. The service itself was greatly improved by the invention of the air brake in 1868 and by the introduction of the sleeping car, the dining car, and the automatic block-signal system soon afterward. As the years passed, however, the railroads began to suffer under competition from newer forms of transportation, especially from the automobile and the commercial airplane.

The revolution in
transportation:
the extension and
improvement of
the railroads

It is impossible to assign credit for invention of the automobile to any one person, though various individuals have claimed it. Both Daimler and Benz made gasoline vehicles in Germany as early as the 1880's, but their original inventions were little more than motorized tricycles. The first man to apply the principle of the internal-combustion engine to a carriage seems to have been the Frenchman Émile Levassor. About 1890 he designed a vehicle with the engine in front and with the power transmitted to the rear wheels by means of a clutch, a shaft, and reduction and differential gears. So far as the evidence shows, this was the first true automobile in history. Obviously, many other inventions were necessary in order to ensure the success of the motorcar as a comfortable and efficient means of travel. Not the least of these were the pneumatic tire developed by J. B. Dunlop in 1888 and the electric self-starter by Charles Kettering about 1910. But the automobile might have remained indefinitely a toy for the rich had it not been for the determination of Henry Ford to produce a car that could be bought by persons of moderate incomes. In 1908 he began the manufacture of his Model T on the basis of the theory that he could make more money by selling a great quantity of cheap cars on a small margin of profit than by turning out an expensive product for the wealthy few. Other companies followed his example, with the result that eventually the automobile industry grew into the largest single branch of manufacturing in the United States.

No more than the perfection of the automobile can the invention of the airplane be credited to any one person. The idea that some day man might be able to fly is an old one indeed. Not only was it suggested by Roger Bacon in the thirteenth century, but it was actually embodied in some definite plans for flying machines conceived by the fertile mind of Leonardo da Vinci. Nevertheless, the birth of aviation as a mechanical possibility really dates from the 1890's. It was about that time that Otto Lilienthal, Samuel P. Langley, and others began their experiments with heavier-than-air machines. The work of Langley was carried forward by the Wright brothers, who, in 1903, made the first successful flight in a motor-driven plane. From that point on advancement was rapid. In 1908 the Wright brothers flew nearly 100 miles. The following year Louis Bleriot crossed the English Channel in the monoplane he had recently invented. During World War I each of the belligerent nations made strenuous efforts to utilize the possibilities of the airplane as a weapon of slaughter. As a consequence, improvements in design and in efficiency came thick and fast. However, it should be remembered that, even without the war, progress would still have been rapid; for, once an invention has been successfully launched, improvements follow in a kind of geometric ratio.

The early Industrial Revolution, or the age of coal and iron, resulted in but one important advance in communication. This, as we have seen, was the invention of the telegraph, which was already in extensive use by 1860. The age of electricity and the internal-combustion engine were accompanied by the perfection of a number of devices that went far toward annihilating both time and distance in the dissemination of news and in communicating with far-off places. First came the telephone, for which the credit is commonly given to

Wireless telegraphy, radio, and television

The First Successful Airplane Flight. The Wright brothers' motor-driven craft takes to the air at Kitty Hawk, North Carolina, on December 17, 1903.

Alexander Graham Bell, though only a few hours after Bell had applied for a patent in Washington on February 15, 1876, Elisha Gray appeared with practically the same idea.[2] Next came the invention of the wireless telegraph by Guglielmo Marconi, on the basis of discoveries by Heinrich Hertz and others relative to the transmission of electromagnetic waves through the ether. In 1899 Marconi dispatched a wireless message across the English Channel and two years later across the Atlantic. The invention of wireless telegraphy paved the way for the development of radio, the wireless telephone, and television.

4. THE NEW CAPITALISM

The growth of finance capitalism

The Second Industrial Revolution was distinguished from the First not merely by technological advances, but even more strikingly by the development of new forms of capitalist organization. The age of coal and iron was also, generally speaking, the age of small enterprise. Until the middle of the nineteenth century, at least, the partnership was still the dominant form of business organization. To be sure, many of these partnerships did business on a considerable scale, but they were hardly to be compared with the giant corporations of later years. Their capital came mainly from profits plowed back into the business, and their owners generally took an active part in the work of management. Many joint-stock companies had also been formed, but, except for their attributes of permanence and limited liability, they differed little from the partnerships. All of these types of business organization, insofar as they were concerned with manufacturing, mining, or transportation, may be designated as forms of *industrial capitalism*. During the Second Revolution, especially after 1890, industrial capitalism was largely superseded by *finance capitalism*, one of the most crucial developments of the modern age. Finance capitalism has four outstanding characteristics: (1) the domination of industry by investment banks and insurance companies; (2) the formation of huge aggregations of capital; (3) the separation of ownership from management; and (4) the growth of holding companies.

The domination of industry by investment institutions

One of the earliest examples of the domination of industry by investment bankers was the formation of the United States Steel Corporation in 1901 with the aid of J. P. Morgan and Company. Thenceforth financial institutions gained control over an increasing number of corporations. Of course they did not own all of the stock, or any considerable fraction of it. Many corporations had tens of thousands of stockholders. But these people were chiefly absentee owners; they had little to do with influencing corporate policy, and some of their shares did not even carry voting privileges.

[2] Clive Day, *Economic Development in Modern Europe*, p. 26.

Banks and insurance companies wielded control in some cases through ownership of a majority of the *voting stock* and in others through floating loans under terms which provided the lenders with extensive powers or with representation on boards of directors.

Another element in finance capitalism was the separation of ownership from management. The real owners of industrial enterprises were the thousands of men and women who had invested their savings in shares of stock; management was in the hands of a group of officers and directors, chosen by a minority of shareholders who had monopolized the voting stock or collected the proxies of absentee owners. In some cases the officers were little more than salaried employees, owning but a tiny percentage of the company's capital. Indeed, it was not unknown that some of them preferred to invest their surplus earnings in sounder enterprises than the ones over which they presided.

Lastly, finance capitalism included the growth of the holding company as a basic form of capitalist organization. The holding company is a device whereby a number of producing units are united under the control of a company that owns their stock. The holding company does not engage in production but receives its income from management fees and from dividends paid by the producing units. Though sometimes justified on the ground that it promotes integration of industry and facilitates business expansion, it is really a symbol of the triumph of the financier over the old-fashioned type of productive capitalist.

In addition to the foregoing changes in the structure and organization of capitalism, the fundamental character of the system underwent a transformation with the advent of the Second Industrial Revolution. The 100-year period from 1770 to about 1870 was the heyday of the free market economy. Free trade, free competition, and freedom of contract were the golden calves that the business establishments in nearly all countries theoretically worshiped. Monopolies, tariffs, and other special privileges conferred by governments were gradually abolished. Every manufacturer and merchant was supposed to compete on equal terms with his rivals. If success did not crown his efforts, he had nothing but the laws of bankruptcy to save him from disaster. The rule that he who does not work shall not eat was ruthlessly applied to the working classes, not necessarily to those who lived by owning. Strikes and collective bargaining were almost universally condemned. Labor unions were few and weak in opposing the system. Nothing resembling the welfare state was tolerated lest a premium be given to indolence and improvidence. The success of the free market economy depended, in theory at least, upon the use of a uniform monetary standard. In 1821 Great Britain put into operation the gold standard, a device whereby the value of all other commodities was measured in terms of gold. The other leading countries gradually adopted it, and most of them clung to it until the Great Depression of the 1930's. The financial classes preferred it because it placed obstacles in the path of government manipulation of currencies and served as a convenient means of balancing accounts between nations.

Such was the ideal economic system during what is often thought of as a golden age of economic liberalism, when Britain led the world in the development of industry and finance. Some authorities, however, maintain that it never really existed except as a British utopia. Perhaps it was not even that. Instead of a smoothly functioning machine, it was subject to interruptions and frequent breakdowns. Years of prosperity were followed by panics and depressions. Jobless men stood in bread lines or begged handouts from door to door. Little was done by governments to help them, and public welfare was unknown. The prevailing theory held that only a sufficient amount of "bloodletting" could effect a cure. When enough businesses and industries had been put through the wringer, the wheels of industry would start turning again. Prosperity would gradually return, and all would be well, until . . . When the workers became desperate enough, they frequently struck. Owners of the plants appealed to the police to defend their property. The powers of the police were often supplemented by the National Guard or private "detective" agencies. Bitter conflict was generally the rule until late in the nineteenth century. The owning classes were left with fruits of victory until labor came into its own on the eve of World War II.

In addition to the class conflict that punctuated the history of the late nineteenth and early twentieth centuries, the economic history of that time departed widely in other respects from the classical model. There was perhaps never a time when all the features of the system remained unchallenged. Great Britain herself did not adopt free trade until 1846. Prussia established protectionism in 1818 and laid the foundations soon afterward for a customs union, or *Zollverein*, for all of Germany. United States tariff policy became strongly protectionist in 1816. It may be noted also that most of the railroads in Continental Europe were built and operated under government ownership. These modifications, however, were pygmy deviations compared with those that were to follow after 1870. Increasing attention was now given to government subsidy and sponsorship. In France, for example, the tobacco and match industries became government monopolies. In practically all countries except Great Britain tariffs for the protection of domestic manufacturers were boosted sky-high. Labor unions waxed in power, and the right of collective bargaining was increasingly recognized. Most important of all, perhaps, a trend toward the welfare state made definite progress. In the 1880's Bismarck inaugurated his program of social insurance, and other governments, including even that of Great Britain, gradually followed suit. Even in the early 1900's some leaders, notably Louis D. Brandeis,

*The ideal and
the reality*

*Wider departures
in countries
other than
Britain*

ENGLAND AT THE START OF
THE INDUSTRIAL REVOLUTION

Population centers

Principal manufacturing cities

Coal fields

Iron ore deposits

Glasgow

Edinburgh

SCOTLAND

NORTHUMBERLAND

Newcastle

Gateshead

CUMBERLAND

DURHAM

Middlesbrough

WESTMORELAND

Ouse R.

NORTH

SEA

I. OF MAN

YORK

York

IRISH

SEA

Leeds

Hull

LANCASTER

Wakefield

Liverpool

Manchester

Grimsby

ANGLESEY

Northwich

Rotherham

Lincoln

CHESTER

DERBY

NOTTINGHAM

LINCOLN

Trent R.

Stoke

Nottingham

STAFFORD

LEICESTER

Norwich

WALES

Walsall

Leicester

RUTLAND

NORFOLK

SALOP

Aston Manor

NORTHAMPTON

Great Yarmouth

Cardigan Bay

Birmingham

WORCESTER

WARWICK

HUNTINGDON

CAMBRIDGE

SUFFOLK

HEREFORD

Avon R.

Northampton

BEDFORD

Ipswich

Gloucester

OXFORD

BUCKING-
HAM

HERTFORD

ESSEX

Swansea

MONMOUTH

GLOUCESTER

Oxford

Newport

BERKS

MIDDLESEX

London

Cardiff

Bristol

WILTS

Reading

Thames R.

Bristol Channel

Bath

Devizes

SURREY

Chatham

SOMERSET

KENT

Taunton

HANTS

DEVON

DORSET

Southampton

SUSSEX

Brighton

Portsmouth

Eastbourne

Hastings

Bournemouth

I. OF WIGHT

Strait of Dover

CORNWALL

Plymouth

ENGLISH CHANNEL

0   50   100 miles

The Massacre of Chios, Eugène Delacroix (1798–1863).
During the Greek war for independence, Turks slaughtered more than 20,000 Greeks in 1822, depicted in this
famous painting. (Louvre)

*Liberty Leading the Peo-
ple*, Eugene Delacroix
(1798–1863). Delacroix was
a colorful painter of dramatic and emotional
themes, as exemplified by
this imaginary scene from
the Revolution of 1830.
(Louvre)

later Associate Justice of the United States Supreme Court, were boldly proclaiming the need of a guaranteed annual income. In many quarters it was coming to be recognized that poverty is not always the fruit of laziness and improvidence, but may often be the product of conditions beyond the individual's control. These it may be the duty of the state to reduce or correct.

Basic organizations of capital rapidly emerged to take advantage of new economic opportunities and to serve in part as a checkmate to the power of labor. By the middle of the nineteenth century partnerships and joint-stock companies were giving way to trusts. These in turn were followed by mergers and cartels. Trusts are combinations of all or nearly all of the producers of certain articles in order to control their price and production. Mergers are combinations of companies producing the same or related articles. They differ from trusts in the fact that their constituent units generally lose their identity and are "merged" into a controlling corporation. Cartels may be defined as loose associations of independent companies for the primary purpose of restricting competition in the sale of their products. They differ from both trusts and mergers in not being corporate entities. They do not generally issue any stock or bonds of their own. The first cartels originated in Germany about 1870, but they did not become extensive until the decade before World War I. They flourished because they enabled German producers to gain great leverage in world trade. They did this by keeping domestic prices high and selling at a loss in foreign markets.

Trusts, mergers, and cartels

During the age of coal and iron, mechanized production was restricted primarily to Great Britain, France, Belgium, and the United States; and Great Britain was far in advance of the others. After 1860 industrialization spread until every one of the major powers had reaped a full harvest of its benefits and evils. The adoption of the new methods was especially conspicuous in Germany. Before 1860 the German states had been predominantly agrarian, with at least 60 per cent of their people obtaining their living from the soil. By 1914 the empire of the Kaisers was the greatest industrial nation in Europe, producing more steel than Great Britain and leading the world in the manufacture of chemicals, aniline dyes, and electrical and scientific equipment. For such remarkable expansion there were several main explanations. In the first place, Germany had no tradition of laissez faire. Her economists had been preaching for years that the state should intervene in every way possible to promote the economic strength of the nation. As a consequence it was easy for the government to bolster up feeble industries, to nationalize the railroads and operate them for the benefit of business, and even to encourage the growth of trusts. As a second reason may be mentioned the German emphasis upon applied science in the schools, resulting in an abundant supply of technicians who could be hired by industrial corporations for a low wage. The famous Krupp

The spread of industrialization: the Industrial Revolution in Germany

Industrialization in Germany. The Krupp munitions works at Essen in 1876.

munitions works at Essen employed a larger staff of trained scientists than any university in the world. Last, but by no means of least importance, was the fact that Germany acquired, as a result of her victory over France in 1870, the rich iron deposits of Lorraine, which ultimately supplied her with three-fourths of the ore for her basic industry of steel manufacture.

The industrialization of Russia, Italy, and Japan

Industrialization did not spread into eastern Europe quite so soon as it did into Germany, nor did it proceed as far. Nevertheless, by 1890 a considerable development of the factory system and of mechanized transportation had begun in Russia. The Industrial Revolution in Russia, like that in Germany, was in part the result of governmental encouragement. Through the influence of Count Serge Witte, able but domineering minister under Alexander III and Nicholas II, the government of the Tsars levied prohibitive tariffs and borrowed money from France to subsidize railroads and numerous industrial enterprises. These and other efforts bore some amazing fruit. By 1914 Russia was producing more iron than France, her coal production had more than doubled, and in textiles she ranked fourth in the world. No fewer than 3,000,000 people were engaged directly in manufacturing, while some of her industrial establishments employed as many as 10,000 workers.[3] The Industrial Revolution in Italy and Japan was also advanced largely by state intervention, at least in its earlier stages. In both countries the movement began about 1880 and had completed a cycle of definite progress by the outbreak of World War I. In Italy the government extended the railway system and fostered the growth of silk and cotton manufactures in such measure that Italian exports increased nearly 300 per cent between 1895 and 1914. The achievements of Japan were even

626   [3] Clive Day, *op. cit.,* p. 388.

more remarkable. By 1914 the little island empire had 6000 miles of railroad, almost entirely owned by the state. Her textile industry almost equaled that of Great Britain, while her foreign commerce had risen in value from virtually nothing to nearly $700,000,000.

5. THE PERSISTENCE OF SOCIAL AND ECONOMIC PROBLEMS

The First Industrial Revolution left numerous economic and social problems in its wake. The Second Revolution continued and accentuated some of these and brought others in its train. In some cases the source of these problems was largely economic, but in a goodly number it was basically social.

Notable among these problems essentially social was an enormous increase in population. Between the French Revolution and World War I the population of nearly every civilized country grew at an unprecedented rate. Some evidences of this phenomenon were noticeable as early as 1800, especially in England, where the increase was about 50 per cent in the second half of the eighteenth century. But in the main the spectacular growth came later. Between the Battle of Waterloo and the outbreak of World War I the population of England and Wales nearly quadrupled. That of Germany rose from about 25,000,000 in 1815 to almost 70,000,000 a hundred years later. The number of inhabitants in France almost doubled between the overthrow of Napoleon and the Franco-Prussian War, and the total of Russians more than doubled in the fifty years preceding 1914. In spite of such adverse factors as famine in Ireland and Russia, emigration to America, and disease resulting from congestion in cities, the population of Europe as a whole mounted from an estimated 190,000,000 in 1800 to 460,000,000 in 1914. During the same period the population of the United States increased from 5,000,000 to almost 100,000,000.

627

To discover the reasons for this unprecedented growth in numbers we must look to several factors. First, it was due in some measure to the effects of the Commercial Revolution in improving the vigor of peoples by providing a more abundant and a more varied diet. Second, it was a consequence of the establishment of infant and maternity hospitals and of advancements in medical science and sanitation, which led to the practical elimination of smallpox, scurvy, and cholera, at least from western Europe and America. A third cause was the influence of nationalism, of the growth of racial, pride and patriotic obsession. Peoples with a solid conviction of their own superiority and buoyant with hopes of victory in future struggles are almost certain to reproduce very rapidly. These were the qualities that characterized most of the nations in the nineteenth century. An equally important cause in Europe at least, was the influence of the industrial revolutions in making it possible for limited areas to support large numbers of people. This increase in population came about not only because the mechanization of agriculture increased the yield from the land, but also because the factory system enlarged the opportunities for earning a living away from the soil. Thus it became possible for countries rich in industrial resources to support several times as many people as ever could be done on an agrarian basis.

Closely related to growth of population as an effect of the industrial revolutions was an increasing urbanization of Western society. By 1914 the artificial conditions of city life had come to be the accepted norm for a large percentage of the inhabitants of industrialized nations. Growth in urbanization was particularly striking in such countries as Germany and England. In the former as late as 1840 there were only two cities of 100,000 inhabitants or more; in 1910 there were forty-eight. In England during the last thirty years of the nineteenth century, approximately one-third of the agricultural population withdrew permanently from the land. The English census of 1901 revealed that the number of persons engaged in farming was only about 20 per cent of the number employed in industrial pursuits. In the United States, despite its wealth of agricultural resources, there was a similar movement away from the land, albeit at a slower pace. By 1915 the proportion of Americans living in urban areas had risen to about 40 per cent. The causes of this drift to the cities and towns were the increasing attractions of urban life and the steady decline in need for agricultural labor as a result of mechanized farming. The effects were a mixture of good and evil. Escape from the soil freed large numbers of men and women from the isolation of rural life, from the tyranny of the weather, from the idiocies of primitive folkways, and from a humdrum existence of lonely toil on stubborn acres. But at the same time it transformed many of them into pawns or tools of their employers. It made some of them robots, who performed their tasks automatically with little sense of responsibility or comprehension of their place in the economic

Wentworth Street by Gustav Doré. The artist was much concerned with the overcrowding squalor which resulted from early industrialization in London.

scheme, and with nothing to inspire their efforts but the hope of a living wage. If it rescued them from the hazards of blight and drought, it plunged them into new dangers of loss of employment from overproduction and forced them to live pell-mell like rats in wretched slums.

A third great result of the Second Revolution was the creation of two new classes: an industrial bourgeoisie and a proletariat. The industrial bourgeoisie, composed of the owners of factories, mines, and railroads, cast in its lot with the old middle class of merchants, bankers, and lawyers. Thus strengthened in numbers and in influence, the combined bourgeoisie soon ceased to be merely a middle class and became for all practical purposes the ruling element in society. In some cases this rise to power was accomplished by pushing the old landed aristocracy into the background; in others, by joining with it. But no sooner had the capitalists and entrepreneurs gained the ascendancy than they began to divide among themselves. The great bankers and magnates of industry and commerce came to constitute an upper bourgeoisie with ambitions somewhat distinct from those of the lower bourgeoisie, made up of small merchants, small industrialists, and professional men. The tendency was for the upper bourgeoisie to become more and more deeply absorbed in finance capitalism. Its members were interested in stock-jobbing operations, in launching new ventures for an immediate profit, and in reorganizing businesses already in existence for purposes of monopolistic or speculative control. To the leaders of this class most forms of government intervention, except protective tariffs and suppression of strikes, were anathema; they insisted that free enterprise was absolutely essential to vigorous economic growth. The lower bourgeoisie began to show signs of an interest in economic stability and security.

The emergence of the industrial bourgeoisie

629

In some countries members of this class were to be found advocating measures to curb speculation, to fix prices, and even to provide for state ownership of public utilities.

The industrial revolutions also brought into existence a proletariat, which ultimately attained sufficient strength to challenge the supremacy of the bourgeoisie. In a sense the proletariat has existed since the dawn of civilization, for the term includes all persons who are dependent for their living upon a wage. The free workers in ancient Greece and Rome were proletarians, and so were the journeymen and the crofters and cotters in the Middle Ages. But prior to the First Industrial Revolution the wage earners were a small proportion of the working class, since the majority of those who toiled for a living were engaged in agriculture, originally as serfs and later as tenant farmers and sharecroppers. Further, the few proletarians who did exist were scarcely conscious of their identity as a class. The industrial revolutions, by concentrating large numbers of workers in the cities and subjecting them to common abuses, infused into wage earners a degree of solidarity and imbued them with a sense of common grievances. Nevertheless, their power as an economic class was limited for many years by stringent legislation. The right to strike, for instance, was not granted by any Western nation until after 1850. And not until late in the nineteenth century were the organized workers able to exert much influence upon the policies of governments.

That the industrial revolutions bestowed both social and material benefits upon the inhabitants of Western nations is a conclusion which few critics would flatly deny. Without question they supplied modern man with tremendous quantities of goods and with an astounding number of useful appliances. But whether the various classes participated in these benefits in anything like a just ratio is a different question. There seems little doubt that real wages, or wages in terms of purchasing power, rose quite rapidly during the nineteenth century. A leading economist, Sir Josiah Stamp, estimated that the ordinary Englishman in 1913 was four times as well off, in relation to the amount his income would buy, as were his ancestors in 1801. Evidences of improvement in standards of living were indicated by substantial increases in the consumption of quality foods, notably meat and milk. The per capita consumption of meat in Germany, for example, advanced from 38 pounds in 1816 to 115 pounds in 1912.

On the other hand, it is at least open to doubt that the mechanization of industry contributed as much to the well-being of the laboring classes as is commonly supposed, as during the First Revolution the introduction of machines often meant that able-bodied men were thrown out of employment by the cheap labor of women and children. Moreover, many of the factories and mines were dangerous and unsanitary. As a result, many British factory employees

*The rise of
the proletariat*

*The uneven
material benefits
of the industrial
revolutions*

*Early effects
upon living
conditions*

were scarcely much better off than the slaves on American plantations. But against these evils must be reckoned the fact that the industrial revolutions did facilitate the organization of workers, thus enabling them to use the power of collective action to improve their condition. Besides, the common people undoubtedly benefited from lower prices made possible by mass production.

6. THE DECLINE OF LAISSEZ FAIRE

Before the Second Industrial Revolution had run its course, it had begun to exert an influence toward economic democracy. That cabinets should be responsible to parliaments, and that every citizen should be entitled to vote, seemed to be matters of comparatively small moment so long as workers were at the mercy of a ruthlessly competitive industrial system. As generally defined, economic democracy implies that all men shall have a substantially equal opportunity to make the most of their latent abilities, and that no one shall suffer needlessly from the misfortunes of life. It is not synonymous with the old liberal concept of equality before the law, which, as Anatole France scornfully remarked, "forbids the rich man as well as the poor man to sleep under bridges, to beg in the streets, and to steal bread." Economic democracy means that little children shall not be exploited by selfish employers, that old people shall not be thrown on the human scrap heap when no longer able to work, and that the poor and helpless shall not be compelled to bear the whole burden of industrial accidents, unemployment, and disease. In short, it involves a somewhat drastic modification of the ideal of laissez faire, which appeared to be so firmly entrenched during most of the nineteenth century.

On the other hand, it should be remembered that the decline of laissez faire was not exclusively the result of the movement for economic democracy. The original form which modification of laissez faire often took on the Continent of Europe was protectionism, prompted by the desire of the rising industrial bourgeoisie to stave off competition from England. Protectionism was sometimes followed by outright subsidies, illustrated by the bounties given by the Italian and French governments to the silk industry and to various branches of agriculture. In such nations as Germany, Italy, and Russia the railroads and telegraph and telephone lines were either built by the state, or nationalized afterwards, primarily for purposes of military efficiency. In France the tobacco and match manufacturing industries were taken over by the state as sources of public revenue, and were operated as government monopolies. Even a great deal of the social legislation enacted in Continental countries was inspired by factors of nationalism, militarism, and paternalism. Governments desired to win the loyalty of all classes of their subjects and to make sure of a healthy supply of cannon fodder in time of war.

The first of the great powers to enact a comprehensive program of social legislation was Germany, under the guidance of her shrewd but dictatorial Chancellor, Prince von Bismarck. The reasons why Germany should have taken the lead are not difficult to fathom. Unlike Great Britain and France she had never been deeply affected by eighteenth-century liberalism; hence she had no strong traditions of individualism or laissez faire. While her political philosophers were persistently affirming the subjection of the individual to the state, her economists were preaching doctrines of national self-sufficiency and paternalism. Bismarck himself maintained that it was the duty of the state to regulate all functions of society in the national interest and to look after the weaker citizens, "that they may not be run over and trampled under foot on the highway of life." But he had other reasons also for engaging in what appeared to be a defense of the workers' rights. He was anxious to undermine the growing popularity of socialism by stealing a portion of its thunder. In a speech in the Reichstag he frankly avowed his purpose of insuring the workingman against sickness and old age so that "these gentlemen [the Social Democrats] will sound their bird call in vain." In addition, he had military purposes in mind. He was desirous of making the German proletarian a loyal soldier and of safeguarding his health in some measure from the debilitating effects of factory labor. Bismarck's program of social legislation was initiated in 1883–1884 with the adoption of laws insuring workmen against sickness and accidents. These acts were soon followed by others providing for rigid factory inspection, limiting the employment of women and children, fixing maximum hours of labor, establishing public employment agencies, and insuring workers against incapacity on account of old age. By 1890, when Bismarck was forced to retire, Germany had adopted nearly all the elements, with the exception of unemployment insurance, in the pattern of social legislation that later became familiar in the majority of Western nations.

Bismarck

Other countries on the Continent of Europe soon followed the German example. A French law of 1892 not only regulated the employment of women and children but prescribed a maximum day of ten hours for all workers; in 1905 this limit was reduced to nine hours. Other acts of the French parliament ensured free medical attendance for laborers and their families, accorded protection to the activities of labor unions, and compelled employers to compensate workers for injuries. The capstone of this system of legislation was added in 1910 with the passage of a law providing old-age pensions. The series of laws enacted in Italy was much the same, except for the absence of the provision regarding free medical attention. The Italian laws were supplemented, however, by an act of 1912 providing for nationalized life insurance and also by measures encouraging cooperative stores.

Because of her strong individualist traditions, Great Britain lagged behind the other great powers in western Europe. To be sure, there had been some early progress, illustrated by laws prohibiting the employment of women and children in underground labor in the mines. But the British government adopted no extensive measures of social reform until after the rejuvenated Liberal party came into power in 1905. The old generation of Liberals under Gladstone, representing primarily the business classes, had been committed to principles of laissez faire. Their energies had been absorbed very largely in problems of political reform and of home rule for Ireland. But in 1898 Gladstone died, and control over his party passed into younger hands. Several of the new leaders—Herbert Asquith, David Lloyd George, and Winston Churchill—were enthusiastic idealists, resolved to wage "implacable warfare" against misery and squalor. Upon coming to power in 1905 these ardent reformers determined to throw the old-fashioned doctrines of their party to the winds and transform Britannia into a paradise of fair treatment for all. During the years that followed, down to the beginning of World War I, they succeeded in having written into the statutes the most remarkable schedule of reform legislation since the Glorious Revolution. First came the Workmen's Compensation Act of 1906 and the Old Age Pensions law of 1908. Next came the Trade Boards Act of 1909, authorizing special commissions to fix the minimum pay for workers in sweatshops. In 1911 the Liberal cabinet procured the passage of the great National Insurance Act introducing a system of contributory insurance against sickness for all wage earners.

To this list of more conventional social reforms of the Liberal government must be added certain others for which there was almost no precedent. In 1909 the Liberal Parliament enacted a law permitting the clearance of slum areas and authorizing local authorities to provide respectable housing for the poor. This law set a precedent for an enormous amount of public housing construction in later years, especially in the period after 1918. Among the most significant of all the social reforms of the Liberal regime were certain provisions incorporated in the Lloyd George budget of 1909. In this remarkable fiscal program David Lloyd George proposed not only to increase the regular income taxes but to levy in addition a super-tax on the incomes of the rich. He recommended also that the government should confiscate 20 per cent of the unearned increment of land values, and that a heavy tax should be imposed on all undeveloped land appraised in excess of £50 per acre. The object of these measures was twofold: to raise revenue for old-age pensions and for various forms of social insurance and to level down great fortunes. It was hoped that the tax on unearned increment and on undeveloped lands would help to break the land monopoly of the richer nobles—of such magnates as the Duke of Westminster, who owned

Social reform in Britain, 1905–1914

New departures in economic and social reform

600 acres in London, and the Marquess of Bute, who owned one-half of the area of Cardiff. Thrown out by the House of Lords, the Lloyd George budget was finally enacted into law after the Liberals were returned to power in the January election of 1910.

SELECTED READINGS

· Items so designated are available in paperbound editions.

THE FIRST INDUSTRIAL REVOLUTION

· Ashton, T. S., *The Industrial Revolution, 1760–1830*, New York, 1948 (Galaxy). A clear introductory account of the First Revolution.

Bowen, Frank, *A Century of Atlantic Travel*, Boston, 1930.

Day, Clive, *Economic Development in Modern Europe*, New York, 1933. Interesting and well-written.

Dietz, F. C., *The Industrial Revolution*, New York, 1927. Good on technological progress.

Heaton, Herbert, *Economic History of Europe*, New York, 1936, Chs. 21–30.

· Mantoux, Paul, *The Industrial Revolution in the Eighteenth Century*, New York, 1947 (Torchbook).

· Mumford, Lewis, *Technics and Civilization*, New York, 1934 (Harbinger). Stimulating.

Ogg, F. A., and Sharp, W. R., *Economic Development of Modern Europe*, New York, 1929.

Reid, W. S., *Economic History of Great Britain*, New York, 1956.

· Tawney, R. H., *The Acquisitive Society*, New York, 1920 (Harvest).

Taylor, George, *The Transportation Revolution, 1815–1860*, New York, 1956.

Toynbee, Arnold, *Lectures on the Industrial Revolution of the Eighteenth Century in England*, London, 1937. Valuable for the early history.

THE SECOND INDUSTRIAL REVOLUTION

Barnes, H. E., *An Economic History of the Western World*, New York, 1937.

Bonbright, J. C., and Means, G. C., *The Holding Company, Its Public Significance and Its Regulation*, New York, 1932.

· Briggs, A., *The Age of Improvement*, London, 1960 (Torchbook).

Edwards, G. W., *The Evolution of Finance Capitalism*, New York, 1938.

· Feis, Herbert, *Europe, the World's Banker, 1870–1914*, New Haven, 1930 (Norton Library).

Giedion, S., *Mechanization Takes Command*, New York, 1948.

Hobson, J. A., *The Evolution of Modern Capitalism*, New York, 1926.

Levy, H., *The New Industrial System*, London, 1936.

Polakov, W. N., *The Power Age*, New York, 1930.

· Rostow, W. W., *The Stages of Economic Growth*, New York, 1960 (Cambridge University Press).

CHAPTER 22

Critics and Apologists of Industrialization

If a man does not keep pace with his companions, perhaps it is because he hears a different drummer. Let him step to the music which he hears, however measured or faraway.
—Henry Thoreau, *Walden*, XVIII, *Conclusion*

The First Industrial Revolution produced its full complement of economic theory—part of it to justify the new order, part of it for critical analysis, and the remainder as a gospel of social reform. No sooner had the factory system been well established and profits begun to flow into the coffers of the new lords of creation than some of the more articulate rose up to defend their privileges. In doing so they often displayed a coldness toward the plight of the masses and a confidence in their own right to inherit the earth which the nobles of the *ancien régime* might well have envied. Indeed, some of the apologists for the new system evolved into a type of economic Bourbons, learning nothing from the past and closing their eyes to the dangers of the future. This attitude was expressed in the doctrines that private property is sacred, that every man has a right to do what he will with his own, and that poverty is invariably the result of laziness and incompetence. Several of the high priests of the new capitalism went so far as to declare that poverty was a good thing for the masses since it taught them to respect their superiors and to be grateful to Providence for such blessings as they did receive.

Economic Bourbonism

I. THE ECONOMIC LIBERALS

But some of the economic theory in defense of the capitalist ideal was more disinterested. Of this type were the teachings of the classical economists, or economic liberals, as they are often called. The founder of classical economics was Adam Smith, whose work was

635

discussed in a preceding chapter. Though Smith wrote before industrial capitalism had reached its full stature, and though some of his teachings did not harmonize well with a strict interpretation of laissez faire, there was nevertheless enough in the general implications of his theory to cause him to be acclaimed the prophet of capitalist ideals. The specific doctrines of classical economics, however, were largely the work of Smith's disciples—including such eminent writers as Thomas R. Malthus, David Ricardo, James Mill, and Nassau Senior. The chief elements in the theory subscribed to by most of these men may be summarized as follows:

(1) Economic individualism. Every individual is entitled to use for his own best interests the property he has inherited or acquired by any legitimate method. Each person must be allowed to do what he likes with his own so long as he does not trespass upon the equal right of others to do the same.

(2) Laissez faire. The functions of the state should be reduced to the lowest minimum consistent with public safety. The government should shrink itself into the role of a modest policeman, preserving order and protecting property, but never in any wise interfering with the operation of economic processes.

(3) Obedience to natural law. There are immutable laws operating in the realm of economics as in every sphere of the universe. Examples are the law of supply and demand, the law of diminishing returns, the law of rent, and so on. These laws must be recognized and respected; failure to do so is disastrous.

(4) Freedom of contract. Every individual should be free to negotiate the best kind of contract he can obtain from any other individual. In particular, the liberty of workers and employers to bargain with each other as to wages and hours should not be hampered by laws or by the collective power of labor unions.

(5) Free competition and free trade. Competition serves to keep prices down, to eliminate inefficient producers, and to ensure the maximum production in accordance with public demand. Therefore no monopolies should be tolerated, nor any price-fixing laws for the benefit of incompetent enterprisers. Further, in order to force each country to engage in the production of those things it is best fitted to produce, all protective tariffs should be abolished. Free international trade will also help to keep prices down.

Several of the disciples of Adam Smith made distinctive contributions of their own. For example, Thomas R. Malthus (1766–1834) introduced the element of pessimism which caused the new economics to be branded as "the dismal science." A clergyman of the Anglican church, rector of a small parish in Surrey, Malthus published his memorable *Essay on Population* in 1798. Issued originally in pamphlet form, the *Essay* grew out of some discussions which the author had with his father concerning the perfectibility of man. The elder Malthus was a disciple of Rousseau, but he was so impressed with his son's arguments against the superficial optimism of the Frenchman that he urged him to put them in writing. The pamphlet created an immediate sensation and provoked discussion for many years afterward. In 1803 it was expanded into a book on the basis of extended researches which the author undertook to refute his critics. The substance of the Malthusian theory is the contention that nature has set stubborn limits to the progress of mankind in happiness and wealth. Because of the voracity of the sexual appetite there is a natural tendency for population to increase more rapidly than the means of subsistence. To be sure, there are powerful checks, such as war, famine, disease, and vice; but these, when they operate effectively, augment still further the burden of human misery. It follows that poverty and pain are inescapable. Even if laws were to be passed distributing all wealth equally, the condition of the poor would be only temporarily improved; in a very short time they would begin to raise larger families, with the result that the last state of their class would be as bad as the first. In the second edition of his work Malthus advocated postponement of marriage as a means of relief, but he continued to stress the danger that population would outrun any possible increase in the means of subsistence.

The main teachings of Malthus were taken over and elaborated by David Ricardo (1772–1823), an English Jew who embraced Christianity at the age of twenty-one and married a Quaker. By the

The Launderers by Honoré Daumier. In his paintings and drawings Daumier's insight as a social critic equaled his abilities as an artist.

time he was twenty-five he had accumulated a fortune on the Stock Exchange and soon became one of the richest men in Europe. As an economist Ricardo is famous, first of all, for his subsistence theory of wages. According to this theory, wages tend toward a level which is just sufficient to enable the workers "to subsist and perpetuate their race, without either increase or diminution." This he held to be an iron law, from which there is no escape. If wages should rise temporarily above the subsistence standard, the population would increase, and the ensuing competition for jobs would quickly force the rate of pay down to its former level. Ricardo is noted, in the second place, for his teachings in regard to rent. He maintained that rent is determined by the cost of production on the poorest land that must be brought under cultivation, and that consequently as a country fills up with people an ever-increasing proportion of the social income is taken by the landlords. Though a great proprietor himself, he denounced the recipients of rent as the real enemies of both the capitalists and the workers. Finally, Ricardo is important for his labor theory of value, which influenced one of the main doctrines of the Marxian socialists. However, he attached some significance also to the role of capital in determining value—an idea which was abhorrent to Marx.

In his later years Ricardo frequently associated himself with an interesting group of reformers in England known as the philosophical radicals. The foremost economist among them was James Mill (1773–1836), who, as already mentioned, enjoyed some reputation as a Utilitarian philosopher. While the teachings of James Mill would now be considered far from radical, they were nevertheless liberal enough to show that the classical economics was not hopelessly benighted and reactionary. The doctrines he incorporated in his *Elements of Political Economy* included the following: (1) the chief object of practical reformers should be to prevent the population from growing too rapidly, on the assumption that the wealth available for productive purposes does not naturally increase as fast as the number of inhabitants; (2) the value of commodities depends entirely upon the quantity of labor necessary to produce them; and (3) the unearned increment of land, or the increase in the value of land which comes exclusively from social causes, such as the building of a new factory in the vicinity, should be heavily taxed by the state. This last doctrine, based upon Ricardo's theory of rent, was destined for a wide popularity in England. In modified form it became part of the gospel of the Liberal party in the early 1900's, and was a feature of the celebrated Lloyd George budget of 1909.

Probably the ablest of the classical economists who came after Ricardo was Nassau William Senior (1790–1864). The first professor of political economy at Oxford, he was also a distinguished lawyer. Like most of his predecessors, Senior regarded economics as a deductive science. He maintained that its truths could all be derived from a limited number of great abstract principles. His main contribution was his theory that *abstinence* creates a title to wealth. He admitted that labor and natural resources are the primary instruments of value, but he contended that abstinence is a secondary instrument. Therefore he argued that the capitalist who has refrained from enjoying all of his wealth in order to accumulate a surplus for investment has a claim on the profits of production. His abstinence involves sacrifice and pain just as does the work of the laborer. Consequently it is unfair to give the entire reward to the latter. The evil reputation of Senior comes primarily from the fact that he condemned the demands of the trade unions for a reduction of the working day. He had an honest but mistaken conviction that the whole net profit of an industrial enterprise is derived from the last hour of operation. Hence to shorten the working day would eliminate profits and thereby result in closing the factories. For this doctrine he was dubbed by his critics "Last Hour" Senior.

2.   DOUBTERS AND REBELS

Most of the leading classical economists or economic liberals were citizens of Great Britain. This was true partly because economic liberalism harmonized well with political liberalism, which was stronger in Britain than in any other European country, and partly because British industrialists were beginning to perceive notable advantages from a policy of free trade with the rest of the world. On the Continent of Europe, however, conditions were entirely different. There the old traditions of strong government still lingered. Moreover, Continental manufacturers were attempting to build up industrial establishments which would be able to compete with the British. To achieve this, it was desirable to have the patronage and protection of the state. Hence we should not be surprised to find that the majority of the opponents of economic liberalism were natives of countries on the Continent. Nevertheless, at least one of its abler critics was an Englishman—the brilliant Utilitarian philosopher, John Stuart Mill (1806–1873). Though Mill as an economist is often considered a member of the classical school, he actually repudiated a number of its most sacred premises. First, he rejected the universality of natural law. He admitted that there are unchangeable laws governing the field of production, but he insisted that the distribution of wealth can be regulated by society for the benefit of the majority of its members. Second, he advocated more radical departures from laissez faire than any recommended by his forerunners. He did not oppose legislation, under certain conditions, for shortening the working day, and he believed that the state might properly take preliminary steps toward the redistribution of wealth by taxing inheritances and by appropriating the unearned increment of land. In the fourth book of his *Principles of Political Economy* he urged the abolition of the wage system and looked forward to a society of producers' cooperatives in which the workers would own

John Stuart Mill

639

the factories and elect the managers to run them. On the other hand, it should not be forgotten that Mill was too much of an individualist ever to go very far in the direction of socialism. He distrusted the state, and his real reason for advocating producers' cooperatives was not to exalt the power of the proletariat but to give to the individual worker the fruits of his labor.

Friedrich List

The most noted of the German economists who wrote in direct opposition to the theories of the classical school was Friedrich List (1789–1846), who derived inspiration for some of his ideas from seven years' residence in America. List condemned the doctrines of laissez faire and freedom of international trade. Contending that the wealth of a nation is determined less by natural resources than by the productive powers of its citizens, he declared that it is the duty of governments to further the arts and sciences and to see to it that every individual makes the most of his talents in cooperating for the general good. He stressed the well-rounded development of the nation as all-important regardless of the effects upon the immediate fortunes of particular citizens. Holding that manufactures are essential to such a development, he demanded protective tariffs until the new industries should be able to compete with those of any other country. He believed that the government should regulate and plan the development of industry so as to balance production and consumption. It is interesting that List was also an imperialist. He demanded a German customs union which would extend "over the whole coast from the mouth of the Rhine to the frontier of Poland including Holland and Denmark."[1] He insisted also that Germany had a mission to lead in world affairs and to civilize barbaric and benighted countries. He was one of the earliest exponents of German expansionism and of Germany's destiny as a world power.

The utopian
socialists

We come next to a group of theorists who were more interested in social justice than in discovering economic laws or in laying the foundations of national prosperity. The earliest exemplars of this more radical attitude were the utopian socialists, who take their name from the fact that they proposed idealistic schemes for cooperative societies, in which all would work at their appropriate tasks and share the results of their common efforts. To a considerable extent the utopian socialists were the heirs of the Enlightenment. Like the philosophers of that movement they believed that all crime and greed were the results of an evil environment. If men could be freed from vicious custom and from a social structure which facilitates enslavement of the weak by the strong, then all might live together in harmony and peace. Accordingly, the utopian socialists recommended the establishment of model communities, largely self-contained, where most of the instruments of production would be collectively owned and where government would be mainly on a

[1] S. S. Lloyd (trans.), *The National System of Political Economy*, p. 143.

New Lanark. In his textile mill and workers' town, Robert Owen proved that productivity could increase with a reduction of working hours from fourteen a day to ten. The factory town was a showplace for visitors from abroad during the early nineteenth century.

voluntary basis. Among the original propagators of such plans was the Frenchman Charles Fourier (1772–1837), but the soundest and most realistic of them all was Robert Owen (1771–1858). A native of Wales, Owen rose from an artisan apprentice to co-proprietor and manager of a great cotton mill at New Lanark in Scotland. Here he built new houses for his workers, reduced their hours of work from fourteen to ten, and established free schools for their children. The severe depression that followed in the wake of the Napoleonic wars convinced him that the economic order was in need of reform. Like many others since his day, he concluded that the profit system was the cause of all the trouble. The existence of profit, he maintained, makes it impossible for the worker to buy all the things he has produced. The result is overproduction, periodic crises, and unemployment. As a solution, Owen proposed the organization of society into cooperative communities, in which the sole reward to each member would be payment in proportion to his actual hours of labor. A number of such communities were set up, the most famous being the ones at Orbiston, Scotland, and New Harmony, Indiana. For a variety of reasons all of them failed within a very short time.

A more influential form of socialism was the so-called "scientific socialism" of Karl Marx (1818–1883). The son of a Jewish lawyer who had turned Christian for professional reasons, Marx was born at Trèves near Coblenz in the Rhineland. His father planned for him a career as a conventional bourgeois lawyer and, with that end in view, sent him to the University of Bonn. But young Marx soon displayed a distaste for the law and abandoned his legal studies for the

Karl Marx

641

Friedrich Engels

pursuit of philosophy and history. After a year at Bonn he went to the University of Berlin, where he fell under the influence of a group of disciples of Hegel who were giving the teachings of their master a slightly radical twist. Though Marx earned the degree of doctor of philosophy at the University of Jena in 1841, his critical views prevented him from realizing his ambition of becoming a university professor. He turned to journalism, editing various radical periodicals and contributing articles to others. In 1848 he was arrested on a charge of high treason for participating in the revolutionary movement in Prussia. Though acquitted by a middle-class jury, he was soon afterward expelled from the country. In the meantime he had formed an intimate friendship with Friedrich Engels (1820–1895), who remained his lifelong disciple and *alter ego*. In 1848 the two men issued the *Communist Manifesto*, the "birth cry of modern socialism." From then until his death in 1883 Marx spent nearly all of his years in London, struggling against poverty, occasionally writing a few articles (some of which he sold to the New York *Tribune* for $5 apiece), but giving most of his time to poring over dusty manuscripts in the British Museum, gathering material for a great work on political economy. In 1867 he published the first volume of this work under the title of *Das Kapital*. Two other volumes were issued after his death from manuscripts revised and edited by some of his disciples.

Not all of the teachings of Karl Marx were entirely original. For some of his ideas he was indebted to Hegel; for others to the French socialist, Louis Blanc (1811–1882), and probably to Ricardo. Nevertheless, it was Marx who first combined these ideas into a comprehensive system and gave them meaning as an explanation of the

The Communist Manifesto. A facsimile of the cover of the 1848 edition.

facts of political economy. Since Marxist theory has been one of the most influential bodies of thought in modern times, it is necessary to understand its doctrines. Fundamental among them are the following:

(1) The economic interpretation of history. All of the great political, social, and intellectual movements of history have been determined by the economic environment out of which they arose. Marx did not insist that the economic motive is the sole explanation of human behavior, but he did maintain that every fundamental historical development, regardless of its character on the surface, has been the result of alterations in methods of producing and exchanging goods. Thus the Protestant Revolution was essentially an economic movement; the disagreements over religious belief were mere "ideological veils," concealing the actual causes.

The economic
interpretation
of history

(2) Dialectical materialism. Every distinct economic system, based upon a definite pattern of production and exchange, grows to a point of maximum efficiency, then develops contradictions or weaknesses within it which produce its rapid decay. Meanwhile the foundations of an opposing system are being gradually laid, and eventually this new system displaces the old, at the same time absorbing its most valuable elements. This dynamic process of historical evolution will continue by a series of victories of the new over the old, until the perfect goal of communism has been attained. After that there will doubtless still be change, but it will be change within the limits of communism itself.

Dialectical ma-
terialism

(3) The class struggle. All history has been made up of struggles between classes. In ancient times there was a struggle between masters and slaves; in the Middle Ages there was a conflict between lords and serfs; now there has been a narrowing down to a struggle between the class of capitalists and the proletariat. The former includes those who derive their chief income from *owning* the means of production and from exploiting the labor of others. The proletariat includes those who are dependent for their living primarily upon a wage, who must sell their labor power in order to exist.

The class
struggle

(4) The doctrine of surplus value. All wealth is created by the worker. Capital creates nothing, but is itself created by labor. The value of all commodities is determined by the quantity of labor power necessary to produce them. But the worker does not receive the full value which his labor power creates; he receives a wage, which ordinarily is just enough to enable him to subsist and reproduce his kind. Most of the difference between the value he produces and what he receives is *surplus value*, which goes to the capitalist. In general, it consists of three elements: interest, rent, and profits. Since the capitalist creates none of these things, it follows that he is a robber, who appropriates the fruits of the laborer's toil.

Surplus value

(5) The theory of socialist evolution. After capitalism has received its death blow at the hands of the workers, it will be followed by the stage of socialism. This will have three characteristics: the dictatorship of the proletariat; payment in accordance with

work performed; and ownership and operation by the state of all means of production, distribution, and exchange. But socialism is intended to be merely a transition to something higher. In time it will be succeeded by communism, the perfect goal of historical evolution. Communism will mean, first of all, the classless society. No one will live by owning, but all men solely by working. The state will now disappear; it will be relegated to the museum of antiquities, "along with the bronze ax and the spinning wheel." Nothing will replace it except voluntary associations to operate the means of production and provide for social necessities. But the *essence* of communism is payment in accordance with needs. The wage system will be completely abolished. Each citizen will be expected to work in accordance with his faculties and will be entitled to receive from the total fund of wealth produced an amount in proportion to his needs. This is the acme of justice according to the Marxist conception. Psychologically, Marx was one of the original exponents of "alienation." He conceived of modern man as divorced from the conditions of his natural life, a wanderer in a strange land with no sense of his mission or destiny.

The influence of Karl Marx upon the nineteenth and twentieth centuries can only be compared with that of Voltaire or Rousseau upon the eighteenth. His doctrine of the economic interpretation of history is a popular theory even among historians who are not his followers. He numbers his disciples in every civilized nation of this planet and in a great many underdeveloped countries besides. He is almost a god in Russia, where his dogma of dialectical materialism is accepted not only as a foundation of economics but as a test to which science, philosophy, and art must also conform. In every industrialized nation before World War I there was a socialist political party of considerable importance, the one in Germany having the largest representation in the Reichstag after 1912. Nearly everywhere the growth of socialism was a vital influence in furthering the enactment of social insurance and minimum wage laws and in promoting taxation of incomes and inheritances for the purpose of redistributing wealth. Marx, of course, was not interested in these things as ends in themselves, but the ruling classes were eventually persuaded to adopt them as a convenient tub to be thrown to the socialist whale. Socialists have also quite generally lent their support to the co-operative movement, to government ownership of railroads and public utilities, and to innumerable schemes for protecting workers and consumers against the power of monopoly capitalism.

Toward the end of the nineteenth century the followers of Marx split into two factions. The majority in most countries adhered to the doctrines of a group known as the revisionists, who, as their name implies, believed that the theories of Marx should be *revised* to bring them into line with changing conditions. The other faction was made up of the strict Marxists, who insisted that not one jot or tittle of the master's teachings should be modified. In addition to this cleavage in general attitude there were also specific differences. Whereas the revisionists advocated the attainment of socialism by peaceful and gradual methods, the strict Marxists were revolutionists. The revisionists concentrated their attention upon immediate reforms; the strict Marxists demanded the dictatorship of the proletariat or nothing. The leaders of the majority faction were willing to recognize the interests of separate nations; they were prone to talk about duty to the fatherland, and they frequently supported the demands of their governments for increased armaments and for lengthened terms of military service. The strict Marxists, on the other hand, were uncompromising internationalists; they held to the contention of Marx that the world proletariat is one great brotherhood, and they frowned upon patriotism and nationalism as capitalist devices to throw dust in the eyes of the workers. On the whole, it was the revisionists who gained control of the socialist parties in the majority of Western nations. The Social Democratic party in Germany, the Unified Socialist party in France, and the Socialist party in the United States were all largely dominated by the moderate faction. In Britain leadership of the Labour party was supplied in most cases by the Fabian socialists, so named from their policy of delay in imitation of the tactics of Fabius, a Roman general in the wars against Carthage. Prominent among the Fabians were Beatrice and Sidney Webb, the novelist H. G. Wells, and the dramatist George Bernard Shaw.

Revisionists and strict Marxists

3. ANARCHISTS AND SYNDICALISTS

Not all critics of the economic and social regime produced by the First Industrial Revolution were socialists. Quite a few became anarchists. Strictly defined, anarchism means opposition to all government based upon force. The followers of this philosophy have generally conceded that some form of social organization is necessary, but they condemn the coercive state as absolutely incompatible with human liberty. As to the problem of what should be done with the economic system, the anarchists have sharply disagreed. Some have been pure individualists, holding that man's right to acquire and use property should be subject only to the laws of nature. The father of anarchism, William Godwin (1756–1836), believed that if the land were made as free as the air, no further change in the economic structure would be necessary. In the judgment of the French anarchist, Pierre Proudhon (1809–1865), an arrangement whereby society would provide every man with free and unlimited credit would be a sufficient means of ensuring economic justice. Such a plan, he thought, would prevent anyone from monopolizing the resources of the earth and would guarantee to the citizen who was thrifty and industrious the full reward of his labors.

Anarchism

But the first of the anarchists to exert much influence were those who combined their hatred of the state with a definite philosophy of collectivism. Foremost among them were the three Russian aristocrats, Mikhail Bakunin (1814–1876), Peter Kropotkin (1842–1921), and Leo Tolstoi (1828–1910). Though often classified as a communistic anarchist, Bakunin was really much closer to socialism. Indeed, for a time he was associated with the followers of Marx in the International Workingmen's Association, organized in London in 1864. His program for a new society included collective ownership of the means of production, abolition of surplus value, and payment in accordance with work performed. In other words, it was much like that of the socialist stage of the Marxists, except, of course, that it did not involve the preservation of the state. Bakunin is also sometimes regarded as the father of terroristic anarchism. He advocated the overthrow of the state and of capitalism by violence. His followers were alleged to have been responsible for assassinating President McKinley, President Carnot of France, and King Humbert I of Italy. But most anarchists of the collectivist school condemned these tactics. For example, Prince Kropotkin denounced the use of individual violence under any conditions. He believed that a final revolutionary effort would be necessary, but he preferred that the state should be weakened by peaceful methods, by gradually convincing people that it is an unnecessary evil, that it breeds wars, and that it exists primarily to enable some men to exploit others. From the standpoint of economic reform, Kropotkin was a communist. He insisted that all property except articles of personal use should be socially owned, and that payment should be on the basis of need.

The most noted of all the collectivistic anarchists and one of the most interesting figures of modern times was Count Leo Tolstoi. Best known for his novels, which will be discussed in a later connection, Tolstoi was also one of the greatest of Russian philosophers. His ideas were born of strenuous emotional conflict and of an almost despairing search for a way of life that would satisfy his restless intellect. He indulged for a time in fashionable dissipation, attempted to relieve his troubled mind by philanthropic activities, and then finally abandoned it all for the life of a simple peasant. He came to the conclusion that no progress could be made in remedying the ills of society until the upper classes renounced their privileges and adopted the humble existence of men who toil for their bread. Tolstoi based much of his philosophy upon the New Testament, especially upon the Sermon on the Mount. He found in Jesus' teachings of meekness, humility, and nonresistance the essential principles of a just society. Above all, he condemned the use of violence, regardless of the purpose for which it is employed. Violence brutalizes man; it places its user in the hands of his enemies; and, as long as force is available as a weapon, reliance upon civilized methods is almost impossible.

A third of the great radical philosophies produced by the Industrial Revolution was syndicalism, whose chief exponent was Georges Sorel (1847–1922). Syndicalism demands the abolition of both capitalism and the state and the reorganization of society into associations of producers. It resembles anarchism in its opposition to the state; but whereas the anarchist demands the abolition of force, the syndicalist would retain it, even after the state has been destroyed. Syndicalism also resembles socialism in that both would involve collective ownership of the means of production; but instead of making the state the owner and operator of the means of production, the syndicalist would delegate these functions to associations of producers. Thus all the steel mills would be owned and operated by the workers in the steel industry, the coal mines by the workers in the coal industry, and so on. Further, these associations or syndicates would take the place of the state, each one governing its own members in all of their activities as producers. In all other matters the workers would be free from interference. On the other hand, Sorel entertained no illusions as to the capacity of the masses for self-government. He regarded the average man as very much of a sheep, fit only to be a follower. He believed, therefore, that the ruling authority in the syndicates should be exercised quite frankly by the intelligent few.

The least radical among all the critics of capitalist economics were the Christian socialists. The founder of Christian socialism was Robert de Lamennais (1782–1854), a French Catholic priest who sought to revive the Christian religion as an aid to reform and social justice. From France the movement spread to England and was adopted by a number of Protestant intellectuals. In its early days Christian socialism was little more than a demand for application of the teachings of Jesus to the problems created by industry, but in later years it began to assume a more concrete form. In 1891 Leo XIII, "the workingman's Pope," issued his famous encyclical *Rerum novarum*, in which he revived with a modern slant the liberal economic attitude of St. Thomas Aquinas. Though the encyclical expressly recognized private property as a natural right and vigorously repudiated the Marxist doctrine of the class war, at the same time it strongly discountenanced unlimited profits. It appealed to employers to respect the dignity of their workers as men and as Christians and not to treat them as "chattels to make money by, or to look upon them merely as so much muscle or physical power." By way of specific proposals, it recommended factory legislation, the formation of labor unions, an increase in the number of small landowners, and limitation of hours of employment.[2] The issuance of this encyclical gave a mighty impulse to the growth of Christian socialism among liberal Catholics. In European countries before

Syndicalism

Georges Sorel

Christian socialism

---

[2] The substance of Leo's encyclical was reaffirmed in 1931 by Pope Pius XI in a new encyclical, *Quadragesimo Anno*.

World War I, Catholic parties frequently played an active role, sometimes in combination with the moderate Marxists, in furthering the movement for social legislation.

4. EXPRESSIONS OF ANTIMATERIALISM

In defense of wealth

Most writers in the nineteenth century took it for granted that industrialization was a beneficent thing. Since the Industrial Revolution showed itself capable of producing comforts and luxuries without parallel, it must be a boon to mankind. "Wealth" was commonly given its original meaning of "weal" or "welfare." Even the socialists never questioned its desirability but advocated merely that it be better distributed. They seldom doubted that *their* system would accomplish this goal for the masses.

The Anti-industrialists: (1) Thomas Carlyle

Not everyone agreed that industrial growth and the production and accumulation of goods were unmixed blessings. Tolstoi, we have seen, called upon his followers to renounce material wealth and to cultivate a life close to the soil with freedom from the envy and strife of industrial man. Even earlier suggestions of anti-industrialism were to be found in the writings of Thomas Carlyle (1795–1881). True, he sometimes applauded industry and its marvelous possibilities for the benefit of man. But he deplored the depressions it created and characterized the spectacle of men willing to work and unable to find work as "perhaps the saddest sight" under a regime of unequal justice. Most of all, he deplored the substitution of a "cash nexus" between man and man under the new regime of laissez faire. He called for the revival of chivalry, "a chivalry of labor" that would give to the workingman a status of honor equal to that of his employer. Much of Carlyle's philosophy bore a medieval tinge: his contempt for democrcy and utilitarianism and his worship of a universal spirit that guides all the forces of history. Its real progenitor, however, was the German Idealism of Kant and Hegel. In this he found late in life the spiritual solace to displace the agnosticism and despair of his earlier years.

(2) John Ruskin

More staunchly representative of antimaterialism was Carlyle's younger contemporary, John Ruskin (1819–1900). Like his forerunner, Ruskin had a tendency to look back to the Middle Ages. Neither had much use for democracy. But Ruskin's philosophy was more nearly that of the aesthete and active reformer. He was repelled not only by the poverty and degradation of the industrial system but also by its ugliness. More emphatically than Carlyle, he condemned the ferocious capitalist struggle for profits and urged that workers be treated as partners in industry, entitled to a more generous share of what they produced.

Finally, no account of the nineteenth century revolt against materialism would be complete without some attention to the two extremists William Morris (1834–1896) and Henry David Thoreau

(1817–1862). Both were aesthetes and humanitarians, though neither showed great sympathy for the hurts and ills of mankind. Morris was the prophet of a pre-industrial age, of an England of green fields and neat gardens, of cities "small and white and clean." He detested mechanized production with its stress on quantity and neglect of quality. Even in his socialism, as expressed in *News from Nowhere* and the *Dream of John Ball,* he celebrated the merits of small enterprise and hand work. Yet he abandoned the British Socialism he had been active in founding as anarchist influences within the movement gained strength.

The American essayist and critic Thoreau agreed with Morris in only a few particulars. Both were enemies of industrialism but Thoreau took a more radical stance. He abhorred all work and performed just enough to provide the bare necessities of living. He held to the conviction that the less labor a man did, over and above absolute need, the better it woud be for him and for the community. He thought the order of the week ought to be reversed—one day of work followed by six days of rest. He lived on a diet of potatoes and beans and a few other vegetables in season, and declared that "a man who buys a new suit of clothes every year never knows what it is to have a suit that really fits." Though he was a devoted and keenly observant student of nature, he had no use for science as an organized body of knowledge. In politics he was essentially an anarchist. The state with its taxing and war-making powers is chiefly an instrument of tyranny and exploitation. He did not advocate overthrow of the state by violence, yet he did teach that "that government is best which governs not at all." Finally, he taught a doctrine of individual nullification, that is, a citizen should break any law that commanded him to do injustice toward another individual, no matter how humble. His *Essay on Civil Disobedience* is a masterpiece of protest against the overpowering state.

Henry David Thoreau

SELECTED READINGS

· *Items so designated are available in paperbound editions.*

Bell, John F., *A History of Economic Thought*, New York, 1956.

Cole, G. D. H., *What Marx Really Meant,* New York, 1934.

Ferguson, J. M., *Landmarks of Economic Thought*, New York, 1938. A good summary, clearly written.

Gide, Charles, and Rist, Charles, *A History of Economic Doctrines*, Boston, 1948. A good summary.

Ginzberg, Eli, *The House of Adam Smith*, New York, 1934. Authoritative.

Hook, Sidney, *Towards the Understanding of Karl Marx*, New York, 1933. A stimulating analysis, though difficult in some places.

Laidler, H. W., *History of Socialist Thought*, New York, 1927.

Mitchell, Harvey, and Stearns, Peter N., *Workers and Protest: The European Labor Movement, the Working Classes and the Origins of Social Democracy, 1890–1914*, Itasca, Ill., 1970.

READINGS
Newman, P. C., *The Development of Economic Thought*, New York, 1952. An elementary survey.

Russell, Bertrand, *Proposed Roads to Freedom*, New York, 1919.

· Schumpeter, Joseph, *Capitalism, Socialism, and Democracy*, New York, 1942 (Torchbook). A provocative analysis.

Wagner, D. O., ed., *Social Reformers: Adam Smith to John Dewey*, New York, 1934.

· Wilson, Edmund, *To the Finland Station*, Garden City, N. Y., 1953 (Anchor). An interesting and provocative survey of the history of Marxism.

SOURCE MATERIALS

· Malthus, T. R., *An Essay on Population*, especially Books I and IV (Richard D. Irwin and others).

· Mill, J. S., *Autobiography*, New York, 1924 (Library of Liberal Arts and others).

Owen, Robert, *A New View of Society*, New York.

——, *Report to the County of Lanark*.

· Tolstoi, Count Leo, *The Kingdom of God Is Within You*, New York, 1905 (Noonday Press).

· Tucker, Robert C., ed., *The Marx-Engels Reader*, New York, 1972 (Norton). The essential writings, early and late.

Webster, Hutton, *Historical Selections*, pp. 776–80, Children in Factories.

CHAPTER 23

The Ascendancy of Nationalism
(1830-1914)

Our conscience tells us that we have not fulfilled a single act, not written a single line, not uttered a single word that was not inspired by a warm love for the fatherland. . . . We were guided constantly by the inflexible intention of maintaining intact the national dignity, of preserving pure of all stain . . . that glorious tricolored flag which a generous sovereign has entrusted to our care.

—Count Camillo Benso di Cavour, Speech to the Piedmontese Chamber of Deputies, April 16, 1858

The day of small nations has long passed away. The day of Empires has come.
—Joseph Chamberlain, Speech, Birmingham, May 12, 1904

The history of the world from 1830 to 1914 was marked by a vigorous growth of nationalism and its logical offshoot, an extensive and arrogant imperialism. Nationalism may be defined as a program or ideal based upon a consciousness of nationhood. The feeling or consciousness of nationhood may depend upon a number of factors. A people may consider themselves a nation because of peculiarities of race, language, religion, or culture. In most cases, however, the factors which weld diverse groups together are a common history and common aspirations for the future or a belief in a common destiny. Only such elements as these can explain the fact that Belgium, Switzerland, Canada, and the United States are nations, since in all four there are major differences in language, in religion, or in both—to say nothing of different ethnic backgrounds. Although nationalism was in some respects a beneficent force, particularly in the early days when it often took the form of struggles for liberty, to a large extent it was and still is an evil influence. It is especially evil when it expresses itself in jingoism, in militarism, and in ambitions to conquer and dominate.

The meaning of nationalism

Without question nationalism was one of the most powerful forces that molded the history of the Western world between 1830

651

and 1914. From a vague sentiment during the early centuries of the modern era it grew into a veritable cult. For millions of deluded folk it became a stronger force than religion, surpassing Christianity in its appeal to the emotions and to the spirit of sacrifice in a holy cause. Men died for the honor of the flag as cheerfully as any martyrs had ever laid down their lives for the Cross. Though often co-existent with democracy and liberalism, militant nationalism was more powerful than either, and frequently thwarted or stifled both.

Nurtured by the French Revolutionary ideal of Fraternity, modern nationalism evolved through two stages. From 1800 to about 1848 it was little more than an emotional loyalty to a cultural and linguistic group and a yearning for deliverance from foreign oppression. After 1848 it developed into an aggressive movement for national greatness and for the right of each people united by cultural and ethnic ties to determine its own destinies. Its more extreme manifestations were exemplified by a frenzied worship of political power and a slavish devotion to doctrines of racial superiority and illusions of national honor. In such forms it was virtually synonymous with chauvinism, that species of vainglorious patriotism expressed in the sentiment, "My country, right or wrong."

I.   THE RISE OF NATIONALISM IN WESTERN AND CENTRAL EUROPE

The greatest outpouring of national feeling at the beginning of the nineteenth century occurred in France. The Revolution of 1789 initiated the sentiment. Nearly every major event that followed reflected in great measure the power of that feeling. The July Revolution of 1830, for example, though primarily a revolt of the bourgeoisie against the reactionary policies of Charles X, was inspired also by a desire to revive the glory of France when she wielded supremacy over most of Europe. Of even greater importance as a manifestation of nationalism was the February Revolution of 1848. As in 1830, the movement began as a revolt against reactionary policies. King Louis Philippe had grown indifferent to the demands of the masses, and his ministers were cynical and corrupt. Moreover, he turned a deaf ear to zealous patriots who wanted France to go to the relief of northern Italians who longed to throw off Austrian rule and of Poles who hated the tyranny of Russia.

The strength of nationalism showed itself clearly in the election that followed the deposition of Louis Philippe. France had been made a republic with a constitution modeled after that of the United States. This meant a powerful executive with the title of President. December 10, 1848, was set as the date of the Presidential election. Four candidates competed in this election: a moderate republican, a socialist, a Catholic, and a man who had something for everybody—Louis Napoleon Bonaparte. More than 7,000,000 votes were cast; and out of this total nearly 5,500,000 went to Louis Napo-

Louis Philippe

leon. Who was this man, who enjoyed such amazing popularity that he could poll more than twice as many votes as the other three candidates combined? Louis Napoleon Bonaparte (1808–1873) was the nephew of Napoleon I, his father being Louis Bonaparte, who for a brief period was king of Holland. After his uncle's downfall, Louis Napoleon went into exile, spending most of his time in Germany and in Switzerland. Returning to France after the July Revolution of 1830, he was imprisoned a few years later for attempting to provoke a local uprising. But in 1846 he escaped to England, where he was liberally supplied with funds by both British and French reactionaries. By the summer of 1848 the situation in France was such that he knew it was safe to return. In fact, he was welcomed with open arms by men of all classes. Conservatives were looking for a savior to protect their property against the onslaughts of the radicals. Proletarians were beguiled by his glittering schemes for prosperity in his book, *The Extinction of Pauperism*, and by the fact that he had corresponded with Louis Blanc and with Pierre Proudhon, the anarchist. In between these two classes was a great multitude of patriots and hero-worshipers to whom the very name Napoleon was a matchless symbol of glory and greatness. It was chiefly to this multitude that the nephew of the Corsican owed his astounding triumph. As one old peasant expressed it: "How could I help voting for this gentleman—I whose nose was frozen at Moscow?"

With grandiose dreams of emulating his uncle, Louis Napoleon was not long content to be merely *President* of France. Almost from the first he used his position to pave the way for a higher calling. He enlisted the support of the Catholics by permitting them to

Louis Napoleon

Louis Napoleon as dictator and then Emperor

An Episode in the Place du Palais-Royal. The date is February 24, 1848, a year when revolutionary fervor spread throughout Europe.

regain control over the schools and by sending an expedition to Rome to restore the Pope to his temporal power. He threw sops to the workers and to the bourgeoisie in the form of old-age insurance and laws for the encouragement of business. In 1851, alleging the need for extraordinary measures to protect the rights of the masses, he proclaimed a temporary dictatorship and invited the people to grant him the power to draw up a new constitution. In the plebiscite held on December 21, 1851, he was authorized by an overwhelming majority (7,500,000 to 640,000) to proceed as he liked. The new constitution, which he put into effect in January 1852, made the President an actual dictator. His term of office was lengthened to ten years, and he was given the exclusive power to initiate legislation and to make war and peace. Although the legislative branch was preserved in name, it could not initiate or amend bills or even change any specific provisions in the budget. Still the little Caesar was not satisfied; he would be content with nothing less than the imperial dignity which had graced the shoulders of his famous uncle. After exactly one year Louis Napoleon Bonaparte ordered another plebiscite and, with the approval of over 95 per cent of the voters, assumed the title of Napoleon III, Emperor of the French.

The Second Empire in France endured from December 1852, to September 1870. Its creator and preserver ruled by methods not dissimilar to those of other Caesars both before and since. He stimulated an imposing prosperity by draining swamps, building roads, improving harbors, subsidizing railroads, and constructing a magnificent system of boulevards in Paris. He cultivated the favor of the lower classes by mouthing Revolutionary phrases and by schemes for social welfare. At the same time he strove to make sure that radicals would not become troublesome. He subjected the press to strict surveillance and controlled elections by paying the expenses of *official* candidates and by requiring all others to take an oath of fidelity to the Emperor. Nor did he neglect opportunities to add luster to his regime by an aggressive foreign policy. He annexed Alge-

The regime of Napoleon III

The Crimean War. This photograph taken between 1854 and 1855 is by Roger Fenton. (See the illustration on the opposite page.)

Roger Fenton's Photographic Van. Fenton was one of the first noted European photographers and gained fame by covering the events of the Crimean War.

ria in northern Africa and established a protectorate over Indochina. In 1854 he plunged into the Crimean War with Russia under the pretext of protecting Catholic monks in Turkey. Since Napoleon had the aid of Great Britain and Turkey and also for a time of Sardinia, he managed to emerge from this war on the victorious side. Now more than ever he could rejoice in the plaudits of the mob and pose as the arbiter of the destinies of Europe.

By 1860 the glamour of Napoleon's reputation had begun to wear thin. The first great blow to his prestige was a result of the outcome of his Italian adventure. In 1858 he had formed an alliance with the Italian nationalists to help them expel the Austrians; but as soon as he saw that his erstwhile friends were bent upon consolidating the whole Italian peninsula into a nation-state and upon destroying the temporal sovereignty of the Pope, he promptly deserted them. By so doing, he antagonized thousands of his more liberal followers, who reproached him for abandoning a gallant people to Austrian oppression. In 1862 Napoleon intervened in Mexico. He sent an army into that country to establish an empire and then offered the throne to the Archduke Maximilian of Austria. But at the conclusion of the American Civil War the government of the United States compelled the withdrawal of the French troops, and soon afterward Maximilian was captured and shot by the Mexicans. As a consequence of this tragic adventure, opposition to Napoleon's rule markedly increased. After the elections of 1869 he decided that it would be expedient to make some concessions. He granted to the Assembly the right to initiate laws and to criticize and ratify or reject the budget. But in 1870 he resolved to gamble once more on a bold stroke of foreign policy to retrieve his fortunes. Shortly before this the government of Spain had been overturned, and the revolutionists had offered the crown to Prince Leopold of Hohenzollern, a cousin of the King of Prussia. Militarists and fire-eating "patriots" in France professed to see in this a threat to the security of the French

The decline and
fall of the
Second Empire

nation. Napoleon himself probably did not desire a war. He apparently assumed that vigorous diplomatic measures would give France all she needed in the way of a glorious triumph. But he allowed himself to be dominated by a militant clique that surrounded the Empress Eugénie and included several of his ministers. Members of this clique emphasized the rapid growth of the Prussian nation and its commanding position in central Europe. Accordingly, they advocated a preventive war. Now or never was their motto. France must seize the initiative while she still had an equality in numbers and a superiority, they believed, in military power. They maneuvered Napoleon into sending the French ambassador to meet with King William I of Prussia at the spa of Ems and there to demand that the king *never* allow a member of the Hohenzollern family to become a candidate for the Spanish throne. Though annoyed by this demand, King William wanted peace. But even less than Napoleon III was he master in his own house. The real dictator of policy in Prussia was the minister-president, Otto von Bismarck. And Bismarck lusted for war, if for no other reason than to rally the south German states behind the Prussian standard and unite all Germans in one great nation. France was badly defeated in the ensuing war, which lasted only a few weeks. After the battle of Sedan (September 2, 1870) Napoleon himself was taken prisoner, and two days later his government was overthrown by a group of republicans in Paris.

Following the collapse of Napoleon's empire a provisional government was organized to rule the country until a new constitution could be drafted. Elections were held in February 1871 for a national constituent assembly, resulting in the choice of some 500 monarchists and only about 200 republicans. The explanation lies in the fact that during the electoral campaign the republicans had urged a renewal of the war, while the monarchists took the attitude that France was already defeated, and that she might as well negotiate with her conquerors for the best terms she could get. It was not that the French people overwhelmingly preferred a monarchy, but rather that they longed for peace. Fortunately the monarchists were hopelessly divided. Angry discord among them postponed for almost four years a definite decision as to the permanent form the French government should take. Finally, in January 1875 the National Assembly adopted the first of a series of constitutional laws recognizing the government as republican in form. This action signified the formal establishment of the Third Republic in France.

The founding of the Third Republic

France in this era was not destined to have a happy future. It was almost torn apart by nationalist discord and social conflict from the beginning. The first episode of this kind was the Commune of Paris in 1871. Though this movement is commonly described as a rebellion of dangerous radicals intent upon the destruction of law and order, it was in reality quite different. Most of its members were not socialists or anarchists. They resembled the Jacobins of the First Revolution and were largely members of the middle class. They did

The Paris Commune

The Last of England, Ford Madox Brown (1821–1893). A haunting scene of a couple emigrating from England by one of the most noted Pre-Raphaelites. (The City Museum and Art Gallery, Birmingham, England)

Valley of Aosta—Snowstorm, Avalanche, and Thunderstorm, Joseph M. W. Turner (1175–1851). Turner's complete absorption in light, color, and atmosphere helped to prepare the way for the French impressionists. (MMA)

Portrait of a Gentleman, Jean Auguste Ingres (1780–1867). A student of David, Ingres was a devoted admirer of classical antiquities. But he was also influenced by romanticism. (MMA)

A Woman Reading, Camille Corot (1796–1875). Corot was predominantly a naturalist, a painter of lifelike scenes of innocence and simplicity. He shared the romanticists' sentimental worship of woods and fields. (MMA)

The Port of La Rochelle, Corot. (Louvre)

The Paris Commune. A view of Champs Elysées showing damage resulting from the 1871 uprising. The Arc de Triomphe may be seen in the distance.

not advocate the abolition of private property but rather its wider distribution. The movement was precipitated by the discontent of the Franco-Prussian War—bitterness over the defeat of Napoleon III and exhaustion by the long siege of Paris that followed. Added to these were fears that the central government would be dominated by the rural population to the disadvantage of the urban masses in the capital. After several weeks of frustrating disputation, the Commune turned into a bloody civil war. The Communards killed about sixty hostages, including the Archbishop of Paris. The government numbered its victims by the thousands. The courts-martial which were set up executed twenty-six. Thousands of others were sentenced to imprisonment or banishment in New Caledonia.

The collapse of the Paris Commune did not end the troubles of France that grew out of her defeat in the Franco-Prussian War. Monarchists and clericals charged the Republic with weakness and corruption and longed for a more autocratic government to lead the nation back to the path of glory. Some of them won applause by clamoring for a war of revenge against Germany. By harping on scandals recently exposed in the republican regime, they endeared themselves to the monarchists and also to conservative Catholics, who hated the Republic for its anti-clerical program. In the 1890's the reactionaries adopted anti-Semitism as a spearhead for the advancement of their aims. The fact that certain Jewish bankers had recently been involved in scandalous dealings with politicians lent color to the monarchist charge that the government was shot through with corruption and that money-grabbing Jews were largely to blame. Catholics were persuaded to believe that Jewish politicians had dictated the anticlerical legislation of the republican regime. In the face of such charges it is not strange that anti-Semitism should have flared into a violent outbreak. In 1894 a Jewish captain of

The Execution of a Communard by Government Troops

657

artillery, Alfred Dreyfus, was accused by a clique of monarchist officers of selling military secrets to Germany. Tried by court-martial, he was convicted and sentenced for life to Devil's Island. At first the verdict was accepted as the merited punishment of a traitor; but in 1897 Colonel Picquart, a new head of the Intelligence Division, announced his conclusion that the documents upon which Dreyfus had been convicted were forgeries. A movement was launched for a new trial, which the War Department promptly refused. Soon the whole nation was divided into friends and opponents of the luckless captain. On the side of Dreyfus were the radical republicans, the socialists, people of liberal and humanitarian sympathies, and such prominent literary figures as Émile Zola and Anatole France. The anti-Dreyfusards included the monarchists, the clericals, the Jew-baiters, the militarists, and a considerable number of conservative workingmen and sincere but mistaken patriots. Dreyfus was finally set free by executive order in 1899, and six years later he was cleared of all guilt by the Supreme Court and restored to the army. He was immediately promoted to the rank of major and decorated with the emblem of the Legion of Honor. The outcome of the Dreyfus affair effectively squelched the monarchist movement in France. Thereafter its adherents were gradually reduced to political insignificance—a mere "handful of old nuts rattling in a bag."

As already intimated, the Dreyfus affair was an element in a broader struggle over the issue of church and state, which also had nationalist implications. From the beginning of its history the Third Republic had been tinctured with anticlericalism. Its founders were not necessarily atheists, but they did believe that a powerful church with ambitions to extend its political and social influence was a threat to republican government. The aims of the anticlericals were to curb this influence, to reduce the economic privileges of the

The roots of anticlericalism

Alfred Dreyfus Leaving the Courthouse after His Court-Martial

Catholic Church, and to break the stranglehold the clergy had gained upon education. Anticlericalism was, in part, a result of the Industrial Revolution, which fostered materialistic interest and intensified the struggle between the bourgeoisie and the die-hard conservatives. It was also a product in some measure of the growth of science and of skeptical and liberal philosophies, which were often employed as primary weapons in fighting religious conservatism. Probably the main cause of its growth was the rise of a militant nationalism. The Catholic Church was not only committed to an internationalist outlook, but as late as the 1860's Popes were still asserting their rights to temporal power and pouring out their anathemas upon rulers who would establish omnipotent states. Wherever nationalism gathered powerful momentum, clericalism was almost certain to be regarded as a primary enemy.

Anticlericalism in France reached the peak of its fury between 1875 and 1914. The great majority of the leaders of the Third Republic were hostile to the Church; and naturally so, for the Catholic hierarchy was aiding the monarchists at every turn. Clericals conspired with monarchists, militarists, and anti-Semites in attempting to discredit the Republic during the Dreyfus affair. But in the end they overreached themselves. The outcome of the Dreyfus affair not only sounded the knell of monarchism but led to a furious attack upon the Church. In 1901 the government passed a series of acts prohibiting the existence of religious orders not authorized by the state, forbidding members of religious orders to teach in either public or private schools, and finally, in 1905, dissolving the union of Church and state. For the first time since 1801 the adherents of all creeds were placed on an equal basis. No longer were the Catholic clergy to receive their salaries from the public purse. Although some of these measures were modified in later years, clericalism remained in the minds of most Frenchmen under a heavy cloud of suspicion.

The February Revolution in France touched off a series of revolts in central Europe, beginning with an uprising in Austria on March 13. Mobs of students and workingmen rioted in Vienna and forced the resignation of that last great pillar of the *ancien régime*, Prince Metternich. Frightened by the refusal of his troops to fire upon the rebels, the Emperor promised a constitution for Germanic Austria, excluding Hungary and the Italian possessions. The constitution as finally adopted provided for a cabinet responsible to parliament and for a liberal franchise, and the assembly which drew it up also abolished the remaining feudal obligations of the peasants. Almost immediately the Hungarians took advantage of the turmoil in Vienna to establish a liberal government, and in April 1849, under the leadership of Louis Kossuth, they proclaimed the independence of the Hungarian Republic. But neither of these revolutions was permanently successful, for the reason that they soon became entangled in the discords of nationalism. The Hungarian liberals were no more

The results of anticlericalism in France

The revolution of 1848 in Austria and Hungary

659

willing than the Austrians to grant the privileges to subject nationalities that they claimed for themselves. As a consequence, the Hapsburgs were able to stir up ill feeling among the Slavs and to use
them to good advantage in curbing the ambitions of the dominant
nationalities. By the summer of 1849 the Emperor had succeeded in
overthrowing the Hungarian Republic and in revoking the Austrian
constitution. The discontent, however, continued until a compromise known as the *Ausgleich* was finally worked out between the
Austrians and the Hungarians in 1867. The *Ausgleich* established a
dual monarchy, with the head of the House of Hapsburg serving as
both Emperor of Austria and King of Hungary. Each of the two
parts of the empire was made practically autonomous, with its own
cabinet and parliament. Three joint ministers, of war, finance, and
foreign affairs, looked after the interests of the state as a whole in
their respective spheres. Enabling both the Magyars in Hungary and
the Germans in Austria to rule as master races, this arrangement
survived until the Dual Monarchy was broken into fragments in
1918.

A major drive of nationalists in Germany was unification of their
country. Since 1815 the German states, together with Austria, had
constituted the thirty-eight members of the German Confederation.

*The movement for
German unification*

Influential liberals among the nationalists hoped to unite all of
Germany into a great empire. Many others, however, were more
deeply concerned with advancing *German* ideals and *German* culture. They ardently believed in the superiority of the German *Volk*,
German law, and the concept of a German Reich. Some were
frankly expansionist, proclaiming Germany's right to civilize backward peoples and even to occupy their territories. Most of the
dogmas of these men of violence fitted in with the aims of the later
militants from Bismarck to Hitler.

German nationalism reached its first climax in the Revolution of
1848. Agitation by liberal dissenters forced the German princes to
grant or to promise reforms. In May high-minded leaders convoked

*The Frankfurt
Assembly*

a great national assembly in Frankfurt to draft a constitution for a
united Germany. From the beginning, controversy raged over
numerous issues: should the government be a republic or a limited
monarchy? If the latter, who should be offered the crown? Should
Austria or only the strictly German states be included? Such were
the rocks on which the Frankfurt Assembly foundered. Soon afterward it broke up in disgust with nothing to show for its efforts.
Most of the reforms which had been secured outside of the Assembly likewise gradually melted away, and thousands of the revolutionaries emigrated from the country and took refuge in the United
States.

The unification of Germany was now left to be achieved by the
hard realism of Bismarck. Otto von Bismarck (1815–1898) was
born into the class of Junkers, or landed aristocrats, who for centuries had furnished the Prussian state with the bulk of its bureaucrats

Legend:

- Prussia at the accession of Frederick the Great, 1740
- Territory conquered by Frederick from Austria, 1763
- Territories acquired by partitions of Poland, 1772, 1793, 1795
- Territories annexed between 1815 and 1871

and high army officers. During the revolutionary movement of 1848 he served in the Prussian Parliament as a staunch upholder of divine-right monarchy. He was one of a group of intransigent aristocrats who urged the Prussian king not to accept a "crown of shame" from the Frankfurt Assembly. Later Bismarck was instrumental in organizing the Conservative party, dedicated to protecting the interests of the Junker class, the established church, and the army, and to the building of a powerful Prussia as the nucleus of a German nation. In 1862 he was summoned by King William I to become Minister-President of his beloved Prussia.

In consolidating the German states into a united nation, Bismarck followed a succession of steps of almost diabolical cleverness. First he plotted to eliminate Austria from her commanding position in the Germanic Confederation. As a preliminary means to this end

Bismarck

661

Bismarck's preliminary steps in consolidating German unity

he entered into a dispute with Denmark over possession of Schleswig and Holstein. Inhabited largely by Germans, these two provinces had an anomalous status. Since 1815 Holstein had been included in the Germanic Confederation, but both were subject to the personal overlordship of the King of Denmark. When, in 1864, the Danish king attempted to annex them, Bismarck invited Austria to participate in a war against Denmark. A brief struggle followed, at the end of which the Danish ruler was compelled to renounce all his claims to Schleswig and Holstein in favor of Austria and Prussia. Then the very sequel occurred for which Bismarck ardently hoped: a quarrel between the victors over division of the spoils. The conflict which followed in 1866, known as the Seven Weeks' War, ended in an easy triumph for Prussia. Austria was forced to give up her claims to Schleswig and Holstein, to surrender Venetia to Italy, and to acquiesce in the dissolution of the Germanic Confederation. Immediately following the war Bismarck proceeded to unite all of the German states north of the Main River into the North German Confederation.

The Franco-Prussian War

The final step in the completion of German unity was the Franco-Prussian War. We have learned of the part played by French politicians in provoking a crisis with Prussia over the question of succession to the Spanish throne. The attitude of Bismarck was just as provocative. He knew that a war with France would be the best possible means to kindle a *German* nationalism in Bavaria and Württemberg and in the remaining states south of the Main. When he received a dispatch sent by King William I from Ems informing him that the demand of the French for perpetual exclusion of the Hohenzollern family from the Spanish throne had been refused, he decided that the time for action had come. He determined to release the telegram from Ems in such a form as to make it appear that King William had insulted the French ambassador. Bismarck's prediction that this would have the effect of "a red rag upon the Gallic bull" was speedily borne out. When the garbled report of what happened at Ems was received in France, the whole nation was immediately in an uproar. On July 15, 1870, when Napoleon's ministers requested the legislative body to approve a declaration of war, there were only ten dissenting votes. No sooner had the struggle begun than the south German states rallied to the side of Prussia in the belief that she was the victim of aggression. Such was the beginning of a war that was destined to have tremendous effects upon the subsequent history of Europe. From the start the Prussians had the advantage. The disciplined efficiency of their military machine stood out in bold contrast to the ineptitude of the French. The result could have been foretold from the beginning. After the capture of Napoleon at Sedan in September 1870 and the conquest of Paris following a desperate siege four months later, the war was officially

Meeting to Arrange Peace Terms at the End of the Franco-Prussian War. On the left is Otto von Bismarck, chancellor of the new German Empire. In the center is Jules Favre and to his right, Louis-Adolphe Thiers, both representing the provisional government set up after the overthrow of Napoleon III.

ended by the Treaty of Frankfurt. France surrendered the major portions of Alsace and Lorraine and agreed to pay an indemnity of 5 billion francs.

2. THE SPREAD OF NATIONALISM TO SOUTHERN AND EASTERN EUROPE

Events in Italy ran a course almost parallel to that which had led to the unification of Germany. Italy before 1848, it should be remembered, was a patchwork of petty states. The most important of those possessing independence were the Kingdom of Sardinia in the north, the Papal States in the central region, and the Kingdom of the Two Sicilies in the south. The former republics of Lombardy and Venetia were held by Austria, while Hapsburg dependents ruled in Tuscany, Parma, and Modena. As the revolutionary fervor of 1848 swept across the peninsula, one ruler after another granted democratic reforms. Charles Albert of Sardinia outdistanced all the others with his celebrated Fundamental Statute providing for civil liberties and a parliamentary form of government. But it soon became evident that the Italians were more interested in nationalism than in democracy. For some years romantic patriots had been dreaming of the *Risorgimento*—the resurrection of the Italian spirit—which would restore the nation to the position of glorious leadership it had held in ancient times and during the age of the Renaissance. To achieve this, it was universally agreed that Italy must be welded into a single state. But opinions differed as to the form the new government should take. Young idealists followed the leadership of Giuseppe Mazzini (1805–1872), who labored with sincere devotion for the founding of a republic. Religious-minded patriots believed that the most prac-

Giuseppe Mazzini

663

Camillo di Cavour

Giuseppe Garibaldi

ticable solution would be to federate the states of Italy under the presidency of the Pope. The majority of the more moderate nationalists advocated a constitutional monarchy built upon the foundations of the Kingdom of Sardinia. The aims of this third group gradually crystallized under the leadership of a shrewd Sardinian nobleman, Count Camillo di Cavour (1810–1861). In 1850 he was appointed Minister of Commerce and Agriculture of his native state and in 1852 Prime Minister.

The campaign for unification of the Italian peninsula began with efforts to expel the Austrians. In 1848 revolts were organized in the territories under Hapsburg domination, and an army of liberation marched from Sardinia to aid the rebels; but the movement ended in failure. It was then that Cavour, as the new leader of the campaign, turned to less heroic but more practical methods. In 1855, to attract the favorable attention of Great Britain and France, he entered the Crimean War on their side despite the fact that he had no quarrel with Russia. In 1858 he held a secret meeting with Napoleon III and prepared the stage for an Italian War of Liberation. Napoleon agreed to cooperate in driving the Austrians from Italy for the price of the cession of Savoy and Nice by Sardinia to France. A war with Austria was duly provoked in 1859, and for a time all went well for the Franco-Italian allies. But after the conquest of Lombardy, Napoleon suddenly withdrew, fearful of ultimate defeat and afraid of antagonizing the Catholics in his own country by aiding an avowedly anticlerical government. Thus deserted by her ally, Sardinia was unable to expel the Austrians from Venetia. Nevertheless, she did make some extensive gains: she annexed Lombardy, and acquired by various means the duchies of Tuscany, Parma, and Modena and the northern portion of the Papal States. Sardinia was now more than twice her original size and by far the most powerful state in Italy.

The second step in consolidating the unity of Italy was the conquest of the Kingdom of the Two Sicilies. This kingdom was ruled by a Bourbon, Francis II, who was thoroughly hated by his Italian subjects. In May 1860 a romantic free-lance adventurer by the name of Giuseppe Garibaldi set out with his famous regiment of 1000 "red shirts" to rescue his fellow Italians from oppression. Within three months he had conquered the island of Sicily and had then marched to the deliverance of Naples, where the people were already in revolt. By November the whole kingdom of Francis II had fallen to the gay buccaneer. Garibaldi at first apparently intended to convert the territory into an independent republic but was finally persuaded to surrender it to the Kingdom of Sardinia. With most of the peninsula now united under a single rule, Victor Emmanuel II, King of Sardinia, assumed the title of King of Italy (March 17, 1861). Venetia was still in the hands of the Austrians, but in 1866 they were forced by the Prussians to cede it to Italy. All that remained to complete the unification of Italy was the annexation of

THE UNIFICATION OF ITALY

Rome. The Eternal City had resisted conquest thus far largely because of the military protection accorded to the Pope by Napoleon III. But in 1870 the outbreak of the Franco-Prussian War compelled Napoleon to withdraw his troops. The opportunity was too good to be overlooked. In September 1870 Italian soldiers occupied Rome, and in July of the following year it was made the capital of the united kingdom.

The occupation of Rome brought the kingdom of Italy into conflict with the papacy. Indeed, the whole movement for unification had been characterized by hostility to the Church. Such was inevitably the case, with the Pope ruling in the manner of a secular prince over the Papal States and hurling the thunders of his wrath against those who would rob him of his domain for the sake of a united Italy. Following the occupation of Rome in 1870 an attempt was

Anticlericalism in Italy

made to solve the problem of relations between the state and the papacy. In 1871 the Italian Parliament enacted the Law of Papal Guaranties purporting to define the status of the Pope as a reigning sovereign. He was to be granted full authority over the Vatican and Lateran buildings and gardens and the right to send and receive ambassadors. In addition, he was to have free use of the Italian postal, telegraph, and railway systems and was to be paid an annual indemnity of about $645,000. This law the reigning pontiff, Pius IX, promptly denounced on the ground that issues affecting the Pope could be settled only by an international treaty to which he himself was a party. Whereupon he shut himself up in the Vatican and refused to have anything to do with a government which had so shamefully treated Christ's Vicar on earth. His successors continued this practice of voluntary imprisonment until 1929, when a series of agreements between the Fascist government and Pius XI effected what appeared to be a satisfactory settlement of the dispute.

Nationalism in
the Balkans

In eastern Europe during the nineteenth century nationalism partook primarily of a liberation character. This was particularly true of the lands of the Balkans. Before 1829 the entire Balkan peninsula— bounded by the Aegean, Black, and Adriatic Seas—was controlled by the Turks. But during the next eighty-five years a gradual dismemberment of the Turkish empire occurred. In some instances the slicing away of territories was perpetrated by rival European powers, especially by Russia and Austria; but generally it was the result of nationalist revolts by the Sultan's Christian subjects. In 1829, at the conclusion of the first Russo-Turkish War, the Ottoman Empire was compelled to acknowledge the independence of Greece and to grant autonomy to Serbia and to the provinces which later became Rumania. As the years passed, resentment against Ottoman rule spread through other Balkan territories. In 1875–1876 there were uprisings in Bosnia, Herzegovina, and Bulgaria, which the Sultan suppressed with murderous vengeance. Reports of atrocities against Orthodox Christians gave Russia an excuse for renewal of her age-long struggle for domination of the Balkans. In this second Russo-Turkish War (1877–1878) the armies of the Tsar won a smashing victory. The Treaty of San Stefano, which terminated the conflict, provided that the Sultan surrender nearly all of his territory in Europe, except for a remnant around Constantinople. But at this juncture the great powers intervened. Austria and Great Britain, especially, were opposed to letting Russia assume jurisdiction over so large a portion of the Near East. In 1878 a congress of the great powers, meeting in Berlin, transferred Bessarabia to Russia, Thessaly to Greece, and Bosnia and Herzegovina to the control of Austria. Seven years later the Bulgars, who had been granted some degree of autonomy by the Treaty of Berlin, seized the province of Eastern Rumelia from Turkey and in 1908 established the independent Kingdom of Bulgaria.

In the very year when this last dismemberment occurred, Turkey herself was engulfed by the tidal wave of nationalism. For some

THE DISMEMBERMENT OF THE OTTOMAN EMPIRE · 1683-1923

ACQUIRED BY:

Great Britain   France   Italy

Austria-Hungary   Russia

GAINED INDEPENDENCE:

———— Boundary of the Ottoman Empire at its greatest extent

—·—·— 1923 boundaries

0 _____ 1000 miles

time her more enlightened citizens had been growing increasingly
disgusted with the weakness and incompetence of the Sultan's government. In particular, those who had been educated in the universities of England and France were becoming more and more convinced that their country should be rejuvenated by the introduction
of Western ideas of science, patriotism, and democracy. Organizing
themselves into a society known as the Young Turks, they forced
the Sultan in 1908 to establish constitutional government. The following year, when a reactionary movement set in, they deposed the
reigning Sultan, Abdul Hamid II, and placed on the throne his wit-
less brother, Mohammed V, as a titular sovereign. The real powers
of government were now entrusted to a grand vizier and ministers
responsible to an elected parliament. Unfortunately this revolution
did not mean increased liberty for the non-Turkish inhabitants of

The Young
Turk revolution

667

EUROPE AFTER THE CONGRESS OF BERLIN · 1878

the empire. Instead, the Young Turks launched a vigorous movement to Ottomanize all of the Christian subjects of the Sultan. At
the same time the disturbances preceding and accompanying the
revolution opened the way for still further dismemberment. In 1908
Austria annexed the provinces of Bosnia and Herzegovina, which
the Treaty of Berlin had allowed her merely to administer, and in
1911–1912 Italy made war upon Turkey for the conquest of
Tripoli.

Nationalism in Russia amounted to comparatively little until nearly
the end of the nineteenth century. Few national minorities rose in
Nationalism   revolt, and those that did were seldom successful. Discontented
in Russia   ethnic elements did not form any large proportion of the Russian
nation, as was the case in Turkey, Austria, and Italy. As a conse-
668   quence the Tsars did not generally find nationalist revolts a serious

threat within their borders. Russian nationalism moved in the direction of external goals. Its aim was to foster external greatness rather than to cultivate the domestic genius of the people. But there were a few notable exceptions.

One was the Narodnik or populist movement. Originating in the 1860's, it spread rapidly. The nationalism of the populists found expression largely in the work of the Slavophil faction which extolled the culture of the Slavs as one of the finest products of civilization. Populism, in fact, was originally an offshoot of the Slavophil movement. It did not become a radical political party until about 1870.

The Narodniki

The most active of the Pan-Slavists, however, were not populists but nationalists committed to an aggressive foreign policy. Their program had no more to do with internal reform in Russia than the *Rule Britannia* movement or *Deutschland über alles* in their respective countries. The Pan-Slavists sought to uphold for Russia a predominant position among all of the Slavs regardless of the country in which they lived. It was held to be the duty of Great Russia to serve as the guide and protector of the Poles, Bulgars, Montenegrins, and all the subject nationalities of the Austrian and Turkish empires. Under its guise Russian imperialists interfered in the concerns of all these bordering peoples and sought to draw them into the Tsarist orbit. Russian ambitions often constituted a threat to the independence and even the existence of such border states as Austria-Hungary and Turkey.

Pan-Slavism

3. NATIONALISM IN THE WESTERN HEMISPHERE

Nearly every development in American history has closely approximated the pattern adhered to by the nations of Europe. The Revolutionary War, though it involved some social issues, was mainly a struggle for independence. The War of 1812 bore little relationship to its alleged cause, the impressment of American seamen, and turned mainly into a struggle for the conquest of lands of the Indians. The Mexican War and the Spanish-American War were blatantly expansionist, the first against Mexico and the second against Spain. Except for the Louisiana Territory, the vast proportion of new lands annexed by the United States before 1900 were acquired by forcible expansion. Even the American Civil War was waged by the North primarily as a nationalist crusade. President Lincoln declared that his main purpose in continuing the war was not to destroy slavery but to preserve the Union.

Nationalism in
the United States:
American wars

Nearly thirty years before he became President, John Adams declared that he had always considered the settlement of America as "the opening of a grand scheme and design in Providence for the illumination of the ignorant and the emancipation of the slavish part of mankind." Nationalism in the United States was closely associated with ethnic chauvinism, or in some cases, racism. Throughout the nineteenth century doctrines of race superiority were freely propagated and accepted. In the minds of many the classification of superior included only those who would now be called WASPs. The Chosen People did not embrace recent immigrants from Southern and Eastern Europe and certainly not from Asia or Africa. God had given to Anglo-Saxons a mission to organize inferior peoples and to civilize the world.

Manifest Destiny

Worship of national greatness in the United States generally went hand in glove with territorial expansion. The prophets of nationalism were commonly advocates of a manifest destiny. For years they could not avert their hungry eyes from the prospect of conquering Cuba, Canada, the lands of the Indians, and Mexico. Not all of these territories were forcibly annexed, but enough were seized to whet the appetite for further conquests.

4.   THE NEW IMPERIALISM OF THE NINETEENTH CENTURY

The universality
of imperialism

The history of nearly every outstanding nation has had its imperialist phase. Moreover, it is hardly an exaggeration to say that imperialism is the same wherever it is practiced. It is inseparable from domination and exploitation where one nation sets itself up as a superior breed and arrogates to itself the right to rule another without its consent.

The expansion of
imperialism

In the competition for empire among the powers of the Old World, Great Britain led the way. By the end of the nineteenth century more than half of the land area of the world had been brought under the British flag. India, Canada, Australia, New Zealand, South Africa, Burma, the Sudan, and South Africa, together with innumerable islands, made up a vast empire. France came next with possessions almost equal in area but much less thinly populated and poorer in natural wealth. Algeria, French West Africa, Equatorial Africa, and Indochina ranked as the principal stars in her imperial crown.

"*The Rhodes Colossus.*" The ambitions of Cecil Rhodes, the driving force behind British imperialism in South Africa, are satirized in this cartoon appearing in *Punch*.

POSSESSIONS OF EUROPEAN POWERS:

British

French

Belgian

Portuguese

Italian

Spanish

GER. German colonies prior to World War I

- - - - Boundaries of the Union of South Africa

Independent native states

IMPERIALISM IN AFRICA TO THE EVE OF WORLD WAR II

Germany and Italy entered the race for colonies late. Both were preponderantly interested in such internal problems as national unification, industrial development, and quarrels between Church and state. Nevertheless, by 1880 both nations were ready to enter the imperial scramble. Though Bismarck at first had scoffed at the acquisition of colonies, he was eventually persuaded to enter the contest for an empire in Africa. Extensive areas were carved out of the southern area of the continent, although most of them proved of limited value. Italy also embarked on a quest for African colonies, but her efforts were even more discouraging than those of Germany. Italian armies were cut to pieces in 1896 when they attempted the conquest of Abyssinia (Ethiopia). The imperialist ambitions of

Late comers in the imperial scramble

671

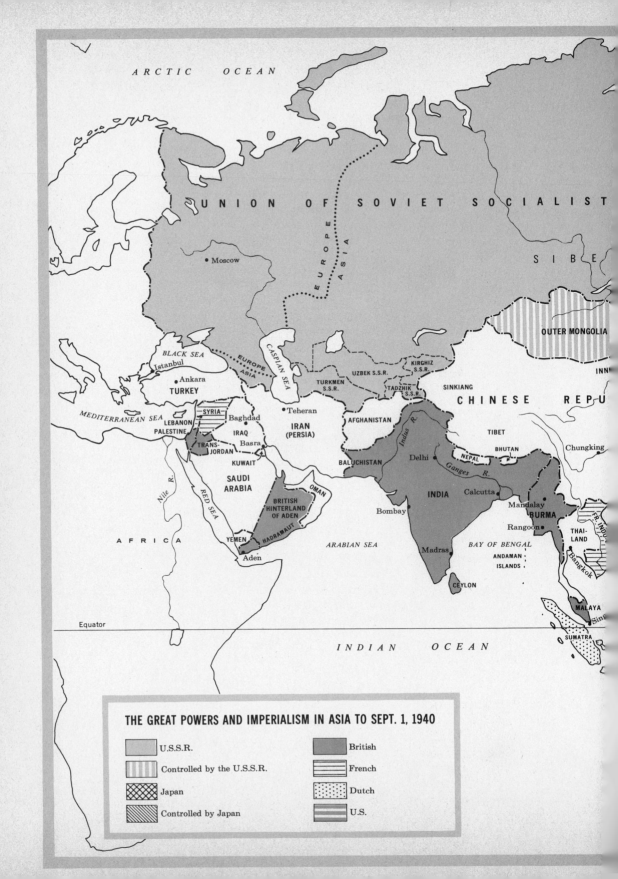

ARCTIC OCEAN

UNION OF SOVIET SOCIALIST

SIBE

• Moscow

OUTER MONGOLIA

EUROPE
ASIA

INN

BLACK SEA

Istanbul

EUROPE
ASIA

CASPIAN SEA

KIRGHIZ
S.S.R.

SINKIANG

• Ankara

UZBEK S.S.R.

CHINESE   REPU

TURKEY

TURKMEN
S.S.R.

TADZHIK
S.S.R.

MEDITERRANEAN SEA

SYRIA

• Baghdad

• Teheran

AFGHANISTAN

TIBET

Chungking

LEBANON

IRAN
(PERSIA)

BHUTAN

PALESTINE

IRAQ

Basra

NEPAL

TRANS-
JORDAN

BALUCHISTAN

Delhi

Ganges   R.

Calcutta

KUWAIT

Indus R.

Nile R.

SAUDI
ARABIA

OMAN

Bombay

INDIA

Mandalay

BURMA

RED SEA

BRITISH
HINTERLAND
OF ADEN

Rangoon

THAI-
LAND

FR. IND.

AFRICA

YEMEN

HADRAMAUT

ARABIAN SEA

Madras

BAY OF BENGAL

Bangkok

Aden

ANDAMAN
ISLANDS

MALAYA

CEYLON

Sing

Equator

SUMATRA

INDIAN   OCEAN

THE GREAT POWERS AND IMPERIALISM IN ASIA TO SEPT. 1, 1940

	U.S.S.R.		British
	Controlled by the U.S.S.R.		French
	Japan		Dutch
	Controlled by Japan		U.S.

ARCTIC OCEAN

REPUBLICS

I A

ALASKA

BERING SEA

SEA OF
OKHOTSK

Amur R.

MANCHUKUO
Harbin

NGOLIA

Vladivostok

SEA OF JAPAN

Peiping

Tientsin

CHOSEN
(KOREA)

JAPAN
Tokyo
Yokohama
Osaka

I C

Nanking

Shanghai

ngtze

Wenchow

E. CHINA SEA

Amoy

Foochow

nton

Swatow

TAIWAN
(FORMOSA)

Hong Kong (Br.)

PACIFIC

OCEAN

INAN

CHINA SEA

Manila

PHILIPPINE

ISLANDS

WAK

NEO

CELEBES

MOLUCCAS
(SPICE ISLANDS)

NEW GUINEA

0   1000 miles along the equator

AUSTRALIA

Tsarist Russia did not take the form of a struggle for overseas colonies. Instead, the Russians concentrated on expansion into contiguous areas. As early as 1582 they began the penetration of Siberia, and in less than a century had extended their domain to the Pacific. Finally, during the closing years of the nineteenth century imperialism blossomed in Japan. In 1894–1895 she made war upon China and forced her to cede Formosa and to grant Korea independence. It must not be thought that only the major powers of the world engaged in the quest for colonies. In 1885 Belgium acquired the Belgian Congo, a territory several times as large as the homeland itself. The Netherlands found rich prizes in the East Indies as early as 1600 and gradually transformed them into a Dutch empire.

Causes of the new imperialism

The causes of the new imperialism did not differ greatly regardless of the country by whom it was practiced. A major one was nationalism. As the new imperialists saw it, the prestige of a nation was largely determined by the size of the yellow, pink, or blue patch on the map indicating the size of its territory. Outranking nationalism was a collection of economic causes. The spread of industrialization to various countries after 1870 produced an intense competition for markets and for new areas of investment of surplus capital. As production continued to grow, the belief prevailed that nothing short of external territories would suffice as dumping grounds for articles the home market could not absorb. It was dimly realized that the prosperity of all rested upon a nicely adjusted balance of imports and exports. But the trouble was that everyone wanted to export as much as possible and import as little as possible. A final cause of the new imperialism was the desire to find homes for surplus inhabitants. It was considered essential that they should not be lost as citizens and therefore potential soldiers of the fatherland.

The balance sheets of the new imperialism seldom present a very creditable record. Its aim of providing homes for the surplus population of the mother country was not often realized. More Japanese

The Transvaal Gold Fields. The combination of low-cost labor plus high-yield mines results in enormous profits for some companies and individuals.

emigrants sought homes in Hawaii and California than in Korea or Manchuria. Emigrants from Italy greatly preferred New York and Chicago to Eritrea and Somaliland. A similar story can be told regarding economic results. With the exception of some parts of the British Empire, colonial possessions did not absorb any large proportion of the surplus production of the mother country. To illustrate, less than 1 per cent of Germany's exports went to her colonies. The bulk of exports from the United States did not go to her colonies but to other independent countries such as Great Britain, Canada, and Japan. Economically developed countries preferred to trade with other developed countries where they could find the richest markets and the most eager demand for their goods. In sum, the economic advantages of colonial empires were mainly an illusion. This is not to say that no one gained from the acquisition of colonies. Individual citizens often reaped rich rewards: investors, merchants, owners of mines and railways. But nations as a whole seldom benefited. They made great sacrifices fighting and dying to conquer and hold some obscure territory in Africa or Asia and had little to show for their pains except a feeling of power and pride.

SELECTED READINGS

· Items so designated are available in paperbound editions.

NATIONALISM

· Binkley, R. C., *Realism and Nationalism*, New York, 1935 (Torchbook). A stimulating account of the period 1852–1871.

· Eyck, Erich, *Bismarck and the German Empire*, London, 1950 (Norton Library). The best one-volume study of the Iron Chancellor.

Eyck, Frank, *The Frankfurt Parliament, 1848–1849*, New York, 1968.

Gewehr, W. M., *The Rise of Nationalism in the Balkans, 1800–1930*, New York, 1931. Brief but scholarly.

Griffith, G. O., *Mazzini, Prophet of Modern Europe*, New York, 1932.

Guérard, A. L., *Napoleon III*, New York, 1958. A laudatory account.

Hayes, C. J. H., *The Historical Evolution of Modern Nationalism*, New York, 1931.

· Kohn, Hans, *The Idea of Nationalism*, New York, 1944 (Macmillan). A perceptive analysis.

· ———, *Basic History of Modern Russia*, New York, 1957 (Anvil).

Noether, E. P., *Seeds of Italian Nationalism, 1700–1815*, New York, 1951.

Siegfried, A., *France, a Study in Nationality*, New Haven, 1930. An interesting interpretation.

Simpson, F. A., *The Rise of Louis Napoleon*, New York, 1925.

Snyder, L. L., *From Bismarck to Hitler*, Williamsport, Pa., 1935. A thorough and scholarly account.

· ———, *Basic History of Modern Germany*, New York, 1957 (Anvil).

· Thompson, J. M., *Napoleon and the Second Empire*, Oxford, 1954 (Norton Library.

· Whyte, A. J., *The Evolution of Modern Italy*, Oxford, 1944 (Norton Library). A good introductory study.

· Williams, Roger L., *The French Revolution of 1870–1871*, New York, 1969 (Norton).

Angell, Norman, *The Great Illusion*, New York, 1933.

· Beisner, Robert L., *Twelve against Empire: The Anti-Imperialists, 1898–1900*, New York, 1968.

Beloff, Max, *Imperial Sunset; Britain's Liberal Empire, 1897–1921*, Vol. I, New York, 1970.

· Betts, Raymond F., *Europe Overseas: Phases of Imperialism*, New York, 1968 (Basic Books).

Carroll, E. M., *Germany and the Great Powers, 1866–1914*, New York, 1938.

Chubb, O. E., *20th Century China*, New York, 1964.

Clark, Grover, *The Balance Sheets of Imperialism*, New York, 1936. A good study of results.

Elletson, D. H., *The Chamberlains*, New York, 1966.

· Feis, Herbert, *Europe, the World's Banker, 1870–1914*, New Haven, 1930 (Norton Library). An interesting economic analysis.

Fraser, H. F., *Foreign Trade and World Politics*, New York, 1926.

Graham, Gerald S., *Great Britain in the Indian Ocean*, New York, 1967.

Harris, N. D., *Europe and Africa*, New York, 1927.

———, *Europe and the East*, New York, 1926.

Hoffman, Ross, *Great Britain and the German Trade Rivalry, 1875–1914*. Philadelphia, 1933. A perceptive account.

Hoskins, H. L., *European Imperialism in Africa*, New York, 1930.

Langer, W. L., *The Diplomacy of Imperialism*, New York, 1950. A standard work.

May, Ernest R., *American Imperialism*, New York, 1968.

Moon, P. T., *Imperialism and World Politics*, New York, 1926.

Owen, D. E., *Imperialism and Nationalism in the Far East*, New York, 1929.

Platt, D. C. M., *Finance, Trade, and Politics in British Foreign Policy*, New York, 1968.

Simon, W. M., *Germany in the Age of Bismarck*, New York, 1968.

Somervell, D. C., *The British Empire*, London, 1948.

· Tan, C. C., *The Boxer Catastrophe*, New York, 1955 (Norton Library). The most recent scholarly account.

Tuveson, Ernest Lee, *Redeemer Nation: The Idea of America's Millennial Role*, Chicago, 1968.

Willcox, W. B., *Star of Empire*, New York, 1950.

SOURCE MATERIALS

Bismarck, Otto von, *Bismarck, the Man and the Statesman, Written and Dictated by Himself*, London, 1899, 2 vols.

Renan, Ernest, *What Is a Nation?*

Ruskin, John, *The Crown of Wild Olive.*

Schurz, Carl, *Reminiscences*, pp. 163–65. Failure of the Frankfort Assembly.

· Tocqueville, Alexis de, *Recollections*, pp. 79–89, February Revolution in France, New York, 1949 (Meridian).

CHAPTER 24

The Maturing of Democracy in Europe and America (1810-1914)

The people, consequently, *may* desire to oppress a part of their number; and precautions are as much needed against this as against any other abuse of power. . . . "The tyranny of the majority" is now generally included among the evils against which society requires to be on its guard.

—John Stuart Mill, *On Liberty*

At no time, at no place . . . had the American people officially proclaimed the United States to be a democracy. The Constitution did not contain the word or any word lending countenance to it. . . . When the Constitution was proclaimed no respectable person called himself or herself a democrat.

—Charles A. and Mary R. Beard, *America in Midpassage*

After the revolutions of 1830 many nations of the Western world experienced a rebirth of democracy. In Europe, Great Britain took the lead while France, Germany, and Italy lagged behind. But even Spain, Turkey, and the Balkan kingdoms ultimately adopted at least some of the forms of democratic rule. What most of these countries were interested in was governmental or political democracy, exemplified by parliaments, universal manhood suffrage, and the cabinet system. Not until after the beginning of the twentieth century was there much concern with social or economic democracy.

The rebirth of democracy

In order to understand the true meaning of democracy, we need to consider its historical origins. As a political ideal, democracy had its roots in the philosophy of Rousseau. It was Rousseau's doctrine of the absolute sovereignty of the majority, together with his and the other romanticists' deification of the common man, which more than anything else gave us our ideal of the voice of the people as the voice of God. Historically, political democracy meant, above all, that the majority of the people should be entitled to speak for the entire nation, and that in forming that majority the votes of all the citizens should be equal. The machinery of the democratic state therefore included universal suffrage and such provisions as frequent elections and adequate popular control over the officers of

The meaning of political democracy

government. In order that this machinery operate effectively, the citizens must have the right to organize political parties and to choose freely among them. Freedom of speech and freedom of the press were also considered essential components of the democratic ideal. But none of these rights was regarded as absolute and beyond the control of the majority. To be sure, if they were destroyed entirely, democracy would cease to exist; but the majority could most certainly limit them when there was a clear and immediate danger to the public safety. Historically, all that democracy has really required is that all ideas unaccompanied by threat of violence be tolerated and that *peaceful* minorities be allowed to strive to become the majority. The political ideal which affirms the *absolute* right of the citizen to write or speak or live as he pleases, so long as he does no actual harm to his neighbor, is not democracy but individualism, or, as some would call it, liberalism.

I.   THE EVOLUTION OF DEMOCRACY
IN GREAT BRITAIN

The evolution of democracy in Great Britain includes primarily three different stages: the extension of the suffrage, the development of the cabinet system of government, and the growth of the supremacy of the House of Commons. Prior to 1832 the system of voting and representation in England was exceedingly undemocratic. Only in a very few boroughs could the majority of the citizens vote. In the rural areas the franchise was restricted to a mere

The undemocratic character of the British government in the early 19th century

Interior of the House of Commons. The government and opposition members sit on opposite sides of this chamber. Those supporting the government, or cabinet, sit to the right of the Speaker, who occupies the canopied throne. Her Majesty's Loyal Opposition sits on the Speaker's left. The cabinet and the "shadow cabinet" of the opposition sit on the front benches.

handful of the larger proprietors. Out of a total membership of about 650 in the House of Commons no more than a third could be said to have been elected in any proper sense. The rest were appointed by local magnates or selected by petty groups of the richest property-holders or by members of favored guilds. In some cases the positions were openly sold or offered for rent for a term of years. To make matters worse, the distribution of seats had been thrown out of balance by the shift of population to the industrial centers of the north. While many of the new cities, such as Birmingham and Manchester, with more than 100,000 people in each, were denied representation entirely, villages in the south which had been almost depopulated continued to send as many as two and three members to the House of Commons. One of these villages (Old Sarum) was a deserted hill; another (Dunwich) had slipped beneath the waves of the sea; yet both were still represented in Parliament, by that remarkable British capacity for preserving a fiction long after the facts have disappeared.[1]

Despite the smug assurance of the Duke of Wellington that the political system described above was "perfectly satisfactory," there was much agitation against it. Not only the common people but also members of the middle class were thoroughly dissatisfied with an arrangement which gave almost a monopoly of power to the landed aristocracy. Emboldened by the success of the July Revolution of 1830 in France, the British Whigs under the leadership of Lord John Russell and Earl Grey inaugurated a movement for electoral reform. Strong opposition and vigorous agitation forced Wellington to resign as Prime Minister. Earl Grey then formed a new ministry, and the famous Reform Bill of 1832 became a law. Though its provisions were much more moderate than many of the radicals would have liked, it was still a noteworthy gain. The bill enfranchised most of the adult males of the middle class and nearly all of the smaller landholders and tenant farmers; but the great masses of agricultural laborers and industrial workers in the cities were still excluded from the suffrage. The proportion of voters was increased from about 1 out of every 100 inhabitants to 1 out of 32. In addition, the bill provided for some sweeping reforms in representation. Villages with a population of less than 2000 were deprived of their right to elect representatives to the House of Commons, while towns of slightly larger size had their representation cut in half. The seats in the Commons thus set free were distributed among the great industrial cities of the north.

The movement for
political reform

---

[1] The prize example of these "rotten boroughs" was the village of Bute in Scotland. Here there was only one inhabitant left who was qualified to vote, but the village retained its right to send a representative to Parliament. On election day this solitary voter regularly appeared at the polling place, "moved and seconded his own nomination, put the question to the vote, and was unanimously elected" to a seat in the House of Commons.

Results of the
Reform Act of
1832

The Reform Act of 1832 definitely established the supremacy of the middle class. In the elections that followed soon afterward, the Whigs, who now began to call themselves Liberals, captured a majority of seats in the House of Commons. The Tories, henceforth more commonly known as Conservatives, also began to bid for capitalist support. The result was a wave of parliamentary enactments distinctly favorable to bourgeois interests. One appropriated money to private societies for the maintenance of schools. Another, the celebrated Poor Law of 1834, abolished "outdoor" relief, except for the sick and the aged, and provided that all able-bodied paupers be compelled to earn their keep in workhouses. This law was based upon the theory that poverty is a man's own fault, and that consequently the poor should be forced to work as a punishment for their shiftlessness. The crowning achievement of this period of bourgeois legislation was the repeal of the Corn Laws in 1846. The Corn Laws were a form of protective tariff for the benefit of the landowning class. Their effect was to give a rich bounty to the British landowners and at the same time to keep the price of bread exceedingly high. For more than twenty years industrial capitalists had clamored for repeal of these tariffs, on the double ground that they necessitated the payment of higher wages and limited the sale of British manufactures in foreign markets. It was not, however, until 1846 that their efforts were successful. The repeal of the Corn Laws started Britain on the road to her free-trade policy, which was continued in force until after World War I.

The Chartist
movement of
1838–1848

None of these results of middle-class supremacy conferred much immediate benefit upon the working class. Hours in the factories were still unconscionably long; and, despite the rapid expansion of industry, periods of hard times still punctuated the rising prosperity. Moreover, Parliament was deaf to all the pleas of the lower classes for a share in the franchise. The great Liberal statesman, Lord John Russell, flatly declared that the reforms granted in 1832 were "final." In the face of such resistance many urban workers decided that the only hope of relief was to strive for a complete democratization of the British government. Accordingly, they enlisted with great enthusiasm under the banner of Chartism, a movement organized in 1838 under the leadership of Feargus O'Connor and William Lovett. Chartism derived its name from its celebrated People's Charter, a program of six points. They included demands for universal manhood suffrage, the secret ballot, abolition of property qualifications for members of the House of Commons, and payment of salaries to members of Commons. Though some of the Chartists advocated violence, most of them confined their activities to mass demonstrations and to the drafting of petitions to be presented to Parliament. In 1848, under the stimulus of the February Revolution in France, the leaders prepared for a giant effort. A procession of 500,000 workers was to march to the Houses of Parliament for the purpose of presenting a monster petition and overawing the members into granting reforms. The ruling classes were badly frightened. The pugnacious old Duke of Wellington was again summoned to command the troops. In addition to the regular army, he was provided with a special force of 170,000 constables. But on the day scheduled for the demonstration there was a heavy downpour of rain. Instead of the 500,000 workers who were to march in the parade, only a tenth of that number appeared. When the petition was presented to Parliament, it was found to contain less than half of the vaunted 6,000,000 signatures, and some of these were fictitious.

Though Chartism ended in failure, the spirit it represented lived on. It is significant that most of the six points, with the single exception of the demand for annual Parliaments, have since been incorporated in the British constitution. In the years following the fiasco of 1848 the forces of democracy gradually recouped their strength and succeeded under the guidance of more practical leaders in achieving considerable progress. In 1858 they wrung from a Conservative government the abolition of property qualifications for members of the House of Commons. By 1866 the democratic movement had gained such headway that the leaders of both parties were ready to compete with each other for popular support. The result was the Reform Act of 1867, maneuvered through Parliament by the Conservative Benjamin Disraeli when the old generation of Liberals refused to go along with William E. Gladstone in enacting the more moderate bill of the preceding year. The Reform Act of 1867 conferred the franchise upon nearly all men in towns and cities who made up the class of industrial workers. In 1884 the Liberals had a turn at extending the franchise. The Reform Act of that year, the third in the series of great electoral reform measures, was sponsored by Gladstone. Its main provision was to extend the voting requirements hitherto adopted for the cities and towns to the counties. The result was to enfranchise nearly all the agricultural

The Reform Acts of 1867 and 1884

A Chartist Demonstration in London

laborers. All that remained was to give the suffrage to women, migratory laborers, and the very poor who could not meet any of the residence or property requirements previously set up. These final concessions were not made until 1918.

The second of the chief factors in the evolution of democracy in Great Britain was the development of the cabinet system. Without the growth of this system Britain might well have remained simply a limited monarchy. It must be understood that the cabinet is not merely a council of ministers but is the supreme organ of the government. It is a committee of Parliament, responsible to the House of Commons, which exercises in the name of the crown the supreme legislative and executive authority. Not only does it decide all questions of general policy, but it originates nearly all legislation; and, as long as it remains in office, it determines what bills shall be passed. If it is defeated in the House of Commons on a fundamental issue, it must either resign forthwith or "go to the country"—that is, dissolve Parliament and order a new election to test the opinion of the voters. In other words, the cabinet has full responsibility for the management of public affairs, subject only to the will of the people and to that of their representatives in the House of Commons. When Englishmen speak of "His (or Her) Majesty's Government," it is the cabinet they have in mind. When the party in power loses an election and thereby control of the House of Commons, the leader of the opposition party immediately forms a new cabinet. While awaiting his turn to become Prime Minister he receives a salary as leader of His (or Her) Majesty's Loyal Opposition.

The British cabinet system

As almost everyone knows, the cabinet system was the product of a slow evolution of precedent. No statute or great charter brought it into being, and to this day it rests solely upon custom. Its history goes back no farther than the Glorious Revolution. Not until after the supremacy of the king had been superseded by the supremacy of Parliament was the principle established that the chief ministers of the crown should be responsible to Parliament. Upon coming to the throne in 1689, William and Mary acceded to the demand that their choice of advisers should be satisfactory to the legislature. For a time they selected their ministers from both of the major parties, but as the need for harmonious relations with Parliament grew more urgent, they gradually restricted their choice to the party which held the majority. In this way the precedent was set that all the chief ministers should possess the confidence of the dominant group in Parliament. But the cabinet was not yet a very powerful body. It did not become so until the reign of George I (1714–1727). George was a dull-witted prince from the German state of Hanover. Since he could neither speak nor understand the English language, he entrusted the whole work of governing to his ministers. He stayed away from meetings of the cabinet entirely and allowed that body to pass under the direction of Sir Robert Walpole. Though he persistently disclaimed the title, Walpole was the first Prime Minister in

The early evolution of the cabinet system

the modern sense. He was the first to perform the double function of head of the cabinet and leader of the majority party in the House of Commons. When in 1742 he suffered defeat in the House of Commons, he resigned immediately, notwithstanding the fact that he still possessed the full confidence of the king.

Such was the early evolution of the cabinet system. Though most of the precedents upon which it rests had already been set by the middle of the eighteenth century, it still had a rocky road to travel. Some members of Parliament disliked the system, since it appeared to involve a partial surrender of Parliamentary supremacy. Not until about the middle of the nineteenth century was the cabinet system universally accepted or fully comprehended as an integral part of the British constitution. Its operation was first clearly described by Walter Bagehot in his *English Constitution*, published in 1867. In more recent years a number of new precedents were added, the most important of them being that when the cabinet is defeated in the House of Commons, the Prime Minister and his colleagues shall have the option of resigning immediately or of dissolving Parliament and appealing to the country in a great national referendum.

Scarcely less important in the evolution of political democracy in Great Britain was the emergence of the House of Commons as the more powerful branch of Parliament. Down to the eighteenth century the House of Lords, composed of hereditary peers and the princes of the church, enjoyed much greater dignity and influence. The first step toward the supremacy of the representative chamber was the establishment of the principle, during Walpole's ministry, that the cabinet should be responsible exclusively to the Commons. In the early nineteenth century the precedent became fixed that the lower house should have final authority over matters of finance. But still the Lords had enormous power. They had a veto over general legislation, which was limited only by the fear of public resentment and by the authority of the Prime Minister in an emergency to threaten the creation of new peers.[2] Furthermore, since the upper chamber was invariably a Tory stronghold, the favorite schemes of Liberal cabinets were often balked. Matters reached a crisis in 1909 when the Lords threw out the budget prepared by David Lloyd George, Chancellor of the Exchequer, and backed by the Asquith cabinet. The Prime Minister dissolved Parliament and appealed to the voters. Though his party won but a modest victory, he was convinced that the nation was on his side and began preparation of a bill to clip the wings of the House of Lords. The measure, known as the Parliament Act of 1911, was finally passed after a threat to swamp the upper house with a majority of Liberal peers. The Parliament

The later evolution of the cabinet system

The emergence of the House of Commons as the more powerful branch of Parliament

---

[2] In Britain the monarch has the authority to elevate an unlimited number of men to the peerage. But since the crown acts only upon the advice of the Prime Minister, it is this official who has the actual power to create new members of the House of Lords. If necessary, he could use this power to pack the upper house with his own followers.

Act provided that money bills should become laws one month after they had been passed by the House of Commons, whether the Lords approved them or not; in the case of other legislation the House of Lords was given only a suspensive veto: if ordinary bills were passed by the Commons in three consecutive sessions, they became laws at the end of two years, despite the opposition of the upper house. It is therefore accurate to say that the popularly elected branch of Parliament was henceforth, for all practical purposes, the real legislative body in Great Britain.

2.   DEMOCRACY ON THE CONTINENT OF EUROPE

The first major country on the Continent of Europe to undergo a movement toward democracy was France. The process began during the reign of Louis Philippe (1830–1848). Louis Philippe professed to rule with the consent of the people, but he really took his cue from the bourgeoisie and systematically ignored the lower classes. However, the movement stopped short of its goal. When completed, only 200,000 Frenchmen could vote. By 1848 the king and his ministers had so aroused the disgust of a large number of their subjects that the latter were ready to incur the risks of a new revolution to overthrow the monarchy.

The insignificant progress of democracy in France before 1848

The French revolution of 1848 is known as the February Revolution. Its causes were several. One was the demand of all but a small minority of the people for more democracy. Another was disgust with the corruption of Louis Philippe and his intimate circle; convinced, like Louis XV in an earlier day, that soon would come the deluge, they strove to enrich themselves as fast as possible at public expense. A third cause was discontent of Catholics with the apparent anticlerical bias of Louis Philippe. He had appointed as his chief minister the Protestant Guizot and had allowed him to discriminate against Catholic schools. A fourth cause was the spread of socialism through the ranks of the industrial proletariat. During the lean months of the depression which began in 1847, many of the workers had been converted to the socialism of Louis Blanc, with its scheme for national workshops to give employment and prosperity to all. But the February Revolution was also a product of nationalism, and in the end this factor was destined to dwarf all the others. As "king of the bourgeoisie" Louis Philippe had placed business above everything else. His chief capitalist supporters were determined that France should not become involved in any war lest their trade and investments be imperiled. Consequently they refused to yield to the clamor for intervention on behalf of the Poles against Russia or of the Italians against Austria. This angered patriotic Frenchmen who thirsted for national glory and for the restoration of France to a position of leadership among the powers of Europe.

Causes of the Revolution of 1848

By 1847 the government of Louis Philippe had alienated the sympathies of nearly all but a wealthy minority of its subjects. However, the most defiant opposition came from patriotic republicans and monarchists and from the socialists. In 1847 these groups organized huge demonstrations designed to impress upon the king the need for reform. When the government took alarm and prohibited a demonstration scheduled for February 22, 1848, barricades were thrown up in the streets, and two days later Louis Philippe was forced to abdicate. A provisional government of republicans and socialists took over control of the state, and in April elections were held for a constituent assembly. The results of the voting were a disappointment to the socialists, for the reactionaries and middle-class parties had combined to protect the interests of private property. A revolt broke out which was finally crushed after bloody fighting in the slums of the capital. The way was now cleared for the bourgeois majority in the Constituent Assembly to complete a constitution for the Second Republic. The document as it finally emerged was copied in part from that of the United States. It contained a bill of rights and provided for universal manhood suffrage and for the separation of powers. There was to be a President elected by the people for a four-year term, and the people were also to choose a single-chambered legislative assembly. Having finished their work, the authors of the constitution set December 10, 1848, as the date for the election of the first President.

As we learned in a previous chapter, the outcome of this election was the choice of Louis Napoleon Bonaparte, nephew of Napoleon I, as President. Though he had ample powers as a constitutional executive, he was not satisfied with a less grandiose title than that of his famous uncle. Accordingly, in 1851, he made himself dictator and a year later Emperor of France. Thereafter most remnants of democracy disappeared, though following the collapse of his Mexican venture the Emperor found it expedient to restore to the Assembly the power to initiate laws and to ratify or reject the budget. Further concessions might also have been made in time had it not been for the Franco-Prussian War. Napoleon III allowed himself to be dragged into this war, with disastrous results. Following the defeat of his armies in the Battle of Sedan (September 2, 1870) and his capture soon afterward, his government was overthrown by an uprising in Paris. A National Assembly was elected and a provisional republic set up which later came to be called the Third Republic.

The constitution of the Third Republic consisted of three organic laws adopted by the National Assembly in 1875. Though amendments and precedents effected some changes, its essential form continued until the dissolution of the Third Republic on July 9, 1940. The government established by this constitution was about as

The overthrow of
Louis Philippe

Drawing of a Medallion by Daumier. The inscription reads "Louis Philippe, the Last King of France." It reflects a popular sentiment of the time.

Beginning of the
Third Republic

685

democratic as any in the world. There was a parliament, with a lower house elected by universal manhood suffrage, and a President chosen by parliament. The cardinal feature, however, was the cabinet system, copied in part from Great Britain. The most important powers of the government were exercised by a ministry responsible to parliament. The President was about the nearest approach to a nonentity that it would be possible to find among heads of state. His every official act had to be countersigned—which is to say, approved—by a member of the ministry. On the other hand, there were several important differences between the cabinet system in France and that in Great Britain. The French cabinet was responsible not only to the lower house or Chamber of Deputies but also to the Senate, which was elected indirectly by the people; the cabinet in Great Britain was responsible exclusively to the House of Commons. The most important difference consisted in the fact that the French Premier had no effective authority to dissolve parliament. This meant that members of parliament could overturn cabinets at will, with no risk of being forced to stand for reelection. If defeated on the floor of either house, the Premier and his colleagues had no alternative but to resign. With the possible exception of the multiplicity of parties, nothing contributed so much to the instability of the French system. Cabinets were sometimes unable to hold the support of a majority in parliament for more than a few weeks or even a few days. Although this instability was often deplored, it was really the product of a natural reaction of the French people against previous dictatorial regimes.

Meanwhile, as a result of the Franco-Prussian War, events were moving toward a new climax in Germany. A great outburst of patriotism across the Rhine made it possible for Bismarck to absorb the south German states into a North German Confederation. Treaties negotiated during the course of the war stipulated that all of Germany should be united into a Hohenzollern empire. These agreements were given formal effect by an impressive ceremony staged in the palace of Louis XIV at Versailles on January 18, 1871, in which King William I of Prussia was invested with the title of German Emperor. Bismarck, now raised to the dignity of prince, became the first Imperial Chancellor. The government thus created had only two features which could positively be considered democratic. First, there was universal manhood suffrage in national elections; second, there was a parliament with a lower house, or Reichstag, elected by popular vote. In other respects the system was well adapted to conservative rule. In place of the cabinet system, the Chancellor and the other ministers were responsible solely to the Emperor. The Emperor himself was no figurehead; he was vested with extensive authority over the army and navy, over foreign relations, and over the enactment and execution of the laws. Besides, he could declare war if the coasts or territory of the Empire were at-

William I of Prussia

tacked, and as King of Prussia he controlled one-third of the votes in the upper house, or Bundesrat, of the imperial parliament.

Yet the government of the German Empire was not a complete autocracy. Although the Kaiser could influence the enactment of legislation, he had no veto power. All treaties he negotiated had to be approved by the Bundesrat, and he could get no money without the consent of the Reichstag. Indeed, the latter body was far from a mere debating society, as was so often alleged by Germany's enemies during World War I. On the contrary, it had law-making powers virtually the equivalent of those of the Bundesrat, and it was strong enough to extort concessions from several Chancellors.

It should be recognized, further, that the government of the German Empire was a constitutional government and not a party dictatorship like that of the Nazis in the twentieth century. The laws were extensive and complete and, for the most part, were strictly observed. Every little bureaucrat had a code to follow, and no one, not even the Emperor, was above the law. The chief defect of the system, aside from the absence of ministerial responsibility to parliament, was the inability of the representatives of the people to originate legislation. Their power was essentially negative: they could veto proposals of the Kaiser and his ministers, but they could rarely initiate measures of their own. Finally, it should be borne in mind that the German Empire was a federal state. Though it was described by President Lowell of Harvard as a union comprising "a lion, a half-dozen foxes, and a score of mice," the division of powers made by the constitution was essentially the same as in the United States. That is, all powers not granted to the central government were reserved to the states. All of the states had control over their own forms of government, relations of church and state, public education, highways, and police. In addition, certain of the larger southern states were given special privileges when they entered the Empire. Even the enforcement of the laws was left primarily in the hands of the state governments, since the government of the Empire had no courts or police and no other machinery for applying the laws against individuals.

Like the republic of France, the new German Empire also had trouble with the Catholic Church. The motivating forces in the two countries were different. French anticlericalism was mainly a liberating movement against the government in league with the Catholic Church. The German movement was chiefly government inspired and directed against the Catholic Church. Called by the pretentious name of *Kulturkampf*, or "struggle for civilization," it was initiated by Bismarck with some help from intellectual liberals, in 1872. Bismarck's motives were almost exclusively nationalistic. He was neither a skeptic nor a materialist but a staunch Lutheran. Nevertheless, he perceived in some Catholic activities a threat to the power and stability of the Empire he had just created. He resented, first of all, the support Catholic priests continued to give to the states'-rights movement in southern Germany and to the grievances of Alsatians and Poles. He was alarmed also by recent assertions of the authority of the Pope to intervene in secular matters and by the promulgation in 1870 of the dogma of papal infallibility. For these reasons he resolved to deal such a blow to Catholic influence in Germany that it would never again be a factor in national or local politics. His weapons were a series of laws and decrees issued between 1872 and 1875. First, he induced the Reichstag to expel all the Jesuits from the country. Next, he forced through the Prussian Landtag the so-called May Laws, which placed theological seminaries under state control and permitted the government to regulate the appointment of bishops and priests. No one was allowed to be appointed to any position in the Church unless he was a German citizen and then only after a state examination. At the same time civil marriage was made compulsory, even though a religious ceremony had already been performed. In the enforcement of these measures, six of the ten Catholic bishops in Prussia were imprisoned, and hundreds of priests were driven from the country.

The failure of the
Kulturkampf

Although Bismarck won some of the chief battles of the *Kulturkampf,* he lost the war. The causes of his failure were several. First, he antagonized his progressive followers by refusing to consider their demands for ministerial responsibility. Second, the Catholic or Center party appealed so effectively on behalf of the persecuted clergy and adopted so enlightened an economic program that it grew into the largest political party in Germany. In the elections of 1874 it captured nearly a fourth of the seats in the Reichstag. Third, Bismarck was alarmed by the growth of socialism, and he was even more dismayed when the chief sponsors of this philosophy, the Social Democrats, formed an alliance with the Centrists. At their current rate of growth these two parties would soon have a majority in the Reichstag. To prevent this Bismarck gradually relaxed his persecution of the Catholics. Between 1878 and 1886 nearly all of the obnoxious legislation was repealed, and the *Kulturkampf* passed into the limbo of statesmen's blunders. The Catholic Church was thus restored practically to its former position in Germany.

Democracy in
Italy

As in Germany, the advancement of democracy in Italy was closely tied in with a nationalist movement for unification. By a series of revolutions, wars, and diplomatic maneuvers, this movement attained its goal, accomplished, as we have seen, between 1848 and 1871. As the revolutionary fervor of 1848 swept across the peninsula, one ruler after another granted reforms. Charles Albert, King of Sardinia, outdistanced all the others with his celebrated Fundamental Statute providing for civil liberties and a parliamentary form of government. Ultimately, this Statute became the constitution of a united Italy, as the various states were brought under the rule of the House of Savoy, the reigning dynasty of the Kingdom of Sardinia.

Some of the smaller states of central and west central Europe actually made more progress in democracy than did most of their large neighbors. For example, all had the cabinet system of government by the eve of World War I. In addition, universal manhood suffrage had been adopted in Switzerland, in Belgium, and in the Scandinavian countries. Norway and Denmark had taken the next logical step of extending the franchise to women. Belgium, Sweden, and Switzerland had adopted proportional representation, and Switzerland had made extensive use of the initiative and referendum. Proportional representation is a device for guaranteeing representation to minorities as well as to the majority. Each political party is awarded a number of representatives in the legislative body in direct proportion to its voting strength. The initiative and referendum are instruments of *direct* democracy. Under the initiative a certain percentage of the voters can initiate legislation and compel a legislature or parliament to take action upon it. The referendum is a device for submitting legislation to the people for their final approval or rejection. With the exception of proportional representation, which was adopted for limited use in local elections in Great Britain, none of these devices produced much appeal in the larger countries.

3. EQUALITARIAN DEMOCRACY IN THE UNITED STATES

The United States did not begin its history as a democracy. Although a few early leaders like Roger Williams and Samuel Adams professed democratic ideals, these were not the doctrines of the most prominent. The Fathers of the Constitution were definitely not interested in the rule of the masses. James Madison thought the people were too prone to impetuous and violent impulses ever to be trusted with unlimited power. The primary aim of the fathers of our government was not to enthrone the masses but to establish a *republic* that would promote stability and protect the rights of property against the leveling of tendencies of majorities. For this reason they adopted checks and balances, devised the Electoral College for choosing the President, created a powerful judiciary, and entrusted the selection of Senators to the legislatures of the several states. In spite of these features the political system the fathers created was liberal in comparison with other governments of that time. The President, at least, was not a monarch, nor was the Senate a chamber of nobles.

Following the establishment of a new government in 1789, ideals of a viable democracy began to make headway in the United States. Until 1801 the Federalist party held the reins of power, representing the big landowners, the money power, and the conservatives generally. In the latter year the Democratic-Republicans gained control as a result of the election of Thomas Jefferson to the Presidency

689

Thomas Jefferson. Painting by
Gilbert Stuart.

in 1800. This event is often referred to as the Jeffersonian Revolution, on the supposition that Jefferson was the champion of the masses and of the political power of the underprivileged. There is danger, however, in carrying this interpretation too far. In several respects Jefferson's ideas were far removed from democracy in its historic meaning. Instead of being a follower of Rousseau, he was a disciple of Locke. He believed that that government is best which governs least, and he strenuously opposed the unlimited sovereignty of the majority. His conception of an ideal political system was an aristocracy of "virtue and talent," in which respect for personal liberty would be the guiding principle. Furthermore, he compared the mobs of great cities to sores on the human body and despised the mass of industrial workers as "panders of vice, and instruments by which the liberties of a country are generally overturned." [3]

Yet it cannot be denied that the Jeffersonian movement had a number of democratic objectives of cardinal importance. Its leaders were vigorous opponents of special privilege, whether of birth or of wealth. They worked for the repeal of primogeniture and entail and the abolition of established churches. They led the campaign for the addition of a Bill of Rights to the Federal Constitution and were almost exclusively responsible for its success. Although professing devotion to the principle of the separation of powers, they actually believed in the supremacy of the representatives of the people and viewed with abhorrence the attempts of the executive and judicial branches to increase their power. Three of the most typical ideals of Jefferson himself were decentralized government, periodic revisions of constitutions and laws, and the importance of public education. He stressed the value of local government to the extent of advocating primary assemblies similar to the New England town meetings for the exercise of a large proportion of the public powers. He urged that constitutions and laws be submitted to the people for their approval or rejection every nineteen or twenty years, on the theory that no one generation has the right to bind its successors for the indefinite future. In later life he completed plans for an elaborate system of public education. There was to be free instruction for all children in the elementary schools, and scholarships were to be provided in district colleges and in the state university for a limited number of students selected on the basis of intelligence and achievement. By this method Jefferson sought to ensure opportunity for all, not simply for the well-born and the rich. The persons thus educated would be available for selection as natural aristocrats by enlightened citizens who had received enough knowledge to recognize good men when they saw them.

By the end of the War of 1812 the force of Jeffersonian Democracy was almost entirely spent. Any democratic movement of the

[3] *Writings of Jefferson* (Washington ed.), I, 403.

future would have to proceed from different premises and rest upon new foundations. Not only did the war create new problems and divert men's interests from the need for reform, but the economic aspect of the country had undergone numerous changes. The common people in the cities had grown conscious of their political importance and had begun to demand privileges. More important, the dominance of the Old South, the stronghold of Jeffersonian Democracy, had passed into history. As a result of the Louisiana Purchase and the settlement of the Northwest Territory, a new frontier had come into existence. Life in the new areas was characterized by a rugged freedom and independence that left no room for snobbishness or class distinctions. In the struggle to survive, the things that counted most were hard work and sharp wits. Birth and education were of little value. As a consequence, a new democracy, which eventually found its leader in Andrew Jackson, rapidly crystallized around the major principle of equality. The Jacksonian Democrats considered all men politically equal, not merely in rights but in privileges. They therefore stood for universal manhood suffrage, for making all public offices elective, and for rotation in office. Since they considered one man as good as another, they rejected the idea that special knowledge or ability was required for government positions. They even threw open to ordinary citizens such offices as county surveyor and superintendent of schools. Paradoxically, the Jacksonian Democrats approved of a strong executive. They restored the veto power to the state governors, lengthened their terms of office, and acclaimed the President of the United States as the real representative of the people's will. The explanation seems to lie in the fact that they had come to regard legislative bodies as strongholds of "special interests."

The most powerful influence affecting the growth of American democracy in the nineteenth century was the Civil War, or War between the States, as it is sometimes called. The most obvious cause of the war, of course, was slavery. The first Negro slaves were brought to Virginia from Africa in 1619. Thereafter for nearly two centuries their numbers increased slowly. But in 1793, with the invention of the cotton gin, the picture was changed radically. The production of cotton was transformed from a minor activity into a tremendously profitable enterprise. Output grew from 4000 bales in 1790 to 4,000,000 in 1860. The plantation system based on slave labor became firmly fixed in the South.

Yet it would be a mistake to assume that slavery was the sole cause of the Civil War. Sentiment in favor of abolition was far from unanimous even in the North. Abolitionists were commonly regarded as fanatics and were sometimes brutally mistreated. Even lynching was not unknown. The majority of citizens in the North seemed perfectly willing to tolerate the continued existence of slav-

Jeffersonian Democracy superseded by Jacksonian Democracy

Political consequences of slavery

Slavery as a cause of expansionism

691

ery in the South. But they opposed its extension into the Louisiana Purchase or into the regions of the Southwest conquered from Mexico in 1848. Such areas they hoped to organize into free states to be settled by land-hungry migrants from New England and the Middle Atlantic region. Leaders of the South were just as anxious to organize as much of these territories as possible into slave states, and thereby to prevent the reduction of their section to a status of permanent inferiority with the North. This conflict over the extension of slavery was probably the basic cause of the Civil War.

Consequences of
the Civil War

The Civil War ushered in epochal changes in the political and social environment of the United States. By the Thirteenth Amendment slavery was legally abolished. Two succeeding amendments gave the former slaves citizenship and prohibited their disfranchisement because of race, color, or previous condition of servitude. Yet these amendments appeared to grant more than they actually accomplished. Although the former slaves were no longer the property of a master, they were often doomed to a kind of wage slavery that made a mockery of their so-called freedom. In like manner the Fifteenth Amendment gave no one the right to vote but simply prohibited denial of the vote on account of race or previous condition of servitude. The makeshift character of these arrangements was eventually ratified by the "compromise of 1877." This compromise was an understanding between Northern Republicans and Southern Democrats by which troops were to be withdrawn from the South, the seceding states were to be readmitted to the Union, and the South was to be left largely to its own devices in observing the Fourteenth and Fifteenth Amendments. Fundamentally, it was a conservative agreement, and one of its primary purposes was to enlist the cooperation of Southern agrarians with Northern businessmen in opening the South to capitalist exploitation.

Efforts for the
widening of
democracy

Movements toward the broadening of democracy flourished between 1880 and 1914. Again, the motivation was largely economic. Severe economic crises punctuated the 1870's, 1880's, and 1890's. Collapse of agricultural prices and shutting down of factories caused great suffering in both rural and urban areas. Political adventurers convinced many people that a restricted money supply was the root of the evil. Accordingly, demands arose for the issue of greenbacks to supplement inadequate quantities of gold and silver. In the 1890's the pressure for greenbacks was replaced by a demand for the coinage of silver in a much larger ratio to gold than had hitherto existed. Not only did the depression parties of the late nineteenth century advocate currency inflation; both the Greenback party and the Populist party urged an income tax, government ownership of railroads and telegraph and telephone lines, and direct election of United States Senators. Both parties went down to defeat in the Presidential elections, although the Populists rolled up a total of 6,500,000 votes in the election of 1896.

Theodore Roosevelt. The candidate of the Progressive party, or Bull Moose party, is shown campaigning in Vermont, 1912.

Though Populism declined with the end of the century, the movement it represented did not die. It sprang to life anew with the organization of the Progressive party in the early 1900's. In general, it had a broader appeal than either of its immediate forerunners. It was not essentially an agrarian movement but sought the support of liberal reformers from all classes. Its leaders sidetracked the currency reforms of Greenbackers and Populists and concentrated on political objectives. Among these were the initiative, referendum, and recall, the secret ballot, the direct primary, the short ballot, and proportional representation. The high-water mark of the movement was the election of 1912, when Theodore Roosevelt ran as the Progressive candidate for President against William H. Taft, the regular Republican, and Woodrow Wilson. Though Wilson himself was in many ways a Progressive, he ran under the Democratic label and was victorious in the three-cornered contest.

Populism graduates to Progressivism

Democratic evolutionary movements in the United States generally fell upon evil days before they were completely successful. They usually managed to attain some of their goals before they went down into the dust of history but none achieved its full program. Nearly all were defeated by some extrinsic factor. In the vast majority of cases that factor was war. Jeffersonian democracy was killed by the War of 1812. Jacksonian democracy came to an untimely end with the Mexican War. Any chance that the better elements of Populism might have survived was stifled by the Spanish-American War. Finally, the most promising of the democratic reform movements of the early twentieth century, the Progressive movement, received a crushing blow by the outbreak of World

The doom of Populism and Progressivism by war

693

War I. Though the United States did not enter that war immediately, the fear and suspicion engendered by the conflict in Europe fostered an environment hostile to democratic progress everywhere. As in previous instances advancement was not resumed until after hostilities had ceased.

SELECTED READINGS

· *Items so designated are available in paperbound editions.*

DEMOCRACY

Bernstein, Samuel, *Blanqui*, Paris, 1970.

Brogan, D. W., *France under the Republic*, New York, 1940.

· Cole, G. D. H., and Postgate, R., *The British Common People, 1746–1946*, New York, 1947 (Barnes & Noble).

· Derry, J. W., *A Short History of Nineteenth-Century England*, New York, 1963 (Mentor).

· Gordon, Donald C., *The Moment of Power: Britain's Imperial Epoch*, Englewood Cliffs, N.J., 1970 (Prentice-Hall).

Hovell, M., *The Chartist Movement*, New York, 1925.

Karpovich, M., *Imperial Russia, 1801–1917*, New York, 1932. An excellent short treatise.

Lindsay, A. D., *The Essentials of Democracy*, Philadelphia, 1929.

——, *The Modern Democratic State*, New York, 1947.

· Maynard, John, *Russia in Flux*, New York, 1948 (Collier).

· Mayo, H. B., *An Introduction to Democratic Theory*, New York, 1960 (Oxford).

Neumann, Robert G., *European and Comparative Government*, New York, 1960.

· Pares, Bernard, *A History of Russia*, New York, 1928 (Vintage). A standard work.

Postgate, Raymond, *1848: Story of a Year*, London, 1955.

Reid, J. H. S., *The Origins of the British Labour Party*, Minneapolis, 1955.

Riasanovsky, N. V., *A Short History of Russia*, New York, 1963.

Robinson, G. T., *Rural Russia under the Old Regime*, New York, 1932.

Seymour, Charles, *Electoral Reforms in England, 1832–1885*, New Haven, 1915.

· Thompson, J. M., *Louis Napoleon and the Second Empire*, New York, 1955 (Norton Library). A valuable summary based on scholarly works.

SOCIAL REFORM

· Hobsbawm, E. J., *Primitive Rebels,* London, 1959 (Norton Library).

Keep, J. L. H., *The Rise of Social Democracy in Russia*, New York, 1963.

Laski, H. J., *The Rise of Liberalism*, New York, 1936. A critical study from a Marxist viewpoint.

Pipkin, C. W., *Social Politics and Modern Democracies*, New York, 1931.

· Robertson, Priscilla, *Revolutions of 1848: A Social History*, Princeton, 1952 (Torchbook). A stimulating account written from the viewpoint of the people who lived at that time.

· Thompson, E. P., *The Making of the English Working Class*, New York, 1964 (Vintage).

Woodward, Ernest, *The Age of Reform, 1815–1870*, Oxford, 1938. Great Britain during the Age of Democracy.

CHAPTER 25

Intellect and the Arts in the Age of Democracy and Nationalism

If a single cell, under appropriate conditions, becomes a man in the space of a few years, there can surely be no difficulty in understanding how, under appropriate conditions, a cell may, in the course of untold millions of years, give origin to the human race.
—Herbert Spencer, *Principles of Biology*

The advancement of learning in the seventeenth and eighteenth centuries is often referred to as *the* Intellectual Revolution. It would be just as accurate to apply this term to the intellectual progress between 1830 and 1914. Never before in so short a time had the mind of man yielded discoveries and provocative ideas in such profusion. And certainly a large proportion of these were quite as revolutionary in their effects as any that had come down from the past. But in several respects the intellectual revolution from 1830 to 1914 was different from that of the seventeenth and eighteenth centuries. The deductive or rationalist tradition was now almost entirely dead, and the decay of rationalism was reflected in a marked decline in the relative importance of philosophy. Indeed, in the new age philosophy was often little more than an echo of science. It was not that the problems of the universe had finally been solved, or that men had lost the ability to think, but rather that the sciences had come to be accepted as the only worthwhile sources of knowledge. To be sure, there were some seekers of wisdom who rebelled against the new tendency; but there were few who had the hardihood to advocate a revival of pure deduction or the viewpoint of the mystic in discovering truth. In other words, the victory of empiricism, or that philosophy which derives its truths from concrete experience rather than from abstract reasoning, was almost complete.

The character of the new intellectual revolution

695

The nature and
causes of the
tremendous sci-
entific progress

Compared with all preceding epochs, the period from 1830 to
1914 marked the zenith of scientific progress. The attainments of
this period were not only more numerous, but they probed more
deeply into the hidden mysteries of things. Each of the older
branches of science was greatly developed, and a dozen or more
new ones were added to the list. The phenomenal scientific progress
of this era was the result of various factors. It was due in some
measure to the stimulus of the First Industrial Revolution, to the rising standard of living, and to the desire for comfort and pleasure.
But to think of modern science as essentially a species of practical
knowledge is to misunderstand its import. The contemporary pure
physicist or chemist is no more concerned with problems of the
workaday world than was St. Thomas Aquinas or Albert the Great.
In fact, pure science occupies a position in the modern age somewhat similar to that of Scholasticism in the thirteenth century. It is
at once a substitute for logic as a discipline for the mind and an expression of an insatiable desire for the conquest of all knowledge,
for an intellectual mastery of the universe.

Explanations of
organic evolution:
the hypothesis of
Lamarck

Although none of the sciences was neglected between 1830 and
1914, it was the biological sciences and medicine which underwent
the greatest development. The outstanding achievement in biology
was the development of new explanations of the theory of organic
evolution. We have seen that this theory was at least as old as Anaximander in the sixth century B.C., and that it was accepted by many
of the great minds of antiquity. We have learned also that it was
revived in the eighteenth century by the scientists Buffon and
Linnaeus. But neither of these men offered much proof or explained
how the process of evolution works. The first to develop a systematic hypothesis of organic evolution was the French biologist, Jean
Lamarck (1744–1829). The essential principle in Lamarck's hypothesis, published in 1809, is the inheritance of acquired characteristics. He maintained that an animal, subjected to a change in environment, acquires new habits, which in turn are reflected in
structural changes. These acquired characteristics of body
structure, he believed, are transmissible to the offspring, with the result that after a series of generations a new species of animal is eventually produced. Lamarck's successors found little evidence to con-
firm this hypothesis, but it dominated biological thought for upwards of fifty years. Though still not absolutely discredited, it is
admitted to have no more than a partial validity.

A much more scientific hypothesis of organic evolution was that
of Charles Darwin, published in 1859. Darwin was born in 1809, the
son of a small-town physician. Though he lived to be seventy-three,
he was of frail constitution, and during most of his adult life he
seems never to have enjoyed a day of the health of ordinary men. In

accordance with his father's wish, he began the study of medicine at Edinburgh, but soon withdrew and entered Cambridge to prepare for the ministry. Here he gave most of his time to natural history and was graduated only tenth in his class among those not seeking honors. In 1831 he obtained an appointment as naturalist without pay on H.M.S. *Beagle*, which had been chartered for a scientific expedition around the world. The voyage lasted nearly five years and gave Darwin an unparalleled opportunity to become acquainted at first hand with the manifold variations of animal life. He noted the differences between animals inhabiting islands and related species on nearby continents and observed the resemblances between living animals and the fossilized remains of extinct species in the same locality. It was a magnificent preparation for his life's work. Upon returning from the voyage he happened to read Malthus' *Essay on Population* and was struck by the author's contention that throughout the world of nature many more individuals are born than can ever survive, and that consequently the weaker ones must perish in the struggle for food. Finally, after twenty more years of careful and extensive research he issued his *Origin of Species,* which has probably done as much to influence modern thinking as any other single book ever written.

Charles Darwin

Darwin's hypothesis as contained in his *Origin of Species* (1859) is known as the hypothesis of natural selection. This involves the idea that it is nature, or the environment, which selects those variants among the offspring that are to survive and reproduce. Darwin pointed out, first of all, that the parents of every species beget more offspring than can possibly survive. He maintained that, consequently, a struggle takes place among these offspring for food, shelter, warmth, and other conditions necessary for life. In this struggle certain individuals have the advantage because of the factor of *variation,* which means that no two of the offspring are exactly alike. Some are born strong, others weak; some have longer horns or sharper claws than their brothers and sisters or perhaps a body coloration which enables them better to blend with their surroundings and thus to elude their enemies. It is these favored members of the species that win out in the struggle for existence; the others are eliminated generally before they have lived long enough to reproduce. He regarded variation and natural selection as the primary factors in the origin of new species. In other words, he taught that individuals with favorable characteristics would transmit their inherited qualities to their descendants through countless generations, and that successive eliminations of the least fit would eventually produce a new species. Finally, it should be noted that Darwin applied his concept of evolution not only to plant and animal species but also to man. In his second great work, *The Descent of Man* (1871), he attempted to show that the human race originally sprang from some apelike ancestor, long since extinct, but probably a common forebear of the existing anthropoid apes and man.

The Darwinian hypothesis of natural selection

The Darwinian hypothesis was elaborated and improved by several later biologists. About 1890 the German August Weismann (1834–1914) flatly rejected the idea that acquired characteristics could be inherited. He conducted experiments to show that body cells and reproductive cells are entirely distinct, and that there is no way in which changes in the former can effect the latter. He concluded, therefore, that the only qualities transmissible to the offspring are those which have always been present in the germ plasm of the parents. In 1901 the Dutch botanist, Hugo De Vries (1848–1935), published his celebrated mutation hypothesis, based in large part upon laws of heredity discovered by the Austrian monk, Gregor Mendel (1822–1884). De Vries asserted that evolution results not from minor variations, as Darwin has assumed, but from radical differences or mutations, which appear in more or less definite ratio among the offspring. When any of these mutations are favorable to survival in a given environment, the individuals possessing them naturally emerge triumphant in the struggle for existence. Not only do their descendants inherit these qualities, but from time to time new mutants appear, some of which are even better adapted for survival than their parents. Thus in a limited number of generations a new species may be brought into existence. The mutation theory of De Vries corrected one of the chief weaknesses in the Darwinian hypothesis. The variations which Darwin assumed to be the source of evolutionary changes are so small that an incredibly long time would be necessary to produce a new species. De Vries made it possible to conceive of evolution as proceeding by sudden leaps. [1]

Next to the exposition and proof of organic evolution, the most important biological achievement was probably the development of the cell theory. The German biologist Theodor Schwann (1810–1882) pointed out about 1835 that not only plants but animals also are composed of cells, and that all but the simplest of living things grow and mature by the division and multiplication of these tiny structural units. A few years later it was discovered that all cells are composed of essentially the same combination of matter, to which Hugo von Mohl (1805–1872) gave the name *protoplasm*. Another of the important biological achievements of this period was the development of embryology. The father of the modern science of embryology was the German-Russian Karl Ernst von Baer (1792–1876), who, about 1830, set forth his celebrated law of recapitulation. This law, which was subsequently elaborated by Ernst Haeckel (1834–1919), states that during the embryonic period each individual recapitulates or reproduces the various important stages in the life history of the species to which it belongs.

Illustrations from Darwin's First Edition of *The Descent of Man*. The drawings were used to point up the similarity between a human embryo (top) and that of a dog (bottom).

[1] It must be understood that the hypothesis of De Vries is not complete in itself, but is based upon Darwin's main principle of natural selection.

Louis Pasteur at Work in His Laboratory

Embryology was not the only subdivision of biology to be developed during the nineteenth century. About 1865 Louis Pasteur (1822–1895) laid the basis for the science of bacteriology by his epochal attack upon the theory of spontaneous generation. Hitherto it had been commonly supposed that bacteria and other microscopic organisms originated spontaneously from water or from decaying vegetable and animal matter. Pasteur succeeded in convincing the scientific world that all existing forms of life, no matter how small, are reproduced only by living beings. This was his famous law of biogenesis (all known forms of life come from pre-existing life).

Cytology and bacteriology

Even more spectacular than the achievements in biology was the progress in medicine. Following the discovery of vaccination for smallpox by Jenner in 1796, the next great landmark in the development of modern medicine was the introduction of ether as a general anaesthetic. Credit for this achievement was formerly given to William T. G. Morton, a Boston dentist, but it is now known that a Georgia physician, Crawford W. Long, performed the earliest operation with the use of ether in 1842. This discovery not only diminished the anguish of the patient, but enabled the surgeon to take his time and thereby increased the number of successful operations. But still many people died as a consequence of the bungling practice of physicians. Mortality was especially high in obstetrical cases, until methods were discovered of controlling the possibilities of infection. In 1847 the Hungarian physician Ignaz Semmelweiss found out that by washing his hands in antiseptic solutions he could reduce the death rate in obstetrical operations by more than four-

Landmarks of progress in medicine

699

fifths. This discovery was extended to the whole field of surgical practice about 1865 by the Englishman Joseph Lister (1827–1912), who is considered the father of antiseptic surgery. Lister achieved sensational results in preventing infection by cleansing wounds and surgical instruments with carbolic acid and by introducing carbolized catgut for surgical sewings. He was rewarded by the British government with a baronetcy in 1883 and was elevated to the peerage in 1897.

The germ theory of disease

The most significant milestone of medical progress during the second half of the nineteenth century was undoubtedly the germ theory of disease. Certainly few other accomplishments have contributed so much to the conquest of the most deadly maladies which afflict mankind. The germ theory of disease was mainly the work of Louis Pasteur and Robert Koch. Pasteur had been practically certain of the germinal origin of disease ever since he had established his biogenetic law, but he was unable to convince the medical profession. Because he was a chemist, physicians were inclined to be scornful of his work. They admitted the existence of germs, but they regarded them as more probably the results of disease than the cause. The opportunity to prove the validity of the theory came with the spread of an epidemic of anthrax, a disease which was carrying off hundreds of thousands of cattle and sheep in Germany and in France. About 1875 Robert Koch (1843–1910), an obscure country physician of East Prussia, began a series of experiments to prove that anthrax was the result of the tiny rodlike organisms found in the blood of the diseased animals. He inoculated mice with this contaminated blood and noticed that they soon sickened and died. He made cultures of the germs, breeding them on potatoes, and found that the germs alone, when introduced into the bodies of animals, were just as deadly as the blood. Meanwhile Pasteur had also been engaged in researches on anthrax. In 1881 he was challenged by his medical opponents to make a public test on cattle. He divided the animals into two groups. Half of them he inoculated with weakened germs of anthrax, and the remainder he left untreated. A few days later he injected malignant germs into all of the cattle. To the discomfiture of his opponents, every one of the animals that had not been inoculated died, while all of the others survived. The theory that germs were the cause of the disease could no longer be disputed.

The conquest of diseases produced by germs

Once the germ theory was positively established, achievements in medicine multiplied rapidly. The talents of Pasteur and Koch were still by no means exhausted. The former in 1885 evolved a method of treating persons afflicted with hydrophobia, one of the most horrible diseases known to humanity. As a result of this accomplishment, the death rate from a malady hitherto almost always fatal was reduced to less than 1 per cent. In 1882–1883 Koch discovered the bacilli of tuberculosis and of Asiatic cholera. Within a few years the germs of yet other diseases were isolated—of diphtheria, of the bubonic plague, of lockjaw, and of sleeping-sickness. For the prevention and treatment of several of these diseases, antitoxins or serums were developed, the first being the diphtheria antitoxin produced in 1892 by Emil von Behring. About the end of the century effective means of combating malaria and yellow fever were made possible by the discovery that both are spread by particular varieties of mosquitoes. Much advancement was made also in the treatment of syphilis. After the germ had been identified in 1905, August von Wassermann (1866–1925) devised a test for revealing its presence in the human body. In 1910 Paul Ehrlich developed a new drug, known as salvarsan, which proved to be an efficient specific for the disease in its primary and secondary stages. Still later the Austrian pathologist Julius Wagner von Jauregg (1857–1940) found out that a fever temperature induced by malaria or by other means has remarkable effects in alleviating advanced stages of the disease, such as syphilis of the brain or paresis.

Finally, it should be noted that by the outbreak of World War I a beginning had been made in the study of the ductless glands and in the discovery of the vitamins. The first step toward an understanding of the ductless or endocrine glands was taken in 1901 when the Japanese scientist Takamine isolated adrenalin, secreted by the suprarenal glands, and showed that it was useful in regulating the action of the heart. About 1912 it was revealed that the pituitary gland yields a substance vitally necessary for regulating the other glands of the body. These discoveries paved the way for a considerable development of glandular therapy in more recent years, including methods of curing certain forms of idiocy by supplementing the hormone secretion of the thyroid gland. On the eve of World War I it was demonstrated by a British biochemist that a healthful diet requires not merely starches, fats, sugars, and proteins but "accessory factors" found only in particular foods. These factors were soon named vitamins, and research was begun to determine their character. In 1915 an American scientist at Johns Hopkins, E. V. McCollum, proved that there are at least two vitamins: Vitamin A, contained in butter, egg yolks, and fish-liver oils; and Vitamin B, which is found most abundantly in yeast, lean meats, whole cereals, and green vegetables. Later investigations have disclosed the existence of at least twenty of these mysterious substances, all of them essential to growth or repair or to the prevention of disease. The discovery of the vitamins has been especially significant in the conquest of illnesses of malnutrition, such as beri-beri, scurvy, and rickets.

The discovery of hormones and vitamins

701

Achievements in
the physical
sciences

The record of attainment in the physical sciences is somewhat less impressive until practically the final quarter of the nineteenth century. Nevertheless, three achievements stand out in the earlier period. About 1810 the English Quaker schoolmaster, John Dalton, revived the atomic theory of matter and defended it so assiduously that it was soon adopted as a basic premise of scientific thought. In 1847 Hermann von Helmholtz formulated the principle of the conservation of energy, or the first law of thermodynamics. This law states that the total energy in the universe is constant, that it can be changed from one form into another but can neither be created nor destroyed. In 1851 came the second law of thermodynamics, or the law of the dissipation of energy. Explained systematically for the first time by William Thomson (Lord Kelvin), this law maintains that, while the total energy of the universe remains constant, the amount of *useful* energy is being steadily diminished. Few discoveries have been more fruitful in influencing the conclusions of astronomers and also of certain philosophers.

Probably it would be safe to say that the period from about 1870 to 1914 surpassed all others since the age of Copernicus in the number of revolutionary developments in the physical sciences. Indeed, it may be doubted whether there was ever a period when so many time-honored scientific conceptions were seriously challenged or overthrown. First of all, there were some extensive revisions of older theories of light, electricity, and energy. About 1865 Clerk Maxwell (1831–1879) showed that light appears to behave in much the same way as electromagnetic waves. The discovery of the X-ray by Wilhelm von Röntgen in 1895 led scientists to wonder whether similar rays might not be given off spontaneously in nature. This suspicion was confirmed by the discovery of uranium in 1896 and of the much more active element, radium, by Madame Curie two years later. About 1903 the British physicists, Ernest Rutherford and Frederick Soddy, developed their disintegration theory, explaining how various radioactive elements break down to form less complex elements, giving off at the same time emanations of electrical energy. The net result of these several discoveries was the conclusion that light, electricity, the X-ray, and all other forms of energy are essentially the same.

Madame Curie

Revisions of the
conception of
matter

From this conclusion it was a comparatively easy step to fundamental revisions of the conception of matter. As early as 1892 Hendrik Lorentz advanced the contention that matter is not composed of solid, indivisible atoms, but that the atom itself is made up of smaller units of an electrical nature. About 1910 Ernest Rutherford and the Danish scientist Niels Bohr presented a picture of the atom as a kind of miniature solar system, composed of a nucleus containing one or more positively charged *protons* around which revolve a number of negatively charged *electrons*. As we shall see, this conception has been modified in more recent years, but its main implication still stands—that electricity is the fundamental constituent of matter.

The years from 1830 to 1914 were characterized also by an extensive development of the social sciences. Most of these subjects are of comparatively recent origin. Before the nineteenth century nearly all of man's efforts to analyze his social environment were restricted to history, economics, and philosophy. The first of the new social sciences to be developed was sociology, originated by Auguste Comte (1798–1857) and elaborated by Herbert Spencer (1820–1903). Next came the founding of anthropology. Though sometimes defined very broadly as "the science of man," anthropology is more commonly restricted to such matters as man's physical evolution, the study of existing human types, and the investigation of prehistoric cultures and of primitive institutions and customs. About 1870 psychology was broken off from philosophy and cultivated as a separate science. Following its origin in Germany under the guidance of Wilhelm Wundt (1832–1920), it was given a new orientation in the 1890's by the work of the Russian Ivan Pavlov (1849–1936). By experiments with animals Pavlov discovered what is known as the conditioned reflex, a form of behavior in which natural reactions are produced by an artificial stimulus. He showed that if dogs were fed immediately following the ringing of a bell, they would eventually respond to the sound of the bell alone and secrete saliva exactly as if confronted by the sight and smell of the food. This discovery suggested the conclusion that the conditioned reflex is an important element in human behavior and encouraged psychologists to center their attention upon physiological experiment as a key to understanding the mind.

The founding of new social sciences

After the opening of the twentieth century, psychologists divided into a number of conflicting schools. A group of disciples of Pavlov inaugurated a type of physiological psychology known as behaviorism. Behaviorism is an attempt to study the human being as a purely physiological organism—to reduce all human behavior to a series of physical responses. Such concepts as *mind* and *consciousness* are relegated to the scrap heap as vague and meaningless terms. For the behaviorist nothing is important except the reactions of muscles, nerves, glands, and visceral organs. There is no such thing as an independent psychic behavior; all that man does is physical. Thinking is essentially a form of talking to oneself. Every complex emotion and idea is simply a group of physiological responses produced by some stimulus in the environment. Such was the extremely mechanistic interpretation of human actions offered by followers of Pavlov. Subject to a number of modifications, it remains the dominant approach for those who believe that psychology should be as objective a science as physics or chemistry.

New types of psychology: (1) behaviorism

Sigmund Freud

Herbert Spencer

The other most important school of psychology to make its appearance after the turn of the century was psychoanalysis, founded by Sigmund Freud (1856–1939), an Austrian physician. Psychoanalysis interprets human behavior mainly in terms of the subconscious or unconscious mind. Freud admitted the existence of the conscious mind, but he avowed that the subconscious is much more important in determining the actions of the individual. He considered man as exclusively an egoistic creature propelled by basic urges of power, self-preservation, and sex. These urges are much too strong to be overcome; but inasmuch as society has branded their unrestrained fulfillment as sinful, they are commonly driven into the subconscious, where they linger indefinitely as suppressed desires. Yet they are seldom completely submerged; they rise to the surface in dreams, or they manifest themselves in lapses of memory, in fears and obsessions, and in various forms of abnormal behavior. Freud believed that most cases of mental and nervous disorders result from violent conflicts between natural instincts and the restraints imposed by an unfortunate environment. His investigations and the theories he evolved from them vitally affected the treatment of mental ailments and exerted a profound influence upon literature and the arts.

2. THE TWILIGHT OF METAPHYSICS

Most of the philosophic movements in the later decades of the nineteenth century and in the early years of the twentieth were deeply influenced by the progress of science. Characteristic examples are to be found in the evolutionary philosophies of Spencer, Huxley, and Haeckel. The first of this trio, Herbert Spencer (1820–1903), was one of the most influential figures of modern times. Born into a family of English Methodists and Quakers of modest means, he refused the offer of relatives to send him to Cambridge and determined to educate himself and live his own life. He worked for a time as a civil engineer on the London and Birmingham railway. Later he became an assistant editor of the *Economist*, but resigned that position upon inheriting $2500 from an uncle. Despite his humble background, he cared little for wealth or power. Moreover, he was inclined to be indolent, reading but haphazardly and neglecting serious books that failed to arouse his interest. For years his life was ill-planned and his ambitions erratic. He spawned ideas for inventions at every turn and cluttered his notebooks with plans for candle-extinguishers, patent saltcellars, wheel chairs, and other ingenious contraptions. His earliest writings were on political and social problems, the most important of them being his *Social Statics*, published in 1850. Not until he was about forty did he develop a serious interest in philosophy. He completed his three-volume work, *Synthetic Philosophy*, at the age of seventy-six.

The keynote of Spencer's philosophy is his idea of evolution as a universal law. He was deeply impressed by Darwin's *Origin of Species* and enriched the hypothesis of natural selection with a phrase that has clung to it ever since—"the survival of the fittest." He contended that not only species and individuals are subject to evolutionary change, but also planets, solar systems, customs, institutions, and religious and ethical ideas. Everything in the universe completes a cycle of origin, development, decay, and extinction. When the end of the cycle has been reached, the process begins once more and is repeated eternally. Strange as it may seem, Spencer was not a mechanist. He argued that back of the evolutionary process there must be some kind of supernatural Power, and he generally assumed that in the long run evolution is synonymous with progress. But he referred to this Power as the Unknowable and declared that it should be dismissed from scientific consideration. Man's capacity for knowledge is limited to matter and motion, to the facts of sensory experience; these alone should constitute the field of his speculation. As a political philosopher, Spencer was a vigorous champion of individualism. He condemned collectivism as a relic of primitive society, as a feature of the earliest stage of social evolution when individuals had not yet been separated from the undifferentiated mass. He held the state in such great abhorrence that he delivered his manuscripts to his publisher in person rather than entrust them to any such agency of tyranny as the post office.

The other philosophers of the evolutionist tradition accepted a great many of the fundamental suppositions of Spencer's theory. Thomas Henry Huxley (1825–1895) defended the doctrine of evolution, not only with logical arguments but with a convincing array of scientific facts; for he was a brilliant biologist as well as philosopher. A "square-jawed man, greedy of controversy," he gloried in the title, "Darwin's bulldog." His celebrated book, *Man's Place in Nature*, was almost as influential in converting the world to evolutionary principles as the *Origin of Species*. But Huxley had broader interests than merely defending organic evolution. Like Spencer, he proposed to extend the evolutionary concept to all of the great problems that trouble man's dreams. He argued that social institutions and moral ideals, instead of being divinely ordained, are simply products of a biological heritage. "The actions we call sinful are part and parcel of the struggle for existence." [2] While he did not reject the possibility of a supernatural power, he averred that "there is no evidence of the existence of such a being as the God of the theologians." [3] He pronounced Christianity to be "a compound of some of the best and some of the worst elements of Paganism and Judaism, moulded in practice by the innate character of certain people of the

Spencer's evolutionary philosophy

Other evolutionist philosophers: T. H. Huxley

[2] Leonard Huxley, *The Life and Letters of Thomas Henry Huxley*, II, 282.
[3] *Ibid.*, II, 162.

Western World." [4] A large part of his philosophy is embraced in his famous doctrine of *agnosticism,* a word which he invented to express his contempt for the attitude of dogmatic certainty symbolized by the beliefs of the ancient Gnostics. [5] As propounded by Huxley, agnosticism is the doctrine that neither the existence nor the nature of God nor the ultimate character of the universe is knowable. It is not atheism, but simply an affirmation that man does not know and never can know whether a God exists and whether the universe is governed by purpose or is merely a blind machine.

Ernst Haeckel

The most uncompromising of the evolutionist philosophers was Ernst Heinrich Haeckel (1834–1919). Originally a physician in Berlin, he became disgusted with crotchety patients and soon turned to the more congenial occupation of a professor of zoology. He was the first outstanding scientist on the Continent of Europe to subscribe wholeheartedly to Darwinism. At the age of sixty-five he summarized his conclusions in a book which he entitled *The Riddle of the Universe.* The philosophy of Haeckel comprises three main doctrines: atheism, materialism, and mechanism. He would have nothing to do with Huxley's agnosticism or with Spencer's assumption of an Unknowable Power; on the contrary, he dogmatically affirmed that nothing spiritual exists. The universe, he maintained, is composed of matter alone in a process of constant change from one form into another. This process is as automatic as the ebb and flow of the tides. There is no fundamental difference between living and nonliving matter, except that the former is more complex. The first life originated from the spontaneous combination of the essential elements of protoplasm. From these earliest forms of protoplasm all the complex species of the present have gradually evolved through the process of natural selection. Haeckel regarded the mind of man as just as much a product of evolution as his body. The human mind differs only in degree from the minds of the lower animals. Memory, imagination, perception, and thinking are mere functions of matter; psychology should be considered a branch of physiology. Such was the compact philosophy of materialism and determinism which appeared to Haeckel and his followers to be a logical deduction from the new biology.

Friedrich Nietzsche

The writings of another German—Friedrich Nietzsche—also reveal a decided influence of the idea of evolution. Nietzsche was not a scientist, nor was he interested in the nature of matter or in the problem of truth. He was essentially a romantic poet glorifying the struggle for existence to compensate for his own life of weakness and misery. Born in 1844, the son of a Lutheran minister, he was educated in the classics at Leipzig and Bonn and at the age of twenty-five was made a professor of philology at the University of

[4] T. H. Huxley, *Collected Essays,* V, 142.
[5] See p. 73

Basel. Ten years later he was forced to retire on account of ill health. He spent the next decade of his life in agony, wandering from one resort to another in a fruitless quest for relief. If we can believe his own statement, each year was made up of 200 days of pain. In 1888 he lapsed into hopeless insanity, which continued until his death in 1900.

Nietzsche's philosophy is contained in such works as *Thus Spake Zarathustra*, *A Genealogy of Morals*, and *The Will to Power*. His cardinal idea is the notion that natural selection should be permitted to operate unhindered in the case of human beings as it does with plants and animals. He believed that such a constant weeding out of the unfit would eventually produce a race of supermen—not merely a race of physical giants but men distinguished above all for their moral courage, for their strength of character. Those who should be allowed to perish in the struggle are the moral weaklings, the ineffective and craven ones, who have neither the strength nor the courage to battle nobly for a place in the sun. Before any such process of natural selection could operate, however, religious obstacles would have to be removed. Nietzsche therefore demanded that the moral supremacy of Christianity and Judaism should be overthrown. Both of these religions, he alleged, are Oriental cults glorifying the virtues of slaves and of other downtrodden folk. They exalt into virtues qualities which ought to be considered vices—humility, nonresistance, mortification of the flesh, and pity for the weak and incompetent. The enthronement of these qualities prevents the elimination of the unfit and preserves them to pour their degenerate blood into the veins of the race. Nietzsche admired the ancient Germanic virtues of bravery, strength, loyalty, honor, and cunning. He defined *good* as "all that heightens in man the feeling of power, the desire for power, power itself." *Bad* he characterized as "all that comes from weakness." [6]

Toward the end of the period we are considering, philosophy began to reflect some of the confusion creeping into the sciences. The revolution in physics accomplished by the discoveries regarding the structure of matter caused a number of thinkers to lose confidence in the optimism of Spencer and in the mechanistic universe of Haeckel. Some renounced mechanism and materialism entirely; others embraced attitudes of skepticism and hopelessness or sought refuge in the worship of beauty. Symptomatic of the new trend was a popular American philosophy known as Pragmatism. Founded by Charles Peirce (1839–1914), it was developed in comprehensive form by William James (1842–1910) and John Dewey (1859–1952). Pragmatism takes its name from its central teaching that any idea which meets the pragmatic test—that is, gives practical results —must be accepted as true, provided, of course, it does not conflict

Nietzsche's philosophy

Friedrich Nietzsche

The antimaterialist interlude

---

[6] Quoted by E. A. Singer, *Modern Thinkers and Present Problems*, p. 204.

with experience. In other words, if a belief in a personal God—or in a multitude of gods—gives mental peace or spiritual satisfaction to any individual, that belief is true for him. The Pragmatists scoffed at all efforts to discover absolute truth or to determine the ultimate nature of reality. They abandoned metaphysics as futile and taught that knowledge should be sought after, not as an end in itself, but as an *instrument* for improving conditions on earth. It should be mentioned also that the Pragmatists rejected all forms of determinism. They denounced interpretations of the universe that reduced man to a slave of some rigid principle or placed him at the mercy of an all-powerful fate.

A much more determined protest against the mechanism and materialism of the nineteenth century came from the New Idealists.

The New Idealism

Among the leaders of this school were the Italian Benedetto Croce (1866–1952), the Englishman F. H. Bradley (1846–1924), and the American Josiah Royce (1855–1916). The New Idealism was essentially a compound of the doctrines of Hegel and of Kant. From the former came the tendency to glorify the state and to subordinate the individual to the group; from the latter was derived the idea of parallel truths in religion and science which never conflict because they belong in two separate realms. The New Idealists admitted that the universe revealed by science is a gigantic machine which grinds on relentlessly, and that man is a helpless atom. But this revelation did not trouble them, for they contended that it is only part of the picture. Science is but a feeble instrument which enables us merely to see as in a glass darkly. We have other methods of knowing which enable us to perceive not merely surface appearances but reality. If we make up our minds to follow the deepest convictions of our being, we shall see the universe as a star-domed city of God, ruled by benevolent purpose and replete with hope for bewildered man. Truths such as these gained by intuition are more valid than any discovered by the telescope of the scientist. Thus did the New Idealists manage to preserve their faith in religion and in ultimate perfection against the onslaughts of skeptics and materialists.

Certain other philosophers drew far different conclusions. A group known as the New Realists despised the tendency to seek

The New Realists

refuge in faith or in any other form of retreat from reason. They conceded that the evidence from science may not be the complete or final truth; but they argued that it is the only truth substantial enough to be taken as a guide for living. They felt that the divorce of philosophy from science was an unmitigated disaster, and that a large proportion of the world's woes could be traced to the growth of mysticism. Though recognizing that science confronts man with a cold and alien universe, they saw in this no need for clinging to the skirts of faith. Even if man is no more than a bundle of atoms, whose gift of immortality is merely to mingle with the dust of centuries, this does not prevent him from living nobly and from waging a good fight to overcome such evils as are within his power. He can at least preserve his self-respect by striving to direct the forces of nature to the good of himself and his fellows, by avoiding any action which may be the cause of suffering to others, and by cherishing "the lofty thoughts that ennoble his little day; disdaining the coward terrors of the slave of Fate, to worship at the shrine that his own hands have built." [7] Such in particular was the philosophy of the Englishman Bertrand Russell (1872–1970), later Lord Russell, one of the most prominent of the New Realists and a leading philosophical writer of the twentieth century.

3. THE TRIUMPH OF REALISM IN LITERATURE

The dominant literary trend in the Western world from about 1830 to 1914 was *realism*. Classicism was now practically defunct. Romanticism continued as a secondary trend, and even enjoyed a revival of popularity toward the end of the nineteenth century. In truth, realism and romanticism had elements in common. Both believed in the affirmation of human freedom, though the realists emphasized much more than the romanticists the obstacles standing in the way of that freedom. Both were idealistic, striving for a better world, however they might differ as to the means of attaining their goals. Literary realism before World War I was distinguished by a number of extraordinary qualities. First, it was a protest against sentimentality and emotional extravagance. The realists sought to portray life in accordance with the hard facts revealed by science and philosophy. Second, realism was distinguished by an absorbing interest in psychological and social problems—in analyzing in detail the conflicting tendencies of human behavior and in depicting the struggles of individuals to overcome the frustrations of their environment. Finally, it should be noted that realists were quite generally governed by one or another of the popular scientific or philosophic conceptions of their time. Perhaps the majority were determinists, holding to the view that mortals are the irresponsible victims of heredity and environment. Others were guided by the evolutionary concept, interpreting man's nature as made up very largely of bestial qualities inherited from his animal ancestors. Still others were swayed by the fervor for social reform and pictured the inequities of the human scene against a sordid background so as to point the need for abolishing poverty, for eliminating war, or for treating those who had broken the laws of society more justly.

Realism as a distinct literary movement made its initial appearance in France. Its leading exponents were four great novelists who ex-

The decline of classicism and the emergence of realism

[7] Bertrand Russell, "A Free Man's Worship," *Mysticism and Logic*, p. 57.

Honoré de Balzac

Gustave Flaubert

erted an influence far beyond the confines of their native land. First in order of time was Honoré de Balzac (1799–1850). In his stupendous *Human Comedy*, Balzac uncovered with brutal frankness the stupidity, greed, and baseness of men and women, chiefly of the bourgeoisie. He delighted in laying bare the hidden springs of human action and in revealing the rottenness behind the polished exterior of respectable society. An even more precise expression of the realist tradition is to be found in the work of Gustave Flaubert (1821–1880). His foremost novel, *Madame Bovary*, is a cool analysis of human degeneration. It is a study of the tragic conflict between romantic dreams and the dreary realities of ordinary existence. Though the book was condemned as salacious, and its author prosecuted for publishing an immoral work, it has been acclaimed by some critics as one of the greatest novels in modern literature.

Realistic writing of a somewhat different brand flowed from the pen of Émile Zola (1840–1902). Indeed, Zola is sometimes classified as a naturalist rather than a realist, to convey the idea that he was interested in an exact, scientific presentation of the facts of nature without any coloring of personal philosophy. But in actual truth Zola did have a definite philosophic viewpoint. His years of wretched poverty in early life imbued him with a deep sympathy for the common man and with a passion for social justice. Though he portrayed human nature as weak and prone to vice and crime, he was not without hope that a decided improvement might come from the creation of a better society. Many of his novels dealt with such social problems as alcoholism, bad heredity, poverty, and disease. He was an aggressive champion of the Third Republic and toward the end of his life took an active part in exposing the hypocrisy of the Dreyfus affair. The fourth of the great figures in French realism before World War I was Anatole France (1844–1924), who preached a gospel of wise and tolerant cynicism. Though he satirized human folly, he seldom gave vent to righteous wrath. His goddess was Irony, a gentle and kindly deity who "teaches us to laugh at rogues and fools whom, but for her, we might be so weak as to despise and hate." [8] Yet his tolerance of evil was by no means unlimited. He joined with Zola in a vigorous attack upon the persecutors of Dreyfus and lent his support to many other unpopular causes. In his later years he became so firmly convinced of the injustice of modern society that he allied himself with the socialists. His works included a varied collection of skeptical essays, mischievous short stories, and pungent satires on religion and politics. Among them are *Penguin Island*, *The Revolt of the Angels*, and *The Garden of Epicurus*.

Realist literature in England included the writings of the vast majority of the Victorian novelists and dramatists. [9] Among the first

[8] Alfred Allinson (trans.), *The Garden of Epicurus*, p. 94.
[9] The Victorian period is named, of course, from the reign of Queen Victoria (1837–1901).

of the novelists to employ the methods of realism were William Makepeace Thackeray (1811–1863) and Charles Dickens (1812–1870). Thackeray was the novelist of the elegant world of the aristocracy, though he was far from admiring all of its qualities. He delighted in exposing the scandals of people in high places and in ridiculing their foibles. Like most of the early Victorians, he was inclined toward a self-satisfied moralizing on the evils of mankind. As Thackeray was the representative of the upper class, so Dickens was the spokesman for the lower. In such novels as *Oliver Twist*, *Dombey and Son*, and *David Copperfield* he wrote with poignant sympathy of the bitter lot of the poor. He denounced the horrors of the workhouses and scathingly portrayed the delays in the courts and the inhuman treatment of prisoners for debt. Though he was often swept into excesses of sentimentality, his books exerted considerable influence in hastening the progress of social reform.

The writings of Thackeray and Dickens were forerunners of the deeper realism expressed by English novelists toward the end of the Victorian Age. The most renowned of late Victorian realists was undoubtedly Thomas Hardy (1840–1928). In such well-known narratives as *The Return of the Native*, *Jude the Obscure*, and *Tess of the D'Urbervilles* he expressed his conception that men are the playthings of inexorable fate. The universe is beautiful, he thought, but in no sense friendly, and the struggle of individuals with nature is a pitiable battle against almost impossible odds. If any such being as God exists, He simply watches with indifference while the helpless denizens of the human ant-heap crawl toward suffering and death. It is to be noted that Hardy's attitude was essentially one of pity for his fellow creatures. He regarded man not as a depraved animal but as an atom of dust caught in the wheels of a cosmic machine.

The Title Page of *David Copperfield* by Charles Dickens

George Bernard Shaw at His
Typewriter

'With the beginning of the twentieth century, realism in English literature took a decidedly different turn. The period from 1900 to 1914 was an era of great progress in social reform and of magnificent dreams for the future. It was natural that this spirit of confidence and hope should be reflected in the leading writings. The first literary genius to sound the clarion call of the new age was George Bernard Shaw (1856–1950). Born in Dublin of Anglo-Irish parents, Shaw betook himself to London at the age of twenty, where he earned his living as a journalist-critic of art and the drama. He soon became interested in socialism and emerged as a leader of the Fabian Society dedicated to the advancement of a modified Marxism. He combined his enthusiasm for socialism with a devotion to materialistic philosophy, an abiding faith in the value of science, and an acid contempt for the artificialities of bourgeois society. By 1900 he had found his true place in literature as the author of realistic dramas. From then on he wrote an amazing number of plays, on subjects ranging from prostitution to socialism and from the Salvation Army to creative evolution. For the most part, his works were not dramas at all in the conventional sense. They were vehicles for the expression of his ideas, in which the plot was completely overshadowed by witty and incisive dialogue. Likewise didactic in tone was the realism of H. G. Wells (1866–1946). The son of a professional cricket player, Wells devoted his early career to teaching science in a private school. As in the case of Shaw, it was a mixture of socialism and faith in the beneficence of science that provided the inspiration for his work as a writer. Most of the novels he published before 1914 depicted scientific utopias, in which toil and poverty would be eliminated by marvelous improvements in technology, while superstition and war would be banished by proper education. His conception of the tragedy of life was not that of a hopeless struggle against nature but the slavery of individuals to outworn institutions and perverted ideals. Among the best-known of his earlier novels are *Tono Bungay*, *Anne Veronica*, and *The History of Mr. Polly*.

Realism was also a virile movement in many other countries. In Germany it was exemplified in the dramas of Gerhart Hauptmann (1862–1946) and in the first great novel of Thomas Mann (1875–1955). Hauptmann was a social dramatist who chose his main themes from the age-long struggle of the working classes against poverty and ill treatment at the hands of their masters. He also wrote satires and symbolical plays of psychological conflict. The first great novel of Thomas Mann was published in 1903. Entitled *Buddenbrooks*, it relates the story of the rise and decline of a great merchant family of Lübeck. The narrative is presented with the same lingering fondness for significant detail that distinguishes the author's later works.

Doubtless the most eminent of all the realists of Teutonic nationality was Henrik Ibsen (1828–1906). Though born in Norway,

Henrik Ibsen

Ibsen was descended from ancestors who were mainly Danish and German. Years of poverty and drudgery in his early life produced a lasting impression upon his mind and left him resentful and bitter. Until the age of twenty-two nearly all of his education had been acquired by assiduous reading. His early dramas were not very favorably received, and while still a young man he decided to abandon his native country. Residing first in Italy and then in Germany, he did not return permanently to Norway until 1891. His writings were characterized most of all by bitter rebellion against the tyranny and ignorance of society. In such plays as *The Wild Duck*, *Hedda Gabbler*, and *An Enemy of the People* he mercilessly satirized the conventions and institutions of respectable life. Along with this scorn for hypocrisy and social tyranny went a profound distrust of majority rule. He despised democracy as the enthronement of unprincipled leaders who would do anything for the sake of votes to perpetuate themselves in power. He makes one of his characters in *An Enemy of the People* say: "A minority may be right—a majority is always wrong."

Notwithstanding the strength of the Puritan tradition in the United States, realism as a literary movement was far from unimportant in that country. Traces of it were to be found as early as the middle of the nineteenth century in the novels of Herman Melville (1819–1891). His masterpiece, *Moby Dick*, combined marvelous descriptions of the wonders and terrors of nature with a profound searching into the mysteries of the universe and of man. But realism scarcely became a dominant force until many years later. Toward the end of the nineteenth century a group of young novelists began writing frankly of political and social abuses, often in such manner as to awaken a desire for reform. Stephen Crane described some of the less romantic aspects of war in his *Red Badge of Courage*. Mark Twain pilloried sham and hypocrisy in a series of novels, the most famous of which was *Adventures of Huckleberry Finn*. The cutthroat speculation of high financiers furnished the theme for Frank Norris's *Octopus*. But the most typical of the realists before 1914 was Theodore Dreiser (1871–1945). His first novel, *Sister Carrie*, was followed by two others of similar type—*Jennie Gerhardt* and *The Genius*. Dreiser's novels were characterized by a rigid determinism that recognized neither purpose in the universe nor meaning in life. But he suffused his writings with a quality of sympathy for his puny figures in their hopeless struggles against the forces of disaster.

Another of the great literatures which came into its own during the age of realism was that of the Russians. However, the boundaries separating particular movements in Russian literature are far from distinct. Several of the great novelists combined their realism with attitudes essentially romantic, others were incorrigible idealists. Among the names that stand out are Ivan Turgeniev (1818–1883),

Henrik Ibsen

Realism in
American
literature

713

Leo Tolstoi in His Study Dictating to His Secretary

Feodor Dostoievski (1821–1881), and Leo Tolstoi (1828–1910). Turgeniev, who spent much of his life in France, was the first of the Russian novelists to become known to western Europe. His chief work, *Fathers and Sons*, describes in brooding and delicate gloom the struggle between the older and younger generations. The hero is a nihilist (a term first used by Turgeniev), who is convinced that the whole social order has nothing in it worth preserving. Dostoievski was almost as tragic a figure as any he projected in his novels. Condemned at the age of twenty-eight on a charge of revolutionary activity, he was exiled to Siberia, where he endured four horrible years. His later life was harrowed by poverty, by family troubles, and by epileptic fits. As a novelist, he chose to write of the seamy side, exploring the anguish of miserable creatures driven to shameful deeds by their raw, animal emotions and by the intolerable meanness of their lives. He was a master of psychological analysis, probing into the motives of distorted minds with an intensity that was almost morbid. At the same time he filled his novels with a broad sympathy and with a mystic conviction that the soul of man can be purified only through suffering. His best-known works are *Crime and Punishment* and *The Brothers Karamazov*.

It is generally conceded that the honor of being Russia's greatest novelist must be divided between Dostoievski and Tolstoi. As a communistic anarchist and an earnest champion of the simple life of the peasant, Tolstoi was somewhat less deterministic than the author of *Crime and Punishment*. Yet in his *War and Peace*, a majestic epic of Russian conditions during the period of the Napoleonic invasion, he expounds the theme that individuals are at the mercy of Fate when powerful elemental forces are unleashed. His other most celebrated novel, *Anna Karenina*, is a study of the tragedy which lurks in the pursuit of selfish desire. The hero, Levin, is really Tolstoi himself, who eventually finds refuge from doubt and from the vanities of worldly existence in a mystic love of humanity. As Tolstoi grew older he became more and more an evangelist preaching a social gospel. In such novels as *The Kreutzer Sonata* and *Resurrection* he condemned most of the institutions of civilized society and called upon men to renounce selfishness and greed, to earn their living by manual toil, and to cultivate the virtues of poverty, meekness, and nonresistance. He set the example by deeding his property to his wife and by adopting the dress and humble fare of the peasant. His last years were devoted mainly to attacks upon such evils as war and capital punishment and to the defense of victims of persecution.

THE TRIUMPH OF
REALISM IN LITERATURE

Realism was by no means the only movement to hold the allegiance of the literary world between 1830 and 1914. Romanticism continued to be exceedingly popular, especially in the realm of poetry. Notable among the poets of this age whose attitudes were essentially romantic were Robert Browning (1812–1889) and Alfred Tennyson (1809–1892). Browning is noted for his sense of the dramatic and for his penetrating studies of human character; but, like a true Victorian, he conceived of man as a moral being and the universe as governed by benevolent purpose. His optimism stands out in bold contrast to the fatalism and pessimism of so many of the realists. He understood the baseness of human passions, but he never lost faith in the ultimate triumph of goodness and truth. A poet of much greater fame in his own lifetime was Alfred Tennyson. In 1850 he was made poet laureate, and in 1884 he became Lord Tennyson. His merit, however, consists primarily in his wizardry with words. The majority of his poems are distinguished for their pictures and music rather than for the expression of ideas. His mastery of color and rhythm enabled him to invest the most commonplace thoughts with a power and brilliance that seemed to endow them with lofty and original meaning. Though he tried hard to be a thinker, he seldom did more than reiterate some of the popular ideas of the Victorian Age. He sang the praises of virtue and of patriotism and delved into medieval legends to revive the glories of King Arthur's court. His nearest approach to profundity is *In Memoriam*, written after the death of a beloved friend. It is a series of lyrics in which the author passes from moods of doubt and despair to a final confident hope in "one far-off divine event, To which the whole creation moves."

The surviving influence of romanticism: Browning and Tennyson

The Manuscript Title Page of Tennyson's Translation of *Claudian*

Three other English authors may also be considered as representatives of the romantic tradition. The first two, Thomas Carlyle (1795–1881) and John Ruskin (1819–1900), were essayists and critics; the other, Rudyard Kipling (1865–1936), was a poet and a writer of popular stories. Thomas Carlyle is perhaps best known for his theory that heroic individuals are the makers of history and for his trenchant criticisms of nineteenth-century culture. Industrialism, democracy, materialism, science, and utilitarianism were the objects of his special fury. A victim of chronic dyspepsia, he often appeared

Work by Ford Madox Brown. Brown, a member of the pre-Raphaelite movement, often chose common people as his subjects. Notable exceptions in this grouping are Carlyle and Frederick Dennison Maurice, standing to the right.

The romanticism of Carlyle, Ruskin, and Kipling

to be crabbed and unreasonable. Yet he was not a mere pessimist and faultfinder. He had a keen perception of the real weaknesses of many modern institutions, and he anticipated some contemporary European ideas of the right of the strong to rule. Carlyle and Ruskin had several attributes in common. Both had a tendency to look back to the Middle Ages. Neither had much use for democracy. Ruskin as much as Carlyle detested the factory regime and abhorred the crude materialism of nineteenth-century science. But Ruskin's philosophy was more nearly that of the aesthete and social reformer. He was repelled not only by the poverty and degradation of the industrial system but also by its ugliness. He condemned the ferocious capitalist struggle for profits and urged that workers be treated as partners in industry, entitled to a more generous share of what they produced. The romanticism of Rudyard Kipling was of an altogether different sort. He had no interest in either the social or the artistic implications of the industrial regime. In his poetry he trumpeted the glories of British imperialism, representing the subjugation of Hindus and Africans as a glamorous missionary enterprise to rescue the heathen from darkness. His prose narratives are mainly

stories of adventure, rich in sentimental fondness for the enchant-
ments of India but not very significant from the standpoint of ideas.

4.   THE BIRTH OF MODERN ART

From 1830 to about 1860 the leading trend in painting was undoubtedly romanticism. Its most significant expressions were to be
found in the work of the Pre-Raphaelites and of Jean François Millet
(1814–1875). The chief figure in the Pre-Raphaelite movement was
Dante Gabriel Rossetti (1828–1882), an Englishman of Italian ancestry who is better known as a poet than as a painter. Rossetti and
his followers aimed to restore painting to the simplicity, directness,
and naturalism which they believed it to have possessed in the Middle Ages and in the early Renaissance. All of the artificial and decorative tendencies that had appeared since the time of Raphael they
deeply deplored. Repudiating the ideal of pure beauty, they insisted
that art, in order to be worthy of the name, must be directly related
to life; it must be useful, either in ministering to the needs of man or
in conveying intellectual meaning.

Romanticism in
painting: the
Pre-Raphaelites

A much greater painter than any of the members of the Pre-Raphaelite group was Jean François Millet. Though associated with the
Barbizon school,[10] Millet did not always follow the Barbizon tradition of romantic landscape painting. His paramount interest was in
depicting the struggles of humble toilers against poverty and the
cruel whims of nature. In *The Man with the Hoe* and *The Sower* he
interpreted the bitter life of the peasant in a manner worthy of his

Millet

[10] See p. 602

The Annunciation by
Rossetti

INTELLECT AND THE ARTS
IN THE AGE OF
DEMOCRACY AND
NATIONALISM

The realist
painters, Courbet
and Daumier

realist successors, but in *The Angelus* and in *The Path through the Wheat* he betrayed the romantic fondness for sentimental piety and for intensity of color.

The development of realism in nineteenth-century painting is generally associated with the work of Gustave Courbet (1819–1877) and Honoré Daumier (1808–1879). Both were concerned with presenting the facts of life as they saw them, often in a coarse or satirical fashion. They were rebellious against classical and romantic traditions and intensely conscious of the social significance of art. Profoundly sympathetic toward the lower classes, especially the poor of the cities, they delighted in portraying scenes of squalor and misery and in pillorying the vices and foibles of the comfortable bourgeoisie. Daumier, in particular, was a powerful satirist of social and political evils. He ridiculed the corruption of petty officials, the pompous blundering of lawyers and judges, and the hypocritical piety of the rich. Courbet won great popularity by scornfully refusing the cross of the Legion of Honor offered to him by Napoleon III. Both Courbet and Daumier were zealous champions of the victims of oppression and exploitation, performing a function in art somewhat similar to that of Dickens and Zola in literature. Of course, not all of their painting took the form of social indictment. Much of it was mild and sympathetic portrayal of homely scenes from the lives of the poor. Whatever the subject, they strove to present it without the sentimental embellishments of the romantic schools.

The first completely original movement in nineteenth-century painting was *impressionism*. In a sense, the impressionist was a realist, for he was determined to paint only what he saw, and he was vitally interested in the scientific interpretation of nature. But his technique was different from that of the older realists. He did not depict scenes from the world around him as they would appear after careful study or thoughtful analysis. On the contrary, he sought to present the immediate impressions of his senses, leaving it to the mind of the observer to fill in additional details. This often resulted in a type of work appearing at first glance to be nonnaturalistic. Figures were commonly distorted; a few significant details were made to represent an entire object; and dabs of primary color were placed side by side without a trace of blending. Convinced that light is the principal factor in determining the appearance of objects, the impressionists fled from the studio to the woods and fields in an attempt to capture the fleeting alterations of a natural scene with each transitory shift of sunlight and shadow. From science they had learned that light is composed of a fusion of primary colors visible in the spectrum. Accordingly, they decided to use these colors almost exclusively. They chose, for example, to achieve the effect of the green in nature by placing daubs of pure blue and yellow side by side, allowing the eye to mix them. Some of their paintings appear at close view to be nothing but splotches of color, but if studied from across the room, they gradually reduce themselves to a natural design, in which mountains, trees, houses, and the like are more or less clearly discernible.

Like so many of the other artistic movements of modern times, impressionism originated in France. It was founded about 1870 by Édouard Manet (1832–1883), who had been deeply affected by a study of the old Spanish masters, especially Velásquez. Probably the greatest of the impressionists were Claude Monet (1840–1926) and Auguste Renoir (1841–1919). Monet was perhaps the leading exponent of the new mode of interpreting landscapes. His paintings have no structure or design in the conventional sense; they do not depict, but subtly suggest, the outlines of cliffs, trees, mountains, and fields. Intensely interested in the problem of light, he would go out at sunrise with an armful of canvases in order to paint the same subject in a dozen momentary appearances. It has been said of one of his masterpieces that "light is the only important person in the picture." The work of Renoir exhibited a greater variety than that of any of his compeers. His subjects include not only landscapes but portraits and scenes from contemporary life. He is famous most of all for his pink and ivory nudes, done in a manner reminiscent of Titian or Rubens. Renoir made use of the familiar device of spots of sunlight for the purpose of bringing certain parts of a picture into high relief, but he presented his subjects with much more solidity of form than did the other members of his group. To this day he is the most popular of the impressionists.

The impressionist painters

See color plates at page 784

For upwards of twenty years impressionism flourished as the dominant style of painting in nearly all countries of the Western world. But in the 1890's it yielded its popularity to a new movement, which is called for want of a better name *postimpressionism*. The postimpressionists criticized the formlessness and lack of volume of their predecessors. They contended that the figures of the painter's art should be as solidly and completely molded as statues. They objected also to the impressionist's preoccupation with the casual and momentary aspects of nature, and they deplored his indifference to ideas. The expression of meaning, they argued, should be the fundamental purpose of art; form and method are not ends in themselves but are important only insofar as they contribute to the expression of meaning. Postimpressionism was not only a reaction against impressionism, but in its ultimate tendencies, at least, it was a revolt against all of the hidebound formulas of the past. It was an expression of the chaos and increasing complexity of the machine age. It symbolized the restlessness and bewilderment that accompanied the emergence of a new society during the closing years of the nineteenth century. It was the beginning of nearly all that we now understand by *modern* art.

Postimpressionism

The artist who laid the foundations of postimpressionism was Paul Cézanne (1839–1906), now recognized as one of the greatest painters who ever lived. A native of southern France, Cézanne wan-

719

Cézanne

Gauguin and
Van Gogh

*See color
plates at pages
752, 784*

dered through the world of art as in a dream. Ever hopeful of reaching some higher goal of achievement, he cared little for the works he had finished. His son cut out the windows of some of his masterpieces for amusement, and his servant used others to clean the stove. Cézanne viewed these disasters quite calmly, for he was convinced that he would produce much better work in the future. His aim as a painter was to represent nature in such a way that objects on a flat canvas would appear to have the roundness and depth of sculpture. To accomplish this he practiced mild distortion, applied paint in thick layers, and modeled his figures with meticulous care. So well did he succeed that it has been said that since Cézanne there is no longer any excuse for sculpture.

The influence of Cézanne was reinforced and extended by two other great artists of the postimpressionist manner. One was the half-Peruvian Frenchman Paul Gauguin (1848–1903), and the other was the Dutchman Vincent Van Gogh (1853–1890). Both were revolutionary in their methods. Gauguin threw off all the restraints of conventional painting. Declaring that the artist should not be the slave either of nature or of the past, he introduced into his work an exotic symbolism and the most startling adaptations of color. His cardinal purpose was to emotionalize nature, to portray the world in accordance with his own subjective feelings. Gauguin is important also as a symbol of the disillusionment which spread through intellectual and artistic circles toward the end of the nineteenth century. Dismayed by the complexity and artificiality of civilization, he fled to the South Sea islands and spent the last decade of his life painting the hot and luscious colors of an unspoiled, primitive society. He was the forerunner of an extensive primitivist movement in twentieth-century art. For a time Gauguin was a friend of the Netherlands painter Van Gogh, but the friendship abruptly ceased when he awoke one night to find the Dutchman advancing upon him with a knife. Van Gogh was unquestionably demented; he cut off one of his ears and carried it to a woman who had offended him, and he finally took his own life. Yet there can be no denying his genius. In order to express the intensity of his feelings, he worked with feverish haste, applying directly to his canvas little worms of violent color which he squeezed from his tubes of paint. Van Gogh has been the chief inspiration for nearly all those modern painters who see in the expression of subjective ideas the exclusive function of art. paint. Van Gogh has been the chief inspiration for nearly all those modern painters who see in the expression of subjective ideas the exclusive function of art.

In the years between 1900 and World War I modern art underwent still further revolutionary development. First, Henri Matisse (1869–1954) greatly extended Cézanne's use of distortion and gradually evolved a type of painting that definitely repudiated fixed ideas of aesthetic merit. This tendency was carried much farther by

Beatrice and Dante, William Blake (1757–1827). This painting is from Blake's series for *The Divine Comedy*. (The Tate Gallery, London)

The Gleaners, Jean François Millet (1814–1875). Sensuous colors and love of natural settings typifies Millet's work. (Louvre)

Above: *The Guitarist*, Édouard Manet (1832–1883). Right: *Émile Zola*, Manet. Though Manet is called the "father of impressionism," he was also a rebel against the traditions of sweetness and artificiality that dominated the XIX cent. He liberated painting, as his friend Zola emancipated literature. (MMA) (Louvre)

Village Girls, Gustave Courbet (1819–1877). One of the first of the realists, Courbet often portrayed life in a bitter and disparaging light. He eschewed imagination and painted only what he saw. (MMA)

The Third-Class Carriage, Honoré Daumier (1808–1879). Though Daumier was noted for his realistic caricatures and satires, his attitude toward common folk was one of sympathy and understanding. (MMA)

Above: *Iris beside a Pond*, Claude Monet
(1840–1926). Monet called some of his
paintings Impressions, and the name soon
came to designate a school. (The Art
Institute of Chicago) Right: *Pink and
Green*, Edgar Degas (1834–1917). Degas
was an impressionist to the extent of his
interest in fleeting motion. But as an admirer of the classicist Ingres, he emphasized line and careful composition.
(MMA)

Still Life, Cézanne. It has been said that when the impressionists painted a haystack, there was light, but there was no haystack. When Cézanne painted an apple, there was the play of light; there was also the apple. (MMA)

Montagne Sainte-Victoire with Aqueduct, Paul Cézanne (1839–1906). This landscape has been a source of inspiration for many of the tendencies of so-called "modern" art. The composition is as structurally balanced and proportioned as a Greek temple. (MMA)

The Card Players, Cézanne. Here are exemplified Cézanne's skill in composition, his discriminating sense of color, and the sculptured qualities of solidity and depth he gave to his figures. (Stephen C. Clark)

The Japanese Divan, Henri de Toulouse-Lautrec (1864–1901). Toulouse-Lautrec found his chief source of inspiration in the night life of Paris. *Divan Japonais* was a noted Paris café. (MMA)

Nude Descending a Staircase. This painting by Marcel Duchamp was first displayed at the Armory Show in New York in 1911. The cubist-surrealist style was roundly criticized at the time.

Pablo Picasso (born 1881), a Catalan Spaniard who came to Paris in 1903 and developed *cubism,* a style that takes its name from the attempt to resolve each figure or object into its underlying geometric elements. It is based upon a doctrine once casually enunciated by Cézanne that the fundamental ideas of form could best be expressed through such shapes as cubes, cones, and cylinders. Picasso took this doctrine literally. But cubism is much more than this. It involves not only distortion but in some cases actual dismemberment. The artist may separate the various parts of a figure and rearrange them in other than their natural pattern. The purpose is partly to symbolize the chaos of modern life but also to express defiance of traditional notions of form—to repudiate the conception of art as mere prettiness. In the opinion of leading authorities cubism represented the real break with nineteenth-century art. Its influence extended beyond painting to sculpture, literature, and music.

Another of the main offshoots of postimpressionism that made its appearance before World War I was *futurism.* The spiritual father of futurism was a poet, F. T. Marinetti, who later took an active part in launching Italian Fascism. In 1910 Marinetti and a group of disciples issued a stirring manifesto calling for relentless war against the aesthetic ideals of the past. They condemned the worship of old masters, the slavish devotion to Roman ruins and to the art of the

Cubism

See color plates at page 785

Futurism

Renaissance, "the erotic obsession," "purism," sentimentality, quietism, and nature-worship. As painters the futurists aspired to glorify the machine and the achievements of modern science. They regarded it as imbecilic that an artist surrounded by the wonders of the modern scientific age should spend his time mooning over pastoral landscapes or attempting to recapture the beauty of classical mythology. Taking their cue from the discovery in physics that the ultimate fact of nature is energy, they insisted that *movement* should be the principal theme of art. Accordingly, they proceeded to break up form in such a manner as to produce the illusion of shimmering and vibration. They loved to depict the motion of a racing animal, the speed of an automobile, or the power and beauty of some complicated machine in a factory. Futurism has exerted a decided influence, especially upon the interior decoration of modern skyscrapers, railroad stations, and government buildings.

Sculpture in the age of democracy and nationalism

Although sculpture flourished in abundance during the age of democracy and nationalism, there was comparatively little that could be considered significant. Most of it was an imitation of the baroque—grandiose, heavy, and exuberantly decorative. It was developed largely for patriotic purposes, to embellish monuments celebrating national greatness. But in the later years of the nineteenth century there was at least one sculptor whose work stands out as original. He was the Frenchman Auguste Rodin (1840–1917), and his achievements have been compared not unfavorably to those of Michelangelo, by whom he was strongly influenced. Rodin was preeminently a realist, but he also reflected the currents of romanticism and impressionism. He was interested in psychological analysis and in man's animal origins and his struggle against the forces of nature. His most elaborate work was *The Gate of Hell*, inspired by Dante's *Inferno*. It is a tragedy depicting the sufferings of the great mass of mankind, damned by the passions of their animal natures. Rodin is perhaps even better known for his statue, *The Thinker*, which suggests the evolution of man from lower species. Soon after the dawn of the twentieth century, sculpture began to exemplify certain traits of postimpressionist painting. It grew more and more abstract and distorted, indicating the strength of the revolt against prettiness and sentimentality.

Architecture

As in sculpture, so in architecture the influence of the past was exceedingly strong. Until nearly the end of the nineteenth century the builder's art continued to be governed by classical and medieval principles. In general, it was the classical that predominated, exemplified especially by the survival of the ponderous and ornate baroque. Monuments of this style included the National Opera in Paris

The Gate of Hell by Rodin. Incorporated in this composite sculpture are many of the artist's other figures. Prominent is *The Thinker*, top center.

The Carson Pirie Scott Building. Designed by Louis Sullivan and constructed in Chicago, it typified the purity of design resulting from the "form follows function" philosophy.

and the Reichstag building and Protestant cathedral in Berlin. Accompanying this development of the baroque, there was a vigorous revival of the Gothic. The renewal of interest in Gothic architecture was a product of the romantic tendency to glorify everything medieval. Just as old legends of knights in armor had been refurbished by poets, so there had to be a return to the building style of the thirteenth century. Consequently Gothic was adopted on a generous scale for churches, universities, and even for some parliament and office buildings.

Development of functional architecture

Between 1880 and 1890 certain architects in Europe and America awoke to the fact that the prevailing styles of building construction were far out of harmony with the facts of modern civilization. The result was the launching of a new architectural movement known as *functionalism*. Its chief pioneers were Otto Wagner (1841–1918) in Germany and Louis Sullivan (1856–1924) and Frank Lloyd Wright (1869–1959) in the United States. The basic principle of functionalism is the idea that the appearance of a building shall proclaim its actual use and purpose. There must be no addition of friezes, columns, tracery, or battlements merely because some people consider such ornaments beautiful. True beauty consists in sincerity, in an honest adaptation of materials to the purpose they are intended to serve. Functionalism also includes the idea that architecture shall express either directly or symbolically the distinguishing features of contemporary culture. Ornamentation must therefore be restricted to such elements as will reflect the age of science and the machine. Modern man does not believe in the Greek ideas of harmony, balance, and restraint or in the medieval virtues of piety and chivalry, but in power, efficiency, speed, and comfort. These are the ideals which should find a place in his art.

There would seem to be little doubt that the functional style of building construction is one of the most significant architectural developments since the Renaissance. Among all of the styles which have been adopted during the last 300 years, it is the only one that is really original. Known also as *modern* architecture or the *international* style, it is the best approach that has yet been made to an efficient use of the tremendous mechanical and scientific resources of the contemporary world. It permits an honest application of new materials—chromium, glass, steel, concrete—and tempts the builder's ingenuity in devising others. Though many people dislike its stark simplicity and its angular, cubist lines, functional architecture has undoubtedly won an established place for the future. It has been adopted for countless new apartment houses, hotels, office buildings, stores, and factories not only in the United States but also in nearly every other civilized nation of the world.

The significance of functional architecture

5. MUSIC IN THE AGE OF DEMOCRACY AND NATIONALISM

Romanticism did not die out in music nearly so early as it did in literature and in the other arts. It was at its height during the middle of the nineteenth century, and it has continued as an important tendency far into the twentieth. Many of the changes in musical expression and ideals in the later nineteenth century are comparable to the trends in literature and the fine arts, but exact parallels can be drawn only with difficulty. For example, although realism asserted itself, it could not be pushed to extremes in an art which is essentially neither descriptive nor pictorial. So productive was this period

Romanticism in music

Taliesin East by Frank Lloyd Wright (1911–1925). A famous example of functional style with the pattern of the house conforming to the natural surroundings.

INTELLECT AND THE ARTS
IN THE AGE OF
DEMOCRACY AND
NATIONALISM

Schumann and
Mendelssohn

that space will permit discussion of only its most salient features and its most eminent composers.

Romanticism was emphasized in the work of the two contemporary German composers and friends, Robert Schumann (1810–1856) and Felix Mendelssohn (1809–1847). Schumann excelled in songs and in chamber and piano music, though he also composed symphonies. While he was one of the most romantic of composers, he was at the same time one of the most intellectual. As an editor and writer he urged the development of musical scholarship and an appreciation of the history of musical achievement. Among his services was the publicizing of the neglected wealth in the songs of Schubert. The insanity which darkened the last two years of Schumann's life was particularly tragic in view of the fineness of his character and influence. Felix Mendelssohn was the grandson of the Jewish philosopher, Moses Mendelssohn. Not the least among his gifts, as in the case of Schumann, were those of his personality. Mendelssohn was at home in all forms of music except opera, and all of it is informed by a classicist elegance and remarkable knowledge of the craft of composition. Mendelssohn's piano music, found too sentimental a generation or two ago, has regained a measure of esteem. His chamber music is the best of the age between Schubert and Brahms. Two of his symphonies and the violin concerto are played everywhere, as is his fine oratorio *Elijah*. The incidental music composed to Shakespeare's *A Midsummer Night's Dream* is unique in that literature.

Franz Liszt (1811–1886) spent his long life moving his place of residence from Paris, to Weimar, to Budapest, to Rome, the model of the modern international musical personality. He early distinguished himself as a concert pianist, and is commonly regarded as the greatest performer upon that instrument who ever lived. Later he turned intensively to composition, with results which were dazzling if not often of lasting import. Schumann and Mendelssohn had cultivated romanticism with restraint; Chopin brought it to the border of sentimentality; Liszt was the first of the romantic realists whose music could be bombastic and sensational but was always highly original. His flair for exotic effects is most successfully revealed in his treatment of native Hungarian themes. Liszt was acquainted with many French literary figures and showed considerable interest in the revolutionary currents of his day. His chief influence derives from his piano playing and teaching, orchestral conducting, and philanthropic activities on behalf of needy musicians. His kindly assistance to Wagner when the latter was being hounded out of Germany was an incalculable service.

Richard Wagner (1813–1883), the outstanding musical figure of the later nineteenth century, was a thoroughgoing revolutionary in the world of art. His initial interest was in the drama, and when he

Richard Wagner

turned to music it was primarily for its dramatic possibilities. His musical training came comparatively late and was largely self-administered, but was nonetheless remarkable. In his operas—which he preferred to call music-dramas—he applied a technique of blending together action, words, music, and scenic effects; his ideal was really a fusion of all the arts into an integrated whole. The result was something different from the conventional opera. Wagner dispensed with the arbitrary division of acts into scenes and discarded all artificial trappings; he took wide liberties with harmony and departed from stereotyped melodic patterns. He sought for a continuous flow of music, not subject to the tyranny of form but sensitive to every demand of expression. In several ways his operas, especially the later glorifying a cult of brutality and egoism. There is no other instance in the history of music where a man's political and aesthetic ideas as well as his music exerted such pervasive influence on generations of musicians. Wagner's operatic ideals became binding—even in France. His harmonies and his magical orchestra enslaved practically every musician, and it was with difficulty that composers were able to liberate themselves from his overwhelming personality even in, the earlier part of our century.

Such a pervasive force as nationalism could not help making its imprint upon music. In most European countries and even in the United States, folk music came under the scrutiny of scholars or found its way into the compositions of the learned. Many composers were fervent patriots. The early operas of Verdi (d. 1901), dedicated to the cause of Italian liberation, were sufficiently inflammatory to arouse the ire of the Austrian authorities. But Verdi, who lifted the opera to new artistic heights, was no narrow patriot. He drew his mature inspiration from a wide variety of sources, including the plays of Shakespeare. Nationalism is typified in the Bohemians Smetana (d. 1884) and Dvořák (d. 1904) and in the Norwegian Grieg (d. 1907). However, most of the devotees of national music did not deviate widely from accepted idioms of expression, but added their bit to the common European store. César Franck (d. 1890), a Belgian by birth and the founder of a modern French school of composers, is distinguished by a quality of otherworldly mysticism. The Finn, Jean Sibelius (1865–1957), although celebrating national sentiments in his tone poem *Finlandia*, displays in his seven symphonies capacities too universal to classify him as a mere nationalist.

One of the most remarkable of the national schools of music to appear was the Russian. Throughout the greater part of the nineteenth century Russian musicians had been content to follow the lead of the Italians, French, and Germans. Even such a brilliant composer as Tchaikovsky (1840–1893) introduced no real innovations. However, fresh paths were opened up by Borodin, Moussorg-

Tchaikovsky

MUSIC IN THE AGE OF DEMOCRACY AND NATIONALISM

The revolutionary achievements of Wagner

Nationalism in music

INTELLECT AND THE ARTS
IN THE AGE OF
DEMOCRACY AND
NATIONALISM

The Russian
school

The classicism of
Brahms and
Richard Strauss

sky, and Rimsky-Korsakov, the last of whom lived into the twentieth century. With the exception of Tchaikovsky, none was trained as a professional musician, a fact which makes their achievement all the more impressive. While they did not throw overboard the familiar European scales and harmony, they brought to composition a fresh point of view, an indifference to orthodoxy, and an enthusiastic appreciation of Slavic folk songs and dances. These qualities won a place for Russia in the very front rank of modern music.

Soon after the close of the last century several divergent tendencies had begun to assert themselves, indicating dissatisfaction with old forms which characterized all the arts. Some of these trends constituted new departures and others a return to the ideals of the past. The flowering of romanticism did not mean that the classical tradition had withered away. A classicist line runs through the romantic age to the end of the century, its most distinguished representative being Johannes Brahms (1833–1897). Though palpably a romantic, Brahms shows a discipline of mind and an understanding for the principles that actuated the old masters. These qualities, as well as his devotion to the symphonic style, made him the successor of Beethoven. Although Richard Strauss (1864–1949) began as a Wagnerian, his fondness for experiment soon became evident and was given free rein, first in his skillfully orchestrated symphonic poems and then in his music-dramas. The latter, in spite of resemblances, are essentially different from the operas of Wagner. While Wagner was romanticism incarnate, Strauss was a realist who summoned all the resources of the modern orchestra to convert music into a pictorial medium capable of evoking concrete and often commonplace images in the listener. Not content with stimulating intangible emotions, as the romanticists had done, he undertook to paint meticulous pictures, asserting that it should be quite possible to depict even a teaspoon by means of musical sounds. The content of his determined realism ranges all the way from the bleating of sheep and the whirring of windmills in *Don Quixote* to abstract philosophic ideas in *Thus Spake Zarathustra* (based on a text of Nietzsche's).

Another manifestation, perhaps of more enduring significance than Strauss's realism, was impressionism, created by the French composer, Claude Debussy (1862–1918). Like the impressionist painters, Debussy abandoned rigidity of design and intellectuality in the attempt to translate into tone the ecstasy or pathos of a particular mood or moment. Also like the impressionists of the brush he moved freely from one tone color to another without blending. Debussy was probably at his best when he applied his sensitive imagination directly to evoking the imagery implicit in the expanse of the sea, the play of moonlight, or the amorous reverie of a faun on a midsummer afternoon. Rejecting precise form and abstract beauty as artistic imperatives, he sought satisfaction not in the realism of life but in a fantastic world of dreams and shadows.

Claude Debussy

728

Items so designated are available in paperbound editions.

PHILOSOPHY

· Barzun, Jacques, *Darwin, Marx, Wagner*, Boston, 1941 (Anchor). Thoughtful and stimulating.

· Bober, M. M., *Karl Marx's Interpretation of History*, Cambridge, 1927, 1948 (Norton Library).

· Brinton, Crane, *English Political Thought in the Nineteenth Century*, Cambridge, Mass., 1949 (Torchbook).

——, *Ideas and Men*, Englewood Cliffs, N.J., 1950.

Burns, E. M., *Ideas in Conflict*, New York, 1960.

· Hayes, C. J. H., *A Generation of Materialism*, New York, 1941 (Torchbook).

· Hofstadter, Richard, *Social Darwinism in American Thought*, Philadelphia, 1949 (Beacon). The standard work on the subject.

Joad, C. E. M., *A Guide to Modern Thought*, New York, 1933.

Mosse, G. L., *The Culture of Western Europe: The Nineteenth and Twentieth Centuries*, Chicago, 1961.

· Perry, R. B., *The Thought and Character of William James*, Cambridge, Mass., 1948 (Torchbook, briefer version).

Randall, J. H., Jr., *The Making of the Modern Mind*, New York, 1926, Chs. XVIII–XXI. A lively summary.

· Reichenbach, Hans, *The Rise of Scientific Philosophy*, Berkeley, 1951 (University of California Press). A book for the student with some knowledge of philosophy.

· Russell, Bertrand, *History of Western Philosophy*, New York, 1945 (Simon & Shuster). Good for both summary and interpretation.

Sabine, G. H., *A History of Political Theory*, New York, 1961. Good for the first half of the nineteenth century.

· Tucker, Robert, ed., *The Marx-Engels Reader*, New York, 1972 (Norton).

· ——, *The Marxian Revolutionary Idea*, New York, 1969 (Norton Library).

SCIENCE

· Butterfield, H. B., *The Origins of Modern Science*, Glencoe, Ill., 1957 (Free Press).

Conant, J. B., *On Understanding Science: An Historical Approach*, New Haven, 1947.

· De Kruif, Paul, *Microbe Hunters*, New York, 1926 (Pocket Book).

· Eddington, A. S., *The Nature of the Physical World*, New York, 1946 (Ann Arbor).

· Himmelfarb, Gertrude, *Darwin and The Darwinian Revolution*, New York, 1959 (Norton Library).

· Jones, Ernest, *The Life and Work of Freud*, New York, 1953 (Anchor, abr.). The best biography of the founder of psychoanalysis.

McKenzie, A. E. E., *The Major Achievements of Science*, New York, 1960.

Robinson, Victor, *The Story of Medicine*, New York, 1936.

· Russell, Bertrand, *The A B C of Relativity*, New York, 1925 (Mentor).

Sears, Paul, *Charles Darwin: The Naturalist as a Cultural Force*, New York, 1950.

Singer, Charles, *A History of Biology*, New York, 1950.

Singer, Charles, and Underwood, A. E., *A Short History of Medicine*, 2d ed., New York, 1962.

READINGS LITERATURE

Brandes, Georg, *Main Currents in Nineteenth Century Literature*, New York, 1901–06.

· Young, G. M., *Victorian England: Portrait of an Age*, Garden City, N.Y., 1954 (Oxford).

· Wilson, Edmund, *Axel's Castle: A Study in the Imaginative Literature of 1870–1930*, New York, 1931 (Scribner Library).

ART

Faure, Elie, *History of Art*, New York, 1937, Vol. IV. A lucid and instructive account.

Gardner, Helen, *Art Through the Ages*, fourth edition, New York, 1967.

Hitchcock, H. R., *Modern Architecture*, New York, 1929.

Janson, H. W., *The History of Art*, New York, 1969.

Wright, W. H., *Modern Painting*, New York, 1927. An excellent interpretation of the leading movements.

MUSIC

Abraham, Gerald, *A Hundred Years of Music*, New York, 1938.

Einstein, Alfred, *Music in the Romantic Era*, New York, 1947.

Lang, Paul, *Music in Western Civilization*, New York, 1941.

Machlis, Joseph, *The Enjoyment of Music*, third ed., New York, 1970.

Newman, Ernest, *The Life of Richard Wagner*, New York, 1937.

SOURCE MATERIALS

· Appleman, Philip, Editor, *Darwin*, New York, 1970 (Norton).

Baumer, F. L. V., *Main Currents of Western Thought*, New York, 1952.

· Darwin, Charles, *The Origin of Species*, especially Chs. IV, XV, Cambridge, 1964 (Collier and others).

———, *The Descent of Man*, especially Ch. XXI.

Dewey, John, *Human Nature and Conduct*, New York, 1930.

· ———, *Reconstruction in Philosophy* (Beacon, 1957).

· Freud, Sigmund, *An Outline of Psychoanalysis*, New York (Norton Library).

· Huxley, T. H., *Man's Place in Nature*, Ann Arbor, 1959 (Ann Arbor).

James, William, *The Philosophy of William James*, New York, 1925.

· ———, *The Will to Believe*, Gloucester, Mass. (Dover).

· Mill, J. S., *Autobiography; Utilitarianism*, Urbana, Ill., 1961 (Library of Liberal Arts and others).

Spencer, Herbert, *Social Statics*, New York, 1954.

CHAPTER **26**

Foretastes of Political and Social Revolution

Man is stark mad; he cannot make a worm, and yet he will be making gods by dozens.

—Montaigne, *Essays,* Book II

That a period as turbulent as the nineteenth century should have been a period of political and social upheaval was a fact unlikely to deceive many observers. Not all of the upheavals and threatened upheavals burst into full-fledged revolution. Some partook of the character of half-baked sorties against the government. Others were outbreaks against social institutions with only incidental threats against the state. Yet all reflected the growth of discontent and the inability of millions to adjust to the rapidity of social and economic change. As the century advanced, conditions paving the road for deeper rumblings of discontent quickly emerged.

Rumblings of discontent

I. THE WEAKENING OF SURVIVING ESTABLISHMENTS

It is a distressing fact of history that periods of turbulence have generally exceeded periods of tranquillity. Even the so-called Golden Ages—the Age of Pericles in Greece, the Augustan Age in Rome—were really not exceptions. Some ages, though, were more plagued by violence than others. This condition was clearly true of the nineteenth century. The century was born of violence. The Wars of Napoleon did not terminate the age of conflict that had marked their beginning. Instead, they gave rise to new antagonisms that kept the Western world in turmoil for many years. France had no fewer than three outbreaks. Belgium, Poland, and Russia had one each. Spain, Hungary, and Italy had a like number. Not all of the uprisings were successful. Several should be classified as revolts

Signs of an uneasy society

731

rather than true revolutions. Yet all were symptoms of a discontent that marked the emergence of an uneasy society.

Economic and
social causes of
discontent

The weakening of reigning establishments occurred partly because of economic chaos—panics and depressions, displacement of skilled workers by advances in technology, conflicts between capital and labor, and inability of the masses to keep pace with the demands of a system they could neither understand nor control. Social factors also contributed to revolutionary ferment. Rapid growth of population created problems hitherto nonexistent. Overcrowding in cities left hordes of poor people living in filth, assailed by vermin, and subject to the ravages of transmissible disease. The burden of guilt, in so far as it was recognized, was generally divided between rulers and the members of the new owning class. Not all of the impoverished, of course, languished in misery, and not all of the proprietors and bosses lived off the fat of the land, but the gulf that separated the two classes was wide enough to be a major cause of discontent.

Political
causes

Obviously, not to be denied as factors precipitating the disturbances of the nineteenth century were the political causes. Many of these reflected economic grievances, but others were products of the stubbornness of rulers and failure to keep pace with the needs of the times.

2. THE SPREAD OF DOMESTIC VIOLENCE

Aside from the Paris Commune, already discussed in Chapter 23, the most serious outbreaks of domestic violence in the Second In-

Tenements in Glasgow. This photo, taken during the 1860's, shows the filthy conditions in which city dwellers often lived their lives. The narrow courtyard was both the source of water (the standpipe at the lower right of the photo) and the dumping ground of garbage and sewage.

The Haymarket Square Riots. A bomb is seen exploding among the police in this illustration by a contemporary artist.

dustrial Revolution were the Haymarket Square riots of 1886 and the Russian revolutionary movement of 1905. The former grew out of an attempt by organized labor to foment a strike among the McCormick Harvester workers in Chicago. A meeting was called at which radical speakers harangued the crowd. One policeman considered the behavior of the multitude dangerous and led a detachment of armed officers against them. A bomb was thrown, no one knows by whom. Anarchists and socialists were widely blamed for the tragedy. Chicago officials rounded up eight of them and accused them of murder. Seven were condemned to death and four were actually hanged. Though the proceedings were of doubtful legality, organized labor in America received a blow from which it did not fully recover for many years.

The Russian Revolutionary Movement of 1905 had numerous forerunners. Waves of discontent broke out several times during the nineteenth century. Threatened uprisings around 1850–1860 persuaded Tsar Alexander II to grant local self-government, to reform the judicial system, and, most of all, to liberate the serfs. Yet he failed to carry through on all these reforms. A wave of reaction followed. Radicalism revived and the number of sects increased. New and well-organized revolutionary parties, Social Democrats and Social Revolutionaries, dominated the scene. The former comprised Marxists while the latter was a peasant party committed to the principle, "The whole land to the whole people." Allied with either or both parties were the nihilists who tended to condemn the whole political and social system. Nihilism originated about 1860 as a movement to solve Russian problems by spreading enlightenment among the peasants. In general it denounced everything that did not lend itself to critical and scientific analysis. Its leaders were mostly

The Haymarket Square riots

The Revolutionary Movement of 1905 in Russia

733

students and mature intellectuals who did not belong to the aristocracy. Their major prophets were Charles Darwin, Karl Marx, and some of the anarchists. Failing to win much support by propagandist methods, they turned more and more to terrorism. The culminating act of this terrorism was the assassination of the Tsar in 1881.

Alexander III and
Nicholas II

The years that followed the death of Alexander II marked the flood tide of reaction against the entire policy of reform. The new Tsar, Alexander III (1881–1894), governed under the theory that Russia had nothing in common with western Europe, that her people had been nurtured on despotism and mystical piety for centuries and would be utterly lost without them. Such Western ideals as rationalism and individualism would undermine the childlike faith of the Russian masses and would plunge the nation into the dark abyss of anarchy and crime. In like manner, Western institutions of trial by jury, parliamentary government, and free education could never produce other than the most hideous fruits if planted in Russian soil. With such doctrines as his guiding principles, Alexander III enforced a regime of stern and vengeful repression. He curtailed in every way possible the powers of the local assemblies, increased the authority of the secret police, and even subjected the governments of the villages to wealthy nobles selected by the state. These policies were continued, though in somewhat less rigorous form, by his son, Nicholas II, who was a very much weaker man. Both Tsars were ardent proponents of Russification and used it with a vengeance to strengthen their power. Russification was simply the more ruthless counterpart of similar nationalistic movements in various countries. Its purpose was to extend the language, religion, and culture of Great Russia, or Russia proper, over all of the subjects of the Tsar and thereby to simplify the problem of governing them. It was aimed most of all at the Poles, the Finns, and the Jews, since these were the nationalities considered most dangerous. Inevitably it resulted in some cruel oppression. The Finns were deprived of their constitution; the Poles were compelled to study their own literature in Russian translations; and high officials in the Tsar's government connived at *pogroms* against the Jews.

The growth and
decline of the
revolutionary
movement

The immediate cause of the revolutionary movement was the calamitous outcome of Russia's war with Japan. As reports came in telling how the armies of the Tsar had been routed time after time on the fighting front in Manchuria, it was impressed upon the Russian people as never before that the system of tyranny under which they lived was rotten and incompetent. Members of the middle class who had hitherto refrained from association with the revolutionists, now joined in the clamor for change. Radical workingmen organized strikes and held demonstrations in every important city. By the autumn of 1905 nearly the whole urban population had enlisted in a strike of protest. Merchants closed their stores, factory owners shut down their plants, lawyers refused to plead cases in court, and even valets and cooks deserted their wealthy employers. It was soon evident to the slow-witted Tsar that the government would have to yield. On October 30, he issued his famous October Manifesto pledging guaranties of individual liberties, promising a moderately liberal franchise for the election of a Duma, or national legislature, and affirming that henceforth no law would be valid unless it had the Duma's approval. This was the high-water mark of the revolutionary movement. During the next two years Nicholas issued a series of sweeping decrees which made the October Manifesto virtually a dead letter. He deprived the Duma of most of its powers and decreed that it be elected indirectly on a class basis by a number of electoral colleges. Thereafter the legislative body was pretty well packed with obedient followers of the Tsar.

The reasons for this setback to the revolutionary movement are not hard to discover. In the first place, the army remained loyal to its commander-in-chief. Consequently, after the termination of the war with Japan in 1905, the Tsar had an enormous body of troops who could be counted upon if necessary to decimate the ranks of the revolutionists. An even more important reason was the split in the ranks of the revolutionists themselves. After the issuance of the October Manifesto, large numbers of the bourgeoisie became frightened at threats of the radicals and declared their conviction that the revolution had gone far enough. Withdrawing their support altogether, they became known henceforth as Octobrists. The more liberal merchants and professional men, under the name of Constitutional Democrats, or Cadets, maintained that opposition should continue until the Tsar had been forced to establish a government modeled after that of Great Britain. This fatal division rendered the middle class politically impotent. Finally, disaffection appeared within the ranks of the proletariat. Further attempts to employ the general strike as a weapon against the government ended in disaster.

Causes of the decline

Bloody Sunday. Led by Father Gapon, a group of workers went to demonstrate their grievances to the Tsar on January 22, 1905. They were met and gunned down by Russian guard troops.

But the Russian revolutionary movement of 1905 was not a total failure. The cruel vengeance taken by the bloodhounds of the Tsar convinced many people that their government was not a benevolent autocracy, as they had been led to believe, but a stubborn and brutal tyranny. The uprising revealed to the masses their principal mistakes and taught them what sources of strength they should rely upon for success in the future. Even a few of the concessions actually obtained were not completely wiped out. The Duma, for instance, was not abolished. It continued to serve as a means by which at least scattered remnants of opponents of reaction could make themselves heard. Significantly enough, the revolution of 1917 actually began in the Duma. But this was not all. The revolt of 1905 persuaded some of the more sagacious advisers of the Tsar that last-ditch conservatism was none too safe. The result was the enactment of a number of reforms designed to conciliate the troublesome classes. Among the most significant were the agrarian reforms sponsored by Premier Stolypin between 1906 and 1911. These included: (1) the transfer of 5,000,000 acres of crown lands to the peasants; (2) permission for the peasant to withdraw from the *mir* and set himself up as an independent farmer; and (3) cancellation of the remaining installments owed by the peasants for their land. Nor were the working classes altogether forgotten. Decrees were issued permitting the formation of labor unions, providing for a reduction of the working day (to not more than ten hours in most cases), and establishing sickness and accident insurance. Yet the hopes of some liberals that Russia was on the way to becoming a progressive nation on the Western model proved illusory. The Tsar remained stubbornly autocratic. Few of the peasants had enough money to buy the crown lands offered for purchase. In view of the rising cost of living, the factory workers considered their modest gains insufficient and lapsed into a sullen passivity. A new revolutionary outbreak merely awaited a convenient spark.

Yet another outbreak of violence in this period was the Easter Rebellion in Ireland. At the beginning of World War I, Irish nationalists, who resented the rule of their country by the British, were ripe for revolt. They had actually been promised self-rule on the eve of the war, but the British later reneged on the ground that a national emergency must take preeminence over everything else. This greatly displeased the people of southern Ireland. They scheduled Easter Monday, 1916, as a day for revolt. British forces quelled the uprising, but not until after a hundred people had been killed. Sporadic outbreaks kept the island in turmoil for years thereafter but were finally brought almost to an end by an agreement constituting Southern Ireland as a Free Republic. The Northern counties, or the province of Ulster, were to continue subject to the British Crown. On the surface the revolt in Ireland was a protest against

British rule with undercurrents of religious conflict. The British Protestants in Ulster were and still are determined to maintain their sovereignty over Northern Ireland.

3. THE REVOLT IN RELIGION

Both Protestant and Catholic branches of Christianity suffered dissension within their ranks during the nineteenth and early twentieth centuries. For a time the Catholic Church was more deeply affected. The reason lay partly in sharp disagreements over Papal policy. In 1864 Pope Pius IX issued a *Syllabus of Errors* condemning what he regarded as the principal religious and philosophical "errors" of the time. Among them were materialism, free thought, anticlericalism, Freemasonry, nationalism, and "indifferentism," or the idea that one religion is as good as another. Though the *Syllabus* was generally accepted by the Church, it was condemned by some critics as a "crusade against civilization."

While heated discussions continued over the *Syllabus of Errors* Pope Pius convoked a Church Council, the first to be summoned since the Catholic Reformation. The name given to the new council was the Vatican Council, to distinguish it from Vatican II convoked by John XXIII a hundred years later. The most noted pronouncement of Vatican I (1869) was the dogma of Papal Infallibility. In the language of this dogma the Pope, when he speaks *ex cathedra*—that is in his capacity "as pastor and doctor of all Christians"—is infallible in regard to all matters of faith and morals. Though generally accepted by pious Catholics, the dogma of Papal Infallibility evoked a storm of protest in many circles. Governments of several Catholic countries denounced it, including France, Spain, and Italy. Even in Germany the enunciation of the dogma was a paramount cause, or at least an excuse, for beginning the *Kulturkampf*. The death of Pius IX in 1878 and the accession of Pope Leo XIII brought a more genial climate to the Church. The new Pope was ready to concede that there was "good" as well as "evil" in modern civilization. He added a scientific staff to the Vatican and opened archives and observatories. However, he made no concessions to "liberalism" or "anticlericalism" in the political sphere. He would go no farther than to urge capitalists and employers to be more generous in recognizing the rights of organized labor. Whatever Leo XIII's intentions may have been, they seemed to have little effect in abating the force of anticlerical opposition to the universal Church. Drastic legislation was enacted, especially in France, but also in Italy and Spain and some countries of Latin America.

Disaffection among Protestants scarcely equaled that in the Catholic Church. For one reason Protestants did not constitute a compact body with a single authority over its members. They were themselves rebels against an older establishment and later found it easy to

Pope Pius IX

Pope Leo VIII

737

The turmoil
among
Protestants

fall into habits of dissension. Their custom of revering an "inerrant
Bible" instead of an infallible Church left them a prey to shifting
winds of doctrine. Defections from among their orthodox midst had
been characteristic of most of the nineteenth century. The most
serious resulted from the scientific revolution. New discoveries in
biology and physics provoked doubts in the minds of many Protestants who had hitherto been satisfied with a literal interpretation of
the Scriptures. Foremost among these discoveries were the conclusions of Charles Darwin. Darwin was in no sense a theologian. He
made no pretense of being able to interpret the divine will or purpose. He did not profess to know *why* species had appeared on the
earth, but merely to discover how they had evolved and what their
probable destinies would be in the future. Yet he threw most of the
world of orthodox belief into a quandary. The Darwinian theory
forced the faithful to abandon much of their accepted doctrine or
to explain it away by a figurative interpretation. The latter alternative led to the formation of a "Modernist" wing in the leading
Protestant denominations. Darwin, of course, was not alone responsible for the "culture shock" inflicted upon Protestantism. Also important were the teachings of such radical evolutionists as Thomas
H. Huxley and August Weismann. Some Modernists rejected the
idea of an infallible Bible and taught that the Scriptures were a
product of evolution like any other religious writings. Others went
so far as to question the Trinity, the Virgin Birth, and even the
divinity of Christ Himself.

The Social
Gospel

But challenging the validity of Protestant theology was by no
means the only objective of those who sought to transform the
Christian epic. Toward the end of the nineteenth century there came
into prominence a movement called the Social Gospel. Its leaders
were Modernists in every sense. Needless to say, they rejected the
Trinity, the Virgin Birth, the Incarnation, the miracles, but also much
later excrescences as original sin, eternal punishment, and infant
damnation. Love of one's neighbor as one's self was usually their
highest ethical slogan. The Social Gospel derived its name from the
fact that its ministers proclaimed the importance of aiding the working man in his struggles for justice. Accordingly, they defended the
worker's right to organize and strike, and they urged the enactment
of numerous laws for the benefit of the working classes. At the same
time, they refused to endorse socialism. The most they would
countenance was a limited form of government ownership together
with cooperatives to keep down the cost of living and strengthen the
laborer's security. "The Kingdom of God," one of them wrote, "is
expressed in cooperation rather than in competition."

Most exponents of the Social Gospel were content with pro-
claiming a humanitarian message of benevolence and justice to the
less fortunate. Such was the goal of middle-of-the-road liberals like
Washington Gladden and their followers in both England and the
United States. But other Social Gospelers had broader conceptions.
A famous "sky pilot" and Secretary of the Home Mission Society,

Josiah Strong, published books and articles warning of the dangers of concentrated wealth and calling upon the church to recognize its responsibilities to the poor. But he was no soapbox radical. He was much more deeply concerned with issues of national and racial destiny. From some of the Aryanists of his day he had imbibed notions of ethnic superiority. The mighty Anglo-Saxon race, he taught, is destined to hold sway over all the peoples of the earth. In fulfilling this mission the people of the United States will perform the most glorious role. It is possessed of such a wealth of resources and such wondrous traditions that it can scarcely escape a glowing destiny. Moreover, the fate of its people is sealed by the fact of their Anglo-Saxon stock. This stock is destined to populate and rule the entire earth. With the Americans as their vanguard, nothing can stop them. They will spread themselves "down upon Mexico, down upon Central and South America, out upon the islands of the sea, over upon Africa and beyond." No one spoke more eloquently as the voice of racism and American imperialism. The fact that Strong's books sold so widely indicated the capacity of evangelical Protestantism to fit itself into the new pattern of aggrandizement and wealth. It was frequently not difficult to translate the Social Gospel into the Gospel of Wealth made famous by John D. Rockefeller and Andrew Carnegie.

Protestantism and Catholicism were not alone involved in the revolt in religion. Only less seriously affected was Judaism. Although the Jews had no Pope or Church councils to issue authoritarian decrees, a substantial basis of unity prevailed among them. The Old Testament, the Talmud, and the forms of synagogal worship were powerful unifying symbols. Besides, the Jews had a common heritage, veneration of scholarship, a vast array of laws and customs, and for the most part a belief in a common destiny. Yet even Judaism had not escaped the kind of conflicts that had beset the other religions. Dissension between die-hards and liberals, between conservatives and modernists, and between dogmatists and rationalists was just as rife as in any of the branches of Christianity.

A liberal wing of the Jewish faith came into prominence during the Enlightenment. Its leaders were Gotthold Lessing and Moses Mendelssohn. Renouncing many of the beliefs of their fathers, they taught all religions should be judged by their effects upon their followers. Unlike the general run of their successors, they rejected the Chosen People idea and the notion of themselves as a superior race. Gradually a body of doctrines and usages developed as a major branch of the Jewish religion. Known as Reform Judaism, it took its place beside the Orthodox and Conservative branches, which had divided the religion for more than a century. Reform Judaism was not chiefly a product of the eighteenth- and nineteenth-century awakening. Instead, it was mainly inspired by rationalist influences. Its idols were the major Prophets of ancient times, Maimonides in the Middle Ages, Spinoza, and the leaders of the Enlightenment. Reform Judaism emphasized ethical content rather than legal forms and requirements. In this it was not a defiance of the best traditions of Judaism. The Hebrew religion in its prime had always been an ethical religion.

Divisions among Hebrews in the Western World were not exclusively religious and ethical. No one could ignore the politico-religious movement known as Zionism. The most active founder of Zionism was Theodor Herzl, a native of Hungary, who lived for a time in Paris but spent most of his life in Vienna. As a journalist in Paris at the time of the Dreyfus affair, he was horrified by the persecution of the Jews and became convinced that they could find no solution for their problem except in "a land of their own." He did not insist at first that this land be Palestine; he thought that some portion of East Africa might be preferable. Later under the influence of some Eastern European followers he adopted the view that nothing less than the true Jewish homeland of their ancestors would suffice. Just as ancient Jews longed for a return to Zion and a rebuilding of the temple in Jerusalem, so their modern descendants yearned for a reconstitution of the ancient homeland. The true Zion would not be primarily political; instead it would be essentially religious, based upon Biblical prophecy and grandiose dreams for the future. By the beginning of World War I it was already one of the most vigorous movements among the Jewish people.

4. THE REVOLT IN EDUCATION

Education has seldom been an arena of violent rebellion or even of peaceful, deep-rooted change. The reasons lie close to the surface. Educational institutions are generally pillars of the established order. They take their cue from those in positions of authority over them. Usually this means the government, although in occasional instances the Church is supreme. The nineteenth century witnessed the triumph of secular education. France took the lead during the Great Revolution and even more definitely during the time of Napoleon. Prussia joined in the movement in the regeneration following the overthrow of Napoleon. Enthusiasm spread rapidly through Germany during the upsurge of patriotism accompanying the founding of the Empire. Britain fell in arrears of most other West European states. The nation had no comprehensive system of public education until 1870. It was not made compulsory until 1880, and fees were not abolished until 1891. Developments in the United States were not much different from those in Great Britain. If anything, the greater number of churches strengthened the notion that schools should be under private control. Some states took steps to combat this notion by appointing state superintendents with powers of visitation and inspection. Still education was not free, public, or universal. Educational facilities were inadequate, and as late as 1900 only about 10 per cent of high-school-age youth were actually in school.

Education all over the world suffered grievously from barbarous practices and outworn philosophies. Nearly everywhere the time-

English Schoolboys. In the early part of this century, these students of the Bluecoat School, marching through the cloisters, were regimented both in dress and action.

honored objective was to make faithful believers out of the children, or if not that, at least dutiful citizens. Little attention was given to the varying psychologies of children, or to the reasons why some children fail. The welfare of the children themselves received scant consideration. Uppermost were the interests and requirements of church and state. Yet a few bold spirits challenged this system. The most eminent among them was the French-Swiss philosopher and author of the *Social Contract*, Jean Jacques Rousseau. The educational ideas of this unusual man were contained in his novel *Émile.* They revolved around the doctrine that man is fundamentally good. This does not mean that human beings are angels. Neither are they devils. It is simply that there is no such thing as original sin. Yet men in society are bad and unhappy. What makes them so? The answer, according to Rousseau, is the whole social environment, the state, the church, and the schools. Banish the corrupting influence of these, and every individual will have an equal chance to develop in peace and happiness.

It was inevitable that other leaders should join the vanguard of educational reform after Rousseau. First in line was the Swiss Johann Pestalozzi. Unlike Rousseau, Pestalozzi was not a philosopher. Instead he devoted himself to practical efforts for the benefit of destitute and neglected children. His basic educational principle was the importance of "sense impression." He doubted the value of any learning not founded upon accurate observation of concrete objects. With this observation he exerted a deep influence upon Prussia during her period of regeneration following the defeat of Napoleon's armies. The second of the great educational reformers who followed Rousseau was the Italian Maria Montessori. Educated as a doctor of medicine, she did not attract attention as an educator until after 1900. She began her system of instruction with supposedly "de-

Maria Montessori

741

fective" children and showed that they could be trained in habits of alertness and persistence as well as youngsters of more gifted qualities. Lessons ranged from a quarter of an hour to an hour in length, and only so much was assigned as the child could readily master. Instruction began at an early age and continued into the high-school years. Regardless of the subject, the instruction was given almost exclusively on an individual basis. Discipline constituted no problem since each pupil moved at his own pace and not at the demands of a slave driver anxious to please his own boss.

Efforts to reform education culminated in the Progressive Education movement at the end of the nineteenth century. Its roots could be traced back many years not only to Rousseau but even to Sir Francis Bacon. However, its main inspiration was the American philosopher John Dewey. Dewey sought to infuse into education the approach and methods of the pragmatist or "instrumentalist" philosophy. That is, he strove to make education yield a truth that would meet the pragmatic test and serve as an instrument for the solution of social problems. He would place the emphasis upon sciences and other utilitarian subjects and relegate ancient history and the classics to the background. The program of the school should be student-centered and not subject-centered. In so far as any approach or viewpoint should be inculcated, Dewey insisted that this should be the scientific method. Nothing else would provide the key to sound knowledge.

Progressive Education in full reign did not survive much longer than fifty years. Though it spread to England and Germany, it enjoyed great influence only in the United States. Its strength waned everywhere as the icy fingers of blood and suspicion tightened their grip upon the nations. Armaments competition, national hatreds, industrial rivalry, and wars produced an environment decidedly inhospitable to a movement that fostered freedom and exalted the individual above the state. Humanists and conservatives criticized its aversion to discipline and indifference to classical literature and ancient languages. Religionists, both Catholic and Protestant, castigated its materialism and demanded more emphasis on spiritual values. Finally, hardheaded patriots condemned its radicalism and failure to worship at the shrine of national virtue. All that was left was for the hysteria surrounding World War I and the fears that came in its wake to seal the doom of the more meaningful kinds of educational reform. And what was true of elementary and secondary schools was no less true of colleges and universities.

Higher institutions in most countries were more likely to be ossified and moth-eaten than those of lower grade. Improvements were far apart and generally of small importance. They included the admission of women to some universities in England and to a few colleges in the United States. Dozens of medieval rules and requirements were abolished all over Europe. The first state universities, mostly Western, were established in America and were paralleled by

The Progressive Education movement

The decline of Progressive Education

the "Redbrick" universities in Britain. Both were under the control of the state, though in Britain they were generally governed and maintained by a major industrial city. They were among the first universities to provide an exclusively secular education. In some of the "Redbrick" universities the teaching of religion was forbidden. Aside from these departures, higher education changed but little. The majority of colleges and universities continued the line of development they had followed since they were founded. In many cases, notably Great Britain, this meant loyalty to the heritage of the Renaissance. In America traditions were carried over from the colonies. The result was an educational pattern dominated by the churches. Doctors of divinity were generally the governing officials. The chief subjects of study were almost invariably Bible, ethics, the classical languages, and literature. The sciences were quite largely neglected. Where they were introduced, as in Russia under Alexander II, they were often considered dangerous to the state and to religion. Nearly everywhere the functions of higher education were "polite letters" and divinity. Until late in the nineteenth century not a single American or British university granted degrees in advanced professional work. Doctors and lawyers obtained their training by studying with some experienced practitioner or in some "fly-by-night" vocational school. About 1880 the German system of advanced professional training and graduate degrees in law, medicine, and philosophy was imported into the United States. Britain steered clear of the custom until much later.

5. MOODS OF OPTIMISM VERSUS DECLINE

By common supposition the period from the French Revolution to the outbreak of World War I was a period of optimism. Men were disposed to think of it as a time when God was in His Heaven, and all was right with the world. The progress in science, and perhaps most of all the progress in technology, seemed to impugn the sanity of all who questioned this belief. Pulpit orators, popular writers, lecturers, and college presidents vied with one another in acclaiming the grandeur of the new order. Optimism flowered into a national religion. Everything that happened seemed to be a herald of a glorious dawn. The growth of population, the acquisition of territory, the expansion of production, the conquest of disease, and the extension of empire into distant lands across the seas—who could deny that the Sun of Heaven conferred its smiles upon such "progress"?

Yet there were some who did deny it in no unmistakable terms. Carlyle, Ruskin, and William Morris questioned the basic assumptions of industrial civilization. Thoreau and Tolstoi went even further. Still others worked out complete philosophies of pessimism stark to the point of despair. First among this inglorious company was the German Arthur Schopenhauer. His cardinal idea was the

Problems of
higher
education

The prevailing
mood of
optimism

notion that a single force directs all growth and movement in the universe. This force he taught is "will," a blind, unconscious craving of individuals and species to survive. Since the will to live is present in all animate forms, and since it leads the strong to devour the weak, this world is the worst of all possible worlds. Since misery and pain are inseparable from life itself, happiness for man consists in as complete a denial of life as possible. The Oriental ascetic has a better chance of finding Nirvana than has Western man of finding the mythical pot of gold at the end of a rainbow.

Equally distinguished among prophets of "doom and gloom" was another German philosopher, Friedrich Nietzsche. Educated partly in Switzerland, Nietzsche was given an appointment as professor of classical philology at the University of Basel. But with the outbreak of the Franco-German War he returned to Germany and spent the remainder of his life in that country. His philosophy in general is discussed elsewhere.[1] As a pessimist he was not so dyed-in-the-wool as Schopenhauer. He did not preach defeatism or take refuge in Oriental quietism. On the contrary, he glorified strength, bravery, courage, and the other ancient Germanic virtues which he believed should distinguish the Overman. The passive virtues of Christianity and Judaism he regarded as relics of a slave morality. Nietzsche allowed at least one element of optimism to creep into his philosophy. He believed that an unhindered natural selection would ultimately produce a race of Overmen.

Pessimistic views of life were by no means confined to German philosophers. Such conceptions were not unknown in other countries. In America the two Adams brothers, Henry and Brooks, could find little to inspire confidence and hope even in the glittering decades at the turn of the century. Both foresaw the decay of civilizations mainly as a result of depletion of energy. Nothing can save them except an infusion of "barbarian blood," or perhaps a return to the simple faith of the twelfth century. Pessimism made only a limited appeal to other philosophers in America and almost none in England and France. Yet by a curious coincidence it drew its converts by the dozens from the ranks of poets and novelists. Nathaniel Hawthorne, for example, was preoccupied with the problem of original sin and sharply critical of bigotry and intolerance. Herman Melville was concerned with the isolation of man, baffled with the search by inquiring minds, and hopeful of solving problems he could never fathom. British and French writers plumbed the depths of utter hopelessness in some of the things they wrote. James Thomson in his *City of Dreadful Night* wrote of

> A mockery, a delusion: and my breath
> Of noble human life upon this earth
> So racks me that I sigh for senseless death.

[1] See pp. 706–07

It was, of course, not merely minor representatives of Western letters who wrote in such a doleful vein. Matthew Arnold spoke of the world as "a darkling plain" where there is "neither joy, nor love, nor light, nor certitude, nor peace, nor help for pain." Even the great Poet Laureate of the British Empire, Lord Tennyson, did not always sing of pompous generals, brave warriors, and "flowers in crannied walls." He could express poignancy and even fleeting moods of despair, as in one of his alternating sentiments in *In Memoriam:*

> O weary life! O weary death!
> O spirit and heart made desolate!
> O damned vacillating state!

SELECTED READINGS

· *Items so designated are available in paperbound editions.*

Demerath, N. J., and Peterson, Richard A., eds., *System Change and Conflict,* New York, 1961.

· Derry, J. W., *A Short History of Nineteenth-Century England,* New York, 1963 (Mentor).

De Vries, Egbert, *Man in Rapid Social Change,* New York, 1961.

· Fanon, Frantz, *The Wretched of the Earth,* New York, 1968 (Evergreen Black Cat Edition).

Graham, Stephen, *Tsar of Freedom: The Life and Reign of Alexander II,* New Haven, 1935.

· Hobsbawm, E. I., *Primitive Rebels,* London, 1959 (Norton Library).

· Horowitz, David, *Empire and Revolution: A Radical Interpretation of Contemporary History,* New York, 1970 (Vintage).

Hovell, M., *The Chartist Movement,* New York, 1925.

Hughes, H. Stuart, *The Obstructed Path: French Social Thought in the Years of Desperation, 1930–1960,* New York, 1968.

Jones, Peter d'A., *The Christian Socialist Revival, 1877–1914,* Princeton, 1968.

Karpovich, M., *Imperial Russia, 1801–1917,* New York, 1932. An excellent short treatise.

Keep, J. L. H., *The Rise of Social Democracy in Russia,* New York, 1963.

Orth, S. P., *Socialism and Democracy in Europe,* New York, 1913.

· Pares, Bernard, *A History of Russia,* New York, 1928 (Vintage). A standard work.

Pipkin, C. W., *The Idea of Social Justice,* New York, 1928.

Postgate, Raymond, *1848: The Story of a Year,* London, 1955.

· Raeff, Marc, *Origins of the Russian Intelligentsia,* New York, 1966 (Harcourt, Brace and World).

· Robertson, Priscilla, *Revolutions of 1848: A Social History,* Princeton, 1952 (Torchbook). A stimulating account written from the viewpoint of the people who lived at that time.

Robinson, G. T., *Rural Russia under the Old Regime,* New York, 1932.

· Thompson, E. P., *The Making of the English Working Class,* New York, 1964 (Vintage).

· Thompson, J. M., *Louis Napoleon and the Second Empire,* New York, 1955 (Norton Library). A valuable summary based on scholarly sources.

Wagar, W. Warren, *Good Tidings, The Belief in Progress from Darwin to Marcuse,* Bloomington, Ind., 1972.

Woodward, Ernest, *The Age of Reform, 1815–1870,* Oxford, 1938. Great Britain during the Age of Democracy.

Younger, Carlton, *Ireland's Civil War,* New York, 1969.

PART VII

The Contemporary World, 1914-: The Age of Deepening Conflict

From the beginning of the Renaissance to the outbreak of World War I in 1914, Europe held the scepter over practically the entire world. European culture and technology set the standards for the majority of nations in both East and West, except for the more isolated ones like China and Japan. Near the end of the nineteenth century a struggle ensued among Western European Powers for control of the outside world. But they did not have the field to themselves. They were soon confronted with formidable competition from the United States, Japan, and eventually Russia. Indeed, the history of the twentieth century thus far has been occupied largely by contentions for mastery over the hundreds of millions of people in Asia, Africa, and the islands of the Pacific. The great question has been, who shall rule the world? Before 1914 a varied collection of candidates vied for the honor—Britain, France, the Netherlands, Germany, Russia, Japan, and the United States. Between 1918 and 1933 the list was narrowed principally to Germany, Russia, the United States, and Japan. The defeat of 1945 eliminated, for the time being at least, Germany and Japan, leaving the world a bipolar structure with the Soviet Union and the United States competing for the right to rule it. After 1949 the collision course followed by these two giants was modified by the emergence of a new colossus, Communist China, with claims to inherit the remains of European empires.

747

A Chronological Table

	INTERNATIONAL	**THE AMERICAS**

1900

Triple Alliance, 1882–1914
Diplomatic Revolution, 1890–1907
Berlin-to-Baghdad Railway, 1890–1914

Entente Cordiale, 1904–1923
Triple Entente, 1907–1917
Bosnian Crisis, 1908
Balkan Wars, 1912–1913
Assassination of Archduke Francis Ferdinand, 1914
World War I, 1914–1918
U.S. enters World War I, 1917

1919

Treaty of Versailles, 1919

League of Nations, 1920–1946

John Dewey, *Reconstruction in Philosophy*, 1920
Eugene O'Neill, *Strange Interlude*, 1920
Renaissance of painting in Mexico, *ca.* 1921
Discovery of insulin, 1922

French invasion of Ruhr Valley, 1923

Locarno Agreements, 1925

1929

Pact of Paris, 1928

Great Depression 1929–1934

Regionalism in art, U.S., ca. 1930

Japan invades Manchuria, 1931

Cancellation of German reparations, 1932

U.S. abandons gold standard, 1933
NRA, 1933–1935
New Deal 1933–1939

World Economic Conference, 1933

Anglo-German naval pact, 1935
Franco-Soviet alliance, 1935
Italy conquers Ethiopia, 1935–1936
Hitler remilitarizes Rhineland, 1936
Rome-Berlin Axis, 1936
Germany absorbs Austria (*Anschluss*), 1938
Appeasement at Munich, 1938

BRITAIN	WESTERN EUROPE	CENTRAL AND EASTERN EUROPE	
		Pan-Slavism, 1890–1914 Expressionism in art, 1893 Pan-Germanism, 1895–1914 Greater Serbia movement, 1900–1914 Industrial supremacy of Germany, 1900–1914	1900
A. N. Whitehead, *The Organization of Thought*, 1916			
	Impressionism in music, 1918 Surrealism, 1918	Overthrow of Tsar, 1917 Bolshevik Revolution, 1917 Expressionism in music, 1918 Revolution in Germany, 1918 O. Spengler, *Decline of the West*, 1918 First Communist regime in Hungary, 1919 Weimar Republic, 1919–1933	1919
		NEP in Russia 1921–1929 Fascist Revolution in Italy, 1922 Runaway inflation in Germany, 1923 Death of Lenin, 1924 Thomas Mann, *The Magic Mountain*, 1924 Dictatorship of Stalin, 1924–1953	
First Labour Government, 1924 General strike, 1926 Second Labour Government, 1929–1931 Discovery of penicillin, 1930		First Five-year Plan in Russia, 1929–1933	1929
Abandonment of gold standard, 1931 Discovery of neutrons, 1932 Abandonment of free trade, 1932	Overthrow of monarchy in Spain, 1931	Nazi Revolution in Germany, 1933	
	Development of sulfa drugs, 1935 Popular Front in France, 1936–1938 Civil War in Spain, 1936–1939 Existentialism, *ca.* 1938		

	INTERNATIONAL	THE AMERICAS
1940	Nazi-Soviet Pact, 1939 World War II, 1939–1945	Discovery of streptomycin, *ca.* 1940
	Atlantic Charter, 1941 Attack on Pearl Harbor, 1941 Cairo Conference, 1943 Teheran Conference, 1943 Establishment of United Nations, 1945	Fair Deal in the U.S., 1945–1953
	Atomic bombs dropped on Japan, 1945 Yalta Conference, 1945 Potsdam Conference, 1945 Cold War of East and West, 1946– Truman Doctrine, 1947	
	European Recovery Program (Marshall Plan), 1948	Discovery of cortisone, 1948
	NATO, 1949	
1950	Korean War, 1950–1953	
	Schuman Plan, 1952	Hydrogen bomb, 1952 Return of Republicans to power in U.S., 1953–1961
	Summit Conference, Geneva, 1955	Overthrow of Peron regime in Argentina, 1955
	Suez Crisis, 1956	
		Establishment of Castro regime in Cuba, 1959 Election of John F. Kennedy, Democrat, as President of U.S., 1960
1960		The New Frontier, 1961–1963 Cuban missile crisis, 1962 Assassination of President Kennedy and the beginning of the presidency of Lyndon B. Johnson, 1963
	Vietnamese War, 1964–	Black revolt, 1965
	Revolt of youth, 1966 6 Day War, 1967 First human heart transplant, 1967 Women's liberation movement, 1968–	Assassination of Martin Luther King, 1968 Assassination of Robert F. Kennedy, 1968 Election of Richard M. Nixon, Republican as President of U.S., 1968
	Man lands on moon, 1969	
1970		Election of Salvador Allende, a Marxist, as President of Chile, 1970
	China admitted to U.N., 1971	
	U.S.-Soviet trade agreements, 1972	Re-election of Richard M. Nixon, 1972
	SALT agreements, 1972	

BRITAIN	WESTERN EUROPE	CENTRAL AND EASTERN EUROPE	
	Franco regime in Spain, 1939–	Atomic fission, 1939 Neo-Orthodoxy, *ca.* 1940	**1940**
Third Labour Government, 1945–1950			
Dissolution of Empire in India, 1947	Fourth Republic in France, 1946–1959	Communist coup in Hungary, 1947 Communist coup in Czechoslovakia, 1948 Division of Germany into East and West zones, 1948 Establishment of German Federal Republic and German Democratic Republic, 1949	
			1950
Return of Conservatives to power, 1950			
		Death of Stalin, 1953 Russia develops hydrogen bomb, 1953 Revolt in Hungary, 1956	
	Fifth Republic in France, 1959–	Dictatorship of Khrushchev, 1958–1964	**1960**
Fourth Labour Government, 1963–		Breshnev-Kosygin regime, 1964–	
		Military coup in Greece, 1967 Russian occupation of Czechoslovakia, 1968 Soviet-Chinese border clashes, 1968	
Protestant-Catholic civil war in Ulster, Northern Ireland, 1968–	Student and worker's rebellion in France, 1968 Defeat of Charles de Gaulle, 1968		
Conservative Government of Edward Heath elected, 1970		Bonn-Warsaw Pact, 1970	**1970**
		Massacre of Israeli Olympic team, 1972	

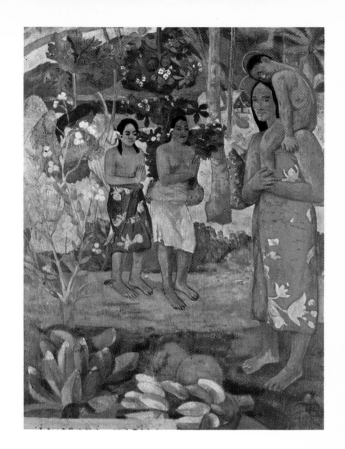

Above: *Portrait of the Artist*, Vincent van Gogh (1853–1890). This self-portrait shows a deep seriousness and intense concentration. (V. W. van Gogh) Right: *Ia Orana Maria*, Paul Gauguin (1848–1903). Gauguin revolted not only against the complexity and artificiality of European life, but against civilization itself. He finally fled to Tahiti to paint the lush, colorful life of an uncorrupted society. (MMA) Below: *The Starry Night*, van Gogh. This painting gives vivid expression to van Gogh's bold conceptions. (Mus. Mod. Art) Below Right: *Sunflowers in a Vase*, van Gogh. The feverish technique seems to have endowed the flowers with rhythmic motion. (V. W. van Gogh)

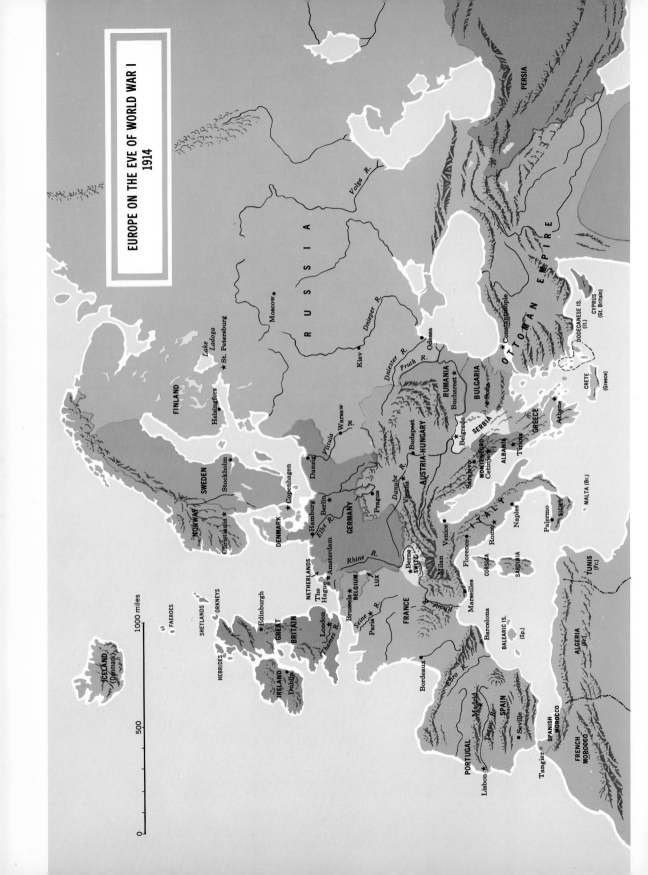

EUROPE ON THE EVE OF WORLD WAR I
1914

1000 miles

500

0

ICELAND
(Denmark)

HEBRIDES

FAEROES

SHETLANDS

ORKNEYS

Edinburgh ★

IRELAND
Dublin ●

GREAT
BRITAIN
London ★
Thames R.

NETHERLANDS
The
Hague ★
Brussels ★
BELGIUM
LUX.

FRANCE
Seine R.
Paris ★

Bordeaux ●

PORTUGAL
Lisbon ★
Tagus R.
Madrid ★
SPAIN
● Seville

Tangier ●

SPANISH
MOROCCO

FRENCH
MOROCCO

Barcelona ●

BALEARIC IS.
(Sp.)

Ebro R.

ALGERIA
(Fr.)

TUNIS
(Fr.)

NORWAY
Christiania ★

SWEDEN
Stockholm ★

Copenhagen ★
DENMARK

Hamburg ●
Berlin ★
GERMANY
Elbe R.
Prague ●

Amsterdam ●

Rhine R.

Berne ★
SWITZ.

Milan ●
ITALY
Venice ●
Florence ●
Rome ★
Naples ●

CORSICA
(Fr.)

SARDINIA

Palermo ●
SICILY

Marseilles ●

Rhone R.

MALTA (Br.)

FINLAND
Helsingfors ●

Lake
Ladoga
★ St. Petersburg

Moscow ●

RUSSIA

Volga R.

Kiev ●

Dnieper R.

Odessa ●

Dniester R.

Pruth R.

Danzig ●
Vistula R.
Warsaw ●

AUSTRIA-HUNGARY
Vienna ●
Budapest ●
Danube R.

RUMANIA
Bucharest ★

BULGARIA
Sofia ★

SERBIA
Belgrade ★

MONTENEGRO
Cetinje ★
ALBANIA
Scutari ●

GREECE
Athens ★

Trieste ●

OTTOMAN EMPIRE

Constantinople ★

PERSIA

DODECANESE IS.
(It.)

CYPRUS
(Gt. Britain)

CRETE
(Greece)

CHAPTER 27

World War I

Victory! Victory!
　On with the dance!
Back to the jungle!
　The new beasts prance!
God, how the dead men
　Grin by the wall,
Watching the fun
　Of the Victory Ball.
　　　—Alfred Noyes, "A Victory Dance,"
　　　Collected Poems, 1919

The war that broke out in 1914 was one of the most extraordinary in history. Though it was not really the "first world war," since such conflicts as the Seven Years' War and the Napoleonic Wars had also been global in extent, it had an impact far exceeding either of these. It quickly became a "people's war" in which civilians as well as soldiers in the trenches participated in violent demands for extermination of the enemy. It bore fruit in an epidemic of revolutions and sowed the dragon's teeth of new and even more venomous conflicts in the future. In such ways it set the pattern for an age of violence that continued through the greater part of the twentieth century. Even more extraordinary was the fact that World War I marked the close of a long era of peace. For almost a century after the end of the Napoleonic Wars in 1815, Europe experienced no major conflicts. True, there were the Crimean War in 1854–1856, the Franco-Prussian War in 1870–1871, and the Russo-Turkish War in 1878–1879, but these were minor affrays compared with those that were to follow. That no more serious conflicts occurred until 1914 must be attributed chiefly to the celebrated balance of power, established by Great Britain about 1818 with the cooperation of Austria, Prussia, and France. Essentially it was a *Pax Britannica*, since it rested upon British economic supremacy and the power of the British navy. When war threatened or broke out in Europe, Britain

End of the
Hundred Years'
Peace

753

generally threw her weight into the scales on the side of the weaker country, thereby restoring or redressing the balance.

1. UNDERLYING CAUSES OF THE WAR

But the balance of power was never in perfect adjustment. It was threatened by Napoleon III in mid-century, by Bismarck in 1870, and by Russia in 1878. Much more serious threats came after 1900. By that date Germany had emerged as the most powerful state on the European Continent. France was no longer a match for her, and even Russia could not hold a candle to her in military might and efficiency. The Germans cultivated grandiose schemes for enlarging their power in world affairs. Under Kaiser William II, who came to the throne in 1888, they developed ambitions for control of North Africa, for economic imperialism in Turkey, and for the building of a navy able to throw down a challenge to that of Great Britain. That they might speedily attain these goals was evidenced by their phenomenal economic growth after 1871. By 1914 Germany was producing more iron and steel than Britain and France combined. In chemicals, in aniline dyes, and in the manufacture of scientific equipment she led the world. She threw down a challenge to the supremacy of Britain in the carrying trade and produced some of the largest and fastest ships on the Seven Seas. Bursting with pride in these accomplishments, she was impatient with the refusal of other nations to accord her a dominant position on the European Continent. Indeed, many historians have drawn the conclusion that it was Germany's threat to the European balance of power that constituted the real and primary cause of the two world wars of the twentieth century.

Threats to the balance of power were implicit in the aims of a number of principal states. By 1900 six great powers in Europe—Germany, France, Russia, Italy, Austria-Hungary and Great Britain—were competing for power, security, and economic advantage. Each had specific objectives, the fulfillment of which it regarded as essential to its national interest. Germany built her ambitions around eastward expansion. After 1890 German capitalists and imperialists dreamed of a *Drang nach Osten* (Drive to the East) and planned the construction of a railway from Berlin to Baghdad to facilitate economic control of the Ottoman Empire. Austria also looked to the east, but to the Balkans rather than to any part of western Asia. Her hold on Trieste and other portions of the Adriatic coast was precarious, since much of this territory was inhabited by Italians. If she could carve a highroad through the Balkans to the Aegean, her access to the sea would be more secure. As time passed, Austria and Germany became more dependent upon each other, the former because of trouble with the Slavs both inside and outside her borders, and the latter because of a growing fear of encirclement. In 1879

Bismarck entered into an alliance with Austria, which was renewed and strengthened in subsequent years. It was an alliance with a corpse, but the Germans clung to it more and more desperately as international tensions deepened.

To a large degree the objectives of France were dictated by a desire to curb or counterbalance the growing might of Germany. France hoped to recover Alsace and Lorraine, which had suddenly become very valuable as the result of a discovery by Sidney Thomas and P. C. Gilchrist in 1878 of a method of converting low-grade iron ore into steel. But recovery of the lost provinces was not the only French objective. The French were determined to add Morocco to their African empire regardless of the interests of other powers in that sadly misgoverned country. The motives of the Paris statesmen were both economic and political. Morocco contained rich mineral deposits, but it would be valuable also for strategic reasons and as a reservoir from which troops might be drawn to offset the manpower shortage at home.

A paramount ambition of Russia was to gain control of the Bosporus and the Dardanelles. She had regarded this as her "historic mission" since early in the nineteenth century. Achievement of this mission would prevent her fleet from being bottled up in the Black Sea in the event of war with some naval power or powers. Besides, it would give her unquestioned access to the Mediterranean and probably possession of Constantinople. Turkey would be eliminated from Europe, and Russia would fall heir to the Balkans. In addition, if the Tsar's agents could get to Constantinople before the Germans, they could turn the Berlin-to-Baghdad railway into an empty dream. But Imperial Russia had other ambitions. She coveted access to the Persian Gulf and Indian Ocean and tried for years to make Persia a Russian protectorate. She strove also for better outlets to the Pacific and attempted to extend her control over Manchuria. Finally, through Pan-Slavism she aspired to play the role of guide and protector of all the Slavic peoples of eastern Europe, including those who were under the rule of Austria-Hungary. That each of these ambitions constituted a threat to the status quo scarcely needs emphasis.

The power policies of Great Britain and Italy were somewhat less closely related to the specific actions of other countries. The policy of Britain, in fact, was directed against almost everyone. She was no less suspicious of the Russian ambitions at Constantinople than she was of the German. Until after the beginning of the twentieth century she distrusted France. Her cardinal aims were (1) to maintain the life lines of her empire, (2) to keep open the sea lanes to her sources of imports and her foreign markets, and (3) to preserve a balance among the nations on the European Continent so that no one of them would ever become strong enough to attack her. If the actions of any other country threatened to interfere with these car-

Ambitions of France

Ambitions of Russia

Great Britain and Italy

dinal aims (as they often did), the hostility of Britain would instantly be aroused. She would seek to put the offending nation in its place by diplomatic pressure, forming an alliance against it, or by going to war, as she finally did against Germany in 1914. Italian policy was mainly based on hopes of aggrandizement at the expense of Austria and Turkey. Austria continued to hold territories which Italy regarded as rightfully hers: the so-called *Italia Irredenta* (unredeemed Italy) as late as 1915; while Turkey blocked Italy's acquisition of Tripoli and other territories in North Africa.

Militarism and the armed peace

One of the clearest expressions of the realities of power politics before 1914 was the growth of militarism. Since the nations of the world were living in a condition of international anarchy, it was almost inevitable that their fears and suspicions should lead to competition in armaments. Europe in particular became an armed camp. After 1870 every one of its chief powers, with the exception of Great Britain, adopted conscription and universal military training. Not only that, but they adopted the belief that national security depended almost entirely upon the extent of military and naval preparedness. After every war scare the size of armies and navies increased until, by 1914, all of the important countries, and many of the smaller ones also, were staggering under a burden which, in a saner world, would have been regarded as intolerable. There were, of course, men of humanity and wisdom who recognized the danger and did all in their power to ward it off. But there were far too many others who not only denied that any danger existed but stoutly maintained that militarism was a positive benefit. Theodore Roosevelt argued that training for war was necessary to preserve the "manly and adventurous qualities" in a nation. Field Marshal von Moltke and Heinrich von Treitschke saw in military conflict one of the divine elements of the universe and a "terrible medicine" for the human race. The French philosopher, Ernest Renan, justified war as a condition of progress, "the sting which prevents a country from going to sleep." Although the propagation of such doctrines was not the chief cause of militarism, it undoubtedly strengthened the position of those who believed in armaments and war as the best methods of solving a nation's problems.

Field Marshal von Moltke

Nationalism: the Greater Serbia movement

Power politics and the failure of the balance of power may be regarded as perhaps the paramount underlying causes of World War I. Prominent also among these causes was nationalism. This factor, as previously explained, had roots extending at least as far back as the French Revolution. By the early twentieth century, however, nationalism had come to assume a variety of particularly dangerous forms. Foremost among them were the Greater Serbia scheme, the Pan-Slav movement in Russia, the revenge movement in France, and the Pan-German movement. The first two were closely related. Since the beginning of the twentieth century at least, little Serbia had dreamed of extending her jurisdiction over all the peoples alleged to be similar to her own citizens in race and in culture. Some of these peoples inhabited what were then the two Turkish provinces of Bosnia and Herzegovina. Others included Croatians and Slovenes in the southern provinces of Austria-Hungary. After 1908 when Austria suddenly annexed Bosnia and Herzegovina, the Greater Serbia scheme was directed exclusively against the Hapsburg Empire. It took the form of agitation to provoke discontent among the Slav subjects of Austria, in the hope of drawing them away and uniting the territories they inhabited with Serbia. It resulted in a series of dangerous plots against the peace and integrity of the Dual Monarchy. And the fateful climax of these plots was the murder of the heir to the Austrian throne on June 28, 1914.

In many of their activities the Serbian nationalists were aided and abetted by the Pan-Slavists in Russia. The Pan-Slav movement was founded upon the theory that all of the Slavs of eastern Europe constituted one great family. Therefore, it was argued that Russia as the most powerful Slavic state should act as the guide and protector of her little brother nations of the Balkans. The latter were to be encouraged to look to Russia whenever their interests were endangered. Serbs, Bulgarians, and Montenegrins, in their struggles with Austria or with Turkey, were to be made to understand that they always had a powerful and sympathetic friend on the other side of the Carpathians. Pan-Slavism was not merely the wishful sentiment of a few ardent nationalists, but was really a part of the official policy of the Russian government. It went far toward explaining Russia's aggressive stand in every quarrel that arose between Serbia and Austria.

The influence of Pan-Germanism as a species of nationalism before 1914 is difficult to assess. The name of the movement is generally taken to refer to the ideas of the Pan-German League, founded about 1895. Specifically, the League advocated the expansion of Germany to incorporate all of the Teutonic peoples of central Europe. The boundaries of the Empire should be extended to take in Denmark, the Netherlands, Luxemburg, Switzerland, Austria, and Poland as far east as Warsaw. A few of the leaders were not even satisfied with this but demanded a large colonial empire and a vast expansion into the Balkans and western Asia. They insisted that such peoples as the Bulgars and the Turks should at least become satellites of the German Reich. Although the Pan-German League made a great deal of noise, it could scarcely claim to represent the entire German nation. As late as 1912 it had a membership of only 17,000, and its violent criticism of the government was widely resented. Nevertheless, a large number of its doctrines had been latent in German thinking for upwards of a century. The philosopher Fichte had taught that the Germans, because of their spiritual superiority, had a mission to impose peace upon the rest of Europe. Ideas of Aryanism and of Nordic supremacy also contributed to the notion that the Germans had a divine destiny to persuade or compel "inferior races" to accept their culture. Finally, the efforts of philosophers

Pan-Slavism

The Pan-German movement

757

like Heinrich von Treitschke to deify the great state and to glorify power as the instrument of national policy helped to impregnate the minds of many Germans of the middle and upper classes with an intolerance of other nations and a belief in the right of Germany to dominate her weaker neighbors.

Nationalism of the types described would have been almost sufficient in itself to have plunged a considerable number of European nations into the maelstrom of war. But the conflict might well have remained limited in character had it not been for the system of entangling alliances. It was this system which transformed a local squabble between Austria and Serbia into a general war. When Russia intervened on behalf of Serbia, Germany felt obliged to come to the defense of Austria. France had close ties to Russia, and Great Britain was drawn in at least partly on account of her commitments to France.

The evolution of the system of entangling alliances goes back to the 1870's, and its original architect was Bismarck. In the main his purposes were peaceful. Prussia and her German allies had emerged victorious in their war with France, and the newly created German empire was the most powerful state on the Continent. Bismarck was anxious, above all, to preserve the fruits of this victory; there is nothing to indicate that he planned any further conquests. However, he was disturbed by fears that the French might start a war of revenge. There was little prospect that they would attempt such a thing singlehanded, but they might with the help of some other power. Therefore Bismarck determined to isolate France by attaching all of her potential friends to Germany. In 1873 he managed to form an alliance with both Austria and Russia, the so-called League of the Three Emperors. But this combination was of a precarious nature and soon went on the rocks. With the League of the Three Emperors defunct, Bismarck cemented a new and much stronger alliance with Austria. In 1882 this partnership was expanded into the celebrated Triple Alliance when Italy was added as a member. The Italians did not join out of love for either Germany or Austria but from motives of anger and fear. They resented the French occupation of Tunisia (1881), a territory which they regarded as properly theirs. Moreover, the Italian politicians were still at odds with the Church, and they feared that the clericals in France might gain the upper hand and send a French army to defend the Pope. In the meantime, the Three Emperors' League had been revived. Though it lasted for only six years (1881–1887), Germany managed to hold the friendship of Russia until 1890.

Thus after little more than a decade of diplomatic maneuvering, the Iron Chancellor had achieved his ambition. By 1882 France was cut off from nearly every possibility of obtaining aid from powerful friends. Austria and Italy were united with Germany in the Triple Alliance, and Russia after a three-year lapse was back once more in

The effects of the system of entangling alliances

The evolution of the system of alliances

the Bismarckian camp. The only conceivable quarter from which help might come was Great Britain; but, with respect to Continental affairs, the British had returned to their traditional policy of "splendid isolation." Therefore, so far as the danger of a war of revenge was concerned, Germany had little to fear. But if either Bismarck or anyone else imagined that this security would be permanent, he was headed for disillusionment. Between 1890 and 1907, Europe went through a diplomatic revolution which practically annihilated Bismarck's work. To be sure, the Germans had Austria still on their side; but they had lost the friendship of both Russia and Italy, and Britain had abandoned her isolation to enter into agreements with Russia and France. This shift in the balance of power had fateful results. It convinced the Germans that they were surrounded by a ring of enemies, and that consequently they must do everything in their power to retain the loyalty of Austria—even to the extent of supporting her reckless foreign adventures.

The diplomatic revolution of 1890–1907

The first of the major results of the diplomatic revolution was the formation of the Triple Entente. This came about through a series of stages. In 1890 Russia and France began a political flirtation which gradually ripened into a binding alliance. The secret military convention signed by the two countries in 1894 provided that each should come to the aid of the other in case of an attack by Germany, or by Austria or Italy supported by Germany. This Dual Alliance of Russia and France was followed by the *Entente Cordiale* between France and Great Britain. During the last two decades of the nineteenth century the British and the French had frequently been involved in sharp altercations over colonies and trade. The two nations almost came to blows in 1898 at Fashoda in the Egyptian Sudan. But suddenly the French withdrew all of their claims to that portion of Africa and opened negotiations for a broad compromise of other disputes. The result was the conclusion in 1904 of the *Entente Cordiale*. It was not a formal alliance but a friendly agreement, covering a variety of subjects. The final step in the formation of the Triple Entente was the conclusion of a mutual understanding between Great Britain and Russia. Again there was no formal alliance. The two powers simply came to an agreement in 1907 concerning their ambitions in Asia. The core of it provided for the division of Persia into spheres of influence. To Russia was assigned the northern portion and to Great Britain the southern. A middle section was to be preserved, temporarily at least, as a neutral area under its legitimate ruler, the Shah.

Results of the diplomatic revolution; formation of the Triple Entente

Thus by 1907 the great powers of Europe had come to be arrayed in two opposing combinations, the Triple Alliance and the Triple Entente. Had these combinations remained stable and more or less evenly matched, they might well have promoted the cause of peace. But no such condition prevailed. Each grew weaker and less stable with the passage of time. The Triple Alliance declined in strength because of a growing coolness between Italy and Austria. Moreover, Italian nationalists coveted territory in North Africa, notably Tripoli, which they believed they could obtain only by supporting French ambitions in Morocco. Meanwhile, the Triple Entente was threatened by discord between Britain and Russia. Because their lifeline to the East might be imperiled, the British could not view with equanimity the cardinal aim of Russia to "open the Straits" and gain control of Constantinople. Disharmony in the Triple Entente also increased when Britain and France refused to support Russia in her dispute with Austria over the latter's annexation of Bosnia and Herzegovina. In short, conflicts were so numerous that the members of neither alliance could be quite sure where their opposite numbers might stand in case of a real threat of a European war.

Between 1905 and 1913 five serious international crises endangered the peace of Europe. In a sense they were not so much causes as they were symptoms of international animosity. Yet each of them left a heritage of suspicion and bitterness that made war all the more probable. In some cases hostilities were averted only because one of the parties was too weak at the time to offer resistance. The result was a sense of humiliation, a smoldering resentment that was almost bound to burst into flame in the future. Three of the crises were generated by disputes over Morocco. Both Germany and France yearned for control of that unhappy country, mainly because of the mineral wealth and trading opportunities it was supposed to contain. In 1905, 1908, and 1911 the two powers stood on the brink of war. Each time the dispute was smoothed over but not without the usual legacy of suspicion and resentment.

The Near
Eastern Crises:
1) the annexa-
tion of Bosnia
and Herze-
govina

In addition to the clash over Morocco, two crises occurred in the Near East. The first was the Bosnian crisis of 1908. At the Congress of Berlin in 1878 the two Turkish provinces of Bosnia and Herzegovina had been placed under the administrative control of Austria, though actual possession was still to be vested in the Ottoman Empire. Serbia also coveted the territories, since they would double her kingdom and place her within striking distance of the Adriatic. Suddenly, in October, 1908, Austria annexed the two provinces, in flat violation of the Treaty of Berlin. The Serbs were furious and appealed to Russia. The Tsar's government threatened war, until Germany addressed a sharp note to St. Petersburg announcing her firm intention to back Austria. Since Russia had not yet fully recovered from her war with Japan and was plagued by internal troubles, she finally informed the Serbs that they would have to wait until a more favorable time.

Still more bad blood between the nations of Eastern Europe was created by the Balkan Wars. In 1912 Serbia, Bulgaria, Montenegro, and Greece, with encouragement from Russia, joined in a Balkan alliance for the conquest of the Turkish province of Macedonia. The war was started in October, 1912, and in less than two months the resistance of the Turks was shattered. Then came the problem of dividing the spoils. In secret treaties negotiated before hostilities began, Serbia had been promised Albania, in addition to a generous slice of Macedonia. But now Austria, fearful as always of any increase in Serbian power, intervened at the peace conference and obtained the establishment of Albania as an independent state. For the Serbs this was the last straw. It seemed that at every turn their path to western expansion was certain to be blocked by the Hapsburg government. From this time on, anti-Austrian agitation in Serbia and in the neighboring province of Bosnia became ever more venomous.

2. THE ROAD TO ARMAGEDDON

It is generally held that the immediate cause of World War I was the assassination of Archduke Francis Ferdinand on June 28, 1914. This was the match thrown into the powder-keg of accumulated suspicion and hate. Nevertheless, it was not quite so trivial an event as many people think. Francis Ferdinand was not simply a useless member of the Austrian nobility; he was soon to become Emperor. The reigning monarch, Francis Joseph, had reached his eighty-fourth year, and his death was expected momentarily. The murder of the heir to the throne was therefore considered as in a very real sense an attack upon the state.

The actual murderer of Francis Ferdinand was a Bosnian student by the name of Princip. But this does not tell half of the story. Princip was merely the tool of Serbian nationalists. The murder, though committed in Sarajevo, the capital of Bosnia, was the result of a plot hatched in Belgrade. The conspirators were members of a secret society officially known as Union or Death but commonly called the Black Hand. What were the motives of the conspirators? If there is any one answer, it would seem to lie in the plan which Francis Fer-

The assassination of Francis Ferdinand

Motives of the assassins

The Archduke Francis Ferdinand. He and his wife are leaving the Senate House in Sarajevo shortly before the assassination, June 28, 1914.

dinand was known to be developing for the reorganization of the Hapsburg Empire. This plan, designated as *trialism*, involved a proposal for changing the Dual Monarchy into a triple monarchy. In addition to German Austria and Magyar Hungary, already practically autonomous, there was to be a third semi-independent unit composed of the Slavs. This was exactly what the Serb nationalists did not want. They feared that if it were put into effect their Slovene and Croatian kinsmen would be content to remain under Hapsburg rule. Therefore they determined to get Francis Ferdinand out of the way before he could become Emperor of Austria-Hungary.

The Austrian ultimatum to Serbia

In the weeks immediately following the tragedy, Austrian officials conducted an investigation which confirmed their suspicions that the plot was of Serbian origin. Consequently, on July 23, they dispatched to the Serbian government a severe ultimatum consisting of eleven demands. Among other things Serbia was to suppress anti-Austrian newspapers, to crush the secret patriotic societies, to eliminate from the government and from the army all persons guilty of anti-Austrian propaganda, and to accept the collaboration of Austrian officials in stamping out the subversive movement against the Hapsburg Empire. On July 25, in accordance with the time limit of forty-eight hours, the Serbian government transmitted its reply. Of the total of eleven demands, only one was emphatically refused, and five were accepted without reservations. The German Chancellor regarded it as almost a capitulation, and the Kaiser declared that now all reason for war had fallen to the ground. The Austrians, however, pronounced it unsatisfactory, severed diplomatic relations, and mobilized parts of their army. The Serbs themselves had been under no illusions about pleasing Austria, since, three hours before transmitting their reply, they had issued an order to mobilize the troops.

Russia and France assume a belligerent attitude

At this point the attitude of other nations becomes important. In fact for some time before this, several of the rulers of the great powers had assumed very belligerent attitudes. As early as July 18 Sazonov, the Russian Foreign Minister, warned Austria that Russia would not tolerate any effort to humiliate Serbia. On July 24 Sazonov exclaimed to the German ambassador: "I do not hate Austria; I despise her. Austria is seeking a pretext to gobble up Serbia; but in that case Russia will make war on Austria." [1] In the adoption of this attitude, Russia had the support of France. About the twentieth of July, Raymond Poincaré, who was now President of the French Republic, paid a visit to St. Petersburg. He kept urging Sazonov to "be firm" and to avoid any compromise which might result in a loss of prestige for the Triple Entente. He warned the Austrian ambassador that "Serbia has very warm friends in the Russian people. And Russia has an ally, France." [2]

[1] S. B. Fay, *The Origins of the World War*, II, 300.
[2] *Ibid.*, II, 281.

The attitude of Germany in these critical days was ambiguous. Although the Kaiser was shocked and infuriated by the assassination, his government did not make any threats until after the actions of Russia gave cause for alarm. Unfortunately, both the Kaiser and the Chancellor, von Bethmann-Hollweg, adopted the premise that stern punishment must be meted out to Serbia without delay. They hoped in this way to confront the other powers with an accomplished fact. The Kaiser declared on June 30: "Now or never! Matters must be cleared up with the Serbs, *and that soon.*" On July 6 Bethmann-Hollweg gave to the Austrian Foreign Minister, Count Berchtold, a commitment which was interpreted by the latter as a blank check. The Austrian government was informed that the Kaiser would "stand true by Austria's side in accordance with his treaty obligations and old friendship." In giving this pledge Bethmann and his imperial master were gambling on the hope that Russia would not intervene for the protection of Serbia, and that therefore the quarrel would remain a mere local squabble.

The attitude of Germany

Austria declared war against Serbia on July 28, 1914. For a fleeting, anxious moment there was a possibility that the conflict might be localized. But it was quickly transformed into a war of larger scope by the action of Russia. On July 29 Sazonov and the military clique persuaded the Tsar to issue an order to mobilize all of the troops, not only against Austria but against Germany as well. Their argument was a logical one. Such a vast country as Russia would require considerable time to get her military machine into operation. But before the order could be put into effect, Nicholas changed his mind, having just received an urgent appeal from the Kaiser to help in preserving peace. On July 30 Sazonov and General Tatistchev, the Chief of Staff, went to work to induce the Tsar to change his mind again. For more than an hour they sought to convince the reluctant autocrat that the entire military system should be set in motion. Finally, General Tatistchev remarked: "Yes, it is hard to decide." Nicholas retorted with a show of irritation: "I will decide," and signed an order for immediate mobilization. Sazonov hurried to the telephone to communicate the news to the Chief of Staff. The next morning in a remote Siberian village an English traveler was awakened by a commotion outside his window, followed by the query of an excited peasant: "Have you heard the news? There is war." [3]

Russian mobilization

There was now no drawing back from the abyss. The Germans were alarmed over Russian preparations for war. The latest action of the Tsar's government made the situation far more critical, since in German military circles, and also in French and Russian, general mobilization meant war. Upon learning that the Tsar's decree had gone into effect, the Kaiser's government sent an ultimatum to St. Petersburg demanding that mobilization cease within twelve hours.

The German ultimatums to Russia and France

[3] *Ibid.,* II, 472–73.

August 1, 1914. A German officer reading the declaration of war in the streets of Berlin.

On the afternoon of August 1 the German ambassador requested an interview with the Russian Foreign Minister. He appealed to Sazonov for a favorable answer to the German ultimatum. Sazonov replied that mobilization could not be halted, but that Russia was willing to continue negotiations. The ambassador repeated his question a second and a third time, emphasizing the terrible consequences of a negative answer. Sazanov finally replied: "I have no other answer to give you." The ambassador then handed the Foreign Minister a declaration of war and, bursting into tears, left the room.[4] In the meantime, the Kaiser's ministers had also dispatched an ultimatum to France demanding that she make known her intentions. Premier Viviani replied on August 1 that France would act "in accordance with her interests," and immediately ordered a general mobilization of the army. On August 3 Germany declared war upon France.

All eyes now turned in the direction of Britain. What would she do, now that the other two members of the Triple Entente had rushed headlong into war? For some time after the situation on the Continent had become critical, Britain vacillated.

The attitude of Britain

It is difficult to believe that the British would have long remained out of the war, even if the neutrality of Belgium had never been violated. In fact, as early as July 29, Sir Edward Grey had given the German ambassador in London a "friendly and private" warning that if France were drawn into the war, Great Britain would enter also.[5] Nevertheless, it was the invasion of Belgian territory which

Britain enters the war

[4] G. P. Gooch, *Before the War: Studies in Diplomacy*, II, 368.
[5] B. E. Schmitt, "July, 1914: Thirty Years After," *Journal of Modern History*, XVI (1944), 193.

provided the immediate cause of Britain's unsheathing the sword. In 1839, along with the other great powers, she had signed a treaty guaranteeing the neutrality of Belgium. Moreover, it had been British policy for a century or more to try to prevent domination of the Low Countries, lying directly across the Channel, by any powerful Continental nation. But the famous Schlieffen Plan of the Germans provided for attacking France through Belgium. Accordingly, they demanded of the Belgian government permission to send troops across its territory, promising to respect the independence of the nation and to pay for any damage to property. When Belgium refused, the Kaiser's gray-coated legions began pouring across her frontier. The British Foreign Secretary immediately went before Parliament and presented the idea that his country should rally to the defense of international law and to the protection of small nations. He argued that peace under the circumstances would be a moral crime, and declared that if Britain should fail to uphold her obligations of honor in this matter she would forfeit the respect of the civilized world. The next day, August 4, the cabinet decided to send an ultimatum to Berlin demanding that Germany respect Belgian neutrality, and that she give a satisfactory reply by midnight. The Kaiser's ministers offered no answer save military necessity, arguing that it was a matter of life and death for Germany that her soldiers should reach France by the quickest and easiest way. As the clock struck twelve, Great Britain and Germany were at war.

Other nations were quickly drawn into the terrible vortex. On August 7 the Montenegrins joined with their kinsmen, the Serbs, in fighting Austria. Two weeks later the Japanese declared war upon Germany, partly because of their alliance with Great Britain, but mainly for the purpose of conquering the German possessions in the Far East. On August 1 Turkey negotiated an alliance with Germany and in October began the bombardment of Russian ports in the Black Sea. Thus most of the nations definitely bound by alliances entered the conflict in its early stages on one side or the other. Italy, however, though still technically a member of the Triple Alliance, proclaimed her neutrality. The Italians insisted that Germany was not fighting a defensive war, and that consequently they were not bound to go to her aid. Italy maintained her neutrality until May, 1915, when she was bribed by secret promises of Austrian and Turkish territory to engage in the war on the side of the Triple Entente.

The conflagration spreads

The tumult and excitement that accompanied the beginning of the great holocaust of 1914 have long since died away. But the questions of how and why the conflagration occurred are still vital ones. Historians who have studied the evidence are generally of the opinion that no one nation was solely responsible. Perhaps none of the great powers really wanted war; they would have preferred to achieve their aims by other means. But in pursuing these aims they followed policies that made war virtually inevitable. The most dan-

The question of war guilt

gerous of national objectives were probably those of Germany. This was true not because they were more selfish than those of Russia or Austria but because they posed a more serious threat to the balance of power in Europe. Germany was attempting to achieve on the Continent of Europe objectives that Britain and France succeeded in attaining in Asia and Africa. Fritz Fischer has shown that, from the beginning of the war, some of Germany's rulers were thinking in terms of a vastly enlarged German empire that would include as satellite states, Poland, Belgium, Holland, the Balkans, and Turkey. Thus would be established a great sphere of influence comparable to that of the United States in the Western Hemisphere and of Russia in the heartland of Eurasia. How many of these territories would be annexed was not made clear; in any event they would constitute a gigantic *Mitteleuropa* dominated by Germany.[6] Fears of what this German scheme would do to the European balance of power produced nightmares in the chancelleries of London and Paris.

The guilt of individuals

During the war and for years afterward there was a tendency among many historians to blame the conflict on the stupidity or criminality of rulers. The villain most commonly singled out was Kaiser Wilhelm II. Count Berchtold, Foreign Minister of Austria, and Alexander Sazonov, Foreign Minister of Russia, were also frequently named. It is doubtful, however, that any of these individuals acted with malevolent intent. For the most part, they did what they felt they had to do. They responded to pressure from various groups within their own countries—industrialists and financiers eager for new economic opportunities, and organizations of expansionists and chauvinists such as the Pan-German League and the Navy League in the Hohenzollern Empire. In some cases they feared revolution if they did not follow a bellicose foreign policy. Like numerous politicians throughout history they sensed the efficacy of a belligerent stand against foreign enemies as the best means of allaying dissension at home. Doubtless the motive that prompted most of them, though, was conformism with the prevailing system of power politics. This system involved suspicion and fear of neighboring countries. The world of nations was assumed to be a jungle, and the only way of preserving peace in that jungle was to curb the predations of warlike states with a balance of power. Whenever that balance was disturbed, it was taken for granted that the rulers of threatened nations must always be ready to throw down the gage of battle. No potential aggressor must be allowed to gain an advantage by springing a surprise of any kind. In some military circles it was argued that to preclude such a possibility launching a preventive war would be justified.

[6] *Germany's Aims in the First World War*, pp. 348–349. Prof. Fischer is concerned primarily with German war aims formulated after the beginning of the war. He pays little regard to the fact that the objectives of a nation at war are almost invariably expanded *during* the conflict. Evidence for this can readily be found in the statement of Allied war aims contained in the notorious Secret Treaties, 1915–1917.

3. THE ORDEAL OF BATTLE

In the prophetic gospel known as Revelation it is related that the forces of good and evil shall be gathered together on "the great day of God" to do battle at Armageddon. The unknown author might almost have been thinking of the titanic conflict which engulfed the nations of Europe in 1914. For World War I was seldom admitted to be a struggle between rival imperialist powers or a product of nationalist jealousy. Instead, it was represented by spokesmen for both sides as a crusade against the forces of evil. No sooner had the war begun than social and political leaders in England and France pronounced it a gallant effort to safeguard the rights of the weak and to preserve the supremacy of international law and morality. Prime Minister Asquith on August 6, 1914, declared that Britain had entered the conflict to vindicate "the principle that smaller nationalities are not to be crushed by the arbitrary will of a strong and overmastering Power." Across the Channel, President Poincaré was pompously assuring his countrymen that France had no other purpose than to stand "before the universe for Liberty, Justice and Reason." Later, as a consequence of the inspiring preaching of such eloquent writers and orators as H. G. Wells, Gilbert Murray, and Woodrow Wilson, the crusade of the Entente powers became a war "to end all wars," to "make the world safe for democracy," and to redeem mankind from the curse of militarism. In the opposing camp the subordinates of the Kaiser were doing all in their power to justify Germany's military efforts. The struggle against the Allies was represented to the German people as a crusade on behalf of a superior *Kultur* and as a battle to protect the Fatherland against the wicked encirclement policy of the Entente nations.[7]

World War I was unique in several respects. Not only were scores of new weapons introduced, but methods of fighting differed quite radically from those in most earlier conflicts. Open warfare disappeared from the Western Front almost at the beginning. After the first few weeks the opposing armies settled down in a vast network of trenches, from which attacks to dislodge the enemy were launched usually in the murky hours just before dawn. For the most part, the struggle was an endurance contest, in which victory depended mainly upon natural resources and upon the ability of the Entente nations to obtain almost unlimited supplies of money, food, and munitions from across the sea. Probably it is safe to say that World War I was fought with greater savagery than any preceding military engagement of modern times. The use of poison gas, of the machine gun, of liquid fire, and of explosive bullets took a toll in lives and in ghastly wounds unprecedented even in the much longer campaigns of Napoleon. It is an interesting sidelight on this savagery

The holy war of the principal powers

Unique features of World War I

[7] The quotations in this paragraph are taken from J. S. Ewart, *The Roots and Causes of the Wars*, I, 16, 104. See also I. C. Willis, *England's Holy War.*

Modern Warfare. Top: After the first few battles, World War I on the Western Front settled into static or position warfare. During the four-year period veritable cities of mud, stone, and timber sprang up behind the trenches. Left: British armored trucks move toward the front. Above: A British tank and field ambulance.

that the number of civilians killed in air raids, in massacres, in famines, and in epidemics exceeded the number of soldiers killed in battle. Finally, the war was unique in the tremendous size of its armies. Altogether about 65,000,000 men fought for longer or shorter periods under the flags of the various belligerents. This was the climax of the steady trend toward mass warfare that had had its beginning during the French Revolution.

As the conflict dragged on through four appalling years, more and more nations threw down the gage of battle on one side or the other. We have seen that Italy postponed her entrance until the spring of 1915. Bulgaria joined the Central Powers in September, 1915, and Rumania entered on the opposite side about a year later.

But the event which finally tipped the scales in favor of an Entente victory was the declaration of war against Germany by the United States on April 6, 1917. The United States entered the war for a variety of reasons. All sorts of moral arguments were avowed by President Wilson and other high officials of the government—to "make the world safe for democracy," to banish autocracy and militarism, and to establish a league or society of nations in place of the old diplomatic maneuvering. Undoubtedly, the primary reason, though, was the concern of the American government over maintenance of the balance of power in Europe. For years it had been a cardinal doctrine in the State Department and among military and naval officers that the security of the United States depended upon a balance of forces in the Old World. No one power must be allowed to establish its supremacy over all of Europe. So long as Great Britain was strong enough to prevent that supremacy, the United States was safe. Some authorities believe that American officials had grown so accustomed to thinking of the British Navy as the shield and buckler of American security that they could hardly tolerate the thought of any different situation. Germany, however, presented not merely a challenge to British naval supremacy but threatened to starve the British nation into surrender and make herself dominant over all of Europe.

The direct cause of United States participation in World War I was the submarine warfare of the Germans. Some historians regard it as the most important of all the factors, on the ground that without it the United States would not have entered the war at all. When the war began, Germany had only a small fleet of submarines, but she rapidly increased their number. On February 4, 1915, the Kaiser's government announced that neutral vessels headed for British ports would be torpedoed without warning. President Wilson

Wartime Leaders. Left: Haig, Joffre, and Lloyd George discuss strategy. Right: Reviewing a map are members of the German high command, Hindenburg, William II, and Ludendorff.

The Lusitania Leaving New York Harbor. In February of 1915 the Lusitania was torpedoed and sunk by a German U-boat. Among the nearly 1200 people drowned were 119 Americans. The disaster was one step in the chain of events which led to the entry of the United States into the war on the side of Britain and France.

replied to this challenge by declaring that the United States would hold Germany to "a strict accountability" if any harm should come to American lives or property. The warning had little effect. The Germans were convinced that the U-boat was one of their most valuable weapons, and they considered themselves justified in using it as an answer to the British blockade. They violated pledges to respect American rights and continued occasional sinkings of passenger vessels, in some cases causing the deaths of American citizens. When the Kaiser's ministers announced that, on February 1, 1917, they would launch a campaign of unrestricted submarine warfare, Wilson cut off diplomatic relations with the Berlin government. On April 2 he went before a joint session of the two houses of Congress and requested a declaration of war. The declaration was approved four days later with only six negative votes in the Senate and fifty in the House of Representatives.

While fighting on the several fronts raged through four horrible years, various attempts were made to bring about the negotiation of

Peace proposals

peace. In the spring of 1917 Dutch and Scandinavian socialists decided to summon an international socialist conference to meet at Stockholm in the hope of drafting plans for ending the fighting which would be acceptable to all the belligerents. The Petrograd Soviet embraced the idea and on May 15 issued an appeal to socialists of all nations to send delegates to the conference and to induce their governments to agree to a peace "without annexations and indemnities, on the basis of the self-determination of peoples." The socialist parties in all the principal countries on both sides of the war accepted this formula and were eager to send delegates to the conference; but when the British and French governments refused to permit any of their subjects to attend, the project was abandoned. That the rulers of the Entente states were not afraid of these proposals merely because they emanated from socialists is indicated by the fact that a similar formula suggested by the Pope was just as emphatically rejected. On August 1 of this same year Pope Benedict XV appealed to the various governments to agree to the renunciation of claims for indemnities, to the future settlement of international disputes by arbitration, to a reduction of armaments, to the restoration of all occupied areas, and to the holding of plebiscites to determine what should be done with such territories as Alsace-Lorraine, Poland, and the Trentino. Nowhere was there a disposition to take these proposals seriously. Woodrow Wilson, as spokesman for the Allies, declared that negotiation of peace *under any conditions* was impossible so long as Germany was ruled by the Kaiser. The Central Powers professed to regard with favor the general import of the papal suggestions, but they refused to commit themselves on indemnities and restorations especially the restoration of Belgium.

The most famous of all the peace proposals was President Wilson's program of Fourteen Points, which he incorporated in an address to Congress on January 8, 1918. Summarized as briefly as possible, this program included: (1) "open covenants openly arrived at," or the abolition of secret diplomacy; (2) freedom of the seas; (3) removal of economic barriers between nations; (4) reduction of national armaments "to the lowest point consistent with safety"; (5) impartial adjustment of colonial claims, with consideration for the interests of the peoples involved; (6) evacuation of Russia; (7) restoration of the independence of Belgium; (8) restoration of Alsace and Lorraine to France; (9) a readjustment of Italian frontiers "along clearly recognizable lines of nationality", (10) autonomous development for the peoples of Austria-Hungary; (11) restoration of Rumania, Serbia, and Montenegro, with access to the sea for Serbia; (12) autonomous development for the peoples of Turkey, with the Straits from the Black Sea to the Mediterranean "permanently opened"; (13) an independent Poland, "inhabited by indisputably Polish populations," and with access to the sea; (14) a League of Nations. On several other occasions throughout 1918 Wilson reiterated in public addresses that this program would be the basis of the peace for which he would labor. Thousands of copies of the Fourteen Points were scattered by Allied planes over the German trenches and behind the lines in an effort to convince both soldiers and people that the Entente nations were striving for a just and durable peace.

By the close of the summer of 1918 the long nightmare of carnage was approaching its end. A great offensive launched by the British, French, and United States forces in July dealt one shattering blow after another to the German battalions and forced them back almost to the Belgian frontier. By the end of September the cause of the Central Powers was hopeless. Bulgaria withdrew from the war on September 30. Early in October the new Chancellor of Germany, the liberal Prince Max of Baden, appealed to President Wilson for a negotiated peace on the basis of the Fourteen Points. But the fighting went on, for Wilson had returned to his original demand that Germany must drop the Kaiser. Soon afterward Germany's remaining allies were tottering on the verge of collapse. Turkey surrendered at the end of October. The Hapsburg Empire was being

World War I Posters Held Back Little in Their Appeal to Emotions.

The approaching end of the struggle

cracked wide open by the revolts of the Slavs. Moreover, an Austrian offensive against Italy had not only failed but had incited the Italians to a counteroffensive, with the consequent loss to Austria of the city of Trieste and 300,000 prisoners. On November 3 the Emperor Charles, who had succeeded Francis Joseph in 1916, signed an armistice which took Austria out of the war.

The signing of the armistice

Germany was now left with the impossible task of carrying on the struggle alone. The morale of her troops was rapidly breaking. The blockade was causing such a shortage of food that her people were in danger of starving. The revolutionary tremors that had been felt for some time swelled into a mighty earthquake. On November 8 a republic was proclaimed in Bavaria. The next day nearly all of Germany was in the throes of revolution. A decree was published in Berlin announcing the Kaiser's abdication, and early the next morning the neurotic old gentleman was hustled across the frontier into Holland. In the meantime, the government of the nation had passed into the hands of a provisional council headed by Friedrich Ebert, leader of the socialists in the Reichstag. Ebert and his colleagues immediately took steps to conclude negotiations for an armistice. The terms as now laid down by the Allies provided for acceptance of the Fourteen Points with three amendments. First, the item on freedom of the seas was to be stricken (in accordance with the request of the British). Second, restoration of invaded areas was to be interpreted in such a way as to include *reparations*. Third, the demand for autonomy for the subject peoples of Austria-Hungary was to be changed to a demand for *independence*. In addition, troops of the Entente nations were to occupy cities in the Rhine valley; the blockade was to be continued in force; and Germany was to hand over 5000 locomotives, 150,000 railway cars, and 5000 motor trucks, all in good condition. There was nothing that the Germans could do but accept these terms. At five o'clock in the morning of November 11, two delegates of the defeated nation met with Marshal Foch in the dark Compiègne forest and signed the papers offi-

German Supplies Moving toward the Somme Front during the Last German Offensive in 1918

cially ending the war. Six hours later the order, "cease fire," was given to the troops. That night thousands of people danced through the streets of London, Paris, and Rome in the same delirium of excitement with which they had greeted the declarations of war.

Victory had been won at last, but what a grim tragedy it turned out to be. Of a total of over 42,000,000 men mobilized by the Entente allies, at least 7,000,000 had been slaughtered. Five million of these had been killed in action or had died of wounds; the remainder had been reported "missing" after the battles were over. More than 3,000,000 others had been totally disabled. Thus it will be seen that almost one out of every four of the soldiers enlisted in the Allied armies suffered a major casualty. This would have been a terrific price even if all the results which were supposed to flow from an Entente victory had really been achieved. But few indeed were the permanent gains. The war which was to "end all wars" sowed the seeds of a new and more terrible conflict in the future. The autocracy of the Kaiser was indeed destroyed, but the ground was prepared for new despotisms which made the empire of William II look like a haven of liberty. In addition, World War I did nothing to abate either militarism or nationalism. Twenty years after the fighting had ended, there were nearly twice as many men under arms as in 1913; and national rivalries and racial hatreds were as deeply ingrained as ever.

The price of victory

4. THE VICTORS' PEACE

The peace concluded at the various conferences in 1919 and 1920 resembled more closely a sentence from a court than a negotiated settlement. The explanation may be found primarily in the fact that the war became a peoples' war rather than a war of governments. Mob passions raged during the conflict and inhibited rational judgments. Politicians pandered to these passions and, in some instances, cultivated them zealously. Thus David Lloyd George campaigned during the election of 1918 on the slogan, "Hang the Kaiser!", while one of his partisans demanded "Squeeze the German lemon until the pips squeak!". In all the Allied countries nationalism and democracy combined to make compromise impossible and to interpret the war as a crusade of Good against Evil. The peace settlement drafted by the victors inevitably reflected these feelings.

Character of the Allied peace settlement

Had the Central Powers emerged victorious in the war, the world might well have seen an even harsher peace. The major examples leading to such a conclusion are the treaties of Brest-Litovsk and Bucharest. The former was concluded by Germany with Russia in March 1918. Its terms required the Russians to surrender control over Estonia, Latvia, Lithuania, and Russian Poland, to recognize the independence of Finland and the Ukraine, and to pay an indemnity of $1,500,000,000. The treaty of Bucharest, imposed upon Rumania in February 1918, provided for the cession of territory to Bulgaria

The Treaties of Brest-Litovsk and Bucharest

The Council of Four. Meeting to draft a peace treaty in Paris were Orlando of Italy, Lloyd George of Britain, Clemenceau of France, and U.S. president Wilson.

and Hungary and gave to the Central Powers such extensive control over the Danube and over the railways and oilfields that Rumania would have been placed in a condition of economic vassalage for years to come. The final defeat of Germany and her allies resulted in the abrogation of both of these treaties, though most of the territories taken from Russia were not restored to her because of antagonism in Western countries toward the new Soviet rulers.

The Paris Conference

The conference convoked in Paris [8] to draft a peace with Germany was technically in session from January until June of 1919, but only six plenary meetings were ever held. Most of the delegates might just as well have stayed at home. All of the important business of the conference was transacted by small committees. At first there was the Council of Ten, made up of the President and Secretary of State of the United States, and the premiers and foreign ministers of Great Britain, France, Italy, and Japan. By the middle of March this body had been found too unwieldy and was reduced to the Council of Four, consisting of the American President and the English, Italian, and French premiers. A month later the Council of Four became the Council of Three when Premier Orlando withdrew from the conference in a huff because Wilson refused to give Italy all she demanded.

The Big Three: Wilson and Lloyd George

The final character of the Treaty of Versailles was determined almost entirely by the so-called Big Three—Wilson, Lloyd George, and Clemenceau. These men were about as different in personality as any three rulers who could ever have been brought together for a common purpose. Wilson was an inflexible idealist, accustomed to dictating to subordinates and convinced that the hosts of righteousness were on his side. When confronted with unpleasant realities, such as the secret treaties among the Entente governments for division of the spoils, he had a habit of dismissing them as unimportant

[8] The conference did most of its work in Paris. The treaty of peace with Germany, however, takes its name from Versailles, the suburb of Paris in which it was signed.

and eventually forgetting that he had ever heard of them. Though he knew little of the devious trickeries of European diplomacy, his unbending temperament made it difficult for him to take advice or to adjust his views to those of his colleagues. David Lloyd George was a canny little Welsh attorney who had succeeded Asquith as Prime Minister of Britain in 1916. His cleverness and his Celtic humor enabled him to succeed, on occasions, where Wilson failed; but he was above all a politician—shifty, ignorant of European conditions, and unconcerned about even his most critical mistakes. Clemenceau said of him: "I suppose that man can read, but I doubt that he ever does."

The third member of the great triumvirate was the aged and cynical French Premier, Georges Clemenceau. Born when the nineteenth century was still young, Clemenceau had been a journalist in the United States just after the Civil War. Later he had won his nickname of "the Tiger" as a relentless foe of clericals and monarchists. He had fought for the French Republic during the stormy days of the Boulangist episode, the Dreyfus affair, and the struggle for separation of church and state. Twice in his lifetime he had seen France invaded and her existence gravely imperiled. Now the tables were turned, and the French, he believed, should take full advantage of their opportunity. Only by keeping a strict control over a prostrate Germany could the security of France be preserved.

Clemenceau

From the beginning a number of embarrassing problems confronted the chief architects of the Versailles Treaty. The most important was what to do about the Fourteen Points. There could be no doubt that they had been the basis of the German surrender on November 11. It was beyond question also that Wilson had represented them as the Entente program for a permanent peace. Consequently there was every reason for the peoples of the world to expect that the Fourteen Points would be the model for the Versailles settlement—subject only to the three amendments made before the armistice was signed. But what was the result? Not a soul among the highest dignitaries at the conference, with the exception of Wilson himself, gave more than lip service to the Fourteen Points. In the end, the American President was able to salvage, in unmodified form, only four of the parts of his famous program: point seven, requiring the restoration of Belgium; point eight, demanding the return of Alsace and Lorraine to France; point ten, providing for independence for the peoples of Austria-Hungary; and the final provision calling for a League of Nations. The others were ignored or modified to such an extent as to change their original meaning.

Emasculating the Fourteen Points

By the end of April 1919 the terms of the Versailles Treaty were ready for submission to the enemy, and Germany was ordered to send delegates to receive them. On April 29, a delegation, headed by Count von Brockdorff-Rantzau, Foreign Minister of the provisional republic, arrived in Versailles. A week later the members of the delegation were commanded to appear before the Allied representa-

Germany sentenced

tives to receive the sentence of their nation. When Brockdorff-Rantzau protested that the terms were too harsh, he was informed by Clemenceau that Germany would have exactly three weeks in which to make up her mind whether to sign or not to sign. Eventually the time had to be extended, for the heads of the German government resigned their positions rather than accept the treaty. Their attitude was summed up by Chancellor Philip Scheidemann in the pointed statement: "What hand would not wither that sought to lay itself and us in those chains?" The Big Three now made a few minor adjustments, mainly at the instance of Lloyd George, and Germany was notified that seven o'clock on the evening of June 23 would bring either acceptance or invasion. Shortly after five a new government of the provisional republic announced that it would yield to "overwhelming force" and accede to the victors' terms. On June 28, the fifth anniversary of the murder of the Austrian Archduke, representatives of the German and Allied governments assembled in the Hall of Mirrors at Versailles and affixed their signatures to the treaty.

The main provisions of the Treaty of Versailles

The provisions of the Treaty of Versailles can be outlined briefly. Germany was required to surrender Alsace and Lorraine to France, northern Schleswig to Denmark, and most of Posen and West Prussia to Poland. The coal mines of the Saar Basin were to be ceded to France, to be exploited by her for fifteen years. At the end of this time the German government would have the privilege of buying them back. The Saar territory itself was to be administered by the League of Nations until 1935 when a plebiscite would be held to determine whether it should remain under the League, be returned to Germany, or be awarded to France. Germany's province of East Prussia was cut off from the rest of her territory, and her port of Danzig, almost wholly German, was subjected to the political control of the League of Nations and to the economic domination of Poland. Germany was, of course, disarmed. She gave up all of her submarines and her navy of surface vessels, with the exception of six small battleships, six light cruisers, six destroyers, and twelve torpedo boats. She was forbidden to have any airplanes, either military or naval, and her army was limited to 100,000 officers and men, to be recruited by voluntary enlistment. To make sure that she would not launch any new attack upon France or Belgium, she was forbidden to keep soldiers or maintain fortifications in the Rhine valley. Lastly, Germany and her allies were held responsible for all the loss and damage suffered by the Entente governments and their citizens, "as a consequence of the war imposed upon them by the aggression of Germany and her allies." This was the so-called war-guilt provision of the treaty (Article 231), but it was also the basis for German reparations. The exact amount that Germany should pay was left to a Reparations Commission. In 1921 the total was set at $33,000,000,000.

For the most part, the Treaty of Versailles applied only to Germany. Separate pacts were drawn up to settle accounts with

Germany's allies—Austria, Hungary, Bulgaria, and Turkey. The final form of these minor treaties was determined primarily by a Council of Five, composed of Clemenceau as chairman and one delegate each from the United States, Great Britain, France, and Italy. The settlement with Austria, completed in September, 1919, is known as the Treaty of St. Germain. Austria was required to recognize the independence of Hungary, Czechoslovakia, Yugoslavia, and Poland and to cede to them large portions of her territory. In addition, she was compelled to surrender Trieste, the south Tyrol, and the Istrian peninsula to Italy. Altogether the Austrian portion of the Dual Monarchy was deprived of three-fourths of its area and three-fourths of its people. In several of the territories surrendered the inhabitants were largely German-speaking—for example, the Tyrol, and the region of the Sudeten Mountains awarded to Czechoslovakia. The Austrian nation itself was reduced to a small, land-locked state, with nearly one-third of its population concentrated in the city of Vienna.

The second of the minor treaties was that of Neuilly with Bulgaria, which was signed in November 1919. Bulgaria was forced to give up nearly all of the territory she had gained since the First Balkan War. The Dobrudja went back to Rumania, western Macedonia to the new kingdom of Yugoslavia, and western Thrace to Greece. All of these regions were inhabited by large Bulgarian minorities. Since Hungary was now an independent state, it was necessary that a separate treaty be imposed upon her. This was the Treaty of the Trianon Palace, signed in June 1920. It required that Slovakia should be ceded to the Republic of Czechoslovakia, Transylvania to Rumania, and Croatia-Slavonia to Yugoslavia. In few cases was the principle of self-determination of peoples more flagrantly violated. Numerous sections of Transylvania had a population that was more than half Hungarian. Included in the region of Slovakia were not only Slovaks but almost a million Magyars and about 500,000 Ruthenians. As a consequence, a fanatical irredentist movement flourished in Hungary after the war, directed toward the recovery of these lost provinces. It may be pertinent to add that the Treaty of the Trianon Palace slashed the area of Hungary from 125,000 square miles to 35,000, and her population from 22,000,000 to 8,000,000.

The settlement with Turkey was a product of unusual circumstances. The secret treaties had contemplated the transfer of Constantinople and Armenia to Russia and the division of most of the remainder of Turkey between Britain and France. But Russia's withdrawal from the war after the Bolshevik revolution, together with insistence by Italy and Greece upon fulfillment of promises made to them, necessitated considerable revision of the original scheme. Finally, in August 1920, a treaty was signed at Sèvres, near Paris, and submitted to the government of the Sultan. It provided that Armenia be organized as a Christian republic, that most of Tur-

The Treaty of St. Germain

The Treaties of Neuilly and the Trianon Palace

The Treaties of Sèvres and Lausanne with Turkey

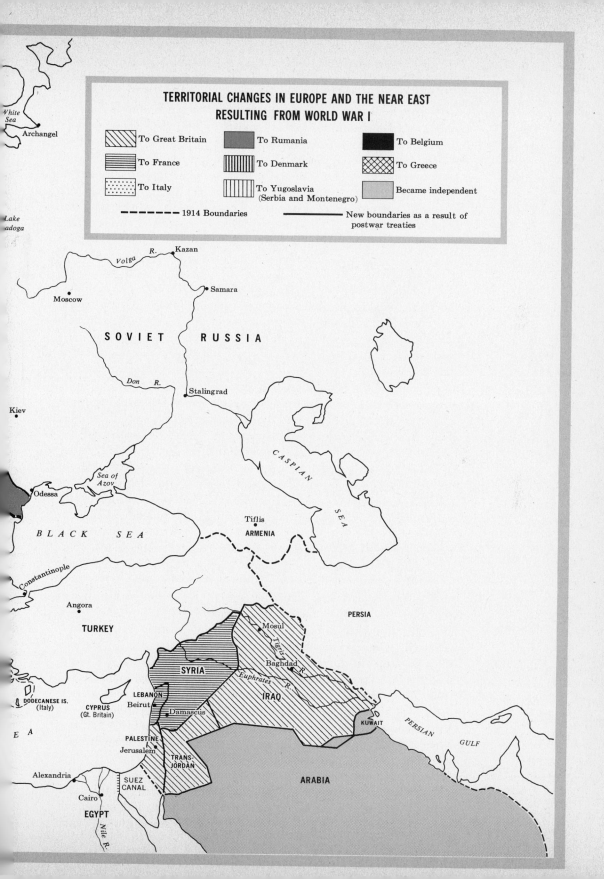

TERRITORIAL CHANGES IN EUROPE AND THE NEAR EAST
RESULTING FROM WORLD WAR I

To Great Britain To Rumania To Belgium
To France To Denmark To Greece
To Italy To Yugoslavia (Serbia and Montenegro) Became independent

– – – – – 1914 Boundaries ———— New boundaries as a result of postwar treaties key in Europe be given to Greece, that Palestine and Mesopotamia become British mandates, that Syria become a mandate of France, and that southern Anatolia be set apart as a sphere of influence for Italy. About all that would be left of the Ottoman Empire would be the city of Constantinople and the northern and central portions of Asia Minor. The decrepit government of the Sultan, overawed by Allied military forces, agreed to accept this treaty. But a revolutionary government of Turkish nationalists, which had been organized at Ankara under the leadership of Mustapha Kemal (later called Ataturk), determined to prevent the settlement of Sèvres from being put into effect. The forces of Kemal obliterated the republic of Armenia, frightened the Italians into withdrawing from Anatolia, and conquered most of the territory in Europe which had been given to Greece. At last, in November 1922, they occupied Constantinople, deposed the Sultan, and proclaimed Turkey a republic. The Allies now consented to a revision of the peace. A new treaty was concluded at Lausanne in Switzerland in 1923, which permitted the Turks to retain practically all of the territory they had conquered. Though much reduced in size compared with the old Ottoman Empire, the Turkish republic still had an area of about 300,000 square miles and a population of 13,000,000.

The League of Nations

Incorporated in each of the five treaties which liquidated the war with the Central Powers was the Covenant of the League of Nations. The establishment of a League in which the states of the world, both great and small, would cooperate for the preservation of peace had long been the cherished dream of President Wilson. Indeed, that had been one of his chief reasons for taking the United States into the war. He believed that the defeat of Germany would mean the deathblow of militarism, and that the road would thenceforth be clear for setting up the control of international relations by a *community* of power instead of by the cumbersome and ineffective balance of power. But in order to get the League accepted at all, he felt himself compelled to make numerous compromises. He permitted his original idea of providing for a reduction of armaments "to the lowest point consistent with domestic safety" to be changed into the altogether different phrasing of "consistent with *national* safety." To induce the Japanese to accept the League he allowed them to keep the former German concessions in China. To please the French he sanctioned the exclusion of both Germany and Russia from his proposed federation, despite his long insistence that it should be a combination of *all* the nations. These handicaps were serious enough. But the League received an even more deadly blow when it was repudiated by the very nation whose President had fathered it.

Established under such unfavorable auspices, the League was never a brilliant success in achieving the aims of its founder. In only a few cases did it succeed in allaying the specter of war, and in each of these the parties to the dispute were small nations. But in every

League of Nations Buildings, Geneva, Switzerland. Since the dissolution of the League in 1946, its main building has been occupied by the International Labor Office.

dispute involving one or more major powers, the League failed. It did nothing about the seizure of Vilna by Poland in 1920, because Lithuania, the victimized nation, was friendless, while Poland had the powerful backing of France. When, in 1923, war threatened between Italy and Greece, the Italians refused to submit to the intervention of the League, and the dispute had to be settled by direct mediation of Great Britain and France. Thereafter, in every great crisis the League was either defied or ignored. Its authority was flouted by Japan in seizing Manchuria in 1931 and by Italy in conquering Ethiopia in 1936. By September 1938, when the Czechoslovakian crisis arose, the prestige of the League had sunk so low that scarcely anyone thought of appealing to it. On the other hand, the point must be made that Wilson's great project justified its existence in other, less spectacular, ways. It reduced the international opium traffic and aided poor and backward countries in controlling the spread of disease. Its agencies collected invaluable statistics on labor and business conditions throughout the world. It conducted plebiscites in disputed areas, supervised the administration of internationalized cities, helped in finding homes for racial and political refugees, and made a notable beginning in codifying international law. Such achievements may well be regarded as providing a substantial groundwork for a later effort at international organization, the United Nations, formed after World War II.

> Successes and failures of the League

SELECTED READINGS

· *Items so designated are available in paperbound editions.*

WORLD WAR I

Chambers, Frank, *The War behind the War, 1914–1918: A History of the Political and Civilian Fronts*, London, 1939. A graphic portrayal of civilian attitudes and political and economic problems.

READINGS • Dehio, Ludwig, *Germany and World Politics in the Twentieth Century*, London, 1959 (Norton Library).

Earle, E. M., *Turkey, the Great Powers and the Bagdad Railway*, New York, 1924.

• Fay, S. B., *The Origins of the World War*, New York, (Free Press), 2 vols.

• Feis, Herbert, *Europe: The World's Banker, 1870–1914*, New Haven, 1930 (Norton Library).

• Fischer, Fritz, *Germany's Aims in the First World War*, New York, 1967 (Norton).

• ———, *World Power or Decline: The Controversy over Germany's Aims in the First World War*, New York, 1973 (Norton).

• Gregory, Ross, *Origins of American Intervention in the First World War*, New York, 1971 (Norton).

• Lafore, Laurence, *The Long Fuse: An Interpretation of the Origins of World War I*, Philadelphia, 1965 (Lippincott). A discriminating account.

• Lee, D. E., *The First World War—Who Was Responsible?* New York, 1963 (Heath, rev. ed.).

Link, A. S., *Wilson: The Struggle for Neutrality*, Princeton, 1961. A well-balanced, scholarly account.

• Mayne, Richard, *The Community of Europe*, New York, 1963 (Norton).

Morgenthau, Hans, *Politics among Nations*, New York, 1954.

Read, J. M., *Atrocity Propaganda, 1914–1919*, New Haven, 1941.

Remak, Joachim, *Sarajevo*, New York, 1959. Fascinating and scholarly.

Tansill, C. C., *America Goes to War*, Boston, 1938. A scholarly and very critical account.

Taylor, A. J. P., *The Struggle for Mastery in Europe, 1848–1918*, New York, 1954. A well-balanced account.

Thomson, G. M., *Twelve Days, 24 July–4 August*, London, 1964. Thorough and scholarly.

• Turner, L. C. F., *Origins of the First World War*, New York, 1970 (Norton).

Vagts, Alfred, *A History of Militarism*, New York, 1937.

• Wheeler-Bennett, J. W., *Brest-Litovsk: The Forgotten Peace, March 1918*, New York, 1938 (Norton Library).

THE PEACE OF 1919–1920

• Bailey, T. A., *Woodrow Wilson and the Lost Peace*, New York, 1944 (Quadrangle).

Birdsall, Paul, *Versailles Twenty Years After*, New York, 1941.

Mayer, Arno J., *Politics and Diplomacy of Peacemaking: Containment and Counter-revolution at Versailles, 1918–1919*, New York, 1967.

Nicolson, Harold, *Peacemaking, 1919*, New York, 1946.

SOURCE MATERIALS

Baker, R. S., and Dodd, W. E., eds., *The Public Papers of Woodrow Wilson*, 6 vols.

Carnegie Endowment for International Peace, *The Treaties of Peace, 1919–1923*, 2 vols.

Gooch, G. P., and Temperley, H., eds., *British Documents on the Origins of the War, 1898–1914*.

Grey of Fallodon, Edward Grey, 1st viscount, *Twenty-five Years*, New York, 1937, 2 vols.

Hendrick, B. J., ed., *The Life and Letters of Walter Hines Page*, 2 vols.

CHAPTER 28

The Challenge of Totalitarianism

Revolution, *n*. In politics, an abrupt change in the form of government.
> —Ambrose Bierce, *The Devil's Dictionary*

Poverty is the parent of revolution and crime.
> —Aristotle, *Politics*, II.vi (Jowett trans.)

Though republicanism had made some progress in Europe by 1914, the same could not be said for democracy. France was a thriving republic and so was Switzerland. Moreover, quite a number of governments headed by monarchs were republics in everything but name. The list included Great Britain, Sweden, Denmark, Norway, Belgium, the Netherlands, Italy, and in some respects Germany and Austria-Hungary. Yet few of these could be considered democracies in the political sense, and almost none of them in a social and economic sense. The real issue in most parts of Continental Europe was whether control of the government and the economic system should continue in the possession of feudal aristocracies, industrialists, and financiers, or a combination of all of them. None of these elements had gone very far in providing the masses with rights and privileges. It was inevitable, therefore, that the war in many countries should have taken on the character of a "war within a war," that the masses should have seen in the emergency an opportunity to dethrone their oppressors. In some cases, the opportunity was not grasped until after the international conflict had ended. But in Russia the bourgeoisie overturned the autocracy in March 1917, and were themselves overturned by the Bolsheviks later in the same year. Socialists in Germany overthrew the Kaiser in early November 1918. The British and French governments had serious trouble with striking workmen, and Britain passed under control of the Labour party a few years after the conflict had ended. Nearly everywhere the right

Struggles of the masses

783

of the old ruling classes to govern became a major issue. The gravest challenge to that right after the war was thrown down by Italy and Germany. Each adopted compulsory military training openly or in secret, and Germany began a program of naval expansion in 1935. Perverted though their fascist regimes were, they had many of the characteristics of mass movements.

I. THE EMERGENCE OF FASCISM

The first of the nations of Western Europe to turn its back on the old ruling class was Italy. This may seem strange in view of the fact that the Italians emerged from World War I on the winning side. But the point must be kept in mind that Italy had been the victim of frustrated nationalism for many years. Time after time her aspirations for power and for empire had been shattered. The effect was to produce a sense of humiliation and shame, especially in the minds of the younger generation, and to foster an attitude of contempt for the existing political regime. Members of the old ruling class were held up to scorn as cynical, vacillating, defeatist, and corrupt. Even before World War I there was talk of revolution, of the need for a drastic housecleaning that would deliver the country from its incompetent rulers.

But the establishment of a Fascist dictatorship in Italy would never have been possible without the demoralizing and humiliating effects of World War I. The chief business of the Italian armies had been to keep the Austrians occupied on the Southern Front while the British, French, and Americans hammered Germany into submission along the battle lines in Flanders. To accomplish her purpose Italy had to mobilize more than 5,500,000 men, and of these nearly 700,000 were killed. The direct financial cost of her participation in the struggle was over $15,000,000,000. These sacrifices, of course, were no greater than those made by the British and the French; but Italy was a poor country. Moreover, in the division of the spoils after the fighting was over, the Italians got less than they expected. While Italy did receive most of the Austrian territories promised her in the secret treaties, she maintained that these were inadequate rewards for her sacrifices and for her valuable contribution to an Entente victory. At first the nationalists vented their spleen for the "humiliation of Versailles" upon President Wilson, but after a short time they returned to their old habit of castigating Italy's rulers. They alleged that such men as Premier Orlando had been so cravenly weak and inept that they had allowed their own country to be cheated.

The war contributed to the revolution in a multitude of other ways. It resulted in inflation of the currency, with consequent high prices, speculation, and profiteering. Normally wages would have risen also, but the labor market was glutted on account of the return

Balzac, Auguste Rodin (1840–1917). Rodin was the great realist of XIX-cent. sculpture. He concentrated most of his attention upon facial detail, no matter how unflattering the result might be. (MMA)

Above: *A Young Woman in the Sun*, Auguste Renoir (1841–1919). Though Renoir used impressionist techniques, the results sometimes bore little resemblance to the work of other impressionists. He believed that "a picture ought to be a lovable thing, joyous and pretty." (Jeu de Paume) Right: *Luncheon of the Boating Party*, Renoir. (Phillips Memorial Gallery)

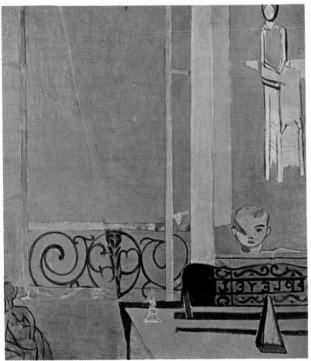

The Piano Lesson, Henri Matisse (1869–1954). Matisse conveyed a freshness of approach and a vitality of line and color. (Mus. Mod. Art)

Portrait of Gertrude Stein, Pablo Picasso (1881–). Picasso seems to have given this portrait of the great experimenter in poetry some elements of the distortion of form characteristic of the work of both. (MMA)

Three Musicians, Pablo Picasso. This painting, regarded by many as the masterpiece of cubism, sums up the final stage of the movement. (Mus. Mod. Art)

to civilian life of millions of soldiers. Furthermore, business was demoralized, owing to extensive and frequent strikes and to the closing of foreign markets. Perhaps the most serious consequence of the war, to the upper and middle classes at least, was the growth of socialism. As hardship and chaos increased, the socialists embraced a philosophy akin to Bolshevism. In 1918 they voted as a party to join the Moscow International. In the elections of November 1919, they won about a third of the seats in the Chamber of Deputies. During the following winter socialist workers took over about a hundred factories and attempted to run them for the benefit of the proletariat. Radicalism also spread through the rural areas, where the so-called Red Leagues were organized to break up large estates and to force landlords to reduce their rents. The owning classes were badly frightened and were therefore ready to accept Fascism as a less dangerous form of radicalism that might save at least part of their property from confiscation.

How much the Fascist movement depended for its success upon the leadership of Mussolini is impossible to say. Benito Mussolini was born in 1883, the son of a socialist blacksmith. His mother was a schoolteacher, and in deference to her wishes he entered a normal school and eventually became a teacher. But he was restless and dissatisfied and soon left Italy for further study in Switzerland. Here he gave part of his time to his books and the rest of it to begging his bread and writing articles for socialist newspapers. He was finally expelled from the country for fomenting strikes in factories. Upon returning to Italy he took up journalism as a definite career and eventually became editor of *Avanti*, the leading socialist daily. His ideas at this time were a mixture of contradictory forms of radicalism. He professed to be a Marxian socialist, but he mingled his socialism with doctrines taken from the syndicalists. In fact, the great syndicalist leader Sorel once referred to him as his most promising disciple.

Rather than a thinker or a sincere believer, Mussolini was essentially a rebel against the status quo. No man with a definite philosophy could have reversed himself so often. He not only condemned the imperialism which he later practiced so zealously, but at one time or another before the war he defamed the Church, vilified the king, and called the Italian flag "a rag to be planted on a dung hill." [1] When World War I broke out in August 1914, Mussolini insisted that Italy should remain neutral. But he had scarcely adopted this position when he began urging participation on the Entente side. As early as October 1914, he had gone over bag and baggage to the interventionist camp. Deprived of his position as editor of *Avanti*, he founded a new paper, *Il Popolo d'Italia*, and dedicated its columns to whipping up enthusiasm for war. The decision of the government

[1] For these and other contradictions between his earlier and later teachings, see Gaudens Megaro, *Mussolini in the Making*.

the following spring to go in on the side of the Entente allies he regarded as a personal victory.

The word Fascism had a dual origin. It derives in part from the Latin *fasces*, the ax surrounded by a bundle of rods representing the authority of the Roman state; it comes also from the Italian *fascio*, meaning group or band. *Fasci* were organized as early as October 1914, as units of agitation to swing Italy over to the Entente cause. Their membership was made up of young idealists, futurists, fanatical nationalists, bored white-collar workers, and misfits of every description. The original platform of the Fascist movement was prepared by Mussolini in 1919. It was a surprisingly radical document, which demanded, among other things, universal suffrage; abolition of the Senate; the establishment by law of an eight-hour day; a heavy capital levy; a heavy tax on inheritances; confiscation of 85 per cent of war profits; acceptance of the League of Nations; and "opposition to all imperialisms." This platform was accepted more or less officially until May 1920, when it was supplanted by another of a more conservative character. Indeed, the new program omitted all reference to economic reform. On neither of these platforms did the Fascists achieve much political success. Even after the elections of 1921 they had only thirty-five representatives in the Chamber of Deputies.

The Fascists made up for their lack of numbers by disciplined aggressiveness and strong determination. And when the old regime became so decrepit that it practically abdicated its functions, they prepared to take over the government. In September 1922, Mussolini began to talk openly of revolution and raised the cry, "On to Rome." On October 28 an army of about 50,000 Fascist militia occupied the capital. The Premier resigned, and the following day Victor Emmanuel III invited Mussolini to form a cabinet. Thus without firing a shot the blackshirted legions had gained control of the Italian government. The explanation is to be found, not in the strength of Fascism, but in the chaos created by the war and in the weakness and irresolution of the old ruling classes. By the end of the next three years Mussolini's revolution was virtually complete. He had abolished the cabinet system, made the political system a one-party system, and reduced the functions of the parliament to ratifying decrees. The leading doctrines of Fascism may be summarized as follows:

(1) Totalitarianism. The state incorporates every interest and every loyalty of its members. There must be "nothing above the state, nothing outside the state, nothing against the state."

(2) Nationalism. The nation is the highest form of society ever evolved by the human race. It has a life and a soul of its own apart from the lives and souls of the individuals who compose it. There can never be a real harmony of interests between two or more distinct peoples. Internationalism is therefore a perversion of human progress.

Left: *"On to Rome."* Mussolini (wearing a suit) and uniformed Fascists march into Rome in October 1922. Right: *Mussolini Addressing a Crowd of His Followers from the Balcony of the Palazzo Venezia in Rome*

(3) Authoritarianism. The sovereignty of the state is absolute. The citizen has no rights but simply duties. What nations need is not liberty, but work, order, prosperity. Liberty is "a putrefying corpse," an outworn dogma of the French Revolution.

(4) Militarism. Strife is the origin of all things. Nations which do not expand eventually wither and die. War exalts and ennobles man and regenerates sluggish and decadent peoples.

Germany succumbed to fascism much later than Italy, mainly for the reason that the forces of nationalism and militarism were temporarily discredited as a result of her defeat in World War I. From 1918 to 1933 Germany was a republic. The revolution which overthrew the Kaiser in November 1918, brought into power a coalition of Socialists, Centrists, and Democrats. In 1919 the leaders of these parties drafted the Weimar Constitution, an instrument of government remarkable for its progressive features. It provided for universal suffrage; the cabinet system of government; and for a bill of rights, guaranteeing not only civil liberties but the right of the citizen to employment, to an education, and to protection against the hazards of an industrial society. But the republic set up under this constitution was beset with troubles from the start. Reactionaries and other extremists plotted against it. Moreover, the German people had had little experience with democratic government. The Weimar Republic did not spring from the desires of a majority of the nation. It was born of a revolution forced upon Germany in her hour of defeat.

The factors which led to the eventual triumph of German fascism were many and various. First was the sense of humiliation arising from defeat in the war. Between 1871 and 1914 Germany had risen to lofty heights of political and cultural prestige. Until 1900, at least,

The era of the republic in Germany

787

Depression in Germany. Following the defeat in World War I, inflation was rampant and food in short supply. Here a fallen horse is torn to shreds by hungry citizens.

she was the leading power on the European Continent. Her universities, her science, her philosophy, and her music were known and admired all over the world. She had likewise attained a fabulous prosperity, and by 1914 she had surpassed even Britain and the United States in several fields of industrial production. Then came the crushing blow of 1918. She was toppled from her pinnacle and left at the mercy of her powerful enemies. It was too much for the German people to understand. They could not believe that their invincible armies had really been worsted in battle. Quickly the legend grew that the nation had been "stabbed in the back" by Socialists and Jews in the government. There was, of course, little truth in this charge, but it helped to salve the wounded pride of German patriots.

A few other causes of the rise and growth of National Socialism may also be mentioned. There was the fact that Germany had always been a military state, imbued with traditions of discipline and order. To many of the people the army was the symbol not merely of security but of national greatness. The qualities of obedience and regimentation, which the military life represented, were virtues most dear to the German heart. As a consequence, many patriotic citizens were seriously disturbed by the laxity and irresponsibility that appeared to distinguish the republican regime. It was alleged that Berlin had displaced Paris as the most frivolous and immoral city of Europe. A cause of more than minor importance was the fear of Bolshevism. The followers of this philosophy in Germany originally called themselves Spartacists. Subsequently they changed their name to Communists. In the Presidential election of 1932 the Communist party polled about 6,000,000 votes, or over one-seventh of the total. As had happened in Italy, a number of capitalists and property owners took alarm at what they regarded as a growing danger of Bolshevik revolution and secretly gave their support to the triumph of fascism as the lesser of two evils.

Yet the factor that gave the Nazi movement the proportions of an avalanche was the Great Depression. This conclusion is

Causes of the triumph of German fascism: (1) defeat in the war

(2) militarism and fear of Bolshevism

788

supported by the fact that the party was never able to win more than 32 seats (barely $\frac{1}{20}$) in the Reichstag prior to the election of 1930. In the early days the movement had drawn its converts chiefly from dissatisfied and uprooted members of the lower middle class and from former army officers unable to adjust to civilian life. After 1929 it received much broader support from a large segment of the German people who felt themselves disinherited and at odds with the ruling elements. Some were farmers angered by the collapse of agricultural prices and by their crushing burdens of debt and taxes. Others were university students who saw little prospect of gaining a place in the overcrowded professions. Undoubtedly the most numerous of all were the unemployed, whose ranks had swelled to 6,000,000 by 1932. Members of all these classes were groping in bewilderment and terror. By no means were they all Nazis, but their despair was so great as to induce them to accept almost any demagogue who promised to deliver them from confusion and fear. Never in the history of the nation had the future appeared so dark.

The origins of German fascism go back to 1919 when a little group of seven men met in a beer hall in Munich and founded the National Socialist German Workers' party.[2] Presently the most obscure of the seven emerged as their leader. His name was Adolf Hitler, born in 1889, the son of a petty customs official in the Austrian civil service. His early life was unhappy and maladjusted. Rebellious and undisciplined from childhood, he seems always to have been burdened with a sense of frustration. He wasted his time at school drawing pictures and finally decided that he would become an artist. With this purpose in view he went to Vienna in 1909, hoping to enter the Academy. But he failed the required examinations, and for the next four years he was compelled to eke out a dismal existence as a casual laborer and a painter of little sketches and watercolors which he sometimes managed to sell to the humbler art shops. Meanwhile he developed some violent political prejudices. He became an ardent admirer of certain Jew-baiting politicians in Vienna; and since he associated Judaism with Marxism, he hated that philosophy also. When World War I broke out, Hitler was living in Munich, and though an Austrian citizen, he immediately enlisted in the Bavarian army.

The founding of the Nazi party; the early career of Hitler

The Nazi revolution began in what appeared to be a quite harmless fashion. During the summer of 1932 the parliamentary system broke down. No Chancellor could retain a majority in the Reichstag; for the Nazis declined to support any cabinet not headed by Hitler, and the Communists refused to collaborate with the Socialists. In January 1933, a group of reactionaries—industrialists, bankers, and Junkers—prevailed upon President von Hindenburg to designate Hitler as Chancellor, evidently in the belief that they

The Nazi revolution; the Reichstag fire

[2] The name of the party was soon abbreviated in popular usage to Nazi.

One Step Away from Power. President von Hindenburg followed by Hitler, Göring on the extreme right, and other Nazi party members.

could control him. It was arranged that there should be only three Nazis in the cabinet, and that Franz von Papen, a Catholic aristocrat, should hold the position of Vice Chancellor. But the sponsors of this plan failed to appreciate the tremendous resurgence of mass feeling back of the Nazi movement. Hitler was not slow in making the most of his new opportunity. He persuaded von Hindenburg to dissolve the Reichstag and to order a new election on March 5. When the new Reichstag assembled, it voted to confer upon Hitler practically unlimited powers. Soon afterward the flag of the Weimar Republic was hauled down and replaced by the swastika banner of National Socialism. The new Germany was proclaimed to be the Third Reich, the successor of the Hohenstaufen Empire of the Middle Ages and of the Hohenzollern Empire of the Kaisers.

Consolidation of Nazi rule

Of course, these events marked only the initial stage of the Nazi revolution. Within a few months, other and more sweeping changes were added. Germany was converted into a highly centralized state with the destruction of the federal principle. All political parties except the Nazi party were declared illegal. Totalitarian control was extended over the press, over education, the theater, the cinema, radio, and many branches of production and trade. Drastic penalties were imposed upon the Jews: they were eliminated from government positions, deprived of citizenship, and practically excluded from the universities. With the passing of the years, the entire regime seemed to shift more and more in a radical direction. The new tendency approached its climax in 1938 with the extension of party control over the army and with the institution of a fanatical crusade against the Jews to expel them from the Reich or to annihilate them entirely.

So far as its ideology was concerned, German fascism resembled in a great many of its essentials the Italian variety. Both were collectivistic, authoritarian, nationalistic, militaristic, and romantic (in the sense of being anti-intellectual). Yet there were some outstanding differences. Italian Fascism never had a racial basis. True, after the formation of the Rome-Berlin Axis, Mussolini issued some anti-Jewish decrees; but most of them appear not to have been enforced very strictly. By contrast, National Socialism made the factor of race a central pillar of its theory. The Nazis argued that the so-called Aryan race, which was supposed to include the Nordics as its most perfect specimens, was the only one ever to have made any notable contributions to human progress. They contended further that the accomplishments and mental qualities of a people were actually determined by blood. Thus the achievements of the Jew forever remained Jewish, or Oriental, no matter how long he might live in a Western country. It followed that no Jewish science or Jewish literature or Jewish music could ever truly represent the German nation. Obviously, most of this racial doctrine was mere rationalization. The real reason why the Nazis persecuted the Jews seems to have been that they needed a scapegoat upon whom they could place the blame for the nation's troubles. Before this extremism had run its course millions of Jews had been exterminated by brutal SS men and Gauleiters.

There were also other differences, both in theory and in practice. Despite the fact that Germany was one of the most highly industrialized countries in the world, National Socialism had a peculiar peasant flavor which Italian Fascism did not possess. The key to Nazi theory was contained in the phrase *Blut und Boden* (blood and soil). The word *soil* typified not only a deep reverence for the beautiful homeland but an abiding affection for the peasants, who were considered to embody the finest qualities of the German race. No class

Blood and soil; the state and the economy

A Nazi Party Rally. Hitler at the height of his power, followed by other Nazi party officials.

of the population was more generously treated by the Nazi government. This high regard for country folk came partly no doubt from the circumstance that they were the most prolific of the nation's citizens and therefore the most valuable for military reasons. It was explainable also by the reaction of the Nazi leaders against everything that the city stood for—not only intellectualism and radicalism but high finance and the complicated problems of industrial society. As upstarts of obscure origin, the Nazis strove to compensate for their sense of inferiority by glorifying the simple life. Finally, it may be said that National Socialism was more frenzied and fanatical than Italian Fascism. It was comparable to a new religion, not only in its dogmatism and its ritual, but in its fierce intolerance and its zeal for expansion.

The significance of fascism, whether German or Italian, is still a subject of controversy among students of modern history. Some argue that it was simply the enthronement of force by big capitalists in an effort to save their dying system from destruction. It is true that the success of both movements in gaining control of the government depended in some measure upon support from great landowners and captains of industry. A second interpretation of fascism would explain it as a reaction of debtors aaginst creditors, of farmers against bankers and manufacturers, and of small businessmen against high finance and monopolistic practices. Still other students of the movement interpret it as a revolt against communism, a reversion to primitivism, a result of the despair of the masses, a protest against the weaknesses of democracy, or a supreme manifestation of chauvinism. Undoubtedly fascism was all of these things combined and a great many others besides. An increasingly popular view in recent years holds that fascism was simply an extreme expression of tendencies prevalent in all industrialized countries. Though most of these tendencies were minority movements, they nevertheless exerted a wide influence. Indeed, official policies in most Western countries in the 1930's took on more and more of a fascist semblance—a tightly controlled economy, limitation of production to maintain prices, and expansion of armaments to promote prosperity. In brief, nearly all nations in that period were beset with similar problems. Had it not been for the expansionist dynamics of the German Reich and its threat to the balance of power, perhaps little opposition would have developed, in the outside world, to Nazi policies.

The complex significance of fascism

2.   THE COMMUNIST UTOPIA (?) IN RUSSIA

Although Russia fought in World War I on the side of the powers that eventually triumphed, she was the first of the belligerent nations to be engulfed by revolution. The reasons for the initial explosion, at least, seem fairly obvious. The Russian government's conduct of the war was not distinguished for brilliance. The weak-

Left: *Tsar Nicholas II and His Family on the Eve of the Revolution.* Right: *An Open-Air Market in Petrograd.* In the foreground for sale are items taken from the home of the Russian aristocracy.

willed Tsar came more and more under the influence of the superstitious Tsarina, who was putty in the hands of an infamous "holy man," Gregory Rasputin. In some instances soldiers were sent to the front without rifles and were inadequately supplied with suitable clothing. There were seldom enough surgeons or hospital facilities to take care of the wounded. The Russian railway system broke down, producing a shortage of food not only in the army but in the congested cities as well. Added to these troubles was a series of crushing defeats by the Germans. Though Russia mobilized 15,000,-000 men, she was unable to hold up her end of the fight on the Eastern Front. By the end of 1916 her power of resistance had practically collapsed.

Effects of the war in causing the initial outbreak of revolution

The revolution in Russia followed a succession of stages somewhat similar to those of the great French Revolution of 1789. The first of these stages began in March 1917 with the forced abdication of the Tsar. For this the principal cause was disgust with the conduct of the war. But there were also many other factors—the inflation and consequent high prices, and the scarcity of food and of coal in urban areas. With the overthrow of the Tsar, the authority of the government passed into the hands of a provisional ministry organized by leaders in the Duma in conjunction with representatives of the Petrograd workers. With the exception of Alexander Kerensky, who was a Social Revolutionary, nearly all of the ministers were bourgeois liberals. Their conception of the revolution was mainly to transform the autocracy into a constitutional monarchy modeled after that of Great Britain. In accordance with this aim they issued a proclamation of civil liberties, released thousands of prisoners, and made plans for the election of a constituent assembly.

The overthrow of the Tsar

The downfall of
Milyukov and the
accession of
Kerensky

The provisional government proved itself inadequate to deal with its problems. Its leaders did not seem to understand the new conditions created by the war or even some of those arising in the prewar period. Among them were congestion in the cities, the emergence of a proletariat, and the inevitable harshness of the class conflict in the initial stages of industrialization. Further, the heads of this provisional government made the mistake of attempting to continue the war on the old basis of 1914–1917. They were just as imperialistic as the Tsar and his minions. They hoped to get Constantinople and everything else that had been promised in the secret treaties. But the masses of the people were desperately weary of the years of hardship and struggle. What they wanted was peace and a chance to return to a normal life. Consequently, in May, when the leaders renewed their pledge of support for the Allies, criticism was so strong that they were forced to resign. A new government was organized which managed to stay in power until September. Its head was Alexander Kerensky, and it consisted primarily of moderate socialists. The ultimate failure of this regime may be ascribed chiefly to the insignificant role played by the middle class in Russia at that time. In no sense can it be compared as a revolutionary force with the bourgeoisie in France in 1789. It was much smaller in size and lacked the prestige and wealth of the elements that destroyed the absolute monarchy of Louis XVI. Moreover, it had little support from the masses.

The triumph of
the Bolsheviks

The downfall of Kerensky's regime marked the end of the first stage of the Russian revolution. The second began immediately after with the accession of the Bolsheviks to power on November 7, 1917. The Bolsheviks were originally members of the Social Democratic party, but in 1903 this party had split into two factions: a majority or Bolshevik faction of Marxist revolutionists and a minority faction of Mensheviks, who contended that the time for revolution was not yet ripe. Soon after the overthrow of the Tsar the Bolsheviks began laying plans for a socialist revolution. They worked their way into the Petrograd Soviet, or Council of Workers' and Soldiers' Deputies, and quickly gained control of it from the Mensheviks and Social Revolutionaries. They organized an armed Red Guard and took possession of strategic points throughout the city. By November 7 everything was ready for the grand *coup*. Red Guards occupied nearly all the public buildings and finally arrested the members of the government, though Kerensky himself escaped. Thus the Bolsheviks climbed to power with scarcely a struggle. Their slogan of "Peace, Land, and Bread" made them heroes to the soldiers disgusted with the war, to the peasants hungry for land, and to the poor of the cities suffering from the shortage of food.

The chief actor in the Bolshevik drama was Vladimir Lenin, whose real name was Vladimir Ulianov (1870–1924). His father was an inspector of schools and a state counsellor and therefore entitled to rank in the petty nobility. An older son, Alexander, was

Lenin Speaking to Crowds in Moscow. At the right of the platform, in uniform, is Trotsky.

hanged for participating in a plot to assassinate the Tsar. In the very same year Vladimir was admitted to the University of Kazan. However, he was soon afterward expelled for engaging in radical activity. Later he was admitted to the University of St. Petersburg and in 1891 obtained a degree in law. From then on he devoted his entire life to the cause of socialist revolution. From 1900 to 1917 he lived principally in Germany and England, acting much of the time as editor of the Bolshevik journal *Iskra* (*The Spark*). Like most of the Russian revolutionists, he wrote under a pseudonym, signing his articles N. Lenin.[3] When the revolution broke out in March 1917, he was living in Switzerland. With the aid of the Germans he made his way back to Russia and immediately assumed leadership of the Bolshevik movement. Lenin had all of the qualities necessary for success as a revolutionary figure. He was an able politician and an exceedingly effective orator. Absolutely convinced of the righteousness of his cause, he could strike down his opponents with the zeal and savagery of a Robespierre. On the other hand, he cared nothing for the fleshpots of wealth or of personal glory. He lived in two rooms in the Kremlin and dressed little better than an ordinary workman.

Vladimir Lenin

The most prominent of Lenin's lieutenants was the brilliant but erratic Leon Trotsky. Originally named Lev Bronstein, he was born in 1879 of middle-class Jewish parents in Ukrainia. He seems to have been the stormy petrel of revolutionary politics during most of his life. Before the revolution he refused to identify himself with any particular faction, preferring to remain an independent Marxist. For his part in the revolutionary movement of 1905 he was exiled to Siberia; but he escaped, and then for some years led a roving existence in various European capitals. He was expelled from Paris in 1916

Leon Trotsky

[3] The "N." did not stand for anything in particular, though many people have assumed that it was a symbol for Nikolai.

for pacifist activity and took refuge in the United States. Upon learning of the overthrow of the Tsar, he attempted to return to Russia. Captured by British agents at Halifax, he was eventually released upon the plea of Kerensky. He arrived in Russia in April and immediately began plotting for the overthrow of the provisional government and later of Kerensky himself. He became Minister of Foreign Affairs in the government headed by Lenin and later Commissar for War.

Revolutionary political and economic changes

No sooner had the Bolsheviks come to power than they proceeded to effect some drastic alterations in the political and economic system. On November 8 Lenin decreed nationalization of the land and gave the peasants the exclusive right to use it. On November 29 control of the factories was transferred to the workers, and a month later it was announced that all except the smallest industrial establishments would be taken over by the government. Banks also were nationalized soon after the Bolshevik victory. But the problem of greatest urgency was termination of the war. After vain attempts to induce the Allies to consent to a peace without annexations or indemnities, Trotsky signed an armistice with Germany on December 15. This was followed by the peace of Brest-Litovsk in March 1918, which officially ended the war so far as Russia was concerned.

The civil war between Whites and Reds

Scarcely had the Bolsheviks concluded the war with the Central Powers than they were confronted with a desperate civil war at home. Landlords and capitalists did not take kindly to the loss of their property. Besides, the Allies were determined to punish the Russian government and accordingly sent troops into the country to support the armies of reactionary generals. The result was a prolonged and bloody combat between the Reds, or Bolsheviks, on the one side, and the Whites, or reactionaries, and their foreign allies on the other. Both sides were guilty of horrible brutality. At times the government resorted to mass executions, as was done in August 1918,

The Red Army, 1919. This scene near the south front was the celebration of the victory over the counterrevolutionary forces.

after a Social Revolutionary had attempted to assassinate Lenin. But at length the terror abated. By the end of 1920 the civil war was practically over. The Bolsheviks had driven nearly all of the foreign soldiers from the country and had forced the reactionary generals to abandon the struggle.

The civil war was accompanied by an appalling economic breakdown. In 1920 the total industrial production was only 13 per cent of what it had been in 1913. To make up for the shortage of goods the government abolished the payment of wages and distributed supplies among the workers in the cities in proportion to their need. All private trade was prohibited, and everything produced by the peasants above what they required to keep from starving was requisitioned by the state. This system was not pure communism, as is often alleged, but was mainly an expedient to crush the bourgeoisie and to obtain as much food as possible for the army in the field. It was soon abandoned after the war had ended. In 1921 it was superseded by the New Economic Policy (NEP), which Lenin described as "one step backward in order to take two steps forward." The NEP authorized private manufacturing and private trade on a small scale, reintroduced the payment of wages, and permitted the peasants to sell their grain in the open market. The new policy continued in force until 1929 when the first of the famous Five-Year Plans was adopted. It was succeeded by a series of others all designed to make Russia a great industrial country, and to further the evolution of a classless, communist society.

In the meantime, the death of Lenin in January 1924 precipitated a titanic struggle between two of his lieutenants to inherit his mantle of power. Outside of Russia it was generally assumed that Trotsky would be the man to succeed the fallen leader. But soon it was revealed that the fiery commander of the Red Army had a formidable rival in the shaggy and mysterious Joseph Stalin (1879–1953). The son of a peasant shoemaker in the province of Georgia, Stalin received part of his education in a theological seminary. But he was expelled at the age of seventeen for "lack of religious vocation" and thereafter dedicated his career to revolutionary activity. In 1917 he became Secretary-General of the Communist party, a position through which he was able to build up a party machine. The battle between Stalin and Trotsky was not simply a struggle for personal power; fundamental issues of political policy were also involved. Trotsky maintained that socialism in Russia could never be entirely successful until capitalism was overthrown in surrounding countries. Therefore he insisted upon a continuous crusade for world revolution. Stalin was willing to abandon the program of world revolution, for the time being, in order to concentrate on building socialism in Russia itself. His strategy for the immediate future was essentially nationalist. The outcome of the duel was a complete triumph for Stalin. In 1927 Trotsky was expelled from the Communist party, and two years later he was driven from the country. In 1940

Left: *Lenin's Casket Is Carried through the Streets of Moscow.* It was not known with certainty until 1956 that, prior to his death, Lenin had discredited Stalin. Right: *Stalin in the Early 1920's*

he was murdered in Mexico City by Stalinist agents. It is interesting to note that Lenin did not hold either of the two rivals in lofty esteem. In a "testament" written shortly before his death, he criticized Trotsky for "far-reaching self-confidence" and for being too much preoccupied with administrative detail. But he dealt far less gently with Stalin, condemning him as "too rough" and "capricious" and urging that the comrades "find a way" to remove him from his position at the head of the party.[6]

The third stage of the Russian revolution

About 1934 the Bolshevik regime entered a new and in some ways more conservative phase, which should perhaps be considered as the third stage of the Russian revolution. It was characterized by a number of significant developments. For one thing, there was a revival of militarism, of nationalism, and of an interest in playing the game of power politics. The army was more than doubled in size and was reorganized in accordance with the Western model. Patriotism, which the older strict Marxists despised as a form of capitalist propaganda, was exalted into a Soviet virtue. In like manner, there was a growing tendency to discard the internationalism of Marx, to strive to make Russia self-sufficient, and to play an active part in old-fashioned diplomacy. With Nazism firmly established in Germany, the rulers of the Kremlin seemed to have decided that Russia needed friends. Along with their efforts to build up a great army and to make their own country self-sufficient, they adopted a policy of co-operation with the Western powers. In 1934 they entered the League of Nations, and in 1935 they exchanged ratifications of a military alliance with France. It is apparent, however, that the real purpose of these moves was to drive a wedge between Germany on the one side and Britain and France on the other. At any rate, when the Soviet leaders became suspicious in 1938–1939 that Britain and France were encouraging Hitler to expand eastward, they did not

See color map at page 816

hesitate to conclude a nonaggression pact with the Nazi government.[4]

The original philosophy of Bolshevism, now more popularly known as communism, was developed primarily by Lenin. It was not supposed to be a new body of thought but a strict interpretation of the gospel of Marx. Nevertheless, from the beginning there were various departures from the master's teachings. Whereas Marx had assumed that a capitalist stage must prepare the way for socialism, Lenin denied that this was necessary and insisted that Russia could leap directly from a feudal to a socialist economy. In the second place, Lenin emphasized the revolutionary character of socialism much more than did its original founder. Marx did believe that in most cases revolution would be necessary, but he was inclined to deplore the fact rather than to welcome it. Further, in his Amsterdam speech of 1872 he had stated that "there are certain countries such as England and the United States in which the workers may hope to secure their ends by peaceful means." Last of all, Bolshevism differed from Marxism in its conception of proletarian rule. There is nothing to indicate that Marx ever envisaged a totalitarian workers' state as arbitrary and oppressive in its methods of governing as fascism. True, he did speak of the "dictatorship of the proletariat"; but he meant by this a dictatorship of the whole working class over the remnants of the bourgeoisie. Within the ranks of this class, democratic forms would prevail. Lenin, however, set up the ideal of the dictatorship of an *élite*, a select minority, wielding supremacy not only over the bourgeoisie but over the bulk of the proletarians themselves. In Russia this *élite* is the Communist party, whose membership has varied from 1,500,000 to 13,000,000.

In 1936, eighteen years after coming to power, the rulers of Communist Russia drafted a new constitution for the entire country to replace earlier ones that had proved inadequate. It was adopted by popular vote and went into effect January 1, 1938. The official name retained for the state was the Union of Soviet Socialist Republics. It provided for a union of eleven (later fifteen) republics, each supposedly autonomous and free to secede if it chose. The constitution established universal suffrage for all citizens eighteen years of age and over. They were to vote not only for the local soviets but for members of a national parliament. The highest organ of state power was declared to be the Supreme Soviet of the U.S.S.R., composed of two chambers—the Soviet of the Union and the Soviet of Nationalities. The former was to have 600 members elected by the people for four-year terms. The Soviet of Nationalities was to consist of 400 members chosen for similar terms by the governments of the several republics. Both chambers were given equal legislative powers. To represent it between sessions, the Supreme Soviet was to elect a committee of thirty-seven members known as the Presidium. This

The philosophy of Bolshevism

The constitution of 1936

[4] See p. 815

799

body also was empowered to issue decrees, to declare war, and to annul the acts of administrative officials which did not conform to law. The highest executive and administrative agency was to be the Council of Ministers, likewise elected by the Supreme Soviet. Each Minister was to be head of a department, such as War, Foreign Affairs, Railways, Heavy Industry, Light Industry, and so forth. Finally, the constitution of 1936 contained a bill of rights. Citizens were guaranteed the right to employment, the right to leisure, the right to maintenance in case of old age or disability, and even the traditional privileges of freedom of speech, of the press, of assemblage, and of religion.

The party the
real power in
the U.S.S.R.

The constitution of 1936 was, and still is, more of a sham than a reality. Its provisions for universal suffrage, for the secret ballot, and for a bill of rights looked good on paper but had little meaning. The explanation lies in the fact that the real power in the Soviet Union rests with the Communist party, the only party allowed to exist. The organs of the government are little more than the vocal mechanisms through which the party expresses its will. It is noteworthy that the very period in which the constitution was being put into effect witnessed an eruption of mass arrests and executions of persons alleged to be "Trotskyists, spies, and wreckers." Nearly all the old war-horses who had worked with Lenin to make the revolution a success, with the exception of Stalin, fell victims in the frenzied purges. Altogether at least fifty prominent theoreticians and party leaders were put to death, in most cases with little evidence except the accused's own confessions. In addition, about 9,000,000 other persons were arrested and imprisoned or sent to Siberia.

Economic and
social results of
the Soviet
upheaval

Perhaps enough has been said to indicate that the Soviet upheaval was not merely political in character but had profound economic and social results. By 1939 private manufacturing and private trade had been almost entirely abolished. Factories, mines, railroads, and public utilities were exclusively owned by the state. Stores were either government enterprises or producers' and consumers' cooperatives. Agriculture also had been almost completely socialized. State farms included about 10 per cent of the land; collective farms, organized on a cooperative basis, occupied nearly all of the remainder. No less revolutionary were the developments in the social sphere. Religion as a factor in the lives of the people declined to a place of small importance. To be sure, Christianity was still tolerated; but churches were reduced in number, and were not permitted to engage in any charitable or educational activities. Furthermore, members of the Communist party were required to be atheists. Communism not only renounces all belief in the supernatural but attempts to cultivate a new ethics. The primary aim is to create a *positive* morality, based upon duty to society, in place of the old negative morality, founded upon a notion of personal sin. The cardinal virtues in this positive morality are industry, respect for public property, willingness to sacrifice individual interests for the good of society, and loyalty to the Soviet fatherland and to the socialist ideal at all times.

By the outbreak of World War II the Soviet regime had undeniable accomplishments to its credit. Among the principal ones may be mentioned the following: (1) the reduction of illiteracy from a proportion of at least 50 per cent to less than 20 per cent; (2) a notable expansion of industrialization; (3) the establishment of a planned economy, which at least operated successfully enough to prevent unemployment; (4) the opening of educational and cultural opportunities to larger numbers of the common people; and (5) the establishment of a system of government assistance for working mothers and their infants and free medical care and hospitalization for most of the citizens.

Accomplishments
of the Bolshevik
regime

But these accomplishments were purchased at a very high price. The program of socialization and industrialization was pushed at so dizzy a pace that the good of individual citizens was almost overlooked. It must not be forgotten either that the Soviet regime fastened upon Russia a tyranny just as extreme as that of the Tsar. Indeed, the number of its victims sentenced to slave-labor camps probably exceeded the number consigned by the Tsars to exile in Siberia. This tyranny, it may be noted, was relaxed considerably in later years. Under the co-dictatorship of Leonid Brezhnev and Aleksei Kosygin labor camps as agencies of punishment were largely abolished (1964).

The price of
revolution

3. THE DEMOCRACIES BETWEEN TWO WARS

By 1939 only three of the chief powers—Great Britain, France, and the United States—remained in the list of democratic countries. Among the lesser states democracy survived in Switzerland, the Netherlands, Belgium, the Scandinavian countries, a few republics of Latin America, and the self-governing dominions of the British Commonwealth. Nearly all of the rest of the world had succumbed to despotism of one form or another. Italy, Germany, and Spain were fascist; Russia was communist; Hungary was dominated by a landowning oligarchy; Poland, Turkey, China, and Japan were essentially military dictatorships. For the most part, this cleavage represented a division between the so-called Have and Have-not nations—the former including the democracies, and the latter the dictatorships. Great Britain, France, and the United States were sated countries, comparatively rich in territorial empire and in mineral resources. Italy, Germany, and Japan were "hungry nations," coveting more lands in the belief that greater amounts of soil and other natural resources would solve their economic problems. They were disgruntled also with their power status, considering it inferior to that of other nations with large empires. Evidence is far from convincing that the citizens of the so-called Have-not coun-

Division of the
world into de-
mocracies and
dictatorships

801

The struggle of classes in Britain, France, and the U.S.A.

tries were really worse off than the inhabitants of states with more extensive territory. But politicians greedy for power used this alleged inequality for propaganda purposes. They overlooked the fact that standards of living bear little relation to extent of territory. The average citizen of Sweden or Switzerland was just as prosperous as the citizens of France or Great Britain notwithstanding his country's total lack of imperial possessions.

It will be impossible to describe minutely internal developments in all the democracies. In general, events in the principal states ran closely parallel. Preeminent among them was a struggle between wealthy bankers and industrial monopolists, on the one side, and organized labor and the lower middle class, on the other. In some countries members of the old order were able to hold their supremacy until after the onslaught of the Great Depression in 1929. In the United States and France, for example, there was little difference between the type of rule in the 1920's and that which had prevailed before the war. Great Britain, however, experienced the triumph of a Labour government as early as 1924. Its tenure was brief and its accomplishments few, but two years later the strength of the working class was sufficient to tie the whole national economy in knots by a general strike, which lasted for nine days. During most of the 1920's France was firmly under the thumb of such arch-conservatives as Georges Clemenceau and Raymond Poincaré. The years 1924–1926, though, witnessed a brief tenure of power by the Radical Socialists under the leadership of Édouard Herriot; better than any other party they represented the interests of small business and the lower middle class. The United States was undoubtedly the most impregnable fortress of conservative power among the democracies. The Presidents elected during the 1920's—Warren G. Harding, Calvin Coolidge, and Herbert Hoover—upheld a social philosophy formulated by the barons of big business in the nineteenth century, and the Supreme Court used its power of judicial review to nullify progressive legislation enacted by state governments and occasionally by Congress.

Labor Troubles in Britain. Mounted police escorting delivery wagons through a mob of angry strikers during the general strike of 1926.

The Stock Market Crash, October 24, 1929. Crowds milling outside the New York Stock Exchange the day of the big crash.

The depression that began in 1929 was one of the most shattering experiences in the economic history of the modern world. It was not limited to any one country, nor can the policies of any one nation be blamed for its origin. Nevertheless, the role of the United States in bringing it on cannot be discounted. At the end of World War I America was the richest nation in the world. While the states of Europe had been mauling each other on the battlefield, Americans had been capturing their markets, penetrating their fields of investment, and expanding their own industry and agriculture enormously. Yet much of the prosperity stimulated by these practices rested upon foundations of sand. It had been fostered in the beginning by the high prices of the war era. Farmers in the mid-West had plunged head over heels into debt to buy land in the arid regions of western Nebraska, eastern Colorado, and western Oklahoma, in the expectation that wheat would always be selling for more than $2.00 a bushel. When the price dropped to 93 cents in 1923, they found themselves stuck with their mortgages. But farmers were not the only ones who had been tempted into overexpansion by fantastic prices; many more coal mines and factories were opened than were necessary to supply the normal demand. A second weakness in American prosperity was the fact that it was based quite largely upon foreign loans. By 1930 American private loans in foreign countries amounted to about $16,000,000,000. Many of these were founded upon inadequate security or mere promises to pay. As a consequence, defaults were widespread. Nor should it be forgotten that United States tariff policy made it difficult for foreign nations to sell their products in American markets and thus to acquire the resources with which to pay their debts. Even as late as 1930 President Hoover, against the advice of more than 1000 economists, signed the Hawley-Smoot bill, which raised the duties on many commodities to the highest levels in the nation's history. Since this was followed by retaliatory tariffs elsewhere, the effect was virtually to strangle international trade.

The depression
of 1929

Results of the
depression

Leon Blum

The severity of
the depression in
the United States

The results of the depression took varied forms in different countries. In 1931 Great Britain abandoned the gold standard, and the government of the United States followed suit in 1933. This action was the forerunner of a broad program of currency management, which became an important element in a general policy of economic nationalism. By way of illustration, President Franklin D. Roosevelt informed the London Economic Conference of 1933 that "the sound internal economic system of a nation is a greater factor in its well-being than the price of its currency in changing terms of the currencies of other nations." As early as 1932 Great Britain abandoned completely her time-honored policy of free trade. Protective tariffs were raised in some instances as high as 100 per cent. Of the European democracies France went farthest in the direction of a controlled economy, though little change occurred until 1936. In that year the nation came under the rule of the so-called Popular Front, headed by Leon Blum, and composed of Radical Socialists, Socialists, and Communists. The Popular Front nationalized the munitions industry and reorganized the Bank of France so as to deprive the 200 largest stockholders of their monopolistic control over credit. In addition, it decreed a 40-hour week for all urban workers and initiated a program of public works. For the benefit of the farmers it established a Wheat Office to fix the price and regulate the distribution of grain.

The most spectacular changes in policy after the depression occurred, not in Europe, but in the United States. The explanation was twofold. The United States had clung longer to the economic philosophy of the nineteenth century. Prior to the depression the business classes had adhered firmly to the dogma of freedom of contract and insisted upon their right to form monopolies and to use the government as their agent in frustrating the demands of both workers and consumers. The depression in the United States was also more severe than in the European democracies. Industrial production shrank by about two-thirds. The structure of agricultural prices and of common stocks collapsed. Thousands of banks were forced to close their doors. Unemployment rose to 15,000,000, or to approximately one-third of the total labor force. Had it not been for widespread feelings of hopelessness and despair, revolution might well have swept the country. Millions were deterred by fear from taking any action that might jeopardize what little security they already had. Rescue from disaster was finally provided by a program of reform and reconstruction known as the New Deal. The chief architect and motivator of this program was Franklin D. Roosevelt, who succeeded Herbert Hoover in the Presidency on March 4, 1933.

Few historians would deny that the New Deal was one of the most significant events in the history of modern nations. Since its results were mainly in the direction of preserving rather than destroying capitalism, it can scarcely be called a revolution. Nevertheless, it probably did more for the farmer and the wage earner than any of the so-called revolutions in American history. Under the New Deal the incomes of these classes increased nearly 100 per cent compared with their level during the depression. Perhaps more important, these classes gained a degree of economic security they had never known before. On the other hand, a number of crucial problems remained unsolved. The most serious was unemployment. In 1939, after six years of the New Deal, the United States still had more than 9,000,000 jobless workers—a figure which exceeded the combined unemployment of the rest of the world. Ironically, it seemed that only the outbreak of a new world war, with its wholesale destruction of wealth and consumption of manpower, could provide the full recovery and full employment that the New Deal had failed to assure. In other words, the New Deal was hardly more than a stop-gap solution that would sooner or later break down under the strain of crucial events.

SELECTED READINGS

· *Items so designated are available in paperbound editions.*

FASCIST ITALY

Ebenstein, William, *Fascist Italy*, New York, 1939.

Schneider, H. W., *Making the Fascist State*, New York, 1928. A penetrating analysis.

NAZI GERMANY

· Bullock, A. L. C., *Hitler: A Study in Tyranny*, London, 1952 (Bantam). A good biography.

Carr, E. H., *German-Soviet Relations Between the Two World Wars, 1919–1939*, Baltimore, 1951.

Deutsch, Harold C., *The Conspiracy against Hitler in the Twilight War*, Minneapolis, 1968.

· Halperin, S. W., *Germany Tried Democracy, 1918–1933*, New York, 1946 (Norton Library). A dependable history of the Weimar Republic.

Neumann, Franz *Behemoth, The Structure and Practice of National Socialism*, New York, 1942.

Orlow, Dietrich, *The History of the Nazi Party*, Pittsburgh, 1969.

Rothfels, H., *The German Opposition to Hitler*, Hinsdale, Ill., 1948.

Scheele, Godfrey, *The Weimar Republic: Overture to the Third Reich*, London, 1946.

Schweitzer, Arthur, *Big Business in the Third Reich*, Bloomington, Ind., 1964. Contends that big business held Nazi regime in check in early days.

· Waite, Robert G. L., *Vanguard of Nazism: The Free Corps Movement in Postwar Germany, 1918–1923*, Cambridge, 1952 (Norton Library).

SOVIET RUSSIA

· Brinton, Crane, *The Anatomy of Revolution*, New York, 1952 (Vintage, rev. ed.). Includes a suggestive comparison of the Russian Revolution with earlier revolutions in Western Europe.

READINGS

- Curtiss, J. S., *The Russian Revolution of 1917*. (Anvil).
- Daniels, R. V., *The Nature of Communism*, New York, 1962 (Vintage). An objective study.
- ———, *Russia*, Englewood Cliffs, N. J., 1964 (Spectrum). Emphasizes period of the U.S.S.R.
- Hunt, R. N. Carew, *The Theory and Practice of Communism*, New York, 1951 (Penguin). A splendid introductory study.
- Pares, Sir Bernard, *A History of Russia*, New York, 1953 (Vintage). One of the best short histories.
- Shub, David, *Lenin*, New York, 1948 (Mentor, abr.). Perhaps the best biography.

  Shukman, Harold, *Lenin and the Russian Revolution*, New York, 1967.
- Von Laue, T. W., *Why Lenin? Why Stalin? A Reappraisal of the Russian Revolution, 1900–1930*, Philadelphia, 1964 (Preceptor).
- Wolfe, B. D., *Three Who Made a Revolution*, New York, 1948 (Beacon). A penetrating study of Lenin, Trotsky, and Stalin.

THE DEMOCRACIES

- Burns, J. M., *Roosevelt: The Lion and the Fox*, New York, 1956 (Harvest). A thoughtful interpretation.
- Feis, Herbert, *The Diplomacy of the Dollar, 1919–1932*, Baltimore, 1950 (Norton Library).

  Friedel, Frank, *Franklin D. Roosevelt: The Triumph*, Boston, 1956. A stimulating and scholarly account.

  Fusfield, D. R., *The Economic Thought of Franklin D. Roosevelt and the Origins of the New Deal*, New York, 1956.
- Graves, Robert and Alan Hodge, *The Long Weekend: A Social History of Great Britain, 1918–1939*, London, 1940 (Norton Library).

  Gregg, Pauline, *The Welfare State: An Economic and Social History of Great Britain, 1945 to the Present Day*, Amherst, Mass., 1969.
- Hofstadter, Richard, *The American Political Tradition: and the Men Who Made It*, New York, 1948 (Vintage).

  Mitchell, Broadus, *Depression Decade; from New Era through New Deal, 1929 to 1941*, New York, 1947.

  Nevins, Allan, *The United States in a Chaotic World*, New Haven, 1950.

  Schlesinger, A. M., Jr., *The Age of Roosevelt: The Crisis of the Old Order, 1919–1933*, Boston, 1957.

  Warren, Sidney, *Battle for the Presidency*, Philadelphia, 1968.

SOURCE MATERIALS

Columbia University, *Introduction to Contemporary Civilization in the West*, Vol. II, pp. 1062–66, 1077–86, Soviet Constitution of 1936 and Weimar Constitution.
- Hitler, Adolf, *Mein Kampf*, especially Vol. I, Chs. II, IV, XI; Vol. II, Chs. II, XIII, XIV, New York, 1962 (Sentry).
- Lenin, Vladimir, *The State and Revolution* (International Publishers).

  Stalin, Joseph, *Leninism*, 2 vols.

  ———, *Problems of Leninism*.

  Trotsky, Leon, *History of the Russian Revolution*, Ann Arbor, 1957, 3 vols.

  von Mohrenshildt, Dimitri, ed., *The Russian Revolution of 1917; Contemporary Accounts*, New York, 1970.

CHAPTER 29

The Origins and Legacy of
World War II

The President [Roosevelt] and the Prime Minister [Churchill],
after a complete survey of the world situation, are more than ever
determined that peace can come to the world only by a total
elimination of German and Japanese war power. This involves
the simple formula of placing the objective of this war in terms
of an unconditional surrender by Germany, Italy, and Japan.
    —Franklin D. Roosevelt, Casablanca, January 24, 1943

In September 1939, Europe plunged again over the rim of the abyss.
The peace of 1919–1920 had turned out to be only an armistice,
and millions of people were now locked in a conflict that surpassed
in frightfulness any that had occurred heretofore. As had happened
in 1914–1918, the new struggle soon became worldwide. Of course,
World War II was not merely a continuation of, or a sequel to,
World War I. Yet the similarity in causes and characteristics was
more than superficial. Both were precipitated by threats to the
balance of power. Both sprang in some measure out of rivalry between the sated and the dynamic nations—the first resolved to keep
what they had already gained, and the others determined to conquer
living space for their burgeoning populations and to gain new
sources of wealth and power. Both were conflicts between peoples,
whole nations, rather than between governments. The lineup of the
two sides, in the beginning, was similar, with Great Britain and
France opposing Germany, and with Italy remaining temporarily
neutral. On the other hand, there were notable differences. Japan
aligned herself with Germany instead of with the Western powers,

A comparison of
the two world
wars

807

and Russia did not enter the conflict until two years after it began. The methods of warfare in World War II had little in common with those of the earlier conflict. Trench warfare was largely superseded by aerial bombing and by blitzkrieg attacks with highly mobile armies. It seems safe to say that the distinction between soldiers and civilians was more completely obliterated in the second conflict than it had been in the first.

1. UNDERLYING AND IMMEDIATE CAUSES

The causes of World War II went back a great many years. To some extent they were related to the failure of the peace of 1919–1920. That peace, while perhaps as good as could be expected in view of the passions and hatreds engendered by the war, created almost as many problems as it solved. By yielding to the demands of the victors for annexation of territory and the creation of satellite states, the peacemakers sowed new seeds of bitterness and conflict. Had the League of Nations they set up been better organized, it might have relieved some of the tensions and prevented clashes between nations still unwilling to relinquish their absolute sovereignty. Moreover, it was not a league of all nations. Both Germany and Russia were excluded, thereby pushing them into the role of outcasts.

Although President Wilson and other sponsors of the League acclaimed it as a means of eliminating the balance of power, it did nothing of the sort. It merely substituted a new and more precarious balance for the old. The signatures on the peace treaties had scarcely dried when the victors began the construction of new alliances to maintain their supremacy. A *cordon sanitaire* consisting of the Baltic states, Poland, and Rumania was created as a buffer against Soviet Russia. A Little Entente composed of Czechoslovakia, Yugoslavia, and Rumania was established to prevent a revival of Austrian power. These combinations, together with a Franco-Belgian alliance and a Franco-Polish alliance would also serve to isolate Germany. Thus the old system of power politics was reconstituted along essentially the same lines it had had before World War I. Even the League itself was fundamentally an alliance of the victors against the vanquished. That there would be fears and anxieties over a disturbance of the new power arrangement could hardly be unexpected. The first sign of such a disturbance appeared in 1922 when Germany and Russia negotiated the Treaty of Rapallo. Though disguised as a mere trade agreement, it opened the way for political and, according to some accounts, even military collaboration between the two states. In 1935 the German government under the direction of Hitler tore up the disarmament provisions of the Treaty of Versailles. It announced the revival of conscription and the return to universal military training. By threatening the creation

Defects of the peace of 1919–1920

Threats to the balance of power

The Krupp Shipworks in Germany. Seen here are German submarines in the final stages of assembly.

of a huge air force Hitler hoodwinked the British into signing a naval agreement permitting Germany to build war vessels up to 35 per cent of the strength of Britain's navy. Finally, in 1936, he flouted the peace settlement by sending troops into the Rhineland to occupy the area of Germany demilitarized by the Treaty of Versailles.

Apostles of peace made various attempts to preserve or restore international amity during the 1920's and 1930's. Some saw in disarmament the most promising means of achieving their purpose. Accordingly, a succession of conferences was called in the hope of limiting at least the competition in armaments. The results were negligible. In 1925 representatives of the chief European powers met at Locarno and acted on the suggestion of the German Foreign Minister, Gustav Stresemann, that Germany and France pledge themselves to respect the Rhine frontiers as established in the Versailles Treaty. They agreed also that they would never go to war against each other except in "legitimate defense." More widely celebrated than the Locarno Agreements was the Pact of Paris, or Kellogg-Briand Pact, of 1928. Its purpose was to outlaw war as an international crime. Eventually nearly all the nations of the world signed an agreement renouncing war as "an instrument of national policy" and providing that the settlement of international disputes "of whatever nature or of whatever origin" should never be sought "except by peaceful means." Neither the Locarno Agreements nor the Pact of Paris was much more than a pious gesture. The signatory nations adopted them with so many reservations and exceptions in favor of "vital interests" that they could never be effective instruments for preserving peace.

Attempts to preserve international amity

As Germany recovered strength during the 1930's, the victorious powers adopted varying attitudes. France, for a time, remained inflexible in her determination to hold Germany down. Her government, however, tolerated Japan's invasion of Manchuria in 1931 and even encouraged Italy's conquest of Ethiopia in 1936. As a trading

Members of the Council of the League of Nations. In the front row from the right are Chamberlain of Great Britain, Vandervelde of Belgium, Stresemann of Germany, and Briand of France.

nation anxious to rebuild her markets in central Europe, Britain favored a policy of leniency toward Germany. Although she had a good legal case for doing so, she refused to take any action against the military occupation of the Rhineland. She was tolerant also toward the Japanese invasion of Manchuria and the Italian conquest of Ethiopia. Like France, she declined to take positive steps to assist the Spanish Republic when Germany and Italy intervened in the Spanish Civil War to guarantee a victory of the Spanish fascists under General Franco. Not until Germany revealed, in 1939, that she had definite ambitions for conquests in Eastern Europe did Britain and France show serious concern over enforcing the balance of power. Their action came too late, for the balance had already been badly upset by the gains Germany and Italy had made through their aggressive policies.

If we look for economic causes of World War II, we can consider, first of all, division of the world into Have and Have-not powers. The former included Great Britain, the United States, France, and Russia. Britain had the smallest homeland, but her empire extended over 13,000,000 square miles, one-fourth of the land area of the earth, and was inhabited by 500,000,000 people, or one-fifth of the population of the globe. France had a total empire of 4,000,000 square miles and 100,000,000 inhabitants. Neither the United States nor Russia owned vast overseas possessions, but both had extensive home areas rich in natural resources. The former ruled over 3,735,000 square miles with a population of 130,000,000. The Union of Soviet Socialist Republics extended over an area of 8,000,000 square miles and was inhabited by no fewer than 170,000,000 people. The position of the Have-not powers—Germany, Italy, and Japan—seemed poor indeed by comparison. The three of them combined had an area of less than 1,500,000 square miles, to accommodate a home population that exceeded the total for Great Britain and the United States. German patriots could point out that the average German citizen had only .004 of a square mile of living space at his disposal, whereas the average Briton could draw upon the wealth and economic opportunities of almost three square miles of imperial territory.

The fallacies in this view of the matter were seldom noticed. It seemed sufficient for the German nationalist to reflect upon the fact that standards of living in Britain were higher than in his own country to prove to him that the existing division of the earth's surface was unjust. He was therefore ready to disrupt the status quo by any means in his power. Perhaps diplomatic cunning would be sufficient, but if not, he would resort to war. Italians and Japanese seemed to have even weightier evidence of the injustice of the existing order, since standards of living in their countries were lower than in Germany. None of them appeared to recognize the fact that living standards in some small European countries, totally or almost completely lacking colonial empires, were just about equal to the average in Britain. But Germany, Italy, and Japan had a sense of grievance for a number of reasons, and presenting themselves before the world as Have-not nations helped to justify their bellicose foreign policies.

Perhaps the most serious economic cause of World War II was the Great Depression. The depression contributed to the coming of the war in several ways. First and foremost, it intensified economic nationalism. Baffled by problems of unemployment and business stagnation, governments resorted to high tariffs in a frenzied attempt to preserve the home market for their own producers.

The depression also had other effects perhaps more difficult to assay. For one thing, it was responsible for a marked increase in armaments. Armaments expansion, on a large scale, was first undertaken by Germany about 1935. The results in a few years were such as to dazzle the rest of the world. Unemployment disappeared and business boomed. It would have been too much to expect that other dissatisfied nations would not copy the German example. Similarly, the depression resulted in a new wave of militant expansionism directed toward the conquest of neighboring territories as a means of solving economic problems. Japan took the lead in 1931 with the invasion of Manchuria. A primary cause was the decline of Japanese exports of raw silk and cotton cloth. Since the nation as a consequence was unable to pay for needed imports of coal, iron, and other minerals, Japanese militarists were furnished with a convenient pretext for seizing Manchuria, where supplies of these commodities could then be purchased for Japanese currency.

Most important of all, the depression was primarily responsible for the triumph of Nazism in Germany. The Nazi party would probably have remained weak and ineffectual had it not been for the influx of millions of followers from the ranks of the farmers and the unemployed and from frightened members of the white-collar classes. The whirling spiral of economic decline had overwhelmed these people with a sense of despair. Convinced that capitalism, socialism, and democracy had all failed, they were ready to grasp at

811

almost any straw that would save them from sinking deeper into the quicksands of depression.

It may be well before leaving this subject of underlying causes to look at the matter from the standpoint of a different interpretation. According to an important school of thought, which may be called the power-politics school, only a few of the factors mentioned above deserve more than slight consideration. Doubtless leaders of this school would accept the economic causes, but most of the others they would dismiss as inconsequential. They place nearly all of the emphasis upon power politics. They maintain that power rivalries and power struggles have been the real causes of international wars since the beginning of modern history. Such forces as nationalism, militarism, and imperialism have simply been instruments for achieving the ends of a quest for power. The seventeenth century, they point out, was marked by a great power struggle between France and Austria, in which France was victorious. During the eighteenth century a primary struggle raged between Britain and France and culminated in the Seven Years' War, with a decisive victory for Britain. The French attempted to recover their power during the wars of the Revolution and under Napoleon, but the effort failed, and Britain gradually emerged as the dominant nation on the earth. Toward the end of the nineteenth century, however, Germany rose to challenge British supremacy, and the result was World War I. After the war conflicting ambitions among the victors permitted a revival of Teutonic power, with the consequence that, by 1939, Germany was ready to challenge again the ability of the dominant nations to continue ruling the world. The fact that Germany and her allies had fascist governments had little to do with the case. According to the power-politics theorists, fascism was simply a by-product of an age-old struggle among nations to gain advantages at their neighbors' expense.

That there is much truth in the foregoing hypothesis seems almost indisputable. The existence of the modern state system practically guarantees that nations shall be engaged in either cold or hot wars nearly all of the time. Under it the relation among states is the same as that among individuals in the supposed state of nature, which philosophers like Locke and Rousseau believed to have existed before the formation of political society. In other words, there is no law or order except that which results from agreements between sovereign units. In making these agreements, the units retain their full sovereignty, and therefore may repudiate them whenever they choose. Another element in the hypothesis which is difficult to refute is the contention that ideologies are not fundamental causes of wars. If British politicians had been gravely concerned about the evils of fascism they could never have pursued their policy of appeasement, for they must have known that its effect would be to strengthen Italy and Germany. Indeed, there is evidence that Neville Chamberlain was perfectly willing to collaborate with

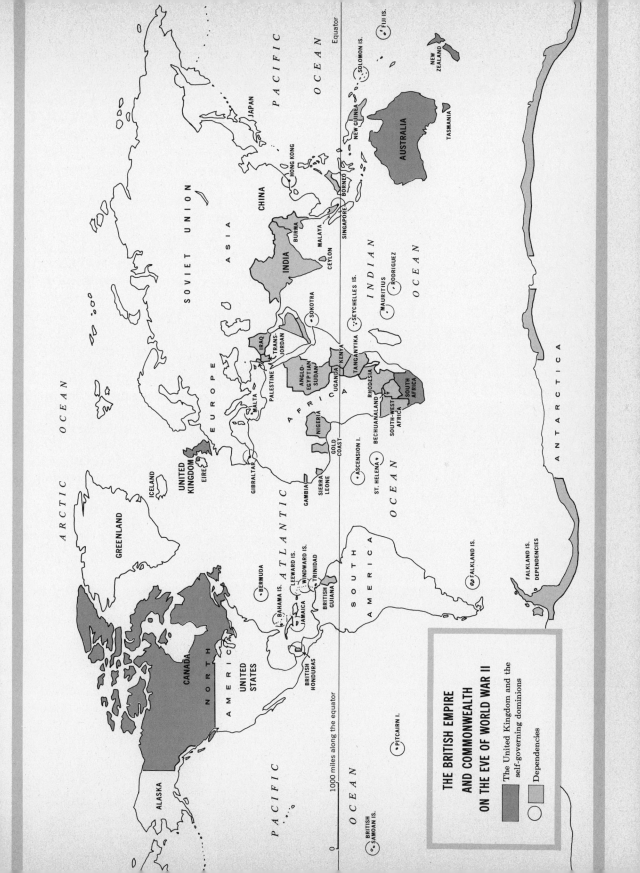

THE BRITISH EMPIRE
AND COMMONWEALTH
ON THE EVE OF WORLD WAR II

The United Kingdom and the
self-governing dominions

Dependencies

fascist governments for his own purposes. One of his chief reasons for going to Munich was to bring Germany, Italy, France, and Britain into a four-power alliance to determine the destinies of Europe. It is significant also that Germany and the Soviet Union became allies in 1939, despite the fact that, shortly before, Hitler had described the Bolsheviks as "scum of the earth," while Stalin had referred to the Nazis as "bloody assassins of the workers." The power-politics hypothesis would appear to suffer, not from inaccuracy, but, like most specialized theories, from a failure to give proper recognition to all of the factors. If nationalism and militarism are not originally primary causes of wars, they often become so as international tension increases.

If there was any one immediate cause of World War II, it could doubtless be found in the appeasement policy of Britain and France. Appeasement may be defined as a policy of granting concessions to an aggressive and unscrupulous nation from motives of fear or indolence. Invariably, the concessions are made at the expense of a weaker country. Appeasement has nothing to do with either benevolence or justice. Appeasement was used several times during the 1930's. It characterized the policy of Britain with regard to Japan in 1931 when the Japanese invaded Manchuria, technically a part of China. Though China appealed to the League of Nations, the British would allow nothing to be done since they feared retaliation against their own interests in the Far East and hoped to use Japan in the future as a counterweight against Russia.

The classic example of appeasement, however, was the Munich Agreement of 1938. By September of that year Hitler had pushed

The appeasement policy

The Munich Conference, 1938. Left: Hitler, Chamberlain, partially hidden behind Hitler, Mussolini with his back to the camera, and Daladier on the far right. Right: Prime Minister Chamberlain addressing a crowd on his return from the Munich conference. In this speech, September 30, 1938, he proclaimed that "peace in our time" would result from the agreement.

German Troops Entering Prague, April 2, 1939. While Nazi motorized units passed by, some Czechs sang "Where Is My Home" and others wept.

his drive to the East so far that only one obstacle, Czechoslovakia, stood in his way. Earlier in the year he had annexed Austria, which left Czechoslovakia almost surrounded by German territory. From that point on he exerted relentless pressure against the Slav republic. Convinced of the imminent danger of war, the British Prime Minister, Neville Chamberlain, determined to leave nothing undone to pacify the German dictator. Frantic appeals came also from other sources, including France, Italy, and the United States. Finally, on September 28, the Fuehrer agreed to meet with Chamberlain, Premier Daladier of France, and Mussolini in a four-power conference in Munich. The result was a complete surrender to the violent, browbeating Chancellor. During the next few months Hitler not only annexed the Sudetenland, or western portion of Czechoslovakia (as the Munich Agreement had permitted him to do), but he annihilated the entire Czech republic. Instead of bringing peace to a frightened Europe, this action intensified the crisis. The Soviet government was convinced that the Munich settlement was a diabolical plot by Britain and France to save their own skins by diverting Nazi expansion eastward. In August 1939, Stalin and his colleagues entered into a pact of their own with the Nazi government. Its effect was to give Hitler the green light for an attack on Poland. Apparently, there was an understanding that the two dictators would divide Poland between them. In going to Munich, Britain and France had thought of nothing but their own interests; Russia would now look to hers.

The Munich Agreement

2. THE OUTBREAK OF HOSTILITIES

Following the extinction of Czechoslovakia, Hitler turned his aggressive designs against Poland. He demanded the abolition of the Polish Corridor and the return of Danzig to Germany. Convinced finally that the Fuehrer's appetite for power was insatiable, Chamberlain announced that Britain would give Poland armed assistance. Soon afterward he declared that his government would come to the aid of *any* country that felt itself menaced by Hitler's ambitions. In

The beginning of World War II

815

The Beginning of World War II. A long line of German tanks speeding into Poland.

the weeks that followed, both Britain and France gave definite guaranties not only to Poland but to Greece, Rumania, and Turkey. Hitler apparently believed that these pledges were worthless. With the Soviets drawn into his camp, he probably thought that Poland would quickly capitulate, and that the Western allies would back down once more as they had done at Munich. When Poland stood firm, the Fuehrer decided to attack. On September 1, 1939, a long column of German tanks crossed the Polish border. Upon learning of the attack, Britain and France sent a joint warning to Germany that she must cease her aggression. To this there was no reply. September 3 brought a radio announcement by Neville Chamberlain that Britain was at war with Germany. He spoke of the "bitter blow" it was to him that his "long struggle for peace" had failed. He asserted that it was evil the British nation would be fighting against —"brute force, bad faith, injustice, oppression, and persecution." Later the same day France also entered the war.

World War II passed through several stages. The conflict with Poland proved to be a brief encounter. In less than three weeks the Polish armies had been routed, Warsaw had been captured, and the chiefs of the Polish government had fled to Rumania. For some months after that the war resolved itself into a kind of siege, a "phony war" or "sitzkrieg," as it was sometimes called. Such fighting as did occur was largely confined to submarine warfare, aerial raids on naval bases, and occasional battles between naval vessels. In the spring of 1940 the sitzkrieg was suddenly transformed into a Blitzkrieg. The Germans struck lightning blows at Norway, Denmark, Belgium, the Netherlands, and France, conquering them one after another. Following these disasters the war entered a new stage, the so-called Battle of Britain. Instead of launching an invasion across the Channel, the Nazis decided to attempt the reduction of Britain to submission by air raids. From August 1940 to June 1941 thousands of planes smashed at British ports, industrial centers, and air defenses throughout the country. Despite the fact that whole sections of cities were laid in ruins and more than 40,000 citizens

Stages of the war

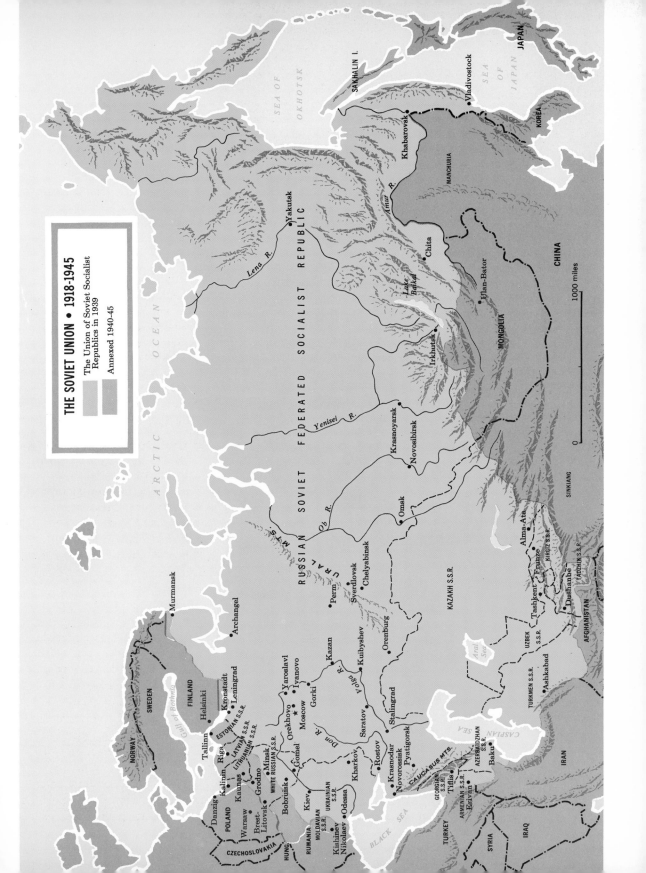

THE SOVIET UNION • 1918-1945

The Union of Soviet Socialist
Republics in 1939

Annexed 1940-45

JAPAN

SEA OF OKHOTSK

SAKHALIN I.

SEA OF JAPAN

Vladivostock

KOREA

MANCHURIA

Khabarovsk

Amur R.

Chita

CHINA

Yakutsk

Lake Baikal

Irkutsk

Ulan-Bator

MONGOLIA

1000 miles

SOVIET   FEDERATED   SOCIALIST   REPUBLIC

Lena R.

Yenisei R.

Krasnoyarsk

Novosibirsk

Omsk

Ob R.

SINKIANG

ARCTIC   OCEAN

Murmansk

Archangel

R U S S I A N

U R A L   M T S.

Perm

Sverdlovsk

Chelyabinsk

KAZAKH S.S.R.

Alma-Ata

Frunze

KIRGIZ S.S.R.

Tashkent

Dushanbe

TADZHIK S.S.R.

UZBEK S.S.R.

Ashkabad

TURKMEN S.S.R.

AFGHANISTAN

Aral Sea

CASPIAN SEA

IRAN

SWEDEN

NORWAY

FINLAND

Helsinki

Gulf of Bothnia

Kronstadt

Leningrad

Tallinn

Riga

ESTONIAN S.S.R.

LATVIAN S.S.R.

LITHUANIAN S.S.R.

Kalinin

Kaunas

Grodno

Minsk

WHITE RUSSIAN S.S.R.

Gomel

Bobruisk

Kiev

UKRAINIAN S.S.R.

Odessa

Nikolaev

Kishinev

MOLDAVIAN S.S.R.

RUMANIA

HUNG.

CZECHOSLOVAKIA

Danzig

POLAND

Warsaw

Brest-Litovsk

Kazan

Yaroslavl

Ivanovo

Orekhovo

Moscow

Gorki

Saratov

Kuibyshev

Orenburg

Volga R.

Don R.

Kharkov

Rostov

Stalingrad

Krasnodar

Novorossisk

Pyatigorsk

CAUCASUS MTS.

GEORGIAN S.S.R.

Tiflis

AZERBAIDZHAN S.S.R.

Baku

ARMENIAN S.S.R.

Erivan

TURKEY

SYRIA

IRAQ

BLACK SEA

Baku

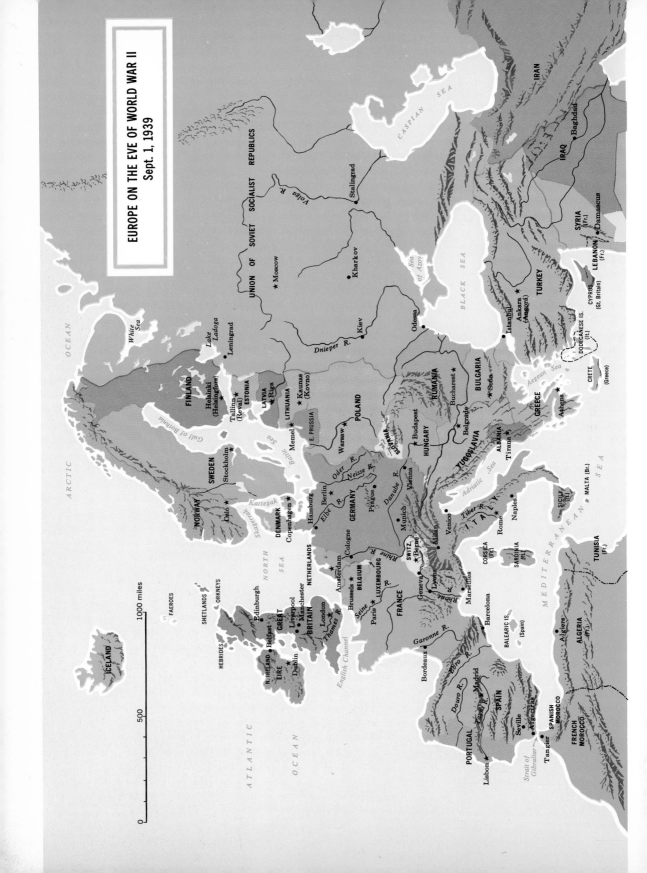

EUROPE ON THE EVE OF WORLD WAR II
Sept. 1, 1939

killed, the British held firm and finally were able to retaliate by even more devastating attacks upon German cities.

Frustrated in his attempt to subjugate Britain, Hitler turned eastward, on June 22, 1941, with a massive invasion of Russia. Before the end of the year his armies had smashed their way to the very gates of Moscow but never succeeded in capturing it. Meanwhile, the war was converted into a global war when Japan struck a deadly blow at Pearl Harbor on December 7 of the same year. The Japanese were already involved in a costly war with China. To wage it successfully they needed the oil, rubber, and extensive food resources of the Netherlands Indies, the Malay Peninsula, and Indochina. Before attacking these areas they apparently considered it necessary to lock the back door by crushing American naval and air power on the great base of Pearl Harbor. The next day the United States Congress recognized a state of war with Japan, and on December 11 Germany and her fascist allies declared war upon the United States.

The course of the war was marked by several turning points. The first was the stubborn defense of Moscow by Stalin's armies in November and December, 1941. The second was the defeat of the Germans in North Africa, which opened the way for the Allied invasion of Italy and the overthrow of Mussolini. The third was the Battle of Stalingrad in 1943, when the Germans failed in their attempt to cut northern Russia off from the food-producing region of the Ukraine and from the oil resources north and south of the Caucasus. The turning points in the Pacific war came during the

THE OUTBREAK OF HOSTILITIES

A German V-2 Rocket. Used in the latter years of the war, it was the forerunner of the early space launch vehicles.

Below: *French Refugees Driven from Their Home during the Early Years of the Nazi Occupation.* Right: *London during the Blitz.* This picture gives a vivid impression of the agony which the British capital suffered during the Battle of Britain from August 1940 to June 1941. In back of the tumbling ruins brought down by fire bombs is St. Paul's Cathedral.

Pearl Harbor, December 7, 1941. This photo shows American battleships sunk at their moorings following the Japanese raid on what President Franklin D. Roosevelt declared was "the day that will live in infamy."

spring of 1942 with the defeat by the United States Navy of Japanese forces in the battles of the Coral Sea and of Midway. These defeats spelled the doom of Japanese attempts to capture Australia and the Hawaiian Islands and thereby deprive the United States of advance bases for a counteroffensive against Japan.

End of the war in Europe

By the winter of 1944–1945 World War II was nearing its end. On June 6, 1944 (D-Day), American forces had crossed the English Channel and landed successfully in northern France. On August 25 they liberated Paris. In September advance detachments drove to the Rhine, and eventually whole armies penetrated to the heart of Germany. Meantime, Soviet troops were approaching from the east. On April 21 they hammered their way into the suburbs of Berlin. During the next ten days a savage battle raged amid the ruins and heaps of rubble. On May 2 the heart of the city was captured, and the Soviet red banner flew from the Brandenburg Gate. A few hours earlier Adolf Hitler killed himself in the bomb-proof shelter of the Chancellery. On May 7 representatives of the German High Command signed a document of unconditional surrender. Peace had come at last to an exhausted Europe after five years and eight months of slaughter and barbarism.

V-J Day

The end of the war in the Pacific was delayed for another four months. Victory over the Japanese empire had to be achieved by savage naval battles and by bloody assaults upon almost impregnable islands. In June 1945, Okinawa was taken, after eighty-two days of desperate fighting. The Americans now had footholds less than 500 miles from the Japanese homeland. The government in Tokyo was nervously anticipating an invasion and calling upon the citizens for supreme endeavors to meet the crisis. On July 26 the heads of the United States, British, and Chinese governments issued a joint proclamation calling upon Japan to surrender or be destroyed. In the absence of a reply the highest officials of the United States government resolved to make use of a new and revolutionary weapon to end the war quickly. This weapon was the atomic bomb recently developed in great secrecy by American scientists. Though many high military and naval officers contended that use of the bomb was not necessary, on the assumption that Japan was already beaten, President Harry S. Truman decided otherwise. On August 6 a single atomic bomb was dropped on Hiroshima, completely obliterating about 60 per cent of the city. Three days later a second bomb was dropped, this time on Nagasaki. That night President Truman warned that the United States would continue to use the deadly new weapon as long as might be necessary to bring Japan to her knees. On August 14 Tokyo transmitted to Washington an unconditional acceptance of the Allied demands. As the news spread through the victorious nations millions of people danced and cheered and paraded in the streets amid the screaming of horns and the shrieking of sirens. Some of the more thoughtful assembled in churches the following day to give thanks that the terrible ordeal was over.

3. THE PEACE SETTLEMENT

The peace settlement at the end of World War II, if such it can be called, was a fragmentary accomplishment. The first statement of Allied objectives in the event of victory was the Atlantic Charter, issued by President Roosevelt and Prime Minister Winston Churchill on August 14, 1941. Its essential principles were as follows:

(1) No territorial changes that do not accord with the wishes of the people concerned.

(2) The right of all peoples to choose the form of government under which they will live.

The Atlantic Charter and the United Nations Declaration

Below: *D-Day*. Cargo ships are seen pouring supplies ashore during the invasion of France. Balloon barrages float overhead to protect the ships from low-flying enemy strifers. Right: *Signing the German Surrender, May 7, 1945*

View of Hiroshima after First Atom Bomb Was Dropped, August 6, 1945. This photo, taken one month later, shows the utter devastation of the city. Only a few steel and concrete buildings remained intact.

(3) All states to enjoy access, on equal terms, to the trade and raw materials of the world.

(4) Freedom to traverse the seas without hindrance.

(5) Disarmament of all nations that threaten aggression.

The Atlantic Charter acquired a broad significance when it was reaffirmed by the United Nations Declaration on January 2, 1942. Twenty-six nations signed this Declaration, including Great Britain, the United States, the Soviet Union, and the Republic of China. Subsequently about fourteen others added their signatures.

As the war progressed, high officials of the leading United Nations met in various conferences for the purpose of determining the conditions of peace. The first of outstanding importance was the **The Cairo Declaration** conference that met in Cairo in November 1943, to discuss the fate of the Japanese empire. The participants were President Roosevelt, Prime Minister Churchill, and Generalissimo Chiang Kai-shek. They agreed that all of the territories taken by Japan from China, with the exception of Korea, were to be restored to the Chinese Republic. Korea was to become free and independent. They agreed, further, that Japan was to be stripped of all the islands in the Pacific which she had seized or occupied since 1914, and of "all other territories which she had taken by violence or greed." What disposition was to be made of these islands and territories was not specified.

The second important conference to determine the conditions of peace met in Yalta, in the Crimea, in February 1945. This time the **The Yalta Agreement** chief participants were Roosevelt, Churchill, and Stalin. A formal report issued at the close of the conference declared that the Big Three had agreed upon plans for the unconditional surrender of Germany, upon methods of controlling Germany and her allies after the war, and upon the establishment of a United Nations

820

Organization to keep the peace. In addition, it was announced that Poland would surrender her eastern provinces to Russia and be compensated by "substantial accessions of territory" in the north and west—to be taken, of course, from Germany. The existing government of Poland, set up under Soviet auspices, was to be reorganized with the inclusion of democratic leaders from among the Poles. The government of Yugoslavia was also to be broadened in similar fashion. Regarding the Far East, it was agreed that Russia should enter the war against Japan and receive as her reward all the territories taken from her by Japan in the war of 1904–1905.

The surrender of Germany on May 8, 1945 seemed to require yet another conference of the victorious powers. On July 17 Joseph Stalin, Winston Churchill, and Harry S. Truman, who had succeeded Franklin D. Roosevelt as President of the United States on April 12, met in Potsdam, a suburb of Berlin. Before the conference had finished its work, Churchill was replaced by Clement Attlee, the new Labour Prime Minister of Great Britain. The most important provisions of the formal Declaration, issued on August 2, were 1) East Prussia to be divided into two parts, the northern part to go to the Soviet Union, and the southern part to be assigned to Poland; 2) Poland to receive the former free city of Danzig; 3) all German territory east of the Oder and Neisse rivers to be administered by Poland, pending a final settlement; 4) the military power of Germany to be totally destroyed; and 5) Germany to be divided into four occupation zones to be governed, respectively, by the U.S.S.R., Great Britain, the United States, and France.

The Potsdam Declaration

After the end of the war the victorious states drafted peace treaties with Japan and with Germany's satellites. The treaty with Japan deprived her of all the territory she had acquired since 1854—in other words, her entire overseas empire. She gave up the southern half of Sakhalin Island and the Kuril Islands to Soviet Russia, and the Bonins and Ryukyus to control by the United

The Treaty with Japan

The Yalta Conference. Below: Roosevelt at the airport. Right: Churchill, Molotov, Secretary of State Stettinius (left), and Stalin (center) with glasses raised in a toast. To Stalin's left, Roosevelt, Churchill, and Molotov.

The Potsdam Conference. Two of the Big Three had changed: Clement Atlee had replaced Churchill as British prime minister, and Harry Truman had succeeded U.S. president Roosevelt.

States. She also renounced all rights to Formosa, which was left in a status still undefined. She yielded to the United States the right to continue maintaining military installations in Japan until the latter was able to defend herself. The treaty went into effect in April 1952, against the opposition of the Russians, who had hoped that Japan would be crippled by drastic punishments and thereby left an easy prey to communism.

Establishment of the United Nations

As in the case of the Versailles Treaty one of the most significant elements in the World War II settlement was its provision for international organization. The old League of Nations had failed to avert the outbreak of war in 1939, and in April 1946, it was formally dissolved. Allied statesmen had long recognized the need for a new organization. In February 1945, they agreed at Yalta that a conference to implement that need should be convoked for April 25 in San Francisco. Despite the tragic death of President Roosevelt two weeks earlier, the conference met as scheduled. A charter was adopted on June 26, providing for a world organization to be known as the United Nations and to be founded upon the principle of "the sovereign equality of all peace-loving states." Its important agencies were to be 1) a General Assembly composed of representatives of all the member states; 2) a Security Council composed of representatives of the United States, Great Britain, the U.S.S.R., the Republic of China, and France, with permanent seats, and of six other states chosen by the General Assembly to fill the nonpermanent seats; 3) a Secretariat consisting of a Secretary-General and a staff of subordinates; 4) an Economic and Social Council composed of eighteen members chosen by the General Assembly; 5) a Trusteeship Council; and 6) an International Court of Justice.

By far the most important functions of the new organization were assigned by the Charter to the Security Council. This agency has the "primary responsibility for the maintenance of international peace and security." It has authority to investigate any dispute between nations, to recommend methods for settlement, and, if necessary to preserve the peace, to employ diplomatic or economic measures against an aggressor. If, in its judgment, these have proved, or are likely to prove, inadequate, it may "take such action by air, naval, or land forces" as may be required to maintain or restore international order. The member states are required by the Charter to make available to the Security Council, on its call, armed forces for the maintenance of peace.

The Security Council was so organized as to give almost a monopoly of authority to its permanent members. It was the belief of the Big Three who assembled at Yalta, and of President Roosevelt especially, that the peace of the world depended upon harmony among the states primarily responsible for winning the war. Accordingly, they agreed that when the Security Council should be set up, no action of any kind could be taken without the unanimous consent of Great Britain, France, the United States, the Republic of China, the Soviet Union, and two other members besides. This absolute veto given to each of the principal states had none of the hoped-for effects. Instead of bolstering the peace of the world, its chief result was to cripple the Council and to render it helpless in the face of emergencies. The primary cause was the growth of distrust between Soviet Russia and the West. Each has opposed most of the demands of the other with respect to disarmament, the control of nuclear weapons, and the admission of new states.

The remaining agencies of the U.N. were given a wide variety of functions. The Secretariat, composed of a Secretary-General and a numerous staff, is chiefly an administrative authority. Its duties, though, are by no means routine, for the Secretary-General may bring to the attention of the Security Council any matter which, in his opinion, may threaten international peace. The functions of the Economic and Social Council are the most varied of all. Composed of eighteen members elected by the General Assembly, it has au-

THE PEACE SETTLEMENT

The Security
Council

The veto power
of the Big Five

Other agencies
of the U.N.

The United Nations. Buildings of the permanent headquarters in New York are the General Assembly building (foreground) and behind it the thirty-eight-story Secretariat.

ARCTIC OCEAN

GREENLAND

ICELAND

ALASKA

CANADA

IRELAND UN
KING

FRA

PORT. SPAIN

PACIFIC

UNITED   STATES

ATLANTIC

MOROCCO

SP. SAHARA

AL

MEXICO

CUBA

HAITI
DOMINICAN REP.

MAURITANIA

JAMAICA

MALI

GUATEMALA
EL SALVADOR
NICARAGUA
COSTA RICA
HONDURAS

BARBADOS

GAMBIA
PORT. GUINEA

SENEGAL

UPPER
VOLTA

TRINIDAD AND TOBAGO

GUINEA

VENE-
ZUELA

GUYANA

SIERRA LEONE

LIBERIA

TOGO

PANAMA

SURINAM
FR. GUIANA

IVORY COAST

DAHO

COLOMBIA

0   2000 miles at the equator

ECUADOR

OCEAN

PERU

BRAZIL

OCEAN

BOLIVIA

PARAGUAY

CHILE

URUGUAY

ARGENTINA

THE UNITED NATIONS

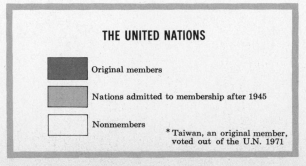

Original members

Nations admitted to membership after 1945

Nonmembers

*Taiwan, an original member,
  voted out of the U.N. 1971

thority to initiate studies and make recommendations with respect to international social, economic, health, educational, cultural, and related matters, and may perform services within such fields at the request of U.N. members. Under its jurisdiction are such specialized agencies as: the World Health Organization (WHO), which works to control epidemics and to assist backward nations in stamping out cholera, typhus, and venereal disease and in raising standards of health and sanitation; and the Food and Agriculture Organization (FAO), which seeks to promote increases in food production by finding remedies for agricultural depressions, for plant and animal diseases and insect pests, and by projecting plans for mechanizing small farms and for the more efficient distribution of food.

Achievements of the U.N.

During the first three decades of its history the achievements of the U.N. constituted a modestly impressive record. It induced Soviet Russia to withdraw her troops from Iran, and Britain and France to take their forces out of Syria and Lebanon. It appointed a commission to investigate the infiltration of foreign Communists into Greece. It terminated a bloody war between Dutch and native forces in Indonesia. It induced the British to agree to the partition of Palestine, and it persuaded the warring Jews and Arabs to conclude a truce. It assisted in arranging a cease-fire agreement between India and Pakistan, which temporarily prevented war from inundating some 400 million people. But against these accomplishments must be recorded several failures. It failed in its efforts to establish control of nuclear weapons. Despite the specific requirements of Article 26 of the Charter, it did nothing to provide for a general reduction of armaments. It failed also to curb the increasing friction between the U.S.S.R. and the United States, which was certainly a threat to international peace. It was powerless in the face of Soviet suppression of the Hungarian revolt in 1956. It has been argued, however, that one of the main contributions of the U.N. was the prevention of a direct clash between the U.S. and the U.S.S.R. By providing makeshift solutions as well as a forum for the discussion of grievances, the U.N. helped to keep the two giants from a head-on collision. As a consequence, crises mounted to a crescendo of bitterness without resulting in a holocaust that would destroy the world.

Other forms of internationalism: (1) the movement for a world republic

In the light of conditions obtaining after World War II, it was perhaps inevitable that internationalism should assume a number of forms. Some thoughtful observers criticized the United Nations as a mere replica of the old League of Nations. Both, it was said, were leagues of governments, not federations of peoples. Those who felt this way argued for nothing less than a world federal republic similar in structure to the United States, with an actual transfer of sovereign powers to a central government. They believed that the government of this republic should include not merely a court to hear disputes and a world executive with police authority, but, above all, a world parliament representing peoples rather than governments and capable of enacting laws which would apply directly to individuals. It was not argued that the functions of the world state should entirely supersede those of national governments. On the contrary, only such sovereign powers as control over armaments, tariffs, and colonial areas should be transferred to the central authority; the rest would be reserved to the national units.

Less idealistic statesmen and publicists held to the belief that the U.N. should be supplemented by military and political alliances. Convinced that the U.S.S.R. was bent upon world conquest, they could think only in terms of a combination of force for the "containment" of Soviet power. Such was the opinion of President Truman and his advisers in the United States, and they seem to have converted to similar views most of the governments of the Atlantic region. In April 1949, a group of representatives of North Atlantic states together with Canada and the United States signed an agreement providing for the establishment of the North Atlantic Treaty Organization (NATO). Subsequently Greece, Turkey, and West Germany were added as members. The treaty declared that an armed attack against any one of the signatory parties would be regarded as an attack against all, and that they would combine their armed strength to whatever extent necessary to repel the aggressor. It was decided also that the joint military command, or NATO army established in 1950, should be increased from thirty to fifty divisions in 1953, and that West Germany should be rearmed and invited to contribute twelve of the divisions. It was thereby hoped that NATO would be ready for any emergency that might arise as a consequence of the expansionist policies of Soviet Russia. By 1966, however the status of the alliance had been compromised by disharmony between France, on the one side, and Great Britain and the United States on the other. Whereas Britain generally supported the policies of the United States, France under de Gaulle aspired to organize Western Europe as an independent entity opposing the threat of communist expansion. He seemed anxious to exclude the United States from a dominant role in European affairs. Western European nations, he believed, were capable of saving themselves and taking care of their own future. To accomplish his aims he was ready for a reconciliation with Germany and practically forced the withdrawal of NATO troops from French soil.

(2) NATO

SELECTED READINGS

· *Items so designated are available in paperbound editions.*

· Aron, Raymond, *The Century of Total War*, Boston, 1955 (Beacon).
· Bailey, T. A., *Woodrow Wilson and the Lost Peace*, New York, 1944 (Quadrangle).
· Carr, E. H., *The Twenty Years' Crisis*, London, 1946 (Torchbook). Stimulating but somewhat dogmatic.

827

READINGS · Chadwin, Mark Lincoln, *The Warhawks: American Interventionists before Pearl Harbor*, Chapel Hill, 1968 (Norton Library).

Coox, A. D., *Year of the Tiger*, Tokyo, 1964. A study of the beginning of the Sino-Japanese War in 1937–1938.

Divine, Robert A., *Roosevelt and World War II*, Baltimore, 1969.

· Eyck, F. Gunther, *The Benelux Countries: An Historical Survey*, Princeton, 1959 (Anvil).

· Feis, Herbert, *The Road to Pearl Harbor*, Princeton, 1950 (Atheneum).

· ———, *Churchill-Roosevelt-Stalin: The War They Waged and the Peace They Sought*, Princeton, 1957 (Princeton).

Finer, Herman, *America's Destiny*, New York, 1947.

Gay, Peter, *Weimar Culture: The Outsider as Insider*, New York, 1968.

Géraud, André, *The Gravediggers of France*, New York, 1944. A critical and impassioned account.

Holborn, Hajo, *The Political Collapse of Europe*, New York, 1951. A penetrating analysis.

Lafore, Laurence, *The End of Glory: An Interpretation of the Origins of World War II*, Philadelphia, 1970. Asserts that that war resulted from efforts of European powers to run affairs with institutions and ideas made obsolete by World War I.

· Langer, William L., *Our Vichy Gamble*, New York, 1947 (Norton Library).

Lifton, Robert J., *Death in Life: The Survivors of Hiroshima*, New York, 1967.

Morgenthau, H. J., *Politics among Nations: The Struggle for Power and Peace*, New York, 1948. A provocative analysis from the viewpoint of a realist.

Neumann, William L., *After Victory: Churchill, Roosevelt, Stalin and the Making of the Peace*, New York, 1967.

· O'Connor, Raymond G., *Diplomacy for Victory: FDR and Unconditional Surrender*, New York, 1971 (Norton).

· Reves, Emery, *The Anatomy of Peace*, New York, 1945 (Compass). An eloquent plea for a world federal republic.

Robertson, E. M., ed., *Origins of the Second World War*, New York, 1970.

· Rowse, A. L., *Appeasement: A Study in Political Decline, 1933–1939*, New York, 1961 (Norton Library).

· Taylor, A. J. P., *The Origins of the Second World War*, New York, 1961 (Fawcett).

· Trevor-Roper, H. R., *The Last Days of Hitler*, New York, 1947 (Collier).

Viorst, Milton, *Hostile Allies: FDR and Charles de Gaulle*, New York, 1965.

Wittner, Lawrence S., *Rebels against War*, New York, 1969.

· Wolfers, Arnold, *Britain and France between Two Wars*, New York, 1940 (Norton Library).

SOURCE MATERIALS

· Churchill, W. S., *Blood, Sweat, and Tears*. Also available in paperback under the title *The Years of Greatness* (Capricorn).

· ———, *The Second World War*, New York, 1960, 6 vols. (Bantam, 1962, 6 vols.).

· Eisenhower, D. D., *Crusade in Europe*, New York, 1948 (Dolphin).

Grew, J. C., *Report from Tokyo*, New York, 1942.

Liebling, A. J., ed., *The Republic of Silence*, New York, 1947. A collection of materials on the French Resistance movement.

Maurois, André, *Tragedy in France: An Eyewitness Account*.

U.N. Dept. of Public Information, *Yearbook of the United Nations*.

CHAPTER 30

New Power Relationships

If we don't have peace and the nuclear bombs start to fall, what difference will it make whether we are Communists or Catholics or capitalists or Chinese or Russians or Americans? Who will be left to tell us apart?

> —Nikita Khrushchev in interview with Norman Cousins, January 1963

Mankind must put an end to war—or war will put an end to mankind. . . . Let us call a truce to terror. Let us invoke the blessings of peace. And as we build an international capacity to keep peace, let us join in dismantling the national capacity to wage war.

> —President John F. Kennedy, September 25, 1961, Address to the General Assembly of the United Nations

World War II left the political world of Europe, Asia, and the United States in a state of disorder. Of course, no such result was intended by those who fought to destroy fascism and to reorganize the world under a new system to take the place of the League of Nations. However, their calculations went awry. The new United Nations proved to be no more effective than the old League. The war itself spawned nationalist revolts all over the world. As victory approached, wartime allies buried their hatchets in each other's backs. With the conclusion of peace, wars broke out on three continents. Some were nationalist struggles to gain independence for former colonies of dying empires. The success of some of these struggles seldom brought peace but merely a continuation of strife in new forms. Still other clashes took the form of conflict between the superstates or some of their satellites. These were among the bloodiest and most destructive of all the outbursts of savagery that marked the period after World War II. Several eclipsed the savagery of that war itself and did much to brand our own age as one of the most barbarous in history.

The new world of disorder

An outstanding phenomenon of the period that followed World War II was the decline of Europe. Ever since the last centuries of the pre-Christian era, a small peninsula of Eurasia—for that is what Europe is—had dominated the civilized world. This limited area had most of the technological advances, the bulk of the wealth, and most of the science, philosophy, literature, music, art, and other embellishments that go to make up the total of civilization. Many of these achievements were based on a hard-driving expenditure of energy that had its origin in religion. Many others sprang from conquest of less enterprising peoples and from enslavement of the least fortunate.

1. THE SECOND HUNDRED YEARS' WAR

The years 1337–1453 marked the period of the so-called Hundred Years' War. The name leaves much to be said from the standpoint of accuracy. In the first place it suggests a continuous conflict, which did not prevail. Instead, there were numerous truces or suspensions of hostilities while the two sides jockeyed for position or bargained for advantages. A similar period in world history began in 1870 and has continued, with interruptions, until the present day. Some observers think it will not terminate before the end of the twentieth century. It began with the Franco-German War in 1870 and continued with the Sino-Japanese War in 1895, and the Russo-Japanese War in 1904–1905. It reached its first great climax in the two World Wars of 1914 and 1939. But destructive though these conflicts were, they did not bring peace to an exhausted world. Instead, they spawned new violence on a more limited scale but with steadily increasing brutality.

The initial armed clash of the post–World War period was the Korean War of 1950–1953. To most people in the West this seemed an obvious attempt of the Russians to use their allies, the North Koreans, as agents for extending Soviet power in the Far East. Most of them were unaware of the conflicting ambitions of North and South Korea. The South Korean President, Syngman Rhee, openly proclaimed his ambition to unite the whole country, by force if necessary. Open warfare began on June 25, 1950 when troops from North Korea crossed the 38th parallel to attack the non-communist republic of South Korea. Soon afterward President Truman sent armed assistance to the South Koreans. Theoretically, the United States forces were fighting merely as representatives of the United Nations. Actually, they were waging an old-fashioned power struggle not essentially different from that between Russia and Japan in 1904–1905. By 1951 the Korean War had reached a stalemate, and two years later a *pro forma* peace settlement was concluded.

The second major example of international violence in the wake of World War II has been the Indochina conflict. This subject will be discussed in full in the next chapter. Suffice it to emphasize now that the Indochina War grew out of a kind of last gasp of nineteenth-century imperialism. The peninsula of Indochina had been

War in Korea. U.S. Marines firing into a bleak hillside.

organized as a French colony in the time of Napoleon III. Over the years it became one of the most valuable of French possessions. When, in 1941, the Japanese extended their aggressions into Southeast Asia, the made Indochina a major target of attack. They set up puppet rulers and governed the peninsula as a colony of Japan. With the defeat of Japan and the end of the war, native nationalists sought to prevent their country from falling into the grasp of the imperialists. Foremost among the native nationalists was a Vietnamese party known as Viet Minh. Their leader was a Moscow-trained Communist, Ho Chi Minh. The rebels resorted to guerrilla warfare and inflicted such costly defeats upon the French that they were forced to abandon the struggle in 1954.

The beginning of war in Indochina

2. THE DECLINE AND REVIVAL OF IDEOLOGY

Despite all the talk about the threat of world communism and the imminence of ideological conquest, the danger of either seems clearly to have diminished in the past decade. Most Communist haters of a bygone age have mellowed and bent over backward to give their blessings to the Soviet Union. Some did this during World War II when Russia was an ally of Britain and the United States. The most famous were Franklin D. Roosevelt and Winston Churchill. In the honeymoon that followed briefly the defeat of Germany, President Truman confessed that he "rather liked Old Joe." Most interesting of all the reversals of attitudes toward communism was that of Richard M. Nixon. Foremost among leaders of anticommunism in the United States during the Cold War, he had gained national fame by goading the prosecution of such Russian sympathizers as Alger Hiss. He referred to the State Department scornfully as Dean Acheson's College of Cowardly Communist Containment. As President, however, Mr. Nixon set himself up as a champion of Communist China, forgetting all the harsh comments

The changing complexion of anticommunism

831

he and his subordinates had been making in the recent past regarding Peking as the regal propagator of the Indochina War. He visited China in 1972 and pushed for its membership in the United Nations. This was to be done, he asserted, without sacrificing the interests of "our old friends," the Nationalist Chinese on the island of Taiwan. His motives are not entirely clear. While probably political, they may also have been to develop Red China as a counterpoise against Russia, and perhaps even against Japan for the long pull.

But America was not the only nation to substitute a shrewd political realism for the Communist-baiting of the past. Orthodox gospels of Marxism have almost disappeared from the scene all over the world. A few proponents can still be found in Russia and Albania and doubtless also in Mainland China. Communist parties exist under compulsion in Poland, Czechoslovakia, and Yugoslavia, but few could vouch for the sincerity of what they believe. Several of their leaders have adopted so many elements of production for profit and for the satisfaction of consumer demands that they have drifted far from the orthodox teachings of Marx and Lenin. A Polish wit has distinguished thus between capitalism and communism: "Capitalism is a system wherein man exploits man. And communism is vice versa." [1] The story of international communism seems little different from that within the several countries. No world communism has swept the globe, despite the dire prediction of many conservatives. In every country west of the Iron Curtain Communist parties have shrunk to insignificance. Italy is an exception, where the Communists constitute the second largest party with a third of the votes cast. In the new states of Africa, which seemed for a time to be such a fertile ground for both Russian and Red Chinese agents, the movement has lost ground. Even in Egypt many of the Kremlin's representatives have been thrown into jail in defiance of whatever dreams they may have had of using the land of the pyramids as a fulcrum of Soviet power in the Middle East. What is true of communism in most countries of the world seems scarcely less true of socialism. Socialists no longer advocate collective ownership of the means of production; they have faded into exponents of the welfare state. It is not uncommon to hear from them slighting references to "baggy-pants Marxism." Defenders of capitalism still exist in theory but few would recognize it if they saw it in full swing. For capitalist economies are no longer free enterprise systems but "mixed" economies, involving government controls, managed currencies, and forced distribution of profits. The small-time capitalist, at least, is permitted to gloat over his gains for a period before turning them over to the government to finance its wars and armaments and public relief.

The causes of the decline of ideology have been several. Many of the architects of utopias were naïve. They believed in the

[1] Daniel Bell, *The End of Ideology*, p. 16.

inherent goodness of human nature and assumed that new and better institutions would provide the open sesame to a perfect society. Rising incomes and the increasing availability of luxuries for members of the lower middle class fostered a disinterest in reform movements. Instead, workers and their families began dreaming of houses in the suburbs, luxury automobiles, and expensive vacations. Even in the Soviet Union, according to Nikita Khrushchev, near the end of his regime, what the Russian masses wanted was not more doctrine but "better goulash." The decline of ideology can also be illustrated by the history of the Socialist party in the United States since World War I. In the Presidential election of 1920 the party polled about 1 million votes. By 1928 the vote had dwindled to 267,000. By 1960 the fortunes of the party were at so low an ebb that it did not even nominate a candidate for President. A final cause of the diminishing importance of ideology was disillusionment with radicalism itself, especially in Western countries. Socialists failed to present a united front against World War I. Though a few remained steadfast in opposing the conflict, most of them were nationalists first and socialists second. Even more disenchanting were the attitudes of Communists in the years that followed. In Germany members of the party collaborated with the Nazis to assist the latter's accession to power. They more or less openly mouthed the slogan, "After Hitler, Our Turn." Communist rulers of the Soviet Union entered into a virtual alliance with Nazi Germany in 1939 which practically assured that Hitler would attack Poland and plunge Europe into World War II.

No account of the decline of ideology would be complete without some further mention of what has been happening in the Soviet Union. Roughly, a situation has developed not unlike that which characterized the intelligentsia in the nineteenth century. A considerable number of writers, scholars, scientists, and artists have emerged who have no sympathy whatever with the Soviet government. The major change came in 1953 with the "timely" death of Stalin. His tyranny had been so deadly and irksome that intellectuals continued to hate it even after he was gone. Among the leaders of the reaction have been Andrei Amalrik, Aleksandr Solzhenitsyn, and Boris Pasternak. Their methods have consisted in staging protests against such events as the occupation of Czechoslovakia and the publication abroad of anti-Soviet books. Although their movement is called a "democratic movement," its aims so far have not gone beyond insistence that government officials adhere strictly to Soviet law.

Ideology experienced a partial revival in the sixties and seventies. Its scope and duration, however, were impossible to predict. It found voices in the writings and speeches of Fidel Castro, his disciple Ernesto Guevara, Herbert Marcuse, Frantz Fanon, and the Weathermen. Although the philosophies of most of these leaders

Causes of the
decline of
ideology

Fidel Castro

833

Latter-day
radicals: Castro,
Guevara, and
Marcuse

were heavily tinctured with communism, they bordered more
closely upon anarchism. Such was true of Fidel Castro and even
more true of Ernesto "Che" Guevara, who fled from Cuba to the
mainland of South America in the hope of fomenting revolutions
against militarists and exploiters. He was killed in 1967 by Bolivian
soldiers. Most popular of the radicals, among intellectuals at least, is
the German-American philosopher Herbert Marcuse. His philosophy is a compound of Marxism and Freudianism with an apparent
predominance of the latter. He is so far removed from Marx that he
condemns modern technological society as "tyrannical." Despite
threats on his life by the Ku Klux Klan, he is not in all cases an advocate of violence. He believes in "subverting" the social order because of its "tyranny," but he has opposed campus demonstrations
because he thinks of the universities as oases of freedom and critical
thinking.

What Herbert Marcuse has been to radical intellectuals of the
present generation, Frantz Fanon has been to the helpless and disinherited of the Third World. As Fanon used the term, the Third
World comprised the victims of capitalist dominance wherever
they might live. They were inhabitants of the developing nations of
Africa, Asia, and the Pacific islands. But others lived in independent
countries of the Western Hemisphere where forms of enslavement
were just as rife though under different names. Fanon himself was a
black, born on the French island of Martinique, though he did not
confine his sympathies to his own race. He championed the cause of
the downtrodden everywhere, and at one time numbered as many
Arabs among his followers as he did blacks. He served in the Algerian war for liberation from France as a psychiatrist from 1954 to
1960, and as a guerrilla fighter by night. As he saw the modern
world, imperialism or colonialism was its most glaring evil. He
would take all measures possible to accomplish its overthrow. Methods he would employ include revolutionary violence, demand for
reparations, and measures to effect the rebirth of the native cultures.
On the other hand, he was not a nihilist. Though he recognized the
necessity of abrupt and violent change, he was more interested in
building a better world than he was in destroying. Fanon's influence
has grown by many cubits since his death from leukemia in 1961.
He was deified by some of the more violent upheavals in Europe
and the United States in the 1960's, especially by those in Paris and
at Columbia. The most lasting influence has been that of the Black
Panthers. They gave him a place among their saints and heroes soon
after publication of the American edition of his *Wretched of the
Earth* in 1963.

"Che" Guevara

3.   THE THREAT TO WESTERN HEGEMONY

Prior to 1914 the list of world powers included no fewer than
eight states. Of these, Great Britain, France, Germany, Austria-
Hungary, Russia, and Italy were generally the real arbiters of world

affairs. The United States and Japan were sometimes accorded a grudging position but they generally did not weigh very heavily in the international scale. After World War I the number of powers shrank to five. Austria-Hungary was eliminated permanently and Germany and Russia for a period of years. On the other hand, the United States and Japan rose to positions much higher than they had previously occupied, while Britain and France sank a bit lower. The effects of World War II upon power relationships were far more upsetting. Germany, Italy, and Japan were defeated so overwhelmingly that they seemed destined to be relegated permanently to the background. They recovered more quickly than expected, however, and regained positions nearly comparable to those they had occupied before the war. Officially, the list of great powers included five states—the U.S.S.R., the United States, Great Britain, France, and the Republic of China. These were the famous Big Five that seemed fated to rule the world. However, China was soon overwhelmed by Communist revolution, while Britain and France became increasingly dependent upon the United States. As a consequence, the world of nations took on a bipolar character, with the United States and the U.S.S.R. contesting for supremacy and striving to draw the remaining states into their orbits.

As had happened several times in the afterglow of victorious wars, America, in the 1950's and 1960's, basked in a kind of Golden Age unparalleled in history. From the standpoint of economic power she had far outdistanced the rest of the nations. Since 1939 her people had doubled their national income and quadrupled their savings. Though they constituted only 7 per cent of the world's population, Americans enjoyed over 30 per cent of the world's estimated income. For the first time in her history the United States was in a position to be the arbiter of the destinies of at least half of the earth. Japan was virtually her colony; she controlled both the Atlantic and Pacific Oceans, policed the Mediterranean, and shaped the development of international policy in Western Europe. But it must not be imagined that her people had found for themselves an earthly paradise. The national debt in 1945 stood at $260,000,000,000, and it has since risen to over $370,000,000,000. More money was required to pay the interest on this debt than had been necessary to defray the entire cost of government before the war. By 1948 the cost of living had risen to 172 per cent of the 1935–1939 average, and one family out of every four was spending in excess of its earnings. Moreover, despite her sacrifice of billions of dollars and 350,000 lives, the United States had not gained security. For years after the war, her citizens lived in as much dread of a new attack as they had felt at almost any time while the war was in progress. Without exception they embraced a policy of success through superior strength. They believed that the United States should never suffer a diminution of this strength which she had inherited from World War II. Moreover, her rulers

Changing status of the great powers

The illusion of American power and prosperity

835

did not seem to believe that such a diminution would ever be likely. America had a perpetual monopoly of death-dealing atomic weapons, and she could use them in accordance with what she conceived as her noble purposes. When the Soviet Union cracked this monopoly in 1949, it might well have plunged America's rulers into a slough of despair. They remained convinced, however, that the policy of superior strength was still completely valid. All that was now necessary was to add new and more deadly weapons and thereby to make sure that no rival could successfully challenge the United States. A chip-on-the-shoulder attitude dominated American policy thenceforth.

Containment

The foreign policy of the United States followed a remarkable consistency throughout the 1950's and 1960's. Regardless of the party in power, the cornerstone of that policy was really the "containment" of communism. At least, it was called that in polite diplomatic circles. Its actual purpose may have been a bit more cynical. It apparently included the protection of American business in Western Europe, the extension of trade with all countries of the "free" world, and the safeguarding of American oil interests in the Middle East and in the dying empires of Asia and Africa.

Origin of
containment
policy

The containment policy actually originated during the Presidency of Harry S. Truman. It was first formulated by a State Department official, George F. Kennan, in 1947. According to Kennan, the U.S.S.R. under Stalin did not rightfully belong in the family of nations. Her national system was not a state in the proper meaning of the term but a religion stamped with demonology and Oriental mysticism. The adoption of this viewpoint by President Truman and his subordinates marked the beginning of the so-called Cold War. Its aim was to isolate the Soviet Union and render it harmless against the West. Soon afterward he decided to speed the development of a hydrogen bomb and recommended increasing "defense" expenditures to $20 billion.[2] The containment policy has continued under Truman's successors.

Kennedy's action
against Cuba

In April 1961 John F. Kennedy approved a plan for the invasion of Cuba to overthrow the government of Fidel Castro. The plan, conceived under Eisenhower by the CIA, called for the training of Cuban exiles and refugees in Florida and Guatemala followed by a secret landing on the Bay of Pigs. The attempted execution of the plot ended in disaster. Few of the participants escaped death or capture. In October 1962 Kennedy aspired to set Russia back on her heels when he instituted a naval blockade of Cuba in order to prevent the Soviet government from supplying "offensive" weapons to that country. The Soviet government took alarm at the threat of a new world war and agreed to remove their missiles and bombers from Cuban soil. The full story of this affair is still locked in the archives of the State Department in Washington.

[2] See George F. Kennan, "The Sources of Soviet Conduct," *Foreign Affairs*, vol. XXV, no. 4 (July 1947), 576.

President Kennedy also applied his vigorous containment policy to other areas. He served notice on the Soviet government that it must respect the rights of the United States in its treaty rights in West Berlin, and that the American stand with regard to those rights was not "negotiable." In 1961 he went so far as to announce that "in some circumstances we might have to take the initiative" in using nuclear weapons against our enemies. His successors chose to accent Kennedy's policy rather than to tone it down. Lyndon Johnson proceeded to "escalate" the Indochina War whenever he thought that increased pressure might bring the enemy to heel. Richard Nixon professed a determination to "wind down" this war, but it was not clear whether he meant a real change or merely a re-direction that would give the appearance of victory.

Soviet Russia emerged from World War II as the second strongest power on earth. Though her navy was small, her land army and possibly her air force by 1948 were the largest in the world. Her population was climbing rapidly toward 200,000,000, and this in spite of the loss of 7,000,000 soldiers and about 8,000,000 civilians during the war. In mineral wealth her position compared favorably with that of the richest countries. After 1946 she claimed a large percentage of the world supply of petroleum. On the other hand, there can be no doubt that her industrial machine had been badly crippled by the war. No fewer than 1700 of her cities and towns had been totally destroyed and about 40,000 miles of railway and 31,000 factories. Stalin declared in 1946 that it would probably require at least six years to repair the damage and rebuild the devastated areas.

It seems reasonable to suppose that much of the hostility displayed by the U.S.S.R. in her dealings with other nations was attributable in some measure to the losses she sustained during the war. Resentful of the fact that she had been compelled to make such sacrifices, she became obsessed with security as a goal that must be attained regardless of the cost to her neighbors. Fearful that poverty and hardship might make her own people rebellious, her rulers adopted a chip-on-the-shoulder attitude in their foreign policy. Soviet citizens must be led to think that their country was in imminent danger of attack by capitalist powers. For similar reasons they must be induced to believe that their rulers were entitled to a kind of worship hitherto reserved for divine-right monarchs. In accordance with a new nationalism designed to bolster the people's courage, the Russians laid claim to a majority of the inventions and scientific discoveries of modern times—from the electric light and wireless telegraphy to penicillin.

The tenseness of Soviet attitudes seemed to relax a bit after the death of Joseph Stalin in March 1953. Stalin was succeeded within twenty-four hours by Georgi M. Malenkov, a dominant figure in the party apparatus. Soon after his elevation to power he declared that there was no dispute or unresolved question between the Soviet

Union and any other nation which could not be settled by "mutual
agreement of the interested countries." Prospects for better relations
between the Soviet Union and the West were further enhanced in
1955 when Malenkov resigned and the supreme power passed into
the hands of Nikita S. Khrushchev. Though he did not immediately
become Premier, he held the all-important position of Secretary of
the Communist party. Khrushchev seemed more anxious than his
predecessor to create the impression that the Soviet government was
ready to repent of the error of its ways. He denounced Stalin for his
paranoid suspicions of everyone around him and for his brutal
tyranny. He and his colleagues announced their approval of the
doctrine of "more than one road to socialism." They concluded
peace with Austria and withdrew their occupying troops. In 1955
they agreed to a "conference at the summit" with the chiefs of government of Great Britain, France, the United States, and the
U.S.S.R. as the participants. The conference was held in Geneva,
and the utmost cordiality prevailed. Repeated pledges of trust and
friendship were given by both sides.

This policy of the "Great Thaw," as it was called, was undoubtedly prompted by discontent within the country. The Russian
masses had no zest for another war, and they were weary of the
restrictions and rigidities imposed by the Stalin regime. They believed that the time had come for less emphasis on the production of munitions and capital goods and more on providing
the amenities of life. The most genial of Soviet dictators, Khrushchev was disposed to sympathize with these demands. The new
policy, however, soon ran into heavy weather. The first sign of
change was the suppression of revolts in Poland and Hungary in
1956. The Poles were let off rather lightly when they promised to
remain within the Soviet orbit in return for permission to make
various modifications in their socialist system. The Hungarians were
repressed with bloody violence when they attempted not merely to
change the economic system but to break all ties with the Soviet

*Nikita Khrushchev Visiting
East Berlin Accompanied by
Walter Ulbricht*

Revolt in Hungary. By 1956 discontent with Soviet domination manifested itself in several of the satellite states. Violent revolt broke out in Poland and Hungary. Left: The photograph indicates the extent of the violence in Budapest. Right: A group of Hungarian freedom fighters

Union. At the beginning of another "summit" conference in Paris in May 1960, Premier Khrushchev erupted violently when he learned that the United States was sending U-2 planes far over Soviet territory to discover the location of bases and other military installations. Though at first Washington officials denied these flights, they later admitted them and sought to justify them as necessary for the military security of the United States. The summit conference terminated immediately, with nothing but a poisoned atmosphere to mark its effects, despite the subsequent suspension of U-2 flights. Yet Khrushchev was not ready to abandon completely his policy of conciliation. Later in 1960 he enunciated his principle of "peaceful coexistence." Though he did not renounce the ultimate triumph of communism, insisting that "we will bury you," he refused to admit that this triumph must be accomplished by force of arms.

With respect to Germany, until recently the Soviet leaders remained unyielding. They nurtured the fear that Germany might launch a new war, aided and abetted by her capitalist allies. For this reason they staunchly opposed unification of the country and insisted upon recognizing East Germany as one of their satellites. In 1961 they ordered the East German government to build a high wall separating the two sectors of Berlin, in order to cut off the escape of thousands of East Germans to West Berlin and then to western Germany. Many did make their escape, but the wall remained as a symbol of Soviet determination to prevent the formation of a united Germany. The development of nuclear weapons fixed in the minds of the Soviet leaders another obsession regarding Germany. They feared that West Germany might be given a finger on the trigger of some project that could be used to destroy the Soviet Union.

Intransigent attitude toward the problem of Germany

The genial Khrushchev did not survive as Soviet dictator indefinitely. In 1964 he was deposed and reduced to the level of an "unperson." The reins of power then passed into the hands of a joint

The Occupation of Czechoslovakia. In 1968 the liberalized regime of Alexander Dubcek was suppressed by the Soviets. The violent response by the citizens was put down by military force.

dictatorship of Aleksei Kosygin as Premier and Leonid Brezhnev as Secretary of the Communist Party. The government did not return to Stalinist policy, but some of the new trends moved noticeably in that direction. A cardinal example was the occupation of Czechoslovakia in 1968. The Soviet dictators accused the Czechs of flirtation with West Germany to such an extent as to threaten the Soviet system and weaken its ties over Eastern Europe. In particular, they resented the economic and social privileges allowed by the Czech government to its own citizens. Accordingly, they sent in armored troops and puppet rulers to take over the country. They followed this action by issuance of the Brezhnev Doctrine, which asserted the right of Moscow to interfere in the affairs of any satellite that strayed from the path of Soviet leadership.

The downfall of Khrushchev and the accession of a new regime in Russia

4. THE IMPOTENCE OF POWER

One of the amazing assumptions of our contemporary age is the doctrine that "God is for the big battalions," as Voltaire expressed it; or in the words of Mao Tse-tung, "Power proceeds from the muzzle of a gun." No doubt, these are keen observations, but they are not universally true. In the past ten to fifteen years they have been much less true than they were in the bloody afterglow of World War II. It did not take long for some of the world's discontented to demonstrate the hollowness of Allied victory.

The emptiness of great power supremacy

By 1970 the one-time great powers had been reduced to pale imitations of their former selves. On the surface this was not true. States that belonged to the "Nuclear Club" seemed to have acquired a weapon that would enable them to impose their will on their neighbors for an indefinite time to come. But this was as empty as any imaginable illusion. A balance of terror canceled their power to wage war against each other. They could not even dictate to their satellites or to any two-bit nation that wished to defy them.

How have the mighty fallen

The United States, theoretically the greatest military power the world had ever seen, found itself stymied by a primitive nation of peasants in North Vietnam. Such fourth-rate powers as North Korea (backed by Soviet threats) and Peru have also made the giant United States military and diplomatic machinery look ridiculous by their defiance. The status of the U.S.S.R. does not benefit by comparison. The Soviets have not been able to control absolutely their own satellites. Poles, Czechs, and Rumanians have managed to gain considerable independence in following their own devices by secret or open defiance of Moscow's authority. An eminent American journalist has said that the world has had only two great powers for the past decade—Israel and South Vietnam. They have wielded more influence in determining the course of recent history than any other nations regardless of size or deadliness of weapons.

Thus it may be noted that attempts to maximize power have in nearly every instance been marked by its concomitant of impotence. States both great and small have yielded to superior force and sometimes almost no force at all in the domain of external relations. But there has been one outstanding exception. At the end of World War II the victorious states bound themselves to unprecedented legal and moral restraints and then proceeded to ignore or flout them completely. These restraints are known as the Nuremberg Principles, unanimously endorsed by the General Assembly of the United Nations in 1946. Embodied in these principles was the Nuremberg Judgment, which condemned all those wars undertaken except in strict self-defense. All wars in this category were classified as wars of aggression and therefore the supreme international crime. Few except legal hairsplitters could exclude from the ban of the Nuremberg Judgment Ho Chi Minh's slaughter of his enemies in North Vietnam, the murder of hundreds of Indian nationalists by the British at Amritsar in 1947, the massacre of guerrilla fighters by the French in Algeria in 1957–1958, and the indiscriminate B-52 bombings by the United States in the Indochina War.

The Nuremberg Judgment

Characteristic examples of the impotence of power have not been rare in modern history. We shall see in other connections how it was illustrated by the struggle against the British in India, the revolt in Algeria, and the war in Indochina. Conspicuous also has been strife in Ireland. We have noted already that violence against British oppression flared at intervals during the eighteenth and nineteenth centuries and reached its climax in the Easter Rebellion of 1916. It died down after the war when the British agreed to the establishment of an Irish Free State.

The beginnings of strife in Ireland

It would be a mistake to consider the roots of conflict in Ireland as entirely religious. In a broader sense they are political and social. The majority of the Irish still consider the British intrusion into their land as a form of invasion and occupation. Such feelings, moreover, are heightened by social cleavage. The workers, especially in the large cities, whether Catholic or not, are mostly im-

Social and economic cleavage

poverished and insecure. Their willingness to work for starvation wages has made them targets of fear and hatred as despised classes invariably are. The wealthy, who are mainly Protestant, strive to keep their status as overlords of a privileged society. Even if religion were not a divisive influence, economics and politics would keep the two classes bitterly antagonistic.

The recent polarization

The most deadly polarization in Ireland began in 1968, that year of bitter turmoil all over the world. The major arena of conflict has been Ulster, especially the cities of Londonderry and Belfast. Ulster was established in the seventeenth century originally as a kind of British Colony. The Irish natives were driven back into the hills while their lands were absorbed by English invaders. Monopolization of economic advantages by these invaders and their descendants gave rise to a series of violent altercations. The first in our own time occurred when a march of demonstrators was stopped by a line of police supported by an angry horde of Protestants armed with clubs and sticks. Insulting taunts and threats were exchanged by both sides. Although there was no bloodshed, passions smoldered for another time.

Later confrontations in Ulster

The attitude of the British throughout the United Kingdom seems to have been one of general sympathy with their kinsmen in Ulster. When the Free State was formed, Ulster remained part of the United Kingdom. The final authority over it was the Home Secretary in London. British policy toward malcontents in Ulster was sometimes conciliatory, but there was usually a gloved hand concealing a mailed fist. New confrontations were not long delayed. The first involving serious violence started on New Year's Day, 1969. A march protesting official tyranny was ambushed by Protestant extremists on the road from Belfast to Londonderry. Scores of men, women, and girls, many of them students at Queen's University, were brutally clubbed, while the police pursued a hands-off policy. Catholic workers shut themselves into their Bogside ghetto and prepared for revenge. New ruptures of the peace

Strife in Ireland, 1916. British troops raiding the office of a Dublin printer who supported the rebellion.

A Renewal of "The Troubles" in Ireland. British soldiers congregate near the ruins of a bar which was blasted by terrorists in August of 1972. As in other parts of the world, bombing had become one of the chief instruments -of political terrorism and rebellion.

were inevitable. The next major battle began in the summer of 1969 when extremists of both sides engaged in savage violence. In three nights of rioting five persons were killed and more than 200 injured. The British seemed unable to think of any means of control except to send in more troops. By February 1972 at least 15,000 British soldiers with armored vehicles were stationed in Ireland. The interval of peace came to an end when some of these soldiers fired into a demonstration of Irish civilians, killing thirteen of them. Radicalism took on new life as defiant parades and a general strike spread through Ulster. Government buildings were destroyed in Belfast, the British embassy in Dublin was burned, and mobs stormed the Prime Minister's residence in London. The regime of violence continued through most of 1972. Even the establishment of direct rule from London did not terminate the disorders. Sporadic attacks from both sides continued. The violence of the Irish Republican Army was invariably matched by the fanaticism of the Protestants, who generally controlled the government in Belfast even after the transfer of authority to representatives of the British Crown.

SELECTED READINGS

· *Items so designated are available in paperbound editions.*

· Acheson, Dean, *The Korean War*, New York, 1971 (Norton).
——, *The Struggle for a Free Europe*, New York, 1971 (Norton).
· Almond, G. A., *The Appeals of Communism*, Princeton, 1954 (Princeton University Press).
· Aron, Raymond, *The Century of Total War*, Boston, 1955 (Beacon). The world today in historical perspective.
Barghorn, F. C., *Soviet Russian Nationalism*, New York, 1956.

READINGS

Barnett, A. Doak, *A New U.S. Policy toward China*, Brookings Institution, 1971.

Berger, Earl, *The Covenant and the Sword: Arab-Israeli Relations, 1948–1956*, Toronto, 1965. Impartial.

Cady, J. F., *Southeast Asia: Its Historical Development*, New York, 1964.

Drucker, P. F., *The End of Economic Man*, New York, 1939. A really profound study of modern man's predicament.

Fairbank, J. K., *The United States and China*, Cambridge, Mass., 1971. A revised and updated edition.

· Fanon, Frantz, *The Wretched of the Earth*, New York, 1968 (Evergreen).

Fleming, D. F., *The Cold War and Its Origins, 1917–1960*, Garden City, N.Y., 1961, 2 vols. A radical interpretation. Places the blame for the Cold War on the Western allies.

· Gatzke, H. W., *The Present in Perspective*, 3d ed., New Haven, 1965 (Rand McNally).

Gregg, Pauline, *The Welfare State: An Economic and Social History of Great Britain, 1945 to the Present Day*, Amherst, Mass., 1969.

· Halpern, Manfred, *The Politics of Social Change in the Middle East and North Africa*, Princeton, 1963 (Princeton University Press).

Issawi, Charles, *Egypt in Revolution: An Economic Analysis*, New York, 1963.

· Kolko, Gabriel, *The Politics of War*, New York, 1970 (Vintage).

Laski, H. J., *Reflections on the Revolution of Our Time*, New York, 1943. A discerning analysis not seriously marred by a Marxist viewpoint.

· Leckie, Robert, *Conflict: The History of the Korean War*, New York, 1962 (Avon). Emphasizes military history.

Lenczowski, George, *The Middle East in World Affairs*, Ithaca, N.Y., 1956.

Lyon, Peter, *Neutralism*, New York, 1963.

McCune, Shannon, *Korea's Heritage: A Regional and Social Geography*, Tokyo, 1956.

Macmillan, W. M., *Bantu, Boer, and Briton*, New York, 1963.

Mannheim, Karl, *Diagnosis of Our Time*, New York, 1944. A thoughtful study.

Marcuse, Herbert, *Counterrevolution and Revolt*, Boston, 1972.

· Mosely, Philip, *The Kremlin and World Politics*, New York, 1961 (Vintage).

· Popper, K. R., *The Open Society and Its Enemies*, New York, 1962 (Torchbook). A vigorous comparison of the totalitarian and democratic philosophies.

· Reves, Emery, *The Anatomy of Peace*, New York, 1945 (Compass). The most eloquent of pleas for a world republic.

Robinson, R. D., *The First Turkish Republic*, Cambridge, Mass., 1963.

· Seton-Watson, Hugh, *Neither War nor Peace: The Struggle for Power in the Post-War World*, London, 1960 (Frederick A. Praeger, rev. ed.).

· Spanier, John W., *The Truman-MacArthur Controversy and the Korean War*, Cambridge, 1959 (Norton Library).

Warth, R. D., *Soviet Russia in World Politics*, New York, 1963.

Wilmot, Chester, *The Struggle for Europe*, New York, 1952.

Young, Crawford, *Politics in the Congo: Decolonization and Independence*, Princeton, 1965.

SOURCE MATERIALS

Roosevelt, F. D., "The Four Freedoms," *Congressional Record*, Vol. 87, pp. 46–47.

U.N. Dept. of Public Information, *Yearbook of the United Nations*.

CHAPTER **31**

New Nations and Forces

There are some defeats more triumphant than victories.
—Montaigne, *Essays,* Chapter 30

Africa, all I ask from you is the courage to know: to look about you and see what is happening in this old and tired world; to realize the extent and depth of its rebirth and the promise which glows on your hills.
—W. E. B. Du Bois, *Autobiography*

It is a truism that the essence of the contemporary world is change. In a sense this has been true of all ages. But except for the Protestant Revolution and the French Revolution, few ages have witnessed so many drastic and sweeping changes as the time in which we now live. Few people in the present age can remember anything other than turbulence and confusion. And though they may glamorize the past as a time of tranquillity, a knowledge of recent history soon convicts them of self-deception.

Protracted change

I. THE ANTICOLONIAL REVOLT

One of the most conspicuous areas of change in recent times has been the revolt of colonies against their former rulers. Again, as it must be emphasized repeatedly in history, this development is nothing new. Colonies have rebelled against their mother countries since the American Revolution. The Irish revolt of 1798, though unsuccessful, was another example. So were the Greek revolt in 1821 and the Belgian revolt against the Dutch in 1830. This is not to forget the numerous revolutions in Latin America against both Spain and Portugal or the rebellion of the Southern states against the North in the 1860's. Yet numerous though these uprisings were, they did not match in intensity the revolutions of our time. Moreover, many of them were unsuccessful.

The early revolutions for independence

The Early Stirrings of Anticolonial Revolt. At first defeated in their efforts to subdue the Boer Republic, British might eventually won out in 1902 but not without considerable loss of prestige. The photo shows a line of Boer commandos.

The anticolonial revolt in the present age has taken the form in some cases of wars for independence, and in other cases of struggles within a country by discontented elements against a dominant group. Examples of the latter would include the revolts of the Czechs, Hungarians, and Poles against Soviet oppression in 1956, and the recent Irish revolt against British rule, which has raged from 1910 to the present. A number of revolts in our time have had a double character. The Algerian revolution affords an example. It began as an outbreak against greedy and domineering landlords in 1954. When the French came to the rescue of their kinsmen as a beleaguered master class, the rebels turned their revolt against the French government. The result was an independent Algeria in 1961.

Multifaceted revolts of the present age

2. THE DESTRUCTION OF THE BRITISH, DUTCH, AND FRENCH EMPIRES

From the standpoint of the old ruling classes the most serious of the upheavals after World War II was the liquidation of the British, Dutch, and French empires. This event was often regarded as a greater catastrophe than the threat of world communism. In fact, it was commonly thought of as a mere prelude to such a disaster. World communism, it was supposed, provided the drive and inspiration for most of the local revolutions. They could not have succeeded, it was argued, without generous external support.

Agitation to break up the old empires actually began before Russian communism cut much of a figure in world politics. Nationalism as far back as World War I was its genesis. The Allied doctrine

The liquidation of old empires

of "self-determination" produced an upsurge that eventually sealed the doom of most world empires. The peace conferences added encouragement to this upsurge when they granted independence to Czechs, Slovaks, Yugoslavs, and Poles. World War II provided an even stronger influence. Winston Churchill and Franklin D. Roosevelt parroted the Wilsonian doctrine when they drafted the Atlantic Charter. It was not strange that many a struggling "half-naked" and half-starved colony should have come to envisage itself as a full-fledged member of the family of nations.

The first empire to undergo liquidation in the anticolonial struggle was the British. Its main problem child was India. Rebel movements had harassed the representatives of British *raj* in that country throughout the nineteenth century. The flames of revolt burned more fiercely during World War I and after. World War II added more tinder. By 1945 anti-British resentment reached such a pitch that the country was ripe for revolution. Resolutions by nationalist bodies such as the Indian National Congress called upon Britain to "Quit India." The Congress took the position that India would fight only as a free nation without limitations imposed by the mother country. Protests and disturbances mounted more strongly than ever. It is noteworthy, however, that the foremost Indian nationalist leader, Mohandas K. Gandhi, did not approve of attacks on rulers and their institutions by violence. His methods were noncooperation and civil disobedience. By 1947, he and his friend and disciple, Jawaharlal Nehru, had gained such support that the British found it expedient to grant autonomy to India and her neighboring area, Pakistan. In 1950 the two countries organized themselves as independent republics. Meanwhile, an appalling tragedy overtook the Indian nationalists. Their saintly leader, Gandhi, was shot and killed by a reactionary chauvinist. The shocking deed should have brought the fanatics on all sides to their senses. Temporarily this was true, but the fire-eaters among both Hindus and Moslems soon renewed

THE DESTRUCTION OF THE BRITISH, DUTCH, AND FRENCH EMPIRES

The genesis of liquidation

The tragedies of Indian independence

Gandhi and Nehru at a Meeting of the All-India Conference in 1946

their frightful hatreds. Crazed fanatics, inflamed by religious bigotry and fearful of what their own future might be, set upon each other and beat and murdered indiscriminately. The most unfortunate victims were the refugees fleeing from one section to another after the Hindu-Pakistan partition had begun. Disorders continued to plague the two countries, finally resulting in a bloody civil war in 1971. East Pakistan seceded from West Pakistan, and became recognized as the independent nation of Bangla Desh.

In the meantime Great Britain had been constrained to give up most of the remaining portions of her empire. Over a period of years she liberated Ceylon, Malaysia, Mauritius, Fiji, Singapore, and Nauru, together with the New World territories of Guyana, Trinidad and Tobago, and Antigua. More significant was the forced liquidation of Egypt. In 1951 Egyptian nationalists compelled the British to withdraw all their troops from Egyptian territory. A year later a clique of nationalist army officers seized control of the government. They deposed the playboy king, Farouk, alleged to be subservient to the British, and proclaimed the state a republic. Soon thereafter the government passed under the control of Lieutenant Colonel Gamal Abdel Nasser, who ruled as a kind of benevolent dictator until his death in 1970. Though his domestic policies contributed somewhat to the benefit of his people, he was almost universally hated outside of the Arab and Soviet worlds for his belligerent and frightening foreign policies. With the collapse of British power in India and Egypt, to say nothing of the long chain of smaller dependencies, little was left of the grand empire on which "the sun never set" except Hong Kong, British Honduras, Gibraltar, Aden, and Southern Rhodesia—and even the status of some of these was uncertain.

The second of the European colonial empires to go down the drain was Indonesia. Known for more than two centuries as the Netherlands Indies, it was the most valuable jewel of the Dutch imperial crown. Indeed, it was one of the richest countries in the world in natural resources. When Japan extended her aggressions to Southeast Asia in 1941, the empire of the Dutch was one of her prize conquests. But toward the end of the war, nationalists, under the leadership of Sukarno, a one-time architect and flamboyant politician, rebelled and proclaimed Indonesia an independent republic. Although the Dutch attempted for four years to regain their sovereignty, the opposition of the natives proved too strong. In 1949 the kingdom of the Netherlands recognized the independence of their former colony.

Downfall of the
French empire:
the revolt of
Algeria

During the nineteenth century France pursued a strenuous effort to keep up with the British and the Dutch in building an overseas empire. On the whole she was successful. By exploiting the wealth and labor of her conquered possessions she managed to hold rich portions of Western and Central Africa and Southeast Asia. But her good fortune could not have been expected to last. Two of her richest colonies rebelled almost simultaneously: Algeria and Indochina. Algeria was inhabited by about 1,000,000 immigrants, mainly

EUROPE IN 1973

Members of NATO

Members of the Communist Bloc

THE MIDDLE EAST AND FAR EAST IN 1973

Members of the Communist Bloc

Members of the Southeast Asia
Treaty Organization

Anti-imperialist Revolt in Algeria, 1960. At Dar-es-Saada, Moslems take furniture from the homes of Europeans and burn it in the streets.

Frenchmen, in a total population of 10,300,000. These immigrants monopolized not only the government positions but also the best economic opportunities in industry, trade, and finance. The Arab and Berber inhabitants were chiefly peasants and laborers, though some, of course, maintained small shops in the native quarters of the large cities. In 1954 Arab and Berber nationalists rose in revolt when their demand for equal status with the French was denied by the government. The revolt continued its bloody course for seven years. It was complicated by the fact that many of the European settlers hated the French government almost as much as they did the Algerian nationalists. They were determined to keep Algeria "French" and feared a sellout by President Charles de Gaulle that would make the former colony independent and subject the immigrant governing class to the rule of the Arabs and Berbers. The upshot was a revolt by four French generals. They seized government buildings, arrested French officials, and threatened to invade France. De Gaulle proclaimed a state of emergency and ordered a total blockade of Algeria. In the face of such determined opposition the revolt collapsed. On a promise of self-government the nationalists laid down their arms in 1962. Additional sections of the French empire in North Africa were also whittled away after World War II. In 1955 the French gave up their protectorate over Morocco and allowed it to be organized as an independent kingdom. A short time afterward they renounced their protectorate over Tunisia, except for a naval and air base at Bizerte. The Tunisian government resisted and after a brief interval the U.N. commanded the French to give up the Bizerte base.

The struggle over Indochina was the most dramatic episode in the extinction of the French empire. We have noted before that Indochina was a casualty of Japanese conquests during World War II.

ARCTIC OCEAN

GREENLAND
(Den.)

ICELAND

ALASKA

CANADA

NEWFOUNDLAND

FR

SPAIN

PACIFIC

UNITED   STATES

BERMUDA
(Br.)

AZORES
(Sp.)

MOROCCO

HAWAII

MEXICO

BAHAMA IS. (Br.)

CUBA   HAITI
      DOMINICAN REP.
JAMAICA   PUERTO RICO (U.S.)

ATLANTIC

CANARY IS.
(Port.)

SP. SAHARA

AL

MAURITANIA   MALI

BR. HONDURAS

TRINIDAD AND
TOBAGO

GAMBIA
PORT. GUINEA

SENEGAL

UPPER
VOLTA

VENE-
ZUELA

GUYANA

SURINAM (Du.)

FR. GUIANA

GUINEA
SIERRA LEONE
LIBERIA

GHANA

COLOMBIA

IVORY COAST

TOGO
DAH

0   2000 miles at the equator

GALAPAGOS IS.
(Ecuad.)

ECUADOR

OCEAN

OCEAN

PERU

BRAZIL

ASCENCION I.
(Br.)

ST. HELENA I.
(Br.)

BOLIVIA

CHILE   PARAGUAY

URUGUAY

TRISTAN DA CUNHA
(Br.)

ARGENTINA

FALKLAND IS.
(Br.)

SOUTH GEORGIA I.
(Br.)

BOL
(

SOUTH SANDWICH IS.
(Br.)

THE DECLINE OF COLONIALISM AFTER WORLD WAR II

Territories gaining independence during postwar period

ARCTIC OCEAN

UNION OF SOVIET SOCIALIST REPUBLICS

MONGOLIA

SAKHALIN

ALEUTIAN IS.

TURKEY
LEBANON
ISRAEL
SYRIA
IRAQ
IRAN
AFGHAN-
ISTAN
PAKISTAN

N. KOREA
S. KOREA
JAPAN

PEOPLE'S REPUBLIC OF CHINA

PACIFIC

JORDAN
U.A.R.
(EGYPT)

BYA

SAUDI
ARABIA

NEPAL
E. PAK.

INDIA

RYUKYU IS. (Jap.)

TAIWAN

PACIFIC TRUST TERRITORY
OF THE U.S.

CHAD

SUDAN

BURMA
LAOS
N. VIET.

THAILAND

CAMB.
S. VIET.

PHILIPPINES

GUAM (U.S.)

FR. SOMALILAND

CENT.
AFRICAN
REP.

ETHIOPIA

CEYLON

SOMALIA

MALAYSIA

Equator

RWANDA
UGANDA
DEM. REP.
OF THE
CONGO
KENYA
BURUNDI

INDIAN

NEW HEBRIDES

INDONESIA

SOLOMON
IS.

OCEAN

TANZANIA

OCEAN

TIMOR

GOLA
'ork)

ZAMBIA

MALAWI

MALAGASY

NEW CALEDONIA

RHODESIA
BOTSWANA

MOZAMBIQUE
(Port.)

AUSTRALIA

SOUTH
AFRICA
SWAZILAND

LESOTHO

NEW ZEALAND

PRINCE EDWARD I.
(S. Afr.)

CROUZET IS.
(Fr.)

EUROPE

FAEROE JS.
(Den.)

SWEDEN

NORWAY

FINLAND

IRELAND

UNITED KINGDOM

DENMARK

NETH.
BELG.
W.
GER.
E.
GER.
POLAND

UNION OF SOVIET
SOCIALIST REPUBLICS

LUX.
CZECHO.

FRANCE

SWITZ.
AUST.
HUNG.
ROMANIA

YUGOSLAVIA

ITALY

BULGARIA

PORT.
SPAIN

ALB.

GREECE

TURKEY

After the defeat of Japan in 1945 France sought to recover her lost empire. Her efforts ended in failure. She was immediately confronted by a rebellion of Vietnamese nationalists under the leadership of Ho Chi Minh. The rebels resorted to guerrilla warfare and inflicted such costly defeats upon the French that the latter decided to abandon the struggle. An agreement was signed at Geneva in 1954 providing for the division of Vietnam into two zones, pending elections to determine the future government of the entire country. Ho Chi Minh became President of North Vietnam and established his capital at Hanoi. His followers, who came to be called Viet Cong, were numerous in both halves of the country. Had elections been held as provided by the Geneva Agreement, Ho Chi Minh would probably have been elected President of all of Vietnam. But the government of South Vietnam, backed by the United States, refused to permit the elections to be held.

From this point on, involvement by the United States in the Vietnamese civil war steadily increased. President Kennedy seemed to be convinced that the Chinese Communist juggernaut would soon roll over all of Southeast Asia. The first victims would be Vietnam, Laos, Cambodia, Malaysia, and Singapore. Then would come Thailand, Burma, and India. How far Kennedy would have gone in his crusade against communism had he escaped the assassin's bullet in 1963 is impossible to say with certainty. Kennedy's successor, Lyndon B. Johnson, seemed to think that a relatively small force of perhaps 100,000 men would be sufficient to defeat the enemies of the South Vietnamese and drive them back into their own country. No consideration was given to the fact that these enemies were solidly entrenched in both states of Vietnam, and that they had been waging a bitter national struggle for upwards of eighteen years. They had succeeded in driving out the French in 1954 and were not likely to surrender to a new invader, as they conceived the Americans to be. The Viet Cong and the North Vietnam regulars were poorly armed and poorly equipped. They had no air force or navy and little or no artillery. Nevertheless, they fought the South Vietnamese and their American allies to a standstill on several occasions. During the Tet offensive of 1968 they came close to capturing Saigon, the South Vietnamese capital.

Exasperated by failure to win an easy victory in South Vietnam, the American civilian and military chiefs determined upon aerial bombing. A series of incidents in 1964 provided the justification. Reports, of doubtful veracity, indicated that North Vietnamese ships had attacked American naval vessels in Tonkin Gulf. President Johnson pronounced these incidents acts of war and immediately obtained from Congress authorization to use whatever measures necessary to repel Communist aggression. Soon afterward the first American bombers unloaded their first cargoes upon towns and villages occupied by the North Vietnamese and the Viet Cong. Although evidence increased casting doubt on the efficacy of these raids, they continued to be used. It has been estimated that at least as much tonnage in bombs was dropped on tiny Vietnam as was unloaded by the Allied forces on all of Germany in World War II. But still the deadly onslaught continued. The only answer of those responsible for strategy in Washington and Saigon seems to have been "Cover up the failure by escalating the war." As the struggle entered its fifth year, with no end in sight, disillusionment spread throughout the United States. Criticism of President Johnson was so harsh in 1968 that he was forced to abandon his plans to run for a second term.

Johnson's successor, Richard M. Nixon, was elected on the strength of promises to end the war. But this turned out to be a shadowy promise. While ground troops were being withdrawn from Vietnam, in May 1970, the United States invaded Cambodia and a few months later the kingdom of Laos. In April 1972, the North Vietnamese, with massive aid from Russia and China, launched a powerful counteroffensive with the apparent objective of conquering South Vietnam and driving all foreign armies out of the country. A number of South Vietnamese strongholds were captured and the offensive seemed more dangerous than the famous Tet offensive of 1968. Nixon countered with increased bombing of North Vietnam's factories and railroads and by mining its harbors. The stalemate continued until a few weeks before the United States presidential election in November 1972, when Nixon's adviser, Henry Kissinger, was sent to hold secret negotiations with North Vietnamese officials. A few days before the election, Nixon was able to declare that "peace was at hand." How quickly after his re-election peace would be a reality remained to be seen.

The Nixon policies

3. THE THIRD WORLD

Closely related to the extinction of the old empires has been the growth of what is often called the Third World. The expression "Third World" was originally popularized by Charles de Gaulle, who used it around 1949 to designate his followers who opposed the Fourth Republic. When he came to power a short time later, he endowed the expression with a broader meaning. The expression has since come to be restricted to the emergent, underdeveloped countries of the world, especially of Africa and Asia. Examples would include India, West Pakistan, Bangla Desh, and Indonesia. Most countries of the Third World have been products of the revolutionary conditions that followed World War II. For this reason many were inclined for a time to throw in their lot with the Communist half of the postwar world. Latterly, however, most of these attitudes have faded, leaving each state with discretion to go its own way.

Origin of the term "Third World"

Standards of living and stages of economic development are by no means uniform throughout the world. This has been nortoriously true since the end of World War II. A relatively small number of nations, mostly in Europe and the Western Hemisphere but including also Japan, sit on top of the world and enjoy the fruits of modern science and technology. Their wealth enables them to command the resources of the earth whether the tin of Bolivia, the fruits of the tropics, or the oil of Arabia and Indonesia. Illustrations can be found in the Gross National Product and the literacy figures for various nations. At the end of the 1960's Great Britain and West Germany each had a GNP of $1500 per capita. The less developed countries for the same period had an average per capita GNP of about $200. Comparative literacy figures for developed and underdeveloped countries also have significant meaning. Percentages of literacy for such countries as Denmark, the Netherlands, and the United States were 100 per cent or slightly lower. For such underdeveloped nations as India it was 30 per cent, for the Sudan 19 per cent, and for Pakistan 16 per cent. Obviously these percentages must be qualified by the effects of immigration and emigration and in some cases by the tyranny and neglect of former rulers. Yet poverty has doubtless been the major influence holding back economic and cultural progress.

4.   THE UPSURGE OF AFRICA

For some years after World War II it appeared that the most volatile countries of the world would turn out to be the new states of Africa. Most of them were imbued with a new consciousness of their importance and determined to win for themselves a place befitting their destiny. They had been influenced by talk of independence at the end of the war and by the success of several struggles for self-rule in other parts of the world.

If any one country could be considered the leader of the African colonial revolt, it was Ghana, formerly called the Gold Coast, a colony of Great Britain. In 1954 Britain granted self-government, and in 1960 Ghana became a republic. Leadership of the Ghana independence movement was at that time supplied by Kwame Nkrumah. The son of an illiterate goldsmith, he obtained an education in the United States and in England. He returned to his homeland in 1948 and became a nationalist agitator. Though he classified himself as a Marxist, he denied being a Communist. Yet he admired Lenin and generally looked to Moscow for support of his policies rather than to London or Washington. Apparently the key to his thinking was opposition to imperialism. He considered it preposterous that the Negroes of Central Africa, with their proud traditions of an ancient culture, should be ruled by Europeans. He regaled his followers with stories of a Golden Age in Africa, whose cultural center was in Timbuctoo, with a great university manned by distinguished scholars. For a time Nkrumah ruled benevolently even after converting the nation into a one-party state. He established hospitals and schools and raised the literacy standards. Accused of extravagance and cor-

Kwame Nkrumah (center, seated) and Members of His Government in Ghana

ruption, he was deposed by a revolt of army officers in 1966. He was driven from his homeland and forced to take refuge in Guinea. He died there in 1972.

The most violent of the revolts in Central Africa occurred in the Congo, where there was not simply one previous colony but two. The smaller is now the People's Republic of the Congo. Though granted nominal independence in 1960, it is still under the influence of France and the People's Republic of China. Conditions in the larger Congo, now called Zaire, which was at one time a colony of Belgium, have been more serious. Fearing an outbreak of violence among her disaffected colonial subjects, Belgium, in 1960, granted them independence. This was the signal for the beginning of a series of rebellions and assassinations that raged for more than five years. A chief cause of the flaming disorders centered in the southeastern province of Katanga. Here were located rich copper resources controlled by Belgian capitalists. At one time the copper mines of Katanga had produced revenues sufficient to defray one-half the costs of the colonial government. In July 1960, Katanga seceded and attempted to gain control of the entire country. In the revolt several former premiers and other high officers were murdered. The U.N. Security Council sent a contingent to guard against revival of civil war. Strong-man rule was revived by President Mobutu, and a degree of stability was ultimately restored.

In most other sections of Central and Eastern Africa there was at least the illusion of tranquillity. Such countries as Nigeria and Kenya seemed like good examples. Both were former British colonies. Some authorities held that British colonial administration was wiser than that of most other European empires. Whereas the French and Belgians withheld self-government as long as they could, and then granted it suddenly, the British brought their colonies to independence more gradually. Many local leaders were trained in administration and knew how to deal with intricate problems before they actually arose. Yet even in Nigeria the familiar charges of corruption and inefficiency led to the murder of the Premier and the overthrow of the government in 1966. After more assassinations a military government seized control. Within a year the Eastern Region seceded and proclaimed itself the Republic of Biafra. Civil war followed and harassed the country for three years. The total of casualties was enormous. More than 1,000,000 people lost their lives. Thousands were killed in battle, but many more died of starvation. The rebels capitulated in 1970. From every standpoint the war was a tragedy. Nigeria is one of the most richly endowed of African countries. Its natural resources include oil and natural gas, coal, and the world's greatest abundance of columbium (used in steel manufacturing).

Also hovering on the verge of tragedy has been the recent history of Kenya, a country of East Africa lying athwart the Equator. Unlike Nigeria, Kenya is a poor country. The whole northern three-

The revolt in the Congo

Civil War in Nigeria

855

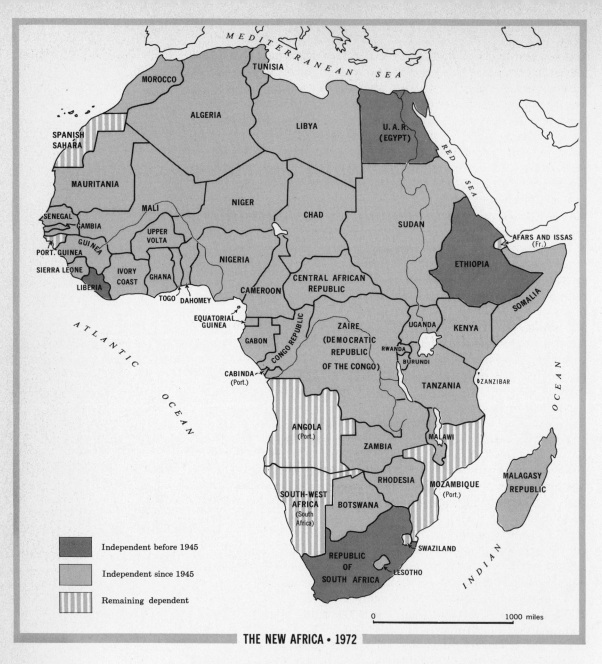

THE NEW AFRICA · 1972

Independent before 1945

Independent since 1945

Remaining dependent

0   1000 miles

**Conditions
in Kenya**

fifths of the territory is barren and almost waterless. Sections can
be found in which there is no rainfall whatever for years at a time.
The only well-watered sections are in the South and along the coast.
It follows that agricultural resources are limited. The staple crops
include coffee, sisal, tea, and wheat. Sugar cane, maize, tobacco, and
cotton are also grown. Most of the farms are small, and white men
often work alongside the Negroes in order to make farming succeed.
World War II brought in thousands of Indians as settlers in Kenya.
They did not become farmers or artisans, but settled in the cities

856

and towns as petty traders. Despite their low standard of living and their meager profits they encouraged the indifferent Negroes to substitute a money economy for the age-old system of barter. By 1970 there were 65,000 Indians in Kenya in a total population of 10½ million.

The population of Kenya has never been closely unified. Tribal jealousies are rampant and sometimes break into open conflict. These jealousies seem not to be based on economic competition or greed. They appear rather to spring from ancient differences rooted in cultural characteristics and hatreds from the past. The most serious of these conflicts broke into the open in 1952 when the Mau Mau rebellion occurred. The Mau Mau were an offshoot of the Kikuyu tribe who believed that their tribe had been restricted in its need for land. They instituted a reign of terror throughout the country against white settlers and all of their kinsmen who sympathized with the colonial government. By 1958 the revolt was suppressed, and five years later the country obtained independence.

The Mau Mau

The native leader who has done most to promote the growth and progress of Kenya has been Jomo Kenyatta, President of his country since 1963. Now over eighty years of age, he has devoted a long career to the defense of his homeland against the white man's exploitation. In 1952 he was thrown into prison for seven years as a Mau Mau leader and a dangerous enemy of the state. His imprisonment seems to have done more to educate him in the realities of politics than to imbue him with hatred of his captors. While in prison he developed his philosophy of African socialism. Although for a time Kenyatta had studied at Moscow University, he adopted almost none of the trappings of Soviet communism. Instead his socialism bore a closer resemblance to that of the British or the Scandinavian countries. He urged his followers to forget the wrongs of the past and to concentrate on building a better world for the future. This future would be found in avoiding affiliations with either the East or the West. The African way has little in common with either capitalism or communism. The sharp antagonisms of class that exist in Europe and America have not been conspicuous elements in the African tradition. African socialism, according to Kenyatta, cannot be based on a dictatorship of the proletariat or any other form of class rule. Rather, its aim should be to prevent the seizure of power by individuals or groups armed with economic power. Its aim should be to enable every mature citizen to participate fully and equally in political affairs. Such is the essence of democracy and also of African socialism, according to Kenyatta's conception.

Jomo Kenyatta Addressing an All-Africa Congress in London

What will happen to Kenya when the aging Kenyatta passes from the scene, no one can predict. He is undoubtedly one of the greatest statesmen East Africa has produced. In his attitude toward guns and swords as the foundation of power, he resembles no one so much as the late Indian statesman Jawaharlal Nehru. Yet Kenyatta has not been able to solve the problem of tribalism in his own country. He

The uncertain future of Kenya

has preached that every man has the right to take pride in the culture and customs of his tribe. But apparently this sentiment must not be carried so far as to endanger the unity of the state. In 1969 his government was forced to deal with a violent revolt by the Kikuyu representing the impoverished North. After threats to disrupt national unity, their political party, the KPU, was banned and a number of its leaders confined in prison. More recently, disgruntled politicians are accused of plotting to seize Kenyatta's mantle of power whenever he is forced to surrender it by death or disability.

5. THE GROWTH OF BLACK MILITANCY

The growth of insurgency among blacks has been predominantly an American movement. Through most of the years from the Civil War to 1900 Negroes were an abject and docile race. Emancipation and the Thirteenth and Fourteenth Amendments brought little change in this attitude. Such changes might have been postponed indefinitely had it not been for the migration of Southern Negroes northward in search of more freedom and better employment opportunities. Thousands came around 1910 and many more thousands during World War I. For the most part, their fate was deplorable. During the war years they benefited from the shortage of labor in industrial cities, but during the postwar depression they were the first to be trampled underfoot.

The year 1919 saw the rise to prominence of the first Negro Messiah. He was Marcus Garvey, a native of Jamaica. Toward the end of the war he made his way to New York City and gained fame among the downcast members of his race for his torrential eloquence. His philosophy had a broad appeal, especially to those outside the "mulatto aristocracy." He fought to gain for the depressed masses a resplendent place in the sun. He rejected the very term "Negro" and taught his followers to refer to themselves as "blacks." He claimed that they were descendants of the "greatest and proudest race who ever peopled the earth." He whipped up enthusiasm for a vast empire in Africa to which Negroes would emigrate. But he closed his career under a cloud. He was convicted of using the mails to defraud, spent two years in the Atlanta penitentiary, and was deported.

Marcus Garvey

Yet Garvey's life was not a failure. He encouraged the Negro Renaissance, or Harlem Renaissance, in the 1920's. Several of its leaders derived inspiration from him, notably Langston Hughes and Countee Cullen. Garvey's philosophy also extended indirectly to the Black Muslim movement through his influence on the father of its most vigorous proselytizer, Malcolm X. Malcolm X was converted in prison by his brother to the religion of Islam. After his release he became a spokesman for Elijah Muhammad, founder of the movement. Most of his followers were people of the same background who had flocked to Garvey's standard—recent migrants from the Deep

South who now lived in hopeless poverty in the black ghettos of Northern cities. Malcolm X attempted to overcome their feeling of helplessness by giving them a new religion to take the place of the white man's Christianity and by restoring black pride. This new religion was Islam, which Malcolm X described as the true faith of Africans. Though he and his followers were firm believers, they were not generally fanatics. They did not renounce worldliness as a life of sin. They urged Negroes to pool their resources and establish black-owned businesses. This would help them to overcome their weakness and lack of status. They taught their adherents to avoid aggression and to fight only when attacked. Their charismatic minister broke with the Black Muslims in 1964. In February 1965 he was shot and killed as he started to speak at a rally in Harlem. The Black Muslim movement rapidly declined.

In the meantime black militancy branched out into new forms. One was the Congress of Racial Equality (CORE) founded by James Farmer, a leader of the Fellowship of Reconciliation, in 1942. His announced aim was to translate "love of God and man" into specific crusades against injustice. By 1950 it began to combine its efforts with those of other protest organizations seeking to end discrimination against Negroes. It helped in promoting "Freedom Rides" for civil rights and boycotts against stubborn whites. After 1955 Farmer often collaborated with Martin Luther King, Jr., a young Baptist minister with a Ph.D. from Harvard. Like Farmer, King also embraced the Gandhian philosophy of nonviolence. For more than ten years he was widely regarded—and feared—as the most effective defender of Negro rights. However, his career was brought to an end by an assassin's bullet as he stood on the balcony of a motel in Memphis in 1968.

Important successors to King, Farmer, and in a sense the Black Muslims, were the Black Panthers. Their story is not simple, mainly because they have been the product of varying influences. The movement began during the civil rights confrontations of the 1950's and 1960's in Alabama and Mississippi. From there it rapidly spread northward and about 1968 established its headquarters in Oakland, California. Its leaders—such men as Huey Newton, Bobby Seale, and Eldridge Cleaver—adopted for their party the name of Black Panthers. They saw in the panther an animal slow to take the aggressive but fierce in retaliation when attacked by its enemies.

The Black Panthers differed from other Negro militants in a number of ways. First of all, they were frankly revolutionary. They believed that only by seizing power could they redress society's wrongs. They adopted Mao Tse-tung's slogan that "All power comes from the mouth of a gun." Second, the Black Panthers, unlike so many of their forerunners, are not pro-African. They struggle for a free America, not for some mythical empire in Africa. Finally, the Black Panthers profess a kind of internationalism similar to that of other revolutionaries. They will not fight for any white empire, re-

THE GROWTH OF BLACK MILITANCY

Martin Luther King, Jr.

Rise of the Black Panthers

Other doctrines of the Black Panthers

859

gardless of how benevolent it may claim to be. In connection with the United States draft, they seem to have originated the slogan "Hell no, we won't go!"

The chief factor in the growing dynamism of the Black Panthers was disillusionment with the failures of conciliation and nonviolence. Other leaders had attempted, during the 1950's, to gain rights for the Negroes, and even the privilege of registering to vote in Southern states, by peaceful means; and to what avail? Scores of marchers and demonstrators were beaten and murdered. Neither the age nor the sex of the victims mattered. Four small girls were killed when a segregationist mob bombed a Negro church in Birmingham. No effective attempt was made by law enforcement authorities to bring the murderers to justice. But while disillusionment helped add to the Black Panthers' ranks, the movement has not been an unqualified success. It has suffered from constant harassment from the police, and as a revolutionary organization it has been torn by conflicts over methods and objectives. Several of its leaders have been caught in the bloody crossfire of internal warfare and by the savage persecution of external opponents. Recently many Panthers have turned their attention to self-improvement and raising the social and intellectual status of their own members.

6. CONFLICT IN THE MIDDLE EAST

When World War I ended, the country now known as Israel was a province of Turkey. Its population was about 70 per cent Arab and 30 per cent Jewish and Christian. By the defeat of Turkey in 1918, it was made a mandate of the League of Nations under the guardianship of Great Britain. In the meantime, Zionists in Britain and the United States worked zealously to convert Palestine into a national home for the Jewish people. In return for their labors the British government issued the famous Balfour Declaration promising to view with favor the establishment in Palestine of a national home for Jewish people. At the same time provision would be made for safeguarding the rights of non-Jewish communities in Palestine.

On the basis of the Balfour Declaration, Britain accepted the mandate for Palestine. She promised as she did so not merely to establish a Jewish National Home, but "to secure the preservation of an Arab National Home and to apprentice the people of Palestine as a whole in the art of self-government." It was an optimistic ambition, but at the time optimism seemed justified. In fact, for a period of ten years there was every reason to expect that the undertaking would be successful. Palestine prospered as never before in its history. Factories were built, land was reclaimed, irrigation works were constructed, the Jordan River was harnessed for electric power, and unemployment disappeared from the face of the land. Except for rioting in Jaffa in 1921, no incident of violence occurred to disturb the general tranquillity. The aspect of the country was so peaceful that in 1926 the British reduced their armed forces to a single RAF squadron and two companies with armored cars.

By 1929, however, evidences of disharmony had begun to appear in the land that was holy to three great religions. The Jews were too prosperous and well-educated and were arousing the envy and fears of the Arabs by their high standard of living and their more strenuous competition. Their purchases of land, in many cases from absentee owners, had resulted in the displacement of thousands of Arab cultivators and had thrown them into the cities at a time when the Great Depression was beginning to make unemployment a serious problem. But the major cause of Arab foreboding was the steady increase in the Jewish population. The opportunity to emigrate to Palestine had offered a greater temptation than the Arabs had expected. As a consequence, some of them foresaw a relentless advance and expansion of Europeans and Americans, backed by foreign capital and flaunting a culture that was alien to the ways of the Arab majority. In 1929, 1930, and 1931 armed attacks were waged upon Jewish settlements followed by terrorist murders.

But these episodes paled into insignificance when compared with the bloody violence that followed. When the mandate was established, no one could have foreseen the desperate plight that was to overtake the European Jews with the accession of the Nazis to power in Germany. As news of the persecutions spread, it was inevitable that pressure should be brought upon the British government to relax the barriers against immigration into Palestine. During the period 1933–1935 the admission of more than 130,000 Jewish immigrants was authorized, and uncounted thousands more came in illicitly. From this time on Palestine was a seething caldron of violence and warfare. The Arabs rose in open rebellion against the mandate. Organized terrorism swept the country. Guerrilla at-

The development of conflicts between Jews and Arabs

Rebellion of the Arabs against the mandate

Immigration to Palestine. Left: British soldiers guard the shore as a ship loaded with unauthorized refugees attempts to land in 1947. Right: A view of the unbearably crowded conditions aboard ships bringing refugees to Palestine.

Termination of the
mandate and
establishment of
the State of Israel

tacks in the rural areas and looting, burning, and sabotage in the towns and cities kept the whole population in turmoil. By 1938 Britain had 20,000 troops in Palestine, and even these were unable to maintain order.

The early years of World War II were characterized by relative quiet in Palestine. Both sides were subdued in some measure by fears that the war would spread, but the primary reason was the White Paper of 1939, which the British government issued a few months before the conflict began. In this document Britain envisioned the "establishment within ten years of an independent Palestine State," with protection for the "essential interests" of both Jews and Arabs, and a government in which both peoples would share. Meanwhile, land purchases from Arabs were to be restricted, and the number of Jews admitted to Palestine was to be limited to 75,000. Though the plan was unfavorably received by the Mandates Commission of the League of Nations, it seemed to allay the fears of the Arabs and to give them a ray of hope that their interests would be protected. But trouble broke out anew when a conference of American Zionists at the Biltmore Hotel in New York, in May 1942, adopted the so-called Biltmore Program, repudiating the White Paper of 1939 and demanding the establishment of a Jewish state and a Jewish army in Palestine. Soon afterward both Jews and Arabs prepared for war to the hilt. Fanatical Zionists, as well as Arabs, resorted to the use of terrorist methods. Illegal military organizations sprang up on both sides and devoted their energies to raiding, burning, and assassination.

In April 1947 the British government referred the Palestine problem to the United Nations and announced that a year later it would terminate the mandate and withdraw all its troops from the country. On May 15, 1948, the British mandate came to an end, and on the same day a Jewish provisional government proclaimed the establishment of an independent State of Israel. Elections were held for a Constituent Assembly, which met in February of the following year and adopted a temporary constitution for a democratic republic. Its chief features were a weak president, a strong cabinet, and a powerful parliament. It was clearly intended that the last two agencies should really govern the country. The cabinet was vested with general direction of the legislative process as well as with executive authority. But the parliament, or Knesset, would exercise independent legislative power, and could overturn cabinets which no longer enjoyed its confidence. The constitution also provided for proportional representation, a unicameral parliament, and universal suffrage for Jews and Arabs alike. A unique element in the system was the close association of religion with the state. Marriage and divorce were placed under the exclusive jurisdiction of religious courts—Jewish, Christian, or Moslem as the affiliation of the parties might require.

Israeli Tanks Move into Jerusalem. A scene during the second Arab-Israeli War, June 1967.

Meanwhile, from the day of proclaimed independence until the spring of 1949, Israel and its Arab neighbor countries were at war. United Nations efforts brought about truces several times, but nothing lasting was achieved until Israel and Egypt signed a general armistice agreement in February 1949; Jordan and Syria also signed armistices in April. The United Nations peace effort was at first under the direction of Count Folke Bernadotte of Sweden; when he was assassinated in September 1948, by Israeli extremists in Jerusalem, it was continued by Dr. Ralph Bunche of the United States. The status at the cease-fire was regarded as a victory for Israel and a defeat for the Arab powers; neither, however, accepted it as final. Violent incidents continued to occur, including retaliatory massacres.

The Arab-Israeli wars

Despite her troubles with the Arabs, Israel strengthened her economy, and many new industries were created. Large sums of money flowed into the country as a result of West German restitution for the outrages of Nazism. Agriculture advanced to a stage sufficient to supply the needs of the home market while export crops such as olives, melons, and citrus fruits were rapidly developed. Land under cultivation more than doubled between 1955 and 1967. The index of industrial production increased from 100 in 1963 to 185 in 1969. The nation had seven universities, two with more than 10,000 students each. Total enrollment in all state schools had increased from 130,000 in 1948 to approximately 800,000 in 1970.

Progress of Israel

Yet the fate of Israel was not a happy one. Trouble brewed in Sinai in 1967 until President Nasser resolved to teach the Jewish nation a lesson. He formed alliances with Jordan and Syria and vowed that Israel must be wiped from the map. Nasser closed Aqaba, Israel's only direct outlet to the Red Sea. The Israelis responded with a lightning war against Egypt and her Arab allies. The Egyptian and

The Six-Day War

863

Syrian forces were routed in six days, and the Syrians accepted a cease-fire a short time later. But cease-fire did not spell peace. New outbreaks flared sporadically for more than two years. The conditions for peace were really nonexistent. The Arabs were tormented by loss of confidence and fearful of their own future as a result of their staggering defeat. The Israelis were obsessed with security and determined to preserve it regardless of cost. It was an impasse from which no one could be sure of a way of escape. Until that impasse could be ended, the two sides would doubtless continue hurling their desperate threats against each other. But how long the two peoples could live under the condition of a "high-noon showdown" no one could predict.

SELECTED READINGS

· *Items so designated are available in paperbound editions.*

Cady, J. F., *Southeast Asia: Its Historical Development*, New York, 1964.

Duncanson, Dennis J., *Government and Revolution in Vietnam*, New York, 1968.

· Erikson, E. H., *Gandhi's Truth: On the Origins of Militant Nonviolence*, New York, 1969 (Norton).

· Fontaine, Andre, *History of the Cold War*, New York, 1970–1971 (Vintage), 2 vols.

· Gettleman, Marvin E., ed., *Viet Nam: History, Documents, and Opinions on a Major World Crisis*, New York, 1965 (Fawcett).

Hammer, E. J., *The Struggle for Indochina*, Stanford, 1954.

Hensler, Robert, *The British in Northern Nigeria*, New York, 1968.

Hoskins, H. L., *The Middle East*, New York, 1954.

Issawi, Charles, *Egypt in Revolution: An Economic Analysis*, New York, 1963.

July, Robert W., *A History of the African People*, New York, 1970. An excellent history of Black Africa.

· Kahin, George M., and Lewis, John W., *The United States in Vietnam*, New York, 1967 (Delta).

Khouri, Fred J., *The Arab-Israeli Dilemma*, Syracuse, N.Y., 1968.

Kochanek, Stanley A., *The Congress Party of India*, Princeton, 1968.

Lenczowski, George, *The Middle East in World Affairs*, Ithaca, 1956.

Low, Francis, *The Struggle for Asia*, New York, 1956.

McCune, Shannon, *Korea's Heritage: A Regional and Social Geography*, Tokyo, 1956.

Macmillan, W. M., *Bantu, Boer, and Briton*, New York, 1963.

Nogueira, Franco, *The Third World*, London, 1968.

Okpaku, Joseph, *Nigeria, Dilemma of Nationhood: An African Analysis of the Biafran Conflict*, Westport, Conn., 1970.

Payne, Robert, *The Life and Death of Mahatma Gandhi*, New York, 1969.

Rossi, Mario, *The Third World*, New York, 1963.

· Ward, Barbara, *The Rich Nations and the Poor Nations*, New York, 1962 (Norton).

Weisbord, Robert G., *African Zion. The Attempt to Establish a Jewish Colony in the East Africa Protectorate*, Philadelphia, 1968.

Wingo, Lowdon, Jr., *Africa: Social Change and Mental Health*, London, 1959.

Worsley, Peter, *The Third World*, 2d ed., Chicago, 1970.

Young, Crawford, *Politics in the Congo: Decolonization and Independence*, Princeton, 1965.

· Zinn, Howard, *Vietnam: The Logic of Withdrawal*, Boston, 1967.

CHAPTER 32

The Revolution of Our Age

The love of money as a possession . . . will be recognized for
what it is, a somewhat disgusting morbidity, one of those semi-
criminal, semi-pathological propensities which one hands over with
a shudder to the specialists in mental disease.
—John Maynard Keynes, *Essays in Persuasion*, Part V

Revolutions have never lightened the burden of tyranny; they
have only shifted it to another shoulder.
—George Bernard Shaw, *Revolutionist's Handbook*

When World War I broke out Sir Edward Grey, British Foreign
Secretary, stood at the window of his office in Whitehall and com-
mented sadly to a friend, "The lamps are going out all over Europe."
Sir Edward Grey, later Viscount Grey, lived until 1933. Had he
survived a few more decades, he might well have considered his
early comment increasingly appropriate. The lamps have been going
out not only all over Europe but all over the world. Revolutions,
violent uprisings, degradation of long-standing customs and institutions, and frightening rivalries between superstates all emphasize the
prevailing uncertainty and confusion. Even as late as the 1970's fears
and anxieties had little abated. To a host of questions no one knew
the answers. Would economic stability eventually be restored? Or
was it merely a flimsy product of war and armaments expansion?
Would the balance of terror postpone indefinitely World War III,
or, as more and more countries crashed their way into the "Nuclear
Club," would some power-hungry dictator precipitate a conflict
that would engulf the globe? These and many similar issues tormented the minds of a whole generation, especially those who distrusted the past and doubted the possibilities of the future.

*The world of
uncertainty and
discouragement*

I. POLITICAL REVOLUTION

The political world of the 1970's bore only a faint resemblance to
that which had existed in the nineteenth century, or even to that
before World War II. It was sometimes assumed that the only

865

essential difference was a change in the relationships among the great powers. A mere handful of powerful nations, under the leadership of Great Britain, had kept the world in order and dictated the terms of existence to the non-Caucasian peoples. But this system began to break down with the two world wars of the twentieth century. By 1970 it was little more than a memory. Britain's empire was gone, and so were the empires of France, Belgium, and the Netherlands. Some Americans think that *their* country should take over the one-time role of Great Britain as arbiter of the destinies of the globe, but they fail to realize that the role is extinct, and that no one nation or small group of nations is capable of reviving it. The spread of nuclear weapons and the fact of mutual destructiveness have put an effective end to that.

The replacement
of trust and
confidence by
suspicion and fear

Before 1914 a balance of power among the strongest nations was, as we have seen, the world's chief reliance for preserving the peace. World Wars I and II substituted international organization for the balance of power. Now for all practical purposes both are gone. Attitudes of distrust have poisoned the relations of those formerly embarked on similar aims. The revival of a nationalism based on suspicion and hatred and motives of aggrandizement have precluded more than minimal cooperation in raising standards of living and educational advancement. The new attitude of the chief nations was illustrated by what happened on the twenty-fifth anniversary of the United Nations. The day was signalized by the resumption of massive nuclear testing by the United States, the U.S.S.R., and the People's Republic of China. The event was probably a coincidence but a most unfortunate one. It symbolized not only the preoccupation of the chief powers with military strength but also their "indifference to the principles of the United Nations." [1]

By an interesting paradox governments of recent times with the strongest commitments to democracy have often been just as autocratic in their actual operation as governments making no pretense to popular rule. The government of the Third Republic in France was no more wise and temperate in dealing with its enemies, whom it sent to Devil's Island, than was the Tsar of Russia in exiling political prisoners to Siberia. The government of Imperial Germany was hardly much more autocratic than some of the governments of its wartime opponents. Though far removed from democracy, it was preserved from rank autocracy by the rule that every German official must exercise his powers in conformity with definite codes of law. But the zenith of arbitrary rule by so-called civilized governments has been reached in the years since World War II.[2] Most governments have been offenders and the gravity of the offenses has usually varied in direct proportion to the wealth and proportion of the nation committing them. To illustrate, the occupation of Czecho-

---

[1] James Reston, *New York Times*, Oct. 16, 1970.

[2] Mr. Justice Douglas has described today's Establishment as "the new George III." *Points of Rebellion*, New York, 1971, p. 85.

slovakia by the Soviets in 1968 had no more legal justification than did the similar actions committed by the Nazis in 1938–1939. In like manner the practice of waging war without the formality of a declaration by the legislative body, as was done by the United States in Korea, Vietnam, Cambodia, and Laos, exemplifies the growing power of the executive at the expense of the legislative, even to the extreme of usurpation. Executive power has mounted in other areas also. Both the President of the United States and the Prime Minister of Great Britain can rule virtually in defiance of Congress and Parliament. The latter have become mere ratifying bodies, with power over both the making and execution of laws concentrated in the hands of the executive.

Executives have undergone accretions of power in a number of other ways. Presidents of the United States, for instance, assumed the sponsorship, each in his turn, of some broad and colorful program for the national welfare. For John F. Kennedy it was the New Frontier, for Lyndon B. Johnson, the Great Society, and for Richard M. Nixon, the New Federalism. Regardless of its label, a President's program covers almost everything he might want the government to adopt during his term of office. It would include his tariff and internal revenue policies, his plans for the national budget and for increasing or reducing the public debt, his hopes for dealing with relief and unemployment and his schemes for subsidizing agriculture and crippled industries. In recent years, however, the majority of these programs have been tied in closely with the military, and their nature has been conditioned by the needs of rearmament and hostile combat.

The increase of executive power

None but extremists woud agree with Tolstoi that the modern state is nothing but "Genghis Khan with the telegraph." For the rulers of nearly every government now in existence profess to be ruling with an eye to the welfare of their subjects. The impression is carefully cultivated that without the fostering care of the government, prosperity would be impossible, education and health would suffer neglect, science and the arts would languish, and crime would run riot in the streets. How much of this doleful picture is true is difficult to determine. Since World War II the welfare state all over the globe has become a cliché. Capitalists vie with Communists and even military dictators in claiming the beneficence of their purposes. Such claims may serve to disguise the destruction of citizens' rights by a General Franco in Spain or the ironclad Colonels of Greece. They make further invasions of civil liberties easy to accomplish and increase the worship of the rulers' own majestic presence.

The great White Father image of rulers

A good measure of the capacity of modern governments to fulfill their functions is their ability to provide for the requirements of the welfare state. These include provisions for the health, safety, and a reasonable prosperity for the citizens. Under the subject of health would come protection from sickness and disability in places of employment and in traveling to and from work. The prevalence of "black lung" among the coal miners of Appalachia would not fit in with a decent compliance with such a standard. Neither would the construction of elaborate freeways leading to excessive speed and reckless driving. Of course, some of the high-speed traveling is done by travelers over long distances, but statistics show that most of the fatal accidents occur within twenty-five miles of the victim's home. Contrary to general opinion, the rate in the United States is not the highest in the world. Some West European countries have a better claim to that "honor." Of course, the replanning and reconstruction of a national highway system would be tremendously expensive, but it would hardly equal more than two days' cost of the Indochina War or a single year of space exploration. It must be granted, of course, that significant accomplishments have occurred in medicine and public health in recent years. In the United States, for example, the death rate declined to 7.3 per thousand in 1967 from 9.0 per thousand twenty years earlier. Even more dramatic was the decline in the infant mortality rate in Sweden of more than 20 per cent.

The majority of American citizens would almost certainly classify crime as the most dangerous menace threatening the dissolution of our civilization. But few topics in the annals of modern states are more loaded with misapprehension. Crime may be taken to include every kind of social maladjustment from premeditated murder to possession of marijuana or even marijuana paraphernalia. Ordinarily in the infliction of penalties distinctions are made on the basis of the gravity or supposed gravity of the offense. But the distinction is often artificial. An offense involving bodily harm to another individual may not draw any stiffer penalty than nude bathing or the sale of an indecent postcard. Persons are sometimes held indefinitely for minor crimes when often it is their politics which threaten the Establishment. Most modern nations still have a distance to go before giving full recognition to the special category of "victimless" crimes. Meanwhile, our judicial machinery is clogged with miscellaneous offenses that never come to trial. It has been estimated that more than half of the alleged criminals in the United States have never laid a hand on any victim or stolen any other citizen's property. What they have done in many cases is to drink in public, engage in illicit sex, take part in the numbers racket, or to be caught in homosexuality. No doubt some of these acts deserve punishment, or at least condemnation, but no police authority can cover the entire waterfront and rake in every loafer or vagrant whom someone might consider a dangerous character. No modern state has the prison facilities to accommodate these hordes of minor offenders. As it is, the State of California spends $100 million a year rounding up its marijuana users. Penal laws are weird and often grotesque. In some states parole cannot be granted for certain violations until after thirty years, while in others murderers are eligible for parole after seven years. The Chief of Police of Washington, D.C., has said, "It's simply not worth arresting the street peddler of narcotics or the petty gambler. We should be going after the top men in the organization." [3]

2.   THE THIRD INDUSTRIAL REVOLUTION

Each economic revolution in modern history has been marked by cataclysmic changes through prosperity and panic and back again. The revolution that began about 1914 has been no exception. The years of the 1920's completed a fabulous cycle in 1929. Never had the prospects appeared more rosy. Prosperity seemed to have established a permanent base in the years that followed. A short time after the great stock market crash of 1929 President Hoover declared that the fundamental business of the country was "on a sound and prosperous basis." Informed economists knew better.

The initial phase of prosperity

The distinguishing feature of the Third Industrial Revolution has been the substitution of synthetic products for natural ones in many processes of manufacturing. The production of synthetics actually began at the end of the First Revolution when William H. Perkin discovered that coal tar could be converted into an infinite variety of products. The process continued apace during the Second Revolution, but it did not reach its full potential until about 1940. Today it is probably safe to say that the number of goods produced synthetically exceeds the number derived from natural materials. Most automobile tires, for instance, are made from petrochemicals. Rubies, sapphires, and other gems can be produced so perfectly in factories as to be scarcely distinguishable from the genuine precious stones. Even many foods, such as whipped cream, salad oil, coffee "cream," butter substitutes, flavoring, and preservatives consist wholly or partially of synthetic substitutes. A reflective Chinese woman said recently: "When I was a little girl in China, I ate dirt; now that I am a grown-up woman in America, I eat chemicals." Yet, the results have not been a total loss. Margarine can be made to look and taste like butter but without the high cholesterol content of the natural product. The same can be said of salad oils made from peanuts or soybeans, which contain only vegetable fat. On the other hand, the use of chemicals to fatten poultry and cattle may be a detriment to the health of the ultimate consumer.

The production of synthetics

The electronics industry has been one of the economic miracles of the Third Industrial Revolution. Electronics derives from that branch of physics which deals with the behavior and effects of electrons, or negative constituents within the atom. Electronic devices have multiplied in staggering profusion since World War II. Among them are devices to measure the trajectory of missiles, to give warnings of approaching missiles or aircraft, to make possible

Electronics

[3] *Wall Street Journal*, Aug. 25, 1971.

The Age of Television. Left: The first working television pickup camera, 1929. Right: The Telstar communications satellite. Weighing only 170 pounds, and measuring 34 inches in diameter, it is powered by 3600 solar cells. It circles the earth at a speed of 1600 miles per hour at a height of from 500 to 3000 nautical miles.

"blind" landings of airplanes, to store and release electrical signals, to amplify and regulate the transmission of light and sound images, and to provide the power for photoelectric cells that open doors and operate various automatic machines. The spacecraft industry, which has made possible the exploration of outer space, including voyages to the moon, is closely dependent upon electronics.

Automation

Scarcely any two developments in modern industry could be more closely related than electronics and automation. Indeed, it was the use of electronic devices for radio reception that led to the initial progress in automation. Automation should not be confused with mechanization, though it may be considered the logical extreme of that process. More correctly conceived, automation means a close integration of four elements: (1) a processing system; (2) a mechanical handling system; (3) sensing equipment; and (4) a control system. Though all of these elements are necessary, the last two are the most significant. Sensing equipment performs a function similar to that of the human senses. It observes and measures what is happening and sends the information thus gained to the control unit. It employs such devices as photoelectric cells, infra-red cells, high-frequency devices, and devices making use of X-rays, isotopes, and resonance. It operates without fatigue and much faster and more accurately than do the human senses. Moreover, its observations can be made in places unsafe for, or inaccessible to, human beings. A control system receives information from a sensing element, compares this information with that required by the "program," and then makes the necessary adjustments. This series of operations is continuous, so that a desired state is constantly maintained without any human intervention, except for that initially involved in "programming." This revolution has been greatly extended by the invention of lasers. A laser is a device for amplifying the focus and intensity of light. High energy atoms are stimulated by light to amplify a beam of light. Lasers have demonstrated their value recently in medicine. They have been used effectively in arresting hemorrhaging of the retina in eye afflictions. Through automation expensive and complicated machines are constantly taking the place of much human labor. Data processing machines and electronic computers are employed to control switching operations in railroad yards, to operate assembly lines, to operate machines that control other machines, and even to maintain blood pressure during critical operations in hospitals.

The Third Industrial Revolution has gone beyond the Second in the adoption of new materials in the manufacturing process. Foremost among them have been plastics, manufactured from various substances, such as casein, phenol, and coal and petroleum derivatives. Plastic steering wheels, plastic machinery housings, and plastic bottles are only a few of them. To a considerable extent aluminum is taking the place of steel and copper, and in some instances where an even lighter material is required, as in airplane construction, magnesium is being substituted for aluminum. Other new metals have been adopted, not principally as substitutes for older metals, but to give toughness and strength or rust-proof qualities to steel. Notable among these are the ferro-alloys, which include tungsten, manganese, nickel, molybdenum, and chromium. Found largely in such countries as Turkey, Russia, China, India, Canada, and Rhodesia, they are indispensable to modern industry. Together with other widely scattered critical materials, they furnish excellent examples of the economic interdependence of the contemporary world.

New materials

That the Third Industrial Revolution would germinate problems affecting labor was a foregone conclusion. The most obvious was technological unemployment. Though new industries absorbed many workers, others were bound to be displaced by automation. In the mid-1960's no one could be quite sure of the extent of this displacement. Apparently, most of those whose jobs were taken found new opportunities with the development of new industries. In any case unemployment, in the United States, had declined by February 1966, to 3.7 per cent of the labor force. But this was a condition of a war economy. What would happen when peace returned, no one could say. Moreover, it was a fact that while the demand for skilled labor remained high, the so-called "entry jobs" as helpers, sweepers, and miscellaneous unskilled workers were fast disappearing. They were being eliminated not by computers so much as by fork-lift trucks and motorized conveyors and sweepers. Mechanization of agriculture also knocked out thousands of jobs for unskilled and un-

Problems affecting labor

educated workers. The mechanical cotton picker in the South and Southwest and the combine on the great wheat farms of the West displaced innumerable field hands who fled to the cities to lead lives of misery and despair in the slums. The problem of the future seemed to be not so much a repetition of the mass unemployment of the 1930's as a dearth of jobs at the bottom, and a surplus of engineers and technical workers.

That the Third Revolution would involve further changes in the nature of capitalism goes almost without saying. Though holding companies had been largely eliminated in the public utility industry by New Deal legislation in the United States, in other industries they continued and even proliferated. They usually took the form, not of trusts but of mergers, composed of dozens of subsidiaries, more or less closely related, and formerly independent companies. The object usually was to strive for product diversification and thereby guard the parent company against shifting patterns of consumer demand. Thus Eastman Kodak continued to manufacture cameras and photographic materials but also acquired subsidiaries extensively engaged in the production of plastics, chemicals, and synthetic fibers. A trend toward consolidation characterized the railroad industry, merchandising, and even banking. The largest bank in New York City, the Chase Manhattan—itself the result of a merger of two giant banks—acquired 130 branches in the Greater New York area, to say nothing of 33 overseas branches throughout the free world.

Along with this trend toward consolidation has gone, strange as it may seem, a diffusion of ownership. In 1970 it was estimated that 1 out of every 6 of the people of the United States was a shareholder in one or more American corporations. This was true despite the bear market of 1968–1970. The amount they owned was usually an infinitesimal fraction of the total shares outstanding and therefore precluded any control over the affairs of the companies. The bulk of the stock in large corporations generally came into the possession of investment trusts, insurance companies, and pension funds, colleges and universities, and foundations. Yet another characteristic of ownership in the Third Revolution has been the virtual disappearance of the old "dynastic" capitalism. The DuPont and Ford families are among the few exceptions. The name Rockefeller is no longer synonymous with oil or the name Carnegie with steel. Management has become increasingly separate from ownership. Presidents and board chairmen of modern corporations are not proprietors but financiers and bureaucrats who made their way up as lawyers or bankers or as successful heads of smaller companies. In some cases they have little direct knowledge of the basic operations of the firms over which they preside. It has been said that a recent chairman of the board of one of our largest steel corporations never saw a blast furnace until "after he died."

Changes in the nature of capitalism: (1) consolidation and diversification

(2) diffusion of ownership

872

3. KEYNES AND THE NEW ECONOMICS

It would be difficult to exaggerate the influence of John Maynard Keynes (later Lord Keynes) in shaping the theory that has underlain the economic programs of modern states. Keynes was born in 1883 and died in 1946. He was thoroughly educated in mathematics and the classics before being sent to Cambridge University. When only twenty-three he passed the British Civil Service examination with the second highest honors. He would have ranked first except for a low grade in economics. At the Paris Peace Conference of 1919 he was the chief economic adviser of the British delegation. He spent a good part of his time castigating the ignorance and indifference of the chief delegates, including Woodrow Wilson. After the war he devoted his talents to lecturing and also to a business career. He became manager of an investment company, chairman of an insurance company, and Director of the Bank of England. He amassed a large fortune, evidently with some qualms, if we can judge from his later writings.

John Maynard Keynes

John Maynard Keynes

But Keynes was far from being a socialist. He wondered how any doctrine so "illogical and so dull' could have exercised so powerful and lasting an influence over the minds of men. Moreover, he believed that capitalism with its inner faults corrected could provide all the justice and efficiency reasonable men could expect. Capitalism, though, would require a "face-lifting" that some of its old-time defenders would consider drastic. First, the idea of a perpetually balanced budget would need to be abandoned. Keynes never advocated continuous deficit financing. He would have the government deliberately operate in the red whenever private investment was too scanty to provide for the needs of the country. But when depression gave way to recovery, private financing could take the place for most purposes of deficit spending. He is supposed to have urged the "euthanasia of the rentier," or the extinction of the no-risk investor. This would leave the road clear for venture capital, which is the only socially productive form of capital. Finally, Keynes recommended monetary control as a means of promoting prosperity and full employment. He would establish what is commonly called a "managed currency," regulating its value by a process of contraction or expansion in accordance with the needs of the economy. Prosperity would thus be assured in terms of the condition of the home market, and no nation would be tempted to "beggar its neighbor" in the foolish pursuit of a favorable balance of trade.

Though he numbered his critics in the thousands, Keynes was an enthusiastic proponent of much of what is generally accepted today as the new economics. He was strongly convinced, especially in his later years, that an economic system could not be grounded on the gold-standard, laissez-faire principles of the nineteenth century. He held that full employment could be achieved only if governments

The influence of Keynes

deliberately encouraged investment in new capital goods, and he sponsored cheap money as one of the best means of accomplishing this. He had no patience with the old negative conception which required the state to spend as little as possible lest businessmen be frightened into a loss of confidence. In his opinion it was better that a moderate number of men be put to work digging holes and filling them up again than that a large number should be unemployed. Although Keynes did not have a high opinion of the economic literacy of some of his followers, many of his doctrines were idolized by statesmen and others of fiscal authority. In the 1930's they strongly influenced the policies of President Franklin D. Roosevelt and formed a major ingredient of his recovery program. Since the beginning of World War II nearly all Western nations, the United States and Britain in the vanguard, have paid homage to Keynesian economics in one form or another.

4. THE CRISIS OF ECOLOGY AND THE POPULATION EXPLOSION

The meaning of ecology

Ecology is the science which concerns the interrelationships of organisms and their environments. The word is often used primarily to refer to man and his environment, but it is much broader than that. Ecologists think of man as a link in a vast chain of life which extends all the way back through mammals, amphibians, invertebrates, and the simplest microorganisms which may be either plants or animals. In popular usage ecology may be synonymous with pollution problems. Again this is an oversimplification. The causes and prevention of pollution make up important elements in the study of ecology, but they are not the whole subject. Equally important

Industrial Pollution. The photo shows the Bethlehem Steel Company's plant at Sparrow Point, Maryland. While polluting gases and particular matter are released into the air, industrial wastes, both thermal and chemical, are released into the water.

An Oil Spill off the Coast of Santa Barbara, California, 1969. Offshore oil drilling has been responsible for numerous spills. Here, at a view from 1800 feet, spreading oil can be seen moving from the offshore rig to pollute the nearby shores.

is man's use of his environment in ways that will safeguard his heritage of fertile soil, pure air, fresh water, and forests for those who come after him.

Ecological violations consist not merely of poisoning the atmosphere and contaminating oceans, rivers, and lakes by dumping wastes into them but by any assault upon them that makes them less valuable for human survival. The excessive construction of dams, for example, causes the silting of rivers and the accumulating of nitrates at a faster rate than the surrounding soil can absorb. The use of insecticides, especially those containing DDT, may result in upsetting the balance of nature. An example in the recent history of Malaysia illustrates such an occurrence. The Malaysian government resorted to extensive spraying of remote areas with DDT in the hope of stamping out malaria. The DDT killed the mosquitoes but also poisoned the flourishing cockroaches. The cockroaches in turn were eaten by the village cats. The net result was a multiplication of rats formerly kept from a population explosion by their natural enemies, the cats. So badly disturbed was the balance of nature that a fresh supply of cats had to be airlifted from more settled regions. Other assaults upon the balance of nature have been even more serious. The Aswan High Dam of Egypt, undoubtedly valuable for increasing the water supply of that country, has at the same time cut down the flow of algal nutrients to the Mediterranean with damaging effects on the fishing industry of various countries. From the

Other assaults upon nature

875

ecological standpoint the fantastic development of industry in modern times is almost an unmitigated disaster. For thousands of years the human race introduced into the environment no more waste substances than could easily be absorbed by the environment. But modern technological man has introduced into nature a variety of wastes never abundant before. Among them are carbon monoxide, sulfur dioxide, and nitrogen oxides. And this is to say nothing of the discharge into nature of pesticides, the great host of synthetic products that are not biologically degradable, and the fruits of nuclear weapons testing.

Diminishing land resources

It is not simply the destruction of our environment by the dumping of harmful and nondegradable products but it is also the wastage of land as our most valuable natural resource. In many parts of the world rivers run brown because they are filled with earth washed from the fields bordering them. In some of the largest American cities two-thirds to three-quarters of the land area is paved with streets and parking lots. Meanwhile, the nation's crop land is shrinking at an alarming rate. Ecologists say that much of this land will probably have to be abandoned. Yet the mad race continues, and optimists stumble over each other in their worship of progress. Growth, speed, ingenuity, mobility have become fetishes in a nation that does not know what to do with these ends when it has achieved them. President Eisenhower hailed the $41 billion highway project launched during his administration as the greatest public welfare undertaking in history. The President made no justification of his project in terms of what it might mean for the public good. Nor did he raise any questions as to ultimate costs in case the passion for growth mounted still higher, as it almost certainly would.

Ecology and the population explosion

A close link exists between the problems of ecology and the population explosion. Indeed, if population control had remained a reality, the problems of ecology might well have passed unnoticed for many years. For example, New York City on the eve of the Civil War had a total population of 700,000. The area was not essentially different from what it is now. Yet the inhabitants of the five boroughs constituting the city have multiplied ten times over. This increase has been accompanied by physical transformations that have facilitated crowded living by masses of people. Oil lamps were replaced by gas light and then by electricity, horse-drawn wagons and carriages by trolley cars and "gas buggies." While some of these contraptions eliminated a few forms of pollution, the general effect was to multiply sources of contamination and abuse of the natural environment. The example of New York City can be duplicated in many other overcrowded areas, not only in America but especially in Asia. Calcutta now has a population of 5 million compared with 3 million in 1961. Tokyo has grown from 9 million to over 11 million in little more than ten years. In some cities of the Orient, though not in Japan, thousands of the inhabitants sleep in the streets, and children compete with dogs and rats for scraps of refuse thrown into the discard by more "affluent" citizens.

Radical environmentalists teach that unless we stop the population from growing and start its eventual decline, we haven't a chance to solve our ecological problems. As the population increases, man creates more and more problems and the damage done by each person escalates rapidly. Conditions in Los Angeles illustrate the danger. Despite excellent laws the city makes little progress in carrying them out. Increases in the number of smog-producers nullify every victory the control experts succeed in gaining. The worst offenders in vitiating ecological progress are the big industrial powers. For one thing they combine exhaustion of natural resources with contamination of the environment by nuclear poisons and their by-products. But aside from their quest of military superiority, the industrial powers consume hundreds of times more natural products than do most of the inhabitants of the Third World. An American, for instance, will consume 300 times as much steel per capita as a native of Indonesia. Paul Ehrlich, the renowned population authority at Stanford, claims that every American baby born is 50 times more of a disaster than an Indian baby because of the vast difference in standards of consumption.

All nations of the contemporary world are in danger of being overwhelmed by a population explosion. Its major cause has been what the experts call the demographic revolution. By this is meant an overturning of the ancient balance between births and deaths, which formerly kept the population on a stationary or slowly rising level. This balance is a biological condition common to nearly all species. For thousands of years of his history man was no exception. It is estimated, for example, that the total population of the earth at the beginning of the Christian era was about 250 million. More than sixteen centuries passed before another quarter billion had been added to the total. Not until 1860 did the population of the globe approximate 1 billion. From then on the increase was vastly more rapid. The sixth half billion, added about 1960, required scarcely more than ten years.[4] According to United Nations projections, the total population of the world by 1975 will be 4 billion. To add the last half billion will require only seven or eight years.

What have been the causes of this radical imbalance known as the demographic revolution? Fundamentally, what has happened has been the achievement of a twentieth-century death rate alongside a medieval birthrate. Medicine and the other health sciences have made such rapid strides that the span of life has been substantially lengthened all over the world. Infant mortality rates have markedly declined. Deaths of mothers in childbirth have also diminished. The great plagues, such as cholera, typhus, and tuberculosis, take a much

[4] P. M. Hauser (ed.), *The Population Dilemma*, pp. 8–11.

smaller toll than they did in earlier centuries. Wars and famines still number their victims by the millions, yet such factors are insufficient to counteract an uncurbed rate of reproduction. Though the practice of contraception has been approved by the governments of such nations as India, China, and Japan, only in the last have the effects been worthy of notice. In some countries the desire of adults to have numerous offspring to care for them in old age has stood as an obstacle. In others poverty, religion, and abysmal ignorance have made the widespread use of contraceptives impossible.

The uneven growth of world population

Of course, the demographic revolution has not affected all countries uniformly. Its incidence has been most conspicuous in the underdeveloped nations of Central and South America, Africa, and Asia. Whereas the population of the world as a whole will double, at present rates of increase, in thirty-five years, that of Central and South America will multiply twofold in only twenty-six years. An outstanding example is that of Brazil. In 1900 its population was estimated to be 17 million. By 1970 this total had grown to 94 million, more than a fivefold increase. Mexico and Venezuela have two of the highest birthrates in the world. The population of Asia (excluding the U.S.S.R. and Japan) grew from 813 million in 1900 to approximately 2 billion in 1970. By way of summary, at midcentury, the population of the underdeveloped portions of the globe was more than twice that of the developed portions. Their total land areas were about equal.

Some would-be authorities contend that the population explosion, though a crucial problem for underdeveloped countries, is not a matter of serious moment to the United States. True, the rate of growth in America is only half as fast as the world average and only one-third as great as many underdeveloped countries. Yet America with less than 6 per cent of the world's population consumes 40 per cent of its wood pulp, 36 per cent of its fossil fuels, 20 per cent of its cotton, and 10 per cent of the world's food products. Few other industrialized nations lag far behind. As a consequence, according to Gerald Leach in the *London Observer*, most talk about the developing nations catching up with the advanced nations of the West is a "gigantic swindle." Wherein lies the remedy? Correcting or eliminating pollution is not enough. No underdeveloped nation is going to refrain from building factories to abate the smog nuisance for the benefit of nations already wallowing in luxurious living. Nor are they interested in protecting their own rivers and lakes in order to enable rich exploiters to hog the last scenery for themselves. Indeed, it often seems that environmentalism standing alone is really a kind of class warfare. Rich nations show no signs of a willingness to share the resources in their possession. Moreover, it is the well-heeled nations that have led in recent years the strongest campaigns for population control. Not a few leaders of the non-Caucasian peoples have denounced these campaigns as efforts to promote white supremacy.

Margaret Sanger, a Leader in the Movement to Awaken the World to the Necessity of Birth Control

Despite these criticisms most environmentalists continue to advocate population control as one of the two indispensable means of saving our planet. Paul Ehrlich thinks almost exclusively of limitation of offspring. He believes that that is the goal toward which every family should strive, with zero population growth the aim for as many as possible. He admits that stopping population growth will not necessarily solve all our problems, but unless we stop the growth and start the decline in the very near future, it may already be too late. We cannot wait for the underdeveloped countries to take the lead. They are too undernourished, too afflicted by disease, and too harassed by wars and exploitation to do much of anything to save themselves. If they go down, however, they will not perish alone. Other environmentalists go even beyond the population factor. They contend that the ecology of the world can be cleared up only by radical changes in every economic, social, and political sphere that seems to the existing power structure as important. The conception of unlimited profit and material success, and, above all, growth and expansion as national fetishes must go by the board. Robert Heilbroner of The New School for Social Research has described our dilemma as tantamount to asking the world's privileged classes to "agree to euthanasia." But what other way of escape is there? The hopes of some optimists that a Green Revolution involving the introduction and cultivation of new and better crops is only a possible answer. After four years of improved grains, better fertilizers and farming techniques, food production in the Third World is still lagging. Primary reasons are the conversion of valuable lands into dust bowls by overuse of fertilizers and excessive grazing, and destruction of water resources.

Recent statistics provide a slender reed of encouragement on which to lean. The United States Census Bureau has published figures showing a record decline in births in the past decade. One might assume that these figures would be a universal cause of rejoicing. But not so. Manufacturers of toys, clothes, automobiles, motorcycles, and even builders feel themselves threatened. Other observers seem deeply disturbed because the decline did not occur in one of the crowded and unprogressive countries of the Orient instead of in a nation as industrially advanced as the United States. Their attitude was reminiscent of that of Secretary of Commerce Sinclair Weeks, who rejoiced when the population of America hit 170 million in 1957. He was "happy to welcome this vast throng of new customers for America's goods and services." They would "help insure a rising standard of living. . . ." [5] Eleven years later the population hit the fantastic total of 205 million. Obviously, an end would be reached sometime. But what fantastic "boon" would bring it to pass? Some

The need for drastic remedies

Crumbs of comfort

[5] David Lyle, "The Human Race Has, Maybe, Thirty-five Years Left," *Esquire Magazine*, Sept. 1967.

Urban Congestion. A traffic jam of major proportions in the market district of London during the early part of the twentieth century.

new version of the Black Death, perhaps, or some weird and unanticipated misuse of nuclear energy.

5. GALLOPING URBANIZATION

The increase in urban living

Closely allied to the population explosion has been the rapid growth of urban areas in nearly all countries. Though the highest birthrates are generally found in agricultural nations, the pressure of increased numbers and falling incomes forced thousands to flee from the land to the cities. The core population of many American cities is already made up of refugees from the cotton fields of the South or from the sugar plantations of West Indian islands. The urban explosion has been much more rapid than the population explosion in general. The population of the United States in 1920 was slightly less than 106 million, with only a little more than half of this total living in urban centers. By 1970 the total had grown to 200 million, with 68 per cent living in other than rural communities. Urbanization, of course, was not confined to the United States. During the first half of the twentieth century, as world population increased by 49 per cent, the inhabitants of cities increased by over 200 per cent.

l and the Village, Marc Chagall (1889–). The subject refers to the artist's childhood and youth in Vitebsk, Russia. The profile on the right is probably that of the artist himself. (Mus. Mod. Art)

The Table, Georges Braque (1881–). An example of later cubism showing the predominance of curvilinear form and line instead of geometric structure. (Mus. Mod. Art)

The Persistence of Memory, Salvador Dali (1904–). The Spaniard Dali is the outstanding representative of the surrealist school. Many objects in his paintings are Freudian images. (Mus. Mod. Art)

Sea and Gulls, John Marin (1870–1953). A native of New Jersey, Marin was a gifted abstract painter. His objects are sometimes recognizable, sometimes not. He painted not the likeness of nature, but *about* nature. (MMA)

Barricade, José Clemente Orozco (1883–1949). The Mexican muralist Orozco was one of the most celebrated of contemporary painters with a social message. His themes were revolutionary fervor, satire of aristocracy and the Church, and deification of the common man. (Mus. Mod. Art)

Around the Fish, Paul Klee (1879–1940). Klee is recognized as the most subtle humorist of XX-cent. art. The central motif of a fish on a platter suggests a banquet, but many of the surrounding objects appear to be products of fantasy. (Mus. Mod. Art)

Concentration of population in large cities has been almost an unmitigated disaster. Most of the influx crowds into the core cities where welfare is available and a life of profitable crime is at least a possibility. The more prosperous and better educated inhabitants then leave the older sections and flee to the suburbs. The whole character of a city may thus be changed with radical transformations of its social and economic life. Studies made of social conditions in the "Inner City" of Washington reveal incredible truths. The area is a center of unemployment, infant mortality, and venereal disease. Thirty-six per cent of all young men between twenty and twenty-four years of age are heroin addicts, and 24 per cent of those between nineteen and twenty-four. Ramsey Clark emphasized the point graphically: "In any city when you put poor education, poor employment, poor housing, and probably poor health on the map, you have marked the same place every time." [6]

In some respects it would be more accurate to speak of galloping "metropolitanization" instead of an urban explosion. Actually, the so-called growth of cities, especially in the United States, has consisted of the growth of large urban areas, each comprising a central city and surrounding suburbs. In a few instances the central city and its suburbs sprawl over so large an area that it is difficult to tell where one metropolis ends and another begins. Some observers predict the development, in the United States, of the "megalopolis," a huge aggregation of cities and suburbs formerly maintaining independent existences. One such megalopolis would be an area extending from Boston to Washington, taking in Providence, New Haven, New York, Philadelphia, and Baltimore. A second would be the Milwaukee–Chicago–South Bend area. Still another would stretch all the way from San Francisco to Los Angeles and San Diego.

Rapid urbanization has had a profound impact upon contemporary society. As in past ages, cities have been the principal means of fostering cultural growth. They provide the art museums, centers of learning, scientific institutes, the great libraries, and other cultural and educational facilities. It is almost a commonplace that without cities civilization can neither grow nor flourish. At the same time, it appears also to be true that metropolitan cities pose a threat to the very existence of civilization. In recent times, particularly, they present problems that almost defy solution. Made possible originally by the automobile, such cities today face strangulation by traffic congestion. Overcrowding combined with industrialization results in smog and miscellaneous pollution and in an environment favorable to the spread of disease. Blight and decay in the older areas magnify the problem of finding sufficient revenue to provide for essential services. These must be constantly expanded because of the increasing numbers of indigent, unemployed, and ignorant who pop-

Consequences of population congestion

Metropolitanization

The impact of urbanization

[6] *New York Times*, Feb. 7, 1971.

Urban Congestion. One of the many curses of urbanization is the automobile. Its use is perpetuated at the expense of sensible mass transit systems as a result of spreading affluence and the feeling that each individual must be able to move about where and when he or she pleases.

ulate the widening slums. So grave were these problems that, in the 1970's, most municipal rulers were urgently pleading with Washington to come to their rescue.

6. THE REVOLT OF YOUTH

Origins of the youth revolt

The years from 1964 onward through 1970 were marked by protest and upheaval by the younger generation more rampant than the world had witnessed in many decades. The agitation was not confined to any one country. It was most far-reaching in the United States, but it did not begin there. Disturbances were common in Japan, France, Italy, and Latin America. About the only nations to escape were those under communism or under the iron heel of dictatorship like Greece and Spain. In the opinion of some observers the youth revolution was nothing new. Attempts have been made to see the current movement as a mere replica of the Beat Generation of Jack Kerouac and Allen Ginsberg. Their predecessors were the Bohemians and anti-Babbitts, who fulminated against the conformists and lame brains of the 1920's. Even long in advance of them were the Thoreaus and Whitmans of the nineteenth century. Such modern exponents of the anti-youth movement as Bruce Cook, Book Editor of the *National Observer*, presents the "hippies as just second-generation Beats." [7] Although the author has a good understanding of background, he seems only dimly aware of the full significance of the current movement. He appears to classify every youth in revolt as a hippie, a confusion which no informed critic would be likely to commit.

The youth revolt of the past few years has often been associated with vandalism and violence. Few newspaper readers have forgotten the uprisings at the University of Paris in 1968, the violence at Columbia, Berkeley, and San Francisco State, and the wild disorders at the Democratic National Convention at Chicago in the same year. Some commentators portray participants in the youth rebellion as engaged in a deadly war with the adult world. *Adult* repression they consider as the primary cause of the violence that accompanies this war. Most of this violence, at least when it takes the form of bloodshed, they credit to overzealous police action. They point out that none of the participants in the outbreaks at Kent State, Jackson (Miss.) State, and Orangeburg, S.C., was armed. Young rebels are sometimes portrayed as unwitting belligerents in an uneven war. Governments marshal against them many of the weapons and techniques used by armed forces against guerrilla fighters in Vietnam. Helicopters, gas warfare, search-and-destroy operations, hit-and-run bombings, and mass arrests are only a few of them. [8] Emphasis by the news media on these picturesque and sometimes tragic clashes between the generations gives a distorted view of the violence and disorder. Many adults have gained the impression of a mass uprising in

The violent phase of the youth revolt

[7] *The Beat Generation*, New York, 1971, p. 205.
[8] John R. Seeley, "Youth in Revolt," Special Report, *Britannica Book of the Year*, 1969.

Students of the University of Paris during the Uprisings of 1968. Of interest is the student in the center who with his right hand throws a paving brick and in his left clutches a camera to record the event.

which only small minorities of students have remained passive or neutral. Undoubtedly some rebellions have reached such a crescendo of frenzy that they have drawn the majority of the student body into their orbit. More often it is clear that the fire-eating dissenters have remained a minority with the body of students intent upon other things or giving no more than verbal support. Competent observers have recently estimated that only about 1 per cent of college and university students have ever engaged in violence.[9]

The apolitical or
quietist revolution

But the real youth revolution does not consist in the violent upheaval of rock throwing, window-smashing attacks upon venerable institutions and the men who run them. Rather it is in the minds and hearts of its authors who renounce the values of conventional society but do not advocate wrecking its institutions. Instead of activists, most of them are quietists living their own lives as individuals or as members of primitive groups. Most of them are strongly apolitical. They consider politics to be self-defeating. It merely substitutes one form of authoritarian domination for another. In particular, they decry political revolutions. Political revolutions even more than shifts of parties result in changes of masters—Napoleon and later the restored Bourbons for the First Republic in France; the Bolsheviks for the Romanoffs in Russia. Human aggrandizement "is a determining factor in human behavior. . . ."[10] Youth leaders believe that this evil must be annihilated and new goals substituted for it.

Achievements
of the youth
rebellion

It is easy to fault the youth movement of our time. Its most obvious deficiency is indifference to creative achievement. Only in music and to a limited extent in art do its leaders show much interest in equaling or surpassing the accomplishments of the past. Science leaves them cold or even antagonistic because of its association with war-making activities. Literature has little appeal except for caustic novels and dramas and satiric poetry. Social sciences, by contrast, evoke a more positive response. Sociology, anthropology, and environmental studies seem more relevant to a threatened world than ancient history, languages, and advanced mathematics. Yet against these generally negative attitudes must be ranked some outstanding achievements. One of these is a more constructive view of race relations. Young people, with few exceptions, regard notions of racial superiority and inferiority as a mass of baseless prejudice. Many have suited their actions to their principles by campaigning for desegregation and civil rights, by free racial association, and sometimes by intermarriage. Finally, it is not too much to credit the youth rebellion with frustrating the designs of certain great powers in many parts of the Third World. It was this rebellion that exposed the inhumanity and hypocrisy of the American adventure in Southeast Asia. Long before adult liberals lifted a finger against the bombing

[9] Charles A. Wells, *Between the Lines*, Sept. 15, 1971.
[10] Jean-François Revel, "Without Marx or Jesus," *Saturday Review*, July 24, 1971.

raids and body counts of that war, students in colleges and universities stormed the institutions of the Establishment in angry protest. Although they did not stop the war, they brought the Johnson administration to its downfall in March 1968. Their compeers in France a year later contributed much to bringing about the defeat of President Charles de Gaulle.

7. EDUCATION IN TRAVAIL

The education system as a whole did not escape the tribulations of students and administrators. All was tranquil enough until 1957. That was the year of Sputnik, when Soviet scientists became the first to place an artificial satellite in orbit around the earth. The unexpected Russian triumph shocked Western educators out of their complacency. Soon everyone was asking how the West could have been brought so low as to suffer defeat by a nation whose mathematicians are still using the abacus. What had gone wrong with Western systems of education? Had they failed because of an excess of "permissiveness," too many frills? These and many other questions were symptomatic of the anxieties of the generation caught up in the Cold War.

It was probably inevitable that the first reaction to the perplexities raised by Sputnik should be a demand for stiffer requirements in secondary schools and colleges, more emphasis on mathematics, languages, and the sciences. But this did not last. The world of the educational conservatives was thrown into confusion by the introduction of the "New Math," which seemed to call into question the convenient assumption that mathematics was the basis of all reasoning. "Relevant" subjects like sociology, ecology, and political science attracted larger enrollments than literature, philosophy, and the physical sciences. More significant was the revival of democratization in the schools. This trend had already begun in the early part of the century. In England and America it was symbolized, as we have learned, by the Progressive Education movement under the leadership of John Dewey. The movement evoked a great deal of criticism from educational traditionalists, and it fell into such disrepute that it almost died out. Now in spite of Communist scares and threats of war it was revived. Western European countries took the lead, although even some Eastern ones did not lag far behind. In 1967–1968 Denmark removed the last traces of corporal punishment from its schools, thus making the prohibition of physical penalties complete throughout Scandinavia. Surprising as it may seem, the Greek government in 1968 declared corporal punishment an anachronism and banned it from its schools. Similar efforts were made in Great Britain, but teacher opposition prevented them from being completely successful. Further efforts at democratization included dilution of educational authoritarianism and movements for the Open University. France was the pioneer in the former. In 1968 Edgar Faure, Minister

Students at Work at the Lenin State Library, Moscow

of Education, promulgated a new system of governance for the schools of the nation. Each would be under the control of a council made up of representatives of three groups approximately equal in size. The groups would be (1) the administration of the school with a contingent of distinguished citizens; (2) teachers and other employees of the school; and (3) pupils and parents.

The first Open University to be established was set up in England in 1962. Its founder was Jennie Lee (now Lady Lee), wife of Aneurin Beven, sometime Minister of Health in the Labour Cabinet after the war. Its purpose was to combat élitism in higher education. Nearly all the previous requirements for university admission were abolished. The Open University is free to all. The course of study, however, is not unlimited. The object is the training of "generalists" rather than specialists. About 1969 the City University of New York began a transformation into an open university. As in England nearly all the old requirements for admission were broken down. About all that was left was the single condition that the aspiring student live within the boundaries of the city.

Many of the new developments, including the one just mentioned, were products of agitation by racial minorities. Blacks in the Northern cities of the United States were the most active. For years they contended that they had been deprived of privileges rightfully theirs on the basis of their numbers and contributions to the national life. Some, of course, did meet the standards of white colleges and succeeded in graduating, in a few instances with brilliant records. The majority, however, were relegated to Negro colleges of indifferent quality maintained by churches in the Southern states. Often these were the only colleges the black students were qualified to enter. Black leaders admitted that this was true, although they contended that in many cases exclusion from the better institutions was likely to be founded on race. Spokesmen for the blacks insisted that in either case their kinsmen were almost certainly being penalized for lack of opportunity—for being born black or for being deprived of the chance to get the rudiments of an education in their very early lives. They therefore urged that colleges admit black students under provisions that would equalize this disparity of opportunity. In response to these demands many colleges adopted relaxed admission standards for the benefit of minorities. Curricula were changed also to provide for new courses on Afro-American Studies, African History, Swahili, and more emphasis on such "relevant" subjects as ecology and sociology.

However the winds of change buffeted the educational systems of most countries, one nation stood as a bulwark against them. This was the Soviet Union. Leonid Brezhnev, General Secretary of the Communist Party, made the official position of the Soviet regime startlingly clear. The revolutionary disturbances in the West he characterized as signs of the deepening crisis of capitalism. He commanded Soviet students to maintain firm discipline and to remember Lenin's advice: "Firstly to study, secondly to study, and thirdly to study." But he rejected all conceptions of objectivity in education. He would not have the schools follow the path of truth wherever it might lead. It was the duty of the Soviet teacher to produce "ideologically convinced fighters for the Communist cause." Could anyone doubt that this was a march backward straight into the arms of Stalin?

SELECTED READINGS

· *Items so designated are available in paperbound editions.*

Banfield, Edward C., *The Unheavenly City*, Boston, 1970.
· Bell, Daniel, *The End of Ideology*, Glencoe, Ill., 1960 (Free Press).
· Brodine, Virginia, and Selden, Mark, eds., *Open Secret: The Kissinger-Nixon Doctrine in Asia*, New York, 1972.
Crowe, F. E., ed., *Collection: Papers by Bernard Lonergan*, New York, 1967.
Drucker, P. F., *The End of Economic Man*, New York, 1939. A really profound study of modern man's predicament.
· Ehrlich, Paul R., *The Population Bomb*, New York, 1968.
Galbraith, John, *The Liberal Hour*, New York, 1960.
———, *The New Industrial State*, Boston, 1967.
· Harrington, Michael, *The Other America: Poverty in the U.S.*, New York, 1962 (Penguin).
———, *Socialism*, New York, 1972. A penetrating recent analysis.
· Hauser, P. M., ed., *The Population Dilemma*, Englewood Cliffs, N.J., 1963 (Spectrum).
———, *Population Perspectives*, New Brunswick, N.J., 1960.
Laski, H. J., *Reflections on the Revolution of Our Time*, New York, 1943. A discerning analysis not seriously marred by a Marxist viewpoint.
Mannheim, Karl, *Diagnosis of Our Time*, New York, 1944. A thoughtful study.
Neumann, Sigmund, *The Future in Perspective*, New York, 1943.
Schapiro, J. S., *The World in Crisis*, New York, 1950.
Snow, C. P., *The Two Cultures and A Second Look*, Cambridge, 1965.
· Toffler, Alvin, *Future Shock*, New York, 1971 (Random House).

READINGS · Tugwell, Rexford G., *Constitution for a United Republics of America*, Santa Barbara, Calif., 1970 (Center for the Study of Democratic Institutions).

· Ward, Barbara, *The Rich Nations and the Poor Nations*, New York, 1962 (Norton).

· ———, *Nationalism and Ideology*, New York, 1966 (Norton).

——— , *The West at Bay*, New York, 1948.

· Wheeler, Harvey, *Democracy in a Revolutionary Era*, Santa Barbara, Calif., 1970 (Center for the Study of Democratic Institutions).

Wingo, Lowden, Jr., ed., *Cities and Space*, Baltimore, 1963.

SOURCE MATERIALS

Dolivet, Louis, *Handbook of the United Nations*, Charter of the United Nations.

Proposed Constitution for a World Republic, *Saturday Review of Literature*, Vol. 31 (April 3, 1948).

CHAPTER 33

Twentieth-Century Culture

I believe that man will not merely endure: he will prevail.
—William Faulkner, Speech upon
receiving the Nobel Prize, Stockholm, December 10, 1950

Occident, *n*. The part of the world lying west (or east) of the
Orient. It is largely inhabited by Christians, a powerful tribe of
the Hypocrites, whose principal industries are murder and cheating, which they are pleased to call "war" and "commerce." They
also are the principal industries of the Orient.
—Ambrose Bierce, *The Devil's Dictionary*

The twentieth century thus far has constituted one of the most critical periods of modern history. It has been an age of wars and upheavals that have threatened the destruction of some of our most
basic ideals and institutions. Some, in fact, did virtually go under in
the devastating flood of barbarism and unreason that have characterized much of the period so far. The early years of the century saw
a continuation of many of the trends begun during the late decades of the nineteenth century. Perhaps one can say that this
was true of ideals such as optimism, confidence in reason as an
instrument of knowledge, and faith in the beneficience of science. To be sure, philosophies such as Pragmatism had attacked the old metaphysics hallowed from the time of Aristotle,
and had cast doubt on the ability of the human mind to discover
ultimate truth. Yet philosophers like F. H. Bradley could still write
of the universe as a "star-domed city of God ruled by benevolent
purpose," if only bewildered man would follow the proper methods
of apprehending its reality. The novelist H. G. Wells and the playwright George Bernard Shaw exuded a sublime confidence in science and in social reform to reshape man's environment and to
enable him quickly to solve his most serious problems. But there
were rumblings of a distant thunder which forced men to question
their views along many of these lines. As time went on, issues of the
most fundamental kind were examined and challenged. Nothing

Trends in the
early twentieth
century

889

escaped, and often the conclusions drawn were profoundly disturbing in nature. No one could accuse contemporary man of being
naïve. At least, he himself would be the last to admit it.

I.   THE DECLINE OF PHILOSOPHY

The history of philosophy since early in the twentieth century presents in large part a record of pessimism and confusion.
To the majority of thinkers who have lived during this period
the events taking place around them justified the deepest anxiety.
World War I seemed the beginning of a new dark age. Later
the onrush of fascism and the plunge into a second world conflict appeared to leave little hope that civilization would ever
recover. To be sure, few of the philosophers gave way to despair, but an increasingly large number lost confidence in the ability of man to save himself without the support of authority or the
aid of supernatural powers. George Santayana fled from the materialist world in disgust and established himself for his declining years
in the Convent of the Blue Nuns in Rome. An even more spectacular change of views was accomplished by the English philosopher
C. E. M. Joad. Agnostic, advocate of polygamy and euthanasia, and
author of the Oxford Oath, which pledged its signers never to fight
for king and country, he turned before his death in 1953 into a
staunch upholder of original sin and a defender of the Christian
faith as a light to live by in a darkening world.

One of the most important of the philosophies that tended to give
a pessimistic view of man and his world was the Protestant conservatism of the Swiss-German theologian Karl Barth and the American
Reinhold Niebuhr. In form a system of theology, it presented profound philosophical conclusions concerning the nature of life and the
destiny of man. Barth and Niebuhr discussed the universe and
its problems in something approaching Calvinist terms. They
believed the world to be governed by an all-powerful Diety, who
controls all things for His own purposes. They considered man to
be a moral being, created in the divine image, and responsible to
God for the use that he makes of this life. Above all, they emphasized what they regarded as the fundamental fact of sin in the
world. Although man is capable of sympathy and benevolence, his
nature is sadly corrupted by pride and self-love. These commonly
take the form of a will to power, which is the primary source of
war, race conflict, tyranny, and exploitation. Sin can be conquered
only as men humble themselves before God, acknowledge the evil in
their own natures, and accept the redeeming power of the Christian
religion. By such means alone can they achieve that love and respect
for others which are the essence of democracy. The fatherhood of
God is the essential foundation of the brotherhood of man.

In the view of some contemporary philosophers, a more satisfying
concept of the nature of man and the problems of the world is being

expressed in the work of some twentieth-century Jesuit thinkers. Their foremost leader is the French Canadian Bernard Lonergan (born 1904). Lonergan is not a philosopher in a really broad sense of the term. He has devoted most of his life thus far to building and defending a system of theology. He has shown little interest in such topics as freedom versus authority, the primacy of faith over knowledge, and the supposedly sinful nature of man. From time to time he has touched upon such doctrines as the Assumption of Mary in an unusually broad and suggestive fashion. He has incorporated with the Assumption doctrine such concepts as the role of suffering, death, and resurrection in the total scheme of the universe. But here he has stopped short of any broad speculation. He seems never satisfied with partial answers and would rather wait for complete solutions no matter how long they must be delayed.

The depths of pessimism in philosophy were reached by a movement known as Existentialism, the most popular form of which originated in France about 1938. Founded by Jean-Paul Sartre, a teacher of philosophy in a Paris *lycée* and subsequently a leader of the Resistance against the Germans, it takes its name from its doctrine that the *existence* of man as a free individual is the fundamental fact of life. But this freedom is of no help to man; instead, it is a source of anguish and terror. Realizing, however vaguely, that he is a free agent, morally responsible for all his acts, the individual feels himself a stranger in an alien world. He can have no confidence in a benevolent God or in a universe guided by purpose, for, according to Sartre, all such ideas have been reduced to fictions by modern science. His only way of escape from forlornness and despair is the path of "involvement," or active participation in human affairs. It should be noted that in addition to the atheistic Existentialism of Sartre, there was also an older, Christian form, which had its origin in the teachings of Sören Kierkegaard, a Danish theologian of the middle nineteenth century. Like its atheistic counterpart, Christian Existentialism also teaches that the chief cause of man's agony and terror is freedom, but it finds the source of this freedom in original sin. It is not difficult to detect the influence of Kierkegaard and his followers upon the Neo-Orthodoxy of Karl Barth and Reinhold Niebuhr. Since 1930 the leading exponent of Christian Existentialism has been Karl Jaspers, philosophy professor at the University of Heidelberg.

Jean-Paul Sartre in Front of His Portrait by Picasso

At least two philosophers of the contemporary age retained their optimism amid the welter of gloom and uncertainty. One was Alfred North Whitehead. Born in England, the son of a clergyman of the Church of England, he spent the most fruitful years of his life as Professor of Philosophy at Harvard. Originally a mathematician, he turned to philosophy in an effort to harmonize modern thinking with the revolutionary discoveries of the new age of science. The system of thought he rapidly developed owed much to Plato, Kant, and Einstein. Like the first two, at least, he regarded intuition as just

The optimistic philosophy of Whitehead

as valid a method of knowing as reason or sensory experience. He rebuked the hardheaded positivists who heaped scorn upon the mystic, the artist, and the romantic poet. A liberal in politics and in social theory, he had a firm belief in the certainty of progress. He had an abiding faith also in a benevolent God. But Whitehead refused to think of this God as a divine autocrat handing down tables of laws and punishing men eternally for trespassing against them. Instead, he conceived of Him as a God of love, as "the poet of the world, with tender patience, leading it by his vision of truth, beauty, and goodness." [1] The defect of most religions, Christianity included, has been to represent God as a God of power. God is not omnipotent, else He would be the author of evil. His primary function is to save human beings from the evil which necessarily arises in connection with their struggle for the good. Such was Whitehead's conception of a friendly universe in which God and man are partners in striving toward perfection.

John Dewey

The second of the philosophers whose thinking was basically optimistic was the American John Dewey. Born in 1859, Dewey had already achieved renown before 1918 as a philosopher of Pragmatism. He never abandoned his allegiance to that movement, but after World War I he gave more and more attention to specific human problems. In his celebrated *Reconstruction in Philosophy*, published in 1920, he urged that philosophy should abandon its dealings "with Ultimate and Absolute Reality" and "find compensation in enlightening the moral forces that move mankind." [2] Unlike most of his contemporaries, he retained a healthy confidence in the powers of the human intellect. He believed that man, making use of the resources acquired by reason and experience, could solve his own problems without any assistance from the supernatural. In common with the Humanists of the past, he considered human beings to be the most important creatures in the universe, and he refused to concede that their nature was corrupt or depraved. Amid the rising tide of totalitarian oppression in the 1930's, he stressed increasingly the importance of freedom. This, together with a belief in equality and in the capacity of men to form intelligent judgments when guided by experience and education, he held to be the essence of democracy.

Bertrand Russell

The Pragmatism of John Dewey was one of the first of modern philosophies that can be classified as antimetaphysical. By some it has been called anti-intellectual, for it denies the possibility of finding conclusive answers to any of the great questions of life—the nature of the universe, the meaning of life, the possibility of a God as the source of the moral law and the architect of human destiny. Dewey had an able ally in Bertrand, Lord Russell, who continued the development of his New Realism into the twentieth century. One of Russell's disciples, Ludwig Wittgenstein, participated in the founding of Logical Positivism, the most extreme of all the antimetaphysi-

---

[1] *Process and Reality*, p. 526.
[2] Pp. 26–27.

cal philosophies. Developed further by the so-called Vienna Circle, whose leader was Rudolf Carnap, Logical Positivism emerged as an uncompromisingly scientific philosophy. It is not concerned with values or ideals except to the extent that they may be demonstrable by mathematics or physics. In general, the Logical Positivists reject as "meaningless" everything that cannot be reduced to a "one-to-one correspondence" with something in the physical universe. In other words, they reduce philosophy to a mere instrument for the discovery of truth in harmony with the facts of the physical environment. They divest it almost entirely of its traditional content and use it as a medium for answering questions and solving problems. They are concerned especially with political theory, for they regard that subject as particularly burdened with unproved assumptions and questionable dogmas.

Included among the social and political philosophies after 1918 were the theories of some who despised democracy and therefore contributed to the deepening crisis. Foremost among them were the Italian Vilfredo Pareto and the German Oswald Spengler. Their forerunner was the Frenchman Georges Sorel, who has already been discussed as the founder of Syndicalism. For the most part, all of them agreed in their contempt for the masses, in their belief that democracy was impossible, in their anti-intellectual viewpoint, and in their admiration for strong and aggressive leaders. Spengler was, in many respects, more extreme than Pareto. Although he completed about 1918 an erudite and in some respects brilliant philosophy of history, which he entitled *The Decline of the West*, his later writings were as full of prejudice as the books of the Nazis. In his *Hour of Decision*, published in 1933, he fulminated against democracy, pacifism, internationalism, the lower classes, and the colored races. He sang the praises of those "who feel themselves born and called to be masters," of "healthy instincts, race, the will to possession and power." He despised the cold, analytical reasoning of urban intellectuals and called upon men to admire the "deep wisdom of old peasant families." Human beings, he maintained, are "beasts of prey," and those who deny this conclusion are simply "beasts of prey with broken teeth."

Antirationalist and antidemo-cratic philosophies

The years following World War II witnessed an increasing popularity of conservative political and social philosophy. The creeping shadow of communism was undoubtedly largely responsible, but the trend had been initiated while the U.S.S.R. was still an ally of the West. The paternity of the new movement should perhaps be ascribed to Frederick A. Hayek, an Austrian political economist who had taken up residence in London. In *The Road to Serfdom*, Hayek condemned all forms of collectivist interference with capitalism, on the ground that they would lead to socialism and eventually to communism or fascism. Destruction of economic freedom, he contended, must surely lead to the destruction of all freedoms, for the right of the individual to unhampered choice in the pursuit of

The New Conservatism

tastes and interests is the very essence of freedom. A more strictly political variety of the new conservatism is exemplified by the work of Peter Viereck, Eric Voegelin, and Russell Kirk. All three espouse a philosophy essentially reactionary and antirational. Viereck, for example, describes himself as one who "distrusts human nature and believes (politically speaking) in Original Sin which must be restrained by the ethical traffic lights of traditionalism." According to Voegelin, Western society can be saved by venerating its tradition-rooted institutions and by abandoning the belief that knowledge, rather than faith, is the greatest good. Russell Kirk demands a revival of family piety, the defense of property, and recognition that a "divine intent rules society" and that "Providence is the proper instrument for change."

2.   THE CHANGING FACE OF RELIGION

The dominance of religion

In the early twentieth century religion seemed the most solidly entrenched of institutions. Scarcely anyone appeared to challenge its authority or to question its right to prescribe public and private morality and what should be taught in the schools. As late as 1925 a teacher in Tennessee was convicted and sentenced to a $100 fine for teaching the theory of evolution to his high school class in biology. Although he won an appeal two years later, the law was not overturned until 1967. Bible-reading and public prayers were not only universal requirements in Western schools, but courses in religion were quite often mandatory even in nondenominational colleges and universities. In the United States the typical college president was a Doctor of Divinity. He might also be a professor—of philosophy in the larger institutions, or of something called Christian Evidences in the smaller ones.

The reign of Pope John XXIII

For the most part religion followed a straight and narrow path until well into the twentieth century. To be sure, as we have seen, factional movements sprang up in both the Catholic and Protestant churches. Each had its modernist revolt fostered by the growth of science and the new emphasis on that subject as the key to human welfare. Dissension mounted within the economic system involving conflicts between capital and labor and between rich and poor. But none of these dissensions continued long in full swing. All gave way in time to more conservative tendencies. The succession of Popes illustrated the trend in the Catholic Church. The liberal Pope Leo XIII was followed in turn by a series of moderately conservative successors. Then came the reign of the tolerant peasant, John XXIII, who presided over the Church from 1958 to 1963. Although seventy-seven years old at the beginning of his reign, he proved himself one of the most vigorous leaders of the Church in modern times. Just before he mounted the throne he announced that he would summon a great Church council to be called Vatican II to revise and update the decrees of an earlier council that had met 100 years before. It was

Pope John XXIII

arranged that the new council should open in October 1962 and that it should be the most representative since the Fourth Lateran Council in 1215. Vatican II marked a milestone in the liberalization of the Church. Pope John urged the fathers to practice freedom of discussion and to find new means of making the fath live in the minds and hearts of the people. He insisted that the present-day Church in opposing errors should use compassion instead of harshness. Pope John XXIII left much of his work unfinished when death overtook him at the age of eighty-one. His successor, Paul VI, announced that meetings of the Council would be resumed in September 1963.

Pope Paul VI

Pope Paul VI has seemed anxious to return to the conservative paths marked out by his earlier predecessors of the twentieth century. Though he has initiated changes, he has confined these to liturgical and formal matters. At his instigation the Vatican Council has authorized the use of vernacular languages instead of Latin exclusively in the services of the Church. He has provided for changes in the Roman Curia, limiting the terms of its members and authorizing early retirement. On the other hand, he has refused to modify the Church's position on birth control and on celibacy of the clergy, except in some cases to permit deacons to marry. But modifications of the Catholic religion outside the central hierarchy have been more important than those made by Popes and Church Councils. In France forty-four priests left the ministry in 1970 declaring that they could no longer accept the rule forbidding priests to marry. Later the same year an international assemblage of clerics dissatisfied on the same

895

subject convened in Amsterdam. In some Latin American countries and in parts of Spain the Church ran into heavy weather because of its tendency to support military regimes and semifascist governments.

As for the United States, disaffection among Catholics has developed peculiar characteristics. Much of it has grown out of a rigorous dogmatism handed down from the past and solidified by a dominant clergy. A good portion was politically motivated. The tendency of some members of the higher clergy to endorse the foreign adventures of the United States government, as illustrated by Cardinal Spellman's blessing of the Vietnam War, annoyed liberal Catholics. The action of the two Berrigan brothers and their associates in burning draft records evoked considerable applause, even though they went to prison for their deeds. Most other deviations from the official Catholic position have been the work of laymen rather than members of the clergy. A poll conducted by *Newsweek* in the early 1970's indicated social and moral heresies among Catholics that a few years ago would have been considered scandalous. Sixty-three per cent had not gone to confession in the past eight weeks. Sixty per cent did not regard a divorced Catholic who remarries as living in sin. Fifty-three per cent believed that priests should be permitted to marry. Doubtless similar questionnaires given to adherents of other religions would bring out answers not greatly different.

Despite the tendencies of organized churches to resist change, they have not been wholly successful in doing so. Protest denominations have generally been less successful than the Church of Rome. Methodists, Baptists, Presbyterians have suffered heavy losses by the growth of Pentecostal movements within their borders. The aim of these movements has been to encourage emotional, revivalistic religion for the poorer classes. In many cases new denominations readily took shape in response to the emotional environment. Many bore unusual names: Church of God, Church of God in Christ, Assembly of God, Church of the Open Bible, Church of the Nazarene, Four Square Gospel Church, and many others. Nearly all appealed to the poor and disinherited classes, and some made a special bid for the support of blacks.

Similar to the Pentecostal movements are the religions associated with contemporary youth. The new religions resemble the Pentecostal movements in rejecting the stiffness and formality of the Establishment churches. There are significant differences, however. The campus religions do not represent the poor and downtrodden; many of their members are affluent and could easily find "spiritual" homes in the rich denominations of their parents. More significant, the campus groups have no ecclesiastical affiliations or membership requirements. Anyone may join who wishes to take part in the kind of "celebrations" they regard as important. The participants may be Catholics, Methodists, Presbyterians, Hindus, Buddhists, or atheists. "Worship" may consist of a small group sitting on the floor with legs crossed and attempting to probe the mysteries of life through won-

Catholic disaffection in the United States

Pentecostal movements

Campus religions

der and awe. Chants may be repeated for hours at a stretch while the aid of rock music, psychedelic lights, and even drugs may be invoked. Obviously, the forms and ceremonies of the new youth religions bear little resemblance to those of the Establishment churches. Their origin and significance are quite different. Their values, also, have little in common with the religions of the past generation. Although they consider themselves Christians, they do not think of this in any official sense. Jesus to them is a man with a perfect understanding and rapport with God. Rather than his being a "King of Kings" or a "Son of God who goes forth to war," they think of him as an unconventional rebel like themselves.

3. SCIENCE — THE HOPE OF THE WORLD?

For much of the twentieth century thus far science has proved to be the savior of mankind. Although its practitioners did not generally turn their backs on religion, they no longer placed their trust in faith or miracles to give them the answers. Science had its own miracles and solutions that made many Biblical legends seem childish. The prestige of science, however, did not continue untarnished. Too many research institutes and the men who worked within them were devoting their careers to the production of weapons of death to arouse much sympathy. Science and technology were made to shoulder the blame for air and water pollution, for the destruction of forests, for the devastation of the land and exhaustion of irreplaceable mineral resources like the fossil fuels. Of course, scientific progress has helped in the conquest of disease, enlarging food supplies, and in maximizing comfort and pleasure; however, in the opinion of many contemporary citizens these effects are counterbalanced by the ambition and greed of the rich and powerful.

The tarnished reputation of science

The most significant climax in the physical sciences in the twentieth century was reached with the publication of the Einstein theories. Originally issued in limited form in 1905, they were expanded with a more general application ten years later. Einstein challenged not merely the older conceptions of matter but practically the entire structure of traditional physics. The doctrine for which he is most noted is his principle of relativity. During the greater part of the nineteenth century, physicists had assumed that space and motion were absolute. Space was supposed to be filled with an intangible substance known as *ether*, which provided the medium for the undulations of light. The planets also moved in it like ships sailing in definite courses over the bounding main. The motion of the heavenly bodies was therefore to be measured by reference to this more or less static ether, just as the speed of a vehicle could be measured in terms of the distance traveled on a highway. But elaborate experiments performed by English and American physicists near the end of the century virtually exploded the ether hypothesis. Einstein then set to work to reconstruct the scheme

Albert Einstein

897

of the universe in accordance with a different pattern. He maintained that space and motion, instead of being absolute, are relative to each other. Objects have not merely three dimensions but four. To the familiar length, breadth, and thickness, Einstein added a new dimension of *time* and represented all four as fused in a synthesis which he called the *space-time continuum*. In this way he sought to explain the idea that mass is dependent upon motion. Bodies traveling at high velocity have different proportions of extension and mass from what they would have at rest. Included also in the Einstein physics is the conception of a finite universe—that is, finite in space. The region of matter does not extend into infinity, but the universe has limits. While these are by no means definite boundaries, there is at least a region beyond which nothing exists. Space curves back upon itself so as to make of the universe a gigantic sphere within which are contained galaxies, solar systems, stars, and planets.

The Einstein theories had a major influence in precipitating other revolutionary developments in physics. By 1960 it had been discovered that the conception of the subatomic world as a miniature solar system was much too simple. The atom was found to contain not only positively charged protons and negatively charged electrons, but *positrons*, or positively charged electrons; *neutrons*, which carry no electric charges; and *mesons*, which may be either negative or positive. Mesons, it was discovered, exist not only within the atom (for about two millionths of a second) but are major components of the cosmic rays that are constantly bombarding the earth from somewhere in outer space. A recent hypothesis assumes the existence of a *neutral* meson that has a "life" of only one one-hundredth of a sextillionth of a second, but which, in disintegrating, is converted into the energy that holds the universe together.

Several of the developments in physics outlined above helped to make possible one of the most spectacular achievements in the history of science, the splitting of the atom to release the energy contained within it. Ever since it became known that the atom is composed primarily of electrical energy, physicists had dreamed of unlocking this source of tremendous power and making it available for man. As early as 1905 Einstein became convinced of the equivalence of mass and energy and worked out a formula for the conversion of one into the other, which he expressed as follows: $E = mc^2$. E represents the energy in ergs, m the mass in grams, and c the velocity of light in centimeters per second. In other words, the amount of energy locked within the atom is equal to the mass multiplied by the square of the velocity of light. But no practical application of this formula was possible until after the discovery of the neutron by Sir James Chadwick in 1932. Since the neutron carries no charge of electricity, it is an ideal weapon for bombarding the atom. It is neither repulsed by the positively charged protons nor absorbed by the negatively charged electrons. Moreover, in the

More recent discoveries regarding matter and energy

Releasing the energy within the atom

process of bombardment it produces more neutrons, which hit other atoms and cause them in turn to split and create neutrons. In this way the original reaction is repeated in an almost unending series.

In 1939 two German physicists, Otto Hahn and Fritz Strassman, succeeded in splitting atoms of uranium by bombarding them with neutrons. The initial reaction produced a chain of reactions, in much the same way that a fire burning at the edge of a piece of paper raises the temperature of adjoining portions of the paper high enough to cause them to ignite. The potential of the neutrons employed in the splitting was only one-thirtieth of a volt, but the potential released was 200,000,000 volts. It was soon revealed that not all forms of uranium are equally valuable for the production of energy. Only the isotope 235, which forms only a tiny fraction of natural uranium, will split when bombarded with neutrons. Uranium 238, which constitutes over 99 per cent of the world supply, absorbs the neutrons and transmutes itself into neptunium and plutonium. The latter, however, behaves very much like uranium 235. That is, it does split and release great quantities of energy. More recently, the practice has developed of manufacturing plutonium in a structure known as an atomic pile, in which large quantities of uranium 238 are exposed to neutrons from uranium 235.

Atomic fission

It is a sad commentary on modern civilization that the first use made of the knowledge of atomic fission was in the preparation of an atomic bomb. The devastating weapon was the achievement of a galaxy of scientists working for the War Department of the United States. Some were physicists who had been exiled by Nazi or Fascist oppression. By 1945 their work was completed, and in July of that year the first atomic bomb was exploded in a test conducted in the New Mexican desert near the War Department laboratory at Los Alamos. On August 6 the first atomic bomb used in warfare was dropped on the Japanese city of Hiroshima. A second bomb was unloaded on Nagasaki on August 9. The deadly effects of the new weapon almost passed belief. It was estimated that a single bomb had the explosive force of 20,000 tons of TNT. More than 100,000 people were killed in the two cities, large portions of which were literally wiped from the map. Man had at last acquired control over the basic forces of the universe, but whether he had created a Frankenstein's monster which might ultimately destroy him, no one could predict. Doleful queries were raised about what would happen in the future when the ability to produce atomic weapons would be no longer a monopoly of Anglo-Americans. This monopoly was brought to an end in the fall of 1949, when the U.S.S.R. exploded an atomic bomb. Since then Great Britain and France have acquired atomic weapons, and so has Communist China.

Atomic weapons

Even more disturbing were the first tests of a hydrogen bomb by the United States Atomic Energy Commission in November 1952. The tests were conducted at Eniwetok Atoll in the South Pacific,

899

An H-Bomb Mushrooms. The cloud spreads into a huge mushroom following a 1952 explosion of a hydrogen bomb in the Marshall Islands of the Pacific. The photo was made 50 miles from detonation site at about 12,000 feet. The cloud rose to 40,000 feet two minutes after the explosion. Ten minutes later the cloud stem had pushed about 25 miles. The mushroom portion went up to 10 miles and spread 100 miles.

and according to reports an entire island disappeared after burning brightly for several hours. The hydrogen bomb, or H-bomb, is based upon fusion of hydrogen atoms, a process which requires the enormous heat generated by the splitting of uranium atoms to start the reaction. The fusion results in the creation of a new element, helium, which actually weighs less than the sum of the hydrogen atoms. The "free" energy left over provides the tremendous explosive power of the H-bomb. The force of hydrogen bombs is measured in *megatons*, each of which represents 1,000,000 tons of TNT. Thus a 5-megaton H-bomb would equal 250 times the power of the A-bombs dropped on Hiroshima and Nagasaki. By 1962 both the Soviet Union and the United States were conducting experimental tests, including high-altitude explosions and devices of unparalleled destructive force. In 1966 China produced her fourth atomic bomb, this time in the form of a nuclear missile that flew 400 miles to its target.

The hydrogen bomb

On October 4, 1957, the government of the Soviet Union inaugurated a new stage in man's control of his physical environment by rocketing into space the first artificial satellite, which began circling the earth at a speed of about 18,000 miles an hour. Though it weighed nearly 200 pounds, it was propelled upward higher than 500 miles. This Russian achievement gave the English language a new word—*Sputnik*, the Russian for *satellite* or *fellow traveler*. A month later the Soviet scientists surpassed their first success by sending a new and much larger Sputnik to an altitude of approximately 1000 miles. Sputnik II weighed more than half a ton and contained elaborate scientific instruments and even a live dog.

The exploration of space

900

These Sputniks were simply the forerunners of others of greater significance. In April 1961, the Russians succeeded in sending the first man into orbit around the earth. Four months later the Soviets achieved an even greater triumph when they sent another of their army officers in a space capsule around the earth. He remained in orbit 25 hours and encircled the earth 17½ times. Meanwhile, scientists and military specialists in the United States had been working hard on the problem of space satellites. After a number of successes with animals and "uninhabited" capsules, they finally succeeded, on February 20, 1962, in launching the first American manned spaceship into orbit around the earth. The successful astronaut was Lieutenant-Colonel John H. Glenn, Jr., and he encircled the globe three times at a top speed of over 17,000 miles per hour. In 1966 a United States Navy officer left the cabin of his spacecraft and walked in space for forty-four minutes, hundreds of miles above the earth. His feat was surpassed in 1969, when Neil Armstrong left his lunar landing module and walked a measurable distance on the moon's surface. All over the world these successful voyages were hailed as events of capital importance. They at least promised an extension of our knowledge of outer space and would doubtless prepare the way for exploration of the moon and eventually of distant planets. But they also had sinister aspects. In addition to depriving possible social welfare programs of billions of dollars, the purpose that inspired them was almost exclusively to gain military advantage. It was assumed, for example, that giant spaceships or artificial satellites hurled into orbit might enable the nation that controlled them to dominate the earth. A disturbing factor for the United States and its allies was thus added to the armament race between East and West. Although space activity continued into the 1970's, emphasis was reduced.

SCIENCE—THE HOPE OF THE WORLD?

Moon exploration

Space aeronautics

Calder Hall. Built in 1956 in England, this is the world's first large-scale atomic power station. The two towers on the left are for cooling.

The Earth. This view taken from the moon by astronauts John W. Young and Charles M. Duke, Jr., of the Apollo 16 mission, shows the west coast of the North American continent, the Gulf of Mexico, Florida, and, below it, Cuba.

Advances in biology

Notable advances in the biological sciences also occurred after World War I. An outstanding one was the discovery of the viruses. Viruses are organisms so small that they pass through ordinary filters. Only by means of special filters made of collodion films, or by the use of ultraviolet or electron microscopes, can their presence be detected. They are the cause of a multitude of dread diseases, including smallpox, measles, infantile paralysis, influenza, rabies, yellow fever, and the common cold. No one has yet been able to say whether they should be classified as animate or inanimate objects. In some ways they appear to have the properties of living creatures, including the capacity to reproduce. But they are closely dependent upon their living host, and remain completely dormant except when they come into contact with living tissue. They seem to occupy a kind of intermediate stage between the inorganic and organic worlds, and are sometimes referred to as "the bridge between Life and Death." Perhaps Aristotle was right more than twenty-two centuries ago when he wrote: "Nature makes so gradual a transition from the inanimate to the animate kingdom that the boundary lines which separate them are indistinct and doubtful."

Antibiotics

From time to time during the history of medicine, discoveries have been made which can justifiably be described as epochal, in the sense that they open up new and much greater possibilities for the conquest of disease. One example was the discovery of vaccination for smallpox by Sir Edward Jenner in 1796. Another was the development and proof of the germ theory of disease by Louis Pasteur and Robert Koch about 1881. After 1918 a series of such epochal

902

discoveries laid the foundations for another new era of medical progress. In 1935 a German named Gerhard Domagk discovered the first of the sulfa drugs, which he called sulfanilamide. Soon others were added to the list. Each was found to be marvelously effective in curing or checking such diseases as rheumatic fever, gonorrhea, scarlet fever, and meningitis. About 1930 Sir Alexander Fleming described the first of the antibiotics, which came to be known as penicillin. Antibiotics are chemical agents produced by living organisms and possessing the power to check or kill bacteria. Many have their origin in molds, fungi, algae, and in simple organisms living in the soil. Penicillin was eventually found to be a kind of miracle drug producing spectacular results in the treatment of pneumonia, syphilis, peritonitis, tetanus, and numerous other maladies hitherto frequently fatal. About 1940 the second most famous of the antibiotics —streptomycin—was discovered by Dr. Selman A. Waksman. Streptomycin seems to hold its greatest promise in the treatment of tuberculosis, though it has been used for numerous other infections that do not yield to penicillin. Still other antibiotics are neomycin, also discovered by Dr. Waksman; aureomycin, effective against Rocky Mountain fever; and chloromycetin, valuable in the treatment of typhus and typhoid fever. Many antibiotics are now used in powerful combinations against a wide variety of human ailments. Yet another category of so-called "miracle drugs" were the tranquilizers. Introduced in 1955, they came to be used in the treatment of mental disorders and achieved success in making violent patients more tractable. They thus eliminated to some extent the "snake pits," the old-fashioned mental institutions with barred windows and locked doors. Although these drugs do not themselves effect cures, they help make the patient more accessible to other forms of therapy. Tranquilizers, of course, also gained comparatively widespread usage among the population at large as antidepressants and tension relievers. Indiscriminate use by the ill-informed led to some glaring evils.

Of almost equal importance with the discovery of new drugs has been the development of means of preventing disease. For the most part these have taken the form of vaccination. A characteristic example has been the development of two types of vaccination against poliomyelitis, or infantile paralysis. The first type was discovered by Dr. Jonas Salk of the Salk Institute for Biological Studies at San Diego. Salk used "killed" viruses of the disease to assist the bodies of human beings to build up immunity against infection. About five years later Dr. Albert B. Sabin of the University of Cincinnati developed a second type of vaccination using "live" but weakened viruses administered orally. The respective advantages of the two types of vaccination continued for some time to be a matter of controversy. During World War II a remarkable insecticide was perfected which gave promise of the ultimate elimination of two of the most ancient ene-

Dr. Jonas Salk in His Laboratory

mies of mankind, malaria and typhus. Popularly known as DDT, it destroys the lice and mosquitoes that transmit these diseases. Recent years have witnessed also the development and wide though not universal acceptance of the fluoridation process for preventing tooth decay in young people. It consists of the simple expedient of adding sodium fluoride to the water supply of municipalities. So impressive was the progress in these and other aspects of preventive medicine that some scientists incautiously predicted that in the comparatively near future every infectious disease known to man would be finally and completely conquered. Their optimism received a shock, however, about 1960, when it was discovered that "new" bacteria, resistant to antibiotics, were making their appearance. Whether they were mutants or older organisms formerly held in check by the balance of nature and now released through the destruction of their natural "enemies" by antibiotics, their menace was serious. This destruction of the balance of nature has recently become the source of great alarm among conservationists. They have procured the enactment of laws prohibiting the use of DDT and other pesticides by farmers and horticulturists in all developed countries. Farm bloc leaders took a different view. Banning of powerful insecticides like DDT and dieldrin would boost the cost of agricultural production almost to prohibitive levels.

Other medical achievements

No account of medical achievements since 1914 would be complete without mention at least of the following: the development of insulin by the Canadian scientist Frederick Banting for the treatment of diabetes; the perfection of radiation treatments for cancer; the discovery that malignant tumors develop their own fluids essential for growth, and that when these fluids are inhibited, tumors fail to grow and soon actually die or become harmless; the discovery of new methods of detecting cancer and other diseases by the use of radioactive isotopes as "tracers"; the development of techniques for storing blood and blood plasma for transfusions; the discovery of the hormone ACTH and its application to asthma and to inflammatory diseases of the eye; the development of artificial kidneys and mechanical hearts to assist and even partially to supplant natural organs weakened by injury or disease; the discovery of atabrine as a substitute for quinine in the treatment of malaria; and the development of psychosomatic medicine based upon a recognition of the importance of anxiety, fear, and other psychological factors in causing ulcers, asthma, high blood pressure, and diseases of the heart. By 1970 the people of the world ought to have enjoyed the most abundant health since the dawn of medicine. Statistically, perhaps they did, taken as a whole. But many parts of the world still suffered from the health problems associated with war, social upheaval, poverty, and famine. Depressing reports of understaffed hospitals, or even hospitals with no staff at all in certain departments, made a mockery of high standards of medical practice even in advanced countries.

In the great majority of the "advanced" nations the issue was one of priorities. Nearly everywhere the military budget took the lion's share of public appropriations. In Soviet Russia expenditures for defense amounted to 8.5 per cent of the Gross National Product. In the United States 8.6 is the percentage. Only in France do expenditures for education exceed those for national defense. In smaller countries the fraction of expenditures to the Gross National Product is 4.0 for Sweden, 2.2 for Switzerland, 2.6 for Denmark.[3]

The record of scientific development in the twentieth century requires consideration of the social sciences. Most of these disciplines were already in existence when the century began, but new interpretations were added and some of the older conceptions were reversed. The two sciences most susceptible to radical change were anthropology and sociology. Originally a study of races and the physical characteristics of man, anthropology was broadened later into a science of "cultures." The pioneers in promoting this transformation were Franz Boas and Bronislaw Malinowski. Both were born and educated in Europe, and both died after years of lecturing in the United States. Their contributions lay principally in the advancement of racial equality. Boas denied the alleged superiority of the Caucasians on the ground of the proved inability of the colored races to resist the white man's diseases. Some of Boas' disciples went even farther than their master in repudiating notions of the inequality of races. A notable example was Ruth Benedict, who taught in the 1940's that the assumed superiority of races by nature was largely a myth. She showed that during World War II Negro children transferred from the Southern states to the North soon revealed themselves the equal of their Northern classmates under conditions of approximately equal opportunity. Malinowski was mainly interested in the emancipation of primitive man from the stigma of brutality and tyranny that rested upon him. He did not describe the "noble savage" as an angel in disguise, but neither did he regard him as "to his fellow man a wolf." Rather he thought of the earliest societies as founded on a basis of need and convenience in getting things done. Such considerations he found among the extremely primitive Trobriand Islanders in the South Pacific, and he assumed them to have been typical of all peoples only remotely touched by civilization.

The great names in sociology were borne by men who began their careers early in the twentieth century, although some have lived to our day. The pioneer among them was Max Weber. Born in Germany before World War I, he served as a professor of law and society at the University of Munich. After Germany became a republic in 1918 he was appointed a member of the commission that drafted

Overemphasis upon military expenditures

Anthropology

Sociology: Max Weber

[3] *The Military Balance*, Institute for Strategic Studies, London, 1970–1971.

the Weimar Constitution. As a sociologist Weber won fame for a book entitled *The Protestant Ethic and the Spirit of Capitalism*. In it he placed a heavy burden of guilt upon Protestantism for alienating man from a benevolent God and a kindly universe. It made work a cardinal virtue and idleness a supreme vice. After the Protestant Revolution man could gain happiness only by driving himself with the fury of the damned. A distressing product of the Protestant Revolution, according to Weber, was revival of the doctrines of original sin and total depravity. He found such doctrines as lingering remnants in the writings of Soren Kierkegaard, Karl Barth, and Reinhold Niebuhr. One of their forerunners, Joseph deMaistre, taught that "men cannot help killing each other."

Sociology in our time has made a special appeal to blacks, both in the United States and abroad. Quite a number of their scholars who began their careers in other fields have switched to sociology because of the opportunities it provides for the study and analysis of racial problems. The greatest expounder of black racial attitudes in the twentieth century was probably William E. B. Du Bois. Though proud of his French and Dutch ancestry, he identified himself with the black race. He gloried in the name of Negro and was "proud of the black blood that flowed in his veins." He attended Fisk University and graduated with second honors. In 1895 he became the first Negro to win a Ph.D. from Harvard. For many years he was head of the Department of Sociology at Atlanta University. Toward the end of his life, however, he devoted himself largely to Pan-African unity. In 1961 he applied for membership in the Communist Party and left the United States to live in Ghana. From his early years Du Bois ranked as a strong advocate of the uniqueness of the black man and his culture. He rejected the approach of Booker T. Washington and his advocacy of industrial education. He believed the Negro to be the intellectual equal of the white man, and he would accept no inferior position for black culture. He held that the Talented Tenth, regardless of race, must always provide the vanguard of every new civilization. Throughout his life he was subject to rising and falling tides of vilification. At fifty he wrote that the occurrence of his death would have been hailed with approval; at seventy-five his "death was practically requested." [4]

Another black sociologist of recent times was Martin Luther King, Jr. Better known for his defense of civil rights than for his scholarship, King was the most active spokesman in the cause of desegregation in both North and South. Although he was educated for the ministry, his interests gravitated principally to sociology. He led marches and demonstrations and made countless speeches in behalf of racial justice. For years he was the foremost exponent of nonviolent resistance in the United States. In 1964 he was awarded a

William E. B. Du Bois

Martin Luther
King, Jr.

[4] *Autobiography of W. E. B. Du Bois*, New York, published posthumously in 1968, p. 414.

Nobel Peace Prize. It was one of the last great triumphs of his career. Already he had begun to divert his attention from Negro rights to crusading against the Vietnam War. On April 4, 1968 he was assassinated outside his motel room in Memphis, Tennessee.

4. CONTEMPORARY MAN AND HIS WORLD AS REFLECTED THROUGH LITERATURE

Literary movements during the period of the depression and the two world wars showed tendencies similar to those in philosophy. Indeed, in many instances, it was difficult to tell where philosophy ended and literature began. The major novelists, poets, and dramatists were deeply concerned about social and political problems and about the hope and destiny of man. Like the philosophers, they were disillusioned by the brute facts of World War I and by the failure of victory to fulfill its promises. Many were profoundly affected also by the revolutionary developments in science and especially by the probings of the new psychology into the hidden secrets of the mind. Instead of a being created by God just "a little lower than the angels," man seemed now to be a creature just a bit higher than the apes. Finally, of course, literary men were influenced by the Great Depression and by the return to war in 1939. Both these developments led to a searching of methods and, among many writers, to a partial revision of objectives.

Major tendencies in literature

Much of the literature of the interwar period revolved around themes of frustration, cynicism, and disenchantment. It was the era of the "lost generation," of young men whose ideals had been shattered by the brutal events of their time. Its mood was set by the early novels of Ernest Hemingway, by the poetry of T. S. Eliot, and by the dramas of Eugene O'Neill. In *A Farewell to Arms* Hemingway gave to the public one of its first insights into the folly and meanness of war and set a pattern which other writers were soon to follow. T. S. Eliot in his poem, *The Waste Land* (1922), presented a philosophy that was close to despair. Once you are born, he seemed to be saying, life is a living death to be ground out in boredom and frustration. The pessimism of Eugene O'Neill appeared to be somewhat different from that of his contemporaries. His tragedies depicted man not so much as a victim of society but rather as the pitiable slave of his own abnormal nature. Most critics would probably agree that O'Neill's greatest dramas were *Strange Interlude* (1927) and *Mourning Becomes Electra* (1931). His own story of his tortured life, *Long Day's Journey into Night*, was not published until after his death. By general consent O'Neill is regarded as America's greatest playwright. By conviction he was a dyed-in-the-wool pessimist. All the old gods were dead, and no new ones were likely to appear. There was no salvation except resignation to a stoic fate no one could explain or understand. Other tendencies manifest-

T. S. Eliot (1888–1965). Noted author of *The Waste Land* and *Murder in the Cathedral* in his London study. He was awarded the Nobel Prize for Literature in 1948. American born, he had been a citizen of Great Britain since 1927.

Noel Coward and Ernest Hemingway in Havana

ing themselves during this era were determinism and stream-of-consciousness writing. Theodore Dreiser brought determinism to a climax in *An American Tragedy* (1925). Deeply influenced by psychoanalysis, James Joyce became the leading exponent of stream-of-consciousness writing. His greatest novel, *Ulysses* (1922), was essentially a study of reverie rather than action.

Influence of the Depression: literature with a serious purpose

The Great Depression of the 1930's forced a reexamination of the methods and purposes of literature. In the midst of economic stagnation and threats of fascism and war, the theory evolved that literature must have a serious purpose, that it should indict meanness, cruelty, and barbarism and point the way to a society more just. The new trend was reflected in the works of a diversity of writers. John Steinbeck depicted the sorry plight of impoverished farmers fleeing from the "dust bowl" to California only to find that all the good earth had been monopolized by big land companies that exploited their workers. Pervading some of the plays of Robert Sherwood and the novels of André Malraux was the strong suggestion that man's struggle against tyranny and injustice is the chief thing that gives meaning and value to life. A similar theme may be said to have characterized Ernest Hemingway's *For Whom the Bell Tolls* (1940). Here also was the strong implication that the individual, in sacrificing himself for the cause of the people, gives a meaning and dignity to life that can be achieved in no other way.

Literature with a serious purpose tended later to emphasize the lonely and tragic life of the common man and to protest ever more

908

strongly against cruelty and injustice. A warm affinity for the plain folk of rural New England was expressed by Robert Frost, greatly beloved American poet. Nobel-prize winner William Faulkner devoted superb artistic talents to portrayals of crude elemental behavior in backward areas of the Deep South. The tragedy of World War II brought a series of novels dealing with the conflict itself, with the heroism of those who resisted Nazi tyranny, or with the brutality and inefficiency of military systems. Foremost among such writings were Norman Mailer's *The Naked and the Dead* and James Jones' *From Here to Eternity*. Both portrayed the coarseness and cruelty of military life with a ruthless realism. But along with these trends toward warm sympathy and stark realism as means of conveying hatred of injustice and oppression, there were also some new manifestations. One was a turning to religion to compensate for a sense of overwhelming tragedy or to prevent calamities which seemed certain to flow from allowing science to get out of control. T. S. Eliot, who in the 1920's had found the universe a barren wasteland with no fruits but boredom and despair, now discovered that life could be meaningful when ennobled by the ageless truths of the Church. His new mood was exemplified by *Murder in the Cathedral* and *The Cocktail Party*. In spite of the different directions of their thinking, most of the postwar writers seemed to have much in common. They were expressing with one voice their concern over the loneliness of man. They saw human beings in an age of mass thinking and mass actions as helpless and pitiable creatures, craving assistance from whatever source it might seem available.

Most of the literary moods of midcentury continued into the 1960's and 1970's. Especially marked was the revolt against the complexities of modern life. There was the same protest against injustice and maltreatment of the weak and unfortunate. Significantly, some of these trends made themselves evident in the Soviet Union, especially after the death of Stalin in 1953. Soon after that date a novel written by Boris Pasternak and bearing the title *Dr. Zhivago* was promptly acclaimed as one of the best to be written in modern times. Though it was allowed to be published only in Italian and English translations, there could be no question of the author's understanding of Russian life and Russian culture. He wrote a burning indictment of the Soviet campaign to pour every citizen into the same mold. Interesting parallels to the life of Pasternak are to be found in the career of Aleksandr Solzhenitsyn. Both were novelists entitled to rank with the world's greatest. Each was awarded the Nobel Prize for Literature, Pasternak in 1958 and Solzhenitsyn in 1970. Both were blacklisted in their own country and neither considered it wise to go to Stockholm to receive the Nobel award. Each produced at least one novel of outstanding merit—Pasternak's *Dr. Zhivago* and Solzhenitsyn's *The First Circle*. The two works defended the right of the individual to live his own life and threw much

Aleksandr Solzhenitsyn

909

light on internal conditions in the Soviet Union. Interestingly enough Solzhenitsyn's works have not been popular among the workers of the Soviet Union. They seem to be regarded with much the same attitude that "hard hats" in most countries take toward the achievements of intellectuals.

The plight of
Western man in
a hostile world

As one would expect, the literature of protest has been more conspicuous in Western countries than in Soviet Russia. It has often involved not simply a castigation of human baseness but an indictment of the whole scheme of the universe. The foremost exponent of bitter discontent in the literature of the early twentieth century was the German novelist Franz Kafka. Educated in the German schools of Prague, he fought the stubborn tyranny of a violent father in striving to gain a foothold as a writer. To his other sufferings was added a raging lung disease which brought an end to his life at the age of forty. Kafka's novels present a vision of man in a hostile universe hopelessly striving to come to terms with a remote and unknown power. It is not so much a dream as it is a nightmare composed of weird, fantastic details brought together in a terrifying pattern. His best-known work, *The Castle*, is at once a satire on bureaucracy and a philosophical representation of the isolation of man in the universe.

Yet another movement has distinguished the literary developments of our age. This is the movement known as the Literature of the Absurd. It is so called from the fact that its authors see individuals as trapped in a nonsense world which moves with its own mad logic. The movement has been inspired by the plays of the German Bertolt Brecht, and the Rumanian Eugène Ionesco. The great master of the movement, however, is Samuel Beckett. Born in Ireland but removing as a young man to Paris, he lived almost entirely as a recluse. Though he recognized the hopelessness of man's condition, he contended that the human animal must go on striving after rays of light that might have the faintest chance of penetrating the dusk and gloom. In 1969 he was awarded the Nobel Prize in Literature but like several others who had been similarly honored, he refused to travel to Stockholm to receive the award. His best-known play is *Waiting for Godot*, published in 1952.

A principal forerunner of the literature of the absurd was the French-Algerian Albert Camus. Though enough of an idealist to participate in the Resistance during World War II, he really had no faith in anything. He sought for some years to work out the tenets of an atheistic humanism; yet in his books he stressed the irrational nature of the universe, even to the extent of its irrationality and proneness to suicide. His death in an auto accident in 1963 brought an end to his stormy but brilliant career.

Most black literature is American largely because in America blacks have been most conscious of their race and most sensitive to the ebb and flow of their racial hopes. It had its origin primarily in the 1920's, in a movement known as the Harlem Renaissance. Such writers as Countee Cullen sought to invest the Negro with a culture at least equal to that of the white man. Their poetry did not generally foreshadow the fiery wrath of their later protagonists but sought to idealize the Negro's past and portray his dreams of equality with whites. The Great Depression brought an end to the dreams of the Harlem Renaissance. In the 1930's Langston Hughes gave a high place to themes of working-class life in his poetry and lauded the spirit of protest in his "Brass Spitoons," a bitter account of a hotel porter's daily rounds.

American leadership in black literature

The major disenchantments and searing indictments in black literature did not begin until the revolutionary era that followed in the wake of the Depression and World War II. The initiator of the new trend was Richard Wright, a product of the misery and squalor of rural Mississippi. As a youth he drifted to Chicago and became a resident of and spokesman for the black ghetto. In his *Native Son* and in his autobiography, *Black Boy*, he portrayed with scathing realism the oppression of working-class Negroes. Despite the pretensions of the New Deal he found that the burdens of that class had not been appreciably lightened. As a novelist Wright has been compared with Dostoievski, but in his social and psychological determinism he bore a closer kinship with Theodore Dreiser. He seems to have been the first American black to preach the liberating effect of killing an enemy. In *Black Boy* the hero (Wright himself) experienced a sense of freedom because he "had done something the white man would notice." He seemed to be saying, though, that a youth reared in the ghetto is almost doomed to ruin. The frenzied pursuit of money and sex, and the wretchedness of poverty, combined with "neurosis-producing" racial suppression, can be guaranteed to accomplish that result.

Complete disenchantment and furious indictment

The most talented black writers of the postwar generation have probably been James Baldwin and Lorraine Hansberry. James Baldwin was born in Harlem, the son of a clergyman, a rigid and embittered man with few gifts of leadership. At the age of fourteen James became a Pentecostal preacher. But his heart was not in it. He left home and drifted into whatever odd employments he could find. After World War II he lived for ten years in Paris. Perhaps his greatest work was *Go Tell It on the Mountain*, which he published in 1953. The dominant theme of his novels was whatever demeans the black man by its very nature demeans the white man who is the author of it. Baldwin was an articulate spokesman of the black American revolution, but he wrote also in defense of deviants and nonconformists generally. Such was true especially of *Another Country* and *Nobody Knows My Name*. One of the most sensitive contemporary black writers was Lorraine Hansberry. She was not primarily a novelist but essentially a poet and dramatist. She won distinction in her brief lifetime for her play *Raisin in the Sun*. Her dramatic talent was shown even more clearly in *To Be Young, Gifted and Black*, presented on the New York stage four years after her death. Unlike

James Baldwin

911

many of her contemporaries, she was not an exponent of black revolution. Nevertheless, she could write in defiance, and sometimes in bitterness, when the delight she saw in life was swallowed up by bigotry and repression. In common with scores of great artists, she was torn between hope and despair. But she never lost faith in the greatness of the human spirit. She believed that the human race does command its own destiny, and that that destiny can "eventually embrace the stars." Her own destiny was to die of cancer at the age of thirty-four.

5. THE FULFILLMENT OF TRENDS IN ART AND MUSIC

The revolt
against impressionism

As in literature, so in art the twentieth century was marked by revolt against exquisiteness and artificiality. In the closing decades of the preceding century this revolt had taken the form of a reaction against impressionism. Cézanne and Van Gogh criticized the formlessness and insubstantiality of the work of the impressionists and held that the figures of the painter's art should be as solidly and completely molded as statues.

Cubism

The work of Cézanne and Van Gogh, we have noted, led directly to *cubism*, the most revolutionary art of the twentieth century. It was developed about 1905 by Pablo Picasso, and continues to be a popular mode of artistic expression. Cubism began as an art of realism *par excellence*. It endeavors to present life, not in accordance with a nicely adorned conventional pattern, but as a jumble of arms, legs, heads, and bodies caught in motion and having no arrangement among themselves except that given by the observer. But disorder and disorganization are not for the cubist ends in themselves. They are intended partly to reflect notions of form—to repudiate the conception of art as mere prettiness.

Surrealism

An even more violent movement of rebellion against traditional standards of art and of life was *surrealism*, whose high priest since 1929 has been the Spaniard Salvador Dali. Originating about 1918 under the combined influence of the war and psychoanalysis, surrealism flourished during the age of nihilism that followed that war. The aim of its followers was not to represent the world of nature but to portray the reactions of the human mind. For this purpose they delved into the subconscious and attempted to depict the content of dreams and the weird impressions of reverie. This commonly resulted in a technique quite different from that of traditional art. In general, the surrealists paid little attention to the conventional standards of beauty and form. They argued that, in the light of the new psychology, naturalism was impossible if art were to have any value as an accurate expression of meaning.

For a time after 1930 the bizarre and anarchic painting of the extreme modernist schools went into a partial eclipse. Its place

Above: *Little Big Painting*, Roy Lichtenstein (born 1923). Oil on canvas. (The Whitney Museum of American Art). In the 1960's and early 1970's, American artists dominated the new movements, particularly "Pop," "Op," and "the New Realism." The works on this and the following page are by some of the best-known contemporary artists. Below: *Summer Rental No. 2*, Robert Rauschenberg (born 1925). Oil on canvas. (Collection Whitney Museum of American Art). Gift of the Friends of the Whitney Museum of American Art.

Top Left: *Girl in Doorway*, George Segal (born 1924). A life-size construction in plaster, wood, glass, and aluminum paint. (Collection Whitney Museum of American Art). Top Right: *Green Coca Cola Bottles*, Andy Warhol (born 1931). Oil on canvas. (Collection Whitney Museum of American Art). Gift of the Friends of the Whitney Museum of American Art. Left: *Gran Cairo*, Frank Stella (born 1936). Synthetic polymer paint on canvas. (Collection Whitney Museum of American Art). Gift of the Friends of the Whitney Museum of American Art.

was taken to an extent by a virile and popular art of the common man.[5] Among the chief representatives of the new movement were the Mexicans, Diego Rivera and José Clemente Orozco, and the United States painters Thomas Benton, Adolph Dehn, William Gropper, and Grant Wood. The fundamental aim of these artists was to depict the social conditions of the modern world and to present in graphic detail the hopes and struggles of peasants and toilers. While they scarcely adhered to any of the conventions of the past, there was nothing unintelligible about their work; it was intended to be art that anyone could understand. At the same time, much of it bore the sting or thrust of social satire. Orozco, in particular, delighted in pillorying the hypocrisy of the Church and the greed and cruelty of plutocrats and plunderers.

Around 1950 another innovating movement in painting began to attract considerable attention. Known by different names, it is perhaps most accurately called *abstract expressionism*. Thus far its chief exponents have been Jackson Pollock, Willem de Kooning, and Franz Kline. So far as the past is concerned it owes most to cubism and surrealism. But the abstract expressionists prefer to repudiate nearly all the traditions of the past. They believe in innovation, experimentation, and the use of bold and startling devices to achieve effects. Some of the work of their minor disciples hardly appears to be painting at all, but seems rather a hodgepodge of daubs of paint interspersed with scraps of metal, bits of cloth and paper, and similar objects. Some who cannot draw achieve interesting results with coffee grounds and bread crumbs.

[5] The art of the common man is also called regional art, especially in the forms developed in the United States.

The new art of the common man

Abstract expressionism

See color plates at pages 880–881

Mahoning by Franz Kline. An attempt by an abstract expressionist to convey the quality of brute power he feels to be characteristic of modern industrial society. Original in the Whitney Museum of Art, New York.

The chief trends
in contemporary
music

Impressionism

Igor Stravinsky

Expressionism:
atonality

It was inevitable that music should reflect the spirit of disillusionment that reached a climax following World War I. The more original developments were closely parallel to those in painting. Most fundamental of all was the revolt against the romantic tradition, especially as it had culminated in Wagner. Many, although by no means all, composers went so far as to repudiate the aesthetic ideal entirely, relying upon complexity and novelty of structure or on a sheer display of energy to supply interest to their works.

Deviations from the classical and romantic formulas have been generally of two types, designated broadly as impressionism and expressionism. The former seeks to exploit the qualities of musical sound to suggest feelings or images. The latter is concerned more with form than with sensuous effects and tends toward abstraction. The most perfect exponent of impressionism was Claude Debussy, its originator, whose work was described in an earlier chapter. Even in France impressionism did not prove to be an enduring school. With Maurice Ravel (1875–1937), most celebrated of the composers who reflected Debussy's influence, it became less poetic and picturesque and acquired a degree of cold impassivity together with greater firmness of texture.

Expressionism, more radical and more influential than impressionism, comprises two main schools: *atonality*, founded by the Viennese Arnold Schoenberg (1874–1951), and *polytonality*, best typified by the Russian Igor Stravinsky (1882–1971). Atonality implies the repudiation of the concept of fixed tonal relationships; it abolishes *key*. In this type of music, dissonances are the rule rather than the exception, and the melodic line commonly alternates between chromatic manipulation and strange unsingable leaps. In short, the ordinary principles of composition are reversed. However, emancipation from the bonds of tradition has enabled the atonalists to give undivided attention to the development of their own subjective ideas with the utmost originality. They attempt, with some success, to let musical sound become a vehicle for expressing the inner meaning and elemental structure of things. Odd as it may appear, some atonal works are deeply emotional in effect. They betray a kinship with symbolism and also show the influence of the theories of the subconscious derived from psychoanalysis. Most of the distinctive features of the atonal school are vividly incorporated in Schoenberg's *Pierrot Lunaire*. This fantasy, in which the singer intones her part in a special "song-speech," somewhat between singing and reciting, has been described as creating "a whole world of strange fascination and enchantment, of nameless horrors and terrible imaginings, of perverse and poisonous beauty."[6]

Polytonality, of which Stravinsky is the most famous exponent, is essentially a radical kind of counterpoint, deriving its inspiration

[6] Cecil Gray, *A Survey of Contemporary Music*, p. 176.

partly from baroque practices of counterpoint that were placed in
the service of new ideas. However, it is not content simply to inter-
weave independent melodies which together form concord, but un-
dertakes to combine separate keys and unrelated harmonic systems,
with results that are highly discordant. It is thus another example of
revolt against the European harmonic heritage and differs from
atonality more in technique than in ultimate aim. But while the
atonalists have retained elements of romanticism, the polytonalists
have tried to resurrect the architectural qualities of pure form,
movement, and rhythm, stripping away all sentimentality and
sensuous connotations. Stravinsky affirmed that his intention was
to produce music in which acoustic properties were the only consideration and which would appeal to the physical ear alone. His
coldly detached, anti-aesthetic experiments have much in common
with cubism and similar tendencies in modern painting. The application of his theories to such purposes conveys the sardonic impression of human beings who are mere automatons, manipulated by
their own physical urges or by the grim hand of a mechanical fate.
Stravinsky's style and interests have undergone successive changes;
in recent years he has turned from the theater to more distinctly
concert forms. Without sacrificing his intense individuality, he has
achieved an increasing clarity of expression and an almost classical integration of structural design.

Polytonality

    The twentieth century produced other great composers who,
though touched by neoclassicism and the other prevailing trends,
went their own individual ways. Mention should be made of the
Hungarian Béla Bartók (1881–1945), the German Paul Hindemith
(1895–1963), and the Russian Serge Prokofiev (1891–1953). In the
meantime American music also came of age. After a period largely
dominated by German romanticism, in the third decade of the
twentieth century there emerged a "school" of music which, though
representing various shades of modernism, can rightfully be called
American. Aaron Copland (born 1900), Roger Sessions (born 1896),
and William Schuman (born 1910), as examples, can take their place
among the best composers active in Europe.

*Other twentieth-
century composers*

6. EPILOGUE

    No one can do more than strike a tentative balance of good and
evil in the long record of human history. The clouds of ignorance
and mystery hang so low as to be almost impenetrable. Time was
when the skies were brighter. John Milton wrote of *Paradise Lost*,
and then perhaps with slightly more confidence sang of the delights
of *Paradise Regained*. The socialists of the nineteenth century, from
Owen to Marx, recognized man as a victim of oppression and
poverty, but believed that a golden day would dawn with a new
freedom from exploitation.

*The balance of
good and evil*

915

The remaining years of the nineteenth century did not greatly alter the scene. A few outbursts of sadness and dejection punctuated the general environment, but the prevailing atmosphere was suffused with confidence and hope. World War I, however, brought signs of a bitter reaction. The cruelty and waste of that war, to say nothing of its egregious folly, persuaded young men who were its actual or probable victims to view it with nothing but disgust and horror.

Many young people today have only a limited sense of history. The great events of the past seem too remote to bear much significance. In like manner the future is too uncertain to be a guide to hapless man. The consequence, then, has been a revival of some of the caustic views of history popular in the eighteenth century. History in those days had almost no standing as a scientific appraisal of the past or a possible guide to the future. For Herbert Spencer history was "worthless gossip." To Napoleon it was a "fable agreed upon." To Edward Gibbon it appeared to be "little more than a register of the crimes, follies, and misfortunes of mankind." The German philosopher Hegel maintained in one of his darker moments that "the only thing that peoples and governments learn from the study of history is that they learn nothing from the study of history."

Does history repeat itself sufficiently to enable us to predict the future? A large proportion of the philosophers of history have conceived of a uniform pattern characterizing the growth and decline of civilizations over thousands of years. Toynbee attributes the growth primarily to a condition of adversity and the decline to such factors as militarism and war, barbarization from within, and the rise of an "internal proletariat." By the last term he means a class like the city mob of ancient Rome who are "in" but not "of" a given society. Despised and disinherited, they nurse grievances against the society and gradually undermine it. Oswald Spengler saw the growth and decay of civilizations, or cultures as he called them, paralleling the four seasons or the life of an organism. Each had its spring or youth phase, its summer or early maturity phase, its autumn or late maturity phase, and its winter or senility phase.

Even in periods of the brightest optimism writers who have done much thinking about the meaning of history have generally assumed that decay and disintegration will follow prosperity and progress. For example, the Founding Fathers in the United States viewed the future of their own country with grave misgivings. So long as the nation remained predominantly agricultural, with an abundance of cheap land, all would be well. But increasing population in a few generations would result in the growth of large cities, with their slums, corrupt politicians, and a dependent mob ready to sell its votes to the highest bidder. The ultimate outcome would be the rise of Catilines and Caesars, who would seek, with the support of the proletariat, to overthrow the republic. In the late nineteenth century, when the age of science and industry in the United States was still facing the rising sun, Brooks Adams and his brother Henry described with accents of gloom the ultimate decay of Western culture. Henry Adams sought to interpret civilization in terms of a scientific law—the second law of thermodynamics, or the law of the dissipation of energy. He predicted that the civilization of Western man would expend its vital force and die of exhaustion by 1932.

There seems little doubt that civilizations do grow old and die from a number of causes. A major one apparently is urbanization, carried to the point where a large proportion of the population is crowded into huge metropolitan areas. This condition adds so much to the complexity of social problems that human intelligence is unable to solve them. Crime, disease, boredom, insanity, corruption, poverty in the midst of plenty are only a few of these critical problems. Pollution of water and air threaten to make large portions of the earth uninhabitable. Excessive concentration of industry results in overproduction and leads to depressions and to exhaustion of natural resources. Whether our own civilization has reached this stage is a question impossible to answer. There are, of course, many ominous portents tempered by a few rays of hope. Disease in the form of several of the great pestilences seems on the way toward extinction. Cholera is largely confined to the Third World and to a few other areas where standards of sanitation are low. Smallpox in advanced countries is becoming so rare that health departments no longer insist upon wholesale vaccinations. Tuberculosis also is nearing extinction as a major disease. On the other hand, much work remains to be done to advance medical progress in other fields. Cardiac and circulatory ailments continue as the principal killers of human beings despite all the recent progress in open heart surgery, "pacers," and transplants. Cancer, emphysema, and venereal diseases continue as troublesome maladies even in countries most widely known for medical advancement. We can only conjecture what may be happening in those parts of the world where famine stalks the land and overpopulation and erosion rule out most chances of a better day.

Despite all the efforts of world leaders, the ghastly threat of annihilation still hangs over the human race. No one can gauge the extent of this threat. It may take the form of defense against a nuclear attack, or more probably the use of a nuclear threat as a means of intimidation. In either case the effect is almost certain to be catastrophic war. Through the entire course of history war has been the chief enemy of civilization. Its principal fruits have been inflation, impoverishment, revolution, and chaos. It has destroyed the best blood of nation after nation and left the weaklings to become the fathers of the new generation.

War, of course, should not be regarded as an insoluble problem. Other evils in the past have been corrected or eliminated even

The fate of our own civilization

Signs of hope tempered by darker shadows

The most ghastly threat of all

917

Basic evils
then and now

though long established or deeply entrenched. Few reformers would have foreseen the abolition of slavery in the early nineteenth century in the British Empire and the United States or the emancipation of the serfs in Russia in 1861. But none of these evils had the powerful backing of governments themselves in keeping them alive. Organized Catholic and Protestant forces keep the caldron boiling in Northern Ireland. Similar hatreds, fostered by religious differences but actually based on demands for political aggrandizement by Arab and Jewish rulers in the Middle East, threaten to drag outside powers into the conflict. Perhaps even more distressing was a violent clash between India and Pakistan. Both are desperately poor, overpopulated, and harassed by a bitter heritage of colonial misrule. They appeared at times to be looking for war as a respite from national problems and a relief from boredom and despair. Yet it would be a mistake to consider any of these nations as having sovereign control over its own destiny. Invariably they were used by great powers to pull one another's chestnuts out of the fire. Pakistan became an instrument of the United States with India as a counterpart for Russia in Southern Asia. In the winter of 1971 Pakistan and India went to war, supported by their two patrons among the great powers. The result was a victory for India, and the subsequent division of Pakistan into two states, West Pakistan and the republic of Bangla Desh.

SELECTED READINGS

· *Items so designated are available in paperbound editions.*

Barzun, Jacques, *Romanticism and the Modern Ego*, Boston, 1945. A discerning interpretation.

Boulding, Kenneth, *The Meaning of the 20th Century*, New York, 1964.

· Bracey, John H., Jr., Meier, August, and Rudwick, Elliot M., *Black Nationalism in America*, New York, 1970 (Bobbs Merrill).

Brisbane, Robert H., *The Black Vanguard*, Valley Forge, Pa., 1970. Scholarly but skimpy for the period since 1960.

Bruun, Geoffrey, *The World in the Twentieth Century*, New York, 1948.

Burns, E. M., *Ideas in Conflict*, New York, 1960. A survey of contemporary thought.

· Copland, Aaron, *The New Music*, New York, 1968 (Norton Library).

· Frazier, Thomas R., *Afro-American History, Primary Sources*, New York, 1970 (Harcourt, Brace, Jovanovich).

· Hecht, Selig, *Explaining the Atom*, New York, 1947 (Compass, rev.).

Heilbroner, Robert, *The Future as History*, New York, 1959.

· Jeans, Sir James, *The Universe Around Us*, New York, 1944 (Cambridge University Press).

Lang, Paul, *Music in Western Civilization*, New York, 1941. An excellent, inclusive account.

Logan, Rayford W., ed., *W. E. B. Du Bois, A Profile*, New York, 1971.

Machlis, Joseph, *The Enjoyment of Music*, third ed., New York, 1970.

Marcus, John T., *Heaven, Hell and History. A Survey of Man's Faith in History from Antiquity to the Present.* New York, 1967.

Mead, Margaret, *Continuities in Cultural Evolution*, New Haven, 1964.

Meier, August, and Rudwick, Elliot M., *From Plantation to Ghetto: An* *Interpretive History of American Negroes*, New York, 1966.

Moore, Wilbert E., *Social Change*, Englewood Cliffs, N.J., 1964.

· Muller, H. J., *The Uses of the Past*, New York, 1952 (Mentor).

· Northrop, F. C. S., *The Meeting of East and West*, New York, 1946 (Collier).

Ogburn, William F., *On Culture and Social Change: Selected Papers*, Chicago, 1964.

Peeks, Edward, *The Long Struggle for Black Power*, New York, 1970. An excellent account by a black liberal.

Schapiro, J. S., *The World in Crisis*, New York, 1950.

Singer, Charles, *A History of Biology*, New York, 1950.

· Slochower, Harry, *No Voice Is Wholly Lost*, New York, 1945. Also available in paperback under the title *Literature and Philosophy between Two World Wars* (Citadel, 1964).

· Snow, C. P., *The Two Cultures and A Second Look*, Cambridge, 1965 (Mentor).

· Storing, Herbert, J., ed., *What Country Have I? Political Writings by Black Americans*, New York, 1970 (St. Martin's).

· Wilson, Edmund, *Axel's Castle*, New York, 1958 (Scribner Library). An interpretative study of recent trends in literature.

· Wittels, Fritz, *Freud and His Time*, New York, 1948 (Universal Library).

SOURCE MATERIALS

Baumer, F. L. V., *Main Currents of Western Thought*, New York, 1952.

· Dewey, John, *Reconstruction in Philosophy* (Beacon, 1957).

· ———, *Liberalism and Social Action* (Capricorn, 1963).

· Niebuhr, Reinhold, *The Children of Light and the Children of Darkness*, New York, 1960 (Scribner Library).

Spengler, Oswald, *The Decline of the West*, Introduction, New York, 1945, 2 vols.

Rulers of Principal European States since 700 A.D.

―――――――――― *The Carolingian Dynasty* ―――――――――

Pepin, Mayor of the Palace, 714
Charles Martel, Mayor of the Palace, 715–741
Pepin I, Mayor of the Palace, 741; King, 751–768
Charlemagne, King, 768–814; Emperor, 800–814
Louis the Pious, Emperor, 814–840

WEST FRANCIA
Charles the Bald, King, 840–877; Emperor, 875
Louis II, King, 877–879
Louis III, King, 879–882
Carloman, King, 879–884

MIDDLE KINGDOMS
Lothair, Emperor, 840–855
Louis (Italy), Emperor, 855–875
Charles (Provence), King, 855–863
Lothair II (Lorraine), King, 855–869

EAST FRANCIA
Ludwig, King, 840–876
Carloman, King, 876–880
Ludwig, King, 876–882
Charles the Fat, Emperor, 876–887

―――――――――― *Holy Roman Emperors* ―――――――――

SAXON DYNASTY
Otto I, 962–973
Otto II, 973–983
Otto III, 983–1002
Henry II, 1002–1024

FRANCONIAN DYNASTY
Conrad II, 1024–1039
Henry III, 1039–1056
Henry IV, 1056–1106
Henry V, 1106–1125
Lothair II (of Saxony), King, 1125–1133; Emperor, 1133–1137   **921**

HOHENSTAUFEN DYNASTY

Conrad III, 1138–1152
Frederick I (Barbarossa), 1152–1190
Henry VI, 1190–1197
Philip of Swabia, 1198–1208 ⎫
Otto IV (Welf), 1198–1215 ⎬ Rivals
Frederick II, 1220–1250
Conrad IV, 1250–1254

INTERREGNUM, 1254–1273
EMPERORS FROM VARIOUS DYNASTIES

Rudolf I (Hapsburg), 1273–1291
Adolf (Nassau), 1292–1298
Albert I (Hapsburg), 1298–1308
Henry VII (Luxemburg), 1308–1313
Ludwig IV (Wittelsbach), 1314–1347
Charles IV (Luxemburg), 1347–1378
Wenceslas (Luxemburg), 1378–1400
Rupert (Wittelsbach), 1400–1410
Sigismund (Luxemburg), 1410–1437

HAPSBURG DYNASTY

Albert II, 1438–1439
Frederick III, 1440–1493
Maximilian I, 1493–1519
Charles V, 1519–1556
Ferdinand I, 1556–1564
Maximilian II, 1564–1576
Rudolf II, 1576–1612
Matthias, 1612–1619
Ferdinand II, 1619–1637
Ferdinand III, 1637–1657
Leopold I, 1658–1705
Joseph I, 1705–1711
Charles VI, 1711–1740
Charles VII (not a Hapsburg), 1742–1745
Francis I, 1745–1765
Joseph II, 1765–1790
Leopold II, 1790–1792
Francis II, 1792–1806

—————Rulers of France from Hugh Capet—————

CAPETIAN KINGS

Hugh Capet, 987–996
Robert II, 996–1031
Henry I, 1031–1060

Philip I, 1060–1108
Louis VI, 1108–1137
Louis VII, 1137–1180
Philip II (Augustus), 1180–1223
Louis VIII, 1223–1226
Louis IX, 1226–1270
Philip III, 1270–1285
Philip IV, 1285–1314
Louis X, 1314–1316
Philip V, 1316–1322
Charles IV, 1322–1328

House of Valois

Philip VI, 1328–1350
John, 1350–1364
Charles V, 1364–1380
Charles VI, 1380–1422
Charles VII, 1422–1461
Louis XI, 1461–1483
Charles VIII, 1483–1498
Louis XII, 1498–1515
Francis I, 1515–1547
Henry II, 1547–1559
Francis II, 1559–1560
Charles IX, 1560–1574
Henry III, 1574–1589

Bourbon Dynasty

Henry IV, 1589–1610
Louis XIII, 1610–1643
Louis XIV, 1643–1715
Louis XV, 1715–1774
Louis XVI, 1774–1792

After 1792

First Republic, 1792–1799
Napoleon Bonaparte, First Consul, 1799–1804
Napoleon I, Emperor, 1804–1814
Louis XVIII (Bourbon dynasty), 1814–1824
Charles X (Bourbon dynasty), 1824–1830
Louis Philippe, 1830–1848
Second Republic, 1848–1852
Napoleon III, Emperor, 1852–1870
Third Republic, 1870–1940
Pétain regime, 1940–1944
Provisional government, 1944–1946
Fourth Republic, 1946–1958
Fifth Republic, 1958–

ANGLO-SAXON KINGS

Egbert, 802–839
Ethelwulf, 839–858
Ethelbald, 858–860
Ethelbert, 860–866
Ethelred, 866–871
Alfred the Great, 871–900
Edward the Elder, 900–924
Ethelstan, 924–940
Edmund I, 940–946
Edred, 946–955
Edwy, 955–959
Edgar, 959–975
Edward the Martyr, 975–978
Ethelred the Unready, 978–1016
Canute, 1016–1035 (Danish Nationality)
Harold I, 1035–1040
Hardicanute, 1040–1042
Edward the Confessor, 1042–1066
Harold II, 1066

ANGLO-NORMAN KINGS

William I (the Conqueror), 1066–1087
William II, 1087–1100
Henry I, 1100–1135
Stephen, 1135–1154

ANGEVIN KINGS

Henry II, 1154–1189
Richard I, 1189–1199
John, 1199–1216
Henry III, 1216–1272
Edward I, 1272–1307
Edward II, 1307–1327
Edward III, 1327–1377
Richard II, 1377–1399

HOUSE OF LANCASTER

Henry IV, 1399–1413
Henry V, 1413–1422
Henry VI, 1422–1461

HOUSE OF YORK

Edward IV, 1461–1483
Edward V, 1483
Richard III, 1483–1485

Tudor Sovereigns
Henry VII, 1485–1509
Henry VIII, 1509–1547
Edward VI, 1547–1553
Mary, 1553–1558
Elizabeth I, 1558–1603

Stuart Kings
James I, 1603–1625
Charles I, 1625–1649

Commonwealth and Protectorate, 1649–1659

Later Stuart Monarchs
Charles II, 1660–1685
James II, 1685–1688
William III and Mary II, 1689–1694
William III alone, 1694–1702
Anne, 1702–1714

House of Hanover
George I, 1714–1727
George II, 1727–1760
George III, 1760–1820
George IV, 1820–1830
William IV, 1830–1837
Victoria, 1837–1901

House of Saxe-Coburg-Gotha
Edward VII, 1901–1910
George V, 1910–1917

House of Windsor
George V, 1917–1936
Edward VIII, 1936
George VI, 1936–1952
Elizabeth II, 1952–

———————— *Prominent Popes* ————————

Silvester I, 314–335
Leo I, 440–461
Gelasius I, 492–496
Gregory I, 590–604

Nicholas I, 858–867
Silvester II, 999–1003
Leo IX, 1049–1054
Nicholas II, 1058–1061
Gregory VII, 1073–1085
Urban II, 1088–1099
Paschal II, 1099–1118
Alexander III, 1159–1181
Innocent III, 1198–1216
Gregory IX, 1227–1241
Boniface VIII, 1294–1303
John XXII, 1316–1334
Nicholas V, 1447–1455
Pius II, 1458–1464
Alexander VI, 1492–1503
Julius II, 1503–1513
Leo X, 1513–1521
Adrian VI, 1522–1523
Clement VII, 1523–1534
Paul III, 1534–1549
Paul IV, 1555–1559
Gregory XIII, 1572–1585
Gregory XVI, 1831–1846
Pius IX, 1846–1878
Leo XIII, 1878–1903
Pius X, 1903–1914
Benedict XV, 1914–1922
Pius XI, 1922–1939
Pius XII, 1939–1958
John XXIII, 1958–1963
Paul VI, 1963–

Rulers of Austria and Austria-Hungary

*Maximilian I (Archduke), 1493–1519
*Charles I (Charles V in the Holy Roman Empire), 1519–1556
*Ferdinand I, 1556–1564
*Maximilian II, 1564–1576
*Rudolph II, 1576–1612
*Matthias, 1612–1619
*Ferdinand II, 1619–1637
*Ferdinand III, 1637–1657
*Leopold I, 1658–1705
*Joseph I, 1705–1711
*Charles VI, 1711–1740
 Maria Theresa, 1740–1780
*Joseph II, 1780–1790

* Also bore title of Holy Roman Emperor.

*Leopold II, 1790–1792
*Francis II, 1792–1835 (Emperor of Austria as Francis I after 1804)
Ferdinand I, 1835–1848
Francis Joseph, 1848–1916 (after 1867 Emperor of Austria and King of Hungary)
Charles I, 1916–1918 (Emperor of Austria and King of Hungary)
Republic of Austria, 1918–1938 (dictatorship after 1934)
Republic restored, under Allied occupation, 1945–1956
Free Republic, 1956–

Rulers of Prussia and Germany

*Frederick I, 1701–1713
*Frederick William I, 1713–1740
*Frederick II (the Great), 1740–1786
*Frederick William II, 1786–1797
*Frederick William III, 1797–1840
*Frederick William IV, 1840–1861
*William I, 1861–1888 (German Emperor after 1871)
Frederick III, 1888
William II, 1888–1918
Weimar Republic, 1918–1933
Third Reich (Nazi Dictatorship), 1933–1945
Allied occupation, 1945–1952
Division into Federal Republic of Germany in west and German
Democratic Republic in east, 1949–

* Kings of Prussia.

Rulers of Russia

Ivan III, 1462–1505
Basil III, 1505–1533
Ivan IV, 1533–1584
Theodore I, 1584–1598
Boris Godunov, 1598–1605
Theodore II, 1605
Basil IV, 1606–1610
Michael, 1613–1645
Alexius, 1645–1676
Theodore III, 1676–1682
Ivan V and Peter I, 1682–1689
Peter I (the Great), 1689–1725
Catherine I, 1725–1727
Peter II, 1727–1730
Anna, 1730–1740
Ivan VI, 1740–1741
Elizabeth, 1741–1762

Peter III, 1762
Catherine II (the Great), 1762–1796
Paul, 1796–1801
Alexander I, 1801–1825
Nicholas I, 1825–1855
Alexander II, 1855–1881
Alexander III, 1881–1894
Nicholas II, 1894–1917
Soviet Republic, 1917–

—Rulers of Italy—

Victor Emmanuel II, 1861–1878
Humbert I, 1878–1900
Victor Emmanuel III, 1900–1946
Fascist Dictatorship, 1922–1943 (maintained in northern Italy until 1945)
Humbert II, May 9–June 13, 1946
Republic, 1946–

—Rulers of Spain—

Ferdinand { and Isabella, 1479–1504
and Philip I, 1504–1506
and Charles I, 1506–1516
Charles I (Holy Roman Emperor Charles V), 1516–1556
Philip II, 1556–1598
Philip III, 1598–1621
Philip IV, 1621–1665
Charles II, 1665–1700
Philip V, 1700–1746
Ferdinand VI, 1746–1759
Charles III, 1759–1788
Charles IV, 1788–1808
Ferdinand VII, 1808
Joseph Bonaparte, 1808–1813
Ferdinand VII (restored), 1814–1833
Isabella II, 1833–1868
Republic, 1868–1870
Amadeo, 1870–1873
Republic, 1873–1874
Alfonso XII, 1874–1885
Alfonso XIII, 1886–1931
Republic, 1931–1939
Fascist Dictatorship, 1939–

Index

Guide to Pronunciation

The sounds represented by the diacritical marks used in this Index are illustrated by the following common words:

āle	ēve	īce	ōld	ūse	bōōt
ăt	ĕnd	ĭll	ŏf	ŭs	fŏŏt
fâtality	évent		ôbey	ûnite	
câre			fôrm	ûrn	
ärm					
àsk					

Vowels that have no diacritical marks are to be pronounced "neutral," for example: Aegean = ê-jê'an, Basel = bäz'el, Basil = bă'zil, common = kŏm'on, Alcaeus = ăl-sē'us. The combinations ou and oi are pronounced as in "out" and "oil."

A

B

C

D

Cato Street conspiracy, 589
Cato the Elder, 185
Caucasus Mountains, 817
Cavaliers, 471
Cavendish, Henry, 510
Cavour (kä-vōōr'), Count Camillo di, 651, 664
Cell theory, 698
Celsus, 201, 378
Celts, 231
Cens, 289
Center party, in Germany, 688, 787
Central America, 439, 590
Central Intelligence Agency (U.S.), 836
Central Powers, 771, 773, 774, 780, 796
Cervantes (thĕr-vän'tâs), Miguel de, 386
Ceylon (sê-lŏn'), 848
Cezanne (sā'zän'), Paul, 719–20f., 912
Chadwick, Sir James, 898
Chalcis (kăl'sĭs), 120
Chaldeans, 50, 51, 71, 79, 105, 171; religion, 62–63, 64; literature, 63–65; morality, 64; science, 64; Persian conquest of, 65–66
Chamber of Deputies: in France, 686; in Italy, 785, 786
Chamberlain, Joseph, 651
Chamberlain, Neville, 812ff., 815, 816
Chamberlayne, Edward, 449
Charlemagne, 235, 236–38, 240, 281, 291, 298, 324
Charles Albert, king of Sardinia, 663, 688
Charles I, emperor of Austria-Hungary, 772
Charles V, Holy Roman Emperor, 369, 410, 420, 428, 442, 459, 480–81, 488
Charles I, king of England, 469–71, 516, 527
Charles II, king of England, 473–74
Charles VII, king of France, 294
Charles VIII, king of France, 368–69
Charles X, king of France, 589, 591–92, 652
Charles I, king of Spain, 379n, 480, 488n
Charles II, king of Spain, 489
Charter of 1814—582, 584, 589
Chartered companies, 446
Chartist movement of 1838–1848—680–81
Chartres (shàr'tr') : cathedral school, 330; Cathedral of, 338
Chase Manhattan Bank, 872

Chateaubriand (shä'tō'brē'än'), François de, 600–1
Chaucer, Geoffrey, 272, 336, 389
Checks and balances, 549–50, 689
Chemistry, 168f.; Saracenic, 268; Intellectual Revolution, 510–11; synthetic, 619–20
Chiang Kai-shek (jyäng' kī'shĕk'), 820
Chicago, 733, 883
China, 7, 72, 204, 271, 438, 439, 484, 485, 747, 780, 801, 814, 817, 820, 822f., 835, 878; *see also* Communist China; Manchuria
Chinese Nationalists, 832
Chippendale, Thomas, 528
Chivalry, 285–86; literature of, 334–35
Chopin (shô-păn'), Frédéric, 726
Chretien de Troyes (krä'tyän' de trwä'), 334
Christian IV, king of Denmark, 488
Christian Existentialism, 891
Christian Fathers, 208, 305
Christian humanists, *see* Humanism
Christian Renaissance, 394–95, 399
Christianity, 70, 72, 73, 75, 79, 88–90, 166, 172, 217, 253, 254, 256, 305, 507, 565, 600, 652, 705, 707, 744, 800, 860, 892; Roman civilization and, 203–4, 207–8, 225–26; Judaism and, 225; early development of, 222–31; early medieval theology, 241–44; Byzantine, 250; Islamic faith and, 263; late medieval, 310–14, 398, 406; *see also* individual sects
Chrysaloras (krī'sà-lôr'us), Manuel, 352
Church, Byzantine, 253–55
Church, Roman Catholic, 213, 235, 296, 376ff., 394f., 468, 474, 577, 593, 601, 653–54, 658–59, 687, 737, 758; organization of, 227–29, 231, 312; feudal system and, 284–85, 286; medieval commerce and, 305–6; late medieval theology, 310–12; reform movements, 313–15; abuses in, 399–401ff.; Reformation in, 422–25; secularization of in France, 557–58; contemporary developments in, 894–96
Church of England, 420ff., 426, 474
Church Fathers, 241–43, 305, 325, 326, 327, 334, 379
Churchill, Winston, 633, 819ff., 831, 844
Cicero, 189–90, 191, 193, 206, 213, 242, 344, 362, 380
Cimabue (chē-mà-bōō'ä), 355

Cinquecento (chǐng'kwê-chen'tō), 343n, 352–53, 359
Cistercian (sǐs-tûr'shăn) order, 314
Cities, 292; growth of, 162, 279, 290, 297, 345; medieval life in, 300–7
City University of New York, 886
City-states, 52, 105; Greek, 119–21, 154, 158; in Italian Renaissance, 347–50; urban explosion and, 880–92
Civil Constitution of the Clergy, 558
Civil rights, 859f., 884, 906
Civil wars: in England, 470–71; in United States, 564, 655, 669, 691–92, 845, 858; in Russia, 796–97; in Spain, 810; in Nigeria, 856; in Pakistan, 848
Civilizations: defined, 18–19; origins and growth of, 19–21; beginning of earliest, 21–25; growth and decline of, 916–17
Clark, Ramsay, 881
Class struggle, 903–4; doctrine of, 643
Classicism, 513–25, 601–2, 709; in painting, 515–18; in literature, 518–19; in music, 523–25, 728
Cleaver, Eldridge, 859
Cleisthenes (klǐs'the-nēz), 126, 127
Clemenceau (klä'män'sō'), Georges, 774, 775, 776, 777, 802
Clement VII, Pope, 420, 423
Clement of Alexandria, 242
Cleopatra, 188
Clermont (klär-mōn'), Council of, 319–20, 321
Clientage, 202–3, 280
Climate, influence of, 19–21, 23–24
Clive, Robert, 4
Clovis, 235, 245
Cluny movement, 313, 318, 337
Code Napoléon, 577
Coffee, 460–61
Coinage, 193, 210; Lydian, 68, 93, 105; Greek, 125; Roman, 181
Coke, Sir Edward, 469
Colbert (kôl'bâr'), Jean Baptiste, 450–51, 477
Cold War, 831, 836, 885
Coleridge, Samuel Taylor, 520, 599
Collectivism, 646, 705
Collectivistic anarchists, 646
College of Cardinals, 312
Cologne, 326, 376; University of, 330
Colonate, 280
Coloni, 232, 280
Colonialism, 440, 448–51, 453, 454, 490f.; revolts against, 845–64; *see also* Imperialism

E

F

H

I

Geometry, 139, 170
George I, king of England, 475n, 682
Georgian architecture, 515
Germ theory of disease, 700–1, 902
German Confederation, 589, 660, 661–62
Germans, ancient, 153, 198, 222, 231–34, 238, 250, 251
Germany, 7, 194, 290, 291, 301, 304, 324, 375–76, 393, 394, 404, 405f., 407, 408–15, 424, 426, 427, 430, 440, 441, 442, 446, 450, 452, 456, 461f., 489, 505, 520f., 577, 589, 600, 617, 620, 624, 627f., 630, 631, 632, 640, 644, 645, 657, 712, 737, 740, 747, 758ff., 783, 784, 795, 801, 810f., 812–15, 833, 834f., 866; feudal system, 283, 284; medieval empire, 298–300; Renaissance in, 376–79; Industrial Revolution in, 625–26; unification of, 660–63; imperialism, 671, 675; Hohenzollern empire, 687–88; World War I and, 754–55, 757–58, 762, 763ff., 773f., 775f., 787f.; Weimar Republic, 787, 790; Nazi regime in, 787–92, 798–99, 808–9, 810, 811–12; World War II and, 807f., 815–17f., 819ff.
Ghana (gä′nà), 855
Ghent (gĕnt), 301
Gibbon, Edward, 519, 916
Gibraltar, 490, 848
Gilbert, William, 509
Gilchrist, P. C., 755
Gilgamesh epic, 81
Ginsberg, Allen, 882
Giocondo, Francesco del, 357
Giorgione (jōr-jō′nāy), 357
Giotto (jôt′tô), 355
Girondists (jĭ-rŏn′dĭsts), 562ff.
Gizeh, 41
Gladden, Washington, 738
Gladiators, 192, 203
Gladstone, W. E., 633, 681
Glasgow College, 552
Glenn, John H., Jr., 901
Glorious Revolution, 474–75, 547, 610, 682
Gluck (glook), C. W., 523–24
Gnosticism, 73, 171–72, 224, 226, 229, 242
Godwin, William, 600, 645
Goethe (gû′tĕ), Johann Wolfgang von, 520, 521, 600
Gogh (gō), Vincent van, 720, 912
Gold, 440–41, 448, 481, 692
Gold Coast, 855
Gold standard, 623–24; abandoned by Great Britain, 804

Golden Age of Greece, 140, 147–51, 157f., 167
Golden mean, 138
Golden rule, 70–71, 224
Goldsmith, Oliver, 520, 599
Goliards (Goliardi), 332–33, 344
Golias (go-lī′as), 333
Gordon, Cyrus H., 101n
Gospel of Wealth, 739
Gospels, 224, 398
Gothic architecture, 337, 338–40, 344, 345, 361, 382, 437, 573, 602, 724
Goths, 232
Gournia, 99
Goya, Francisco, 517, 518
Gracchi (gräk′ē), Revolt of, 186–87
Gracchus, Gaius, 186–87
Gracchus, Tiberius, 186
Granada, 480
Grand Armée, 581
Grand jury, 236, 296
Gravitation, law of, 367, 508–9
Gray, Elisha, 622
Gray, Thomas, 520, 599
Great Britain, 211, 213, 489, 490, 491, 563, 568, 578f., 580, 586ff., 589, 590f., 592, 633–34, 638, 639, 655, 664, 666, 686, 689, 736f., 740, 742f., 753f., 759f., 781, 783, 788, 793, 801, 802, 803, 810f., 812f., 815, 826f., 834f., 842, 854, 860, 866, 874, 885, 886, 899, 918; Industrial Revolution in, 609–11ff., 617, 618, 620, 623–24, 625; imperialism, 670, 675; evolution of democracy in, 678–84; World War I and, 754, 755–56, 758, 764ff., 774f.; World War II and, 807, 815–16ff., 819–20ff.; Irish question, 841–43; anticolonial movement and, 846, 847–48; increase of executive power in, 867
Great Depression, 624, 788f., 802, 803–5, 811–12, 907, 908, 911
Great Lakes, 439, 477
Great Mother, cult of, 192, 203
Great Powers, 834–35, 840–41
Great Revolt in England, 458
Great Schism (grāt sĭz′m), 403
Great Society, 867
"Great Thaw," 838
Greater Serbia movement, 756–57
Greco-Persian War, 127, 144
Greece, ancient, 66, 175f., 181f., 198, 217, 249, 513; see also Hellenic civilization
Greece, 591, 630, 666, 760, 777f., 781, 826, 827, 882; World War II and, 816; revolt of 1821—845; military junta, 867

Greek civilization, see Hellenic civilization
Greek Orthodox church, 258
Greeks: ancient, 66, 68, 93, 96ff., 398
Greenback movement, 692
Gregorian chant, 340
Gregory I (the Great), Pope, 240–41, 310, 340
Gregory VII, Pope, 312, 313, 316, 317, 319, 423
Gregory of Nyssa, 253
Gregory of Tours, 245
Grey, Earl, 679
Grey, Sir Edward, 764, 865
Grieg, E. H., 727
Gropper, William, 913
Grotius (grō′shĭ-us), Hugo, 493, 526
Guadeloupe (gwäd′loōp′), 491
Guatemala, 20
Guevara, Ernesto (Che), 834
Guiana, 491, 587
Guicciardini (gwēt′chär-dē′ne), Francesco, 354
Guilds, 330, 374, 407, 438, 557n, 570; Byzantine, 252; Saracenic, 272; medieval, 303–7; economic theory of, 305–7; Commercial Revolution and, 443–44
Guinea, 439
Guiscard (gēs-kär′), Robert, 319
Guise, Duke of, 429
Guizot (gē′zō′), Premier of France, 684
Gunpowder Plot, 468–69
Gustavus Adolphus, 478–79, 488, 489
Gutenberg, Johann, 346n

Hades, realm of, 117
Hadrian, Roman emperor, 256
Haeckel (hĕk′el), Ernst, 704, 706f.
Hahn, Otto, 899
Hals, Frans, 517–18
Halys (hăl′ĭs) River, 104
Hamath, 94
Hamburg, 307
Hamilton, Alexander, 548
Hammurabi, 50, 62; Code of, 49, 53, 57, 61, 76, 84
Hampden, John, 470
Handel, G. F., 522–23
Hannibal, 184
Hanoi, 852
Hanover, House of, 475n
Hansberry, Lorraine, 911–12
Hanse, 306–7, 484
Hanseatic League, 307, 438
Hapsburg Empire, 757, 762, 771–72
"Hapsburg ring," 478

J

Hapsburgs, 375, 415, 478, 480, 561, 586, 587, 660, 663, 664; struggle with Bourbons, 487–91
Harding, Warren G., 802
Hardy, Thomas, 711
Hargreaves, James, 611–12
Harlem Renaissance, 858, 910–11
Harold, king of England, 239
Harun-al-Raschid (hä-rōōn'äl'rǎ-shēd'), 264
Harvard University, 906
Harvey, Sir William, 5, 367, 368, 463, 512
Hastings, Battle of, 239
Hattusas, 94
Hauptmann (houpt'män), Gerhart, 712
Hawaii, 818
Hawkins, Captain John, 459
Hawley-Smoot Act, 803
Hawthorne, Nathaniel, 744
Haydn (hī'd'n), Joseph, 524, 525
Hayek (hī'ĕk), Frederick A., 893
Haymarket Square riots (1886), 733
Hébert (ā'bâr'), J. R., 566
Hebrew civilization, 75–90, 153; importance of, 75; origins and early history, 75–76; law, 76, 84–85, 90; political history, 77–80; religion, 76, 80–84, 88–89; Lost Ten Tribes, 78–79; Babylonian captivity, 79; Diaspora, 79; art, 84; science, 84; literature, 85–88; philosophy, 87–88; influence of, 88–90
Hebrews, 60, 63, 570; see also Jews
Hedonism (hē'dŏn-ĭzm), 500
Hegel (hā'gĕl), Georg Wilhelm F., 595–96, 642, 648, 708, 916
Hegira (hē-jī'ra), 262
Heidelberg, 376; University of, 330
Heilbroner, Robert, 879
Heine (hī'ne), Heinrich, 600
Helen of Troy, 96
Heliocentric theory, 5, 365–66
Hellenic civilization, 113–54, 222; Mycenaean period, 113–14; writing, 114; Dark Ages, 113, 114–19; culture, 115; government, 115–16; social and economic life, 116, 120; religion, 116–19, 154; citystates, 119–21; Sparta, 121–24; Athens, 124–30, 147–51; Persian war, 127; Peloponnesian war, 127–28; political disintegration of, 128–29; Macedonian conquest, 129–30; philosophy, 131–38; science, 139–40; literature, 140–44; architecture and sculpture, 144–47; achievements and significance of, 151–54; tragic flaw in, 154
Hellenistic Age, 145n, 146, 268

Hellenistic civilization, 109, 130, 139, 145n, 146, 157–73, 192, 198ff., 209–10, 213, 222, 268; Hellenic civilization and, 157–58; political history and institutions, 158–59; economic and social developments, 159–63; philosophy, 163–66; literature, 166–67, sculpture and architecture, 167–68; science, 168–71; religion, 171–72; compared with modern age, 172–73; Roman conquest of, 185
Hellespont, 66
Heloïse (ā'lō'ēz'), 325
Helots (hĕl'ots), 123, 124
Hemingway, Ernest, 907, 908
Henry I, king of England, 295
Henry II, king of England, 295–96, 494
Henry III, king of England, 297
Henry VII, king of England, 298, 374–75, 466
Henry VIII, king of England, 369, 375, 378, 387, 419–20, 421, 466
Henry IV, king of France, 429, 467, 476–77, 478
Henry IV, German emperor, 316
Henry of Navarre, see Henry IV, king of France
Hepplewhite, George, 528
Heracleitus (hĕr-a-klī'tŭs), 113, 164
Herbert of Cherbury, Lord, 507
Heredity, laws of, 698
Hero or Heron (hē'rŏn), of Alexandria, 171, 613
Herod I, 222
Herodotus (hē-rŏd'ō-tŭs), 41, 65, 144
Herophilus (hē-rŏf'i-lŭs), 170
Herriot (ĕ'ryō'), Édouard, 802
Hertz, Heinrich, 622
Herzegovina (hĕr'tsâ-gô'vē'nä), 666, 668, 757, 760
Herzl, Theodor, 740
Hesse, Elector of, 584
Hetaera (hĕ-tē'rē), 151
Hieroglyphic writing, 39, 101
Highway systems, 868
Hildebrand, 313
Hindemith, Paul, 915
Hindus, 847f., 856f.
Hipparchus, 169, 170
Hippies, 883
Hippocrates of Chios (hǐ-pŏk'rà-tēz, kī'ŏs), 139
Hippocrates of Cos (kŏs), 139, 140
Hiram, king of Tyre, 78
Hiroshima (hē-rŏsh''mä), 819, 899f.
Hiss, Alger, 831
History: defined, 3; theories concerning, 4–5; prehistory and, 5–6;

economic interpretation of, 643, 644; contemporary attitudes toward, 916
Hitler, Adolf, 569, 660, 789, 808–9, 814ff., 818, 833; career of, 789–90
Hittite civilization, 94–96; significance of, 93, 96; discovery and history of, 94; economic system, 94–95; art, 95; law and literature, 95; religion, 96
Hittites, 76, 84, 99, 104, 105
Ho Chi Minh, 831, 841, 852
Hobbes, Thomas, 449, 492–93, 499, 500, 501, 502
Hohenstaufen dynasty, 298–300, 790
Hohenzollern dynasty, 450, 482, 491, 662, 686, 766, 790
Holbein (hōl'bīn), Hans, 377–78
Holding companies, 623
Holland, 291, 426, 429, 452, 489f., 490, 495, 578, 586–87, 592, 766; see also Netherlands; Low Countries
Holstein (hōl'shtīn), 662
Holy Alliance, 587
Holy Land, 318ff.
"Holy League," 369
Holy Roman Empire, 298–300, 317, 347, 369, 375–76, 410, 415, 426, 428, 480–81, 488f., 495, 578
Holy Synod (sīn'ud), Russia, 485, 486
Homer, 97, 115, 118
Homo sapiens (hō'mō sā'pǐ-enz), 8
Homosexuality, 203, 868
Honduras, 20
Hong Kong, 848
Hooke, Robert, 511
Hoover, Herbert, 802, 803, 869
Horace, 175, 197
Hormones, 701
Horse, 50
Hortensian Law, 181
Hortensius, 242
Horus, 34f.
Hosea, 82
Hrozny (hrôz'nē), Bedrich, 94
Hudson, Henry, 439
Hudson's Bay Company, 446
Hughes, Langston, 911
Hugo, Victor, 601
Huguenots, 419, 429, 475ff., 479, 611
Humanism, 167, 277, 387, 397, 398–99, 508, 513; in Greek art, 144–47; in Italian Renaissance, 350–63; in German Renaissance, 376–78; in Renaissance in Low Countries, 379–82; in English Renaissance, 387–92; Christian, 394–95, 419

K

L

Jay, John, 548
Jeanne d'Arc (zhän' därk') (Joan of Arc), 294
Jefferson, Thomas, 475, 507, 548, 689–90
Jeffersonian Revolution, 689–90
Jehovah, *see* Yahweh
Jenner, Sir Edward, 513, 699, 902
Jerusalem, 77, 78, 79, 84, 322
Jesuits, 386, 424–25, 426, 427, 460, 688, 890
Jesus of Nazareth, 72, 88, 90, 221, 229, 242, 263, 314, 380, 646, 897; career and crucifixion of, 222–24; teachings, 224
Jews: in ancient times, 51, 65, 148, 169, 172; in Middle Ages, 222f., 240, 250, 262, 266, 319, 323, 441; in modern world, 385, 407, 480, 483, 505, 508, 657–58, 734, 788, 790, 791, 826, 860, 918
Joad, C. E. M., 890
Joan of Arc (jōn uv ärk'), *see* Jeanne d'Arc
Joanna, 480
Job, Book of, 58, 86–87
John, king of England, 296–97, 317–18, 494
John XII, Pope, 298
John XXIII, Pope, 737, 894–95
John the Baptist, 223
John of Leyden, 414–15
John of Meun, 336
John of Salisbury, 328, 344
Johnson, Lyndon B., 837, 852f., 867, 885
Joint-stock companies, 446, 610, 622
Joliet (zhō-lyä'), Louis, 439
Jones, James, 909
Jonson, Ben, 390
Jordan, 863
Joseph II, emperor of Austria, 483–84
Journeymen, 304
Joyce, James, 908
Judah, kingdom of, 51, 78–79
Judaism, 83, 225, 263, 707, 739–40, 744, 789; Reform, 505
Judicial review, U.S., 469
Julian, Roman emperor, 207–8
Julius II, Pope, 345, 349, 360, 362, 369
Julius Caesar, *see* Caesar, Gaius Julius
July Revolution, 591–92, 652, 679
Junkers (yŏŏng'kĕrs), 660f., 789
Jupiter, 182
Juries: Athenian, 126–27; Roman, 205; medieval, 296
Jus civile (yŏŏs sĭ-vēl'ê), 256

Jus gentium (yŏŏs gĕn'tĭ-ŭm), 206, 207, 493
Jus naturale (yŏŏs năt'ûr-äl'ĕ), 206–7, 256–57
Justification by faith, 409
Justinian, 235, 240, 249, 251, 253–54, 256, 257; Code of, 212, 256, 257
Juvenal, 198, 209

Kaaba (kä'ba), 260, 261
Kafka, Franz, 910
Kant, Immanuel, 594–95, 648, 708, 891
Karnak, 41, 42, 69
Kassites, 50–51
Katanga, 856
Kato Zakros, 98
Keats, John, 599–600
Kellogg-Briand Pact, 809
Kempis, Thomas à, 394–95
Kennan, George F., 836
Kennedy, John F., 829, 836–37, 852, 867
Kent State, 883
Kenya, 856–58
Kenyatta, Jomo, 857–58
Kepler, Johann, 461, 478
Kerensky, Alexander, 793, 794, 796
Kerouac, Jack, 882
Kettering, Charles, 620
Keynes, John Maynard, 873
Khrushchev (krŏŏsh-chôf'), Nikita S., 829, 833, 838–39
Khufu, pyramid of, 41
Kierkegaard (kĭr'kĕ-gôr), Sören, 891, 906
Kikuyu, 857, 858
King, Martin Luther, Jr., 859, 906–7
Kipling, Rudyard, 715, 716–17
Kirk, Russell, 893f.
Kline, Franz, 913
Knossos, 97f., 101, 103, 114
Koch (kôkh), Robert, 700, 701, 902
Koran (kôr-än'), 249, 263f.
Korea, 674, 820, 867
Korean War, 830
Kosygin (kô-sē'gĭn), Aleksei N., 801, 840
KPU, 858
Kremlin, 485, 580
Kropotkin, Peter, 646
Krupps, 625–26
Ku Klux Klan, 834
Kulturkampf (kŏŏl-tŏŏr'kämpf'), 687–88, 737
Kuraish (kû-rīsh'), 260f.
Kuril (kŏŏ'rĭl) Islands, 821

Labor/Labor unions, 304, 560, 623, 624, 625, 632, 639, 733, 737, 738, 871–72
Labour Government, in Great Britain, 645, 783, 802
Lacedaemonia (lăs'ê-de-mō'nĭ-a), *see* Sparta
Lacedaemonians, 121n
Laconia, 121
Lafayette, Marquis de, 544, 562n
Laibach (lī'bäkh), Congress of, 588
Laissez faire (lĕ'sä'fâr'), 552–53, 625, 631–34, 636, 639, 640, 648
Lamarck, Jean, 696
Lamennais (lä'mĕ'nĕ'), Robert de, 647
Landini, Francesco, 392
Landtag, Prussia, 688
Langley, Samuel P., 621
Laos (louz), 852, 853, 867
La Salle, René Robert, 439
Lasers, 871
Lassus, Roland de, 393f.
Last Judgment, 70, 84
Later Middle Ages, 277–341, 406, 407; agriculture, 286–87; commerce, 290, 292, 297–98, 300–1; secular *vs.* spiritual authorities, 315–18; urban life, 300–3; guild system, 303–7; Christianity, 309–15; philosophy, 324–27; political theory, 327–28; science, 328–29; education, 329–32; literature, 332–37; architecture, 337–40; music, 340–41
Latin America, 737, 801, 845, 882, 895
Latin language, 332–33, 344
Latium, 177
Latvia, 773
Laud (lôd), William, 470
Lausanne (lō'zăn'), Treaty of, 780
Lavoisier (lä'vwä'zyä'), Antoine, 510–11
Law, 52; primitive, 17; Egyptian, 29, 47; Sumerian, 53–54, 57; Old Babylonian, 56–57; Assyrian, 61; Hebrew, 76, 84–85, 90; Hittite, 95; Roman, 178f., 180f., 186–87, 190, 194, 205–7, 212, 256, 259, 318, 405, 412; early medieval, 234, 236; Byzantine, 256–57, 259; common, 295–96; late medieval, 328
Law, John, 452
Law of nature, 547, 548, 645
Lay investiture, 316
Leach, Gerald, 878
League of Nations, 495, 771, 775, 776, 780–81, 786, 798, 808, 814, 822, 826, 829, 860

M

N

O

Minerva, 182
Ministeriales (mĭn'ĭs-têr-ĭ-ăl'êz), 284
Minnesingers, 334, 341
Minoan-Mycenaean civilization, 106, 113, 114; discovery of, 96–97; economic life, 97–98, 99; rise and downfall of, 98; government and social order, 99–100; religion, 100–1; writing, 98, 101; science, 101; art, 101–2; Egyptian civilization and, 102–3; influence of, 103
Minos (mī'nŏs), 99
Mirabeau (mē'rá'bō'), Marquis de, 544, 555, 562n
Miracle drugs, 903
Miracle plays, 305
Mirandola (mê-rän'dô-lä), Pico della, 362
Mississippi, 859
Mississippi Bubble, 452–53
Mississippi Company, 452
Mississippi valley, 439, 477
Mithraism, 71–72, 171–72, 192, 203, 225
Mithras (mĭth'răs), 71
Mitylene (mĭt''l-ē'nē), 119
Mobutu, President, 856
Model Parliament, 297
Modena, (mô'dâ-nä), 587, 663, 664
Mohammed (Muhammad), 261ff.
Mohammed V, sultan of Turkey, 667
Mohammedanism, *see* Islam
Mohl, Hugo von, 698
Molière (mô'lyâr'), 518
Moloch (mō'lŏk), 105
Moltke, Field Marshal von, 756
Mommsen, Theodor, quoted, 181
Monarchists, in France, 656, 657–58, 659, 685
Monasteries/Monasticism, 229–31, 337, 411; schools, 245–46, 279, 330; reform movements, 313–14; dissolution of, 420; *see also* individual orders
Monet (mô'nē'), Claude, 719
Money: Egyptian, 46; in Commercial Revolution, 438, 446–47; *see also* Coinage
Money economy, 161, 446
Mongols, 250–51, 485
Monism in religion, 70, 100
Monody, 521
Monophysite (mô-nôf'i-sīt) movement, 253–54
Monotheism, 36, 47, 50, 70, 82
Montagu, Lady, 512
Montaigne (môn'tĕn'y'), Michel de, 373, 383–85, 463
Monte Cassino, 231

Montenegro, 669, 757, 760, 765
Montesorri, Maria, 741–42
Montesquieu (môn'tĕs-kyû'), Baron de, 19, 544, 547, 548, 549–50, 558, 559
Monteverdi, Claudio, 522
Montfort, Simon de, 297
Montpellier (môn'pĕ'lyä'), University of, 330, 383
Moors, 236, 281, 319, 375, 385, 438, 480
Morales (mō-rä'läs), Louis de, 385
Morality: during Reformation, 459–60; during Age of Enlightenment, 527–28
More, Sir Thomas, 387, 395, 419, 463
Moret (mô'rä'), Alexandre, 24
Morgan, J. P., and Company, 622
Morocco, 267, 271, 755, 760, 849
Morse, Samuel F. B., 617
Morton, William T. G., 648–49, 743
Mosaics, 258
Moscow, 817; Grand Duchy of, 485
Moscow International, 785
Moscow University, 857
Moses, 76, 81–82, 85
Moslems, 251, 281–82, 322, 407, 441, 847f.; *see also* Saracens
Mosul, 271
Motet, 393
Mount Olympus, 117
Mount Sinai, 81
Moussorgsky (mōō-sôrg'skī), Modeste, 727–28
Mozart (mō'tsärt), Wolfgang, 524–25
Muhammad, Elijah, 858
Mun, Thomas, 437
Munich, 376
Munich Agreement, 814–15
Münster (mün'stēr), 414–15
Münzer, Thomas, 413–14
Murray, Gilbert, 767
Music: in Later Middle Ages, 340; in Renaissance, 392–94; in Intellectual Revolution, 521–25; classicism in, 523–25; romanticism in, 603–5; in Age of Democracy and Nationalism, 725–28; contemporary, 914–15
Mussolini (mōōs'sô-lē'nē), Benito, 569, 791, 815, 817; early career of, 785–86
Mustapha Kemal (mōōs-tä-fä' kĕ-mäl'), 780
Mutation hypothesis, 698
Mycenae (mi-sē'nē), 97f., 114, 115
Mycenaeans, 98, 102, 121
Myron, 147
Mystery cults, 151, 192, 203–4

Mystery plays, 305
Mystery religions, 171–72, 225, 227
Mysticism, 73, 171–72, 196, 208, 226, 227, 268, 327, 403–4, 708

Nabopolassar (năb'ô-pô-läs'er), 51
Nagasaki (nä'ga-sä'kē), 819, 899f.
Nanshe, 54
Nantes (nänt), Edict of, 429, 477, 479
Naples, 175, 177, 341, 347, 350, 368, 490, 578, 580, 664; University of, 329, 330
Napoleon I, 158, 300, 447, 564, 571, 586, 601–2, 653, 812, 884, 916; French Revolution and, 568–69, 574f.; *coup d'état*, 568, 574f.; early career of, 574–75; regime set up by, 575–76; statecraft of, 576–77, 579; legal reforms, 577; as military commander, 577–79, 580–81; causes of downfall, 579–83; significance of, 583–84
Napoleon III, 601, 652–56, 657, 662, 664, 665, 685, 718, 754, 831
Napoleonic Wars, 641, 731, 753
Narodniki, 669
Nasser (nä'sēr), Gamal Abdel, 848, 863
National Assembly, in France, 554–58f., 577n, 655, 656, 685
National Convention, in France, 561–67, 570–71, 575, 577
National Insurance Act, 633
National monarchies, 323; in France, 291–95, 476–80; in England, 295–98; in Spain, 480–82; in Prussia, 482–83; in Russia, 484–87
National Socialism, *see* Nazi regime, in Germany
National Socialist German Workers' party, 636; *see also* Nazi party
Nationalism, 533, 570–71, 584, 596, 601, 628, 631, 684, 773, 786, 812; economic, 448, 450; evolution of, 651–52; in France, 652–59; in Italy, 663–66; in Eastern Europe, 666–69; in United States, 669–70; new imperialism and, 674; in music, 727–28; World War I and, 756ff.; in Asia, 831; contemporary, 866
NATO (North Atlantic Treaty Organization), 827
Natural law, 636, 639
Natural selection, 697
Naturalism, 912
Nauru, 848
Navigation, 105–6
Navigation Acts, 449–50

P

Q

R

T

U

Secularism, 109, 344
Security Council of United
  Nations, 822–23, 856
Sedan (sē-dän'), Battle of, 656, 662
Seleucia (sê-lū'shǐ-a), 162
Seleucid (sê-lū'sǐd) empire, 159, 161
Seleucus (sê-lū'kus), 158
Self-determinism, doctrine of,
  846–47
Seljuk Turks, 251, 267, 321f.
Semites, 53, 59
Semmelweiss (zěm'el-vīs), Ignatz,
  699–700
Senate: Roman, 178, 179f., 184,
  187, 188f., 190, 195, 206, 207;
  Carthaginian, 183; French, 686;
  United States, 689
Seneca, 123, 196, 197, 201, 337, 344
Senior, Nassau William, 638–39
Sennacherib (se-năk'er-ĭb), 51
Separation of church and state,
  565–66, 570, 658–59
Separation of powers, 549–50, 558,
  594, 690
Separatists, 468, 471
September massacres, 559
Serbia, 591, 666, 758, 760–61;
  World War I and, 756–57, 761ff.
Serbs, 251, 757, 765
Serfdom, 161, 162, 210–11, 232,
  570; among ancient Germans,
  234; in early Middle Ages, 240,
  241; in Byzantine and Saracenic
  civilizations, 253, 255, 272; in
  feudal system, 280, 287, 288–90,
  291; in Austria, 483; in Russia,
  486, 487, 590, 733, 736; in 18th
  century, 529; in France during
  Revolution, 546, 557; in Prussia,
  584
Sermon on the Mount, 646
Servetus (sûr-vē'tus), Michael,
  367–68, 430
Sessions, Roger, 915
Set, 34f.
Seven Cardinal Sins, 70
Seven Liberal Arts, 245–46
Seven Weeks' War, 662
Seven Years' War, 490–91, 541, 610,
  753, 812
Sèvres (sâ'vr'), Treaty of, 777f.
Sforza (sfôr'tsä), Francesco, 348
Sforza family, 345, 356
Shaftesbury, Lord, 507
Shakespeare, William, 142, 389, 390,
  391–92, 457, 518, 726, 727
Shamash, 54
Shaw, George Bernard, 645, 712
Shelley, Percy Bysshe, 152, 589,
  599–600
Sheraton, Thomas, 528

Sherwood, Robert, 908
Shiites (shē'īts), 263f., 265f.
Ship money, 470
Short ballot, 693
Sibelius (sǐ-bā'lǐ-ōōs), Jean, 727
Siberia, 484, 592, 674
Sicily, 105, 120, 128, 183f., 298,
  299, 301, 322, 369, 644
Sickingen (sǐk'ĭng-en), Franz von,
  411–12
Sidon (sī'd'n), 105
Siena (syâ'nä), 338
Sieyès (syâ'yâs'), Abbé, 539, 555,
  562n, 564, 575
Silesia (sǐ-lē'shǐ-a), 482, 483, 491
Silver, 440–41, 448, 481, 692
Silver, Age of, 452
Simeon Stylites (sǐm'ê-un stī-li'tēz),
  St., 299–300
Simons, Menno, 415
Simony (sǐm'ô-nǐ), 313
Sinai Peninsula, 863
Singapore, 848, 852
Sino (sǐn'ô)-Japanese War of
  1894–1895—674
Sistine (sǐs'tēn) Chapel, 359
Sitzkrieg, 816
Six Articles, 420
Six Day War, 863–64
Sixtus V, Pope, 423
Skepticism, 38, 134, 135, 165–66,
  171, 269, 327, 363, 366, 384,
  505, 707
Slave trade, 490, 526
Slavery, 99, 134, 508, 526, 565, 570,
  577; in Egypt, 43–44; in Assyria,
  61; in Athens, 148f.; in Hellenistic
  civilization, 162; in Roman civili-
  zation, 180, 185, 190, 191–92,
  202–3, 205, 206; in Later Middle
  Ages, 287, 288; revival of, 453;
  American Civil War and, 691–92
Slavophil movement, 669
Slavs, 231, 250f., 319, 660, 669, 754,
  755, 762, 772
Slovakia, 777
Slovaks, 847
Slovenes, 757, 762
Smetana (smě'tà-nà), Bedrich, 727
Smith, Adam, 527, 552–53, 635–36
Social contract, 551
Social Democrats: in Germany,
  645, 688; in Russia, 733, 794
Social Gospel movement, 738–39
Social reform, movements for,
  631–34
Social Revolutionaries, 733, 793,
  794
Social sciences, development of,
  702, 884, 905
Socialism, 598, 632, 649, 684, 688;

Utopian, 640–41; Marxian,
  641–45; Christian, 647–48;
  Fabian, 712; in Italy, 785;
  decline of ideology and, 832f.;
  African, 857
Socialist Party: in United States,
  645, 833; in Italy, 785; in
  Germany, 787, 789; in France,
  802, 804
Socialists, 685, 783, 788, 794;
  World War I peace proposals,
  770
Society of Jesus, see Jesuits
Socrates, 134–35, 136, 137, 144,
  152, 380
Soddy, Frederick, 702
Soil-exhaustion theory, 20–21
Solomon, 77–78, 84, 87
Solon (sō'lun), 125
Solutré (sô-lū-trā'), 9
Somerset, Duke of, 421
Song of Songs (Song of Solomon),
  86
Sophia, Electress of Hanover, 475
Sophists, 133–34, 135, 144, 166,
  498
Sophocles, 142, 151, 352
Sophrosyne (sō'frŏs'ĭ-nē), 138
Sorel (sô'rěl'), Georges, 647, 785,
  893
South Africa, 587, 670
South America, 439, 440, 452, 590,
  878
South Korea, 830
South Sea Bubble, 452, 453
South Sea Company, 452
South Vietnam, 841, 852ff.
Southeast Asia, 848, 852, 884
Southern Rhodesia, 848
Soviet regime, 258
Soviet Russia, see U.S.S.R.
Soviet Union, see U.S.S.R.
Space, exploration of, 900–1
Space-time continuum, 898
Spain, 105, 176, 194, 266, 267, 272,
  319, 322, 364, 369, 382, 393f.,
  395, 421, 425, 426, 438f., 441,
  448, 449, 452, 468, 473, 476, 477,
  478, 488, 489–90f., 586, 588–89,
  590, 655f., 662, 731, 737, 801,
  845, 867, 882, 895; ancient, 183f.;
  early medieval, 235; Renaissance
  in, 375, 385–86; Reformation in,
  422; Revolt of 1808—580;
  absolutism in, 480–82; civil war of
  1936–1939—810
Spanish Armada, 482
Spanish Succession, War of, 489–90
Spanish-American War, 669, 693
Sparta, 65, 119, 121–24ff., 129, 130;
  population, 119; militarism,

W

Y

Z